Contents

KU-779-539

Introduction to
Kenya

Lapped by the Indian Ocean, straddling the equator, and with Mount Kenya rising above a magnificent landscape of forested hills, patchwork farms and wooded savanna, Kenya is a richly rewarding place to travel. The country's dramatic geography has resulted in a great range of natural habitats, harbouring a huge variety of wildlife, while its history of migration and conquest has brought about a fascinating social panorama, which includes the Swahili city-states of the coast and the Maasai of the Rift Valley.

Kenya's world-famous national parks, tribal peoples and superb beaches lend the country an exotic image with magnetic appeal. Treating it as a succession of tourist sights, however, is not the most stimulating way to experience it. If you get off the beaten track, you can enter the world inhabited by most Kenyans: a ceaselessly active scene of muddy farm tracks, corrugated-iron huts, tea shops and lodging houses, crammed buses and streets wandered by goats and children. Both on and off the tourist routes, you'll find warmth and openness, and an abundance of superb scenery – rolling savanna dotted with Maasai herds and wild animals, high Kikuyu moorlands grazed by cattle and sheep, and dense forests full of monkeys and birdsong. Of course Kenya is not all postcard-perfect: start a conversation with any local and you'll soon find out about the country's deep economic and social tensions.

Where to go

The **coast** and major **game parks** are the most obvious targets. If you come to Kenya on an organized tour, you're likely to have your time divided between these two attractions. Despite the impact of human population pressures, Kenya's **wildlife spectacle** remains a compelling experience. The million-odd annual visitors are easily absorbed in such a large country, and there's nothing to prevent you escaping the predictable tourist

ABOVE LAKE NAKURU **OPPOSITE** MORNING IN NAIROBI

bottlenecks: even on an organized trip, you should not feel tied down.

The major **national parks and reserves**, watered by seasonal streams, are mostly located in savanna on the fringes of the **highlands** that take up much of the southwest quarter of the country. The vast majority of Kenyans live in these rugged hills, where the ridges are a mix of smallholdings and plantations. Through the heart of the highlands sprawls the **Great Rift Valley**, an archetypal East African scene of dry, thorn-tree savanna, splashed with lakes and studded by volcanoes.

The hills and grasslands on either side of the valley – Laikipia and the Mara conservancies, for example – are great walking country, as are the high forests and moors of the Central Highlands and Mount Kenya itself – a major target and a feasible climb if you're reasonably fit and take your time.

Nairobi, at the southern edge of the highlands, is most often used just as a gateway, but the capital has plenty of diversions to occupy your time while arranging your travels and some very worthwhile natural and cultural attractions in its own right.

In the far west, towards **Lake Victoria**, lies gentler countryside, where you can travel for days without seeing another foreign visitor and immerse yourself in Kenyan life and culture. Beyond the rolling **tea plantations** of Kericho and the hot plains around the port of Kisumu lies the steep volcanic massif of **Mount Elgon**, astride the Ugandan

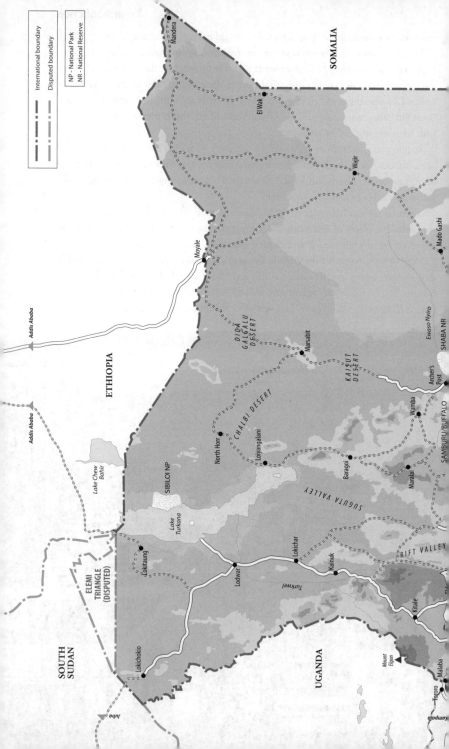

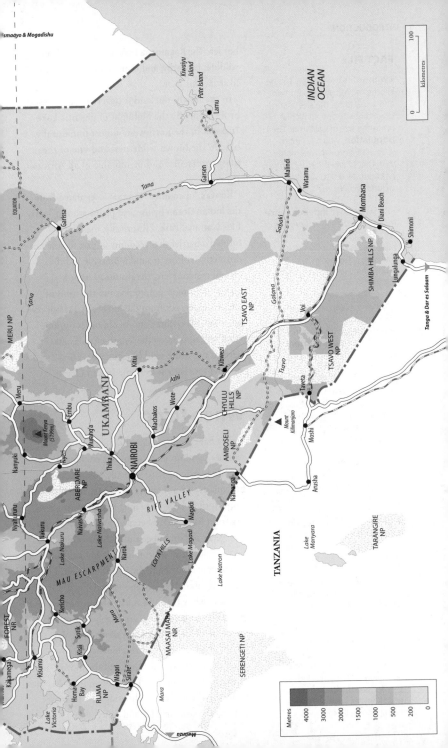

FACT FILE

• With an area of 580,400 square kilometres, Kenya is about two and a half times the size of the UK and nearly one and a half times the size of California. The **population**, which for many years had a growth rate higher than that of any other country, has now started to stabilize at around 40 million.

• Kenya regained **independence** in 1963 after nearly eighty years of British occupation and colonial rule. The Republic of Kenya is a multiparty democracy with more then twenty registered political parties.

• With few mineral resources (though potentially viable oil reserves were confirmed in 2012), most of the **foreign currency** Kenya needs for vital imports is earned from coffee and tea exports, and tourism. Most Kenyans scrape a living through subsistence agriculture and remittances from one or two family members in paid employment.

• Kenyan **society** consists of a huge, impoverished underclass, a small but growing middle class and a tiny elite whose success often owes much to nepotism and bribery. Unbridled **corruption** percolates every corner of the country and affects every aspect of the economy.

• More positively, around three out of four Kenyans has a **mobile phone**, an exceptionally high figure for a developing country. The mobile money service M-Pesa, allowing anyone with a mobile phone to send money to another phone user, is one of the most advanced in the world, and has transformed the lives of many poor Kenyans working far away from their families.

border. The **Kakamega Forest**, with its unique wildlife, is nearby, and more than enough reason to strike out west.

In the north, the land is **desert** or semi-desert, broken only by the highlight of gigantic **Lake Turkana** in the northwest, almost unnaturally blue in the brown wilderness and one of the most spectacular and memorable of all African regions.

Kenya's "upcountry" interior is separated from the **Indian Ocean** by the arid plains around Tsavo East National Park. Historically, these have formed a barrier that accounts in part for the distinctive culture around **Mombasa** and the coastal region. Here, the historical record, preserved in mosques, tombs and the ruins of ancient towns cut from the jungle, marks out the area's **Swahili civilization**. An almost continuous **coral reef** runs along the length of the coast, beyond the white-sand beaches, protecting a shallow, safe lagoon from the Indian Ocean.

When to go

Kenya has complicated and rather unpredictable weather patterns, and the impact of **climate change** is striking hard. Broadly, the seasons are: hot and dry from January to March; hot and wet from April to June (the "long rains"); warm and dry from July to October; and warm and wet for a few weeks in November and early December – a period called the "short rains". At high altitudes, it may rain at almost any time. Western Kenya has a scattered rainfall pattern influenced by Lake Victoria, while the eastern half of the country, and especially the coast itself, are largely controlled by the Indian Ocean's **monsoon winds** – the dry northeast monsoon (*kaskazi*) blowing in from November to March or April and the moist southeast monsoon (*kusi*) blowing in from May to October. The *kusi* normally brings the heaviest rains to the coast in May and June.

KENYA'S PEOPLES

For Kenya's forty-plus ethnic groups, the most important social marker is language and the best definition of a tribe (a term with no pejorative connotation) is people sharing a common first language. It's not uncommon for people to speak three languages – their own, Swahili and English – or even four if they have mixed parentage.

The largest tribe, the **Kikuyu**, based in the central highlands, make up about 20 percent of the population; the **Kalenjin** from the Rift Valley 15 percent; the **Luhya** of western Kenya 14 percent; the **Luo** from the Nyanza region around Kisumu 12 percent; and the **Kamba** from east of Nairobi 11 percent. Many people from these big ethnic groups have had a largely Westernized orientation for two or three generations and their economic and political influence is considerable. Which isn't to say you won't come across highly educated and articulate people from every tribal background. "Tribes" have never been closed units and families often include members of different ethnic background, nowadays more than ever. Politics still tends to have an ethnic dimension, however: people retain a strong sense of whether they are locals or newcomers. Inter-tribal prejudice, although often regarded as taboo, or at best an excuse for humour, is still quite commonplace and occasionally becomes violent.

Smaller ethnic groups include the closely related **Maasai** and **Samburu** peoples, who make up little more than two percent of the population. Well known for their distinctive and still commonly worn traditional dress and associated with the national reserves named after them, they herd their animals across vast reaches of savanna and, when access to water demands it, drive them onto private land and even into the big towns. Many **Turkana** and some of the other remote northern groups also retain their traditional garb and rather tooled-up appearance, with spears and other weapons much in evidence.

Kenya has a large and diverse **Asian** population (perhaps more than 100,000 people), predominantly Punjabi- and Gujarati-speakers from northwest India and Pakistan, mostly based in the cities and larger towns. Descendants in part of the labourers who came to build the Uganda railway, they also include many whose ancestors arrived in its wake, to trade and set up businesses. There's also a dispersed Christian Goan community, identified by their Portuguese surnames, and a diminishing **Arabic** community, largely on the coast.

Lastly, there are still an estimated 30,000 **European** residents – from British ex-servicemen to Italian aristocrats – and another 30,000 temporary expats. Some European Kenyans maintain a scaled-down version of the old farming and ranching life, and a few still hold senior civil service positions. Increasingly, however, the community is turning to the tourist industry for a more secure future.

AVERAGE DAILY TEMPERATURES AND RAINFALL

	Jan	Feb	Mar	Apr	May	Jun	Jul	Aug	Sep	Oct	Nov	Dec
NAIROBI (ALT 1660M)												
Max/min (°C)	25/12	26/13	25/14	24/14	22/13	21/12	21/11	21/11	24/11	24/13	23/13	23/13
Rainfall (mm)	38	64	125	211	158	46	15	23	31	53	109	86
Days with rainfall	5	6	11	16	17	9	6	7	6	8	15	11
MOMBASA (SEA LEVEL)												
Max/min (°C)	31/24	31/24	31/25	30/24	28/24	28/23	27/22	27/22	28/22	29/23	29/24	30/24
Rainfall (mm)	25	18	64	196	320	119	89	66	63	86	97	61
Days with rainfall	6	3	7	15	20	15	14	16	14	10	10	9
KISUMU (ALT 1135M)												
Max/min (°C)	29/18	29/19	28/19	28/18	27/18	27/17	27/17	27/17	28/17	29/18	29/18	29/18
Rainfall (mm)	48	81	140	191	155	84	58	76	64	56	86	102
Days with rainfall	6	8	12	14	14	9	8	10	8	7	9	8

Temperatures are determined largely by altitude: you can reckon on a drop of 0.6°C for every 100m you climb from sea level. While the temperature at sea level in Mombasa rarely ever drops below 20°C, even just before dawn, Nairobi, up at 1660m, has a moderate climate, and in the cool season in July and August can drop to 5°C at night, even though daytime highs in the shade at that time of year easily exceed 21°C and the sun is scorching hot. Swimming pools are rarely heated, and only those on the coast are guaranteed to be warm.

The main **tourist seasons** tie in with the rainfall patterns: the biggest influxes are in December–January and July–August. Dry-season travel has a number of advantages, not least of which is the greater visibility of wildlife as animals are concentrated along the diminishing watercourses. July and August are probably the best months, overall, for game-viewing, with August almost certain to coincide with the annual wildebeest migration in the Maasai Mara. October, November and March are the months with the clearest seas for snorkelling and diving. In the long rains, the mountain parks are occasionally closed, as the muddy tracks are undriveable. But the rainy seasons shouldn't deter travel unduly: the rains usually come only in short afternoon or evening cloudbursts, and the landscape is strikingly green and fresh even if the skies may be cloudy. There are bonuses, too: fewer other tourists and reduced accommodation prices.

KITENGELA GLASS, NAIROBI

Author picks

Author Richard Trillo first travelled around Kenya in the 1980s on a bicycle. Since then he's hitched on planes and lorries, driven Land Rovers and Suzukis, squashed into countless matatus and buses, and survived River Road, Mount Kenya, and the Lake Bogoria hot springs. He's no less adventurous today, and is never happier than when visiting somewhere new or trying something for the first time. Some of his favourite experiences and encounters include:

Exploring the mountains of the North Climbing from northern Kenya's arid plains into lush highland forests delivers you into a world of gushing streams and cool shade. **See p.527**

Nairobi nightlife Once a virtual no-go zone after dark, Nairobi's Central Business District has reignited at weekends, with dozens of clubs, bars and restaurants shaking until the early hours. **See p.131**

Umani Springs Relax at this affordable and beautifully designed self-catering lodge in the idyllic Kibwezi forest, just minutes from the rush of the Nairobi–Mombasa highway. **See p.322**

Kaya Kinondo The Mijikenda sacred groves are ancient sites in the coastal forest, preserving wildlife as well as cultural traditions. This is the first to open its secrets to visitors. **See p.433**

Nyama choma and beer at Magadi Swimming Pool Club Take a trip south of Nairobi and away from the tourist routes to Magadi soda lake and its excellent public pool. Then flesh out with a Kenyan meat feast. **See p.153**

Umoja Women's Group This cheap and friendly camping/*banda* site at Samburu, one of Kenya's most beautiful reserves, has an inspiring story behind it. **See p.376**

Kitengela Glass The sheer creative energy that emerges from this community of artisans and an endless supply of old bottles has to be seen to be believed. **See p.136**

Karura Forest An astonishingly large sanctuary of highland forest, close to the heart of Nairobi, Karura's stands of giant trees, caves and waterfall – recently opened to visitors – are just a short walk from the busy traffic. **See p.140**

Our author recommendations don't end here. We've flagged up our favourite places – a perfectly sited hotel, an atmospheric café, a special restaurant – throughout the guide, highlighted with the ★ symbol.

19

things not to miss

It's not possible to see everything that Kenya has to offer in one trip – and we don't suggest you try. What follows is a selective and subjective taste of some of the country's highlights, including standout experiences, spectacular sights and unexpected wildlife. All entries have a page reference taking you straight to the relevant place in the book, where you can find out more. The coloured numbers refer to regional chapters in the Guide section.

1 MOUNT KENYA
Page 167

Many climbers consider Africa's second-highest peak a tougher test than Kilimanjaro: it's certainly less of a highway to the top. You'll be glad of the new *via ferrata* on the last morning.

2 MARA NABOISHO CONSERVANCY
Page 369

The newest conservancy in the greater Mara region combines wildlife conservation with community involvement and offers outstanding viewing of big cats, elephants and giraffes.

3 THIMLICH OHINGA
Page 266

Even most Kenyans have never heard of their most impressive upcountry ancient site – huge stone circles in a remote part of western Kenya.

4 GRACEFUL HIPPOS
Page 344

The chain of lakes at Mzima Springs, fed by subterranean meltwater from Kilimanjaro, is a magical location in an exceptionally beautiful park – Tsavo West.

STARS AT BEDTIME
Book a night out in the bush under the stars, on a specially adapted "star bed" atop a secure platform.

LAKE BARINGO
The world record count of bird species seen in 24 hours – 342 – was made at this freshwater lake in the Rift Valley. There's budget accommodation on the shore and luxury lodges on the islands.

CHAMELEONS
These curious, harmless reptiles can be found all over Kenya, but only the highlands are home to the impressive Jackson's three-horn species, like a miniature triceratops.

FRESH COCONUTS
If you've never had a fresh coconut, you're in for a treat – try one at any coast hotel for the price of a tip to the intrepid tree climber.

LAKE TURKANA CULTURAL FESTIVAL
Join twelve local tribes for three days of traditional song and dance in a chilled, international atmosphere.

13

10 WARRIOR TRAINING
Page 369

Head to an eco-camp and learn the ways of Maasai warriorhood – which you'll soon discover involves playfighting with sticks and much singing and jumping.

11 LAKE NAIVASHA
Page 203

The perfect getaway from Nairobi: excellent backpackers' hostels, boating, a music festival, hippos and the secluded and atmospheric Green Crater Lake.

12 LOLLING IN THE LAGOON
Page 415

The Indian Ocean coast is sheltered by a coral reef for nearly its entire length: you can drift among shoals of fish or skim around on a kite- or surfboard.

13 NAIROBI NATIONAL PARK
Page 141

On the city's doorstep, the park is home to nearly all Kenya's big mammals, including the largest of Kenya's antelopes, the eland.

14 DESERT LAKE
Page 511

Venture to the shores of Lake Turkana in the barren lands close to the Ethiopian border where the climate is harsh, life precarious and the landscapes searingly beautiful.

14

Itineraries

The following itineraries include the biggest and most important parks and lakes as well as some little-known gems, plus the highlands and the northern deserts. Join them together – by public transport, in a rental car, or on a tailor-made safari – and you'd have an unforgettable ten-week tour of the country, taking in wildlife, energetic towns and a clutch of reef-protected beaches. NP: National Park; NR: National Reserve.

NORTHERN FRONTIERS

From the capital's contrasts to the highs and lows of the highlands, this route is about extremes – nowhere more so than where the Jade Sea cuts through the desert. Allow two to four weeks for some or all of this loop.

❶ Nairobi Wildlife, parks and forests bring balance to East Africa's biggest city, where urban life – from museums and crafts workshops to cutting-edge restaurants and clubs – sets the agenda. **See p.96**

❷ Mount Kenya NP Scale Africa's second-highest peak on one of four different routes, but take time to enjoy the wildlife-rich forests and frenetically active towns on the lower slopes. **See p.167**

❸ Laikipia Challenging the Maasai Mara as Kenya's best wildlife destination, Laikipia offers rare rhinos and opulent conservancy stays as well as wild dog-tracking and budget camping. **See p.500**

❹ Maralal This semi-desert, alternately dusty and muddy cowboy outpost, the unofficial capital of the Samburu people, hosts an annual camel derby. **See p.520**

❺ Samburu NR Watered by the forest-fringed Ewaso Nyiro, this is a relaxing area to encounter northern wildlife – from reticulated giraffe to Somali ostrich. **See p.374**

❻ Marsabit NP A true desert oasis, this mountainous outburst of volcanic craters and rich soil stands thick with misty, creeper-swathed forest. **See p.542**

❼ Lake Turkana Getting to the fabled Jade Sea is half the fun, but the annual Lake Turkana Festival is a huge incentive. And at any time of year, expect colourful cultural adventures. **See p.511**

WESTERN LAKES, SAVANNAS AND FORESTS

Strike out across the Great Rift Valley to freshwater and soda lakes, then climb to the Mara basin's rolling grasslands, one of the last rainforests in Kenya and giant Lake Victoria. Some of this journey could be done in a fortnight, but allow three weeks to do it all.

❶ Lake Naivasha Head into the Rift Valley for a breezy escape from Nairobi, with country retreats and backpackers' camps and walks in Hell's Gate and austere Mount Longonot. **See p.203**

❷ Maasai Mara NR Only in the Mara can you experience a wildlife panorama stretching from horizon to horizon. Stay on a community wildlife conservancy and see the herds without the crowds. **See p.354**

❸ Lake Victoria Spend a day or two in characterful Kisumu and catch musicians and markets. Then head for one of the islands to see rock paintings and watch fishermen. **See p.251**

ABOVE FROM LEFT FORT JESUS, MOMBASA; RETICULATED GIRAFFES, SAMBURU NR; FISHING BOATS ON LAKE VICTORIA

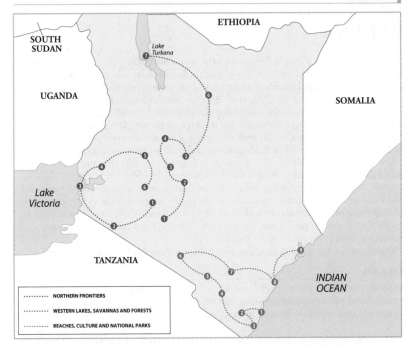

○ Kakamega Forest NP The bird and reptile hotspot of western Kenya, this stranded piece of central African rainforest is a joy for independent travellers. **See p.303**

○ Lake Baringo On one side the changing lake colours, crocs and hippos and Njemps fishermen of the lake; on the other the green lawns, backpacker haunts and safari camps of the shores and islands. **See p.236**

○ Lake Nakuru NP This Rift Valley soda lake is famous for black and white rhinos, leopards and (sometimes vast) flocks of flamingos. **See p.222**

BEACHES, CULTURE AND NATIONAL PARKS

Historic sites dot Kenya's coast behind the coral beaches, while inland, vast national parks offer the classic safari experience. Allow three weeks for this loop, and don't stint on days in Lamu.

❶ Mombasa This island city, dating back more than a thousand years, is best explored on foot. Don't miss Fort Jesus Museum and the narrow streets of the Old Town. **See p.388**

❷ Shimba Hills A park of forested hills – Shimba is the only place to see sable antelope in Kenya – is less than an hour's drive from shimmering Diani Beach. **See p.424**

❸ Kaya Kinondo The first Mijikenda sacred forest to be opened to visitors, this hidden jungle treat is packed with buttress-rooted trees and woodland wildlife. **See p.433**

❹ Taita Hills Off the tourist routes, the people of these fertile peaks have preserved some of their culture – including fascinating caves of ancestors' skulls. **See p.329**

❺ Tsavo West NP Prepare to be enchanted by Tsavo's landscapes, including lava flows and the magical Mzima Springs. **See p.342**

❻ Amboseli NP Magnificent Kilimanjaro rises behind plains and marshes roamed by huge herds of elephants and other wildlife. **See p.334**

❼ Tsavo East NP Kenya's biggest national park is home to brick-red elephants, lions and cheetahs, crocs, hippos and superb birdlife. **See p.348**

❽ Malindi Diving, kitesurfing, eating out and nightlife are all big here, and it's close to the small resort of Watamu and fascinating Gedi ruins. **See p.460**

❾ Lamu A cultural as well as a physical island, Lamu's unmissable combination of historic town and laidback beaches is the best place to finish a Kenya trip. **See p.472**

Wildlife

Kenya has more than a hundred species of large, native **mammals** and its plains are home to the world's last surviving community of megafauna: the giant animals – including elephant, rhino, lion and giraffe – that dominated the earth approximately one to two million years ago. The so-called "Big Five" (elephant, black rhino, buffalo, lion and leopard) were the hunter's trophies of the early twentieth century, but are still a fixation in the minds of many driver-guides and their clients. But don't ignore the less glamorous animals: there can be just as much satisfaction in spotting a serval or an uncommon antelope, or in noting rarely observed behaviour, as in ticking off one of the more obvious status symbols.

This field guide provides a quick reference to help you identify the larger mammals you're likely to encounter in Kenya – and despite huge losses since the early twentieth century, Kenya still teems with wildlife. While visiting some of the country's forty-odd parks and reserves can almost guarantee sightings, if you travel fairly widely, even outside the parks, you're almost certain to see various gazelles and antelopes, zebra and giraffe – and even hippo, buffalo and elephant. Monkeys and baboons can be seen almost anywhere and are a regular menace.

Swahili names are given in brackets. NP: National Park; NR: National Reserve.

BIG CATS

Kenya's **big cats** are some of the most exciting and easily recognizable animals you'll see. Although often portrayed as fearsome hunters, pulling down plains game after a chase, many species do a fair bit of scavenging and all are content to eat smaller fry when conditions dictate or the opportunity arises.

LION *(SIMBA) PANTHERA LEO*

Of the large cats, lions are the easiest species to find. Lazy, gregarious and very large – up to 1.8m in length, not counting the tail, and up to 1m high at the shoulder – they rarely make much effort to hide or to move away. They can be seen in nearly all the parks and reserves, and their presence is generally the main consideration in determining whether you're allowed out of your vehicle or not. "Man-eating" lions appear from time to time but seem to be one-off misfits. Normally, lions live in prides of three to forty (usually six to twelve) hunting cooperatively, in the day as well as at night, preferring to kill very young, old or sick animals, and making a kill roughly once in every two attacks. They will happily steal the kills of cheetahs or hyenas. Lions can manage in most habitats, except desert and thick forest, but habitat disturbance can cause them to move into pastoral areas where they often kill goats or cattle and are then killed in turn by herding communities. With fewer than 2000 lions left in Kenya, the problem of keeping *Panthera leo* and *Homo*

sapiens apart is a daily struggle for the Kenya Wildlife Service.

LEOPARD *(CHUI) PANTHERA PARDUS*

Possibly the most feared animals in Kenya, and intensely secretive, alert and wary, leopards live – usually solitarily – all across the country except in the most treeless zones. Their unmistakeable call, which sounds something like a big hand saw being pulled back and forth, is unforgettable. Although often diurnal in the parks, they are strictly nocturnal wherever there is human pressure: they sometimes survive on the outskirts of villages, carefully choosing their prey to avoid a routine. They tolerate nearby human habitation and rarely kill people unprovoked. For the most part, leopards live off any small animals that come their way, pouncing from an ambush and dragging the kill up into a tree where it may be consumed over several days – the so-called "leopard's larder". Melanistic leopards are known as black panthers, and seem to be more common in highland areas, such as Mount Kenya and the Aberdare range.

SMALLER CATS

CHEETAH *(DUMA) ACINONYX JUBATUS*

In the flesh, the cheetah is so different from the leopard, it's hard to see how there could ever be any confusion. Cheetahs are lightly built, finely spotted, with very long legs, small heads and a dark "tear mark" running from eye to jowl. Unlike leopards, which are highly arboreal, cheetahs rarely climb trees – though where accustomed to

vehicles, they climb on them to scan the horizon. They live alone, or sometimes briefly form a pair during mating. Hunting, too, is normally a solitary activity, dependent on eyesight and an incredible burst of speed that can take the animal up to 100kph (70mph) for a few seconds. Cheetahs can be seen in any of Kenya's large parks, and are usually out and about during the day.

SERVAL *(MONDO) FELIS SERVAL*

The beautiful part-spotted, part-striped serval is found in most of the parks, though it's uncommon and always a special sighting. They normally prefer reed beds or tall grassland near water, and while often nocturnal and solitary, they can sometimes be seen setting off on hunting forays on roadsides or at water margins at dawn or dusk.

CARACAL *(SIMBA MANGU) CARACAL CARACAL*

The aggressive, tuft-eared caracal resembles a lynx, but is more closely related to the serval and the even rarer golden cat. They are seen quite rarely, and while occasionally arboreal, they tend to favour open bush and plains in dry-country zones like Tsavo East NP and Samburu NR. A night drive, however, is the most likely way of seeing one.

SMALLER PREDATORS

GENET *(KANU) GENETTA GENETTA*

Once encountered, never forgotten, the beautifully marked, sinuous genet thrives in light bush country and even arid areas. It's a fairly common, slender, cat-sized, partly arboreal hunter, with short legs and a very long tail. Reminiscent of an elongated domestic cat, they were in fact once domesticated around the Mediterranean, but cats proved better mouse-hunters. You'll often see genets at game lodges, where they frequently become habituated to humans and can be found draped on a rafter above the bar, or mincing along a deck rail.

AFRICAN CIVET *(FUNGO) CIVETTICTIS CIVETTA*

A curious, short-legged, terrestrial prowler, about the size of a small dog, the civet is not to be confused with the smaller genet. And while genets are most likely to be seen around lodges, the civet is a solitary nocturnal omnivore that prefers to keep close to woodland and dense vegetation. They're not often seen, but they are predictable creatures that wend their way along the same paths at the same time, night after night, so if there's one in the neighbourhood, you'll see it.

HONEY BADGER *(NYEGERE) MELLIVORA CAPENSIS*

Also known as the ratel, this widespread, omnivorous, badger-sized animal is notoriously aggressive, even to humans. They sometimes encounter people when raiding beehives or scavenging rubbish dumps – giving rise to one of the possible sources for the myth of the Nandi Bear (see p.284). Honey badgers tolerate a very broad range of habitats, are mainly nocturnal and are usually solitary, although they can also be found in pairs. Primarily an omnivorous forager, they will tear open bees' nests (to which they are led by a small bird, the honey guide), their thick, loose hides rendering them impervious to the stings.

DWARF MONGOOSE *(KITAFE) HELOGALE PARVULA*

An unmistakeable group of animals, made famous by their cutest member, the meerkat (which isn't found in Kenya), mongooses are often seen and always delightful to watch. The main Kenyan species, in order of size, are the dwarf, black-tipped or slender (*Galerella sanguinea*), banded (*Nguchiro; Mungos mungo*), large grey (*Herpestes ichneumon*) and white-tailed (*Kicheche; Ichneumia albicauda*), which is a good-sized, shaggy beast, with surprisingly long legs. Mongooses' snake-fighting reputation is greatly overplayed: in practice they are mostly social foragers, fanning out through the bush like beaters on a shoot, hunting out anything edible – mostly invertebrates, eggs, lizards and frogs.

KENYA'S WILDLIFE WEBSITES

East African Wildlife Society ⓦeawildlife.org. Influential Kenya-based group, centrally involved in the movement to ban the ivory trade. Publishes the excellent Swara magazine.

Ecotourism Society of Kenya ⓦecotourismkenya.org. This local organization promotes sustainable tourism by awarding ratings to lodges, tented camps and tour operators.

Friends of Nairobi National Park ⓦfonnap.wordpress.com. Works to keep open the migration route into the park, and raise awareness about the remarkable environment on Nairobi's doorstep.

Green Belt Movement ⓦgreenbeltmovement.org. Grassroots conservation and women's movement founded by the Nobel Peace Prize winner Wangari Maathai, who died in 2011.

Kenya Forests Working Group ⓦkenyaforests.org. Promotes sound forest management and conservation.

Nature Kenya ⓦnaturekenya.org. The website of the East African Natural History Society organizes regular activities and has a good online newsletter.

Wildlife Direct ⓦwildlifedirect.org. Chaired by Richard Leakey, this is where conservation fundraising meets a network of conservationists, including more than 50 bloggers from the field in Kenya.

---

1 GENET; 2 AFRICAN CIVET; 3 HONEY BADGER; 4 DWARF MONGOOSE >

DOGS AND ALLIED SPECIES

AFRICAN HUNTING DOG *(MBWA MWITU)*
LYCAON PICTUS

The unusual and rather magnificent hunting dog is still extremely rare in Kenya, having been present in reasonable numbers 50 years ago. Its decline was partly due to canine distemper and partly because of human predation and habitat disruption. The good news is that hunting dogs, also known as wild dogs or painted dogs, seem to be on the increase. There are now quite a few packs around the country, and in the last couple of years they have been spotted in the Maasai Mara NR and neighbouring conservancies, in Tsavo West NP and even in Lake Nakuru NP, as well as in the Laikipia range lands where they have held out for decades. They are diurnal, highly nomadic and can range hundreds of kilometres, but if the opportunity exists to see them you'll hear about it.

BLACK-BACKED JACKAL *(BWEHA) CANIS MESOMELAS*

The commonest members of the dog family in Kenya are the black-backed and side-striped jackal. Both species can be seen just about anywhere, usually in pairs, in a broad range of habitats from moist mountain regions to desert, but drier areas are preferred. The black-backed jackal has a distinctive dark "saddle" flecked with white, so it's sometimes known as the silver-backed jackal. Although they usually live in pairs, you can often see family packs of these smartly coated canids playing in and around their dens, and even hunting – a much more common activity than the scavenging after lions with which they're normally associated. The shyer side-striped jackal (*C. adustus*) has smaller ears and a lateral stripe that can be more or less distinctive, while the unmarked golden or common jackal (*C. aureus*) is otherwise very similar, though in Kenya it is mostly restricted to the Maasai Mara and Laikipia.

SPOTTED HYENA *(FISI MADOA) CROCUTA CROCUTA*

Kenya's biggest carnivore after the lion is the spotted hyena; it is also, apart from the lion, the meat-eater you will most often see. Although considered a scavenger *par excellence*, the spotted hyena is a formidable hunter, most often found where antelopes and zebras are present. Highly social, usually living in extended family groups,

spotted hyenas are exceptionally efficient consumers, with immensely strong teeth and jaws, and they eat virtually every part of their prey, including hide and bones (which explains their distinctive, white droppings). Where habituated to humans, they sometimes steal leather shoes, unwashed pans and trash from tents and villages. Although they can be seen by day, they are most often active at night – when they issue their unnerving, whooping cries. Clans of twenty or so animals are dominated by females, which are larger than the males and compete with each other for rank. Curiously, female hyenas' genitalia are hard to distinguish from males', leading to a popular misconception that they are hermaphroditic. Not surprisingly, in view of all their attributes, the hyena is a key figure in local mythology and folklore.

STRIPED HYENA *(FISI MIRABA) HYAENA HYAENA*

Shy, solitary, largely silent and infrequently seen, the striped hyena is a shyer and less common animal than its spotted cousin, although apparently widespread in dry country and occasionally glimpsed very early in the morning trotting along park roads. The stripes can be a good identification guide, but the most obvious identifier is the pointed ears and erect mane of hair or crest along the shoulders.

AARDWOLF *(FISI NDOGO) PROTELES CRISTATA*

This is a much smaller hyena cousin, though it's easily mistaken for a small striped hyena. Widespread but shy and largely nocturnal, it lives all over Kenya, wherever it can find its unusual food supply – harvester termites and other insects, for which it forages solitarily while usually pairing for life.

BAT-EARED FOX *(MBWEHA MASIKIO) OTOCYON MEGALOTIS*

Bat-eared foxes aren't uncommon, and they're unmistakeable in appearance. Their distribution coincides with that of termites – their favoured diet. Monogamous pairs spend many hours every night foraging, using their sensitive hearing to pinpoint their underground prey. In the cooler months they can also be seen out and about during the day.

ELEPHANTS AND HIPPOS

AFRICAN ELEPHANT *(NDOVU) LOXODONTA AFRICANA*

Elephants are found throughout Kenya: almost all the big mountain and plains parks have their populations. These are the most engaging of animals to watch – their interactions, behaviour patterns and even individual personalities have so many human parallels. Babies are born after a 22-month gestation, with other cows in close attendance. A calf will suckle for up to three years, from the mother's two breasts between her front legs, and grows from helpless infancy, through self-conscious adolescence, to adulthood. The basic family unit is a group of related females, tightly protecting their babies and young, and led by a venerable matriarch. It's the matriarch that is most likely to bluff a charge, and occasionally she may get carried away and actually tusk a vehicle or person. Seen in the flesh, elephants seem even bigger than you would imagine – you'll need little persuasion from those flapping, warning ears to back off if you're too close – but they are at the same time surprisingly graceful, silent animals on their padded, carefully placed feet. In a matter of moments, a large herd can merge into the trees and disappear, their presence betrayed only by the noisy cracking of branches as they strip trees and uproot saplings. Old animals die in their seventies or eighties, when their last set of teeth wears out and they can no longer feed. Grieving elephants pay much attention to the disposal of their dead relatives, often dispersing the bones and spending time near the remains.

HIPPOPOTAMUS *(KIBOKO) HIPPOPOTAMUS AMPHIBIUS*

Hippopotamuses are highly adaptable and found wherever rivers or lakes are deep enough for them to submerge and have a surrounding of suitable grazing grass – from the humid estuary of the Tana River to the chilly mountain district of Nyahururu, including briny Lake Nakuru in the central Rift Valley and saline Lake Turkana in the semi-desert of the northwest. They spend most of the day in water to protect their thin, hairless skin from dehydration. After dark, they move onto land and spend the whole night grazing, often walking up to 10km in one session. In the Maasai Mara, they wander across the savanna; at Lake Naivasha they plod through farms and gardens; and everywhere they are rightly feared. Hippos are reckoned to be responsible for more human deaths in Africa than any other large animal (mosquitoes being by far the most deadly). Deaths occur mostly on water, when boats accidentally steer into hippo pods, but they can be aggressive on land, too, charging and slashing with their fearsomely long incisors. They can run at 30km/h if necessary and have a small turning circle. Although uncertain on land (hence their aggression when cornered), they are supremely adapted to long periods in water. Their nostrils, eyes and ears are in exactly the right places and their clumsy feet become supple paddles – as can be seen, if you're lucky, from the underwater observatory at Mzima Springs in Tsavo West National Park.

ELEPHANTS AND THE ENVIRONMENT

Local overpopulation of **elephants** is usually the result of old migration routes being cut off, forcing the elephants into reserves – like the Maasai Mara and its neighbouring conservancies – where their massive appetites can appear destructive. Adults may consume up to 170kg of plant material daily, so it's estimated that several thousand tonnes of foliage pass through the Maasai Mara elephant population's collective gut each month. This foliage destruction puts new life into the soil, however, as acacia seeds dunged by elephants are released when dung beetles tackle the football-sized droppings, breaking them into pellets and pulling them into their burrows where the seeds germinate. Elephants also dig up dried-out waterholes with their tusks, providing moisture for other animals. Elephants are **architects of their environment**, setting the inter-species agenda by knocking over trees, creating deadwood habitats for invertebrates and causing hundreds of other impacts, all of which are natural functions in a dynamic ecosystem. The jury is still out on how it works when the wildlife corridors are closed, or the parks fenced in. What is not in doubt is that their **ivory** is increasingly valuable and poaching is on the rise again (see p.350). And when they are closely managed and secured in safe sanctuaries, the elephant populations quickly reach unsustainable levels. The Kenya Wildlife Service is getting proficient at translocating elephants, moving them around to balance the numbers.

RHINOS

There are two, highly endangered species of rhinoceros in Africa, the hook-lipped or **black rhino**, and the much heavier wide-lipped or **white rhino**, which has two distinct subspecies, southern and northern white rhinos. The shape of their lips is far more significant than any colour difference, as it indicates their respective diets (browsing for the black rhino, grazing for the white) and favoured habitats (thick bush and open grassland respectively). Both species give birth to a single calf, after a gestation period of fifteen to eighteen months, and the baby is not weaned until it is at least a year or sometimes two years old. With a calf only every three to four years, their population growth rate is slow compared with most animals – another factor contributing to their rarity.

BLACK RHINOCEROS *(FARU OR KIFARU) DICEROS BICORNIS*

Black rhinos, which are slightly smaller than white, were a fairly common sight in most of Kenya's parks until the early 1970s. Amboseli, for example, had hundreds of magnificent black rhinos, some with graceful, upper horns more than 1m in length. But poaching decimated the population (see p.350), and today there are around six hundred black rhinos in Kenya, distributed between Nairobi, Lake Nakuru, Aberdare, Meru and Tsavo West national parks, Maasai Mara NR, and increasingly in the Laikipia conservancies. Black rhinos prefer thick bush, at altitudes up to 3500m. They are solitary and active day and night, taking rests between periods of activity. Notoriously bad-tempered, they have good hearing and sensitive smell, but bad eyesight, making them dangerous at close quarters.

WHITE RHINOCEROS *(FARU OR KIFARU) CERATOTHERIUM SIMUM*

Native northern white rhinos ("white" from the Afrikaans *wijd* for the wide mouth) have been extinct for several hundred years in Kenya, but reintroduced southern white rhinos, mostly from South Africa, can be seen in several parks and wildlife sanctuaries. At Ol Pejeta in Laikipia, Kenya also has four of the world's last seven northern white rhinos, brought here from a Czech zoo in 2009, and it's hoped the subspecies can be saved here. Docile grazers, white rhinos are a savanna species, active day and night like black rhinos. Males tend to be solitary, but females often cluster in small same-sex herds or nursery groups.

ZEBRAS

PLAINS OR BURCHELL'S ZEBRA *(PUNDA MILIA) EQUUS BURCHELLI GRANTI*

The plains zebra (the Kenya subspecies, is called Grant's) has thick stripes and small ears and is found in savanna in most parts of Kenya up to about 4000m. In the far north, they tend to have a very short mane. In Tsavo West and other parts of southern Kenya, they often exhibit the "shadow striping" typical of the species in southern Africa, with fawn stripes alternating between the black ones. Their usual social set-up is a harem of several mares and foals led by a dominant stallion, active day and night, resting intermittently. In Amboseli and Maasai Mara, they gather in migrating herds several thousand strong, along with wildebeest and other grazers.

GREVY'S ZEBRA *(PUNDA MILIA) EQUUS GREVYI*

Grevy's zebra is a large, fairly rare equid with very fine stripes and big, saucer-like ears, restricted to arid regions in Tsavo East and the northern parks and reserves. These zebras are largely diurnal and live in small territorial herds. Mares with foals and stallions generally keep to separate troops.

PIGS

WARTHOG *(NGIRI OR GWASI) PHACOCHOERUS AETHIOPICUS*

The commonest wild pig in Kenya is the warthog, seen all over the country at altitudes up to 2000m. Flighty and nervous, warthogs are notoriously hard to photograph as they're generally on the run through the bush, tails erect, often with their young in single file. They shelter in tunnels (often using old aardvark burrows), and live in family groups, usually of a mother and her litter of two to four piglets. They're diurnal, and principally grazers of grass and herbs, though they also root for tubers. Boars join the group to mate, and are easily distinguished from sows by their big warts, which protect their heads during fights.

BUSH PIG *(NGURUWE MWITU) POTAMOCHOERUS PORCUS*

Two nocturnal pigs, both much rarer than the warthog, are also found in Kenya. The red river hog or bush pig, which resembles a long-haired domestic pig with tasselled hair on its ears and a white-crested back, is found in dense forest, close to agriculture and river margins, and lives in groups of up to twenty pigs. The huge, dark-coloured giant forest hog (*Hylochoerus meinertzhageni*), is a bristly, big-tusked pig that lives in the highlands and is very occasionally seen from tree hotels on Mount Kenya or the Aberdare range.

GIRAFFES

The tallest mammals on earth, **giraffes** are relatively common and unmistakeable and found widely across Kenya in wooded savanna and thorn country. Mild-mannered and non-territorial, they gather in loose, leaderless herds and spend the day browsing on the leaves of trees too high for other species (acacias are favourites), while at night they lie down and ruminate. Bulls test their strength while in bachelor herds by "necking" – using their powerful necks like broadswords. When a female is in heat, which can happen at any time of year, the dominant male mates with her. She gives birth after a gestation of around fourteen months. More than half of all young fall prey to lions or hyenas in their early years.

GIRAFFE *(TWIGA) GIRAFFA CAMELOPARDALIS*

Kenya has three types of giraffe, differentiated from each other by their pattern and the configuration of their short horns. Most often seen is the Maasai giraffe (*G. c. tippelskirchi*), with two horns and a very broken pattern of dark blotches on a buff or fawn background. This is the giraffe you will see in Maasai Mara, Amboseli and Tsavo West. In northern Kenya, and eastern Kenya roughly northeast of the Tana River, lives the dramatically patterned reticulated giraffe, which normally has three or five horns and boldly defined chestnut patches on a very pale background. The reticulated subspecies (*G. c. reticulata*) is seen in the Samburu reserves, Meru NP and Lewa and Ol Pejeta in Laikipia. The more solidly built Rothschild giraffe (*G. c. rothschildi*) which has a pattern more like crazy paving (also with well-defined blotches), plain white lower legs, like socks, and usually two horns, is largely restricted in Kenya to Lake Nakuru NP and the Nairobi Giraffe Centre. They all appear able to interbreed, but because they are geographically separated, they very rarely do. There is disagreement among zoologists over whether any of the giraffe's subspecies should be accorded the status of separate species – particularly concerning the reticulated giraffe – but some, like the Rothschild, are extremely rare and in need of protection.

WILDEBEEST AND RELATIVES

The rather ungainly **hartebeest** family includes one of Kenya's rarest antelopes, the hirola or Hunter's hartebeest (*Damaliscus hunteri*) of the lower Tana River. The Coke's hartebeest, however, is found widely in southern Kenya, and topi are practically emblematic of the Maasai Mara, their main habitat. The **wildebeest** is also particularly associated with the Mara.

COKE'S HARTEBEEST *(KONGONI) ALCELAPHUS BUSELAPHUS COKII*

Hard to confuse with any other antelope except the topi, the Hartebeest has several subspecies, distinguishable by horn shape, two of which live in Kenya – Coke's and Jackson's (*A.b. jacksoni*), which is darker and lives only in western Kenya. Coke's hartebeests live in a wide range of grassy habitats. They're diurnal and the females and calves live in small, wandering herds, while the territorial males are solitary.

TOPI *(NYAMERA) DAMALISCUS LUNATUS*

An extremely fast runner, once it accelerates out of bouncy, hartebeest gear, the topi is largely restricted in Kenya to the Maasai Mara, where the subspecies (one of four found across the continent) is *D. l. jimela*. They show a marked preference for moist savanna grasslands, near water, and the females and young form herds with an old male. These male topis are very characteristic of the Mara landscape: often seen standing sentry on abandoned termite hills, they're actually marking their territories against rival males, rather than nobly defending the herd against predators.

BLUE WILDEBEEST OR BRINDLED GNU *(NYUMBU) CONNOCHAETES TAURINUS*

With its long tail, mane and beard, the blue wildebeest is an unmistakeable, nomadic grazer. An intensely gregarious animal, it lives in a variety of associations within "mega-herds" that can number more than a million animals. During the breeding season, the territorial bulls gather cows into their areas and defend their harems against rivals. Strictly grazers, dependent on pasture and preferring short grass, they are always found near water. It is that dependence that drives their continuous migration, forming mega-herds that shape into columns of animals to follow each other on the scent of new grass, only to dissolve and spread out again when good grazing is reached. With the East African climate changing rapidly, their movements are less and less regular, and hundreds of thousands of wildebeest can be months "early" or "late" in locations along the route that was typical of the mid-twentieth century.

GAZELLES AND ALLIED SPECIES

THOMSON'S GAZELLE (SWALA TOMI) GAZELLA THOMSONI

The most obvious of the gazelles, the Thomson's gazelle is smaller than the similar Grant's, and distinguished by the black band on its flank. The female has tiny horns. This gregarious, diurnal grazer prefers flat, short-grass savanna near water, and is quite often seen at the roadside in southern Kenya. Thomson's gazelles live in a wide variety of social structures, often massing in the hundreds with other grazers.

GRANT'S GAZELLE (SWALA GRANTI) GAZELLA GRANTI

Larger than the very similar Thomson's gazelle, Grant's is distinguished from it by the white rump patch which extends onto the back. The female's horns are smaller than the male's but not the tiny spikes of female "Thommies". Grant's gazelles thrive on wide grassy plains with good visibility, where they live in small, territorial harems. They can range much further from water than Thomson's, and their geographic range extends further north to encompass the northern parks of Samburu and Meru where Thommies are absent.

GERENUK (SWALA TWIGA) LITOCRANIUS WALLERI

The unmistakeable gerenuk is an unusual browsing gazelle able to nibble from bushes standing on its hind legs (its name means "giraffe-necked" in Somali). Although considered an arid-land specialist, its range encompasses most of Kenya east of the Rift Valley and it's not uncommon. Gerenuks are usually solitary or live in small, territorial harems. Females are hornless.

IMPALA (SWALA PALA) AEPYCEROS MELAMPUS

The impala, although technically not one of the gazelles, is closely related to them and common in many parts of Kenya. The only antelope with a black tuft above the hooves, the males have long, lyre-shaped horns and the females are hornless. Usually found in open savanna with light woodland cover, impalas are diurnal and make distinctive, high, graceful leaps when fleeing danger. Females live grouped together in large herds that overlap with several male territories. During the breeding season, the males become territorial and separate out breeding harems of up to twenty females, which they vigorously defend from rivals.

GRAZING ANTELOPES, REEDBUCKS AND WATERBUCKS

ORYX (CHOROA) ORYX GAZELLA CALLOTIS

Ranging from open grasslands into waterless wastelands, and tolerant of prolonged drought, this distinctive, rapier-horned antelope is nocturnal as well as diurnal. They live in highly hierarchical mixed herds of up to fifteen, led by a dominant bull. The O. g. callotis subspecies, which lives in Tsavo and Amboseli, is easily distinguished by its luxuriantly tufted ears from the Beisa oryx (O. g. beisa), found in northern Kenya.

SABLE ANTELOPE (PALAHALA) HIPPOTRAGUS NIGER

This very large, handsome antelope lives only in Shimba Hills NP, inland from the south coast. Here it finds its preferred mix of open woodland and tall grassland near water. Sables are hard to confuse with any other antelope:

the females are tan-coloured while the males are glossy black, and both have white bellies and facial markings, stiff manes and huge curved horns that reach 1m or more in length in the males. Active by day and night, sable antelopes live in territorial herds of females and young, dominated in breeding season by the bulls.

ROAN ANTELOPE (KIRONGO) HIPPOTRAGUS EQUINUS

The massive roan antelope, a close relative of the sable but with much shorter horns, is fairly common in much of west and south-central Africa, but restricted in Kenya to Ruma NP south of Kisumu – a sanctuary of tall grassland with plenty of water. Small herds are usually led by a dominant bull, but immature bachelor herds and seasonal pairs are also common.

WATERBUCKS AND REEDBUCKS

COMMON OR BOHOR REEDBUCK (TOHE) REDUNCA ARUNDINUM

Reedbucks and waterbucks are related, and both spend much time in or near water. The medium-sized common reedbuck has a patchy distribution in southern Kenya, living in monogamous pairs or family groups in territories defended by the (horned) male. They subsist on a specialist plant diet that is generally unpalatable to other herbivores.

WATERBUCK (KURO) KOBUS ELLIPSIPRYMNUS

The rather deer-like waterbuck is relatively common in many

parts of central and southern Kenya, living in open woodland and savanna, near water. There are two subspecies in Kenya: the ringed waterbuck, east of the Rift Valley, which has a white circle on its rump, and the Defassa waterbuck of western Kenya, whose rump is solid white. They are large antelopes, with a tendency to look a bit shaggy and unkempt, and like the reedbuck, its plant diet is unpalatable to other grazers (and can give it a distinctive smell, according to some authorities). Only the males have horns, and they either lead a territorial herd of females and young or maintain a territory that is visited by wandering female herds.

1 THOMSON'S GAZELLE; 2 GRANT'S GAZELLE; 3 IMPALA; 4 ORYX; 5 SABLE ANTELOPE; 6 GERENUK; 7 COMMON REEDBUCK;
8 RINGED WATERBUCK; 9 ROAN ANTELOPE >

DWARF ANTELOPES

KIRK'S DIK-DIK *(DIGIDIGI OR DIKA) MADOQUA KIRKII*

Found all over Kenya, Kirk's dik-dik measures no more than 40cm at the shoulder, and usually pairs for life. You frequently see pairs of this hare-sized antelope, named after its alarm cry, at the roadside in national parks and reserves, and all over Laikipia and northern Kenya. They have quite a distinctive, swollen snout that looks like the beginning of a short trunk. Adults are sometimes accompanied by a single youngster, and occasionally by an older sibling too. If you do a bush walk, you'll come across their territorial boundaries, marked by piles of droppings and black secretions from their facial glands, deposited on grass stems like tiny drops of engine oil.

SUNI *(SUNI) NEOTRAGUS MOSCHATUS*

The suni is much less common than the dik-dik, and frequently mistaken for it, though it is even smaller, at just 35cm, and doesn't have the dik-dik's proboscis. Like the dik-dik, they live in monogamous pairs, sometimes with additional non-breeding females forming a small group. They can be encountered almost anywhere there's good, dry forest cover, but their distribution is extremely patchy: forested coastal hills have the largest populations. Sunis tend to be nocturnal and crepuscular, hiding in shade by day, and will habitually freeze when threatened or surprised, before darting into the undergrowth.

SHARPE'S GRYSBOK *(DONDOO OR DONDORO) RAPHICERUS SHARPEI*

This is a rarely seen antelope, around 50cm high at the shoulder. It's distinguished from the slenderer steenbok by its light underparts. Only the males have short horns, using them to defend their territories. They pair loosely, not monogamously or for life, and are most likely to be seen in dense thicket adjacent to open grassland where they rest during the day and feed by night.

ORIBI *(KASIA) OUREBIA OUREBIA*

This small antelope (the biggest of this group at about 60cm at the shoulder) is patchily distributed in Kenya, mostly in the southwest and the coast north of the Tana, but it's not hard to see where common as it's diurnal and favours open grassland. The oribi is distinguished from the smaller grysbok and steenbok by a black tail and dark skin patch, like a stain, below the eye. Their territorial harems consist of one to four females led by a horned male. Males are noted for their charming foreplay: when the female is in heat, the male pushes his head under her hindquarters and shoves her along on her forelegs like a wheelbarrow.

KLIPSPRINGER *(MBUZI MAWE) OREOTRAGUS OREOTRAGUS*

With their raised hooves wonderfully adapted for scaling near-vertical rock faces ("rock goat" is the translation of their Swahili name), klipspringers are a distinctive sight in many rockier parts of the country, or wherever there are cliffs and *kopjes*. Being browsers, and not dependent on pasture, they can often be seen far from water in remote, desolate districts, and out and about in the heat of the day. A territorial male (with horns; though occasionally females are also horned) lives with his mate or a small family group, and they often have quite restricted, long-term territories.

STEENBOK *(DONDOO OR DONDORO) RAPHICERUS CAMPESTRIS*

Despite a height of only 50cm at the shoulder, the surprisingly aggressive steenbok – an inhabitant of dry savanna – defends itself furiously against attackers or, in extremis, dashes down any available hole. Male steenboks have horns, but the species is normally solitary, waking and feeding intermittently by day and night, using its huge ears to warn of the first sign of danger.

DUIKERS

The **duikers** (from the Dutch for "diver", referring to their plunging into the bush) are larger than the dwarf antelopes though they appear smaller because of their hunched posture. Uniquely among antelopes and allied species, duikers are omnivorous, feeding not just on leaves, fruit and fungi but also on a range of insects and other invertebrates – and even catching frogs and lizards and snatching birds when the opportunity arises.

COMMON DUIKER *(NYSA) SYLVICAPRA GRIMMIA*

The 60cm-high common duiker is found throughout the country in many habitats, but most species are choosier and prefer plenty of dense cover and thicket. The red duiker and blue duiker are quite widespread, but the tiny Zanzibar duiker is restricted in Kenya to the Arabuko Sokoke Forest near Malindi, the black-fronted duiker to Mount Kenya and Mount Elgon and the yellow-backed duiker to the Mau forest.

1 ORIBI; 2 SHARPE'S GRYSBOK; 3 SUNI; 4 KIRK'S DIK-DIK; 5 COMMON DUIKER; 6 KLIPSPRINGER; 7 STEENBOK >

BUFFALO AND SPIRAL-HORNED ANTELOPES

Kenya's **big antelopes** are the twisted-horn bushbuck types (*Tragelaphinae*; after the Greek for "billy goat"), though they are all related, surprisingly perhaps, not to goats or the smaller antelopes, but to cattle and **buffalos**.

AFRICAN OR CAPE BUFFALO *(NYATI OR MBOGO)* SYNCERUS CAFFER

The buffalo itself is very common and closely related to the domestic cow. Buffalos tolerate a wide range of habitats, up to altitudes of 4000m, but always near water. Their scent is much more acute than other senses. Active day and night, they rest up during the heat of the day. They live in large herds of cows and calves that can number up to three hundred and rarely make much effort to move when vehicles approach. Young bulls often form small bachelor herds, whereas older bulls are usually solitary and can sometimes be dangerous. Although usually ambivalent to the presence of humans, they are often destructive: you don't have to read the papers long before finding an example of buffalos trampling crops or goring a farmer trying to protect his harvest.

COMMON ELAND *(MPOFU OR MBUNGU)* TAUROTRAGUS ORYX

Spotted almost as easily as the buffalo, in most parks and reserves, is the huge, cow-like eland, with its distinctive dewlap. This highly adaptable mega-antelope – the biggest in Africa – is happy from semi-desert to mountains, but it prefers scrubby plains for its 24hr life, punctuated intermittently with brief periods of sleep. Non-territorial herds of up to sixty elands is the norm, but temporary gatherings of as many as a thousand aren't unheard of. Despite being so huge, and relatively common, it's still a shy animal, and usually turns and moves away when you stop to say hello. Indeed, elands can be quite skittish, and they're surprisingly good jumpers for a half-tonne beast. Both sexes have straight horns with a slight spiral.

GREATER KUDU *(TANDALA MKUBWA)* TRAGELAPHUS STREPSICEROS

This is another impressively big antelope (up to 1.5m at the shoulder) with very long, spiral horns in the male. Strikingly handsome and extremely localized, it is shy of humans, tends to be nocturnal and is not often seen in the daytime unless its territory is secure, as on some of the Laikipia conservancies. Your best bet for seeing them is Lake Bogoria NR and semi-arid, hilly or undulating bush country in northern Kenya, sometimes far from water. Male greater kudus are usually solitary; females live in small troops with the young.

LESSER KUDU *(TANDALA MDOGO)* TRAGELAPHUS IMBERBIS

The lesser kudu isn't infrequently seen, where it exists at all, but, like its greater cousin, it's localized and a threatened species. You're most likely to see lesser kudu in Tsavo West NP or Tsavo East NP, where they inhabit dense scrub. Like the greater kudu, lesser kudu females clump together with the young, while the adult males are more solitary. Like the eland, both species are startlingly good jumpers – which somehow ties in neatly with their spring-like horns.

BUSHBUCK *(KULUNGU OR MBAWALA)* TRAGELAPHUS SCRIPTUS

Another notoriously shy antelope – the only usual evidence of a bushbuck in the area is its noisy crashing through the undergrowth and a flash of a chestnut rump as it takes off. With their very variable appearance, even in the same close locality (there are as many as 29 subspecies, and some zoologists consider that the bushbuck is actually at least two different species), they can sometimes be hard to identify: look out for randomly white-spotted or sometimes white-broken-striped flanks. Thick bush and woodland close to water is their principal habitat, and even with this protection they are mostly nocturnal. They tend to be solitary. The male has fairly short, straight, spiralled horns.

SITATUNGA *(NZOHE)* TRAGELAPHUS SPEKEI

This large, hirsute, semi-aquatic relative of the bushbuck is found only in one or two remote corners of western Kenya (including Saiwa Swamp NP, where they are easy to see), and at Lewa Conservancy in Laikipia. They are very localized and are not likely to be mistaken for anything else. Usually seen half submerged, it's a challenge to spot their remarkable hooves, up to 18cm long and widely splayed – exactly as if a marsh-dwelling antelope were taking on the characteristics of a lily-trotter. As usual in this genus, only the males have horns.

BONGO *(BONGO OR NDONGORO)* TRAGELAPHUS EURYCERUS

The bongo is a particularly impressive member of this group, now confined to the highlands of Mount Kenya, the Aberdare range and possibly the Cherangani Hills and Mau Escarpment. Your best chance of seeing these stocky, robust, splendidly marked creatures is at Mount Kenya Safari Club, at Nanyuki, which has successfully bred and reintroduced them on the mountain.

1 AFRICAN BUFFALO; 2 BONGO; 3 COMMON ELAND; 4 SITATUNGA; 5 BUSHBUCK; 6 LESSER KUDU; 7 GREATER KUDU >

PRIMATES

Excluding *Homo sapiens*, there are twelve species of primates in Kenya, most of them diurnal. They range from the pint-sized, slow-motion, lemur-like potto (*Perodicticus potto*), found in Kakamega Forest, to the baboon. Other rare or more localized monkeys include the stocky but distinguished-looking De Brazza's monkey (*Cercopithecus neglectus*), with its white goatee, found almost exclusively in Saiwa Swamp National Park; the Tana River crested mangabey (*Cercocebus galeritus galeritus*), a partly ground-dwelling monkey with a characteristic Mohican-style crest of hair; and the terrestrial Patas monkey (*ngedere*; *Erythrocebus patas*), a moustachioed plains runner of Laikipia and the dry northwest. Kenya no longer has any great apes (the family to which the gorilla and the chimpanzee belong), although they probably only became extinct in the western forests, of which Kakamega is a relic, in the last 500 years, during the period when the region was being widely settled by humans. There's a large chimpanzee welfare sanctuary in Ol Pejeta conservancy, but it isn't engaged in breeding.

VERVET MONKEY *(TUMBILI) CHLOROCEBUS PYGERYTHRUS*

Widespread, common and occasionally a nuisance where used to humans (they will steal food and anything else that looks interesting), the primate you are certain to see almost anywhere in Kenya, given a few trees, is the vervet monkey. This small monkey lives in troops led by a dominant male (easily identified by his sky-blue scrotum), and they have no difficulty adjusting to the presence of humans and their food. The vervet is one of the guenons – typical African monkeys – every species of which has distinctive facial markings and hairstyles.

BLUE OR SYKES' MONKEY *(NYABU, KIMA OR NCHIMA) CERCOPITHECUS MITIS*

Almost as common as the vervet in certain areas, notably on the coast, is Sykes' monkey, also known as the blue monkey. Naturally a monkey of the forests, a number of Sykes' troops at Diani Beach have become notoriously accustomed to stealing food from hotel dining tables, and large males will even raid bedrooms. Upcountry populations of Sykes' monkey seem to be more timid.

EASTERN BLACK-AND-WHITE COLOBUS MONKEY OR GUEREZA *(MBEGA) COLOBUS GUEREZA*

You are most likely to see the beautiful, leaf-eating black-and-white colobus monkey in the Kenya highlands, where the Eastern species lives. Strictly diurnal, and almost entirely arboreal (their missing thumb is a distinctive characteristic that aids swinging; "kolobos" means "mutilated" in Greek), they live in small troops and are dependent on thick forest habitat, but also live along water courses and around lake margins in otherwise arid savanna districts. You can see them in the Aberdare and Mount Kenya national parks, in patches of forest among the tea hills northwest of Nairobi, at lakes Naivasha and Nakuru and around Maasai Mara NR. A second, smaller species, the Angolan black-and-white colobus (*C. angolensis*), can

also be spotted in the Diani forest on the coast south of Mombasa. Both species are usually seen high in the tree canopy; look out for the pure-white babies. The Tana River red colobus (*Procolobus rufomitratus rufomitratus*) is only found in the remote Tana River National Primate Reserve north of Malindi.

GREATER BUSHBABY OR THICK-TAILED GALAGO *(KOMBA) GALAGO CRASSICAUDATUS*

In some Kenyan coastal lodges, where there's enough nearby forest, you're quite likely to see this appealing, cat-sized primate – the largest of Kenya's three species of bushbabies – as they sometimes visit dining rooms and verandas. They're strictly nocturnal, roosting in small family groups during the day, and very active hunters and foragers after dark, when their wailing "baby" cries are such a distinctive sound. The tiny Senegal bushbaby (also *komba*; *G. senegalensis*) is a shy, tree-leaping sap- and insect-eater: it's the big species that wants your bread roll or fruit.

YELLOW BABOON *(NYANI) PAPIO CYNOCEPHALUS*

On safari you'll have plenty of opportunities to watch baboon troops up close. Large males can be intimidating – disconcertingly so towards women, whom they identify as less physically threatening than men. Troops, averaging 40–50 individuals, spend their lives, like all monkeys, in clear but mutable social relationships. Rank and precedence, physical strength and kin ties all determine an individual's position in this mini-society led by a dominant male. They favour open country with trees and cliffs, always near water, and their days revolve around foraging and hunting for food (baboons will consume almost anything, from a fig tree's entire crop to a baby antelope found in the grass). There are two species, whose distributions overlap in Kenya: the slenderer yellow baboon in the east and south, and the stockier, heavily maned olive baboon (also *nyani*; *P. anubis*) in the west and north. Both adapt quickly to humans, are frequently a nuisance and occasionally dangerous.

OTHER MAMMALS

It's unlikely **rodents** will make a strong impression on safari, unless you do a night game drive. In that case you may see the frenzied leaps of a spring hare, dazzled by headlights or a torch. In rural areas off the beaten track you may occasionally see hunters taking home giant rats or cane rats – shy, vegetarian animals, which make good eating.

Kenya has several species of **squirrel**, of which the most widespread are the two species of ground squirrel – striped and unstriped – which are often seen, dashing along the track in front of the vehicle on game drives. The most spectacular squirrel, however, is the giant forest squirrel, with its splendid bush of a tail, and the nocturnal flying squirrel – which glides from tree to tree on membranes between its outstretched limbs. Both are most likely to be seen in Kakamega Forest. Kenya's true flying mammals will usually be a mere flicker over a waterhole at twilight, or sometimes a flash across your headlights. The only **bats** you can normally observe in any meaningful way are fruit bats hanging from their daytime roosting sites. The hammer-headed fruit bat, sometimes seen in Kakamega Forest, has a huge head and a wingspan of more than 1m.

ROCK HYRAX (PIMBI) PROCAVIA CAPENSIS

Rock hyraxes, which you are certain to see at Hell's Gate NP, on Mount Kenya and in Nairobi NP, look as if they should be rodents. But one of the most memorable bits of safari knowledge imparted by guides is the fact that they share the same prehistoric ancestor as the elephant. Present-day hyraxes are pygmies compared with some of their prehistoric ancestors, which were as big as a bear in some cases. Rock hyraxes live in busy, vocal colonies of twenty or thirty females and young, plus a territorial male. Some areas swarm with the adults and the playful and very independent young. The tree hyrax (pembere; Heterohyrax brucei) is quite similar, but largely nocturnal: this is the hyrax making the painfully wheezing cry that you sometimes hear at night.

AARDVARK (MHANGA) ORYCTEROPUS AFER

The aardvark is one of Africa's – indeed the world's – strangest mammals, a solitary termite-eater weighing up to 70kg. Its name, Afrikaans for "earth pig", is an apt description, as it holes up during the day in large burrows – excavated with remarkable speed and energy – and emerges at night to visit termite mounds within a radius of up to 5km, to dig for its main diet. It is most likely to be seen in bush country, well scattered with tall termite spires, when you're out on a night drive.

PANGOLIN (KAKAKUONA) MANIS TEMMINCKII

Pangolins are also very unusual – nocturnal, scale-covered mammals, resembling armadillos and feeding on ants and termites. When frightened, they secrete a noxious liquid from anal glands and roll into a ball with their scales erect (pangolin is Malay for "rolling over"). The ground pangolin, the only species found in Kenya (most pangolins are arboreal), lives mainly in savanna and woodland districts.

CRESTED PORCUPINE (NUNGU OR NUNGUNUNGU) HYSTRIX CRISTATA

This is a really large rodent (up to 90cm in length), rarely seen, but common away from croplands, where it's hunted as a pest, or for its quills. Porcupines are adaptable to a wide range of habitats and often hide in caves during the day, where several may gather, coming out only at night to forage for roots and tubers along their routine pathways.

GOLDEN RUMPED ELEPHANT SHREW (SENGI) RHYNCHOCYON CHRYSOPYGUS

The insectivorous elephant shrews are worth looking out for, simply because they are so weird. Your best chance of a sighting is of the golden-rumped elephant shrew, at Gedi ruins on the coast, near Watamu, or in the nearby Arabuko Sokoke Forest NP. This fascinating insect-eater is a creature of many parts: the size of a small cat, but built like a giant mouse, running on stilts, it has a soft, elongated snout, like a short trunk. "Elephant shrew" captures the look fairly well.

DUGONG (NGUVA) DUGONG DUGON

The rarest of all of Kenya's "other mammals" is the dugong, the mermaid-prototype, of which there are believed to be a handful of individuals remaining in Kenyan waters, drifting in the shallows around the Lamu Archipelago, part of a much depleted population – threatened by deliberate hunting and accidental trawling – that lives all along the Indian Ocean coast, feeding on seagrass that is also vulnerable to habitat destruction, and coming up for air every few minutes. Adults usually weigh around half a tonne and reach about 3m in length, and the females give birth, in very shallow water, to metre-long, 30kg calves that suckle for eighteen months.

CURIO STALL

Basics

Getting there

Flying is the only straightforward way of getting to Kenya, unless you're travelling overland from southern Africa. Flights to Kenya are generally most expensive from late June to mid-August, and from mid-December to mid-January.

Cheaper tickets generally have fixed dates that you won't be able to change without paying an extra fee. Some airlines offer various **restricted eligibility fares** for students and under-26s which may be cheaper and more flexible than ordinary adult fares.

Charter flights to Mombasa, available from Britain and Europe, are often cheaper than scheduled flights, but there's usually a maximum stay in Kenya of two to four weeks.

Make **reservations** as far in advance as possible, especially if you want to travel in high season, as flights frequently fill up.

An inclusive **package trip** can make a lot of sense. Some packages, based around Mombasa charter flights and mid-range coast hotels, are relatively inexpensive and, if you choose carefully, you shouldn't feel too constrained. Based on your flight, plus a week of half-board accommodation (dinner, bed and breakfast) they cost from around £800 from the UK. Beach hotels vary greatly in price, atmosphere and amenities, so choose carefully. It's worth remembering that you aren't obliged to stay at your hotel all the time: you could use it as a base to make independent trips around the country.

Adding some **safari** travel to a beach package holiday will increase the price by at least £200 per person per day of safari. If you have more time and flexibility, book a safari in Kenya – recommended companies are listed in the relevant sections of the book (see p.76, p.117 & p.406).

Flights from the UK and Ireland

London Heathrow is the only British airport with **direct flights to Nairobi**, operated by Kenya Airways (Ⓦkenya-airways.com) and British Airways

(Ⓦba.com), and taking around nine hours. **Fares** for flights on fixed dates start from under £500 return in low season and rise to above £1000 on key dates in high season. It may well be cheaper to take an **indirect flight**, changing planes in the airline's hub city in Europe or the Middle East (see below).

There are also several **charter operators** with whom you can sometimes get "seat-only" deals to Mombasa, out of London (and sometimes one or two UK regional airports) from around £500. Any online or high-street agent can give you a quote.

Flying from Ireland, your easiest bet is to fly to Heathrow, connecting there for a BA or Kenya Airways flight. Flights should cost between €650 and €1300, depending on the season.

Flights from the US and Canada

There are still no direct flights from the US or Canada to East Africa. The fastest routes to Nairobi are usually two non-stop legs via **London** on British Airways (Ⓦba.com), or Amsterdam on KLM (Ⓦklm.com) and Kenya Airways (Ⓦkenya-airways.com). Other possible connections are available with European and Middle Eastern airlines (see below). **Fares** start from around $1300 for a low-season round-trip ticket out of New York, and from $2000 in high season.

West-coast travellers might want to consider Korean Air's new route to Nairobi (Ⓦkoreanair.com), though there's an all-day layover in Seoul between flights. It's the only via-Asia option.

Flights via Europe, Africa and the Middle East

Airlines that fly from New York and London and **connect to Nairobi** – though layovers may be inconvenient – include Brussels Airlines (Ⓦbrussels airlines.com), Egyptair (Ⓦegyptair.com.eg), Emirates (Ⓦemirates.com), Ethiopian Airlines (Ⓦethiopian airlines.com), Etihad (Ⓦetihadairways.com), KLM (Ⓦklm.com), Saudia (Ⓦsaudiairlines.com), Lufthansa (Ⓦlufthansa.com), Qatar Airways (Ⓦqatarairways .com), Swiss (Ⓦswiss.com) and Turkish Airlines (Ⓦturkishairlines.com).

A BETTER KIND OF TRAVEL

At Rough Guides we are passionately committed to travel. We believe it helps us understand the world we live in and the people we share it with – and of course **tourism** is vital to many developing economies. But the scale of modern tourism has also damaged some places irreparably, and **climate change** is accelerated by most forms of transport, especially flying. All Rough Guides' flights are carbon-offset, and every year we donate money to a variety of environmental charities.

Scheduled flights to **Mombasa** include Kenya Airways, Ethiopian Airlines (**W** ethiopianairlines .com), Brussels Airlines and Qatar Airways, connecting in Nairobi, Addis Ababa, Brussels and Doha respectively.

Flights from Australia and New Zealand

There are no direct flights to Kenya from Australia or New Zealand. From **Australia**, South African Airways (**W** flysaa.com) has some good connections to Nairobi via Johannesburg, while Emirates (**W** emirates .com) also offers decent connections and fares. From **New Zealand**, Emirates via Dubai is your most obvious bet, but Air New Zealand (**W** airnewzealand .co.nz) and Qantas (**W** qantas.com) can get you to Kenya in combination with other airlines, such as South African from Johannesburg. Another option, with a potential bonus stopover, is Australia or New Zealand to Mauritius, followed by a direct flight to Nairobi, all on Air Mauritius (**W** airmauritius.com).

Except for the Christmas period, when you will have to pay more, **fares** to Kenya from Australia and New Zealand are generally not seasonal. The lowest-priced return tickets bought from a discount agent or direct from the airline cost around Aus\$2000–3500 from Australia or NZ\$2400–4000 from New Zealand.

Flights from South Africa

There are several daily **direct flights** to Nairobi from Johannesburg on South African Airways (**W** flysaa .com) and Kenya Airways (**W** kenya-airways.com). Round-trip fares start at around R4000.

DISCOUNT FLIGHT AGENTS

Africa Travel UK **W** africatravel.co.uk. Experienced and resourceful.
Airfares Flights Aus **W** airfaresflights.com.au. Fare-comparison site.
Airtech US **W** airtech.com. Airline consolidator fares and standby-seat broker.
Airtreks US **W** airtreks.com. Specialist in round-the-world and multi-sector tickets.
Best Flights Aus **W** bestflights.com.au. Well-priced and user-friendly agent.
Flight Centre Worldwide **W** flightcentre.com. Flights and safari packages and some of the best Nairobi fare deals.
North South Travel UK **W** northsouthtravel.co.uk. Excellent personal service and discounted fares, with all profits going to grassroots development charities.
Spector Travel of Boston US **W** spectortravel.com. African flights and tours agent, with some great prices.

STA Travel Worldwide **W** statravel.com. Specialists in flights and tours for students and under-26s, though others are catered for.
Trailfinders UK & Ire **W** trailfinders.com. Long-established, reputable agent, with good-value flights and a small range of Kenya accommodation.
Travel Bag UK **W** travelbag.co.uk. Discount flight deals.
Travel Cuts Can/US **W** travelcuts.com. Popular, long-established student travel organization.
USIT Ire **W** usit.ie. Irish and Northern Irish student and youth specialists.
World Express Travel UK **W** worldexpresstravel.co.uk. Consolidators for Kenya Airways, Brussels Airlines and Ethiopian.
World Travel Centre Ire **W** worldtravel.ie. Cheap flight deals.

KENYA AND AFRICA SPECIALISTS

In addition to the agents and operators listed, you can book an itinerary through companies in Nairobi (see p.117) and elsewhere in Kenya. Most companies will be able to assist you, regardless of your home country, though international flights will generally have to be booked with a company in the country you are departing from.

Australia

African Travel Specialists **W** africantravel.com.au. Well-established agent, with an excellent reputation and a team of experienced staff, many of whom know Kenya well.
Classic Safari Company **W** classicsafaricompany.com.au. Tailor-made safaris ranging from comfortable to luxurious including mobile camping, riding and walking options.

UK

Aardvark Safaris **W** aardvarksafaris.co.uk. Committed and enthusiastic tailor-made Africa specialists who spend a lot of time getting to know the high-end camps and lodges they work with – there are more than sixty in Kenya alone.
Adventure Alternative **W** adventurealternative.com. Small, personal operator, with a strong sense of responsibility and reciprocation, run by a committed founder and dedicated local staff, with fixed-date tours including Mt Kenya climbs and budget safaris from £150/day.
Africa Odyssey **W** africaodyssey.com. Tailor-made tours in east and southern Africa featuring safaris, beach holidays and small lodges off the beaten track.
Africa Sky **W** africasky.co.uk. Very well-established and knowledgeable agent-operator with a helpfully clear website and a host of offerings in Kenya, most of them responsible and mid-priced.
Cazenove & Loyd **W** cazenoveandloyd.com. Intelligently designed, entirely tailor-made, private safaris, relying on clients who know what they're looking for.
Exodus **W** exodus.co.uk. Long-established overland and adventure company, with an interesting selection of Kenya tours, including a photographic trip to the Mara, a Mount Kenya climb on the Sirimon route and a Kenya/Rwanda combination.
Expert Africa **W** expertafrica.com. Specialists in tailor-made trips, with very strong local knowledge. The Kenya programme is run by Richard Trillo, author of the Rough Guide to Kenya since 1987, and the team includes other guidebook writers.

Extreme-Safari Ⓦ extreme-safari.com. Adventure and adrenaline sports travel operator specializing in Kenya.

Footloose Adventure Travel Ⓦ footlooseadventure.co.uk. Enthusiastic independent outfit offering a selection of treks and safaris; they'll tailor-make a safari to fit your budget and interests, offer advice and track down flights.

Freeman Safaris Ⓦ freemansafaris.com. Personal, specialist photographic safari operator, using Land Rovers and a raft of experience to deliver exceptional trips.

Gane & Marshall Ⓦ ganeandmarshall.com. Africa specialists, with responsible travel credentials and a good Kenya programme, including Mount Kenya and Laikipia.

Hartley's Safaris Ⓦ hartleys-safaris.co.uk. Highly rated safari specialists creating bespoke tours.

Imagine Africa Ⓦ imagineafrica.co.uk. Well-established and reliable outfit with a good reputation for organizing mid- to high-end safaris.

IntoAfrica Ⓦ intoafrica.co.uk. Small, good, eco-minded tour operator, whose trips give a genuine insight into the country while having minimum negative impact on people and environment.

Intrepid Guerba Ⓦ intrepidtravel.com. Guerba, the acknowledged African truck-travel experts, now part of Intrepid Travel, run a string of Kenya trips, many of which include Tanzania.

Natural High Safaris Ⓦ naturalhighsafaris.com. Very cool consultancy, safari-planner and booking agent, with highly experienced staff.

On The Go Tours Ⓦ onthegotours.com. Lively and competitively priced range of Kenya tours from a no-frills camping trip to a safari that includes the gorillas in Uganda.

Rainbow Tours Ⓦ rainbowtours.co.uk. Award-winning small operator with long-standing links with Africa, some unusual Kenyan properties and keen and experienced staff.

Safari Consultants Ⓦ safari-consultants.co.uk & Ⓦ safariconsultants.co.uk. Long-established and very personal Africa specialists who know their stuff and rely on direct contact with clients.

Steppes Travel Ⓦ steppestravel.co.uk. Innovative company with a personal approach, specializing in tailor-made trips, based in luxury lodges.

Theobald Barber Ⓦ theobaldbarber.com. Experienced, bespoke safari planners, offering a very personalized service.

Tim Best Travel Ⓦ timbesttravel.com. Eco-luxurious holiday company with a great reputation for delivering off-the-beaten-track arrangements.

To Escape To Ⓦ toescapeto.com. Property rental and accommodation agent, offering more than sixty hotels, lodges and camps in Kenya, including mid-priced options.

Tourdust Ⓦ tourdust.com. Out-of-the-ordinary and competitively priced treks in the Loita Hills and Mt Kenya as well as safaris and good-value beach extensions.

Tribes Travel Ⓦ tribes.co.uk. Highly recommended small company in the vanguard of responsibly operated and traded tourism, including more than ninety places to stay in Kenya, all individually reviewed and rated.

Wild Frontiers Ⓦ wildfrontiers.co.uk. Adventure travel specialist highlighting the travel as much as the destination, with some excellent Kenya tours.

US and Canada

Africa Tours Ⓦ africasafaris.com. A choice of seven off-the-peg – but customizable – Kenya safaris.

African Adventure Company Ⓦ africa-adventure.com. One of the best agencies in the business, offering eight safari options in Kenya, including a "voluntourism" trip to Kasigau.

African Horizons Ⓦ africanhorizons.com. Decent range of well-priced Kenya safaris with flexible departures.

Bicycle Africa Ⓦ ibike.org/bikeafrica. Easy-going small-group cycling tours visiting many parts of Africa, including Kenya.

Born Free Safaris Ⓦ safaris2africa.com. Plain-speaking operator established in the 1970s, with good-value safaris on offer.

GAP Adventures Ⓦ gapadventures.com. Long list of off-the-peg Kenya tours from basic camping trips to luxury short breaks from this Canadian company.

Good Earth Tours Ⓦ goodearthtours.com. Very good-value safaris, starting at $210/day for minibus camping trips, excluding air travel.

Journeys International Ⓦ journeys-intl.com. Award-winning ecotourism operator with a handful of Kenya trips, including a mainstream nine-day safari and an unusual eleven-day culture-and-wildlife safari that ventures off the beaten track into Ukambani.

Ker & Downey Ⓦ kerdowney.com. Renowned and much-commended upmarket travel company, working closely with top Kenya property groups Cheli & Peacock and Bush & Beyond.

Micato Safaris Ⓦ micato.com. Multi-award-winning Kenyan-American tour operator with a variety of Kenya offerings.

Mountain Madness Ⓦ mountainmadness.com. Seattle-based adventure travel firm, offering really good-value, well-planned, well-paced Mount Kenya climbs.

Mountain Travel Sobek Ⓦ mtsobek.com. Wonderful foot safaris through Tsavo East and the Rongai Route up Kili from the Kenyan side.

Nature Expeditions Ⓦ naturexp.com. Good-value, flexible educational tours – one just in Kenya, one including Tanzania – with optional lectures on wildlife, natural history and culture. Good for older kids and teens.

Premier Tours Ⓦ premiertours.com. Environmentally sound upmarket safaris in Eastern and southern Africa.

Uncharted Outposts Ⓦ unchartedoutposts.com Highly recommended operator, with many Kenya options, particularly focusing on boutique camps and small lodges.

WILDLIFE AND BIRDWATCHING SPECIALISTS

African Wildlife Safaris Aus Ⓦ africanwildlifesafaris.com.au. Upmarket lodge- and camp-based safaris, many run by renowned Nairobi-based operator Origins Safaris.

Naturetrek UK Ⓦ naturetrek.co.uk. Natural-history holidays, including four in Kenya.

Wildlife Worldwide UK Ⓦ wildlifeworldwide.com. Tailor-made trips for wildlife enthusiasts including a "Big Cat Weekend" and "Adventure Camping".

Birdfinders UK Ⓦ birdfinders.co.uk. Expertly guided birdwatching tours, including an annual 18-day Kenya extravaganza.

Ornitholidays UK Ⓦ ornitholidays.co.uk. Birdwatching in the Rift Valley and the Maasai Mara.

VOLUNTOURISM & CHARITY CHALLENGES

If you're interested in voluntary work or doing a charity challenge in Kenya, check out Ⓦ charityfacts.org and Ⓦ intelligentgiving.com.

Adventure Alternative Northern Ireland Ⓦ adventurealternative .com. A good clutch of Kenyan professional electives and gap year "voluntourism" opportunities.

Africa Venture UK Ⓦ aventure.co.uk. Gap year and team-building projects aimed at students, graduates or older travellers, near Machakos, lasting 10–12 weeks.

Amanzi Travel UK Ⓦ amanzitravel.co.uk. Agent offering a range of voluntourism and adventure holidays in Kenya, among other countries.

Camp Kenya UK Ⓦ campsinternational.com. Expertly run, community-facing, gap-year, school-team and career-break programmes for people of all ages, doing genuinely useful work.

Worldwide Experience UK Ⓦ worldwideexperience.com. Predator research placements at Koiyaki Guiding School in the Maasai Mara's Naboisho Conservancy.

Overlanding to Kenya

With plenty of time and a sense of adventure, **travelling overland** can be a rewarding way of getting to Kenya. Central African conflicts have effectively closed routes from West Africa for the time being, and while adventurous **self-drive** overlanders are heading to Kenya from Egypt, taking a boat from Aswan to Wadi Halfa in Sudan, crossing into Ethiopia at Metema and entering Kenya at Moyale or at the northern end of Lake Turkana, this route is not an easy one.

Currently the only advisable route is from **southern Africa**. You can drive by various routes, take the train up through Zambia and Tanzania, go overland by local transport, or hook up with any number of overland operators from Cape Town to Nairobi. Scrutinizing their websites gives an indication of their preparedness and know-how; if the blurb looks cheap or hasty, you should probably give them a wide berth.

Most of the **recommended operators** (see below) offer five- to ten-week Nairobi–Cape Town trips, which are usually possible in the other direction too. Prices vary widely: for a six- to ten-week Cape Town–Nairobi trip, taking in Namibia, Victoria Falls, Uganda and other highlights, you're looking at anything from $50–100/day, including the local kitty. As usual, you tend to get what you pay for.

OVERLAND COMPANIES

Absolute Africa UK Ⓦ absoluteafrica.com. Budget overland operator with trips in East and southern Africa.

Acacia African Adventures UK Ⓦ acacia-africa.com. Expensive but good-value overland operator.

INFORMATION FOR TAKING YOUR OWN VEHICLE

CAA US/Can Ⓦ bit.ly/CAA-carnet.

Horizons Unlimited Bulletin Board
Ⓦ bit.ly/TheHUBB-paperwork. Excellent motorcycle and driving information and forums.

RAC UK Ⓦ bit.ly/RAC-carnet.

African Trails UK Ⓦ africantrails.co.uk. Well-regarded budget overland operator with a trans-continental range of tours.

Dragoman Overland UK Ⓦ dragoman.com. Highly experienced responsible tourism operator offering extended overland journeys in purpose-built expedition vehicles.

Gecko's Grassroots Adventures UK Ⓦ geckosadventures.com. Budget brand of Australian company Peregrine, with some down-to-earth Kenya and overland tours.

Getting around

There's a wide range of travel options in Kenya. If you want to be looked after throughout your trip, you can travel on a shared or exclusive road safari where you sign up to an off-the-shelf or tailor-made itinerary; alternatively you can take an air safari, via scheduled domestic airlines (often in small planes with great visibility), or chartering a light plane for your own use. If you want more independence, you can easily rent a vehicle for self-drive or with a driver. If you're on a budget, you'll find a wide range of public transport – though, to be clear, it is all privately operated – from air-conditioned buses run by large operators to smaller companies and "saccos" (cooperatives) with a single battered minibus. In towns of any size, crowds of Nissan minibuses, operating as shared taxis and referred to as matatus, hustle for business constantly. Kenya's railway "network" appears to be in terminal decline, but the Nairobi–Mombasa line still runs several services a week.

Flying

Domestic flights in Kenya – normally by turbo-prop plane – are thoroughly enjoyable, especially to the national parks, with animals clearly visible below as you approach each airstrip.

The main operators are SafariLink (Ⓦsafarilink -kenya.com), Kenya Airways (Ⓦkenya-airways .com), Airkenya (Ⓦairkenya.com), Mombasa Air Safari (Ⓦmombasaairsafari.com), 540 Aviation (Ⓦfly540.com) and Jetlink (Ⓦjetlink.co.ke). The destinations served include the main **towns and cities** (Nairobi, Mombasa, Kisumu, Eldoret, Kitale and Nanyuki), **coastal resorts** (Diani Beach, Malindi, Lamu and Kiwayu) and airfields serving safari clients in the main **parks and reserves** of Amboseli, Maasai Mara, Meru, Tsavo West and Samburu-Shaba, and at Lewa Downs and Loisaba north of Mount Kenya. Most services are daily and in some cases there are several flights a day, though frequencies on certain routes are reduced in low season. Same-day connections can be a problem, however. For some ballpark return **fares**, reckon on Nairobi–Maasai Mara costing $330, Nairobi–Lamu $390 and Nairobi–Diani Beach (Ukunda) $300. **Baggage allowances** on some internal flights are 15kg – though excess baggage charges are nominal.

Chartering a small plane for trips to safari parks and remote airstrips is worth considering if money is less important to you than time. Costs for a two-seater are typically around $3/km, or $7/km for a 5-seater. Remember that the plane has to make a round trip, even if you don't. Two of the best charter companies are Tropic Air (Ⓦtropicairkenya.com), based at Nanyuki airfield, and Boskovic Air Charters (Ⓦboskovicaircharters.com), based at Wilson Airport in Nairobi.

Car rental and driving

All the parks and reserves are open to private vehicles, and there's a lot to be said for the freedom of choice that **renting a car** gives you. Unless there are more than two of you, though, it won't save you money over one of the cheaper camping safaris. If you're going to be in Kenya for some time, buying a **secondhand** vehicle in Nairobi is a realistic possibility, though prices are high. Check the poster boards at any big mall or shopping centre such as Village Market or the Sarit Centre.

Before renting, shop around for the best deals and try to negotiate as you might with any purchase, bearing in mind how long you need and the season. July, August and Christmas are busy, so you might want to book ahead. **Rates** vary greatly: some are quoted in Kenyan shillings and some in dollars or euros; some include unlimited mileage while others don't. The minimum age to rent a car is usually 23, sometimes 25.

You can often rent a vehicle with a **driver or driver-guide** supplied by the rental company, which can be more relaxing and a great introduction to the country. This should add around Ksh1000/day to your bill for the driver's salary, and up to another Ksh1000/day for his daily living expenses. Obviously fuel is still extra. Be clear precisely what the arrangements are before you set off: it's best to have things in writing.

Check the insurance details and always pay the daily **collision damage waiver (CDW)** premium, sometimes included in the price; even a small bump could be very costly otherwise. **Theft protection waiver (TPW)** should also be taken. Even with these, however, you'll still be liable for an **excess**, usually $500–1000, for which you are liable if there is any claim. You're also required to leave a hefty deposit, roughly equivalent to the anticipated bill, normally on a credit card. Assuming you return the vehicle, this should not be debited from your account.

If stopped at a police checkpoint, you may be asked to produce evidence that the rental car has a **PSV** (passenger service vehicle) licence. You should have a windscreen sticker for this as well as the letters "PSV" written somewhere on the body; if in doubt, check this out with the rental company before you leave. All PSV vehicles are, in theory, fitted with speed governors, physically limiting your top speed to the speed limit of 80km/h. In practice, few companies leave them operational.

Being **stopped by the police** is a common occurrence. Checkpoints are generally marked by low strips of spikes across the road, with just enough room to slalom through. Always stop, greet the officer and wait to be waved through. If they accuse you of breaking any law, then politely accept what you are told, including the possibility of a court appearance (highly unlikely). Being set up for a bribe still happens, but more often you'll be asked "What did you bring for me?" or something similar. Unless you're happy to participate in Kenya's ongoing institutionalized petty corruption, you should always respond with bemused propriety, and pay nothing.

If you have a **breakdown**, before seeking assistance, you should pile bundles of sticks or foliage 50m or so behind and in front of the car. These are the universally recognized "red warning triangles" of Africa, and their placing is always scrupulously observed, as is the wedging of a stone behind at least one wheel to stop it rolling away.

You might consider joining **AA Kenya** (Ⓦaakenya.co.ke), which offers temporary membership for up to six months for Ksh2000, which

DISTANCE CHART

Figures are given in kilometres

	Busia	Eldoret	Embu	Garissa	Isebania	Isiolo	Kakamega	Kericho	Kisii	Kisumu	Kitale	Lamu (Mokowe)	Lodwar	Loiyangalani	Malaba
Busia	–	157	537	794	305	534	87	195	223	110	149	1120	445	692	33
Eldoret	157	–	393	650	275	390	97	161	193	117	72	975	365	536	128
Embu	537	393	–	329	460	194	476	344	442	428	463	654	687	566	520
Garissa	794	650	329	–	720	461	710	608	661	699	733	355	966	895	794
Isebania	305	275	460	720	–	526	242	186	87	193	350	1077	649	747	328
Isiolo	534	390	194	461	526	–	437	339	438	423	534	787	711	428	517
Kakamega	87	97	476	710	242	437	–	133	161	49	110	1074	406	640	85
Kericho	195	161	344	608	186	339	133	–	101	82	229	926	530	554	216
Kisii	223	193	442	661	87	438	161	101	–	111	269	984	566	649	246
Kisumu	110	117	428	699	193	423	49	82	111	–	157	1029	455	639	135
Kitale	149	72	463	733	350	534	110	229	269	157	–	1047	299	600	119
Lamu (Mokowe)	1120	975	654	355	1077	787	1074	926	984	1029	1047	–	1313	1223	1100
Lodwar	445	365	687	966	649	711	406	530	566	455	299	1313	–	720	417
Loiyangalani	692	536	566	895	747	428	640	554	649	639	600	1223	720	–	662
Malaba	33	128	520	794	328	517	85	216	246	135	119	1100	417	662	–
Malindi	1032	910	726	345	940	874	992	861	905	945	956	218	1207	1169	1037
Maralal	460	299	338	665	517	198	405	331	426	409	371	970	495	230	428
Marsabit	798	646	406	668	784	256	729	597	696	680	716	1045	797	228	772
Meru	522	385	98	409	524	51	469	337	437	421	457	740	704	413	514
Mombasa	931	794	607	463	874	755	877	745	785	826	863	334	1112	1051	920
Moyale	1125	898	653	969	1035	505	977	845	946	928	965	1297	1054	477	1021
Nairobi	478	313	130	366	343	279	395	264	306	345	380	695	630	569	462
Naivasha	391	224	205	443	325	301	308	177	275	260	305	767	545	484	353
Nakuru	302	157	272	507	296	231	240	108	210	192	227	834	475	453	284
Namanga	619	474	287	523	505	436	650	424	465	510	541	926	794	731	600
Nanyuki	456	311	117	447	449	78	394	263	360	344	382	775	631	431	439
Narok	324	261	259	499	203	365	262	157	164	212	319	823	584	580	347
Nyahururu	362	218	176	505	356	173	299	169	311	250	286	833	536	396	345
Nyeri	464	315	74	405	456	137	403	269	368	353	387	730	637	480	447
Sekenani Gate	338	346	345	584	173	453	279	175	181	231	388	908	680	664	364
Shimoni	1018	874	686	543	899	834	956	824	867	908	945	414	1194	1141	999
Taveta	763	619	431	728	645	580	701	569	611	652	684	575	936	883	742
Voi	784	640	452	622	715	599	722	592	632	672	711	469	959	901	768

includes the usual breakdown and rescue services, where available.

Choosing and running a vehicle

A high-clearance **four-wheel drive** (4WD) vehicle is always useful, and often essential, thanks to the dire state of many roads. Even when you're not planning any off-road driving, and expect to stick to tarmac, entrance roads and access tracks are often not surfaced and can become impassable quagmires after rain. Most car rental companies will not rent out non-4WD vehicles for use in the parks, and park rangers will often turn away such cars at the gates, especially in wet weather. Maasai Mara and the mountain parks (Mount Elgon, Mount Kenya and the Aberdare range) are the most safety-minded.

Four-wheel drive **Suzuki jeeps** are the most widely available vehicles, but ensure you get a long wheelbase model with rear seats, room for four people (or five at a pinch) and luggage space at the back. These are more stable than the stumpy short-wheelbase versions. Suzukis are light and dependable, capable of great feats in negotiating rough terrain, and can nearly always be fixed by a local repair workshop. Beware, however, of their notorious tendency to tip over on bends or on the dangerously sloping gravel hard shoulders that line so many roads.

You shouldn't assume that the vehicle is roadworthy before you set off. Have a good look at the engine and tyres, and don't set off without checking the spare wheel (preferably two spare

Malindi	Maralal	Marsabit	Meru	Mombasa	Moyale	Nairobi	Naivasha	Nakuru	Namanga	Nanyuki	Narok	Nyahururu	Nyeri	Sekenani Gate	Shimoni	Taveta	Voi
1032	460	798	522	931	1125	478	391	302	619	456	324	362	464	338	1018	763	784
910	299	646	385	794	898	313	224	157	474	311	261	218	215	346	874	619	640
726	338	406	98	607	653	130	205	272	287	117	259	176	74	345	686	431	452
345	665	668	409	463	969	366	443	507	523	447	499	505	405	584	543	728	622
940	517	784	524	874	1035	343	325	296	505	449	203	356	456	173	899	645	715
874	198	256	51	755	505	279	301	231	436	78	365	173	137	453	834	580	599
992	405	729	469	877	977	395	308	240	650	394	262	299	403	279	956	701	722
861	331	597	337	745	845	264	177	108	424	263	157	169	269	175	824	569	592
905	426	696	437	785	946	306	275	210	465	360	164	311	368	181	867	611	632
945	409	680	421	826	928	345	260	192	510	344	212	250	353	231	908	652	672
956	371	716	457	863	965	380	305	227	541	382	319	286	387	388	945	684	711
218	970	1045	740	334	1297	695	767	834	926	775	823	833	730	908	414	575	469
1207	495	797	704	1112	1054	630	545	475	794	631	584	536	637	680	1194	936	959
1169	230	228	413	1051	477	569	484	453	731	431	580	396	480	664	1141	883	901
1037	428	772	514	920	1021	437	353	284	600	439	347	345	447	364	999	742	768
–	939	1035	725	118	1292	600	687	756	708	805	742	784	756	827	195	382	249
939	–	345	250	821	577	340	251	212	505	196	345	154	253	429	900	653	663
1035	345	–	309	1010	247	535	620	495	696	335	621	429	394	705	1091	835	858
725	250	309	–	702	557	225	302	372	381	76	357	168	133	442	782	525	548
118	821	1010	702	–	1269	481	568	637	597	692	625	668	640	711	80	265	157
1292	577	247	557	1269	–	783	845	739	939	583	869	679	642	953	1337	1082	1103
600	340	535	225	481	783	–	85	155	161	205	143	185	164	227	560	305	328
687	251	620	302	568	845	85	–	70	252	193	126	98	238	210	651	395	418
756	212	495	372	637	739	155	70	–	322	158	132	64	162	217	720	465	486
708	505	696	381	597	939	161	252	322	–	368	301	348	100	387	672	417	439
805	196	335	76	692	583	205	193	158	368	–	286	94	58	370	763	508	528
742	345	621	357	625	869	143	126	132	301	286	–	191	287	86	234	109	469
784	154	429	168	668	679	185	98	64	348	94	191	–	102	277	747	490	514
756	253	394	133	640	642	164	238	162	100	58	287	102	–	372	712	448	467
827	429	705	442	711	953	227	210	217	387	370	86	277	372	–	788	533	554
195	900	1091	782	80	1337	560	651	720	672	763	234	747	712	788	–	343	235
382	653	835	525	265	1082	305	395	465	417	508	109	490	448	533	343	–	109
249	663	858	548	157	1103	328	418	486	439	528	469	514	467	554	235	109	–

wheels) and making sure that you have a few essential tools. Always carry a tow rope and spare water and ideally spare fuel in a jerrican (it's not uncommon for petrol stations to run out). You might also take a spare fan belt and brake fluid. You are responsible for any **repair** and **maintenance work** that needs doing while you're renting the vehicle, but good car rental companies will reimburse you for spare parts and labour, and expect you to call them if you have a breakdown, in which case they will often send out a mechanic to help.

When you get a **flat tyre**, as you will, get it mended straight away: it costs very little (Ksh100–200) and can be done almost anywhere. Local mechanics are usually very good and can apply ingenuity to the most disastrous situations. But spare parts, tools and proper equipment are rare off the main routes. Always settle on a price before work begins.

At the time of writing, the **price of petrol** (gasoline, always unleaded) ranges from roughly Ksh110–130/litre (£0.85–£1.00/litre or $5–6/US gallon), depending on the retailer, the remoteness of the town and Kenya's latest oil imports. The vast majority of petrol stations charge similar prices at the lower end of the range. There is occasionally a choice of regular or premium, but the latter is the norm. **Diesel** is five to ten percent cheaper. When filling, which is always done by an attendant, check the pump is set to zero. In city petrol stations you can sometimes pay by credit card, but don't count on it as their card reader may be out of action.

Driving on the roads

You can drive in Kenya with either a valid **driving licence** from your home country, or an international one. A **GPS** SatNav device or smart phone is very useful as there are very few road signs and no detailed, accurate road maps.

Be cautious of abrupt changes in road surface. On busy **tarmac roads**, "tramlines" often develop, parallel with the direction of travel. Caused by heavy trucks ploughing over hot blacktop, these can be deep and treacherous, making steering difficult. Slow down.

Beware of animals, people, rocks, branches, ditches and potholes – any combination of which may appear at any time. It is accepted practice to honk your horn stridently to warn pedestrians and cyclists. **Other vehicles** are probably the biggest menace, especially in busy areas close to towns where matatus are constantly pulling over to drop and pick up passengers. It's common practice to flash oncoming vehicles, especially if they're leaving you little room to pass. Try to **avoid driving at night**, and be extra careful when passing heavy vehicles – the diesel fumes can cut off your visibility without warning.

Officially Kenya **drives on the left**, though in reality vehicles keep to the best part of the road until they have to pass each other.

You should recognize the supplementary meanings of **left and right** signals particularly common among truck drivers. A right signal by the driver ahead of you means "Don't try to pass me", while the left signal which usually follows means "Feel free to pass me now". Do not, however, automatically assume the driver can really see that it is safe for you to pass. In fact, never assume anything about other drivers.

Beware of **speed bumps**, found wherever a busy road has been built through a village, and on the roads in and out of nearly every town. Try to look out for small bollards or painted rocks at the roadside, but usually the first you'll know of speed bumps is when your head hits the roof.

Driving in towns, you may need to adopt a more robust approach than you would use at home, or risk waiting indefinitely at the first busy junction you come to. There is no concept of yielding or giving way in Kenya: most drivers occupy the road forcefully and only concede when physically blocked by another vehicle or someone in uniform with a weapon. Although it sounds highly confrontational, incidents of "road rage" seem few and far between.

Finding somewhere to **park** is rarely a problem, even in Nairobi or Mombasa. There are council traffic wardens in most large towns from Monday to Saturday, from whom you can buy a 24-hour ticket (the only option) for Ksh50–150. If you don't, your car may be clamped or towed away. Be careful not to inadvertently park on yellow lines, which are often faded to near-invisibility.

Off-road driving

Although there are few parts of Kenya where 4WD vehicles are mandatory, you would be well advised not to go far off tarmac in a two-wheel-drive vehicle, if only because a short cloudburst can transform an otherwise good dirt road into a soft-mud vehicle trap. Take local advice if attempting unsurfaced roads in the rainy season, when mud pits with a smooth and apparently firm surface can disguise deep traps. A covering of vegetation usually means a relatively solid surface.

If you have to go through a large muddy puddle, first kick off your shoes and wade the entire length to check it out (better to get muddy than bogged down). If it's less than 30cm deep, and the base is relatively firm (ie your feet don't sink far), you should be able to drive through. Engage 4WD, get into first gear, and drive slowly straight across, or, if there's a sufficiently firm area to one side, drive across at speed with one wheel in the water and one out (beware of toppling over in a Suzuki). For smaller puddles, gathering up speed on the approach and then charging across in second gear usually works.

It's harder to offer advice about approaching **deep mud**. Drive as fast as you dare, never over-steer when skidding, and pray.

On a mushy surface of "**black cotton soil**", especially during or after rain, you'll need all your wits about you, as even the sturdiest 4WDs have little or no grip on this, and some – Land Cruisers for example – are notoriously useless. It's best to keep your speed down and stay in second gear as much as possible. Try to keep at least one wheel on vegetation-covered ground or in a well-defined rut.

If you do **get stuck**, stop immediately, as spinning the wheels will only make it worse. Try reversing, just once, by revving the engine as far as you can before engaging reverse gear. If it doesn't work, you'll just have to wait for another vehicle to pull you out.

Buses, matatus and taxis

Safety should be your first concern when travelling by public transport: matatus, and to a lesser extent buses, have a bad **safety record**. The most dangerous matatus are those billed as "express" (they mean it). Don't hesitate to ask to get out of the vehicle if you feel unsafe, and to demand a partial refund, which will usually be forthcoming.

Whatever you're travelling on, it's worth considering your general **direction** through the trip and which side of the vehicle will be shadier. This is especially important on dirt roads when the combination of dust, a slow, bumpy ride and fierce sun through closed windows can be unbearable.

Note that in more remote areas, where a service has no clear **schedule**, if a driver tells you he's going somewhere "today", it doesn't necessarily mean he expects to arrive today.

Inter-city bus and matatu **fares** are typically around Ksh2–5/km (or if the vehicle is "deluxe" in some way, up to Ksh7/km). Even the longest journey by matatu, the 300km, six-hour journey from Nairobi to Kisumu, should cost no more than Ksh1000 (or Ksh1500 by "deluxe" vehicle). Rarely does anyone attempt to charge more than the approved rate. Baggage charges should not normally be levied unless you're transporting a huge load. If you think you're being overcharged, check with other passengers.

Buses

Buses cover almost the whole country. Some, on the main runs between Nairobi and Mombasa, and to a lesser extent the centre and west, are fast, comfortable and keep to schedules; you generally need to **reserve** seats in advance. The large companies have ticket offices near the bus stations in most towns, where they list their routes and prices. Their parking bays are rarely marked, however, and there are no published timetables except on the occasional website. The easiest procedure is to mention your destination to a few people at the bus park, and then check out the torrent of offers. Keep asking – it's virtually impossible to get on the wrong bus. Once you've acquired a seat, the wait can be almost a pleasure if you're in no hurry, as you watch the throng outside and field a continuous stream of vendors proffering wares through the window.

Matatus

Along most routes the matatus these days are Nissan **minibuses** (in rural areas one or two old-style **pick-up vans**, fitted with wooden benches and a canvas roof, still ply their trade). The Nissans can be fast and are sometimes dangerous: try to sit at the back, to avoid too graphic a view of blind overtaking. And, at the risk of being repetitious, always ask to get out if you're scared of the driving.

After new **regulations** were introduced by the Kibaki government in 2003, all seats were supposed to be fitted with seat belts (they are often broken); loud music was banned (it is often still played, and is the one saving grace for some passengers); and electronic speed governors are supposed to prevent speeds above 80km/h (they are often broken or deliberately disabled). Passenger numbers are, in theory, strictly limited, but on many routes, especially off the main roads, the old maxim of "room for one more" still applies. *Kitu kidogo*, a "little something" for police officers at roadblocks, ensures blind eyes are turned towards many infringements. There's more on bribery elsewhere (see p.49), but it's worth pointing out that passengers are never expected to contribute directly (though sudden fare increases on a particular route may sometimes amount to the same thing).

Matatus can be an enjoyable way of getting about, giving you close contact, literally, with local people, and some hilarious encounters. They are also often the most convenient and sometimes the only means of transport to smaller places off the main roads.

When it comes to making a **choice of matatu**, always choose one that is close to full or you'll have to wait inside until they're ready to go, sometimes for hours. Beware of being used as bait by the driver to encourage passengers to choose his vehicle, and equally of a driver filling his car with young touts pretending to be passengers (spot them by the newspapers and lack of luggage). Competition is intense and people will tell brazen lies to persuade you the vehicle is going "just now". Try not to hand over any money before you've left town. This isn't a question of being ripped off, but too often the first departure is just a soft launch, cruising around town rounding up more passengers – and buying petrol with the fare you've just paid – and then going back to square one.

If your destination isn't on a main matatu route, or if you don't want to wait for a vehicle to fill up (or, indeed, if you just want to travel in style), drivers will happily negotiate a price for the **charter** or rental of the whole car. The sum will normally be equivalent

MATATU TERMS

The following terms are worth knowing: a **stage or stand** is the matatu yard; a **manamba or turn boy** is the tout who takes the fares and hangs on dramatically; and **dropping** is what you do when you disembark, as in "I'm dropping here".

to the amount they would receive from all the passengers in a full vehicle over the same distance.

Taxis and other vehicles

Transport in towns often comes down to **private taxis**. You'll need to discuss the fare in advance: most drivers will want to be earning something like Ksh500/hour and at least Ksh100/km, but would baulk at driving anywhere for less than Ksh200–300. In some towns, there's also the option of using a **tuk-tuk** (three-wheeled vehicles imported from Asia, on which fares are around half the price of an ordinary taxi). Alternatively, many areas have the two-wheel taxis consisting of a motorcycle which can carry one or two people without luggage (known as a **piki-piki**), or a bicycle with a padded passenger seat for one (known as a **boda-boda**). Most drivers/cyclists will be straight with you (if surprised to be taking a fare from a foreigner), but if you're in doubt about the correct fare, which is generally around Ksh25/km, asking passers-by will invariably get you a quick sense of the proper price to pay.

Trains

Rift Valley Railways runs Kenya's few passenger train services. The overnight **Nairobi–Mombasa** train leaves three times a week in each direction, taking around 14–17 hours to complete the journey. There's also a thrice-weekly **Nairobi–Kisumu**

TRAIN TIMETABLES

As explained (see opposite), this schedule is very much a theoretical framework rather than a reliable guide.

NAIROBI–MOMBASA

Nairobi Depart Mon, Wed, Fri 7pm, arrive Mombasa 10am.

Mombasa Depart Tues, Thurs, Sun 7pm, arrive Nairobi 10am.

Fares, including bedding, dinner and breakfast: first class Ksh4405, second class Ksh3385, third class (seat only) Ksh680.

NAIROBI–KISUMU

Nairobi Depart Mon, Wed, Fri 6.30pm, arrive Kisumu 9am.

Kisumu Depart Tues, Thurs, Sun 6.30pm, arrive Nairobi 9am.

Fares, including bedding, dinner and breakfast: first class Ksh3010, second class Ksh2210, third class (seat only) Ksh500.

---

service, which takes a similar time. On both routes, the train can pull in anything up to eight hours late. Frustrating though the almost routine delays are, they at least mean you are likely to have a few hours of daylight to watch the passing scene: approaching Nairobi from Mombasa, the animals on the Athi Plains; approaching the capital from Kisumu, the Rift Valley; approaching Mombasa, the sultry crawl down to the ocean.

The Rift Valley Railways website (W riftvalleyrail .com), includes schedules and fares, but is not always entirely accurate. The Man in Seat 61 (W seat61.com) is a much more reliable and up-to-date source of information.

If you want to book tickets before you arrive in Kenya, the agents Let's Go Travel (W uniglobelets gotravel.com) do a reliable job, but you pay a little extra. You can always book at the local station, ideally the day before.

Trains have three **seat classes**, but only first and second offer any kind of comfort. In first class, you get a private, two-berth compartment; second class has four-berth compartments, which are usually single-sex, though this may be disregarded if, for example, all four people are travelling as a party; third class has hard seats only and is packed with local passengers because it's half the price of the cheapest bus.

The carriages and compartments aren't luxurious, and the toilets are not all European-style, but the train usually starts its journey clean, and in a reasonably good state of repair. **Meals and bedding**, available in first and second class only, cost a little extra, and must be paid for when you buy your ticket, though it's normally assumed you will take them: they are included in the fares in our timetable box (Mombasa service dinner Ksh700, breakfast Ksh470; Kisumu service dinner Ksh350, breakfast Ksh250). The linen (Ksh320) is always clean, washing water usually flows from the compartment basins, meals are freshly prepared and service is good. On the Mombasa train, dinner is served in two sittings (7.15pm & 8.45pm). You should go for the first sitting for the best food and service, and the second if you'd rather take your time. Breakfast is served from 6am. Singles and couples will usually have to share their tables with other diners.

You can usually rely on getting **drinks** – bottled water, cold beers and sodas, and sometimes wine, all at fairly standard prices. It's a good idea to **take some snacks** with you – you'll be glad of them if the train rolls in eight hours late, as it occasionally does.

In recent years, the Nairobi–Kisumu service has often been suspended for weeks or months at a time, while the Nairobi–Mombasa service has generally kept going – the Wednesday/Thursday service seeming to be the first to go when there are problems.

There are **disused railway tracks** in several parts of Kenya and occasionally sections are refurbished: a Nairobi–Nanyuki service ran every Saturday in 2009, but seems to have failed again. There are also one or two **suburban commuter services** in Nairobi, and a new service is expected to start to the international airport in the near future.

Boats and ferries

Kenya has no rivers navigable for any distance by anything bigger than a canoe, and there's no passenger **shipping** along the Kenya coast apart from the small vessels connecting the islands of the Lamu archipelago. Informally, you can sometimes get lifts with dhow captains, though there are few working dhows left. On Lake Victoria, the network of steamer routes was suspended when the lake became clogged up with water hyacinth, and although there are occasional services, there's nothing you can rely on.

Hitchhiking

Hitchhiking is how the majority of rural people get around, in the sense that they wait by the roadside for whatever comes, and will pay for a ride in a passing lorry or a private vehicle, the cost being close to what it would be in a matatu. Private vehicles with spare seats are comparatively rare, but Kenyans are happy enough to give lifts, if often bemused by the idea of a tourist without a vehicle. Hitching rides with other tourists at the gates of national parks and reserves is also sometimes possible, but only if you have lots of time on your hands – and a plan for where you'll spend the night if you get a lift. Highway hitching **techniques** need to be fairly exuberant: beckon the driver to stop with a palm-down action, then quickly establish how much the ride will cost. And be sure to choose a safe spot with room to pull over. Alternatively, use a busy petrol station and ask every driver. That's the most likely way to get a ride. In terms of **safety**, it's highly unlikely you would run into any unsavoury characters, but do not get in if you think the vehicle is unroadworthy, or the driver unfit to drive.

Cycling

Kenya's climate and varied terrain make it challenging and interesting **cycling** country, and you can rent bikes or go on organized tours, or sign up for one of the charity-fundraising rides that regularly take place.

With a bike, given time and some determination, you can get to parts of the country that might otherwise be hard to reach. Several of the smaller game parks allow bikes, including Hell's Gate at Naivasha, Kakamega Forest and Saiwa Swamp. You need to consider the **seasons**, however, as you won't make much progress on dirt roads during the rains. On **main roads**, a mirror is essential, and, if the road surface is broken at the edge, give yourself plenty of space and be ready to leave the road if necessary.

As well as renting, you can take a bike with you to Kenya, or buy one locally. Most towns have bicycle shops selling basic mountain bikes and trusty Indian three-speed roadsters, starting from around Ksh7000. We've mentioned some outlets in Mombasa (see p.407) and Nairobi (see p.117). Whatever you take, and a mountain bike is certainly best, it will need low gears and strongly built wheels, and you should have some essential spare parts.

If you're taking a bike with you, then you'll probably want to carry your gear in **panniers**. These are inconvenient, however, when not on the bike, and you might instead consider strapping your luggage onto the rear carrier. It's possible to adapt your carrier locally with furniture cane and lashings of inner-tube strips (any market will fix you up for pennies), thus creating your own highly un-aerodynamic touring carrier, with room for a box of food and a gallon of water underneath.

If you're taking a bike from home, take a battery **lighting system**: with darkness falling at around 6.30pm all year round it's surprising how often you'll need it. The front light will double as a torch, and getting batteries is no problem. Also take a **U-bolt cycle lock**. In situations where you have to lock the bike, you'll always find something to lock it to (out in the bush, locking is less important). Local bikes can be locked with a padlock and chain passed through a length of hosepipe, which you can buy and fix up in any market.

Buses and matatus with **roof racks** will always carry bicycles for about half the regular fare, even if flagged down at the roadside. Trucks will often give you a lift, too. The trains also take bikes at a low fixed fare.

Accommodation

There's a huge diversity of accommodation in Kenya, ranging from campsites and local lodging houses for a few hundred shillings a night to luxury lodges and boutique tented camps that can easily cost many hundreds of dollars a night.

If you're planning a trip to Kenya using mid-range or expensive accommodation, a lot of money can be saved by not going in the **high season**. Most resort hotels and safari lodges and tented camps have separate high-, mid- and low-season (sometimes called "green-season") rates. There's sometimes a peak season too, just covering the Christmas and New Year break from December 21 to January 2. Low-season rates can be anything from 30 to 50 percent of the high-season rates.

Some of the smaller camps and lodges close for a couple of months some time between mid-March and mid-April (as soon as Easter has passed) and June, and sometimes also in November. The seasons vary widely across different operators and lodge-owners, depending on their markets (February can be high, for example). Listings throughout the guide show the latest details on months of closure, though these can vary from year to year. Closures are not just due to lack of demand or less-than-ideal weather conditions, but to allow for maintenance and refurbishment.

Hotels, lodges and tented camps

The term **hotel** covers a very broad spectrum in Kenya (the word *hoteli* means a cheap café-restaurant, not a place to sleep). At the top end are the big tourist and business-class establishments. In the game parks, they're known as lodges. Some establishments are very good value, but others are shabby and overpriced, so check carefully before splurging. Try to reserve the more popular places in advance, especially for the busiest season (Dec & Jan).

At the mid-price level, some hotels are old settlers' haunts that were once slightly grand and no longer quite fit in modern Kenya, while others are newer and cater for the Kenyan middle class.

A few are fine – charmingly decrepit or fairly smart and semi-efficient – but a fair few are just boozy and uninteresting.

As a rule, expect to pay anything from Ksh3000–10,000 for a decent double or twin room in a town hotel, with bathroom en suite, known in Kenya as "self-contained" (and abbreviated throughout this book to s/c). Breakfast is usually included, but if you want to have breakfast elsewhere, the price will be deducted. Features such as TV – often with DSTV (satellite) service – floor or ceiling fans and air conditioning will all put the price up, and are sometimes optional, allowing you to make significant savings at cheaper hotels.

Older **safari lodges** may show their age with rather unimaginative design and boring little rooms, but those which date back to the 1960s were built when just having a hotel in the bush was considered an achievement. Today, the best of the big lodges have public areas offering spectacular panoramas and game-viewing decks, while the rooms are often comfortable chalets or *bandas*. The vogue in the most expensive, boutique lodges tends to be Tarzan-like, eschewing straight lines wherever possible and incorporating bare rock and reclaimed branches of dead wood. Some places have just half a dozen "rooms", constructed entirely of local materials, ingeniously open-fronted yet secure, with stunning views, and invigorating open-air showers.

If you want to experience the fun of camping without the hassle, opt for a **tented camp**. These consist of large, custom-made tents erected over hard floors. The walls flap in the breeze and large areas of mosquito screening can be uncovered to allow maximum ventilation. All the usual lodge amenities, including electricity, comfy beds, clothes storage and floor coverings, are installed. Floor coverings can include carpets or rugs, and the furniture is what you'd expect to find in a comfortable hotel, though often with a nod to bush life, with canvas chairs on the deck and antique-style lock-up chests rather than room safes. At the back, the bathroom is usually more of a solid-walled structure, with a flush toilet – though the "safari shower" or "bucket shower" using hot water delivered on request by staff to a pulley system outside the bathroom, is a popular anachronism that works very well and saves water. At night, the tents zip up tight to keep the insects out. In the centre of the camp, the usual public areas will include a dining room and bar, or in smaller camps a luxurious "mess tent" with sofas and waiters proffering drinks, where you'll eat together with your hosts and the other guests and share the day's

---

SEASONS (APPROXIMATE)

High Dec 21 to Jan 2, July 1 to Sept 30.
Mid Jan 3 to Easter, Oct 1 to Dec 20.
Low/Green/Closed After Easter to May 31.

experiences in an atmosphere that always has a little *Out of Africa* in it.

Because tented camps are relatively easy to construct and re-configure, they're at the vanguard of Kenya's **environmentally responsible tourism** movement (see p.24). The most innovative camps limit their use of electricity to what can be generated by solar panels, provide "safari showers" to order, using a reservoir and pulley system, rather than permanent hot water, and take care to limit their footprint in other ways, for example by composting their organic waste and trucking out non-biodegradable trash rather than burning it. Scavenging **marabou storks** at camps and lodges are a sure sign of poor waste management.

Some lodges and camps are surrounded by a discreet, or not so discreet, **electric fence**. This gives you the freedom to wander at will, but detracts from the sense of being in the wild. Places that don't have such security may ask you to sign a disclaimer to limit their liability in the event that a large mammalian intruder should abruptly terminate your holiday. In practice, although elephants, buffaloes and other big animals do sometimes wander into camps, serious incidents are exceptionally rare and you have nothing to worry about. After dark, unfenced camps employ escorts – usually traditionally dressed, spear-carrying *askaris* (see box, p.58) – to see you safely to and from your tent.

Meals in the lodges and camps are prepared in fully equipped kitchens and served by waiters who are often knowledgeable about local wildlife and

> ## TOILETS
> There are very few public **toilets** (*wanawake* for women; *wanaume* for men). Hotels and restaurants are unlikely to turn you away if you ask to use their facilities.

customs. Although the food can be repetitive, the best places have their own organic vegetable gardens and prepare gourmet dinners, fresh bread and excellent pastries in the middle of nowhere.

Most of the more expensive hotels, lodges and tented camps quote their **rates** in US dollars or sometimes euros – a hangover from the days when the Kenya shilling was not a convertible currency. You can always settle your bill in Kenya shillings, but the exchange rate is often poor.

It's always worth trying to negotiate a **discount**. Many cheap hotels will bend over backwards to remind you that their rates can be discussed. And in the more expensive places which usually apply a two-tier tariff for **residents and non-residents**, it's a perfectly acceptable negotiating tactic to claim to be a resident, though you may have to eat humble pie if they demand to see proof.

Kenya's upmarket hotels are generally good at providing internet services. Where **wi-fi** is mentioned in the listings in the guide, that means free wi-fi. Internet services that are chargeable are usually not mentioned: there's likely to be a cybercafé round the corner offering connections for a tenth of the price.

ACCOMMODATION PRICES AND SEASONS

The **accommodation rates** given in this guide are for double- or twin-bed occupancy during the high season (usually Dec 21 to Jan 2 and July 1 to Sept 30).

All cheap lodgings, all Nairobi hotels and most town hotels (unless they're on the coast) are **non-seasonal**. All coastal resort hotels, safari camps and lodges operate **seasonal** rates.

The rates have been provided directly by the property and are the non-resident "rack rates" – in other words the regular walk-in rates that you will pay for the night, including taxes (16 percent VAT and 2 percent training levy). If there is more than one class of room, the standard or cheapest option is the one quoted.

For **dorm beds** and **campsites**, the price per person has been given, while for **self-catering** cottages, houses and *bandas*, the price given is for the whole unit.

Agents, online booking services and the property's own reservations desk may offer cheaper deals for advance bookings. And you can, of course, always ask if they can offer you a discount – for paying by cash; because you're a first-time visitor; because you're a repeat visitor; or for any other plausible reason you care to invent.

Cheap hotels quote their rates in Kenyan shillings, while hotels aimed at the tourist market tend to quote their rates in dollars.

Residents' rates for Kenyan citizens and residents, including expat workers (typically around 30–40 percent discount), are offered at most establishments above the budget bracket. There's no hard-and-fast rule, but most places charging above $80–100 a room have a two-tier pricing.

Boarding and lodgings

In any town you'll find basic guesthouses called **boarding and lodgings** (for which we've coined the abbreviation "B&L"). These can vary from a mud shack with water from the well to a multistorey building of en-suite rooms, complete with a bar and restaurant, and usually built around a lock-in courtyard/parking area. Most B&L bathrooms include rather alarmingly wired "instant showers", giving a meagre spray of hot water 24 hours a day.

If you want a **double bed**, ask for a room with "one big bed". If you ask for a "double room" you will normally get a room with two beds. What matters is how many beds will be used, not the number of people sleeping in them. So a couple sharing a double bed will nearly always pay the same price as a single guest, though they'll have to pay for an extra breakfast. At about the price point where residents' and non-residents' rates come into play, and rates are set in dollars rather than shillings, the international language of "doubles", "twins" and "single room supplements" is usually spoken.

While you can find a room for under Ksh1500 – and sometimes much less – in any town, **prices** are not a good indication of quality. If the bathrooms don't have instant showers, then check the water supply and find out when the boiler will be on. The very cheapest places (as little as Ksh500 or less) will not usually have self-contained rooms, so you should check the state of the shared showers and toilets. You won't cause offence by saying no thanks.

The better B&Ls are clean and comfortable, but they tend to be airless and often double as informal brothels, especially if they have a bar. If the place seems noisy in the afternoon, it will become cacophonous during the night, so you may want to ask for a room away from the source of the din. Moreover, if it relies on its bar for income, security becomes an important deciding factor. Well-run B&Ls, even noisy, sleazy ones, always have uniformed security staff and gated access to the room floors. You can leave valuables with the manager in reception (usually a small cell protected by metal grills), though use your judgement. Leaving valuables like cameras in your room is usually safe enough if they're packed away in your bags. It's money and small items left lying around that tend to disappear.

Cottages and homestays

Increasingly, it's possible to book **self-catering** apartments, villas or cottages. Langata Link Holiday Homes (☎+254 (0)20 891314 or +254 (0)721 556031, ⓦholidayhomeskenya.com) are agents for a wide range of houses especially on the coast. Kenya Beach

---

ACCOMMODATION TERMS

a/c air-conditioned
AI all-inclusive
askari or soja guard, security officer
banda cottage or chalet
BB bed & breakfast
B&L boarding and lodging, a cheap guesthouse
FB full board (lunch, dinner, bed and breakfast)
fly camp mobile camp
HB half board (dinner or lunch, bed and breakfast)
hoteli cheap restaurant or café, not a hotel
lodge safari hotel in the bush
long-drop non-flushing toilet – a hole over a deep pit
mabati corrugated-iron roof
package the usual full-board arrangement in high-end safari camps and lodges, with all drinks and activities included
rondavel small, round hut, containing beds but no bathroom
safari shower also known as a bucket shower, a refillable reservoir of hot water above the shower area, in eco-friendly tented camps
s/c "self-contained" room, with en-suite bathroom
star-bed four-poster bed mounted on vehicle wheels, pulled onto a deck at night and guarded by askaris
tented camp a camp in the bush, or in a game park, consisting of large, walk-in safari tents with solid bathrooms
tree-hotel animal-viewing lodge on stilts, after the style of *Treetops* (see p.191)

Rentals (Ⓦkenya-beachrentals.com) specializes in coastal properties. Uniglobe Let's Go Travel (☎+254 (0)20 2678646 or +254 (0)722 331899; Ⓦuniglobelets gotravel.com) is a highly recommended agent for accommodation across the spectrum, including homestays, cottages and villas.

Youth hostels

Only two Kenyan **youth hostels**, at Nairobi (see p.122) and Naro Moru (see p.167), are affiliated to Hostelling International (Ⓦhihostels.com). Both are fairly basic, and *Nairobi Youth Hostel* isn't much used by budget travellers. Non-members pay Ksh120 per night in addition to the normal rate (Ksh700 in dorms). The hostels can be booked through HI or the local association (Ⓦyhak.org). There are also **YMCAs**, **YWCAs** and **church-run hostels** in a number of towns. The better ones are mentioned in accommodation listings.

Camping

If you're on a budget and have a flexible itinerary, there are enough **camping sites (campgrounds)** in Kenya to make it worthwhile carrying a tent, and camping wild is sometimes a viable option, too. Bring the lightest tent you can afford and remember its main purpose is to keep insects out, so one made largely of mosquito netting could be ideal.

Campsites in the parks are usually very basic, though a handful of privately owned sites have more in the way of facilities. **Kenya Wildlife Service** (KWS) manages all the campsites in national parks, for which the current rate ranges from $15–25/ person per day. For that hefty price, you often get little more than a place to pitch your tent and park your vehicle. Showers and toilets are often rudimentary and the other normal camping site features, such as a shop or café, non-existent.

The so-called **special campsites**, found in a number of national parks, are in reality simply campsites which have to be reserved on an exclusive basis for private use. Some of them are in particularly attractive locations, but unlike standard campsites they have no facilities whatsoever: you need to be entirely self-sufficient to use them. To reserve a special campsite, which costs a flat fee of Ksh7500 for up to one week, plus the daily per-person rates ($30, or $40 in Amboseli and Lake Nakuru), contact ☎+254 (0)726 610508, ✉reservations @kws.go.ke or visit KWS headquarters at Nairobi National Park Main Gate in Nairobi. Camping fees in the major national parks (Aberdare, Amboseli,

Nairobi, Lake Nakuru, Tsavo East and Tsavo West) are normally deducted from your pre-paid Safari Card (see p.71).

Opportunities for **wild camping** depend on whether you can find a suitable, safe site. In the more heavily populated and farmed highland districts, you should always ask someone before pitching in an empty spot, and never leave your tent unattended. Camping near roads, in dry river beds or on trails used by animals going to water, is highly inadvisable (see p.84), as is camping on the beach.

Far out in the wilds, hard or thorny ground is likely to be the only obstacle. During the dry seasons, you'll rarely have trouble finding dead wood for a fire, so a stove is optional. You can buy camping gas cartridges in a few places in Nairobi (see p.122).

Eating and drinking

For the vast majority of Kenyans, meals are plain and filling. Most people's living standards don't allow for frills, and there are no great national dishes. For culinary culture, it's the coast, with its long association with Indian Ocean trade, that has produced distinctive regional cuisine, where rice and fish, flavoured with coconut, tamarind and exotic spices, are the major ingredients. For visitors, and more affluent Kenyans, the cities and tourist areas have no shortage of restaurants, with roast meat, seafood and Italian restaurants the most common options among a range of cuisines that runs the gamut from Argentine to Thai. The Language section (see p.595) contains a list of useful terms (see p.595).

In the most basic local restaurant, a decent plate of food can be had for less than Ksh200. Fancier meals in touristy places rarely cost more than Ksh2000 a head, though there are a number of establishments where you could easily spend Ksh5000 or more. When checking your bill, remember there's a 16 percent value added tax (VAT) on food and drink and a 2 percent government training levy in all but the smallest establishments. In most establishments, taxes are included in the prices on the menu, but in some they are extra, basically adding nearly one-fifth to the bill. An "optional" service charge can be added, too, and of course you may want to add a tip (see p.91).

Many restaurants on the coast serve halal fare, and elsewhere in the country you'll usually be able to find a Somali-run *hoteli* that has halal meat.

Home-style fare and nyama choma

In any **hoteli** (small restaurant) there is always a list of predictable dishes intended to fill customers' stomachs. Potatoes, rice and especially **ugali** (a stiff, cornmeal porridge) are the national staples, eaten with chicken, goat, beef, or vegetable stew, various kinds of spinach, beans and sometimes fish. Portions are usually gigantic; half-portions (ask for *nusu*) aren't much smaller. But even in small towns, more and more cafés are appearing where most of the menu is fried – eggs, sausages, chips, fish, chicken and burgers.

The standard blow-out feast for most Kenyans is a huge pile of **nyama choma** (roast meat). *Nyama choma* is usually eaten at a purpose-built *choma* bar, with beer and music the standard accompaniments, and *ugali* and greens optional. You go to the kitchen and order by weight (half a kilo is plenty), direct from the butcher's hook or out of the fridge. There's usually a choice of *nyama* – goat, beef, mutton. After roasting, the meat is brought to your table on a wooden platter, chopped to bite-size with a sharp knife, and served with crunchy salt and *kachumbari* – tomato and onion relish.

Snacks and breakfast

Snacks, which can easily become meals, include samosas, chapattis, miniature kebabs (*mishkaki*), roasted corncobs, *mandaazi* (sweet, puffy, deep-fried dough cakes) and "egg-bread". *Mandaazi* are made before breakfast and served until evening time, when they've become cold and solid. Egg-bread (misleadingly translated from the Swahili *mkate mayai*) is a light wheat-flour "pancake" wrapped around fried eggs and minced meat, usually cooked on a huge griddle. While you won't find it everywhere, it's a delicious Kenyan response to the creeping burger menace (McDonald's, happily, is still not here). Snacks sold on the street include cassava chips and, in country areas, at the right time of year, if you're lucky, roasted termites (which go well as a bar snack with beer).

Breakfast varies widely. Standard fare in a *hoteli*, or in the dining room of a boarding and lodging house, consists of sweet tea and a chapatti or a doorstep of white bread thickly spread with margarine. Modest hotels offer a "full breakfast" of cereal, eggs and sausage, bread and jam, and a banana, with instant coffee or tea. If you're staying in an upmarket hotel or safari lodge, breakfast is usually a lavish acreage of hot and cold buffets that you can't possibly do justice to.

At upmarket lodges and safari camps, you will usually be offered nibbles or appetizers – **"bitings"** as they are usually called – with your pre-dinner drink, as part of your package. Look out for the excellent feta and coriander samosa with chilli jam, which has spread from Nairobi to become a bit of an obsession among foodies.

Restaurant meals

Kenya's seafood, beef and lamb are renowned, and they are the basis of most restaurant meals. **Game meat** used to be something of a Kenyan speciality, most of it farmed on ranches. Giraffe, zebra, impala and warthog all regularly appeared at various restaurants. These days, only captive-farmed ostrich (excellent, like lean beef) and crocodile (disappointingly like gristly fish-tasting chicken) are legal.

Indian restaurants in the larger towns, notably Nairobi and Mombasa, are generally excellent, with *dhal* lunches a good standby and much fancier regional dishes widely available too. When you splurge, apart from eating Indian, it will usually be in

---

VEGETARIAN AND VEGAN FOOD

If you're a **vegetarian** staying in tourist-class hotels you should have no problems, as there's usually a meat-free pasta dish, or various egg-based dishes. In more expensive establishments, vegetarian cooking is taken seriously, with creative options increasingly available that are more just stodge. If you're on a strict budget you'll gravitate to Indian vegetarian restaurants in the larger towns where you can often eat well and cheaply. Otherwise, it can be tricky, because meat is the conventional focus of any meal not eaten at home, and *hotelis* rarely have much else to accompany the starch; even vegetable stews are normally cooked in meat gravy.

If you're a **vegan**, you'll find there are nearly always good vegetables and lots of fruit at safari lodges and the more expensive hotels. Once again, where you'll struggle is if you're on a strict budget and eating local restaurant food.

hotel restaurants, with food often very similar to what you might be served in a restaurant in Europe or North America. The **lodges** usually have buffet lunches at about Ksh1200–2000, which can be great value, with table-loads of salads and cold meat.

Fruit

Fruit is a major delight. Bananas, avocados, pawpaws and pineapples are in the markets all year, mangoes and citrus fruits more seasonally. Look out for passion fruit (the familiar shrivelled brown variety, and the sweeter and less acidic smooth yellow ones), cape gooseberries (*physalis*), custard apples and guavas – all highly distinctive and delicious. On the coast, roasted **cashew nuts** are widely available, but not cheap. Never buy any with dark marks on them. **Coconuts**, widely seen at roadside stalls in their freshly cut, green-husked condition, are filling and nutritious. At this stage, when the nuts are young, they're full of coconut water and the flesh is like soft-boiled egg white. If left to ripen on the tree until the husk goes brown, the liquid reduces, and the flesh becomes firm.

Drinking

The national beverage is **chai** – tea. Universally drunk at breakfast and as a pick-me-up at any time, the traditional way of making it is a weird variant on the classic British brew: milk, water, lots of sugar and tea leaves are brought to the boil in a kettle and served scalding hot (*chai asli*). It must eventually do diabolical dental damage, but it's quite addictive and very reviving. The main tea-producing region is around Kericho in the west, but the best tea tends to be made on the coast. These days, tea is all too often a tea bag in a cup, with hot water or milk brought to your table in a thermos.

Coffee, despite being another huge Kenyan export, doesn't have the same place in people's hearts, and if you order it in a cheap restaurant it's invariably instant coffee granules. Local chains of American-style coffee shops have sprung up in Nairobi in recent years, however, and it's steadily getting easier to order a latte or cappuccino, while breakfast with a good *cafetière* of the excellent local roast is also increasingly the norm, especially in upmarket places.

Soft drinks (sodas) are usually very cheap, and crates of Coke, Fanta and Sprite find their way to the wildest corners of the country. Krest, a bitter lemon, is not bad, and Krest also makes a ginger ale, but it's watery and insipid; Stoney ginger beer has more of a punch. Sometimes you can get plain soda water. A newer drink is Alvaro, a malty, pineapple-flavoured non-alcoholic alternative to beer, which is very popular but too sweet for some tastes.

Fresh fruit **juices** are available in the towns, especially on the coast (Lamu is fruit-juice heaven). Passion fruit, the cheapest, is excellent, though nowadays it's likely to be watered-down concentrate. Some places serve a variety: you'll sometimes find carrot juice and even tiger milk, made from a small tuber (the tiger nut or Spanish *chufa*). Bottled Picana mango juice is also available at some shops that sell sodas.

Plastic-bottled **spring water** is relatively expensive but widely available in 300ml, 500ml and one-litre bottles. Mains water used to be very drinkable, and in some places still is, but it's safer to stick with bottled (see p.64).

Beer

If you like **lager**, you'll find Kenyan brands generally good. The main lagers are Tusker and White Cap (both 4.2 percent) and Pilsner (4.7 percent), sold in half-litre bottles, with Tusker Malt (5.2 percent) in 300ml bottles. They all cost from a little over Ksh100 in local bars up to about Ksh400 in the most expensive establishments. Brewed by East African Breweries, they are fairly inconsistent in flavour: try a blind taste test. While Tusker Malt is fuller-flavoured, Tusker, White Cap and Pilsner are all light, slightly acidic, fairly fizzy, well-balanced beers that most people will find very drinkable when well chilled. You can also get a head-thumping 6.52 percent-alcohol version of Guinness.

Occasionally you can get keg Tusker **on tap** at roughly the same price, and more rarely the cheaper Senator beer, which is only sold in kegs and costs around Ksh50 per half litre.

In **cheap bars**, the bar counter itself is usually protected by a metal grill, putting the staff in a kind of cage. In this sort of place, you'll need to specify whether you want your beer cold or warm. Warm is the usual local preference. A point of drinking **etiquette** worth remembering is that you should never take your bottle away. As bottles carry deposits, this is considered theft and surprisingly ugly misunderstandings can ensue.

Other alcoholic drinks

Most of the usually familiar **wines** sold in Kenya come from South Africa and Chile, with Italy, California, France and Spain also featuring. Locally made wines struggle a little, but Richard Leakey's Pinot Noir vineyard is finally breaking through with Zabibu

(Wzabibu.org), and Rift Valley Winery makes the increasingly well-known Leleshwa (Wleleshwa.com).

Kenya Cane (white rum) and **Kenya Gold** (a coffee-flavoured liqueur) deserve a try, but they're nothing special. One popular Kenyan cocktail to sample is the **dawa** ("medicine") – a highly addictive vodka, white rum, honey and lime juice mix, poured over ice and stirred with a sugar stick.

There's a battery of laws against **home brewing** and distilling, perhaps because of the loss of tax revenue on legal booze, but these are central aspects of Kenyan culture and they go on. You can sample *pombe* (bush beer) of different sorts all over the country. It's as varied in taste, colour and consistency as its ingredients: basically fermented sugar and millet or banana, with herbs and roots for flavouring. The results are frothy and deceptively strong.

On the coast, where coconuts grow most plentifully, merely lopping off the growing shoot produces a naturally fermented, milky-coloured **palm wine** (*mnazi* or *tembo*), which is indisputably Kenya's finest contribution to the art of self-intoxication. It's bottled, informally, and usually drunk through a piece of dried grass or straw with a tiny filter tied to the end. There's another variety of palm wine, tapped from the doum palm, called *mukoma*.

Although there is often a furtive discretion about *pombe* or *mnazi* sessions (in fact, *mnazi* was recently legalized, at least on the coast), consumers rarely get busted.

Not so with home-distilled spirits: think twice before accepting a mug of **chang'aa**. It's treacherous firewater, and is also frequently contaminated with industrial alcohol, regularly killing drinking parties en masse. Sentences for distilling and possessing *chang'aa* are harsh, and police or vigilante raids common.

Health

Disease is an ever-present threat to most Kenyans, but health should not be a big issue for visitors. Malaria is endemic and HIV infection rates are high, but so long as you take sensible precautions – remember your malaria pills, clean any cuts or scrapes, and avoid food that has been left out after cooking – you should have no problems beyond the chance of minor tummy trouble.

One of the biggest hazards is the fierce **UV radiation** of the equatorial sun. Brightness rather than heat is the damaging element, so wear a hat

and use high-factor **sunblock**, especially in your first two weeks. If you're going to be on the road for a long time, it may be worth considering taking some **vitamin** tablets with you, though they are no substitute for a balanced diet with plenty of fresh fruit and vegetables. If you're going to Kenya for longer than a short holiday, get a thorough **dental checkup** before leaving home. A freshly cut "toothbrush twig" (*msuake*) is a useful supplement, and some varieties contain a plaque-destroying enzyme. You can buy them at markets.

Sexually transmitted diseases, including **HIV**, are rife. Four out of five deaths among 25- to 35-year-olds are AIDS-related. Using a condom will help to protect you from this and other STDs, including **hepatitis B**, which is quite widespread and can lead to chronic liver disease.

Medical resources

Your doctor is your best first source of advice and probable supplier of jabs and prescriptions. Depending on your doctor and your health provider, you may get your requirements free of charge, or have to pay.

INTERNATIONAL AND EMERGENCY

IAMAT W iamat.org. A free-membership non-profit organization, providing travel health info and lists of approved participating hospitals and clinics in Kenya.

International SOS Assistance W internationalsos.com. Emergency evacuation and assistance to members.

MEDJET Assistance W medjetassist.com. Medical evacuation specialists.

UK

MASTA W masta-travel-health.com. Clinic locations throughout the UK, but expensive.

NHS Choices Travel Health W bit.ly/NHSChoicesTravel. Detailed, free advice.

NHS Scotland Fit for Travel W fitfortravel.nhs.uk. Scottish NHS website on travellers' health.

Nomad Pharmacy W nomadtravel.co.uk. Three locations in London, plus Bristol, Southampton and Manchester.

Ireland

Tropical Medical Bureau W tmb.ie. More than a dozen clinics across Ireland.

US and Canada

Centers for Disease Control and Prevention W cdc.gov/travel. US government official site for travel health.

Public Health Agency of Canada W bit.ly/YFCanada. Complete listing of yellow fever vaccination centres across Canada.

Travel Health Online ⓦ bit.ly/TripPrep. Well-updated, US, private-sector health and safety site with substantial Kenya information.

Australia, NZ, Asia, South Africa

The Travel Doctor TMVC ⓦ traveldoctor.com.au. Travellers' medical & vaccination centres across Australia, New Zealand, Asia and South Africa.

Inoculations

For arrivals by air direct from Europe and North America, Kenya has **no required inoculations**. Entering overland from Uganda or Tanzania, though (or flying via another African country), you may well be required to show an International Vaccination Certificate (IVC) for **yellow fever**. If you intend to enter Kenya by land or to break your journey to Kenya elsewhere in Africa, plan ahead and start organizing your jabs at least six weeks before departure. A yellow fever certificate only becomes valid ten days after you've had the jab, but is then valid for ten years. If you are returning home to a country that requires an IVC for yellow fever in the case of travellers who have been in Kenya (Australia is one), then you should get your vaccination before departure.

You should ensure that you are up to date with your childhood **tetanus** and **polio** protection: boosters are necessary every ten years and it's as well to check before travelling.

Although not necessary for an ordinary safari-and-beach holiday, if you're going to be exposed to unhygienic conditions, doctors recommend jabs for **typhoid**, **hepatitis A** and **hepatitis B** (or a combined vaccination course). Effective protection takes some time to develop after the vaccination, so again, if you're going to be working locally or travelling extensively, talk to your doctor as far ahead as you can.

Malaria

Malaria is endemic in tropical Africa and has a variable **incubation period** of a few days to several weeks, meaning you can get it long after being bitten. It's caused by a parasite called *Plasmodium*, carried in the saliva of the female *Anopheles* mosquito. *Anopheles* prefers to **bite** in the evening, and can be distinguished by the eager, head-down position as she settles to bite. *Anopheles* is rarely found above 1500m, which means Nairobi and much of central Kenya is naturally malaria-free, but infected humans are vectors for the disease, meaning that an uninfected *Anopheles* mosquito

that bites an infected person can pass malaria on to someone else, so you should assume the whole country is risky. Recent research has spotlighted a number of areas as having relatively **high levels of malaria transmission**, including the far south coast, around Shimoni, and the Lake Victoria shoreline and the plains inland from it. It can't be stressed enough, however, that you can catch malaria virtually anywhere in Kenya.

Though not infectious, the disease can be very dangerous and sometimes fatal if not treated quickly. The destruction of red blood cells by the *Plasmodium falciparum* parasite can lead to **cerebral malaria** (blocking of the brain capillaries) and is the cause of a nasty complication called **blackwater fever** in which the urine is stained by excreted blood cells.

Wherever you travel, mosquito bites are almost a certainty and protection against malaria is essential. The best and most obvious method is to reduce your risk of being bitten. Keep your arms, legs and feet covered as much as possible after dusk (long, light-coloured sleeves and trousers are best), and cover exposed skin with a strong repellent. **Deet-based repellents** ("deet" is the insecticide diethyltoluamide) are best; citronella oil is considered much less effective, and has the disadvantage that elephants are attracted to the smell, and have been known to break into cars and tents to get at it. Sleep under a **mosquito net** (if you're using your own, you might want to impregnate it with Deet) and burn **mosquito coils**, or mosquito-repellent **tablets** on a plug-in electric burner, both readily available in Kenya. Electronic buzzers have been shown not to work.

However much you can avoid being bitten, most medical professionals consider it essential to take **anti-malaria tablets**. The commonly recommended preventatives are the weekly mefloquine (sold as **Lariam**), which has a poor record for side effects, the antibiotic **doxycycline**, taken daily, and atovaquone-with-proguanil, taken daily (sold as **Malarone**), which, while expensive, has few, if any, side effects and can be started just two days before you leave. Your doctor may be able to advise further on which of these pills is the best one for you, and what the various side effects can be. It's important to maintain a careful routine and cover the period **before and after** your trip with doses.

If you do get a **dose of malaria**, you'll soon know about it: the fever, shivering and headaches are something like severe flu and come in unpleasant waves, making you pour with sweat for half an hour and then shiver uncontrollably. If you suspect anything, go to a hospital or clinic immediately. You will be rapidly tested and sold the appropriate treatment. If you can't get to a doctor, seeing a pharmacist is a good plan B.

If you're visiting Kenya for an extended period, it makes sense to **buy anti-malarial tablets in Kenya**. You can buy all of them over the counter and they can be much cheaper than at home – a box of one hundred doxycycline, for example, costs less than Ksh1000. You may be offered loose tablets in ordinary pharmacies, but the risk of being sold counterfeit drugs means you should stick to properly packed tablets or capsules. In the case of doxycycline, the value should be too low to be worth the effort of counterfeiting the pills.

Waterborne diseases

Serious stomach upsets don't afflict a large proportion of travellers. That said, Kenya's once fairly safe **tap water** is increasingly unfit to drink and the supply can be particularly suspect during periods of drought or heavy flooding. Where there is no mains supply, be very cautious of rain- or well-water. To purify water intended for drinking, use purifying tablets or, better, iodine (six drops per litre of water, then wait for half an hour), or boil it (if at high altitude, for thirty minutes).

If your stay in Kenya is short, you might as well stick to **bottled water**, which is widely available. For longer stays, think of **re-educating your stomach**; it's virtually impossible to travel around the country without exposing yourself to strange bugs from time to time. Take it easy at first, don't overdo the fruit (and wash it in clean water), don't keep food too long, and be wary of salads. It is also wise to eat food that is freshly cooked and piping hot.

Should you go down with **diarrhoea**, it will probably sort itself out without treatment within 48 hours. In the meantime, and especially with children, for whom it may be more serious, it's essential to replace the fluids and salts lost, so drink lots of water with oral rehydration salts (if you can't get them from pharmacies, use half a teaspoon of salt and eight teaspoons of sugar in a litre of water). It's a good idea to avoid greasy food, heavy spices, caffeine and most fruit and dairy products. Plain rice or *ugali* with boiled vegetables is the best diet. Drugs like Lomotil and Imodium simply plug you up, undermining the body's efforts to rid itself of infection, though they can be useful if you have to travel.

Avoid jumping for antibiotics at the first sign of trouble: they annihilate what's nicely known as your "gut flora" and will not work on viruses. But if your diarrhoea continues for more than five days, seek medical help. You should be aware of the fact that diarrhoea reduces the efficacy of malaria and contraceptive pills as they may pass straight through your system without being absorbed.

Bilharzia (medical name schistosomiasis) is a dangerous disease. It comes from tiny worm-like flukes, the schistosomes, that live in freshwater snails and which burrow into animal or human skin to multiply in the bloodstream. The snails only favour stagnant water and the chances of picking up bilharzia are small. The usual recommendation is never to swim in, wash with, or even touch, lake water that can't be vouched for as schistosome-free. The stagnant and weed-infested parts of Kenyan lakes and rivers often harbour bilharzia, but the danger of crocodile attack means you're unlikely to want any close contact with most inland waters in any case. If you suffer serious fatigue and pass blood, which are the first symptoms of bilharzia, see a doctor: it's curable.

Heat and altitude

It's important not to underestimate the power of the **equatorial sun**: a hat and sunglasses are strongly recommended to protect you from the bright light. The sun can quickly burn, or even cause **sunstroke**, so a high-factor sunblock is vital on exposed skin, especially when you first arrive (and it's expensive in Kenya, particularly in hotel shops, so take it with you). Be aware that overheating can cause **heatstroke**, which is potentially fatal. Signs are a very high body temperature, without a feeling of fever but accompanied by headaches and disorientation. Lowering the body temperature (by taking a tepid shower, for example), and resting in a cool place, are the first steps in treatment.

The sun's radiation is stronger at higher altitudes, but the biggest risk if you climb to over 2500m above sea level is **altitude sickness** (see p.169), which may affect climbers on Mount Kenya, and even walkers in the Cherangani Hills.

On the coast, many people get occasional **heat rashes**, especially at first. A warm shower to open the pores, and loose cotton clothes, can help, as can zinc oxide powder. **Dehydration** is another possible problem, so make sure you're drinking enough fluids, especially when you're hot or tired, but don't overdo alcoholic or caffeinated drinks. The

MEDICINE BAG

Various items worth taking on a trip include:
- **Alcohol swabs** Invaluable for cleaning minor wounds and insect bites.
- **Antihistamine cream** Apply immediately after insect bites to reduce itchiness.
- **Anti-malaria tablets** Essential.
- **Antibiotics** If you are likely to be far from medical help for any length of time, your doctor should be able to prescribe you suitable antibiotics in case you need to treat a serious lower bowel crisis or dysentery.
- **Antiseptic cream**
- **Aspirin or paracetamol**
- **Iodine tincture, with dropper, or water purifying tablets** If you can't get clean water, these will do the trick.
- **Lip-salve/chap stick**
- **Tampons** Available in town chemists but expensive, so bring your own supplies.
- **Thermometer** Get a plastic one that sticks on your forehead.
- **Zinc oxide powder** Useful anti-fungal powder for sweaty crevices.

main danger sign of dehydration is irregular urination, and dark urine definitely means you're not drinking enough water.

Cuts and bites

The most likely way to hurt yourself on a trip to Kenya is while swimming or snorkelling, as old coral rock can be very sharp. Wear fins or swimming shoes. You should also take more care than usual over minor **cuts and scrapes**. In the tropics, the most trivial scratch can quickly become a throbbing infection if you ignore it. Take a small tube of antiseptic cream with you.

As for animal bites, **dogs** are usually sad and skulking, and pose little threat, but rabies does exist in Kenya, and can be transmitted by a bite or even a lick, so it's best to avoid playing with pets or strays unless you know the owner and are sure they are safe. On the smaller scale, **scorpions and spiders** abound, but are hardly ever seen unless you deliberately turn over rocks or logs. Scorpion stings are painful but rarely dangerous, while spiders – even the big ones – are mostly harmless. **Snakes** are common but, again, the vast majority are harmless. To see one at all, you need to search stealthily. If you walk heavily they obligingly disappear. Larger animals, especially elephants, pose a potential risk to safari-goers, but not one that you need to worry about if you follow the rules (see p.75).

Medical treatment

For serious treatment Kenya has too few well-equipped hospitals, and in most you're expected to pay for all treatment and drugs. The Consolata Sisters' Nazareth Hospital on Riara Ridge, northwest of Nairobi (☎+254 (0)20 2017401), and in Nyeri (☎+254 (0)61 2031010), are well run and modestly priced, as is Kijabe Hospital on the east side of the Rift Valley near Naivasha (☎+254 (0)20 3246500). The best local hospitals are mentioned in relevant parts of the guide.

Kenya's **flying doctors** air ambulance service (☎020 6993000, ⓦflydoc.org) offers free evacuation by air, which is very reassuring if you'll be spending time out in the wilds. Tourist membership costs $16/person per month to cover Kenya and Tanzania. The income goes back into their outreach programme and the African Medical Research Foundation (AMREF) behind it. They have an office at Wilson Airport, from where most of their rescue missions take off.

The media

The press in Kenya is lively and provides reasonable coverage of international news, while the BBC, CNN and European sports stations are available on satellite TV.

Radio and TV

The Kenya Broadcasting Corporation has three main **radio** services, broadcasting in English, Swahili and local languages, as well as a 24-hour Nairobi reggae station Metro FM (101.9FM), competing with the independent Capital FM (98.4Mhz; ⓦcapitalfm.co.ke). Better for music is another independent station, Kiss 100 (100.3FM). The *Nation* newspaper runs a news station, Nation FM (96.4FM). The BBC World Service can be picked up on FM in Nairobi (93.7MHz) and Mombasa (93.9MHz). Most radio stations are available on the **internet** – good for pre-departure immersion.

Kenyan **television**, much of it imported, carries a mix of English and Swahili programmes. There are three main channels: the stuffy and hesitant state-run KBC, which carries BBC World for much of the day; the upbeat, mainly urban KTN owned by the Standard newspaper group, which carries CNN during the night and much of the morning; and the *Nation* newspaper's channel, NTV. An increasing number of homes, bars and hotels have **satellite dishes**, usually on the South African DSTV service (Ⓦdstv.com), giving access to Britain's Sky TV, Eurosport and other foreign channels.

The press

Kenya is a nation absorbed in its press, though the papers, as everywhere, struggle to hold their own against online media. The leading mainstream **newspaper** is the *Daily Nation* (Ⓦnationmedia .com), part-owned by the Aga Khan, which has reasonable news coverage, including international news and European football results, and a letters page full of insights into Kenyan life. Its main competitor is *The Standard* (Ⓦeastandard.net). Both papers are available on **digital subscription**. Unfortunately, sharp analysis is in short supply and many editorials and opinion pieces lack bite. For a more critical take on the news, turn to *The Star* (Ⓦthe-star .co.ke) which is much more outspoken but tends to be gossipy.

Of the **foreign press**, weekly editions of the UK's *Daily Telegraph* and other papers reach areas with substantial white populations, and you can find a fair number of foreign papers in busy areas on the coast in high season. *Time* and *Newsweek* are hawked widely and, together with old *National Geographics* and copies of *The Economist*, filter through many hands before reaching the second-hand booksellers.

Online, apart from newsfeeds from the Nation and the Standard, BBC Focus on Africa (Ⓦbbc.in /FocusonAfrica) has monthly news and features from the BBC World Service; the fortnightly Africa Confidential (Ⓦafrica-confidential.com) provides solid inside info on politics and business; and the hugely popular Kumekucha (Ⓦkumekucha .blogspot.com) has a scurrilous and entertaining mix of inside scoops and rants.

Cultural and arts resources include the sprawling Ⓦartmatters.info, lively blog Ⓦkenyanpoet.com, which has events flagged up in good time, and Ⓦkwani.org, Kenya's pre-eminent literary website.

Public holidays and festivals

The main Christian religious holidays and the Muslim festival of Id al-Fitr are observed, as well as secular national holidays. Other Muslim festivals are not public holidays but are observed in Muslim areas. Local seasonal and cyclical events, peculiar to particular ethnic groups, are less well advertised.

On the coast, throughout the northeast, and in Muslim communities everywhere, the lunar **Islamic calendar** is used for religious purposes. The Muslim year has 354 days, so dates recede against the Western calendar by an average of eleven days each year. Only the month of fasting called **Ramadan**, and the festival of **Id al-Fitr** – the feast at the end of Ramadan, which begins on the first sighting of the new moon – will have much effect on your travels. In smaller towns in Islamic districts during Ramadan, most stores and *hotelis* are closed through the daylight hours, while all businesses will close in time for sunset, to break the daily fast. Public transport and most government offices continue as usual. **Maulidi**, the celebration of the prophet's birthday, is worth catching if you're on the coast at the right time, especially if you'll be in Lamu, where it is celebrated in great style.

There are fewer **music and cultural festivals** than you might expect. Nairobi has a number of regular events (see p.131), usually publicized on Facebook. On the coast, the Mombasa carnival used to take place in November, but has not happened for several years, but the Lamu Cultural Festival (see p.475) is a highly recommended regular fixture. Less than two hours west of Nairobi, Kenya's first annual outdoor music festival, the Rift Valley Festival, has taken root on the shores of Lake Naivasha in late August (see p.208) and makes a great tie-in with a Maasai Mara migration safari. Finally, if you're visiting in May, do everything possible to catch the extraordinary Lake Turkana Festival – a hugely enjoyable tribal gathering at Loiyangalani (see p.529).

PUBLIC HOLIDAYS AND ISLAMIC FESTIVALS

Note that if a public holiday falls on a Sunday, the following Monday is usually declared a public holiday.

January 1	New Year's Day	**October 20**	Mashujaa Day**
March/April	Good Friday	**December 12**	Jamhuri Day†
March/April	Easter Monday	**December 25**	Christmas Day
May 1	Labour Day	**December 26**	Boxing Day
June 1	Madaraka Day*	**Shawwal 1**	Id al-Fitr (see opposite)
October 10	Moi Day		

* Self-rule Day
** Heroes' Day, formerly Kenyatta Day
† Republic Day & Independence Day

ISLAMIC FESTIVALS: APPROXIMATE DATES

Maulidi/Mouloud (12th Rabia I)	Jan 24 2013	Jan 13 2014	Jan 3 2015	Dec 23 2015
Beginning of Ramadan (1st Ramadan)	July 9 2013	Jun 28 2014	Jun 18 2015	Jun 6 2016
Id al-Fitr/Id al-Saghir (1st Shawwal)	Aug 8 2013	Jul 28 2014	Jul 17 2015	Jul 6 2016
Tabaski/Id al-Adha (10th Dhu'l Hijja)	Oct 15 2013	Oct 4 2014	Sep 23 2015	Sep 11 2016
Muslim New Year's Day (1st Moharem)	Nov 4 2013*	Oct 25 2014**	Oct 14 2015†	Oct 2 2016††
Ashoura (10th Moharem)	Nov 13 2013	Nov 3 2014	Oct 23 2015	Oct 11 2016

*1435 **1436 †1437 ††1438

Agricultural shows

The Agricultural Society of Kenya (ASK; ⓦ ask.co.ke) puts on a series of annual **agricultural shows**, featuring livestock and produce competitions, beer and snack tents, as well as some less expected booths, such as family planning and herbalism. These can be lively, revealing events, borrowing a lot from the British farming-show tradition, but infused with Kenyan style.

ASK SHOW DATES

Eldoret Early March
Kakamega Late June
Meru Early June
Nanyuki Late June
Embu Mid-June
Machakos Late June/early July
Nakuru Mid-July
Kisii Mid-July
Kisumu Late July/early Aug
Garissa Sept
Mombasa Late Aug
Nyeri Mid-Sept
Nairobi Early Oct
Kabarnet Mid-Oct
Kitale Late Oct/Early Nov

Entertainment and sport

Kenya's espousal of Western values has belittled much traditional culture, and only in remote areas are you likely to come across traditional dancing and drumming which doesn't somehow involve you as a paying audience. If you're patient and a little adventurous, however, you're likely to witness something more authentic sooner or later, especially if you stay somewhere long enough to make friends. On a short visit, popular music and spectator sports are more accessible.

Dance

The hypnotic swaying and displays of effortless leaping found in **Maasai and Samburu dancing** are the best-known forms of Kenyan dance. Similar dance forms occur widely among other non-agricultural peoples. **Mijikenda dance troupes** (notably from the Giriama people) perform up and down the coast at tourist venues, while all-round dance troupes perform a range of "tribal dances" for tourists in hotels all over the country. It's best to ignore any purist misgivings you might have about the authenticity of such performances and enjoy them as distinctive and exuberant entertainments in their own right.

Music

Your ears will pick up a fair amount of current music (see p.576) on the streets or on buses and matatus, but the live spectacle of **popular music** is mostly limited to Nairobi, a few coastal entertainment spots, and various upcountry **discos** and "**country clubs**". The indigenous music scene is somewhat overshadowed by soul and hip-hop, reggae (especially in the sacred image of Bob Marley) and a vigorous Congolese contribution, often called **Lingala**, after the language of most of its lyrics.

Theatre and film

Theatrical performances are effectively limited to one or two semi-professional clubs in Nairobi and Mombasa and a handful of upcountry amateur dramatic groups.

Cinema in Kenya revolves almost entirely around imports. The big towns have a few cinemas, including an Imax in Nairobi, but DVDs are how most people get their movies, with US and Bollywood box-office hits the staple diet. Homegrown Kenyan cinema has barely got off the ground, though the new Kenya Film Commission (🆆 kenyafilmcommission.com) may stimulate an industry that up to now has mostly been about servicing foreign productions, from *Out of Africa* to *African Cats*.

Sport

Kenya's ongoing **Olympic success story** is internationally recognized, with a regular clutch of gold and silver in the **track events** – though 2012 didn't match their success in 2008 in Beijing. Kenya's athletes are among the continent's leaders and the country's long-distance runners are some of the best in the world. It has even been suggested that certain Kalenjin communities may have a genetic make-up which makes them more likely to be strong athletes, but Kalenjins as much as anyone else have played down this idea. What is indisputable is that Kenya has possibly the most successful athletics training school in the world in St Patrick's High School at Iten, up at an altitude of 2400m in the Rift Valley (see p.240).

Football is wildly popular, with English Premiership teams having millions of devoted fans. You'll see plenty of matatus decorated with the colours of Arsenal or Liverpool, and any small bar with a satellite TV will show all the big games from Europe and will always be packed. Kenya's national team, the Harambee Stars, have won the East and Central African CECAFA Cup several times, most recently in 2002, and hosted it in 2009. While the team have never qualified for the World Cup, their star performers are held in high regard and the names Victor Wanyama and Dennis Oliech are known in most villages across the country.

A slow increase in sponsorship money made available to Kenyan football teams over the last decade has allowed the **Kenyan Premier League** to develop into one of the more financially stable leagues in East Africa. Crowds are still low (often no more than 2000) but more and more teams are turning professional and the title has been won by several different teams in the last few years.

Kenyan **cricket** received a boost when Kenya beat the West Indies at the World Cup in 1996 and came third overall in 2003. Most matches are played in the Nairobi area. Check out CricInfoKenya 🆆 bit .ly/CricInfoKenya.

Other spectator sports include: **racing** at the racecourse in Nairobi (see p.145), which dates from early colonial times; and **camel-racing**, spotlighted annually at the international camel derby in Maralal (see p.521) and now co-promoted with **mountain-bike racing** at the same event.

Car rallies

Once considered "the world's toughest rally", but dropped by the World Rally Championship in 2003, the **KCB Safari Rally** (🆆 safarirally.net) blazes a smaller trail across Kenya than it used to, doing a couple of "clover leaf" routes out from Nairobi and back. The rally is usually held on a weekend between Easter and June and uses public roads. Depending on weather conditions, drivers either spin through acres of mud or chase each other blind in enormous clouds of dust.

Another annual motor event, usually held in June, is the **Rhino Charge** motor race (🆆 rhinocharge .co.ke), which attracts 4WD-drivers from across the globe, though these days it's largely restricted to those who can raise the most funds. Registrations usually close about a year ahead. The funds raised go to the Rhino Ark Charitable Trust, which has already fenced Aberdare National Park to protect its rhinos (🆆 rhinoark.org). The challenge is to reach ten control posts in remote locations, whose whereabouts are revealed to the entrants only the night before the event.

Outdoor activities

Kenya has huge untapped potential for outdoor activities, with hiking and climbing particularly good inland and diving and snorkelling the outstanding coastal activities. Walking, running, horseriding, fishing, windsurfing, kitesurfing, rafting and golf also have strong local followings and are easy for visitors to take part in. Cycling is increasingly popular, and there are some good cave systems.

It's worth seeking advice from the Mountain Club of Kenya (see opposite), not just on climbing but on outdoor pursuits in general. For detailed descriptions of various climbing, hiking and caving locations in Kenya, see the "East Africa Mountain Guide" section of Executive Wilderness Programme's website (Ⓦewpnet.com).

Walking and running

If you have plenty of time, **walking** is highly recommended and gives you unparalleled contact with local people. In isolated parts, it's often preferable to waiting for a lift, while in the Aberdare, Mau and Cherangani ranges, and on mounts Kenya and Elgon, it's the only practical way of moving away from the main tracks. You will sometimes come across animals out in the bush, but buffaloes and elephants (the most likely dangers) usually move off unless they are solitary or with young. Don't ignore the dangers, however, and stay alert. You'll need to carry several litres of water much of the time. You might prefer to go on an organized **walking safari**, at least as a starter. Such trips are offered by a number of companies in Nairobi (see p.117) and by most of the smaller lodges and camps in the private game sanctuaries, especially in Laikipia (see p.508).

Popular parks where lions are normally absent and you can hike include Hell's Gate and Lake Bogoria. Parks inhabited by lions, but in which you can generally hike, include Aberdare and Mount Kenya.

Kenya produces some of the world's top long-distance runners, and **jogging** and **running** are popular. If you're a **marathon** runner, there are several events to tie your trip in with, which usually offer fun runs and half-marathons too. The Safaricom marathon (Ⓦsafaricom.co.ke/safaricommarathon) is the best known, on account of its location, in the prestigious Lewa conservancy north of Mount Kenya, and altitude (an average of more than 1600m), both of which make for a tough and exciting race. Marshals ensure your safety in the wildlife areas, but you'll be running on dirt tracks through the bush. It usually takes place in June. The Nairobi marathon (Ⓦnairobimarathon.com) takes place in October, running on roads. The Mombasa marathon takes place in August.

Climbing

Apart from Mount Kenya (see p.167), there are **climbing** opportunities of all grades in the Aberdare, Cherangani and Mathews ranges, in Hell's Gate National Park and on the Rift Valley volcanoes, including Longonot and Suswa. If you intend to do any serious climbing in the country, you should make contact with the **Mountain Club of Kenya** (Ⓦmck.or.ke; clubhouse at Wilson Airport; $30 joining fee, plus $30 annual membership). They're a good source of advice and contacts. Don't expect them to answer detailed route questions, however; leave that until you arrive. Safari companies in Nairobi offer everything from a simple hike to technical ascents of Mount Kenya.

Cycling

Cycling is more popular in Kenya than you might expect, given the often steep terrain, and you will even see hardy road riders and mountain bikers – both locals and expats – braving the traffic-clogged streets of Nairobi. But the real joy of cycling in Kenya is out in the bush, on quiet roads in the Rift Valley or Laikipia, or on the coast. Hell's Gate National Park is a popular place to cycle with the wildlife (see p.212). A number of companies offer tours (see p.118) and you can usually rent bikes at several places on the coast, notably in Diani Beach, Malindi and Watamu; some visitors even bring their own (see p.55).

Caving

Kenya's big attractions for cavers are its unusual **lava tube caves**, created when molten lava flowing downhill solidified on the surface while still flowing beneath. Holes in the surface layer allowed air to enter behind the lava flow, forming the caves. Lava tubes in Kenya include the Suswa caves near Narok, and Leviathan cave in the Chyulu Hills, one of the world's biggest lava tube systems, with more than 11km of underground passages. For more information, contact one of the lodges in the Chyulu area (see p.341).

Riding

There are good opportunities for **horseriding** in the Central Highlands and Laikipia, and there's an active equestrian community in Nairobi and scattered throughout the country. Bush & Beyond (see p.118), Safaris Unlimited (see p.119) and Safari & Conservation Company (see p.119) offer riding safaris in the Amboseli area, the Chyulu Hills and the Mara, and Offbeat Safaris (Ⓦ offbeatsafaris.com) do horseback safaris in the Mara. The African Horse Safari Association (Ⓦ africanhorse.com) is a useful resource. **Camel safaris** are popular too, though the best operators to contact tend to change from year to year (see p.525).

Fishing

Some of the highlands' streams are still stocked with **trout**, imported early in the twentieth century by British settlers. A few local fishing associations are still active. The Fisheries Department, next to the National Museum in Nairobi (☎ +254 (0)20 3742320), can supply more details and **permits**. For **lake fishing**, it's possible to rent rods and boats at lakes Baringo, Naivasha and Turkana (Loiyangalani), and there are luxury fishing lodges on Rusinga, Mfangano and Takawiri islands on Lake Victoria.

Kenya's superb offshore coral reef, with its deep-water drop-offs and predictable northerly currents, is ideal for **near-shore angling**. For **ocean fishing**, Watamu and Malindi are the most popular centres (see p.460).

Diving and snorkelling

Kenya's coastal waters are warm all year round so it's possible to **dive** without a wetsuit and have a rewarding dip under the waves almost anywhere, though the best period is October to April with October, November and March ideal. Most of the dive bases located at Malindi, Watamu, the coast north of Mombasa or Diani Beach, will provide training from a beginner's dive to PADI leader level. For underwater photographers, in particular, the immense coral reef is a major draw. The undersea landscape is spectacularly varied, with shallow coral gardens and blue-water drop-offs sinking as deep as 200m, and as there are few rivers to bring down sediment, visibility is generally excellent. There are some useful **guidebooks** (see p.590) and, if you plan to do a fair bit of **snorkelling**, it makes sense to bring your own mask and snorkel, though they can always be rented.

Wind- and kite-surfing

Windsurfing has been a feature of the Kenya coast since the 1970s, while Diani Beach (see p.438) and Che Shale north of Malindi (see p.469) are increasingly popular among **kitesurfing** enthusiasts. The coast has excellent conditions from December to February, with the northeast monsoon tending to get up in the afternoon, blowing between 16 and 22 knots (Force 4 to 5 Beaufort), which is ideal for both beginners and experienced riders. While the southeast monsoon, blowing from June through to September, isn't as reliable as the northeasterly, it can offer some exceptional conditions.

Rafting

Both the Tana and Athi rivers have sections that can be **rafted** when they're in spate. Approximate dates are early November to mid-March, and mid-April to the end of August. Savage Wilderness Safaris is the main operator (see p.164), and offers single- and multi-day trips.

Golf

Kenya has almost forty **golf clubs**, notably around the old colonial centres of Nairobi, Naivasha, Thika, Nanyuki and Nyeri in the central highlands, and Kisumu and Kitale in western Kenya. There are also several courses on the coast, and – the most bizarre – on the scorched moonscape shore of Lake Magadi (see p.151). Green fees vary widely, usually from about $30/person per day. Details for all of these can be had from the Kenya Golf Union (Ⓦ kgu.or.ke). For organized upmarket **golfing safaris**, contact Tobs Golf Safaris Ltd (Ⓦ kenya-golf-safaris.com).

National parks and reserves

Kenya's national parks are administered by the Kenya Wildlife Service (KWS) as total sanctuaries where human habitation, apart from the tourist lodges, is prohibited. National reserves, run by

local councils, tend to be less strict on the question of human encroachment. Increasingly, the conservation effort is also being supported by private sanctuaries and community wildlife conservancies, where private operators work with the local community to conserve wildlife and the environment while bringing landowners a direct income from tourism.

Most parks and reserves are not fenced in (Lake Nakuru, Aberdare and the north side of Nairobi National Park being exceptions). The wildlife is free to come and go, though animals do tend to stay within the boundaries, especially in the dry season when cattle outside compete for water.

All the parks and reserves are open to **private visits** (though foreign-registered commercial overland vehicles are not allowed in). A few parks have been heavily developed for tourism with graded tracks, signposts and lodges, but none has any kind of transport at the gate for people without their own transport (Nairobi National Park is the one partial exception, with a weekend bus service taking visitors around the park).

In general, without your own transport, you'll have to go on an organized safari. The largest and most frequently visited parks are covered in depth in Chapter 5, with others covered in regional chapters. Our table (see p.72) gives you some idea of what to expect from the major parks.

It's important to bear in mind some simple facts to ensure that you leave the park and the animals as you found them. **Harassment** of animals disturbs feeding, breeding and reproductive cycles, and too many vehicles surrounding wildlife is not only unpleasant for you, but also distresses the animals. If you're camping, collecting **firewood** is

strictly prohibited, as is picking any flora. If you **smoke**, always use an ashtray. Cigarette butts start numerous bush fires every year.

Entry fees

Park and reserve **entry fees** are set in US dollars and payable either in dollars (the best approach) or in pounds, euros or Kenya shillings (all often converted at rather poor rates). They are charged per person per 24-hour visit, and you are expected to know exactly how long you plan to stay. Your ticket will indicate your time of arrival. One **re-entry** is allowed per 24 hours, meaning you can leave the park to stay overnight outside and return again the next morning.

For most parks and reserves, you pay – usually in cash only – at the gate where you enter. However, entry to the six most popular national parks – Aberdare, Amboseli, Lake Nakuru, Nairobi, Tsavo East and Tsavo West – is by a pre-loaded **smartcard** called the Safari Card. You can obtain Safari Cards at various **Points of Issue and Points of Sale (POIPOS)** (see box opposite) with proof of identity. The card costs Ksh1000 to issue. You need to be over 18 (under-18s' fees go on adult cards). Once you've got your smartcard, you load it with credit, which you can do in cash or with a credit card – the precise sum determined by which park or parks you're visiting and for how long. If you have sufficient credit, your smartcard is good for entry by any entrance to any Safari Card park. Unused credit is non-refundable, and the card is retained as soon as credit runs out – meaning you have to go to a point of sale to get a new one if you want to make further visits to smartcard parks. The whole system seems somewhat complicated, but it's designed to stop large sums of money being held at the gates.

If you're visiting the parks on an organized safari, all this is handled and paid for on your behàlf. But if you're travelling independently, it does require some planning and makes last-minute changes of itinerary potentially problematic. Happily, there seems to be enough **flexibility** in the system to allow most gates to process independent visitors who turn up hoping to pay in cash. If your itinerary has gone awry, or you're entering through a minor gate, you can also usually persuade KWS rangers to allow you to travel through the park to a gate where you can rectify your status. Likewise, if you decide to stay another day, you can usually pay the balance owing on departure.

Note that if you **overstay**, even by a few minutes, you will very likely have to pay the full 24-hour fee (for a group that could easily be more than $300). If

SMARTCARD POINTS OF ISSUE AND POINTS OF SALE
Aberdare National Park Park HQ, Mweiga
Amboseli National Park Iremito Gate
Lake Nakuru National Park Main Gate
Malindi Marine Park Park HQ, Malindi
Mombasa Marine Park Park HQ, Mombasa
Nairobi National Park Main Gate and East Gate
Tsavo East National Park Voi Gate
Tsavo West National Park Mtito Andei Gate

National Park/ National Reserve	Description	Main attractions	Accommodation
Aberdare NP $50 Safari Card (see p.187)	Forest and montane grassland, access by 4WD only	Hiking; elephant, buffalo, black rhino, giant forest hog, rare bongo antelope	*Treetops* and *The Ark*, KWS cottage, camping
Amboseli NP $80 Safari Card (see p.334)	Small, flat, marshy, dominated by Kilimanjaro	Kilimanjaro; elephant, hyena, buffalo, zebra, hippo, giraffe, cheetah, lion	Lodges, KWS cottages, camping
Arabuko Sokoke NP $20 (see p.450)	Coastal forest, home of pioneering community conservation projects	Walking; Aders' duiker, elephant shrew, birds and butterflies	Camping in the park, hotels in Watamu
Buffalo Springs NR $70 (valid for Samburu & Shaba) (see p.374)	Smallish reserve adjacent to Samburu	Ewaso Nyiro River; lion, elephant, reticulated giraffe, Somali ostrich, gerenuk, crocodile	Lodges
Chyulu Hills NP $20 (see p.341)	Rarely visited volcanic hills near Tsavo West	Hiking, horseriding, cloud forest; black rhino, elephant, buffalo, eland	One lodge and one tented camp outside the park, camping
Hell's Gate NP $25 (see p.212)	Small, scenic park next to Lake Naivasha	Walking, cycling, rock-climbing; zebra, giraffe, buffalo, Thomson's gazelle	KWS campsites
Kakamega Forest NR $20 (see p.303)	Last stand of lowland tropical forest in western Kenya	Walking, birdwatching; great blue turaco, monkeys, chameleons	KWS *bandas*, camping, small lodges nearby
Lake Bogoria NR Ksh2500 (see p.233)	Rift Valley soda lake with limited facilities	Hot springs; flamingos, greater kudu	Hotel outside reserve, camping
Lake Nakuru NP $80 Safari Card (see p.222)	Soda lake, accessible by taxi	Lakeshore circuit; flamingos, pelicans, lion, leopard, buffalo, white and black rhino	Lodges, KWS cottage, camping
Maasai Mara NR $80 ($70 if staying in reserve) (see p.354)	Best park for game-watching, and often very busy, surrounded by conservancies with fewer tourists	Wildebeest migration (Aug–Sept); big cats, huge variety of savanna wildlife	Dozens of lodges and tented camps, some budget accommodation and camping outside the gates

you are genuinely delayed through no fault of your own, it's a good plan to alert the rangers and ask them to radio ahead, as the gate you exit through is more likely to waive the excess fee if they have been notified. Don't, however, expect to use this plan to do an extra game drive or stay for lunch: they watch the clock.

Non-residents' fees range from $15 to $80. Residents' rates range from Ksh300 to Ksh1000.

Children's rates apply to anyone over 3 but under 18, while students under 23 can apply for student discounts in advance direct to KWS (ⓦ kws.go.ke). Students need to be studying or researching in Kenya to get the reductions: leisure trips don't count.

Throughout the guide, we have *only* quoted adult, non-residents' rates. Over the last decade, KWS park fees have increased roughly every two

National Park/ National Reserve	Description	Main attractions	Accommodation
Meru NP $65 (see p.379)	Beautiful landscapes, relatively few visitors, increasingly good wildlife	Lion, cheetah, elephant, buffalo, reticulated giraffe, Grevy's zebra, black and white rhino	Lodges and tented camps, KSW *bandas*, camping
Mount Elgon NP $25 (see p.294)	Kenyan slopes of an extinct volcano on the Ugandan border	Hiking; salt-lick caves, hot springs, scenery, elephants	KWS cottage and *bandas*, camping
Mount Kenya NP $55 (see p.167)	Kenya's highest mountain, an extinct volcano	Hiking and climbing; high-altitude afro-alpine flora; buffalo, elephant	Hiking huts, hotels around the base
Nairobi NP $40 Safari Card (see p.141)	Close to downtown Nairobi, with a great variety of savanna, streams, gorges and forest	Full variety of plains game, including giraffe, lion, cheetah, black and white rhino (no elephants)	Tented camp, lodge, camping
Saiwa Swamp NP $20 (see p.290)	Smallest park in Kenya, access on foot only	Walking on boardwalks; sitatunga antelope, birdlife	Small treehouse, Sirikwa Safaris guesthouse (11km)
Samburu NR $70 (valid for Buffalo Springs & Shaba) (see p.374)	Peaceful and beautiful park of arid lowlands north of Mt Kenya	Ewaso Nyiro River; leopard, elephant, reticulated giraffe, Grevy's zebra, Somali ostrich, gerenuk, cheetah, Beisa oryx, crocodile	Lodges, tented camps, camping
Shaba NR $70 (valid for Samburu & Buffalo Springs) (see p.377)	Better watered and less visited than Samburu with striking landscapes	Ewaso Nyiro River; elephant, jackal, lion, Grevy's zebra, reticulated giraffe	One lodge, one tented camp
Shimba Hills NP $20 (see p.424)	Forested hills near Diani Beach, with pleasant climate	Views; elephant, sable antelope, leopard, bushbabies	Tree-hotel, KWS *bandas*, camping, luxury lodges nearby
Tsavo East NP $65 Safari Card (see p.348)	Biggest park in Kenya, popular for short safaris from the coast	Mudanda Rock, Lugard's Falls; elephant, hippo, crocodile, lion, zebra, cheetah	Lodges and tented camps, camping
Tsavo West NP $65 Safari Card (see p.342)	Busy and popular core area, surrounded by wilderness	Mzima Springs (underwater hippowatching), lava flows; elephant, zebra, giraffe, lion, buffalo, lesser kudu	Lodges and tented camps, KWS *bandas*, camping

years, to great opposition from tour operators and agents. It is very likely that the fees quoted here, set in 2012, will increase again during the lifetime of this edition.

In the **national reserves** (the main ones are Maasai Mara, Samburu, Buffalo Springs and Shaba), revenue is not controlled by KWS but by rangers employed by the local county councils. Fees are comparable to national park fees, and

strictly for periods of 24 hours, but transactions usually take place only at the gates. In 2012, Narok County Council began an experiment with a pre-payment smartcards system for the Maasai Mara National Reserve through select branches of Equity Bank in Nairobi, Mombasa and Narok. As of late 2012, rangers at the gates and airstrips were still accepting fees from independent travellers in cash.

Seasons

Most of the parks get two **rainy seasons** – brief rains in November or December, more earnest in April and May – but these can vary widely. As a general rule, you'll see more animals during the dry season, when they are concentrated near water and the grasses are low. After the rains break and fill the seasonal watering places, the game tends to disperse deep into the bush. Moreover, if your visit coincides with the rains, you may have to put up with mud and stranded vehicles, making for frustrating game drives. The effects of climate change have led to several temporary closures over recent years, and park conditions are often unpredictable. By way of compensation, if your plans include upmarket accommodation, you'll save a fortune at lodges and tented camps in the low season. Most places reduce their tariffs by anything from a third to a half between April and June. And, when the sun shines in the rainy season, the photographic conditions can be perfect.

Getting around the parks

If you're travelling on a **shoestring budget** and don't have access to a vehicle or a tour, then with a lot of luck you *may* be able to get a lift at one of the busier park gates with visitors in a private vehicle, but this is not a common option and you could wait a very long time, even at a relatively popular park. And you still need a plan for where you will stay once you're in the park. The best gates to try are **Voi Gate** of Tsavo East National Park and **Mtito Andei Gate** of Tsavo West National Park. In both cases, if you have to give up, you can easily pick up public transport to get away again by walking back to the highway or into town. You can also use public transport to reach the **Talek or Sekenani gates** of Maasai Mara National Reserve, making arrangements to do game drives with local vehicle owners or budget tented camps located just outside the reserve (see p.365).

If you're **self-driving**, or renting a vehcle with a driver, a 4WD vehicle (see p.49) is close to essential in the parks. None of the park roads are paved; most car rental companies will insist you have 4WD to visit them, and rangers on the gates may not allow you to enter in a 2WD vehicle, especially in wet weather. A night spent stuck in Maasai Mara mud isn't to be recommended; nor is trying to reverse down a boulder-strewn slope in Tsavo West. In any case, a normal saloon will be shaken to bits on the average park road.

Be sensitive to the great damage that can be done to delicate ecosystems by **driving off marked roads**. Even apparently innocent diversions can scour fragile, root-connected grasslands for years, spreading dust, destroying the lowest levels of vegetation and hindering the life cycles and movements of insects and smaller animals, with consequent disruption to the lives of their predators.

The effects of this are especially visible in Amboseli and Maasai Mara, both of which are now ecologically at risk. Use only the obvious dirt roads and tracks (admittedly, it can sometimes be hard to judge whether you're following a permitted route, or simply the tyre marks of others who broke the rule), and if you have a driver, ask him to do the same. Stick to the official maximum **speed limit** posted at the gates, usually 30km/h. **Night driving** between 7pm and 6am is not allowed in Kenyan parks and reserves without permission from the warden.

Park accommodation

If you're travellng independently on a **medium-to-high budget** and staying in lodges or tented camps, it's very wise to make advance reservations as there is often heavy pressure on beds, especially during the peak seasons. Besides their **campsites** (see below) KWS have a limited range of self-catering cottages, houses and *bandas* in most of the parks. See Ⓦ kws .org for reservations or take a chance at the gate.

If you're visiting the parks on a **shoestring budget** it may well be worth bringing a **tent** – consider renting or buying one in Nairobi (see p.122). If you don't have one, you will find the budget options fairly limited, and in some parks and reserves a campsite may be the only affordable place to stay, as well as significantly adding to the adventure.

Game drives

If you're on an organized drive-in (road) safari, your driver will conduct morning and afternoon **game drives** – two- to three-hour excursions from wherever you are staying, slowly heading around the park, looking for animals to watch and photograph. If you fly in, you'll use the services of the driver/guides and vehicles at your lodge or camp. Invariably, two game drives per day are included in your safari.

If you've booked a lodge or camp yourself, and made your own travel arrangements, you may have to pay extra for game drives (usually around $40–80/person for 2–3hr). If you want exclusive use of the vehicle, expect to pay $150–200 for a drive and up to $350 for a full day. Lodge or camp-based drives are usually very worthwhile because the drivers know the animals and the area.

The usual pattern is two game drives a day: at dawn and late afternoon, returning just after sunset. In the middle of the day, the parks are usually left to the animals. While the overhead sunlight makes it a poor time to take photos, the animals are around, if sleepy. If you can put up with the heat while most people are resting back at the lodge, it can be a tranquil and satisfying time.

Rangers can usually be hired for the day: the official KWS rates are Ksh3000 for a full 24-hour period, or Ksh1500 for six hours. If you have room in your vehicle, someone with intimate local knowledge and a trained eye is a good companion.

There are some fairly obvious **rules** to adhere to when watching animals. If you're stopping, switch off your engine and be as quiet as possible, speaking in low murmurs rather than whispering. Obviously, never get out of the vehicle except at the occasional (often rather vaguely designated) parking areas and viewpoints. Never feed wildlife, as it upsets their diet and leads to dependence on humans (habituated baboons and vervet monkeys

KENYA'S HABITATS

Kenya's **location** and range of **altitude** and its **climate**, dominated by the Indian Ocean's monsoon winds, have given rise to a diverse range of **ecosystems**. From lowland rainforest to savanna grassland, high-altitude moorland to desert, and coral reef to mangrove swamp, these zones provide equally varied habitats for its extraordinary fauna and flora. With few large **rivers**, Kenya's riverine habitats are restricted, but those that exist – notably the Tana and the Athi-Galana-Sabaki – are extremely attractive to wildlife. The vast, relatively shallow expanse of **Lake Victoria**, fed mainly by rainwater rather than rivers, is low in nutrients, but ideal for papyrus beds and marshes, harbouring birds found nowhere elsewhere in Kenya.

LOWLAND FOREST AND WOODLANDS

West of the Rift Valley, the 240 square kilometres of the Kakamega Forest, and a few adjacent outliers, are examples of the "Guineo-Congolan" **equatorial forest**, usually found only in central Africa and home to many animal and plant species encountered nowhere else in Kenya. Beyond Kakamega, Kenya's once widespread **forests** are now limited largely to the highlands, notably Mount Kenya (see p.167) and the Aberdare range (see p.187), and to a much smaller extent the coast (see p.387), where patches of old forest often correspond to the sacred groves or cultural villages of the Mijikenda, known as kaya (see p.449).

GRASSLANDS

The **wooded savanna** of grassland with scattered trees – East Africa's archetypal landscape – covers large areas of Kenya between about 1000m and 1800m. The main grasslands are in the Lake Victoria basin, which includes the Maasai Mara (see p.354), and east and southeast of Mount Kenya, where the savanna is protected by the national parks of Meru (see p.379) and Amboseli (see p.334) and the better watered areas of Tsavo East (see p.348) and Tsavo West (see p.342). Dry-season **fires** are quite common – whether natural or deliberately set to encourage new pasture with the first rain – and many of the often broad-leaved and deciduous trees are protected by their cork-like bark. The savanna of the Great Rift Valley is dotted with bird-rich **lakes** – ranging from freshwater Naivasha and Baringo to intensely saline Magadi and Bogoria – which act as a magnet for wintering migrants from Europe and northern Asia.

ARID AREAS

Starting just 30km inland from the Indian Ocean, a vast region known as the **nyika** – "wilderness" – stretches west across the drier areas of Tsavo East and West to the edge of the central highlands. Nyika is characterized by an impenetrably thick growth of stunted, thorny trees with scaly bark, such as acacias and euphorbias. Grey for most of the year, they sprout into a brilliant palette of greens during the rainy season. Where the land is lower than around 600m and there's unreliable rainfall and strong winds, the vegetation is sparse and scrubby, with tufts of grass, scattered bushes and only occasional trees, mainly baobab and acacia. In these **semi-arid areas**, where much of the ground is bare and soil is easily removed by the wind, long droughts are common. Kenya's true **desert** habitats are drier still, with very limited plant life and only dwarf trees and bushes. Large areas of northern Kenya consist of bare, stony or volcanic desert with thin, patchy grasses and the odd bush along seasonal watercourses.

can become violent if refused handouts). Remember that animals have the right of way, and shouldn't be disturbed, even if they're sitting on the road in front of you. This means keeping a minimum distance of 20m away, having no more than five vehicles viewing an animal at any one time (wait your turn if necessary), and not following your subjects if they start to move away.

To see as much game as possible, stop frequently to scan with binoculars, watch what the herds of antelope and other grazers are doing (a predator will usually be watched intently by them all), and pause to talk to any drivers you pass along the way. Most enthusiastic wildlife-watchers agree the best time of day is just before sunrise, when nocturnal animals are often still out and about, and you might see that weird dictionary leader, the aardvark.

Safaris

At the heart of most visits to Kenya, the safari is the wildlife-watching part of the trip, and usually implies at least an overnight stay. Before anything else, bear in mind that the professionalism and experience of your guide can transform any visit to the parks. Then think about whether you want comfort or a grittier experience, and whether you want the convenience of having it pre-booked as part of a package holiday, or the independence of picking and choosing online, or once you're in Kenya. Remember that the parks can be visited privately, allowing you to arrange your own itinerary. If you have the time, this is a good alternative to an organized trip.

Types of safari

Air safaris, using internal flights to get around, will add significantly to the cost and comfort of your trip and give you spectacular views, but a much less intimate contact with Kenya. A week-long air safari will work out in the range of $500–1000/person per day, assuming four scheduled flights and three different camps or lodges, but will depend on the quality of your accommodation and, to a lesser extent, the size of your party. With air safaris, your actual wildlife viewing – your game drives – will be organized with the vehicles and guides of the lodge or camp you are staying at, which usually means good local knowledge of the park and the

particular area, and specially adapted, often largely open, 4WD vehicles.

On a **road safari**, on the other hand, the long drives require minibuses or other closed vehicles with pop-up roof hatches, and your game drives will be conducted in the same vehicle. The journeys can be exhausting, while hours of your time are eaten away in a cloud of dust. Moreover, opportunities to see much of the landscape or communities through which you're passing can be somewhat limited, though this will depend on the route you take, the quality of your vehicle and the level of engagement of your guide, and thus the cost of the trip.

Most road safaris take you from one lodge or camp to another, staying two or three nights at each lodge, in two or three parks. Samburu–Nakuru–Maasai Mara would be a typical route. Make sure you have a window seat and ask about the number of passengers and whether the vehicle is shared by several operators or is for your group only. A week's safari by road, staying at lodges or tented camps, will cost in the range of $300–700 per person per day, assuming at least five or six clients.

The alternative to a standard lodge safari is a **camping safari**, again usually in a minibus, where the crew (or you, if it's a budget trip) pitch your tents each day. With this kind of trip you have to be prepared for a degree of discomfort along with the self-sufficiency: insects can occasionally be a menace; you may not get a shower every night; the food won't be so lavish; and the beer not so cold. The price should be in the range of $200–300 per person per day, depending on the itinerary.

It's common on camping safaris to spend the hot **middle of the day** at the campsite. Some of these are shady and pleasant, but that's not always the case and, where there are nearby lodges with swimming pools, cold beer and other amenities, it's worth spending a few hours in comfort. Similarly, if you want to go on an early game drive, or spend the whole morning out, don't be afraid to suggest to the tour leader that you skip breakfast, or take sandwiches. Too often, the itinerary is a product of what tour operators think customers want (passed from management to drivers and cooks), constrained by the driver's fuel allowance. In practice, daily routines may be altered to suit the clients easily enough if you ask, though going over-budget on fuel is likely to be an issue.

On better camping safaris, you travel in a more **rugged vehicle** that's higher off the ground – a 4WD Land Rover or Land Cruiser or even an open-sided lorry – giving more flexibility about where you go and how long you stay. The most **expensive camping safaris** come very expensive indeed: you can easily expect to pay $600–1000 per person per day. But you'll be guided by expert guides (you want a silver guide, or a gold guide if possible: see p.78) and usually looked after superbly, with top-quality tents ready for your arrival at your fly-camp every evening, good meals, cold drinks and informed safari chat.

Horseriding, **camel-assisted**, **walking** and **cycling** safaris are also available, and are generally comparable in price with mid-range or expensive conventional safaris.

Note that the **balloon safaris** you see advertised are short balloon flights, not complete tours. They take place at dawn and last a couple of hours. They can be done in the Maasai Mara (and sometimes one or two other parks), and the bill is a big one, around $500/person (see p.363).

Booking safaris direct

If you want the flexibility of booking your **own safari**, rather than having a travel agent or operator at home organize the whole trip for you, you will probably be dealing with agents or operators in Nairobi or on the coast, although you could piece the whole trip together yourself direct with camps/lodges and local airlines or car rental companies. It's worth noting that the **minibus safaris** that are included in inexpensive Mombasa-based charter packages venture no further afield than the three national parks easily accessible from the coast, Tsavo East, Tsavo West and Amboseli. Trips north to Samburu or west to the Maasai Mara are cheaper if arranged from Nairobi.

If you have the budget to organize a **tailor-made, exclusive safari**, your only constraints will be the availability of staff and vehicles at the companies you approach. Choosing a **budget safari company**, however, can feel fairly hit-or-miss. Unless you have the luxury of a long stay, your choice will probably be limited by what is available during your visit. If you're booking at the last minute, many companies are willing to offer a

discount in order to fill unsold seats; some outfits will also give student or other discounts if you ask.

This is not to recommend the very **cheapest outfits**. Some camping operators sell safaris that undercut the competition just to get seats filled, and then have to cut corners to make any kind of profit. The easiest way for disreputable operators to cut costs is to avoid paying park entry fees, or to disguise a one-day, 24-hour park stay, as a **"3-day safari"**: Day 1: leave Nairobi, drive slowly to camp outside park doing "game drive"; Day 2: enter park after breakfast for all-day game drive; Day 3: enter park again for early game drive, leaving for breakfast before ticket expires, followed by a slow drive back to Nairobi.

Some companies make a habit of failing to deliver on their promises, knowing that a combination of their clients' goodwill and inadequate legal recourse will allow them to get away with it. Before signing up, always ask for a **full breakdown** of what is included in the proposed itinerary, including the number of park tickets and the exact locations and names of the places you will be staying.

You should be somewhat suspicious of any safari to the main parks and reserves that comes in under $200 per day. Some such itineraries are run by legitimate small operators content to make very narrow margins. But some are crooks.

KATO

Some **recommended operators** are listed in the Nairobi section (see p.117), but it's difficult to find a company that's absolutely consistent, and this is particularly the case among the budget operators. While unpredictable factors such as weather, illness and visibility of animals all contribute to the degree of success of the trip, and group relations among the passengers can assume great significance in a very short time, it's the more controllable factors like breakdowns, food, equipment and competence of the staff, that really determine reputations. If anything goes wrong, reputable companies will do their best to compensate you on the spot.

The Nairobi grapevine and social media are probably your best guide to the latest good deals.

RESPONSIBLE TOURISM

Kenya's diverse and fragile environments, its traditional lifestyles and its reliance on tourism make it especially vulnerable to exploitation by insensitive visitors and the local tourist industry. We give an account of wildlife, the environment and responsible tourism elsewhere in this section (see p.57). As a first port of call, check out Kenya's main **responsible tourism** body, Ecotourism Kenya (ⓦecotourismkenya.org), which awards bronze, silver and gold eco-ratings to hotels and operators.

Membership of **KATO**, the Kenya Association of Tour Operators (🌐katokenya.org), is a good sign, but don't take it as a guarantee. KATO, based in Longonot Rd, off Kilimanjaro Ave, in Upper Hill, Nairobi (☎+254 (0)20 2713348 or (0)722 434845, 🌐katokenya.org; see map, p.102), publishes full lists of its members, and can offer advice if you have problems with any of them. The KATO website runs a quotation service, which forwards your needs and interests to their members who then contact you directly by email.

Guides and tips

Leaving aside your choice of itinerary, transport, and standard of accommodation, the one aspect of your safari that is right out of your hands once you've booked is the calibre of your **guide**. Since the late 1990s, the Kenya Professional Safari Guides Association (🌐safariguides.org) has taken the lead in setting benchmarks for professional guides in Kenya. They hold monthly exams and there are now more than a thousand accredited KPSGA bronze guides in the country. Of these, nearly two hundred have also passed their silver exam and a dozen have reached gold.

It's highly rewarding to go out **game-watching with a silver or gold guide**. They can offer memorable insights into animal behaviour and can be astonishingly adept at tracking animals and interpreting their observations: a good guide will know, for example, why two male lions are being chased by a lioness, and what you might expect to find if you discreetly follow the lioness later. And all silver and gold guides have a wealth of knowledge about natural history in general, not just big game.

Bronze guides can be very good, too: they have to wait three years before they can take their silver exam, and many bronze guides will spend hours every day reading the literature. Many, too, will have worked for many years before thinking about getting qualified: a thoroughly proficient and experienced bronze or unqualified guide is likely to be as good in most respects as a young and eager silver student. You can check the association's bronze, silver and gold members at the KPSGA website, and it's perfectly fair to ask your company if they have any accredited guides and if so whether they will be guiding your safari.

Good guides are far more than animal-spotters: they are often gifted linguists, highly practical in every way, and excellent bush companions. Many visitors become close friends of their guides and are drawn back to the same company repeatedly to renew the friendship.

Guides earn reasonable salaries by Kenyan standards, but clients' tips still make up a large proportion of their income, accounting sometimes for more than half their earnings. **Tipping** – of guides, drivers and other staff – can often cause misunderstandings between clients, who are usually expected to organize themselves to give collective gratuities on the last day. Some companies even make suggestions in their briefing packs. You should budget for Ksh500, or around $5–10 per member of staff per day from each client, slightly more for a small group of two or three, and less for a very large group, or one that includes children. If you are a couple, in a group being looked after by a driver/guide and an animal spotter or second-in-command, then you might give $200 in tips at the end of a week's safari. If this sounds like a lot, especially in Kenyan terms, bear in mind that the guides may spend many weeks each year not working.

Sooner or later, a Kenyan safari operator will start offering **tip-free safaris**, paying salaries that fully reflect the income expectations of their staff instead of relying on a system of ad hoc contributions from clients in lieu of proper wages.

Crafts and shopping

Kenya's most important crafts traditions are metal-working (for jewellery and tools), basketware, beadwork and gourd utensils, all of which go back centuries. The wonderful carvings you'll see all over are usually made specifically for the tourist market. It's often easier to feel you're buying something that comes from the community when you buy the textiles that local people wear.

It's a good idea if possible to buy from **cooperatives and development organizations**. Places such as Kazuri Beads (p.136), Makindu Handicrafts Cooperative (p.320), Akamba Woodcarvers Village (p.404), Bombolulu (p.412) and Malindi Handicraft Co-operative (p.468) provide their employees with above-average rewards.

What you take home will depend somewhat on how much you can transport. It's easy to get carried away when bargaining: some wooden and soapstone carvings are heavy as well as fragile, and can be hard to cart home. Bigger shops and large cooperatives will ship items for you.

Carvings

Kenya is one of the world's biggest manufacturers of **wooden carvings**. From the ubiquitous animals of doubtful appearance to finely chiselled bowls and plates, carvings are created here in the millions, mostly by Kamba carvers (see p.313). The most striking carvings are in the dramatic makonde style (after the Makonde people of Mozambique and Tanzania, a group of whom live west of the Taita Hills). Makonde carvings are ostensibly made from endangered ebony, but most are fortunately carved from blackened rosewood or something similar. The other popular carving material is steatite, or **soapstone** – a soft, lustrous stone mined from one area, Tabaka near Kisii (see p.274). Apart from its tendency to snap (which makes soapstone hippos more popular than giraffes), soapstone is one of the most versatile materials, and the industry encompasses a wide variety of plates, bowls, boxes and utensils, as well as decorative items such as chess sets and candlesticks.

Baskets

The Kamba are also big basket-makers (see p.312): **sisal baskets** (*chondo*, or *vyondo* in the plural) come in a huge variety of patterns and can be made from nylon string as well as sisal and, much more rarely, baobab bark twine, with beads woven in. The baskets are all light and functional and, since becoming international fashion accessories, are much more expensive than they were: buying direct from weavers, especially when leather straps and other decorations have still to be added, can be an excellent deal for all.

Beads, tribal items and weapons

Beadwork (*ushanga*, *mkufu*) and tribal **regalia** – weapons such as spears and clubs, shields, drums (*ngoma*), carved stools and headrests, traditional utensils made from gourds (sometimes beaded), cowhorn keepsafes and metal jewellery – are fairly common, but often more expensive when they're the genuine article rather than made for the tourist industry. The best region if you want to buy metal goods is the north: Turkanaland can yield some fairly spectacular examples of lethal weaponry, crafted indiscriminately for murderous assault or apartment wall. The bracelet-like wrist knives, or *aberait*, used to slash an enemy, are particularly impressive. You can buy **traditional weapons** – clubs, knives, swords, spears and bows and arrows – almost anywhere, and sometimes it can be hard to distinguish between an authentic weapon and an item made for tourists: the old man wandering the streets of Machakos with two bows and a quiver full of beautifully flighted arrows for Ksh20 each is not thinking of your souvenir requirements but of local hunters and security guards.

Toys

Look out for beautifully fashioned, push-along **buses**, **cars** and **lorries** made entirely of wire. These used to have tall rods, fitted with steering wheels, and would be given to lucky boys in rural areas by older brothers and uncles. Today, they're vastly outnumbered by mass-produced (though still hand-made) wire vehicle toys, manufactured as tourist souvenirs. Also widely available are amusing, push-along birds, monkeys and cyclists, that flap, bob or crank as they're rolled.

Textiles and sandals

Fabrics, although usually imported, bear a certain stamp of authenticity in that they are worn locally and make good-value, practical souvenirs. On the coast, the printed women's wraps – **kanga** – in cotton, and the heavier-weave men's sarongs – **kikoi** – are really good buys, and older ones represent collectable items worth seeking out. *Kangas* are always sold in pairs and are printed with intriguing Swahili proverbs. Local tailors will make them into garments for you at reasonable prices. You can also buy pretty, beaded, leather **sandals**, and the much tougher and more local sandals made from discarded vehicle tyres known as "five-thousand-mile shoes".

Musical instruments

It's hard to buy traditional musical **instruments** – for example a *nyatiti*, a Luo lyre (see p.577) – rather than souvenir facsimiles, but always worth trying. As for **drums**, the ones designed to be held under

> ## IVORY
>
> Although you are very unlikely to be offered it, it's worth knowing that possession of **ivory** is strictly illegal in Kenya, and most countries have banned all trade. If it's found by customs you are likely to be heavily fined and imprisoned.

one arm, most common on the coast, are the most practical as souvenirs. Lamu has its own wind instrument called a **siwa**, a huge side-blown thing traditionally made from an elephant tusk, but these days carved from wood.

Culture and etiquette

Although it's not essential on a short visit, understanding something of the subtle rituals and traditions that underpin everyday life will make a big difference to your appreciation of Kenyan culture. And if you're staying for an extended period, you'll need to make some adjustments yourself. There's more detailed information about Kenya's tribes and cultural traditions in boxed sections throughout the guide, as well as a dedicated language section (see p.602).

Greetings

Every contact between people in Kenya starts with a greeting. Even when entering a shop, you shake hands and make polite small talk with the shopkeeper. **Shaking hands** upon meeting and departure is normal between all the men present. Women shake hands with each other, but with men only in more sophisticated contexts. Soul-brother handshakes and other, finger-clicking variations are popular among young men, while a common, very respectful handshake involves clutching your right arm with your left hand as you shake or, in Muslim areas, touching your left hand to your chest when shaking hands.

Traditionally, **greeting exchanges** last a minute or two, and you'll often hear them performed in a formal manner between two men, especially in rural areas. Long greetings help subsequent negotiations. In English or Swahili you can exchange something like "How are you?""Fine, how's the day?""Fine, how's

business?""Fine, how's the family?", "Fine, thank God". It's usually considered polite, while someone is speaking to you at length, to grunt in the affirmative, or say thank you at short intervals. Breaks in conversation are filled with more greetings.

Hissing ("Tsss!") is an ordinary way to attract a stranger's attention, though less common in more sophisticated urban situations. You may get a fair bit of it yourself, and it's quite in order to hiss at the waiter in a restaurant: it won't cause any offence.

If you're **asking questions**, avoid yes/no ones, as answering anything in the negative is often considered impolite. And when making enquiries, try not to phrase your query in the negative ("Isn't the bus leaving?") because the answer will often be "Yes" (it isn't leaving).

If you'll be staying in Kenya for some time and really want to prepare, print a batch of **photos** of you and your family with your contact details on the back. Personalized "business cards" like this are greatly appreciated.

Body language, gestures and dress

You are likely to notice a widespread and unselfconscious ease with close **physical contact**, especially on the coast. Male visitors may need to get used to holding hands with strangers as they're shown around the guesthouse, or guided down the street, and, on public transport, to strangers' hands and limbs draped naturally wherever is most comfortable, which can include your legs or shoulders.

It's good to be aware of the **left-hand rule**: traditionally the left hand is reserved for unhygienic acts and the right for eating and touching, or passing things to others. Like many "rules" it's very often broken, at which times you have to avoid thinking about it.

Unless you're looking for a confrontation, never **point** with your finger, which is equivalent to an obscene gesture. For similar reasons, **beckoning** is done with the palm down, not up, which if you're not familiar with the action can inadvertently convey a dismissive gesture.

Don't be put off by apparent shiftiness in **eye**

"KENYA" OR "KEENYA"?

Although you'll hear "Kenya" most of the time, the second pronunciation is still used, and not exclusively by the old settler set. The colonial pronunciation was closer to the original name of Mount Kenya, "Kirinyaga". This was abbreviated to "Ki-nya", spelt Kenya, which came to be pronounced with a short "e". When Jomo Kenyatta became president after independence, the pure coincidence of his surname was exploited.

contact, especially if you're talking to someone much younger than you. It's normal for those deferring to others to avoid a direct gaze.

In coastal towns, wearing **shorts and T-shirts** (which are considered fine on the beach) won't get you into trouble, as people are far too polite to admonish strangers, but it's better to dress in loose-fitting long sleeves and skirts or long trousers. Lamu calls more for *kikoi* and *kanga* wraps for both sexes and, because it's so small, more consideration for local feelings.

For **women**, even more than men, the way you look and behave gets noticed by everyone, and they're more important if you don't appear to have a male "escort". Your **head and shoulders** and everything from **waist to ankles** are the sensitive zones, particularly in Islamic regions. Long, loose hair is seen as extraordinarily provocative, and doubly so if it's blonde. It's best to keep your hair fairly short or tied up (or wear a scarf) and wear long skirts or very baggy long pants. **Topless sunbathing** is only possible in private villas or beach houses, not in hotels.

You'll also need to be suitably attired to enter **mosques** and in practice you should take advice from your guide – you can't enter unaccompanied, and women often won't be able to enter mosques at all.

Beggars

In central Nairobi and Mombasa **beggars** are fairly common. Most are visibly destitute, and many are disabled, or homeless mothers with children. While some have regular pitches, others keep on the move, and all are harassed by the police. Kenyans often give to the same beggar on a regular basis: to the many Kenyans who are Muslim, alms-giving is a religious requirement. This kind of charity is also an important safety net for the destitute in a country with no social security system.

Sexual attitudes

Although there is a certain amount of ethnic and religious variation in attitudes, **sexual mores** in Kenya are generally hedonistic and uncluttered. Expressive sexuality is a very obvious part of the social fabric in most communities, and in Muslim areas Islamic moral strictures tend to be generously interpreted. The age of consent for heterosexual sex is 16.

Female **prostitution** flourishes almost everywhere, with a remarkable number of cheaper hotels doubling as informal brothels. There are no signs of any organized sex trade and such prostitution appears to merge seamlessly into casual promiscuity. If you're a man, you're likely to find flirtatious pestering a constant part of the scene, especially if you visit bars and clubs. With HIV infection rates extremely high, even protected sex is extremely inadvisable. On the coast there's increasing evidence of child prostitution and, apart from the odd poster, little effort by the authorities to control it.

Sex between men is illegal in Kenya, and **homosexuality** is still largely a taboo subject; lesbianism doubly so, although no law specifically outlaws it. Many Kenyans take the attitude that gay sex is an un-African practice. While there is barely any gay scene as such, male homosexuality is generally an accepted undercurrent on the coast (*msenge* is the Swahili for a gay man) – though attempts by local gay couples to hold wedding ceremonies have resulted in violent protests. Nairobi's nightclubs are *relatively* tolerant (see p.132) and the Lake Victoria region has a fairly relaxed attitude, but if you are a gay couple you may have to be discreet. Public displays of affection are out of the question, and while holding hands may not bother anyone (see p.80), you might be unlucky so it's best to avoid even doing that. Fortunately, gay couples seem to experience no more problem sharing a room (even when opting for one double bed) than straight travelling companions, and the prevailing mood about gay tourists seems to be "don't ask, don't tell".

Gay Kenya Trust (Ⓦgaykenya.com) is a human rights and advocacy organization for the LGB community, and **Identity Kenya** (Ⓦidentitykenya .com) is an informative news agency. A long-established and reliable, **gay-friendly travel company** in Nairobi is Magical Africa (see p.118).

Crime and safety

There's no denying that petty crime is a problem in Kenya, and you have a higher chance of being a victim in touristy areas, where pickings are richer. It's important to bear in mind, though, that most of the large number of tourists who visit the country each year experience no difficulties. Wildlife should not compromise your safety either if you act sensibly (see p.75).

For **official government warnings**, check the travel advisories on the websites of the UK Foreign Office (Ⓦbit.ly/FCOKenya), the US State Department

(W bit.ly/USSDKenya) or the travel advisory service of your own country. But bear in mind that travel advisories have an inherent tendency to be somewhat cautious and nannying, and are only as good as the information fed into them on the ground.

In Kenya, the **Kenya Tourism Federation** is an umbrella organization uniting a number of tourist industry associations. They have a sporadically updated website with security news (W ktf.co.ke).

Avoiding trouble

After **arriving** in Kenya, a fair few people get robbed on their first day or two in Nairobi, before they've had a chance to get used to the place. Try to be acutely conscious of your belongings: never leave anything unguarded even for five seconds; never take out cameras or other valuables unless absolutely necessary; and be careful of where you walk, at least until you've dropped off your luggage and settled in somewhere.

It's hard not to look like a tourist, but try to **dress like a local**, in a short-sleeved shirt, slacks or skirt and sunglasses, and try not to wear anything brand-new. Wearing **sunglasses** lessens your vulnerability, as your inexperience is harder to read.

In Nairobi, the rush hour at dusk is probably the worst time for pickpockets, but it's a good idea to be alert when getting off a night bus early in the morning, too. When you're out and about, avoid carrying a **bag**, particularly not a day-pack over your shoulder, that will instantly identify you as a tourist. And don't wear fancy earrings or any kind of chain or necklace. There's usually less risk in leaving your valuables, tucked in your luggage in a locked hotel room, than in taking them with you.

The only substantial **risks** outside Nairobi are down at the coast, where valuables often disappear from the beach or occasionally get grabbed, and in a few tourist-traffic towns such as Naivasha, Nakuru, Nanyuki and Isiolo.

If you're **driving**, it's a good idea never to leave your vehicle unguarded, even if it's locked, if it has anything of value in it. In towns, there's usually someone who will volunteer to guard it for you for a tip (Ksh100 is plenty), but again, don't leave any valuables inside.

When you have to carry **cash and other valuables**, try to put them in several places. A money belt or pouch tucked into your trousers or skirt is invisible and the most secure, while pouches hanging around your neck are easy targets for grab-and-run robberies and ordinary wallets in the back

pocket are an invitation to pickpockets. Similarly, the voluminous "bum bags", worn back to front by many tourists over their clothing, invite a slash-and-grab mugging. You'll be carrying around large quantities of low-value banknotes, so make sure you have a reasonably safe but accessible purse or zip pocket to stuff it all in.

All of this isn't meant to induce paranoia, but if you flaunt the trappings of wealth where there's poverty and a degree of desperation, somebody will try to remove them. If you clearly have nothing on you, and look like you know what you're doing, you're unlikely to feel, or be, threatened.

Cons and scams

On public transport, **doping scams** have occasionally been a problem, with individuals managing to drug tourists and relieve them of their belongings. It's best not to accept gifts of food or drink on public transport, even at the risk of causing offence.

Approaches in the street from "schoolboys" with **sponsorship** forms (only primary education is free, and even then, books, uniforms and even furniture have to be bought) and from "refugees" with long stories are not uncommon and probably best shrugged off, even though some, unfortunately, may be genuine. Also beware of people offering to **change money** on the street, especially in Nairobi, which is usually a trick to get you down an alley where you can be relieved of your cash.

Gangs of scammers who pick on gullible visitors in the Nairobi CBD to work elaborately theatrical cons are another occasional problem, and surprisingly successful to judge by the number of tourists who fall for their deceptions. If you find yourself surrounded by a group of "plain clothes policemen" insisting you have been seen talking to a "known terrorist" following a conversation you've had with someone who claimed to be a "student" or "refugee", and you need to "discuss the matter" with them, you should agree to nothing and go nowhere. Call their bluff and don't be afraid to cause a scene and involve passers-by. The group will quickly melt away.

A particularly unpleasant new scam on the **coast** involves a male tourist being approached by children who start a brief conversation, which is then followed up by an adult minder accusing the tourist of soliciting for sex. He then demands a payment or threatens a visit from the police. As with the "terrorist" scams, never agree anything or pay any money.

WOULD-BE HELPERS

It's very easy to fall prey to **misunderstandings** in your dealings with people (usually boys and young men) who offer their services as guides, helpers or "facilitators" of any kind. You should absolutely never assume anything is being done out of simple kindness. It may well be, but if it isn't you must expect to pay something. If you have any suspicion, it's best to deal with the matter head-on at an early stage and agree a price – or more rarely apologize for the offence caused. What you must never do, as when bargaining, is enter into an unspoken contract and then break it by refusing to pay for the service. If you're being bugged by someone whose help you don't need, just let them know you can't pay anything for their trouble. It may not make you a friend, but it always works and it's better than a row and recriminations.

Police and thieves

If you get mugged, **don't resist**, as knives and guns are occasionally carried. It will be over in an instant and you're unlikely to be hurt. But the hassles, and worse, that gather when you try to do anything about it make it imperative not to let it happen in the first place. Thieves caught red-handed are usually mobbed, and often lynched, so avoid the usual Kenyan response of shouting "Thief!" ("*Mwizi!*" in Swahili), unless you're ready to intercede instantly once you've retrieved your belongings.

Usually you'll have no chance of catching the thief, and if you've lost something valuable, the first reaction is to go to the **police**. Unless you've lost irreplaceable property, however, think twice about doing this. They rarely do something for nothing, and even stamping an **insurance form** will probably cost you, though you will need it to make a claim from the insurance company. And never agree to act as a decoy in the hope that the same thing will happen again in front of a police ambush. Police shootings take place all the time and you may prefer not to be involved in a cold-blooded murder.

If you have **official business** with the police, which is only likely at police roadblocks when you are the driver, then politeness, smiles and handshakes always help to limit the damage. If they claim you have committed a misdemeanour, whether or not you really have (for example, exceeding the speed limit, committing a driving error, talking on your mobile while at the wheel, or having something wrong with your vehicle) and you think you are being solicited for a bribe (*chai*, meaning "tea", or *kitu kidogo*, "something small"), to be allowed to go on your way ("Are you in a hurry?"), and if you're prepared to get into that, then haggle over the sum as you would any payment. Calling their bluff usually works just as well, however: agree that this is all unfortunate but you need to be sure it's being dealt with in the proper way, and if they would just explain the procedure to you, you will be happy to oblige. Of course, court appearances and official fines are rarely on their radar. And if you, and they, know you've done nothing wrong and you're not in any rush, then politely refusing to play their game will only cost a short delay until they give up on you and try another potential source of income.

In **unofficial dealings**, the police, especially in remote outposts, can go out of their way to help you with food, transport or accommodation. Try to reciprocate. Police salaries are low and they rely on unofficial income to get by. Only a completely new police force and realistic salaries could alter a situation that is now entrenched.

Drug and other offences

Though **illegal**, marijuana (*bhang* or *bangi*) is widely cultivated and smoked, and is remarkably cheap. However, with the authorities making efforts to control it and penalties of up to ten years for possession (or 20 years for trafficking), its use is not advisable. Official busts result in a heavy fine and deportation at the very least, and quite often a prison sentence, with little or no sympathy from your embassy. Heroin is becoming a major problem on the coast, and possession of that, or of anything harder than marijuana, will get you in a lot worse trouble if you're caught. The herbal stimulant *miraa* or *qat* (see p.184) is legal and widely available, especially in Meru, Nairobi, Mombasa and in the north, but local police chiefs sometimes order crackdowns on its transport, claiming it is associated with criminality.

Be warned that failure to observe the following points of behaviour can get you arrested. Always stand on occasions when the national anthem is playing. Stand still when the national flag is being raised or lowered in your field of view. Don't take photos of the flag or the president, who is quite often seen on state occasions, especially in Nairobi. And if the presidential motorcade appears, pull off the road to let it pass. Smoking in a public place is prohibited (it's usually okay to smoke outdoors, though not advisable to do so on the street; check before lighting up). It's also a criminal offence to tear or deface a banknote of any denomination, and, officially, to urinate in a public place.

Sexual harassment

Women travellers will be glad to find that machismo, in its fully-fledged Latin varieties, is rare in Kenya and male egos are usually softened by reserves of humour. Whether travelling alone or together, women may come across occasional **persistent hasslers**, but seldom much worse. **Drinking** in bars unaccompanied by men, you can expect a lot of male attention, as you can in many other situations. Universal basic rules apply: if you suspect ulterior motives, turn down all offers and stonily refuse to converse, though you needn't fear expressing your anger if that's how you feel. You will, eventually, be left alone. These tactics are hardly necessary except on the coast, and then particularly in Lamu. Some women mitigate unwelcome attention by adapting their dress (see p.81).

Fortunately you will usually be welcomed with generous hospitality when travelling on your own. On **public transport** a single woman traveller causes quite a stir and fellow passengers don't want to see you treated badly. Women get offers of **accommodation** in people's homes more often than male travellers. And, if you're staying in less reputable hotels, there'll often be female company – employees, family, residents – to look after you.

Terrorism and kidnaps

Kenya has a porous border with Somalia, where there was no functioning government for two decades until 2012. In two highly publicized **kidnapping incidents** in the Lamu archipelago in 2011 – at *Kiwayu Safari Village* (see p.473) and on Manda Island (see p.489) – a British woman was kidnapped and her husband murdered (she was subsequently released when her family paid a ransom), and a French woman in poor health was kidnapped and died from lack of medication. These incidents – which appear to have been driven by criminal rather than ideological motives – led to UK and US travel advisories against visiting the Lamu area and a downturn in tourism (see p.473). But the

warnings were soon lifted after the Kenyan military entered Somalia and better security was brought into the area.

The mood in Kenya at the end of 2012, after a number of Islamist extremist grenade and gun attacks in northeastern Kenya and low-income parts of Nairobi and Mombasa, was one of stoicism. Life goes on, you'll be told, and you are still far more likely to be injured in a road traffic accident or catch malaria (both quite remote possibilities) than you are to be caught up in a terrorist attack. You could never rule out the possibility, but terrorism is an international threat which is no more likely to affect you during a visit to Kenya than it would were you to stay at home. Needless to say, security at shopping malls and big hotels is high-profile, with airport-style baggage scanners and metal detectors widely in use.

Wildlife dangers

Although **wild animals** are found all over Kenya, not just inside the parks, dangerous predators like **lions** and **hyenas** rarely attack unprovoked, though they are occasionally curious of campfires. More dangerous are **elephants** and **buffaloes**, and you should stay well clear of both, especially of solitary bulls. In the vicinity of lakes and slow-moving rivers you should watch out for **hippos**, which will attack if you're blocking their route back to water, and **crocodiles**, which can be found in most inland waters and frequently attack swimmers and people at the water's edge. Never swim in inland lakes or rivers. More generally, follow park and conservancy rules and, unless signs indicate an area is specifically designated as a nature trail and you're allowed to leave your vehicle, never walk unaccompanied in areas where large mammals are present.

A persistent and growing problem is the continued, unstoppable damage done by those loutish hooligans, **baboons**. A locked vehicle might be safe but an unwatched tent or an open-fronted lodge room certainly isn't.

Travel essentials

Bargaining and receipts

Bargaining is an important skill to acquire, and you'll need to get into it quickly; once you do, you'll rarely end up paying more than the going rate for food, transport or accommodation. If you do pay an unreasonable price for goods or services, you

RULES OF BARGAINING

Don't begin if you're in a hurry; don't show interest if you're not thinking of buying; and never offer a price you are not prepared to pay.

contribute to local inflation, so be cautious over your purchases until you've established the value of things.

It's surprising how little is sold at a fixed price: even hotel rooms are often negotiable and it's always worth making an offer. You're expected to knock down most negotiable prices by anything from ten percent to a half. **Souvenirs** are sometimes offered at first prices ten times what the vendor is actually prepared to accept. You can avoid the silly asking prices by having a chat and establishing your streetwise credentials. The bluffing on both sides is part of the fun; don't be shy of making a big fuss and turning on the comedy. Where prices are marked, they are generally fixed, which you'll quickly discover if you walk away and aren't called back.

Petty bureaucracy is deeply ingrained in Kenya and you will often be given a **handwritten receipt** after making the most elementary payment. If you doubt whether the sum you're being asked to pay is officially sanctioned, however – for example, an obscure entrance fee, a fee for a guide, or on occasions when police try to impose an on-the-spot fine – just asking for a receipt before you pay will often clarify matters.

Costs

Kenya can be expensive for **budget travellers** if you want to rent a car or go on organized safaris, especially in high season. By staying in B&Ls, eating in local places and using public transport, you can get by okay on $25–40 a day, though $50 would be more comfortable. It's always cheaper per person if you're travelling with others. Getting around by bus and matatu is inexpensive, but you can't use public transport to visit the game parks. Renting a vehicle, and paying for fuel, will add at least $100 a day to your costs. If you're in a group of three or more, it starts to become more reasonable. Don't be tempted, however, to use the very cheap camping safari companies touted on the street (see p.117).

If you're travelling on a more **comfortable budget** then once you've forked out for your accommodation and transport (bearing in mind all-inclusive safari

prices of around $300–1000 per person per day) you're likely to find daily expenses refreshingly modest. Drinks in most hotels, tented camps and lodges run from around Ksh200–400 ($2.50–5) for a beer or a glass of house wine, and a main course in a restaurant generally costs around Ksh800–2000 ($8–25). Taxis are reasonably priced, but you need to establish the fare in advance (see p.54).

Customs and duty-free

Duty-free allowances on entering Kenya are one bottle of spirits or wine and one carton of 200 cigarettes (or 50 cigars or 225g of tobacco). If you're stopped at customs, you may be asked if you have any cameras, camcorders or the like. Unless you're a professional with mountains of specialist gear, there should not be any question of paying duty on personal equipment, though some officials like to note it down in your passport to ensure it is re-exported. If you are taking presents for friends in Kenya, however, you are likely to have to pay duty if you declare the items.

Electricity

The mains electricity supply (220–240V) from **Kenya Power and Lighting** is inconsistent and unreliable, and all but the most basic establishments have backup generators and/or solar panels. Most hotels have electric-shaver sockets in the bathrooms. Wall sockets are the square, three-pin variety used in Britain. Appliances using other plug fittings will need an adaptor to fit Kenyan sockets (available in major supermarkets), while North American appliances that work only on 110V (most work on 110–240V) will also need a transformer.

Emergencies

For police, fire and ambulance dial ☎999. They often take ages to arrive. There's also a national disaster line ☎911.

Entry requirements

Most nationals, including British, Irish, US, Canadian, Australian and EU passport-holders, need **visas** to visit Kenya, either obtained in advance or at the immigration counter on arrival. A number of Commonwealth nationals are exempt (New Zealand and South African passport-holders should be allowed a visa-free stay of up to thirty days, though the rules on this do not seem to be well established), while citizens of certain African and Middle Eastern nations must apply in advance. Children of the relevant nationalities also require visas and pay exactly the same. It's a good idea, however, to check with a Kenyan embassy website to confirm the current situation. Also ensure that your passport will remain valid for at least six months beyond the end of your projected stay and that you have at least a couple of pages clear for the stamps.

Visas and visitor's passes

Visas can be obtained in advance from Kenyan embassies, consulates or high commissions. Applications take up to three weeks to process, and require two passport-size photos. A single-entry tourist visa costs $50 or equivalent, multiple-entry visas $100 (valid for a year) and transit visas, if you're simply changing planes or making a brief connection, $20. Remember that Kenyan diplomatic missions are closed on Kenyan public holidays (see p.67). Visas are variously valid for entry to Kenya within three months or six months of the date of issue, depending on which embassy you use.

It's usually easier and cheaper to get your **visa on arrival** (no postage or delays and no photos required). If you're doing this, it's a good idea to download the application form from an embassy website, and have it filled in and ready on arrival, in order to reduce your waiting time.

Once you have your visa, your passport will be stamped with a **visitor's pass**. Various factors may influence the length of time actually granted, including your appearance, how much money you have and, fortunately, how long a stay you ask for. The maximum length of a visitor's pass is three months.

A valid visitor's pass issued on a single-entry visa allows **re-entry** to Kenya after a visit to Uganda or Tanzania. For other trips outside Kenya, unless you have a multiple-entry visa, you'll need another visa to get back in.

If you intend to stay beyond the visitor's pass date stamped in your passport, you should renew it before it expires, assuming your visa is still valid. Confusion over expiry dates can arise if, for example, you can't decipher KVP5W/H ("Kenya Visitor's Pass 5-Week Holiday") – if you're in any doubt, ask. If your visa is also about to expire, you'll need to get a new one. You can stay in Kenya for a maximum of six months as a tourist, after which time you'll have to leave East Africa. Visitor's pass and visa **renewals** can be done at the immigration

offices in Nairobi, Mombasa, Lamu, Malindi and Kisumu. Addresses for these are given in the relevant sections in the guide.

KENYAN EMBASSIES

The Kenyan diplomatic missions that readers are likely to find most useful are listed here. There's a full, official list at Ⓦ bit.ly /KenyaEmbassies.

Australia 33–35 Ainslie Ave, Canberra ☎ 02 6247 4788, Ⓦ kenya.asn.au.

Canada 415 Laurier Ave E, Ottawa, K1N 6R4 ☎ 613 563 1773, Ⓦ kenyahighcommission.ca.

Ethiopia Fikre Mariam Rd High 16, Kebelle 01, Addis Ababa ☎ 011 661 0033, ⓔ kengad@telecom.net.et.

Ireland 11 Elgin Rd, Ballsbridge, Dublin 4 ☎ 01 613 6380, Ⓦ kenyaembassyireland.net.

New Zealand Closest representation: Australia.

South Africa 302 Brooks St, Menlo Park, Pretoria 0081 ☎ 012 362 2249, Ⓦ kenya.org.za.

South Sudan Hai-Neem, Juba ☎ 0811 823 664.

Sudan Plot 516 Block 1, West Giraif, Street 60, Khartoum ☎ 0155 772 800, Ⓦ kenembsud.org.

Tanzania 127 Mafinga St, Kinondoni, Dar-es-Salaam ☎ 022 266 8285, Ⓦ kenyahighcomtz.org.

Uganda Plot 41, Nakasero Rd, Kampala ☎ 041 258 232.

UK 45 Portland Place, London W1B 4AS ☎ 020 7636 2371, Ⓦ kenyahighcommission.net.

US 2247 R St NW, Washington DC 20008 ☎ 202 387 6101, Ⓦ kenyaembassy.com; Los Angeles consulate, Park Mile Plaza, 4801 Wilshire Boulevard, CA 90010 ☎ 0323 939 2408.

Insurance

You'd do well to take out a **travel insurance policy** prior to travelling to cover against theft, loss, illness and injury. It's worth checking, however, that you won't duplicate the coverage of any existing plans you may have. For example, many private medical schemes include cover when abroad.

A typical travel insurance policy usually provides cover for loss of baggage, tickets and cash up to a certain limit, as well as cancellation or curtailment of your journey. Most of them exclude so-called dangerous sports unless an extra premium is paid: in Kenya such sports could mean scuba-diving, windsurfing and climbing, though not vehicle safaris. If you take medical coverage, check there's a 24-hour medical emergency number. When securing baggage cover, make sure that the limit per article, which is typically less than $1000, will cover your most valuable possessions, like a camera. If you need to make a claim, you should keep receipts for medicines and medical treatment, and in the event you have anything

ROUGH GUIDES TRAVEL INSURANCE

Rough Guides has teamed up with WorldNomads.com to offer great **travel insurance** deals. Policies are available to residents of more than 150 countries, with cover for a wide range of **adventure sports**, 24-hour emergency assistance, high levels of medical and evacuation cover and a stream of **travel safety information**. Roughguides.com-users can take advantage of their policies online 24/7, from anywhere in the world – even if you're already travelling. And since plans often change when you're on the road, you can extend your policy and even claim online. Roughguides.com-users who buy travel insurance with WorldNomads.com can also leave a positive footprint and donate to a community development project. For more information go to ⓦ **roughguides.com/shop.**

stolen, you must obtain an official statement from the police validating the circumstances as explained by you to them.

Internet access

Internet cafés are increasingly widespread in Kenya, but they can still be thin on the ground in rural areas and connections can be painfully slow. Mornings are the best time to get a fast connection. If you can't find a cybercafé, many post offices have internet facilities where you buy credit on a prepaid card. The **browsing charge** in most cyber cafés is Ksh1 per minute, though you'll pay much more (up to Ksh25 per min) in hotel "business centres". **Wi-fi** hot spots have yet to take off in a big way, but some hotels offer them, either as an extra, or increasingly as one of the benefits of staying with them.

With a **3G mobile phone**, you can get online either roaming with your home service provider (which may prove extremely expensive) or using a local SIM card (see p.89). Alternatively, if you have your **laptop** with you, you can buy a local internet service provider's modem and SIM card to give you mobile broadband access. The set-up cost, currently around $20, is coming down all the time. Connectivity and speeds are improving, but be prepared for some frustration if you're aiming to do more than email and browse. Whatever you select, ensure everything is working before you leave the shop: fortunately most mobile shops are very professional and the staff will ensure you are fully set up.

Laundry

There are virtually no launderettes in Kenya, but all hotels, lodges and tented camps run a **laundry service** for guests. Female underwear is normally excluded except where they have a washing machine (soap powder is provided for guests to do their own). In cheap hotels, you'll easily find people offering the same service (*dobi* in Swahili), but again

they often won't accept female, and sometimes male, underwear. If you're camping, you'll find small packets of washing powder widely available, and clothes dry fast in the sun. Beware of **tumbu flies**, however, which lay their eggs on wet clothes where the larvae subsequently hatch and burrow into your skin. As the larva grows, it's painful but harmless, reaching the size of a grain of rice after a few days until it breaks out, leaving a small, round scar. Not quite *Alien*, but still very unpleasant, and most people don't wait to find out, but burst the early swelling and clean it with antiseptic. A good, hot iron should kill the eggs, which is why every item of your clothing will be returned neatly pressed. Don't leave swimming costumes drying outside, but hang them in your shower.

Mail

There are main **post offices** in all the towns and, except in the far north, sub-post offices throughout the rural areas. Post offices are usually open Mon–Fri 8am–5pm, Sat 9am–noon. Letters and airmailed parcels take a few days to reach Europe and around ten days to North America, Australia and New Zealand. If you want speedy delivery, pay a little extra for express. Times from these places to Kenya are slightly longer, and things go missing fairly frequently. The internal service, like the international one, is not particularly reliable.

There is no mail delivery service in Kenya: recipients have to collect their mail and all **postal addresses** comprise a post office box number and the name of a town or city. Some post offices now have five-number postal codes (the Nairobi GPO is 00100).

If you want to receive a letter, the **Poste Restante** (general delivery) service is free, and fairly reliable in Nairobi, Mombasa, Malindi and Lamu. Have your family name marked clearly, followed by "Poste Restante, GPO" and the name of the town. You'll need to show your passport. Packages can be received, too, but many go missing, and expect to haggle over import duty when they're opened in your presence. Ask the sender to mark the package "Contents To Be Re-exported From Kenya". For large or valuable items, always use a courier. FedEx, DHL and UPS have branches or agents in all large towns.

Maps

There are very few good **road maps** of Kenya. The best available, without flattering ourselves, is the Rough Guide Map: Kenya & Northern Tanzania (1:950,000; 2004) printed on rip-proof, waterproof plastic paper, which is designed to work alongside this guide. If you can't find the Rough Guide Map, the Reise Know-How Map: Kenia (1:950,000) is for the most part identical, although the 2012 update had some strange errors, including showing the whole of the Nairobi-Mombasa highway as a "route under construction".

A local company (Ⓦtouristmapskenya.com) has also licensed some of the Survey of Kenya material and published a number of **maps of parks and reserves**, which are available in bookshops and at park gates. Nairobi and Mombasa **A-Z street atlases**, available in bookshops, are being superseded by the all-enveloping **Google Maps**, which has already covered most of Kenya in impressive detail.

Money

Kenya's currency, the Kenyan shilling (Ksh), is a colonial legacy based on the old British currency (as in pre-decimal Britain, Kenyans occasionally refer to shillings as "bob"). There are notes of Ksh1000, 500, 200, 100 and 50, and coins of Ksh20, 10, 5, 1 and 50 cents (half a shilling). Some foreign banks stock shillings should you wish to buy some before you leave, but you'll get rates about five percent less than what you might find in Kenya. You can import or export up to Ksh100,000 (you need the exchange receipts if exporting).

Because the Kenya shilling is a weak currency, prices for anything connected to the tourist industry tend to be quoted in **US dollars**. Cash dollars, together with British pounds and euros, are invariably acceptable, and often preferred, as payment. People often have calculators and know the latest exchange rates. At the time of writing, the **rates of exchange** were approximately Ksh135 to £1, Ksh85 to $1 and Ksh110 to €1. If you take **$100 bills** to Kenya, be sure they are less than five years old as they won't be exchangeable in many places otherwise.

While most **prices** in this book are given in Kenyan shillings or US dollars, the occasional use of euros or pounds sterling reflects the way hotels and tour operators price their services.

Credit and debit cards, and ATMs

The best way to carry your money is in the form of **plastic**. This is not so much because you can use credit or debit cards to buy things (though increasingly you can), but because they're more secure than cash, and you can use them at **ATMs**. Most bank branches have ATMs inside a secure booth and guards on the street outside. There's often a line of local people waiting to withdraw cash, though you rarely have to wait long.

Many banks have 24-hour ATMs, including most branches of Barclays (Ⓦbit.ly/BarclaysKenyaATMs), Standard Chartered (Ⓦbit.ly/SCBKenyaATMs), Kenya Commercial (Ⓦbit.ly/KCB-ATMs) and Equity (Ⓦequitybank.co.ke) banks. The machines variously accept cards with Visa, Visa Electron, MasterCard, Plus or Cirrus symbols. You'll have to ask your own bank what charge they make per withdrawal: the cost varies. Many banks also give **cash advances** in Kenya shillings (and, if you're in Nairobi or parts of the coast, in US dollars or pounds) on Visa and MasterCard credit cards. The maximum amount you can withdraw per day is usually Ksh40,000 from an ATM, or Ksh50,000 over the counter.

Visa **credit cards** are widely accepted for tourist services such as upmarket hotels and restaurants, flights, safaris, and car rental; MasterCard and others are more limited. There's usually a two- to five-percent mark-up on top of the price for the cost of the transaction to the company. Chip-and-pin transactions have barely arrived in Kenya, and **credit card fraud** is not uncommon, so if you're paying a sum in shillings, make sure you've filled in the leading digits with zeros and the voucher specifies the currency before you sign. If it doesn't, it's all too easy for the vendor to fill in a $, € or £ sign in front of the total after you've left.

Exchanging money

You can **exchange** hard currency in cash at banks and foreign exchange ("forex") bureaux all over the country, and also at most large hotels, though for a substantially poorer rate. US dollars, British pounds and euros are always the most easily changed. Always check the commission and any charges, as they may vary mysteriously, even within branches of the same bank.

Cash invariably attracts better rates than **travellers' cheques** which, in the age of the ATM, are rarely worth the trouble, especially as you need to have the original receipts as well as your passport and the patience of a saint when waiting in the bank to cash them.

Banks are usually open Mon–Fri 9am–3pm, Sat 9–11am (some branches are not open every Sat). In out-of-the-way places, you may have to wait until the rates arrive from Nairobi.

Foreign exchange (forex) bureaux usually offer better rates of exchange than banks. The Central Bank of Kenya publishes a list of licensed independent forex dealers: Ⓦ bit.ly/KenyaForexBureaux.

Street moneychangers in Nairobi, Mombasa and Malindi may offer slightly better than official rates, but this **black market** is illegal, and many of them are chancers aiming to rip you off or even muggers looking to lure you into an alley. An exception is when entering Kenya by land from Uganda or Tanzania, where moneychangers in the border towns will give Kenyan shillings for Ugandan or Tanzanian shillings or cash US dollars. Local authorities turn a blind eye, but always count the shillings very carefully before handing over your hard currency.

Wiring money

Having **money wired** from home is not cheap, but it is relatively easy. You can have it sent with Western Union (Ⓦ westernunion.com) to branches of PostBank and KCB, or with MoneyGram (Ⓦ moneygram.com) to branches of the Co-op Bank and some forex bureaux. The transfer is instantaneous, and fees depend on the amount being transferred. Wiring $1000, for example, will cost around $65.

At the time of writing, **M-Pesa**, the much more affordable mobile-to-mobile money transfer system that has transformed Kenya's rural economy, was planning to go international. Operated by Safaricom, M-Pesa could allow Kenyans to make payments overseas and, potentially, enable overseas mobile-phone users to make payments to people with mobiles in Kenya.

Museums and historical monuments

Kenya's **museums** are always worth visiting if you're in the neighbourhood, although perhaps only the National Museum in Nairobi, Fort Jesus in Mombasa and Lamu Museum deserve a special visit. They're run by the National Museums of Kenya (Ⓦ museums.or.ke), which also coordinates archeological digs and looks after various sites and monuments – several of which, such as the ruins of

Gedi on the coast, and **Thimlich Ohinga** near Lake Victoria, are impressive and highly recommended. If you're visiting Nairobi, it's worth getting the **special-rate pass** that entitles you to free entry to all the sites and museums for a month (see p.110).

Opening hours

Opening hours tend to follow patterns you're likely to be familiar with. In larger towns, major stores are open Mon–Sat 8am–5pm or 9am–6pm, often with a break for lunch. Large supermarkets are increasingly open late in the evenings and big towns often have at least one 24-hour Nakumatt hypermarket. Tourism businesses such as travel agents, car rental firms and airline offices are usually open Mon–Fri 8am–5pm or 9am–6pm, plus Sat 9am–noon. Banks are usually open Mon–Fri 9am–3pm, and Sat 9–11am. Museums are usually open seven days a week. Post offices are usually open Mon–Fri 8am–5pm, Sat 9am–noon. Most other offices are closed all weekend. In rural areas, small shops can be open at almost any hour. Some petrol stations stay open late, but very few are open all night.

Phones and mobiles

Kenya's conventional **landline telephone system**, run by Telkom (operator ☎900), appears to be in terminal decline. Where it works, people use it because it can be the cheapest way to make a call, but in many towns, the local phones, including the call boxes, are all but defunct. If you borrow someone's phone, or you can find a working payphone (some large post offices have working boxes), then you should be able to call internationally (see box, p.90) as well as in Kenya. The easiest way is with a Telkom Kenya scratch card, available in various values and durations. The cards can be used for local and international calls from any landline phone with tone dialling, including call boxes.

Kenya's **area codes** are all three figures, comprising 0 plus two digits. The subscriber numbers are five, six or seven digits, with all numbers moving (in theory) to seven digits.

Kenya also has CDMA **wireless lines**, which are vastly more reliable than land lines. Like Nairobi land lines, wireless lines always have the code ☎020, followed by a seven-digit number.

Mobile phones

Mobile (cell) phones outnumber landlines in Kenya, and most of the country has coverage. The main exception is the far north, but reception can also be patchy in thinly populated rural areas.

Mobile phone services are provided by **Safaricom** (the biggest operator), and its rivals **Airtel** and **Orange**. All Safaricom and Airtel numbers begin with a four-digit code starting 07, followed by a six-digit number.

Unless your mobile is very old, it is almost certain to work in Kenya, but very high charges make using it on **roaming** unattractive for anything but emergencies.

There are two easy options: either buy a cheap handset from any mobile phone shop, which will cost around $20, or buy a Kenyan **pay-as-you-go SIM card** (around Ksh100) and temporarily replace the SIM card in your mobile. As well as standard mini-SIMs, the cut-down micro-SIMs for iPhones and other smart phones are widely available. Check with your home service provider that your phone is not locked to their network (unlocking, if necessary, can be done anywhere).

Once you have your Kenyan SIM installed (any phone shop, from the airport onwards, will sell you one and put it in your phone), you can buy **airtime** cards literally anywhere, rubbing a scratch number, which you use to key in the top-up. Most Kenyans top up with Ksh50 or Ksh100, a deeply resented pricing structure that gives them poor rates per minute. Ksh1000 will give you very low-price calls (as low as Ksh3 per minute and Ksh2 per text on the same network) and should last you for a short holiday.

For most short-term visitors to Kenya, it's fairly immaterial whether you choose an Airtel, Orange or Safaricom SIM card. They continually outbid each other for value and flexibility. If, however, you're travelling more widely in **East Africa**, you'll find Airtel's One Network service handy. It allows you to use the same SIM card throughout Kenya, Tanzania, Uganda and several other countries, while topping up in the local currency.

International calls

To **call Kenya from abroad**, dial your country's international access code followed by 254 for Kenya, then the Kenyan area code or mobile-phone code (omitting the initial 0), and then the number itself.

Kenya, Uganda and Tanzania have a special telephone code agreement, used just between them, which replaces their international access and country codes with a single three-digit code, ☎005 for Kenya, ☎006 for Uganda and ☎007 for Tanzania. So, if you're calling Kenya from Uganda or Tanzania, you dial ☎005, then the Kenya area code (omitting

---

INTERNATIONAL CODES WHEN CALLING FROM KENYA

Australia ☎000+61
Canada ☎000+1
Ireland ☎000+353
Netherlands ☎000+31
New Zealand ☎000+64
South Africa ☎000+27
Tanzania ☎000+255 (☎007 from East African landlines)
Uganda ☎000+256 (☎006 from East African landlines)
UK ☎000+44
US ☎000+1

---

the initial zero), then the number. Note, however, that on mobiles, no matter where you're dialling from, the codes for Kenya, Tanzania and Uganda are the usual, international +254, +255 and +256.

To **call out of Kenya**, the international access code is 000, followed by the country code followed by the number, omitting any initial 0 (this includes calls to mobiles being used with foreign-registered SIM cards in Kenya).

Photography

Kenya is immensely photogenic, and with any kind of camera you'll get beautiful pictures. But if you want good wildlife shots, you'll need a **camera** with an optical magnification of at least 10x on a point-and-shoot camera or 400mm-equivalent on a DSLR. Such telephoto capabilities are essential if you want pictures of animals rather than savanna. **Wildlife photography** is largely about timing and patience. Keep your camera always to hand and, in a vehicle, always turn off the engine.

Keep your camera in a dust-proof bag. If it uses a rechargeable **battery**, take a spare – you will always run out of power at the critical moment if you don't. If you intend to email digital pictures home or store them online, note that cybercafés don't always have computers with USB ports, and that uploading can take a very long time. The lack of USB also means you may have difficulty archiving your photos to CD (at least you can buy CDs and DVDs widely), so it pays to take plenty of memory cards with you, or a separate storage device.

When **photographing local people** you need to be sensitive and always ask permission first. If you don't accept that some kind of interaction and exchange are warranted, you won't get many pictures. Though most people are tolerant of cameras, the superstition that photos capture part of the soul is still prevalent in some areas, and there can be a special objection to photography of children or animals, whose souls may be considered especially vulnerable. The idea that your photos may show Kenya in a poor light is also common. The Maasai and Samburu, Kenya's most colourful and photographed people, are usually prepared to do a deal (bargain over the price, as you would for any payment), and in some places you'll even find professional posers making a living at the roadside. Other people may be happy to let you take their picture for free, but will certainly appreciate it if you take their name and address, and send a print when you get home, or email the shot to them.

Note that it's always a bad idea to take pictures of anything that could be construed as strategic, including any military or police building, prisons, airports, harbours, bridges and the president or his entourage.

Place names

Place names in Kenya can be confusing to outsiders. In some parts, every town or village seems to have a name starting with the same syllable. In the Kenya highlands, you'll find Kiambu, Kikuyu, Kiganjo, Kinangop and so on. Further west you confront Kaptagat, Kapsabet, Kapenguria and Kapsowar. If you find this problematic, just get into the habit of "de-stressing" the first syllable and remembering the second.

A more practical problem all over rural Kenya is the vague use of names to denote a whole district and, at the same time, its nucleus, be it a small town, a village, or just a cluster of corrugated-iron shops and bars. Sometimes there'll be two such focuses. They often move in a matter of a few years, so what looks like a junction town on the map turns out to be away from the road, or in a different place altogether. Ask for the "shopping centre" and you'll usually find the local hive of activity and the place with the name you were looking for. Note that **Makutano**, a very common name, just means "junction" in Swahili.

Time

Kenya's **time zone** is three hours ahead of Greenwich Mean Time (UTC) all year round (thus two hours ahead of British Summer Time). It's eight hours ahead of North American Eastern Standard Time, and eleven hours ahead of Pacific Standard Time. Take off an hour from these (ie seven hours

and ten hours respectively) during summer daylight saving time. Kenya is seven hours behind Sydney and nine hours behind New Zealand; add an hour to these during summer daylight saving time.

Sunrise comes between 6am and 6.40am and **sunset** between 6.10pm and 6.50pm throughout the year. Dawn arrives earliest on the coast and the sun sets latest on Lake Victoria. Because of its equatorial location, there are no short days or long evenings in Kenya.

If you're learning Swahili, remember that "Swahili time" runs from dawn to dusk to dawn rather than midnight to midday to midnight: 7am and 7pm are both called *saa moja* (one o'clock) while midnight and midday are *saa sita* (six o'clock). It's not as confusing as it first sounds – just add or subtract six hours to work out Swahili time (or read the opposite side of your watch).

Tipping and gifts

If you're staying in tourist-class establishments, **tipping** is expected, though ironically, in the cheapest establishments, where employees are likely to be on very low wages, it is not the custom. In expensive hotels, Ksh100 wouldn't be out of place for seeing you to your room with your bags (and £1, $1 or €1 would also be very acceptable, though the employee has to change the money, which can be difficult; shillings are always better). It isn't necessary to tip waiting staff constantly while staying in a hotel. Fortunately, many hotels have a **gratuities box** in reception, where you can leave a single tip for all the staff – including room staff and backroom staff – when you leave, in which case Ksh500 or Ksh1000 per room per day is about right. In tourist-class restaurants, tips aren't essential, but leaving a tip equivalent to ten percent of the bill for your waiter would be generous. Note that on safaris, tips are considered very much part of the pay and you're expected to shell out at the end of the trip (see p.78).

As for **gifts**, ballpoint pens and pencils are always worth taking and will be appreciated by children as well as adults. Many visitors take more clothes with them than they intend to return with, leaving T-shirts and other items with hotel staff and others along the way: there's even a website devoted to this concept where your philanthropic instincts can be more precisely honed (W stuffyourrucksack .com). Bear in mind, however, that all this largesse deprives local shops and businesses of your surplus wealth and perpetuates a dependency culture. Assuming you can spare a little, it's always better to make a positive gift of cash to a recognized institution which can go into the local economy while providing local needs in a school, clinic or other organization.

Tourist information

The **Kenya Tourist Board** (KTB ⓦmagicalkenya .com) doesn't run any walk-in offices abroad, but has franchised its operations to local PR companies, who are often very helpful. In addition to the UK and US offices (see below), there are KTB representative offices in Düsseldorf, Dubai, Hong Kong, Madrid, Milan, Netherlands, New Delhi, Paris, Prague, Rome, Stockholm, Sydney, Tokyo and Toronto (addresses at ⓦmagicalkenya.com).

There are several good arts and culture blogs and **websites** (see p.66) and you can always ask practical questions and expect a useful reply – often from the author of this Rough Guide – at the very good online Kenya forums at ⓦsafaritalk .net, ⓦbit.ly/FodorsKenya, ⓦbit.ly/ThorntreeKenya, ⓦbit.ly/TA-Africaforums or the Rough Guide to Kenya blog itself at ⓦbit.ly/ExpertKenya.

Once you're in Kenya, the only official tourist offices are in Eldoret (see p.285), Mombasa (see p.400) and Malindi (see p.465).

KENYA TOURIST BOARD OFFICES

UK c/o Hills Balfour, Colechurch House, 1, London Bridge Walk, London SE1 2SX ☎020 7367 0900, ⓦhillsbalfour.com.
US c/o Myriad Marketing, 1334 Parkview Avenue Suite, 300 Manhattan Beach, CA 90266, ☎310 545 3047, ⓦmyriadmarketing.com.

Travelling with children

Wherever you go, local people will be welcoming to your **children**, and only in exceptional cases are under-7s barred from certain lodges (the tree-hotels, for example). Babies, if they're easy-going, can be relatively straightforward, but taking toddlers and young children to Kenya can be quite a hassle in terms of supervision and organization. It obviously helps if they are huge animal fans: if they're not enchanted by the wildlife and environment, you may find the overall adventure isn't enough reward for journeys that can be long and tiring.

Health issues (see p.62) figure most prominently in most people's minds, but you can largely discount fears about your children getting a tropical disease in Kenya (remember how many healthy expat children have been brought up there: the biggest health problem for Kenyan children is poverty). It can, however, be very difficult to persuade small children to take **malaria pills**. Be sure to cover children carefully with a Deet-based mosquito repellent early each evening and ensure they sleep under secure nets. Every morning, smother them in factor forty sunscreen, insist they wear hats, and make sure they get plenty of fluids.

In terms of what to bring, disposable **nappies/ diapers** are available from supermarkets, as are **baby foods**, and hotel kitchens usually have a good variety of fresh food and, given some warning, staff will happily prepare it to infants' tastes. If you have a light, easily collapsible **buggy**, bring it. Many hotels and lodges have long paths from the central public areas to the rooms or cottages. A **child-carrier** backpack is another very useful accessory. Unless you're exclusively staying on the coast, bring some **warm clothing** for upcountry mornings and evenings, when temperatures can drop quite low. If the children are old enough to enjoy spotting animals, make sure they have their own **binoculars**.

For a young family, going on a group **safari** with other travellers is probably inadvisable. Renting a vehicle and driving yourself, or taking a driver, is quite feasible, however, and gives you the flexibility and privacy you need for toilet stops and other interruptions. For babies and young children you'll need a car seat, which, if you have the right model, also works as an all-purpose carrier, poolside recliner and picnic throne.

Some **parks** are more child-friendly than others. At Nairobi and Lake Nakuru distances are small and the animals close, and Amboseli is usually a hit, too, for its manageable size and large numbers of elephants.

Given a few hours' notice, most tourist hotels and lodges can organize a **babysitter** from the housekeeping staff, who should cost around Ksh500– 1000 for an evening, though few hotels will have anyone with a childcare qualification. In safari camps and lodges, you can speak to the restaurant manager and arrange for an *askari* (night watchman) to sit outside to keep an ear open for the little ones at your room or tent while you're having dinner.

Travellers with disabilities

Although by no means easy, Kenya does not pose insurmountable problems for **people with disabilities**. While there is little government support for improving access, travel industry staff and passersby are usually prepared to help whenever

THINGS TO TAKE

- **Binoculars** for each member of your party
- **Cotton clothes** (loose and few), plus a warm, light, jacket or fleece
- **GPS** (basic handheld version), or GPS-enabled smart phone, immensely useful in the bush
- **Multipurpose penknife** (be sure to put it in your checked luggage)
- **Sheet sleeping bag**, essential in the very cheapest accommodation
- **Torch** (flashlight), ideally a wind-up one
- **Water shoes** (easy to swim in) to protect your feet

necessary. For wheelchair-users and those who find stairs hard to manage, many hotels have ground-floor rooms, a number on the coast have ramped access, and larger hotels in Nairobi have elevators. While the vast majority of hotels, lodges and tented camps have at least some rooms that are ramped or with only one or two steps, most only have showers, not bathtubs, and few have any properly adapted facilities.

The majority of safari vehicles, too, are not ideal for people with impaired mobility. **Off-road trips** can be very arduous and you should take a pressure cushion for game drives.

If you're flying from the UK, you can avoid a change of plane by going with BA or Kenya Airways direct from London to Nairobi. All charter flights are direct (if they're not always non-stop, at least you won't need to change), but they only go to Mombasa.

If you're looking for a **tour**, contact the disabled and special needs travel specialists Go Africa in Diani Beach (W go-africa-safaris.com) and the highly recommended Mombasa-based Southern Cross (see p.406; W southerncrosssafaris.com), who are one of the few mainstream companies to offer special safaris for people with mobility impairments.

Work and volunteering

Unless you have lined up a job or voluntary work before arriving in Kenya, you have little chance of getting **employment**. Wages are extremely low – for school teachers, for example, they start at the equivalent of less than $200 per month, while hotel staff wages can be less than half that – and

there is serious unemployment in the towns. Particular skills are sometimes in demand but the employer will need to arrange the necessary papers. It's illegal to obtain income in Kenya while staying on a visitor's pass.

An international **work camp** is no holiday, and conditions are usually primitive, but it can be a lot of fun, too, and is undoubtedly worthwhile. One group to contact is the Kenya Voluntary Development Association (W kvda.or.ke), a locally inspired organization bringing Kenyans and foreigners together in a number of locations across the country – digging irrigation trenches, making roads, building schools, or just producing as many mud bricks as possible. The minimum age is 18 and there's no formal upper age limit, but volunteers older than 25 are unusual. The groups are very mixed in terms of nationality. The programmes, which include basic accommodation, meals and transport in Kenya, start at around €250 for two weeks – not including flights.

Other groups employing volunteers in community projects are **Volunteer Kenya** (W volunteerkenya.org), whose main focus is on AIDS awareness, education and women's income generation, and **Kenya Voluntary Community Development Project** (W kvcdp.org), which works in a variety of fields and in Kenya is known as Inter-Community Development Involvement (ICODEI). Both organizations have bases in western Kenya and the fees for a month are around $1200.

An alternative would be to compromise and take a **working holiday** with a commercial "volun-tourism" organization. One of the better companies is Camp Kenya (see p.48).

Nairobi and around

CURIO STALL, NAIROBI MARKET

1

Nairobi and around

Easily the largest city in East Africa, Nairobi is also the youngest, the most modern, the fastest growing, the largest and, at nearly 1700m altitude, the highest. The superlatives could go on forever. "Green City in the Sun", runs one tour-brochure sobriquet, "City of Flowers" another. Less enchanted visitors growl "Nairobbery". The city catches your attention, at least: this is no tropical backwater. Most roads in Kenya, particularly paved ones, lead to Nairobi and, like it or not, you're almost bound to spend some time here. Strolling around the malls in Westlands or negotiating Kenyatta Avenue at rush hour, it's also perhaps easy to forget how quickly you can leave the city and be in the bush.

Apart from being the safari capital of the world, Nairobi is an excellent base for Kenyan travel in general. To the coast, it's as little as six hours by road, an overnight train journey, or an hour if you fly. It takes about the same time to get to the far west and barely two hours to get to the great trough of the **Rift Valley** or the slopes of **Mount Kenya**.

An excellent day-trip, literally on the city's doorstep, is **Nairobi National Park**, a wild attraction where you'd expect to find suburbs. And a much overlooked trip due south, to **Lake Magadi**, takes you into a ravishingly beautiful and austere part of the Rift Valley.

Nairobi

NAIROBI is one of Africa's major cities: the UN's fourth "World Centre", East Africa's commercial, media and NGO hub, and a significant capital in its own right, with a population of between three and four million, depending on how big an area you include. As a traveller, your first impressions are likely to depend on how – and where – you arrive. If you've come here overland, some time resting up in comfort can seem an appealing proposition. Newly arrived by air from Europe, though, you may wonder – amid the rash of roadside ads persuading you to upgrade your mobile-phone package or catch the latest TV offering – just how far you've travelled. Nairobi, little more than a century old, has real claims to Western-style sophistication but, as you'll soon find, it lacks a convincing heart. Apart from some lively musical attractions – some of East Africa's busiest clubs and best bands – there's little here of magnetic appeal, and most travellers stay long enough only to take stock, make some travel arrangements and maybe visit the **National Museum**, before moving on.

If you're interested in getting to know the real Kenya, though, Nairobi is as compelling a place as any and displays enormous vitality and buzz. The controlling ethos is commerce rather than community, and there's an almost wilful superficiality in the free-for-all of

Highlights

❶ Kibera Take away some added awareness and leave a little extra cash behind on a tour of Kenya's biggest slum district – a sobering but not a depressing experience. **See p.108**

❷ National Museum By far the biggest and best museum in the country and a good introduction to Kenyan culture and natural history. **See p.110**

❸ Markets From the bewildering, muddy maze of Gikomba to the tourist-oriented Maasai markets, these are excellent places to sample a slice of Nairobi life, eat street food or pick up souvenirs. **See p.136**

❹ Nairobi National Park On Nairobi's doorstep, the park is home to most of Kenya's big mammals, and the place for classic photos of plains animals against a backdrop of skyscrapers. **See p.141**

❺ David Sheldrick Trust Highly regarded elephant and rhino orphanage where you can get on petting terms with tiny pachyderms. **See p.144**

❻ Olorgasailie prehistoric site Stark site in the southern Rift Valley, with huge numbers of early hominin stone tools preserved *in situ*. **See p.150**

HIGHLIGHTS ARE MARKED ON THE MAP ON P.98

1

commuters, shoppers, police, hustlers, security guards, hawkers and tourists. It's hard to imagine a city with a more fascinating variety of people, mostly immigrants from the rural areas, drawn to the presence of wealth. On the surface the city accepts everyone with tolerance, and, in any downtown street, you can see a complete cross section of Kenyans, every variety of tourist, and migrants and refugees from many African countries.

Nairobi's rapid growth, however, inevitably has a downside. Watch the local TV news, read any paper or talk to a resident and you'll hear jaw-dropping stories of crime and police shootings. Although the city has become safer in recent years, you should certainly be aware of its reputation for **bag-snatching and robbery**, frequently directed at new tourist arrivals (see the box on security on p.106). If you plan to stay in Nairobi for any length of time, you'll soon get the hang of balancing reasonable caution with a fairly relaxed attitude: thousands of visitors do it every year. If you're only here for a few days, you're likely to find it a stimulating city.

Brief history

Nairobi came into being in May 1899, an artificial settlement created by Europeans at Mile 327 of the Uganda Railway, then being systematically forged from Mombasa on the coast to Port Florence – now Kisumu – on Lake Victoria. Although called the "Uganda Railway" there was no connection to Kampala until 1931; before that, Lake Victoria ships provided the link.

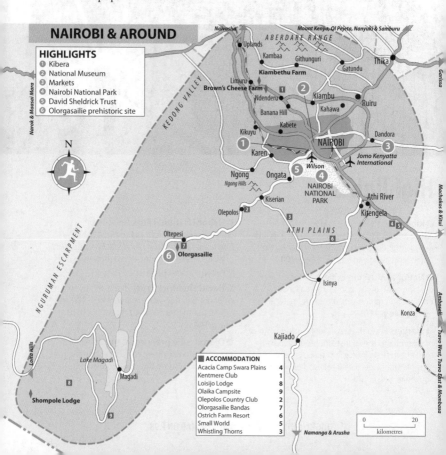

NAIROBI & AROUND

HIGHLIGHTS
1. Kibera
2. National Museum
3. Markets
4. Nairobi National Park
5. David Sheldrick Trust
6. Olorgasailie prehistoric site

■ ACCOMMODATION	
Acacia Camp Swara Plains	4
Kentmere Club	1
Loisijo Lodge	8
Olaika Campsite	9
Olepolos Country Club	2
Olorgasailie Bandas	7
Ostrich Farm Resort	6
Small World	5
Whistling Thorns	3

0		20
	kilometres	

GETTING ORIENTED IN NAIROBI

Nairobi has widespread suburbs but the downtown area of the **Central Business District** – known simply as "town" to many Nairobians – is relatively small: a triangle of shops, offices and public buildings, with the railway station on the southern flank and the main bus stations to the east. The triangle of downtown Nairobi divides into three principal districts bisected by the main thoroughfares of **Kenyatta Avenue** and **Moi Avenue**. The grandest and most formal part of the CBD is the area around **City Square**, in the southwest. This square kilometre is Nairobi's heart: government buildings, banks and offices merge to the north and east with upmarket shopping streets and major hotels. The area's big landmarks are the **Kenyatta International Conference Centre**, with its huge cylindrical tower and artichoke-shaped convention hall, and the blue-glass skyscraper of **Lonrho House**. To the south of this area, towards the train station, stands the **Memorial Park** on the site of the bombed US Embassy.

North of Kenyatta Avenue, there's a shift to smaller scale and lesser finance. The **City Market** is here, surrounded by a denser district of modest shops, restaurants and hotels. The modest-sized **Jeevanjee Gardens** are a welcome patch of greenery, and a little further north is the university district and Nairobi's oldest establishment, the *Norfolk Hotel*, contemporary with the original 1907 rebuilding of the city.

East of Moi Avenue, the character changes more radically. Here, and down towards the reeking trickle of the Nairobi River, is the relatively poor, inner-city district identified with **River Road**, its main thoroughfare. The River Road quarter is where most long-distance **buses and matatus** start and terminate, and where you'll find the capital's cheapest restaurants and hotels, as well as the highest concentration of African-owned businesses. It's also a somewhat notorious area, with a traditional concentration of sharks and pickpockets (see box, p.106). The reputation is exaggerated, but you can still meet residents of Nairobi who five minutes' walk away and in all their years in the city have never been to this part of town.

If you're not on a shoestring budget and/or you're not eager to become acquainted with the city centre's gritty soul, then your time in Nairobi is more likely to be spent in one of the **suburbs**: the busy inner suburb of **Westlands** just north of the CBD; the forest-swathed ridges of **Runda** or **Spring Valley** further north; or the well-fed lawns and gardens of **Karen** or **Langata** in the southwest. Many of the city's attractions and most popular hotels, restaurants and bars are also found in these suburbs.

Nairobi was initially a supply depot, switching yard and camp ground for the thousands of Indian labourers employed by the British. The bleak, partly swampy site was simply the spot where operations came to a halt while the engineers figured out their next move – getting the line up the steep slopes that lay ahead. The name came from the local Maasai word for the area, *enkare nyarobi*, "the place of cold water", though the spot itself was originally called *Nakusontelon*, "Beginning of all Beauty".

Surprisingly, the unplanned settlement took root. A few years later it was totally rebuilt after the burning of the original town compound following an outbreak of plague. By 1907, it was so firmly established that the colonists took it as the capital of the newly formed "British East Africa" (BEA). Europeans, encouraged by the authorities, started settling in some numbers, while Africans were forced into employment by tax demands (without representation) or onto specially created **reserves** – the Maasai to the Southern Reserve and the Kikuyu to their own reserve in the highlands.

Nairobi's districts and suburbs

The capital, lacking development from any established community, was somewhat characterless in its early years – and remains so. The **original centre** retains an Asian influence in its older buildings, but today it's shot through with glassy, high-rise blocks. Surrounding the core of the old **Central Business District** is a vast area of suburbs: wealthiest in the west and north, increasingly poor to the south and east.

Limuru ▲
Limuru & Brown's Cheese Farm ▲
Nazareth Hospital ▲

Ndenderu ●

LIMURU ROAD

Banana Hill ●

GIGIRI

Village Market
US Embassy

Canadian
HC

Sigiria
Forest

KITISURU

LOWER KABETE ROAD

Kikuyu ●

LORESHO

WAIYAKI WAY

SEE "WEST NAIROBI" MAP FOR DETAILS

WESTLANDS

Arboretum

Railway
Museum

Lenana
Forest
Centre

War
Cemetery

Junction Mall

HILL

Motherland
Centre

Racecourse

Forest HQ

Jamhuri
Park

KIBERA

Wilson
Business
Park

Ngong Road Forest

Uhuru Gardens
National Monument

KAREN

Nakumatt Crossroads

Karen Office Park

Lengal
House

Wilson

Mamba
Village

Nairobi Safari Walks &
Animal Orphanage

Splash!

Main Gate

Hillcrest
School

Bomas of
Kenya

KWS
HQ

Hyena Dam

Symbion House

Karen
Club

LANGATA

Galleria Mall

Langata
Gate

Ivory
Burning Site

Karen Blixen
Museum

No.
Dam

Oloolua
Forest

Oloolua
Forest Gate

BOGANI ROAD

USHIRIKA ROAD

Langata
Link

Banda
Gate

Narogomon
Dam

Impala
Hill

River Kisembe

MUKOMA ROAD

AFEW Giraffe
Centre

Mbagathi
Gate

**HYRAX
VALLEY**

DSWT Elephant
Orphanage

River Empakasi

Ngong ●

Ongata
Rongai

MAGADI ROAD

**NGONG
HILLS**

N

GREATER NAIROBI

0   2
kilometres

▼ 24 25 26 27 & Magadi

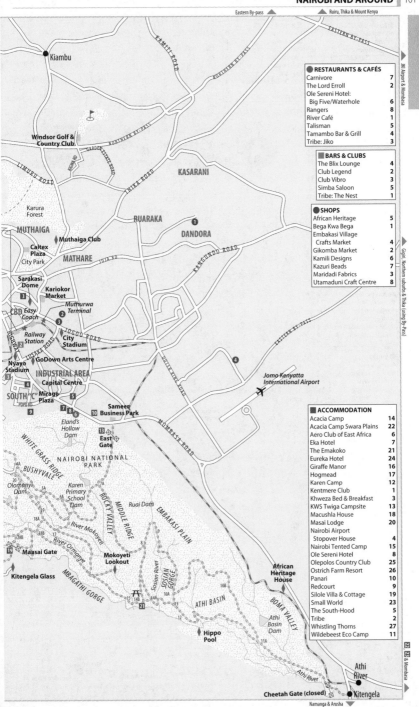

Eastern By-pass
Ruiru, Thika & Mount Kenya

Kiambu

Windsor Golf &
Country Club

Karura
Forest

MUTHAIGA
Caltex
Plaza
City Park
Sarakasi
Dome
Kariokor
Market
CBD Easy
Coach
Railway
Station
Nyayo
Stadium
INDUSTRIAL AREA
Capital Centre
SOUTH "C" Mirage
Plaza
Sameer
Business Park

KASARANI

RUARAKA

DANDORA

Muthaiga Club
MATHARE

Muthurwa
Terminal
JOGOO ROAD
City
Stadium
GoDown Arts Centre

Eland's
Hollow
Dam
East
Gate

WHITE GRASS RIDGE
BUSHYVALE
NAIROBI NATIONAL
PARK
Olompanyi
Dam
Karen
Primary
School
Dam
ROCKY VALLEY
MIDDLE RIDGE
Ruai Dam
EMBAKASI PLAIN
River Mokoyeti
River Ormaye
Maasai Gate
Mokoyeti
Lookout
Kitengela Glass
MBAGATHI GORGE
SOSIAN GORGE
Sosian River
ATHI BASIN
Athi
Basin
Dam
BOMA VALLEY
Hippo
Pool

Jomo Kenyatta
International Airport

African
Heritage
House

Athi
River

Cheetah Gate (closed)
Kitengela
Namanga & Arusha

RESTAURANTS & CAFÉS
Carnivore	7
The Lord Erroll	2
Ole Sereni Hotel:	
Big Five/Waterhole	6
Rangers	8
River Café	1
Talisman	5
Tamambo Bar & Grill	4
Tribe: Jiko	3

BARS & CLUBS
The Blix Lounge	4
Club Legend	2
Club Vibro	3
Simba Saloon	5
Tribe: The Nest	1

SHOPS
African Heritage	5
Bega Kwa Bega	1
Embakasi Village	
Crafts Market	4
Gikomba Market	2
Kamili Designs	6
Kazuri Beads	7
Maridadi Fabrics	3
Utamaduni Craft Centre	8

ACCOMMODATION
Acacia Camp	14
Acacia Camp Swara Plains	22
Aero Club of East Africa	6
Eka Hotel	7
The Emakoko	21
Eureka Hotel	24
Giraffe Manor	16
Hogmead	17
Karen Camp	12
Kentmere Club	1
Khweza Bed & Breakfast	3
KWS Twiga Campsite	13
Macushla House	18
Masai Lodge	20
Nairobi Airport	
Stopover House	4
Nairobi Tented Camp	15
Ole Sereni Hotel	8
Olepolos Country Club	25
Ostrich Farm Resort	26
Panari	10
Redcourt	9
Silole Villa & Cottage	19
Small World	23
The South-Hood	5
Tribe	2
Whistling Thorns	27
Wildebeest Eco Camp	11

JK Airport & Mombasa

Gigiri, Northern suburbs & Thika

Gigiri, Northern suburbs & Thika (using By-Pass)

26 & Mombasa

22 & Mombasa

1

RESTAURANTS & CAFÉS

Alan Bobbe's Bistro	7
Amaica	1
Amani Garden Café	10
Bombay Chowpaty	4
Cedars	13
Furusato	2
Golden Spur	6
Habesha	14
Le Rustique	3
Little Sheep Hot Pot	18
Mediterraneo	16
Milimani Café	15
Misono	17
Moonflower Restaurant	11
Mughal's	19
Osteria del Chianti	12
Peppers	8
Seven Seafood Bar & Grill	5
Spice Roots	9

BARS & CLUBS

Black Parrot	7
Brew Bistro	8
Caribea	6
Casablanca	5
Klub House	2
The Loft	3
Lord Delamere Terrace	4
Mercury Lounge	1
Tree House	3

ACCOMMODATION

Boulevard Hotel	5
Country Lodge	15
Fairview Hotel	14
Heron Hotel	13
Jungle Junction	11
Mennonite Guest House	1
Milimani Backpackers	12
Miti Mingi Guest House	3
Nairobi Youth Hostel	16
Norfolk Hotel	6
Parklands Shade Hotel	4
Serena Hotel	10
Southern Sun Hotel	2
Upper Hill Backpackers	8
Woodmere Apartments	9
YMCA	7

SHOPS

Amani ya Juu	2
Mikono Craft Shop	4
Spinner's Web	1
Textbook Centre	3
Woodley Weavers	5

SPRING VALLEY

Westlands Office Park

Safaricom HQ2

AACC Building

ABC Place

Bishop Josiah Kibira House

Almont Park

KYUNA ROAD

KYUNA CRESCENT

SHANZU ROAD

KYUNA CRESCENT

BROOKSIDE DRIVE

MUKABI RD

WAIYAKI WAY

MANYANI ROAD

KANJATA CRESCENT

NJTHANGUNI DR

ST MICHAEL ROAD

KANJATA ROAD

BHAPTA ROAD

Nairobi River

WAIYAKI WAY

EWASO NGIRO PARK

TABARASHAN AVE

MUHOYA AVE

JAMES GICHURU ROAD

MZIMA SPRINGS RD

MZIMA SPRINGS LANE

RIVERSIDE DRIVE

Ludwig Krapf House

THE PADDOCKS

MUKOMA AVE

MBUTHI AVE

MZIMA SPRINGS RD

LAVINGTON

CONVENT ROAD

MZIMA SPRINGS RD

MANYANI WAY

TENDE DRIVE

TEMBO DRIVE

ISAAC GITHANJU RD

NDOTO ROAD

OLENGURUONE ROAD

Lavington Green Shopping Centre

MASHIKA ROAD

HOLORI RD

MUCUMO ROAD

NYERI ROAD

JATI ROAD

LIKONI LANE

MWINGI ROAD

Dallago

CONVENT ROAD

JAMES GICHURU ROAD

MUTHANGARI ROAD

MAGETA ROAD

MATUNI ROAD

MUGUMO RD

Kuona Trust

JAMES GICHURU ROAD

MUTHANGARI GARDENS RD

KAPTEI ROAD

SUGUTA ROAD

KILELESHWA

KAYAHWE ROAD

AMBOSSELI ROAD

GITANGA ROAD

KIKAMBALA ROAD

LENANA ROAD

Roshanmaer Place

TURBO ROAD

Yaya Centre

KINGARA ROAD

MBAZI AVE

VANGA ROAD

HENDRED ROAD

KUNDE ROAD

KOROSHO ROAD

OLE ODUME ROAD

ARGWINGS KODHEK ROAD

KIRICHWA ROAD

MUGUMO RD

OTHAYA ROAD

KING'ARA ROAD

CHANIA

KINGARUMA

RIARA ROAD

KINGARA ROAD

Junction Mall

Piedmont Plaza

MAKINDU ROAD

RIARA ROAD

MURINGA ROAD

OLE DUME ROAD

KILIMANI ROAD

DAGORETTI CORNER

NGONG ROAD

Adam's Arcade

The Greenhouse

Prestige Plaza

WOODLEY

NGONG

RING ROAD

Kibera

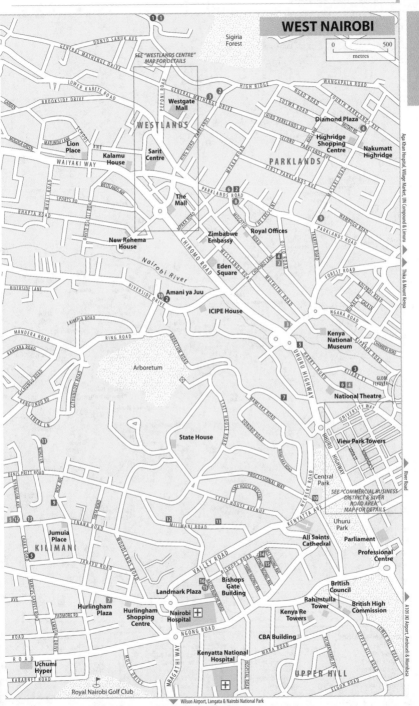

WEST NAIROBI

COMMERCIAL BUSINESS DISTRICT AND RIVER ROAD AREA

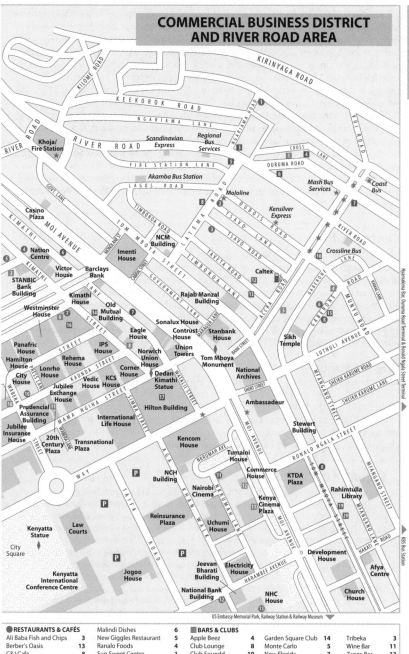

● RESTAURANTS & CAFÉS		Malindi Dishes	6	■ BARS & CLUBS		Garden Square Club	14	Tribeka	3
Ali Baba Fish and Chips	3	New Giggles Restaurant	5	Apple Beez	4	Monte Carlo	5	Wine Bar	11
Berber's Oasis	13	Ranalo Foods	4	Club Lounge	8	New Florida	7	Zanze Bar	13
C&J Cafe	8	Sun Sweet Centre	1	Club Soundd	10	Simmers	9		
Fiesta	9	Tamarind	12	Dolce	2	Stanley:		
Hewhay Fastfood	2	Thorn Tree Café	7	Fameland	1	Exchange Bar	6		
Home Park	11	Trattoria	10	Florida 2000	12				

US Embassy Memorial Park, Railway Station & Railway Museum

The names of these **suburbs** – Karen, Parklands, Eastleigh, Spring Valley, Kibera, among many others – reflect the jumble of African, Asian and European elements in Nairobi's original inhabitants, none of whom were local. The term "Nairobian" is a relatively new one that still applies mostly to the younger generation. Although it has a predominance of Kikuyu, the city is not the preserve of a single ethnic group, standing as it does at the meeting point of Maasai, Kikuyu and Kamba territories. Its choice as capital, accidental though it may have been (the Kikuyu town of Limuru and the Kamba capital, Machakos, were also considered), was a fortunate one for the future of the country.

Since the 1990s, the Central Business District has seen the steady flight of businesses into the suburbs, particularly to **Upper Hill** and the surrounding districts to the west of the CBD; to the booming satellite city of **Westlands**, just a couple of kilometres to the northwest; and for kilometre after kilometre out along the **Mombasa road** to the south. Just in the last few years, however, regeneration efforts in the CBD have begun to pay off. It's not quite like the rebirth of central Johannesburg, but businesses and nightlife are returning to a district that feels safer and more habitable than at any time in the last two decades.

Central Nairobi

The "old" heart of **downtown Nairobi** may only date back a little over a century, but there is still enough here to while away a morning or afternoon while you decide what you think of modern Kenya. The **Central Business District** is not the most cosmopolitan part of the city – that dubious honour would have to be shared between several suburban malls – but after the dark, anti-democracy period in the 1980s and the collapse of security in the 1990s, twenty-first-century central Nairobi is beginning to feel like a world-class city again. One advantage of strolling around here in the daytime is that if you choose to check out the CBD's nightlife (p.131), you'll have some idea of where you are.

Kenyatta Avenue

The obvious place to start looking around Central Nairobi is **Kenyatta Avenue.** Originally designed to allow a twelve-oxen team to make a full turn, the broad, multi-laned thoroughfare, planted with flowering trees and shrubs, remains – along with the Kenyatta Conference Centre – the capital's favourite tourist image. The avenue is smartest – and most touristy – on its south side, with would-be money-changers, itinerant souvenir hawkers and safari touts assailing you from every direction.

SECURITY IN NAIROBI

Nairobi isn't nearly as bad as its **"Nairobbery"** reputation would suggest. The city has cleaned up considerably over the past few years: the city centre is less threatening, there are fewer street children, beggars and touts, and a dedicated tourist police force patrols the streets. That said, it pays to take some precautions against crime. It helps to memorize any route you're walking, as lost-looking tourists are easier targets. Keep your hands out of reach, as a handshake can sometimes throw you off guard, and be – rationally – suspicious of everyone until you've caught your breath. It doesn't take long to get a little streetwise. Every rural Kenyan coming to the city for the first time goes through exactly the same process.

At night, be extra vigilant if you're walking in the city centre and don't wander outside the CBD unless you're really clued-up. Be especially wary in the **River Road district**, which in practical terms means anything east of Moi Avenue, and indeed sometimes includes the avenue. Even some locals avoid walking there and taxi drivers are quite often reluctant to venture into certain parts of the district. Obviously don't walk through the **parks** at night.

All the main **bus** and **matatu stations** are somewhat chaotic and ideal for pickpockets and snatch-and-run robberies. If you're **driving or being driven**, avoid displaying phones and cameras and laptops, and keep your windows rolled up, especially at traffic lights.

The focus of the avenue's eastern end is the *Sarova Stanley Hotel*'s **Thorn Tree Café**, on the corner of Kimathi Street. The CBD's one proper pavement café, the *Thorn Tree*, is an enduring meeting place – despite its prices and a clientele largely made up of *wazungu* and rich business types (see p.128). The thorn tree in question was once Nairobi's main information exchange, with notice boards fixed to its trunk. It was felled in 1997 and replaced with a new sapling and purely ornamental message boards.

Off Kenyatta Avenue, close to Uhuru Highway, is **Koinange Street**, named after the Kikuyu Senior Chief Koinange of the colonial era. The peculiar, caged **Galton-Fenzi Memorial**, just here on the left, is a monument to the man who founded, of all things, the Nairobi branch of the Automobile Association. In 1926, Galton-Fenzi was also the first motorist to drive from Nairobi to Mombasa.

The former **Provincial Commissioner's Office**, the low grey-red building with the dome, on the corner of Kenyatta Avenue, in the shadow of Nyayo House, was the register's office for births, marriages and deaths during the colonial period. It is now the **Nairobi Gallery**, but doesn't have a regular programme of exhibitions, so you'll just have to call by and see what's on, if anything.

Uhuru and Central parks
Western side of Uhuru Highway • Daily 24hr • Free

Central and **Uhuru** parks – not to be confused with Uhuru Gardens, the independence park on Langata Road (see p.140) – are unfenced and never closed (though it's a distinctly bad idea to visit after dark when they have a reputation for muggings). There are rowing boats for rent in the small murky lake in Uhuru Park, which are very popular at weekends and holidays. A poignant **memorial** to the many lives lost in political violence over the past decade can be seen at the roadside verge of **Uhuru Park** at Kenyatta Avenue, also known as "Freedom Corner", where the Green Belt Movement (see p.24) have planted "Trees of Peace", each bearing a simple wooden cross with the name of a victim and the words "Saba-Saba", meaning "Seven-Seven", after the crackdown on pro-democracy demonstrators on July 7, 1990.

City Square
Heading south down Koinange Street and on to Kaunda Street, passing the *InterContinental* on your right and Holy Family Cathedral on your left, you cross City Hall Way and enter **City Square**. Jomo Kenyatta's statue sits benevolently, mace in hand, on the far side of the wide, flagstoned court; his mausoleum, with flickering eternal flames, is on the right as you approach the Parliament building further on. When the flags are out for a conference it all looks very bright and confident.

Parliament
Parliament Rd • Parliamentary sessions usually mid-Oct to mid-July Wed & Thurs at 2.30pm

The legend over the main doors of Kenya's **Parliament** reads: "For a Just Society and the Fair Government of Men". The motto seems finally to be losing its edge of irony, the government having been forced by both national and international pressures to allow greater democracy and accountability in its business. A host of contentious motions is openly debated here, concerning corruption and ethnic violence, and there's even the occasional vote of no confidence in the government.

To sit in the **public gallery** you first have to register for a visitor's permit at the gatehouse on the corner of Parliament Road and Harambee Avenue, leaving all your belongings with the attendant outside. The gallery tends to be full of schoolchildren who are very well behaved – which of course is more than can be said of the members of parliament. Try to get hold of a copy of the Orders of the Day – there may be a juicy question or two worth anticipating. The guards at the gate can tell you how to get a tour of the building when Parliament is not in session. If you are assigned a guide, make sure you agree about exactly how much you'll pay for the tour.

1

The Kenyatta International Conference Centre

Harambee Avenue • Daily 6am–6pm • Ksh400 • ☎ 020 2247247, ⓦ kicc.co.ke

From Parliament, walking down Harambee Avenue along the shady pavement, you come to Nairobi's pride and joy – the thirty-storey, 105m-high **Kenyatta International Conference Centre** or KICC. This, for a long time the tallest building in Kenya, is capped by a revolving restaurant, now closed. It's still worth going to the top, as the view of Nairobi is without equal and a firm reminder of the vastness of Africa. Just 4km to the south, the Mombasa road can be seen trailing through the suburbs and out towards the coast; northwards, hills of coffee and tea roll into the distance towards the Aberdare range. On a clear day you really can see Mount Kenya in one direction and Kilimanjaro in the other. Immediately below you, the traffic swarms, and **Jogoo House**, containing government offices, is suddenly seen to be built remarkably like a Roman villa. In 2000, the KICC was overtaken by the nearby 38-storey **Times Tower**, the tallest building in East Africa at 140m, but occupied by Kenya's tax authority and inaccessible to tourists.

National Archives

Moi Ave, junction with City Hall Way • Mon–Fri 9am–4.30pm, Sat & Sun 9am–4pm • Ksh200 • ☎ 0722 599212, ⓦ archives.go.ke

Housed in the striking old Bank of India building on the bend of Moi Avenue across from the *Hilton*, the **National Archives** amount to a museum and art gallery in the heart of the city that few visitors to Nairobi know about. If you want to see the locked archives themselves (mainly books, papers, correspondence and some recordings) you can pay a token fee for a year's access.

The ground floor is a **public gallery** with a range of paintings from Kenya and throughout the African continent; an enormous display of Maasai, Luo, Turkana,

---

KIBERA

Said to be the largest shanty town in sub-Saharan Africa, **Kibera** is a sprawling mass of shacks, just a few kilometres west of Nairobi's city centre. Although it's perhaps best not to just wander down there, it is safe to visit if you're accompanied by local residents or NGO workers, and is now an option as a morning excursion, offered by a number of local operators. The slums were a flashpoint during the post-election violence in January 2008. Protestors torched buildings and uprooted the Nairobi-Nakuru railway line that runs right through the slum. Few Kibera residents buy newspapers or own TVs: the Kibera community radio station **Pamoja FM** (99.9 FM; ⓦ bit.ly/Pamoja) provides a vital "glue" that helped prevent Kibera from ripping apart.

Kibera started at the end of World War I as a village housing Sudanese Nubian soldiers of the demobilized armies of British East Africa. Subsequently, as rural-to-urban migration increased, people moved into the area and began putting up mud-and-wattle structures. Today, Kibera is home to several hundred thousand residents (no one knows exactly how many), most of whom live in makeshift huts. The typical home in Kibera measures 3m by 3m, with an average of five people per dwelling. Access to electricity, running water and sanitation ranges from zero to very minimal – the occasional makeshift pit latrines are shared between anything from ten to one hundred homes, though foreign donors have constructed some new toilet blocks. The streets are a mass of seemingly endless trenches, alleyways and open gutters clogged with waste and sewage. As well as lacking even the most basic services, Kibera has an HIV infection rate of more than twenty percent and the number of orphans rises daily. However, the slum somehow works and is full of small **businesses**, from video cinemas to bakeries.

Several tour operators now run escorted visits to Kibera. Make sure before you sign up that you know exactly where your money is going: some businesses are not above running "pro-poor" tourism as part of their activities while pocketing much of the cash supposed to be supporting slum projects. As you visit various premises and community projects, you should find the experience deeply affecting, if not enjoyable, and not without its lighter moments. Contact: Kibera Tours (ⓦ kiberatours.com), Chocolate City Tours (ⓦ bit.ly/ChocolateCityTours) or Explore Kibera Tours (ⓦ explorekibera.com).

Luhya and Ethiopian weaponry; and a wall of tribal photographs. In the centre of the floor there's also a jumbled collection of African ethnographia – musical instruments, masks, weapons and domestic artefacts.

Past the first floor and its photograph library, the second floor houses a photographic exhibition of the struggle for **independence** – compelling not just for its content but because this is one of the few public places in the country where Kenyans can be reminded of the period in their history euphemistically called "The Emergency".

Tom Mboya Monument

Facing the National Archives, the new (2011) **Tom Mboya Monument** commemorates the life of the left-leaning Luo government minister who was assassinated in 1969 close to this spot on Moi Avenue. Mboya's statue, sculpted by Oshoto Ondula, depicts him in Ghanaian robes as presented to him by the first president of Ghana, Kwame Nkrumah, and surrounded by pink flamingos – a curious reference not to his family's lakeside origins but to the plane tickets he bought for students to study abroad after independence.

August 7th Memorial Park

Corner of Haile Selassie and Moi Ave • **Park**: daily 7am–6pm • Ksh20 • **Memorial centre**: daily 9am–6pm • Ksh100

The **August 7th Memorial Park** occupies the site of the former American embassy, which was bombed by al-Qaeda in 1998 (see p.569). The park is a peaceful refuge from the free-for-all of downtown Nairobi, with grassy lawns and statues built from the rubble. It is also a chilling reminder of the horror perpetrated here. In the centre of the park, near the fountain, a wall commemorates each of the 218 victims of the blast. The memorial centre displays artefacts from the bombing and a video about the atrocity.

Dedan Kimathi Memorial

Opposite the *Hilton Hotel*, on the corner of Kimathi Street and Mama Ngina Street, stands a statue honouring **Dedan Kimathi**, the Mau Mau freedom fighter who was executed by the British in 1957. The statue – an imposing 2m bronze sculpture atop a 3m base – is hard to miss. Kimathi, sporting the dreadlocks typical of Mau Mau fighters, holds a gun in one hand and his *rungu* (club) in the other. The statue was erected in February 2007 on the fiftieth anniversary of his death.

The Jamia Mosque

The **Jamia Mosque** stands near the City Market, north of Kenyatta Avenue. The ornate green-and-white exterior contrasts strikingly with the simple interior, and the central dome appears far larger from beneath than it does from the courtyard outside. Although most Kenyan towns now have at least one mosque, often financed by Saudi patrons, few are as large or as beautiful as Nairobi's Jamia. It's unlikely that non-Muslims will be allowed in, although polite requests, a genuine interest in Islam and the usual modesty of attire may help.

Jeevanjee Gardens

Corner of Muindi Mbingu St and Moktar Daddad St • Daily dawn to dusk • Free

In a reasonably reputable part of the city, **Jeevanjee Gardens** are always worth a visit, especially during a weekday lunchtime when you can picnic on a bench and chat with the office workers not thronging the nearby restaurants. It seems to be an acceptable place to have a **cigarette** in a public place, too. You can also listen to the preachers who have made Jeevanjee their church and the bemused picnickers their congregation. The park contains a curiously small statue, just about recognizable, of **Queen Victoria**, presented to Nairobi by the nineteenth-century business tycoon A. M. Jeevanjee, who founded the *Standard* newspaper. And there's a rather good sculpture of the tycoon himself, crafted from heavy, iron wire.

1

The Railway Museum

1km west of the railway station (signposted) • Daily 8.15am–5pm • Ksh400, including guided tour

Nairobi's privately run **Railway Museum** is a natural draw for rail fans and of more than passing interest for anyone else. The main hall contains a mass of memorabilia, including photos of early stations, of the "Lunatic Express" East African Railway from Mombasa to Lake Victoria being built, pictures of the engineering feats involved in getting the carriages up and down the escarpment, and of strange pieces of hardware, such as the game-viewing seat mounted at the front of the train. Passengers who risked this perch were reminded that "The High Commissioner will not be liable for personal injury (fatal or otherwise)". In the museum annexe, the motorized bicycle inspection trolley is quite a sight, but, as the write-up explains, the experiment in the 1950s "was not really successful", as the wheels kept slipping off the rail.

Outside, exposed to the elements, is the museum's collection of old **locomotives**, most of them built in Britain. You can clamber inside any of the cabs to play with the massive levers and switches. The restriction on forward visibility in some of the engines seems incredible; the driver of the *Karamoja Express* couldn't have had any idea what was in front of him while steaming down a straight line.

Lions figure prominently in the early history of the railway. Look in the shed for first-class coach #12 to learn the story of Superintendent C. H. Ryall. In 1900, two years after the hunt for the "Man-eaters of Tsavo", lion-hunter Ryall had been sent to Kima station to shoot another suspected man-eater. He readied his gun one evening, settled down in the carriage and offered himself as bait. Unfortunately, he nodded off and was dragged from this carriage and devoured while colleagues sat frozen in horror. The coach, together with the repainted loco #301, was used in the filming of *Out of Africa* at Kajiado.

If the museum fills you with nostalgic delight, you should also note that Nairobi and Mombasa stations both have **locomotive graveyards**, which, with persistence, you should be able to look around.

The National Museum

Museum Hill • Daily 8.30am–5.30pm • Ksh800 (or Ksh1200 combined ticket with the snake park; also see below for temporary membership) • ⓦ museums.or.ke • 30min walk from Kenyatta Ave or a few minutes by bus (#21, #23 or #119)

In 2008, the **Nairobi National Museum** reopened its doors after a three-year, Ksh800 million facelift. The refurbished result is a still partly sparkling, showpiece attraction and a good prelude to any tour around the country. It's easy to reach from the centre of town and provides a solid overview of Kenya's culture, history and wildlife.

Hall of Kenya

This expansive entry hall into the museum is sparsely appointed with some of Kenya's most impressive and unusual artefacts and artworks. In one display case is a Swahili

---

MUSEUMS IN KENYA

To keep up with developments in Kenya's museums, contact the Kenya Museum Society (☏ 020 3743808, ⓦ kenyamuseumsociety.org), based off Kipande Road, behind the National Museum. As well as publishing the excellent annual journal *Kenya Past and Present*, they organize a one-week "Know Kenya" course (Ksh5000) in October or November every year, featuring behind-the-scenes access to museums, visits to places of historical or environmental interest and lectures by well-known Kenyan writers and academics. You can take out **one-month temporary membership** of KMS for Ksh800, which entitles you to free entry in all NMK museums and sites around the country – a very good deal.

1

siwa from the 1680s. The *siwa*, a ceremonial horn intricately carved from an elephant tusk, was traditionally blown on celebratory occasions as a symbol of unity and was considered to possess magical powers. There is also a **sambu**, a Kalenjin elder's cloak made from the skins of Sykes' monkeys. Beautiful photos of some of Kenya's animals adorn the wall of this hall, and prepare you for the next gallery.

The Great Hall of Mammals

Dedicated to Africa's charismatic, endangered **megafauna**, and the plains animals that are still found in some abundance in Kenya, this hall features some impressive dioramas. In the centre of the room are examples of a giraffe, an elephant, a buffalo, a zebra and an okapi, the strange forest-dwelling relative of the giraffe found only in the jungles of the Democratic Republic of Congo. Along the walls are displays of most of Kenya's mammals, including the big cats, primates and antelopes, with explanations of their habitats, diets and life cycles. Also displayed in this gallery is the skeleton of **Ahmed**, the most famous of the giant-tusked bull elephants of Marsabit, in the north of the country. In the 1970s, when poaching was rampant in northern Kenya, conservationists feared that Ahmed would be targeted because of his enormous tusks. Kenya's first president, Jomo Kenyatta, assigned two rangers to track Ahmed day and night until he died of natural causes at the age of 55. His tusks weighed in at 68kg (150lb) each. There's a life-size replica of Ahmed in the courtyard between the entrance and the shop.

Just off the Hall of Kenya gallery is a room devoted to **ornithology**, featuring 1600 specimens in glass cases. Kenya's birdlife usually makes a strong impression, even on non-birdwatchers. Look out for the various species of hornbill, turaco and roller, and for the extraordinary standard-wing nightjar, which is frequently seen fluttering low over a swimming pool at dusk, hunting for insects.

The Cradle of Human Kind

The unique interest of the Nairobi museum lies in the **human origins** exhibit, where palaeontology displays are housed. Along the walls, skeletons and skull casts of ancient hominins trace primate diversity and the evolution of the human species back millions of years. Of particular importance is the almost complete skeleton of "Turkana Boy", the 1.6-million-year-old remains of an immature male hominin found near Lake Turkana. Hardcore palaeontology fans will want to visit the **Hominin Skull Room**, which contains the skulls of some of our ancient ancestors and non-ancestral cousins, such as *Homo erectus*. The understanding of human evolution is itself a rapidly evolving field, with new theories about human origins and ancestry appearing almost yearly, but East Africa is invariably its field-research location.

Cycles of Life

Upstairs, next to the temporary galleries of local art, the **Cycles of Life** exhibit covers Kenya's tribes and cultures, in neatly laid out displays of artefacts telling the story of each ethnic group from childhood through adulthood to ancestor status. If you're planning on travelling through any of the areas inhabited by pastoral peoples (especially Pokot, Samburu, Maasai or Turkana), then seeing some old and authentic handicrafts beforehand is a good idea.

The room begins with a display of traditional birthing methods and child-rearing techniques, including a traditional Pokot child carrier made from monkey skin and children's toys made from discarded scraps of metal. The exhibit moves on to explain initiation and circumcision rituals. On display here is a Maasai warrior outfit, complete with spear and shield. The adulthood display contains various clothing and beauty products including beaded necklaces and earplugs used by some of the semi-nomadic tribes to stretch the earlobes. A display of grave markers and artefacts used to send someone into the afterlife marks the end of the exhibit.

The Snake Park
Museum campus • Daily 8.30am–5.30pm • Ksh800–1200 combined ticket with the National Museum • monthly pass available (see p.110) • 🌐 museums.or.ke

The **Snake Park**, a reptile exhibit in the museum grounds, is not nearly as interesting as it should be, with the majority of the serpents housed in dark, glass-fronted tanks and pretty much invisible under their rocks and branches. Only the **pythons**, **tortoises** and an inappropriate American **alligator** have large, well-lit enclosures. Nevertheless, it's worth getting the most out of the visit by taking an informative tour with one of the very willing **guides** hovering around: their services are free (note the "Report corruption" signs everywhere). Perhaps you could ask your guide to explain how the central, open-air enclosure – the one that warns "Trespassers will be Poisoned" – manages safely to house highly venomous **boomslangs** – whip-fast tree snakes that the guide gleefully points out, not much more than an arm's length from the crowds of school children jostling around.

City Park
Limuru Rd • Daily 6.30am–6.30pm • Free • Matatu #11 from Globe Terminal

The biggest and best park in the city centre is **City Park** in the north, a half-hour stroll from the National Museum down Forest Road and Limuru Road. City Park has a wealth of tropical trees and birdlife, including hornbills, several troops of vervet and Sykes' monkeys, a small stream with wooden bridges, gravel paths, shady lawns, and the city's Jewish, Goan and World War I memorial cemeteries. At the weekend, it gets crowded with families. During the week it's delightful, though it's best for women not to visit it alone.

The Arboretum
Arboretum Rd, off State House Rd • Daily dawn–dusk • Free; guides Ksh500 (and a guided walk, last Mon of each month – call to check and arrive at the gate by 9.30am) • ☎ 020 3746090 or 0723 833045, 🌐 naturekenya.org • Matatu #48

Close to the city centre, northwest of Uhuru Park on Arboretum Drive, the **Arboretum** is a lovely place to wander or picnic and, of course, a must if you're botanically inclined. Somewhat overgrown, almost jungly in parts, it contains more than two hundred varieties of tree, and even the odd monkey. There are security notices everywhere, so don't take any valuables, but it's guarded and fenced and, since its makeover and the paving of its paths by the Friends of Nairobi Arboretum (☎ 020 2725471 or 0727 300933), it has become essentially another safe area of the city. The Arboretum Café, in the car park just outside the gate, has drinks and snacks.

BIRDWATCHING IN NAIROBI

Birdwatching need not be exclusively a bush pursuit. For any visitor staying in central Nairobi, an impressive sight during the early morning and late evening is groups of **black kites** circling as they move between feeding and roosting sites, and among these are readily identified black-and-white **pied crows**. **Marabou storks**, **sacred ibises** and **silvery-cheeked hornbills** can sometimes be seen flying over the city (dramatically large marabous may also be seen in the thorn trees on Uhuru Highway, near Nyayo Stadium), while flocks of **superb starlings** call noisily from office buildings. The leafier areas of the city are likely to produce even more birds.

The gardens in the grounds of the National Museum are an interesting and relatively safe area to start birding. Here, keen birdwatchers may encounter **sunbirds** (variable and Hunter's) and the **cinnamon-chested bee-eater**. Another bird of the gardens is the **African paradise monarch**, a species of flycatcher. In breeding plumage, the rufous males have long tail streamers, which trail behind them like ribbons as they flit from tree to tree.

Nature Kenya organizes bird walks from the National Museum every Wednesday morning at 8.45am for a temporary membership fee of Ksh200. They usually proceed to another part of Nairobi. Longer trips are also held at least once a month. For more information, contact Nature Kenya at the museum (☎ 020 3537568 or 0771 343138, 🌐 naturekenya.org).

1

BY PLANE

JOMO KENYATTA AIRPORT

International flights and domestic Kenya Airways, Jetlink and Fly540 services use **Jomo Kenyatta International** Airport (☎020 6611000, ⓦ kenyaairports.co.ke), commonly abbreviated to JKA or JKIA, 15km southeast of the city centre, off the Mombasa highway. If you're dropping or picking up, there's easy parking, but remember to pay at a booth before you leave again (Ksh70 short-stay, Ksh700/24hr).

Arrivals JKIA arrivals are normally straightforward; for visa information, see Basics (p.85). There's normally a cursory customs check, where you may be asked what you're bringing into the country, but obvious tourists are usually waved through. If at any stage someone asks you for a bribe, or "a little something", refuse politely. If you have a long layover you may want to use the air-conditioned First/Business Class lounge ($20) near Gate 10, which gives you a comfy sofa to curl up on, papers and TV, and unlimited snacks and drinks. The airport's sleep-and-shower facility was dismantled during recent refurbishments and, at the time of writing, there was no sign of a new facility reopening.

Baggage store There's a left-luggage store (Ksh300 per bag) at the domestic terminal.

Money There are Barclays and Equity Bank ATMs outside the arrivals hall, and one or two other bank exchange desks and forex bureaux. Count notes carefully if you're exchanging money.

Mobile phones The airport has mobile phone shops where you can buy a local SIM card.

Food, drink and toilets There's little choice in terms of food and drink: airside, the always busy branch of *Java House* coffee shop near Gate 14 is most people's retreat. There are also cafés between Gates 8/9 and 3/4. The quietest toilets are by Gate 13.

Children There's a children's play room by Gate 11.

Information and assistance There are Kenya Airports Authority customer care counters by Gates 6 and 11.

Airport taxis Once you're out of the arrivals hall, a horde of private taxi touts invariably assails new arrivals. Ignore them and walk straight to the waiting cabs lined up outside, or else go to the Kenatco office on the right of the small concourse. If you'd prefer to be met, contact Kenatco direct (ⓦ kenatco.com) or a travel agent like Uniglobe Let's Go Travel (p.118), who can organize a cab. There's a range of generally agreed prices to the city centre, currently around Ksh1500–2000, depending on which hotel you want to go to. Karen and the northern suburbs are more expensive. Taxis don't have meters, so always agree the exact price before getting in (see p.54).

Airport buses There is no public airport shuttle, but some hotels will pick you up if you make prior arrangements. The

local Citi Hoppa bus #34 leaves from outside the arrivals hall (roughly every 20min; daily 6am–9pm; Ksh70), entering the city through the eastern suburbs (rather than running straight up Uhuru Highway) and stopping on Accra Road or at the nearby *Ambassadeur Hotel*.

WILSON AIRPORT

If you fly into Nairobi on a domestic flight with Airkenya or SafariLink, you'll probably arrive at Wilson Airport (☎020 501941), 5km from the city centre between the CBD and the National Park. It's a small facility, right by Langata Road, and there are always taxis awaiting passengers. Airkenya and SafariLink both have departure lounges with café-restaurants, and there's a branch of I&M bank with an ATM.

REGIONAL DESTINATIONS

Wilson Airport: WIL; Jomo Kenyatta International Airport: NBO.

Amboseli NP lodges (2 daily; roughly 45min; WIL); Diani Beach (2 daily; 1hr 30min; WIL); Eldoret (3 daily; 45min–1hr 45min, depending on route; NBO); Entebbe, Uganda (2 daily; 1hr 20min; NBO); Juba, South Sudan (2 daily; 1hr 45min; NBO); Kilimanjaro (2 daily, more in season; 45min–1hr 10min; NBO); Kisumu (6–7 daily; 50min; NBO); Kitale (2–3 daily; 50min; WIL); Lamu (daily; 2hr; NBO); Kiwayu (SafariLink; 1 daily; 2hr; WIL); Lamu (2 daily; 1hr 10min–2hr, depending on route; WIL, NBO); Lewa Downs (2–3 daily; 1hr; WIL); Loisaba (daily; 1hr 45min; WIL); Lokichokio (4 weekly; 1hr 45min; WIL); Maasai Mara NR lodges (4-plus daily; 1hr, depending on lodge; WIL); Malindi (3-plus daily; 1hr–2hr, depending on route; NBO, WIL); Meru NP (1 daily; 50min; NBO, WIL); Mombasa (at least 12 daily; 1hr–1hr 10min; NBO); Naivasha (1 daily; 15min; WIL); Nanyuki (3 daily; 40min; WIL); Samburu NR (3 daily; 1hr 10min, depending on route; WIL); Shaba NR (2 daily; 1hr 10min, depending on route; WIL); Tsavo West NP lodges (1 daily; 50min, depending on route; WIL); Zanzibar (2–3 daily; 2hr 20min; NBO).

BY TRAIN

The railway station is virtually in the city centre, with one of Nairobi's biggest matatu stages right in front. Arriving on the train, you can just walk straight out and follow Moi Avenue into town. Watch out for taxi drivers and porters who will more or less kidnap your luggage if you don't prevent them. Otherwise, the main attention you'll attract is from safari touts, who are persistent, but friendly enough, and useful if you need an escort to one of the cheaper River Rd addresses. A small tip agreed between you (say Ksh100) would be appreciated.

Leaving Nairobi If you're planning to take the train from Nairobi, it's important to make a reservation, especially if you want a first-class compartment. While you may get away with leaving this until a couple of hours before departure, it's always advisable to reserve well in advance, especially during busy travel periods like Christmas and New Year. It's best, and cheapest, to buy tickets in person at the station (☏ 020 2044476 or 0728 787301), but agents (see p.139) can also obtain tickets for you.

Destinations Kisumu (3 weekly; 13hr); Mombasa (3 weekly; 14hr); Nakuru (3 weekly; 5hr); Voi (3 weekly; 9hr); all in theory (see p.54).

BY BUS

Most bus companies have their booking offices or parking areas in the River Rd district, especially around Accra Rd (see map, p.104). The smaller companies operate out of the Country Bus Station (aka "Machakos Airport"), 1.5km east of the city centre just past Wakulima market, between Pumwani Rd and Landhies Rd (buses #4, #18 or #28 from the *Ambassadeur Hotel* bus stage). There is often a wide range of prices, depending on the vehicle and the services on board, which may include video, snacks and a/c. Always reserve tickets in advance. Note that whatever you may hear, the Tanzanian Scandinavia Bus company stopped services to Kenya a number of years ago, while Kenya's most famous bus line, Akamba, also sadly went bust in 2012.

DESTINATIONS

Arusha (8 daily; 6hr); Chogoria (6 daily; 4hr); Eldoret (6–8 daily; 8hr); Embu (6 daily; 2hr 30min); Isiolo (4 daily; 6hr); Kakamega (12 daily; 8hr); Kampala (6 daily; 12hr); Kericho (10–20 daily; 4hr); Kisumu (10–30 daily; 7hr); Kitale (10–15 daily; 7hr); Kitui (4 daily; 3hr); Machakos (frequent; 1hr 30min); Maralal (4 daily; 8hr); Meru (8 daily; 5hr); Mombasa (frequent, especially around 7am and 7pm; 7–9hr); Moshi (6 daily; 5hr 30min); Naivasha (20–40 daily; 1hr 30min); Nakuru (10–15 daily; 2hr 30min); Namanga (8 daily; 3hr); Nanyuki (frequent; 3hr 30min); Narok (6 daily; 5hr); Nyeri (8 daily; 2hr 30min); Thika (frequent; 40min).

DOMESTIC BUS COMPANIES

Coast Bus (aka Coast Air, Coastline, Coast Express, Modern Coast) corner of Accra Rd and Cross Lane ☏ 020 3577104 or 0722 206448, ⊛ coastbus.com. One of the best companies, running multiple daily services between Mombasa (and Malindi) and Nairobi, plus Kisumu, Kakamega, Kitui and points in between. "Oxygen " is their a/c service.

Crown Bus Lagos House, Monrovia St ☏ 020 2212253 or 0722 719944, ⊛ crownbus.co.ke. Nairobi to Mombasa plus western Kenya.

Easy Coach Haile Selassie Ave ☏ 020 2212711 or 0738 200301, ⊛ easycoach.kbo.co.ke. One of Kenya's biggest bus companies, running services principally to the Rift Valley, western Kenya and Kampala, including many of the

defunct Akamba bus company's former routes.

Kensilver Express Dubois Rd ☏ 020 2120935 or 0722 509918. Popular bus services to the Central Highlands, especially Embu and Meru.

Mash Corner of Accra Rd and Duruma Rd ☏ 0723 663133 or 0733 929626, ⊛ mash.ssanics.com. Mash (short for Mashuru) is a major competitor of Easy Coach, running services principally along the Mombasa (and Malindi)–Nairobi–Malaba–Kampala axis.

ARUSHA BUS COMPANIES

The following all offer – in theory – daily services from city-centre hotels via JKIA to Arusha, although in practice, the number of buses actually running depends on demand. If you're boarding at JKIA, you should contact the company well in advance with flight details. Most services leave the CBD at approximately 7am and JKIA at 9am, arriving in Arusha at 2pm. Prices range from $25–35.

Davanu Shuttle Oluvimu Rd, South "C", off Mombasa Rd ☏ 020 6007415 or 0722 787182, ⊛ davanushuttle .com.

East Africa Shuttles House Suite 403, 4th Floor, Portal Place, Muindi Mbingu St ☏ 020 2248453 or 0722 348656, ⊛ eastafricashuttles.com.

Impala Shuttle No walk-in office; pick-ups from Parkside Hotel, Monrovia St (see p.121) ☏ 0800 2219000 or 020 2730953, ⊛ impalashuttle.com.

Riverside Shuttle Room 1, 3rd Floor, Panafric House, Kenyatta Ave ☏ 0725 999121 or 020 2229618, ⊛ riverside-shuttle.com.

BY MATATU

Matatus leave from various terminals (see map p.104) as detailed below. There are no matatus to the coast.

Accra Rd Terminal (between River Rd and Duruma Rd) Embu (frequent; 2hr 30min); Isiolo (4–5 daily; 5hr).

Accra Rd Terminal (between River Rd and Tsavo Rd) Meru (frequent; 4hr 30min); Nanyuki (frequent; 3hr).

Accra Rd Terminal (Dubois Rd area) Busia (hourly; 9hr); Kakamega (8 daily; 7hr); Kericho (hourly; 6hr); Kisii (hourly; 6hr); Kisumu (hourly or more; 7hr).

Accra Rd Terminal (River Rd end) Archers Post (1 or 2 daily; 6hr); Nyeri (10 daily; 2hr 30min).

Muthurwa Terminal (by Wakulima Market) Machakos (frequent; 1hr 30min).

Globe Terminal (by Globe Flyover) Thika (frequent; 1hr).

Latema Rd Terminal Nyahururu (2 daily; 3hr).

Nyamakima Bar, Duruma Rd Terminal Eldoret (frequent; 5hr 30min); Gilgil (hourly; 2hr); Kitale (hourly; 7hr); Maralal (4 daily; 7hr); Naivasha (frequent; 1hr 30min); Nakuru (frequent; 2hr 30min); Narok (6 daily; 4hr).

Railway Station Terminal Magadi (3 daily; 2hr).

Ronald Ngala St Terminal Kajiado (8 daily; 1hr 30min); Namanga (6 daily; 3hr).

1

INFORMATION

Tourist Information Nairobi has no official tourist information service, but the *Standard* and *Nation* newspapers are useful sources of current information and special offers, and the free and widely circulated magazines *Go Places*, ⓦ goplaceskenya.com and *Kenya Buzz* ⓦ kenyabuzz.com are always worth a look.

Maps If you need a detailed map of the city, buy the Nairobi *A–Z*, available from bookshops. Alternatively, the city has now been comprehensively Google-mapped, so if you're prepared to put up with roaming charges or you've got an unlocked phone and a local SIM card (see p.90) your GPS-enabled 3G mobile phone will be able to guide you around.

GETTING AROUND

Getting around Nairobi has been a headache for decades: the lack of transport planning and the absence of any light rail transport means **traffic jams** for four or five hours on weekday mornings and evenings, and serious delays in getting from one suburb to another, except late at night and before dawn. Getting **around the CBD** is so straightforward you won't need much assistance. By day, you'll probably want to walk; by night, you'll want to take a taxi. If you're on any kind of budget, though, it's certainly worth getting to know what passes for the city's public transport system: and look out for the **bus and matatu map** published by Kenya Buzz (ⓦ kenyabuzz.com).

BUSES AND MATATUS

The green Citi Hoppa buses which roar around Nairobi all day are cheap (Ksh20–100; pay the conductor) and very unpredictable. Buses are numbered, but bus stops aren't and routes change frequently. Nairobi's matatus – which, like the city's taxis, must bear a yellow stripe – tend to take the same routes as buses and often display the same route numbers. They're generally faster, more dangerous and even more packed, though serious accidents are rare.

TERMINALS

City buses and matatus save you money on getting around, certainly for longer trips out of the city centre, but take some figuring out. They all start and finish their routes at terminals ("stages" or "stands") in the city centre, where they fill up and then head out on their routes – although they are not supposed to drop off or pick up anywhere in the CBD. The terminals are marked on the CBD map (p.104). From north to south they are:

Globe Roundabout East and southeast suburbs.
Khoja/Fire Station West and northwest suburbs.
Latema Rd West and northwest suburbs.
Accra Rd Embakasi.
Kencom House Kibera, Ngong, southwest suburbs.
Ambassadeur Hotel JKI Airport.
Ronald Ngala St Eastern suburbs.
KBS Bus Station Kiambu and northern suburbs, Dagoretti, southern suburbs.
Railway Station Magadi Rd, Ongata, Kiserian, Kikuyu, Limuru.
Muthurwa Lane Eastern suburbs.

TAXIS AND TUK-TUKS

By Kenyan standards, Nairobi's private taxis – the registered ones all bear a yellow stripe – are expensive. Cabs, licensed by the Kenya Taxi Cabs Association, crowd around key spots in the city and have generally agreed prices for well-known routes, with the lowest fare for any

trip in the city centre around Ksh300. A reliable company is Kenatco, who have a 24hr office at Uchumi House on Aga Khan Walk (☎ 020 2225123, ⓦ kenatco.com), and a branch at the airport (☎ 0720 108222). Tuk-tuks (auto-rickshaws) imported from Asia are also available. They cost a little less than regular taxis, though bargain hard. They're being supplanted, however, by motorcycle taxis, known as *piki-pikis* or *boda-bodas*, which carry one or two passengers, charge around half the taxi fare, and are best used only for short hops.

COMMUTER TRAINS

On weekday mornings and evenings, there are several slow and packed commuter rail services between the suburbs of Ruiru, Kahawa, Embakasi, Kikuyu and Stony Athi and the city centre. These aren't much help to most travellers, but a brand-new station which opened in 2012 at Syokimau, just south of the international airport, signalled the start of an expansion of services which should include a new airport shuttle rail service within the lifetime of this book.

DRIVING

Avoid driving in or through the city if you can. The congestion has to be seen to be believed, and your average speed can be as little as 3km/h – commuting has become nightmarish, and many city workers spend four hours a day behind the wheel. If you're hiring a car, if possible, pick it up at the airport, or have it delivered there, which gives you time to get used to the vehicle and the traffic before joining the city-centre madness. For general driving advice, see Basics (p.52). The driving itself can be a nerve-wracking experience, too, though you do get used to it. Watch out for matatus, which lurch into the fray as suddenly as they stop to pick up fares. And beware of roundabouts (traffic circles). These labour under "priority traffic" regulations, which in theory means cars already on the roundabout have priority, but in practice means chaos as nobody is prepared to give way. Try to stay in lane.

Parking Parking in the CBD can be difficult during business hours, though there's usually space at the Loita Street Car Park, next to Barclays Plaza (Ksh150/day), or at the Kenyatta International Conference Centre (entrance off City Hall Way (Ksh150/day). If you park on the street, assuming you can find a legal space, you'll need to buy a daily parking ticket from one of the city's many uniformed parking wardens (Ksh150; valid until 8am the next morning).

Car repairs Stantech Motors, Shimo la Tewa Rd, off Lusaka Rd, Industrial Area ☎020 530662, ⓦstantechmotors .co.ke, is reliable and recommended.

Leaving Nairobi Driving out of Nairobi, allow plenty of time to get clear of the city traffic. The first bypass, the Northern By-Pass, has been more or less completed, and runs roughly from Gigiri to JKIA, but there are as yet no other ring roads so most vehicles, including trans-continental trucks, go through the city centre.

CAR RENTAL

Avis College House, University Way ☎020 336074, ⓦbit.ly/2C1Gr.

Budget Muindi Mbingu St ☎020 223581, ⓦbudget -kenya.com.

Central Rent-A-Car 680 Hotel, Muindi Mbingu St ☎020 2222888, ⓦcarhirekenya.com.

Concorde Car Hire Shell Petrol Station, Lower Kabete Rd, Westlands ☎020 4448953, ⓦconcorde.co.ke.

Cruising Cruisers Ground floor, Motherland Centre, corner of Ngong Rd and Karen Rd ☎0736 219639, ⓦcruisingcruisers.com.

Market Car Hire Ground Floor, Chester House ☎020 2225797.

Sunworld Riverside Lane, off Riverside Drive, Westlands ☎020 4445669 or 0722 525400, ⓦsunworld-safari.com.

BICYCLES

If you plan to cycle in Nairobi, you won't be alone, but you need to keep your wits about you and mirrors are essential. To connect with other urban cyclists, visit ⓦshecyclesnairobi.wordpress.com. Kenya Cycle Mart, the best parts, repair and sales shop in the city, is on Butere Road, Industrial Area; Cycleland, lower ground floor, Sarit Centre, Westlands (Mon–Fri 9.30am–6.15pm, Sun 10.30am–3pm), offers bike rental (Ksh800/day; Ksh10,000 deposit). If you want to buy a bike, a half-decent mountain bike will cost you around Ksh26,000.

SAFARI TRANSPORT AND OPERATORS

Nairobi is the travel hub of Africa, with a mass of opportunities for **safaris** around Kenya and hundreds of safari operators, car-rental outlets and travel agents to provide you with everything you need for your trip. See the "Safaris" section in Basics (p.76) for general information about safaris and guides. If you're organizing your own self-drive safari in Kenya (with or without a driver), see the list of **car rental** companies (above). One possibility not often considered is **cycling**: Hell's Gate at Naivasha, Kakamega Forest and a number of other small parks allow bikes, and there's a lot of wonderful cycling country besides these areas. At the other end of the budget spectrum, **chartering a plane** offers unequalled opportunities for seeing the country. A few small operators, mostly based at Wilson Airport, will oblige; see "Air charter companies" (p.138) for details.

SAFARI OPERATORS

You can pick up plenty of leaflets about safaris from most travel agents, the best of whom are honest and reputable. Many belong to KATO (see p.77), but some who don't are still very good. It's always a good idea to meet staff from the operator you are travelling with in advance of departure. Safari touts who hang around on the street, or at various hotels and lodgings, are keen to take you to operators' offices, but should be avoided – no reputable company uses them. Check whether the advertised safari is actually run by the company in question, as the practice of one company sub-contracting a safari to another is common. Take your time, ask to see their vehicles, ask about the KPSGA qualifications of their guides (see p.78), demand everything in writing including a detailed breakdown of the costs, and don't be pressured into making any decisions until you are ready. Pay particular attention to how many 24hr park/reserve tickets your safari will use. Every other business in Nairobi seems to be a safari

outfit, and in the challenging environment of Kenya, spotless reputations are hard to maintain. The following businesses, however, rarely come in for criticism. The pricing categories are only a rough guide – per person, all-inclusive except drinks.

UNDER AROUND $300 PER DAY

African Home Safaris Nairobi Youth Hostel, Ralph Bunche Rd ☎0722 760661, ⓦ africahomeadventure .com; map pp.102–103. Budget safari operator affiliated to Hostelling International – they also run the Enchoro Wildlife Camp in the Mara (see p.365). They have seven minibuses and can usually run safaris with seven passengers for an average of $150/day.

Best Camping 2nd floor, Amee Arcade, corner of Muthithi Rd and Parklands Rd, Westlands ☎0733 630053 or 0733 603090, ⓦbestcampingkenya.com; map p.128. Long-established operator whose budget camping trips are generally recommended.

1

Dallago Convent Drive, Lavington ☎020 3872845 or 0786 351000, ⬤dallagotours.com; map p.102. One of the few budget companies to have KPSGA-certified guides, Dallago offers good-value camping safaris to Maasai Mara, Lake Nakuru, Samburu and Amboseli.

★ **Gametrackers** 5th floor, Nginyo Towers, corner of Koinange and Moktar Daddah streets ☎020 2222703, ⬤gametrackersafaris.com; map p.104. Long-established, popular and consistently good operator with strong northern Kenya credentials.

Green Belt Safaris Adams Arcade, Kilimani Lane, off Elgeo Marakwet Rd ☎020 3873057, ⬤bit.ly /GreenBeltSafaris ; map p.102. Community homestays, where the guests participate in rural activities (seed collection, tree planting, harvesting) for up to a week.

Ice Rock Mountain Treks and Safaris 4th floor, NCM Building, Tom Mboya St ☎020 2244608 or 0722 301306, ⬤icerockclimbing.com; map p.104. A small professional setup with knowledgeable guides, mainly dealing with safaris to Mount Kenya, Kilimanjaro and Hell's Gate. The owner, who used to be a member of the Mount Kenya rescue team, organizes and leads most trips.

Kenia Tours and Safaris Suite No. 26, 2nd floor, Royal Offices, Mogotio Road, Westlands ☎0721 474814 or 0729 163545, ⬤keniatours.com; map p.102. Keenly priced, budget camping safaris specialist.

★ **Savage Wilderness Safaris** Sarit Centre, Westlands ☎020 7121590, ⬤whitewaterkenya.com; map p.128. Excellent programme of technical climbing and walking trips on Mount Kenya, rafting, and cycling and walking safaris.

Savuka Tours & Safaris 4th floor, Panafric House, Kenyatta Ave ☎020 2215256 or 0722 415643, ⬤savuka-travels.com; map p.104. Good-value camping safaris that get favourable recommendations from budget travellers for their good food and driver/guides, though accommodation is basic.

★ **Uniglobe Let's Go Travel** ABC Place, Waiyaki Way, Westlands (branches at Triad House in Muthaiga and at Karen crossroads) ☎020 4447151 or 0722 331899, ⬤letsgosafari.com; map p.102. Consistently impressive, Let's Go are the first and best port of call for independent travellers in Kenya, agents for a large number of homestays and independent lodges throughout the country and operators of well-organized camping safaris.

AROUND $300–500 PER DAY

Africa Expeditions Ngong Racecourse, Ngong Rd ☎020 3002711 or 0722 203115, ⬤africaexpeditions .com; map p.102. Photographic safari specialists, with a good record and highly professional approach, offering largely tailor-made trips and their own camps in the Mara and (unusually) the Loita Hills.

Eastern & Southern Safaris 6th Floor, Finance House, Loita St ☎020 2242828 or 0716 500001, ⬤essafari .co.ke; map p.104. Highly regarded safari company that has built a reputation on delivering a very reliable service.

★ **Gamewatchers** UN Crescent, behind Village Market ☎0774 136523, ⬤porini.com; map p.100. Innovative, eco-conscious operators with a strong list of bronze and silver guides among their staff. As well as running excellent safaris, they also own and manage the outstanding *Porini* eco-camps in the Mara, Amboseli area and Ol Pejeta. Highly recommended.

Magical Africa Lavington Green Shopping Centre (next to Post Office) ☎020 4348444 or 0722 608169; map p.102. General operator, in business since 2003, billing itself as Kenya's only gay-friendly safari operator.

Southern Cross Symbion House, Karen Rd ☎020 8070311, ⬤southerncrosskenya.com; map p.100. Considering they have a number of silver as well as bronze guides, their lodge and tented camp safaris offer extremely good value for money.

Steenbok Safaris Suite 1G, 1st Floor, Sunrise Plaza, Ruiru (behind Bushgate/Oilibya) ☎020 2432452 or 0733 775763, ⬤steenboksafaris.com; map p.198. Reputable mid-budget safari outfitter with a decent fleet of vehicles and a car-rental operation.

★ **Sunworld** Riverside Lane, off Riverside Drive ☎020 4445669 or 0722 525400, ⬤sunworld-safari .com; map p.102. Extremely proficient 4WD specialists with a good fleet of vehicles, bronze and silver driver-guides and a well-organized, walk-in bookings operation.

OVER $500 PER DAY

★ **Bush & Beyond** Wilson Business Park, Wilson Airport ☎020 6000457 or 020 6005108, ⬤bush-and -beyond.com; map p.100. Very good bespoke safari organizers (including riding safaris) and reservations agents for a short list of superb camps and lodges. If you know what you want, they know how to deliver.

★ **Cheli & Peacock** Lengai House, Wilson Airport ☎020 6003090, ⬤chelipeacock.com; map p.100. As owners and agents for some of Kenya's very best small lodges and tented camps, C&P have a savvy and personal approach that keeps them at the forefront of safari operation and lodge design: you tend to see it here first. They also have a good number of bronze and silver guides among their staff.

Ker & Downey Safaris Ndalat Rd (south of Langata Link), off Langata South Rd, Karen ☎020 8058032 or 0724 252606, ⬤kerdowneysafaris.com; map p.100. The archetypal old-style safari outfitter (Kenya's oldest, dating from 1946), Ker & Downey are the people to choose if you want a no-expense-spared, tailor-made safari, either fully mobile or using lodges and camps. Many silver and bronze guides work for them.

★ **Origins Safaris** 5th floor, Landmark Plaza, Argwings Kodhek Rd ☎ 020 2042695, ⓦ originsafaris .info; map p.102. Excellent birdwatching trips and a huge range of other safaris, for all interests, with more than twenty bronze and silver guides and one of only four gold guides in the country. Not cheap, but very highly recommended if you have specific interests, with accommodation at well-selected lodges and tented camps.

Micato Safaris 2nd Floor, Almont Park, Church Rd, Westlands ☎ 020 4445220 or 020 4445218, ⓦ micato .com; map p.102. Much lauded Kenyan-American tour operator with off-the-peg and tailor-made trips run by crews who include more bronze and silver safari guides than any other operator in the country – all trips are run by a driver-guide with at least a bronze certificate.

Safari & Conservation Company Wilson Business Park, Wilson Airport ☎ 020 2115453 or 0712 579999, ⓦ thesafariandconservationcompany.com; map p.102. Safari organizers and agents for a short list of beautiful, owner-managed camps and lodges in some of Kenya's most remote and exciting corners.

Safaris Unlimited 328 Langata Rd, near Hillcrest Schools, 3km west of Bomas turning ☎ 020 8890435 or 0727 535019, ⓦ safarisunlimited.com; map p.102. Horseriding safari specialists, for confident riders only, covering the Maasai Mara, Loldaiga Hills, Laikipia and other wilderness areas.

Tropical Ice 98 Marula Lane, Karen ☎ 020 2405573 or 0712 282793, ⓦ tropical-ice.com. High-end adventure safaris combining 4WD vehicles with foot safaris in Tsavo East's elephant country, led by expert safari guides, operating traditional-style, mobile camps.

ACCOMMODATION

It isn't difficult to find **accommodation** in Nairobi, but it can be very expensive. The main question is which area fits your needs. The Central Business District is useful for accessing shops and some offices on foot (though many businesses, embassies and other offices are not located here), while if you base yourself further afield, you're likely to need transport or have to rely on the nearest mall. Travellers congregate at a number of different spots around the city and many visitors never set foot in the downtown Central Business District. If you're arriving in town in the small hours or early in the day, it's worth knowing that most places won't be able to offer you a room before 10am. It's also worth knowing, if you're used to air conditioning in hotels, that it's not considered essential in Nairobi's climate and you'll only find it at top-end addresses, which also uniformly offer free room safes.

Parking All the top-of-the-range places and most backpacker haunts have guarded or enclosed parking – only cheap, city-centre lodgings are a problem in this respect. Naturally, leave nothing of value in the vehicle, or attached to it – such as spare wheels, jerricans or roof boxes.

MOMBASA ROAD AND AIRPORT AREA

There are no hotels at JKIA itself and only limited options in the area. The following can be convenient as they are largely clear of city-centre traffic jams, but none is as close to the airport as they would have you believe (the distances below are correct). If you're driving, remember the Mombasa Highway is divided along this street, and there are relatively few turning points. As an alternative, consider one of the options in – or just outside – Nairobi National Park (see p.124) – though you will usually have to pay park fees on top – or the excellent Acacia Camp near Athi River (see p.148).

Eka Hotel Mombasa Highway, 12km from JKIA ☎ 0719 045000 or 0732 105000, ⓦ ekahotel.com; map p.100. New business and tourist hotel aiming to outdo the neighbouring *Ole Sereni* as a relatively convenient airport address at very competitive rates. Pool and wi-fi. BB $169

Nairobi Airport Stopover House Oluvimu Rd, South C ☎ 0722 787182, ⓦ nairobiairportstopoverhouse.com; map p.100. Half the name is true – it's definitely a place to stop over. But the bit about the airport is misleading, since it's only 3km from the city centre – not close enough to be within easy walking distance but still likely to be affected by rush-hour traffic. Nevertheless, a clean, reliable overnight base at a good price, with dorm beds and s/c rooms with nets. Dorm beds $12, BB $35

Ole Sereni Hotel Mombasa Highway, 12km from JKIA ☎ 020 3901000 or 0731 436405, ⓦ ole-serenihotel .com; map p.100. Glitzy and flamboyant hotel cramming 134 rooms into a limited space directly on the boundary of the Nairobi National Park, with views across the savanna from the pool terrace. Public areas are busy and pound with dance music. There's also excellent food, a pool and free wi-fi. BB $360

Panari Mombasa Highway, 11km from JKIA ☎ 020 3946000 or 0725 694600, ⓦ panarihotels.com; map p.100. Even leaving aside the tired opulence, standard rooms here are absurdly overpriced. Assuming you can't get into one of its neighbours, then you should be looking for a major discount. Lower floors include a small shopping mall, gym, pool and famous ice rink (see p.138). Wi-fi in rooms. BB $390

Redcourt Hotel Kenya Red Cross Complex, Red Cross Rd, off Popo Rd, off Mombasa Highway, 13km from JKIA ☎ 020 604528 or 0728 606476, ⓦ redcourt.co.ke; map p.100. Surprisingly smart sixty-room hotel owned by the Kenya Red Cross. Rooms are on the small side, but stylish enough, with DSTV, and there's a gym, sauna, and wi-fi in rooms. BB $270

1

The South-Hood House #54, Balozi Estate, off Mombasa Highway, 12km from JKIA ☎0712 652280, ⓦsouthhood.com; map p.100. Smart, recently opened BB offering a more affordable alternative to the hotels on the highway. BB $100

RIVER ROAD AREA

The very cheapest lodgings in Nairobi are around River Road, the main drag through the city centre's poorest quarter. Despite the constant worry about safety, River Road is central Nairobi's most stimulating and animated area, and offers a plunge into a world you pass by if you stay in the CBD or out in the suburbs. Choose carefully, as some places have rowdy bars and clubs attached to them, their rooms aren't always terribly clean or secure, and they may not be ideal for solo female travellers.

INEXPENSIVE

Destiny Hotel Duruma Rd ☎0724 954999; map p.104. This four-storey block is conscientiously run, with airy rooms and electric showers. Particularly good value for friendly couples as only single rooms with modestly sized beds are available. There's a TV lounge and cold sodas but no bar or restaurant. Room only Ksh850

Evamay Lodge River Rd, at the junction with Duruma Rd ☎020 2216218 or 0703 949680; map p.104. Very good value for the price, the s/c rooms have phones, TVs and mosquito nets, and the whole place is clean and has good security. BB Ksh2000

Mercury Hotel 18 Tom Mboya St ☎0720 553820; map p.104. With its walls hung with moth-eaten game trophies, this seems to hark back to the 1970s. Rooms have sporadic hot showers, and there's a pleasant courtyard bar-restaurant (beer Ksh140, soda Ksh60) with a *nyama choma* bar and a bizarre miniature rockery. Room only Ksh$1860

Mid-View Central Hotel Latema Rd ☎0720 484496; map p.104. Fifty cramped rooms with nets, TVs and phones, spotless bathrooms with electric showers and a no-prostitution policy. BB Ksh2500

★ **Nawas Hotel** Nawas Building, corner of Latema Rd & River Rd ☎020 2243148 or 020 2218569; map p.104. Thirty-six small, neat rooms with sporadic hot water and a good, friendly restaurant on the first floor. Excellent value all round. BB Ksh1800

New Kenya Lodge River Rd, at the top of Latema Rd ☎020 2222202 or 0733 925208, ⓦnksafari.com; map p.104. A long-established backpackers' haunt, with six small dorms, three s/c twin rooms with electric showers and one non-s/c single. Popular communal area, book exchange, two common showers (though don't expect hot water), nets and roof terrace. Budget safaris can be organized here, but check all the details and "what ifs" before committing. Dorm beds Ksh600, room only Ksh1300

New Swanga Lodge Corner of Duruma Rd and Accra Rd ☎0721 620127 or 0734 912379; map p.104. The rooms here, though not large, are comfy enough, with nets and electric showers, and are securely bolted away behind spectacular, time-consuming, triple locks. Convenient for buses and good value, with a decent breakfast, though hardly quiet. BB Ksh1400

Hotel Princess 20 Tom Mboya St ☎020 2214640; map p.104. Busy establishment, with a restaurant and bar ("No idle sitting"). The rooms are rather cramped but have nets and good showers. Basic but adequate, and it fills up quickly so they must be getting it mostly right. Breakfast Ksh200, beer Ksh140, soda Ksh60. Room only Ksh1400

Samagat Hotel Park House, Taveta Rd ☎020 2250211; map p.104. In a former apartment block, this has spacious rooms with nets and TVs, the upper ones with views of the CBD's high-rises. Elevators get you to your room and the ninth-floor dining room/TV lounge. BB Ksh2500

Sirikwa Lodge Munyu Rd, on the corner of Accra Rd ☎020 2226687; map p.104. Reasonable rooms above a *miraa* shop, with evenings-only hot water. Ideally located for enjoying the chaos of the Accra Road matatu stands, but overpriced compared to similar places. BB Ksh2300

MODERATE

Abbey Hotel Gaberone Rd ☎0727 865625; map p.104. A noisy, boozy place, rather pricey for what it offers, but the rooms have nets, TVs and are mostly clean and fresh, with tiled bathrooms and electric showers. Unlovely, and has an awful lot of stairs to climb, but adequate, and there's a cybercafé, bar and restaurant. BB $50

★ **Khweza Bed & Breakfast** South side of Ngara Rd, 200m west of Sarakasi Dome ☎020 2672116 or 0717 060045, ⓦkhweza.com; map p.100. Popular and funky alternative to central Nairobi's cheap hotels, with brightly decorated rooms, a roof terrace and other travellers to meet. BB Ksh3900

Sandton Palace Hotel Taveta Rd ☎020 342104 or 0720 629985, ⓦsandtonhotels.co.ke; map p.104. One of the best hotels in the district, although rather overpriced. All 102 rooms, accessed by lift, have TV with in-house video, direct-dial phones, safes, ceiling fans and electric showers in proper shower cubicles. Basement parking. The similarly appointed and priced sister hotel *Sandton City* is on nearby Duruma Rd. BB $90

CENTRAL BUSINESS DISTRICT

The following listings cover the more affluent parts of the city centre, roughly north as far as the museum and west as far as Central and Uhuru parks. Even at the lower end, it's always worth discussing the price, and rates on the websites of the international groups can be cheaper by as much as fifty percent if you book online and pay in advance.

INEXPENSIVE

Downtown Hotel Moktar Daddah St ☎0721 417832 or 0738 787787, ✉downtownhotel2000@yahoo.com; map p.104. A clean and (in some rooms) quieter alternative to its neighbour, the better-known *Terminal*. Rooms are a bit small, but it remains good value in the Jeevanjee Gardens area. Rooms only Ksh2400

Hotel Embassy Tubman Rd, right behind the City Market ☎020 2224087 or 0722 521651, ⓦhotelembassy-kenya.com; map p.104. Very decent place, with a reliable restaurant and well-maintained, if rather tired, rooms with nets, fans and electric showers. BB $45

Parkside Monrovia St ☎020 2214154 or 0720 885545; map p.104. Facing Jeevanjee Gardens and convenient for buses to Arusha, the *Parkside* is large, secure, and has clean, airy and reasonably pleasant rooms with nets and electric showers. It can be noisy, however. Room only Ksh2700

Terminal Hotel Moktar Daddah St ☎020 2228817 or 020 2228818; map p.104. A long-time backpackers' favourite, with large, well-kept rooms, all with nets and electric showers. No guests after 7pm. Good value, but bring some earplugs to counter the noise from the neighbourhood. Room only Ksh2200

MODERATE

680 (Six-Eighty) Corner of Kenyatta Ave and Muindi Mbingu St ☎020 315680 or 0722 207361, ⓦsentrim-hotels.com; map p.104. Getting run-down but very convenient if you want to be right in the CBD, and better value than many other central hotels – assuming you bargain hard for a good rate. Rooms have DSTV and bathtubs, but old-style plumbing, and there's safe basement parking. Be sure to ask for a room at the back unless you want to be kept awake by the racket from *Simmers*, opposite. BB $170

Boulevard Hotel Harry Thuku Rd, next to the National Museum ☎020 2227567, ⓦsentrim-hotels.com; bus #21, #23 or #119, matatu #104; map p.102. On the fringes of the CBD, and functional rather than extravagant, this well-cared-for hotel has a garden setting, a good pool (unfortunately on the traffic side of the building), tennis court, TV in all rooms and ample parking. It's always lively with mid-market tour groups. To avoid the noise of Uhuru Highway, get a room at the back in the middle, overlooking the garden. BB $200

Kenya Comfort Hotel Corner of Muindi Mbingu St and Monrovia St ☎0722 608866, ⓦkenyacomfort.com; map p.104. Handily located, this large hotel is popular with budget safari operators, and staff are used to arrivals in the middle of the night. The reasonable rooms come with nets and DSTV, and there's a rooftop terrace, 24hr bar and restaurant, although the place has perhaps begun to rest on its laurels. Room only $65

Oakwood Hotel Kimathi St ☎020 2220592 or 0722 208905, ⓦmadahotels.com; map p.104. An endearing oddity lost amid the skyscrapers, this older two-storey hotel has wood panelling, a wonderful antique lift and good security, and you can't beat the price for this location. On the downside, the rooms need some serious updating. There's a relaxing first-floor bar looking across to the touristy *Thorn Tree Café*. BB $80

EXPENSIVE

Hilton Mama Ngina St ☎020 2790000 or 020 2288000, ⓦhilton.com; map p.104. The iconic cylindrical tower is unmistakeable, and the lobby impressive, but the impersonal *Hilton* caters more for expense-account travellers than for leisure visitors. Rooms get better the higher you climb, but they all need refurbishing. The "rooftop pool" is nice, but somewhat overshadowed as it's located on the second floor. Facilities include a health club, spa, sauna and steam room, and four restaurants. BB $340

InterContinental City Hall Way ☎020 3200000, ⓦichotelsgroup.com; map p.104. More than forty years old and working hard to keep up with its newer competitors, the 376-room *InterContinental* has some surprisingly secluded corners in the grounds, many amenities, including a heated pool, health club, casino, Italian and Indian restaurants, 24hr bar, an ATM in the lobby, and good disabled access. BB $275

Norfolk Hotel Harry Thuku Rd ☎020 2265000 or 020 2265555, ⓦfairmont.com/norfolkhotel; map p.102. Nairobi's oldest hotel has had the Canadian Fairmont treatment, which has lightened and freshened it all over, improving standards while diminishing the reason you'd want to stay here – the Edwardian atmosphere. The very comfortable rooms have good beds and flat-screen TVs; facilities include a pool, health club, sauna and wi-fi. BB $292

Stanley Hotel Corner of Kimathi St and Kenyatta Ave ☎020 2757000 or 020 2714444, ⓦsarovahotels.com; map p.104. Complete with its famous *Thorn Tree Café*, this is as central as you can get, and a popular base for tourists and business travellers alike. The rooms are equipped with DSTV, minibar and noise-excluding double glazing, and some are designed for disabled guests. Facilities include a modern gym and sauna and a heated rooftop pool and bar, plus wi-fi. BB $505

WESTLANDS AND PARKLANDS

Jacaranda Hotel Off Waiyaki Way, Westlands ☎020 4448713 or 0733 601613, ⓦjacarandahotels.com; map p.128. Strong selling points include the great location, a couple of minutes' walk to the Sarit Centre mall and other Westlands amenities, plus a good pool in a pleasant garden. Rooms (all with fan and DSTV) are on the small side and don't have a/c, while the "Garden" rooms are getting very tired – get a "Pool" room instead. BB $312

1

Mennonite Guest House 71 Church Rd, Westlands ☎020 4444790 or 0723 161935, ⊛mghkenya.com; map p.102. If you want clean, safe, comfortable and quiet, this is worth booking far ahead. The nice gardens and decent meals (Ksh400) are added incentives, and there's an exchange library and wi-fi. As well as standard rooms with shared bathrooms, they also have more expensive s/c rooms. No smoking or alcohol are allowed on the premises. BB $60

★ **Miti Mingi Guest House** Terrace Close, off Rhapta Rd ☎0713 860900, ⊛mitimingi.com; map p.102. Charming, small, secure, owner-managed guesthouse in a tree-filled garden above the Nairobi River that gurgles nightly with a frog chorus. Accommodation is in four simple and individually decorated s/c rooms – "Sky", "Sea", "Sun" and "Shade" – with DSTV, nets, fans, safes, plus free use of a kitchen (with basic supplies on an honesty basis) and wi-fi. BB $95

Parklands Shade Hotel Klub House entertainment complex, Ojijo Rd, Parklands ☎0717 969500, ⊛bit.ly /ParklandsShade; map p.102. The tiled, no-frills s/c rooms with double beds here are quite decent and serve their purpose of providing a resting place for exhausted Klub House refugees (though not all guests are principally interested in sleep, as you may discover). BB Ksh4000

★ **Sankara** Woodvale Grove ☎020 4208000 or 0703 028000, ⊛sankara.com; map p.128. The standout accommodation in Westlands, and indeed one of Nairobi's most consistently good new hotels, the *Sankara* is efficiently managed and has all the facilities of a five-star establishment, including a glass-bottomed rooftop pool and an *Angsana* spa, while giving off the vibe of a boutique hotel. The 156 rooms are impeccably comfortable, light and well thought-out. Wi-fi. BB $410

Southern Sun Hotel Parklands Rd, next to the Mayfair casino ☎0722 3740920 or 0722 205508, ⊛tsogosun hotels.com; map p.102. Classy, well-maintained, very likeable establishment in a pastiche of Edwardian and Art Nouveau styles (the original building, the *Mayfair*, opened in 1949). The 171 rooms come with a/c, safe and DSTV, while facilities include two pools, spa, gym and plenty of other amenities – all set in several acres of tropical gardens. BB $324

UPPER HILL, LAVINGTON & KILELESHWA

Many of Nairobi's better-value mid-range and upmarket hotels – often independently owned – are located in the relatively affluent suburbs west of the city centre, while the area also has a good selection of backpacker places.

INEXPENSIVE: CAMPING, BACKPACKERS AND HOSTELS

All the following offer long-stay discounts – often close to fifty percent for a month or more. Nairobi is a good place to buy camping equipment. Try the following outlets: Atul's, Biashara St ☎020 2225935 (map pp.104–105); Kenya

Canvas, Kirinyaga Rd ☎020 2226854 or 0722 511349; Xtreme Outdoors, 1st Floor, Yaya Centre, Hurlingham ☎020 2722224 or 0736 411527, ⊛xtremeoutdoors.co.ke.

Jungle Junction Amboseli Rd, Lavington, near Dagoretti Corner ☎0722 752865 or 0723 392014, ⊛c_handschuh_68@yahoo.com; map p.102. Legendary overlanders' garden hangout and campsite, where you can get your vehicle fixed – or find out who can do it for you. There are facilities for long-term vehicle storage and a large garden for camping, with clean, communal toilets, showers, kitchen area, washing machine and wi-fi, plus dorm beds and s/c rooms. Camping from Ksh550 per person, dorm beds Ksh1000, BB Ksh5000

★ **Milimani Backpackers** Milimani Rd ☎020 2724827 or 0718 919080, ⊛milimanibackpackers .com; map p.102. Clean and friendly, with nets for some beds, hot showers (the female dorm is s/c), some s/c and non-s/c rooms and a self-service bar (beer Ksh160, soda Ksh50). Good meals are available, and there's also wi-fi (Ksh200/day) and a cybercafé (Ksh2/min). Dorm beds Ksh750, camping Ksh600 per person, room only Ksh2000

Nairobi Youth Hostel Ralph Bunche Rd, near Nairobi Hospital ☎020 2738046 or 0722 656462, ⊛yhak.org; map p.102. Rather dingy and institutional, and it's not clear how much linkage there is with Hostelling International, but the staff are nice. There's internet access (Ksh1.50/min), a passable café (see p.130) and a popular roof terrace, and the hostel is also the base of reliable budget operator African Home Safaris (see p.117) and a good place to meet Kenyan students and foreign interns based at nearby Nairobi Hospital. Dorm beds Ksh700, room only Ksh1800

★ **Upper Hill Campsite & Backpackers Campsite** Othaya Rd, Lavington ☎020 2500218 or 0721 517869, ⊛upperhillcampsite.com; map p.102. They moved from Upper Hill, but this small, relaxed campsite is still very popular with backpackers and motorized overlanders. There are dorms, s/c doubles and eight small three- and four-bed cabins, all with shared hot showers, plus the *Drunken Geko* bar-restaurant, use of the kitchen and good security. Camping Ksh600 per person, dorm beds Ksh840, cabins from Ksh2920, room only Ksh4200

YMCA State House Rd, 300m from Uhuru Highway ☎020 2606239 or 0729 152816, ⊛kenyaymca.com; map p.102. On the edge of the CBD, the well-equipped Central YMCA is popular with female as well as male travellers, offering a choice of dorms and s/c rooms with nets. There's well-priced if average food (breakfast Ksh400, main meals Ksh600), and secure parking, but the clincher is the facilities, including a pool and tennis and squash courts. BB dorm beds Ksh1100, BB Ksh3100

MODERATE

Country Lodge 2nd Ngong Ave ☎020 2881600, ⊛countrylodge.co.ke; map p.102. Stylish and affordable hotel, and a popular alternative to its more expensive, co-owned neighbour the *Fairview*. Rooms can feel a bit sterile, like a small private hospital, but it's very clean, and in keeping with *Fairview* tradition security is positively airtight. A pleasant garden, gym and free wi-fi complete the amenities and you can use the *Fairview's* restaurants and pool. BB **Ksh11,400**

Heron Hotel Milimani Rd, Nairobi Hill ☎020 2720740, ⓦheronhotel.com; map p.102. Close to the city centre but on a leafy, relatively quiet street, this is a bit of a bargain since its conversion from apartments. Smart, comfortably functional rooms – with neat bathrooms, flat-screen DSTV and room safes – rise on five floors around a central atrium. Staff are helpful; there's an adequate restaurant, *TJ's*, with a large balcony overlooking Milimani Rd, and a nice pool, gym and sauna, plus free cable internet. Great value for Nairobi. BB **Ksh12,000**

Woodmere Apartments Rose Ave, off Lenana Rd, three blocks from the Yaya Centre ☎020 2712511 or 0722 344778, ⓦwoodmerenairobi.com; map p.102. Well-guarded premises with a small pool, sauna, gym and garden. Accommodation ranges from fully furnished, serviced studios with tiny kitchen and loft sleeping area to spacious apartments. Monthly rates for budget studios from **$1500**, four-bed apartments from **$4000**

EXPENSIVE

★ **Fairview** Bishops Rd, Nairobi Hill ☎020 2711321 or 0733 636561, ⓦfairviewkenya.com; map p.102. A peaceful, rambling country-style place with spacious grounds that are great for birding, plus unusually good security and a wide variety of accommodation across the 100-odd rooms – each of which is guaranteed to cost the same price no matter where you book it. The pool and relaxed atmosphere make it popular with families (family rooms have bunk beds for kids), and there's excellent food by one of Nairobi's best chefs, the celebrated Eamon Mullen. Reserve far ahead. Wi-fi. BB **Ksh17,300**

Serena Processional Way, between Nyerere Rd and Kenyatta Ave, facing Central Park ☎020 2822000 or 020 2822354, ⓦserenahotels.com; map p.102. Dating from the mid-70s, the 183-room *Serena* is impeccably decked out in Pan-African style, replete with sculptures and wall hangings. Rooms are very comfortable and feature carved furniture, marble bathrooms and African art. Amenities include a health club, pool, shops and wi-fi. A comfortable, safe bet, though don't venture out of the grounds on foot after dark. BB **$460**

KAREN AND LANGATA

INEXPENSIVE

Acacia Camp Magadi Rd, 1.5km south of Langata Rd ☎0733 603501, ⓦafricatravelco.com; map p.100. Not

to be confused with the tented camp at Swara Plains near Athi River (see p.100), this is one of the best-equipped campsites in Nairobi, base of a South African overland company, with single and double rooms and some dorm beds. The site is secure, and the bar is a good place to talk to staff from a number of safari operators. Food is available, and there are laundry facilities and DSTV. Camping **$7** per person, dorm beds **$10**, room only **$36**

Aero Club of East Africa Wilson Airport ☎020 600482, ⓦaeroclubea.com; map p.100. If you're taking an early flight from Wilson, where better to stay than this old flying club? It's far from fancy – and being close to Langata Rd the traffic noise continues until late at night – but it's safe, decent and reliable and you can get solid fare from the bar-restaurant and eat on the deck as the planes buzz in and out. Pool. Rates include temporary membership. Room only **Ksh4600**

Karen Camp Marula Lane, Karen ☎020 8833475 or 0723 314053, ⓦkarencamp.com; map p.100. A B&B-cum-overlanders' camp with pleasant s/c and non-s/c rooms, permanent tents, dorms and a big lawn for camping, as well as good food and a bar. Quiet and peaceful, but a long way from town. Camping **$6** per person, BB **$40**

★ **Wildebeest Eco Camp** 151 Mokoyeti Rd West, Langata (1.4km west of Galleria Mall, then 1.5km north) ☎020 2103505 or 0734 770733, ⓦwildebeest ecocamp.com; map p.100. Close to the Ngong Road Forest, this exceptional, family-run house and garden caters across the range, from backpackers to more upmarket guests. Pitch your own tent, take a bed in a dorm tent, stay in a non-s/c room or one of their non-s/c "garden" (Ksh4500) or s/c "deluxe safari" (Ksh9000) tents. There's a great deck over the pond – superb for birders – and a bar-restaurant. BB: dorm beds **Ksh1250**, camping **Ksh1000** per person, room **Ksh3500**

EXPENSIVE

★ **Giraffe Manor** Koitobos Rd, adjacent to the AFEW Giraffe Centre, Langata ☎020 2316756, ⓦgiraffemanor.com; map p.100. Neck and shoulders above Nairobi's other places to stay is this wonderfully eccentric Scottish-style manor house in the grounds of the Giraffe Centre, whose inhabitants like to share your breakfast through the windows. Rates include airport transfers and Giraffe Centre entry. Wi-fi. Closed May. Package **$1010**

Hogmead Corner of Mukoma and Kikenni rds, Langata ☎020 2115453, ⓦhogmead.com; map p.100. Where *Giraffe Manor* has twigas through the window, *Hogmead* has ngiris on the lawn. Large 1970s residence, lavishly reinvented and beautified as a contemporary country-house hotel in ten acres of grounds. The large and sumptuous rooms in the house have fans, floor-to-ceiling

1

nets and DSTV. The simpler garden rooms are in a converted stable block. Wi-fi. HB $\underline{\$400}$ (garden room), $\underline{\$770}$ (main house)

★ **Macushla House** Nguruwe Rd, Langata ☎ 020 891987 or 0733 706178, ⓦ macushla.biz; map p.100. Delightfully unpretentious, owner-managed boutique hotel in a forested and secluded part of Langata. Although the grounds are small, the rooms are large and comfortable, and the tightly organized gardens are attractively funky with their quirky ornaments and have more than sixty species of birds. Good meals are available in the bar-restaurant (tasty fusion-style dishes from Ksh1000), and there's a pool and wi-fi. BB $\underline{\$230}$

NAIROBI NATIONAL PARK

Park fees are payable if you're staying at most of the following, but a huge benefit to overnighting in the park if you're using one of the airports is the dramatic reduction in driving time. East Gate is a reliable 15min drive from JKIA at any time of day, while Main Gate is just 5km from Wilson airport, or about an hour's drive in a worst-case scenario.

★ **The Emakoko** Mbagathi Gorge, Nairobi National Park, accessed exclusively through the park ☎ 0774 309752, ⓦ emakoko.com (reservations ☎ 020 6000457, ⓦ bush-and-beyond.com); map p.100. Very attractive new owner-managed designer lodge on the south side of the national park, on the banks of the Mbagathi River near the confluence of the Emakoko and Mokoyeti streams, with very large, light, cottage rooms, plus pool and wi-fi. Rates include very convenient airport transfers, game drives, all drinks and excellent meals. Park fees payable. Package $\underline{\$840}$

KWS Twiga Campsite East Gate, Nairobi National Park (reservations – not normally necessary – with KWS ☎ 0726 610508, ✉ reservations@kws.go.ke); map p.100. Pleasant and secure campsite with good showers and toilets, cooking area and helpful rangers. You will probably need a vehicle to camp here, as walking the 200m from the gate is not allowed. Park fees payable. $\underline{\$15}$ per person

Masai Lodge Just outside the park, between the Kiserian and Mbagathi gorges, less than 2km west of Maasai Gate, or accessible from Ongata Rongai ☎ 020 3003846 or 0736 160888, ⓦ masailodge.com; map p.100. Minutes from the park, in a pre-eminent position in the steep, rocky valley of the Mbagathi, looking north across the gorge. This long-established lodge is no longer on the safari circuit but is popular for Nairobi weekenders, weddings and parties. Distinctly old-school, it delivers good value for money – on a good day – with haphazard service, reasonable rooms (some with great views), a good pool, well-stocked bar and a kitchen that needs plenty of

advance notice (order meals the day before). Double-check your reservation. BB $\underline{\$120}$

★ **Nairobi Tented Camp** In the densely wooded western part of the park ☎ 020 2603337 or 0733 884298, ⓦ nairobitentedcamp.com; map p.100. Traditional-style tented camp (the only one in the park) with top-notch meals in the lovely mess tent and excellent spotters and guides available for 4WD game drives (extra). It's also very convenient for the DSWT elephant orphanage, just 5km away (see p.144). Rates include soft drinks and meals. Park fees payable. FB $\underline{\$630}$

★ **Silole Villa & Cottage** Above Kingfisher Gorge, Silole Sanctuary, outside the park, west of Maasai Gate ☎ 0721 646588, ⓦ silolesanctuary.com; map p.100. Set in a private, four-hundred-acre wildlife sanctuary that extends to the riverside boundary of the park. Choose between the three-bedroom villa (sleeping five), either self-catering or with private chef, plus all meals and soft drinks; and the purely self-catering, thatched cottage, with two s/c double rooms, plus loft space for adventurous kids to bed down. Whole cottage $\underline{\text{Ksh8000}}$, whole villa $\underline{\text{Ksh15,000}}$ (self-catering) or $\underline{\text{Ksh30,000}}$ (FB)

THE NORTHERN SUBURBS

With the opening of the Northern Bypass, Gigiri can now be reached from JKIA in as little as 45min – or up to around 90min during rush hours.

Kentmere Club Limuru Rd, 20km northwest of Nairobi ☎ 020 3585511, ⓦ kentmereclub.com; map p.98. Situated amid the tea and coffee plantations of the Tigoni highlands, this small, friendly country inn – all beams and wood-tile roofs – has 16 adequate s/c rooms in cosy cottages with fireplaces, surrounded by beautiful gardens. You'll meet various Anglo-Kenyan and Kikuyu locals who pop in for a drink (beer Ksh200, wine Ksh250) or a bite at the restaurant, which serves traditional English meals (mains around Ksh1000), including a good Sunday roast. BB $\underline{\$120}$

Tribe Next to Village Market, Gigiri ☎ 020 7200000, ⓦ africanpridehotels.com/tribe; map p.100. Basking in its reputation as Nairobi's most chic hotel, *Tribe* is popular for its proximity to the UN headquarters and many embassies, but its location isn't ideal for regular trips around the city. The plunging, angular atrium and generous displays of African art are impressive, and the well-selected lounge music and outdoor swimming pool/water feature/sun terrace are fun, but sponsored poolside events can make for very noisy evenings and there are no gardens as such. Standard rooms are super-comfortable, with orthopaedic mattresses, flat-screen DSTV and glass-walled bathrooms. Food in the *Jiko* restaurant (see p.131) can be good, but it's not the gastronomic experience you might expect. Wi-fi. BB $\underline{\$360}$

EATING

Nairobi has no shortage of eating places. Their diversity is one of the city's best points, and eating out is an evening pastime that never dulls. Admittedly, anything like authentic Kenyan food is generally not highlighted in most restaurants, which concentrate on offering a range of Asian and European cuisines, and spectacular quantities of meat. Included below are one or two of the city's fancier **hotels**, where the food has a good reputation. For further eating-out **listings**, check out the bars and nightlife section (see p.131), which includes a number of venues that double as restaurants. When assessing **prices** (or checking your bill) remember there's a two percent training levy and sixteen percent value-added tax (VAT) on food and drink in all but the smallest establishments. Some include or add a variable service charge as well, which could raise the actual food and drink price by a further eight to ten percent. A lot of places include these taxes and charges in their menu prices, but some don't. Some long-established restaurants still don't take **credit cards**, either. At the more upmarket restaurants in the following listings, it's often a good idea to **reserve a table** or, as an alternative to calling yourself, try the free services of **Eat Out Kenya** (ⓦeatout.co.ke), a Nairobi-based online startup that makes restaurant bookings for you via your mobile.

CITY-WIDE CHAINS

Many of Nairobi's best-known eating and drinking venues have multiple venues in the city. This isn't to say that each branch maintains consistent standards, but they're generally fairly predictable. American-style **coffee shops**, in particular, have caught on in a big way, with *Java*, *Dormans* and now *Artcaffé* all slugging it out for market share.

Artcaffé Village Market, Westgate, Junction and Galleria malls. The newest kid on the coffee block, *Artcaffé* bakes very good bread and pastries to munch over your emails (free wi-fi) and does tasty pizzas (around Ksh800), light meals (around Ksh1000), and excellent coffee (espresso Ksh130), plus drinks (beer Ksh250, wine Ksh350). Daily 7.30am–10pm or later.

Creamy Inn Union Towers, corner of Moi Ave and Mama Ngina St, plus branches around the city. Serves great ice cream, including a spectacular honey crunch waffle sundae (cones from Ksh100). Hours vary.

Dormans Jubilee Exchange House, Mama Ngina St, plus branches at Airkenya at Wilson Airport, Junction Mall, Karen Nakumatt, Sarit Centre, Village Market, Westgate and Yaya Centre ⓦdorman.co.ke. Always full of cool young Nairobians and business people, *Dormans* is among the best of Nairobi's many coffee shops, serving an excellent range of regular and flavoured coffees and home-made cakes – and they usually have free wi-fi too. Daily 7am–8pm.

Kengeles Koinange St, plus other branches at Lavington Green shopping centre on James Gichuru Drive and at the Yaya Centre. Fast-food joint serving burgers, steaks, toasted sandwiches and Kenyan dishes washed down with beer or wine to a loud, nonstop music accompaniment. There's a pleasant balcony at the Koinange St branch. You could eat well and have a couple of drinks for Ksh1500. Daily 8am–midnight.

★ **Nairobi Java House** Transnational Plaza, Mama Ngina St, plus a dozen other branches, including ABC Place on Waiyaki Way, Adams Arcade on Ngong Rd, Capital Centre on Mombasa Rd and at Gate 14, JK International Airport; ⓦnairobijavahouse.com. This hugely popular coffee shop has some of the best breakfasts in Nairobi, good-value lunches (home fries, cheese, guacamole and salsa for Ksh380), and a great variety of coffees (large cappuccino Ksh210). Daily, with minor branch variations, 7am–9pm.

Savanna Coffee Lounge Loita St, between Market St and Koinange Lane, plus branches on Kenyatta Ave at the corner of Wabera St, Ralph Bunche Rd in Milimani, at the National Museum and at Sameer Business Park on the Mombasa Road, just east of the Ole Sereni Hotel. Great coffee, excellent sandwiches and a little more space to kick back than at some of the competitors. Mon–Fri 7am–9pm, Sat & Sun 7am–8pm.

Steers Muindi Mbingu St opposite Jeevanjee Gardens, plus other branches including Wabera St, The Mall in Westlands, Uchumi Hyper on Ngong Rd and Village Market ⓦsteers.co.ke. It's something of a miracle that a certain well-known global burger chain doesn't already have three hundred outlets in Kenya, so despite hit-and-miss service and quality, respect to the South African fast-food chain for venturing into Kenya with all their usual beef-based offerings (cheeseburger and chips from Ksh230), plus toasted sandwiches, salads, shakes, juices and great caramel ice cream. Daily 9am–10pm.

NAIROBI'S DRINKING WATER

Nairobi's **tap water**, once fine, is now either unfit to drink or too unpredictable to be worth the risk. Most people, even those on very low incomes, boil their water, and the more affluent drink only bottled water. If in any doubt, or if eating in cheap places where bottled water is not offered, stick to sodas.

1

RESTAURANTS & CAFÉS
MOMBASA ROAD AND AIRPORT AREA

There's a very limited choice of places to eat at the airport itself: the *Nairobi Java House* (see p.125) by Gate 14 of the international terminal is reliable, has a bar, and is open 24hr. There's a branch of *Home Park* (see opposite) nearby. For something a little more upscale, try the *Simba Restaurant* on the top floor of the arrivals building.

Ole Sereni Hotel Mombasa Highway, 12km from JKIA ☎020 3901000 or 0731 436405, ⓦole-serenihotel .com; map p.100. There are two main places to eat here: the Big Five restaurant and the Waterhole snack bar and terrace – both surprisingly good considering their essentially captive customers. Nibble on sides and starters (Ksh200 and up) or tuck into something mouthwateringly good like the Jack Daniels beef fillet with a baba ghanoush and mustard sauce (Ksh1350). Daily 6.30am–midnight.

RIVER ROAD

The River Road area has one *hoteli* after another on most streets, generally dishing up standard meals of fried fish, chicken or sausages with chips or *ugali*.

Ali Baba Fish and Chips Tsavo Rd; map p.104. Cheap, greasy and satisfying: where else in the city centre will you get a large pile of chips for Ksh70, kebabs for Ksh35 each or fried fish for just Ksh60 a portion? Squeeze onto a stool at the counter or carry out. Daily 7am–11pm.

C&J Cafe Gaberone Rd; map p.104. Cheerful and well-run mini café-diner serving breakfasts (Ksh115–180), good fish curries and meat stews with a choice of rice, *ugali* or chapatti (Ksh200–350), and takeaway chips with salad (Ksh60). Daily 6am–midnight.

Hewhay Fastfood Latema Rd, opposite Mid-View Central Hotel; map p.104. Next to the charms of the Maximum Miracle Evangelical Centre, this tiny and very cheap place delivers hole-in-the-wall happiness, such as a quarter chicken, chips and cold soda for Ksh200. Daily 6.30am–11pm.

Malindi Dishes Gaberone Rd ☎0722 103410; map p.104. Self-service cafeteria with good cheap Swahili dishes. They've been here for more than thirty years and they know their business: mutton or beef pilau costs Ksh150, or there's chicken tikka or fish masala for Ksh220. Daily 6.30am–midnight.

Sun Sweet Centre Ngariama Rd; map p.104. Indian place, large, sparse and slightly lacking in atmosphere, but with excellent vegetarian food and tempting sweets. Mon–Sat, variable hours until late.

CENTRAL BUSINESS DISTRICT

⭐ **Berber's Oasis** Mezzanine Floor, NHC Building, Aga Khan Walk ☎051 8016089 or 020 6004666; map p.104. Definitely worth an outing for its good, filling African dishes – *kisamvu na karanga* (cassava leaves with

groundnuts), *githeri*, beef curry and rice (Ksh450) – served in a quirky dining room, plus beer (Ksh170), wine (Ksh250) and cheap cocktails (from around Ksh350). See if they have any *muratina* (home-made honey beer, Ksh120). Wi-fi. Daily 6.30am–11pm (last orders 10pm).

Fiesta 3rd floor, Chester House, Koinange St ☎020 2240326; map p.104. Despite the name and the hacienda-gone-wrong interior, this is a reliable standby, often used by journalists based in the same building. There's a very nice rooftop terrace, affordable drinks (beer Ksh170, wine Ksh250) and standard fare such as pastas and salads (under Ksh500), grills, and one or two more interesting dishes, such as a succulent chicken curry with spinach and coriander (Ksh700). Daily 7am–11pm.

Home Park Tumaini House, Nkrumah Lane, plus a branch at JKI airport ☎020 2248376; map p.104. Wholesome, reliable, rather old-school bar and restaurant, competently run by nice, informal staff and with a flat-screen DSTV providing the entertainment. As well as all the usual greasy-spoon stuff, they do a good range of African dishes: try the sautéed bean stew with rice (Ksh250) or stir-fried chicken coconut with chapatti (Ksh500). Mon–Sat 6.30am–11pm.

New Giggles Restaurant Banda St, corner of Kimathi St; map p.104. It's not obvious what's so funny – unless it's the action unleashed nightly across the street at the Tribeka club. Pavement tables are set up for tired revellers – and the odd waiting driver – for beers (Ksh140), samosas, saveloys and other tasty snacks. Stuff yourself for Ksh200. Daily 7am–late, depending on business.

⭐ **Ranalo Foods** 1st floor, Balfour House, Kimathi St, near the Nation building ☎020 2249728 or 0721 323238; map p.104. Long-established (formerly *Kosewe*, after the owner) yet still surprising, this big upstairs self-service dining hall and bar, with a rooftop terrace, majors on Luo dishes from western Kenya. Fish in coconut, roast beef stew (*athalo*), millet *ugali* and several indigenous vegetables are all recommended – and you can eat well for under Ksh500. It's invariably packed, and there's always music, often dancing, and occasional live bands. Daily 8am–10pm (later at weekends).

⭐ **Tamarind** National Bank Building, Harambee Ave ☎020 2217990, ⓦtamarind.co.ke; map p.104. Nairobi's best seafood restaurant, with a kitchen run by Julius Mugo, head chef here for more than 20 years, and waiting staff overseen by Alex Mtundo, who has been here 30 years. Highly rated for its superb food, which is just as well, because it doesn't score highly for ambience or decor and is fairly cramped. Nevertheless, if you want to rub shoulders (literally) with government ministers and TV presenters, this is the place. The bill will depend on whether your tastes are simple or you tuck into the oysters and lobster, but don't expect much change from Ksh5000 per person, without drinks. Wines (from Ksh2400/bottle) include a

1

good selection from South Africa. Reservations essential (reserve crab or oysters specifically). Mon–Sat noon–2pm & 6.30–10pm, Sun & holidays 6.30–10pm.

Thorn Tree Café Stanley Hotel, Kimathi St; map p.104. A welcome refuge from street hustlers and a handy meeting place, partly screened from the street by beautiful Kitengela glass (see p.136). The famous notice board is still there (see p.107), though not much used. A pot of coffee costs Ksh300, beer Ksh330, and snacks go from Ksh300. Daily 7.30am until around 11pm.

Trattoria Corner of Wabera St and Kaunda St ☎020 2340855; map p.104. This still gets enthusiastic reviews – and not just from budget travellers having a splurge – and it's great to find a place that's stuck it out in the CBD for more than thirty years and has helped to bring about the area's rejuvenation. The pasta dishes and pizzas (around Ksh1000) are the real thing, and the cakes and ice cream magnificent. Daily 7am–11pm.

WESTLANDS AND PARKLANDS

Behind the Oilibya petrol station on Lower Kabete Rd, there's a useful 24hr food court with branches of *Pizza Inn*, *Creamy Inn*, *My Shop* and *Chicken Inn* – and a terrace on which to consume your calories and admire the traffic trying to get onto Waiyaki Way. *My Shop* sells Vasili's very good bread (Vasili's bakery was one of the first shops at Westlands roundabout) plus beer, wine and spirits from 10am–8.30pm.

★ **Alan Bobbe's Bistro** Andrews Apartments, far west end of Rhapta Rd, Westlands ☎020 4252000, ⓦ andrews.co.ke; map p.102. Opened in 1962 in the CBD, Nairobi's oldest bistro is still devotedly patronized. Tempted by home-baked bread and pastries, apartment residents come for breakfast (Ksh750) and a swim in the pool (changing rooms available), and blackboards display the day's lunch and dinner offerings, such as salade niçoise (Ksh500) followed by ragout of rabbit (Ksh1350). Count on around Ksh2500 per head without drinks, which are decent value (beer Ksh250, litre of house wine Ksh1800). Daily 6am–10am, noon–3pm & 6–9pm.

Bombay Chowpaty Diamond Plaza, Masari Rd ☎020 3748686 or 0713 293338; map p.102. The best location in Nairobi for south Indian, exclusively vegetarian meals, with a huge and inexpensive menu (most dishes Ksh300–500), or indulge in a full thali for Ksh450. Daily 10.30am–11pm.

Dass (also spelled Daas) Woodvale Grove, Westlands, above Havana ☎020 4441632 or 0721 208843; map p.128. Up two flights of stairs, this large dining room, with seating around low drum-tables, is the real deal in the heart of Westlands: authentic Ethiopian *injera* flat bread covered in dollops of different *wat* (stew; most around Ksh500–600) accompanied at weekends by musicians, poets and other performers. Sun–Wed 10.30am–11pm, Thurs–Sat 10.30am–2am.

Fogo Gaucho Viking House, Waiyaki Way, Westlands ☎020 3544037 or 0729 243202, ⓦ fogogauchonbi.com; map p.128. Recommended and convenient all-you-can-eat meat palace – a Brazilian churrascaria – that gives *Carnivore* a run for their money, with lunch at Ksh1400 and dinner at Ksh1800. There's also a mostly vegetarian buffet

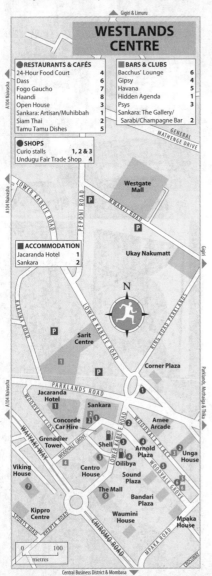

▲ Gigiri & Limuru

WESTLANDS CENTRE

● RESTAURANTS & CAFÉS
24-Hour Food Court	4
Dass	6
Fogo Gaucho	7
Haandi	8
Open House	3
Sankara: Artisan/Muhibbah	1
Siam Thai	2
Tamu Tamu Dishes	5

■ BARS & CLUBS
Bacchus' Lounge	6
Gipsy	4
Havana	5
Hidden Agenda	1
Psys	3
Sankara: The Gallery/ Sarabi/Champagne Bar	2

■ SHOPS
| Curio stalls | 1, 2 & 3 |
| Undugu Fair Trade Shop | 4 |

■ ACCOMMODATION
| Jacaranda Hotel | 1 |
| Sankara | 2 |

A104 Nairobi

GENERAL MATHENGE DRIVE

LOWER KABETE ROAD

PEPONI ROAD

MWANZI ROAD

Westgate Mall

P

P

Ukay Nakumatt

Gigiri

N

LOWER KABETE ROAD

NJUGU ROAD

RING ROAD PARKLANDS

Parklands, Muthaiga & Thika

Sarit Centre

P

Corner Plaza

PARKLANDS ROAD

Jacaranda Hotel

Sankara

Amee Arcade

Concorde Car Hire

WOODVALE CLOSE

WOODVALE GROVE

LOWER KABETE ROAD

WOODVALE PLACE

Grenadier Tower

Shell

Arnold Plaza

Unga House

Viking House

Centro House

Oilibya

WOODVALE GROVE

Sound Plaza

WAIYAKI WAY

The Mall

Bandari Plaza

Kippro Centre

Waumini House

Mpaka House

SPORTS ROAD

RHAPTA ROAD

CHIROMO ROAD

MPAKA ROAD

CROSSWAY

0   100
metres

▼ Central Business District & Mombasa

(lunch Ksh800, dinner Ksh1200) and salad bar. Mon–Sat 12.30–3pm & 6.30–10.30pm, Sun 12.30–10.30pm.

Furusato Corner of Ring Rd Parklands and General Mathenge Drive ☎020 3743007 or 0722 488706; map p.102. One of Nairobi's most popular Japanese restaurants – affordable and unpretentious. Choose from the counter and either eat in the restaurant or garden. They do a "sashimi boat" for Ksh1550, à la carte sashimi from around Ksh600 for nine pieces and a vegetarian sushi menu for Ksh900. There's a Korean menu, too, including tofu kimchi with pork (Ksh750). Takeaway available. Daily 12.30–3pm & 6.30–11pm.

Golden Spur Southern Sun Hotel, Parklands Rd ☎0724 253804; map p.102. US-style grill house, complete with huge triptych menus. The decent meals include good ribs and a 500g steak with chips and onion rings (Ksh1490) and a main-course salad buffet (Ksh680). Daily 11am–11pm.

★ **Haandi** Mezzanine floor, The Mall, Westlands ☎020 4448294, ⓦhaandi-restaurants.com; map p.128. Nairobi's best north Indian restaurant (now with branches in London) specializes in tandoori (clay oven) cooking – on display through the glass – with a huge variety of vegetarian and meat dishes from around Ksh600. Try the Diwani Haandi (peas, beans and cauliflower cooked in ginger and garlic; Ksh545) or Haandi Saag (mutton and spinach; Ksh685). Daily 12.30–2.30pm & 7.30–10.30pm.

★ **Open House** Ground floor, Centro House, Westlands ☎020 4445902 or 0735 621824; map p.128. Usually packed with local Indian families and not at all touristy, this place serves up delicious and well-prepared Indian dishes such as ginger chicken masala (Ksh650), pulao (pilau) of crunchy steamed vegetables (Ksh350) and light, crispy, buttery naans, all washed down with beers (Ksh225) or wine (Ksh1000/litre of house wine). Daily 11am–2.30pm & 6–10.30pm.

Peppers Parklands Rd, opposite the Southern Sun Hotel, Parklands ☎020 3755267 or 0722 201880; map p.102. Big parties who don't know what they want to eat are well catered for at this busy restaurant "specializing" in Indian, Chinese, seafood, barbecue and the dreaded Continental. They do a good job at most dishes, with great grills and a nice line in cocktails served with style by knowledgeable bar staff. There's a good-value Afghan chicken (the whole bird, Ksh1290), and drinks are reasonably priced (beer Ksh250, wine Ksh270). Popular with families for the huge garden and indoor and outdoor kids' play areas. Mon–Fri noon–3pm & 6–10pm, Sat, Sun & holidays noon–10.30pm.

★ **Le Rustique** General Mathenge Drive, Westlands ☎020 2622927 or 0721 609601 ⓦlerustique.co.ke; map p.102. Idiosyncratic, owner-operated Mediterranean restaurant and crêperie, with a pretty garden and gallery space. Very popular at weekends when you can have a very good brunch for around Ksh1000. Dinner, which features different dishes each week (look ahead online), comes in at around Ksh2000. Mon, Tues & Thurs–Sun 9am–7pm, Wed 9am–10pm.

Sankara ☎020 4208000 or 0703 028000, ⓦsankara .com; map p.128. There are two main places to eat here: the *Artisan* restaurant and the open-kitchen fusion/noodle bar *Muhibbah*. *Artisan* has a very good, pricey wine list and equally pricey food that varies from okay to sublime (burgers, sandwiches and salads around Ksh1000, choice of daily Kenyan two-course menus Ksh2500), while *Muhibbah* does lively curries (from Ksh1000), Asian salads (from Ksh700) and reliable noodles. *Artisan* daily 6am–11pm; *Muhibbah* daily noon–11pm.

Siam Thai 1st floor, Unga House, Muthithi Rd, Westlands ☎0707 180832; map p.128. Run by an Indian family in love with Thai food, this is probably the best Thai in town, despite the uninspired decor. Try the chicken cashew nut (Ksh870) or *larb gai* – spiced chicken mince with onions, mint and lemon grass (Ksh870), or share an Ahan Talay of mixed seafood (Ksh1450). Mon–Sat 10.30am–2.30pm & 6–10.30pm, Sun & holidays 11am–3pm & 6–10.30pm.

★ **Seven Seafood Bar & Grill** ABC Place, Waiyaki Way, Westlands ☎0737 776677, ⓦexperienceseven .com; map p.102. Very appealing, slick and well-presented seafood and salads, and always busy. The fish and crustacea are top-drawer, including an excellent, crunchy fish and chips (Ksh780) and several other daily fish dishes, and there's also a range of burgers and salads, including their own delicious interpretation of a salade niçoise (Ksh900) and a bigger dinner menu, with very good grills. Daily 11am–11pm.

Spice Roots Corner of Masari Rd and Parklands Rd, Parklands ☎020 3752658 or 0725 161126; map p.102. *Koroga* spot (self-cooking) that also does very good north Indian tandoori clay oven cooking, much cheaper than the more prestigiously located *Haandi*, and open incredibly late. Count on Ksh1000 a head. They also have a bar (beer Ksh195, wine Ksh250). Daily 10am–5am.

Tamu Tamu Dishes Woodvale Grove, Westlands ☎0728 872944; map p.128. Cheap and cheerful Swahili-centric food (fish and chapatti Ksh270, beef matoke Ksh240). Open 24hr.

UPPER HILL, LAVINGTON & KILELESHWA

Amani Garden Café Riverside Drive ☎020 4449071, ⓦamaniafrica.org; map p.102. Nice salads Ksh500–600) – including plenty of vegetarian and one or two vegan options – plus bagels and other snacks, and a children's menu, in a very pleasant shady garden with children's play equipment. Mon–Sat 10am–4.30pm (last orders 3.30pm).

Cedars Lenana Rd, Kilimani ☎020 2710399 or 0700 045521; map p.102. Excellent Lebanese food, if a little

1

pricey, at Ksh1900 a head for the full mezze. There's a balcony and terrace, and the dining room – with understated Middle Eastern decor – often has a roaring fire for chilly July evenings. Daily noon–11pm.

★ **Habesha** Argwings Kodhek Rd, Hurlingham ☎ 020 5213990 or 0733 730469; map p.102. Arguably the best yet least expensive Ethiopian food in town, *Habesha* serves large portions of spicy wat (stew) of various kinds on huge spongy *injera* flat breads, shared by the whole table. Dessert is traditionally popcorn, served with coffee, deliciously Ethiopian-style. The best tables are outside in the garden next to the fire pits. Allow Ksh1000 per person. Beers Ksh170, Ethiopian wine Ksh1000/bottle. Daily 11am–11pm.

Little Sheep Hot Pot Ngong Rd between Adams Arcade & Prestige Plaza ☎ 0736 113333 or 0706 304448; map p.102. Great Mongolian hot-pot place, popular with Chinese expats, where you cook your choice of raw veg, fish and meat ingredients in a steaming pot of stock and eat with tasty home-made wheat noodles and soy, ginger, garlic and chilli sauces. Allow Ksh900 per person. Daily 11am–11pm.

★ **Mediterraneo** Junction Mall, Ngong Rd ☎ 020 3878608 or 0734 845077, ⓦ mediterraneorestaurant .co.ke, plus branches at Pamstech House, Woodvale Grove, Westlands and UN Ave, Gigiri; map p.102. Popular and lively Italian, with a good wine list, serving everything from pasta to seafood and meat dishes, as well as excellent desserts. Not that cheap, though: with most antipasti and mains around Ksh1000 and up, you're looking at around Ksh3000/head, without drinks. Wi-fi. Daily noon–11pm.

Milimani Café Nairobi Youth Hostel, Ralph Bunche Rd; map p.102. Outside the YH itself, this isn't the cheapest hoteli in Nairobi, but it's convenient and wholesome – the beans and chapatti (Ksh150) and fruit salad (Ksh80) are good deals. There's also a great row of fruit stands just around the corner on Argwings Kodhek Rd. Daily 7am–8pm.

★ **Misono** Ground floor, The Greenhouse, Ngong Rd, Kilimani ☎ 020 3868959 or 0722 511229; map p.102. Japanese venue, famous for its avocado sauce, with tasty teppanyaki hot plate options downstairs as well as sushi and sashimi. It's popular at lunchtime with nearby office workers and does good set menus and lunchtime specials, including bento boxes. Allow Ksh2000 per person. Mon–Sat 12.30–3.30pm & 6.30–11.30pm.

Moonflower Restaurant at the Palacina Hotel, Kitale Lane, off Denis Pritt Rd, Kilimani ☎ 020 2715517 or 0720 493747; map p.102. Stylish and expensive little restaurant with attentive staff, where grills, lobster and Asian dishes are the principal focuses, while the Ksh3200 choma platter will feed you enough meat for a week. There are also vegetarian options (around Ksh1000) like eggplant

parmigiana or a satisfying chick pea and lentil korma, plus beer (Ksh300) and wine (from Ksh1950/bottle). The outdoor, tented setting by the pool is fun (or you can eat at the upper terrace), and there's live jazz Wed, Fri & Sat 8–11pm. Daily 11.30am–10.30pm.

Mughals Above Java Coffee House, Adams Arcade, Ngong Rd ☎ 0721 667711 or 0733 667711; map p.102. Very good, authentic Tandoori cuisine, with chicken tikka paneer and the like in the Ksh450–650 range. A must-try is the dense and creamy frozen *kulfi*. Daily noon–10pm.

Osteria del Chianti Lenana Rd, Kilimani ☎ 0724 277332 or 0734 472778, plus branches in Village Market and on Windy Ridge, Karen; map p.100. Occupying a large compound attached to the enjoyable *Casablanca* bar (see p.134), Osteria is a lively and straight-up Italian decorated with plenty of bottles and sausages. They do a brisk trade in wood-fired pizzas (Ksh450–800), either eaten in or delivered. Most other dishes – chicken, pasta – barely break the Ksh1000 barrier, though taxes are extra. Daily noon–11pm (last orders 10pm).

KAREN AND LANGATA

Carnivore Langata Rd ☎ 0733 611608 or 0722 204647, ⓦ tamarind.co.ke; map p.100. Nairobi's most famous restaurant no longer serves game meat (Kenya banned it in 2004), and seats more than 400, so it's not a refined experience, but go in a party frame of mind and you'll probably enjoy it. The all-you-can-eat menu (lunch Mon–Sat Ksh2920; Sun lunch & dinner Ksh3265; under 12s half-price; under 6s free) includes farmed samples of chewy camel and fishy-chicken crocodile, but the very good ostrich, beef and lamb, carved off the roasting sword, are usually excellent, and what you should fast for. There's an all-you-can-eat fish and vegetarian menu, too (lunch Ksh2370; dinner Ksh2625), plus beers at Ksh350. Reserve ahead, go early to choose a good table, and don't be tempted by early-evening distractions of sausages. Daily noon–2.30pm & 6.30–10.30pm.

Talisman 320 Ngong Rd, Karen ☎ 020 8092220 or 0733 761449, ⓦ thetalismanrestaurant.com; map p.100. One of Nairobi's best restaurants, with pleasant gardens children can run around in, artworks on show, a really nice terrace and funky colonial-oriental decor. The menu features a diverse variety of international dishes – their celebrated feta-and-coriander samosa starter is almost a Kenyan foodie cliché, and turns up all over the country. Reserve ahead and allow about Ksh3000 per person. Tues–Sat 8.30am–11pm, Sun 10am–9pm.

NAIROBI NATIONAL PARK

Rangers Main Gate, Nairobi National Park ☎ 020 2357470 or 0723 457480, ⓦ rangersnairobi.com; map p.100. You don't visit *Rangers* for the food, but for its very cool location, with its Twiga Terrace literally poking into a wooded part of the national park. Test current standards and quality by getting a quick snack and a drink before committing to a meal. Mains Ksh500–800, beers Ksh200. Mon–Fri 8am–11pm, Sat 8am–midnight or later, Sun 8am–10pm.

THE NORTHERN SUBURBS

★ **Amaica** Getathuru Gardens, off Peponi Rd ☎ 0724 477663, ⓦ amaica.co.ke; map p.102 (plus another, smaller branch in Milimani). Just above the Getathuru Stream, near the Sigiria Forest, is this excellent restaurant specializing in Kenyan regional and Pan-African cuisine. Try the smoked beef, Luhya bean soup or Luo omena fish in peanut sauce. Mains around Ksh1000. Daily 9am–11pm.

The Lord Erroll Ruaka Rd, Runda Estate, behind Village Market, Gigiri ☎ 0721 920820 or 0733 579903, ⓦ lord-erroll.com; map p.100. Colonial-style house with an old-fashioned, mahogany-panelled bar, the *Highlander*, two dining rooms and a terrace. Food and service are excellent, and there are good imported wines to accompany the French-with-a-touch-of-Swiss menu. Starters from Ksh500, mains from Ksh1500, vegetarian mains from Ksh1000. Daily noon–2.30pm (Sun 3pm) & 7.30–9.30pm (last orders).

★ **River Café** Off Limuru Rd, Rosslyn ☎ 020 2033340 or 0725 969891, ⓦ bit.ly/RiverCafé; map p.100. Based at a garden centre, with a children's play area and peaceful lakes, this popular outdoor café-restaurant is often packed for Saturday or Sunday brunch, with affluent Nairobians and UN-types digging into eggs Benedict (Ksh950) and French toast with crème Chantilly. It's a good idea to book a table. Daily 7am–6pm (last orders 5pm).

★ **Tamambo Bar & Grill** Top floor, Village Market, Gigiri ☎ 020 7124005 or 0722 200069, ⓦ tamarind .co.ke; map p.100. Modern African brasserie serving very good African and European food (try the crab cigars or the Kachos – Kenyan nachos made with cassava). There's an appealing terrace as well as the main restaurant, and the bar serves excellent frozen *dawas*. Live music some weekends. Daily 11am–3pm & 6.30–10pm.

Tribe Next to Village Market, Gigiri ☎ 020 7200000, ⓦ africanpridehotels.com/tribe; map p.100. The *Jiko* is the *Tribe* hotel's main restaurant, with a choice of *menus du jour* for lunch (Ksh1500) and a straightforward carte (mains Ksh1200–2500), including some nicely chosen local side dishes (like black-eyed peas and sukuma) at Ksh250, plus luscious desserts. Reputation and setting considered, it's not overpriced, but the food can be hit and miss. Daily breakfast, lunch and dinner.

BARS, CLUBS AND MUSIC VENUES

Promoting bands in Nairobi is as precarious a business as anywhere and, given the volatile nature of the music business, **venues** and bands change at a moment's notice. Check out ⓦ nairobinow.wordpress.com and ⓦ facebook.com (most clubs and bands have a Facebook account even if they have no website) and look at the *Nation* newspaper on a Friday and Saturday for one-off gigs. Most **clubs** are open nightly and often on weekend afternoons – and in some cases never close at all. Starting times vary considerably for live music: on weekdays, 8pm wouldn't be too early to turn up, while at weekends even the warm-up act may not begin before 10pm, and some shows may not get rolling until midnight. Earthy, local clubs have free entry or very cheap entrance fees, while in the glitzier places, men still sometimes pay more than women; around Ksh200–400 as against Ksh100–200. Included in the listings below are one or two of the more interesting **bars** in the city's fancier hotels, where there may be a minimum bill.

Security In recent years, downtown Nairobi's after-dark reputation as a dead zone, where nobody moved except by taxi, has been transformed by more street lighting and simple numbers: the clubbier streets are often streaming with people, especially at weekends, so there's no reason to feel threatened. Take the usual precautions you would in any city, by not carrying anything with you that you don't need or would hate to lose. Other than that, make the most of a rejuvenated night-time Nairobi. Do be warned though that, male or female, if you're not accompanied by a partner of the opposite sex, you soon will be.

BLANKETS AND WINE

Leisure Gardens, Mamba Village, Langata North Rd (map p.100) • First Sun of the month • Ksh1500 (Ksh400 children) • ⓦ blanketsandwine.com

This monthly festival, founded in 2009, has become one of Nairobi's biggest regular **music events** and looks set to spread its wings and spawn similar monthly outdoor music days in other parts of Kenya and neighbouring countries. Showcasing new bands, old favourites and anyone the organizers like, the mood is mellow and family-centric, featuring local singer-songwriters and rock and roots bands, accompanied by BYO picnics, plus a bar and food and crafts stalls.

1

GAY NAIROBI

Homosexuality is illegal (see p.81), but that doesn't stop gay men and lesbians coming out – and going out – and Nairobi is increasingly tolerant of lesbian, gay, bisexual and transgendered people. Progress takes two steps forward and one back, however: a number of the otherwise recommended clubs and bars in our listings were closing their doors to LGBT people in 2012. The following were extending a cautious welcome, or at least turning a blind eye: *Club Soundd* (see below); *Simmers* (see opposite), the *Exchange Bar* at *The Stanley* (see p.121) and the *Wine Bar* in 20th Century Plaza, Mama Ngina St (map p.104).

MOMBASA ROAD

Club Legend Baricho Rd, off Uhuru Highway, by Nyayo Stadium ☎0723 920436; map p.100. Flash bar with sports screens, music theme nights, a lot of rumba and occasional live music, including Congolese bands. Daily until late.

Club Vibro Mai Mahiu Rd, Nairobi West (off Langata Rd between Nyayo Stadium and Wilson Airport) ☎0728 826628; map p.100. Live music of various stripes at the weekend at a fine old barn of a place that has hosted some big names over the years. Daily until late.

RIVER ROAD

Apple Beez Gaberone Rd, corner of Luthuli Ave ☎0707 0749712; map p.104. Cheap beer, friendly staff, slightly kitsch decor, and a lively soundtrack of mostly Lingala music. Can be a congenial spot for a drink, though it has evolved into something of a strip joint and lap-dancing venue in recent years: beware you don't stray into the Ksh1000 "VIP section". Free entry by day; Ksh300 at night; Happy Hour (4–6pm) beers Ksh100. Open 24hr.

Fameland Duruma Rd; map p.104. There are good DJs – and occasional live bands – at the weekend in this dingy and weathered "day and night club". Thursday is African disco night, with plenty of hip-gyrating rhythms to grind to, and you can usually get *nyama choma* with *ugali*, washed down with a beer (Ksh140) or soda (Ksh50). Open 24hr.

Monte Carlo Club Accra Rd; map p.104. A cavernous place with a good atmosphere, very cheap food to soak up the booze (steak and chips Ksh220) and music featuring a mix of reggae sessions (Wed from 8pm, Sat & Sun from 3pm; Ksh100), and Lingala sounds on other days (free entry). "No weapons or *miraa*", say the signs – a necessary notice, judging from a few unsavoury types lurking within. Daily until 4.30am.

CENTRAL BUSINESS DISTRICT

Club Lounge Eagle House, Kimathi St ☎0723 785879; map p.104. An exuberant, young crowd packs this bar, one of several at this end of Kimathi St, and spills out onto the balcony. There's an infectious mix of Kenyan and international hip-hop and pop, and, as the night wears on, tables and chairs are pushed aside and the venue becomes

an impromptu dancefloor. Daily until late.

Club Soundd 2nd floor, Hamilton House, corner of Kaunda St and Standard St ☎0722 571382; map p.104. Upmarket and relatively sophisticated for the CBD, featuring live bands, poetry readings, open mic sessions, and Sun afternoon salsa lessons, followed by salsa club night. Entry free–Ksh300. Daily 4pm–midnight.

Dolce Club Cianda House, Koinange St ☎020 2218298, ⊛dolcetheclub.com; map p.104. Slick, smooth *Lingala* and soul dinner-dance place for a glitzy crowd, with a deafening sound system. Fun if you're in the right mood, but quite pricey. Daily 5pm–1am.

Florida 2000 1st floor, Commerce House, Moi Ave ☎020 2229036 or 0726 110968, ⊛floridaclubskenya .com; map p.104. Also known as *F2*, the sister establishment of the *New Florida* (see below) attracts similar clients and offers equally unambiguous entertainment, pumped up with what they call "most exotic floor shows". For some local ladies, this means grabbing drunken *wazungu* and persuading them to part with their money. Be relaxed, but beware. Daily 9pm–6am.

Garden Square Club City Square, City Hall Way, opposite the Holy Family Cathedral; map p.104. Laidback bar-restaurant with live music on Fri & Sat. Daily 7pm–2am.

The Loft Westlands Rd, by Museum Hill Overpass; map p.102. Cool, 18-plus DJ club upstairs behind *Tree House* (see p.133) playing pop and dance music. Lounges, sheesha. Fri & Sat only, 9pm–6am.

Lord Delamere Terrace Norfolk Hotel, Harry Thuku Rd ☎020 2265000 ext. 2056, ⊛fairmont.com/norfolk hotel; map p.102. Sooner or later, a people-watching drink and snack at this century-old bar is a must – though at times it can feel a bit stuffy and there's not much flavour of 1904 about it. It does, however, offer the full range of local drinks as well as expensive imports, and the snacks aren't as pricey as you might expect. Daily 6.30am–10.30pm.

New Florida Chai House, Koinange St ☎020 2215014, ⊛floridaclubskenya.com; map p.104. Popularly known as *F1*, *Mad House or Maddi* and irresistible for its tackiness, this big red-and-white mushroom of a building above a Total filling station is always full of prostitutes and rather desperate-looking business types, but staff ensure the atmosphere stays steamy, never heavy. There's a floor show at midnight, and Reggae nights every Wed; entrance Ksh300. Daily 8pm–6am.

Simmers Corner of Muindi Mbingu St and Kenyatta Ave ☎020 2217659 or 0722 593185; map p.104. Large and laidback, the CBD's only *nyama choma*-style joint, and thus very popular (especially with office workers deferring the misery of commuting home). Music, dancing and frequent live bands. Daily 7am–midnight.

Tree House Westlands Rd, by Museum Hill Overpass ☎0736 597057, ⓦtreehousenairobi.wordpress.com; map p.102. On weekend nights up to two thousand people pack into this landmark venue built around the giant mahogany tree, lured by live music, reasonable prices (beer Ksh250, wine Ksh300, jungle burger Ksh500, Caesar salad Ksh550) and guaranteed crowds. Tues–Sat 11am–4am, closed Sun & Mon.

Tribeka Corner of Banda St and Kimathi St ☎0708 322222; map p.104. Very busy double-storey bar-resto, flashing with sports screens, banging with sounds and heaving with sweaty, and mostly young, bodies – and with a balcony overlooking this lively corner (Triangle Below Kimathi). Theme nights include karaoke (Tues), live music (Wed) and reggae (Thurs). To escape for a breather or a cheaper bite to eat, grab a table at *Giggles*, opposite (see p.126), and you can keep an eye on the action. Daily 24hr.

Zanze Bar 5th floor, Kenya Cinema Plaza, Moi Ave ☎020 2222568 or 0722 787250; map p.104. A good place for a beer (Ksh150) in the afternoon, accompanied by TV news and a game of pool, before it gets disco-feverish with the house DJs in the evening. They do food (beef stew Ksh280, chapatti Ksh40, goat leg choma Ksh480/kg) and there's live music on Wed, Fri and Sun from 7pm (Ksh300). Daily 11am–3am.

WESTLANDS AND PARKLANDS

Bacchus' Lounge Woodvale Grove, Westlands ☎0724 441964; map p.128. Popular music club, relaxed, welcoming and air-conditioned. Music includes hip-hop (Sun–Tues), slow sounds (Wed), techno (Thurs) and dance music (Fri & Sat). Beers Ksh200, wine Ksh250. Daily 4pm–4am/last customer leaves.

Gipsy Woodvale Grove, Westlands ☎020 4440836; map p.128. As well being a friendly and not too hustly terrace bar, rendezvous and hang-out, *Gipsy* is a good place to eat late, with a vaguely Spanish-styled menu, including steaks (Ksh1200), seafood (Ksh1000) and burgers and veggie meals (Ksh700–1000). Mon–Sat 11.30–2.30pm & 5pm–2am.

Havana Opposite Bandari Plaza, Woodvale Grove, Westlands ☎020 4450653, ⓦhavana.co.ke; map p.128. Dark and smoky Latin restaurant and bar, with a chic young crowd attracted by good snacks and cheap cocktail pitchers. Daily noon–3am.

Hidden Agenda 1st Floor, Sarit Centre, Westlands ☎0714 129997 or 0737 444810; map p.128. Upmarket café and bar, popular with Westlands youth, with smart leather decor and tables out in the mall. Bar meals, such as calamari and salad, go for under Ksh1000 and there are happy hours (Mon–Thurs 4–6pm) and music theme nights. Daily noon–late.

Klub House Junction of Chiromo Rd and Ojijo Rd ☎020 3749870 or 020 3742149, ⓦklubhouse.co.ke; map p.102. Huge, gated, quintessentially Kenyan drive-in entertainment complex (part of the highly successful Kahama empire). Inside you'll find the double-storey wooden *Klub House* itself ("Paradise" downstairs, and "Heaven" upstairs with six pool tables and beers for Ksh200); the *Karwash* snack bar where the menus have valeting services on one side and snacks on the other; the *Pitcher & Butch* live music venue, pub and *nyama choma* grill (mbuzi arm Ksh1450/kg), which sometimes has working wi-fi; and a hotel, the *Parklands Shade* (see p.122), for when you just have to crash. Daily 24hr.

Mercury Lounge ABC Place, off Waiyaki Way, Westlands ☎020 4451875 or 0722 309947, ⓦmercurylounge.co.ke; map p.102. Cool designer watering hole with a curved wooden bar and dark green and purple leather furniture. In keeping with the retro feel, the DJs tend to spin 1970s funk and soul, and there's regular live music. Cocktails cost from Ksh300, and there's tapas-style food and light dishes such as Caesar salad (Ksh700). Sun–Thurs 4pm–midnight, Fri & Sat 4pm–4am.

Psys Unga House, Woodvale Place ☎0710 574419; map p.128 (plus another branch at Hamilton House, Kaunda St, in the CBD, above Club Soundd). With welcoming staff, a different music theme and DJs every night, and cheap drinks (beer Ksh180, wine Ksh200), *Psys* is going down well. Sun–Thurs 5pm–midnight, Fri & Sat 5pm–5am.

Sankara Hotel ☎020 4208000 or 0703 028000, ⓦsankara.com; map p.128. There are three bars in this hotel (see p.122): The *Gallery* wine bar and patisserie on the first floor (with probably the best wine selection in Nairobi); the slick, rooftop *Sarabi* with its glass-bottomed swimming pool; and the seventh-floor *Champagne Bar*. Daily: The Gallery 6am–1am; Sarabi 7am–1am; Champagne Bar 7pm–1am.

UPPER HILL, LAVINGTON & KILELESHWA

Black Parrot Basement, Hurlingham Plaza, Argwings Kodhek Rd, Hurlingham ☎0734 926705, ⓦblack-parrot.net; map p.102. Cheap drinks, regional Kenyan food and Kenyan bands most weekends. Daily until late.

★ **Brew Bistro** Piedmont Plaza, Ngong Rd ☎020 4183382 or 0771 152350, ⓦthebigfivebreweries.com;

1

map p.102. Microbrewery terrace bar and restaurant. Go for the interesting beer, the buzz and the scene of Nairobians paying to be seen – and keep your fingers crossed that the food, when it comes, will be as good as it sometimes can be: waiting staff are frequently swamped. Mon–Fri 4–9pm, Sat & Sun 11am–9pm.

Caribea Komo Lane, off Wood Ave, Hurlingham ⓣ 020 2108579 or 0703 993123; map p.102. Formely *Azalea*, this is now a Koroga restaurant and heavily Bacardi-branded cocktail bar. There's a nice garden for hanging out, drinks aren't expensive (beers Ksh200), and there's a jazz band on Thurs. Daily until late.

Casablanca Lenana Rd, Kilimani ⓣ 020 2723173; map p.102. Stylish Moroccan-themed bar attached to the highly recommended *Osteria* restaurant, with a wonderful oasis-style garden complete with sand, palms, cushions and shishas. The cocktails are expensive (from Ksh700), but delicious and potent. Beers Ksh300. Mon–Thurs 5pm–2am, Fri & Sat 5pm–6am.

KAREN AND LANGATA

The Blix Lounge Karen Plains Arcade, Karen; map p.100. Would the baroness have liked this 18-plus bar-restaurant with sports screens and weekend DJ nights? Possibly not, but today's locals flock to it. Daily 6pm–2am.

Simba Saloon Carnivore restaurant, Langata Rd ⓣ 020 602764, ⓦ tamarind.co.ke; map p.100. A successful melding of bands and DJs in a pleasant outdoor environment with a very spacious dancefloor. There's frequent live music, both Kenyan and international, and big names like Baaba Maal and Youssou N'dour have played here. The adjacent *Carnivore Gardens* concert venue holds up to 15,000. Open during concerts until 2am.

THE NORTHERN SUBURBS

Tribe: The Nest Next to Village Market, Gigiri ⓣ 020 7200000, ⓦ africanpridehotels.com/tribe; map p.100. *The Nest* is the *Tribe* hotel's very comfy, open-air rooftop cocktail (Ksh600) and shisha (Ksh1000) bar. They also do light meals for around Ksh1000. Daily 10am–midnight.

ARTS AND ENTERTAINMENT

After years of stagnation, the Nairobi **arts scene** seems to be finally finding a rhythm of its own, independent of the tourist market, which had previously driven much of it. Although still modest by international standards, it is well worth discovering. Besides checking out the theatres and arts centres listed below, your first base should be the excellent arts-scene blog ⓦ nairobinow.wordpress.com, which posts news of up-and-coming performers, shows and events. Also worth having a look at are the theatre pages in the Thursday edition of the *Standard* and the *Nation* on Friday and Saturday. For **cinema** listings, see Directory (p.138).

Alliance Française Corner of Loita and Monrovia streets ⓣ 0727 600622, ⓦ afkenya.or.ke; map p.104. Constant stream of activity – events, shows and fora.

★ **Banana Hill Art Studio & Gallery** Raini Rd, centre of Banana Hill ⓣ 0733 882660 or 0711 756911, ⓦ bit.ly/BananaGallery; map p.100. Very worthwhile contemporary Kenyan painting and sculpture based around a community of artists.

British Council Upper Hill Rd ⓣ 020 2836000 or 0722 205335, ⓦ britishcouncil.org; map p.102. Good resources, but not as lively as some other national cultural organiszations.

★ **GoDown Arts Centre** Dunga Rd, Industrial Area ⓣ 020 555770 or 0726 992200, ⓦ thegodown artscentre.com; map p.100. A not-for-profit organization including an art gallery, dance studio and performance space presenting everything from classical music by local musicians to visiting overseas artists.

Goethe-Institut Maendeleo House, corner of Loita St and Monrovia St ⓣ 020 2224640, ⓦ goethe.de/ins/ke /nai; map p.104. The German overseas cultural mission.

Italian Institute of Culture 5th floor, Grenadier Tower, 1 Woodvale Close, Westlands ⓣ 020 4451266, ⓦ iicnairobi.esteri.it; map p.128. Beautiful event and exhibition space that does as much to promote African culture as support Kenya's lively and long-settled Italian community.

Kenya National Theatre Opposite the Norfolk Hotel, Harry Thuku Rd ⓣ 020 2086748 or 0712 6008677; map p.102. Built in 1952, the theatre was refurbished in the early 2000s by a combination of government funds and the private sector and has now been restored in all its Art Deco glory, hosting productions with a special emphasis on African theatre, and Kenyan drama in particular.

★ **Kuona Trust** Likoni Close, off Likoni Lane, off Dennis Pritt Rd, Hurlingham ⓣ 0721 262326 or 0733 742752, ⓦ kuonatrust.org; map p.102. Active for many years, this visual arts centre brings together Kenyan and international artists and performers for residencies, workshops and events.

Michael Joseph Centre Safaricom HQ2, Waiyaki Way ⓣ 0722 005890, ⓦ safaricom.co.ke/michael josephcentre; map p.102. Gallery and performance space, funded by the mobile phone company, that increasingly hogs the limelight in Nairobi's arts universe, with an eclectic variety of shows from classical European music to Kenyan hip-hop and theatre.

Professional Centre/Phoenix Players Parliament Rd ⓣ 020 2225506, ⓦ phoenixtheatre.co.ke; map p.102. This small theatre has assumed the mantle of Nairobi's leading playhouse, and is highly recommended. Its energetic repertory company, the Phoenix Players, formed in 1948, stages contemporary works by Kenyan and foreign playwrights and classics adapted for Kenya – always worth catching and sometimes outstanding.

★ **Sarakasi Dome** Ngara Rd, opposite the post office ☎ 020 2694026 or 0722 814133, ⊛ sarakasi.org; map

p.100. Built in 1952 as a circus (*sarakasi*) venue, then the Shan Cinema for many years, this is now a Dutch-owned venue and renovated performance space for the very active Sarakasi Trust and their vibrant Sarakasi Players, promoting contemporary African art, music and dance.

SHOPPING

It doesn't take long to realize that commerce is Nairobi's *raison d'être*. Nairobi is the best place in East Africa to buy **handicrafts**, with the widest, if not the cheapest, selection, and the city also has some lavish **produce markets**, enjoyable even if you only want to browse. The upper part of Moi Avenue is Nairobi's busiest ordinary shopping street, with some colonnaded shop-fronts still remaining. A certain amount of **bargaining** is expected at all Nairobi's markets and many independent shops.

SHOPPING MALLS AND SUPERMARKETS

Nakumatt Branches all over the city; some are open 24hr including Nakumatt Ukay in Westlands, Nakumatt Ngong Road at Prestige Plaza, and Nakumatt Lifestyle on the corner of Monrovia and Moktar Daddah streets near Jeevanjee Gardens in the CBD. There's no bargaining at Nakumatt, Kenya's number one supermarket and hypermarket chain, where you can buy everything from beans to solar panels, but the erstwhile Nakuru Mattresses Co. does deliver on variety and – usually – price.

Shopping malls Nairobi now has the dubious distinction of having more shopping malls – over twenty, and counting – than any other African city outside South Africa, providing a hassle-free environment for getting on with ordinary shopping and business. You'll find most of them stuffed into the western and northern suburbs where they cater to the expat and wealthy Kenyan markets. All include banks, travel agents, specialist food suppliers and an assortment of cafés and restaurants. The biggest and most popular – Westgate in Westlands, Village Market in Gigiri, Junction and Yaya Centre on Ngong Rd, Galleria in Langata – are major landmarks. Shops in the malls generally don't open until 9am or even 10am and then remain open until 7pm or 8pm. The malls themselves are usually open by 7am for breakfast and coffee outlets.

CRAFTS AND FABRICS

For the exhausting business of buying crafts and curios, it's advisable to be quite focused and decide what sort of items you're interested in buying before stepping into a shop or looking at a stall: if you merely browse you'll often be hassled mercilessly by the majority of shopkeepers and stallholders (see p.85). There are dozens of curio shops and you might get a good deal at almost any of them, though you should never accept their first price, and always bargain hard. Upmarket places are increasingly relocating to the city's suburban malls. In the CBD they're clustered on Standard, Kaunda and Mama Ngina streets. At some of the fancier places you can browse for ages undisturbed, but at cheaper outlets dilly-dallying is not encouraged and the pressure may be on to part with your money. As well as the

following shops, City Market has a number of crafts stalls, but the sales pressure can be intense. For fabrics, **Biashara Street** ("Commerce Street") is the traditional home in Nairobi of cloth merchants, and many of them are still there.

African Heritage Carnivore, Langata; map p.100. A selection of curios and crafts from across the continent, representing some of the large collection at African Heritage House. Daily 10am–10.30pm.

★ **African Heritage House** Mombasa Rd ☎ 0721 518389, ⊛ africanheritagebook.com; map p.100. This appointment-only treasure trove of beautiful items collected by an American Africaphile and Kenya resident includes superb musical instruments such as thumb pianos and lyres – well worth a special visit.

Batik Heritage Muindi Mbingu St; map p.104. Similar to Kashmir Crafts.

Embakasi Village Crafts Market Mombasa Rd, towards the airport (second left after City Cabanas Restaurant); matatu #110 or bus #33; map p.100. One of the most organized craft markets in Kenya, and most items here are much cheaper than in other Nairobi markets. You can also watch carvers at work, and commission individual carvers. Daily 8am–5pm.

Haria's Stamp Shop 38 Biashara St ⊛ hariastamp .com; map p.104. This old place has an excellent and very reasonably priced range of fabrics, including *kikois* and *kangas*. Mon–Sat 9am–6pm.

Kamili Designs Langata Rd, Karen, near Karen Hospital ☎ 020 2430495 or 0733 607025, ⊛ kamili designs.com; map p.100. This textile workshop sells locally designed, hand-printed fabrics in typically bold and colourful patterns, available both by the metre and as cushions, bedspreads and the like. Mon–Fri 9am–5pm.

Kashmir Crafts Biashara St; map p.104. If you are in no hurry and after something unique, but not necessarily Kenyan, this is worth a visit, with a great selection of carvings, masks and jewellery from across the continent at very reasonable prices. Daily 8am–5pm.

Shah's Moktar Daddah St, west of Muindi Mbingu; map p.104. Another general crafts store worth visiting.

1

★ **Zanzibar Curio Shop** Moi Ave; map p.104. To browse and to establish comparative values, pay a visit to this excellent shop, which has a huge range of stuff at fixed and realistic prices. You'd be hard-pressed to match its prices by bargaining anywhere else. Mon–Sat 9am–6pm.

COMMUNITY CRAFT CENTRES

Nairobi has a number of craft shops with charitable status, or associated with development or self-help projects. Although sometimes a little expensive (and they don't go in for bargaining), they often have unusual and well-made stock, some of which finds its way into charity catalogues overseas. A few are a little way out of town, but well worth making special journeys to visit, and they can be good tonics if you're suffering from curio shop fatigue.

Amani ya Juu Riverside Drive ☎020 4449071, ⓦamaniafrica.org; matatu #48; map p.102. This project employs fifty women who have been marginalized by poverty and war. It's great for gifts, including colourful handmade clothes and bags. Mon–Fri 9am–4pm, Sat 10am–4pm.

Bega Kwa Bega Korogocho Projects ☎0720 234228, ⓦbegakwabega.com; map p.100. Federation of small handicrafts producers from the Korogocho slums of eastern Nairobi, offering sisal bags, necklaces, batiks, furniture and cloth puppets. Mon–Fri 9am–4pm.

★ **Kazuri Beads & Pottery Centre** Mbagathi Ridge, Karen ☎020 2328905 or 0720 953298, ⓦkazuri.com; map p.100. Kazuri, which means "small and beautiful", employs nearly a hundred formerly destitute women who make an extraordinary variety of handmade, mostly ceramic, jewellery and beads. You can watch the whole process from shaping and colouring to firing, and there's also a pottery showroom. It's expensive, but the stuff is lovely. Workshops: Mon–Fri 8am–4.30pm, Sat 8am–1pm; shop: Mon–Sat 8am–5pm, Sun 9am–5pm.

★ **Kitengela Glass** Off the Magadi road, south of Nairobi National Park ☎020 6750602 or 0734 287887, ⓦkitengela-glass.com; map p.100. Inspiring community of glass-blowers and craftspeople in a photogenic creative village. Visitors are welcome and you can observe, browse and buy unhassled lots of beautiful work, and plenty of quirky rejects, although you'll need your own transport to get here. Mon–Sat 8am–5pm, Sun 11am–4pm.

Maridadi Fabrics City Stadium roundabout, Landhies/Jogoo Rd, 2km east of the train station ☎020 6750454; bus #34 or #36; map p.100. Church-based Maridadi was created in 1966 as an income-generating community project for women in one of Nairobi's oldest slum areas – Pumwani and Shauri Moyo. The main workshop is a delight if you're into making your own clothes, with a large screen-printing workshop (on view from the visitors' gallery) producing the wide range of prints for sale in the shop. Especially appealing are the bark cloth prints – a natural

weave used for clothing by many East African peoples until the end of the nineteenth century. Mon–Fri 8am–5pm.

Mikono Craft Shop Gitanga Rd, Lavington ☎020 3877498, ⓦjrsea.org; bus #46 or #46B; map p.102. The outlet of the Jesuit Refugee Service, with well-made work (including especially beautiful patchwork textiles) from refugees, and superb Mozambican carvings. Mon–Fri 8.30am–1pm & 2–5pm, Sat 9am–3pm.

Spinner's Web Getathuru Gardens, off Peponi Rd, Westlands ☎020 2072629 or 0731 168996, ⓦspinnerswebkenya.com; map p.102. A large shop selling a lot of good stuff – crafts, textiles, woollen goods and jewellery, much of it made by self-help groups and individuals, including Meru's Makena Textile Workshop and Spinner's Web in Nanyuki (see p.179). Mon–Fri 9.30am–6.30pm, Sat & Sun 9.30am–5.30pm.

★ **Undugu Fair Trade Shop** 5th Floor, Arnold Plaza, Woodvale Grove, Westlands ☎0733 610100, ⓦundugukenya.org; map p.128. With its roots in the church, Undugu ("fraternity") is the most vigorous society of its kind in the country and organizes regular guided visits to their slum projects. Their shop sells a good selection of well-priced, high-quality crafts with some more unusual items, such as Ethiopian jewellery, basketwork, and crafts from DRC, Tanzania and Uganda. You may also be able to have a look around the workshops. Mon–Fri 9am–6pm, Sat 9am–3pm.

Utamaduni Crafts Centre Bogani East Rd, Langata ☎020 891798, ⓦutamaduni.com; bus/matatu #24; map p.100. Eighteen individual craft shops in one large house, opened by Richard Leakey in 1991 (a portion of the profits goes to the Kenya Wildlife Service). It has everything you might want, much of it made on site or from street-kid projects. Quality and prices are high, and the attached *Verandah* restaurant is excellent. Daily 9.30am–6pm.

Woodley Weavers Chaka Rd, Hurlingham ☎020 3873759 or 0733 612028, ⓦwoodleyweavers.com; map p.102. Known to many as the "rug gallery", this place has a variety of rugs made by local women, often single mothers from the Kibera slum, using local wool, cotton and plant dyes. Mon–Fri 9am–5pm.

MARKETS

City Market Muindi Mbingu St; map p.104. Though it doesn't offer the city's lowest prices, for a colourful and high-quality range of fruit and vegetables (plus separate meat and fish sections) this is the obvious option in the CBD, though many erstwhile greengrocer's stalls have switched to overpriced crafts. Beware of bag-snatching while browsing. Mon–Fri 7.30am–6.30pm, Sat 7.30am–3pm, Sun 8.30am–noon.

Gikomba Market Off Landhies Rd, past the Country Bus Station; take any bus or matatu for Jogoo Rd and get off at Gikomba; map p.100. The largest general market in Nairobi, this is a spot that few tourists ever see, a labyrinth of muddy alleyways, courtyards and open sewers. It's also a place to experience an exhilarating slice of Nairobi life, and just about anything can be found on sale, from school uniforms to industrial-size ovens. Come with someone who knows the place, though; it's very easy to get lost and Gikomba can be unsafe.

Kariokor Market Ring Road, Ngara; bus/matatu #4, #6, #14, #15, #30, #31, #32, #40, #42 or #46/46B; map p.100. Named after the wartime "Carrier Corps", Kariokor is closer to an oriental bazaar than most markets in Kenya, with permanent booths for the traders. Inside, there's as much manufacturing and finishing going on as selling – you'll find sisal weavers, leather workers, makers of tyre-rubber sandals ("5000-mile shoes" – about Ksh300 a pair and surprisingly comfortable), carpenters, toy-makers (look out for locally made wire-and-fabric contraptions – cars, bicycles, flapping birds – which are sometimes beautiful works of art), tailors, and traditional healers with various remedies and charms. Kariokor is the best place in Nairobi to buy baskets (*vyondo*), made with sisal, coloured with natural or artificial dyes; with garish plastic; or with cord manufactured from the bark of the baobab tree. The cord baskets can be truly exquisite, with tiny beads included in the tight weave.

Maasai markets If you're after Maasai crafts (whether traditional beaded jewellery or items made up for the tourist industry), or carvings and crafts in general, the city's various "Maasai Markets" are recommended, though they are no longer the cheap, hot tip they once were. Initiated downtown opposite the post office in the mid-1990s, the original group of Maasai and other women from rural areas (as well as a number of men) were moved several times by city council *askaris* and now convene to display their wares at various places throughout the week. You'll sometimes find prices well below those in the tourist markets, with good deals on the simpler designs of beaded jewellery, baskets and gourds. But more usually you'll have to bargain hard to get what seems like an acceptable price. Tues: Kijabe St, behind the *Norfolk Hotel*, map p.102; and

Westgate Mall in Westlands, map p.128; Thurs: Junction Mall, Ngong Rd, map p.102; Fri: rooftop car park at Village Market, Gigiri, map p.100; Sat: Law Courts car park off City Hall Way, map p.104; and Galleria Mall, Langata; map p.100; Sun: Yaya Centre, Hurlingham, map p.102; all markets open roughly 8am–3pm.

CLOTHES AND MATUMBA

You'll find clothes shops all over the city, but more interesting for visitors is the *matumba* phenomenon, the secondhand clothes stalls that are found in markets and spilling over roadsides across the city. These are entirely supplied through a murky chain of international connections whose first link is the donation of unwanted clothes to "charity" clothes collection companies in Europe and the USA. *Matumba* is big business and a serious challenge to local clothing manufacturers: the vast majority of Kenyans buy most or all of their clothes at these stalls.

BOOKSHOPS

Just a few years ago there was barely a handful of decent bookshops in Nairobi. Now they're everywhere, with most malls having at least one. The shelves tend to be packed with school and college books, but the best of them have excellent ranges of local and imported fiction, gift books, travel and maps. In the CBD, the best bookshop is probably Bookpoint in Loans House, Moi Ave. In Westlands, the Textbook Centre at the Sarit Centre mall is also good. Further out, the best branch of Books First is at the Village Market mall, Gigiri.

MUSIC

The huge volume of music on CD makes Nairobi a great place for music fans, especially if you have a taste for Kenya's stunning variety of ethnic musical strands, not to mention the plethora of recordings from elsewhere in east and central Africa, especially Congo. The famous Assanand's on Moi Avenue sadly closed in 2010, but Musikland on Moi Avenue, Melodica on Tom Mboya Street or any of a host of shops around the River Road district are all worth a browse.

SPORT

Diving Nairobi Sailing and Sub-Aqua Club, off Langata Rd, opposite Wilson Airport ⓦdiveclubkenya.com. BSAC training and trips to coastal and lake diving sites.

Football (soccer) Nyayo Stadium, at the junction of Uhuru Highway and Langata Rd ☎020 201 3704, is the national stadium as well as being the headquarters of the Football Kenya Federation (ⓦfkf.co.ke) and home ground of Nairobi's top premier league team, AFC Leopards. The season runs from Feb–Nov and seats start at Ksh200.

Golf Karen Golf & Country Club, Karen Rd ☎020 3882801, ⓦkarencountryclub.org; Muthaiga Golf Club, Muthaiga Rd ☎020 3761280, ⓦmuthaigagolfclub.com; map p.100;

Royal Nairobi Golf Club, Mucai Drive, off Ngong Rd ☎020 2721630, ⓦroyalnairobigc.com; Windsor Golf & Country Club, Kigwa Rd ☎020 8562300.

Horse racing The Kenya Jockey Club's racecourse is on Ngong Road ☎0722 414598; bus #24 or matatu #111. Races are held every Sun, with general viewing free or grandstand entry for Ksh200.

Horseriding Karen Riding School, Marula Lane, Karen ☎0712 292630, ⓔgarycattermole@yahoo.com (Tues–Sun 8am–6pm).

Jogging & Hash House Harriers The jogging trails through the golf course at the *Windsor* hotel (map p.100)

1

are useful, and you can also jog in many parks and suburban streets, often in the company of others; contact the Nairobi Hash (ⓦnhhh.co.ke) for information about running with them.

Karting GP-Karting, next to *Carnivore* ☎020 6008444 or 0710 883991, map p.100 (Tues–Sun 10am–7pm), has a 500m circuit, with rides from Ksh1300.

Skating Panari Sky Centre, Mombasa Rd. Ksh700/hr, including skates (daily 11am–10pm).

Swimming Many hotel pools are open to the public for a fee. Alternatively, Nyayo Stadium (see above) has a 50m pool, or try *Splash!* water park next to *Carnivore* (see p.130) ☎020 603777 (Wed–Sun 10am–5.30pm; adults Ksh400, children aged 2½-plus Ksh350).

DIRECTORY

Air charter companies SafariLink (see below) offer charter flights from $3.50/mile for a two-seater Cessna 182. Other charter companies include: Blue Bird Aviation, Wilson Airport ☎020 6002338 or 0720 251000, ⓦbluebird aviation.com; Boskovic Air Charters Ltd, Wilson Airport ☎020 6006364 or 0733 600208, ⓦboskovicaircharters .com; East African Air Charters, Wilson Airport ☎020 6003860, ⓦeaaircharters.co.ke; Mission Aviation Fellowship, Wilson Airport ☎020 6007051, ⓦmaf.org (flights to Marsabit).

Airlines, domestic Airkenya Express, Wilson Airport ☎020 3916000, ⓦairkenya.com; ALS, Wilson Airport ☎020 6000019, ⓦals.co.ke; East African Airlines, Wilson Airport ☎020 233441 or 0720 600700; Fly540, ABC Place, Waiyaki Way, Westlands ☎020 4453252 or 0722 540540, ⓦfly540.com; Jetlink, JKI Airport ☎020 8021444 or 0737 222444, ⓦjetlink.co.ke; SafariLink, Wilson Airport ☎020 6000777 or 0734 338888, ⓦflysafarilink.com.

Airlines, international Air Madagascar, 1st floor, Hilton Building, City Hall Way ☎020 2225286; Air Tanzania, Mezzanine floor, International Life House, Mama Ngina St ☎020 2227486; British Airways, 4th Floor, The Citadel, Muthithi Rd, Westlands ☎020 3277400; Brussels Airlines, 5th floor, Bandari Plaza, Woodvale Grove, Westlands; ☎020 4443070; Delta (KLM to Amsterdam), Sound Plaza 10, Woodvale Grove, Westlands ☎020 4445500; Egyptair, Hilton Building, City Hall Way ☎020 2226821; Emirates, 20th Floor, View Park Towers, Monrovia St ☎020 3290000; Ethiopian Airlines, Bruce House, Muindi Mbingu St ☎020 2217558; Etihad, Block 1, 1st Floor, Eden Square, Westlands ☎020 3673234; Kenya Airways, Ground Floor, Sarit Centre ☎020 6422465 & 1st Floor, Barclays Plaza, Loita St ☎020 3274100 (plus Yaya Centre & Village Market); KLM, Barclays Plaza, Loita St ☎020 3274210; Qatar Airways, 2nd Floor, Barclays Plaza, Loita St ☎020 2800000; South African Airways, Mezzanine Floor, International Life House ☎020 2247342; Swiss Airlines, 1st floor, Regal Plaza, Limuru Rd, Parklands ☎020 3744045.

American Express Hemingways House, Karen Office Park, Langata Rd ☎020 2295000, ⓦexpresstravel.co.ke.

Banks and foreign exchange There are branches of Barclays, Equity Bank, Kenya Commercial Bank (KCB) and Standard Chartered everywhere, most with ATMs. All banks are closed on Sun except those at the airport, but most ATMs operate 24/7. The Central Bank of Kenya publishes a list of licensed independent forex dealers at ⓦbit.ly /KenyaForexBureaux.

Camera Repairs Try Camera Clinic (Kamae Lane, off Luthuli Ave ☎020 2222492) or Spectrum Colour Lab (ABC Place, Westlands ☎020 4448352).

Cinemas The major malls all have modern multiplex movie theatres showing recent mainstream releases. Seats cost around Ksh200–500. Daily programmes can be found in the *Nation* and the *Standard* newspapers. Venues include: Fox Cineplex, Capital Capital Centre, Mombasa Rd ☎020 3753026 or 0733 968243, ⓦfoxtheatres.co.ke (map p.100); Fox Cineplex Sarit, Sarit Centre, Westlands ☎0736 703063 or 0736 703063, ⓦfoxtheatres.co.ke (map p.128); IMAX, 20th Century Plaza, Mama Ngina St ☎0737558802 or 0737 558785, ⓦimax.or.ke (map p.104); Planet Media, Westgate Nakumatt, Westgate Mall, Westlands (map p.128); Star Flix Prestige, Prestige Plaza, Ngong Rd ☎0721 279030 (map p.102); Star Flix Village, Village Market Mall, Gigiri ☎0720 602222 (map p.100).

Dentists Peter Griffiths & Associates, Kolloh Rd, off James Gichuru Rd, Lavington ☎020 4443391 or 0722 736439, map p.102; Skye Dental, 4th floor, Junction Mall, Ngong Road ☎0734 816470, map p.102.

Doctors and hospitals Aga Khan Hospital, Third Parklands Ave ☎020 3662020, map p.102; Nairobi Hospital, Argwings Kodhek Rd ☎020 2722160, map p.102; Nazareth Hospital, Riara Ridge, outside Nairobi off the Limuru road ☎020 2017401, map p.98.

Embassies, high commissions and consulates Australia, ICIPE House, Riverside Drive, off Chiromo Rd ☎020 4277100; map p.102; Burundi, 1st Floor, Co-op Trust House, Lower Hill Road off Bunyala Road, ☎020 2719200, map p.102; Canada, Limuru Rd, Gigiri ☎020 3663000, map p.100; DR Congo, 12th floor, Electricity House, Harambee Ave ☎020 2229772, map p.104; Egypt, 24 Othaya Rd (south), off Gitanga Rd, Kileleshwa B ☎020 3870298, map p.102; Eritrea, 2nd floor, New Rehema House, Rhapta Rd ☎020 4443164 (Mon–Fri 9am–noon; visa $25; 10 days notice), map p.102; Ethiopia, State House Ave, Nairobi Hill ☎020 2732052 (visas only issued for entry by air), map p.102; France, 9th floor, Barclays Plaza, Loita St ☎020 2778000 ⓦambafrance-ke.org (can issue visas for some francophone countries in West Africa), map p.104; Germany, Ludwig Krapf House, 113 Riverside Drive ☎020 4262100, ⓦnairobi.diplo.de, map p.102; Ireland, Hon.

Consulate, Waumini House, Westlands ☎020 2444367; Italy, 9th floor, International Life House, Mama Ngina St ☎020 2247750 ⟨w⟩ambnairobi.esteri.it, map p.104; Madagascar, Ground floor, Bishop Josiah Kibira House, Waiyaki Way, Westlands ☎020 4452410, map p.102; Malawi, Sports Rd, off Waiyaki Way, Westlands ☎020 4440569, map p.102; Mozambique, 3rd floor, Bruce House, Standard St ☎020 2214191, map p.104; Netherlands, Riverside Lane, off Riverside Drive ☎020 4288000 ⟨w⟩kenia .nlembassy.org/; New Zealand, Hon. Consul, Room 2C, 2nd Floor, Mirage Plaza, Mombasa Rd, (next to Bellevue Cinema) ☎020 6001074, map p.100; Rwanda, Limuru Rd, Gigiri ☎020 7121321, ⟨w⟩kenya.embassy.gov.rw, map p.100; Seychelles, Professional House, Denis Pritt Road, Kilimani ☎020 2016322, map p.102; Somalia, Likoni Lane off Dennis Pritt Road, Kilimani ☎020 2736618, ⟨w⟩somaliaembassynairobi.com, map p.102; South Africa, 3rd floor, Roshanmaer Place, Lenana Rd ☎020 2827100, map p.102; Spain, CBA Building, 3rd Floor corner of Mara & Ragati Roads, Upper Hill ☎020 2720222, map p.102; South Sudan, 6th Floor, Bishops Gate Building, 5th Ngong Ave ☎020 2711384, map p.102; Sudan, Kabarnet Rd, off Ngong Rd, Woodley ☎020 3875118, map p.102; Tanzania, 9th floor, Reinsurance Plaza, Taifa Rd ☎020 2311948, map p.104; Uganda, Riverside Paddocks, off Riverside Drive ☎020 4445420 (visa section: Uganda House, Kenyatta Av, map p.104); UK, Upper Hill Rd, off Haile Selassie Ave ☎020 2844000, ⟨w⟩ukinkenya.fco.gov.uk, map p.102; USA, United Nations Ave, Gigiri ☎020 3636000, ⟨w⟩nairobi.usembassy.gov, map p.102; Zambia, Nyerere Rd, by Central Park ☎020 2724796, map p.102; Zimbabwe, 2 Westlands Close, Westlands Rd ☎020 3744052 (Mon–Fri 9am–noon), map p.128.

Internet There are internet cafés all over the city and plenty of wi-fi hotspots, too. In the CBD, try the many places round the junction of Loita St and Monrovia St. Most coffee-shop chains (see p.125) offer free wi-fi.

Libraries British Council Library, Upper Hill Rd ☎020 2836000 (Tues–Fri 10am–5pm, Sat 9am–noon); McMillan Memorial Library, Banda St ☎020 2224281 ext 2253 (Mon–Fri 9am–6pm, Sat 9.30am–4pm); British Institute in Eastern Africa, Laikipia Rd, off Arboretum Drive, Kileleshwa ☎020 4343190, ⟨w⟩biea.ac.uk (visits by arrangement).

Optician Maclins Sight Consultancy, Hurlingham Shopping Centre, Hurlingham Plaza ☎0720 465237.

Pharmacies Mimosa Pharmacy, Ground Floor, Junction Mall (plus branches) ☎020 3873763, map p.102; Acacia Pharmacy, ICEA Building, Kenyatta Ave ☎020 2213551, map p.104.

Post Office The GPO is on Kenyatta Ave (map p.104), offering poste restante and the usual services (Mon–Fri 8am–6pm, Sat 9am–noon).

Travel agents for airline bookings Most travel agents can book you international airline seats, but the following should be able to offer discounted seats: Akarim Agencies, ground floor, Kenyatta International Conference Centre ☎020 2218880, ⟨w⟩akarim.net, map p.104; Bunson Travel, 2nd Floor, Park Place, Limuru Rd ☎020 3685990, ⟨w⟩bunsontravek.com, map p.100; Kambo Travel, 1st floor, Mpaka House, Mpaka Rd, Westlands ☎020 4448505 or 0735 299461, ⟨w⟩kambotravels.com, map p.100.

Vaccinations Cholera, yellow fever, typhoid and hepatitis jabs can be obtained from the Inoculation Centre, City Hall, City Hall Way ☎020 2224281 ext. 2526 (Mon–Fri 8.30am–12.30pm & 2–4.30pm).

Visitor's passes/visas Visitor's pass extensions can be obtained at Nyayo House, Posta Rd, behind the GPO ☎020 2222022 (Mon–Fri 8.30am–12.30pm & 2–3.30pm).

Around Nairobi

NAIROBI PROVINCE, an area of some 690 square kilometres, ranging from agricultural and ranching land to savanna and mountain forest, used to stretch way beyond the city suburbs, but the city is increasingly filling the whole province. For visitors, most of the interest around Nairobi lies to the **south and southwest**, in the predominantly Maasai land that begins with **Nairobi National Park** and includes the watershed ridge of the **Ngong Hills** – just outside Nairobi in neighbouring Rift Valley Province. It's a striking landscape, vividly described in Karen Blixen's *Out of Africa* (see p.591).

North of the city, the land is also distinctive, with narrow valleys twisting up into the Kinangop plateau, some still filled with jungle and, it's said, leopards. In spite of that, the steep slopes here are high-value real estate, still being developed as exclusive suburbs, planted with shady gardens and festooned with security signs. To the **northwest** lies largely Kikuyu farmland, densely cultivated with corn, bananas, tea and the cash crop insecticide plant, pyrethrum.

Southeast, beyond the shanty suburb of Dandora, are the wide Athi plains, which are traditionally mostly ranching country but nowadays increasingly invaded by the spread of Nairobi's industrial and residential satellites.

1

Uhuru Gardens National Monument

Langata Rd, 2km west of Wilson Airport • Daily 8am–6pm • Free entry to pedestrians, parking Ksh100 • Take any matatus to Langata, Karen and Ongata

The point of having a place like **Uhuru Gardens** – not to be confused with Uhuru Park (see p.107) in the CBD – is presumably to provide a location for national events when required. There isn't any obvious reason to make a special trip here, but if you're killing an hour between flights or appointments – or you've simply had enough of sitting in traffic on Langata Road – then it's certainly somewhere to stretch your legs and inspect some examples of triumphalist post-independence architecture. Most locals come here for a picnic or just to doze.

On the east side of the park is the more striking of the two Uhuru edifices, a towering 24m **obelisk**, opened in December 1986. Its base is decorated with sculptures of a dove of peace perched on the clasped hands of unity, a group of citizens cooperating to put up a flagpole and a barrel-chested worker standing ready to defend the nation with his bare hands.

On the other side of the park, an ambitious **water feature** constructed in 1978 marks a quarter century of independence in the year that saw the passing of the first president, Jomo Kenyatta. Abstract figures cooperate to hold up a monstrous, black-tiled diamond, but the lack of running water may be taking something away from the meaning.

Nairobi's forests

A colour map of Nairobi suggests a multitude of cool green spaces around the fringes of the city and, happily, over the last decade, the pretty picture has become more of a reality. Two of the most important of Nairobi's forests – the **Ngong Road Forest Sanctuary** in the west and the **Karura Forest** in the north – have been fierce battlegrounds between environmentalists and developers who had hoped to move onto these public lands amid a morass of corruption. As a new road snakes through it, the future of the Ngong Road Forest is still under some doubt, but the safety of Karura and the fine rainforest at **Olooloua**, in the southwest corner of the city, seems assured.

Karura Forest

Main entrance off Limuru Rd, 5.2km from the National Museum (map p.100); the Sigiria entrance is at the end of Thigiri Lane, off Thigiri Ridge Rd, 4.4km from Westlands roundabout • Daily 6am–6pm • Ksh600, parking Ksh100, guide Ksh300/hr • ☎ 0724 215423, ⓦ bit.ly /KaruraForest, ⓦ friendsofkarura.org • Matatus to Gachie, Denderu and Limuru serve the main entrance • Ten square kilometres

Where Nairobi's exclusive northern suburbs are divided by forest-flanked ridges and gurgling brown streams, the stretch of indigenous rainforest, gum-tree plantation and marshland that comprises **Karura Forest** has been secured and opened to visitors. Formerly notorious as a refuge for muggers and bush-meat hunters, the "squatters" who used to live in the forest were talked into moving out and taking jobs as rangers under an initiative headed up by the wife of the former British High Commissioner.

The forest is now a popular area for **jogging**, **dog-walking**, **biking** and **horseriding**. You can buy a map showing the clearly cut trails at the entrance (Ksh500), and although it's a peaceful escape from the city, you won't be alone, as several hundred local residents every day make use of it. The waterfall that is such a feature of Karura publicity is no Niagara, but for a city, it's an impressive asset, especially after heavy rain, and you can even swim in the clean pools at the bottom. Some of the grand rainforest trees near the waterfalls have been labelled, so you won't miss the giant sycamore fig, nor the steeple-like Newtonia. Most of the forest's **wildlife** is on the small side, and fairly secretive, but duikers abound and there are three species of monkeys, genets, monitor lizards and more than two hundred species of birds.

Ngong Road Forest Sanctuary

Main entrance on Ngong Rd, 1.5km west of Junction Mall, before you pass Nairobi War Cemetery (map p.100) • Daily 8am–6pm • $10 on foot, $15 with a bicycle, $20 with a horse • ☎ 020 2113358 or 0729 840715, ⊛ ngongforest.org • Take any matatus to Woodley, Dagoretti and Ngong • Six square kilometres

Formerly off-limits to all but timber thieves, medicinal bark strippers and outnumbered forest guards, the **Ngong Road Forest Sanctuary** is now safe to walk, jog, cycle or ride a horse through, thanks to increased ranger patrols and perimeter fencing. It's a particularly impressive achievement, considering that the Kibera slum (see p.108) presses up hard against the forest on its eastern flank – and, indeed, bringing Kibera residents into the forest and engaging people with conserving their natural heritage has been intrinsic to the success of the sanctuary.

This is one of the world's few indigenous forests within a capital city, harbouring more than 300 species of tree and plant, at least 120 species of birds, and mammals including bushbuck, porcupine, aardvark – and, it's said, even hyenas and leopards, unlikely as that seems. One spectacular species you probably will see is the forest's breeding **crowned eagles**, whose unmistakeable bonfire-shaped nests are often visible, high in a tree fork.

As you stroll through the glades, beneath towering, buttress-rooted forest giants, you'll also spot **red duiker** and tiny **suni** antelope and, floating near the treetops, handsome **swallowtail** butterflies marked with azure and brown that swoop down to visit damp mud patches on the paths. The forest is also the habitat of some of the best **timber** for sculpting tourist souvenirs – and that as much as the new Southern Bypass is a threat to its long-term future.

Oloolua Forest and Nature Trail

Entrance at the far southern end of Karen Rd (map p.100) • Mon–Fri 9am–4pm, Sat & Sun 9am–5.30pm • Ksh400 • ☎ 020 882571 or 0722 387137, ⊛ primateresearch.org • Citi Hoppa #24 • One square kilometre

Although not quite as extensive as Nairobi's other city forests, **Oloolua Forest** is a very attractive area in a part of the city suburbs that is conveniently close to other attractions like the AFEW Giraffe Centre and the Karen Blixen Museum. The forest serves principally as a primate sanctuary, where the **Institute of Primate Research** looks after a protected zone where they study the habits of olive baboons and vervet and colobus monkeys, as well as breeding and studying other species in captivity as the focus of tropical disease research.

You can drive into the forest reserve, or leave your car at the barrier and walk. You immediately come to a picturesque bridge over the jungle-swathed Mbagathi River. The forest reserve contains caves (Mau Mau hiding places, naturally), bamboo thickets, a waterfall, papyrus groves and a campsite and picnic area. The marked, 3km **nature trail** takes about ninety minutes to walk, with regular stops to watch monkeys, birds and butterflies. Or you could drive round slowly in about half an hour.

Nairobi National Park

Daily 6am–7pm (map p.100) • $40 with Safari Card (see p.71) or $65 "package" including the Animal Orphanage and Safari Walk • Park and Kenya Wildlife Service Headquarter ☎ 020 2423423 or 020 2587435, ⊛ bit.ly/NairobiNP

Despite the hype, it really is remarkable that the plains and woodland making up **Nairobi National Park** should exist almost uncorrupted within earshot of Nairobi's downtown traffic, complete with more than eighty species of large mammals, including all the giant savanna species with the exception of the elephant. It boasts the greatest density of **megafauna** of any city park in the world. There is, in fact, no comparable park anywhere. In contrast to the pitted streets of the city, gridlocked with traffic, the park is a haven of tranquil wilderness where humans have only temporary landing rights.

The park is a good place to spend time during a flight layover, or before an afternoon or evening flight, and you have a high chance of seeing certain species, especially black rhino, which might well elude you in the bigger Kenyan parks. Although it is fenced along its northern perimeter, the park is open to the south, in theory allowing migrating herds, and the predators that follow them, to come and go more or less freely. For all the low-flying planes and minibuses, you have a greater chance of witnessing a kill here than in any other park in Kenya.

Around the park

The first couple of hours after dawn are always best for **game-watching**. Try asking the rangers on arrival and you'll get the latest news: "Number 12 for a cheetah; mother and baby black rhino at 6A; lions at number 20...", the numbers referring to the road junctions, marked on every map of the park. The highest point in the western part of the park, **Impala Hill**, is a good spot to pause and scan the park with binoculars. It's also a picnic site, with toilets.

The Mbagathi or Athi River, forming the park's **southern boundary**, is its only permanent river and fringed with the yellow acacias that early explorers and settlers dubbed "fever trees" because they seemed to grow in the areas where malaria was most common. Flowing into the Mbagathi, several of the park's seasonal streams are dammed to regulate the water supply; in the dry season, these **dams** – all located on the northern side of the park where the streams come down off the Embakasi plain to the north – draw the densest concentrations of animals. **Hippos** can usually be viewed at a pretty pool at the confluence of the Mbagathi and Athi rivers (junction #12), beyond the "Leopard Cliffs", which has the added attraction of a **nature trail** and **picnic site** where you can leave your vehicle and disappear into the thickets for closer communion with nature (there's usually an armed ranger on guard). As you're wandering, look out for **crocodiles** in the river, which look little different from submerged logs to an untrained eye, and **monkeys** in the bushes.

Cheetah Gate, in the far southeast of the park, is permanently closed, but it's worth driving down here to visit the lovely **Mokoyeti picnic site** at junction #14B, near the Leopard Cliffs where the Mokoyeti stream flows into the Mbagathi, just below Mbagathi gorge. This route gives you a chance to drive through the open savanna country favoured by **zebra** and **antelope**. Impossibly tall **giraffe** browse from the underside of flat-topped acacia trees; bevies of graceful, high-heeled **impalas** vault across the track ahead of your vehicle; stocky **eland** munch the sward; **ostriches** appear to float above the landscape like giant feather dusters; and fearsome phalanxes of **buffalo** turn and face as you drive by.

The Ivory Burning Site

If you're looking for a spot to **picnic**, go a couple of kilometres in from the main gate, to the first fork. There's a shady site on the left, beside the **Ivory Burning Site**, the location of the public burning of twelve tonnes of ivory, in 1989, by President Moi to mark the start of a major, very successful offensive on ivory poaching and smuggling, led by the then-director of the Kenya Wildlife Service, Dr Richard Leakey.

Big cats

If you arrive early, start if possible at the western end of the park, where most of the woodland is concentrated. If you're very lucky, this is where, just after dawn, you're most likely to see a **leopard**, perhaps back from a nocturnal foray into Langata, hunting for guard dogs. Such forays are becoming a bit of a problem: 2012 saw two lionesses on the loose in this affluent part of suburban Nairobi, one of which, with four cubs, was eventually shot by Kenya Wildlife Service rangers (the cubs were saved).

Lions, usually found in more open country, are generally best located by checking with the rangers at the gate: their excursions into suburban areas are blamed by some authorities on the high proportion of male lions in the park, causing vulnerable females with cubs to leave and pick on domestic animals and livestock. Such a scenario led to

THE NAIROBI MIGRATION

Until the end of the twentieth century, the park witnessed the second-largest **herbivore migration** after that of the Mara and Serengeti, with thousands of wildebeest and zebra streaming in from the south in July and August for the good grazing. Before 1946, when the park was created, only the physical barrier of Nairobi itself diverted what was a general northward migration on towards the Aberdare range and the foothills of Mount Kenya. The erection of fences along the park's northern perimeter closed that migration route, while the steady encroachment of housing, industry, farms and livestock grazing along the southern boundary is also tightening the **wildlife corridor** there. The wildebeest you see nowadays are mostly sedentary individuals that stay in the park all year, and the migration has been reduced, in most years, to a trickle. Conservationists are, however, determined to keep the southern corridor open, claiming that to fence the park (partly a response to fears about lion and rhino poaching) would effectively suffocate its ecosystem, which depends on free-ranging wildlife to be sustainable. The "Friends of Nairobi National Park" (☎0723 690686, ⓦfonnap.wordpress.com) have the full story on this and much more about the park.

the killing, also in 2012, of two lionesses and four cubs in Kitengela, a densely populated area outside the southeast corner of the park, by Maasai youths who were incensed that their livestock had been attacked. With only around 2000 lions in the whole country, the killings caused a public outcry and also drew criticism for KWS for failing to respond quickly enough with a darting team.

There are usually a few **cheetahs** in the park, though seasonal long grass can make seeing them very difficult and they are inclined to move in and out between the park and the big rangelands south of the built-up area around Athi River.

Rhinos

It's much easier than spotting spotted cats to see some of the park's fifty-odd **black rhinos**, which are most often found in the forest glades in the west. The park has one of the largest populations anywhere in Kenya, attesting in part to the perseverance of the David Sheldrick Wildlife Trust (see p.144). You'll also see nice groups of the much more docile and approachable **white rhinos** (again, there are at least fifty), easily distinguished from the other species not by colour but by their grazing habits and consequent wide (*weid*: Afrikaans) mouths compared with the hook-lipped features of the black rhino that likes to lurk in dense bush and uses its almost prehensile upper lip to browse trees and shrubs.

Birdlife

The park's **birdlife** is staggering: four hundred-plus species have been seen here, including migrant rarities from European latitudes as well as the rich local avifauna flitting and chattering all around – babblers, weavers, flycatchers and widow birds. Even if you're fresh off the plane and ornithologically illiterate, the first glimpses of ostrich, secretary bird, crowned crane and the outlandishly hideous marabou stork never fail to impress.

Nairobi Education Centre & Animal Orphanage

Inside the Main Gate • Daily 8am–6.30pm • $15, children $5 • ☎ 020 2587435, ⓦ bit.ly/AnimalOrphanage

Mainly intended for children, the **Animal Orphanage** is moderately interesting if you're fed up with seeing wildlife only from a distance. Here, a motley and shifting collection of waifs and strays, protected from nature, has for some years been allowed to regain strength before being released. That, anyway, was the idea, though many of the inmates seem to be established residents and it appears doubtful whether "this orphanage is not a zoo", as the sign claims. At least it's a zoo with a difference, with as many wild monkeys outside the cages as in them, and good opportunities for meeting and petting the tamer inmates.

1

Nairobi Safari Walk

Inside the Main Gate • Daily 8am–6.30pm • $20, children $10 • ☎ 020 2423423 or 020 2587435, ⓦ bit.ly/SafariWalk

More inspiring than the orphanage is the **Nairobi Safari Walk**. Showcasing Kenya's great ecological diversity, the walk simulates the country's wetlands, savanna and forest in a captivating, semi-natural environment. This is the closest you can come to seeing captive animals behaving as they would in their natural habitats. The boardwalks to the open-air pens, observation points and platforms are clearly signposted and full of useful information about the animals. Also accessible from the walk is the *Rangers Restaurant* (see p.130), which has a veranda in the forest and overlooks a small floodlit water hole.

The David Sheldrick Wildlife Trust

Access via the park's Banda Gate (map p.100), signposted "Sheldrick", a 5min drive (park fees are waived) • Daily 11am–noon and, by private arrangement, from 4pm onwards for "foster parents" sponsoring a minimum of $50; office open Mon–Fri 9am–5pm • Ksh500 • ☎ 020 2301396, ⓦ sheldrickwildlifetrust.org

The **David Sheldrick Wildlife Trust** elephant and rhino orphanage, inside the western end of the park, offers a chance to see staff caring for baby elephants, and sometimes baby rhino, which have been orphaned by poachers, or have been lost or abandoned for natural reasons. The trust is run by Daphne Sheldrick in memory of her husband, the founding warden of Tsavo National Park, and, during the hour-long open house, the elephant keepers bring their juvenile charges up to an informal rope barrier where you can easily touch them and take photos.

After many years of trial and error, Sheldrick and her staff have become the world's experts on hand-rearing baby African elephants, sometimes from birth, using a special milk formula for the youngest infants and assigning keepers to individual 24-hour guardianship of their charges, a responsibility that includes sleeping in their stables. Without the love of a surrogate family and plenty of stimulation, orphaned baby elephants fail to thrive: they can succumb to fatal infections when teething, and, even if they survive, can grow up disturbed and unhappy and badly prepared for reintroduction to the wild.

Rehabilitation is one of the Sheldrick Trust's major preoccupations. For rhinos, which mature at twice the speed of elephants, this involves a year or more of walks with their keeper, introducing the orphan's scent, via habitual dung middens and "urinal" bushes, to the wild population. Many of Nairobi National Park's rhinos grew up in the Sheldrick nursery; the last surviving member of Amboseli's famous long-horned rhino herd was rescued by the Trust in 1987 and is now a successful breeding female, having been released in Tsavo East. In the case of elephants, which mature at about the same rate as humans, the process of reintroduction is more attuned to the individual: outgoing animals are encouraged while young to meet wild friends and potential adoptive mothers, again through walks with their keepers, most often in Tsavo National Park. More traumatized elephants take longer to find their feet. Matriarchs who were Sheldrick orphans them-selves, such as Eleanor at Tsavo East, have been responsible for adopting many returnees.

ARRIVAL AND INFORMATION   **NAIROBI NATIONAL PARK**

The park is accessible via the **Main Gate**, Langata Rd; **Langata Gate**, Magadi Rd; **East Gate**, Mombasa Rd (enabling you to avoid retracing your route from the park's western end if you're going to the airport or the CBD); **Banda Gate**, Magadi Rd (David Sheldrick Wildlife Trust only); and **Maasai Gate**, Ongata–Kitengela Rd. The Mbagathi Gate, Magadi Rd, & Cheetah Gate, Mombasa Rd, are closed to the public.

By matatu and hitchhiking Early birds can get an early #125 bus or #126 matatu to the main gate; after 7am you can use any bus or matatu going down Langata Rd. Once at the main gate, either hitch for a lift (which may take some time), or, on Sun, take the KWS park shuttle (Sun only, 2–4.30pm; $20; advance booking required).

By car You can self-drive in a rental car: 4WD is preferable, but not essential in dry weather, while a satnav or a smartphone with GPS is useful for navigation.
Tours Any tour operator will fix you up with a half-day tour – try East Africa Shuttles (☎ 020 2248453, ⓦ eastafrica shuttles.com), which charges $110 for 4hr, including park fee (see p.115).

The Bomas of Kenya

Forest Edge Rd (400m north of the junction at Galleria Mall; map p.100) • Shows Mon–Fri 2.30–4pm, Sat, Sun & holidays 3.30–5.15pm • Ksh600 • ☎ 020 8068400, ⊕ bomasofkenya.co.ke • Bus/matatu #15, #125 or #126

The **Bomas of Kenya** were originally an attempt to create a living museum of Kenyan culture, with a display of eleven traditional homesteads (*bomas*) and an emphasis on regional dances. Unfortunately, the place has always had a touristy feel, not helped by the huge indoor **amphitheatre** where the dances are performed. In fact the vitality of the Bomas is channelled mainly into souvenir-selling and conferences, most famously the constitutional conference of 2003 leading to the so-called Bomas draft constitution calling for decentralized government. The ethnic homesteads re-creating Kenya's vernacular architecture (a guided tour of which is included in the price) are for the most part sadly unkempt. Even so, if you're looking to fill an afternoon, they can be enjoyable enough, particularly on weekends, when they're busier, and when an evening disco sometimes follows the dance show.

Surprisingly, perhaps, the dances are not performed by the appropriate Kenyan tribes; instead, the **Harambee Dancers** do fast costume changes between acts and present the nation's traditional repertoire as professional performers rather than participants. If the acoustics were better and the whole place less of an amphitheatre, the impression would undoubtedly be stronger. As it is, you at least get a very comprehensive taste of Kenyan dance styles, from the mesmeric jumps and sinuous movements of the Maa-speaking peoples, to the wild acrobatics of some of the Mijikenda dances.

AFEW Giraffe Centre

Koitobos Rd, 3km off Langata Road (signposted; map p.100) • Daily 9am–5.30pm • Ksh1000, children Ksh500 • ☎ 020 8070804 or 0734 890952, ⊕ giraffecenter.org • Citi Hoppa #24

Although it tends to be promoted as a children's outing, the **AFEW Giraffe Centre** has serious aims. Run by the African Fund for Endangered Wildlife, it has successfully boosted the population of the rare **Rothschild's giraffe** from an original nucleus of animals that came from a wild herd near Soy (see p.284). Its other main mission is to educate children about conservation. You'll get some great mug shots from the giraffe-level observation tower, where the giraffes push their huge heads through to be fed the feed pellets you're given to offer them. There are various other animals around, including a number of tame **warthogs**, and a wooded 95-acre **nature sanctuary** across the road – a great birdwatching opportunity. If you really like it here, and have deep pockets, stay overnight at the wonderful, country-house-style **Giraffe Manor** (p.123).

Karen

Always associated with its famous former resident, the author **Karen Blixen** (pen name Isak Dinesen), the suburb of **KAREN** was actually named after her cousin, Karen Melchior, whose father was the chairman of the Karen Coffee Company – the estate that was sold for residential development and named Karen – though most people, including Blixen herself, were not aware of the coincidence.

While the number of African residents is rising steadily, until recently, Karen was the quintessential white suburb – five-acre plots spaciously set on eucalyptus-lined avenues amid fields grazed by horses. Still separated from Nairobi by the dense, bird-filled woodland of the Ngong Road Forest (see p.141), Karen is a reminder of how completely the settlers visualized and created little Europes for themselves. In parts of Karen, you could almost be in the English shires – or, for that matter, northern California.

If you're driving the most direct route to Karen from the city centre, along Ngong Road, you pass **Jamhuri Park**, the Agricultural Society of Kenya showground (see p.67), the **racecourse** (see p.137), and the **Nairobi War Cemetery**, a peaceful and dignified

1

World War II cemetery, set far back from the busy road among shady trees, with pink stonework and carefully tended lawns.

Karen's central **shopping centre**, at the crossroads of the Langata and Ngong roads, officially now called Karen Connection, but usually referred to as Karen *dukas*, includes a growing cluster of safari businesses, banks and other services. The whole area now feels much less like a country crossroads and much more like a town centre, especially with the arrival of the big new **Nakumatt Crossroads**.

Karen Blixen Museum

Karen Rd, 3.5km south of Karen crossroads • Daily 9.30am–6pm • Ksh800, although note that temporary membership of the museum society (see p.110) costs only Ksh500 and allows free entry • ☏ 020 882779, ⓦ museums.or.ke • Citi Hoppa #24; alternatively, organized tours, which may also include the AFEW Giraffe Centre, cost $70–100

The **Karen Blixen Museum** is located in the house where much of the action of Karen Blixen's autobiographical memoir *Out of Africa* (see p.591) took place. The epitome of colonial Africa, the **house** was presented to Kenya by the Danish government as an Uhuru gift at the time of independence, along with the agricultural college built in the grounds – the **gardens**, laid out as in former times, are delightful.

It's a beautiful, well-proportioned home with square, wood-panelled rooms, and the restoration of its original appearance and furnishings has evidently been very thorough. A guided tour is included in the price but can be somewhat rushed, especially at weekends, and there's no guarantee that they'll let you wander around on your own. They certainly don't like you to take photos of the old black and white pictures.

On weekends you may be somewhat suffocated by a surfeit of Mozart (the favourite composer of Karen Blixen's lover, Denys Finch Hatton), and by tour groups complaining about how little Finch Hatton resembles Robert Redford. The fake-1920s Nairobi that was built nearby for the shooting of *Out of Africa* would have been a magnetic attraction, but the dictates of licensing agreements ensured its demolition once the film crews left.

There's a restaurant, bar and cottage rooms at a 1912 Swedish coffee plantation manager's residence, now the Karen Blixen Coffee Garden, 336 Karen Road, 500m north of the museum (ⓦ karenblixencoffeegarden.com).

The Ngong Hills

Walk or drive from Ngong police station • Daily dawn–dusk • Ksh500 (plus negotiable security escort fee) • Matatu or bus #111 or #126

The town of **NGONG**, the jumping-off point for the **Ngong Hills**, is 8km past Karen shopping centre; turn right after the police station in Ngong. If you have the chance, stop on the way at **Bulbul**, 4km from Karen, and take a look at the pretty mosque of this largely Muslim village. As often happened in Kenya, Islam spread here through the settlement of discharged troops from other British-ruled territories, in this case from Nubia in Sudan. Ngong itself is basically just a small junction town with limited shops and services and the rough D523 road trailing out to the west towards the Maasai Mara.

The Ngong Hills are revered by the Maasai, who have several traditional explanations of how they were formed. The best known says that a giant, stumbling north with his head in the clouds, tripped on Kilimanjaro. Thundering to the ground, his hand squeezed the earth into the Ngongs' familiar, knuckled outline. An even more momentous story explains the Ngongs as the bits of dirt left under God's fingernails after he'd finished creating the earth.

The walk along the sharp spine of the Ngong Hills was once a popular weekend hike and picnic outing, easily feasible in a day, although, unfortunately, the hills got a reputation for muggings in the 1980s, curtailing independent expeditions, and KWS rangers usually now provide an escort (negotiable, from Ksh1000 per ranger for 3hr). The views, of Nairobi on one side and the Rift Valley on the other, are magnificent, and despite the wind farm at the northern end of the hills, the forested slopes are still inhabited by buffalo and various species of antelope. With a car – and it has to be

4WD if it's been raining – you can get to the summit, **Point Lamwia** (2459m), which offers a 360-degree view. If you want to walk, and are reasonably fit, allow a minimum of three hours to get to the top and back to your car. Alternatively, you could organize transport to meet you west of Kiserian, on the C58 Magadi road, and spend four to five hours traversing the length of the peaks, a walk of about 15km.

On the ridges below the summit, on privately owned land, almost due east of the highest point, is the **Finch Memorial**, Karen Blixen's tribute to the man who took her flying.

Brown's Cheese Farm

Tigoni, 7km west of the Kentmere Club (map p.98), 30min drive from Village Market • Daily noon–2.30pm (advance booking essential) • Ksh2500 per person including tasting plate, minimum 4 people • ☎ 0728 999654, ⓦ brownscheese.com

This artisanal family **cheese-maker** has cracked the art of producing something exceptional while making its production the basis for a fascinating visit. You can buy a huge variety of their cheeses here, too. Cheese, which you quickly learn is all about keeping the harvest season's calories for the lean season, is created here using biodynamic principles. The explanation of the process rolls around as you stroll through the admirably cottage-sized factory from the warm steel milk pans to the deliciously mysterious storage rooms, all maintained with specific temperatures and humidities depending on their contents.

The tour finishes in the family dining room overlooking the biodynamic kitchen garden, where everything grows by the principles set out by Rudolf Steiner (no artificial additives, planting with the moon, and no tilling or weeding, everything being dug back in). Guests sample a slate of delicious **cheese morsels** with home-made crackers and a glass or two of wine, followed by an excellent three-course **lunch**: you really should skip breakfast if you're visiting Brown's – or perhaps book the slightly more expensive and longer afternoon tour.

Kiambethu Farm

Past Limuru Girl's School, 7km west of the Kentmere Club (map p.98) • Lunch and afternoon tea (advance booking essential) Ksh3000 per person (minimum four people) • ☎ 020 2012542 or 0733 769976, ⓦ kiambethufarm.co.ke

A visit to the working **Kiambethu tea farm** gives you the opportunity to sample the charmingly time-warped settler lifestyle (albeit a third-generation, naturalized one) over a very good lunch. The farmhouse is set in a glorious highland garden, with sweeping lawns and a colourful riot of flowers and tropical birds. To work up an appetite you take a stroll with the owners up the lane, past bushes full of chameleons to the edge of one of the tea fields, where a swathe of neatly plucked shrubs plunges into the valley. A little further, there's a relict patch of highland rainforest – standing proud in a sea of tea bushes – where you'll be escorted on a short forest walk, during which you've a good chance of seeing some of Kiambethu's resident colobus monkeys.

Southeast of Nairobi

Until a couple of decades ago, **Athi River**, 25km southeast of Nairobi, consisted of a railway station and the Kenya Meat Commission processing plant. Then the real-estate marketeers got to work and suddenly the dusty plains around the river became a desirable commuter neighbourhood. But the meat factory was still there, and so the developers invented the new suburb of **Kitengela**, a few kilometres further south, beyond the smell of the factory, where Maasai herders roamed and the wildebeest and gazelle herds – and the odd cheetah – moved in and out of the Nairobi National Park.

Today, driving into Kitengela up the A104 from the Tanzanian border, the new town is a harbinger of Nairobi: what was Maasai pasture lands in the 1990s has become a wide main street lined with canteens, petrol stations and soaring apartment blocks, as well as unplanned shanties. Just as well, then, that a few kilometres outside this

1

burgeoning residential zone, the **Lukenya Plains** are still home to cheetah and most other plains species, and they have some protection in the shape of **Swara Plains Sanctuary** – a former game ranch (see below).

ACCOMMODATION AND EATING
SOUTHEAST OF NAIROBI

★ **Acacia Camp Swara Plains**, 11km southeast of the Kitengela junction (turning for the A104 Namanga and Arusha), turn right at Small World (see below) and follow signs ☎ 0733 812556 or 0733 912994, ⒲ swaraplains.com; map p.98. The former *Hopcraft Ranch*, which once supplied game meat to the *Carnivore* (see p.130), is now a wildlife conservancy and offers the perfect solution if you want to avoid Nairobi on your first or last night. Rustic s/c *bandas*, with decent bathrooms, nets, electricity and plug sockets, encircle a pretty garden, with a pleasant bar-restaurant to one side. Casual meals are available (Ksh1500–2000) – the food is surprisingly good, though you should call a day in advance to book. Overnight

camping and *banda* rates include the conservancy fee of Ksh500 per person. Camping Ksh1000 per person, HB $185
Small World 11km past the Kitengela junction (turning for Namanga and Arusha), signposted on the south side of the highway at the entrance to Swara Plains ranch (see left) ☎ 0734 818340, ⒲ klubhouse .co.ke. A perfectly okay place to spend the night, either as a prelude to driving straight to Tsavo or Mombasa the next morning or because you left it too late to reach Nairobi. The small s/c cottages have double beds and there's also wi-fi, a restaurant and bar, plus live music some weekends. Room only Ksh2500

The southern Rift Valley

The journey south from Nairobi down into the hot, sparsely inhabited southern districts of the **Rift Valley** takes you first to the prehistoric site at **Olorgasailie**, then on to the dramatic salt lake of **Magadi**, and finally to the **Nguruman Escarpment** and the remote nature conservancy at **Shompole**. The scenery opens out dramatically as you skirt the southern flank of the Ngong Hills and descend steeply down the escarpment; if you're travelling by public transport, try to get a front seat, as giraffe and other animals are often seen.

Kiserian and around

KISERIAN, 15km southwest of Nairobi National Park's main gate, is your last chance to buy decent provisions, as there's not much available further south. Once a tiny Maasai trading post tucked below the Ngong Hills, Kiserian is now the final gasp of Nairobi's sprawling suburbs, barely separated from **Ongata** – the burgeoning dormitory suburb south of Karen. The drive south from here, over the southern spine of the Ngongs, is truly spectacular.

ACCOMMODATION AND EATING
KISERIAN AND AROUND

There are several basic B&Ls in the centre of Kiserian, or you can head east to *Whistling Thorns* or the *Maasai Ostrich Farm*, or press on to Olepolos. There's a pleasant picnic site at *Olepolos Country Club* some 12km southwest of Kiserian.

Eureka Hotel Town centre, Kiserian ☎ 020 2522346; map p.98. A lively restaurant and bar with occasional live music, as well as decent s/c rooms. BB Ksh2200
Olepolos Country Club Magadi road, Olepolos, 13km southwest of Kiserian ☎ 0716 737423, ⒲ bit.ly /Olepolos. Pleasant rural picnic and camping site, *nyama choma* garden and bar (sometimes with live music), plus rooms. Camping Ksh500 per person, BB Ksh3400
Ostrich Farm Resort Maasai Ostrich Farm (go 21km southeast of Kiserian junction on the Isinya road then turn left and take the farm road a further 10km; also

accessible from Athi River) ☎ 050 2502128, ⒲ mericagrouphotels.com; map p.98. A curious combination of ostrich farm and Kenyan-country-club-style resort, incorporating pleasant, shady gardens with very overpriced s/c tented chalets with electric showers, and a glittering swimming pool, usually accompanied by country music warbling from speakers through the trees. As well as touring the farm and eating the excellent but pricey low-cholesterol meat, you can also ride the birds (Ksh300), though the warning that "Maasai Ostrich Resort is not liable for any incident that may occur during riding" is

1

probably enough to deter most would-be ostrich jockeys. Camping Ksh800 per person, BB $125

★ **Whistling Thorns** 12km southeast of Kiserian junction on the Isinya road ☎020 3540720 or 0722 721933, ⦿whistlingthorns.com; map p.98. Very pretty country guesthouse, campsite, gardens and restaurant that could practically be in Wales or Oregon if it wasn't for the Maasai jewellery for sale and the prospect of running into wandering elephants in the neighbourhood (a herd walked up here from Amboseli in 2012). While the rooms

are overpriced for what they are (go for a safari tent if one is available), the whole setup is so relaxing that they're worth every penny, while the food, if somewhat hit and miss, is hard to dislike when eaten on the terrace overlooking the garden and delightful swimming pool. There's lots of variety on the menu, including stir-fries and veggie options (Ksh500–1200), good desserts and a reasonably priced bar. Horseriding is Ksh1200/hr, with an accompanying syce. Camping Ksh500 per person, room only Ksh3900

Olorgasailie Prehistoric Site

Signposted 3km south of Oltepesi, then 1.6km from the main road • Daily dawn–dusk • Ksh500 • ⦿museums.or.ke

Between 400,000 and 500,000 years ago, the wide, shallow lake east of what is now **Olorgasailie Prehistoric Site** was inhabited by a species of hominin, probably *Homo erectus* of the Acheulian culture (after St Acheul in France, where it was first discovered). The site is endowed with numerous pathways, boardwalks and informative signs, and is a peaceful place to stay, though most people just stop here for an hour or two. The guided tour around the excavations (included in the entrance charge, tip welcomed) is not to be missed. The museum and accommodation are just above the excavations, on a ridge overlooking the former lake.

The **early people** who lived at Olorgasailie made a range of identifiable stone tools: cleavers for skinning animals; round balls for crushing bones, perhaps for hurling or possibly tied to vines to be used, like gauchos, as *bolas*; and heavy hand axes, for which the culture is best known, but for which, as Richard Leakey writes, "embarrassingly, no one can think of a good use". The guides tell you they were used for chopping meat and digging. This seems reasonable, but some are very large, while hundreds of others (particularly at the so-called "factory site") seem far too small, the theory being that they were made by youngsters, practising their toolmaking.

Mary and Louis Leakey's team did most of the unearthing here in the 1940s. Thousands of the **stone tools** they found have been left undisturbed, *in situ*, under protective roofs. Perhaps the most impressive find, however, is the fossilized leg bone of an extinct **giant elephant**, dwarfing a similar bone from a modern elephant placed next to it. It was long hoped that human remains would also be uncovered at Olorgasailie, but despite extensive digging none has been found – providing more scope for speculation.

Today, sitting with a pair of binoculars and looking out over what used to be the lake can yield some rewarding **animal-watching**, especially in the brief dusk. Go for a walk out past the excavations towards the gorge and you may see baboons, duiker, giraffe, eland and even gerenuk if you're lucky – Olorgasailie is the westernmost extent of their range in southern Kenya.

ARRIVAL AND DEPARTURE	**OLORGASAILIE**

By matatu If you don't have your own transport, find out when the next matatu along the road between Lake Magadi and Nairobi will be passing by, as they are few and far between.

By car If you're driving, the road from Kiserian to Oltepesi, which marks the end of the steep descent to the Rift Valley floor, is badly potholed. Thereafter it's reasonably smooth for most of the way to Magadi.

ACCOMMODATION

Olorgasailie Bandas Olorgasailie Prehistoric Site ⦿bit.ly/Olorgasailie; map p.98. Simple *bandas* – four new and presentable with twin beds, bedding, nets and kerosene lamps; four old and decrepit with beds and bedding only. Separate tepid shower and long-drop toilet

blocks are also available, plus a couple of sit-down loos for site visitors. Maasai ladies sell firewood for Ksh200–300/ bundle, but that is the only commodity available on site apart from occasional sodas. Camping Ksh250 per person, old *bandas* Ksh500, new *bandas* Ksh800

SHOPPING

Contacts with Maasai are good at Olorgasailie and there's jewellery for sale under a sponsored shelter. You can cultivate further friendships – and collect some scant provisions – at the cluster of desolate *dukas* at **Oltepesi**, 3km back along the Nairobi road, where they also have warm beer and soft drinks.

Lake Magadi and around

Lying in a Rift Valley depression 1000m below Nairobi, **Lake Magadi** is a vast shallow pool of soda (sodium carbonate), a sludge of alkaline water and crystal trona deposits, and one of the hottest places in the country. Magadi is also the second-largest source of soda in the world, after the Salton Sea in the USA. At Magadi, the Magadi Soda Company – formerly an ICI business, now owned by the Indian company Tata – operates the very model of a **company town**, on a barren spit of land jutting out across the multicoloured soda. The company's investment here is guaranteed – hot springs gush out of the earth's crust to provide an inexhaustible supply of briney water for evaporation. Everything you see, apart from the homes of a few Maasai on the shore, is owned and run by the corporation. You pass a company police barrier where you sign in and enter over a causeway, past surreal pink salt ponds, often flocked by flamingos. Now on company territory, a sign advises visitors that "it is dangerous to walk across the lake surface", just in case you were contemplating a stroll across the soda. Note that some of the company police are touchy about you taking photos of the factory installations. Despite this, the atmosphere here, somewhat surprisingly because of the nature of the work and harshness of the environment, is relaxed and welcoming. By comparison with the rest of Kenya, the company pays its 700 staff high wages, starting at around Ksh20,000 per month; people tend to get drunk a lot, and staff accommodation and many services are free.

Many visitors come to Magadi specifically for its **birdlife**. There's a wealth of avifauna here, including, usually, large numbers of flamingos at the southern end of the lake. At this end, there are also freshwater swamps, which attract many species.

Around the lake

The lake lies behind the police station, which stands on the highest point of the peninsula. If you look the other way (to the west), the road to the left leads to the "management" end of town, where a dozen or so senior staff live in shady villas and where there's a strange, barren golf course; to the right, the town slopes gently down to a crusty shore where most of the Kenyan employees live in gaunt blocks of apartments. There's also a church, a mosque, schools and a glittering swimming pool, poolside bar and *nyama choma* kiosk.

For most of the year, on the eastern side where you first arrive, you can watch the **sweepers** in rubber boots shovelling the by-product, sodium chloride, or common salt, into ridges on the technicolour "fields" (after heavy rain, the dilute solution removes the need for manual labour in the lake and all the work is done by dredging machines). Common salt crystallizes on top of the sodium carbonate, and is then loaded onto tractor-drawn trailers and taken away to be purified for human and animal consumption.

Magadi **soda**, used principally for glass-making, is Kenya's most valuable mineral resource. The dried soda is exported, first by rail to Mombasa via Kajiado and Konza, thence, much of it, to Japan. Despite the relatively high wages, however, you wonder how anyone can be persuaded to work in this lurid inferno: the first rains here are usually so-called phantom rain, the ground so hot that the raindrops evaporate before hitting the surface. It's important to wear sunglasses and a hat while out in the sun, and bring plenty of drinking water.

1

Magadi Hot Springs

With your own vehicle you can drive south from Magadi town, around the lake to the **hot springs** in the southwest corner. You're very likely to find a local in town who'll offer to guide you there. On the south side of Magadi town, 1km south of Magadi Sports Club, you reach a checkpoint for the **Magadi Community Eco-Tourism Project**. If there's anyone there, you pay Ksh300 per person, Ksh300 per car and Ksh300 per person to camp. If you find the gate open and nobody about, just carry on: somebody will find you at the hot springs and take payment there.

It's a further, straightforward 14–15km to the hot springs (not 10km as the checkpoint sign advises), reached by driving south along the eastern shore of the lake. The precise route you take will depend on how much water is flowing into the lake from the higher ground to the south. Depending on the time of year, you'll be able to cut across sandy, desert-like areas, following other vehicle tracks, but don't venture onto unknown surfaces without a good guide.

At the **hot springs**, you'll be able to park near the water's edge and camp nearby if you are fully equipped. Local Maasai will appear to sell jewellery. The springs bubble up into the shallow waters of the lake itself and create deep pockets of perfectly mixed bathing water. Do take great care to find the right spot, however, and don't attempt to bathe without getting clear confirmation that it is safe to do so.

The **birdlife** here is fascinating, and if you're a photographer you will delight in the contrast of pink flamingos, shimmering water and the austere, background landscape.

Shompole Conservancy

From the Magadi hot springs, you can drive west to the Ewaso Nyiro River at the foot of the Ol Choroi plateau, also known as the **Nguruman Escarpment**. Forget about trying to take a 4WD up the rough track beyond the river, over the escarpment and on to the Mara. People have done that in the past, but the whole area is privately owned Maasai land and, for the moment at least, not accessible.

This whole area focuses around the 142-square-kilometre **Shompole Conservancy**, an ecotourism venture involving the Maasai Shompole Group Ranch. Access to the highly appealing *Shompole Lodge* is usually by chartered plane to their private **airstrip**, but the lodge closed in 2011 after a dispute with the community, and it's not clear when it will reopen.

If you have a guide, it's straightforward enough to drive right **around the lake**, up the west shore, joining the Magadi–Nguruman road after 18km. You then drive east on the good gravel road back to Lake Magadi, crossing the northwest arm of the lake on a causeway and driving right through the industrial part of town – a fascinating clash of railway tracks and furnaces, rusting pipework and traditionally dressed Maasai.

ARRIVAL AND INFORMATION   LAKE MAGADI

By matatu There are matatus between Magadi town and Nairobi (2 daily; 3hr) and Olorgasailie (2 daily; 1hr). The first matatu to Nairobi leaves at 5am. There are no regular vehicles south of Magadi. Everyone waits for lifts either in a passing vehicle, or on the back of a motorbike. If you don't have your own transport, you should wait in town and see what turns up.

By car Apart from along the main Magadi–Nguruman road

(which isn't much used and is in good condition), driving south of the lake it's best to go with a guide: even with GPS, the tracks change so often that you shouldn't rely on satellite imagery or previous tracks – routes around the lakeshore and across areas that have dried out are very unpredictable.

Services There's a Co-operative Bank with ATM on Duka Hill Rd, in the building behind the Total station. Note that there's very patchy mobile coverage in this part of Kenya.

ACCOMMODATION AND EATING

MAGADI TOWN

There are two places to stay (map p.98), but you need to call ahead or send a text in good time – not so much to ensure there is a free room as to make sure the relevant

key-holder is around to meet you and take payment. If you're fully self-sufficient, you could possibly camp almost anywhere south of the town, but it's baking hot during the day and a favourite haunt for baboons, so hardly ideal

1

territory. In a pinch, you're likely to be invited home by employees. For provisions and limited fresh food, Magadi has barely any shops, but there is a daily market. On the western shore of the lake, local Maasai will sell you *pombe* (bush brew), fermented from a base of roots, herbs and honey. It's a lot cheaper than beer, and stronger, too.

Flamingo Club Southern side of Magadi town, signposted east of the road. Mid-market watering hole with food available if ordered well in advance, and a pleasant enough terrace. Daily 7am–10pm.

Lower Guesthouse Opposite the hospital, Magadi, reservations through Magadi Eco-Tourism ☎0721 698052. Simple rooms with shared bathrooms. Room only **Ksh2000**

Magadi Sports Club (MSC) Southern end of Magadi town, reservations through the company ☎020 6999201. The most "upmarket" option in town, with basic rooms, some s/c, plus a bar-restaurant and a nice swimming pool and garden terrace. Room reservations essential. BB **Ksh5000**

★ **Swimming Pool Club** Town centre, Magadi. Far and away Magadi's best option for rest and recuperation, with decent *hoteli* fare (Ksh150–300) and ample cold sodas (Ksh70) and beers (Ksh140) to consume on the terrace – not to mention the large and inviting pool. Daily 7am–midnight.

SHOMPOLE CONSERVANCY

While *Shompole Lodge* remains closed, the only accommodation inside Shompole Conservancy is at *Loisijo Lodge*, or you can camp wild near the hot springs or use the tents at *Olaika Campsite* (map p.98).

Loisijo Lodge Shompole Conservancy ☎020 3533338 or 0722 515377, ⦾loisiijolodgeshompole.org. The former *Shompole Bandas* have been revamped as a beautiful self-catering or catered lodge tucked under fig trees on the banks of the Ewaso Nyiro sleeping a total of 12. If you're self-catering, you get the services of a cook and other staff included, but unless you book the whole lodge ($450/night) you can only confirm a stay within 48 hours of arrival. Self-catering **Ksh4000** per person, FB (minimum 2-night stay) **$240**

Olaika Campsite Oloita village, Shompole Group Ranch, 23km south of the fork ("Shompole Oloika, Hot Spring"), at the southern end of Magadi town ☎0726 956693 (reservations in Kiserian ☎0721 473925). Basic, mosquito-proof safari tents in a field, with limited shade, modern ablutions block and *chai na chapatti* for breakfast. There's plenty of game in the area, including zebra, wildebeest and (apparently) lions. BB **Ksh1500**

The Central Highlands

TRIBAL DANCERS, KATARINA

The Central Highlands

There are some great rewards to travel through the Central Highlands, Kenya's political and economic heartland. Mount Kenya, Africa's second-highest peak, gave the colonial nation its name and offers visitors numerous hiking opportunities. And, while hikes lower down and in the Aberdare range are easier, they are still dramatic, with the added bonus that you might see some wildlife. Travel itself is never dull here, and the range of scenery is a spectacular draw in its own right: primary-coloured jungle and shambas, pale, windswept moors and dense conifer plantations, all with a mountain backdrop. People everywhere are friendly and quick to strike up a conversation, the towns are animated and the markets colourfully chaotic. Most roads are in good shape and bus and matatu journeys invariably packed with interest and amusement.

After the main game-viewing areas and the coast, the circuit provided by the **Mount Kenya ring road** is one of the most travelled in Kenya, and there are always a few tourist vehicles to be seen. Apart from the high forests, moors and peaks, little of this remains wild country, with *shambas* steadily encroaching the ridges. The Kikuyu, Meru and Embu peoples have created an extraordinary spectacle of cultivation on the steep slopes, gashed by the road to reveal brilliant red earth.

As you travel, the mountain is a constant, looming presence, even if you can't often see much of it. With a base 80km across, Mount Kenya is one of the largest free-standing volcanic cones in the world. The twin peaks are normally obscured by clouds, but early in the morning and just before sunset the shroud can vanish suddenly, leaving them magically exposed for a few minutes. To the east and south, the mountain drops steeply away to the broad expanse of Ukambani (Kamba-land) and the Tana River basin. Westwards, and to the north, it slopes away more gently to the rolling uplands of Laikipia.

The **Aberdare range**, which peaks at 4001m, is less well known than Mount Kenya. The lower, eastern slopes have long been farmed by the Kikuyu (and more recently by European tea and coffee planters), and the dense mountain forests covering the middle reaches are the habitat of leopard, buffalo, some six thousand elephants and a few small herds of critically endangered bongo antelope. Above about 3500m, lions and other open-country animals roam the cloudy moorlands. Melanistic forms, especially of leopard, but also of serval cat and even bushbuck, are also present.

The park stretches 60km along the length of the peaks, with the Salient on the lower slopes reaching out east. Like Mount Kenya National Park, it attracts the worst of the weather: rainfall up here is high, often closing the park to vehicles in the wet season, although in the Salient the "tree-hotel" **game lodges** – *The Ark* and *Treetops* – stay open all year. The towns of **Naivasha** and **Nyeri** are the usual bases. **Nyahururu**, the other important town in the region, has **Thomson's Falls** as a postcard attraction, and is also the setting-off point for a wild cross-country journey to Lake Bogoria, 1500m below, in the Rift Valley (see p.232). Also from Nyahururu begins the main route to Maralal and Loiyangalani on the eastern shore of Lake Turkana (see p.519).

MOUNT KENYA

Highlights

❶ **Tana River rafting** Test the class III, IV and V whitewater rapids and bungee jump above Kenya's longest river. **See p.164**

❷ **Trout Tree** Enjoy delicious fresh fish and a treehouse setting among fig trees at this quirky restaurant. **See p.167**

❸ **Climbing Mount Kenya** Africa's second-highest mountain is a highly recommended trekking area, with various routes and diverse flora and fauna. **See p.167**

❹ **Nanyuki** Good hotels and restaurants, a beautiful climate and the best information centre in Kenya. **See p.178**

❺ **Animal orphanage** Find zehorses (zebra-horse crosses), a century-old tortoise, rare, breeding bongos, and Liberian pygmy hippos at the Mount Kenya Safari Club. See p.179

❻ **Aberdare range** Sensational views and a good chance of seeing elephants and buffaloes in a compelling highland environment. **See p.187**

❼ **Horseriding** Take a guided equestrian tour of Mount Kenya's lush green foothills – Sandai offers guided tours and there are a number of other options in and around the area. **See p.194**

HIGHLIGHTS ARE MARKED ON THE MAP ON P.158

2

KENYA'S HIGHLAND FORESTS AND MOORS

Kenya's main **highland forests** are on Mounts Kenya, Elgon and Marsabit, on the Aberdare range and on the Mau Escarpment. The characteristic natural landscape in the highlands is patches of evergreen trees separated by vast meadows of grasses – often wire grass and Kikuyu grass. The true highland forest, typically found only above 1500m, contains different species of trees from lowland forest, and does not normally grow as tall or dense. Typical species include camphor, *Juniperus procera* (the East African "cedar") and *Podocarpus*. The better-developed forests are found on the wetter, western slopes of the highlands. Above the forest line, at altitudes of 2500m and higher, you get stands of giant bamboo, while along the lower, drier edges of the highlands, the stands of trees tend to be interspersed with fields of tall grass, where you commonly also find various species of olive.

Brief history

The Central Highlands are utterly central to Kenyan history. The majority of British and European settlers carved their farms from the countryside around Mount Kenya. Later, and as a direct consequence, this was the region that saw the development of organized anti-colonial resistance culminating in Mau Mau.

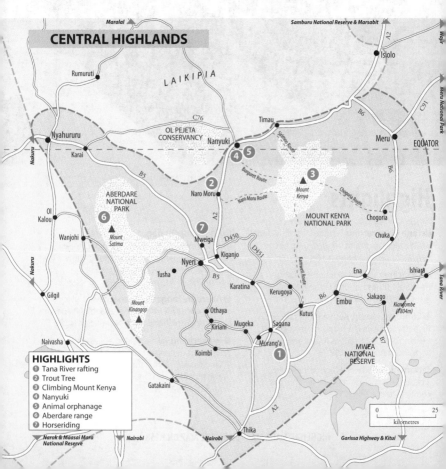

CENTRAL HIGHLANDS

HIGHLIGHTS
1. Tana River rafting
2. Trout Tree
3. Climbing Mount Kenya
4. Nanyuki
5. Animal orphanage
6. Aberdare range
7. Horseriding

Until independence, the fertile highland soils ("A more charming region is not to be found in all Africa," thought Joseph Thomson, exploring in the 1880s) were reserved largely for Europeans and considered, in Governor Eliot's breathtaking phrase, "White Man's Country". The **Kikuyu peoples**, skilled farmers and herders, had held the land for several centuries before the Europeans arrived. They were at first mystified to find themselves "squatters" on land whose ownership, in the sense of exclusive right, had never been an issue in traditional society. They were certainly not alone in losing land,

2

THE KIKUYU

The ancestors of the **Kikuyu** migrated to the Central Highlands between the sixteenth and eighteenth centuries, from northeast of Mount Kenya. Stories describe how they found various hunter-gatherer peoples already in the region (the **Gumba** on the plains and the **Athi** in the forests), and a great deal of intermarriage, trade and adoption took place. The newcomers cleared the forests and planted crops, giving the hunters gifts of livestock, honey or wives in return for using the land.

Likewise, there was trade and intermarriage between the Kikuyu and the **Maasai**, both peoples placing high value on cattle ownership, with the Maasai depending entirely on livestock. During bad droughts, Maasai would raid Kikuyu herds, with retaliation at a later date being almost inevitable. But such **intertribal warfare** often had long-term benefits, as ancient debts were forever being renegotiated and paid off by both sides, thus sustaining the relationship. Married Kikuyu women enjoyed a special immunity that enabled them to organize trading expeditions deep into Maasai-land, often with the help of a *hinga*, a middleman, to oil the wheels.

Like the Maasai, the Kikuyu advanced in status as they grew older, through named age-sets and rituals still important today. For Kikuyu boys, **circumcision** marks the important transition into adulthood (female circumcision, or clitoridectomy, is illegal and rarely performed today). In the past, boys would grow their hair and dye it with ochre in the style of Maasai warriors (in fact, the Maasai got their ochre from the Kikuyu, so it may really have been the other way around). They also wore glass beads around their necks, metal rings on their legs and arms, and pulled their ear lobes out with ear plugs. Women wore a similar collection of ornaments and, between initiation and marriage, a headband of beads and discs, still worn today by most Maasai women.

Traditionally, the Kikuyu had no centralized **authority**. The elders of a district would meet as a council and disputes or important decisions would be dealt with in public, with a party to follow. After their deaths, elders – now known as ancestors – continued to be respected and consulted. Christianity has altered beliefs in the last few decades, though many church-goers still believe strongly in an **ancestor world** where the dead have powers over their living descendants. The Kikuyu traditionally believed that the most likely abode of God (Ngai), or at least his frequent resting place, was Mount Kenya, which they called **Kirinyaga** (Place of Brightness). Accordingly, they used to build their houses with the door always looking out towards the mountain, hence the title of Jomo Kenyatta's book, *Facing Mount Kenya*.

Today, the Kikuyu are at the forefront of Kenyan **development** and, despite entrenched nepotism, are accorded grudging respect as successful business people, skilled media operators and formidable politicians. There is considerable political rivalry between the Kiambu Kikuyu of the tea- and coffee-growing district north of Nairobi and the Nyeri Kikuyu (one of whose number is President Mwai Kibaki), based in the fertile area of Othaya who rely on a more mixed economy.

The **GEMA** (Gikuyu, Embu and Meru Association), created in 1971 to further Kikuyu interests, at first concerned itself primarily with countering Daniel Arap Moi's ascent to the presidency, and although it was banned in 1980, it is believed to continue to operate clandestinely throughout Kenya.

The emergence in Kikuyuland in the early 2000s of the secret and violent **Mungiki** cult, somewhat modelled after the colonial era's Mau Mau independence movement but based primarily around extortion and gangster operations rather than emancipation, brought terror to slum districts in parts of Central Kenya. In a recent twist of jaw-dropping chutzpah, its leader escaped justice, declaring himself a born-again Christian. He is now wooed by mainstream politicians, while Mungiki has become a deeply corrupting force within the political process.

but, by supplying most of the "Mau Mau" fighters for the Land and Freedom Army (see p.560), they were placed squarely in the political limelight. In return, they received a large proportion of what used to be known as the "Fruits of Independence". Today, most of the land is in African hands again, and it supports the country's largest rural population. There's intensive farming on almost all the lower slopes and much of the higher ground as well, beneath the national parks of Mount Kenya and the Aberdare.

Thika

THIKA, a bustling Nairobi satellite just off the main road to Mount Kenya, is not redeemed by the profusion of flame trees you might expect from its famous literary connection, Elspeth Huxley's *The Flame Trees of Thika*, recording her family's move there in 1913. It's a surprisingly laidback, friendly sort of place, with a bit of light manufacturing, but best known for its pineapples. The fruit was introduced in 1905 and thousands of acres flourish here, mostly owned by Del Monte and easily confused with the sisal also grown in the area.

The town centre is compact and straightforward, although there are no major attractions. If you're passing through, it's worth visiting the **Blue Posts hotel**, where the grounds include a small **zoo** (Ksh200), the best viewpoints for the **Chania and Thika Falls**, a clutch of well-stocked, competitively priced **curio shops** and a small children's playground and boating pond.

ARRIVAL AND DEPARTURE   THIKA

By car The recent completion of an eight-lane superhighway connecting Nairobi and Thika has eased congestion along this route – the 50km drive should take around 1hr. The road narrows to one lane after Thika but remains in good condition until past Nanyuki.

By bus and matatu Frequent buses and matatus plough the busy Nairobi–Thika route (30min). Matatu stands line the highway at all major junctions. Most buses and matatus carry on to Murang'a (1hr), Embu (1hr 30min), Nyeri (2hr) and Naro Moru (2hr).

INFORMATION

Services ATMs include Barclays and Standard Chartered, and other services include the Mbambu Cyber Café (Mon–Sat 7.30am–7.30pm; Sun 11am–4pm) on Uhuru St, a Mathai supermarket (daily 8am–7.30pm), a good

pharmacy, The Chemists (Mon–Sat 8am–6pm, Sun 9am–4pm), and a market east of the town centre, past the street stalls at the stadium roundabout.

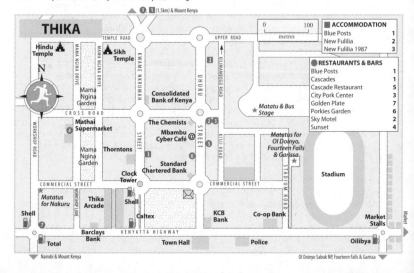

ACCOMMODATION

Thika doesn't offer a wide choice for an overnight stay. The B&Ls are basic and don't have instant showers, while the only "upmarket" option is out of town and somewhat overpriced.

Blue Posts Just to the east of the Nairobi–Murang'a road (no signpost), 1.3km north of the turning to downtown Thika ☎020 2080606 or 0721 578245, ✉blueposthotel @africaonline.co.ke. Dating from 1908, older than Thika itself, this has modest, tourist-class rooms, with good nets and small TVs. Coming from Nairobi, take the slip road signposted "Thika Coffee Mills 3km" and traverse the A2 on the flyover to reach the hotel. The relatively primitive bathrooms do have instant showers but no tubs, and don't expect hot water in your basin. Room only **Ksh4400**, BB **Ksh6000**

New Fulilia Uhuru St ☎0720 003863. Reasonably clean lodgings, though only one of the fifty-odd rooms has two beds. Frenetic bar, plus *nyama choma* and a decent *hoteli*. Room only **Ksh1200**

New Fulilia 1987 Kwame Nkrumah St ☎067 21840. A more basic alternative to its sister establishment, with noisy courtyard-style B&L with plenty of small, windowless singles, only a couple of rooms with two beds, and no guarantee of hot water. Busy, ground-floor *hoteli* and second-floor bar. Room only **Ksh1000**

EATING AND DRINKING

Blue Posts Just to the east of the Nairobi–Murang'a road (no signpost), 1.3km north of the turning to downtown Thika ☎020 2080606 or 0721 578245. Popular local venue, especially at weekends, with its tables on the lawns, and sweeping views of the Chania and Thika Falls. The restaurant offers good lunchtime buffets (Ksh700) and various dinner dishes for around Ksh600. Daily 7am–11pm.

★ **Cascade Restaurant** Uhuru St ☎0726 147655. This clean and crowded local joint is a safe bet for fast food (fish and chips Ksh200, chicken and chips Ksh240) and has a pleasant atmosphere. Daily 6.30am–8.30pm.

Cascades At the Blue Posts Hotel, off the Nairobi–Murang'a road. This big disco turns up its sound system at weekends, but don't expect a crowd to form much before midnight. Daily 10pm–late.

City Pork Center Kisii Rd ☎0728 932960 or 0720 273423. Tiny and basic but friendly butchery with a restaurant specializing in pork. Kilo pork and chips Ksh250. Daily 6.30am–8.30pm.

★ **Golden Plate** Kenyatta Highway, across from Total. Busy, clean, friendly and well-run *hoteli* with plenty on the menu, much of it available. Meals from Ksh200. Daily 7am–7pm.

Porkies Garden Uhuru St. Food is on offer (*bhajia* Ksh100, burger Ksh100), but this is more bar than restaurant. There's a covered courtyard offering live English football, a pool table and balcony. 24hr.

Sunset Bar & Restaurant Mama Ngina Drive. This bar and restaurant includes a busy *hoteli* (chips and quarter chicken Ksh200) serving alcohol on upstairs veranda with a beer cage. Daily 6.30am–8pm.

Fourteen Falls

Daily 9am–5pm • Adults $4, children $2, vehicles $5, cameras $5, camcorders $10 • Head for the village of Kilima Mbogo, 18km east of Thika, along the Garissa road; some matatus stop at Kilima Mbogo, while others go on to the village of Donyo, 4km off to the south, down a dirt track that passes 900m from the entrance to Fourteen Falls

The trip to **Fourteen Falls** on the Athi River, close to Ol Donyo Sabuk National Park, is popular with locals. Donyo, on the south side of the river, is a busy centre, with dozens of *dukas* and *hotelis*.

Fourteen Falls is a broad cascade, plunging 30m over a precipice with many lips, hence the name. The falls are modestly spectacular after rain, when they flood into a single, thundering red cataract. You may end up with breathtaking photos, but will have to experience the stench of what is sadly becoming an increasingly polluted ecosystem due to upstream development. The boat-crossing to the viewpoint to watch locals jump off the falls is well worth the modest entrance fee.

Ol Donyo Sabuk National Park

$20 • ⊕ kws.org/parks/parks_reserves/OSNP.html • Matatus run to Kilima Mbogo village, 18km east of Thika along the Garissa road; the park gate is 2km further on – follow the signpost by the teacher training college

Seen from a distance, **Ol Donyo Sabuk**, "Big Mountain" in Maa, also known as Kilima Mbogo ("Buffalo Mountain" in Kikuyu), is not especially inspiring, and at

2146m it's not high in Kenyan terms. The attractions of the national park become apparent when you approach the gate, as the flat, dry scrubland gives way to red soil, cool air and fine views. The national park encloses the entirety of the mountain, and protects diverse birdlife and indigenous forest, though the mammals – buffaloes, Sykes' and colobus monkeys, and porcupines – make themselves scarce in the thick vegetation.

Walking the 9km track from the gate to the summit requires being accompanied by an armed ranger (Ksh1500). Beyond signboard #8, at the 7km mark, on the left, you come to the grave of Sir William Northrup MacMillan, the fattest of famous settlers, whose intended burial place on the summit had to be abandoned when his modified tractor-hearse's clutch burned out. He rests here with his wife, maid and dog. Between the MacMillans' graves and just below the summit, the track winds steeply up through dense forest. The occasional clearings offer good views, including a huge oxbow in the Athi River and, when the air is clear enough (usually Dec & Jan), Mount Kenya and Kilimanjaro. The vegetation at the summit is more open, with shrubs and grassland, spoiled by a humming grove of communications towers.

ACCOMMODATION   **OL DONYO SABUK**

Lookout campsite 7km up the hill from the gate ☎ 020 2062503, ✉ reservations@kws.go.ke. There are no facilities here, but this is a beautiful spot overlooking Athi Plains, Nairobi and Thika. $25 per person

Sabuk Guest House 1km south of the gate ☎ 020 2062503, ✉ reservations@kws.go.ke. Very large and nicely situated old home, formerly MacMillans' Ranger residence. It's a charming place with satellite TV and full kitchen for up to ten. Whole house $200

Turacco campsite By the gate ☎ 020 2062503 or main KWS reservations ☎ 0726 610508, ✉ reservations @kws.go.ke. Shady lawns, free firewood, rudimentary showers and toilets with nice picnic spot. New bathroom and shower facilities were under construction when we went to press. $15 per person

Murang'a

Established as the administrative outpost of **Fort Hall** in 1900, **MURANG'A** has since come to be thought of as the "Kikuyu Homeland" because of its proximity to Mukuruwe wa Nyagathanga, a sort of Kikuyu Garden of Eden. At the beginning of the twentieth century, Fort Hall consisted of "two grass huts within a stone wall and a ditch". Although a British military base, it was never a settlers' town: Fort Hall district was outside the zone earmarked for white settlement and most of it comprised the "Kikuyu reserve". Colonel Richard Meinertzhagen, an officer in the King's African Rifles, posted here in 1902, found time, when not shooting animals (or people), to write, "If white settlement really takes hold in this country it is bound to do so at the expense of the Kikuyu who own the best land, and I foresee much trouble." That said, Meinertzhagen helped put down some of this trouble, launching "punitive expeditions" from Fort Hall with his African troops (see p.591).

The present-day town, perched above the busy Mount Kenya road, is a small commercial centre, bustling energetically, and outwardly a happy enough place, despite its notoriety as an area of Mungiki gang violence (see p.159). But this won't impact in any way on your visit, and there's no reason not to call in. There's even a bit of sightseeing in the **CPK Cathedral**, formerly the Church of St James and All Martyrs. The cathedral features an unusual mural sequence which depicts the life story of an African Christ in an African landscape. The murals were painted by the Tanzanian artist Rekiya Elimoo Njau in 1955 – the year the church was founded by the Archbishop of Canterbury – as a memorial to the thousands of Kikuyu victims of Mau Mau attacks.

Mukuruwe wa Nyagathanga

In Kikuyu mythology, it was at nearby Mukuruwe wa Nyagathanga that God made husbands for the nine daughters of Gikuyu and Mumbi, spiritual ancestors of all the Kikuyu people. The husbands, who became the ancestors of the nine Kikuyu clans, were found by Gikuyu under a large fig tree. Although the original *mukuruwe* (fig tree) disappeared long ago, you can take a matatu to nearby **Mugeka** and walk from there to **Gakuyu** village if you'd like to see the site.

ARRIVAL AND DEPARTURE MURANG'A

There are three main onward travel options from Murang'a: clockwise around Mount Kenya via Karatina; anticlockwise around the mountain via Embu (see p.185); or up to Nyeri and the Aberdare range (see p.191). The main route from Murang'a to Nyeri goes north via the town of Sagana, where it joins the A2 highway. But if you're not in a hurry, you should take either of the two minor roads leading out of Murang'a to the west. Both in good condition, and much more pleasant to travel on than the main highway, they join at Kiriani. Frequent buses and matatus run from Murang'a to Thika (1hr 30min), Nairobi (2hr 30min), Embu (1hr) and Nyeri (1hr 30min) from the bus station off Gichinga Lane.

INFORMATION

Services Barclays and KCB both have ATMs and there's internet access at the Post Office, off Kenyatta Highway. There's a Mathai supermarket at the western end of Market Street.

ACCOMMODATION

Murang'a has several recommended lodgings providing bed and breakfast at knock-down prices; however, there is nowhere upmarket.

★ **Golden Palm Breeze Hotel** On the highway in Kenol town, about 10km from Thika ☎0712 619342, ⓦgoldenpalmbreezehotel.com. The most modern building en route to Murang'a from Thika, with manicured gardens and small but welcoming rooms. Room only Ksh1500, BB Ksh1900

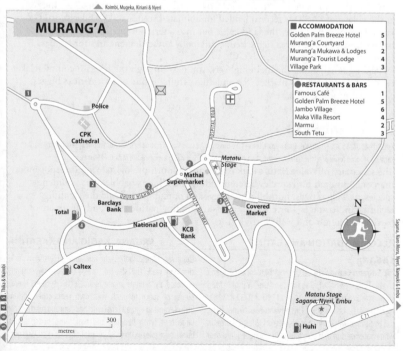

Koimbi, Mugeka, Kiriani & Nyeri

MURANG'A

■ ACCOMMODATION	
Golden Palm Breeze Hotel	5
Murang'a Courtyard	1
Murang'a Mukawa & Lodges	2
Murang'a Tourist Lodge	4
Village Park	3

● RESTAURANTS & BARS	
Famous Café	1
Golden Palm Breeze Hotel	5
Jambo Village	6
Maka Villa Resort	4
Marmu	2
South Tetu	3

Police

CPK Cathedral

Matatu Stage

Mathai Supermarket

UHURU HIGHWAY

Barclays Bank

Total

National Oil

KCB Bank

Covered Market

N

Matatu Stage Sagana, Nyeri, Embu

Huhi

0   300
metres

Thika & Nairobi

Sagana, Naro Moru, Nyeri, Nanyuki & Embu

Murang'a Courtyard Kangema Rd ⓣ0721 166878. Nine small but pleasant and clean rooms, each with a small double bed, over a popular bar-restaurant. Very affordable, but you get what you pay for. BB **Ksh800**

★ **Murang'a Mukawa & Lodges Ltd** Uhuru Highway ⓣ0723 701409. A cut above the other lodgings, with a nice terrace bar with views across the hills. BB **Ksh1400**

Murang'a Tourist Lodge 2km down the Thika road ⓣ0726 495060, ⓔintercity1984@yahoo.com. Somewhat run-down yet clean and agreeable, with dark rooms but good breakfasts (Ksh150). Room only **Ksh1200**

Village Park Market St. Good bet for a dirt-cheap night in the town centre, and relatively peaceful as it has no bar. Rooms are extremely basic, however, with shared bucket showers. Room only **Ksh700**

2

EATING AND DRINKING

Famous Café Uhuru Highway. A good joint for a tea and snacks with samosas and *mandaazi*, though it's a little cramped and surrounded by a cacophony of traffic. Daily 6am–8pm.

Golden Palm Breeze Hotel Off the Thika– Muranga'a highway ⓣ0712 619342. This is a great stop on the way to Murang'a. It's a popular weekend spot for locals, with a full *nyama choma* restaurant, a nice garden and four separate bars featuring live music on weekends. Meals from Ksh250–350, with buffet lunch or dinner for Ksh750. Daily 6am–late.

Jambo Village 300m south of Muranga Tourist Lodge ⓣ0722 896836. Lively *nyama choma* (1kg Ksh450) spot on the outskirts of town that's packed on weekends with a family-friendly atmosphere, music and decent chicken and chips (Ksh220). Daily 8am–11pm.

Maka Villa Resort Club Opposite Total ⓣ0722 304943 or 060 31187. Not a bad place for open-air drinking and cheap *nyama choma* (1kg Ksh450). Daily 10am–3am.

Marmu Restaurant Uhuru Highway. A busy spot with a good range of snacks. Mains from Ksh250. Daily 6.30am–9pm.

South Tetu Day & Night Club Market St. Boozy and friendly, with a pool table, this is the closest you'll get to a nightclub in Murang'a. Daily 10am–late.

Sagana, Kagio and Karatina

SAGANA has some accommodation and a good activities camp nearby (see below), but little else to recommend it. Seven kilometres northeast of here, the market (Tues & Fri) at the village of **KAGIO** is recommended for animated scenes and wonderful fruit and vegetables. South of here, the land levels out into a series of intricately irrigated **rice paddies**, part of the Mwea rice scheme, originally a resettlement area for landless farmers supported by Japanese NGOs.

Heading north along the main highway, you pass through the feverish commercial centre of **KARATINA**. Its market (Sat and Tues–Thurs) is one of East Africa's biggest cattle and produce sales.

Wajee Nature Park

Ksh300 • ⓣ0725 770077, ⓦwajeenaturepark.com • Take the main A2 road from Karatina to Nyeri, turning west 3km northwest of Karatina at Tumu Tumu onto the Gakonya road; then go south about 17km via Mukurweini and Mihuti • 25 acres

The sanctuary of **Wajee Nature Park** is a magnet for ornithologists, who can spot more than one hundred bird species here, including the Hinde's babbler, a rare endemic species, as well as owls, hornbills, monkeys and porcupines. While the camping facilities and cottages are very basic, the surrounding nature trails and apiary are of particular interest and well worth a visit.

ACCOMMODATION AND EATING — SAGANA, KAGIO AND KARATINA

SAGANA

★ **Sagana Camp Site** On the east bank of the Sagana river, 7km south of Sagana on the Nairobi road signposted to the west ⓣ020 7121590 or 0737 835963, ⓦwhitewaterkenya.com. This adventure activities base, run by Savage Wilderness Safaris (see p.118), specializes in whitewater rafting and also has a 60m bungee jump over the river, nature walks, zip line and an artificial rock-climbing wall. The shaded, grassy campsite is entirely powered by a home-made hydroelectric system. There's plenty of space to pitch your own tent; other options include renting a small tent (with bedding and mattress) or large tent (with bedding and two camp beds), and a bunkhouse (sleeps up to 32 people). An extra Ksh2500 gets you breakfast, lunch, dinner and two beers/sodas. Per person: camping Ksh1000, small tent Ksh1350, large tent Ksh1450, whole cottage Ksh4650

KARATINA

Hotel Starbucks Next door to Ibis, off the main road ☎0721 466577, ⓦhotelstarbucks.com. Small, clean rooms, good security and satellite TV. You can eat (6am–midnight) fast food at *Chicken Inn* downstairs, à la carte and buffet at *Stings* restaurant upstairs, and drink at *Casper's Bar*, whose nice veranda looks onto the main street and has a lively atmosphere. Bed only Ksh1500

Ibis Opposite Uchumi supermarket, off the main road ☎0722 701149, ⓔKihuria@ibishotel.co.ke. The hotel

offers the bare necessities with a restaurant, bar and night club next door. Bed only Ksh2000

Safari Treat Restaurant On the main road 100m south of Uchumi supermarket. Cosy local joint with the standard Coca-Cola-branded tables serving up snacks, *mandaazi* and samosa. Full meals Ksh250–350. Daily 6am–9pm.

WAJEE NATURE PARK

Wajee Nature Park Campsite ☎0721 749987 or 0722 453658. The campsite here also offers rather run-down garden accommodation with four self-contained triple rooms, hot water and a kitchen with gas and firewood. Camping Ksh300 per person, whole cottage Ksh1000

Southern Mount Kenya

The *Castle Forest* lodge can arrange a hiking trip for you for $120 a day all-inclusive, regardless of the size of the party, via *Mackinder's Camp* and Point Lenana, terminating either in Naro Moru (4–6 days) or Chogoria (6–9 days)

Relatively few tourists approach Mount Kenya from the park's southern boundary, which offers some excellent accommodation options and great basecamp hiking. If you're keen to try an unusual approach to the summit, consider the **Kamweti route** which begins at the road-head, a steep 8km north of *Castle Forest* (see below). This southern part of the mountain shelters the last remaining wild **bongos** on Mount Kenya, as researchers' night-surveillance cameras proved in 2008.

Thego Fishing Camp

Ksh100 • ☎0716 465831

Along the Chaka route, 7km from the highway, you pass *Thego Fishing Camp*, a pretty spot by the Thego stream with camping allowed and rudimentary *bandas*, but no electricity. If you don't already have a fishing licence, you can get one here for Ksh500, giving you a year's worth of fishing, and allowing you up to six fish per day (if you're lucky).

ACCOMMODATION

SOUTHERN MOUNT KENYA

★ **Castle Forest Lodge** Southern slopes of Mount Kenya, 40km from Sagana via Kagio ☎0721 422908 or 0722 314918, ⓦcastleforestlodge.com. A private home built for British royalty before World War I, this nestles in a fragrantly piney forest clearing at 2100m. Remotely sited and personally managed by its Dutch leaseholder, it is far from the main road and overlooks a waterhole regularly visited by most of the usual suspects. Even if you're simply passing by, there are few nicer ways to spend an afternoon than sitting on the veranda with tea and home-made cakes. The old house has several modest, comfortable rooms with camphor-wood floors. In the grounds there are three bungalows, each sleeping four, an arc of stylish, individually decorated double and twin cottages with fireplaces, a newly built two-bedroom self-catering cottage and the option of DIY camping. *The Lodge* uses an impressive hydro system from the nearby waterfall for electricity, good-value meals are available and there's a

well-stocked bar. In between sleeping and eating, you can walk in the woods, sit by the waterfalls of the Karute stream (a short walk from the house through beautiful thick forest), fish the stream for trout or take a horse out for a ride. Make sure you ask about necessary precautions if venturing deep into the forest – in 2010 two visitors were killed by a charging elephant 5km from the main lodge. To get here from Sagana, take the C73 towards Embu. After 18km, you reach Kutus; continue east on the C73 for 400m, then turn left on the tarmac D458 signposted "Castle Forest Lodge 22km". After 2km, turn left onto an excellent road which eventually becomes a forest track in reasonable condition. Camping $8 per person, BB $120, FB $140

★ **Serena Mountain Lodge** Mount Kenya National Reserve, on the southwest slopes of Mount Kenya ☎061 2030785 or 0733 203078, ⓦserenahotels.com. The best of Kenya's three highland tree-hotels, set at an altitude of 2200m. Reminiscent of an old-style ski lodge in

2

its cosy, dark wood design, it has public balconies facing the forest-encircled, floodlit waterhole, en-suite rooms and excellent food. The lodge is inside the Mount Kenya National Reserve and you pass through KWS's Kihari gate, where you'll need to pay the standard entry fee (see p.167). Visit the underground bunker for close-up waterhole views. It's a 40min drive from the A2: from Karatina, drive 3km northwest and take the right (east)

turning at Tumu Tumu, then follow directions for 31km; from Kiganjo, head north 4km, take the right (east) turning at the market centre of Chaka and drive 27km to the lodge. Both routes are paved and in good shape and join at Sagana State Lodge, a well-guarded presidential retreat with excellent game viewing 14km short of *Serena Mountain Lodge*. BB **$250**

Naro Moru

Heading north up the A2 towards Naro Moru from Kiganjo, you emerge from the folded landscape of Kikuyu cultivation onto a high, windswept plain. Here, you're crossing one of Kenya's great animal migration routes, severed by human population pressure. Until 1948, when the two mountain parks were created, every few years used to see a mass migration of **elephants** from one side to the other. When the parks were opened, it was decided to keep the elephants away from the crowded farmlands in between, so an 8km-long ditch was dug across their route.

The road climbs gently and steadily to nondescript **NARO MORU**, which stands on the watershed between the Tana and the Ewaso Nyiro river basins. Built around its now disused train station, Naro Moru is the most straightforward base for climbing Mount Kenya, either independently or on an organized trek.

ARRIVAL AND DEPARTURE

NARO MORU

By bus and matatu Frequent matatus to and from Nanyuki (30min) and Nyeri (45min) pass through Naro Moru. Transport also connects Naro Moru with Nairobi (3hr).

By car The A2 highway connects Naro Moru with Nanyuki and Nairobi and is in good shape.

INFORMATION

Guided treks *Naro Moru River Lodge* and *Bantu Mountain Lodge* (see below) run guided treks. Another recommended outfit in Naro Moru is Mount Kenya Guides and Porters Safari Club (☎ 020 3524393 or 0723 112483, ⌨ mtkenyaguides

.com), whose office is 6km along the Naro Moru trail, about 3km before the youth hostel.

Services The town has a post office and KCB bank with ATM, but no Barclays.

ACCOMMODATION AND EATING

The area around Naro Moru and the route north to Nanyuki offers a good variety of **accommodation**. If you're camping, the rather exposed campsite at *Naro Moru River Lodge* ($10) is the obvious destination. There's not a lot in the **food** department in Naro Moru; the centre's offerings are strictly in the *karanga* and *chapati* line – besides the *Trout River Restaurant*, your best bet for something classier are the lodges – try the *Naro Moru River Lodge*.

Bantu Mountain Lodge 8km north of Naro Moru ☎ 0728 559364, ⌨ mountainrockkenya.com. A decent mid-range trekking base (also known as *Mountain Rock Lodge*), rated for its grounds full of indigenous trees and for its organized treks using its own mountain bunkhouses – there's also horseriding (Ksh1000/hr) and escorted walks on offer. The lodge's standard rooms are nothing to write home about and you might want to upgrade to "superior" (Ksh3500 B/O or Ksh4000 BB) for the quaintly preferable furnishings and fireplace. You can also camp in the grounds. All rooms have TVs and prices are highly negotiable. Bed only **Ksh3000** BB **Ksh3500**, camping **Ksh600** per person

★ **Colobus Cottages** 1km south of Bantu Mountain

Lodge, then 2km west of the A2 ☎ 0722 840195 or 0753 951720, ⌨ colobuscottages.com. Three delightful solar-powered cottages on the banks of the Burguret stream, built and managed by a former restaurateur. The cottages come with natty decor and fireplaces and perch by a stream for trout fishing, overlooking colobus-laden trees. There's a treetop bar and restaurant. Self-catering two-bedroom cottage **Ksh12,000**, three-bedroom **Ksh18,000**

Mount Kenya Royal Cottages 1km south of Nanyuki airport, just off the A2 ☎ 0721 470008. Newly built highway-side stopover with spacious, nicely furnished rooms with cosy duvets, TV and hot water. There's also a family-friendly restaurant, bar and gardens serving traditional Kenyan dishes. BB Ksh5000

★ **Naro Moru River Lodge** Signposted 1.5km northwest of the town centre ☎ 0724 082754 or 062 2031047, ⓦ naromoruriverlodge.com. The town's upmarket base, this is also the area's main climbing rendezvous, with a pricey but decently stocked kit-rental shop. It has a welcoming atmosphere, pretty gardens along the Naro Moru stream, and superb birdwatching, as well as a sauna, squash, tennis, a pool and riding. Although some rooms need refurbishment, most have fireplaces and balconies and are reasonable value for money, as are the twelve self-service cottages (most sleep 6 or 7 at around $40 per person). The *Lenana Bar*, and *Kinnyaga* restaurant are busy hangouts on the weekend, with hearty breakfasts and lunches ($20), and good dinners for $30. BB $135

★ **Trout Tree Restaurant** About 9km north of Naro Moru, just past Bantu Mountain Lodge ☎ 0726 281704, ⓦ tamtrout.com. Built on wooden platforms among giant fig trees, overlooking trout ponds, the restaurant serves very good fish (Ksh700–800) in a variety of styles. Daily 11am–4pm.

Youth Hostel 9km up the well-signposted track to Mount Kenya National Park's Naro Moru gate ☎ 062 62412, ⓦ hihostels.com. This excellent hostel has comfortable if basic dorms and camping, with hot showers and a well-equipped kitchen. A good place to team up with others for climbing the mountain independently. Dorm Ksh900, camping Ksh500 per person

Mount Kenya National Park

$55 • ⓦ tinyurl.com/mount-kenya • 715 square kilometres

An extinct volcano some 3.5 million years old, **Mount Kenya** is Africa's second-highest mountain, with two jagged peaks. Formed from the remains of a gigantic volcanic plug – it rose more than 7000m above sea level until a million years ago – most of its erupted lava and ash have been eroded by glacial action to create a distinctive, craggy silhouette. The peaks are permanently iced with snow and glaciers, the latter in retreat due to climate change. On the upper slopes, altitude and the equatorial location combine to nurture forms of **vegetation**, seemingly designed by some 1950s science-fiction writer, that exist only here and at one or two other lofty points in East Africa. When you first see them, it's hard to believe the "water-holding cabbage", "ostrich plume plant" or "giant groundsel".

Europeans first heard about the mountain when the German missionary **Johann Ludwig Krapf** saw it in 1849. His stories of snow on the equator were not taken seriously, but in 1883 the young Scottish traveller Joseph Thomson confirmed its existence to the outside world. The Kikuyu, Maasai and other peoples living in the region had venerated the mountain for centuries, and park rangers still occasionally report finding elderly Kikuyu high up on the moorlands, drawn by the presence of God – Ngai – whose dwelling place this is. It is not known, however, whether anyone had scaled the peaks before Sir Halford Mackinder reached the higher of the two, **Batian**, in 1899. Another thirty years passed before **Nelion**, a tougher summit, was conquered. Both were named by Mackinder's expedition after nineteenth-century Maasai *laibon*, or ritual leaders.

The **KWS-managed national park** encloses all parts of the mountain above 3200m plus stretches down the Naro Moru and Sirimon streams. Inside this area fees have to be paid, and strict rules control your activities. Outside this zone, surrounding the national park, lies the Mount Kenya National Reserve, in which your movements are normally only limited by your inclinations and equipment – though on some access roads, such as the one for *Mountain Lodge* (see p.165), fees are payable even in the reserve. There are various specialist **guidebooks and maps** (see p.590).

Climbing Mount Kenya

There are **four main routes** up Mount Kenya. From the west, the **Naro Moru trail** provides the shortest and steepest way to the top. The **Burguret** and **Sirimon trails** from the northwest are less well trodden; Sirimon has a reputation for lots of wildlife, while Burguret passes through a long stretch of dense forest. The fourth trail, **Chogoria**, is a

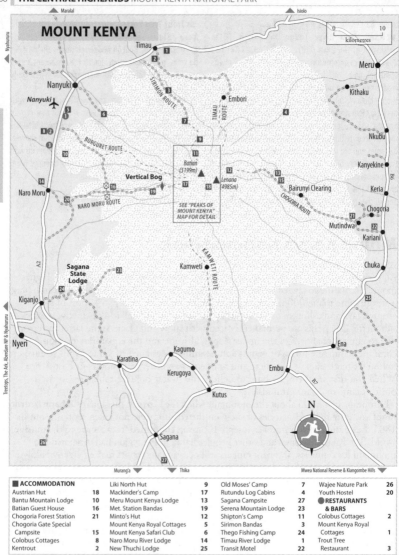

■ ACCOMMODATION		Liki North Hut	9	Old Moses' Camp	7	Wajee Nature Park	26
Austrian Hut	18	Mackinder's Camp	17	Rutundu Log Cabins	4	Youth Hostel	20
Bantu Mountain Lodge	10	Meru Mount Kenya Lodge	13	Sagana Campsite	27	**● RESTAURANTS**	
Batian Guest House	16	Met. Station Bandas	19	Serena Mountain Lodge	23	**& BARS**	
Chogoria Forest Station	21	Minto's Hut	12	Shipton's Camp	11	Colobus Cottages	2
Chogoria Gate Special		Mount Kenya Royal Cottages	5	Sirimon Bandas	3	Mount Kenya Royal	
Campsite	15	Mount Kenya Safari Club	6	Thego Fishing Camp	24	Cottages	1
Colobus Cottages	8	Naro Moru River Lodge	14	Timau River Lodge	1	Trout Tree	
Kentrout	2	New Thuchi Lodge	25	Transit Motel	22	Restaurant	3

beautiful, much longer ascent up the eastern flank of the mountain, on which you have to carry tents. In practice, Naro Moru, Sirimon and Chogoria account for nearly all hikes; if you want to use any other route, you have to inform the warden in advance (this can be done by radio by the rangers at any park gate).

The technical peaks of **Batian** (5199m) and **Nelion** (5189m) are accessible only to experienced, fully-equipped mountaineers, and the easiest route is Grade IV, making them a lot more testing, for example, than most of the routes up the Matterhorn. If you want to climb these peaks, you should join the Mountain Club of Kenya (see p.69), who will put you in touch with the right people, and can give reductions on accommodation charges.

Anyone who is reasonably fit can scale the third-highest peak, **Point Lenana** (4985m). The climb has acquired a reputation for being fairly easy, and lots of people set off quite unprepared for high-altitude living – a quarter of attempts fail for this reason. Above about 4000m the mountain is often foggy or windy and freezing cold, wickedly so after dark. The air is thin, and it rains or snows, at least briefly, almost every day, though most precipitation comes at night.

Mount Kenya's **weather** is notoriously unpredictable. There are days when it's fairly clear even during the rainy seasons, but driving up the muddy roads to the park gates may be nearly impossible. If it's really bad, you probably won't be allowed in anyway. The most **reliable months** are February and August, although January and most of July can be fine, too.

What to bring

Above all, it's essential to have a really **warm sleeping bag**, ideally with an additional liner and/or a Gore-Tex bivouac bag, capable of keeping you warm below freezing point. One **thick sweater**, or better still, several thinner ones, and either a **windproof jacket** or a down- or fibre-filled one are also essential, as is a **change of footwear**, as you're bound to have wet feet by the end of each day. **Gloves** and a **balaclava** or **woolly hat** are also handy. A light cagoule or anorak is good to have, as is a set or two of thermal underwear for the often shivering nights. A **torch**, ideally a wind-up one, is always handy, and essential if you're trekking without a guide. An **emergency foil blanket** is advisable, weighs next to nothing and packs down very small. Another prerequisite is a **stove**, as you'll be miserable without regular hot drinks. Firewood is not available and cannot be collected once you enter the park (no burning is allowed). For **food**, dehydrated soup and chocolate are perhaps the most useful. The *Naro Moru River Lodge* (see p.167) has a **rental** shop where you can get just about anything, though at prices that may make you wish you'd simply bought it in Nairobi (see p.122).

Altitude and health

The various ascents themselves are mostly just steep hikes, if rough underfoot in parts. It's the **altitude** rather than the climb that may stop you reaching the top. Much more relevant than the training programmes that some people embark on is giving yourself enough time to acclimatize, so that your body has a chance to produce extra oxygen-carrying red blood cells.

Above 3000–4000m, you will be well outside your normal comfort zone and are likely to notice the effects of altitude. You may want to take Diamox (acetazolamide) to speed up your acclimatization and keep painkillers handy for headaches, which are fairly normal at first, especially at night. Keeping your **fluid intake** as high as possible will also help – three to five litres a day is recommended. Most water sources on the mountain are reckoned to be safe (one or two exceptions are noted). It's best to avoid alcohol while climbing.

The effects of altitude can be largely avoided if you **take your time** over the trek, as minor symptoms gradually disappear. Going up the Naro Moru route, you shouldn't attempt to climb from the base of the mountain (that is, from Naro Moru town at 2000m) to Point Lenana (just under 5000m) in less than 72 hours. Five or six days is much better, especially if you've just arrived in Kenya and are used to living at sea level. Assuming you allow a day to get down again, giving yourself a week for the whole trip is a good idea. If you can, climb for an hour or two higher than the altitude you are going to sleep, or spend two nights at the same altitude.

The symptoms of **altitude sickness**, also known as acute mountain sickness, vary between individuals, and appear unrelated to how fit you are – indeed, fit young men often suffer the most acute symptoms. If you climb too fast, extreme breathlessness, nausea, disorientation and even slurred speech are all possible. If someone in your group shows signs of being seriously tired and weak, you should descend a few hundred metres. If the symptoms develop into unsteadiness on the feet and drowsiness, **descend rapidly** until the symptoms improve. The effects of altitude, especially on bodies tuned only to sea level, are remarkable, and they can quickly become very dangerous and even fatal if high-altitude pulmonary or cerebral oedema (water in the lungs or brain cavity) develop.

ARRIVAL AND DEPARTURE   MOUNT KENYA NATIONAL PARK

Getting to the Mount Kenya area is an easy trip from Nairobi up a busy highway. If you're not driving, you could buy a bus ticket from Nairobi direct to any of the towns in this section, or make Thika (see p.160) or Murang'a (see p.162) a first destination before heading around the mountain. Naro Moru (see p.166), a popular base for climbing the mountain, lies on its west side, while Nanyuki (see p.178), 25km further north, offers a good alternative hiking base and is the closest commercial airstrip to the park. On the eastern slopes, Chogoria (see p.176), between Meru and Embu, offers arguably the finest route up the mountain. Or you could head up to the southern slopes, where Castle Forest Lodge (see p.165) is an excellent, low-key staging post.

INFORMATION, ENTRY AND COSTS

KWS operates a sign-in/sign-out system and you register your details and plans at your gate of entry. This is where you pay fees for your anticipated stay ($55 per 24hr, $220 for 4-day package, $270 for 5, $320 for 6; no refunds). You can change your plans once on the mountain, or extend your stay and pay the balance on departure, but you must leave by one of the three main gates – Naro Moru, Sirimon or Chogoria – and formally sign out. It's a bad idea to use any alternative exit: KWS will look for you and eventually organize an air search if you don't show up. Stories circulate of people being pursued to Nairobi and beyond for non-payment of huge rescue service bills.

Costs Climbing Mount Kenya is a fairly expensive business, though still significantly cheaper than Kilimanjaro. Doing the trek independently from Naro Moru, the cheapest possible four-day trip (three up, one down) for two people, including park fees, overnight accommodation, transport to the road-head and a basic self-catering food budget of $10/day, but excluding any equipment rental, would cost around $330/person. Organized trips start from around $100/person per day. Note that the multi-day fees (see above) for national park entry include camping fees, which would otherwise cost $15 per night. Note that the smallest party allowed to hike on the mountain is two people, which in practice means solo independent travellers have to team up with others or hire a guide/porter.

Guides and porters Though it's not obligatory to hire a guide or porter, you should always climb the mountain with paid assistance, out of respect for the local community. Expect to pay around $10–20/day per porter, plus Ksh400 for his special-discount park fees. Every guide needs to have an official KWS guiding permit. Ask to see it, and don't be fobbed off with local guiding association cards. It's best to agree terms in writing in advance and to pay half or two-thirds of the wages up front and the balance on safe delivery back to base. You can hire guides and porters in Naro Moru at *Naro Moru River Lodge*, *Bantu Mountain Lodge* or the Mount Kenya Guides and Porters Safari Club (see p.166), in Nanyuki at the *Jambo House Hotel* (see p.180) and in Chogoria at the *Transit Motel* (see p.176).

ACCOMMODATION

With a tent, you can camp anywhere in the park – the only practical advantages of the campsites at the *Met Station Bandas*, *Mackinder's* and various other designated campsites on the mountain are water pipes and long-drop toilets. Accommodation on the mountain includes some basic lodges with limited facilities and a number of rudimentary mountain huts which provide little more than shelter and bare bunks. Accommodation inside the park is given in the relevant route accounts.

KEEPING MOUNT KENYA CLEAN

The Kikuyu and other tribes venerated Mount Kenya as the dwelling place of God. It was believed that if you went up to the peaks you would find him, and medicine men and diviners routinely trekked up the mountain to seek miraculous cures or spiritual inspiration. Nowadays, it's mainly tourists, some 15,000 each year, who tread in their steps. Few of them, it seems, particularly respect, never mind venerate, the old mountain deity, and many tonnes of rubbish are left behind every year. Take all your trash back down with you.

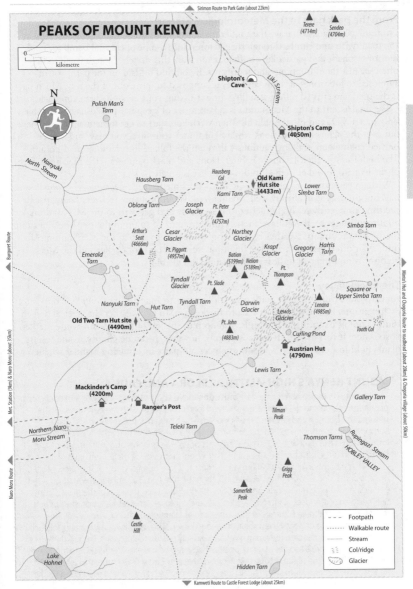

The Naro Moru route

The earth road between **Naro Moru** town (see p.166) and the road-head at the Meteorological Station is a 26km haul. There are no regular matatus; private transport with a driver, booked with *Naro Moru River Lodge*, will set you back $80. If you walk, you may get a paying lift some of the way, but the very light traffic thins out as you head east, and if you don't get transport past the youth hostel after 9km, you should allow five hours to walk the rest of the way. Another 9km beyond the youth hostel, you come to the **park gate** and usually a few buffalo chewing the cud on the lawn.

From the park gate to the Meteorological Station

From the park gate, you leave the conifer plantations and occasional *shambas* behind as the road twists and climbs through shaggy forest into a zone of colossal **bamboo**. Look out for elephant and particularly **buffalo** if you walk this stretch, though you'll more often see just their droppings and footprints. If you find buffalo on the path, you're supposed to lob stones at them, and they're supposed to move out of the way. Much safer is the tried and trusted retreat-steadily-without-taking-your-eyes-off-them approach.

The final ascent to the Met Station is a 3km series of steep hairpins usually driveable only in a 4WD (and often not at all when wet). You start to get some magnificent views out over the plains from up here, while right under your nose you may find a three-horned **chameleon**, stalking cautiously through the foliage like a miniature dinosaur. The high forest is their favourite habitat. **Lions** and **black panthers** – the melanistic form of the leopard found at high altitudes – can occasionally be seen in this area.

With an early start, it's physically perfectly possible to reach *Mackinder's Camp* in one day, but unless you're already well acclimatized, you'll probably feel very below par by the time you get there. It's far better to take it easy and get used to the Met Station's 3050m altitude, or, if you have a tent, climb an hour or so up to the tree line and camp there. The mountain's weather is another good reason to stop at the Met Station. After midday, it often gets foul, and the infamous **vertical bog** (not far beyond the Met Station) is no fun at all in heavy drizzle and 20m visibility.

The Teleki Valley

An early start from the Met Station should see you to *Mackinder's Camp* (see opposite) by lunchtime, before the clouds start to thicken up. In fair weather the vertical bog en route is not as daunting as it sounds: you keep to the left of the red-and-white marker posts where it isn't as wet. In wet conditions, however, it can be ghastly, as the rosette plants hold just enough icy water to reach certain parts in a bracing manner whenever

---

MOUNT KENYA'S HIGH-ALTITUDE FLORA AND FAUNA

The mountain's vegetation is zoned by **altitude**. Above about 2000m, *shambas* and coniferous plantations cease and the original, dense cloud forest takes over, with the best areas on the mountain's southern and eastern, rain-facing slopes. At 2400m, forest gives way to giant bamboo, with clumps up to 20m high. The bamboo, a member of the grass family, appears impenetrable, but dark-walled passages are kept open by elephants and buffalo. Again, it's the south that has the best bamboo areas; on the dry, northern slopes, there's very little of it.

Above the bamboo at about 2800m you come into more open country of scattered, twisted *Hagena* and St John's Wort trees (*Hypericum*), then the tree line (3000m) and the start of peculiar, Afro-Alpine moorlands. Above about 3300m, you reach the land of the giants; giant heather, giant groundsel, giant lobelia. Identities are confusing: the cabbages on stumps and the larger candelabra-like "trees" are the same species, giant groundsel or tree senecio, an intermediate stage of which has a sheaf of yellow flowers. They are slow growers and, for such weedy-looking vegetables, they may be extraordinarily old, up to 200 years. The tall, fluffy, less abundant plants are a species of giant lobelia discovered by the explorer Teleki and found only on Mount Kenya. The name plaque below one of these (there's a little nature trail along the ridge above the Naro Moru stream) calls it an "ostrich plume plant" (*Lobelia telekii*), and it's the only plant that could fairly be described as cuddly. The furriness, which gives it such an animal quality, acts as insulation for the delicate flowers.

Any nights you spend up in the mountain huts will normally be shared with large numbers of persistent **rodents**, which you won't see until it's too late. Remember to isolate your food from them by suspending it from the roof. The familiar diurnal scavengers that you'll see are **rock hyraxes**, which are especially tame at *Mackinder's Camp*; the welfare service provided to them by tourists preserves elderly specimens long past their natural life span. Hyraxes are not rodents; the anatomy of their feet indicates they share a distant ancestry with elephants. You're likely to come across other animals at quite high altitudes, too, notably **duiker antelope** on the moorlands.

you slip. As you reach the bog, you enter another vegetation zone, that of **giant heather**. Beyond and above the bog, the path follows a ridge high above the **Teleki Valley** with the peaks straight ahead, rising brilliantly over a landscape that seems to have nothing in common with the hazy plains below.

For *Mackinder's*, you follow the contours across the valley side and jump, or cross by stepping stones, over the snowmelt Northern Naro Moru stream. The peaks of **Batian** and **Nelion** tower magnificently over the valley, with a third pinnacle, **Point John**, even closer. There's usually a fresh icing of snow every morning, but early sunlight melts most of it by midday.

Point Lenana

If you want to climb straight to **Point Lenana**, you're likely to find at least one group leaving with a guide from around 2am the following morning. Leaving this early, with a three- to five-hour hike ahead of you, allows you to get to the summit by dawn for a fabulous view, in the right conditions, from northern Kenya on one side to Kilimanjaro on the other. If you're planning to go without a guide, it's probably safest to scramble straight up the ridge to Point Lenana from *Austrian Hut* rather than cross the unpredictable vestiges of the Lewis glacier without proper equipment.

On the final ascent to Point Lenana, a 500m **via ferrata** steel cable and ladder system, bolted into the rock, was installed by KWS and Rift Valley Adventures in 2012. This "iron road" – the highest via ferrata in the world – allows safer and steadier climbing, and more route options, on the final stretch – assuming you have a harness and carabiners. Still, it's not advisable to rush into doing this final ascent. For most people, day three is better spent getting acclimatized in the Teleki Valley, and not making the climb to Point Lenana until the morning of the fourth day. Note that spending your third night on the mountain at *Austrian Hut*, just below Point Lenana, is not a good idea if you're not used to the altitude.

The **descent** doesn't take long. After summiting, you can get all the way down to Naro Moru in one day, assuming you have transport arranged at the Met Station or manage to find a lift there. If you're not ready to go straight back down, you might want to do the circular **hike around the peaks** (see p.177).

ACCOMMODATION   NARO MORU ROUTE

As well as the *Austrian* and *Liki North*, there are a number of other huts in various states of repair, owned by the MCK and reserved for their members.

Austrian Hut At 4785m ⓦ kws.go.ke. *Austrian* is usually staffed by KWS rangers. Reserve in advance or pay at the gate. Bed only Ksh1000 per person

Batian Guest House At 2400m near the park gate ☏ 020 3568763, ⓦ kws.go.ke. A KWS-run, self-service guesthouse, once the home of the former park warden. Needs to be booked well in advance. Six beds in four bedrooms.

Liki North Hut At 3990m ⓦ kws.go.ke. This very basic, poorly maintained hut is used by porters and – rarely – by intrepid hikers. Reserve in advance or pay at the gate. Bed only Ksh1000 per person

Mackinder's Camp At 4200m. Book via ☏ 0724 082754, ⓦ naromoruriverlodge.com. Alpine stone hut with bunk beds that's owned by *Naro Moru River Lodge*. Set at 4200m, virtually at the head of Teleki Valley, it's certainly no hotel, but does provide some warmth and the company of other climbers, Kikuyu guides and porters. It can be booked in advance, or on arrival if they have space. $15 per person

Met Station Bandas At 3050m. Book via ☏ 0724 082754, ⓦ naromoruriverlodge.com. Basic self-catering bunk beds. Like *Mackinder's*, it's owned by *Naro Moru River Lodge* and can be booked in advance, or on arrival if there's space. Bed only Ksh15,000

The Chogoria route

The **Chogoria trail** is scenically superior to the others, but it's also the longest route. You should allow a *minimum* of five days from Chogoria village up to Point Lenana and down the west side to Naro Moru, or six days if you're returning to Chogoria. Note that the Chogoria route is a camping-only trek: you have to show you have tents for your party when passing through the park gate.

Chogoria village
The muddy, Land Rover-choked village of **CHOGORIA** off the B6 highway is your first target. Public transport sometimes drops passengers on the highway (a 1km walk into Chogoria village) and sometimes drives into the small centre.

Up to the park entrance
The road from Karaa/Kiriani meets the one from Chogoria 5km west of the highway at a rural junction hamlet called **Mutindwa**. From here, it's about 26km to the park gate. En route, some 2km from Mutindwa at Chogoria Forest Station, there's a decent campsite (see p.176).

If you're driving, 4WD is vital on this steep track, but even with it, getting up to the park gate in wet weather can't be guaranteed. If you haven't got your own vehicle, you can charter transport at the *Transit Motel* or elsewhere in Chogoria. Expect to pay around Ksh1000 for a ride on the back of a motorbike or around Ksh8000 to charter a Land Rover for your group. It's a good idea not to pay in full until you get up to the gate. You may prefer to walk up in any case, as it helps you acclimatize. There's exciting, dense rainforest along much of the road, and you're likely to see colobus monkeys, hyena, buffalo and lots of elephant dung. The next available campsite is the only clearing in the forest, at a place called **Bairunyi Clearing**, 15km further up the track, with no water. The national park's **Chogoria Gate** is 9km further up the increasingly steep and rough track, flanked by giant, creaking bamboo forest.

Meru Mount Kenya Lodge and the road-head
Just before the gate for the camping-only Chogoria Route, there is good *banda* accommodation at *Meru Mount Kenya Lodge* (see p.176); you can also camp by the gate or follow the main track up from here to a special campsite (see p.176).

Both the main track and a side branch, via the site of the old *Urumandi* hut, eventually meet up at the **road-head**, 7km further on. The side branch is the more interesting walk, but tougher on vehicles. The road-head, with a small parking area, is on the north side of the Nithi stream and there's another very pleasant **campsite** here, with good stream water.

There are good walks round about, useful for acclimatizing to the 3000m-plus altitude. Short scrambles from the road-head take you to the four sets of waterfalls at **Nithi Falls**, while longer walks (3–6hr round trip) take you north to **Mugi Hill**, **Lake Ellis** and the flat-topped peak known as the **Giant's Billiard Table** or Mount Kilingo.

Minto's to Point Lenana
From the road-head (a 3hr trek from *Meru Mount Kenya Lodge*), all wheels are abandoned as you slog on foot up towards *Minto's Hut*, a six-hour stint away in the high moorlands. The route tracks along the axis of an ascending ridge, then flattens onto the rim of the spectacular **Gorges Valley**, carved deep by glaciation. There are unobstructed and encouraging views up to the peaks as you hug the contours of the valley wall.

Minto's Hut, at 4300m is, like *Mackinder's* on the west side of the mountain, a three- to five-hour hike from Point Lenana. Situated by the four small **Hall Tarns**, it's perched above the larger **Lake Michaelson** at the head of the valley below – a very beautiful place, inspiringly set off by giant groundsel, lobelia plants and weird volcanic formations inhabited by rock hyraxes. The hut is only for porters. Beware of the tarn water, which is not pure; boiling it at this altitude (water boils at 85–90°C) will kill fewer bugs than usual, so you should use purifying tablets or iodine.

On the morning of day three you have two options. The first is to head up to the ridge west of *Minto's* and follow it, through pretty scenery, to **Simba Tarn**, below Simba Col.

OPPOSITE THOMSON'S FALLS (P.195) >

2

From there, head due south around the peaks and past little **Square Tarn** before turning right to follow the contours for a tough kilometre to the so-called **Curling Pond** (matches have been held on the ice here) and *Austrian Hut*. If you're thinking of a short cut straight up to Square or Upper Simba Tarn, note that it's very steep. Alternatively, from *Minto's* make for the base of the ridge extending east from Point Lenana, then tackle the cruel scree slope to the south for a ninety-minute scramble up to a saddle, followed by a straight drop to the head of the **Hobley Valley** with its two tarns. From here, it's just an hour across to the base of Lenana Ridge, behind which, again, is *Austrian Hut*. Mercifully, whichever route you choose, this day's hike is a short one and at this altitude (over 4000m) you'll be glad to spend the rest of the day at one of the huts, recuperating for the final ascent. Considering the altitude, a safer and probably more comfortable option would be to spend a second night acclimatizing at the base of Simba Tarn, followed by a pre-dawn assault on Point Lenana on day four. As on the Naro Moru approach, the new via ferrata on the approach to Lenana is a big help (see p.173).

After the climb to Lenana, you have a ninety-minute **descent** from *Austrian Hut*, tracking back and forth over miserable scree, to the Teleki Tarn at the head of the Naro Moru stream. *Mackinder's*, and the scent of civilization, is just an hour away down the valley. But if you can resist that lure, and it is still early in the day, *and* if you have enough food and water, you can continue around the west side of the peaks to **Hut Tarn**, then up and down over the ridges to the site of the former *Kami Hut*, at the head of the Sirimon route on the north side. If you want to do it, and you feel acclimatized, there's no problem making it from *Minto's* to Point Lenana and on down to the Met Station in one day.

ARRIVAL AND DEPARTURE
CHOGORIA ROUTE

By bus Buses connect Chogoria with Embu (several daily; 1hr 30min); Meru (several daily; 1hr); Nairobi (several daily; 4hr).

INFORMATION AND TOURS

Services Chogoria has a KCB bank with ATM, but no Barclay's. There are several porter/guide associations in Chogoria, most of whose members are extremely pushy. The most reliable is the Mount Kenya Chogoria Guides Association, based at the *Joywood Hotel* (☎ 064 22266 or 0733 262448). Expect to negotiate a wage of around Ksh500–1000/day per porter.

ACCOMMODATION

Note that *Minto's Hut* is not open to tourists – once you've passed the gate to the park, the only accommodation on the ascent is in your own tent. On your descent, the *Austrian Hut* and *Mackinder's Camp* offer beds (see p.173).

Chogoria Forest Station Campsite 2km from Mutindwa ☎ 0721 744454. Decent site on the edge of the park, dominated by a fine, huge-leaved *Anthocleista zambesiaca* tree. Firewood is available. Camping Ksh600 per person

Chogoria Gate Special Campsite Up the main track from Chogoria Gate, reserve via ☎ 0726 610508, ⓦ kws .go.ke. This is a beautiful place to camp, near *Meru Mount Kenya Lodge*. Camping $15 per person

★ **Meru Mount Kenya Lodge** At 3015m, just before Chogoria Gate ☎ 0729 390686. The very good and beautifully located *bandas* of Meru Mount Kenya Lodge are

just before the gate. Firewood is available for the fireplaces in each *banda*, and there's a basic shop that usually has beer. The lodge is often visited by buffaloes, and you can sometimes see elephants at the nearby waterholes. Whole *banda* Ksh1500 per person, camping Ksh300 per person

Transit Motel 1.5km off the main road south of Chogoria at Karaa Market ☎ 0721 973133, ⓦ transitmotelchogoria.com. By far the best of several lodgings near Chogoria Village, with reasonable self-contained rooms. To get here, alight from your bus or matatu at Kiriani stage, 3km south of the Chogoria turn-off. Double Ksh1900

The Sirimon route

The **Sirimon route** leads up from the A2 highway from a point some 14km east of Nanyuki. The route climbs over the northern moorlands, giving superb views of the main peaks as well as the twin lesser peaks of Terere (4714m) and Sendeyo (4704m), which have small glaciers of their own.

There are certain advantages in using this route: it's the driest route, the scenery is more open, and it's renowned for wildlife. *Bantu Mountain Lodge* (see p.166) offers all-inclusive **guided tours** up to Point Lenana using this route, as do other Naro Moru and Nanyuki operators. Independent trekking is fine if you're in a small group, but if you're looking to team up with others, you're much less likely to find company here than on the Chogoria or Naro Moru routes as, apart from the huddle of *dukas* on the highway, 9km below the park gate, there isn't any real base to start from.

ACCCOMMODATION   **THE SIRIMON ROUTE**   **2**

Accommodation consists of the *Sirimon Bandas* at the gate, *Old Moses Camp* at the road-head (3400m up and accessible only by 4WD), the porters' *Liki North Hut* at 3990m – with camping nearby (see p.173) – and *Shipton's Camp* bunkhouses at 4200m.

Old Moses Camp At 3400m ⓦ mountainrockkenya.com. Alpine huts, formerly known as *Judmeier's Camp*, with basic bunk beds and friendly atmosphere. Both huts have a kitchen and dining area with a clean and well-maintained bathroom. Owned by *Bantu Mountain Lodge*. Bed only ‾S̲4̲0̲
Shipton's Camp At 4230m ⓦ mountainrockkenya .com. Just below the main peak and used often for the

night before the final summit hike, this mountain hut offers basic bunk beds. Owned by *Bantu Mountain Lodge*. Bed only ‾S̲4̲0̲
Sirimon Bandas At 2650m, just outside the gate ☏ 020 3568763, ⓦ kws.go.ke. KWS-run operation with two four-bed *bandas* together with a campsite. Whole *banda* K̲s̲h̲3̲0̲0̲0̲

Treks around the peaks

Though most people head straight up to Point Lenana, trekking round the peaks is an even more exhilarating experience, with the bonus of exploring some of the tarns and glacial valleys on the north side. It is reckoned to be easier to do this anticlockwise in two or three days. If you want to do it in one day, however, set off clockwise from *Mackinder's* via the site of the former *Two Tarn Hut* next to **Hut Tarn**, set in a glorious and eerily silent col beneath the glaciers and scree. The walk from here round to Point Lenana is very much a switchback affair but, as long as the mists stay away, the scenery is fairy-tale. If you're fairly fit and acclimatized, it should take eight to ten hours. Both the *Two Tarn Hut* and *Kami Hut*, on the north side of the peaks, have been demolished, but you can still camp at both sites.

Other routes: Burguret and Kamweti

The trails described above represent only the most obvious and well-trodden of the mountain's possibilities. With time and the right gear, you could **hike** the moorland and peaks area for as long as you liked. Note, however, that you must be fully self-sufficient, you must inform the rangers at the park gate where you buy your tickets of the route you intend to take, and you must exit and sign out via one of three approved gates, paying any fees owed.

Burguret

Bantu Mountain Lodge's preferred route used to follow the **Burguret River** up from the lodge through thick bamboo forest and moorland, but this is now mostly overgrown and hard to follow without a guide. The lower trail passes a clutch of caves described as a "Mau Mau conference centre" (the lodge offers half-day hikes or mountain-bike trips on this trail).

Kamweti

The southern flanks of the mountain seem to have largely escaped the notice of hikers, but there are several forest stations in the vicinity of Embu and plenty of scope for exploration. Most of the southern slopes were a designated "Kikuyu reserve" during the colonial period, so few European climbers created routes up here, but the **Kamweti route** from *Castle Forest Lodge* is becoming more popular (see p.165).

Nanyuki

North of Naro Moru, the A2 runs across the yellow-and-grey downs, scattered with stands of tall blue gums, roamed by cattle and overflown by brilliant roller birds, before dropping to **NANYUKI**. You might be forgiven for expecting something momentous to take place at the **equator**, just south of town. There's a sprouting of curio shops and signs ("This sign is on the Equator") and even an "Equator Professor" who claims to demonstrate the Coriolis effect of the earth's rotation using a bucket of water and a matchstick (aided by sleight of hand). In the northern hemisphere a large body of still water in a perfectly formed vessel would gurgle through a plug hole anticlockwise, whereas in the southern hemisphere it would flow clockwise – though in practice the direction of flow is controlled by the operator because the Coriolis effect is too tiny to

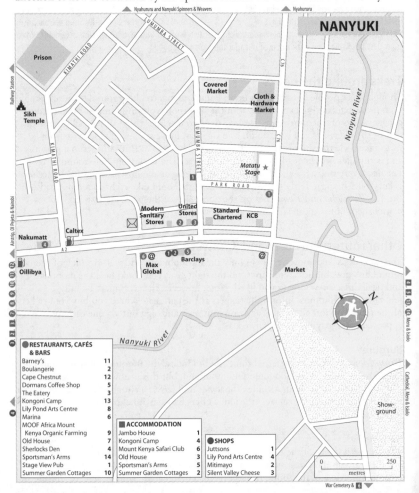

NANYUKI

Nyahururu and Nanyuki Spinners & Weavers

Nyahururu

Prison

Railway Station

Sikh Temple

KIMATHI ROAD

LUMUMBA STREET

Covered Market

Cloth & Hardware Market

C76

Nanyuki River

Matatu Stage

PARK ROAD

Airstrip, Ol Pejeta & Nairobi

Modern Sanitary Stores

United Stores

Standard Chartered   KCB

Nakumatt

Caltex

A2

Oillibya

Max Global

Barclays

A2

Market

A2

C76

Nanyuki River

RESTAURANTS, CAFÉS & BARS

Barney's	11
Boulangerie	2
Cape Chestnut	12
Dormans Coffee Shop	5
The Eatery	3
Kongoni Camp	13
Lily Pond Arts Centre	8
Marina	6
MOOF Africa Mount Kenya Organic Farming	9
Old House	7
Sherlocks Den	4
Sportsman's Arms	14
Stage View Pub	1
Summer Garden Cottages	10

ACCOMMODATION

Jambo House	1
Kongoni Camp	4
Mount Kenya Safari Club	6
Old House	3
Sportsman's Arms	5
Summer Garden Cottages	2

SHOPS

Juttsons	1
Lily Pond Arts Centre	4
Mitimayo	2
Silent Valley Cheese	3

Showground

0   250
metres

Meru & Isiolo

Cathedral, Meru & Isiolo

War Cemetery &

have an impact, especially anywhere near the equator itself where the effect is zero. The demonstration is free; the "certificate" comes for a fee.

Nanyuki has the dual distinction of being Kenya's air-force town and playing host to the British Army's training and operations centre. And although it has taken in thousands of refugees in recent decades, escaping from rural poverty and ethnic violence, it remains very much a country town in atmosphere, and an oddly charming one. Yet the town is becoming popular with foreign and Kenyan investors, and **real-estate prices** have doubled in recent years. The town's modern Nakumatt supermarket, the funky new Lily Pond Arts Centre (see p.181), and assorted coffee shops and restaurants are a sign of things to come.

A wide, tree-lined main street and the mild climate lent by its 2000m altitude bestow an unfamiliar, cool spaciousness that seems to reinforce its colonial character: shops lining the main road include the Modern Sanitary Stores (aka Modsan; they sell camping gas) and the Settlers Store ("1938").

Brief history

The first party of **settlers** arrived in the district in 1907 to find "several old Maasai *manyattas*, a great deal of game and nothing else". Nanyuki is still something of a settlers' town and European locals are always around. The animals, sadly, are not. Although you may see a few grazers on the plains, the vast herds of **zebra** that once roamed the banks of the Ngare Nanyuki (Maasai for "Red River") were decimated by hunters seeking hides, by others seeking meat (particularly during World War II, when eighty thousand Italian prisoners of war were fed a pound of meat each day), but most of all by ranchers protecting their pastures.

Animal Orphanage and Wildlife Conservancy

At Mount Kenya Safari Club, 8km southeast of the town centre • Ksh1000

As the zebra herds dwindled, so lions became a greater threat to livestock and the predators retreated, under fire, to the mountain forests and moors. These days, the non-profit **Animal Orphanage and Wildlife Conservancy** is doing good work with waifs and strays and has an active **bongo breeding programme** which is now working on reintroductions. The orphanage, resembling something out of *Dr. Doolittle*, hosts llamas, zehorse (zebra/horse), pygmy hippos, cheetahs, adorable patas monkeys and even the late William Holden's 100-year-old tortoise.

Nanyuki Spinners and Weavers workshop

Located about 1km down the Nyahururu road, on the left • ☎ 0720 220899, ⓦ www.spinnersandweavers.org

This women's group employs more than 130 local women and sells their rugs and blankets, woven on hand looms, at decent prices (Ksh500–10,000). It's a recommended trip, and they appreciate visitors.

ARRIVAL AND DEPARTURE   NANYUKI

By plane Nanyuki's airfield is 9km south of the town centre on the way to Naro Moru and has several scheduled flights a day to and from Nairobi. It's also the home of local charter company Tropic Air (☎ 020 2033032 or 0722 207300, ⓦ tropicairkenya.com) and has a very pleasant bar-restaurant serving Kenya's best cappuccino, as well as the excellent Laikipia Wildlife Forum info centre and Laikipia Outpost shop, where you can pick up gifts and essential leaflets on regional attractions and

accommodation (Mon–Fri 8am–5pm).
Destinations Maasai Mara (2 daily; 1hr 15min); Nairobi (2 daily; 40min).
By matatu Isiolo (several daily; 2hr); Nakuru (several daily; 5hr); Nairobi (several daily; 3hr 30min); Nyahururu (3hr); Timau (frequent; 30min).
By bus Nairobi (2–3 daily; 3hr 30min); Nakuru (1 daily; 5hr); Naro Moru (2–3 daily; 30min); Nyahururu (1 daily; 3hr); Nyeri (2–3 daily; 1hr 30min).

INFORMATION

Information and tours If you're looking for guides/porters for the Sirimon route up Mount Kenya, try Montana Treks in the *Jambo House Hotel* building (☏06220 32731), but be sure to insist on card-carrying KWS-approved personnel. The airport (see p.179) has some useful information on the area too.

Services There are ATMs at KCB, Barclays and Standard Chartered, all in the town centre. For the internet, try Max Global (Mon–Sat 8am–8pm, Sun 11am–8pm), next to the *Marina Grill*, or the cybercafé at the Equatorial Supermarket.

ACCOMMODATION

You can **camp** at *Kongoni Camp* and usually at the *Sportsman's Arms*. Also bear in mind that Naro Moru (see p.166) is only a 20min drive away, and there are some good places to stay and eat between the two town centres.

Jambo House Lumumba St, opposite the park ☏0729 821218 or 0721 654982. You get what you pay for here, an unembellished place to sleep, and most rooms are dark and airless, albeit with hot water. Breakfast is Ksh100. Room only Ksh700

★ **Kongoni Camp** 1km north of the town centre on the way out to Meru, then 200m off the highway south ☏0702 868888 or 062 2031225, ⓦkongoni camp.com. Campsite, fine-dining restaurant, pizzeria, café and bar, deservedly popular as a celebration spot for returning Mount Kenya trekkers. The *bandas* and hotel rooms aren't huge, but they're clean and cosy, with instant showers, and the overall setting and mood of the place are spot on. Highlights include free wi-fi, stone-oven pizza and a "tented spa". Bed only Ksh8600, camping Ksh650 per person

Mount Kenya Safari Club 8km southeast of the town centre ☏020 2216940, ⓦfairmont.com/kenyasafari club. Founded by Hollywood star William Holden, and recently entirely renovated, this lavish resort hotel offers extraordinary levels of comfort but seems to relate little to its local environment. Plenty of activities and facilities in and around the hotel, including tennis, riding, bird walks, golf, swimming and visiting the stylish art gallery and the not-to-be-missed animal orphanage (see p.179).

Good-value online advance purchase deals available. Bed only $400

★ **Old House** Haile Selassie Rd, 1km south of the town centre ☏0722 697868 or 020 3526007, ⓔoldhousenki@gmail.com. A clutch of cool, clean, modern cottages, overlooking the gardens and the little Nanyuki River, each divided into two comfortable rooms with TVs (but no nets, fans or a/c), with a well-established bar-restaurant. BB Ksh4500

Sportsman's Arms North side of town ☏062 32348 or 0734 944077, ⓦsportsmansarmshotels.com. An old establishment, with various parts renovated, improved or neglected. The old cottages ooze atmosphere but main-block rooms and newer cottages are better equipped, though not with nets or a/c. Decent-sized outdoor pool, hot tub, sauna and fitness centre for Ksh300. The weekend discos can be testing if you're a light sleeper. BB Ksh6900

Summer Garden Cottages South of town just off the highway, by Old House ☏0702 189729 or 0712 626222, ⓔlilmuri50@yahoo.com. Series of tented cottages set up around a spacious open garden with modern bar, lounge and restaurant. There's a good selection of continental meals and a good bar. BB Ksh6500, camping Ksh1000 per person

EATING AND DRINKING

★ **Barney's Bar & Restaurant** Nanyuki airfield, 9km south of the town centre ☏0723 310064, ⓦbarneys nanyuki.com. The people here have created an effortlessly cool ambience on a veranda overlooking lawns next to the runway. Drop in for great coffee or a big English breakfast, or call ahead for a list of the day's specials. It's a little pricey (Ksh550 for chips and salad, Ksh950 steak and chips), but everything is fresh, tasty and really well prepared and they have the nicest loos in Nanyuki – pity it's not open in the evening. Daily 8am–5pm.

Boulangerie Coffee Shop In the town centre ☏0738 342395. Great coffee shop with a trendy ambience in the heart of Nanyuki town. Tempting, expensive coffee, pastries and light dishes. Daily 7.30am–8pm.

Cape Chestnut South of the town centre ☏0705

250650. A popular local rendezvous for English-style home cooking and curries, with wine and beer available; it's known to locals as "LSD". Dishes around Ksh500. To get here, take a left 300m before the road to *Mount Kenya Safari Club* and continue for 700m. Mon–Fri 9am–6pm, Sat 9am–2pm, closed Sun.

Dormans Coffee Shop By Barclays on Main St ☏0702 787890, ⓦdorman.co.ke. Kenya's answer to café culture serves up tasty but pricey smoothies, cakes, sandwiches, and burgers. Daily 7am–7pm.

The Eatery By the corner of Lumumba St and Kenyatta Ave ☏062 2031829. A cosy and quaint boutique-style diner with great selection of fresh and colourful daily specials. Meals from Ksh800. Daily 8.30am–7pm.

★ **Kongoni Camp** 1km north of town on the south

side of the Meru road ☎0702 868888. This popular bar-restaurant specializes in "curries, steaks, pizza and everything". It's quite a big place, with room for sixty, and you can eat in the welcoming high-ceilinged timber and *mabati* bar-fine dining room, or at thatched-roof garden tables. Pizza Ksh650, fillet steak Ksh750. Daily morning–midnight or later.

★ **Lily Pond Arts Centre** Ol Pejeta Rd ☎0726 734493 or 0702 006541, ⓦlilypondartscentre.com. This creative space, restaurant and bar is a wonderful retreat. The open seating areas are spread throughout a series of walkways and a colourful main bar, and the place as a whole is reminiscent of a Frida Kahlo dream set in an eighteenth-century fairy tale. Visit the art gallery showcasing artwork from locals and expats, or try their daily soup, quiche and burger specials (meals from Ksh450). Open late on weekends with a funky well-stocked bar. Movie nights every Sat. Mon–Thurs & Sun 8am–8pm, Fri & Sat 8am–midnight.

Marina Grill & Restaurant Main St, opposite the post office. For a lively drink, and perhaps a meal, try this popular hangout of tourists and soldiers. Something from the snacks and fast-food menu will set you back around Ksh150, with mains taking a lot longer and costing around Ksh300–400. Daily 7am–11.30pm.

MOOF Africa ☎0733 664103, ✉moofafrica@yahoo .com. Mount Kenya Organic Farming's slow-food restaurant serves fresh tilapia, free-range chicken, fresh juices and home-grown organic produce. It's also a great educational visit, with much to teach about permaculture in tropical countries. Fishing and workshops can be organized on the organic farm, which supplies many local restaurants including Dormans and Barney's. You can also camp here for Ksh500 per person. Daily 8am–9pm.

Old House Off Haile Selassie Rd, 1km south of the town centre ☎0722 697868. Pub and restaurant, formerly the popular *Horse's Mouth*, which still does good food, with curries from Ksh400, *nyama choma* at Ksh500 a half kilo and snacks in the Ksh100–300 range. A great spot for a pint with the locals. Daily 8am–midnight.

Sherlock's Den Located upstairs in the new Nakumatt complex on Main St ☎0786 667409. The spacious sports bar and lounge has an extensive and good-value menu including enormous pizzas and Mexican food. Free wi-fi. Daily 7am–1am.

Sportsman's Arms North side of town. Time appears to have stood still for seventy years in the downstairs pub at this old hotel, while their big, upstairs deck bar conforms more to twenty-first-century norms, with table football, pool and discos (Fri, Sat & Sun). Buffet Ksh900. Daily 6am–11pm (later if it's busy).

Summer Garden Cottages South of town just off the highway, by Old House ☎0702 189729 or 0716 626222. Multi-cuisine restaurant and bar serving everything from Indian to Chinese and Italian for Ksh600–700. Daily 7am–midnight.

SHOPPING

Wandering around Nanyuki's small **shops** is quite fun. The *Lily Pond Arts Centre* (see above) has gifts, crafts and art on sale and is worth a look.

Juttsons Main St. The main bookseller and stationer, with good local knowledge. Mon–Sat 8am–5pm.

Mitimayo Craft Shop Main St, next to Barclays. Superior bric-a-brac, crafts and souvenirs.

Silent Valley Cheese Off the highway to Nyeri, to the right. Sample and buy local cheese including their popular mozzarella, cheddar, yoghurt and paneer varieties – the cheeses are delicious even if the office doesn't look like much. Daily 8am–6pm.

Timau

Leaving Nanyuki eastwards, the ring road skirts closer to the mountain than at any other point in its circumference. The extremely fertile land here is for the most part covered by rolling wheatfields and commercial estates; many people work on the acreages of poly-covered flower and vegetable fields.

After 19km you come to the high-altitude village of **TIMAU**, unremarkable but for two outstanding stopover possibilities with accommodation.

ARRIVAL AND DEPARTURE   TIMAU

By public transport Frequent buses and matatus connect Timau with Nanyuki (30min), Meru and Isiolo. Both accommodation options would require a taxi or a long walk from the main road.

By plane The nearest airport is located just south of Nanyuki.

ACCOMMODATION AND EATING

Kentrout Trout Farm 3km to the south of Timau up a rough, signposted track (4WD in rainy weather) ☎ 072 1950691 or 072 0804751. A delightful retreat, the gardens, river and indigenous forest teeming with birdlife and colobus monkeys. The restaurant (daily 8am–5pm) offers delicious alfresco lunch buffets (Ksh1000), the ingredients for which are grown or bred on the farm. There are three rooms in a rambling old ranch house and a number of self-contained, rather run-down *bandas*, plus one self-service stone cottage for rent. HB <u>Ksh7000</u>, FB <u>Ksh8000</u>

★ **Timau River Lodge** 2km east from Timau and 1km off to the south ☎ 0721 331098 or 0716 703111,

✉ timauriverlodge@hotmail.com. The dream of a charming Afghan couple, this lodge (a diverse collection of log, mud and underground houses) was built to run on ecological principles. Every *banda* has its own small kitchen (there's also a communal cooking area with ancient Scottish cast-iron ovens) and children will adore the loft bedrooms in the largest *bandas*. You can camp anywhere you like (tents and bedding are an extra Ksh1500 per person). Trout fishing and mountain climbing are on offer, and there are secluded waterfalls and river pools for bathing in, plus a huge expanse of forest to explore. Per person rates: camping <u>Ksh700</u>, FB <u>Ksh4000</u>, HB <u>Ksh3250</u>, BB <u>Ksh2500</u>, self-catering <u>Ksh2000</u>

East to Meru

After Timau, the scenery acquires a real grandeur as you pass along the southern fringes of the Lewa Wildlife Conservancy (see p.504). The 70km from Timau to Meru couldn't illustrate better the amazing variety of climate and landscape in Kenya. The road climbs steeply to almost 3000m, passing alternative routes to the peaks and giving unparalleled views of them in the early morning. A spectacle you might not have guessed at, however, is the panorama that spreads out to the north as the road drops once again. On a really clear day, after rain has settled the dust, this is devastatingly beautiful. Even on an average day, you can see as far as the dramatic mesa of **Ol Olokwe**, nearly 100km north in the desert. Isiolo (p.537) lies out there, too, first stop on the way to the northern wilderness. East of the Isiolo and Lewa turn-off, the road to Meru suddenly plunges through verdant jungle, with glimpses through the trees of the Nyambeni Hills and volcanic pimples dotting the plain.

ACCOMMODATION   EAST TO MERU

Rutundu Log Cabins About 20km east of Timau you reach the North Imenti petrol station, and 300m beyond that, the hour-and-a-half, 4WD-only track to this rustic retreat on the rarely visited northeast side of Mount Kenya – or you can charter a helicopter from Lewa or Nanyuki. No telephone, but reservations ☎ 0727 232445 or 0731 325797, ⊛ rutundu.com. On the moorland shore of little Lake Rutundu at 3000m,

beneath the dramatically flat-topped Rutundu hill, this is the perfect place for getting away from it all – and even better if you want to have large trout for dinner every night. The comforts are elementary, yet it's exclusive at the same time – and given huge cachet as the place where Prince William proposed to Kate Middleton. Self-catering, sleeping up to 8. Closed Nov & April 15–30. Exclusive use <u>$570</u>

Meru

The moist, jungle atmosphere around **MERU**, with wood smoke curling up against a background of dark forest, is very reminiscent of parts of West Africa, and a change of mood after the dryish grasslands on the northwest side of the mountain. **Meru oak** is the commercial prize of this forested eastern side of the mountain, though judging by the number of active sawmills at the upper end of the town, supplies won't last much longer. The forest still comes almost to the town's edge, however, with tall forest giants still looming high, and paths lead off to cleared *shambas* where, for a year or two, just about anything will grow.

Meru town stretches for several kilometres down the mountain slopes, with great views from the upper (**Makutano**) half of town over the densely settled lower areas. The municipal **market** is large, and it's the obvious place to sample the excellent agricultural

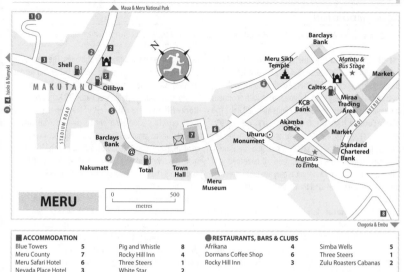

■ ACCOMMODATION					
Blue Towers	5	Pig and Whistle	8		
Meru County	7	Rocky Hill Inn	4		
Meru Safari Hotel	6	Three Steers	1		
Nevada Place Hotel	3	White Star	2		

● RESTAURANTS, BARS & CLUBS			
Afrikana	4	Simba Wells	5
Dormans Coffee Shop	6	Three Steers	1
Rocky Hill Inn	3	Zulu Roasters Cabanas	2

produce of the district: they grow the best **custard apples** in Kenya here, and you won't find cheaper, bigger or better bunches of *miraa* anywhere (see box, p.184).

Meru Museum

Daily 9am–6pm • Ksh500 • Ⓦ tinyurl.com/cletop

The tiny but fascinating **Meru Museum** is a treat. It occupies the oldest stone building in town, a former District Commissioner's office, where you're likely to be the only visitor, except at weekends when they also do special film shows for local children. The emphasis is on the traditional culture of the Meru people: small ethnographic exhibits, pick-up-and-feel blocks of fossilized wood, stone tools from a prehistoric site at Lewa Downs and some woeful stuffed animals. There's a particularly good **herbal pharmacopoeia** – a collection of traditional medicinal plants growing in the garden, where you can see what a *miraa* bush looks like – and the museum's **Meru homestead** is well presented.

If you're interested in the Meru tribe, ask at the museum about the **Njuri-Ncheke traditional courthouse**, approximately 9km north of Meru on the road to Maua. The Njuri-Ncheke is a semi-secret society of elders sworn to preserve and uphold traditional cultural structures and religion.

ARRIVAL AND DEPARTURE   MERU

By bus and matatu Meru is a hub for transport south, west and east. Numerous bus and matatu companies have their offices between the mosque and *miraa* trading area, and most major destinations are served from the main stage, with the exception of Embu, vehicles for which leave from the western end of Moi Avenue.

Bus destinations Embu (several daily; 2hr); Maua (3 daily; 1hr); Mombasa (4 weekly; 12hr); Nairobi (several daily; 5hr); Nanyuki (2–3 daily; 2hr); Thika (several daily; 4hr).
Matatu destinations Isiolo (1hr); Maua (several daily; 1hr); Nairobi (6hr); Nanyuki (2hr).

INFORMATION

Services All three main banks have ATMs here, and you can use the internet at the cybercafés outside Nakumatt (Mon–Sat 8am–10pm, Sun 10am–10pm) and under the

Meru Safari Hotel (Mon–Sat 8.30am–9.30pm, closed Sun), among other places.

ACCOMMODATION

In keeping with its market-town functions, Meru has no shortage of accommodation, but there's nowhere much above adequate.

★ **Blue Towers** At the junction of Meru-Maua Rd in Makutano ☎064 30309 or 064 30225. Decorated with paintings and posters, this offers excellent value, with TVs, nets and safes in every room. Deluxe rooms, with enormous bathrooms, cost a few hundred shillings more. BB Ksh2100

Meru County Near the town centre ☎0700 120910 or 0723 332234, ✉merucountyhtl@gmail.com. Resting on its laurels and now rather tired and overpriced, but most rooms have balconies, and all have nets and satellite TVs. Hot water, however, is only available mornings and evenings. It's managed by Meru Municipal Council. BB Ksh2000

Meru Safari Hotel Tom Mboya St ☎064 31500, ⓦmerusafarihotel.kbo.co.ke. Large hotel, with a rather institutional feel and smallish rooms with instant showers, but clean and pleasant enough, with a nice terrace bar-restaurant and, overall, better value than its County neighbour. BB Ksh2000

Nevada Place Hotel By Makutano's shopping centre, along the Meru-Nanyuki road ☎0715 599999 or 0715 760761, ⓦnevadapalacehotel.co.ke. Large, attractive hotel with conference facilities, next to the Wakulima Market. BB Ksh2800

Pig and Whistle On the lower side of town, on the Meru-Nkubu Rd ☎064 31411, ✉puritykobia@gmail.com. One of the most recognizable hotels in Meru, this is an old colonial-era pub, surprisingly still open. The new rooms attached to the old building are slightly better, but tend to be noisy, while the garden rooms have TVs, nets and big windows but older-style shower-baths. BB Ksh2200

Rocky Hill Inn 8km northwest of Meru on the Nanyuki road ☎0714 190424. An ornate creation with chalets almost hidden among the landscaping and overgrown gardens, this has an unreliable water supply and is perhaps more a weekend *nyama choma* venue than a hotel, but is endearingly weird and worth a visit. The quaint little rooms are non-s/c. BB Ksh3000

Three Steers 2km along the Nanyuki road, past Makutano ☎0728 588005 or 0725 683724, ⓦnairobi pacifichotels.com. This large motel-type complex has good rooms with nets and TVs, though conventional rather than instant showers. There's also a *nyama choma* joint, two bars and a cheap Indian-influenced restaurant. Safe parking. It has comfortable rooms that are good for a short stopover. BB Ksh2300

White Star Moi Stadium Rd ☎064 32989. Sister hotel of the *Blue Towers* at the junction, and similarly decorated with garish artworks and high standards and facilities. Standard rooms are large and airy and include TVs, safes and nets ("Hippo" is the best), while deluxe rooms have four-poster beds with a separate shower and tub. The restaurant doesn't serve alcohol. BB Ksh2000

MIRAA

Throughout Kenya, and especially in the Central Highlands and on the coast, you'll often see people selling and chewing what looks like a bunch of twigs wrapped in a banana leaf. This is **miraa**, more commonly known abroad by its Somali name **qat**, a natural stimulant that is particularly popular among Somalians, Somali Kenyans and Yemenis. The shrub (*Catha edulis*) grows in the hills around Meru (the world centre for its production), and the red-green young bark from the shrub's new shoots is washed, stripped with the teeth and chewed, with the bitter result being something of an acquired taste (it's usually taken with bubble gum to sweeten it). *Miraa* contains an alkaloid called cathinone, a distant relative of amphetamine, with similar **effects**, though you have to chew it for some time before you'll feel them. When they do kick in, they include a feeling of alertness, ease of conversation and loss of appetite. Long-term daily use can lead to addiction. It's not always looked upon favourably, with signs prohibiting the chewing of it in many hotels and bars.

Miraa comes in bundles of a hundred sticks called "kilos" (not a reference to their weight) and various **qualities**, from long, twiggy *kangeta*, which is the ordinary, bog-standard version, to short, fat *gisa kolomba*, which is the strongest. As it loses its potency within 48 hours of picking, it's wrapped in banana leaves and transported at speed. Street stalls selling it often display the banana leaves to show that they have it, and the best place to buy *miraa* in many towns is where the express matatus arrive from Meru. The use of *miraa* by bus, truck and matatu drivers goes a long way towards explaining why they have so many accidents. There are no **legal restrictions** on the use of *miraa* in Kenya, although imams have issued a *fatwa* (legal judgement) condemning it as an intoxicant, like alcohol, which means that it is forbidden to true believers. In fact, in most countries (but not the UK), *miraa* is a controlled narcotic, the possession of which is a criminal offence.

EATING AND DRINKING

Meru doesn't have any outstanding places to **eat**, but everywhere is reasonably cheap. Most of the hotels have good restaurants that serve a selection of African dishes – as well as the ones listed in this section, *Meru Safari Hotel* has good old *nyama choma* and beer, *Gatimene Palm* offers a relaxed garden dining experience, *Blue Towers Hotel* has a great selection from both buffet and à la carte menus and *Westwind Hotel* is popular for its filling English breakfast. If you're **self-catering**, there's a huge new Nakumatt at the upper, Makutano, end of town. Makutano district is also the centre for **nightlife**.

Afrikana Moi Ave. Popular restaurant offering a wide variety of tasty and affordable African dishes in a fresh environment. Most dishes Ksh150–200, *chai* Ksh15. Daily 8am–10pm.

Dormans Coffee Shop This branch of the Kenyan chain offers the best coffee and fresh pastries in Meru. Daily 8.30am–9pm.

Rocky Hill Inn 8km northwest of Meru on the Nanyuki road ☎0714 190424. At the weekend, you might want to venture here for their *nyama choma*. They even do a bring-your-own deal: you supply the animal, they do the rest (goat roast Ksh2500, chicken Ksh200). Daily 7am–9pm.

Simba Wells 50m from the Makutano Junction, along the Meru–Embu Highway. Always jam-packed during the weekends, this is the most famous nightspot in Meru. They have reasonably priced beer, great *nyama choma* and a large dancefloor. Daily 11am–6am.

Three Steers 2km along the Nanyuki road, past Makutano ⓦ nairobipacifichotels.com. This hotel's clean and appetizing restaurant is the most upmarket place in Meru. Their Indian dishes include plenty of vegetarian options. Ksh200–300. Daily 7am–9pm.

Zulu Roasters Cabanas At an outdoor courtyard opposite the mosque. You can't go far wrong with the fast food and drinks here – you can stuff yourself for about Ksh100. Daily 10am–6am.

Embu and around

The fast road from Meru to Embu swoops around the eastern slopes of Mount Kenya through vibrant scenery. Five kilometres south of Meru, you cross the **equator**, and it's indicative of the lack of tourism round here that there's not a single curio stand, let alone a "Professor Coriolis" (see p.178). Hundreds of streams, the run-off from luxuriant rainfall blown in by the southeast monsoon, cut deeply into the volcanic soil of this eastern flank of the mountain. As a result, this side has a much broader covering of jungle, which extends, *shambas* permitting, down to the level of the road and beyond. Driving along, you plunge from one green and tan gorge to the next – early in the morning (the safest time to travel) you can sit back and admire the scenery. Sit on the right side of the vehicle for glimpses of snow-capped peaks, normally visible at this time of day. Most public transport between Meru and Embu stops at **Chogoria**, a base for the eastern Mount Kenya ascent (see p.176), although if you're staying overnight you might consider continuing to the livelier market town of **CHUKA**.

There's very little to get excited about at **EMBU**, and it's not obvious why it was chosen as the capital of Eastern Province. Without the apparatus of a provincial headquarters, the town wouldn't amount to much, although its proximity to Mount Kenya has resulted in a fair range of accommodation, mostly in the form of small motels.

ARRIVAL AND DEPARTURE   EMBU AND AROUND

Most public transport between Meru and Embu stops at Chogoria (50min from Embu) and Chuka (35min from Embu). Heading south, transport from Embu along the Kangonde route goes to Thika, with only a few matatus bound for Kitui (2hr). The trip to Nairobi via Sagana is covered by dozens of buses and matatus. If you want to climb **Mount Kenya** from Embu, the closest route is via the idyllic *Castle Forest Lodge* (see p.165).

By bus from Embu Meru (several daily; 2hr); Nairobi (several daily; 2hr 30min); Sagana (several daily; 1hr); Thika (several daily; 2hr).

By matatu from Embu Isiolo (3hr 30min); Meru (2hr 30min); Nairobi (2hr 30min); Sagana (1hr); Siakago (several daily; 1hr).

ACCOMMODATION

CHUKA

Kimwa Farmer's Hotel On the B6 highway in the centre of Chuka ☎ 020 630570. Has *nyama choma*, a busy disco and sometimes live music at weekends. BB **Ksh2000**

New Thuchi Lodge South of Chuka ☎ 020 2074559 or 0734 465625, ✉ karueinvestco@yahoo.com. Relatively upmarket local haunt with beautifully tended tropical gardens, a large pool, well-kept rooms with nets and TVs and very spacious two-bedroom cottages. To get here, turn off the main B6 road 8km south of Chuka at Kathegeri, and take the easterly direction on the E652 signposted "Kigumo 7km". The lodge is 3km down this decent earth road. BB **Ksh2000**

EMBU

★ **Izaak Walton Inn** At the top end of town, on the way out northwards, towards Meru ☎ 068 31128 or 0712 781810, ⓦ izaakwaltoninn.co.ke. By far the best place in Embu is a colonial-era former farmhouse, now an assemblage of green-*mabati*-roofed and newer buildings, with pleasant gardens, welcoming staff and an enthusiastic local clientele. Rooms are clean and comfortable, with nets and TVs, and mix colonial fixtures and fittings with refurbishments. There's quite a range to choose from, so check several rooms before deciding. It's also a decent place for a drink or meal. BB **Ksh3800**

Highway Hotel Haile Selassie St, off Kenyatta highway ☎ 0722 827700, ⓦ mainahighwayhotel.com. This hotel is distinguished by good modern facilities, a location in the heart of Embu and a pool. BB **Ksh2000**

Kryptonite Hotel Opposite Embu Municipal Council Offices ☎ 068 31090 or 0728 398455, ⓦ thekryptonitehotel.com. Spacious en-suite rooms, high-speed free internet, laundry services and ample, secure basement parking. BB **Ksh3300**

EATING AND DRINKING

Embu has a number of decent *hotelis* doing reliable food. Most of the hotels also have restaurants: the *Izaak Walton Inn* offers the most sumptuous food selection in Embu, and other options include the restaurants in *Kryptonite Hotel* and *Prime Lodge*.

Morning Glory Hotel Opposite the Exhibition Centre, Embu. For chicken and chips and other inexpensive fare.

Rehana's Café A little way up the hill near the post office, Embu. This has been busily serving up excellent spicy samosas for more than 25 years.

The Kiangombe Hills

The relatively modest altitudes of the **Kiangombe Hills** (Kiangombe peak is 1804m) aren't enough to lure climbers, but the unspoilt district, upstaged by Mount Kenya and ignored by tourists and travellers, is worth a visit if you have an interest in mysterious folklore. The hills are the home of the **Mbere**, who are related to the Kikuyu, Embu and Meru, and have a reputation in Kenya as possessors of magical powers. Some villages have elderly sages, **Arogi**, credited with terrifying abilities, though others – the **Ago** – have more beneficent gifts like the ability to foretell the future or find missing goats. The identity of these "witches" is at best a hazy and mysterious one which people aren't in any hurry to talk about and is further confused by the supposed existence in the hills of a race of "**little red men**" whose diminutive size (estimated at 1.2m) and fleeting appearances in the bush have led more imaginative scientists to suppose that they might be *australopithecines*, or ape-men, hanging on into the twenty-first century. They and the Ago-Arogi may be just part of the "old people" mytho-history of central Kenya, which is at least partially based on the real, ancient and probably Cushitic-speaking peoples of two thousand or more years ago. Such, anyway, are the stories that might draw you from the main highway.

Siakago

SIAKAGO is the main centre of the Kiangombe Hills. Siakago isn't a ki-Mbere word and its derivation is uncertain. It may well have derived from "Chicago", after a group of American anthropologists based themselves here in the 1930s and started the ape-men stories. It's a pleasant and relaxed one-street town, all deep-red earth, green vegetation and colourfully painted shop fronts. As well as basic services, there's a noisy little market (main days Tues & Fri), which mostly sells livestock at extortionate prices, and several mission churches set amid the huts and *shambas* on the outskirts.

Exploring the hills

The Kiangombes rise behind Siakago and look deceptively easy to **climb**. In fact, it's a stiff hike to the top, better as a two-day trip with an overnight camp in the hills. You start with a 10km hike to **KUNE**, northeast of Siakago, followed by a 2km walk to a **forest station**, where you'll find the start of the main approach to the summit area. You should pick up a **guide** at the forest station (expect to pay around Ksh1000), which may have to be coordinated in Siakago or Kune the day before. From the forest station, ignore the disused vehicle track winding into the hills; it soon becomes difficult to follow. Instead, use the **footpath** leading straight up from behind the huts, which takes you in about four hours to the peaks area. Much of your way is likely to be impeded by thick vegetation and, if you're alert to every photographic possibility, you'll find following the overgrown trail can be tiresome, so ensure someone in your party has a *panga* to trail-blaze it with. As you climb, human population quickly thins out; this is "red-people" territory and traditionally feared by the Mbere.

2

ARRIVAL AND INFORMATION

THE KIANGOMBE HILLS

By matatu Siakago can be reached from Embu by matatu (5–6 daily; around 30min).

By car From the north, take the B7 road from Embu, turning off at Musonoke, to Siakago. You can also reach

Siakago from Kitui (see p.315) in about 2hr.

Services Siakago has a scattering of *hotelis* (usually combined with butchers), a petrol station and two B&Ls.

Mwea National Reserve

$20 • ☎ 068 20301 or 020 6000800, ⓦ tinyurl.com/mweanationalreserve • 42 square kilometres

The **Mwea National Reserve** is well worth the effort if you're looking for solitude and want to avoid the touristy atmosphere of some other parks and reserves. It's a beautiful area with a wealth of ornithological interest and wildlife including giraffes, buffaloes, antelopes and elephants, though the big beasts can be hard to see. With your own tent you can camp either by the main gate or on the sloping site near the shore of the reservoir, though swimming is highly inadvisable – the crocs have a mean reputation.

ARRIVAL AND DEPARTURE

MWEA NATIONAL RESERVE

By car The easiest way to get to the reserve is via the tarmac B7 Embu–Kangonde road. Some 15km south of Embu, the signposted *murram* road off the B7 to the reserve is passable all year round. Further along the B7, on the south side of the hydroelectric Kamburu dam, another

signposted road heads in via Masinga Dam from just before the village of Kaewa: the first 11km are tarmac, the remaining 12km *murram*, liable to be impassable in wet weather. One kilometre to the left, at the end of the tarmac, is the hilltop Masinga Dam Resort.

ACCOMMODATION

Masinga Dam Resort 1km from Masinga Dam ☎ 020 3417847 or 020 248254, ✉ mdresort@tarda.co.ke. The resort is located on a hilltop, overlooking the reservoir. It

has a pool and a choice of rooms – both prefab tents and suites with better views. BB Ksh4300

Aberdare National Park

$50 with Safari Card (see p.71) • ⓦ tinyurl.com/aberdareNP • 767 square kilometres

Aberdare National Park splits into two different environments: the **high moorland and peaks** which form its bulk, and the lower **Salient** to the east where the vegetation is dense rainforest and there is considerably more wildlife.

In order to protect the park's **wildlife,** in particular its fifty-odd black rhino (one of the largest populations in Kenya), but mainly to arrest the conflict between wildlife and humans, which most visibly manifested itself in the trashing of crops and homes fringing the park by "rogue" or "rampaging" elephants, the KWS has built a 388km

2

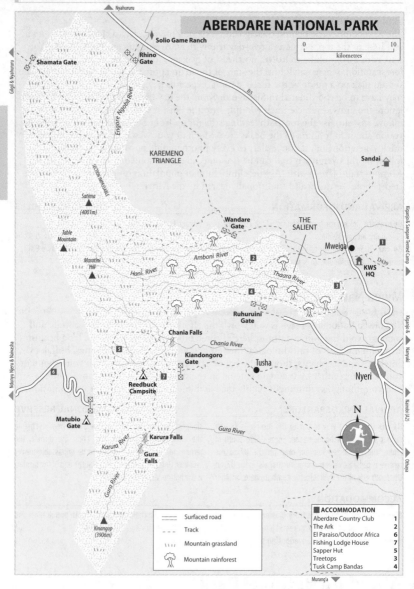

electric fence to encircle the national park and the forests of the Aberdare Conservation Area, with the support of **Rhino Ark** (🌐rhinoark.org) and the annual Rhino Charge **motor race** (see p.68).

The high park

The high moorlands have some exceptional **walking** and include **three peaks**, Lesatima (the highest at 4001m) in the north, Il Kinangop (3906m) in the south, and Kipipiri

HISTORY OF THE ABERDARE RANGE

The Kikuyu called these mountains Nyandarua ("drying hide", for their silhouette) long before Joseph Thomson, in 1884, named them after Lord Aberdare, president of the Royal Geographical Society. In their bamboo thickets and tangled forests, Kikuyu **Mau Mau guerrillas** hid out for years during the 1950s, living off the jungle and surviving thanks to techniques learned under British officers during the Burma campaign in World War II, in which many of them had fought. Despite the manhunts through the forests and the bombing of hideouts, little damage was done to the natural habitat, and Aberdare National Park remains one of Kenya's most pristine forest reserves.

On the western side, the range drops away steeply to the Rift Valley. It was here, in the high Wanjohi Valley, that a concentration of settlers in the 1920s and 1930s created the myth of the glamorous, decadent **Happy Valley** out of their obsessive, and unsettled, lives. There's not much to see (or hear) these days. The old wheat and pyrethrum farms were subdivided after independence and the valley's new settlers are more concerned with making their market gardens pay. The memories live on only among veteran *wazungu*. The Kinangop plateau (p.215) was settled by Europeans, too, but in 1950 the high forest and moorland here was declared **Aberdare National Park**.

2

(3349m), an isolated cone outside the park above the Wanjohi Valley in the west. They can be climbed relatively easily, given good weather conditions. It takes about three hours to climb Lesatima and two hours back down again. *Sandai* (see p.194) organize climbs, or ask the Mountain Club of Kenya in Nairobi for details (see p.69). *El Paraiso* (see p.191) can also arrange guiding. Hiking in the park is allowed only with the approval of the warden, so apply in good time. You may be required to take a guide (whom you'll have to pay).

Unless you're planning several days of walking, fishing or camping, the most straightforward visit to the moorlands is to spend a day driving through from one side to the other between the **main gates**, Matubio and Ruhuruini. There are two other eastern gates further from Nyeri (Wandere and Kiandongoro) and two at the remote north end of the park (Shamata, accessible from Nyahururu, and Rhino Gate, from the B5 Nyeri–Nyahururu road), but there's no reliable route through the park between north and south, and the small circuit of tracks in the north is very rough. Driving via the park from Naivasha to Nyeri (or vice versa) is easy enough in good weather with 4WD. If conditions are less than ideal, however, and you get stuck, you could be in for a long day, or a miserable night. You need to check **road conditions** with the rangers at the park gates. Surfaces are mostly red *murram*, though there are also a few, very steep, rocky sections. It's usually permissible to wander a short distance from your car, though the lion situation changes from time to time.

Naivasha to Matubio Gate

From Naivasha, follow the signs for the national park via the Uplands road as if going to Nairobi, as far as the junction for Kinangop on the east side of town. From here, you climb about 14km, on reasonably intact tarmac, past the National Youth Service camp to Karima, where you turn left onto a good dirt road. After another 5km or so, you reach Kipipiri junction, where you keep right.

At **Ndunyu Njeru** centre, you pass the last chance of fuel and the final stop of matatus up from Naivasha. Back on the route to the gate, the road finally runs out of reasons to continue except to the national park itself, becoming a narrow, quite acceptable, tarmac switchback, and climbs through the vegetation zones, with increasing evidence of elephants (dung everywhere), to pitch out finally through the highest extent of the forest at Matubio Gate, on the threshold of the moorland. Along the last 7km there are some excellent views back down to Lake Naivasha. Allow two to three hours to get this far.

2

Matubio Gate to Ruhuruini Gate

Allowing four hours from Matubio Gate to Ruhuruini Gate gives time enough, in good weather, for visits to Chania Falls and Karura Giant Falls. Proper access to the top of the **Karura Falls** (there's no way down to the bottom) was built only in 1992, by the British Army's Royal Engineers. They've created two superb, dizzy, timber viewpoints, one on each side, from which you can look across through dripping, Afro-Alpine vegetation to the babbling, 4m-wide Karura stream as it plunges over the abyss, dropping nearly 300m in three stages. To the south, the distant veil of the **Gura Falls**, a kilometre or two across the yawning canyon, seems to make for a surfeit of dramatic beauty.

The much lower, sheer drop of the **Chania Falls** has rickety access walks and platforms (be careful), and you can gaze from the top, or the bottom, and even contemplate a swim in the pool. It was near here, in 1984, that an American tourist was badly mauled by a lion, an incident that so unnerved the park's authorities that for many years there were tough rules on unaccompanied walking. In 2000, this was followed by a cull of more than one hundred lions, many of which had been relocated from Solio Ranch. The cull was intended to rebuild the safe reputation of the park and give various herbivores, such as the giant forest hog and bongo, a chance to increase their endangered populations. In the case of the giant forest hogs, that has been rather *too* successful, but the bongos are still recovering only slowly.

The 15km east to **Ruhuruini Gate** descends in a breathtaking helter-skelter through the cloud forest, with stunning views across jungle-cloaked valleys. The road down to Nyeri from the gate is in good condition and you soon reach tarmac.

The Salient and the Tree-hotels

Kenya's most famous hotel, **Treetops**, was hosting Princess Elizabeth in February 1952 when she became **Queen Elizabeth II** on the death of her father George VI. The original tree house she stayed in was burned down in 1955 by Mau Mau freedom fighters; the present, much larger, construction is an ugly box, built on stilts, with a few trees growing through it. The main Nyeri road passes by just 3km away, and *shambas* and villages are easily visible: this is no jungle hideaway. Both tree-hotels, *Treetops* and *The Ark* (see opposite), are located in the controlled area called **the Salient**, a lower-altitude extension of the Aberdare National Park. Depending on the season, mist and low temperatures can affect both lodges: take warm clothes.

The problem at *Treetops* is clear when you survey the scene from the open-air "top deck". It is a victim of its own success. The laying of **salt** by the waterhole guarantees the nightly arrival of heavyweight camera fodder, but has brought about the destruction of all the nearby forest by elephants. The current scene – tree-planting areas enclosed by electric fences and acres of mud – is neither popular with visitors nor good for wildlife. That shy forest antelope, the bongo, hasn't put in an appearance since 1988. Despite the lack of cover, black rhino are seen roughly every other night, and leopard two or three times a month. But efforts to encourage hardwood forest regeneration behind the electric wires seem doomed to fail – they've been trying for more than thirty years.

ARRIVAL AND GETTING AROUND   ABERDARE NATIONAL PARK

Naivasha (see p.189 & p.215) and Nyeri (see opposite) are the usual bases.

By car Driving in the park is beautiful, with waterfalls and sensational views more than compensating for comparatively scarce wildlife. On the west side of the park, Matubio Gate is a 50km drive from Naivasha. On the east, distances from Nyeri are: Ark Gate 28km, Treetops Gate 29km, Ruhuruini Gate 20km, Kiandongoro 30km and Wandare Gate 47km.

By plane The nearest airstrip is located at Mweiga along the Nyeri–Nyahuru road next to Sasini Estate Farm.

By matatu Ndunyu Njeru is the final stop of matatus up from Naivasha, and from the last few kilometres to the park gate you will need to hire private transport. It's relatively easy to get around the lower parts of the range, with regular bus and matatu services between the villages. To head over the mountains and through the park, however, you need your own 4WD vehicle unless you're prepared to wait for a lift for days (you could try the *Outspan Hotel* in Nyeri). Few organized tours venture up there.

ACCOMMODATION

THE HIGH PARK

There are several accommodation options in the high park, including camping at the basic *Reedbuck Campsite* near *Fishing Lodge House*. With the exception of *El Paraiso/Outdoor Africa*, all are reservable in advance through KWS (☎0726 610508 or 0736 663421, ⊛kws.go.ke).

Fishing Lodge House Some 2km inside the Kiandongoro Gate, located on open moors above the Magura River. Two stone-built, *mabati*-roofed cottages, each with three bedrooms and seven beds. Central, open-fire cooking and eating area. You need to take food, warm sleeping bags and firewood; wood-fired boiler tanks outside produce hot water. Whole house $180

Camp Kipipiri/El Paraiso/Outdoor Africa About 9km north of Ndunyu Njeru centre ☎050 2050246 or 0722 715853, ✉kipipiri@gmail.com, ⊛campkipipiri.blogspot .co.uk. A pleasantly rustic, multi-monikered adventure centre, offering camping, meals, guided walks and safaris. Bronze guide. Camping Ksh1000 per person, with tent hire Ksh3000 per person

Sapper Hut Some 10km west of the Fishing Lodge, on a little tributary of the Chania River, at around 3000m. A wooden *banda* with living room, double bedroom, fireplace, veranda, wood-fired boiler and chilly outside bathroom. Paraffin lamps (bring paraffin), bed sheets, firewood and basic cooking facilities are provided, but take bedding, towels, food and drinking water. Collect the key from the *Fishing Lodge*. Ksh2500 per person

Tusk Camp Bandas About 2km inside the park from Ruhuruini Gate, at 2300m. Tucked into a glade surrounded by forest, there are two wooden *bandas* here (one with two double beds, one with four single beds), an ill-equipped kitchen (bring pots, pans and cutlery), a pit latrine with one of Kenya's most regal views, and a caretaker to help you out. Visits from here to the Salient should be possible if you enquire first with the rangers at the gate. Full *banda* $120

THE TREE-HOTELS

The Ark The Salient ☎0736 799990, ⊛thearkkenya .com. The normally good game-viewing here is helped by the wide variety of viewing points. Accommodation is a little more spacious than at *Treetops*, and since recent renovations the lodge has become exceedingly cosy; all rooms are en suite and while being quite small have a healthy dose of charm and luxury. Dinner is usually excellent, and you eat breakfast up here before returning to the affiliated *Aberdare Country Club in Nyeri*. Children under 7 not accepted. BB $290

Treetops The Salient ☎061 2032425 or 0722 207761, ⊛aberdaresafarihotels.co.ke. This tall, thin lodge, only 6m from front to back, has something of the creaking atmosphere of a wooden ship, and the corridors and standard rooms are very cramped. The entire place has recently undergone noticeable renovations (all rooms are now s/c), which have brought the hotel up to par with its royal reputation, but it still brings to mind a *Travelodge* made of wood. Dinner remains notoriously variable – excellent and copious one night, like a school dinner the next. Children under 5 not accepted; unsuitable for wheelchair-users. BB $343

Nyeri

The self-styled capital of Kikuyu-land – a title the Kikuyu of Kiambu might dispute – **NYERI** is the administrative headquarters of Central Province and a lively, chaotic and friendly highland town, whose name derives from the Maa word *nyiro*, meaning "reddish brown", after its earth. An attractive trading centre, it nestles in the green hills where the broad vale between Mount Kenya and the Aberdare range drops towards Nairobi. Tumultuous markets, scores of *dukas*, and even a few street entertainers, lend it an air of irrepressible commercialism.

Another former British military camp, Nyeri emerged as a market town for European coffee growers in the hills and for settlers on the ranching and wheat farms further north. Nyeri was also the last home of Robert **Lord Baden-Powell**, founder of the worldwide scouting movement, whose cryptically named Paxtu cottage, now a small museum ($5), stands in the grounds of the *Outspan Hotel* and whose grave and memorial are to be found on the north side of town in the cemetery. The **Baden-Powell Scouts Information Centre** (optional donation) plans a small museum and guesthouse here, and it's interesting, as ever, to have a look at the old graves in the cemetery.

2

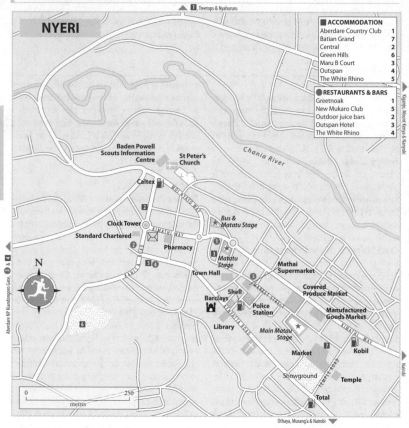

NYERI

■ ACCOMMODATION	
Aberdare Country Club	1
Batian Grand	7
Central	2
Green Hills	6
Maru B Court	3
Outspan	4
The White Rhino	5

● RESTAURANTS & BARS	
Greetnoak	1
New Mukaro Club	5
Outdoor juice bars	2
Outspan Hotel	3
The White Rhino	4

ARRIVAL AND DEPARTURE

NYERI

By bus and matatu The bus stage and main matatu stages are on Kimathi Way.

Bus destinations Eldoret (1 daily; 5hr); Nairobi (2–3 daily; 2hr 30min); Sagana (2–3 daily; 1hr).

Matatu destinations Eldoret (4 daily; 5hr); Kisumu (7hr); Nairobi (3hr); Nakuru (3hr 30min).

By car A signposted route leads west from Nyeri, past the *Outspan* (see opposite), up into the Aberdare range and to the park's Kiandongoro Gate in the high moorland. In the other direction, the road splits out of town, forking south to Murang'a via Othaya, Kiriani and Koimbi (a good road all the way), or continuing east to the A2 highway and the

quickest return route to Nairobi via Sagana. A fourth route takes you northwest out of town, splitting in two after 2km. Take the right fork for the A2 highway for Naro Moru and Nanyuki, via Kiganjo. Fork left to take the B5, which sweeps past the road for Aberdare Park's Ruhuruini Gate, the track for *Treetops*, the turning to the right (east, on the D439) for the *Aberdare Country Club*, Mweiga (8km from Nyeri), and, finally, the track up to *The Ark*. A kilometre or so south of Mweiga, on the east side of the road, is the national park's KWS headquarters, the only point of sale for Smartcards in the highlands.

INFORMATION

Services Nyeri has branches of all the banks, including Barclays, KCB and Standard Chartered, all with ATMs.

Internet access is widely available, especially along Market Street.

ACCOMMODATION

Nyeri's role as a rural business centre and major transport crossroads means there are plenty of cheap places to **stay** in town, as well as the historic *Outspan*.

Batian Grand Market St ☎ 061 2030743 or 0722 265863, ⓦ batianhotel.com. Ageing but acceptable block of small rooms around a central courtyard, with nets and TVs in every room. Conscientiously run but overpriced. BB Ksh3400

Central Kanisa Rd ☎ 061 2030296 or 0722 667437. Secure s/c rooms, all with nets and instant showers, some with balconies and TVs (Ksh300 extra). The newer rooms are good value and breakfast is included. It's the best place in Nyeri for *kienyeji*, and there's occasional live music at weekends. BB Ksh1600

Green Hills Bishop Gatimu Rd, 1km south of town ☎ 061 2030604, ⓦ greenhills.co.ke. A decently run, busy hotel but not as slick as its prices, which for non-residents are nearly twice the residents' rates (ask about their more basic rondavels). Rooms are fine, with nets. This is mostly a conference base, with a big gym and aerobics suite, a pool and extensive gardens and lawns. BB Ksh8000

Maru B Court Off Kimathi Way ☎ 020 2144518. Reasonable, and probably better than the *Batian* for its good security and busy bar-restaurant below the rooms – as long as you don't rule out a place where the rooms have

nets and lime green walls, with no toilet seats or instant showers. Bed only Ksh1600

Outspan Off the Kiandongoro Gate road (2km west of the clock tower on Kanisa Rd) ☎ 061 2032424 or 0722 207762; reservations through ⓦ aberdaresafarihotels .com. Built in 1927 and set in splendid grounds, the stately *Outspan* (the base for visits to *Treetops*) is comfortable enough, but has the irritating flaws of its era which won't endear it to visitors expecting international standards: there are, for example, no fans, nets, a/c or room safes. The showers can be iffy, and some rooms are on the small side. The new (Chania) wing rooms are larger, with better showers, tubs and fireplaces, while the rooms in the old building have the most character (especially those downstairs, with balconies) and lovely garden views. Activities include a chilly pool, guided bird walks, the neighbouring nine-hole golf course and various excursions. FB $400

The White Rhino Kenyatta Rd ☎ 0736 046784, ⓦ whiterhinohotel.com. One of the largest and most reliable hotels in Nyeri. The nightclub within the same compound is busy (the noise isn't too bad) every night but the rooms are nicely finished with satellite TV. BB Ksh7000

EATING AND DRINKING

Nyeri has a number of interesting restaurants and bars, a cheese factory (from which lots of produce is available locally) and a clutch of juice bars near the Standard Chartered bank, which do very nice, tall glasses of avocado, beetroot and regular fruit juices for around Ksh40.

Greenoak Kimathi Way. Very good value, serving up top-quality *nyama choma*, plus stews, curries and fried dishes (Ksh200–400). If the weather's okay, the first-floor terrace-bar, overlooking the commotion below, is fun too, and serves alcohol. Daily 6am–midnight.

New Mukaro Club Opposite the Mathai supermarket. A pleasant boozer (offering meals for about Ksh450)with a balcony. They even serve rabbit. Daily 8.30am–11.30pm.

Outspan Hotel Off the Kiandongoro Gate road (2km west of the clock tower on Kanisa Rd). This atmospheric pile welcomes day-visitors for its excellent buffet lunches

(Ksh1400), or for tea on the lawn and a swim in the pool (Ksh500). The hotel's *Tavern Bar* is pleasant enough for a beer in the evening in civilized surroundings. Daily 11am–late.

The White Rhino Kenyatta Rd. Nyeri's most put-together fast-food joint, selling burgers and pizza – they're nothing special, but it's the cleanest restaurant in the centre. The hotel's restaurant offers lunch buffets, and the bar/nightclub within the same complex is very popular with the locals. Mon–Thurs & Sun 6am–11pm; Fri & Sat 6am–late.

Around Nyeri

The extraordinary density of **cultivation** in the tightly spaced *shambas* around Nyeri (crops include maize, cassava, sugar cane, millet, squash and citrus fruits, as well as tea, coffee and macadamia nuts) is partly a hangover from white settlerdom, when a rapidly growing population was deprived of huge tracts of land and forced to cultivate intensively. Partly, too, it's the result of land consolidation – the "rationalization" of fragmented land holdings into unitary *shambas* that took place in the 1950s, turning people who had held traditional verbal rights into deed-holding property owners. It's also the simple consequence of an excellent climate and soil, plus a birth rate reckoned to be one of the highest in the world.

There's no doubt that the changes which have taken place in Nyeri District have been some of the most profound and rapid anywhere in the country. Even the villages of

2

Kikuyu-land are nearly all innovations of the last sixty years, the irreversible effects of the Emergency. Until then, the Kikuyu had mostly lived in scattered homesteads among their crops and herds. British security forces, unable to contain open revolt in the countryside, began the systematic internment of the whole Kikuyu population into fenced and guarded villages, forcing the guerrillas into the high forests, and the villages of today have mostly grown from such places.

North of Nyeri, the B5 passes several routes into Aberdare National Park, including the tracks for the tree-hotels. Eight kilometres from Nyeri you'll find the hilltop centre of **Mweiga**; several ranches offer good spots to relax and watch wildlife in the vicinity.

Sangare Conservancy

Conservancy fee $55 • ⓦ sangareconservancy.com • From Nyeri, head north towards Mweiga, turn east onto the D439 and drive 5km past the *Aberdare Country Club;* from the Kiganjo side, head via the *murram* D439 road, which branches off the A2 3.5km north of Kiganjo and 20km south of Naro Moru

The main draw of **Sangare Conservancy**, north of Nyeri, is its **birdlife**, with migratory pelicans, glimpses of crowned eagles and black-headed herons squawking loudly in the trees. There are usually some elephants and buffalo in the vicinity, as well as zebra, gazelle, hyena, Sykes' and colobus monkeys, and the occasional leopard, while darkness brings a fantastic chorus of frogs and toads. The low-key and affordable *Sangare Tented Camp*, appealingly located on a lakeshore in the conservancy, was closed at the time of writing.

Solio Game Ranch

$60 • ☎ 020 249177 or 061 2055271 • Well signposted 30km north of Nyeri off the main road to Nyahururu; you can also visit the ranch by joining a trip from Sandai or the Aberdare Country Club • Seventy square kilometres

Solio Game Ranch lies a few kilometres north of Mweiga, off to the right. Privately run, the Solio more or less single-handedly saved the Kenyan black rhino from extinction, breeding them here for subsequent translocation into the national parks and other Kenyan reserves. From an original population of 23 black rhino, there are now 70, and of the original 16 white rhino, imported from South Africa, the population now stands at more than 140.

ACCOMMODATION

AROUND NYERI

Aberdare Country Club 11km out on the Nyahururu road near Mweiga, then signposted 3km along the D439 murram road ☎ 020 2144216 or 0722 205407, ⓦ aberdarecountryclub.com. Parts of this former farmhouse date from 1930, and much of it, such as the dining room in the old house, is still attractive. The 49 rooms are in 25 cottages, built in the 1960s and still furnished comfortably, if not stylishly, while the old "Nursery Wing" has spacious family rooms with older fittings. The whole property, which has just completed significant renovations, sits on the 50-square-kilometre ACC game sanctuary, with warthogs, bushbucks, suni and even the odd leopard, together with 170 species of birds. Activities include an unheated pool, tennis and game walks. They're under the same ownership as *The Ark* (see p.191), and tours often take in both. FB $400

★ **Sandai** 11km northeast of Mweiga ☎ 0733 734619, ⓦ africanfootprints.de. This German-family-run farmhouse is a charming and relaxing rural homestay, with comfortable and very attractive rooms. Activities include horseriding ($60/day), day hikes to the Aberdares, overnight excursions, painting and yoga. The two two-bedroom self-catering cottages (€100) are also beautifully furnished, with fireplaces and kitchens. To get here from Mweiga, head north for 4.2km from the town centre – note the white tyre in the earth on the east side of the road, marked "Sandai 7km" (beneath a sign announcing "St Joseph Mahiga Secondary School"). Follow this for 5.3km, turn left and after a further 600m right, then follow the white tyres to the farmhouse. FB $180, camping Ksh500 per person

Solio Lodge Solio Game Ranch ☎ 020 249177, ⓦ thesafaricollection.com. Only opened in 2010, this exclusive farm and safari getaway on one of Kenya's oldest conservancies has just six large and luxurious cottages, complete with high thatched roofs and modern glass-walled bathrooms. Highly recommended, assuming price is not an issue. Conservation fee $60. Closed Nov. FB $1130

Nyahururu (Thomson's Falls)

Like Nanyuki, **NYAHURURU** is almost on the equator, and it shares much of Nanyuki's character. It's high up (at 2360m, Kenya's highest town), cool and set on open savanna lands with patches of indigenous forest and plenty of coniferous plantation. Since the B5 road to Nyeri was completed, Nyahururu has been less cut off, but it's still something of a frontier town for routes north to Lake Turkana and the desert. A tarmac road goes out as far as Rumuruti and then the fun begins (see p.519).

Joseph Thomson gave the town its original name when he named the nearby waterfall after his father in 1883. Many still call it "T. Falls", and not just the old settlers you might expect. Thomson's Falls was one of the last settler towns to be established. The first sign of urbanization was a hut built by the Narok Angling Club in the early 1920s to allow its members to fish for the newly introduced trout in the Ewaso Narok, Pesi and Equator rivers. In 1929, when the railway branch line arrived, the town began to take shape. The line has closed now, but the hotel built in 1931, *Thomson's Falls Lodge*, is still going strong, and Nyahururu remains an important market town, and not really a tourist centre. The **market** is well worth a browse, especially on Saturdays. It sprawls out over most of the district west of the stadium, an indication of the town's rapid growth over the last couple of decades.

NYAHURURU

RESTAURANTS & BARS
Bettan Hotel & Lodge — 3
Emms Café — 5
Kejo's Stage View Restaurant — 4
Nyahururu Steak House — 2
Suera Flowers — 6
Waterfalls Resort — 1

ACCOMMODATION
Equator Lodge — 4
Laikipia Comfort Hotel — 2
Nyaki — 3
Safari Lodge — 5
Thomson's Falls Lodge — 1
Thomson's Falls Sports Camp and Hostel — 6

The falls

On the northeast outskirts of town, **Thomson's Falls** are pretty rather than spectacular, though they can be dramatic when the Ewaso Narok is in flood after heavy rain. The falls are a popular stopoff for tourists travelling between Samburu and Maasai Mara game reserves, and the hotel lawns above the falls get crowded with picnickers from town at weekends. Uniformed council officials have taken to extracting an "entrance fee" at the turning from unwary tourists: only pay if they can give you an official ticket or receipt, otherwise tell them you have business at the hotel. The path leading down to the bottom of the 75m falls is somewhat dangerous, especially when wet, and you should ensure there have been no recent incidents of robbery. Don't attempt to climb up again by any other route, because the cliffs are extremely unstable.

Excursions around Nyahururu

With a couple of hours to spare, you can search for a longer walk down into the forested valley, following the **Ewaso Narok River**. If you want to try this, cross the road bridge first, then look for a way downstream. The spray-laden trees are shaken periodically by troops of colobus monkeys, and chameleons are always around. The area is also fruitful for ornithologists. A much shorter stroll also takes you over the bridge and then past the electricity substation, beyond which the first trail you come to leads to the top of a hill with a communications tower and a skeletal lookout post. Excellent views from here stretch south towards Ol Kalou and the marshy trough of Lake Ol Bolossat.

A longer excursion takes you in quest of the highest **hippos** in Kenya. A kilometre from the turning off to *Thomson's Falls Lodge* on the Nyeri road, you come to a small cluster of *dukas* on the right. Walk down towards the houses closest to town and, about 300m from the road, you emerge by a swampy area fed by Lake Ol Bolossat. The area immediately by the access path is thick with reeds, but walk round the lake to the clump of trees and you can shin up one of these and select a natural observation platform. Sit and watch and you may see as many as half a dozen or so hippos. If you don't find them here, then they're likely to be in Lake Ol Bolossat itself, which has its north shore some 15km south of Nyahururu on the road to Aberdare National Park's Shamata gate.

ARRIVAL AND DEPARTURE
NYAHURURU

By matatu Matatus run down the fairly fast B5 road to Nyeri (1hr 30min) through forested valleys and over immense plains of swaying grass. Other destinations include Maralal (several daily; 4hr), Naivasha (several daily; 1hr 30min) and Nakuru (several daily; 2hr).

By bus Nairobi (1 daily; 3–4hr); Nakuru (1 daily; 2hr); Nyeri (1 daily; 1hr 30min).

By car The mostly unsurfaced C76 road to Ol Pejeta Conservancy and Nanyuki begins at Karai, 15km east of Nyahururu; the B5 road westwards out of Nyahururu descends the escarpment to Nakuru, via the Subukia valley, following the route to Lake Bogoria (see p.232); and lastly, the reasonably quiet C77 road to Gilgil and the Rift Valley heads south out of town, crossing the equator.

INFORMATION

Services The town has branches of KCB and Barclays, both with ATMs. Internet access is at *Clicks Cybercafé* (Mon–Sat 8am–6pm) in the Mima Centre, among quite a few other places.

ACCOMMODATION

Equator Lodge Sharpe Rd ☎ 0710 205809. Basic, small, dark rooms, with TVs and nets. It also has a very-good-value restaurant and bar, and safe parking in the courtyard. Bed only <u>Ksh1200</u>

Laikipia Comfort Hotel Opposite the Cooperative Bank on the way to Nyahururu Catholic Church ☎ 065 2022326. One of the newer hotels in Nyahururu, this is very clean, with good customer reception. BB <u>Ksh2500</u>

Nyaki North side of town, across from Nyahururu Steak House ☎ 065 2022313. The reasonable rooms are on the top floor, with nets, TVs and instant showers, but are perhaps a little pricey as they don't include breakfast. There's a restaurant on the first floor and a bar on the second. Bed only <u>Ksh3000</u>

Safari Lodge Near the bus stage ☎ 065 2022334 or 0722 305735. Relatively spacious, clean rooms, some with balcony and all with TV and instant shower, but no nets.

There's an alcohol ban here, and safe parking. Probably the best of the cheapies. Bed only <u>Ksh1000</u>

★ **Thomson's Falls Lodge** ☎ 020 2608702 or 0724 775027. Abidingly pleasant, friendly old hotel, with a highlands-farmhouse atmosphere and log fires in the rooms, which include nets, lots of polished floors and old-style bathtub-showers. The camping price (Ksh500) includes hot showers and ample firewood. BB <u>Ksh5100</u>

Thomson's Falls Sports Camp and Hostel 6km south of town on the Gilgil road, then east 1.5km ☎ 0722 275827, ⓦ sportscamp-hostel.com. If you have transport, this is a reasonable place to camp, but it's run-down. As well as weary s/c rooms, there's a large campsite, plus dorm accommodation in an old London bus. Hot water mornings only. Camping <u>Ksh300</u> per person, dorm bed <u>Ksh400</u>

EATING AND DRINKING

Bettan Hotel & Lodge Kenyatta Ave. The balcony here is always full of people drinking *chai* above the bustling commerce below. Good service. 24hr.

Emms Café Below Cyrus Lodging, opposite the market. Next to the main bus station along the busy Nairobi highway, this is very clean with excellent service. Whole chicken Ksh720. Daily 6am–9pm.

Kejo's Stage View Restaurant Near the market. Lively and relaxing atmosphere with good, filling dishes and snacks. Samosas from Ksh30 and whole chicken from Ksh280. Daily 6am–9pm.

★ **Nyahururu Steak House** Located right in town next to St Martin Catholic Church on the road to Nyeri.

A cut above the other places in town – a restaurant, coffee house and bar doing decent steaks (Ksh200–350) and good samosas. Daily 7am–11pm.

Suera Flowers If you're driving south to Gilgil, 5km south of the town centre by the Caltex station. This is a slightly upmarket restaurant and *nyama choma* joint, where you can eat well for Ksh300. There's a nice panoramic view of the Aberdares, and rose scents from the flower gardens next to the tents. Live local music on weekends. Daily 7am–9pm.

Waterfalls Resort Near Thomson's Falls ☎0723 823897. Serves up delicious roast meat with fully stocked bar. Ample space for outdoor dining and large groups. 1kg of *nyama choma* Ksh500. Daily 10am–11pm.

2

The Rift Valley

HELL'S GATE NATIONAL PARK

The Rift Valley

Kenya's Rift Valley is only part of a continental fault system that runs 6000km across the Middle East and Africa from Jordan to Mozambique. Perhaps Kenya's most important topographical feature, it is certainly one of the country's great distinguishing marks, acting as a human and natural divide. With its spectacular scenery of lakes and savanna, it has come to be seen as a monumental valley of teeming game and Maasai herders, a trough of grasslands older than humanity. Although the iconic image is no longer entirely borne out by reality, the valley certainly is magnificent, a literal rift across the country, with all the stunning panoramas and gaunt escarpment backdrops you could wish for, and the plains animals are still abundant in places. Nevertheless, much of the game has been dispersed by human population pressure onto the higher plateaus to the southwest, and today most of the Maasai live farther south.

At least the Rift Valley's **historical influence** cannot be diluted. People have trekked down it, generation after generation, over perhaps the last two or three thousand years, from the wetlands of South Sudan and the Ethiopian highlands. Some of the more recent immigrants were the ancestors of the **Maasai**, who dominated much of the valley and its surroundings for several centuries before the Europeans arrived. Until the beginning of the twentieth century the Maasai lived on both sides of the valley, and the northern **Ilaikipiak** group were a constant threat to trading caravans coming up from the coast. With European settlement, the Maasai were forced from their former grazing grounds in the valley's turbulent bottleneck and confined to the "Southern Reserve" (now Amboseli National Park) for much of the colonial era. Although many have now returned to the valley, and many retain their ancient Maa names, the Maasai are at their most conservative and traditional in southern Kenya (see p.360).

The parts of the Rift Valley covered in this chapter offer several exceptional lakes, lots of rocky, twisting roads, and some of central Kenya's wildest areas. Highlights of the **central Rift Valley** include the scenic freshwater **Lake Naivasha**, the dramatic cliffs of **Hell's Gate** and nearby craggy crater rim of **Mount Longonot**, the shallow, alkaline **Lake Elmenteita**, and the busy **Lake Nakuru National Park** with its almost guaranteed rhinos and less certain huge flocks of flamingos. In addition, there are several interesting **prehistoric sites** in this area with a refreshing rawness about them.

Heading into the **northern Rift Valley** away from Nakuru, the land drops away gently, and, as the road descends, so temperatures rise, the landscape dries up and human population becomes sparser. Although this region isn't far from Nakuru or Nairobi, and is

BLACK RHINO, LAKE NAKURU NATIONAL PARK

Highlights

❶ Lake Naivasha and Hell's Gate National Park A hauntingly atmospheric freshwater lake near the sheer red cliffs of Hell's Gate, where the plains have good wildlife, and whose ravine makes for spectacular hiking. **See p.204**

❷ Lake Nakuru National Park Lake Nakuru's picturesque combination of woods, grasslands and lakeshore offers one of your best chances of seeing flamingos, rhinos and leopards. . **See p.222**

❸ Hyrax Hill If you don't visit any other Stone-Age site in Kenya, try to take an hour out for a wander around the eerily evocative Hyrax Hill, just outside Nakuru. **See p.228**

❹ Lake Bogoria The often overlooked Lake Bogoria – with steaming hot springs, greater kudu antelope and remote campsites – makes a wonderful retreat, and in recent years has been the location for the Rift Valley's vast flocks of flamingos. **See p.233**

❺ Lake Baringo A beautiful freshwater oasis in the dry northern Rift Valley, with plenty of hippos, crocs, more than four hundred bird species and a clutch of excellent places to stay. **See p.236**

HIGHLIGHTS ARE MARKED ON THE MAP ON P.202

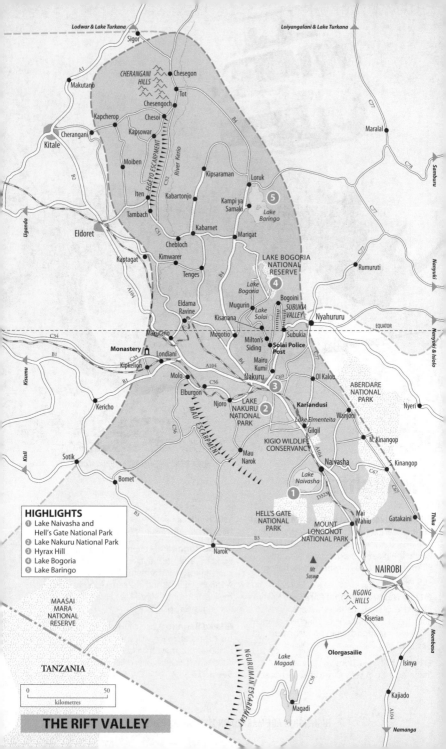

not necessarily a difficult journey, it has a bright, harsh beauty: freshwater **Lake Baringo** and saline **Lake Bogoria** – currently the most likely place in Kenya to see flamingos in their hundreds of thousands – are alluring targets and distinctively different, both from each other and from the lakes further south. This northern region also includes the spectacular **Kerio Valley** (see p.242), which deserves a special recommendation as an unusual route north if you're heading for the west side of Lake Turkana.

Apart from **Naivasha**, **Nakuru** and the string of towns up the western escarpment (**Njoro**, **Elburgon** and **Molo**), the area covered in this chapter contains few places larger than a village. Though there is usually somewhere to lay your head, this is a region where, if you're on a budget, a **tent** will be worth its extra weight, and good walking shoes are a definite advantage. Watch out for the climate too: the northern Rift is lower, and consequently hotter, than most upcountry regions, so be prepared for some very high temperatures and don't underestimate your **water** requirements.

GETTING AROUND   **THE RIFT VALLEY**

Roads and transport are generally fine on the valley floor around Naivasha and Nakuru, but northwards, once you leave the main Nakuru–Baringo–Kabarnet axis, you can expect long waits, next-to-no buses and infrequent matatus.

By car Driving between Nairobi and Naivasha, both the Uplands Road (A104) and the Escarpment or Lower Road (B103) are currently in reasonable shape, though if you're climbing the steep and winding B3 back towards Nairobi on a busy day, it can be slow going in the fumes and traffic. North of Nakuru, there are three possible routes up to Lake Turkana (see p.511), two of them joining with the Kitale–Lodwar road west of the lake,

and the third curving up to Maralal for the east side. You will need a 4WD, spare fuel and water and some flexibility in your schedule.

By matatu or bus Most public transport between Nairobi, Naivasha and Nakuru uses the Uplands Road. North of Nakuru there's reasonable public transport as far as Marigat, though it thins out beyond Lake Bogoria and dries up almost completely north of Lake Baringo.

Nairobi to Naivasha

Many travellers' first proper view of the Rift Valley is from the souvenir-draped **B3 Escarpment Road**, originally built by Italian prisoners-of-war during World War II. This flirts with the precipice before dropping steeply down to the Rift through candelabra euphorbia and spikey agave. The little **chapel** at the bottom, also Italian-built, and often used as a picnic site, seems fitting in this Mediterranean scene.

The alternative route, the **A104 Uplands Road**, goes slightly farther north and joins the B3 at Naivasha. Out of northwest Nairobi, it crosses a broad, bleak plateau, where roadside traders sell rhubarb, plums, carrots and potatoes, and where, in the wet season, you can find yourself driving over a thick carpet of hailstones between gloomy conifer plantations. All this contrasts dramatically with the dusty plains of the Rift Valley. When you start descending, get out your binoculars and you can pick out herds of gazelle, Maasai with their cattle and, bizarrely, a satellite-tracking station.

For years the Uplands Road was the better of the two routes, but they're currently both in reasonable shape, though if you're climbing the steep and winding B3 back towards Nairobi on a busy day, it can be slow going in the fumes and traffic. On the escarpment section, roadside souvenir stands sell crafts and small sheepskins (the latter often excellent value, though they're not always very well cured, so don't last long).

Lake Naivasha

Naivasha, like so many Kenyan place names, is a corruption of a local Maasai name, this time meaning heaving waters, *E-na-iposha*, a pronunciation still used by Maa-speakers in the area. The grassy lakeshore was traditional Maasai grazing land for

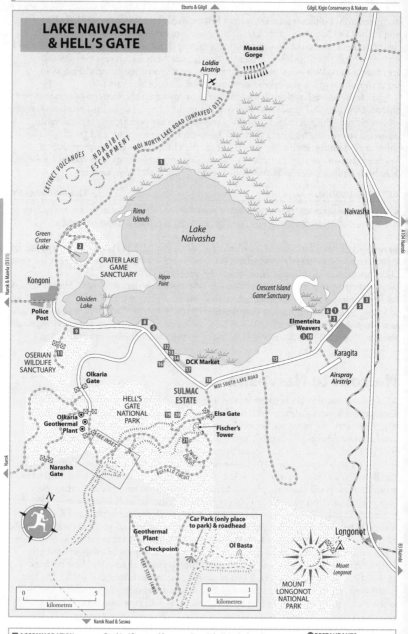

LAKE NAIVASHA & HELL'S GATE

Eberru & Gilgil

Gilgil, Kigio Conservancy & Nakuru

Maasai Gorge

Loldia Airstrip

MOI NORTH LAKE ROAD (UNPAVED) D323

NDABIBI ESCARPMENT

EXTINCT VOLCANOES

Naivasha

A104 Nairobi

Rima Islands

Lake Naivasha

Green Crater Lake

CRATER LAKE GAME SANCTUARY

Hippo Point

Crescent Island Game Sanctuary

Kongoni

Oloiden Lake

Narok & Maiela (D331)

Police Post

Elmenteita Weavers

Karagita

OSERIAN WILDLIFE SANCTUARY

DCK Market

Airspray Airstrip

Olkaria Gate

MOI SOUTH LAKE ROAD

SULMAC ESTATE

HELL'S GATE NATIONAL PARK

Elsa Gate

Olkaria Geothermal Plant

SEE INSET

Fischer's Tower

Narok

YMCA CIRCUIT

Narasha Gate

BUFFALO CIRCUIT

Longonot

B3 Nairobi

Geothermal Plant

Car Park (only place to park) & roadhead

Checkpoint

Ol Basta

VERY STEEP (4WD)

Mount Longonot

0   5
kilometres

0   1
kilometres

MOUNT LONGONOT NATIONAL PARK

Narok Road & Suswa

■ ACCOMMODATION				● RESTAURANTS	
Camp Carnelly's	14	Enashipai Resort and Spa	7	Lake Naivasha Sopa Resort	15	The Club House	3
Chui Lodge	11	Endachata Campsite	19	Nairburta Campsite	20	Geothermal Club	2
Crater Lake Tented Camp	2	Fischers Tower	5	Ol Dubai Campsite	21	Lake Naivasha Country Club	1
Crayfish Camp	17	Fish Eagle Inn	12	Olerai House	1	
Crescent Camp	4	Fisherman's Camp	13 & 16	Sanctuary Farm	10	
Elsamere	8	Kiangazi House	9	Yellow Green Hotel	3	
		Lake Naivasha Country Club	6	YMCA	18	

LAKE NAIVASHA DANGERS

Beware, out on Lake Naivasha. The possibility that underground springs may feed the lake, its location on the floor of the Rift Valley, and its shallowness all combine to produce notoriously fast changes of mood and weather: grey and placid one minute, suddenly green and choppy with whitecaps the next. **Boating mishaps** are all too common and you should be sure your vessel has lifejackets and your "captain" and mate (don't go out with only one crew) have radio contact with the shore, not just a dodgy cellphone connection. Watch out, too, for hippos, which can overturn a small boat easily if frightened or harassed. Although there's no bilharzia in Naivasha, the hippos, the dense weeds, and the occasional sightings of **crocodiles** combine to offset any enthusiasm you might have had for a swim.

two centuries or more, prior to the lake's "discovery" by Joseph Thomson in 1884. Before the nineteenth century was out, however, the "glimmering many-isled expanse" had seen the arrival, with the railway, of the first European settlers. Soon after, the *laibon* Ole Gilisho, whom the British had appointed chief of the Naivasha Maasai, was persuaded to sign an agreement ceding his people's grazing rights all around the lake – and the country houses and ranches went up. Today the Maasai are back, though very much as outsiders, either disputing grazing rights with the many European landowners still left here, working their herds around the boundary fences, or labouring on the vast horticultural farms around the lake.

The **lake**, slightly forbidding but picturesque with its purple mountain backdrop and floating islands of papyrus and water hyacinth, has some curious characteristics. It is fresh water – Lake Baringo is the only other example in the Rift – and the water level has always been prone to mysterious fluctuations. The lake shrunk to half its present size in the 1950s, and although it has recovered since, it remains smaller than it was when the original European settlers arrived (its former extent marked by the outer edge of the fringing band of papyrus, where you can still spot the occasional fence post).

The fast lakeside road has brought tens of thousands of migrant workers to the **farming estates**, where they grow vegetables and flowers, mostly in giant, polythene greenhouses, for export by air to European supermarkets. Since the late 1980s, great stretches of acacia scrub have been cleared for the expansion of the farms, and ugly lines of squalid field-hand housing have sprouted in the dust between the plantations. The mixed, migrant community at impoverished **KARAGITA**, the largest lakeshore settlement, is still scarred by the post-election violence of 2008, which hit it as hard as anywhere in the country, causing thousands to flee.

Despite the development, and the ever-growing encroachment of farms and job-seekers, Lake Naivasha is still a place of considerable natural beauty. The lakeshore retains some patches of fairly unspoilt savanna and woodland, and boasts plenty of local wildlife. Even today, you can still see the odd giraffe as it lopes down to Crescent Island, and the area's climate, with a light breeze always drifting through the acacias, along with the many hiking possibilities around the lake, makes it hard to beat as a first stop out of Nairobi.

On the northeastern side of the lake, **NAIVASHA TOWN** has little to offer as a place to stay, and unless you arrive late in the day, you may as well head straight down to the lake. If you plan to spend any time in the area, however, you may want to go into town to stock up on essentials first.

Elsamere

South Lake Rd • Daily 8am–5pm • Ksh800 • ☎ 050 2021055, ⓦ elsamere.com

Elsamere (see p.209) is the former home of naturalist and painter Joy Adamson, author of *Born Free*, a chronicle of her relationship with a lioness named Elsa. The house is now a field-studies centre and the focus for Lake Naivasha's environmental issues. For visitors, there's a video about Adamson, a small museum and a copious and civilized

> **WILDLIFE OF LAKE NAIVASHA**
>
> One of the lake's most interesting features is its **wildlife**, especially its protected **hippo** population. Despite their bulk, hippos are remarkably sensitive creatures, with good night vision, for never is a camper's guyline twanged. By day you can also, occasionally, still see **giraffes**, floating blithely through the trees, taking barbed wire and gates in their stride. Naivasha has extraordinary **birdlife** of all kinds, from grotesque, garbage-scavenging marabou storks to pet-shop lovebirds, doves cooing in the woods, and splendid fish eagles, whose mournful cries fill the air like seagulls. And Lake Oloiden, once a bay of the main lake, is now a separate, saline lake and frequently has a large flock of several thousand flamingos on its southern shore.

high tea on the lawn. Book ahead if you want to have lunch (Mon–Fri Ksh1200; Ksh1600 at weekends), high tea (Ksh800) or dinner (Ksh1600). While the house and museum are somewhat shrine-like, the garden is a fine place to while away a couple of hours with a pair of binoculars, and a troop of colobus monkeys can be seen in the acacias around the grounds.

Crescent Island Game Sanctuary

Daily 7.30am–6pm • Guides available from 8.30am (free; tips appreciated) – ask the ticket-seller • $25, cars Ksh200, minibuses Ksh300 • ☏ 0733 579935 or 050 2021030, ⓦ crescentisland.co • The island is connected to the shore by a narrow causeway on the private land of Sanctuary Farm, about 2km from Moi South Lake Rd; alternatively, take a boat trip (Ksh2500) from a recognized operator such as the *Lake Naivasha Country Club* and arrange to be picked up later in the day • Horseriding is available at Sanctuary Farm (☏ 0721 346961; Ksh2000/ hr) • Two square kilometres

A very popular short trip is a visit to **Crescent Island Game Sanctuary**. The "crescent" is the outer rim of a volcanic crater, which forms a deep bay, the deepest part of the lake. At first you may think there's nothing much on the island (which has actually been a peninsula for several years), but you'll soon come across a wealth of wildlife, including hundreds of species of birds, as many as four hundred wildebeest and two hundred impala, more than one hundred zebra, a variable-sized herd of giraffe, as well as hippos, waterbuck, Grant's and Thomson's gazelles and some startlingly large, though harmless, pythons.

Oserian Wildlife Sanctuary

Off the southwestern shore of Lake Naivasha • $60 • ☏ 050 2020792, ⓦ oserianwildlife.com • Most visitors come on day or night game drives included in a stay at Oserian's *Kiangazi House* (see p.209), but you could also visit from its sister establishment, *Chui Lodge* (see p.209) • Forty square kilometres

Although it's not on the tourist minibus circuit, and visits are normally restricted to guests at Kiangazi House or Chui Lodge, **Oserian Wildlife Sanctuary** is an accessible and very worthwhile conservation area in a former ranch away from the lakeshore and the road. Judging from the polythene horticulture so prevalent in the area, you might not guess that the same Dutch family behind the biggest flower farm in Kenya – the Zwagers – have set aside this area of land as a sanctuary. There are rarely more than one or two other vehicles visiting, and although the proximity of the lake and its burgeoning population can't be ignored, the reserve comprises an extensive wild area with a good array of big mammals and excellent birdlife (birders won't need reminding about the rare grey-crested helmet shrike that can be seen here).

All guides will be able to find you some of Oserian's impressively long-horned **white rhinos**, a notable conservation success story, now into their second generation and numbering at least fifteen. Look out, too, for species translocated from northern Kenya – greater kudu, Grevy's zebra and Beisa oryx – and for wildebeest and topi from the Mara. One species they are going to have to do something about is the warthog – the sanctuary swarms with them, and there aren't enough leopards, cheetahs and hyenas to keep the numbers down.

THE THORNS OF THE ROSE

Despite the listing of Lake Naivasha as a Ramsar wetland site of global ecological importance in 1995, the future of the lake's delicate ecosystem is far from secure. Naivasha's multimillion-dollar **horticultural industry** is one cause for concern, particularly the use of pesticides on the lakeshore's huge farms and the enormous volumes of water used to irrigate them.

It is becoming increasingly apparent, however, that the survival of the lake and its wildlife depends on a multitude of other factors ultimately linked to the country's growing **population**. Since 1977 the number of people living near the lake has risen at least fivefold, and human waste has become a major problem due to inadequate sewage treatment facilities, with the result that some partially treated effluent is finding its way into the lake. The Malewa and Gilgil rivers (which flow into Lake Naivasha from the north) have also been dammed, rendering the lake even more vulnerable.

Consequently, the lake's wildlife is seriously threatened. Until the exceptional 1997/98 rains raised the lake's level, thereby diluting the pollutants, the **fish eagle** had been especially badly affected, though its numbers now appear to be stable. The birds were not getting enough to eat, and **Louisiana crayfish**, introduced in the 1970s for commercial fishing, were largely to blame. By eating their way through the lake's flora (which, as well as acting as a soak for excess nutrients and a sediment trap, serves as food and cover for some species of fish and birds), the crayfish caused the water to become murkier, making hunting harder for the eagles. Fishermen also complain that tilapia and black bass have sharply declined due to agrochemicals washed into the lake, and many of the area's 350 species of birds, as well as the hippos and other wildlife, are still in danger: the lily-trotter, the great crested grebe and the crested helmet shrike have already all but disappeared.

Some **companies** finally appear to be waking up to their responsibilities. Oserian, the huge Dutch-owned flower exporter, has developed a new way of fighting fungal diseases without resorting to chemicals, using geothermal steam to purge diseases in its greenhouses, while other companies have adopted computerized drip-irrigation to optimize their water efficiency.

Green Crater Lake

17km past Fisherman's Camp and 6km beyond the end of the tarmac and regular transport • $15 • Excellent guides can accompany you from *Crater Lake Tented Camp* (see p.209)

The teardrop-shaped **Green Crater Lake** is a straightforward target for a short trip, but preferably with your own vehicle. A **game sanctuary** has been set up all round the crater, with various tracks you can follow, though the one to the crater rim is only for hikers or 4WD vehicles. The birdlife is exceptional and there's a host of wildlife in the vicinity, including colobus monkeys and bushbuck. The brilliant jade lake is quite breathtaking: the Maasai consider its deep alkaline waters good for sick cattle, and it's also a favourite sacred place. From the main viewpoint on the west rim it's a ten-minute scramble up to the highest point. There are not many places where you can get down to the crater floor – the easiest trails are on the southwest side near the tented camp.

ARRIVAL AND DEPARTURE
LAKE NAIVASHA

A road runs all the way around the lake, branching off from the main A104 Naivasha–Nakuru highway 3km north of Naivasha town. The southern part of this road – the paved, 30km-long **Moi South Lake Road** – is where you'll find most of the lake's accommodation and other facilities. Beyond Kongoni village, you hit the dust and potholes of **Moi North Lake Road**, which loops for 35km (a 1–2hr drive) around the northern side of the lake before rejoining the A104 highway 9km north of Naivasha town.

By plane A daily SafariLink service flies from Nairobi's Wilson Airport to Loldia airstrip on the west side of the lake (continuing to Maasai Mara and then directly back to Nairobi). It's also possible to charter small planes to the short Airspray airstrip on the lake's southeast shore.

By matatu Most matatus crowd in a mass up Kenyatta Avenue in Naivasha town. Those going up to North Kinangop leave from the alley alongside the Sera Centre. Other destinations include Eldoret (6–10 daily; 4hr); Kabarnet (2–6 daily; 2hr); Kericho (6–10 daily; 2hr); Nakuru (20–40 daily; 1hr 15min).

3

THE RIFT VALLEY MUSIC FESTIVAL

Taking its cue from Malawi's increasingly popular Lake of Stars festival, the annual **Rift Valley Music Festival** is Kenya's first international music festival, and has taken place every late August since 2010, at Fisherman's Camp on the shores of Lake Naivasha (☎0715 050588, ⓦbit.ly/FacebookRVFestival; three-day tickets). Energetic and dance-oriented on the Saturday, it turns more low-key and family-friendly on Sunday when the mood is blankets, picnics and beer. The highly recommended festival features mostly Kenyan artists and a few international acts playing from a single, central stage to an audience of a few hundred. Recent line-ups have included Ayub Ogada, DJ Yoda, J Star, Suzanna Owiyo, Frankie Francis, Jesse Hackett from Gorillaz, Joe Driscoll and Felix B from Basement Jaxx. You can stay anywhere around the lake and walk, cycle or get a matatu every day, or book ahead if you want to stay on-site.

GETTING AROUND

By matatu or hitchhiking Regular matatus shuttle between the lake and Naivasha town, and you can also hitchhike down to the lake fairly easily. If you're trying to reach *Olerai House* or Green Crater Lake, however, continuing past Kongoni village along Moi North Lake Road is next to impossible either hitching or using public transport – your only option is to take one of the motorbikes that hang around the junction.

By bike A good way of exploring the lakeshore and Hell's Gate National Park, bicycles can be rented from several of the more independent traveller-oriented camps and a number of roadside operators (around Ksh500/day).

By boat It's possible to go out in a boat at many of the lakeshore establishments, usually for Ksh2500–5000/hr with room for up to eight passengers. Check the life vests before you embark and make sure the crew have radios to contact shore. An hour in a reasonably fast boat will see you over to the main concentration of hippos and back to the south shore.

INFORMATION

Banks There's a full showing of banks with ATMs (including Barclays and KCB) on Moi Ave in Naivasha town. Closer to the lake itself, there's a KCB ATM at Karagita (3.5km from the junction), and KCB and Barclays ATMs at DCK Market (between the *YMCA* and *Carnelly's*).

Internet The Sera Centre on Kenyatta Avenue in Naivasha town is the best place to look for an internet café, or try Mandera Cyber on Moi Ave (daily 8am–midnight; Ksh40/hr).

Post office There's a post office in Naivasha town on Moi Ave.

ACCOMMODATION

There's a wide variety of accommodation **around the lake** along Moi South Lake Road – everything from frugal *bandas* and camping to stately hotels and homestays. The distances mentioned in the reviews below refer to the distance from the lake road junction with the main Nairobi road (which is 3km from Naivasha town itself). Note that a number of lakeshore properties are regularly visited by hippos at night: although accidents are rare, you should take great care and follow local advice. Many of the rooms in **Naivasha town** are surprisingly pricey, and nowhere has fans or air conditioning. There's not much to choose between the many B&Ls, but those below are all at least adequate.

AROUND THE LAKE
BUDGET

★ **Camp Carnelly's** Moi South Lake Rd, 17.9km from the junction ☎0722 260749 or 0722 329465, ⓦcamp carnelleys.com; map p.204. Funky backpacker den with four-person, s/c *bandas* (Ksh12,000), twin rooms, dorm bunks and camping. The welcoming and convivial ambience, with a relaxing bar-dining area decked out in cushions, makes it a firm favourite among the independent and overland crowd. The bar-restaurant does slightly unusual things like smoothies, Camembert samosas and beef wraps. Camping **Ksh600** per person, dorm bed **Ksh800**, BB **Ksh2500**

Crayfish Camp Just before DCK market, Moi South Lake Rd, 17km from the junction ☎0720 226829,

ⓦcrayfishcamp.co.ke; map p.204. Hemmed in by flower farms, this popular budget option is noisy and rather run-down, but what it lacks in atmosphere it makes up for in originality: for the same price as the tatty standard doubles you can sleep in a barely converted boat, bus or lorry cab. There's also horseriding (Ksh600/hr), and a disco at weekends. BB **Ksh3400**

Crescent Camp Moi South Lake Rd, 1.9km from the junction (plus 1km down to the site) ☎020 2732936, ⓦcrescentcamp.com; map p.204. Expansive stretch of grass under acacias, planted with rows of enormous safari tents that give the place a slightly militaristic feel. The tents are very comfortable, however, with huge built-in bathrooms and wood floors. BB **Ksh10,000**

Fischers Tower Moi South Lake Rd, 1km from the junction (200m past the Yellow Green Hotel, right by the main road) ☎0700 000296; map p.204. Friendly place, frequented mainly by Kenyans, with a pleasant garden setting, a large bar and a *nyama choma* joint. There's also more chance of live music here than at the *Yellow Green*, although the rooms aren't as nice, and it's a fair walk from the lake. BB Ksh2500

Fish Eagle Inn Moi South Lake Rd, 18.2km from the junction ☎020 267076, ⓦfisheagleinn.com; map p.204. Big, reasonably well-run, middle-of-the-road, resort establishment with a variety of accommodation options, including dull but well-equipped "standard rooms" (with nets, hot water and spotless toilets) and dorms. Camping is also available, and although most campers head for the nearby *Fisherman's* or *Carnelly's*, the pool, gym, sauna and steam room may appeal. Camping Ksh600 per person, dorm beds Ksh1000, BB Ksh5000

Fisherman's Camp (Bottom Camp) Moi South Lake Rd, 18.2km from the junction ☎020 2139922 or 0726 870590, ⓔfishermanscamp@gmail.com; map p.204. This long-established budget hideaway has one of the best lakeside locations, right by the water's edge and set in a magnificent grove of fever trees. Besides camping (optional tent rental Ksh500 per two-person tent), there's a choice of rather dingy three- and four-person s/c *bandas* (Ksh1300, or Ksh4000 at weekends) and the six-person *Kasuku Cottage* (Ksh2000, or Ksh8000 at weekends). Camping Ksh500 per person, BB Ksh1300

Fisherman's Camp (Top Camp) Moi South Lake Rd, 18.2km from the junction ☎0728 594961 or 020 2139922, ⓔfishermanscamp@gmail.com; map p.204. Up on the cliffs above the lakeshore on the other side of the road from *Fisherman's Bottom Camp*, *Top Camp* offers several rudimentary *bandas* along with a few four-person s/c cottages (Ksh4000) with kitchenettes. BB Ksh1800

Yellow Green Moi South Lake Rd, 0.8km from the junction ☎050 2030269, ⓦyellowgreenhotelnaivasha .co.ke; map p.204. Far from the lake itself, and a little tatty, but with acceptable chalet-style cottages a cut above those at neighbouring *Fischers Tower* (all s/c with hot water), set in rambling, bougainvillea-filled gardens. The owners are charming and helpful, and there's a restaurant and bar that's popular with locals at weekends. BB Ksh2500

YMCA Moi South Lake Rd, 15.1km from the junction ☎0722 840857, ⓦkenyaymca.com; map p.204. Still one of the lake's cheapest (and friendliest) places to stay, a 10min walk from the shore itself – and certainly the easiest base if you're planning an early-morning hike into Hell's Gate National Park, as the Elsa Gate is just up the road. You can camp in the acacia grove, stay in the dorm (you'll need bedding), or rent one of the spartan three- to six-person *bandas*. Firewood, eggs, lake fish and milk are sporadically available, and there's also hot water, and food cooked to

order. Camping Ksh300 per person, dorm beds Ksh500, BB Ksh1000

MID-RANGE TO EXPENSIVE

Chui Lodge Oserian Wildlife Sanctuary ☎050 2020792 or ☎0722 200596, ⓦoserianwildlife.com; map p.204. Set by a waterhole inside the Oserian Wildlife Sanctuary, this intimate, very upscale little lodge features two-person cottages made from local materials and decorated with hand-crafted furniture. There's a heated pool and a lovely terrace restaurant overlooking the waterhole itself – perfect for watching the animals come out around dinner time. Game drives are included in the price. FB $990

Crater Lake Tented Camp Green Crater Lake, off Moi North Lake Rd, 8km from Kongoni ☎0722 203804, ⓦmericagrouphotels.com; map p.204. Tucked at the base of an old crater on the shore of a hidden satellite lake of Lake Naivasha, this once fairly luxurious establishment is in an idyllically peaceful spot. Unfortunately, the twin and double tents and family *bandas* are getting tatty. Still, the birding is superb, with birdbaths everywhere, so your subjects effectively come to you – and don't miss the silent electric boat trip. BB $280

Elsamere Moi South Lake Rd, 20.7km from the junction ☎020 2050964 or 0722 648123, ⓦelsamere.com; map p.204. Joy Adamson's former home (see p.205) offers comfortable, English holiday home-style rooms in spacious cottages, each with a veranda facing the lake. Very friendly and relaxing. Reservations advisable. FB $240

Enashipai Resort & Spa Moi South Lake Rd, 3.6km from the junction ☎051 2130000, ⓦenashipai.com; map p.204. Recently redeveloped luxury complex, with a slightly Mediterranean feel and pretty, well-maintained grounds. The rooms are opulently furnished, with big beds and a nod to African style, while the four- and five-bedroom cottages are large enough to house several families. Facilities include a large heated pool, gym and sauna, along with all the restaurants and bars you might expect. FB $445

★ **Kiangazi House** Moi South Lake Rd, 25.5km from the junction ☎050 2020792 or 0722 200596, ⓦoserian wildlife.com; map p.204. Stylish and personable family-run guesthouse with a strong flavour of the Med and a broad veranda overlooking the southwest corner of the lake. Three artificial pools (one for guests, the other two for buffalo, zebra and antelope) provide entertainment, while day and night game drives into the Oserian Game Sanctuary are included in the price, as are superb meals, accompanied by excellent wines. FB $990

Lake Naivasha Country Club Moi South Lake Rd, 3.8km from the junction ☎020 3589277 or 0736 701653, ⓦsunafricahotels.com; map p.204. Once the best hotel on the lake, the *Lake Hotel* (as it's still usually known) has seen better days, and the flying-boat era (passengers from London landed just offshore between 1937 and 1950) is long past. Like a 1930s English Lake District hotel, with sweeping lawns and a colonial-style lounge, it's a little too old-fashioned (especially in its bathrooms) for some visitors. But it's less ostentatious than *Enashipai* and a good place for families, with a small adventure playground and huge gardens to roam; the tangled undergrowth at the bottom of the garden is still trampled by big beasts, including waterbuck and, at night, hippo. All-ground-floor rooms also make it suitable for visitors with mobility problems. FB $\underline{$280}$

Lake Naivasha Sopa Resort Moi South Lake Rd, 8.6km from the junction ☎050 2050139 or 050 2050140, ⓦsopalodges.com; map p.204. With its ostentatious public areas sprawling from an impressive

euphorbia grove, this total makeover of the 1970s *Safariland Lodge* has 21 cottages, each with four exceptionally spacious rooms with TV and safe. The rooms can be rented independently; the two upstairs come with king-size beds and balconies, and the two downstairs with two double beds, terraces and bathtubs. HB $\underline{$347}$

Olerai House 19km along Moi North Lake Rd from the A104 turn-off 9km north of Naivasha ☎020 8048602, ⓦolerai.com; map p.204. Located in a small, private wildlife sanctuary, this is the former home of Iain and Oria Douglas-Hamilton, who were involved in the struggle to ban the ivory trade (they still live on the estate). There are five double rooms, full of cool touches and idiosyncratic design ideas, in bungalows surrounding the main, flower-covered house. Sanctuary fee $20 ($10 per child). FB $\underline{$680}$

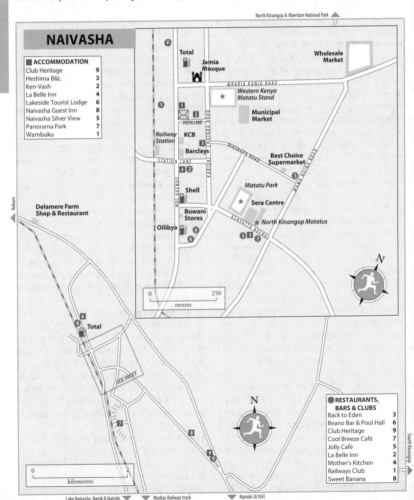

NAIVASHA

■ ACCOMMODATION

Club Heritage	9
Heshima B&L	3
Ken-Vash	2
La Belle Inn	4
Lakeside Tourist Lodge	6
Naivasha Guest Inn	8
Naivasha Silver View	5
Panorama Park	7
Wambuku	1

North Kinangop & Aberdare National Park

Total
Jamia Mosque
Wholesale Market
MBARIA KANIU ROAD
Western Kenya Matatu Stand
Municipal Market
POSTA LANE
Railway Station
KCB
Barclays
STATION LANE
Best Choice Supermarket
Matatu Park
Shell
Sera Centre
Bowani Stores
KENYATTA AVENUE
North Kinangop Matatus
Oilibya
BIASHARA ROAD
MOI AVENUE

Nakuru

Delamere Farm Shop & Restaurant

0   250
metres

Total

SEE INSET

0   2
kilometres

South Kinangop

● RESTAURANTS, BARS & CLUBS

Back to Eden	3
Beano Bar & Pool Hall	6
Club Heritage	9
Cool Breeze Café	7
Jolly Café	5
La Belle Inn	2
Mother's Kitchen	4
Railways Club	1
Sweet Banana	8

Lake Naivasha, Narok & Nairobi ▽   ▽ Markas Railway track   ▽ Nairobi (A104)

★ **Sanctuary Farm** At the head of Crescent Island, 1km down a dirt road off Moi South Lake Rd, 6km from the junction ⓦ sanctuaryfarmkenya.com (enquiries via email only, ⓔ gherkins.julie@gmail.com); map p.204. With its 400 acres of wooded grounds roamed by zebras, giraffes and wildebeest, it's no wonder this place has become a favourite among expats and NGO workers. There are just a handful of rooms in a converted old polo stable, all beautifully decorated and great value, with a sense of privacy that's hard to find elsewhere. Meals cooked to order, or you can self-cater (Ksh8000). Reservations required. FB Ksh12,000

NAIVASHA TOWN

Club Heritage A104 highway, top end of town ⓣ 050 2030101 or 020 2090371, ⓔ clubheritageltd@yahoo .com; map p.210. Attached to this big nightclub are 17 fairly small s/c rooms with instant showers, nets and TV. It's clean and well looked after and decent value for Naivasha, but inclined to be noisy at weekends. BB Ksh3300

Heshima B&L Kariuki Chotara Rd ⓣ 0723 103836; map p.210. The rough facade isn't indicative of the tidy, non-s/c rooms in this extremely cheap B&L, which have nets but no other frills. The shared toilets are all squatters, but there's plenty of hot water in the showers, plus safe parking. Room only Ksh600

Ken-Vash Posta Lane ⓣ 0716 198481, ⓔ gaterin bugua@gmail.com; map p.210. Lacking in atmosphere, but reasonably comfortable and very clean, with good nets, DSTV in all rooms, and – strangely – carpeted throughout. It's a bit old-fashioned, but the service is good and there's safe parking. BB Ksh2500

★ **La Belle Inn** Moi Ave ⓣ 020 3510404, ⓔ info @labelleinn.com; map p.210. Popular and atmospheric old staging post on the main street through town, built in 1922, with a variety of good-value, homely, English-BB-style s/c rooms with nets and TV, set around a garden courtyard. Rooms are mostly spacious and well furnished and the whole place is well looked after, though the

bathrooms are tatty, with old plumbing and hot water in the mornings and evenings. Safe parking. BB Ksh4000

Lakeside Tourist Lodge Moi Ave ⓣ 050 2020856 or 0722 524565, ⓔ lakesidetlodge@yahoo.com; map p.210. Large, pleasant place on the north side of the town centre with good, clean, bright s/c rooms with nets and TV (some on the 1st floor with verandas) and efficient service. Go for a window room, as inside rooms are small and dark – and negotiate on the price, which is a bit steep. BB Ksh4000

Naivasha Guest Inn Kenyatta Ave ⓣ 050 2021227; map p.210. Two kilometres from the town centre, this is handy if you've just been dropped at the junction, but is basically a dressed-up B&L. The cosily furnished, s/c rooms with nets and instant showers (and TV in the doubles) are reasonable, and there's a busy *hoteli* and bar behind. Secure parking. Negotiable rates, which is good as the price is far too high. BB Ksh1000

Naivasha Silver View Kenyatta Ave ⓣ 0716 660022; map p.210. Not much of a step up from an ordinary B&L, but perfectly okay on a budget, with clean rooms (with nets, but no instant showers), a very busy *hoteli* at the front, and safe parking. Room only Ksh600

Panorama Park On the cliff-edge, off Koinange Rd on the south side of town ⓣ 050 2030128 or 0712 091777, ⓦ lakenaivashapanoramapark.co.ke; map p.210. A holiday resort that feels far from the city, this has neat little rooms with nets, TV and instant showers, each occupying half a rondavel, and some larger chalets with boiler-heated showers. The grounds are attractively landscaped with plenty of flowers, and the restaurant boasts gorgeous views across the lake. Rates are somewhat confusing and highly negotiable. BB $105

Wambuku Moi Ave, next to the post office ⓣ 050 2030287; map p.210. Big and impersonal, the *Wambuku* has stuffy, rather cramped s/c rooms with nets, TV and old-style showers (hot water evenings only) ranged around a trough-like courtyard. Still, it's not bad value for Naivasha. BB Ksh1200

3

EATING AND DRINKING

You can drop in for meals and drinks at all the camps and lodges **around the lake**, and it's probably worth calling ahead if possible to see what specials they're offering. Some charge casual visitors an entry fee, usually recoupable from whatever you spend. In **Naivasha town** there's a clutch of cheap, local places to eat on Moi Avenue north of the Total gas station. For **food shopping** in Naivasha town, try the well-stocked Bowani Stores (Mon–Sat 8.15am–6pm) on Moi Ave or the Best Choice Supermarket (Mon–Sat 7am–8pm) at the upper end of Biashara Road. *La Belle Inn* (see above) has good picnic food like sandwiches and pastries, and you can get fruit in the *dukas* across the road.

AROUND THE LAKE

Geothermal Club KenGen complex, 19.6km from the junction; map p.204. A picturesque place to grab a drink or a bite to eat, with great views and a short list of (mostly Kenyan) daily specials, scrawled on a blackboard out front – although the swimming pool is pretty murky. Mains from Ksh270. Daily 7am–11pm.

Lake Naivasha County Club 3.8km from the junction ⓣ 020 3589277 or 0736 701653, ⓦ sunafricahotels .com; map p.204. This hotel (see p.209) remains a favourite spot for lunch, and the buffet meals ($20 per person) are reliable, although always best when the hotel is fairly full. Daily 6.30am–11pm.

The Club House Sanctuary Farm, at the head of Crescent

Island, 1km down a dirt road off Moi South Lake Rd, 6km from the junction 📧 gherkins.julie@gmail.com; map p.204. Set in a characterful old wooden polo club on stilts overlooking a meadow filled with wild game, this intimate restaurant offers fine dining cooked by the owner of *Sanctuary Farm* (see p.211), who is also a professional caterer. Three-course set menus are prepared using lots of locally sourced food and home-grown veggies; expect to pay Ksh2000–3000 per person. Meals (lunch and dinner) are by prior reservation only (email for bookings), but this may change in the future.

NAIVASHA TOWN

★ **Back to Eden** Corner of Mama Ngina Rd and Biashara Rd; map p.210. Wonderful little juice bar with freshly squeezed juices for only Ksh20 per glass and fruit salads to take away. Mon–Sat 6.30am–7.30pm.

Beano Bar & Pool Hall Kariuki Chotara Rd; map p.210. For a game of pool and a few beers with the locals, you could do worse than this spot at the south end of town. Mon–Sat 5–11pm, Sun 2–11pm.

Club Heritage A104 highway, top end of town; map p.210. One of Naivasha's busiest nightspots, with discos and, sometimes, live music. Entry, if you're not staying here, is around Ksh200–300 depending on who's playing (there's no cover charge when it's the house band). Fri–Sun 6.30pm–late.

Cool Breeze Café Kenyatta Ave; map p.210. Sun-filled little wooden box of a café, vaguely reminiscent of an American diner and surrounded by foliage. There's basic Kenyan food on offer for around Ksh150, as well as baked goodies like samosas and mandaazi. A good spot for coffee or breakfast. Daily 6.30am–9.30pm.

Jolly Café Naivasha Silver View Hotel, Kenyatta Ave; map p.210. At the front of the *Silver View* hotel, this lively *hoteli* has lots of reliable staples (main dishes around Ksh200–300) and *chai* for Ksh30. Mon–Sat 6.30am–10pm, Sun 7am–10pm.

★ **La Belle Inn** Moi Ave; map p.210. The terrace bar-restaurant here serves great fried breakfasts and is a good place to while away a few hours. For lunch and dinner the fish – including barbecued tilapia, spiced crayfish, Naivasha bisque and the like, all for around Ksh500 – is particularly good, and there's usually a vegetarian choice as well. They also have a good pastry chef and always have fresh bread and croissants in the shop. Daily 6.30am–10pm.

Mother's Kitchen Kariuki Chotara Rd; map p.210. A big, cheery canteen always heaving with locals, where you can get enormous buffet meals for Ksh400 per heaped plateful (Ksh300 without chicken), or order á la carte. Come hungry. Daily 6am–9pm.

★ **Railways Club** Near the railway tracks, west of the post office; map p.210. An amiable-to-riotous local dive with free entry, beers at Ksh120 and bands on Fridays and Sundays. Note the list of "breakage charges" posted on the wall: "glass Ksh60, window pane Ksh300...". Open 24hr.

Sweet Banana Moi Ave, north of Total; map p.210. The best in this string of cheap *hotelis*, with great *nyama choma* from Ksh100, along with the usual local dishes. Daily 6am–10.30pm.

SHOPPING

There's always a cluster of artists and art salesmen in **Naivasha town** offering various works, some quite good, but if you get tired of their pestering you can get crafts in the *dukas* opposite Shell and *La Belle Inn*. **Around the lake**, the best hotel gift shop for general souvenirs is at *Lake Naivasha Sopa Resort*. As in the accommodation reviews, the number of kilometres noted below refers to the distance along Moi South Lake Road from the junction with the main Nairobi road.

DCK Market (aka Sulmac dukas) 17.6km from the junction, just before Carnelly's; map p.204. Near the main entrance to the Sulmac flower plantation (one of the biggest in the area) is this small shopping centre. Newspapers are on sale every morning and you'll usually find a gathering of ladies selling produce from their *shambas*.

Elmenteita Weavers 4.3km from the junction, and then 800m along the signposted track 📞 0733 603649, 🌐 elmenteitaweavers.com; map p.204. A very friendly weaving shop, with looms behind the showroom. Carpets and rugs, sweaters (some superb), *kangas* and *kikois* compete with various other crafts from Fired Earth and Eastleigh Women's Group, including a line in home-made pickles and chutneys. Most credit cards accepted. Daily except Thurs 7.30am–5pm.

Hell's Gate National Park

$25 • 📞 020 2433037, 🌐 bit.ly/HellsGateNP

Hell's Gate was the outlet for the prehistoric freshwater lake that stretched from here to Nakuru and which, it's believed, would have supported early human communities on its shores. Today it's a spectacular and exciting area, the **Njorowa gorge**'s red cliffs and undulating expanse of grassland providing one of the few remaining places in Kenya where you can walk among herds of **plains game** without having to go a long way off the beaten track. Buffalo, zebra, eland, hartebeest, Thomson's gazelle and baboons are all usually seen, lions and leopards hardly ever, but you might just see a cheetah, and you'll certainly come across their footprints if you scan the trail. There are also servals – one of the most elegant of cats – and, high on the cliffs, small numbers of klipspringer ("cliffjumper") antelope.

The park is also home to **Olkaria Geothermal Plant**, the first productive geothermal installation in Africa. The underground temperature of the super-heated, pressurized water is up to 304°C, one of the hottest sources in the world, and the station is eventually expected to supply half of Kenya's energy requirements. Although the whole complex is working at full tilt, the impact on the local environment appears to be small, and it certainly doesn't spoil the landscape.

The best time **to arrive** is dawn, when most animals are about, and you should try to avoid the midday hours, as the heat away from the lake can be intense. You'll need to carry plenty of water and some food (the only place to buy anything in the park is a simple staff kiosk in the Olkaria Geothermal Area).

The upper gorge

From Elsa Gate, first take a look at the rock known as **Fischer's Tower**, after the German explorer who arrived at Lake Naivasha via Hell's Gate. The rock is a volcanic plug, the hard lava remaining from an ancient volcano after the cone itself has been eroded. It's now the home of a colony of very astute rock hyraxes, who look like large, shaggy guinea pigs and expect to be fed.

Through the gorge along the main track you'll find more and more animals visible on the slopes leading up to the sheer cliffs. Secretary birds are nearly always seen, mincing carefully through the grass at a safe distance.

If you're driving or on a bike, rather than heading straight down to the gorge, you can take the longer Twiga or Buffalo circuits. The **Twiga Circuit** climbs up to the left from just inside Elsa Gate before you reach Fischer's Tower. Branching off Twiga is **Buffalo Circuit**, which ploughs through thick bush. Don't go anywhere near the buffalo, as they can be unpredictable and dangerous. Both tracks are insanely dusty in the dry season,

---

HIKING THE RAVINE FROM OL BASTA

Hiking in the ravine itself is exhilarating, the best expedition in the area. Note that the **trail from Ol Basta** is the only realistic route, and beware of suggestions that there's a path around the south side of Ol Basta, directly above the eastern branch of the ravine: there isn't, and trying to prove otherwise is dangerous. The steep path down into the ravine starts just south of the gorge crossing, near the car park. You need tough walking shoes for this and shouldn't attempt it alone. Once down on the **ravine floor**, it's about a one-hour walk southwards to the point where you can climb up to the road on its west side. Watch out for unexpected slippery surfaces and do not enter the ravine if it's been raining in the Naivasha area – in 2012 seven people died when a flash flood ripped through the ravine.

If you've come equipped for a night out, you can press on, to emerge after a further (and difficult) 12km at the end of the canyon – still 15km short of the Narok road. For orientation, aim for **Mount Suswa** – itself an area of great exploring interest, only properly documented in the last couple of decades. Otherwise, either turn back and retrace your path to Elsa Gate, or else climb up towards the noise and steam of the **Olkaria geothermal station**, which is inside the national park. On the clifftop you can look out over the gorge and a Maasai village below, with your back to the Olkaria Geothermal Plant. Heading for the main buildings through the scrub, and the maze of pipes and hissing steam jets, you meet a perfect **tarmac road**. From here, you shouldn't have any problem getting a ride with employees the 5km down to the lake road at a point 2km west of *Elsamere*. If you hike it (and there are fine views of Oloiden and Green Crater lakes), allow about three hours after leaving the ravine to complete this section.

but when the dust clears, the views out over Hell's Gate and across to the Aberdare range are magnificent.

The lower gorge

Towards the southern end of the gorge (12km from Elsa Gate), a second rock tower – **Ol Basta** – marks its transition into a deep, tangled ravine, through which it is possible to hike (see box, p.213). There's a car park here but nowhere to park on the narrow, rocky track that follows the gorge to the south for a short distance. The nearby **viewpoint** provides a good place to picnic and take shelter from the sun. The best move you can make from this road-head is to cross the gorge and follow the so-called "Nature Trail" round the north side of Ol Basta. There's really nothing nature-trail about it, but it's easy enough to follow as far as the rock tower, where most people turn back.

ARRIVAL AND DEPARTURE   HELL'S GATE NATIONAL PARK

The main entrance road to Hell's Gate is just south of the *YMCA*, with the Elsa Gate a further 1.5km along this track. From Elsa Gate, it's about 25km to the road-head and back; if you need a **lift**, a fair number of vehicles visit at weekends, though there are far fewer during the week. If you're **driving**, be aware of the need for high clearance on some of the tracks. **Cyclists** are better off entering by the Olkaria Gate, which makes for an easier downhill ride to Elsa Gate; the road to Olkaria Gate is 28km from the lake road junction (5km south of Moi South Lake Road). The third entrance to the park is the more remote Narasha Gate, in the southwest corner.

ACCOMMODATION

There are several campsites in the park. Reservations can be made through KWS on ☎ 020 6000800 or at ⓦ kws.go.ke.

Endachata Campsite Across the gorge on the northern cliffs; map p.204. A "special campsite" that must be reserved in advance (for a fee of Ksh7500), this site has no facilities to speak of, but it is exclusive and boasts great views of waterholes frequented by giraffes and zebra. $30 per person

Naiburta Campsite Across the gorge on the northern cliffs; map p.204. Close to Endachata and with similar views of the waterholes, this public campsite is fitted out with cooking sheds, picnic benches, drinking water and latrines, though you have to bring your own wood and food. $15 per person

Ol Dubai On the clifftop south of Fischer's Tower; map p.204. This shady and superbly sited public campsite is probably the nicest place to camp, and the best place for large groups. Facilities include cooking sheds, drinking water and latrines, but carry in your own wood. $15 per person

Mount Longonot National Park

$20 • ☎ 0721 327327, ⓦ bit.ly/Longonot

The prominent cone of the dormant volcano **Mount Longonot** (2777m) looms high above Lake Naivasha, flanked by thorny savanna slopes and visible for many kilometres around. It's a relatively easy ascent, worth climbing for the fabulous views in every direction as you circle the rim.

Up the mountain

Don't try to make the ascent of the mountain from the lake road or Hell's Gate – it's further and steeper than it looks, and the north slopes are covered in dense bush frequented by buffalo. Instead, head for **Longonot village** on the old Nairobi road. About 500m south of the village, just beyond the railway bridge, a 4km dirt road leads to the national park gate at the base of the mountain. You can leave your car safely at the gate and get a drink (remember to take ample water with you).

There's only one straightforward route up to the crater rim, a 3km trail that takes about an hour. At the top you can collapse (the last section is rather steep) and look back over the Rift Valley on one side and the enormous, silent crater on the other. Joseph Thomson, the first *mzungu* up here in 1884, was overcome:

The scene was of such an astounding character that I was completely fascinated, and felt under an almost irresistible impulse madly to plunge into the fearful chasm. So overpowering was this feeling that I had to withdraw myself from the side of the pit.

Avoiding the same urge, it's now possible to scramble down **into the crater**, where exciting encounters with buffalo aren't uncommon: a 1937 guidebook observes that "any attempt to descend into the crater is accompanied by hazard". You should preferably be accompanied by a guide if you want to go down to the crater floor.

Walking the crater rim

Most climbers walk around the **crater rim**. The anticlockwise route is easier because the climb to the summit on the western side is quicker and steep sections easier to negotiate. It doesn't look far, but allow two to three hours to circumnavigate the 2km-diameter bowl. Longonot's name comes from the Maasai *oloonong'ot*, "mountain of many spurs" or "steep ridges", and you soon find out why. The cone is composed of very soft volcanic deposits that have eroded into deep gulches and narrow ridges: much of the path is over crumbly volcanic tufa worn into a channel so deep and narrow that it's difficult to put one foot in front of the other.

Until recently, Longonot's crater was famous for its steam jets; the volcano is classed as "senile", rather than extinct. Although the pockmark-like vents from which steam issues are still visible in several places around the rim and on the crater walls, emissions of steam have decreased since the Olkaria geothermal plant went on line, though the hot-air currents are said to still be sufficient to deflect light aircraft.

ACCOMMODATION	**MOUNT LONGONOT NATIONAL PARK**
Campsite Just outside the national park gate ☏ 050 2020510. There's a spot to pitch your tent just before you enter the park, where you'll find a cooking shed, latrines and drinking water, as well as a few *dukas* selling drinks and basic food. There are no official campsites on the mountain itself, and if you want to sleep there you'll have to get formal permission in advance from the rangers. <u>$15</u> per person	**Swara Mawe Guest House** Longonot Village, just west of the main road behind Adam's Business Centre ☏ 0722 697373. Tiny s/c rooms with hot water in an unexpectedly cute little courtyard, brightly painted with pictures of animals and shaded by passion-fruit vines. There's no sign, but walk through Adam's Business Centre and you'll find it. BB <u>Ksh2000</u>

Naivasha to Thika via the Kinangop

If you're serious about hiking, biking or fairly adventurous expeditionary driving, the route to **Thika** (see p.160) from **North Kinangop** is suitably dramatic, cutting up from the Rift Valley and over the southern flank of the Nyandarua (Aberdare) range – still, in large part, virgin mountain rainforest. The approach **from Naivasha** is quite straightforward, as frequent matatus make the journey up to North Kinangop. Routine though it may be, this part of the journey is still spectacular. The road climbs constantly towards the **Kinangop Plateau**, with the Rift Valley and Lake Naivasha way below. The land hereabouts is Kikuyu farming country, once widely settled by Europeans who were lured by the wide-open moors, rocky outcrops and gushing streams. Sheep and cattle graze everywhere.

North and South Kinangop

NORTH KINANGOP is nowadays a rather isolated rural community, a village of gumboots and raggy sweaters (it can freeze here at night), whose road becomes nearly impassable during the long rains. Transport onwards is usually little problem outside the rainy season – at least as far as South Kinangop. Tractors will pick you up and there are a few old lorries trundling around, too.

SOUTH KINANGOP (also known as **Njabini**) is livelier than its northern counterpart, a small trading centre with regular matatus from Naivasha.

Across the southern Aberdare

South Kinangop to Gatura is approximately 36km, a good eight hours on foot, or a great half-day mountain-bike trip. The dirt road (the C67) has very little traffic, even to begin with, as it switchbacks downwards across a series of streams flowing south from the Aberdare range to the Chania River. The road follows the river, with tremendous scenic variation, though almost always through forest – sometimes indigenous, sometimes conifer plantation.

After the turn-off (left) for **South Kinangop forest station**, the occasional *shambas* and all signs of human habitation stop completely. From here down, the forest is untouched mountain jungle – trees with huge leaves, bamboo thickets, birds shrieking in alarm, the crashing of colobus monkeys, chameleons wobbling across the road and tell-tale elephant dung. After rain, the "road" can become a complete quagmire, really just fit for tractors. If you try this route by 4WD, you'd better have a winch, and a good saw, if not a chain saw, as elephants push a lot of trees across the route, and for months if not years on end it can be all but impassable to motor vehicles (as was the case in 2012). When the foresters can't drive in, the road soon becomes overgrown. On foot or mountain bike, or possibly a good, light, trial motorbike, there's no danger of getting stuck, though you should ensure you have food and water, and ideally a GPS.

Kimakia Forest Station to Gatura

You finally reach human habitation again at the **Kimakia Forest Station**, where there's normally a barrier across the road. If you've arrived by 4WD, someone will unlock it for you. If you're on foot, or two wheels, you can go round. Now on a proper road, you meet some tarmac a few kilometres later outside the Ngere tea factory, but the tarmac road doesn't start properly until you reach the outskirts of **Gatura** (B&Ls, petrol, shops, matatus), the first of a chain of small towns and villages along the scenic road down to Thika, 31km distant.

Kigio Wildlife Conservancy

Between Naivasha and Gilgil, signposted 500m before the Gilgil toll station • $25 • ☎ 020 3748369, ⓦ kigio.com • Fourteen square kilometres

Just 1km off the road between Naivasha and Gilgil lies the **Kigio Wildlife Conservancy**, a former cattle ranch. Established in 1997, Kigio has a good conservation record, with the herd of **Rothschild's giraffe** relocated here in 2002 now breeding. The conservancy is entirely fenced except along its riverbank side and rarely contains any large predators, which means that you can walk or cycle here safely. The large mammal count is very healthy and includes hippo, buffalo, impala, Thomson's gazelle, eland, waterbuck, zebra and warthog, and more than 250 species of birds, including ostriches. The reserve is a great place to visit for a few hours, and you can also stay here (see p.217) as an alternative to basing yourself at Naivasha. As well as wildlife-viewing (by car, on foot or with mountain bikes) and riverside birding, Kigio offers hikes up the densely wooded Kasuki gorge, with river swims and rock-jumping just 1.5km downstream from the *Malewa Wildlife Lodge*.

ACCOMMODATION

KIGIO WILDLIFE CONSERVANCY

Kigio Wildlife Camp Kigio Wildlife Conservancy ☎ 020 3748369, ⓦ kigio.com. Very comfortable suites surrounded by fever trees and perched above the Malewa River, on grounds grazed by buffalo, hippos and giraffes. Nature walks, fishing and bike rental are all included in the price, as are meals. FB S̶502

Malewa Wildlife Lodge Kigio Wildlife Conservancy ☎ 020 3748369, ⓦ kigio.com. This riverside bush eco-lodge offers delightfully eccentric accommodation featuring a mix of reclaimed timber, mud walls and thatched roofs. The main lodge has a public lounge with an open fireplace and dining terrace, and there are five private cottages and four river suites on stilts around the grounds. FB S̶502

Malu South of Kigio Wildlife Conservancy, 15km north of Naivasha (3.7km from the A104 junction, after Kobil, turn right, then drive 11km) ☎ 050 2030181 or 0720 899530, ⓦ malu-kenya.com. Located in an expansive indigenous forest reserve of cedar and olive, with breathtaking views of Lake Naivasha and Mount Longonot, *Malu* has a variety of great-value accommodation in cottages, family villas and a superb "treehouse", plus excellent Italian-inspired food from the farm. Activities include donkey-cart rides, horseriding, mountain biking and visits to the warm-spring plunge pool. BB Ksh9000

Lake Elmenteita and around

Often overlooked by people rushing from Lake Naivasha to Lake Nakuru, the area around **Lake Elmenteita** and up into the lower foothills of the Aberdare range offers some off-the-beaten-track destinations such as **Kariandusi** prehistoric site and other activities, including first-rate **wildlife viewing**, which take advantage of the pretty, lightly wooded hills and lush valley of the Malewa River. In addition, several top-end **lodges** provide an intimate alternative to their more touristy cousins around lakes Nakuru and Naivasha.

Malewa Bush Ventures

On the banks of the Malewa River on the far edge of Kigio Wildlife Conservancy • Ropes courses from Ksh2500 per person • ☎ 020 3535878, ⓦ malewa.co.ke

For those looking for a challenge, the **Malewa Bush Ventures** centre offers a range of activities including a high-ropes course, rock-climbing and abseiling, along with more mainstream wildlife and bird walks and game-viewing excursions (all activities must be booked in advance). You can camp on the site for Ksh750 per person, and food is available if you give them some notice. The centre manages and supports the Malewa Trust, which feeds resources into the local community.

Gilgil

GILGIL, just south of Lake Elmenteita, is as dull a town as you could find anywhere, with fragile-looking *dukas* and dusty streets scavenged by goats. On the outskirts lie the serried, pastel-coloured ranks of housing for the local Gilgil Telecoms Industries workers. Still, you're bound to pass this way en route to Nakuru, and Gilgil can be a good spot to stock up on provisions and take a quick peek at the old war cemetery.

Gilgil War Cemetery

If you have half an hour to spare, have a look on the north side of town at the **Gilgil Commonwealth War Cemetery**. Of more than forty cemeteries in Kenya tended by the Commonwealth War Graves Commission, this is one of the most meticulously kept, and a good place to stop for a picnic and some moments of contemplation. There are about two hundred graves here from the East African campaign of World War II and from the war for independence – "the Emergency" – in the 1950s. Whether by accident (which doesn't seem likely) or design, the African graves are all at the bottom of the slope, and record no personal details apart from name, age and rank. The graves of British soldiers are higher up, the stones inscribed with family messages. As well as graves from World War II, there are also poignant reminders of lives lost between 1959 and 1962, after the British government's futile attempt to prevent the inevitable.

Lake Elmenteita

Beyond the turn-off for Gilgil, the fast A104 sweeps the eastern wall of the Rift Valley and pushes up high above **Lake Elmenteita**. Elmenteita's setting is spectacular and primeval, framed by the broken caldera walls of several extinct volcanoes, which resemble a reclining human figure. The Maasai know these peaks as Elngiragata Olmorani (Sleeping Warrior) – a name that is ironically fitting, since the lake and its lands were expropriated from the Maasai at the start of the colonial period by Lord Delamere (the caldera is now also known as "Delamere's Nose"). You can get a good view from the big "parking lane" viewpoint – if you survive the occasionally desperate assaults by curio sellers.

The shallow soda lake itself, which has been known to shrivel to a huge white salt pond, is a good site for flamingos when Lake Nakuru is out of favour, and always good for pelicans, along with an estimated three hundred bird species in all. Like Lake Nakuru, Elmenteita has no outflow, and its accumulated alkaline salts make it uninhabitable for all but one species of fish, the indomitable *Tilapia grahami*. Nearly all the land around the lake is now part of the private, fenced **Soysambu Wildlife Sanctuary**. In practice, the eastern shoreline is accessible if you're staying at one of the small camps or lodges in the area, such as the *Sleeping Warrior Camp* or *Oasis Eco Camp*.

A number of prehistoric sites are scattered around the lake's once-lush shores, of which **Gambles Cave**, 10km southwest of Elmenteita village at Eburru, is the most famous. The cave can be visited by making arrangements ahead of time – ask at the National Museum in Nairobi.

Kariandusi

Signposted off the A104 highway, 1km south of Lake Elmenteita Lodge and 1.5km east of the highway • Daily 8.30am–5.30pm • Ksh500 • ⓦ bit.ly/Kariandusi

For an easier shot of prehistory, try a visit to **Kariandusi**, an Acheulian site characterized, like Olorgasailie (see p.151), by heavy hand-axes and cleavers. The site is very small, consisting of just two excavated areas cleared by Louis Leakey in 1928–31 and 1947, each displaying a scattered assortment of stone tools, many of them made of the black glassy volcanic rock, obsidian.

The small **museum** explains the formation of the Rift Valley and has comparative skull specimens of various distant human ancestors. Neither Kariandusi nor Olorgasailie demonstrate any signs of permanent habitation, and it's been suggested that they were simply places where the kill was habitually butchered and consumed, the tools being made on the spot and left for the next occasion. Nothing much is known about the toolmakers themselves, apart from the fact that they obviously had a formidable grip. The most likely candidate is a primitive form of *Homo erectus*, an early hominin whose remains have been found at Olduvai Gorge in Tanzania alongside Acheulian artefacts.

ARRIVAL AND INFORMATION	**LAKE ELMENTEITA AND AROUND**
By matatu The best way to get to and from Gilgil by public transport is to catch one of the numerous matatus that ply the route between Naivasha and Nakuru.	**Services** Gilgil town has a Gilgil Mattresses supermarket, a KCB with ATM, a post office and several filling stations and car repair yards, but not much else.

ACCOMMODATION

GILGIL

Hotel Freci On the main road from the highway into town ☏ 020 215524. An outwardly unremarkable motel, but the best place here to stay or eat. Inside, the comfortable pastel-coloured rooms are well insulated against the heat, with instant showers and nets. There's a busy bar-restaurant, with main meals around Ksh400 and plenty of snacks. Come here at the end of the week and you might find a crowd, with live music in the "club room". BB Ksh1000

LAKE ELMENTEITA

Jacaranda Lake Elmenteita Lodge Signposted 1km off the road from Naivasha ☎ 050 2050836 or 0712 237333, ⓦ jacarandahotels.com. Housed in a red-brick building of 1918, this is one of the oldest lodges on the lake and certainly the most historic. There are nice views from the terrace restaurant, though the decor is a bit old-fashioned and there's no direct lake access. Rooms are in brick cottages at the back, or you can camp. Camping Ksh600 per person, HB $276

Oasis Eco Camp 2km off the road from Naivasha, signposted down a dirt path ☎ 0729 910410, ⓦ oasis .co.ke. This is one of the few budget offerings in the area, and its lakeshore location makes it very good value. Accommodation is in thatched, glass-fronted s/c cottages with lake-view lofts, comfortable s/c safari tents (Ksh2500 per person) or dome tents (Ksh1200 per person), or bring your own tent. Bike rental and meals are also available (call ahead for the latter). Camping Ksh1000 per person, BB Ksh6000

Sleeping Warrior Camp Overlooking the south-eastern end of the lake, signposted down a dirt path off the road from Naivasha ☎ 0733 385156 or 0735 408698, ⓦ sleepingwarriorcamp.com. Good-value camp and eco-lodge, down a winding dirt trail, with stone cottages and a collection of comfortable s/c safari tents. With their rustic decor, firepits and African fabrics, the rooms and lounges have the vaguely colonial feel of an old-fashioned safari, and there are game drives, guided walks and atmospheric bush dinners on offer. HB $228

★ **Sunbird Lodge** Past Jacaranda Lake Elmenteita Lodge, at the northeastern end of the lake ☎ 0715 555777 or 020 8000075, ⓦ sunbirdkenya.com. Still the nicest lodge on the lake, though it's got plenty of competition these days, with cute, spectacularly sited cottages on grounds that ramble down the hillside toward the lake. All rooms come with wide balconies boasting the best views hereabouts, while the common areas are comfortably cosy, with soft couches and firepits, and the service is warm and friendly. FB $380

Nakuru

Kenya's fourth-largest city (though it projects a noticeably busier and more energetic image than Kisumu, the third), **NAKURU** is capital of the enormous, sprawling Rift Valley Province that stretches from the Sudanese border to the slopes of Kilimanjaro. A noisy, dusty and hustly place, the town is a major transport hub and the closest jumping-off point for visits to the justly celebrated **Lake Nakuru National Park** and the vast **Menengai crater** (whose *shamba-* and conifer-cloaked southern flank you'll have passed if approaching Nakuru along the main highway from Nairobi), as well as the departure point for trips to **lakes Bogoria** and **Baringo**, and the **northern Rift Valley**.

Nakuru came into existence on the thrust of the Uganda railway and owed its early growth, at least in part, to **Lord Delamere**, the Kenya Colony's most famous figure. In 1903 he acquired four hundred square kilometres of land on the lower slopes of the Mau escarpment, followed by two hundred more at Soysambu, on the other side of the lake. Eager to share the empty vistas with compatriots – though preferably with other Cheshire or Lancashire men – he promoted in England the mile-square plots being offered free by the Foreign Office. Eventually, some two hundred new settler families arrived and Nakuru – a name that as usual could mean various things, including "Place of the Waterbuck" (Swahili) and "Swirling Dust" or "Little Soda Lake" (Maasai) – became their country capital. It lies on the unprepossessing steppe between the lake and the flanks of Menengai crater. This desolate shelf has a nickname: "the place where the cows won't eat grass" (the pasture was found to be iron-deficient). Farmers near the town turned to pyrethrum, the plant used to make insecticide, as a cash crop.

Modern Nakuru is still largely a workaday farmers' town, with unadorned old seed shops and veterinary paraphernalia much in evidence on the main street, like a little Nairobi without the flashy veneer, its streets frequently undergoing ear-shattering repairs. The town can appear intimidating at first, and most visitors on their way to the national park stay in one of the lodges there. Still, Nakuru has some positive aspects: the **market** is animated and a pleasure to look around (though it, too, has its fair share of hassle), and there's a glimmer of charm remaining in the colonnaded old streets and jacaranda-lined avenues at the edge of town.

ARRIVAL AND DEPARTURE

NAKURU

Nakuru's **matatu stages** are packed together at the east end of the town centre, with cheap lodgings all around, although better places to stay can be found within easy walking distance. The national park gate and campsite (5km) is a bit of a slog without transport – take a taxi, *tuk-tuk*, *piki-piki* or *boda-boda*.

By bus The town's bus companies all run regular and frequent services to Nairobi, as well as Eldoret, Kisumu, Kitale, Kisii and other points west (the recommended EasyCoach's office is next to Kobil; ☎0726 354303). Alternatively, you can take the quieter road west (see p.229) through the highland towns of Njoro, Elburgon and Molo.

Destinations Eldoret (4 daily; 2hr 30min); Kakamega (2 daily; 4hr); Kisumu (6 daily; 5hr); Kitale (2 daily; 5hr); Mumias (2 daily; 4hr); Nairobi (5 daily; 2hr 30min).

By matatu Heading southwards, you can get to Narok (for the Maasai Mara) by matatu up the fantastic Mau escarpment (allow a day to get there). In the other direction, matatus make the spectacular climb up to Nyahururu through the Subukia Valley. A string of matatus

run daily to Marigat at Lake Baringo, as well as to Kabarnet in the hills to the west.

Destinations Eldoret (20–30 daily; 2hr 30min); Kabarnet (6–8 daily; 2hr); Kericho (8–12 daily; 2hr); Kisumu (10–20 daily; 4hr); Kitale (3–4 daily; 5hr); Marigat (10–15 daily; 1hr 30min); Nairobi (20–30 daily; 2hr 30min); Narok (3 daily; 5hr); Naivasha (20–40 daily; 1hr 15min); Nyahururu (6–8 daily; 1hr 30min); Subukia (8–10 daily; 1hr).

By car A lavishly scenic route runs to Nyahururu through the Subukia Valley, an ascent of the Rift that, for sheer grandeur, comes close to the Naivasha escarpment. If you're driving this, note that the turn-off 2.5km along the Nairobi road is not signposted – turn left at the Shell petrol station by *Kunste Hotel*.

ACCOMMODATION	
Amoodi's B&L	7
Avenue Suites	3
Bontana Hotel	8
Carnation	9
Kivu Resort	11
Merica	5
Midland	1
Mid-Rift Hotel	2
Pivot	10
Shik Parkview	4
Waterbuck Hotel	6

RESTAURANTS, CAFÉS, BARS & CLUBS	
Club Dimples	2
El-Bethel Cana Metting Place	6
Enigma	4
Guava	1
Nakuru Coffee House	3
Nakuru Sweet Mart	8
Planet Fries	5
Renacom Café	7
Summit Resort	11
Taidy's	10
Tipsy Restaurant	9

NAKURU'S ROADSIDE RIP-OFFS

Nakuru is the **con-mechanic capital of Kenya**, and if you're driving, beware of any likely-looking individuals around Nakuru telling you there's something wrong with your car. Tricksters hang around along the roadside either between the eastern suburb of Lanet and Nakuru town centre or between the town centre and the national park main gate, and have also been seen along the road to Eldoret. They work in teams, pointing one after another at your wheels as you drive past or, if you stop anywhere, "discovering" oil dripping from your engine – anything to get you into their garage for a bogus repair job.

ACCOMMODATION

You're spoilt for choice for **cheap rooms**, though few places stand out, and there are a number of **mid-range hotels** dotted about the western avenues – amazingly good value compared to Nairobi. However, the sewers there can turn even the hardiest stomachs, and the throbbing of discos from Wednesday to Sunday can also be a nuisance. If you're **camping**, go to the national park: you may have to pay entry fees (see p.222) to use the sites inside the gate, but it's worth a try.

Amoodi's B&L Nehru Rd ☎051 2241939. A no-frills B&L with excellent security, plenty of hot water, clean toilets and the cheapest twin beds in town, in shoebox rooms. Cramped but okay, with towels and nets. Room only Ksh500

Avenue Suites Kenyatta Ave ☎051 2210607, ✉avenuesuiteshotel@yahoo.co.uk. Good-value place with over sixty rooms, all with nets, TV and reasonable bathrooms, and most with balconies and views down over Nakuru's main street. BB Ksh1400

Bontana Hotel Tom Mboya Rd ☎0725 145460, ✇bontanahotel-nakuru.com. Located in a quiet, residential part of town, this hotel is restful but rather dull, and its furnishings are slightly the worse for wear. The rooms are a good size, though, and all have balconies, while those on the upper floor enjoy nice views. BB $110

Carnation 1st floor of a building on Mosque Rd ☎051 2215360 or 0720 269002. Well-run establishment with attentive staff and a good restaurant – although beware of the travel companies and tour touts who hang out here. Rooms come with TV and nets, though the showers are old-style. BB Ksh1000

Kivu Resort 1.5km from main park gate ☎0726 026894, ✇kivuretreat.com. Not far from the national park, this secure and good-value (rates negotiable) place has nicely decorated rooms set in a garden, plus a 25m pool (Ksh200 extra) and paddling pool for kids. It's also possible to camp here. Camping Ksh800 per person, BB Ksh4500

Merica Corner of Court Rd and Kenyatta Ave ☎051 2216013, ✇mericagrouphotels.com. Busy town hotel, built on the central-courtyard model, with nearly one hundred large, bright rooms with nets, a good restaurant, large pool and live music at weekends. Rates are highly negotiable. BB $160

Midland GK Kamau Highway ☎051 2212125, ✇midland hotel.co.ke. Terminally dull, 50s-style-institutional Nakuru landmark, but adequate for a comfortable night. The attached bar-restaurant is lively enough, but the food isn't great. Rooms come with nets and TV (though the bathtubs are more reliable than the showers), at very negotiable rates. BB Ksh4250

Mid-Rift Hotel Gusii Rd ☎020 2439270, ✉midrift @gmail.com. One of the best joints in this quarter of town, with light and spacious s/c rooms with nets and TV, good cheap breakfasts and a matatu stage opposite. Very good value, but can be raucous on disco nights (Wed & Fri–Sun). BB Ksh1800

Pivot Lower Factory Rd ☎0714 471111, ✉pivothotel @gmail.com. Recommended, despite its uncanny resemblance to a military hospital, offering seventy clean rooms with nets, DSTV and ample hot water, though no instant showers. Choosing one of rooms #1–15 will lessen the deafening disco din on weekend nights. Ksh1500

Shik Parkview Kenyatta Ave ☎020 2614381. Straightforward B&L, with reasonably airy s/c and non s/c rooms, some on the small side and with squat toilets, but very clean. There's also a very busy restaurant and great views of downtown Nakuru from the roof terrace, and security is good. Room only Ksh600

Waterbuck West Rd ☎051 2215672, ✉waterbuck @waterbuck.co.ke. The *Waterbuck* is a bit of an oddity, its garish reception area with Maasai maiden statues trumpeting rooms that turn out to be plain, well kept and clean, with nets, TV, decent bathrooms and balconies. There's also a lively swimming pool and friendly bar area, often full of Kenyan families at weekends. Safe parking. BB Ksh6400

EATING AND DRINKING

Finding good **food** isn't that easy in Nakuru. As a guide, the older, more down-at-heel establishments are bunched towards the east end of town near the train station, while the west end, especially along Kenyatta Avenue, tends to be more upmarket.

El-Bethel Cana Meeting Place Moi Rd. A cheery eatery that's a good standby for rice, stews and cold sodas (mains around Ksh250). There's also a pleasant outside seating area, and lots of decorative plants. Daily 6.30am–6.30pm.

Guava 4th floor, CBA Building, Kenyatta Ave ☎0722 900103. Polished café, with views of downtown from the terrace, serving some creative Western dishes like vodka-infused pasta alongside Japanese food and a sushi bar (platters from Ksh900). A good spot for a sundowner, too, with a long list of cocktails. Daily 11am–9.30pm, bar till 10.30pm.

Nakuru Coffee House Moi Rd ☎0702 644533. Good venue for real coffee and tasty pastries, as well as mains like roast chicken and pizzas (around Ksh250). Mon–Sat 6.30am–7pm.

★ **Nakuru Sweet Mart** Gusii Rd. Long-established vegetarian Indian establishment serving up massive *dhals*, great *bhajias*, a good range of breads, *masala tea*, *Indian sweets* (0.25kg for Ksh250). Good value, and highly calorific. Daily 8.10am–6.45pm.

Planet Fries Watalii Rd ☎0726 096575. Despite its unpromising name, this sidewalk café boasts a pleasantly leafy outdoor terrace and serves salads, curries and pizzas alongside the expected fried meat. Wildly popular with locals. Mains around Ksh250. Daily 7am–9pm.

Renacom Café Government Rd. Laid-back and friendly bar-café with outdoor seating and food including good chicken, whole grilled fish (Ksh250) and a small selection of European cheeses. Mon–Sat 8am–5.30pm.

Summit Resort Lake Rd, near the national park main gate. A few minutes' drive from town, this large, friendly and mostly open-air complex features several different dining areas serving excellent *mutton choma* (Ksh250 for half a kilo) and grills, plus a dance floor and swimming pool (Ksh200). Daily 8am–midnight.

Taidy's Corner of Oginga Odinga Ave and Gusii Rd. Popular and lively open-air terrace bar and grill overlooking a busy corner, serving mostly platters of meats (mixed grill Ksh500) and Indian dishes. Daily 8am–3am.

Tipsy Restaurant Gusii Rd ☎051 2212493. Owned by the same family as the *Nakuru Sweet Mart*, but offering a wider range of dishes including both veg and meat offerings, with grilled meats and curries for around Ksh300. Daily 8am–7pm.

NIGHTLIFE AND ENTERTAINMENT

Club Dimples Club Rd. Hung with mirrors and disco balls, this club attracts all ages with its mix of rock, rhumba and reggae. Entry Ksh100. Wed–Sun 7pm–late.

Enigma Kenyatta Ave. Glitzy bar and club above the shops, playing a mix of African and Western dance tunes. Mon–Fri 5pm–late, Sat & Sun 2pm–late.

Nakuru Players Kipchoge Ave ☎051 2216993 or 0723 959861. Occasional drama and comedy performances by the Nakuru Players at their dour-looking theatre on Kipchoge Avenue; tickets around Ksh250.

Summit Resort (see above). One of the best places for a night out in Nakuru. The open-air dancefloor gets packed at weekends with patrons of all ages getting down to Western and Kenyan pop and golden oldies. Fri–Sun 6pm–3am.

DIRECTORY

Banks Scattered all over Nakuru, most of them with ATMs.

Clinic Avenue Healthcare, in the Polo Centre on Kenyatta Ave (☎051 2214623; Mon–Fri 8am–8pm, Sat & Sun 8am–2pm), offers a full range of outpatient services.

Internet Cyber Planet, upstairs in the Tropical House on Watalii Rd (Mon–Sat 8am–7pm; Ksh1/min).

Market The main produce market, near the railway station, has the full range of fruit and vegetables, but watch out for pickpockets and petty thieves.

Pharmacy There are lots of pharmacies at the eastern end of Kenyatta Ave, including Care Chemists (☎051 2211954; Mon–Sat 8.30am–6pm).

Supermarkets The best supermarkets in town are Tusky's on Kenyatta Ave (daily 7.30am–midnight) and the big new Nakumatt on the corner of Kenyatta Ave and West Rd (Mon–Sat 8am–10pm, Sun 10am–8pm); or try the smaller Gilani's grocery on Club Rd (Mon–Sat 8.15am–7pm, Sun 10am–6.30pm).

Travel agents Crater Travel, Inder Singh Building, just off Kenyatta Ave (☎051 2215019 or 051 2214896; Mon–Fri 8.30am–1pm & 2–5pm, Sat 8.30am–1pm), can help with air ticketing and visas, and also offers the usual range of tour and safari deals.

Lake Nakuru National Park

Daily 6.30am–6.30pm • $80 Safari Card (see p.71) • ☎020 2664071, ☯ bit.ly/LakeNakuruNP

Just 5km outside Nakuru, **Lake Nakuru National Park** is one of the most popular in the country and a must-see for wildlife enthusiasts, offering one of the best chances in Kenya of spotting black and white rhinos. With more than 300,000 visitors each year, this is one of the Kenya Wildlife Service's two "premier parks" (the other being Amboseli). Though not large, it's a beautiful park, the terra firma mostly under light acacia forest, well provided with tracks to a variety of hides and lookouts. It's also one of the easiest parks to visit, with or without a vehicle, and the contrast and apparent dislocation between the shallow soda lake, with its primeval birds, and the animated woodlands all about give it a very distinctive appeal. The easy-to-follow topography means you really can't get lost and it's a pleasure to drive around, which takes about three hours.

Around the park

The **northeastern shores** of the lake, being close to the Main Gate, are the most accessible and heavily trafficked section of the park, with the route between the gate and *Sarova Lion Hill Lodge* getting relatively busy; the southern parts of the park are usually empty. The vegetation in the north is mostly lightly wooded acacia forest and this area, close to Nakuru town, is the least interesting for wildlife, so if you have the time you'd do well to focus your attention on the south.

Taken clockwise, the main park road runs through the woods, past *Lion Hill* and into an exotic-looking forest of candelabra **euphorbia** – great cactus-like trees up to 15m high. At

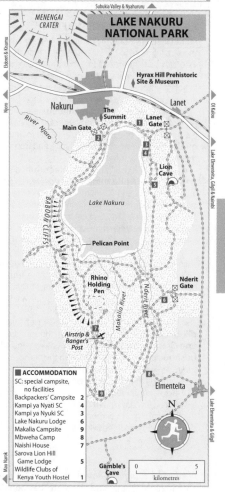

Subukia Valley & Nyahururu

LAKE NAKURU NATIONAL PARK

MENENGAI CRATER

Eldoret & Kisumu

B4

Njoro

Nakuru

River Njoro

Hyrax Hill Prehistoric Site & Museum

Lanet

The Summit

Main Gate

Lanet Gate

1

2

3

4

Lion Cave

5

BABOON CLIFFS

Lake Nakuru

Pelican Point

Rhino Holding Pen

Nderit River

Makalia River

Nderit Gate

6

Airstrip & Ranger's Post

7

8

Elmenteita

9

N

Mau Narok

Ol Kalou

Lake Elmenteita, Gilgil & Nairobi

Lake Elmenteita & Gilgil

3

■ ACCOMMODATION
SC: special campsite, no facilities
Backpackers' Campsite **2**
Kampi ya Nyati SC **4**
Kampi ya Nyuki SC **3**
Lake Nakuru Lodge **6**
Makalia Campsite **9**
Mbweha Camp **8**
Naishi House **7**
Sarova Lion Hill
Game Lodge **5**
Wildlife Clubs of
Kenya Youth Hostel **1**

Gamble's Cave

0   5
kilometres

the southern end of this zone you come into a stretch of more open country, past the turning (left) up to *Lake Nakuru Lodge*, and one or two side tracks down to the mud and the lakeshore (right), after which the road turns west into the southern park's dense acacia jungle. This is where you may see a **leopard** and – if they overcome their shyness – one of the park's sixty-odd **black rhino**. Several kilometres further, the road opens again onto wider horizons with plenty of buffalo, waterbuck, impala and eland all around. You're likely to see one of the park's forty **white rhino** here, looking for good grazing, and this is also the most likely area for seeing the park's herd of introduced **Rothschild's giraffe**.

The **west shore**, especially "Pelican Point", offers the best chance of seeing the **flamingos**, if they've returned (see box, p.225). In places, the road runs on what is virtually a causeway, past the lake's edge, with high cliffs rearing up behind. Finally, the main route leaves the shore and ploughs north, through thick forest with many tall trees and dense undergrowth, back to the Main Gate.

Good **vantage points** around the lake include the northern **mud flats** (follow established tracks across the dry surface); the dead tree **watchtower** (northeast); *Kampi*

3

LAKE NAKURU'S WILDLIFE

Fortunately, in view of the flamingos' here-today-gone-tomorrow caprice (see box opposite), there's a lot more to the lake's spectacle than the pink flocks. Its shores and surrounding woodlands are home to some four hundred other species of **birds** including, during the northern winter, many migratory European species. Towards the end of the dry season in March, the lake is often much smaller than the maps suggest and, consequently, water birds are a greater distance from the park roads.

There's a good number of **mammals** here as well. The lake isn't too briny for **hippos** – a herd of a dozen or more snort and splash by day and graze by night at the northern end. Nakuru has also become a popular venue for introduced species: there are **Rothschild's giraffe** from the wild herd near Kitale, and **lions** and secretive **leopards** from wherever they're causing a nuisance.

In the early 1990s, a number of **black rhinos** were relocated from Solio Game Ranch (see p.194), and ten **white rhinos** were donated by South Africa in 1994; the park now boasts around 60 black and 40 white rhinos, one of the highest concentrations of rhino in the country. Electric fencing has been installed around the entire perimeter of the park – the only park in the country to be so enclosed – with the intention of maintaining a viable number of rhinos in a zone secure from poachers.

Nakuru may be Swahili for "place of the waterbuck", and the park is **waterbuck** heaven. With only a handful of lions and small numbers of leopards to check their population, the large, shaggy beasts number several thousand, and the herds (either bachelor groups or a buck and his harem) are large and exceptionally tame. **Impala**, too, are very numerous, though their lack of fear means you rarely witness the graceful flight of a herd vaulting through the bush.

The two other most often seen mammals are **buffalo** – which you'll repeatedly mistake for rhinos until you get a look through binoculars – and **warthog**, scuttling nervously in singles and family parties everywhere you look. Elephants are absent, but you're likely to see **zebra**, **dik-dik**, **ostrich** and **jackals** and, in the southern part of the park, **eland** and **Thomson's and Grant's gazelles**. More rarely you can encounter **reedbuck** down by the shore and **bushbuck** dashing briskly through the herbage. Along the eastern road, near *Lake Nakuru Lodge*, are several over-tame **baboon troops** to be wary of. The park is also renowned for its very large **pythons** – the patches of dense **woodland** in the southwest, between the lakeshore and the steep cliffs, are a favourite habitat. The star turn of recent years was the arrival for a few days in 2011 of three **wild dogs**, the extremely rare and elusive nomadic hunter, a strong sign of their revival in Kenya.

Lastly, if you tire of the living spectacle, go looking for the **Lion Cave**, beneath Lion Hill ridge in the northeast; it's an excavated prehistoric rock shelter and rarely contains lions.

ya Nyuki and *Kampi ya Nyati* campsites; *Lake Nakuru Lodge*, for a general view across unobstructed savanna; and the high "**baboon cliffs**" in the west.

ARRIVAL AND DEPARTURE   LAKE NAKURU NATIONAL PARK

The park has three gates: Main Gate, Lanet and Nderit. **Main Gate**, the point of issue for Safari Cards, is on the southern edge of Nakuru town, and is the location of the park headquarters, together with a large shop and the main campsite. Entering through **Lanet Gate**, on the northeast side of the park, gives the most direct access from Naivasha or Nairobi to the park's two lodges and allows you to avoid the congestion of Nakuru town. The 1.5km dirt road to Lanet Gate starts opposite the *Stem Hotel*: if you're coming from Naivasha heading towards Nakuru and you cross the railway bridge, you've overshot. **Nderit Gate**, in the southeast corner, is useful only if you're driving cross-country from Lake Naivasha or over the Mau escarpment from Narok.

GETTING AROUND

By car or taxi If you don't have a vehicle, the most straightforward way to see the park is by rented car or taxi – some of the taxi drivers around Nakuru town know the park well. You can rent a six-person 4WD van from KWS ($60/2hr or $250/day; ☎0711 508158), with pick-ups at the *Merica Hotel*. Otherwise, the *Midland Hotel* (see p.221) is as good a place as any to track down a taxi. Reckon on some hard bargaining and count on around $15/hr for a 3hr trip, with park fees on top (including Ksh1300 in fees for the car and driver).

Hitchhiking An alternative – though not always a very practical one – is to hitch for a lift at the Main Gate, about an hour's walk from the town centre. The rangers are usually sympathetic, but there's no guarantee of finding a ride out, so be prepared to spend the night in the park.

ACCOMMODATION

There's limited lodge accommodation in the park, and it's a good idea to reserve well in advance at all the places listed below.

Lake Nakuru Lodge Southeast corner of the park ☎0720 404480, ⓦlakenakurulodge.com. On a wooded rise in the southeast corner of the park, based around an old Delamere Estate house in shady gardens, *Lake Nakuru Lodge*'s main selling point is a good, large pool (non-guests $8) and uninterrupted views across the savanna with a distant glimpse of a corner of the lake. On the downside, most of the rather discordantly decorated *banda*-style rooms are fairly small and dark, though the family rooms are large, with big bathrooms. FB **$300**

★ **Mbweha Safari Camp** Just outside the park, a 15min drive from Nderit Gate ☎020 234192 or 0715 555322, ⓦatua-enkop.com. Nine private cottages tucked among euphorbias, all made from local materials and with private verandas and views of the Eburru and Mau ranges. There's also a sunken lounge and bar area looking out onto a small waterhole, and a fantastic restaurant. A range of activities is on offer including bike rides, game drives, bush dinners and sundowners. FB **$520**

Naishi House Southwest part of the park; bookings through KWS ☎020 6000800, ⓦkws.go.ke. A popular and peaceful little country house surrounded by savanna, with a fully equipped kitchen and four bedrooms to suit a self-catering group of up to eight (two doubles in the main house, and two more in a separate annexe). Firewood is provided and the generator is fired up from 7pm to 10pm (no electricity at other times). There's a good front terrace, and spotlights shine on a small water point at night. Expect to see zebras, black rhino and the occasional lion. Ranger-guided game drives can be organized. Whole house **$200**

Sarova Lion Hill Game Lodge On the park's eastern slopes, high above the lake ☎0728 606584, ⓦsarovahotels.com. One of Sarova's less exciting lodges, with typically high standards but undistinguished (albeit comfortable) rooms in grey block cottages ranged along the hillside among the trees. All come with a large double plus a single bed and good nets, but few other embellishments. Meals are excellent and slightly cheaper than at *Lake Nakuru Lodge*. Pool and sauna (non-residents Ksh400). FB **$260**

Wildlife Clubs of Kenya Hostel 3.5km from the main gate ☎020 2671742, ⓦwildlifeclubsofkenya.org. Set in a renovated old farmhouse, this hostel is aimed at groups

THE MYSTERY OF THE VANISHING FLAMINGOS

Lake Nakuru has always been viewed as a flamingo lake *par excellence*. Several decades ago, up to two million **lesser flamingos** (maybe a third of the world's population) could be seen here massing in the warm alkaline water to feed on the abundant blue-green algae cultivated by their own droppings. In addition, the lake was also home to a small population of the much rarer **greater flamingo**, a species which tips its head upside down to use its beak to sift for small crustaceans and plankton.

Like Lake Elmenteita, Lake Nakuru has no outlet, meaning that its level fluctuates wildly. In 1962, it dried up almost completely, while in the late 1970s, increased rainfall lowered the lake's salinity and raised the water level. The flamingos began to disperse, some to lakes Elmenteita, Magadi and Natron (in Tanzania), some up to Turkana, and the majority to Lake Bogoria. Since then, flamingos have been sporadically seen again in the surreal pink flocks that have become a photographic cliché. There are always hundreds, probably thousands, but the presence of mass flocks is unpredictable.

Over the last twenty years, large areas of forest in the lake's catchment area have been converted to small farms, and Nakuru town has industrialized and grown massively. Sewage and industrial pollution is believed to be a major factor behind the flamingos' decline, as are water diversion, soil erosion leading to siltation and even sand-harvesting along the Njoro River. The introduction in the 1960s of a hardy species of fish, *Tilapia grahami* – partly to control mosquitoes – has encouraged large flocks of **white pelicans**, and it's likely that their presence is another disruptive element (a breeding colony of greater flamingos at Lake Elmenteita was forced off by the pelicans). The Nakuru Wildlife Trust has been studying the ecology of Rift Valley lakes since 1971 in an effort to find some of the answers, and the WWF now organizes educational trips to the park for local children, as well as running a scheme to monitor pollution from individual industries.

of students but is open to anybody, and represents the best (and only) truly budget option in the park. Facilities are simple and most of the rooms are dorms, though there's also a three-person banda on offer for the same price, and a kitchen. All in all, it's good value. BB **Ksh1250** per person

CAMPSITES

Camping rates are high, thanks to Lake Nakuru's standing as one of KWS's top-league parks. Special campsites must be reserved in advance, though it's a good idea to reserve at the public sites as well. Call KWS on ☎ 020 2664071 to book a spot at all the sites below.

Backpackers' Just inside the Main Gate. The park's main public campsite sits on a grassy patch under fine old yellow acacias, but its meagre facilities – cold showers, unpleasant squat toilets and communal tap – are a let-down. Beware the audacious vervet monkeys and baboons here. **$25** per person

Kampi ya Nyati (Buffalo Camp) Northeastern part of the park. One of the park's two "special campsites" (meaning you'll have the place all to yourself), located in a clearing among the trees between the road and the open shore, with splendid private access to quiet vantage points on the shore through driveable tunnels of undergrowth – but no facilities to speak of. **$40** per person

Kampi ya Nyuki (Bee Camp) In the northeastern part of the park. This is the nicer of the two special campsites, with a setting very similar to that of Kampi ya Nyati, but closer to the lake. There are no facilities here, so be sure to bring all your own food, water and fuel. **$40** per person

Makalia Campsite At the southern tip of the park. The other public campsite is the somewhat elusive Makalia, in a wonderful location on either side of the stream of the same name, close to a waterfall. It has the same poor facilities as *Backpackers'*, but the setting is nicer. Very few organized tours come down this way, but should you feel isolated, you may be reassured to know there's a ranger station fairly close by. **$25** per person

Menengai crater

Containing an enormous caldera, **Menengai crater** is 12km across and nearly 500m deep in places, a spectacular sea of bush-covered lava whose black waves are frozen solid. The crater was the site of a battle around 1854 in which the Ilpurko Maasai defeated the Ilaikipiak Maasai, whom they considered upstarts disrespectful to Batian, the *laibon* (paramount chief) of the time, after whom the highest peak of Mount Kenya was named. At intervals throughout the nineteenth century these **Maasai civil wars** flared up over the issue of true Maasai identity. In this case, it wasn't simply a matter of honour but also of grazing rights in the Rift Valley, especially around Lake Naivasha and on the scarp slopes. The Ilpurko were herders, while the Ilaikipiak from the north grew crops as well. Both had been preparing for battle for some time and it is said that hundreds of Ilaikipiak *morani* were hurled over the crater rim to their deaths. The place retains a sinister reputation – even the normally fearless Maasai traditionally consider it to be the dwelling place of devils and evil spirits – and local people prefer not to go near the edge.

A century later, at the highest point of this windy crest, the Rotary Club erected a signpost. Apart from informing you that Nairobi is 140km away and Rome 2997km in the opposite direction, it also points out that the crater wall is 2272m above sea level and its area covers some 90 square kilometres – the whole dramatic extent of which you can see before you descend into the crater itself. You'll also get fantastic views over Lake Nakuru if you walk down the dirt road along the south side of the gum-tree plantation.

ARRIVAL AND DEPARTURE
MENENGAI CRATER

It's 8km from the centre of Nakuru to the rim of the crater. There's no public transport, although at weekends you might be lucky and get a lift.

By car Head up Menengai Drive and take the fourth left turn (Crater Climb) through the suburbs above town towards the telecommunications tower 4.5km up the hill. Turn right at the tower, following the track for 20min to a fire lookout tower on the bare cliff, from where the crater spreads out beneath you.

On foot Allow 3hr to reach the crater rim from Nakuru on foot, and at least another hour to hike down to and up from the crater floor. Try to go up in a group, as muggings are a possibility.

FROM TOP LAKE BOGORIA NATIONAL RESERVE (P.233); LAKE BARINGO (P.236) >

Hyrax Hill

3.5km from Nakuru centre, off the north side of the Nairobi road • Daily 8.30am–5.30pm • Ksh500 • ☎ 051 2217175, ⓦ bit.ly/HyraxHill • Matatus for Lanet and Gilgil will drop you at the turn-off, from where it's a 600m walk to the small museum where you pay the entrance fee • It's usually possible to camp here either free or for a small fee (staff facilities only)

An easy target outside Nakuru, **Hyrax Hill** has been a human settlement site for at least three thousand years, with finds dating from the Neolithic period immediately before the modern era. Named for the hyraxes that once scampered over this ancient tongue of lava, the prehistoric settlement site was discovered by Louis Leakey in 1926, and subsequently excavated by Mary Leakey ten years later and by others between 1965 and 1987. An excellent guide published in 1983 is on sale in the museum.

The Northeast Village

The path leading out to the right of the museum winds its way around the north side of the hill to an excavated pit dwelling or "sunken enclosure", with baulks left in place to show the depth of material that was removed during the digging. There are thirteen similar depressions in this "**Northeast Village**", but it's uncertain exactly how they were used. They have yielded a tremendous quantity of pottery shards, tools made from flakes of obsidian and animal-bone fragments. The absence of postholes normally needed to support a roof suggests they may have been shelters for livestock, but just as plausibly, a roof might have been added whenever needed, leaving no trace, and animals and people may have shared the shelters.

It's believed the inhabitants would have been semi-nomadic Sirikwa- or Nandi-speaking (Kalenjin) herders. Today, the Kalenjin mostly live further west, but they're associated with so-called pit-dwellings elsewhere (see p.243) and, in the case of Hyrax Hill, they may have been forced to flee by an expanding Maasai population from the north.

The fort

Following the path towards the top of the hill, you come to an exposed "**fort**" facing out towards Nakuru, which consists of a circle of hefty boulders enclosing a flattened area. It may have been an Iron Age lookout post, but there's no way of being certain, or of knowing how old it might be, since no artefacts have been found. From here, you can scramble over the volcanic boulders to the summit, where you get a good view of the southern part of the site and the lake. Now several kilometres away, Lake Nakuru once extended, probably as fresh water, right to the base of the hill and across much of the Rift Valley, turning Hyrax Hill into a peninsula or even an island.

Burial sites

A hundred metres down the hillside in a fenced-in shelter, the massive stone slab which sealed a **Neolithic burial mound** has been removed to display part of a skull and some limb bones. The remains of a further nineteen Neolithic skeletons were discovered north of this, beneath a more recent Iron Age occupation area marked by the two stone circles (which were hut foundations). Nineteen Iron Age skeletons were also discovered, overlying the Neolithic graves, mostly of young men, possibly slain warriors, apparently buried unceremoniously or in a hurry, their skulls and limbs in tangled heaps. The coincidence of nineteen skeletons at each level may be just that – coincidence. Or perhaps the Iron Age survivors who buried their young men knew about the ancient Neolithic graves beneath.

The game of bau

For a less dramatic, but more accessible, impression of life at Hyrax Hill, the **game of bau**, cut into the rock just before you get back to the museum, is a delightfully fresh record. *Bau* is the Bantu name for a game of skill and – depending on the rules used – amazing complexity that has been played all over Africa for a very long time. Two people play, moving pieces (cowries, seeds or pebbles) from one hole to another to win. There are a number of these "boards" around the hill; the one near the museum is a particularly good example.

West of Nakuru

West of Nakuru, the **A104** is a busy, often dangerous highway along which lorries, buses and matatus thunder at top speed over a surface which varies, unpredictably, from perfect to perfectly awful and which has been the subject of a massive resurfacing and road-building operation in recent years. It's hair-raising if you're driving yourself or with a driver, and even more wearing on the nerves if you're travelling by public transport.

Heading into Western Kenya, the **C56** offers a scenic and much quieter alternative to the main highway, climbing gradually up to the towns of **Njoro**, **Elburgon** and **Molo**, in ascending order of altitude and size. This is a gentle land of small towns, colonial manors and conifers, and although most travellers see nothing more of it than the road to Kericho, the area offers some of the most charming accommodation in the region, and is well worth a stopover.

THE KALENJIN PEOPLES

The **Kalenjin** form the majority of the population in the central part of the Rift Valley. Their name, actually a recent adoption by a number of peoples speaking dialects of Nandi, means "I tell you". The principal Kalenjin are the **Nandi**, **Terik**, **Tugen**, **Elgeyo**, **Elkony**, **Sabaot**, **Marakwet** and **Kipsigis**, and, more contentiously, the Pokot. They were some of the earliest inhabitants of Kenya and probably absorbed the early bushmen or pygmy peoples who had already been here for 200–300,000 years.

Primarily **farmers**, the Kalenjin have often adapted their economies to local circumstances. The first Kalenjin were probably herdsmen. The pastoral **Pokot** group still spurn all kinds of cultivation and despise peoples who rely on anything but livestock, calling the **Marakwet**, living against the western Rift escarpment, *Cheblong* ("The Poor"), for their lack of cattle. The **Okiek** provide another interesting clue to the past. Hunter-gatherers, they live in scattered groups in the forests of the high slopes flanking the Rift, but unlike most hunter-gatherers, they do very little gathering. Meat and honey are the traditional staples. They consider wild fruits and vegetables barely palatable, though cornmeal and gardening have been introduced, and they now keep some domestic animals too. They may be the descendants of Kalenjin forebears who lost (or ate) their herds. There are other groups in Kenya who live mostly by hunting – Ndorobo or Wanderoo – for whom such a background is very likely, and who are all gradually abandoning their old lifestyles and dislikes amid the inexorable advance of "civilization".

Many Kalenjin played key roles in the founding of the Kenya African Democratic Union (KADU – now disbanded), but the most famous of Kalenjin in recent years was Kenya's second president, Daniel Arap Moi, a **Tugen** from Baringo District. As he was from a small ethnic group, his presidency at first avoided the accusations of tribalism levelled so bitterly against Kenyatta. But Moi's firm grip on the reins of power was increasingly exercised through the Kalenjin-dominated civil service, rather than the more ethnically mixed cabinet. In 1992, when democratic elections first took place, there were **tribal clashes**, often coordinated from behind the scenes, with the "ethnic cleansing" of non-Kalenjin (usually Kikuyu incomers) from the Rift Valley by groups of surprisingly well-organized young men. The same story was repeated at election time in 1997, 2002 and 2007 (see p.571).

Njoro

The turn-off to Njoro and the Mau escarpment lies 5km west of Nakuru, and is usually marked by a police roadblock. From here, it's 13km to **NJORO**, the hometown of **Egerton University** (main campus 5km out of town on the road to Narok), which has several other campuses scattered through the highlands. The jacaranda-fringed main road runs straight past the "centre" of town – a great acreage of mud (or, at best, dust), backed by a humble row of *dukas* and *hotelis*. Beyond the Narok junction, there's another and more soulful Njoro of wooden-colonnaded, tin-roofed, one-storey *dukas*. Here you'll also find a KCB bank and the Njoro Farmer's Petrol Station, a Shell garage. On the other side of town, past timber yards, is flat cereal country, with herds of dairy cattle and racehorses between the lines of gum trees and copses of acacia.

Kenana Knitters

Kembu Farm, 5km from Njoro along the C56 • Mon–Fri 8.30am–5pm, and at other times by prior arrangement • ☎ 0715 262303, ⓦ kenanaknitters.com

Just outside Njoro you'll find the buzzing workshop of **Kenana Knitters**, a non-profit women's cooperative which makes toys and other knitted items primarily for export, although you can see how they put them together (and buy some of the finished products). The handmade clothing and stuffed animals are all made from organic cotton, home-grown wool and plant dyes, and many of them are really quite beautiful.

ACCOMMODATION AND EATING   NJORO

★ **Deloraine House** 34km from Nakuru off the A104; turn right 1km past Salgaa, then right again, and follow signs to the house ☎ 0722 870161, ⓦ offbeatsafaris.com. Exquisitely chilled and stately colonial pile built in 1920 on a vast estate beneath the Mount Londiani forest, just a few kilometres northwest of – but a million miles from – the straggling truck-stop of Salgaa (Rongai). The long shady terrace looks east across luxuriant borders and lawns and there's a large swimming pool, lovingly maintained stables with eighty horses, and a gentle Happy Valley atmosphere. The rooms are baronial and the meals delicious, copious and garden-fresh. It particularly appeals to riders, who often stay here as part of a safari with Offbeat (see p.370). Full-board packages including riding **$700**

★ **Kembu Campsite and Cottages** 5km from Njoro along the C56 to Elburgon, 18km from the A104/C56

junction west of Nakuru, and then 1.2km from the main road (well signposted) ☎ 0722 361102, ⓦ kembu .com. Set on an 800-acre, family-run working farm with great views and wonderful hospitality, with accommodation in a variety of spacious, relaxing cottages, some dating back to the 1920s and '30s, including a delightful "Tree House" and an old wooden railway carriage, "Cobb's Carriage". A good spot to hang out for a few days, it's also popular with overland groups, and has fresh farm produce for sale, excellent food and a convivial bar-restaurant ensuring regular company. *Kembu*, incidentally, is Kikuyu for chameleon, and you can find little Van Hoehnell's chameleons all around the site. Fantastic value, and great for families. Prices range from Ksh3900 for Cobb's up to Ksh13,700 for a fully s/c cottage sleeping four, or you can camp. Three excellent meals will add Ksh3900/ day to your bill. Camping **Ksh400** per person, BB **Ksh3900**

Elburgon and Molo

ELBURGON is a good deal bigger than Njoro, and higher up. You're into seriously muddy, conifer country up here, and the buildings, characteristically chalet-style, are built of dark, weathered planks. It's timber money that gives Elburgon a degree of commercial prosperity and can be the only reason for the massive investment in the *Hotel Eel* (see opposite).

Molo

West of Elburgon, the road winds and dips through patches of Mau forest for several kilometres, with glimpses of railway viaducts across the valleys, until it emerges, still higher up, among the cereals and pyrethrum fields at **MOLO**. Molo straggles for several kilometres down into a broad valley across the rail tracks and up the other side on to Mau Summit Road, where you'll find a post office, banks and several petrol stations.

On towards Lake Baringo

If you're continuing from here towards **Lake Baringo** in your own vehicle, you can avoid doubling back to Nakuru by heading north to the A104 from Molo and turning northwest towards Eldoret. After 5km, when you reach Makutano, take the surfaced road to the right, which goes through some wonderful mountain scenery via **Eldama Ravine** and **Tenges**, up to the C51 where you can turn right and join the B4 to the lake.

ACCOMMODATION · ELBURGON AND MOLO

Highlands Hotel 6km west of Molo, and just over 3km west of the last fuel stop ☎ 0722 501267. This is a fine old property, but desperately run-down, and the huge, wood-floored rooms with fireplaces (s/c, no nets) are long overdue for a major refit – although the whole place may change hands soon, with renovations around the corner. There's a bar and dining room, where lamb with baked potatoes is the speciality (Ksh500, but give them plenty of notice). BB Ksh1500

Hotel Eel East side of town ☎ 0727 078441, ✉ elburgit @yahoo.co.uk. The centre of gravity for local entertainments, this mid-sized hotel is a dull but perfectly acceptable option, offering sizeable, well-maintained s/c rooms with bathtubs (but without nets), and secure parking. BB Ksh1800

The Mau Forest

South of Molo, up into the **Mau forest**, a graded road runs to **Keringet**, where a huge old estate, once owned by Italians, is gradually crumbling, and on to **Olenguerone**. From here, the road tunnels eerily through a forest of huge gum trees, to Bomet (see p.362). There are several daily matatu runs along this route from Molo. The Kenya Wildlife Service has been trying for years to open up the mountain forest, like the Aberdare National Park, but there is stubborn resistance, not least from the forest's indigenous Okiek (Dorobo) hunter-gatherers, as well as from loggers.

Kipkelion Monastery

The **Our Lady of Victoria Abbey** is a Cistercian monastery between Londiani and Kipkelion, in an area formerly known by the Maasai as "Lumbwa", though Kipkelion ("Kif-*kel*-ion") is the original and much-preferred Kipsigis name. Founded in 1956, this is the only Cistercian monastery in Kenya and, deep in this rural hill country, the tall cement-block church is a remarkable sight. The monks make a living from their dairy herd and chickens, and run the only hospital in the area and an important school. During the post-election violence in 2008, they protected hundreds of refugees. The monastery began as a Trappist retreat, with the absolute silence the reformist order stipulates, but later reverted to the rather less stringent code of the older Cistercian order.

ARRIVAL AND DEPARTURE · KIPKELION MONASTERY

By matatu One or two daily matatus service the route from Londiani via Baisheli, 15km west of Londiani (1hr), leaving early in the morning.

By car The easiest approach from the west is via Kipkelion railway station, which is signposted, left, off the main B1 highway 25km east of Kericho. From the signpost, it's 10km to the station, followed by a rocky, 3km climb to the C35. Turning right onto the C35, you drive a further 6km northeast to reach the start of the 11km track on the left (signposted "Monastery Hospital") up to the abbey from the small centre of Baisheli. Approaching from the east, you drive 13km west of Londiani on the C35 to reach the start of the 11km track (on your right) to the monastery. The track to the monastery is rough, narrow and steep in parts, winding through intensively cultivated Kipsigis *shambas*.

ACCOMMODATION

★ **Kipkelion Monastery Guest Rooms** 11km from Baisheli on the C35 (signposted); PO Box 40 Kipkelion ☎ 052 2030096. The international group of brothers talk only when necessary, but are happy to receive visitors – you may receive a surprisingly loquacious welcome. If you like the idea of peace and contemplation in a rural setting, call to let them know you're coming. FB, with a suggested donation of Ksh3000 per person

The Subukia Valley

The **Subukia Valley** was the Maasai's "Beautiful Place" (Ol Momoi Sidai) and its lush pastures were their insurance against the failure of the grass up on the Laikipia plateau. But they were evicted in 1911 to the "Maasai Reserve" and the way was clear for **settler families**. It's easy to see why the Europeans chose this high valley, despite its isolation, with its soft, arcadian beauty far removed from the windy plateaus above or the austere furnace of the Rift Valley floor below.

The village of **SUBUKIA**, just 4km north of the equator, has a scattering of *hotelis* and *dukas*, and a filling station.

Up the valley to Bogoini

If you have your own transport and two or three hours to spare (or a couple of days to walk it), you can take a major diversion up the Subukia Valley to **BOGOINI**, then turn west and cut back south again, past Lake Solai (about 45km in total). From the grubby junction at Subukia village where the main road passes, head north about 700m to an old T-junction, with roads to Nakuru (left) and Lower Subukia (right), then take the latter. The track, consisting of rough dirt and rocks, is easy to follow, but you must be self-sufficient if you're walking it, since sources of food along the way are negligible until you reach Bogoini itself. Transport is also sparse, with only four matatus daily between Subukia and Bogoini. Matatus between Bogoini and Mairu Kumi via Solai are slightly more frequent, but you may still have to wait hours. Travel between Subukia and Bogoini is also possible by *boda-boda*.

Lake Solai

Little **Lake Solai** is a curiously isolated soda lake with a reedy shoreline grazed by cattle and a scattering of sisal plots. For many years it was a seasonal lake, but it has been a permanent feature of the landscape since the early 1980s. South of Lake Solai, the road climbs through scattered euphorbia and acacias to the junction (hard right) at **Solai police post**. Lines of jacaranda streak the scenery at intervals all over this district, bordering old driveways – evidence of the erstwhile community of white settlers.

ARRIVAL AND ACCOMMODATION   **SUBUKIA VILLAGE**

Matatus stop near the T-junction where the Subukia Valley road meets the B5, not far from the *Malindi* hotel, and there's regular transport to Nakuru (1hr) and Nyahururu (30min), for where you shouldn't have to wait any more than an hour.

Malindi Hotel Southern end of the village ☎ 0734 980423. Simple lodgings are available at this friendly, family-run hotel, with modest non-s/c rooms and cold showers. *Uncles's Pub*, next door, is a decent source of beer and *nyama choma*. Room only **Ksh600**

From Subukia to Bogoria's Emsos Gate

The most direct route from Subukia village to Lake Bogoria's **Emsos Gate** begins by climbing 4km out of the valley along the main road back to Nakuru. An unsignposted right turn (or left if you've just come from Nakuru) goes over the hill to the west past the curious **St Peter's** church – a quaint Anglican church that looks as if it just flew in from England – and then drops 15km down to the **Solai police post**. From here, the 50km route to Bogoria is rough in many places, though normally negotiable in a 4WD, for which you should allow at least three hours. Matatus are sparse, though they do run. If you're on foot or bicycle and still want to do it, check your emergency water and food supplies, tighten your bootlaces – or check your brakes – and set off west.

The route

The road descends steeply from the Solai police post to the Solai Valley with its disused railway line, which you cross at a place called **MILTON'S SIDING**. When you reach the tracks, follow the road, parallel to the tracks, to the right, for 1km, and then turn sharp left to cross the tracks. The road descends in a series of steps to a broad, flat valley with a sharp, right-hand bend up the hill on the far side, which it crosses to reach **KISANANA** – life-saving *chai* and a place to stop for the night if necessary, though there's no formal accommodation.

From Kisanana, you turn left at the old signpost and follow decent *murram* tracks for some 5km to a fork around some buildings. Here you head left and are soon pitching up a diabolical slope – rarely used by motor vehicles and by all appearances dynamited out of solid bedrock – which winds up and over a scrub-covered hog's-back ridge for some 7km, eventually twisting north and dropping to a better red *murram*, interspersed with white, rocky stretches. You come to a crossroads (turn left), then after a few hundred metres a T-junction at a place of a few huts called **MUGURIN** (turn right), where you may find a solitary *hoteli* open. From here, you're within the compass of the lake, with Emsos Gate some 25km away. The road descends steadily now as you travel north – there's only the odd signpost but no danger of taking a wrong turn. If in doubt, head right.

Lake Bogoria National Reserve

Daily 6am–7pm • Ksh2500

One of the least-visited lakes in the Rift Valley, despite being a globally recognized Ramsar wetlands site since 2002, **Lake Bogoria** is a sliver of saline water – unbelievably foul-tasting – entrenched beneath towering hills, 60km north of Nakuru. With the increasing pollution of Lake Nakuru, Lake Bogoria has become the adopted feeding ground of tens (at times hundreds) of thousands of **lesser flamingos**, and the lakeshore is one of the few places where **greater kudu** antelope can easily be seen. The chief warden, William Kimosop (☏0720 317760), is a local authority on birds and, with prior arrangement, may be able to accompany you into the reserve. But the lake is worth visiting as much for its physical spectacle as for the wildlife: a largely barren, baking wilderness of scrub and rocks, from which a series of furious **hot springs** erupts on the western shore, and the bleak walls of the Siracho range rise from the east.

The lake

Hidden in its deep bowl, Lake Bogoria – when approached from Mugurin – is only visible when you're almost on top of it. The final stretch of the track leading down to Emsos Gate is steep and rocky as well as being savagely beautiful, the landscape transformed into a strident dazzle of red and blue and splashes of green. The lake itself, a glistening pool of soapy blue and white, usually has a mirage of pink flamingos tinting its shores.

LAKE BOGORIA'S WILDLIFE

Although there's plenty of wildlife in and around Lake Bogoria, it tends to make itself scarce, with the exception of the flamingos at the hot springs. Most animals – including buffalo, hyena, klipspringer, impala, dik-dik, zebra, warthog and Grant's gazelle – prefer the remote and inaccessible eastern shore, though you may see **greater kudu** just about anywhere. The **flamingos**, for some curious reason – possibly chemical – tend to flock in their greatest numbers to the shallows on the western shore, where the hot springs flow into the lake (they appear immune to the heat). The Bogoria **fish eagles** have made a gruesome adjustment to their fierce, fishless environment: they prey on flamingos. Other birds to look out for include avocets, transitory pelicans and migratory steppe eagles.

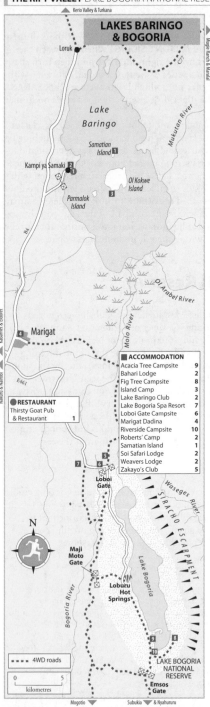

LAKES BARINGO & BOGORIA

Kerio Valley & Turkana

Loruk

Lake Baringo

Samatian Island **1**

Kampi ya Samaki **2**
1

3

Ol Kokwe Island

Parmalok Island

Mogie Ranch & Maralal

Mukutan River

Ol Arabel River

Molo River

Kabarnet & Eldoret

Marigat **4**

Nakuru & Nairobi

E461

■ ACCOMMODATION
Acacia Tree Campsite	9
Bahari Lodge	2
Fig Tree Campsite	8
Island Camp	3
Lake Baringo Club	2
Lake Bogoria Spa Resort	7
Loboi Gate Campsite	6
Marigat Dadina	4
Riverside Campsite	10
Roberts' Camp	2
Samatian Island	1
Soi Safari Lodge	2
Weavers Lodge	2
Zakayo's Club	5

● RESTAURANT
Thirsty Goat Pub & Restaurant	1

7 **6**

Loboi Gate

N

Waseges River

SIRACHO ESCARPMENT

Maji Moto Gate

Lake Bogoria

Bogoria River

Loburu Hot Springs

9 **8**

10

LAKE BOGORIA NATIONAL RESERVE

Emsos Gate

- - - - 4WD roads

0   5
kilometres

Mogotio   Subukia & Nyahururu

While the Bogoria Reserve **paved road** between the Loboi Gate and the Loburu hot springs is in good condition, the **east shore road** has been quite impassable for years, owing to a huge rock fall coupled with higher water levels, so there is no circuit round the lake. If you're driving northwest from Emsos Gate, there's a river bed to negotiate before you reach the tarmac, for which 4WD is essential. It may be best to take a ranger who knows the road: ask at the gate.

The Loburu hot springs

However you enter the reserve, you're bound to want to see the **hot springs**, a series of boiling water spouts on the shore. Although they hardly touch Yellowstone or Rotorua standards, "hot springs" is a tame appellation for this very impressive, terrifying, and photogenic phenomenon. Depending on the lake level, one or more of the springs may break the surface of the lake (while the others show their presence by the agitated green water above them, some steam and a strong smell), or they may all be visible from the shore.

With normal water levels, the springs burst up from huge natural cauldrons of super-heated water not far below the ground and drain into steaming rivulets that cut through the crusty earth, continuously collapsing and reforming their courses down to the lake. Even at midday, when the sun glares like a furnace, clouds of steam drift across this infernal scene. Near the lakeshore, the macabre bleached skeletons of flamingos lie strewn in the sand and, in the background, the dull thundering of the springs fills the air. It's like some water garden in Hell.

There's a **drinks kiosk** at the springs, but no food. Picnickers sometimes think it's fun to boil eggs and heat tins of food in the pools, but the consequences of a fall can be messy and even fatal: over the years a number of people have slipped and

THE CASE OF THE ENDOROIS

The **Endorois** are a small tribe of Kalenjin pastoralists, closely related to the **Tugen**. They used to range over a large area around Lake Bogoria, but were evicted from the narrow shores of the lake when the **reserve** was created in 1974 (see ⓦtinyurl.com/ybezkjt). Although they lost little of their traditional grazing lands within the reserve's narrow confines, what they did lose was precious and fertile, including land along the wooded southern shore, where several streams provided valuable **fresh water**, and at Loboi in the north, where the ill-conceived spa-hotel owned by the family of former president Daniel Arap Moi expropriated the warm springs. They also lost valuable **honey** and sources of **herbal medicine**. Like every one of Kenya's indigenous groups, they had valid claims, and the four percent share of the gate receipts allotted to them was pitifully low – especially since Bogoria rarely figures on safari itineraries. Inspired community leadership saw them pursue restitution of their lands and compensation as far as the African Union's Commission on Human and Peoples' Rights, which ruled in their favour in 2010, setting a new precedent for minority rights across the continent. However, as of 2012 the decision had yet to be implemented, and the Endorois were still waiting to reclaim their land.

3

died as a result. An *askari* has now been posted to watch out for visitors, but if you scald yourself, help might still be a long time coming.

ARRIVAL AND DEPARTURE

LAKE BOGORIA

FROM NAKURU VIA MOGOTIO TO EMSOS GATE

The B4 road north from Nakuru runs 20km to the west of Lake Bogoria and carries little traffic – tortoises in the road present the greatest hazard to motorists. The reserve is signposted to the right, 36km from Nakuru at Mogotio (fill up on petrol here), from where a good *murram* road, easily motorable in the dry season, cuts across to the lake. Some 23km from this junction, shortly after Mugurin (see p.233), you fork left for the western Maji Moto Gate (an incredibly rough 17km further, bringing you to the hot springs and tarmac lakeshore road), or right/straight ahead for the southern Emsos Gate (an equally rough 13km), which brings you to the wooded part of the reserve, from where a further rough track leads to the springs. You'll need 4WD beyond Mugurin, and there's no public transport.

FROM NAKURU TO THE LOBOI GATE

It's easier and quicker to continue northwards up the B4 to the signposted junction a few kilometres before Marigat (see p.236). From here, a fast tarmac road, the E461, takes you straight to the Loboi Gate 20km farther on. There are infrequent matatus from Marigat to Loboi Gate, but if you're staying at Lake Baringo you might try to arrange a lift from there as most vehicles visiting Bogoria come from Lake Baringo.

FROM NAKURU OR NYAHURURU VIA SOLAI TO EMSOS GATE

This route highlights the Rift Valley's striking topography as it drops from one monumental block of land to another, with dramatic changes of climate and scenery. The early part of the route from Nyahururu is particularly stunning, falling in a series of breathtaking steps over the fault lines until it reaches a high scarp above Subukia. When you reach the plain at the bottom of the valley, past Solai police post, you get an indelible impression of the way the earth has split apart and sunk to form the Rift over the last twenty million years. The route is described in more detail in the "From Subukia to Bogoria's Emsos Gate" section (p.232).

By car, bike or on foot Coming from Nakuru, drive or hike 14km past Menengai crater to the small trading centre of Mairu Kumi ("Ten Miles"), where the road divides. The left fork (unsignposted) leads, after 14km, to the Solai police post, while the right fork continues along the tarmac to Subukia and Nyahururu. If you don't have your own transport you'll have to hike the rest of the way down to Bogoria from the Solai police post – a good two days' walk or a fine half-day cycle ride.

By matatu Several buses and matatus run daily between Nyahururu and Nakuru via Subukia, while the police post at Solai is served infrequently by direct matatus from Nakuru, although a better bet for getting there is from Nakuru (or from Nyahururu or Subukia) is to take a matatu to Mairu Kumi and another one from there.

GETTING AROUND

While you're allowed into the reserve on foot or by bicycle, in theory this is only permitted from Loboi Gate as far as the Loburu hot springs. Exceptions may be made, however (and perhaps a ranger provided, for a fee), if you're heading for one of the campsites. You can rent mountain bikes at Loboi Gate (Ksh700/day; ☏0711 318598).

ACCOMMODATION

The rigour of Lake Bogoria's landscape is relieved by three shady **campsites** at the southern end of the lake, though they're difficult to get to unless you have 4WD. There are also a few **accommodation** options just outside the reserve's main Loboi Gate in the north.

LODGES AND RESORTS

Lake Bogoria Spa Resort 3km before Loboi Gate ☎0710 445627, ⌨lakebogoria-hotel.com. Essentially no more than an ordinary town hotel stranded in the bush, this is tasteless and not quite functional enough (a/c and nets, but hand-held showers only in the plain main-block rooms); the pricier cottage rooms (Ksh9300) are larger but only slightly better appointed. If you have a tent, you can camp near the swimming pool for Ksh1200, using the pool bathrooms. The best feature is the naturally replenished thermal spring pool, always a steady 37°C; you can take a dip for Ksh300. BB **Ksh7400**

Zakayo's Club Loboi village, about 500m from the gate ☎0722 153582. A barely adequate fallback, with safe parking, electric sockets (but no guarantee of power) and cold water showers. The funky little courtyard bar outside is a relaxing place for a drink, however. BB **Ksh800**

CAMPING

Acacia Tree Campsite 1.5km past Riverside Campsite, a 30min walk from Emsos Gate. A pretty spot on the lakeshore, shaded by acacias and frequented by kudu. Water and latrines are provided here, which makes the site better equipped than most. **Ksh500** per person

★ **Fig Tree Campsite** 3.5km from Emsos Gate. An absolute delight, though the magnificent glade of giant fig trees that shades the site is a favourite haunt of baboons that gorge themselves day and night. Buffalo also graze near here and are not to be trifled with. Bring your own food – a few basics are usually available just outside Emsos Gate – though water isn't a problem, since a permanent brook, clear and sweet, runs right through the site and provides a natural spa. *Fig Tree* is something of a dead end and, if you're down here and don't have your own vehicle, you may be in for a long wait before someone turns up to give you a lift out. **Ksh500** per person

Loboi Gate Campsite Loboi Gate You can camp at Loboi Gate, next to the Environmental Education Centre, just outside the reserve. It's not the most picturesque place, but there are latrines and usually water, and the handful of small shops at the gate can provide you with basics like eggs, biscuits and drinks; bring any other food and supplies yourself. **Ksh500** per person

Riverside Campsite 2km from Emsos Gate. The most basic of the three campsites, on the banks of a river that serves as the camp's only water source. Weaver birds breed nearby, and you can hear them in the trees at night. The site can be impossible to access during the rainy season – check with the park rangers before you go. **Ksh500** per person

Lake Baringo

An internationally recognized Ramsar wetlands site since 2002, **Lake Baringo** remains a peaceful oasis in the dry-thorn country, rich in **birdlife** and with a captivating character entirely its own. The waters are heavily silted with the red topsoil of the region, and they run through a whole range of colours every day from yellow to coral to purple, according to the sun's position and the state of the sky. On the lakeshore are villages inhabited by the **Il Chamus** (Njemps) people, who live by an unusual mixture of fishing and livestock-herding, breaking the taboo on the eating of fish, which is the norm among pastoralists. Speaking a dialect of Maa – the Maasai language – these fishermen paddle out in half-submerged dinghies made from the spongy and buoyant saplings of the fibrous *ambatch* tree that grows in profusion around the lake.

Marigat

Matatus from Nakuru come up only as far as the small district town of **MARIGAT**. This ought to be the hub of the Baringo–Bogoria tourist circuit, but it's a bland, dust-blown little place. The town's major landmark is an impressive bright green and white **mosque** funded by a wealthy Saudi, with two tiers of large windows and a capacity that obviously exceeds the area's Muslim population. There's also a KCB bank with ATM (but no Barclays) among the tin shacks, and a couple of B&Ls on the main street.

Kampi ya Samaki

Ksh200, vehicles Ksh100 • Regular matatus run between here and Marigat

The lakeside village of **KAMPI YA SAMAKI** ("Fish Camp") is the de facto capital of Lake Baringo, 2km from the main road, past the council-run roadblock where you pay your daily **admission fee** (all above-board and receipted). There are very few facilities in the scruffy little settlement itself; a small post office, but no bank and little in the way of shops. There's not a whole lot to do here, either, apart from a small **reptile park** (daily 8am–6pm; Ksh200), signposted, near the *Island Camp* boat stage, where you can see some local snakes, lizards and tortoises at close range.

Around the lake

Lake Baringo is fresh water (Naivasha being the only other non-saline Rift Valley lake), so its fish support a wide variety of **birds** and there are also sizeable populations of crocodiles and hippos. Though you rarely see much more than ears and snout by day, **hippos** come ashore after dark to graze; on a moonlit night their presence can be unnervingly obvious, though even in pitch darkness they're too noisy to be ignored. Although it used to be commonly understood that Baringo **crocodiles** were too small to pose a danger to swimmers, what constitutes a dangerous size in a Nile crocodile is perhaps a reckless debate. A regular local swimmer was badly mauled in 2008 so swimming is certainly highly inadvisable.

Ruko Wildlife Conservancy

North shore of the lake • Ksh500 per person, plus Ksh3000–4000 to rent a seven-person boat, including guide • Book through Roberts' Camp ☎ 0717 176656, ⍟ rukokenya.org

The new **Ruko Wildlife Conservancy** on the northern shore is still in its infancy, but with support from the Northern Rangelands Trust, *Roberts' Camp* and other local businesses, it's likely to consolidate in the next few years, while the numbers and variety of species will increase with planned KWS trans-locations. Using a small motorboat from *Roberts' Camp*, you can do some basic exploratory bush walks in the area in the company of Pokot and Njemps game scouts during which you're likely to see warthog, ostrich, common (Grant's) zebra, waterbuck, impala and possibly serval.

BIRDWATCHING AT LAKE BARINGO

Baringo's 458 species of **birds** are one of its biggest draws, and even if you don't know a superb starling from an ordinary one, the enthusiasm of others tends to be infectious. Former Baringo ornithologist Terry Stevenson holds the world record "bird-watch" for 24 hours – 342 species. Baringo's bird population rises and falls with the seasons (the dry season is the leanest time for birders), but the lakeshore resounds with birdsong (and frogs) at most times of year. It's surprisingly easy to get within close range of the birds – some species, such as the starlings and the white-bellied go-away bird, are positively brazen – so you'll find rapt amateur photographers lurking behind practically every bush. There are some interesting areas just south of *Lake Baringo Club*, where you should see some unusual species such as the white phase of the paradise flycatcher, grey-headed bush shrike, violet wood hoopoe and various kingfishers. Hippos commonly graze here, too, even in daylight hours. Wherever you're staying, an early-morning, birding boat trip along the lake's reedy shore is likely to be on offer, possibly in combination with a visit to the **Goliath Heronry** and one or two **hippo** and **croc** haunts. Afternoons can profitably be used for a trip out near the main road under some striking red cliffs, an utterly different habitat where, apart from hyraxes and baboons, you can see several species of hornbill, sometimes the massive nest of a hammerkop (wonderful-looking birds in flight, resembling miniature pterodactyls with their strange crests) and, with luck, the rare Verreaux's eagle.

Approaching **from the south**, the lake can be reached by matatu via the town of Marigat. Travelling **north of Baringo** is a hit-or-miss affair without your own transport: there's no public transport either to Maralal or to Tot or Lodwar from here, so try to hitch a ride with other tourists. If you're driving north of Baringo, note that there is **fuel** at Marigat and sometimes at Kampi ya Samaki, but none after that until Maralal or Archer's Post.

From the south: by matatu via Marigat Matatus from Nakuru go only as far as the small district town of Marigat, where you'll have to change to another vehicle. Travelling back from Kampi ya Samaki, there are one or two matatus direct to Nakuru at around 6am. Later in the day you can hail a matatu along the main road to Marigat, from where there are plenty of onward vehicles.

Destinations from Marigat Kabarnet (10–12 daily; 45min), with onward connections to Kampi ya Samaki (3–6 daily; 30min); Loboi (5–6 daily; 30min); Nakuru (6–8 daily; 1hr 30min).

From the north: by road to or from Maralal The highly recommended and not too rough road from Lake Baringo to Maralal (one day) or the rougher continuation to Samburu National Reserve (best done over two days) are only really viable with your own vehicle – there's effectively no public transport on these routes. The Maralal route starts by swinging north from the shore of Lake Baringo, leaving tarmac and tourism behind, and taking you up into the rugged country of the Lerochi plateau, dotted with Tugen and Pokot settlements. When the air is clear, there are stunning views back over Baringo. After two to three hours, you join the Rumuruti–Maralal *murram* road at Mugie Ranch (see p.509), then go north as far as Kisima, where you choose between a short journey onwards to Maralal or some inspiring but wheel-shattering driving along the C78/79 east to Archer's Post and Samburu (see p.540).

ACCOMMODATION AND EATING

Bahari Lodge Kampi ya Samaki, next to the post office ☎ 0726 857947. Run by the vivacious Mama Lina, this warm and welcoming B&L is the best in the village, even if the mattresses are old and the toilets are squatters. The small rooms come with nets and the food is very good, making it a favourite with local drivers, and there's a bar as well. Singles are a bargain at Ksh300. Room only Ksh600

Island Camp On the southern tip of Ol Kokwe Island ☎ 0728 478638 or 0735 919878, ⊕ islandcamp.co.ke. Although not as luxurious as some tented camps, this has real atmosphere and a superb location, dense with birdlife, as well as numerous species of lizard. The 22 small, comfortable tents have expansive views directly over the lake, which lulls you to sleep with its lapping just metres away. Boat trips, waterskiing, guided island walks can all be arranged, and there's a good-sized (if chilly) pool. Rates include boat transfer from their jetty at Kampi ya Samaki. BB $225

Lake Baringo Club 1km south of Kampi ya Samaki ☎ 0788 524801, ⊕ sunafricahotels.com. Struggling to keep going, this former oasis dating from the 1960s is still pleasant and worth a visit, and occasionally hosts birding groups, but either of the island-based camps is infinitely better to stay at. The 49 plain, high-ceilinged, well-insulated rooms with ceiling fans and nets tend to be occupied by conference delegates rather than tourists. Hippos graze the lawns at night, under the watchful eyes of the club *askaris*, and there's also a pool (non-residents Ksh300). FB $180

Marigat Dadina Near the roundabout in Marigat, 19km from Kampi ya Samaki ☎ 0735 359351. Fairly well-kept rooms around a dusty courtyard, though the singles and doubles (both s/c and non s/c) are rather small and cell-like. Still, not a bad option for the price. Room only Ksh500

★ **Roberts' Camp** 1km south of Kampi ya Samaki ☎ 0717 176656, ⊕ robertscamp.com. Lovely campsite in a large, acacia-shaded garden dipping into the lake, with lots of space, good facilities and great birding. Most visitors camp, but there are also four very nice, non-s/c twin *bandas* with electricity, shared kitchen and bathrooms with hot water, plus a comfortable safari tent (Ksh2000), and four self-catering cottages (Ksh8000–10,500 for four). At the heart of the camp is the *Thirsty Goat* pub (see below). Book ahead. Camping Ksh500 per person, BB Ksh4000

★ **Samatian Island** ☎ 0727 232445, ⊕ samatian islandlodge.com. Set on a minuscule private island, this is one of Kenya's very best and most relaxing lodges, with room for ten adults and four children. Birds hop and flit everywhere, and there are fantastic, ever-changing lake views in every direction. Rooms (in individual *bandas*) are very spacious and fully open-plan, with no windows or walls to block out the idyllic natural environment. Food is extra, or you can self-cater. The island can only be privately booked for groups of four or more with a minimum booking of three nights, and you'll also have to pay a daily conservation fee ($60 per adult, $30 per child). Entire island $1000

Soi Safari Lodge Kampi ya Samaki ☎ 0704 411623, ⊕ soisafarilodge-lkbaringo.com. The newest big place by the lake, offering fifty rooms with a/c, nets and TV (but hot water mornings and evenings only). The rooms are airy but plain, there's no direct lakeshore access and the large pool (non-residents Ksh200) is surrounded by about an acre of crazy paving. "Suswa Wing" rooms are nicer, with more of a lake view, but still it's hard to see why you would choose to stay here. HB $180

Thirsty Goat Pub and Restaurant At Roberts' Camp, 1km south of Kampi ya Samaki ☎0717 176656. Occupying a pleasant patio with hippos grazing nearby, this is the one real focus for food and drink in the area. There's always a buzz here, with pizzas or goat curry around Ksh550 and beer and wine Ksh200. Daily 7am– late, kitchen closes at 9pm.

Weavers Lodge On the left of the road through Kampi ya Samaki, behind Bahari Lodge ☎0724 987437. A reasonable fallback with large-ish s/c rooms with nets, but overpriced, and less homely than the *Bahari*. There's a popular TV bar in the same compound. BB Ksh1200

TOURS AND ACTIVITIES

Activities tend to centre around *Roberts' Camp* and the more upmarket lodges and include **motorboat trips** around the shores (Ksh3000/hr for up to seven people), but make sure that life jackets are provided and that no more than seven passengers are carried. It's best not to go if these conditions aren't met, bearing in mind that Baringo can get rough and the boats are rarely what you'd call seaworthy: in 2004, a number of people drowned when their boat capsized on the lake. Many boatmen know their birds and most are old hands at luring fish eagles by tossing them fresh fish – take your camera for spectacular close-ups as the eagles swoop down for the bait. There are also enjoyable boat trips to **Ol Kokwe Island** (Ksh1000) on request from *Island Camp*'s jetty on the north side of Kampi ya Samaki. *Island Camp* (see opposite) also offers **waterskiing** (Ksh1500/15min).

Lake Baringo Boats and Excursions Opposite Roberts' Camp ☎0722 420699. This community run tour company offers similar prices to *Roberts'*, with activities including boat trips, bird walks (Ksh400–500 per person for a 2hr walk) and visits to traditional Pokot compounds (Ksh3000 for a group of seven). They also offer expensive internet access in their office (Ksh4/min). Daily 7am–6.30pm.

Marina Boats Just south of the village ☎0725 937506. Another community-run operation offering boat trips, bird walks and cultural tours, although the usual caveats apply about the boats. Daily 7am–6.30pm.

Roberts' Camp 1km south of Kampi ya Samaki ☎0717 176656, ⓦrobertscamp.com. This appealing camp (see opposite) offers a range of activities including bird walks (Ksh400–500 per person for a 2hr walk), cultural visits to traditional Pokot compounds (Ksh1200 per person), cycle rental (a pricey Ksh400/hr, Ksh2500/day), and visits to *Island Camp* for a buffet lunch and a swim in the pool (Ksh1800 per person; minimum of two), which is a wonderful way to splurge a little if you're on a budget.

Kabarnet

KABARNET has a superb setting on the **Kamasia massif** – the slab also known as the Tugen Hills, which remained upstanding on the brink of the Kerio Valley when the rest of the area sank – and the road up the escarpment offers breathtaking views over the Rift Valley floor to Lake Baringo. The journey between Lake Baringo and Kabarnet mirrors the exciting trip to Lake Bogoria down the eastern side of the Rift. Frequent matatus make the climb from Marigat, the road soaring and plunging through at times almost alpine scenery. Kabarnet has good transport connections to surrounding towns, and makes for a good jumping-off point for excursions into the Kerio Valley.

Despite its dramatic location, the town of Kabarnet itself is fairly featureless and dull. From a small nucleus of administration buildings and *dukas* on the hillside in colonial times, it has expanded in every direction since becoming capital of Baringo District, undoubtedly related to its status as former president Daniel Arap Moi's home town (he was born in Sacho, 30km away). But apart from its post office, banks with ATMs and a few supermarkets, Kabarnet's only point of interest is a small **museum** (daily 9am–6pm; Ksh500) featuring exhibits on human evolution, headdresses from around the country, and artefacts and homesteads of the Tugen, Pokot and Il Chamus peoples who inhabit the region, plus a small snake farm.

ARRIVAL AND DEPARTURE   KABARNET

By matatu Matatus leave from the bustling stage in front of *Hotel Sinkoro*, with frequent connections to a number of towns in the area. Destinations Eldoret (6–8 daily; 1hr 45min); Iten (8–10 daily; 1hr); Marigat (10–12 daily; 45min) with onward connections (see p.238); Nakuru (6–8 daily; 2hr 30min); Tenges (3–4 daily; 1hr).

ACCOMMODATION

Kabarnet Hotel 1km above the town, off the Nakuru road ☎ 053 22094 or 0722 391246. Quiet and a bit tatty, this hotel has seen better days but is still worth a visit for its pool (non-residents Ksh100), mountain views and above-average food. Rooms come with big windows overlooking the garden. BB **Ksh2000**

Hotel Sinkoro By the matatu stage ☎ 0722 718740 or 0720 144829. A rambling place with large, light rooms, though those facing onto the matatu stage are noisy. There's also safe parking, a bar and a passable restaurant, but it's not cheap for what you get. BB **Ksh1300**

The Kerio Valley

From Kabarnet, the C51 runs on to **Eldoret** across the hot and fascinating **Kerio Valley**. The excitement of this route builds only after you leave Kabarnet town and plunge into the valley, a drop of 1000m in not much more than the same distance. There are magnificent views as the road rolls through **Chebloch**, crossing the Kerio River, after which the road turns sharply up the **Tambach escarpment** on the western side of the Kerio Valley. A turn right just before the hamlet of **Biretwo** is the start of the lonely trans-valley route north to Tot (see p.243). Also before Biretwo, look out for the **Torok Falls**, looming high above and to your left at the top of the Tambach escarpment. They're worth a visit if you like waterfalls; count on a good half-day if you're hiking up.

Iten

After a few more hairpins and a spectacular viewpoint (with obligatory curio and drinks stall), the road finally levels out at **ITEN**, a busy little market town on the rim of the escarpment. Iten is the main centre on this west side of the Kerio Valley, with fuel, a KCB bank with ATM and a small market (known for its leather goods). The town is known primarily as a training ground for **runners**: the famous St Patrick's High School (see box below) can be seen just after the main shops on the road north to Kapsowar. Otherwise Iten is just a quiet mountain community, with a cool climate and some beautiful walks in the area.

ACCOMMODATION AND EATING   ITEN

Jumbo Hotel Eastern end of town, in the huge building on the south side of the main road ☎ 0721 223358, ✉ jumborestaurant@yahoo.com. The *Jumbo* has chaotic plumbing and dodgy electrics, but is basically okay and has a good bar and restaurant. You may even meet foreign athletes here, since it's an affordable place to base yourself for a few weeks of high-altitude training. BB **Ksh800**

RUNNING IN ITEN

The remarkable **St Patrick's High School** in Iten must be the world's top school for runners, having produced middle-distance stars such as Peter Rono, Wilson Kipketer and Ibrahim Hussein, while its associated athletics camps have produced female runners such as Lydia Cheromei, Susan Chepkemei and **Lornah Kiplagat**. The phenomenon dates back to the 1970s, when an Irishman, **Colm O'Connell**, recognized the students' potential and set out to turn them into world-class athletes, developing a training programme which Iten's runners still follow to this day. Their remarkable success is something that sports scientists have yet to explain fully, but has a lot to do with climate, altitude and physiological factors, and seems particularly to involve the Nandi. But the town's reputation has spread, and these days elite athletes come from all over the world to do their high-altitude training in Iten, several hundred passing through each year to run up and down the valley and absorb the atmosphere of champions. If you're interested in pursuing some serious athletics, contact the **High Altitude Training Centre** (see p.242), which can arrange coaching, personal training and physiotherapy from Ksh5000 per week.

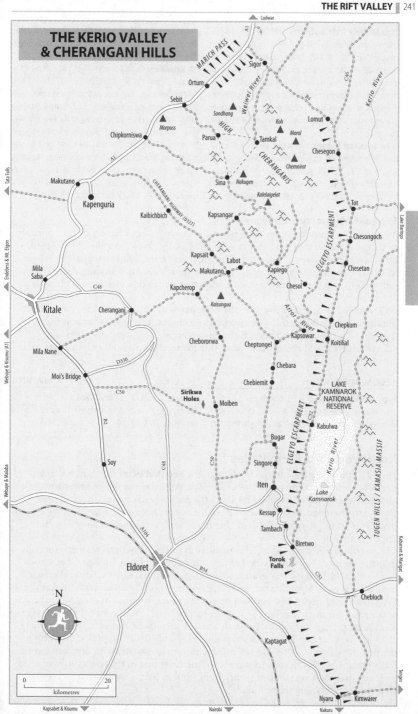

High Altitude Training Centre (HATC) Off the road to Eldoret, just before the red arch marking the entrance to town ☎0705 133878, ⓦlornah.com. If you're an athlete rather than a tourist, you'll already know about Lornah Kiplagat's training camp, but if you'd simply like to stay in Iten and do some running and training, or just relax, it's open to all-comers. There's a 25m pool on site, as well as a gym and sauna, and a single room is only half the price of a double. FB **€66**

Lelin Overland Campsite 6km out on the Kabarnet road, signposted off the main road, just south of Kessup ☎0722 900848, ⓔlelincampsite@yahoo.com. A friendly overlanders' place with magnificent views and the choice of s/c and non s/c *bandas* with wood-fired hot showers, or you can camp ($7 per person). Food is available, though the menu isn't large and you'll need to pre-order. BB **Ksh1200**

★ **Kerio View** About 2.5km south of Iten, 0.8km off the Eldoret road ☎020 2039559 or 0722 781916, ⓦkerioview.com. The best option in the area, with attentive service and an unbeatable location overlooking the valley. The cottages are simply decorated but have stunning views, as does the very cool, glass-fronted bar-restaurant (Mon–Thurs 7am–9pm, Fri–Sun until 10pm). Even if you're not staying here it's a great place for a meal; the menu features Kenyan dishes prepared with European flair, such as Nile perch with Dijon mustard (Ksh680). They also do a great range of activities, including paragliding. BB **€84**

To Iten via Tenges and Kimwarer

An alternative trans-valley route begins at the turn-off east of Kabarnet, running south to **Tenges** on a surfaced road that twists spectacularly along the spine of the Tugen Hills, with lovely views across the valley. You'll find some public transport to Tenges from Kabarnet, but very little when you turn right, west, for Kimwarer down in the valley. Kimwarer is more easily reached via a better road that meets the C51 just west of Chebloch.

KIMWARER is a company town for the **fluorspar mine** at the head of the Kerio River (fluorspar – calcium fluoride – is used in the manufacture of steel, aluminium and cement). With nothing but bush, Kalenjin herders and the occasional party of honey-hunters round about, Kimwarer's tidy managerial villas and staff quarters come as a surprise.

ACCOMMODATION   **KIMWARER**

Sego Safari Lodge 2km west of the Kerio bridge, then turn left (south) ☎0722 407470, ⓦsegosafari lodge.co.ke. Very good-value place, offering s/c cottages, a pool, a restaurant and nice views of the escarpment. You can camp here, too. Camping **Ksh400** per person, BB **Ksh3200**

North down the Kerio Valley

There's a dearth of public transport through the **Kerio Valley** off the main Kabarnet–Iten C51 road. The route north from Chebloch along the east side of **Lake Kamnarok National Reserve** is passable only by 4WD (forget it when it rains). The road from **Biretwo to Chesongoch** on the west side of the reserve has a good *murram* surface passable in an ordinary car; north of Chesongoch, it's very rough as far as Tot, but improves after that.

It's possible to **hitchhike** along this road north to **Tot**, **Lomut** and **Marich**, especially in mango season (Nov–Jan), when lorries come down as far as Tot and Chesongoch for the fruit. Otherwise, transport is sparse until you reach Lomut, where there are regular matatus to Sigor, Marich and Kapenguria, especially on Lomut's market day (Sat). Between Biretwo and Tot, you may well end up "footing" or waiting by the side of the road. No matter, as long as you have several days, for this road, following one of Kenya's most beautiful valleys, is worth a few blisters. Note, however, that the villages along the way have no facilities for travellers, and only limited supplies. For most of the year the valley, wooded and not much cultivated, resonates with dry heat and the rattle of cicadas and crickets. Climatic conditions are best in the few months of vivid greenery after the long rains, in theory from April to June – and fiercest in February and March, just before they break.

By matatu There are very occasional matatus between Tot and Sigor – one or two a day if you're lucky – but transport opportunities improve if you can coincide with weekly markets at Chesegon (Wed), Lomut (Sat) and Sigor (Thurs). Matatus also run between Lomut and Makutano, near Kapenguria on the A1 (see p.293).

ACCOMMODATION

★ **Pokot Village** Lomut, south of Sigor (and north of Chesegon) ☎0736 958294, ✉rgloor@icipe.org. A compound in the style of a Pokot homestead, run by the Lomut Traditional Dancers group with nine newly renovated *bandas*, delicious food and home-baked bread. *PoViLo* is part of Project Cabesi (Camels, Bees, Silk) under the steerage of the International Centre of Insect Physiology and Ecology (ICIPE) which works here on sustainable bee-keeping and silk-production and also helps with camel husbandry. It's a great place to meet Pokot people in an environment far removed from the safari industry, and the dancers usually perform for visitors. FB Ksh1200

Around Iten: the Sirikwa holes

6km west of Moiben • Matatus run daily from Eldoret and Iten to Moiben; you might have to change at the junction where the *murram* road to Moiben leaves the paved C51 • To reach the holes from the crossroads by the upper primary school and chief's office, follow the dirt track past another school on the left and out into farmland – you may need to ask directions, first for Rany Moi Farm and then for the holes themselves

Northeast of Iten, near the village of Moiben, the **Sirikwa holes** (known locally as "Maasai holes" or "Maasai homes") are a collection of depressions, some circular, about 10m across and a few metres deep, others a longer oval shape, all ringed by large stones. Some holes are isolated examples; others are joined by passages dug a metre or so into the ground. They are thought to have been cattle pens rather than dwellings, but would each have had a small hut by the entrance. The Moiben site is relatively undisturbed, but as the pressure from local farms increases, it seems likely that these enigmatic remains will eventually be demolished and ploughed over. You'll find more holes at the *Naiberi River Campsite* near Kaptagat (see p.286), though they're less well preserved, and there are others scattered around the district.

The Northern Elgeyo Escarpment

The long, lush shelf of the **Elgeyo Escarpment** looms over the Kerio River, providing some of the most spectacular panoramic views of the Rift Valley you'll find anywhere. Access to the northern stretches of the escarpment is difficult, and few tourists make it this way, so intrepid souls are likely to have mountain towns like Kapsowar and Chesoi all to themselves.

Heading north from Iten, your first logical destination along the escarpment is picturesque **Kapsowar**, which is also where public transport ends; frequent matatus do the run from Eldoret to Kapsowar, but after that the going gets too tough for the rickety minibuses to handle. **If you're heading to Chesoi** and on to **Tot** along the northern Elgeyo Escarpment, the road is diabolical, and too steep for any but the most steely nerved of drivers. It's a thrilling, gut-wrenching trip in a Land Rover – someone else's preferably – but think twice before driving up this road yourself. It's most easily approached on the return leg of a trip to Turkana, but make sure you have enough petrol as there's no fuel along the way.

Chesoi

The next major settlement along the northern Elgeyo escarpment, **CHESOI** is only 8km away from Kapsowar as the crow flies, but 20km by road – a hike around the highland spurs which is much more easily accomplished in the other direction, making for a fine and easy, mostly downhill, walk. The land here warps and buckles like a rumpled patchwork

THE MARAKWET IRRIGATION SYSTEM

The Marakwet – part of the broadly related Kalenjin group of peoples – may have arrived on these slopes as long as a thousand years ago. They say the **irrigation** channels were there long before their own forefathers arrived, and it is possible the original irrigators were a mysterious group called the **Sirikwa**. These people have disappeared, or more likely been absorbed, and the only reminders of them are their name and a lot of curious **holes**, earthworks and cairns, noticed by archeologists around the Kerio Valley and in other parts of western Kenya (see p.243).

Marakwet elders still remember stories of a small people called the **Terngeng**, who may have lived in pits in the ground something like those at Hyrax Hill and Moiben. Other stories refer to tall, long-haired, bearded men who roamed the Rift Valley. Either or both of these groups might have been responsible for the building of the irrigation system, but perhaps the Marakwet's claim to have inherited the system, but not built it, is just a way of saying how old it really is.

quilt, with the Cherangani Hills (see p.244) stretching away to the west. The area up near Chesoi is the best place to see the area's remarkable **irrigation system** (see box, p.244), which is impressive in scope, if not particularly in appearance when you see the canals close-up.

From Chesoi, you can walk or hitch (but don't count on seeing a vehicle) the 25 breathtaking kilometres down to **Tot**, turning left at **Chesongoch** in the valley.

Around Chesoi: the Marakwet homesteads and irrigation system

The rocky, almost perpendicular slopes around Chesoi are dotted with **Marakwet homesteads**, the huts unusual in being built of stone (there's a limitless supply up here), giving them an ancient-looking permanence rarely seen in Kenyan rural architecture. A thousand metres below, spreading like a grey-green carpet into the haze, are the scrubby, bush-covered plains of Pokot and south Turkana. Dozens of tiny wisps of smoke from charcoal burners combine to smudge out the distant peaks of Mount Kenya to the southeast. The places where the trees grow thicker mark the passage of seasonal streams, which flood and dry up with the rains; Pokot gold-panners still find enough gold in them to trade with anyone passing through.

The escarpment itself is the location of an ancient **irrigation system**, stretching north–south for over 40km, diverting water from the gushing streams of the Cherangani Hills into a branching layout of furrows and aqueducts. Complex, unwritten laws ensure that each Marakwet sub-clan is fairly provided for by the system, which is without parallel anywhere else in the country; the results, as you'll see along the base of the scarp, are spectacular. Indeed, for a considerable distance up the Kerio Valley, there's a band of intensive, luxuriant gardening: tiny *shambas* slotted back-to-back between the spurs and down towards the main river. Magnificent, richly flavoured bananas are on sale everywhere. Many of the irrigation channels now pass under the road, but a few still flow over it and a great deal of ongoing repair work is needed to keep the streams flowing in the right direction. **Chesoi canal** is a major water supply a couple of kilometres behind Chesoi centre, a metre-wide channel clinging to the hillside which any local will show you. In other places, the irrigation system has become almost a piped water supply, with hollow logs used as aqueducts, but the Chesoi channel has been built with cement. Unfortunately, the water in the vicinity, diverted from the Arror River, tastes disgusting even when boiled (a problem you encounter often in the Cheranganis).

The Cherangani Hills

Rolling gently away to the west of the Elgeyo Escarpment, the thickly forested **Cherangani hills** are wild, hardly explored, and still home to a few bongo antelope. Higher up (Kamelogon peak on Mount Chemnirot is 3581m), they merge into mountain moorland and giant Afro-alpine vegetation, superb hiking country where you're very unlikely to meet any other walkers. Parts of the hills are also accessible by car, most notably along the scenic **Cherangani Highway circuit**.

Chesoi to Kapiego

A couple of days' walking from Chesoi will see you over the southern ridges to **Kapcherop**, where you'll have no difficulty picking up transport west to Kitale or Eldoret. For this route, you first climb through Chesoi village and past the mission for about ninety minutes through *shambas*, after which it's an hour's walk through forest, mostly flat; ninety minutes of climbing through bamboo forest; and a further two hours though hilly pasturelands and woods before you reach **Kapiego**. This crossroads centre provides a suitable stop for the night, with a few *hotelis* and at least one daily matatu run to Eldoret. If you're driving, note that the Chesoi–Kapiego part of this route is non-motorable and that you can only drive to Kapiego from the south or west.

Onward routes from Kapiego

From Kapiego, routes lead northwest to **Kalelaigelat summit** (motorable to the base in a couple of hours from Kapiego, but with no matatus and no water); north to the **main Cherangani peaks** (again, motorable in 2–3hr, or a day's walk); and west on a little-used road to **Labot** and – 5km further on – **Makutano**. One or two matatus pass through Makutano most days en route between Kapcherop and Kapsait, and there's also one to Kapiego. There's also usually one matatu a day between Labot (leaving around 7am) and the other Makutano near Kapenguria (leaving there at lunchtime).

South of the Makutano near Kapsait, a quiet road leads down through grassland, then forest, to **Kapcherop** (home of Kenya's former international athletics champion Moses Kiptanui) – about a three-hour walk. From there you'll find matatus to Cherangani, and thence to Eldoret and Kitale.

The central massif

If your hiking plans are more ambitious, try to get hold of the relevant Survey of Kenya 1:50,000m-scale maps and set off, suitably equipped, over the high central districts of the massif. There are several peaks up here, all relatively easy to scale. The best base for exploring this area is *Barnley's Guesthouse* (see p.292), with the *Marich Pass Field Studies Centre* (see p.294) offering a less expensive alternative. You can hire local guides at both.

The Cherangani Highway circuit

The scenic D327 road from Makutano through **Kapsait** and **Kaibichbich** is known as the "**Cherangani Highway**", and the northern stretch forms part of a popular driving circuit. The road does, however, suffer landslides, and you should check on its current condition before setting out – *Barnley's Guesthouse* (see p.292) should be able to advise.

Starting at the junction on the A1 near Kapenguria, you can drive down through Kaibichbich to a junction north of Kapsait, where you take a left, passing through Kapsangar towards the peak of Kalelaigelat. Another left turn takes you northwest through **Sina** and back to meet the A1 at **Chipkorniswa**. The hills between Sina and the villages of **Parua** and **Tamkal** to its north are popular for hiking, with footpaths connecting the three villages, although you'll need a guide to follow them. All three villages are connected to the A1 by *murram* roads. If you are going to Tamkal, it's worth trying to coincide with market day, which is Tuesday.

Western Kenya

KITUM CAVE, MOUNT ELGON NATIONAL PARK

Western Kenya

Like the tiers of a great amphitheatre, western Kenya slopes away from Nairobi, the major game parks and the coast, down to the stage of Lake Victoria. Cut off by the high Rift wall of the Mau and Elgeyo escarpments, this region of dense agriculture, rolling green valleys and pockets of thick jungle is one of the parts of the country least known to travellers. Although more accessible than the far north, or even some of the major parks, it has been neglected by the safari operators – and that's all to the good. You can travel for days through lush landscapes from one busy market town to the next and rarely, if ever, meet other tourists.

It's not easy to see why western Kenya has been so ignored, and there's a great deal more of interest than the tourist literature's sparse coverage would suggest. While the west undeniably lacks teeming herds of game stalked by lions and narcissistic warriors in full regalia, what it offers is a series of delightfully low-key, easily visited attractions. For a start there are **national parks**: at **Kakamega Forest**, a magnificent tract of equatorial rainforest bursting with species found nowhere else in Kenya; at **Saiwa Swamp**, where access on foot allows you to get quite close to the rare sitatunga antelope; at **Ruma**, where a lush valley harbours reticulated giraffe, roan antelope and black rhinos; and at **Mount Elgon**, an extinct volcano to rival Mount Kenya in everything but crowds.

Lake Victoria is the obvious place to make for in the west, sprinkled with out-of-the-way islands, populated by exceptionally friendly people, and with the region's major town, **Kisumu**, on its shores. And there's the offbeat, if admittedly very minor, new attraction of **Kogelo**, the home village of the father of US president Barack Obama. The **Western Highlands** rise all around Lake Victoria in a great bowl, dotted with a string of busy towns. While **Eldoret** and **Kakamega** are essentially route-hubs with little for visitors to do, **Kisii** has a couple of good excursions, the tea capital **Kericho** is certainly worth an overnight stay, and **Kitale** has some museums. Away from the towns, much of the west, even the areas of intensive farming, is ravishingly beautiful: densely animated jungle near Kakamega and Kitale, regimented landscapes of tea bushes around Kericho, and many areas of swamp and grassland alive with birds.

Ethnically, the region is dominated by the **Luo** on the lakeshore, but there are Bantu-speaking **Luhya** in the sugar lands, north of Kisumu, and **Gusii** in the formidably fertile Kisii Hills. Other important groups speak one or other of the Kalenjin languages, principally the **Nandi**, around Eldoret, and the **Kipsigis** in the district around Kericho. And of course there are thousands of migrants from other parts of Kenya.

GIRL WITH NILE PERCH, RUSINGA ISLAND

Highlights

❶ Kisumu Museum Action-packed taxidermy and cultural illumination at one of Kenya's best regional museums. **See p.254**

❷ Ruma National Park Verdant national park, home to rare roan antelope, Rothschild giraffes and black rhinos. **See p.265**

❸ Thimlich Ohinga Like a scaled-down Great Zimbabwe, this is the most impressive site of stone wall enclosures in western Kenya. **See p.266**

❹ Islands in the lake Prehistoric and historical sites vie with Nile perch-fishing trips at Rusinga and Mfangano islands in Lake Victoria. **See p.268**

❺ Tea country Kericho, the most important centre for tea production in the whole of Africa,

is surrounded by an endless rolling sea of brilliant green plantations. **See p.278**

❻ Saiwa Swamp National Park Home to the unusual sitatunga antelope, rare monkeys and a huge variety of birds, Saiwa Swamp can only be explored on foot. **See p.290**

❼ Mount Elgon One of Africa's biggest extinct volcanoes, Elgon's slopes include the mysterious Elkony caves, whose walls are gouged by elephants for minerals. **See p.294**

❽ Kakamega Forest This unique patch of lowland rainforest off the tourist trail preserves wildlife that has more in common with central Africa than Kenya. **See p.303**

HIGHLIGHTS ARE MARKED ON THE MAP ON P.250

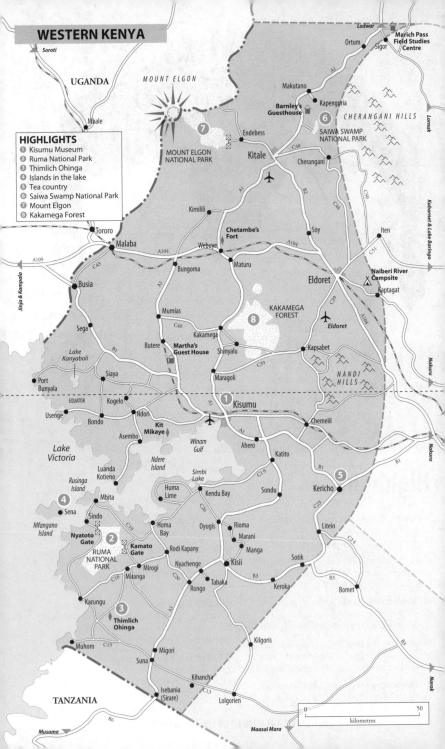

GETTING AROUND   **WESTERN KENYA**

Travel is generally easy. The region has a high population and plenty of roads (though they're often in poor condition), so you'll rarely have long to wait for transport, and although the west has only a handful of luxury or international-class hotels, there is no lack of good, modest **lodgings**. If you like to plan ahead, one obvious circuit begins in Kisumu and runs through **Kisii**, **Kericho**, **Eldoret**, **Kitale** and **Kakamega**. You could also head southwest from Kisumu to **Rusinga Island**, then further south along a spectacular, hilly stretch of the Lake Victoria coast, through **Ruma National Park** and back up to Kisii, or even east to the Maasai Mara.

TRAVEL AROUND LAKE VICTORIA

Lake Victoria is the obvious place to make for in the west, but frustratingly few main roads get really close to its shores – the best drive is the scenic route from Mbita to Sindo. Most travellers arrive in Kisumu, which used to have ferries linking it with several Kenyan ports, as well as ports in Tanzania and Uganda. Unfortunately, all services – apart from a ferry across the mouth of the Winam Gulf between Luanda Kotieno and Mbita – are suspended, because low water levels, and stretches clogged by water hyacinth, make navigation unsafe. Currently, the only transport from Kisumu to other lakeshore towns is by road. If you want to get out on the lake, the best place to head for is Mbita, which has regular matatu-boats to Mfangano Island, one of

the least-visited corners of Kenya, with the added attraction of some wonderful prehistoric rock art.

WALKING IN THE WESTERN HIGHLANDS

There are some good walking areas in the Western Highlands: at Saiwa Swamp National Park and Kakamega Forest National Park, for example, both areas where visiting on foot is essential to appreciate the forest environment. For well-equipped hikers, Mount Elgon is also a major temptation, sharing much of Mount Kenya's flora and fauna, but with very few visitors. There's more wonderful walking country in the high hills of the Cheranganis, though you need to build in some extra time for accessing them.

4

Kisumu

In the sultry atmosphere of **KISUMU**, a distinctive smell from the lake – fish, mud and rotting vegetation – drifts in on a vague breeze from central Africa. More laid-back than any other big town in Kenya, Kisumu was founded as a railway town and lake port, becoming the country's third-largest town as its fortunes rose with the growth of trade in colonial East Africa and the newly independent nations. It suffered badly following the East African Community's break-up, however, and throughout the 1980s and early 1990s the port was mostly dormant. Kisumu's position might lead you to expect a bustling waterfront and a lake-facing atmosphere, although in fact the town has now turned its back on the water, focusing instead on the commercial centre and land links to the rest of Kenya. Although some commercial shipping has resumed, and the port sporadically buzzes with loading or unloading (and people looking for a lift to Uganda or Tanzania), low water levels and water hyacinth have held back progress.

Even if the time-warped atmosphere of a place that's been treading water for three decades may not be much comfort to its inhabitants, Kisumu is one of the few upcountry towns with real character. It's a tranquil, easy-going town, where even the *manambas* at the bus station are unusually calm. Any anticipation of claustrophobia is quickly soothed by the spacious, shady layout. The contrast with Nakuru, if you've just

---

LAKE VICTORIA HEALTH HAZARDS

Although going out on the lake is fun, it is, unfortunately, a disease-ridden body of water, and even though there aren't always clouds of mosquitoes, the **malaria** risk is quite high. Snails carrying **bilharzia** also flourish in the reeds around the fringes of the lake, and although the Luo wash and swim in it and sail their vividly painted, dhow-like mahogany canoes on it, the danger of bilharzia is all too real. It's very rare to get the disease after brief contact with infected water, but you should avoid getting wet, as far as possible, if you're fishing or boating, and don't even think about swimming.

KISUMU

■ **ACCOMMODATION**

The Duke of Breeze	8
Impala Eco Lodge	16
Imperial	10
Joy Guest House	14
Kiboko Bay Resort	15
Kisumu Hotel	11
Lake Side Guest House	7
Lake View	9
Milimani Resort	12
New East View	6
New Victoria	2
Palmers	4
Perch	1
Sooper Guesthouse	5
St Anna Guesthouse	17
Sunset	13
YWCA	3

● **RESTAURANTS & CAFÉS**

The Duke of Breeze	7
Expresso Coffee House	9
Green Garden	4
Haandi	11
Kenshop Cyberstation	8
Kisumu Hotel	12
The Laughing Buddha	5
Oriental	10
Raj Sappy	3
Señorita	6
Simba Club	1
Tilapia Beach	2
The Yacht Club	13

■ **BARS & CLUBS**

Kisumu Social Centre	1
Octopus Bottoms Up	2
Railway Institute	5
Ramogi Bar	4
Signature	3

Map of Kisumu, Western Kenya. Labels include: Nakumatt City, Pendeza Weaving, Apoc Complex, Homa Bay, Kericho & Nairobi; Ondiek Highway; Ochieng Avenue; Library; Nairobi Road; Ring Road; Museum; Busia Road; United Mall; Modern Coast Bus; Triton; Buses & Matatus; Market; National Oil; Olilibya; SAI; Hare Krishna Temple; Kenyatta Avenue; Police; Somken; Law Courts; Aga Khan Hospital; Jamia Mosque; Victoria Bakery; Olilibya; Standard Chartered; Sant Bookshop; University of Nairobi Kisumu Campus; Al-Imran Plaza; Alpha House; KCB; Mega Plaza; Varsity Plaza; Maseno University City Campus; Nyanza Provincial HQ; Barclays; Zaira Tours; Clocktower; Kisumu Travel & Tours; Victoria Forex; Swan Centre; National Oil; Fish Hotelis; Railway Station; Port Entrance; Lake Victoria; Port.

Kick Trading; Varsity Plaza, Kondele, Mamboleo, Kiboso & Busia; Nyanza Golf Club, Airport, Luanda Kotieno, Kogelo & Busia; Impala Sanctuary & Dunga

0 — 500 metres

come from there, is striking. It's a good idea to find somewhere to stay soon after arriving, before starting any energetic wanderings, as it gets tremendously hot here.

Brief history

The **railway line** from Mombasa reached the lake by 1901, reassuring the British public who were having serious doubts that the "Lunatic Line", as it was dubbed, would ever reach completion, but the first train only chugged into the station at **Port Florence**, as Kisumu was originally known, in 1903 when the Mau Escarpment viaducts were completed. By then, European transport had already arrived at the lake in the form of a steamship brought up from Mombasa piece by portered piece, having steamed out from Scotland in 1895. Many of the ship's parts were seized en route from the coast and recycled into Nandi ornamentation and weaponry, and it was five years before a complete vessel could be launched on its maiden voyage across the lake to Port Bell in Uganda.

By all accounts Kisumu was a pretty disagreeable place in the early years. Apart from the endemic sleeping sickness, bilharzia and malaria, the climate was sweltering and municipal hygiene primitive. But it quickly grew into an important administrative and military base and, with the consolidation of the colonies in the 1930s and 1940s, became a leading East African entrepôt and transport hub, attracting Asian investment on top of the businesses that had been set up at the railway terminus when the Indian labourers were laid off. Kisumu's rise seemed unstoppable until 1977, when the sudden **collapse of the East African Community**, more or less overnight, robbed the town of its *raison d'être*. The partial reformation of the community in 1996 brightened prospects, and by 1999 the port was relatively busy, thanks largely to UN World Food Programme transit goods destined for war-torn Rwanda and Congo.

Since then, however, Kisumu has again seen a downturn in its fortunes, due to the decline of the local **sugar** industry, sugar cane being the surrounding region's main cash crop. Dumping of subsidized sugar by the EU led to a worldwide crash in prices, and this in turn forced the closure of sugar refineries at nearby Muhoroni and Miwani, which were the mainstays of the local economy. More recently, parts of Kisumu were badly hit during the post-election **clashes** in 2007–8, though recovery since then has been rapid.

THE LUO

The **Luo** are the second-largest ethnic group and one of the most cohesive "tribes" in Kenya. Their distinctive language, Dholuo, closely resembles the Nuer and Dinka languages of southern Sudan, from where their ancestors migrated south at the end of the fifteenth century. They found the shore and hinterland of Lake Victoria only sparsely populated by hunter-gatherers, scattered with occasional clearings where Bantu-speaking farmers had settled over the previous few centuries. Otherwise, the region was wild: untouched grassland and tropical forest, dense with heavy concentrations of wildlife.

The Luo were swift invaders, driving their herds before them, from water point to water point, always on the move, restless and acquisitive. They raided other groups' cattle incessantly and, within a few decades, had forced the Bantu-speakers away from the lakeshore. Despite the conflict, **intermarriage** (essentially the buying of wives) was common and the pastoral nomads were greatly influenced by their Bantu-speaking in-laws and neighbours, ancestors of the present-day Luhya and Gusii.

The Luo today are best known as fishermen, a lifestyle that had sustained them while migrating along the rivers, but they also cultivate widely and still keep livestock. Culturally, they have remained surprisingly independent, and are one of the few Kenyan peoples who don't perform circumcision. Traditionally, children had six teeth knocked out from the lower jaw to mark their initiation into adulthood, but the operation is hardly ever carried out these days. **Christianity** has made spectacular inroads among the Luo, with an estimated ninety percent being believers, but it does not seem to have destroyed their traditional culture quite as thoroughly as it has elsewhere. Despite the ubiquity of Gospel singing, **traditional music**, especially the playing of the *nyatiti* lyre, is still very much alive and well worth listening out for.

Kisumu Market

By the bus station • Daily dawn to dusk

Kisumu's **market** is the biggest and best in western Kenya, and an absorbing place to wander, crammed with fruit and vegetables (including some oddities like breadfruit) and all the usual household paraphernalia – pots and plates, reed brushes, wickerwork and wooden spoons. The market is such a success that it has mushroomed out into the adjacent municipal park, much to the consternation of the local authorities.

Jamia Mosque

Otieno Oyoo St

The calls to prayer from Kisumu's green-and-white **Jamia Mosque** sound odd in such a heavily Christian region, but Islam is well established here and is an important regional influence dating from well back into the nineteenth century. This orthodox Shafi'ite mosque was built in 1919, though the women's section on the right was only finished in 1984. The beautiful long mats inside are from Saudi Arabia.

The Port

Ksh100 • Paul Waswa (☎ 0720 406954; Ksh200 for a tour) is a helpful guide and can tell you all about water hyacinth and shipping movements

If you're interested in **visiting the port**, it's easy enough to go down there, buy a "port visitor" ticket at the port gates and wander along the dock. There is, in truth, practically nothing to see, although if a ship or two are in port, the scene can be quite animated. Your visit may be improved, however, by having a local guide to stroll with you, especially if you want to take photos.

Kisumu Museum

Busia Rd • Daily 9am–6pm • Ksh500 (see p.110)

Foremost among the town's sights is the engaging and ambitious **Kisumu Museum**. Set in a large garden with carefully labelled trees, the main gallery happily mingles zoological exhibits with ethnographic displays. Apart from the rows of trophy-style game heads around the walls, the **stuffed animals** and preserved insects and crustaceans are displayed with considerable flair and imagination. Particularly good use has been made of old exhibits from Nairobi's National Museum. A free-swinging vulture, for example, spins like a model aircraft overhead while, centre stage, a lion is caught in full, savage pounce, leaping onto the back of a hysterical wildebeest in the most action-packed piece of taxidermy you're ever likely to see.

The **ethnographic** exhibits are illuminating, too. The Maasai aren't the only people who take blood from their cattle for food: Kalenjin peoples like the Nandi and the Kipsigis once did the same, and even the Luo lived mostly on cow's blood mixed with milk before they arrived at Lake Victoria and began to cultivate and fish. In separate halls from the main gallery are a small, but worthwhile **aquarium**, illustrating the problem of fish depletion in the lake (see what your tilapia looked like before it became a curry), and a **snake house** with a fairly comprehensive collection of Kenyan species. Outside, the tortoise pen and croc pond seem rather pointless extras. The crocodiles, getting extremely large, are fed on Monday afternoons at around 4pm.

Impala Sanctuary

3km southwest of town • Daily 6am–6pm • $15 • ☎ 057 2501535, ☏ kws.go.ke

For a fine walk out of town, follow any road heading southwest and you'll pass the entrance to the small **Impala Sanctuary**. Here, more than twenty tame impala (said to be the remnants of wild herds from the early railway days) run free, with vervet monkeys and plenty of birdlife in the dense woodland. A single main footpath (no cars allowed) runs through the kilometre-long sanctuary from end to end, taking you between the lakeshore and a few cramped pens and cages that contain a pair of bored **leopards**, an **ostrich**, and a **hyena** that looks as if it might well escape from its insecure confinement. More of a city park than a nature reserve, the sanctuary is worth a visit for the chance to stretch your legs in the shade and stroll near the lakeshore. And, cages aside, it's a pleasant place for an hour or too and a good escape from the heat. Railway buffs will be pleased to find a bit of old **railway line** along the lakeshore at the far end.

Hippo Point

800m south of the sanctuary, past the yacht club • Boat trips cost around Ksh2500/hr for a boat seating up to six people

Riotously hued sunsets can be seen from the rock-strewn shore at **Hippo Point**. There's a strong, warm breeze at dusk, and it's a curious sensation to experience this giant body of water without the characteristic smell of the ocean in the air. Hippos are still seen here, and the small crowd of friendly local boatmen will offer to take you out to view them. They use "long shaft" outboard motors for manoeuvrability in the shallows and, as well as hippos, can often show you spotted-necked otters in the area. As a contribution to local environmental restoration, they've planted a patch of what they call "freshwater mangrove", or ambatch, as in Lake Baringo.

Dunga

2km beyond Hippo Point, on the headland

Beyond the Impala Sanctuary, most people make for the Luo fishing village of **Dunga**, a picturesque settlement and home to the Dunga Environmental and Eco-Tourism Team (DECTTA), the main focal points of the pleasant little beach. DECTTA have taken a new approach to the problem of earning a sustainable living based on more than just increasingly uncertain fishing, branching out into tourism and educational activities as well. They share a small office, just up the road from the beach, with the **Dunga Wetland Pedagogical Centre** (daily 8am–6.30pm; ☎0726 701042,

---

LAKE VICTORIA'S DISCOVERY AND EXPLORATION

The westward view from Kisumu gives you little sense of the vastness of **Victoria Nyanza** (**Lake Victoria**). From the shores of the narrow Winam Gulf it's difficult to grasp the fact that there's another 300km of water between the horizon and the opposite shore in Uganda, and an even greater distance south to Mwanza, the main Tanzanian port. Victoria, the second-largest freshwater lake in the world after Lake Superior, covers a total area of nearly 70,000 square kilometres – almost the size of Scotland or Nebraska – of which only a fraction is in Kenya.

It was barely five centuries ago that the **Luo** first settled beside the vast equatorial lake they called **Ukerewe**, and the lake remained uncharted and virtually unknown outside Africa until well into the second half of the nineteenth century. Then, in the midst of the race to pinpoint the **source of the Nile**, the lake suddenly became a focus of attention. When English adventurer **John Hanning Speke** first saw Ukerewe in 1858, he was convinced that the long search was over, and promptly renamed the lake after his Queen. In 1862, he became the first person to follow the Nile downstream from Lake Victoria to Cairo, and triumphantly cabled the Royal Geographical Society in London with the words "The Nile is settled". Sceptics, however, doubted the issue was settled, countering that Lake Tanganyika was the true source, and it took a daring circumnavigation of Lake Victoria, led by the American journalist **Henry Morton Stanley**, in 1875, to prove Speke right. Sadly, Speke did not live to enjoy the vindication – he was killed in a shooting accident in 1874.

@wetlandcentre@ecofinderkenya.org), whose friendly staff are happy to provide information on local ecology and assist you with any lake activities you might want to pursue, from night fishing to birdwatching. There's also a gift shop.

ARRIVAL AND DEPARTURE   KISUMU

Kisumu is the west's transport hub, well connected to the rest of the country by **bus** and **matatu** and excellently positioned for exploring the region – all the towns covered in this chapter are within a half-day's journey.

By plane Kisumu airport (☎057 2020056 or 00728 765361) is 4km out of town off the Busia road, and was undergoing renovations and runway expansion at the time of writing. There are always a few cabs around until the last flight of the day arrives; the current standard fare into town (15min) is Ksh1000. There are currently once-daily flights to Nairobi (1hr) with Fly540 (☎057 2025363; $79), Jetlink (☎0714 111888; $77) and Kenya Airways (☎057 2056000; $80), plus flights to Eldoret with Fly540 (2 daily; 20min; $35).

By bus and matatu The bus and matatu stage is on Gumbi Rd, at the intersection of Kenyatta Ave and Otieno Oyoo St, with services to more or less everywhere in western Kenya and further afield to Nakuru, Nairobi and Mombasa. Modern Coast Bus, behind the matatu stage (☎0716 817400), run overnight buses to Mombasa (three nightly; 15hr), via Nairobi, arriving at Mombasa in the early

morning. EasyCoach, United Mall, Gumbi Rd (☎0728 200307), run buses to Nairobi (6 daily; around 7hr).
Matatu destinations Busia (10–40 daily; 2hr 30min); Homa Bay (6–12 daily; 2hr 30min); Kendu Bay (4–6 daily; 2hr); Kericho (10–20 daily; 2hr); Kakamega (20–30 daily; 1hr), some continuing to Kitale (6–12 daily; 3hr); Kisii (10–20 daily; 2hr 30min); Luanda Kotieno (2–4 daily; 2hr 30min); Homa Bay (6–12 daily; 3hr); Mbita (3–6 daily; 4hr); Nairobi (10–30 daily; 7hr); Nakuru (10–30 daily; 5hr).
Bus destinations Kitale (2 daily; 3hr); Mombasa (6 daily; 15hr); Nairobi (roughly hourly; 7hr); Nakuru (roughly hourly; 5hr) via Kericho (2hr).
By car If driving into Kisumu you may run into a few time-wasters trying the "something wrong with your car" trick to lure you into a yard for "repairs" or other scams – there's a group of them on Gor Mahia Rd. Drivers will also run into parking wardens – it costs Ksh100/24hr to park anywhere.

ACCOMMODATION

There's a wide choice of places to stay, with a good number of modest, mid-range **hotels**, though prices tend to be higher than usual. Temperature, humidity and mosquitoes will conspire to give you an uncomfortable night if you don't have a net or a fan (preferably both), so it's worth paying a little more for them. It's worth noting too that most hotels in Kisumu have a 9.30am checkout time.

INEXPENSIVE
The Duke of Breeze Off Kenyatta Ave ☎0717 105444, ⓦthedukeofbreeze.com. A very popular budget option with enormous, clean rooms in a concrete tower block, though it suffers a bit from traffic noise. Rooms come with fans, nets and instant showers, but it's the rooftop bar (see opposite) that makes it such a hit. BB **Ksh2600**
Joy Guest House 1.4km beyond the Impala Sanctuary between Hippo Point and Dunga, by the Kiboko Bay Resort turn-off ☎0715 220485. While nothing special, this European-style house offers reasonable value, with a large double s/c room with TV and four twin non-s/c rooms sharing a bathroom with instant shower. All rooms have nets. BB **Ksh800**
★**Lake Side Guest House** Kendu Lane ☎0725 468797. This cosy little guesthouse is probably the best value in town, offering nicely appointed rooms with ceiling fans, lock-up cupboards and good showers. A pleasant terrace out front overlooks the street and the lake, as do some of the rooms. BB **Ksh800**
Lake View Alego St ☎0721 778287. Despite the name there are no exceptional views here, though with its corner

position, the Lake View does offer some breeze and also has a very congenial bar. Rooms come with nets and hot water but no fans. BB **Ksh1500**
New East View Omolo Agar Rd ☎0722 556721. A quieter alternative to the nearby *Palmers*, with twenty well-kept, scrupulously clean rooms adorned with satin bedcovers, pink walls and bathtubs. Showers are old-style, but there is safe parking. BB **Ksh2300**
★**New Victoria** Gor Mahia Rd ☎057 2021067 or 0734 246615. Perennially popular with travellers, this well-maintained and efficiently run hotel is bright and cheerful inside and out. Most rooms have balconies, and rooms 206–209 have good lake views; there are also a few non s/c singles (Ksh900) for those on a tight budget. The very good breakfasts alone are worth the visit. BB **Ksh1950**
Palmers Omolo Agar Rd ☎057 2024867 or 0722 999691, @hotel.palmers@yahoo.com. Handy for the bus and matatu stand, and with safe parking, this friendly place is nicely furnished, offering rooms with TVs, fans and big windows. There's also a breezy café at the side. BB **Ksh2300**
Perch Corner of Mark Asembo Rd and Obote Rd ☎0722 974607. A cavernous block behind the port area, this is

reasonably comfortable, and the s/c rooms (some with lake views) have nets, TV and instant showers, but no fans. There's a busy bar-restaurant, safe, basement parking and rates that are slightly pricey, but just about acceptable. BB **Ksh3000**

★ **Sooper Guesthouse** Oginga Odinga Rd ☎0725 281733 or 0723 292781, ✉kayamchatur@yahoo .com. Living up to its name, *Sooper* offers some of the best cheap lodgings in Kisumu, with light, clean s/c rooms with instant showers, nets, TV, lock-up cupboards and electric sockets – the best rooms are the two at the front sharing a balcony overlooking the street. Cold drinks, snacks and breakfast are available, and there's a kind of roof terrace. BB **Ksh1500**

St Anna Guesthouse Signposted on the left, 450m south down Tom Mboya Drive next to Care Kenya, Milimani Estate ☎057 2024792 or 0734 600119, ⓦstannaguesthouse.com. Tricky to find, but worth the effort, offering 35 well-kept, value-for-money rooms with solar-heated showers and TV. Although managed by Franciscan sisters, it's open to all and has no guest requirements beyond refraining from alcohol. The top-value restaurant serves filling staples. Safe parking. BB **Ksh2500**

YWCA Off Ang'awa Ave ☎057 2024788 or ☎0733 992982. Friendly, cheap but rather bland, with a canteen, camping facilities (see below), one double room (Ksh1200) and five-bed dorms. It's popular with conference groups, so book ahead. Dorm beds **Ksh450**, BB **Ksh1200**

MID-RANGE AND EXPENSIVE

Impala Ecolodge Inside the Impala Sanctuary ☎057 2533040, ⓦimpalaecolodge.com. A brand-new high-end retreat offering its guests the kind of exclusive safari atmosphere normally found in game parks, and with prices to match. The cottages, all with private wooden decks and lake views, are attractively furnished using local materials, and there's an elegant bar-restaurant on site. BB **$310**

Imperial Jomo Kenyatta Ave ☎057 2020002 or 0721 240515, ⓦimperialhotelkisumu.com. The top hotel in town and the usual choice of expense-account travellers,

offering seventy rooms with big, hanging mosquito nets, DSTV, a/c and proper showers. The modest-sized courtyard pool (10am–12.30pm & 2.30–7pm; non-residents Ksh200) is the cleanest in Kisumu. BB **$216**

★ **Kiboko Bay Resort** 1.5km south of the Impala Sanctuary, between Hippo Point and Dunga ☎0733 532709 or 0724 387738. A very pleasant tented camp with a beautiful location on the lakeshore, offering nine luxurious safari tents equipped with mains electricity, generator backup, nets, fridges, full solid bathrooms and floor fans, plus a pool (non-residents Ksh300) and terrace by the lake. A popular alternative to staying in town, and a great spot for lunch at weekends. BB **$185**

Kisumu Jomo Kenyatta Ave ☎057 2024157, ⓦkisumu hotel.net. Average-sized, carpeted rooms with TV, a/c and old-style baths and showers. There are three bars and a moderately priced restaurant, and the small pool (11am–6pm, non-residents Ksh200) is nicely situated on a shaded terrace. BB **Ksh6500**

Milimani Resort Off Got Huma Rd ☎057 2023245 or 0734 141666, ⓦmilimaniresort.co.ke. Fifty attractive, tile-floored rooms in a quiet, residential street, with nets, a/c, DSTV and good views (from the upper floors). Staff are friendly and facilities include a restaurant, lounge (though no bar) and a large pool (non-residents Ksh150). BB **Ksh4400**

Sunset Aput Lane, 2.5km south of the town centre ☎0733 411001, ⓦsunsethotel.com. Above and behind the Impala Sanctuary, this five-storey complex dating from the 1960s is fraying around the edges but offers great lake views and beautiful sunsets from rooms on floors 2–4, most of which have small balconies as well as TV, floor fans and a/c. The business centre has decent internet, and there's also a pool (11am–6pm; non-residents Ksh200). BB **Ksh5500**

CAMPING

YWCA Off Ang'awa Ave ☎057 2024788 or 0733 992982. A broad, shady expanse of grass on which to pitch a tent, with good facilities available, but it's set on a busy corner near the market so there's a fair bit of traffic noise. **Ksh250** per person

EATING AND DRINKING

Kisumu has lots of good **places to eat**, but it's worth starting early as many places close shortly after dusk. For **budget food**, the best deal in town is the fresh fried tilapia dished up in a series of *hotelis* down by the lakeside at the far northern end of Oginga Odinga Rd, served with either *ugali* or chapattis. There are a number of good **supermarkets** including the 24hr Nakumatt Nyanza at Mega Plaza, as well as several decent **bakeries** – Victoria (Mon–Sat 7am–6.30pm, Sun 7am–2pm), by the *New Victoria Hotel* on Gor Mahia Rd, has probably the best selection of cakes and pastries in western Kenya.

★ **The Duke of Breeze** Top floor, Duke of Breeze hotel, off Kenyatta Ave ☎0717 105444, ⓦthedukeof breeze.com. A breezy rooftop escape from the city, strewn with lounge pillows and wafting music that gets steadily livelier as the night wears on. The eclectic menu ranges from

Mongolian stir-fry to fajitas, or you can get three courses for Ksh1000. Stunning views, and a great spot for sundowners. Daily 11am–11pm, Fri & Sat until midnight.

Expresso Coffee House Otuona Rd. A long menu of fry-ups, but the coffee is instant, despite the name, and the "juice" isn't freshly pressed either. Nevertheless, it's not bad for breakfast (Ksh180) or lunch. Daily 6.30am–6pm.

Green Garden Odera St ☎0727 738000 or 057 2024906. Very popular NGO and traveller haunt on an unpromising side street, serving a long menu of dishes in the pretty courtyard dining area – pizzas, vegetarian and grills for Ksh400–500 – accompanied by a wonderful range of African music. Daily 11am–11pm.

Haandi Ground floor, Mega Plaza, Oginga Odinga St ☎0733 224788, ⌨haandi-restaurants.com. Part of a chain of upmarket Indian restaurants, serving dishes like chicken korma, malai kofta and a range of Punjabi specialities. The food is good, but expect to spend at least Ksh700 per person, without drinks. Daily noon–3pm & 6.30–11pm.

★**Kenshop Cyberstation** Oginga Odinga Rd. An excellent place for breakfast or tea, with real espresso coffee and fresh juices, plus pies, sandwiches, pizzas, snacks and even a very tasty fish burger (Ksh290). It's also right next to Kenshop Supermarket's really good bakery, with nice fresh loaves. Mon–Sat 8.30am–6pm, Sun 9am–3pm.

★**The Laughing Buddha** Swan Centre, Oginga Odinga Rd ☎0728 270013. Sophisticated vegetarian café with a pleasant streetside location, serving a delicious mix of Eastern and Western dishes (think falafel, pasta and sizzling fudge brownies). The desserts and milkshakes are divine, and you can wash it all down with wine or herbal teas. Mains Ksh300–500. Tues–Sun 10.30am–11pm.

Oriental Upstairs, al-Imran Plaza, Oginga Odinga Rd ☎057 2025462 or 0722 289185. All the usual Chinese favourites, like beef with broccoli and chilli garlic prawns,

plus some Thai starters; good but quite pricey, with most dishes Ksh500–900. Daily 11am–11pm.

Raj Sappy Paul Mbuya Rd ☎0722 227333. A casual little vegetarian café serving a small menu of spicy Indian thalis (from Ksh300), as well as a wide selection of syrupy sweets that you can order by the kilo. Daily 7am–7pm.

Señorita Oginga Odinga Rd ☎0733 744588. A long and varied menu of Indian and African dishes (mains around Ksh450), and good for steaks and stews, although there's nothing Spanish or Latino, despite the name. Mon–Sat 8am–7pm.

★**Simba Club** Jomo Kenyatta Ave ☎0734 197050. The Sikh Union's restaurant is open to non-members, with an excellent menu of tandoori dishes and curries. Specialities include Amritsari fish (in a tandoori-style marinade, but fried rather than baked; Ksh500) and fish à la Simba (marinated in coriander and green chilli; Ksh600). Friday evening is the best time to go, when it's full of families relaxing into the weekend. Daily 11am–3pm & 7pm–midnight.

Tilapia Beach Down a dirt road at the northern end of Oginga Odinga Rd. The pick of the fish fry *hotelis*, where you can gorge yourself on fresh tilapia, *ugali* and chips (from Ksh700) in shady lakeside *bandas*. Daily 8.30am–11pm.

The Yacht Club Next to the Impala Sanctuary ☎020 8089040. Gorgeous location with tables overlooking the lake, where you can dine on Indian food or pizza (Ksh400) while watching fishing boats drift by. Visits require temporary membership (Ksh300, or Ksh50 Fri & Wed evenings). Mon–Fri 11am–2pm & 6–11pm, Sat & Sun 11am–11pm.

NIGHTLIFE

Kisumu has good nightlife, with the chance to catch **live bands**, and sometimes even big-name stars. More run-of-the-mill **discos** are plentiful, too. The regional music speciality is *ohangala,* based on Luo folk music, which is just as danceable as the alternatives of Congolese Lingala, or *benga,* which is also largely a Luo creation (see p.580).

Kisumu Social Centre Off Gumbi Rd, by the library. Live bands – this is a hub of *ohangala* – with a bar, though the crowd can sometimes get rough so it's best to go with a local. Entry is usually free, sometimes rising to Ksh200. Daily 6pm–midnight.

The Laughing Buddha Swan Centre, Oginga Odinga Rd ☎0728 270013. With its mood lighting and lava lamps, this modern bar above the restaurant is a good place for cocktails or a sheesha (Ksh500). Tues–Thurs 9pm–midnight, Fri–Sun 9pm–2.30am.

Octopus Bottoms Up Ogada St. A pick-up joint of the first order, so not for the faint-hearted, but relaxed enough if you just want to mingle over a beer or two. The restaurant is often empty, but the disco is always lively, and the roof terrace is a popular, breezy rendezvous, albeit with dire

service. Open 24hr.

Railways Institute New Station Rd. Rough, rowdy and wildly popular local joint by the train station, with a house band playing *benga*. Thurs–Sun 5pm–1am (music from 6pm).

Ramogi Bar Kendu Lane. A satisfyingly seedy and friendly little hole in the wall, with the remains of a vintage jukebox and plenty of local characters eager to share a beer or five. Daily 10am–11pm.

Signature 4th floor of a building on Asembo Rd. Kisumu's poshest new club and the most popular place to dance, featuring a sleek bar, modern sound system and plenty of disco lights. Gets very crowded at weekends. Ksh200 cover on Fri & Sat. Daily 9pm–late.

SHOPPING

HOPE Airport 📞0710 663990. The UN-award-winning Hyacinth Ornament Production Enterprise (HOPE) trains disabled women to create handicrafts out of Lake Victoria's endless supply of water hyacinth, whose fibres are used to fashion bags, jewellery and clothing, which you can purchase at this small stall outside the arrivals hall. Daily 7am–6.30pm.

Pendeza Weaving About 3km along the Nairobi road (go past the chief's camp and look for a small white sign on the right) 📞0734 587253, 🌐globalcrafts.org /partner/pendeza.htm. Another worthwhile visit for hand-woven cotton crafts such as tablecloths, bedcovers, dresses and Christmas ornaments. Daily 8am–6pm.

Sarit Bookshop Oginga Odinga Rd, corner of New Station Rd 📞057 2021222. A selection of novels in English and Swahili, including some African literature, and a few Kenya guidebooks and birding guides. Mon–Fri 8.30am–5.30pm, Sat 8.30am–1.30pm.

Tourist Market By the museum (see p.254). The best place to find craft sellers. Things to buy here include heavy, three-legged Luo stools (the best are intricately inlaid with beads, and dark brown from repeated oiling), plus bangles, carvings and rows of soapstone knick-knacks.

DIRECTORY

Banks and exchange The town is full of banks with ATMs – and there's also a KCB ATM at the airport. In addition, Victoria Forex, on Central Square near Barclays (Mon–Fri 8.30am–4.30pm, Sat 8.30am–12.30pm) and PEL Forex in al-Imran Plaza, Oginga Odinga Rd (Mon–Fri 8.30am–4.40pm, Sat 9am–12.30pm) charge no commission for changing cash or travellers' cheques, with only slightly lower rates for the latter.

Birdwatching Lake Victoria Sunset Birders is the local birding group (📞0734 994938 or 057 2024162, 🌐lvsb.50megs.com). You can join up for Ksh500 and participate in their internationally recognized monitoring work or simply go on one of their regular bird walks – the area along the golf club shore and the 120 acres of Dunga swamp are very productive areas.

Car rental and travel agents Rav4s and similar small 4WDs are available from around Ksh4500/day. Try Piepercaps, Swan Centre, Odinga Rd 📞057 2024249 or 0722 344148, 🌐piepercaps.org; Kisumu Travels, Central Square 📞057 2020785 or 0722 206020; or Helpys Tours & Travels, Varsity Plaza, Kenyatta Highway, opposite the *Kisumu Hotel* 📞057 2024929 or 0721 530856. Zaira Tours, Ogada St (📞057 2524293, 🌐zairatoursafrica.com), offer a range of Obama-themed tours (see p.260), many of which include an exploration of Luo history and culture; Integritour (📞0700 517969 or 0725 790303, 🌐integritour .com) are a very well-regarded new operator and agent, based on the Ground Floor, at the *Duke of Breeze Hotel*, who claim to be the first responsible tourism operator in western Kenya and who offer a number of tours, including safaris to the Maasai Mara.

Golf Nyanza Golf Club (📞0704 133131, 🌐nyanzaclub .com) is on the lakeshore, the first left down the airport road, about 4km from the town centre. A round of 18 holes costs Ksh1000.

Hospitals The main treatment centre is Nyanza Provincial General Hospital, northeast of the centre on Jomo Kenyatta Ave 📞057 2020801. The best private hospital is the Aga Khan Hospital on Otieno Oyoo St 📞057 2020005.

Immigration The Immigration Department, first floor, Reinsurance Plaza, behind Alpha House on Oginga Odinga Rd (📞057 2024935), is generally helpful, usually stamping visitors' pass extensions on the spot.

Internet access There are numerous places around town, and several in the Mega Plaza on Oginga Odinga Rd. Kenshop Cyberstation (see p.258) is good (Ksh1/min), or try Bhavniks on the ground floor of Mega Plaza (Mon–Sat 9am–7pm, Sun 9am–5pm; Ksh1/min).

Kisumu Show The annual Agricultural Society of Kenya show is held in the first week of August, 6km north of town on the Miwani road (off to the east of the Kakamega road).

Library Off Gumbi Rd, behind the bus and matatu station 📞020 2158368 (Mon–Fri 8am–6.30pm, Sat 8am–5pm).

Mobiles Safaricom Service Centre, Mezzanine floor, Mega Plaza, Oginga Odinga Rd 📞0722 002546 (Mon–Fri 8am–6.30pm, Sat 8am–5pm).

Pharmacies Several are open late and on Sundays. Try Winam, Mega Plaza, Oginga Odinga Rd 📞057 2023167 (daily 7am–10pm), and A-Z Pharmacy, Ang'awa Ave, 100m from the clock tower 📞0722 988725 (Mon–Sat 8am–6pm, Sun 8am–noon).

Police Omolo Agar Rd 📞057 2024719.

Swimming Forget the lake – bilharzia, hippos and crocs are all unfriendly – and instead swim at the *Sunset*, the *Milimani*, the *Kisumu* or the *Imperial*. The small fee is usually waived if you have a meal.

Kogelo and the road to Uganda

Heading **northwest out of Kisumu**, down a broad avenue of flame trees, you pass first the Sunni Muslim, Ismailia and Hindu cemeteries, then Nyanza Golf Club and emerge into the rolling plains of Nyanza Province's **Siaya District**, home to herbalists and a reasonable base for exploration. There's a constant stream of matatus and buses to the town of **Busia**, on the Ugandan boarder.

If you're driving to **Kogelo**, you take the left turn at **Kisian**, 10km past the Kisumu airport, where the roads to Usenge (C27) and Busia (B1) split. The **C27** to Bondo and Usenge is a very pretty road, in good shape and well worth the trip, even without the minor justification of Kogelo along the way.

The easy route to **Mbita** (see p.268) ends with a short ride aboard the small car ferry (8am, 11am, 1pm, 3pm & 6pm; 45min) from **Luanda Kotieno**, reached by turning south off the C27 at **Ndori**.

Kit Mikaye

1km south of the C27 highway (signposted off the highway 14km west of Kisian junction)

Kit Mikaye is a locally famous landmark and minor pilgrimage site. Meaning Place (*kit*) of the First Wife (*mikaye*), it's the largest balancing act in a landscape of giant boulders. This scenic, rocky spot is where the first wife of the Luo is supposed to have rested on the tribe's journey south from Sudan, and local women often visit for cures and meditation.

Back on the C27, there's another huge boulder-pile directly by the north side of the road, while on the south side of the highway the mobile-phone operator Zain has taken the trouble to brand another big clump of giant boulders in their subtle pink and yellow colours.

4 Kogelo

KOGELO is exactly 1km south of the equator. The Senator Obama Secondary School apart, there are no outward signs of Kogelo's place in the family history of the US president – and little evidence of the development and investment that the media speculated would transform it after the 2008 US elections. Obama's family roots can be traced back to the **homestead of Mama Sarah Onyango Obama**, third wife of Barack's paternal grandfather, 1km or so out of the "centre" of Kogelo, to the northwest, which is where Barack's father (who died in a car crash in 1982) is buried. The homestead is now a gated and *askari*-guarded plot, with several tents for the security detail in the front garden and Mama Obama herself the host of frequent local delegationsm – although you can take a look from the outside, and possibly even pay a visit. Plans to build an **Obama Museum** here have been put on hold while the competing claim of the village of Kanyadhiang near Kendu Bay – where Obama Senior was born, according to some family members – is considered (see p.263).

ARRIVAL AND INFORMATION   KOGELO

By matatu If you're travelling by matatu from Kisumu you'll have to change vehicles in Ndori (see p.271), with maybe a wait of an hour or two for a connection on to Kogelo. If you want to continue north from Kogelo to reach the B1 Busia road, take one of the occasional matatus from Kogelo to Siaya and points north, then change at the B1 junction.

By car To reach Kogelo, turn right (north) at Ndori onto the C28, 200m west of the turning for Asembo and Luanda Kotieno. Head north for 8km along this *murram* road to reach the Yala River bridge, after which the road winds gently uphill for a couple of kilometres to reach a small junction with a few *dukas* and some shady trees. If you

want to continue driving north, the C28 road from Ndori to Kogelo continues north, across the equator, to meet the C30, which goes west to Siaya (it's 7km from Kogelo to the C30).

Tours Tiny Kogelo isn't a place you can "tour" on your own: the only point to being here is to hire a local to show you around. You may find a guide on the spot, but the best people for the job are Zaira Tours on Ogada St in Kisumu (see p.259), who offer a range of Obama-themed tours, many of which include Kendu Bay and a thorough exploration of Luo history and culture. They will tailor tours to your interests, and may even be able to secure you an audience with Mama Obama if she is available.

ACCOMMODATION

Kogelo Village Resort ☎0714 000011 or 0735 458850, ⓦkogelovillageresort.com. If you want to stay in Kogelo this is really the only option, with spacious *bandas* surrounding a landscaped compound just 100m from the Mama Obama homestead. The s/c rooms come with DSTV, and there's a bar and restaurant as well (order in advance). BB Ksh2500

Siaya

The district capital, **SIAYA**, locally known as Tat Yien ("Roof of Herbs"), has a large community of traditional **herbalists** and is a well-known healing (and bewitching) town. There isn't much to see or do in Siaya itself, but as one of the largest towns in the area it's not a bad base for expeditions to nearby Kogelo and Usenge.

INFORMATION, ACCOMMODATION AND EATING   SIAYA

There's a KCB bank with **ATM**, as well as the useful Siaya Self Service **supermarket** and plenty of **cybercafés** – try the centrally located Jamat Cyber Café, 100m from the market (daily 8am–6pm; 50 cents/min).

Mwisho Mwisho Tourist Hotel Equity Bank building, 1km from the centre on the road to Kisumu ☎0717 553359 or 0736 000363, ✉info @mwishohotel.com. If you're staying overnight you'll probably end up at this noisy place, which offers unexciting but good-value rooms with nets, and the occasional live band. Meal service is rather slow. BB Ksh1500

The Place Next to the law courts. A modest but popular little canteen serving local food for very reasonable prices (pilau for only Ksh100). Look for the chicken roasting out front. Daily 6.30am–8.30pm.

Usenge

USENGE (or Usengi), at the end of the C27 road from Kisumu, is something of a diversion if you're en route to Uganda, but a good target if you're planning an exploration of the district. It's also a town of pre-colonial historical significance in its own right. The nearby hill, **Got Ramogi**, is by tradition the site where the first Luo arrived at the lake from further north. It's not a hard climb to the top for a satisfying view over Yala Swamp, Lake Sare and the land that the Luo fought for and eventually won from the Bantu-speakers at the end of the fifteenth century. Usenge itself is a pretty town, but there are no banks, few services and not much in the way of accommodation.

4

GEM OF AN IDEA

In the early **colonial period**, the Luo benefited from some inspired, if dictatorial, leadership. They had inherited the institution of the *ruoth* (king or chief) from the original immigrants from Sudan. The *ruoth* of Gem, a location just east of Siaya, was Odera Akang'o, an ambitious and perceptive young man with an almost puritanical attitude to his duties. He had a private police force to inspect farms and report any idleness to him, and he regularly had his subjects beaten or fined for "unprogressive" behaviour. He introduced new crops and, under British protection, made himself quite a sizeable fortune. He was widely feared.

In 1915, the colonial government sent him, with two other chiefs, to Kampala. He returned full of admiration for the European education and health standards there, and ashamed of Gem and Luoland in general. Fired with enthusiasm, he applied his style of schooling and hygiene, bullying his subjects into sending their children to classes and keeping their shirts clean, while the British turned a blind eye. The results were rapid educational advances in Gem, which is still considered a progressive district today. Odera, unfortunately for him, was employed by the British to use his methods on the Teso people in Uganda, where they singularly failed. He was accused of corruption and sent into internal exile, where he died.

Busia

The **road to Busia** is getting rather rough in parts, but is lined with colourful scenes of everyday rural life, including women carrying huge head-loads of bananas, sugar cane and baskets, often in brilliantly pleated, floral-print dresses. **BUSIA**, on the Uganda border, is surprisingly bearable for a border town. It boasts more services and less hassle than Malaba, the frontier post on the railway line further north, and is a much more pleasant place to cross.

ARRIVAL AND INFORMATION   BUSIA

Moneychangers on both sides of the border will change Ugandan and Kenyan shillings, or give either for dollars, euros or pounds, but check the rates in advance. There are also Barclays and KCB banks with ATMs.

By bus Several daily from Busia to Nairobi (8hr) via Kisumu (2hr 30min). Most companies run one morning and one evening service.
By matatu There are frequent matatus to Kisumu (anything from 10–40 daily; 2hr 30min), Malaba (4–8 daily; 1hr), some going on to Bungoma (4–8 daily; 3hr), and morning departures to Kitale (1–2 daily; 4hr 30min) and Nairobi (6–20 daily; 9hr 30min). On the Ugandan side, frequent matatus run to Jinja (2hr) and Kampala (4hr).

ACCOMMODATION

Blue York Bulanda Rd, south of the main drag ☏ 0721 696078. Very popular with NGOs, with clean, tidy s/c rooms around a small but well-manicured courtyard. The restaurant is a pleasant place for a meal or a drink, with a bit of outdoor seating. BB **Ksh1600**
Farm View Hospital Rd, 1km south of the main drag ☏ 0711 712861, ✉ hotelfarmview@yahoo.com. The farm on view may be just a field of corn, but this quiet complex has a nice countryside feel to it nonetheless. The good s/c rooms come with nets and TV, and there's a kids' play area in the shady garden. BB **Ksh1800**

South Nyanza

The territory south of Kisumu is interesting to explore and easy enough to get around, if you're willing to go by matatu. Highlights include the agreeable little town of **Kendu Bay**, the main town of **Homa Bay**, the unjustly overlooked **Ruma National Park**, the intriguing ruins of **Thimlich Ohinga**, the islands of **Rusinga and Mfangano** and, down near the Tanzanian border, the one-street town of **Migori**. The **lakeshore** west of Migori is remote and, in parts, beautiful, with **Karungu Bay** and the scenic route via **Sindo** to **Mbita** a rewarding side trip.

Kendu Bay

The best route from Kisumu to **KENDU BAY** is straight along the lakeshore from Katito, south of Ahero. There's a wealth of interest in the surrounding Luo countryside, most of it until recently a rural backwater, with scenes of fishing boats and compounds of square, thatched mud-brick houses (a fairly recent change; traditionally they were round). Although Kendu Bay has a good deal of intrinsic charm, there's little to offer the casual visitor in the town itself. The old part, 500m off the Kisumu–Homa Bay main road, has one notable building in the gorgeous **Tawakal mosque**. You can look around it, though there's not much to see, and climb on the roof. The smaller **Jamia mosque** is less ornate, but older, built in 1902.

Simbi Lake

About 4km west of the centre of Kendu Bay (if you don't have transport it's a 45min walk, or take a *boda-boda*): follow Homa Bay road past the turning to Oyugis and Kisii; 2km beyond, over the river bridge before you reach Kanyadhiang, turn right down the dirt road and continue another 15min along the river's left bank before climbing to the lake's rim

Kendu Bay's local fame comes from the curious **Simbi Lake**. The lake and the nearby

THE LEGEND OF SIMBI LAKE

According to legend, the **origins of Simbi Lake** are to be found in the story of an elderly woman, travelling alone, who was refused hospitality one rainy night at the village that once occupied the site of the lake. A big beer party was going on and she was ignored. Only one woman would allow her to warm herself, and the old woman insisted she and her family leave the village with her. The young woman tried in vain to persuade her husband to come with them, fearing the old lady's revenge for her ill-treatment. So the two women left alone. Later that night there was a tremendous cloudburst and the rain came down so hard that the village was swamped to become Simbi Lake. Further variations on the story (there are many) improve on the theme of drunkenness and debauchery to give a Sodom and Gomorrah ring to the tale. Other lakes in Kenya have similar tales of origin.

Ondago Swamp have been adopted as June and July feeding grounds by a couple of thousand **lesser flamingos**, refugees from Lake Nakuru. Although some locals and officials would like to exploit the attraction, it remains a tranquil beauty spot, with a footpath around the rim, the only commerce being the odd local selling sugar cane. Even without the flamingos, this is unquestionably a weird body of water: around 70 acres of bright green, alkaline water, sunk 20–30m below the surrounding land and less than 2km from Lake Victoria itself. It has no apparent source and its origins are somewhat mysterious: it looks like a huge meteorite crater.

It's only a couple of kilometres around the perimeter path – an easy half-hour walk. The little lake's shores are almost devoid of vegetation. It's of volcanic origin and is apparently extraordinarily deep. According to one local belief, visitors should throw money in to avoid bad luck. Whatever the natural explanation, it seems plausible that the area was inhabited when the lake was formed, and that a natural disaster accounts for the legends.

An interesting new twist on the fame of Simbi is the claim by locals from the hamlet of **KANYADHIANG** (just south of the bridge on the C19 road) that their village is the true birthplace of Barack Obama Senior, rather than Kogelo, and hence the rightful location of any western Kenya Obama museum (see p.260) – a dispute which is likely to run a lot longer than the president's time in office.

ARRIVAL AND INFORMATION
KENDU BAY

By matatu You'll have no difficulty getting a matatu to or from Oyugis or Homa Bay. The obvious alternative route is the lakeshore road from Kendu Bay to Katito, where it meets the A1 between Kisii and Kisumu.

By boat The ferry dock (a pier partly made of concrete-filled barges) is about 1km from the old town, but there were no boat services at the time of writing due to low water levels in the lake.

Services There's a Total petrol station on the main road by the junction with the road to Oyugis, and a post office about 100m west of the junction, but no banks or ATMs.

ACCOMMODATION, EATING AND DRINKING

Hotel Big Five At the petrol station ☎0711 769762. Decorated with Disneyesque concrete trees and animals, this restaurant serves excellent fish (Ksh300) and its nightclub has music (occasionally live) every night, though it's only really busy on Sat. Daily 6.30am–10pm (club open later).
Hotel Maryland Just south of the petrol station ☎0720 892622. Comfortable and reasonably priced s/c rooms, with tiled floors and nets, set behind an

ostentatious-looking restaurant. The showers are cold, but there's hot water in buckets on request. BB Ksh800
Milimani Bar & Lodging In the old town, before the mosque ☎0733 989062. B&L with eight basic, dark, non s/c rooms with bucket showers and solar-powered electric lights. Not terribly comfortable, but dirt cheap (singles are only Ksh250) and bearable for one night. Room only Ksh400

Homa Bay

At first glance a scruffy and unremarkable place, the small port town of **Homa Bay**, the region's main centre, is one of the friendliest towns in Kenya, and also a good base for

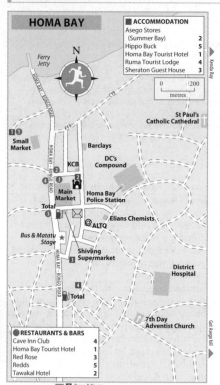

visits to Ruma National Park, Rusinga Island and Simbi Lake. The town, admittedly, has nothing much of interest, just a few potholed streets and the unusual straw-hat-shaped **St Paul's Catholic Cathedral**, atop a low hill behind town, with its central altar-in-the-round and great views from the back of the pews. However, if you're into **traditional Luo music**, Homa Bay is the place to track down tapes of *nyatiti* (lyre), *orutu* (single-stringed bow fiddle) and *onand* (accordion) music, as well as the ubiquitous gospel pop.

Homa Bay used to have a busy port, but in 1997 this, and much of the shoreline, became hemmed in by more than 1km of **water hyacinth**. The weed infestation happened quickly, trapping some boats. Ferries were suspended, and people sold off their vessels. The hyacinth was eventually cleared mechanically, and fishermen keep the remainder at bay by hand, but the port is a shadow of its former self.

Got Asego

The hike up **Got Asego**, the impressive conical hill on the east side of town, is recommended. The hill is the highest of dozens of volcanic plugs (cores of old volcanoes) in the area; from its table-sized summit, you'll have a 360-degree panorama of lakeshore and surrounding plains. It is remarkable how little of the land is not used. Luo thatched huts are interspersed with tin-roofed homesteads, a patchwork of small plots and agave hedges. Take binoculars and you can see more: clumps of papyrus drifting across the lake, and traffic along the road where it snakes east to Kendu Bay.

It takes about an hour to reach the top from the centre of town (actual ascent 30–45min), an easy climb but best tackled late in the afternoon (early morning ascents, though cooler, can be treacherous thanks to dew on the rocks). Head up the Rongo road, turn left 500m south of the Total petrol station and turn right up the *murram* road after Homa Bay School. The hill itself is best approached up the northwest ridge, where there's a well-defined footpath.

ARRIVAL AND DEPARTURE   HOMA BAY

Most of the town is strung out along the main street, the C20, which starts at the jetty and runs uphill. The little town centre fills a small grid of dusty streets between this main road and the higher, residential area to the east.

By bus Numerous bus companies run services to Nairobi (10hr); there are also three daily buses to Kisii (1hr) and Kericho (3hr 30min), as well as two that go as far as Mombasa (14hr).

By matatu Matatus leave Homa Bay from the stage on the main road, serving Kendu Bay (4–8 daily; 30min), Kisii (10–15 daily; 1hr 30min), Kisumu (6–12 daily; 2hr 30min), Mbita (12–15 daily; 1hr 30min) and Migori (5–10 daily; 2hr). If you can't find a direct vehicle to Kisii, then take a Migori matatu and get off at Rongo on the A1 highway, where you can soon find a Kisii-bound vehicle coming up from the south.

ACCOMMODATION

★ **Asego Stores (Summer Bay)** Next to the mosque, opposite the KCB bank ☏0733 268718. Nice, bright lodgings, basic but clean, with large beds, squat loos and bucket showers, all set around a courtyard-style dining area. Great-value, especially the giant double in a turret of sorts. BB Ksh800

Hippo Buck Rongo Rd, 2km south of the town centre ☏0723 262000. Competing with *Homa Bay* (below), the standard rooms are functional and clean, and the dining area, food and staff all improve the stay. The deep canal that gushes through the courtyard after heavy rain is a nice feature, but the place is still a bit overpriced. BB $40

Homa Bay Tourist Hotel Near the old port, just west of the main road ☏0727 112615, ⊕homabaytourist hotel.com. Twenty-three renovated rooms in this formerly state-run hotel (with TVs, nets, floor fans, and instant showers), and six roomy safari tents facing the lake (Ksh5200). The grounds are very attractive, and there's a good restaurant. BB Ksh3900

Ruma Tourist Lodge South end of town backing onto the Total station ☏0701 238422. Small, but clean and pleasant, s/c rooms set apart from a very congenial outdoor bar-restaurant, with safe parking. The enormous, rustically furnished "special rooms" are worth the extra Ksh600. BB Ksh1100

Sheraton Guest House Behind the matatu stage ☏0728 129458. Don't be seduced by the fancy facade of the main house – the non-s/c rooms are ranged around a small vine-covered courtyard at the back, and are small and stuffy, but very clean and cheap as chips. Separate showers and (clean) squat loos. Room only Ksh700

EATING AND DRINKING

For **food**, there are inexpensive *hotelis* everywhere. Homa Bay is not especially hot on **nightlife**, but it does have a few bars worth checking out in the evening.

Cave Inn Club On the main road. Has a disco playing *benga* and other local sounds – a nice spot with a curious wood-panelled interior and a shady terrace for a sundowner. Mon–Fri 5–11pm, Sat & Sun 2–11pm.

★ **Homa Bay Tourist Hotel** Down near the old port, just west of the main road ☏0727 112615, ⊕homabaytouristhotel.com. A gorgeous stretch of lawn sloping down to the lake, sprinkled with tables in patches of shade, with a flamboyant tree growing out of the bar. The perfect spot for a drink cooled by the offshore breeze, or a lunch of European dishes like lamb in mint sauce (Ksh400) or vegetable wraps. Daily 6.30am–11pm.

Redds Across from the Total petrol station. The most sophisticated drinking spot in town, with a little terrace and mirrors on the walls. Mon–Fri 5–11pm, Sat & Sun 2–11pm.

Red Rose Across from Tawakal Hotel. The best spot for a breakfast of tea and delicious fresh *mandaazi*, though it's not bad for other meals as well, and it's open late for dinner. Chicken, fish, beef and curry go for around Ksh200. Mon–Fri 8am–11pm.

Tawakal Hotel KCB Rd. Worth checking out for its "coastal-style" dishes like pilau and biryani (Ksh220), and there's a nice little patio outside to eat it on. Daily 8am–9pm.

4

DIRECTORY

Banks There are Barclays and KCB ATMs, both east of the main road.

Internet ALTQ is small, but it can get you online for Ksh1/min (Mon–Sat 8am–5pm).

Pharmacy Elians Chemists (☏0702 928120; Mon–Sat 7.30am–7pm).

Shopping The shopping chains haven't yet reached Homa Bay, but Shivling Supermarket (daily 8am–7pm) has most of what you might need.

Ruma National Park

25km southwest of Homa Bay • $20 • ☏035 29119 (or contact the park warden in the DC's compound in Homa Bay on ☏020 2332693), ⊕kws.go.ke • 200 square kilometres

The Lambwe valley's tsetse-fly-ridden bush, protected as **Ruma National Park**, is one of the few places in Kenya where you can see **Jackson's hartebeest** and two extremes of the antelope family: the miniature **oribi** and the enormous, horse-like **roan**, which is found only here. Roans are extremely rare, and the best place to see them is among the park's western grasslands, which are often hit by community fires that spread into the park from the west – they like the fresh grazing on burnt ground. Ruma also has about seventy beautiful **Rothschild giraffe** which aren't too hard to see above the tall grass. You'll have more difficulty spotting **leopard**, the park's only large predator, and you'll be very lucky to spot one of Ruma's twenty prize denizens, the **black rhinos** translocated from Mugie ranch in Laikipia in 2012 (see p.509).

ARRIVAL AND DEPARTURE   RUMA NATIONAL PARK

Ruma isn't really practical without your own vehicle and is tricky to reach by public transport – the busiest matatu route, Homa Bay to Mbita, skirts it by 11km – but if you're driving it's worth the effort, as you're virtually guaranteed to have the park to yourself. There are two main gates, **Kamato**, in the east, with the park HQ and the *Oribi Guest House* (signposted, 25km from Homa Bay), and the more remote **Nyatoto** in the northwest, on the road between Mbita and Karungu (24km from Mbita; the road crosses the park). If you're coming along the A1 from Migori or Kisii, a signposted *murram* road leads straight to Kamato gate.

ACCOMMODATION

Fig Tree Campsite 200m from Kamato gate and park HQ. Public campsite on a flat stretch of grass, shaded by a few acacia trees and frequented by buffalo and bush bucks. Bring all your own equipment, food and water. **$15** per person

Nyati Campsite Around 200m from Kamato gate, near the Fig Tree Campsite. Similar to Fig Tree, except that this is a "special campsite" – reserve in advance on

☏ 0717 176709 and pay the booking fee, and you'll have it all to yourself. Bring all your own supplies, as there are no facilities. **$30** per person

Oribi Guest House Just outside the gate ☏ 020 6000800, ✉ reservations@kws.go.ke. Self-catering cottage on the Kanyamwa Escarpment, with three double rooms sharing a bathroom, solar power and a fully equipped kitchen. Room only **$100**

Thimlich Ohinga

Daily • No set hours or entry price, but tips welcome

Thimlich Ohinga is an archeological site of potentially huge significance, considered one of the greatest stone enclosures in East Africa, and for sheer visual impact you won't find a more impressive or atmospheric ancient site anywhere in Kenya away from the coast.

The precise meaning of "thimlich ohinga" in archaic Luo is open to interpretation, but it is generally held to mean "scary, walled enclosures", though some say the "scary" is a reference to the wild bush country from which the occupants of the site were protected. It's estimated the compounds were built around the fifteenth century by a people whose history has been forgotten, but were almost certainly Bantu-speaking predecessors of the Luo. It probably came to be occupied by Luos displaced in inter-clan fighting in the early eighteenth century, within a few decades of their arrival here. Elsewhere in the district, successive generations of various communities have used stone enclosures and, in some places, modern Luo families have their homesteads inside the remnants of such walls.

Covering an area of 52 acres, the site is the most striking example of an architecture whose remnants are scattered across South Nyanza. Similar to the dry-stone enclosures of southern Africa (of which Great Zimbabwe is the classic example), the biggest structure is a **compound** about 150m in diameter, inside which are five smaller enclosures, probably used as cattle pens, and at least six house pits, the sites of former dwellings. The walls, which range in height from 1m to 4.2m, are built from a combination of natural boulders and dressed stone, the latter used particularly in the construction of the low doorways through the walls. A combination of gradual excavation and continued restoration work means it's a little hard to get a clear grasp of the whole layout of the site (and there's no map or guidebook), but there are at least four large walled enclosures, each with smaller enclosures inside them.

OPPOSITE TEA PICKERS NEAR KERICHO (P.278) >

You really need your **own transport** to get to Thimlich Ohinga. If you're very determined and intrepid you could try reaching the site by a combination of matatus and hitchhiking (or walking), but there's nowhere to stay, barely anywhere to eat, and you'll need a tent and supplies in case you can't get there and back in a day.

From Migori The easiest approach to Thimlich Ohinga is from Migori. Follow the Tanzania road for 4km to reach Soma and the junction for Muhoro Bay, where there's a National Cereals and Produce Board depot. Take the turn-off on the right (west) onto *murram* here and continue for a couple of kilometres from the depot to reach another junction. Turn right here and drive straight on via Suna and Macalder, across a big bridge over the Migori River and then (exactly 4.8km further on) over a smaller bridge across the Gucha. A further 800m west is a place called Ayego (or Ombo). Turn right (north) onto a basic farm/bush track, in fair condition and a bit stony in dry weather but liable to be tricky in the wet. Continue north for 12.3km, following the ridge to the west of the Gucha river valley, as far as another junction at another small location, Masara. Turn right here onto a broad stretch of *murram*, following a fence, and 200m further you'll find the entrance to the site (a total of 55km from the Cereals Board

Depot). You can also reach Thimlich Ohinga, using the last part of these directions, by driving east from Karungu (the junction at Ayego is 21.2km east of Karungu). If you don't have your own vehicle, it's possible to get most of the way to the site using the occasional matatus that ply between Migori and Karungu, getting out at Ayego. But you might have to walk that last 12km.

From Kisii or Homa Bay via Miranga From Kisii (105km) or Homa Bay (60km), head for Rodi Kopany on the C20 between Homa Bay and Rongo, where you take the C18 southwest, through Mirogi and Ndhiwa to Miranga. You should be able to make it this far by matatu from the Homa Bay/Rongo road. Just beyond Miranga's shops, a signpost shows the direction of Thimlich Ohinga down a rough *murram* track, driveable in an ordinary car when dry, but requiring 4WD in the wet. The site is about 30km south of here, and there is no public transport.

Rusinga Island and Mbita

Much easier than Ruma National Park or Thimlich Ohinga is the trip to **Rusinga Island**. The narrow channel between **Mbita** and the island was bridged by a **causeway** in 1984, so driving around Rusinga is quite feasible.

Mbita and the causeway

The shabby town of **MBITA**, straddling either side of the causeway, is very unprepossessing indeed, but things improve once you get on to the island. The building of the causeway – partly over two dumper trucks that fell into the lake during the operation and couldn't be recovered – has had some unwanted side effects. Vervet monkeys now move onto the island to raid crops, and fish have become scarce on the

MFANGANO & RUSINGA ISLANDS

Lake Victoria (Elevation 1133m)

N

Mzenzi Is.

Riringiti Is.

Risi Is.

Nyakweri

Ukula

Kaklimba

Abasuba Community Peace Museum

Soklo

Cave Paintings

Mount Kwitutu (1694m)

Ramba

Sena

Mfangano

Ukinga

Takawiri Is.

Ngodha Is.

Rusinga

Wanyama Hill

Kaswanga

Mboya's Mausoleum

Kasmasengere

Nyamuga

Lugongo Hill

Kakrigu

Mbita

Uozi

Mzenzi Is.

| △ Hilltops |
| - - - Footpaths |

■ ACCOMMODATION
Abasuba Community Peace Museum	7
Badilisha Ecovillage	1
Elk Lodge	3
Gethsamane Guesthouse	5
Lake Victoria Safari Village	6
Mfangano Island Camp	4
Patroba Ogweno Lodge	3
Rusinga Island Lodge	2
Viking Rest House	3

0 ___ 5 kilometres

Ruma NP (Kamato Gate); Homa Bay

Kisii & Ksumu

Sindo, Ruma NP (Nyatoto Gate), Karungu & Midori

Kisumu side of Rusinga because the causeway blocks the current, turning the water there into a stagnant pond. A bridge to replace the old chain ferry would have been the best solution to the island's access problem. As it is, the causeway has ended Rusinga's slight isolation at what many local people feel is an unacceptable cost.

Rusinga Island

Rusinga Island itself is small and austerely pretty, with high crags dominating the desolate, goat-grazed centre, and a single dirt road running around the circumference. Life here is difficult, with drought commonplace, and high winds a frequent torment. The occasional heavy rain either washes away the soil or sinks into the porous rock, emerging lower down where it creates swamps. Ecologically, the island is in very dire straits: almost all its trees have been cut down for cooking fuel or to be converted into lucrative charcoal. These conditions make harvests highly unpredictable and most people fish to make ends meet (although the causeway has forced them to make longer fishing trips), either selling the catch on to refrigerated lorries or bartering directly for produce with traders from Kisii. Yet the islanders, in common with their mainland cousins, remain an unfailingly friendly and cheerful bunch, more than happy to make contact with wayward travellers.

LAKE VICTORIA'S ECOLOGY AND ECONOMY

Lake Victoria fills a shallow depression (no deeper than 80m) between the Western and Eastern Rift valleys, yet it is not part of the Rift system. Until the 1960s, it was home to around five hundred different species of brilliantly coloured tropical fish, known as haplochromines or **cichlids**, all of them endemic – unique to the lake. Scientists, puzzling over how such a dazzling variety of species came to evolve in this largely uniform environment in the space of no more than a million years, have suggested that, at some stage in its history, the lake must have dried into a series of small lakes in which the fish evolved separately. Lake Victoria's cichlids are popular aquarium fish, and one of the commonest larger species, the tilapia, is a regional speciality, grilled or fried and served whole.

In the early 1960s, a voracious carnivore, the **Nile perch**, was introduced to the lake, and proceeded to eat its way through the cichlid population, driving some species close to extinction, though many have held on in parts of the lake which were too shallow for perch, or in smaller lakes around the main one. For local people, the introduction of the perch, which can reach a weight of 250kg, has been a bit of a Trojan horse: while they're consumed locally and sold for export (good news for the lakeshore economy), traditional fishing and processing have been hit hard by the arrival of modern vessels and factories joining in the feast and taking their profits elsewhere.

The lake has other problems, however. **Algae** have proliferated, due to industrial and sewage pollution, depriving the lake of oxygen. More than three million litres of human waste drain into the lake every day, and the Swedish development agency, SIDA, estimates that Kenya, with the smallest share of the lake's shoreline, is its main polluter. As well as suffering a dramatic fall in oxygen levels, the lake is becoming so murky that the remaining cichlids are unable to identify mates, so that hybridization is occurring. Meanwhile, the building of the causeway between Mbita and Rusinga Island has turned the Winam Gulf into even more of a pond, with only one outlet, inhibiting currents and making its water even less healthy.

Another threat comes from the **water hyacinth**, originally native to Brazil. This floating weed grows quickly around the lakeshore and spreads like a carpet across the surface, blocking out the light, choking the lake to death and snaring up vessels. Since the mid-1990s, Homa Bay, Kendu Bay and Kisumu have all at times been strangled by kilometre-wide cordons of the weed, inhibiting passage to all but the smallest canoes, with disastrous results for the local economy. Solutions have included the promotion of products (furniture, paper, even building materials) made from harvested hyacinth. In 2001, mechanical clearance enabled passenger ferries to resume, only for falling water levels to cause their suspension once more. There's been a resurgence of the invasive weed since 2006, and the nutrient run-off following heavy rains in 2010 spread the deadly canopy even further.

If you're interested in making a contribution to the welfare and development of the Rusinga community, there's a permaculture project and education centre at **Badilisha Ecovillage** near the lakeshore at Kaswanga, on the north side of the island, 9km from Mbita, that brings together green-minded volunteers from around the world to work with AIDS orphans, in local schools doing support work or working the land on the permaculture project, founded on the principles of sustainability and respect for the environment. You can stay here for a night or a couple of months (see opposite), and the stays make for an excellent way of getting to know local issues in a remote and challenging rural setting.

The island is rich in **fossils**, and was the site of Mary Leakey's discovery of a skull of *Proconsul africanus* (a primitive anthropoid ape), which can be seen in the National Museum (see p.110). It was also the family home of **Tom Mboya** (see p.565), the civil rights champion, trade unionist and charismatic young Luo politician who was assassinated in Nairobi in 1969, a turning point for the worse in Kenya's post-Independence history, sparking off a crisis that led to more than forty deaths in widespread rioting and demonstrations.

Tom Mboya's mausoleum

Daily 8am–7pm • ☎ 0726 670249

Tom Mboya's mausoleum, built in the shape of a bullet to recall the manner of his death, contains various mementoes and gifts Mboya received during his life, including a cup won in a dancing competition and the briefcase he was carrying when murdered. The inscription on the grave reads:

THOMAS JOSEPH MBOYA
August 15th 1930 – July 5th 1969
Go and fight like this man
Who fought for mankind's cause
Who died because he fought
Whose battles are still unwon!

You don't have to know anything about the man to be impressed. In any other surroundings his memorial might seem relatively modest, but on this barren, windswept shore, it stands out like a beacon. Members of Mboya's family live nearby and are happy to see foreign visitors. They maintain the mausoleum themselves so always appreciate donations, though these are not obligatory. If you're interested, take a look at the rather good folder of press cuttings about Mboya.

ARRIVAL AND INFORMATION   TOM MBOYA'S MAUSOLEUM

The mausoleum lies on family land at Kamasengre on the north side of the island, about 7km by dirt road from Mbita, or roughly 5km directly across the island.

On foot or by public transport Two matatus do the circuit around the island daily (at 6am and 6pm); otherwise you'll need to take a *boda boda* (Ksh100 one way) or walk (allow 4hr and take some water). Local residents will show you the way to the mausoleum. From the Mbita causeway, aim for the crags in the centre of the island, skirt them to the right and then walk down to rejoin the road on the other side of the Tom Mboya Memorial Health Centre. From here, it's less than 2km to Mboya's mausoleum, the conical silver roof clearly visible just off the road.

By car If you're driving, turn right 11.7km from the causeway (signposted "Kolunga Beach"), and then right again after 150m, and the mausoleum is 600m further on.

Hippo Bay

Fifty metres past the Tom Mboya Secondary School, on the north side of the island, the path to the right takes you through *shambas* of millet and corn to a seasonally grassy lakeside called **Hippo Bay**. Here you can watch nesting fish eagles as well as, usually, hippos. If you're lucky, you may see the pretty and little-known spotted-necked otters that live around Lake Victoria and nowhere else in Kenya.

ARRIVAL AND DEPARTURE

Apart from the odd matatu that runs around Rusinga Island, and the occasional ones that venture down to Sindo, the town of Mbita is as far as you can go by public road transport. There are, however, some wooden "engine boats" connecting Mbita daily (until around 5pm) with various ports on Mfangano Island, Takawiri Island, as well as the car ferry to Luanda Kotieno.

By matatu A steady stream of matatus plies the Homa Bay–Mbita route throughout the day, but they're often packed, and the road is rough *murram* the whole way, and very difficult when wet. There are some good lakeshore views (and access if you're driving and want a break) for a couple of kilometres south of Luanda (29km from Homa

MBITA AND RUSINGA ISLAND

Bay's Mbita junction). From Kisumu, it can be quicker to get a matatu to Luanda Kotieno (see p.256), from where there are ferries over to Mbita (at 8am, 11am, 1pm, 3pm & 6pm; 45min; matatus leave Kisumu 3–4hr earlier to connect). Matatus complete the journey to Kisumu via Asembo and Ndori – usually a faster way of reaching Kisumu than going via Homa Bay.

By ferry Leaving Mbita, you can take the car ferry across the Winam Gulf for the short 10km ride to Luanda Kotieno. The ferry goes five times a day (currently 7am, 10am, noon, 2pm & 5pm), returning 2hr later (passengers Ksh150, cars Ksh800). There's also a ferry service to Sena on Mfangano Island (3–4 daily; 1hr) via Takawiri Island (45min).

ACCOMMODATION

RUSINGA ISLAND

Badilisha Ecovillage Rusinga Island ☏0738 015009, ⒲ badilisha.net. Local homestays are organized for Badilisha volunteers in which you and your host family agree the terms, which include bed and board. You can also turn up at Badilisha and camp in your own tent or stay in their simple *bandas*. Meals and shared showers and toilets are provided. Suggested donation per person FB `Ksh1000`

Rusinga Island Lodge On the north side of the island, 10.5km from the causeway coming via the north side, or 9.5km via the south side. ☏0716 055924 or 0734 402932, ⒲ rusingaislandtrust.com. A luxurious rustic retreat, most of whose clients fly in from the Maasai Mara to the lodge's airstrip. Part fishing lodge, part spa retreat, part watersports club, part birders' paradise (369 species have been recorded), this is a sumptuous and relaxing escape with comfortable, safari-style cottages and large bathrooms. Much of the produce for the sixteen guests is grown on site. There's also the chance to do a fossil walk to the site where Mary Leakey discovered *Proconsul africanus*. FB package for two including all activities (but not flights) `$1050`

MBITA

Elk Lodge Across the square from the matatu stand ☏0720 716665, ⒲ safarikenya.net/elk.htm. A friendly little guesthouse offering clean s/c doubles and non s/c

singles, set around a patio garden with flowers and pawpaw trees. There's no hot water, but they may be able to provide some in a bucket. Room only `Ksh700`

★ **Lake Victoria Safari Village** 2km down the dirt road toward Sindo ☏0722 829645, ⒲ safarikenya.net. Run by the Norwegian husband of the *Elk*'s landlady, this is an excellent place to stay, with delightfully restful, high-vaulted *bandas* divided to create good, spacious twins and doubles, with clean, well-appointed bathrooms and little terraces overlooking a lakeside beach. There's also a rather magnificent honeymoon suite in a mock-lighthouse. At night you can watch fishermen putting out hurricane lamps to attract tiny *omena* fish (making "more light than Nairobi" as one waiter put it) from the very nice terrace dining room of the "Village", where the food, when it comes, is always good (most dishes around Ksh400). BB `Ksh5500`

Patroba Ogweno Lodge Behind the Elk Lodge ☏0733 731638. Very good-value s/c rooms set around a concrete courtyard. It's not quite as cosy as the *Elk* or *Viking*, but the hot water is on tap and the well-appointed downstairs rooms are nice and cool. Room only `Ksh700`

Viking Rest House 20m from Elk Lodge and run by the same lady ☏0720 716665, ⒲ safarikenya.net/viking .htm. The non s/c rooms here are smaller than the ones at the *Elk*, but they're well maintained and reasonable enough for the price. The bar out front gets lively, but never too loud. Room only `Ksh450`

Mfangano Island

Ksh500/day for a guide

Said to have been inhabited for centuries, enigmatic **Mfangano Island** is out of range of the smallest fishing boats, and, aside from a handful of motorbikes, entirely without vehicles. The island is populated by a curious mixture of immigrants from all over Kenya, administered by a chief and three sub-chiefs with help from a trio of policemen. Monitor lizards swarm on the sandy shores and **hippos** are much in evidence out in the water.

Larger and more populous than Rusinga, with a similarly rugged landscape but better vegetation cover, Mfangano's greatest economic resource is still the lake itself. As on

Rusinga, the local **fishing techniques** are unusual: the islanders fish with floating kerosene lamps hauled shorewards, or towards a boat, to draw in the schools to be netted. At the moment, local residents still rely on a network of temporary **footpaths** that are constantly changing course, but that could soon change with the upcoming completion of a ring road around the island. At the moment you can still use these paths to walk through the interior of Mfangano, though it's always easier if you have a guide.

Sena

The chief's camp and capital of Mfangano, Sena has a couple of small *dukas* and *hotelis* and a post office. About 1km north of the centre lies the **Abasuba Community Peace Museum** (daily 9am–5pm; Ksh200; ☎0723 898406, ⌨abasuba.museum), which displays cultural artefacts such as traditional cooking pots and farming implements. The helpful staff can also organize guided excursions to the island's main sights, and can even arrange transport from Mbita. For further information, contact museum director Jack Obonyo on the number above.

Rock paintings

The main sites (at Kwitone and Mawanga) are close to Ukula on the north coast • Ksh500 guiding fee to be taken to them from Sena, and a Ksh200 entry fee at each site

The island's **rock paintings** are certainly worth the trip alone. Thought to be at least a thousand and possibly four thousand years old, they are believed to have been painted by the island's original hunter-gatherer inhabitants who were displaced in around the sixteenth century by Luo incomers, who were themselves displaced a couple of centuries ago by a Bantu people called the Abasuba.

The Peace Museum, which publishes an excellent pamphlet explaining the local rock art (⌨bit.ly/RockArtPublications), can arrange trips to two sites, **Kwitone** and **Mawanga**, featuring prehistoric rock paintings comprising reddish spirals and whorls, some with rays up to 50cm across, that at first sight could come from any Von Däniken paperback. The paintings were probably used for rainmaking ceremonies, and all kinds of rituals and taboos are still supposed to apply to people visiting them – a period of sexual abstinence, for example, and not telling anybody that you are coming to the site before you actually do so.

ARRIVAL AND DEPARTURE   MFANGANO ISLAND

By boat Unless you fly in, the only way of reaching Mfangano is on the large wooden boats with outboard motors ("matatu" or "engine" boats) that shuttle local people and their produce between Mbita and the surrounding islands and peninsulas. It's a 90min crossing to Sena from Mbita. Most boats stop at Takawiri Island then head around Mfangano in an anticlockwise direction, calling at Sena, Nyakweri and Ukula, though others go around clockwise. The first boat leaves Mbita around 9am, the last around 5pm, with the last boat leaving Sena at around 2pm, so a day-trip isn't really practical unless you have enough money (around Ksh4000) to hire a boat for the day.

ACCOMMODATION

Abasuba Community Peace Museum 1km north of Sena ☎0723 898406, ⌨abasuba.museum. The museum allows camping on its grounds (Ksh500 per person, including tents and mattresses), or you can stay in one of their traditional Abasuba huts. Both options come with drinking and washing water, but no showers. BB **Ksh3000**

Gethsamane Guesthouse On the lakeshore just beyond the museum; boats from Mbita will drop you there directly on request ☎0724 005910. A simple wooden barn of a building crammed with bunk beds, each with a mosquito net, and cold-water showers. It's rustic, but the lakeshore location is lovely. Food can be cooked to order. BB **Ksh1200**

Mfangano Island Camp ☎0733 268888, ⌨governors camp.com. Alternative accommodation, at the other end of the spectrum, is provided by this exclusive camp (sleeping 12) comprising a huddle of clay-and-thatch buildings laid out in the shape of a Luo homestead, but fitted out in deluxe style and overlooking a private bay. Most of the camp's visitors fly in from the Maasai Mara on a day-trip (fishing and birding in the morning, lunching and lounging in the afternoon), but some stay on to enjoy the beautiful setting, gourmet food and attentive service. Closed April & May. FB packages (including a boat with driver at your disposal; flights extra) **$886**

Mbita to Sindo and Karungu

Continuing south beyond Mbita to Sindo and Karungu is slow going by matatu. The road can be very difficult during the rains and, at the best of times, there's only a limited demand, so one daily departure is the norm. Karungu is better linked with Migori: the stretch between Sindo and Karungu, while remote and beautiful in parts, is best done in your own 4WD.

Some of the most scenic landscapes in western Kenya are to be found around the **Gembe Hills**, south of Mbita. As you approach **SINDO** from the north, the little lakeside town, with the impressive towering backdrop of the **Gwasi Hills**, soaring nearly 1000m above the level of the lake, makes for some memorable views which seem to have more in common with the Greek islands than with equatorial Africa.

The road then turns inland, between the Gembe and Gwasi hills, and runs down to **KWOYO** and the northwestern Nyatoto Gate entrance to Ruma National Park (see p.265). The narrow public road, mostly of treacherous black cotton soil, follows the eastern border of the park, just inside the fence line. If you can take your eyes off the road, you're likely to get some excellent free game-viewing and can expect to see Rothschild giraffe and various antelope out on the grassy plain to the east. After you leave the park zone, the road improves to a wider, stonier surface, and you should be able to keep up a decent speed to Karungu.

Seventy kilometres from Mbita, **KARUNGU** is a small town on the lakeshore, greatly occupied with *omena* catching and drying, with one or two basic lodgings and *hotelis*. All the streets in the town seem to have been surfaced, but the road out to the east, to Suna and Migori, is *murram*.

4

Migori

Spread out along the A1 highway for 4km, the "border town" of **MIGORI** is the last major settlement before Tanzania – although the actual border crossing is a further 23km down the road at Isebania. More of a western highlands town than you might imagine, conifer-covered hills rise up to the east. Market days are interesting for the variety of peoples and for traditional activities untainted by tourism. Although Migori is just 80km from the Maasai Mara, the state of the road (see p.362) doesn't make it an ideal jumping-off point for visits to the park. But it can still make for a pleasant stopover en route to Tanzania.

East of Migori to the Maasai Mara

Much of the **C13** road east to the Maasai Mara (see p.362) is in a pretty dreadful state, and, if you're driving, it should only be attempted in a 4WD. Some matatus do parts of this

---

ROLE-PLAY AMONG THE KURIA

Kihancha is the capital of the **Kuria** people, who live in scattered rural communities. The Kuria have an interesting, quasi-matriarchal system found in various parts of Africa which essentially allows women of means to "marry" younger women in order to be provided with children. In practice, an older woman who can't have children may invite a younger woman into her home. The young "bride", in turn, chooses a male partner, often in secret, to father her children, who are brought up by the two women without the involvement of the father or the older woman's husband (if she has one – she may also be a widow, or simply unmarried). In any case, the older woman lives like a male elder – attending to light business affairs but essentially waited upon hand and foot from dawn to dusk. It's a system with much to recommend it, especially when it takes care of unmarried mothers (who are barred from marrying men), who come into the family as "wives" – surrogate mothers – and whose children are automatically adopted. Ironically, despite these apparently female-controlled arrangements, it's male children that women-families want, and men who inherit land.

route, and one or two services go right through to Narok and back, which, if you're on a budget, is one way of visiting the Maasai Mara without paying for the privilege. You won't enter the reserve itself, but you will see some wildlife en route, especially in the great conservancy areas north of the reserve, though it's a long and uncomfortable journey.

The Maasai Mara junction is at **Suna**, 4km south of Migori down the A1, where the *murram* road to Karungu also meets the highway. From here, it's 22km to the **Kihancha** turning (keep on straight: the small town is to the right) and you cross the Migori River 2km later. Halfway between Kihancha and Lolgorien, the road improves to fair-to-good *murram*, with the odd rough patch. You reach **Lolgorien**, 46km from Suna, and another 20km sees you at the top of the escarpment above the Oloololo Gate, with the plains of the Mara spread out to the east. Allow at least two hours to get here.

ARRIVAL AND INFORMATION
MIGORI

By bus and matatu Buses and matatus run to Nairobi (3–12 daily; 8hr) via Kisii (2hr), Kericho (4hr) and Nakuru (6hr) leaving early morning or evening, and there are also morning buses to Eldoret (8hr), and frequent matatus to Homa Bay (5–10 daily; 3hr 30min), Kisumu (2–8 daily; 4hr 30min) and Kisii (8–20 daily; 2hr). Heading down to Tanzania, there are direct buses to Mwanza mornings and evenings, but otherwise you'll have to take a matatu to the border post at Isebania (also called Sirare, and served by direct matatus from Kisumu), or at Kianja, cross on foot and take an onward vehicle from the other side.

Services The town has a Barclays with an ATM, as well as one or two small supermarkets.

ACCOMMODATION AND EATING

There are one or two decent, modest **hotels** in Migoria, but water supplies are sporadic, and even cold water may not be available on tap. If you're looking for something cheaper than the Girango, try one of the B&Ls around the matatu stand and north of the bridge.

Girango At the south end of town ☎0721 273878. Friendly and peaceful, with quiet rooms equipped with couches and TV. Basic local food (mains around Ksh250) is served in the pleasant garden, and there's safe parking. BB __Ksh1500__

Heritage Hotel Near the matatu stage. Once famous for the quality of its food, this restaurant has seen better days, but planned renovations should return it to its former glory. In the meantime, it's still a good option for chicken, fish and meat dishes (all around Ksh350). Sun–Fri 6am–10pm.

Kisii and around

Headquarters of the **Gusii** people, and district town of a region vying with Nyeri in having the fastest-growing population in the country, **KISII** is a prosperous, hard-working trading centre in the hills. Notoriously muddy and rubbish-strewn, with a minor reputation for hassle which really only reflects the friendliness of the locals, the town is undergoing something of a makeover, with its sloping streets gradually being resurfaced with paving blocks. Kisii is most famous for its fine **soapstone**, though there's little to be seen in the town itself. The best locality for watching the carvers and making on-the-spot purchases is **Tabaka**, some way south. One thing you may notice if you stay overnight in Kisii is the occasional **earth tremor** – the town lies on a fault line and minor earthquakes are not uncommon. Wildlife enthusiasts will want to check out the tree full of **giant bats** in the government compound between Moi Highway and Sports Club at the southern end of town.

Tabaka

TABAKA is one of the most important centres in the world for **soapstone** (steatite) production. Most of the carvings are bought up by buyers from curio shops in Nairobi and elsewhere, but shops selling the carvings now line the road through the little town, and are happy to sell directly to visitors.

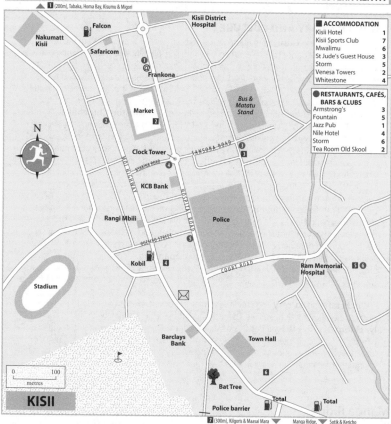

▲ 1 (200m), Tabaka, Homa Bay, Kisumu & Migori

KISII

ACCOMMODATION
Kisii Hotel	1
Kisii Sports Club	7
Mwalimu	6
St Jude's Guest House	3
Storm	5
Venesa Towers	2
Whitestone	4

RESTAURANTS, CAFÉS, BARS & CLUBS
Armstrong's	3
Fountain	5
Jazz Pub	1
Nile Hotel	4
Storm	6
Tea Room Old Skool	2

7 (300m), Kilgoris & Maasai Mara ▼   Manga Ridge, ▼   Sotik & Kericho ▼

Beyond Tabaka centre are four **quarries**, with two main ones, the first on the left, and the other further down on the right. There must, however, be vast reserves of stone under the ground all over the district. The stone emerges in a variety of colours and densities: white is easiest to work, shades of orange and pink harder, and rosy-red the hardest and heaviest. A number of families have become full-time carvers, but for most people it's simply a spare-time occupation after agriculture, a way of making a few shillings. You'll even see children walking home from school carving little animals from chips of stone. The professional carvers often specialize in a variety of designs from chess sets and traditional animals, to vases, cups and human figures. The stone is dampened to bring up the colour and make it easier to work, and then waxed to retain the lustre.

ARRIVAL AND DEPARTURE   TABAKA

By car The turn-off for Tabaka is at Nyachenge, 18km west of Kisii on the A1 Migori road. A sign to the left, if coming from Kisii, points to the St Amillus Tabaka Mission Hospital and Kisii Soapstone Carvers Co-operative Society. From here it's 5km into the village (6km to the Co-operative Society) on a rough dirt road that's treacherous in wet weather, though an ordinary car can make it when it's dry. Coming by matatu from Kisii, it's best to get one that goes direct to Tabaka, even if that means waiting. The alternative is hanging around just as long at the halfway point, or a long walk from Nyachenge. The last matatus from Tabaka back to Kisii leave around 5pm.

GUSII HISTORY AND CULTURE

The Bantu-speaking **Gusii** (after whom Kisii is named) were only awakened to the brutal realities of British conquest in 1905, when they rebelled, pitching themselves with spears against a machine gun. It was "not so much a battle as a massacre", one of the participants recalled, leaving "several hundred dead and wounded spearsmen heaped up outside the square of bayonets". In 1908, after the District Commissioner was speared in a personal attack, the same thing happened again, only this time the Gusii were trying to escape, not attack. Crops were burned and whole villages razed to the ground. **Winston Churchill**, at the time the Under-Secretary of State for the Colonies, telegraphed from the Colonial Office: "Surely it cannot be necessary to go on killing these defenceless people on such an enormous scale."

The Gusii were totally demoralized. In a few brief years, the fabric of their communities had been torn apart, hut taxes imposed, and cattle confiscated to be returned only in exchange for labour. And then came World War I. Kisii was the site of the first Anglo-German engagements in East Africa, and thousands of men were press-ganged into the hated Carrier Corps.

It seems extraordinary that the exceptionally friendly people of Kisii are the grandchildren of the conscripts. The powerful, millennial religious movements that burst among them during the colonial period under the name Mumboism may partly account for the very strong ties of community they've maintained against all odds. Prophets and medicine men have always been important here, and even in today's superficially Christianized society, the Gusii have solidly kept their cultural identity. The practice of **trepanning**, for example, which involves tapping a small hole in the skull to relieve headache or mental illness, seems to be as old as the Gusii themselves. "Brain operations" are still performed, clandestinely, but apparently quite successfully.

Witchcraft and **sorcery** also continue to play important roles in the life of the town and its district, and often make headlines. The growing influence of Christianity has led to spates of **lynchings** of suspected witches. Residents are often reticent to come forward as witnesses, which can lead to an interesting collision of worldviews in the media. On one occasion the local police chief was quoted saying: "We hope we can get them [the witches] and if possible charge them in court. This way we shall save their lives."

Manga Ridge

The lavishly fertile district around Kisii gets rain all year, in remarkable contrast to the semi-arid lowlands of the lakeshore just a few kilometres away. A walk to the dramatic escarpment cliff of **Manga Ridge** is a good way of getting into the countryside. It's a two- to three-hour walk north of the town, wonderful either in the early morning, or, if you can arrange a lift back, the late afternoon.

Leaving Kisii on the Kericho road, turn left into Manga Road at the bottom of the hill, 500m after Barclays, and follow the road as it sweeps you towards and then alongside the ridge. After about 5km you can cut down one of the tracks across the lush valley to your left and continue straight up the escarpment (several hundred metres high). Beware of snakes lurking among the rocks and grass on the upward scramble. Alternatively, you can continue along the road for a further 5km to come up behind the ridge. From here it's a ten-minute hike up to the edge, where a path follows the cliff for a kilometre or two. Magnificent views out over Kisii and down to Lake Victoria are your reward. It's possible to get a matatu to the village of **Manga** from Kisii town (in front of *St Jude's Guest House*), but make it clear you want to get off at the ridge.

Kisii to Sotik and Kericho

The road to Sotik is all roadworks, bumps and dust, and **SOTIK**, when you reach it, is nothing more than a couple of petrol stations. But **KEROKA**, halfway between Kisii and Sotik, has become a sizeable town and has a huge **Sunday market** drawing people from many kilometres around. From Sotik to Kericho, the road is smooth.

Museum of History, Art and Science of the Kipsigis People

Kapkatet, 12km east of Sotik and 150m off the north side of the road • Mon–Fri 9am–5.30pm, Sat & Sun 9am–6.30pm • Ksh500 • ☎ 0721 274453, ✉ tumpaul45@yahoo.com

Travelling along the road to Sotik it's worth stopping at **KAPKATET** to take a look around the little **Museum of History, Art and Science of the Kipsigis People** (see p.229). The museum comprises a diverse little collection of traditional garments, tools, weapons, containers and musical instruments, all well lit and well captioned, with pronunciation guides, putting many of the country's official national-museum collections to shame. Look out for the young girls' circumcision cloaks and for the *chepchingilit* – bells that would have been worn by sheep or goats (and by girls, after their operations and only removed after marriage). Finally, there's a fascinating and pretty successful attempt to recreate a cross section of a traditional Kipsigis home, with wooden sliding door ("with a peephole for anticipating attacks").

ARRIVAL AND DEPARTURE   KISII

Kisii is something of a route hub, with both regional and national bus and matatu services passing through. If you're heading to **Tanzania**, bus and matatu services run throughout the day to the border crossing, variously known as Isebania or Nyabikaye on the Kenyan side, and Serira, Sirare or Siria on the Tanzanian.

By matatu Plenty of matatus run throughout the day, most departing from the main stage in front of the market. These include three or four useful early-morning departures roughly for Narok via the B3, passing the junctions for the C12 and C13 Maasai Mara access roads. Other destinations include Eldoret (4–10 daily; 3hr 30min); Homa Bay (10–15 daily; 1hr 30min); Kericho (10–15 daily; 2hr); Kisumu (10–20 daily; 2hr 30min); Migori (8–20 daily; 2hr); Nairobi (6–12 daily; 6hr); and Rongo (45min).

By bus There are numerous bus services to and from Kisii, with most buses pulling into and departing from the matatu stage. Services include Homa Bay (4 daily; 1hr 30min); Migori (6 daily; 1hr 30min); Mombasa (4 daily; 14hr) and Nairobi (roughly hourly; 5–8hr).

By car If you're driving and are planning to take the route to the Maasai Mara via Kilgoris and Lolgorien, note that the road to the Mara is difficult beyond Kilgoris, even with 4WD, and the section down the Oloolelo Escarpment can be impossible after rain. Heading for the north or east of the reserve, the fastest route is via Sotik and Bomet.

ACCOMMODATION

You'll find plenty of places to **stay**, although some are pretty awful, and most are noisy, especially on Wednesdays and weekends when bars and discos are at their loudest, and women travelling alone will want to avoid cheaper places. Water supplies are notoriously erratic and you should be prepared for power fluctuations during heavy rain, so have some candles handy.

Kisii Hotel Moi Highway, 200m north of Nakumatt on the road to Kisumu ☎ 0725 558154. Ramshackle but quiet, with an agreeable, creaking colonial atmosphere and helpful staff, the *Kisii* belies outward appearances with its twelve spacious, clean s/c rooms with nets, TV and instant showers. There's guarded parking and a huge and beautiful bird-filled garden, perfect for relaxing with a cold beer, though the food in the restaurant isn't great. BB **Ksh1500**

Kisii Sports Club Heading south, turn right 300m past the Total station, then right again ☎ 0725 964164. The club is open to all, with seven good-sized, clean and well-furnished rooms with nets, TV and instant showers. There's a golf course, squash court and pool on site, though it costs extra to use them, and the peaceful grounds have lots of space for kids to run around on the lawns. BB **Ksh2350**

Mwalimu Moi Highway ☎ 058 30357. This 1979 concrete block at the southern end of town was once a teachers' hostel and is still run by the teachers' union. The decent s/c rooms are comfortable and carpeted, with nets and hot water, but they tend to feel like classrooms converted into bedrooms. Strangely, the two-room suites are the same price as doubles. BB **Ksh2700**

St Jude's Guest House Just south of the bus station ☎ 0714 231007. Decent B&L whose rooms have instant showers, nets and TV throughout, though many have inward-facing windows and are quite dark. Rooms #11–19 have good views over the town, but the best, "executive room" #10 (Ksh1500), has magnificent views from a 270-degree balcony and a bit of a honeymoon theme going on, complete with plastic flowers and slightly more mirrors than necessary. There's also a nice, well-lit upper-floor *hoteli*. BB **Ksh800**

Storm Court Rd ☎ 058 30649 or 0727 630021. The quietest hotel in Kisii offers a choice of adequate rooms with nets, TV and instant showers, plus some more

4

expensive suites, and an outside bar and *nyama choma* joint. Good value and well managed. BB **Ksh1800**

Venesa Towers Hospital Rd ☎0721 417000. This six-storey block, with great town views from the roof and upper floors, offers good value, though they're still bringing water (even cold water) in buckets "because the showers get destroyed". All the rooms are s/c with balconies, but some are small and cramped, so be choosy. BB **Ksh800**

Whitestone Moi Highway ☎0721 771500. Cheap, secure and clean with hot water, s/c doubles, and s/c or non-s/c singles. Some of the rooms are dark and rather cramped, but it's still a good deal if you're counting the pennies. **Ksh500**

EATING AND DRINKING

Despite the noxious drain smells, the overflowing **market** is the first base for hungry travellers. Kisii is also blessed with a big **supermarket**, Nakumatt Kisii (Mon–Sat 8.30am–8.30pm, Sun 10am–8pm).

Armstrong's Ground floor, St Jude's Guest House. A long bar with a congenial atmosphere, plus several screens of sports (usually English football) and good music. Daily 10am–10pm.

Fountain Ogembo St. Cavernous, multi-level bar playing African tunes and showing sports on wide-screen TVs. They also serve grilled meats, chicken and fish for around Ksh300. Daily 9am–midnight.

Jazz Pub Hospital Rd. Perennially popular and relaxed venue, with waiter service and an eclectic mix of sounds. Daily 7am–midnight.

Nile Hotel Hospital Rd. A very popular first-floor terrace restaurant, offering huge portions of Kenyan staples, plus a few more unusual items like sandwiches and pizza (Ksh400). The wrap-around balcony is a great place for hanging out and people-watching. Open 24hr.

Storm Restaurant Court Rd ☎058 30649 or 0727 630021. A cheery little courtyard restaurant and bar with checked tablecloths, though there's nothing unusual on the menu. *Nyama choma* costs from Ksh550/kg. Daily 5am–midnight.

Tea Room Old Skool Moi Highway. True to its name, this packed little eatery does a gorgeous cup of milky, sweet *chai*, along with snacks and all the usual local dishes (mains Ksh150). Open 24hr.

DIRECTORY

Banks There's a KCB on Hospital Rd, and a Barclays on Moi Hwy; both have ATMs.

Car repair If you're driving and need advice or assistance, try the very helpful Rangi Mbili parts store and workshop (☎058 30511; Mon–Sat 8am–5pm, Sun 8am–1pm).

Hospitals The main hospital is Kisii District in the northern part of town, at the end of Hospital Rd (☎058 30564); the private option is Ram Memorial Hospital on Court Rd (☎058 30236; Ksh500 consultation fee).

Internet access Frankona, on the second floor of a shopping mall on Moi Avenue (daily 8am–8pm; 50 cents/min).

Kericho and the tea country

Kericho, named after the early English tea planter John Kerich, is Kenya's **tea capital**, a fact that – with much hype from the tourism machine embellished by the presence of the *Tea Hotel* – is not likely to escape you. Its equable climate and famously reliable, year-round afternoon rain showers make it the most important tea-growing area in Africa. While many of the European estates have been divided and reallocated to small farmers since independence, the area is still dominated by giant tea plantations.

Kericho town

Compact **KERICHO** town seems as neat as the serried rows of bushes that surround it. The central square has shady trees and flowering shrubs – a bandstand would make it complete – and even the matatu park has lawns around it. It's a gentle, hassle-free place to wander, the people mild-mannered. In many ways, it's an oddity. Clipped, clean and functional, there's little of the shambolic appearance of most upcountry towns. With so many people earning some sort of salary on the tea plantations or in connection with them, and so few acres under food or market crops, the patterns of small-town life are changed here. Most workers live out on the estates, their families often left behind in their home villages.

Kericho is above all an administrative and shopping centre, and a relay point for the needs of the estates. The produce market is small, trading is limited and most places seem to close early. The town suffered badly during the 2007–8 election violence, with dozens killed and around 20,000 displaced. Things are calm now, but some say the historical resentment behind the violence remains, and that there is still tension between Kipsigis – the original inhabitants – and Kikuyus over land ownership.

There's a substantial Asian population in the town: note the vast Sikh **Gujwara** temple, whose superb gardens are worth a stroll. Many of the streets have a vaguely Oriental feel, with single-storey *dukas* fronted by colonnaded walkways where the plantation "memsahibs" of fifty years ago presumably did their shopping. This curious, composite picture is completed by the grey stone **Holy Trinity Church**, with its small assembly of deceased planters in a miniature cemetery. Straight out of the English shires, it tries so hard to be Norman that it's a pity to point out that it was only built in 1952. Unfortunately (at least from an aesthetic point of view) it is now overshadowed by the modernist **AIC Kericho Town Church**, with its welcoming perimeter of razor wire.

ARRIVAL AND DEPARTURE KERICHO

Kericho has hassle-free travel options in every direction: southwest to **Kisii** and **Migori**, east over the Mau Escarpment to **Nakuru via Molo** (see p.230), or northwest to **Kisumu** and **Kapsabet**. Heading south to the **Maasai Mara**, the first part of the route, to Bomet, follows a good road through splendid farming country and then links with the highway to Narok (see p.231). If you're going east, Nairobi and Nakuru buses and matatus generally originate in Kisumu and Kisii and pass through Kericho throughout the day and night. Kericho is fairly compact, fortunately, since if you don't have your own vehicle, **getting around** town can be a bit of a problem unless you walk, as there are very few town taxis, and no *boda-bodas*.

By matatu Matatus arrive at the main stage, on the north side of the centre opposite the market. Leaving Kericho, there are services to Eldoret (8–12 daily; 3hr 30min); Kisii (10–15 daily; 2hr); Kisumu (10–20 daily; 2hr); Molo (8–12 daily; 2hr); and Nairobi (10–20 daily; 4hr) via Nakuru (10–20 daily; 2hr).

By bus Buses in both directions pass through town on the Moi Highway; you can pick them up around the Total

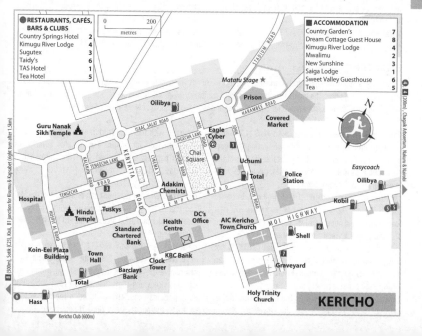

RESTAURANTS, CAFÉS, BARS & CLUBS
Country Springs Hotel	2
Kimugu River Lodge	4
Sugutex	3
Taidy's	6
TAS Hotel	1
Tea Hotel	5

ACCOMMODATION
Country Garden's	7
Dream Cottage Guest House	8
Kimugu River Lodge	4
Mwalimu	2
New Sunshine	3
Saiga Lodge	1
Sweet Valley Guesthouse	6
Tea	5

0   200
metres

STADIUM ROAD

Matatu Stage ★

Prison

Oilibya

HARAMBEE ROAD

Covered Market

Guru Nanak Sikh Temple

ISAAC SALAT ROAD

TENGECHA LANE

Eagle Cyber @

Chai Square

Uchumi

Total

Police Station

Easycoach

Oilibya

KENYATTA ROAD

CHEMASE ST

UHURU ROAD

KERICHO ROAD

Adakim Chemists

Hospital

TENGECHA LANE

MOI ROAD

JOHN

TEMPLE ROAD

Kobil

Hindu Temple

Tuskys

Health Centre

DC's Office

AIC Kericho Town Church

MOI HIGHWAY

Standard Chartered Bank

Shell

Koin-Eei Plaza Building

Town Hall

KBC Bank

Clock Tower

Barclays Bank

Graveyard

Total

Hass

Holy Trinity Church

KERICHO

Kericho Club (600m)

200m); Chagaik Arboretum, Nakuru & Nairobi

(500m); Sotik (C23); Kisii, B1 junction for Kisumu & Kapsabet (right turn after 1.5km)

4

station, where several bus companies also have offices. The EasyCoach office is at OiLibya (☎0726 354306; 24hr). Destinations include Busia (6 daily; 4hr); Kakamega (8–10 daily; 3hr); Kisumu (roughly hourly: 2hr); Nairobi (3–4 day and 3–4 night services; 6hr) via Nakuru (2hr).

ACCOMMODATION

★ **Country Garden's** Signposted down a dirt road behind the AIC Church ☎0721 157321. A wonderfully homely little cottage with a cosy communal sitting room and a handful of bright s/c rooms with flowered bedspreads. It feels just like a private house, with meals cooked on request and an expansive garden. You'll find a similar setup for the same price at *Sweet Valley Guesthouse* (down a dirt road past Shell; ☎0729 561779), which is run by the same family. BB **Ksh2000**

Dream Cottage Guest House Moi Highway, 700m west of Total on the south side of the road ☎0722 647240, ✉thedreamcottage@gmail.com. British-style BB with attentive management, offering ten rooms with big nets, instant showers and DSTV. A safe choice, and all very cosy, but strictly no alcohol served or allowed to be consumed on the premises. BB **Ksh3000**

Kimugu River Lodge Off Moi Highway, opposite the BP station, 700m northeast of the centre ☎0720 861079, ⊛kimuguriverlodge.com. Take the signposted turning and follow the track for 600m to reach this rather downmarket-looking but peaceful place, with a great location above the Kimugu River. The rooms in brick- and wood-panelled alpine-style chalets come with lots of hot water and are simple but comfortable (best are B and D), and there's also a decent bar and reasonable restaurant. BB **Ksh2000**

Mwalimu Moi Rd ☎0722 733663 or 0726 681753. Well-run cheapie in a bustling mini-mall. The 36 rooms are mostly a bit bigger and brighter than its miserable neighbour the *TAS*, but still lack nets or any added comforts – and don't expect hot water except in the mornings and evenings. Room only **Ksh650**

New Sunshine Tengecha Rd ☎052 30037 or 0724 146601. Well-run place that's easily the best in the town centre (though pricier than its neighbours), with small, neat, extremely clean rooms with TV, nets and instant showers. There's a busy *hoteli* downstairs, and safe courtyard parking. BB **Ksh1700**

Saiga Lodge John Kerich Rd ☎051 8011711. A surprisingly large establishment hidden away behind the shops, with a selection of very cheap s/c and non-s/c rooms, hot water, and parking in the yard. Rooms have nets and electric sockets but no fans, and most have inward-facing windows, so they're a bit dark. But decent value given the low price. Room only **Ksh600**

Tea Moi Highway ☎0714 510824, ⊛teahotel.co.ke. Built in 1952 by the Brooke Bond tea company, and at one time the best place in town, the *Tea Hotel* has been in slow decline ever since, though it retains a faded charm. Standard rooms are large and comfortable enough, with instant showers and nets but no fans or a/c, and would be quite overpriced if you weren't also getting the beautiful gardens and large swimming pool (non-residents Ksh100). Choose your room carefully as the main house can be noisy. You can also camp (Ksh500 per person) using room showers or the pool-changing facilities. BB **$95**

EATING AND DRINKING

If you're buying food, you'll find Kericho's **market** is best at weekends, when there's a greater variety of fruit, vegetables, snacks and spices at good prices. The town's best **supermarkets** are Tusky's (Mon–Sat 8am–8.30pm, Sun 9am–8pm) and Uchumi (daily 7.30am–8.30pm). Kericho has its fair share of cheap and fairly ungastronomic *hotelis*, heavy on the chips and *ugali*.

Country Springs Hotel Kenyatta Rd ☎0721 848497. A friendly little diner with family-style seating that gets quite busy at mealtimes, probably because it's one of the best options in town for cheap staples; pilau goes for a mere Ksh120. Daily 6am–9pm.

★ **Kimugu River Lodge** Off Moi Highway, opposite the BP station, 700m northeast of the centre. The best food in town (and not expensive), with an extensive menu of mainly Indian food (most dishes around Ksh400) including chicken *methi*, *malai kofta* and (although not always available) a wonderful crayfish *masala*. You can dine overlooking the Kimugu River. Mon–Fri noon–10pm, Sat & Sun 11am–10pm.

Taidy's Moi Highway, just past the Hass petrol station ☎0712 385555. Branch of the excellent Nakuru restaurant, with the same thick menu of pizzas, burgers and Indian food for around Ksh220, plus a range of decadent pastries. The attached sports bar turns into a fairly classy club on weekends. Restaurant daily 7am–1am, bar daily 11am–2am.

TAS Hotel Moi Rd. The busiest and best-value of the Moi Road *hotelis*, always lively and packed with workers at lunchtime. Tuck into a full breakfast for just Ksh180. Daily 6.30am–9pm.

Tea Hotel Moi Highway ☎0714 510824, ⊛teahotel.co.ke. For an upmarket hotel, the snack menu isn't particularly expensive, and they rarely go far wrong with club sandwiches and chips. Tea for two costs Ksh200; if you'd rather have good strong, boiled-in-the-pot, African tea, ask for *chai majani*. Daily 7am–10pm.

DIRECTORY

Banks The three main banks are on Moi Highway at the Kisumu end of town; all have ATMs.

Hospital Kericho boasts good medical facilities including the superior Central Hospital, 1km past the *Tea Hotel* on the Unilever tea estate.

Internet access There are several cybercafés on Moi Rd, including Eagle Cyber (Mon–Sat 8am–7pm; 65 cents/min).

Pharmacy Adkaim Chemists (☎ 0721 759977; Mon–Sat 7.30am–7.30pm, Sun 8.30am–7pm); there are no late-opening or night pharmacists.

Around Kericho

This is **tea country**: Kenya is the world's third-largest producer after India and Sri Lanka, and the biggest exporter to Britain. As you gaze across the dark green hills, you might pause to consider that the land, now covered in vast regimented swathes of tea bushes, was, until not much more than a century ago, virgin rainforest, only a tiny part of which, the Kakamega Forest, survives. The estates were first set up after World War I with tea bushes imported from India and China.

The tea estates

The factories generally operate daily except Mon (the day after the pickers' day off), though they might be open every day during rainy season; visits to tea factories are best booked several days in advance • Tours last 2hr (Ksh200/person, minimum two people, plus Ksh500 for transport if required); alternatively, you can just take a tour of the tea fields combined with a nature walk (Ksh200/person)

It is possible to **visit the tea estates** on a guided tour (enquire in the lobby of the *Tea Hotel*). The *Tea Hotel*'s guide can also be hired for **birding** excursions in the neighbourhood at Chagaik Arboretum, and to **Lelartet Cliff**, which is also home to a

4

TEA

Tea (*Camellia sinensis*) is a psychoactive shrub originally native to China. Its effects are said to have been discovered by the legendary third millennium BC Chinese emperor Shen Nung, who was apparently taking a cup of hot water in the shade of a shrub when one of the buds fell into it, making him an invigorating drink. For centuries the Chinese had a monopoly on tea, but with its rise in popularity at home, the British were keen for an independent source of supply, and eventually managed to smuggle some cuttings to India. In Kenya, tea was first grown in 1903, though it was nearly twenty years before commercial production got under way. Kenyan teas are known for their strength and full flavour, and are a major component of most commercial blends sold in the UK and Ireland. Kenya's other main customers are Egypt, Pakistan and Afghanistan.

Tea **production**, though not complicated, is very labour-intensive. Picking continues throughout the year, and you'll see the pickers moving through the bushes in their brilliant yellow-and-green (KETEPA) plastic smocks, nipping off the top two leaves and bud of each bush (nothing more is taken) and tossing them into baskets. Working fast, a picker can collect up to 70kg in a day, though half that is a more typical figure; the piece-rate is set at around eight shillings per kilo picked. After withering, mashing, a couple of hours' fermentation and a final drying in hot air, the tea leaves are ready for packing and export. The whole process can take as little as 24 hours.

Tea can be harvested three years after planting, and in the first year of production it must be picked every eight days, then every fourteen days in the second year and every seventeen in the fourth, after which the bush must be pruned to keep it at the right height for picking, which can begin again after three months. Weeding is not necessary as the foliage is sufficiently dense to prevent other plants from growing under it.

The stimulating **effects** of tea are due to the presence of caffeine, and a cup of strong tea can contain as much caffeine as a cup of medium-strength coffee. The effect feels different because it is moderated by other alkaloids such as thebaine, which is a relaxant. Because the human body requires fluid to process caffeine and thebaine, tea depletes the body of water, even though it appears to quench your thirst. Like beer, therefore, strong tea should not be taken as a fluid against dehydration.

large number of red colobus and black-and-white colobus monkeys. There's no fixed price for these trips; just tip as you see fit.

Kimugu Valley

Down in the **Kimugu Valley**, behind the *Tea Hotel* and *Kimugu River Lodge*, you can get some idea of what the land was like before the settlers arrived. Although vast swathes have recently been cleared for cultivation, most of the valley is still a deep, tangled channel of sprawling trees and undergrowth, with shafts of sunlight picking out clouds of butterflies. The cold brown waters of the Kimugu flow down from Chagaik Dam and allegedly harbour **trout**.

Chagaik Arboretum

Drive or get a lift in the Nairobi direction, past the KETEPA buildings, then take the right turn to Chagaik Dam, 6.5km from the *Kimugu River Lodge* (marked with a small white signpost saying "Kericho Forest Station"), then the first left, after which it's a 5min walk to the arboretum • Daily 7.30am–5.30pm • Free

A curious sight amid the closely cropped tea bushes, the graceful **Chagaik Arboretum** consists of acres of beautiful trees from across the tropics and subtropics, tumbling steeply down through well-tended lawns to a lily-covered lake. Inside the arboretum, a plaque reads "Founded by Tom Grumbley, Tea Planter 1946–75". Don't miss the magnificent stands of bamboo on the banks. Entry to this haven of landscaped tranquillity is unrestricted and you can picnic or rest up as long as you like, though there are gardeners around who won't let you camp. It gets quite popular at weekends and holidays when families come out here to enjoy the space and air. Across the lake, thick **jungle** drops to the water's edge. Mysterious splashes and rustles, prolific bird and insect life, and at least one troop of colobus monkeys are a surprising testament to the tenacity of wildlife in an environment hemmed in on all sides by the alien ranks of the tea bushes.

Eldoret and around

The direct journey from Kericho to Eldoret through the **Nandi Hills** is one of the most varied and spectacular in the west, through countryside that is often far wilder than you'd expect, including bleak mountainous scrublands and jungle-packed ravines. Midway, you cross the Kano Plains and you may have to change transport at **Chemelil**, a major crossroads in the Nyando valley, down in the flat sugar lands. Beyond, the road zigzags northwards into high tea country again, the homeland of the **Nandi**, the fiercest early opponents of the British, and the haunt of a crypto-zoological mystery known as the **Nandi bear** (see box, p.284). The only town of any size before Eldoret is **Kapsabet**, which has a couple of banks, a market, and a trio of reasonable lodgings, but nothing to warrant a stopover unless, again, you need to change matatus. If you're driving, you might pause at the **Kingwal swamp**, north of Kapsabet (the road passes right through it), where more than sixty **sitatunga** antelope (see p.290) hang on in an unprotected wetland area.

Although more bustling than Kericho, and somewhat healthier and pleasanter than Nakuru, **ELDORET** really has hardly anything to differentiate it from dozens of other highland centres, though as Kenya's fifth-largest town, it's a good deal bigger. The **Uasin Gishu Plateau** all around is reliably fertile cereal, vegetable and stock-raising country; wattle plantations provide the tannin for the town's leather industry; the Raymond, Rivatex, Raiply and Ken-Knit **textile factories** provide employment; and **Moi University** has proved a shot in the arm for local schools. Eldoret's prosperity is shown clearly enough by the windows of Eldoret Jewellers on the main road.

Though there are no sights as such to keep you here for very long, you may well find Eldoret a useful stopover, and it's refreshingly unthreatening and friendly despite its

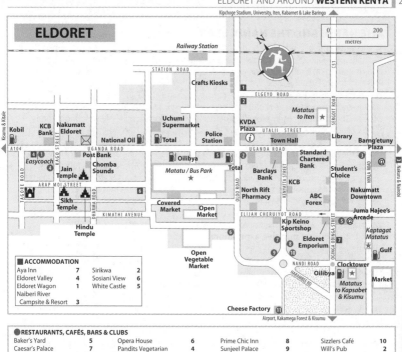

Kipchoge Stadium, University, Iten, Kabarnet & Lake Baringo

ELDORET

Railway Station

STATION ROAD

Crafts Kiosks

ELGEYO ROAD

Uchumi
Supermarket

KVDA
Plaza   UTALII STREET

Matatus
to Iten

Police
Station

Town Hall

Library

Barng'etuny
Plaza

Kobil   KCB   Nakumatt
Bank   Eldoret

National Oil   Total

UGANDA ROAD

UGANDA ROAD

Standard
Chartered
Bank

Post Bank

Easycoach

Chomba
Sounds

Oilibya

Matatu / Bus Park

Total

Barclays
Bank

KCB

Student's
Choice

Nakumatt
Downtown

Jain
Temple

ARAP MOI STREET

North Rift
Pharmacy

ABC
Forex

Juma Hajee's
Arcade

Sikh
Temple

KIMATHI AVENUE

Covered
Market

Open
Market

ELIJAH CHERUIYOT ROAD

Kip Keino
Sportshop

Kaptagat
Matatus

Hindu
Temple

Eldoret
Emporium

Gulf

Open
Vegetable
Market

NANDI ROAD   Clocktower

ACCOMMODATION

Aya Inn	7	Sirikwa	2
Eldoret Valley	4	Sosiani View	6
Eldoret Wagon	1	White Castle	5
Naiberi River Campsite & Resort	3		

Oilibya

Matatus
to Kapsabet
& Kisumu

Market

Cheese Factory

Airport, Kakamega Forest & Kisumu

4

RESTAURANTS, CAFÉS, BARS & CLUBS

Baker's Yard	5	Opera House	6	Prime Chic Inn	8	Sizzlers Café	10
Caesar's Palace	7	Pandits Vegetarian	4	Sunjeel Palace	9	Will's Pub	2
Doinyo Lessos Creamery	11	Places	1	Siam	3		

size. The town's affluence is reflected in a wide variety of places to stay, eat and drink, and enough nightlife to see you through an evening or two.

Brief history

Eldoret was initially a backwoods post office on Farm 64, later chosen in 1912 as an administrative centre because the farm's soil was poor and the deeds were never taken up by the owner. The name started as Eldare (a river), was then Nandi-ized to Eldaret, and finally misprinted in the *Official Gazette* as Eldoret.

Before the town existed, the area was settled by **Afrikaners**. They gave it much of the dour worthiness that seems to have characterized its first half-century and which is perceptible even today – though most of the Boers trekked on after Kenya's independence. In the era of **President Moi**, whose roots were in nearby Kabarnet, Eldoret was a special focus for investment and development: this is when its university was founded and its "international" airport opened. Although most modern inhabitants are Kalenjin-language-speakers from the Elgeyo and Nandi tribes, there are also Somali-speakers, the remnants of the European settler community, and a long-established and respected Asian community (Juma Hajee's supermarket, now a shopping arcade, is the oldest business in the town).

In addition, there are enough immigrants from the rest of Kenya for Eldoret to have been a brutal flashpoint in the **post-election violence** of 2007–8. This culminated in the massacre of more than forty Kikuyu people, including many children, in an arson attack on the Assemblies of God church in the suburb of Kiambaa, where they had taken refuge. Outwardly, Eldoret has already recovered from the trauma of the clashes: most Kikuyu fled the area, as did members of many other non-Rift Valley and non-Western tribes, some of whom seem resigned to staying in internally displaced

4

THE NANDI AND THE NANDI BEAR

At the end of the nineteenth century, the **Nandi** (dialects of whose language are spoken by all the Kalenjin peoples) were probably in the strongest position in their history. Their warriors had drummed up a reputation for such ferocity and daring that much of western Kenya lived in fear of them. Even the Maasai, at a low point in their own fortunes, suffered repeated losses of livestock to Nandi spearsmen, whose prestige accumulated with every herd of cattle driven back to their stockades. The Nandi even crossed the Rift Valley to raid Subukia and the Laikipia plateau. They were intensely protective of their own territory, relentlessly xenophobic and fearful of any adulteration of their way of life. Foreigners of any kind were welcome only with express permission.

With the killing of a British traveller, Peter West, who tried to cross their country in 1895, the Nandi opened a decade of guerrilla warfare against the British. Above all, they repeatedly frustrated attempts to lay the railway line and keep communications open with Uganda. They dismantled the "iron snake", transformed the copper telegraph wires into jewellery, and took whatever livestock and provisions they could find. Despite increased security, the establishment of forts, and some efforts to reach agreements with Nandi elders, the raiding went on, often costing the lives of African soldiers and policemen under the British. In retaliation, a series of **punitive expeditions** shot more than a thousand Nandi warriors (about one young man in ten), captured tens of thousands of head of livestock, and torched scores of villages. The war was ended by the killing of Koitalel Arap Samoiei, the *Orkoiyot* or spiritual head of the Nandi who, having agreed to a temporary truce, was then murdered at a meeting with a delegation led by the British officer Richard Meinertzhagen, who shot him in cold blood (see p.591). As expected, resistance collapsed. His people had believed Koitalel to be unassailable and the Nandi were subsequently hounded into a reserve and their lands opened to settlers.

Traditionally keepers of livestock, the Nandi have turned to agriculture with little enthusiasm and focus instead on their district's milk production, the highest in Kenya. *Shambas*, however, are widespread enough to make your chances of seeing a **Nandi bear**, the source of scores of Yeti-type rumours, remote. Variously said to resemble a bear, a big wild dog or a very large ape, the Nandi bear is believed to have been exterminated in most areas. But in the less accessible regions, on the way up to Kapsabet, many locals believe it still exists – they call it *chemoset*. Exactly what it is is another matter, but it doesn't seem to inspire quite the terror you might expect; the occasional savagely mutilated sheep and cattle reported in the press are probably attributable to leopards. A giant anthropoid ape, perhaps a gorilla, seems the most likely candidate for the original *chemoset*, and the proximity of the Kakamega Forest may account for the stories. This is a surviving tract of the rainforest that once stretched in a continuous belt across equatorial Africa and is still home to many western and central African species of wildlife (though not giant apes). The *chemoset* possibly survived up until the early twentieth century in isolated valleys, even if it is now extinct. Whatever the truth, if you camp out in the Nandi Hills, you won't need reminding to zip your fly-sheet.

person (IDP) camps in the district for years. But the anger released did nothing to resolve the tensions that remain.

Beyond Eldoret

Beyond the small centre of **Kaptagat** and **Kaptagat Forest**, which has a few trails and is a nice place for walks, runs the unpaved route down to the fluorspar mine at **KIMWARER**. Believe it or not, this used to be the main way across the Kerio Valley, and although it no longer sees much traffic, you can usually hitch a ride with a lorry travelling to or from the mine – an incredible hairpin descent that seems to go on forever. Route details for the Kerio Valley continue in the Rift Valley chapter (see p.240).

In the other direction (northwest) out of Eldoret, the only real town is **SOY**, 9km past the B2/A104 junction, formerly a tiny community but now a sizeable centre. Beyond Soy, the road continues through **MATUNDA**, formerly the railway station of Springfield

Halt (18km past Soy and 25km short of Kitale), and the small trading centre of **MOI'S BRIDGE**, 21km short of Kitale.

ARRIVAL AND DEPARTURE ELDORET

Eldoret sprawls widely and inelegantly in all directions, stretching some 10km along the highway. The whole place can be a real bottleneck, and it can easily take 30min to get through town from one end to the other. If you want to **park** here you'll need a ticket, sold by the parking wardens all over town (Ksh100; valid 24hr). Heading directly **to Uganda** by bus or matatu, there's little to delay your progress to Malaba on the border, via Webuye and Bungoma. For the **Kakamega Forest**, take a bus or matatu going to Kisumu via Kapsabet, and get off at the D267 turning about 20km west of Kapsabet (signposted "Kisieni 12km"), from where you might be able to hitch a lift; otherwise it's a walk of about 3hr to the *Forest Rest House*.

By plane Eldoret airport (☎053 2063377) is 16km south of town on the Kapsabet road and has twice-daily flights with Fly540 to Nairobi ($69; 1hr).

By matatu The main matatu stage is at the east end of Arap Moi St. Matatus from the main stage run to Kakamega, Kisumu, Kitale and Kaptagat. Matatus for Iten and Kabarnet (with connections to Lake Baringo and Lake Bogoria) leave from the stage on the corner of Oginga Odinga and Utalii streets using the spectacular Tambach Escarpment route.

Destinations Cherangani (3–6 daily; 2hr); Kabarnet (4–5 daily; 2hr) via Iten (6–8 daily; 45min); Kakamega (6–10 daily; 3hr); Kaptagat (4–5 daily; 30min); Kitale (8–12 daily; 1hr 45min); Malaba (4–6 daily; 2–3hr).

By bus The EasyCoach office is next to the Eldoret Valley on Uganda Road (☎0738 200308), from where buses run twice a day to Nairobi (10am & 10pm; 8hr) via Nakuru (2hr 30min). Destinations Kitale (6 daily; 1hr 45min); Malaba (2 daily; 2–3hr); Nairobi (6–8 daily; 8hr) via Nakuru (2hr 30min).

INFORMATION

Banks Barclays, Standard Chartered and KCB all have ATMs. There's also Safari Forex in KVDA Plaza (Mon–Fri 8.30am–4.30pm, Sat 9am–1pm), but they don't take small bills and give slightly lower rates for travellers' cheques.

Internet There are numerous internet cafés in

Barng'etuny Plaza including U.G. Communications (Mon–Sat 8am–7pm; Ksh1/2min).

Tourist office On the second floor of KVDA Plaza ☎053 2032086. Not much in the way of handouts, but staff are very helpful with information on local attractions. Mon–Fri 8am–5pm.

ACCOMMODATION

ELDORET

Eldoret has no shortage of accommodation, though cheap places tend to be grubby or clearly intended for "short-term guests". Campers should consider heading out to the lovely *Naiberi River Campsite & Resort* (see p.286).

Aya Inn Oginga Odinga St ☎053 2062259, ✉ayainn @africaonline.co.ke. A friendly place with clean rooms (though some are a bit dark), nets and instant showers. There's good security and safe parking, and the two rowdy but good-natured bars aren't bad options for a drink. BB **Ksh900**

Eldoret Valley Uganda Rd ☎053 2032314 or 0722 816108. Small but scrupulously clean rooms in an orderly B&L established more than thirty years ago. The nearby *Places* disco makes rooms at the back noisy, though, so while it's very good value, it won't suit everyone. The restaurant serves decent Kenyan fare and good tea. BB **Ksh900**

⭐ **Eldoret Wagon** Elgeyo Rd ☎053 2062270, ⓦeldoretwagonhotel.co.ke. Helpful, friendly, charmingly old-fashioned but professionally managed, the *Wagon* has 102 light, airy rooms, with nets, TV and instant showers, and a *nyama choma* bar. The Eldoret Jambo Casino is by the front gate and the whole place gets quite lively at weekends.

Unusually, they take most credit cards. Very good value. BB **Ksh3600**

Sirikwa Elgeyo Rd ☎053 2063614 or 0728 680000, ⓦhotelsirikwa.com. The town's "premier" hotel, this monolithic and faintly pompous pile is fairly bright and clean, although rooms are very tired and overpriced – it's supposedly due for a renovation soon. Discounting the pool, which is in good shape (non-residents Ksh200), the more low-key and much cheaper *Eldoret Wagon*, opposite, is a better bet any day. BB **Ksh5800**

Sosiani View Arap Moi St ☎053 2033215. Situated by the transport terminus, this five-storey block has good views – the best are from the fifth floor, which is also the quietest – and nice large s/c rooms with nets, but primitive plumbing. The first-floor bar is a good place for a beer. BB **Ksh800**

White Castle Uganda Rd ☎053 2061362, ✉eldoret whitecastlemotel@yahoo.com. Although first impressions are very unpromising – a bland modern building on the noisy main road through town – the rooms turn out to be better than average, spacious and comfy, with bathtubs (but old-fashioned showers). There's a lift, and even a sauna and health club. Most credit cards accepted. BB **Ksh2650**

BEYOND ELDORET

Kaptagat Hotel 1km off the main road 5km east of Naiberi River Campsite ☎0722 778654. More sedate than the Naiberi River Campsite, this colonial anachronism survives from the days when British aristocrats roamed the neighbourhood. The hotel is set in extensive and beautiful grounds, and there's excellent birdwatching from the terraces of the cottages, which come with wooden floors, open fires and the dodgy bathroom plumbing you'd expect from such an old establishment. There's also a bar and TV lounge and meals can be rustled up (assuming you have plenty of time). BB `Ksh2800`

★ **Naiberi River Campsite & Resort** 16km east of Eldoret, 400m off the Kaptagat Road ☎0722 686512, ⓦnaiberi.com. A very popular stop for independent overlanders and tour trucks heading for Uganda, with a scenic location above the small Naiberi River and comfortable, s/c cabin-style rooms, plus dorm beds (Ksh1100 or Ksh1500 with good, shared showers and toilets) and camping (Ksh500 per person). The centrepiece is a sprawling and enjoyable pub-restaurant built into the hillside, incorporating streams and waterfalls, a central fireplace and the remains of what are said to be Sirikwa holes (see p.243). The chef cooks up excellent, sizzling, hot-plate dishes and other meals. It's a delightfully relaxing place to hang out for a day or two, the hilly grounds leading down to the river, and a sparkling (if chilly) swimming pool making it hard to tear yourself away. Driving here, turn east towards Kaptagat 3km southeast of Eldoret town centre on the Nairobi road then drive 15.3km and *Naiberi* is on your left. Call ahead for a lift from town. BB `Ksh5000`

EATING AND DRINKING

Eldoret has plenty of good places to grab a bite, with a clutch of established snack bars, several options for dinner, and one or two evening haunts. For your own supplies, head for the markets west of Oloo Road, or a branch of the Nakumatt **supermarket**: choose between the big 24hr Nakumatt Downtown in Oginga Odinga St, or Nakumatt Eldoret on Uganda Rd (Mon–Sat 8.30am–10pm, Sun 9.30am–9pm). It's also worth a visit to **Doinyo Lessos Creamery and Cheese Factory** (daily 8am–6pm), at the end of the track south of Kenyatta St. This little place has been making top-quality European-style cheese, yogurt and ice cream since 1964, and although they don't have a shop per se, you can buy their products directly from the factory window (minimum purchase 250g for cheese, at around Ksh500–800/kg).

Baker's Yard Juma Hajee's Arcade, Elijah Cheruiyot Rd. Excellent place that tempts you in with the aroma of warm bread, which is sold alongside biscuits, pies, cakes, pastries (Ksh35–70) and good filter coffee. Mon–Sat 7am–6.30pm.

★ **Pandits Vegetarian** Kago St ☎0729 039099. Charming snacks and sweetmeats shop, and an excellent place for vegetarian Indian meals including thalis and some good lunch specials. Mains around Ksh380. Mon–Sat 8am–6pm, Sun 8am–5pm.

Prime Chic Inn Kenyatta St. Fast-food place with high standards and keen prices, offering chicken, burgers, fry-ups and chips every which way. Half a chicken goes for Ksh400. Open 24hr.

Siam Nyala Rd, corner of Uganda Rd ☎053 2060402. The Chinese dishes, with the accent on chilli, aren't bad, though at around Ksh480 they're a bit pricey. What makes it worthwhile are the great-value lunchtime specials: Ksh460 for a main dish, a spring roll and a drink. Mon–Fri noon–3pm & 6–10.30pm, Sat & Sun noon–4pm & 6–10.30pm.

Sizzlers Café Kenyatta St ☎053 2031259. Popular American-style diner, offering speedy, high-quality burgers (Ksh165), excellent samosas, ice cream and other desserts. Mon–Sat 9am–6pm.

★ **Sunjeel Palace** Kenyatta St ☎053 2030568 or 0720 554747. Operating very much in British-style Indian-restaurant mode, this is where Eldoret's Asian community often comes for a good meal out, usually ordering ahead (allow at least 30min) from a selection of fine curries (veg and non-veg), plus good *naan*. Expect to pay Ksh600–800/head, without drinks. Daily 11.30am–11pm.

Will's Pub Uganda Rd ☎053 2062379. Mostly patronized by local businessmen, this is a good place for a beer, but also for solid Kenyan food and snacks, including tasty meat samosas. Full breakfasts Ksh400, pizzas Ksh450. Sun–Thurs 9am–11pm, Fri & Sat until midnight.

NIGHTLIFE

Most of the following places charge a small entry fee at weekends but are free during the week.

Caesar's Palace Kenyatta St. A revamped disco, loud and enjoyable, with salsa night on Wed. It's generally packed at weekends when they play soul, ragga and hip-hop, with live English and European football on screen. Daily 5pm–late.

Opera House Oloo Rd. Very firmly established nightspot (pronounced "O-pair-a", not "Oprah") playing live reggae on Fri & Sat until dawn. The rest of the week it's basically just a bar. Sun–Thurs 5pm–late, Fri & Sat 1pm–late.

Places Uganda Rd. Sophisticated decor, a sunken dance-floor, and a fairly well-mannered clientele, with snacks available and good DJs. Music is mainly Western disco. Daily 6pm–3am.

SHOPPING

Chomba Sounds Music Store Dharma Rd ☎0722 747675. Offers lots of local sounds. Mon–Sat 8.30am–6.45pm.

Eldoret Emporium Corner of Elijah Cheruiyot and Oginga Odinga streets ☎0711 108694. A good selection of Kenyan books. Mon–Sat 8.30am–6pm.

Kip Keino Sports Shop Kenyatta St ☎0723 878086. Set up by athlete and Christian philanthropist Kepchugi Keino. Keino's double gold at the 1964 Olympics blazed a trail that has since been followed by other Kenyan runners,

mainly from around Eldoret. It's a small place, but still good for sports equipment and clothing. Mon–Fri 8am–5.30pm, Sat 8am–1pm.

Souvenirs Check out the row of crafts traders on Oloo Road, near the station.

Student's Choice Oginga Odinga St ☎053 2063740. Like Eldoret Emporium, has a decent range of Kenyan books – it's also easier to browse and also carries a few foreign titles. Mon–Sat 8.30am–5.30pm.

Kitale

KITALE is smaller than Eldoret, and not much more exciting, but has more going for it from a traveller's point of view, primarily as the base for visits to **Mount Elgon**, Kenya's second giant volcanic cone, and the superb, very underrated hiking country in the area. It's also an obvious springboard for the **Cherangani Hills**, and a straightforward departure point for trips to the west side of **Lake Turkana**. There's a **national park** nearby – the little-known but easily accessible **Saiwa Swamp**, which can only be explored on foot. In addition, the town also has two **museums** and a couple of other sites to visit.

The town's present population is a mix of tribes, including Nandi, Pokot, Marakwet, Sabaot and Sengwer, as well as a few Luhya, Kisii and Kikuyu and an influential Asian community. Like most towns in the Rift Valley and Western provinces, it was seriously affected by the post-election clashes of 2007–8, but managed to make a swift recovery.

Brief history

Originally Quitale, a relay station on the old slave route between Uganda and Bagamoyo in Tanzania, the modern town was founded in 1920 as the capital of Trans-Nzoia District. When the first white settlers arrived after World War I, this vale of rich grasslands between Mount Elgon and the Cherangani Hills was supposedly

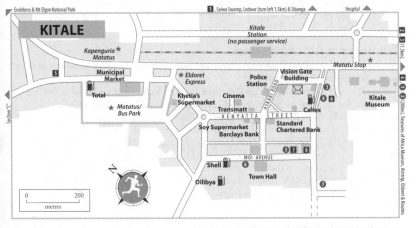

■ ACCOMMODATION					● RESTAURANTS, CAFÉS, BARS & CLUBS			
Barnley's Guesthouse	1		Kitale Highview Hotel	8	Amboseli Ranch	5	Iroko Twigs Café	4
Iroko Twigs Hotel	6		Mid Africa	7	Coffee Shop Kitale	3	Kitale Club	1
Karibuni Lodge	4		Muremba Retreat	2	Elgon View	2	Makuti Club	7
Kitale Club	3		Takrim Lodge	5	Iroko Roots Café	6		

almost uninhabited. But just a few years earlier it had been a Maasai grazing area, and a group of people who consider themselves Maasai still live on the eastern slopes of Elgon. With the arrival of the railway in 1925, the town and the region around it began to flourish, with a fantastic array of fruit, cereals, vegetables and livestock, and all the attendant settler paraphernalia of agricultural and flower shows, church fetes and gymkhanas. This heady era lasted barely forty years, but the region's **agriculture** is still famous; almost anything, including such exotic fruit as apples and pears, can be grown here. The Kitale Show is held each year in late October or early November.

Kitale Museum

Southeast of the town centre on the road to Eldoret • Daily 8.30am–5.30pm • Ksh500 • ☎ 054 30996

Originally the "Stoneham Museum", a collection opened to the public by a lieutenant colonel on his Cherangani farm in 1927, the **Kitale Museum** was transferred here in 1972. For the most part, Stoneham's curious collections are just that: collected curiosities in striking contrast to the recent, more educationally motivated, Kenyan additions.

The main hall contains interesting **ethnographic displays** on Pokot, Elkony (Elgon), Luhya, Maasai, Turkana and Luo, with artefacts such as Kamba carvings (including skin-covered animals and smooth polished abstracts); a Pokot goat bell made from a tortoise shell; and intricate Turkana belts and beadwork. In the small room to the right of the entrance in the main building is an old piano and accordion and a collection of traditional **musical instruments**, which really are becoming museum pieces as younger generations embrace more cosmopolitan musical genres (though you can buy cassettes of traditional Luhya music in town). Outside, the re-creations of Nandi and Luhya **homesteads** make an interesting point of comparison with the realities of present-day villages.

Agroforestry Project

Next to the Kitale Museum (though the entrance is 300m further east) • Daily 8am–5pm • Free • ☎ 020 4180201, ⓦ bit.ly/Agroforestrykitale

The Swedish Co-operative Centre's **Agroforestry Project** was set up to educate cultivators in Trans-Nzoia and West Pokot about the basics of tree planting. This accomplished, it now deals with soil erosion and overgrazing, and offers practical advice to farmers on the selection of species best suited to local conditions. There's a small gallery and demonstration *shamba*, showcasing sound techniques for increasing crop yield.

Treasures of Africa Museum

1.7km from the town centre, northeast of the main road to Eldoret, 200m past the Kitale Club • Hours are irregular, though there's usually someone around to let you in • Ksh500 • ☎ 054 30867

The quirkiest of Kitale's sites is the **Treasures of Africa Museum**. Run by John Wilson, a retired former colonial administrator in Uganda, the museum displays cultural artefacts, mainly from the Karamojong pastoralists of northern Uganda. The exhibits are arranged in robustly un-scientific fashion to illustrate the proprietor's case, based on supposed linguistic parallels between Karamojong and other languages, such as Gaelic, that a single worldwide farming culture existed tens of thousands of years before what is normally believed to be the case. The curator-proprietor is usually on hand to explain his theory in person, but if you want to be sure of a guided tour – and the visit is fascinating – it's best to call in advance of your visit.

Kitale Nature Conservancy

About 5km north of Kitale en route to Saiwa Swamp and Kapenguria • Daily 8am–6pm • $10 • ☎ 0720 309108, ⓦ kitalenature.or.ke

The **Kitale Nature Conservancy** is a small zoo ostensibly geared toward conservation, but the real focus is on its bizarre collection of natural freaks and oddities – five-legged cows and the like – that would normally be slaughtered at birth. It's all a bit grotesque and some locals claims that the animals aren't cared for as well as they should be, but if you can stomach it the place is still morbidly fascinating.

ARRIVAL AND DEPARTURE   KITALE

By plane The airport is 6km southwest of town, off the A1 road to Webuye. There's currently one daily flight to Nairobi with Fly540 ($109; 1hr).

By matatu Matatus spill out from the stage near the municipal market onto the adjoining main road, and there's a smaller gathering of Nissans bound for Eldoret, Kakamega and Kisumu opposite the Kitale Museum on the corner of the Lodwar road. For Mount Elgon, regular matatus (2–3 daily; 1hr) make the trip to *Mount Elgon Lodge* near the national park's Chorlim Gate. Otherwise, the next closest destination is Endebess, reached quickly enough by regular matatus. Southwards, Kisumu is no more than 3hr away down the busy and bumpy A1.

Destinations Cherangani (3–6 daily; 30min); Eldoret (8–12 daily; 1hr 45min); Endebess (6–8 daily; 30min); Kipsaina (10 daily; 30min); Kisumu (6–12 daily; 3hr); Makutano for Kapenguria (10 daily; 40min); Nairobi (10–

15 daily; 7hr) via Nakuru (5hr).

By bus Most buses leave from the bus park in the west of town, or the streets around it. Eldoret Express run regular buses to Nairobi (8hr) via Eldoret (1hr 45min) and Nakuru (4hr 30min), leaving when full – roughly every hour – from the main bus park. There are also services to Lodwar (6 daily; 12hr) and Mombasa (1 daily; 16hr). The road to Lodwar for Lake Turkana (see p.513) is in such an appalling condition beyond Marich that it may as well not be paved at all. There are several buses a day (but no matatus), most in the afternoon. Remember to take water, and also to stock up on provisions, as you'll only find more basic stuff on sale further north (fresh fruit and vegetables are expensive and poor quality in Lodwar).

By car If you're driving yourself, be sure you've got plenty of food and water in case of a breakdown, and note that there is nowhere to get fuel between Ortum and Lodwar.

INFORMATION

Services The local branches of Barclays and SCB banks, both on Kenyatta St, have ATMs. For internet access, try the

Silver Springs Centre at the eastern end of Askari Rd (daily 7.30am–6.30pm; Ksh1/min).

ACCOMMODATION

In town, there are quite a few cheap lodgings, the very cheapest of which are at the grubby north end of town, past the market. For mid-range hotels, you're spoilt for choice, but there's nothing top-end. You can camp at *Karibuni Lodge*. *Barnley's Guesthouse* (p.292) near Saiwa Swamp is also an excellent option for those who don't mind being based a bit further afield.

★ **Iroko Twigs Hotel** Kenyatta St, behind Iroko Twigs Café ☎0773 475884, ✉kmuyundo@yahoo.com. Conveniently located right in the centre of town, these are the most luxurious and sophisticated rooms in Kitale, decked out with wood floors, gleaming new bathrooms, DSTV and enormous double beds. The only down side is that inward-facing windows make them a bit dark. BB **Ksh3500**

★ **Karibuni Lodge** Milimani district, 2km from the town centre (heading for Eldoret, turn left at Total) ☎0706 043618, ⓦkaribunikitale.com. A very nice place catering to NGOs and backpackers, with camping (Ksh400 per person), dorm beds (Ksh750) and s/c rooms with nets and hot water set in pleasingly rustic cabins scattered throughout the garden. The owner does a good line in locally sourced home cooking, including vegetarian options. Guests also have use of the kitchen. BB **Ksh2300**

Kitale Club 1.5km out on the road towards Eldoret ☎0726 610241, ✉ktlclub@rocketmail.com. On the site of the former slave headquarters, offering old cottages with cement floors, a new block with larger rooms and wooden

floors, and new cottages with wooden floors, TVs and fireplaces. The price includes temporary membership and access to club facilities including the golf course (Ksh1000) and pool (Ksh200). Not a bad option if you don't mind wading through the slightly stuffy club rules. BB **Ksh5300**

Kitale Highview Hotel Moi Ave ☎0325 31570, ✉kcchm2010@gmail.com. Friendly high-rise hotel with good, breezy and relatively clean s/c rooms with nets, and a decent balcony restaurant. The luxury rooms, which cost slightly more than the ordinary ones, are much bigger and come with a sitting area. BB **Ksh1800**

Mid Africa Moi Ave ☎0727 277077, ⓦmidafricahotel .com. A relatively slick multistorey hotel popular with business travellers, though these days it's starting to look a bit dour. Still, there's a reasonable restaurant and rooftop *nyama choma* bar, and the s/c rooms (some with balconies) have wi-fi and DSTV. Cheaper non-s/c rooms are available too. BB **Ksh3900**

Muremba Retreat Wamalwa St, Milimani district, 2km out of town ☎0722 716070, ⓦmuremba retreatkitale.com. A cosy house in a big garden with seven rooms, all quite comfortable, though the best are the two rooms in the wooden cottage with a sauna. Staff are attentive, and the breakfast is very good. BB `Ksh4000`

Takrim Lodge Main road, northern end of town ☎0725 496394. Basic but dirt cheap, Somali-run and by a mosque, with quite a Middle Eastern feel. The clean, s/c rooms have cold showers, with hot water provided in a bucket on request. Room only `Ksh250`

EATING, DRINKING AND NIGHTLIFE

Kitale has several quite good **places to eat**, including the local *Iroko* franchise, and after dark a number of places provide for drink and lively conversation. The best places to stock up on provisions are the Transmatt **supermarket** on Kanyatta St (daily 8am–7pm) and Khetia's near the bus park (daily 8am–7.30pm).

Amboseli Ranch Roof of the Mid Africa Hotel, Moi Ave. Cheerful rooftop *nyama choma* bar with views of Mt Elgon plus football matches on TV. Ksh300 for a half kilo of meat. Daily 11am–11pm.

★ **Coffee Shop Kitale** Corner of Kenyatta St and the Eldoret road ☎0717 604068. This very nice establishment is a good spot to start the day, combining a café-bistro with tourist information and crafts sales. Food includes breakfasts, sandwiches (Ksh300) and Mexican, and there's also wi-fi. Mon–Sat 8.30am–4.30pm, Sun 9.30am–4.30pm.

Elgon View Eldoret road, 1km southeast of the centre ☎0722 553144. The most upscale restaurant in town, with views of the mountain from the garden out the back and a menu of Chinese-inspired dishes alongside tasty Indian offerings, including plenty of vegetarian options. Mains around Ksh400. Daily 11.30am–10pm.

★ **Iroko Roots Café** Moi Ave. A perennial favourite for cheap but tasty Kenyan food, always packed with a mix of locals and tourists dining on delicious stews, curries and pilau (Ksh80–200). Open 24hr.

Iroko Twigs Café Kenyatta St ☎0773 475884. Sister establishment to *Iroko Roots*, always busy and equally nice, but with more Western food on the menu – think soups, salads and sandwiches (most dishes around Ksh350). Daily 7am–9.30pm.

Kitale Club 1.5km out on the Eldoret road ☎0726 610241. Serves a mix of Indian and European dishes, all heavy on the meat, in a rather old-fashioned dining room; dishes are around Ksh400, but there's a Ksh500 membership surcharge to eat here. Better value are the two bars, including an atmospheric wood-panelled sports bar and a lounge with expansive views onto the golf course. Daily 6.30am–10pm.

Makuti Club Entrance down a dirt road off Kenyatta St. The most popular club in town, with DJs spinning a mix of East African and Western rock music. Step off the dance-floor for a game of pool or a greasy plateful of *nyama choma*. Daily 5pm–late.

Saiwa Swamp National Park

$20 • ☎0717 672121, Ⓦ kws.go.ke • 1.9 square kilometres

Created specifically for the protection of the **sitatunga**, a rare and vulnerable semi-aquatic antelope, **Saiwa Swamp National Park** is the smallest in the country and is rarely visited, despite its accessibility, which is a pity. The requirement that you walk (rather than drive) around the jungle and swamp, plus the chance of seeing the antelope as well as various monkeys and birds, makes it an exciting and interesting day out. If you're staying at *Barnley's* (see p.292), think about hiring a guide there for the trip, which is worthwhile and not at all expensive.

Wildlife-watching

You're almost bound to see one of the park's **sitatunga**, an unusual species of antelope which lives most of its life partly submerged in water and weed. Similar in size and general appearance to the bushbuck, the sitatunga is reddish-brown with a slightly shaggy coat and very large ears, while the males have spiral horns. The sitatunga's most unusual features (usually hidden in water) are their strangely splayed and elongated hooves, evolved, it's believed, to help prevent them sink as they pick their way gingerly through their native swamps. It's hard to see how much help these feet really are in keeping the antelope from sinking into the swamp, as the hooves are only moderately elongated: the theory makes sense, but evolution has a little more work to do here. Due

BLUE MONKEY, KAKAMEGA FOREST (P.303) >

to poaching, numbers in the park are down from more than seventy in the 1980s to fewer than twenty at the last count.

Sitatunga can be found in scattered locations throughout western and central Africa, but in Kenya they are restricted to Saiwa Swamp, the Kingwal swamp south of Eldoret (see p.282), a few spots around Lake Victoria, and Lewa Downs, which has a translocated group (see p.504). Only at Saiwa Swamp, however, have they grown really used to humans. They can be watched from **observation platforms**, which have been built in the trees at the side of the swamp – two on the east side, two on the west. These somewhat precarious, Tarzan-esque structures enable you to spy down on the life in the reeds, while one of them – *Treetop House* – has been converted into a snug overnight stay (see below). The best times for sitatunga-spotting are early morning and, to a lesser extent, late afternoon.

The drier parts of the park also shelter **bushbuck**, easily distinguished from the sitatunga by their terrified, crashing escape through the undergrowth as you approach. As well as the antelopes, Saiwa Swamp is a magnet for ornithologists, with a number of unusual **bird species**, including several turacos, many kingfishers, and the splendid black-and-white casqued hornbill. Most conspicuous of all are the **crowned cranes** – elegance personified when not airborne, but whose lurching flight is almost as risible as their ghastly honking call.

A delightful, easily followed, **early-morning walk** takes you across the rickety duckboards over the swamp and along a jungle path on the eastern shore. Here you're almost bound to see the park's four species of **monkey**: colobus, vervet, blue, and the distinctively white-bearded de Brazza's monkey.

ARRIVAL AND DEPARTURE   SAIWA SWAMP NATIONAL PARK

By matatu The park is 11km from *Barnley's Guesthouse* (see below), and easily reached by matatu from there or from Kitale. The park lies to the east of the main Kitale–Lodwar road, near the village of Kipsaina, 17.5km from Kitale. Matatus from Kitale will drop you at Kipsaina (10 daily; 30min), from where it's Ksh150 each way by *boda-boda*, or a poorly signposted 4.8km walk to the park gates.
By car If you're driving straight to the park from Kitale, you can also turn right 11.5km north of Kitale (signposted "Sibanga") for Saiwa Swamp's main gate (7km).

ACCOMMODATION

★ **Barnley's Guesthouse** (also known as *Sirikwa Safaris*) Signposted off to the right 23.1km north of Kitale on the A1 ☎ 0723 917953 or 0737 133170, ✉ sirikwabarnley@gmail.com. One of the finest homestays in the country, and the best place to stay around Kitale if you have your own transport or you're heading north anyway. Based around an old farmhouse and superb gardens situated on a tree-covered hill, *Barnley's* offers camping in three furnished tents with electricity (Ksh3000) or rooms in the fine old house, with full-on highlands atmosphere and shared facilities – or you can pitch your own tent in the gardens (Ksh500 per person). Excellent meals (Ksh1000–1500) are cooked to order and eaten with the charmingly informative hosts. Given notice, the Barnleys will organize just about anything, and can also provide excellent guides (Ksh800/ day for a field guide, Ksh2400/day for the ornithologist) – perfect companions for the Saiwa Swamp, or for a trip to the Cherangani Hills for anything from a day to a week. BB <u>Ksh7000</u>
Park campsite Just inside the main gate ☎ 020 6000800, ✉ reservations@kws.go.ke. You can pitch a tent on this stretch of lawn, which has basic facilities including cooking *bandas* and firepits. It's also a good spot for a picnic. <u>$15</u> per person
Treetop House Just inside the main gate ☎ 020 6000800, ✉ reservations@kws.go.ke. A one-bedroom stilted house sleeping three, with great views from the front deck; perfect for dawn birdwatching and animal-spotting. Water tends to go off after 6pm. <u>$50</u>

Kapenguria

KAPENGURIA, off the highway north of Saiwa Swamp, is surprisingly small given its status as the capital of West Pokot District and is notable only for its role of minor notoriety in colonial history. You can find out more about this at the Kapenguria Museum, which is interesting enough to warrant a day-trip.

Kapenguria Museum

Kapenguria town centre • Daily 8.30am–5.30pm • Ksh500

This excellent museum occupies the prison where Jomo Kenyatta and his colleagues were detained during their parody of a trial. Their individually named cells have been restored, and contain copies of contemporary press reports, photos, depositions and the charges laid against each of the "Kapenguria Six" (some almost laughably nebulous). All six defendants were found guilty of belonging to Mau Mau and sentenced to seven years in jail with hard labour. More visually interesting are the **ethnographic displays** of local cultures, including well-described photographs of traditional circumcision dances and initiation groups, musical instruments, and a telling series on the changes wrought by modern life. Look out for the chisel for removing teeth, and the small horn "for sucking after making incisions on both sides of the head if one has a headache". In the museum grounds are some traditional Pokot family compounds, which the museum caretaker will explain to you.

ARRIVAL AND DEPARTURE

By matatu Matatus from Kitale will drop you on the main A1 road at Makutano, 5km from Kapenguria, which is the main town in the western Cherangani Hills and has more services than Kapenguria itself (the turning for Kapenguria is a couple of kilometres further north). If you're heading

KAPENGURIA AND MAKUTANO

towards the Kerio Valley (p.240) on the other side of the Cheranganis you'll find plenty of matatus between Makutano and Lomut, especially on market day in Sigor (Thurs) or Lomut (Sat), with fewer onwards to Tot, unless you coincide with the weekly market at Chesegon (Wed).

INFORMATION AND ACTIVITIES

Banks There's a Barclays, plus a KCB ATM opposite the Total station.

Makutano Fine Arts Studio Makutano, on the Kitale road ☎ 0711 546941. Run by a local artist named Alfred, this little curio shop also hosts art classes (Ksh1000–3000/day) in which you can learn to make your own batiks, carvings, candles and fabric paintings. Classes can

last as long as you want, ranging from one-day workshops to intensive three-month courses; prices vary according to the number of days involved and the cost of the materials. But whether you're looking for a taste of African art or trying to master a craft, this is a good place to start. Daily 9am–4pm.

ACCOMMODATION

Perkau Princess Lodge Makutano, behind an unmarked orange gate next to the Total station ☎ 0721 165534. Owned by Olympic marathon runner Tegla Loroupe, this small B&L offers very simple rooms that are getting pretty tatty and run-down. Their one redeeming quality is the price. Room only Ksh400

Sebit Resort Club Makutano, west of the main road and north of the Total station ☎ 0734 406521. Located

behind a lively bar and restaurant, these s/c rooms are unexceptional, but at least they're clean and well kept, with nets and TV. BB Ksh1300

White House Resort Club Kapenguria, before the museum, signposted down a dirt road on the left ☎ 0713 602710. A bar and nightspot that also provides simple s/c rooms with mosquito nets. Not a bad option if you don't mind a bit of noise. BB Ksh1000

Ortum and the Marich Pass

North of Makutano, the road enters the truly spectacular countryside of West Pokot proper, winding up the western ridge of Lenan forest, then plunging steeply to the Marun (or Moruny) River. After some 45km you reach **ORTUM**, beautifully positioned beneath the heights of the Cheranganis close to the **Marich Pass**, which is a jumping-off point for a hike into the hills. If you're heading north by car, Ortum has the last petrol before Lodwar, though it's better to fill up at Makutano to be on the safe side. **Mount Sekerr** (or Mount Mtelo, 3354m) is the peak that looms to the northwest – it's a three-day hike to the top and back down. Nearer Marich, 3206m **Mount Koh** to the southeast is a one-day hike if you've got 4WD to get halfway up; two full days otherwise.

ACCOMMODATION **ORTUM AND MARICH PASS**

There are several cheap B&Ls in the village (try *Sondany* or *Simotwo*) and no shortage of *hotelis*.

★ **Marich Pass Field Studies Centre** On the banks of the Marun River, signposted 1km down a track south of the Lodwar road, 1km north of the trading centre of Marich (which is at the junction of the A1 road to Lodwar and B4 road to Sigor, Tot and the Kerio Valley) ⊕0722 139151, ⊕gg.rhul.ac.uk/MarichPass. An excellent base, with a lovely shaded campsite (Ksh360 per person), some good cottages with mosquito nets, including two s/c cottages adapted for wheelchair use, and dorm beds (Ksh420 per person). Firewood, stoves and lamps are available for a small charge. The food is basic but wholesome, and mostly vegetarian unless meat is requested (order well in advance; Ksh200–480) and drinking water comes pure from the well. Even if you're not staying, it's well worth dropping in for a picnic (admission Ksh120), as the centre is surrounded by dense bush, quivering with bird and animal life, and there are guides to help you on excursions around the hills, to Pokot homesteads and to the local markets (tours Ksh1000–1500). BB **Ksh1240**

★ **Mount Mtelo View Campsite** 120km north of Kitale, a 4hr hike or 1hr drive from Marich Pass Field Studies Centre ⊕0737 941400, ⊕mbara1.webs.com/mteloviewpointcampsite.htm. For anyone in search of solitude and tranquillity, this campsite and handful of brightly painted *bandas*, all overlooking the broad expanses of the Rift Valley, certainly fit the bill. The garden is slung with hammocks, and you can spend your time relaxing or hiking with guides from the community. Meals are cooked on site. To get there you'll have to drive (4WD only) or hike, or call in advance and the owner will arrange a pickup. Camping **Ksh400** per person, *bandas* **Ksh800**

Mount Elgon National Park

4

$25 • ⊕kws.go.ke

Straddling the Kenya–Uganda border, **Mount Elgon** is hidden in clouds most of the time, its precise outline hard to discern. The name comes from the Maasai **Ol Doinyo Ilgoon**, meaning "Breast Mountain", and, like Mount Kenya, it's an extinct volcano, around whose jagged and much-eroded crater rim the flat-topped peaks crop up like stumpy fingers of an upturned hand. The two mountains are comparable in bulk, but Elgon is lower. It's below the snowline and less precipitous, which is encouraging if the thought of tackling the "loneliest park in Kenya" was putting you off.

The highest of the peaks, **Wagagai** (4321m; there's also nearby Little Wagagai, at 4298m), is across the caldera in Uganda, but the most evocatively shaped peaks (Sudek, 4176m; Lower Elgon, 4301m; Koitoboss, 4187m; and Endebess Bluff, 2563m) belong to Kenya. Part of the east side of the mountain is enclosed within the confines of **Mount Elgon National Park**. Outside this zone is a forest reserve, with some restrictions on movement due to the presence of poachers, cattle rustlers, and the conflict between a local militia and the Kenyan armed forces (see box, p.297). The park itself, however, is open for business.

Exploring the park

The easiest way to visit Elgon is by driving in at the main Chorlim Gate, staying just inside the park and visiting the nearby **caves and forest**. There are several relatively easy circular drives and short hikes in this lower part of the park. On the **moorland** and towards the **peaks**, the smoothing effects of erosion make **hiking** relatively easy, and there's some bracing walking country. **Driving** within the park, it's possible to get to within 4km of Koitoboss peak with a 4WD vehicle, but it needs to be an extremely sturdy, high-clearance vehicle, and you'll need steely nerves as it's a steep, rocky and extremely muddy ride up to the road-head where the summit trail starts. Indeed, the route is often completely impassable (Jan & Feb is the best time), and even the area near Chorlim Gate can be extremely treacherous, with slippery tyre-ruts and ample opportunities to bog down or even roll your vehicle.

The mountain also has good **rock-climbing** – the best routes are on the cliffs of Lower Elgon, Sudek and the nearby pinnacles – but you must be properly equipped. You'll

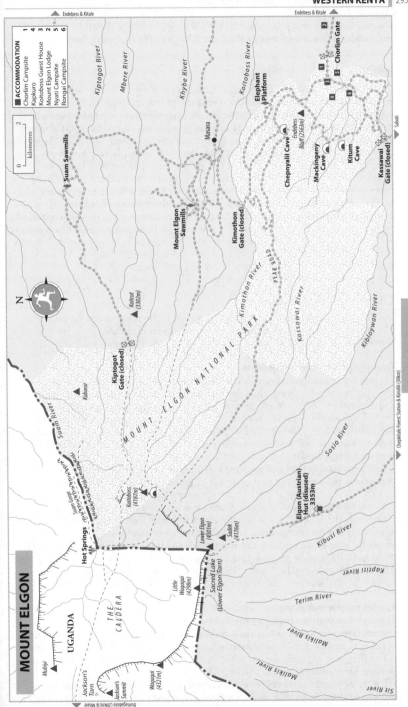

MOUNT ELGON

■ ACCOMMODATION	
Chorlim Campsite	1
Kapkuro	4
Koitoboss Guest House	3
Mount Elgon Lodge	2
Nyati Campsite	5
Rongai Campsite	6

N

0   1   2
kilometres

Endebess & Kitale

Endebess & Kitale

Kiptogot River

Mbere River

Khybe River

Koitoboss River

Chorlim Gate

Elephant Platform

Masara

Suam Sawmills

Mount Elgon Sawmills

Chepnyalil Cave

Endebess Bluff (2563m)

Mackingeny Cave

Kitum Cave

Kassawai Gate (closed)

Saboti

Kimothon Gate (closed)

Kimothon River

PEAK ROAD

Kossowai River

Kiblojwan River

Koitrut (3302m)

Kiptogot Gate (closed)

Suam River

Kuboror

M O U N T   E L G O N   N A T I O N A L   P A R K

Chepkitale Forest Station & Kimilili (30km)

Sosio River

Suam Gorge

Koitoboss (4187m)

Koitoboss

Hot Springs

Lower Elgon (4301m)

Sudek (4176m)

UGANDA

T H E   C A L D E R A

Mubiyi

Jackson's Tarn

Jackson's Summit

Wagagai (4321m)

Little Wagagai (4298m)

Sacred Lake (Lower Elgon Tarn)

Elgon (Austrian) Hut (disused) 3353m

Kibusi River

Kaptiti River

Terim River

Malikisi River

Malikisi River

Sit River

Bumagabula (20km) & Mbale

4

also need to clear your plans with the KWS rangers. Up inside the caldera (technically in Uganda), the **warm springs** by the Suam River provide a tempting bath.

Wildlife

The **vegetation** on Mount Elgon is similar to Mount Kenya's, and equally impressive, with bamboo and podocarpus forests (the latter more accessible than Mount Kenya's) giving way to open moorland inhabited by the strange statues of giant groundsel and lobelia. The **wildlife** isn't easily seen until you get onto the moors, but some elephant and a fair few buffalo roam the forest (be extremely wary of both). The best place to see elephants used to be the **Elephant Platform** north of Chorlim Gate, where herds congregated to browse on the acacias, but many were wiped out by poachers in the 1980s, and the remainder became reclusive. It's very rare to see them at the **Elkony caves**, where they regularly used to gouge salt. The Kenya Wildlife Service is confident that poaching is now under control, and estimates the elephant population to be around two hundred. The lions have long gone and, though there are still **leopards** and **servals**, you're not likely to see one. The **primates** are more conspicuous: blue monkeys and black-and-white colobus crash through the forested areas, troops of olive baboons patrol the scrub, and along the Kimothon River that forms the lower park's northern boundary, there's a scattering of rare de Brazza's monkeys.

Climbing Mount Elgon

In most respects, you should treat a trip up Mount Elgon much as you would one to Mount Kenya. However, **altitude** is less of a problem on Elgon and, given several days to climb it, few people will be badly affected by the ascent. The key is to take your time.

Timing, guides and equipment

Elgon is best from December to March, rather less good in June and July, and probably not worth visiting when the heaviest rains fall during April, May, August and September. This is a lonely mountain and it's probably best not to go up alone. If you hire a **guide** to accompany you at Chorlim Gate, the official KWS ranger fee is Ksh3000/day. You're likely to find locals willing to go up for around Ksh1000/day, but, unlike Mount Kenya, there is no guiding industry here, and finding a good guide is correspondingly harder.

Take a **compass** or GPS and supplies for at least two to three days of self-sufficiency. Suggestions on clothing and equipment can be found in the Mount Kenya section (p.169). You'll need a **tent** if you want to explore beyond the lower park area, and a powerful **torch** if you want to go any distance into the caves. If you are planning more than a short visit, the 1:35,000 KWS map (usually available at Chorlim Gate, but better bought in advance) is better than nothing, and useful for the roads and trails, though it sketchily misses out most of the contours and mixes metric and imperial spot heights. For the high peaks and caldera, it's much more useful to have the topographically accurate *Mount Elgon Map & Guide* published by Andrew Wielochowski (the map of the caldera itself is at a useful 1:50,000; ⓦewpnet.com/maps.htm), though the practical details are dated.

Routes up the mountain

There are five **principal routes** up the Kenyan side of Elgon, but only the route via **Chorlim Gate** is currently open. The **Kimothon** and **Kiptogot** routes on the north side of the park and the **Kimilili** and **Kassawai** routes up the south side have been closed for years. They may physically be accessible, but using them to enter the park (there are no facilities for registering your details or paying) is not permitted.

The only entrance currently open is **Chorlim Gate**, 22km from Kitale. Matatus usually run two or three times a day to *Mount Elgon Lodge* and Chorlim Gate from Kitale

MAYHEM ON MOUNT ELGON

Despite the tranquillity inside the national park, communities around the southern slopes of Mount Elgon have been embroiled in land disputes with the government since colonial times, and wracked by violent episodes over the past two decades. The most recent began in 2005 with the formation of the **Sabaot Land Defence Force**. Formed to resist a forced resettlement programme, the SLDF rapidly degenerated into a brutal **insurgency** that terrorized unsupportive Sabaot villagers and Okiek tribespeople alike, with murder, mutilations and rape, and is estimated to have displaced 66,000 people and killed more than six hundred. Early in 2008, as the world watched the post-election clashes in Eldoret, Kisumu and Naivasha, the Kenyan military went on a **rampage** in the southern Elgon foothills, arresting every Sabaot man over the age of 15, torturing and raping villagers suspected of involvement with the SLDF, and, according to the local MP, Fred Kapondi, killing more than 150 people. As reported by Human Rights Watch, the Red Cross and the UN Special Rapporteur on Extrajudicial, Summary or Arbitrary Executions, Philip Alston, it seemed that the Kenyan armed forces believed they could get away with murder, and, if anyone noticed, the even worse atrocities committed by the SLDF would cover for them. In May 2008, the army cornered and shot the SLDF's military commander, 25-year-old Wycliffe Komon Matakwei, and arrested or killed most senior members of the militia, though questions remain about their funding and political control. For now, the insurgency seems to be over, but the issues of landlessness, official abuses and legal whitewash persist, as do rumours that the SLDF itself remains secretly in operation.

(leaving around 3–5pm, depending on passenger numbers), and there are frequent services to **Endebess**, from where it's a fairly easy two-hour walk if you don't get a lift. Otherwise you can hire a taxi, which costs Ksh3500 either for a full day or for the round trip if you're spending the night on the mountain. If you're driving, fill up with fuel in Kitale, and head northwest towards Endebess along the tarmac road. After 9km, the road splits, with the tarmac continuing to Endebess and a *murram* road bearing left for Chorlim Gate. About 6km further you reach a crossroads (right to Endebess, left to **Saboti** and the A1, straight ahead to Chorlim Gate).

Once inside the park, install yourself near the gate at one of the campsites or *bandas*, or at the self-catering *Koitoboss Guest House*. These are the obvious bases for visiting the **Elkony Caves** (see below). For **Koitoboss Peak** (4187m), follow the driveable track or "Peak Road" into the moorlands to the road-head on the southern border of the park at 3500m, allowing three to four hours to cover the 30km. You leave your vehicle here, and it's a three-hour hike up the upper Kimothon valley to the pass at the southern base of Koitoboss peak, where there are flat (but cold and windy) places where you can camp. You can then make the one-hour scramble to the top, or take a two- to three-hour diversion to the Suam warm springs in the caldera.

The Elkony Caves

Perhaps Elgon's most captivating attraction is the honeycomb of **caves** on the lower slopes. Some of these were long inhabited by one of the loosely related Kalenjin groups, the **Elkony** (whose name, in corrupted form, was given to the mountain), and used both as living quarters and as livestock pens at night. There is evidence that the caves had a ritual function as well – **Chepnyalil Cave** contains a structure that might have served as an altar or shrine, and its walls are painted with a red-and-white frieze of cattle. The caves are also linked with Luhya circumcision ceremonies, in which boys spent their month-long initiation period covered from head to toe in the white diatomite powder found in the area, before returning home as men. The Elkony were officially evicted from the caves by the colonial government, who insisted that they live in the open "where they could be counted for tax", but several caves were still occupied by extended families within living memory.

The largest and most spectacular cave is **Makingeny Cave**, close to the road and marked by a cascade falling over the entrance. It makes a good hike teamed up with its neighbour, **Kitum Cave**, a twenty-minute hike to the south. Early explorers believed that some of the caves were artificial, one report referring to "thousands of chisel and axe marks on the walls". In fact, generations of elephants were responsible: the well-signposted Kitum Cave was the mineral fix of local elephants, and on rare occasions they still walk into the cave at night to gouge the salt-flavoured rock from the walls with their tusks. If you're exceptionally lucky, a night vigil at Kitum Cave may be repaid by a visit from the elephants; but if not, the thousands of bats and the sounds of the forest are good compensation.

ARRIVAL AND DEPARTURE   MOUNT ELGON

Access to the national park is easy, with two or three **matatus** most days from Kitale. If you **drive** in, you can park and hike on your own, but if you don't have your own vehicle you will need to sign a waiver form at the gate.

Crossing into Uganda If you want to cross the mountain into Uganda, you will need to make arrangements in advance with the senior warden (☎020 3539903, ✉menp@swiftkenya.com), who will coordinate with the Ugandan park authorities on the west side of the mountain; you'll be asked to pay park fees on the Ugandan side as well. You'll need to hire a Kenyan ranger to accompany you as far as the warm springs on the border, where you are handed over to the care of a Ugandan ranger (or vice versa if coming the other way), and you will also have to visit Suam to complete border formalities before going through the park. The Suam border post is easily reached by road, and a lot more easy-going than those further south at Malaba and Busia. Suam is accessible by regular matatus from Kitale and Endebess. On the Ugandan side, there are matatus to Kapchorwa and thence to Mbale, where you'll find onward transport to the rest of Uganda.

ACCOMMODATION

Inside the park itself and on the slopes of the mountain, **camping** is the obvious option. The **bandas** and **guesthouse** are more comfortable and are often available on the day, but it's best to book in advance with KWS (☎020 6000800, ✉reservations@kws.go.ke).

Kapkuro 1km from the gate, in a clearing in the woods. Four good *bandas*, each with a bedroom with one double and one single bed, a basic kitchen and a bathroom with hot water delivered in a bucket when required – but no electricity. BB $\overline{\underline{\$25}}$

Koitoboss Guest House Just up from Chorlim Gate. If you want something more comfortable than Kapkuro, and with electricity, there's the old warden's house, which has been converted into a self-catering guesthouse set in a garden full of impala, bushbuck and waterbuck. It comes with six double beds, a well-equipped kitchen with a big fridge, two bathrooms and the generator electricity from 7 to 10pm. A very nice spot, though a little pricey for fairly basic comforts. Whole house $\overline{\underline{\$180}}$

Mount Elgon Lodge 1.5km outside the park on the track between Chorlim Gate from Kitale ☎020 2094643 or 0722 875768. Although it's an interesting old pile, you can't get away from the fact that the main house is desperately run-down and the ten cottage rooms in the garden only slightly less so. Camping in the grounds is an accepted, and very acceptable, alternative to taking a room (Ksh600 per person, including use of bathroom and showers), and the food is actually pretty good. Be sure to order lunch or dinner in advance (Ksh550) and get them to show you round the old house. BB $\overline{\underline{\$65}}$

Public campsites Near Chorlim Gate. There are three public campsites near Chorlim Gate – *Chorlim*, *Rongai* and *Nyati*. Of these, Chorlim has the best facilities. But if you're going to be hiking deep into the park, camping in the wild is your only option. $\overline{\underline{\$15}}$ per person

Malaba and the road to Uganda

Although it's the least interesting part of western Kenya to look at – mostly undulating **grasslands** and Kenya's largest **sugar-cane** fields – the route through Malaba is a good alternative to that via Busia (see p.262) for travellers passing between Kenya and Uganda, and should passenger rail services resume it will undoubtedly become the main border crossing point, as indeed it once was.

ELIJA MASINDE'S CULT OF THE ANCESTORS

In the 1940s and 1950s, there was a resurgence of **Bukusu resistance** and nationalism in the *Dini ya Msambwa* (Cult of the Ancestors) movement, spearheaded by the charismatic prophet-rebel, **Elija Masinde**. The heart of the movement was in the Elgon foothills between Kimilili and the Ugandan border. It called for the eviction of all *wazungu* and the transfer of their property to Africans. As the *Dini* spread, there were violent confrontations with colonial forces, and a number of deaths. Masinde was sent into internal exile but, since he was by then a folk hero, his followers kept the sparks of resistance alive throughout the more organized uprising of Mau Mau in the Central Highlands, until independence was finally obtained. The movement collapsed in the early years of *uhuru*, when Masinde was allowed home to Kimilili and his continued denouncements of all authority and claims to divine inspiration began to lose their coherence. Until his death in the 1990s, he could still be seen on the streets of Kimilili, a rather terrifying figure shouting at the wind.

If you're making your way to the south from this district down towards Kakamega and Kisumu, the busy A1 will take you through some fine stands of tropical forest, heralding the **Kakamega Forest** to the southeast.

Chetambe's Fort

Perched above the drab town of WEBUYE, at the junction of the A1 and the A104, are the lonely remains of **Chetambe's Fort**. This was the site, in 1895, of a last-ditch stand by the Bukusu group of the Luhya tribe against the motley line-up of a British punitive expedition, which had enrolled Ugandan, Sudanese, Maasai and even other Luhya troops. A predictable massacre, in this case by Hotchkiss gun, took place, with negligible losses on the attackers' side and equally few survivors among the defenders. How the British managed to storm the scarp in the first place, however, is a mystery: presumably the Bukusu were all inside their walled fort at the top. Resistance among the Bukusu continued right up until independence (see box above).

The "fort" itself is quite unimpressive, and in fact not easy to make out: all that remains these days is a circular field covering several acres, surrounded by a shallow ditch. The spot where the British placed their deadly gun, opposite the fort's main entrance, is just west of the water tower and is now marked by a small concrete memorial, dated 11.5.88 (the day the emplacement was declared a monument). The people who live nearby are glad to show visitors the site, and can tell you stories from their grandparents of finding bones in the compound area, of women coming here to weep in the evenings, and of animal sacrifices to the dead warriors.

ARRIVAL AND DEPARTURE   **CHETAMBE'S FORT**

The fort sits on top of the steep scarp that rears up beyond Webuye, 8km from the main A104 road.

By car From the *Webuye Falls Resort*, the local *hoteli* north of the A104, keep straight on along the *murram* road, passing the KBC transmitter towers. Bear left at a couple of small junctions, keeping to the top of the ridge. 5.1km from the resort you reach a T-junction. Here you turn sharp left and, after 400m, you reach the end of the track and the site of the fort.

By foot Alternatively, you can hike straight up the steep escarpment on foot. The trail head begins 1.5km north of the A1 Kitale road's junction with the A104, where there's a *murram* turning to the right (east) near a grove of trees and some buildings. Scramble directly up the scrubby hillside for 400m to reach the top of the ridge. The fort is 200m in front of you.

To the border: Bungoma and Malaba

The only town of any size between Webuye and the Ugandan border is **BUNGOMA**, a surprisingly animated commercial town, with its Sharriffs Centre **shopping plaza** and bustling, arcaded main street. There's a Barclays **ATM** (the first you'll find if you're coming from Uganda), but no special reasons to stop.

If you're heading **south from Bungoma** on the C33, the road starts out alright, but seriously deteriorates near Mumias. **West of Bungoma**, the tarmac is smooth and the scenery unexciting until you reach the border crossing at **MALABA**. This is less used by passenger road traffic than Busia, but it's where most freight, as well as the (presently freight-only) railway line, crosses the border with Uganda. Endless lines of lorries choke the roads on both sides; for some, it can take days to get across. Fortunately, pedestrians can cross without difficulty, and a planned upgrade of the border post promises to make the crossing even easier. Official formalities are relatively simple, and moneychangers are on hand on both sides of the border. Try to find out the current rates in advance, watch out for scams and count the currency you're buying carefully before handing yours over.

ARRIVAL AND ACCOMMODATION
MALABA

Whether you're arriving in Kenya or departing for Uganda, you'll find the point where your **bus** drops you on one side of the border to where the bus picks you up on the other side is a long walk and it can be confusing, especially at night: it's a good idea to have a companion for the crossing, especially if you can't find a *boda-boda* or *piki-piki* to speed you across. There are several budget **guesthouses** on the Kenyan side, although few people hang around.

By bus and matatu There are several bus companies doing the run to Nairobi via Eldoret. Matatus on the Kenyan side serve Bungoma, Kisumu and Eldoret; on the Ugandan side, they run to Tororo, Jinja and Kampala.

Jaki Guest Hotel On the south side of the main drag about 500m from the border post ☎ 055 54004. Your best bet in Malaba, quiet and set back from the street, with cheap and simple s/c doubles and singles (singles cost just Ksh300, and some have beds big enough for two). There are also pricier and fancier doubles in the main block. BB Ksh800

Mumias

MUMIAS was originally *Mumia's*, capital of the Luhya-speaking mini-state of **Wanga**, and well established by the middle of the nineteenth century at the head of an important caravan route to the coast. **King Mumia**, who came to power in 1880, was Wanga's last king and the present-day town stands on the site of his capital. His ten-thousand-strong army, half of them dispossessed Maasai from the Uasin Gishu Plateau, was largely responsible for smashing Bukusu resistance at Chetambe's Fort fifteen years later (see p.300).

Even at the beginning of Mumia's reign, Europeans were beginning to arrive in the wake of Arab and Swahili slave-traders, who in turn had been settling in since the 1850s with the full accord of the Wanga royal family. By 1894 there was a permanent British sub-commissioner or collector of taxes posted here. King Mumia had always welcomed strangers, and he allowed the slavers to continue their work on other Luhya groups (notably the Bukusu), but he was unprepared for the swift usurpation of his authority by the British, whom he'd assumed were also there to trade. He was appointed "Paramount Chief" of a gradually diminishing state and then, as an old man, was retired without his real knowledge. He died in 1949, aged 100, and with him expired, almost without notice, Kenya's first and only indigenous upcountry state.

Modern Mumias is now a charming and lively little market town. The central **mosque** (by the junction of the Bungoma and Kakamega roads) was built in King Mumia's honour and its Koran school is just one of about 25 around the town. Mumias has long been a centre of Islam, famous for its coastal ways. Today, however, women in *buibuis* (the long, black coverall of the coast) are rarely seen, and Islam is losing ground to Catholicism, exemplified by the town's impressive Catholic church, 2km down the Kakamega road.

ARRIVAL AND INFORMATION	**MUMIAS**

By matatu Matatus run from Mumias to Kisumu (1hr 30min), Kakamega (40min), Bungoma (30min) and most other places in the district. Leaving Mumias there's a fast new road to Kisumu via Butere.

By bus Buses run to Kisumu (2 daily; 1hr 30min),

Kakamega (4 daily; 40min) and Nairobi (2 daily; 8hr 30min), and there are also two daily services direct to Mombasa (16hr).

Services Mumias has KCB and Barclays banks with ATMs, and a handful of petrol stations.

ACCOMMODATION AND EATING

There are a couple of places to stay and eat, and numerous places to get a drink in the evening – although you might want to give *Club Hookers* a miss.

Crossroads Café Across the street from the matatu stage. "The finest cuisine in Mumias" according to the sign out front, and it just might be true, with breakfasts, snacks, *nyama choma* and chicken (mains Ksh300) served in a room that looks like it's been decorated for Mardi Gras, complete with crenellated pink walls, silk flowers and a non-functional fountain. Daily 5am–10pm.

★ **Martha's Guest House** Mundeku, 25km south of Mumias ☎0723 712538 or 0728 267600, ⓦmarthasguesthouse.com. Built by railway employee James Shiraku Inuyundo in 1935 and officially opened as a guesthouse by Princess Margaret in 1956, this is the quirkiest place to stay between Lake Victoria and Mount Elgon, with charming grounds, attentive service, good food and accommodation in a variety of non-s/c rooms in the main house and creatively themed chalets in the large gardens – pricey, but full of character. There's a fascinating little museum (Ksh50 entry) which crams more into one tiny hut than some of the national museums manage in a large

building. To reach *Martha's*, heading south from Mumias past Butere, ask to be dropped at Khumailo. A signboard on the left indicates "Martha's Guesthouse 5km away". About 4km down this dirt road you'll see another sign pointing down a small track; it's 400m down the track, behind an anonymous green gate. Just 200m further along the dirt road, the grove of large trees on the left is Omulundu, a sacred grove of the Luhya elders, never to be cut. BB Ksh3500

St Mary's Guest House Behind St Mary's Hospital on the Kakamega road just outside town ☎0726 712382. Friendly guesthouse in the quiet hospital grounds. The French windows of the spacious s/c rooms open out onto a garden, and meals can be prepared on request. BB Ksh1600

Wanga Palace Guest House In the red-brick Wanga Castle building, on the main street behind the matatu stand ☎0720 425693. An adequate option for the price, right in the centre with large s/c rooms and instant showers, though the bar downstairs means it's not terribly restful. Room only Ksh600

4

Kakamega

KAKAMEGA is the headquarters of the **Luhya**, a loosely defined group of peoples whose only clear common denominator is a **Bantu language**, spoken in more than a score of vernaculars, which distinguishes them from the Luo to the south and the Kalenjin to the east. Numerically, the Luhya (also spelt Abaluhya or Luyia) are Kenya's second-largest ethnic group, and most are settled farmers.

Kakamega itself was founded as a buying station on the ox trail known as **Sclater's Road**, which reached here from the coast in 1896. Historically, its only fame came in the 1930s, when gold was discovered nearby and more than a thousand prospectors came to the region. However, very few fortunes were made. In the early 1990s, Kakamega became the first town in Kenya to use the bicycle taxis known as *boda-bodas*, now almost a nationwide institution. Today, it's a lively place, but with little to detain casual visitors. If you're passing through in August of an even-numbered year, however, it's worth being aware that some of the Luhya communities in the district are swept up in exuberant boys' **circumcision parties** – though the actual chop is usually done in hospital and the initiates themselves tend not to be the ones doing the partying. A more sedate event, the **Agricultural Society of Kenya annual show**, takes place at the town's showground every November.

ARRIVAL AND DEPARTURE

The obvious routes out of the area lie along the **A1**, heading either north to Kitale or south to Kisumu – the latter is a real roller-coaster drive, particularly the final 8km descent over the Nyando Escarpment. An alternative onward route heads straight through the Kakamega forest via Shinyalu and out to Kapsabet, where you join an excellent tarmac highway, the **C39**, to Eldoret and rejoin the **A104**. There's also a paved road west to Mumias, with regular public transport.

By matatu Most matatus leave from the main stand on Sudi Rd, although those for Mumias have their own stand on the Mumias Rd.
Destinations Kericho (8–10 daily; 3hr); Kisumu (20–30 daily; 1hr); Kitale (2hr 30min); Mumias (12 daily; 40min); Webuye (12–20 daily; 1hr).

By bus Coast Buses (☎0722 206453) run direct daily services to Mombasa at 5.30pm (14hr), while the comfortable Easy Coach (☎056 30837 or 0738 200313) departs for Nairobi at 8.30am and 8pm (8hr). Other destinations include Kisumu (8–10 daily; 1hr); Mombasa (1 daily; 14hr); Nairobi (6–8 daily; 8hr).

ACCOMMODATION

If you arrive here late in the day (or after around 2.30pm in a 2WD vehicle, when the rain often starts to fall), you may want to stay in town rather than arrive in the forest after dark.

Ambwere Alliance Sudi Rd, nearly opposite the Total station ☎0724 227504. This dour-looking place isn't terribly friendly, but the plain rooms are cheap and decent enough, with hot water, mosquito nets and safe parking, while some even come with small balconies. Room only **Ksh700**
Franka Mumias Rd ☎0708 766646. The secure parking, clean s/c rooms (some with good views) and *nyama choma* in the evenings make this a reasonable choice, though the noisy nightclub downstairs is something of a drawback. BB **Ksh800**
Golf Hotel Khasakhala Rd ☎0728 833974,

ⓦgolfhotelkakamega.com. Well-insulated rooms (nets and TVs, bathtubs and old-style showers, but no fans or a/c in a comfortable, tourist-standard hotel from the late 1970s, its pretensions comically clipped by the vultures hopping over the lawns. There's a large pool and gift shop, but rates for non-Kenya residents are too high. BB **$126**
Jionee Guesthouse Cannon Awori St ☎0722 289819. A friendly little place above a local eatery offering simple but spacious rooms with nets. Everything is spick-and-span, though the cheaper rooms share bathrooms. BB **Ksh1200**

EATING AND DRINKING

In addition to the hotel dining rooms, there are some good, cheap **restaurants** in Kakamega. As for **drinking** places with character, you're spoilt for choice. For supermarkets, Tusky's on Kisumu Rd (daily 8am–9pm), and Yako Supermarket on Kenyatta Ave (daily 8am–8pm), should do the job.

Club Bling Mumias Rd. A good bar and nightclub with forest-style decor, which opens up its dancefloor every night for a mix of reggae, rumba and R'n'B. Daily 5–11pm, Fri–Sun till late.
Franka Mumias Rd. Below the guesthouse of the same name, this is one of the town's liveliest drinking holes, with some outdoor seating and a disco that pounds out music until around 3am. Daily 5–11pm, disco until 3am.
Golf Hotel Khasakhala Rd ☎0728 833974. A reasonably priced option, considering its poolside location in the town's most upscale hotel, offering decent à la carte European food, including burgers and fish & chips, plus set menus (Ksh450 or Ksh700). Daily 7.30am–9pm.

★ **Lawino 2000** Cannon Awori St. An innovative eatery specializing in western Kenyan cuisine ("Our mission: to contribute to a healthy and safety nourishment, through indigenous African cuisines"), *Lawino* serves local dishes such as *alya* (smoked beef), ranging from Ksh100 to Ksh300, and even wine. Mon–Sat 6am–8pm.
★ **Wayside Palace Hotel** Kenyatta Ave, next to the clocktower. The warmest, friendliest café in town, with great breakfasts, good music and heaps more atmosphere than most. The food is just local fare, but it's good, especially the tilapia (Ksh350). The sidewalk seating makes for great people-watching. Mon–Sat 6.30am–9pm, Sun 2–8pm.

DIRECTORY

Banks There are Barclays and SCB banks with ATMs, both on Kenyatta Ave.
Books Vaghela bookshop (☎0721 223799; Mon–Sat 8am–6pm, Sun 8.30am–12.30pm), on Mumias Rd, has a reasonable selection of Kenyan and other English-language fiction.
Internet Kakamega Cyber Café (daily 8am–7pm; Ksh1/

min), by the SomKen station on Sudi Rd, has fast connections.
Market The municipal market, next to the bus station, is very lively, particularly on Wed & Sat, when the stalls are swelled by produce from outlying rural areas. Among the local produce on offer you'll find natural remedies and medicines made from forest plants.

Kakamega Forest

The nearby **Kakamega Forest** is one of western Kenya's star attractions, and if you have any interest at all in the natural world, it's worth going far out of your way to see. Fortunately, it's fairly easy to get to Kakamega Forest from Kisumu or, if you've been in the Mount Elgon region, from Webuye along a scenically forested stretch of the A1.

Some 400 years ago, Kakamega Forest would have been at the eastern end of a broad expanse of forest stretching west, clear across the continent, virtually unbroken as far as the Atlantic. Three hundred years later, following human population explosion and widescale cultivation, the forests everywhere had receded, reducing Kakamega to an island of some 2400 square kilometres, cut off from the rest of the Guineo-Congolan rainforest. Today, with an area of less than 230 square kilometres, it's a small patch of relict equatorial jungle, famous among zoologists and botanists around the world as an example of how an isolated environment can survive cut off from its larger body.

Despite a laudable scheme to educate the local population about the forest (see box, see p.306), the lack of any coherent backing or action from the authorities means that its long-term future isn't bright. Pressure from local people, who need grazing for their livestock, land to cultivate, and firewood, amounts to a significant threat. The present area is less than a tenth of what it was in 1900, and its closed canopy cover (which indicates the forest's health and maturity) has dropped from ninety to fifty percent of the total area. This has led to the degradation of the natural habitat, and, inevitably, to some species being threatened, while others, like the leopard, last seen in the forest in 1992, are becoming extinct.

Exploring the forest

The forest is fragmented, interspersed with open fields of grassland, and the larger, central area has cultivated stream margins, small settlements and even tea plantations (which give the locals an alternative to plundering the forest as a source of income). Two main areas can be visited, though one comes with a heaftier entrance fee than the other, and their names are confusingly similar. The first, which has been accessible for many years, is the central **Kakamega Forest Reserve**, lying east of Kakamega town, somewhat off the beaten track, and managed by the Forest Department. Most visitors come to part of one of the densest stands of forest in this area, and often stay at the *Forest Guest House* in the glade at its edge. The second section, the **Kakamega Forest National Reserve**, is northeast of Kakamega town, just off the A1 highway, and very easy to get to. This is a strictly controlled zone of 44 square kilometres, maintained by the KWS more or less like a national park.

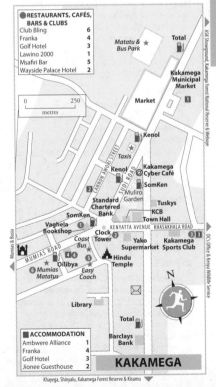

RESTAURANTS, CAFÉS, BARS & CLUBS
Club Bling 6
Franka 4
Golf Hotel 3
Lawino 2000 1
Msafiri Bar 5
Wayside Palace Hotel 2

ACCOMMODATION
Ambwere Alliance 1
Franka 4
Golf Hotel 3
Jionee Guesthouse 2

KAKAMEGA

Kakamega Forest Reserve

Daily 8am–6pm • Daily "recreation" charge of Ksh600 (Ksh150 for children) • Guides cost Ksh500–1000/person, depending on the walk you choose, plus any tip you care to add (Ksh300–500 for 3hr is about right) • ⓦ kakamegarainforest.com

On arrival at the *Forest Guest House* (see p.307) you'll be greeted by an official guide (a member of Kakamega Biodiversity Conservation Tour Operators – KaBiCoTOa for short), whose name should be on the board outside the hut on the path up to the house. You will be given a brief introduction to the region and the conservation being done by KEEP (see box, p.306) – all guides should have a KEEP identity card.

It's best to take up the offer of a **guide**, especially if you're a woman on your own (there are several female guides here). Exceptionally, for a profession that usually attracts hustlers, this lot are professional and knowledgeable; their walks are tremendously enjoyable, and they're happy to tailor them to your particular interests. Expect a wander along the labyrinthine jungle paths, with birds, monkeys, chameleons and other animals pointed out to you, most of which you would miss if you went on your own. A pair of **binoculars** is more or less indispensable if you're out to watch birds.

THE WILDLIFE OF KAKAMEGA FOREST

The Kakamega Forest is a haven of shadowy gloom for more than three hundred species of birds, 45 percent of all the butterfly species ever recorded in Kenya, seven species of primates, as well as snakes, various other reptiles and untold varieties of insects. Many of these creatures are found nowhere else in East Africa because similar habitats no longer exist. The fear now is that even this tiny surviving track of rainforest is in grave danger of being eliminated.

BIRDS

Among the commoner **birds** are the noisy and gregarious black-and-white-casqued hornbill and the very striking, deep violet Ross's turaco. You may also see familiar-looking African grey parrots and, circling above the canopy on the lookout for unwary monkeys, the huge crowned hawk eagle. Kakamega's avian stars, however, are the **great blue turacos**, glossy, turkey-sized birds like dowagers in evening gowns. They're easily located by their raucous calls: a favourite spot at dusk is the grove of very tall trees down by the pump house. They arrive each evening to crash and lurch among the branches as they select roosting sites.

MAMMALS

The forest draws mammal-watchers as well, particularly for its **monkeys**. Troops are often seen at dusk, foraging through the trees directly opposite the *Forest Guest House* veranda. Apart from the ubiquitous colobus, you can see Sykes' monkeys and the much slimmer black-cheeked white-nosed monkey (most easily recognized by its red tail). They're often seen milling around with the hornbills. You may also see pairs of giant forest squirrels capering in the treetops – the deep booming call you sometimes hear in the morning is theirs.

At **night**, armed with a powerful torch, you might catch a glimpse of bushbabies, palm civets, genets or even a potto, a slow-moving, lemur-like animal whose name aptly conveys its appearance and demeanour. The forest is also home to several species of fruit bat, of which the hammer-headed fruit bat (*Hypsignathus monstrosus*) is the largest in Africa, with a wingspan of a metre and an enormous head. Other nocturnal Kakamega specialities are the otter shrew, which lives in some of the forest streams, the tree pangolin (a kind of arboreal scaly anteater) and the flying squirrel.

REPTILES

The forest's reptiles are legendary, but few people actually see any **snakes**, and you're much more likely to come across **chameleons**. Reptiles spend a good deal of time motionless, especially when frightened, and to see snakes in the dense foliage you have to be experienced. Visible or not, however, snakes are abundant and you certainly shouldn't walk in the forest in bare feet or sandals: the sluggish gaboon viper, growing to a metre or more in length, and fatter than your arm, is a dangerous denizen of the forest floor, though not an animal that seeks confrontation. To avoid a serpentine encounter, simply walk heavily: snakes are highly sensitive to vibration and will flee at your seismic approach.

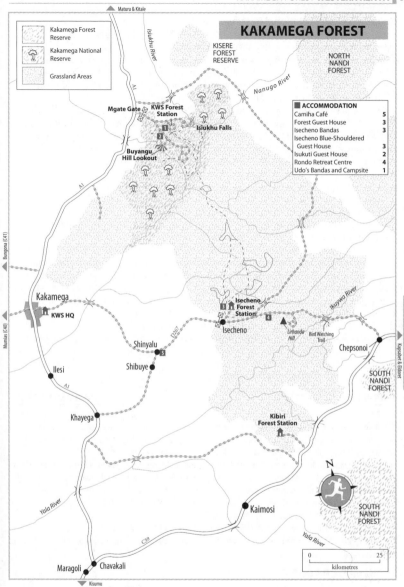

If you have time for more than one daylight walk, you could ask a guide to show you the way to **Lirhanda Hill**, via a trail that's rich in medicinal plants. You will be shown the leaves, berries and saps that forest dwellers chew, swallow or anoint themselves with to treat various ailments. Lirhanda Hill itself is a lookout point, offering fine views over the whole expanse of forest, with the sombre bulk of Mount Elgon glowering in the distance. Cutting into the hillside near the top is a gold-mining shaft, long disused and now home to a large colony of bats. With a powerful torch and a steely nerve you can grope your way along the tunnel to meet them at close quarters.

Kakamega Forest National Reserve

Entrance to the reserve is via a signposted *murram* road some 16km northeast of Kakamega town along the A1, at a junction with a cluster of shops and *hotelis* set back from the road • $20 • ☎ 056 30603, ⓦ kws.go.ke

Driving south down the A1 road to Kakamega from its junction with the A104 at Maturu, you enter the thick forest of the Kakamega forest region after about 14km. Although parts are cleared and there's no lack of people about, it's a very different environment from just about anywhere else in Kenya.

Kakamega Forest National Reserve is the part of Kakamega Forest managed by the Kenya Wildlife Service. If you've got your own vehicle, it's easier to get around this part of Kakamega forest than the Kakamega Forest Reserve central zone. The deepest and most interesting part of the forest is, in fact, a fair walk from the KWS-run *Udo's Bandas and Campsite* (see p.307), though a number of driveable and walkable tracks begin just beyond *Udo's*. You have free run of the national reserve on foot. The main trail is well signposted and there are numerous branches and "exit" trails that allow for a relatively quick return when you've had enough of the deep forest.

The most significant difference between the National Reserve here and the Forest Reserve further south is the age of the growth. Many of the **trees** are colossal. In addition, the climate is generally drier and there's a greater diversity of habitat, including ancient forest, young forest and areas of scrub. It's an impressive area and, as in the southern forest, there's a huge variety of bird and plant life, and many monkeys.

An easy excursion from the forest station is to the **Isiukhu Falls**, a rather feeble waterfall 1.5km away along a rocky path. Alternatively, you could head for **Buyangu Hill viewpoint**, a precipice with a spectacular vista east across the forest to the Nandi Escarpment. To reach the viewpoint tower, don't stop when you get up to the coniferous trees. Walk through them another 100m or so and you'll see it, up a steep rise (an easy scramble).

A longer walk leads to the **Kisere Forest Reserve**, 5km from Mgate Gate: a separate, outlying part of the main reserve, four kilometres square and home to de Brazza's monkeys and other species, as well as some superb examples of the prized Elgon olive timber tree. Ask the rangers for directions.

ARRIVAL AND DEPARTURE

KAKAMEGA FOREST

BY CAR

Whichever of the two approaches described below you take, track surfaces get treacherously slippery in wet weather. Given the predictable afternoon rains, this limits you to arriving between 10am and 2pm, when the road is at its driest. Even so, 4WD is advisable.

From Kakamega via Khayega From Kakamega, the easiest approach road is from Khayega, 7km south of Kakamega on the A1. The junction is marked by signposts for the Arap Moi Girls' School and the Office of the President. From here, an earth road leads 6km to Shinyalu.

Keep right at Shinyalu and continue for another 5.3km to Isecheno, turning left just after the barrier and a signposted arrow. From the barrier, it's less than 1km to the trail to the *Forest Guest House*.

From Eldoret via Kapsabet Approaching from Eldoret via Kapsabet, the road into the forest starts at Chepsonoi, on the C39 where you take the right turning (west), signposted "Kisieni 12km D267".

BY PUBLIC TRANSPORT

From Kakamega From Kakamega, the cheapest way of

"KEEP OUR FOREST"

The Kakamega Environmental Education Programme, or **KEEP** (ⓦ keep-kakamega.or.ke), was set up by the guides at *Forest Guest House* to combine visits to the forest for local schoolchildren with their school lessons. They hope that by convincing the children of the importance of the forest, the message will spread into the community. A tree nursery has been started to demonstrate basic tree-planting techniques, alongside information on waste recycling and efficient use of firewood. In addition, a butterfly farm has been set up, with the aim of breeding local butterflies to frame and sell as souvenirs, generating income for the local community from the forest itself. Other sustainable projects in the pipeline include bee keeping and snake farming (for antivenin). They're always looking for volunteers – contact them through the website above.

reaching the forest on public transport is to catch a matatu to Shinyalu (there are occasional matatus from Khayega to Shinyalu too, or you could take a *boda-boda* from there). Alternatively, a private taxi from Kakamega to Shinyalu (or the *Forest Guest House* if you're lucky) will cost Ksh1500–2000. It's a lovely hour-long walk to Isecheno from Shinyalu, while Shinyalu itself often has a cattle auction and a major

market on Saturdays, when it's worth pausing an hour to soak up the atmosphere of cowboys in the jungle.

From Eldoret, any bus or matatu heading towards Kisumu via Kapsabet, Chavakali and Maragoli will pass the turning for Isecheno at Chepsonoi. From here, if you don't get a lift, it takes about 3hr to walk through the magnificent forest to the Central District HQ at Iescheno.

INFORMATION

For all matters relating to Kakamega Forest visit the Kenya Wildlife Service office in Kakamega (☎ 056 30603; Mon–Fri 8am–5pm): go past the *Golf Hotel*, right at the roundabout, follow the road past the DC's office (which it's behind) to the next junction, turn left and it's on the left after 50m.

ACCOMMODATION

If you stay in one of the Isecheno places (the *Forest Guest House* or *Isecheno Bandas*) the closest reliable **supplies** are at the *dukas* about 3km away on the road to Shinyalu, meaning that it's best to bring your own food. For candles and simple staples – bananas, *chai*, mineral water, biscuits, sodas and sometimes beer – there's a small *duka* (open daily) on the way to the pump house. They also cook inexpensive meals to order, given a few hours' notice.

Camiha Café At the start of the Isecheno road in Shinyalu ☎ 0729 637518. If you want to stay somewhere with beer and music, this might fit the bill, although it's really just a café and bar, with four basic rooms, bucket showers (hot water on request), and music till late. Room only Ksh200

Forest Guest House Central District HQ ☎ 020 2315979 or 0721 711293. If you're not too fussy about comforts this wooden chalet is a delight – a kind of budget *Treetops* without the crowds. There are four s/c twin rooms up on the first floor, with a long veranda facing the wall of forest. There's basic bedding, but you might bring a blanket or sleeping bag, as it can get decidedly chilly early in the morning. You can also camp. There's no electricity, but each room has a functioning bathroom and toilet. Camping Ksh650 per person, BB Ksh1000

Isecheno Bandas Next to the Forest Guest House ☎ 0735 610095 or 0734 523078, ⓦ keep-kakamega .or.ke. KEEP's own *bandas* are located right next to the *Forest Guest House*, but instead of going to the park, the money is used locally for KEEP's ongoing community conservation projects. There are five cute, non-s/c *bandas*, with beds, blankets, sheets and pillows, and a separate shower (hot water on request) and toilet block. As at the *Forest Guest House*, you can either bring food and firewood to self-cater, or make arrangements locally to have meals provided. BB Ksh1400

Isecheno Blue-Shouldered Guest House 500m south of the Central District HQ ☎ 0722 886833, ⓔ blueshouldered@yahoo.com. Quirky little homestay named after the blue-shouldered robin-chat, one of Kakamega's unusual birds. Sleeping five people in three rooms, the house has a veranda from where you can watch monkeys in the trees opposite. There are also ten bunk beds

in a spacious dorm, all with nets and separated from the main house in a well-appointed *banda*. Meals are made to order (or bring food and cook your own in the spotless kitchen), and forest walks available (the owner is a Kakamega guide). Dorm beds Ksh700, BB Ksh1400

Isukuti Guest House 1.2km from the main gate, Just before Udo's as you come into the reserve ☎ 020 6000800, ⓔ reservations@kws.go.ke. This guesthouse has four beds in two rooms, a bathroom and kitchen, and is a good deal more spacious and comfortable than Udo's, but lacks atmosphere. Book in advance with KWS. BB $50

Rondo Retreat Centre 2.5km east of the Isecheno junction ☎ 0735 894474, ⓦ rondoretreat.com. Kakamega Forest's most upmarket option, situated in a fine old sawmiller's house built in 1948. This "Christian sanctuary for nature lovers" – owned by a group called the Trinity Fellowship – has wonderful, bright bedrooms in cottages set among cool lawns. It's fresh and elegant, with just enough clutter and lack of uniformity to make it feel homely. There's great birdwatching, butterfly-spotting and flower-enjoying too, but they don't serve alcohol (though you can bring your own). HB Ksh7800

★ **Udo's Bandas and Campsite** 300m from the northern reserve boundary and under 2km from Mgate Gate ☎ 020 6000800, ⓔ reservations@kws .go.ke. Named after the ornithologist Udo Savalli, these seven simple thatched rondavels (six twins and one quad), with bedding, nets and padlocks on the doors, come with a few pieces of cane furniture, but no other comforts, plus basic cold showers and long-drop toilets nearby. It's basic, but the forest environment touches it with a little magic. Book in advance with KWS. Camping $15 per person, BB $60

4

The National Parks and Mombasa highway

LIONS IN THE MAASAI MARA

5

The National Parks and Mombasa highway

This chapter covers the well-travelled route from Nairobi to Mombasa and a number of detours off it, along with the country's most visited game parks: Maasai Mara, Amboseli, Meru, Chyulu Hills, Tsavo East and West, and a trio of reserves in the north – Samburu, Buffalo Springs and Shaba. The Mombasa highway is Kenya's most important thoroughfare, the subject for many years of a massive resurfacing project, which was more or less completed in 2009. With scenic interest marginal for much of the journey, the temptation is to head straight for the coast, stopping only at the Amboseli or Tsavo national parks. But there are some rewarding diversions off the highway, which are not greatly explored: east into Kamba country and the towns of Machakos, Kitui and Mwingi, or south towards the base of Kilimanjaro and the Taita Hills.

Together with the coast, the **game parks** in this chapter are the most visited parts of Kenya, and the country's archetypal image. This is not to take anything away from their appeal, for visiting any of them is an exceptional experience. In the 24,000 square kilometres covered by the nine parks, animals hold sway. Their seasonal cycles and movements, most spectacularly in the Maasai Mara's **wildebeest migration**, are the dominant plots in the natural drama going on all around. Seeing the wildlife isn't difficult, but it does require some patience and an element of luck that makes it exciting and addictive.

It's likely that you will either already be booked on a safari, or you'll book one once in Kenya, either from the coast or from Nairobi. Popular alternatives are to **rent a vehicle**, with or without a driver, or, if you're alone or there are just two of you, and especially if you're on a limited budget, to take a **no-frills camping safari**. There are details on the ins and outs of booking safaris in Basics (see p.76), and plenty of operators listed in Nairobi (see p.117) and Mombasa (see p.406).

Ukambani

One very good way to start a trip heading towards the coast, if you're in no particular hurry, is to take an excursion right into the heart of **Ukambani**, the land of the Kamba people.

HOT AIR BALLOON OVER WILDBEEST, MAASAI MARA

Highlights

❶ Umani Springs This stunning yet affordable designer lodge nestles deep inside the Kibwezi forest, just a short drive from the Mombasa highway. **See p.322**

❷ The Taita Hills The densely cultivated and untouristy Taita Hills rise steeply from the dry plains. Visit the skull caves, where the heads of Taita ancestors are interred. **See p.328**

❸ Selenkay Conservancy North of Amboseli National Park, this rewarding community conservation initiative, staffed by local Maasai, offers bush walks as the norm. **See p.337**

❹ Mzima Springs A remarkable oasis, bubbling with crystal-clear water and inhabited by hippos, crocodiles and a variety of other species, some of which can be seen from the underwater viewing chamber. **See p.344**

❺ The migration At any time of the year, the Maasai Mara yields an extraordinary wildlife spectacle, but a visit during the annual wildebeest migration can be truly awe-inspiring. **See p.359**

❻ Mara Naboisho Conservancy This new Mara region conservancy sets a shining example, combining conservation with community involvement and superb safari experiences. Attractions include lots of lions, big herds of elephants and all the other stars of the region. **See p.369**

❼ Meru National Park After years off the map, Meru is now a model national park, although it remains little visited. The welcoming Kinna *banda* site includes a swimming pool. **See p.379**

HIGHLIGHTS ARE MARKED ON THE MAP ON P.312

5

Machakos

The biggest town in Ukambani, the bustling, good-natured trading centre of **MACHAKOS**, is, after Nairobi, the main urban focus for the Kamba people. Imperial British East African Company's first upcountry post, established in 1889, Machakos is ten years older than Nairobi, and therefore the first capital of Kenya according to some Kamba people. "Machakos", now the capital of Ukambani, is really a corruption of *Masaku's*, after the headquarters of a Kamba chief of the time. It's a name still seen all over town. The **old fort site** is located near the road in the administrative district, though there is nothing left to see.

Distinctly friendly, and overwhelmingly Kamba, Machakos has a backdrop of green hills and a tree-shaded, relaxed atmosphere to its old buildings that is quickly endearing. The weaving of **sisal baskets** (*vyondo*) is a visible industry and a major

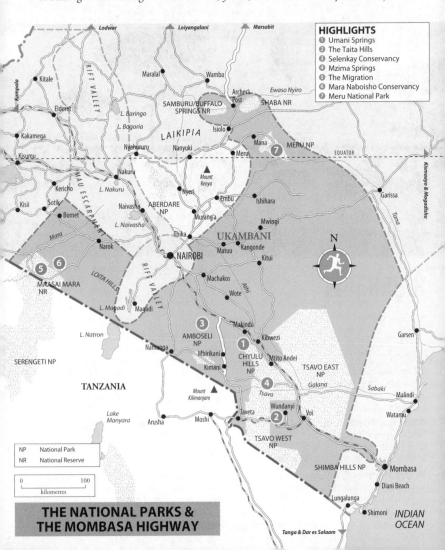

HIGHLIGHTS
1. Umani Springs
2. The Taita Hills
3. Selenkay Conservancy
4. Mzima Springs
5. The Migration
6. Mara Naboisho Conservancy
7. Meru National Park

| NP | National Park |
| NR | National Reserve |

0 — 100 kilometres

THE NATIONAL PARKS & THE MOMBASA HIGHWAY

THE KAMBA

The largely dry stretch of central Kenya from Nairobi to Tsavo and north as far as Embu has been the homeland of the Kamba people for at least five centuries. They moved here from the regions to the south in a series of vague migrations, in search, according to legend, of the life-saving **baobab** tree, whose fruit can stave off the worst famines, and whose trunks hold large quantities of water.

With a diverse economy in better years, including mixed farming and herding as well as hunting and gathering, the Kamba slowly coalesced into a distinct tribe with one (Bantu) language. As they settled in the hilly parts, the population increased. But drier areas at lower altitudes couldn't sustain the expansion, so **trade** for food with the Kikuyu peoples in the more fertile highlands region became a solution to the vagaries of their generally implacable environment.

In return for farm produce, the Kamba **bartered** their own manufactured goods: medicinal charms, extra-strong beer, honey, iron tools, arrowheads and a lethal and much-sought-after hunting poison. In the eighteenth and nineteenth centuries, as the Swahili on the coast strengthened their ties inland, **ivory** became the most important commodity in the trade network. With it, the Kamba obtained goods from overseas to exchange for food stocks with the highlands tribes.

Long the **intermediaries** between coast and upcountry, the Kamba acted as guides to Swahili and Arab caravans, and led their own expeditions. Settling in small numbers in many parts of what is now Kenya, they were naturally enlisted by the early European arrivals in East Africa. Their broad cultural base and lack of provincialism made them confident travellers and employees, and willing porters and soldiers. Serving alongside British troops during **World War I** gave them insights into the ways of the Europeans who now ruled them. Together with the Luo and Kikuyu, they suffered tens of thousands of casualties in the white men's wars. Even today, the Kenyan army has a disproportionately high Kamba contingent, while many others work in the police and as private security guards.

In the early years of **colonialism**, the Kamba were involved in occasional bloody incidents, but these were usually more the result of misunderstandings than any concerted rebellion. Although there was a major ruckus after an ignorant official at Machakos cut down a sacred *ithembo* tree to use as a flagpole, on the whole their trade networks and diplomatic skills helped to ease their relations with the British. As early as 1911, however, a Kamba movement rejecting European ways had emerged. Led by a widow named **Siotune wa Kathake**, it channelled opposition to colonialism into frenetic dancing, during which teenage girls became "possessed" by an anti-European spirit and preached radical messages of non-compliance with the government. Later, in the 1930s, the Ukamba Members Association (one of whose leaders was **Muindi Mbingu**) was formed in order to pre-empt efforts to settle Europeans in Ukambani and reduce Kamba cattle herds by compulsory purchase. Five thousand Kamba marched in peaceful protest to Kariokor market in Nairobi – a show of collective political will that succeeded in getting their cattle returned – and the settlers never came to Ukambani in any numbers.

Wamunyu, midway between Machakos and Kitui, was the birthplace of the modern Kamba **woodcarving industry**. Kamba men who served in World War I were introduced to the techniques of wood sculpture by the Makonde ebony carvers of the Tanganyikan coast. Today, the vast majority of woodcarvings in Kenya are still produced by Kamba artists, often in workshops far from Ukambani.

occupation for many women, either full-time, or behind the vegetable stand in the market. Machakos effervesces and it's a great place to stay for a day or two, especially on Monday and Friday, market days. Look out for (though you can scarcely miss) the truly splendid and quite venerable **mosque** and the fine, upstanding **Catholic cathedral**, Our Lady of Lourdes. Despite its significance, you can walk round the compact centre of Machakos in twenty minutes.

ARRIVAL AND DEPARTURE   MACHAKOS

By bus and matatu For Nairobi (frequent; 2hr), Mombasa (several daily; 7hr) and Voi (several daily; 5hr) head for the main stage in the centre of town. For services to Kitui (frequent; 1hr 30min), which has connections for

5

Embu and Mwingi, the stage is just up on the Embu road, beside the noisy *jua kali* metalworkers' area.

By car Depending on Nairobi traffic, it's a 1hr drive to Machakos.

INFORMATION

Services Barclays, Standard Chartered, Equity and KCB all have ATMs. You can get online at Solanq, Masaku Book Centre and Cyber Café (Ksh1/min). *Lapis Pharmacy* (Mon–Sat 8am–8pm, Sun 11am–6pm), next to Tea Tot Hotel reception, is a good chemist. Apart from the town's many produce markets, there are several supermarkets, including the basic Kutata, in the town centre, and the big Susu shopping centre on the way into town from Nairobi.

ACCOMMODATION

Central Park Guest House Machakos centre ☎0723 836107 or 0722 230932, ⌨bit.ly/CentralParkGH. Large complex whose clean, well-furnished s/c rooms have nets, TV and instant showers. Rates include a solid English-style breakfast. BB **Ksh2500**

Garden Hotel 1km north of the town centre ☎044 20037 or 0722 585637, ⌨gardenhotels.co.ke. With views of the Iveti Hills, this is the most upmarket place in town – a muzak-piped, "international-class" hotel with a health club, sauna and steam bath. The carpeted rooms have nets and TV, but it's getting tired and feels overpriced. BB **Ksh5280**

Ikuuni Hotel Machakos centre ☎0702 334044 or 0711 465344. Large and busy watering hole and restaurant, with five s/c (double bed) and five non-s/c (mix of twin and double) rooms – all well kept, if nothing out of the ordinary, with nets and TVs. Hot water most, or some, of the time. Discos Fri & Sat nights, and occasional entertainment on Wed evenings and Sun afternoons. BB s/c **Ksh2800**

Kavoca Hotel (aka KAFOCA Club) Machakos centre ☎0726 941990. The thirty rooms at this former Kenya

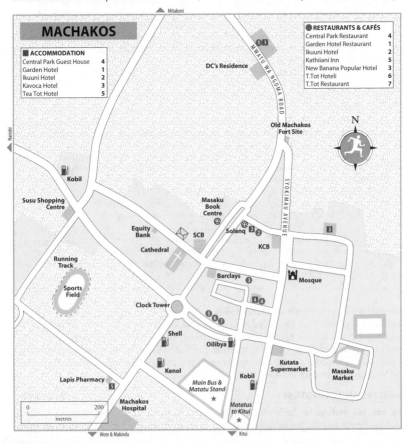

MACHAKOS

■ ACCOMMODATION
Central Park Guest House	4
Garden Hotel	1
Ikuuni Hotel	2
Kavoca Hotel	3
Tea Tot Hotel	5

● RESTAURANTS & CAFÉS
Central Park Restaurant	4
Garden Hotel Restaurant	1
Ikuuni Hotel	2
Kathiiani Inn	5
New Banana Popular Hotel	3
T.Tot Hoteli	6
T.Tot Restaurant	7

Mitaboni

MWATU WA NGOMA ROAD

DC's Residence

Nairobi

Kobil

Susu Shopping Centre

Old Machakos Fort Site

N

Masaku Book Centre @

Equity Bank

SCB

Solanq

KCB

STYOKIMAU AVENUE

Cathedral

Running Track

Sports Field

Barclays

Mosque

Clock Tower

Shell

Oilibya

Kenol

Kutata Supermarket

Masaku Market

Lapis Pharmacy

Kobil

Main Bus & Matatu Stand

Machakos Hospital

Matatus to Kitui

0   200
metres

Wote & Makindu

Kitui

Armed Forces Old Comrades Association club are reasonably well looked after and cheap enough, with nets and old-style showers. Safe parking. Room only s/c **Ksh1000**
Tea Tot Hotel Opposite Machakos Hospital ☎ 044 20577 or 0718 009684, ⓦ teatot.co.ke. To enhance the

confusion of there being two restaurants in town called *Tea Tot*, there's now a hotel of the same name. With its 56 plain, clean rooms with nets and electric showers, this is overpriced at non-residents' rates, but good value (Ksh3000) for residents. BB **$65**

EATING, DRINKING AND NIGHTLIFE

Central Park Restaurant Machakos centre ☎ 0723 836107, ⓦ bit.ly/CentralParkGH. The first-floor restaurant is a popular local pub with flat-screen TV and big meals (plate of bhajias Ksh140, beer Ksh130). Their *Wizards* club gets very lively on Fri & Sat nights with a disco (Ksh200–300 when there's live music). Daily 7am–midnight.

Garden Hotel Restaurant 1km north of the town centre ☎ 044 20037 or 0722 585637. Good-value snacks and main meals, including salads (Ksh100–200), sandwiches (Ksh150–250) and buffets (Ksh900). Daily 10am–11pm.

Ikuuni Hotel Machakos centre ☎ 0702 334044 or 0711 465344. Wide range of dishes, including *mushkaki* (Ksh220), liver and chips (Ksh350) and green salad (Ksh120), though some prices are well above the *hoteli* norm. Beers Ksh140, wine Ksh150. Daily early–late.

Kathiiani Inn Machakos centre. Dishes up good curries

and chapattis. Eat well for under Ksh200. Daily 7am–9pm.
★ **New Banana Popular Hotel** Machakos centre. Basic but very friendly place, serving a range of Kenyan dishes, from *karanga na chapatti* (Ksh160) to chicken biriyani (Ksh220) and a nice line in soups – gizzard, for example (Ksh40). Daily early–late.
★ **T.Tot Hoteli** Machakos centre. The original of two similarly named but separately owned neighbouring *hotelis*. Both are busy, but this one has the edge, with a steady turnover of satisfied customers tucking into pilau (Ksh200), kebab (Ksh80), fruit salad (Ksh60) and the like, served by efficient staff. Daily 6am–9.30pm.

T.Tot Restaurant Machakos centre. The newer neighbour, slightly undercutting the more established *T.Tot Hoteli*, with *sukuma nyama* (Ksh90), chapati and soup (Ksh110), fruit salad (Ksh50) and other dishes. Daily 6am–9.30pm.

Kitui

Like Machakos, **KITUI**, 100km further east, lies in an impoverished area and is often badly hit by drought. Despite its proximity to Nairobi, this district is one of Kenya's least developed. The town is small, but there's a sizeable Swahili population, descendants of the traders and travellers who criss-crossed Ukambani in the nineteenth century. The town's mango trees were planted then, and are a reminder of the trading tradition.

Kitui was the home village of **Kivoi**, the most celebrated Kamba trader, who commanded a large following that included slaves. It was Kivoi who met the German missionary **Ludwig Krapf** in Mombasa, and who guided him to Kitui in 1849, from where he became the first European to set eyes on Mount Kenya.

Although it has no sights, Kitui is a busy trading centre, its streets lined with arcaded shops. Look out for **Kauma Glass Mart**, a quaint little place with an ever-changing stock of musical instruments and drums, knick-knacks, furniture and picture frames.

ARRIVAL AND DEPARTURE   KITUI

By bus and matatu Embu (several daily; 3hr); Kibwezi (several daily; 4hr); Machakos (frequent; 1hr 30min); Mombasa (5 nightly; 8hr; Ksh1000); Nairobi (frequent; 3–5hr; Ksh400).
By car Roads in the area are improving all the time. You

can reach Nairobi in under 3hr, city traffic permitting. The Kitui–Kibwezi road is still a slog of 3hr-plus. Some 20 to 30km at each end is reasonably graded, but the rest is mostly in poor condition.

INFORMATION

Services There are KCB, Barclays and Equity banks, all with ATMs. Happy Family supermarket is well stocked and busy, and Kitui supermarket is a long-serving

standby, but the biggest supermarket in town is the new Naivas in the town centre (Mon–Sat 6.45am–8.30pm, Sun 7.45am–8.15pm).

ACCOMMODATION

Kitui Cottages and Guest House Out of town, about 800m southeast of Kitui centre ☎ 0724 121009 or

0731 121009, ⓦ kituicottages.com. The swankiest, most expensive and least atmospheric place in Kitui.

5

Rooms have nets, DSTV, electric showers. Safe parking and good security. BB $\underline{\$3100}$

M&M Hotel Northwest of Kitui centre ☎0712 204306, ✉info@mmhotelsresorts.com. Reasonable, if somewhat chaotically furnished, lodgings with nets and electric showers, and a large café-restaurant and bar-lounge on the ground floor. BB $\underline{\$1700}$

Parkside Villa Northwest of Kitui centre ☎020 8074405 or 072 275129, ✉kituiparkvilla@yahoo.com. 38 decent, fairly basic rooms in blocks and cottages, with nets, TVs and electric showers, set in a large garden compound. The Kamba Cultural Centre crafts shops (see below) are at the front. BB $\underline{Ksh1300}$

Rosen Guest House Kilungya St ☎0711 772843. Small B&L with a few rooms, of which #5 (very small) and #6 (slightly more room), with a shared balcony overlooking the street, are easily the best, although there is only one barely double bed in each room. Nets, TVs, electric showers. BB $\underline{Ksh700}$

★**Talents Guest House** Northwest of Kitui centre ☎0711 963222 or 0722 672378, ✉talentshotel@yahoo.com. Kitui's nicest and best-value hotel, offering clean if somewhat cramped rooms, with electric showers and fresh-smelling towels and sheets, nets and TVs. Safe courtyard parking and, as it's on a cul-de-sac, a pleasant, paved area to sit outside at the front of the hotel. BB $\underline{Ksh2400}$

EATING

Flavours/Flavas Kitui centre. Co-owned with *Talent Lodge*, this is hands-down the best restaurant in town. Not only are the meals appetizing and well presented by switched-on staff (chicken mixed grill Ksh270, beef stew with *githeri* Ksh200), but the first-floor terrace is Kitui's best people-watching address. Mon–Sat 7am–9pm, Sun closed.

Moonlight Restaurant Kitui centre. Busy Somali establishment, with the usual pilau, *arosto* (roast goat, Ksh300), *aleso* (goat stew, Ksh300), plus *githeri* (Ksh100) and other upcountry dishes. Daily 5am–11pm.

Parkside Hotel Kilungya St. Busy and popular, with a terrace as well as indoor tables and nourishing staples such as bone soup (Ksh50), chips and greens (Ksh150), chicken pilau (Ksh300) and fruit salad (Ksh50). Daily 6am–9.30pm.

Riverside Bar & Hotel Kalundu Market, 1km from central Kitui. A big *nyama choma* joint that's dead during the day, but lively every evening, when they play music. Take your pick of goat (Ksh560/kg) or chicken (Ksh700 whole) with *sukuma* (Ksh50), washed down with cheap beer (Ksh130), soda (Ksh40) or wine (Ksh100). 24 hr.

Shining Glory Hotel Kilungya St. Intriguing *hoteli* with a mission to feed locals properly, serving dishes such as *githeri* with *matoke* (corn, pulse and plantain mix Ksh150), beef with *mukimo* (Ksh230) and brown rice with green beans (Ksh130). Daily 6am–10pm.

Travellers Hotel/Kitui Traveller's Café Hotel Kitui centre. Thriving and lively hotel offering lots of cheap chips and *mandaazi*. Daily 6am–9.30pm.

SHOPPING

Kauma Glass Mart Opposite the bus station. *The* place for drums, *kayamba* musical shakers, religious icons and fine, heavy, three-legged stools. Mon–Sat 8.30am–6pm.

Kitui Kamba Cultural Centre Front grounds of the Parkside Villa Hotel. Row of crafts shops, each selling a particular output of the local crafts industry – including

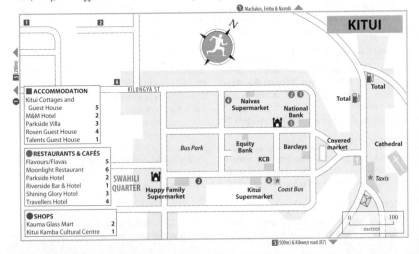

baskets, woodcarvings and jewellery. Prices are fixed but fair (medium *vyondo* sisal baskets: Ksh800), and each item is identified with its creator so the money goes back to the right people. Mon–Sat 8am–5.30pm, Sun 2–6pm.

The Thika-Garissa Road

This important artery to the east is in good condition for most of the way and security along the road is generally good, making it a viable first part of an alternative route to the coast to the obvious, traffic-choked Mombasa highway.

Matuu

A thriving trading centre along the Thika-Garissa road, **MATUU** is busiest at the top of the hill, near the easternmost of the town's two communications masts, where you'll find most shops and businesses.

Mwingi

MWINGI's surprisingly attractive site is an area of rocky hillocks and woodland, 150km east of Thika. Coming from that direction, you first see the town more than 10km before you arrive, spread out across the boulder-dotted hills. Mwingi offers little in the way of sights or entertainment, but plenty of small **places to eat** and an array of **lodgings**.

ARRIVAL AND INFORMATION   **THE THIKA-GARISSA ROAD**

By bus and matatu There's no shortage of vehicles passing along the highway, though as usual pickings thin out in the afternoon. Buses and matatus from Mwingi to Nairobi (or the reverse) take around 4hr. Vehicles from Matuu to Nairobi (or the reverse) take around 3hr.

By car It's an easy drive of around an hour from Thika to Matuu, and a further hour's drive will see you in Mwingi. From there, allow 3hr to reach Garissa (see p.536).

Services Matuu's KCB and Equity banks have ATMs; Mwingi has a KCB ATM.

ACCOMMODATION

MATUU

Ndallas Hotel On the road out towards Thika ☎0733 662537 or 0713 662662, ✉info@ndallashotel.com. The biggest and classiest establishment in Matuu with rooms of varying quality (avoid paying even more for a deluxe room: they have carpets, which are hard to keep clean). None has fans or a/c, but they all have nets, DSTV and hot water (in theory, 6pm–6am). The pleasant terraces, bar and restaurant are prettified by lots of original paintings. Residents' rates (Ksh3900) are more sensible than non-residents'. BB **$75**

MWINGI

Garden Cottage Hotel Exactly 2km north up the C93 Katse road ☎044 822448 or 0710 625599. The best option by far. Popular with local NGOs, this offers pleasant, if slightly unkempt, gardens, a small, shadeless pool (Ksh200 for outside guests), and a bar-restaurant and shaded terrace, which improve value of the rooms and variously equipped cottages. BB **Ksh3000**

Nairobi to Namanga

The A104, which used to be the main route to Amboseli National Park – now mainly accessed via Emali (see p.319) – links Nairobi with Arusha in Tanzania. Going south, the largely dull Kapiti plains are broken only by the **Maasai Ostrich Farm** (see p.148), signposted 7km off to the west, 15km south of Athi River. Further south, in the gentle hills where Maasai country really begins, is the district capital of **KAJIADO**. Set among sisal spikes and acacias, it's a friendly market town, where Maasai in all their gear mix with other Kenyans, and there's a fascinating daily **market**. The scenic interest picks up south of Kajiado, as the road snakes into the hills, giving views of the conical Mount Meru in Tanzania (4565m), and, if the sky is clear, your first glimpses of Kilimanjaro.

5

Namanga

The hot frontier town of **NAMANGA** sits on the Kenya–Tanzania border, nestled in a wooded valley between steep hills, 130km north of Arusha and 85km from Kajiado. It's a big **Maasai** trading centre, and Maasai women hawk armloads of beaded jewellery and other crafts around the town centre. The miniature **glass beads** used in the beadwork are actually manufactured in the Czech Republic, which exports them to Peru and the Native American reservations as well as East Africa. If you want to put a little money into the local economy, then buy some copper bangles, which go for around Ksh50 each, with discounts for bulk purchases.

ARRIVAL AND DEPARTURE   NAMANGA

By bus and matatu There are frequent services to Nairobi (4hr; Ksh500) and Arusha (3hr), plus the Nairobi-Arusha-Nairobi "shuttle" buses passing through, which often have the odd empty seat.

ACCOMMODATION

Namanga River Hotel On the right as you arrive in town ☎0733 440089 or 0722 440089, ⓦriverhotel namanga.com. A colonial-era oddity, composed of wooden cabins set amid pretty gardens, it was the halfway house on the old safari trail between Nairobi and Arusha. The place has a likeable atmosphere, with nets but no fans or a/c, and decent bathrooms, but uncertain hot water. The restaurant is reasonable (lunch Ksh750) and meals are served in the garden. You can also camp in the grounds, using the shower provided and toilet block. Camping **Ksh500** per person, BB **Ksh4700**

Namanga Safari Lodge Next to Namanga River Hotel ☎0735 249543 or 0735 249527. Clean, tidy rooms, which are more affordable but just as good as those at the *River Hotel*, with instant showers, nets and TV. BB **Ksh1200**

The Mombasa highway

The main town on the **Mombasa highway** is the relatively large service town and sisal-processing centre of **Voi**, about two-thirds of the way to Mombasa. There are several wildlife-related places where you might think about stopping over for a day or two, including the **Kibwezi Forest**, **Sagala Game Sanctuary**, **Ngutuni Game Sanctuary** and **Rukinga Ranch** – as well as **Tsavo East** (see p.348) and **Tsavo West** (see p.342) national parks themselves.

However you travel south down the highway, it's worth knowing that the right side of the vehicle is the best place for scenic views. From this vantage you may, in exceptionally clear conditions, see Kilimanjaro, either on the stretch between the small settlements of Sultan Hamud and Kiboko, or to the west of the Tsavo River. Your best chances are in the early morning or late afternoon.

GETTING AROUND   THE MOMBASA HIGHWAY

Although basic **supplies** are increasingly available along the road, **ATMs** are more limited. Barclays, Equity, KCB and SCB all have ATMs at Voi; KCB also has ATMs at Mtito Andei and Kibwezi.

NATIONAL PARKS AND KWS SAFARI CARDS

If you're travelling independently, and plan to visit **Amboseli**, **Tsavo West** or **Tsavo East** **national parks**, it's best to get your **Safari Card** (see p.71) issued and charged with the exact payments you'll need before you set off, at the Kenya Wildlife Service office in Mombasa (see p.406) or Nairobi (see p.141). The only gates in these parks where you can be issued, or top up, a card are the Voi Gate of Tsavo East, the Mtito Andei Gate of Tsavo West, and the Iremito and Meshanani gates of Amboseli. If you want to enter by any other gates, you'll need to have called at a point of sale (see p.71) and have the appropriate funds loaded on the card in advance. None of this applies to **non-Safari Card parks**, such as Chyulu Hills National Park, where you pay in cash on arrival.

By bus and matatu Try to avoid using matatus for travelling on the highway, as their constant stopping for passengers makes them more dangerous than usual. Going by bus, you can always ask to be dropped at the towns and sights along the highway if you want to make a stopover or take a detour. While the vast majority of services run between Nairobi and Mombasa, most buses break their journeys at Voi and Mtito Andei, and most companies will give you a part-refund on the full fare if you drop early.

By car In a reasonably fast private vehicle, you should reach Voi from Nairobi in under 4hr, while Mombasa is roughly a 6hr drive, not counting congestion at either end. The big filling stations at Mtito Andei and Voi always have fuel: otherwise, the stations at Sultan Hamud, Emali, Kiboko, Makindu, Kibwezi, Maungu, Mackinnon Road, Samburu and Mariakani usually have fuel too. The long gap that sometimes catches drivers out, especially those heading for Nairobi, is the 65km stretch between Sultan Hamud and the junction for Machakos. Salama, midway along, has a couple of old-fashioned pumps on the southwest side of the road, but supplies can't be guaranteed.

Athi River to Emali

Accommodation, eating and drinking, and nightlife in this area are covered in our Nairobi chapter (see p.148)

Heading southeast from Nairobi, the road runs along the east side of Nairobi National Park, passing at its end the junction for the A104 to **Athi River**, **Kitengela**, **Namanga** (on the Tanzanian border) and **Arusha**. It then skirts the Kapiti Plains on your right.

After here, there's a long drive to the truckers' stopover of **Salama**, the first of many one-horse towns on the way to Mombasa, providing lodging, food and beers for truckers and lost-looking Maasai. The next settlement, **Sultan Hamud**, isn't much bigger, but does usually have fuel.

The first centre of any real significance, however, is **EMALI**, which lies on the boundary of Kamba and Maasai territory. Three kilometres east of Emali, just after the railway flyover, a sharp turn to the south marks the start of the fine new C102 highway, which heads to Amboseli National Park, the western flanks of the Chyulu Hills, Oloitokitok (on the northern slopes of Kilimanjaro) and the Chyulu

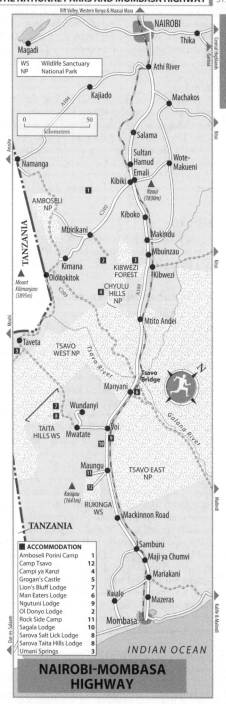

ACCOMMODATION

Amboseli Porini Camp	1
Camp Tsavo	12
Campi ya Kanzi	4
Grogan's Castle	5
Lion's Bluff Lodge	7
Man Eaters Lodge	6
Ngutuni Lodge	9
Ol Donyo Lodge	2
Rock Side Camp	11
Sagala Lodge	10
Sarova Salt Lick Lodge	8
Sarova Taita Hills Lodge	8
Umani Springs	3

NAIROBI-MOMBASA HIGHWAY

5

Gate of Tsavo West National Park. Just beyond the C102 junction, the small centre of **Kibiki** is the regular Friday venue for a major **cattle market**, attracting hundreds of Maasai herders, as well as Kamba people and Kenya Meat Commission buyers. It's an animated scene and worth a pause if your timing is right.

Nzaui

A north turn from Emali leads up into the Machakos Hills with the dramatic rock-mountain peak of **Nzaui** (1830m above sea level, 800m above the plain). If you don't have your own transport, get a matatu from the Emali crossroads to **Matiliku**, some 15km from the main road; Nzaui rears up ahead. With luck, you'll find some schoolchildren to guide you up – it's a popular local trip. From the top of the 500m precipices on the south face there are sweeping views across the Kamba and Maasai plains to Mount Kilimanjaro. If you have a vehicle, there's also a lazy way up Nzaui from the north, approached from the village of **Nziu**, further along the same road.

Kiboko

At the petrol-station oasis of **KIBOKO**, 160km from Nairobi, there's **accommodation** on offer in the shape of *Hunter's Lodge*. If you're travelling on a low budget, the lodge can be a good place to get a lift. The tiny village itself has a handful of rudimentary lodgings.

ACCOMMODATION AND EATING   KIBOKO

Hunter's Lodge Mombasa Mombasa highway ☎ 0727 209509, ⓦ madahotels.com. Named after the J.A. Hunter of rhino-potting notoriety (see p.350), this lodge boasts an acacia-backed garden full of vervet monkeys on the banks of the dammed Kiboko ("Hippo") River, with a tranquil birdlife haven over on the other side. Service can be sluggish but the food (grills from Ksh500, sandwiches from Ksh400, chips Ksh170) is good when it finally arrives. The twelve very serviceable rooms, with old-style showers (hot water available) and DSTV, have verandas overlooking the small reservoir,

and they're reasonably priced for residents (Ksh5500). There's also a simple campsite by the reservoir (Ksh500). BB $\overline{\underline{\$100}}$

Kiboko Safari Campsite 200m west of Hunter's Lodge, then 1km (not "0.1km") north of the highway, ☎ no tel. This new Kenya Wildlife Service facility isn't much more than a clearing in the bush, with showers and long-drop toilets, but it's a pleasant spot and convenient for self-driving campers. KWS rangers live behind the campsite, but you need to be fully self-sufficient to stay here. Camping $\overline{\underline{Ksh300}}$ per person

Makindu

Twenty minutes southeast of Kiboko, you pass the Sikh temple at **MAKINDU**, sometimes strung with what look like Christmas lights, and prettily unmistakeable. The Sikh community here dates back to 1899 and the construction of the railway. The temple was formally opened in 1926 and, in 1998, the Sikh community opened the hospital behind.

The **road from Makindu to Mtito Andei** is unusually scenic, with grand, sweeping views south over the Chyulu Hills and glimpses of lava flows and strange rock outcrops just to the north. The Kibwezi district is well known for its **honey**, which you'll be offered – along with **basket ware** and the usual stacks of **charcoal** – by countless sellers along the road. You may see grass and brick huts, distinguishable from human dwellings by their lack of windows. Each contains up to ten **beehives**, owned and tended by local women's cooperatives. When the honey is good, it's delicious, but if there's a dry spell you may be treated instead to something approximating coloured syrup.

Makindu Handicrafts Co-operative

13km southeast of Makindu • Daily 7am–6pm

In the village of **Mbuinzau**, where the road and railway skirt around the rocky massif of the same name, the **Makindu Handicrafts Co-operative** has grown from small beginnings to provide a trade for more than one hundred active members. You can watch them at work, and there are some nice pieces as well various quirky rejects that are much cheaper.

ACCOMMODATION   MAKINDU

The *gurdwara* gives a warm welcome to travellers who want to call in for a meal, or stay the night. Alternatively, there are several basic B&Ls in Makindu.

Sikh Temple Mombasa highway, corner of Wote Rd ☎ no tel, ⊕ sikhtemplemakindu.org. With sixty clean and comfortable s/c rooms, most with three beds, the temple is rarely full and they welcome tired souls escaping the highway any time up to 9pm. Meals are available too (daily 7am–9pm). There are no formal charges, so you should leave whatever you feel is appropriate: any excess supports the community hospital behind the temple. HB **Donation**

Kibwezi town

KIBWEZI is a growing Kamba trading town off the highway at the junction for the B7 to Kitui. There are a few shops, including a small **supermarket** and a **market** where you can occasionally buy spiky green **soursops**. One of those fruits you either love or loathe, the soursop is related to the custard apple, but larger and tarter.

After Kibwezi, the altitude drops below 900m above sea level and, at this lower altitude, you start to see large **baobabs** along the highway. Some are said to be more than 1000 years old. In the past, they were credited with all manner of spiritual powers and associations (see p.447), and oral history has it that the Kamba were drawn to this area by the sponge-like centres of their trunks, which are a vital source of liquid during droughts. In the low sunlight of early morning or late afternoon, the baobab landscape, with Kamba women working tiny plots of maize between the huge trunks, is one of the highway's most beautiful sights.

INFORMATION   KIBWEZI

Services There's a KCB bank with an ATM. A small branch of Kitui Happy Family supermarket stocks the essentials, and a basic produce market has fruit and veg.

ACCOMMODATION

If you're lucky, you'll be booked at the extraordinary self-catering lodge, *Umani Springs*, in the Kibwezi forest (see p.320).

Kambua Guest House Kibwezi town, 2.3km from the highway (turn left after the railway bridge, then follow the road north around the back of the town for 1.5km; signposted) ☎ 0722 521580 or 0720 260250, ⊕ kambuaguesthouse.com. Bright self-contained rooms with nets and a/c, with a shady terrace and pleasant gardens. They also do meals. HB **Ksh3500**

The Kibwezi forest

Daily dawn–dusk • Ksh1000 • 64 square kilometres

The **Kibwezi forest** is one of the largest groundwater woodlands in Kenya. This tropical forest ecosystem could not be supported by Kibwezi's low rainfall, but is largely dependent on the springs seeping up from the base of the Chyulu Hills through the area's porous bedrock and volcanic soil. The forest is managed by the Sheldrick Wildlife Trust on behalf of the Kenya Forest Service. Despite being just a few kilometres from the highway, it's a gloriously unspoilt area, and the only sounds you'll hear in the dense woodland are the calls of forest birds and the crashing around of the odd large mammal by day and an impressive cacophony of frog and insect noise at night.

Forest wildlife includes a good number of **elephants**, but some of the few **black rhinos** living under KWS guards in the Chyulu Hills move into the forest reserve

5

periodically. Around Umani Springs, you can often see **crocodiles**, and the area has become famous for some exceptionally large rock **pythons**. Even if you don't see any of these, the forest **birdlife** and extraordinary insect life (more then 230 species of **butterflies** have been recorded) make it a compelling area to explore.

ARRIVAL AND DEPARTURE   KIBWEZI FOREST

By bus or matatu You'll need to be dropped off at the Kibwezi junction, or ideally at the forest road entrance, 4km northwest of the Kibwezi junction. From here you'll have to walk or perhaps get a lift with the rangers.

By car The easiest entrance to Kibwezi Forest is signposted off the south side of the highway, 4km northwest of the Kibwezi junction. From here it's 700m to the forest rangers'

gate, where you sign in, then a further 8.6km of rough track to *Umani Springs* lodge, which is sited close to the boundary of the Chyulu Hills National Park. With a high-clearance 4WD you can drive over the hills through the park to *Ol Donyo Lodge* and the C102 road to Amboseli, but you'll need to advise *Umani Springs* in advance so they can arrange for a guide to show you the way.

ACCOMMODATION

★ **Umani Springs** Kibwezi Forest, 9.3km from the Mombasa road ☎ 0733 891996, ⓦ bit.ly/UmaniSprings, Nairobi reservations through ⓦ sheldrickwildlifetrust .org. Once a modest tented camp, *Umani Springs* has been entirely rebuilt as a chic, self-catering designer lodge, and is one of the most graceful and delightful in Kenya. Set deep in the forest, shaded by huge fig and acacia trees, and fully staffed, it combines real bush living with very high levels of comfort, including solar power with generator backup, a

very competent team of staff and an excellent cook (who can prepare anything for which you bring ingredients). Ten beds in three spacious houses are enhanced by extensive decking, dry-stone lava block walls for the outdoor showers, broad lawns, a large spring-fed swimming pool and two comfy tree-swings. You need to bring everything, from drinking water to toiletries and all your food, but it's possible to stock up adequately in Kibwezi. Self-catering, minimum four guests, whole house **Ksh6000**

Mtito Andei

MTITO ANDEI, or "Vulture Forest", is a big sprawl of service stations and snackeries, rising out of the dry country by the northern boundary of Tsavo West National Park.

INFORMATION   MTITO ANDEI

Services Fill up on fuel in Mtito Andei, as the next petrol station is at Voi, 97km further south. There is a Kenya

Wildlife Service sales office and information centre (see p.346) at Mtito Andei Gate.

ACCOMMODATION AND EATING

If you want to stay the night without entering the park, you should find the old way station of *Tsavo Inn* a pleasant enough retreat, but there are also simple lodgings on offer if it's beyond your budget.

Tsavo Inn Next to the Caltex filling station ☎ 0708 253488. This old place has a tempting pool (Ksh300 to non-guests) and more than fifty rather tired, but clean and secure rooms (nets and fans, but no a/c). The 1963 Michelin

map of East Africa, by the lobby, is fascinating. Meals are available (including chicken curry and rice Ksh700, avocado and tomato salad Ksh330), but be prepared to wait if you haven't called ahead. BB **Ksh5800**

The Tsavo River

From Mtito Andei to Voi, the road runs through remote national park country. When you cross the **Tsavo River**, 49km south of Mtito Andei, you're in the spot where two **man-eating lions** played havoc with the building of the railway in 1898, while engineers grappled with the river crossing. The lions seem to have been preternaturally lucky, since they eluded Colonel Patterson's various weapons for nearly a year and killed 28 Indian labourers in that time. The Field Museum in Chicago has the two stuffed man-eaters on display.

You're unlikely to see lions at the roadside these days, but between the Tsavo River and Manyani you may well come across **elephants**, always a brick-red colour, thanks to the soil. The Tsavo bridge marks the northern side of a 10km-wide animal migration corridor linking Tsavo East and Tsavo West, and thus also effectively connecting the northern Kenya ecosystem with that of southern Kenya. Note that **Tsavo**, although marked as a town or village on some maps, is neither; it's just a bridge and a virtually disused, slightly eerie railway station.

ACCOMMODATION AND EATING   TSAVO RIVER

Patterson's Camp (see p.352), in Tsavo East National Park, is accessed opposite the Tsavo Gate of Tsavo West National Park, on the north side of the bridge.

Man Eaters Lodge Off the highway, 1km to the northeast on the south bank of the Tsavo River, accessed by crossing the railway tracks by the old station ☎ 020 2072392 or 0710 467273, ⍾ maneaterslodge.com. Consisting of 31 tents along a bend in the Tsavo River in a private concession just inside the park (no park fees payable), this has tent-style rooms with good nets and verandas, decent bathrooms with electric showers, and generator electricity. You can also stop for lunch (Ksh1000) and a swim in the excellent pool. FB **$226**

Manyani

Some 13km south of the Tsavo bridge, and 2km south of Tsavo East National Park's Manyani Gate (see p.352), the nondescript highway centre of **Manyani** marks the southern side of the animal migration corridor. This has a number of *dukas* and basic *hotelis* refuelling weary travellers. **Manyani prison**, on the west side of the road, was an infamous British Mau Mau detention centre (see p.561).

Voi

The only sizeable town between Nairobi and Mombasa is **VOI**. It's a short way from the highway to the east, connected by two access roads, one from the Nairobi side to the west, and one from the Mombasa side 5km to the southeast. You drive through Voi to reach the Voi Gate of Tsavo East National Park, 5km to the northeast of the town centre, and it's the closest town to several wildlife sanctuaries along the highway to the south. There's no compelling reason to stay here or even stop – though the **Commonwealth War Cemetery**, with its graves from the Anglo-German campaigns of World War I, is interesting. If you do stay, however, you'll find it's a pleasant enough place, especially on the south side of town, where most of the street grid has been neatly block-paved and there are several nice enough places to stay, eat and drink.

ARRIVAL AND DEPARTURE   VOI

By bus and matatu Buses running between Mombasa (2–3hr from Voi) and Nairobi (4–5hr from Voi) come in all day – the heaviest concentration arriving mid-morning and late at night. Some Mombasa-bound buses continue on to Malindi (6hr). Buses from Mombasa to Taveta (2hr) also stop at Voi. Matatus go to Mombasa (2hr) and Taveta (2hr), as well as Wundanyi in the Taita Hills (last departure around 5pm; 1hr 30min). Any Mombasa-bound bus or matatu will drop you at Ngutuni Game Sanctuary, Sagala Game Sanctuary or Rukinga Ranch – or take a taxi from Voi, which should cost a little over Ksh100/km.

By car Voi is around 4hr from Nairobi or 2hr from Mombasa. If you'd rather keep on the road than come into town, but still need a break or a bite to eat, you'll find the smart new 24hr Petro filling station on the east side of the highway, just south of the Nairobi junction, has a useful café-restaurant, *Poa* (also 24 hr), and a shop (daily 7.30am–9pm).

By train The train to Mombasa (4hr; first class Ksh600, second class Ksh400) departs – in theory – at 4am on Tues, Thurs and Sat, while the Nairobi-bound train (9hr; Ksh1300 and Ksh700) passes through town– again, in theory – at 11.20pm on Tues, Thurs and Sun. The station (☎ 043 2030098) is 10min walk from the town centre.

INFORMATION

Services Voi has plenty of filling stations, a couple of supermarkets (though none of the big chains) and several banks with ATMs, a fair few lodgings and budget safari camps, and plenty of cheap bars and *hotelis*.

5

ACCOMMODATION

Voi is a safari and tour-drivers' hub, so there's a bit of hustle around the edges of some of the town **lodgings**. There are several safari lodges and tented camps inside the park (see p.347); if you want something outside the park but fairly park-like, try *Ngutuni Lodge* or *Sagala Lodge* (see p.325 and p.326). Both are just a few minutes' drive from town, on the highway going south. Off the 3.5km road between Voi town and the park gate, there's a string of safari camps and lodges – mostly budget to mid-market places.

VOI TOWN

New Distarr Voi centre ☎043 203 0277 or 0715 160678. A busy, well-managed warren of a place, with clean, basic s/c rooms, with nets, TVs and electric showers (but no fans) and some with balconies. BB `Ksh1500`

Oasis Guest House Voi centre ☎0724 540257. Good-value, clean, s/c rooms. Popular enough to fill up quickly, so call ahead. Room only `Ksh1000`

Tsavo Park Hotel Opposite the bus and matatu stage ☎0721 328567. Decent rooms, with nets, fans, TVs, electric showers and little balconies. Overpriced, even for residents (Ksh3000). BB `$50`

Vision Guest House Voi centre ☎0722 660113. Very basic but cheap s/c rooms with nets, plug sockets and electric showers. Ask for an upstairs room. Room only `Ksh700`

★**Zion Plaza Guest House** Voi centre ☎0729 844018 or 0726 039439. Clean, secure and breezy rooms with fans, nets and TV. Safe parking and good value all round. Room only `Ksh1200`

BETWEEN VOI TOWN AND TSAVO EAST VOI GATE

Augustine George Resort 1km from Voi town junction ☎0723 455370 or 0721 919925, ⊛bit.ly /AugustineFB. Pleasant, local, Christian-style place, with conference facilities. Rooms have fans and electric showers, and TVs – most have double beds only. Good-value meals from Ksh350, but no alcohol. BB `Ksh4000`

Impala Safari Lodge 1km from junction ☎020 2108174 or 0731 669577, ⊛impalasafarilodge.com. Budget safari camp on a cramped plot, with six closely

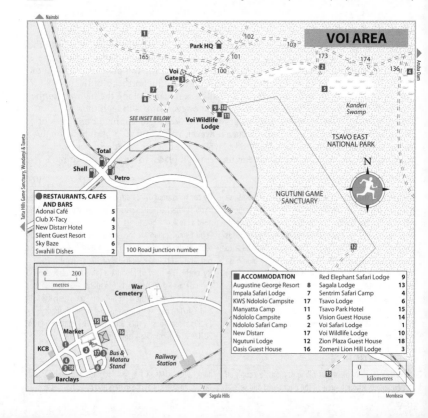

VOI AREA

Nairobi

Park HQ 🏠
165   102   103
101   173   174
100   136
Voi
Gate
Kanderi
Swamp

Voi Wildlife
Lodge

SEE INSET BELOW

TSAVO EAST
NATIONAL PARK

Total
Shell
Petro

N

NGUTUNI GAME
SANCTUARY

● **RESTAURANTS, CAFÉS AND BARS**

Adonai Café	5
Club X-Tacy	4
New Distarr Hotel	3
Silent Guest Resort	1
Sky Baze	6
Swahili Dishes	2

100 Road junction number

Taita Hills Game Sanctuary, Wundanyi & Taveta

0   200
metres

War
Cemetery

Market

KCB
Bus &
Matatu
Stand

Barclays

Railway
Station

■ **ACCOMMODATION**

Augustine George Resort	8	Red Elephant Safari Lodge	9
Impala Safari Lodge	7	Sagala Lodge	13
KWS Ndololo Campsite	17	Sentrim Safari Camp	4
Manyatta Camp	11	Tsavo Lodge	6
Ndololo Campsite	5	Tsavo Park Hotel	15
Ndololo Safari Camp	2	Vision Guest House	14
New Distarr	17	Voi Safari Lodge	1
Ngutuni Lodge	12	Voi Wildlife Lodge	10
Oasis Guest House	16	Zion Plaza Guest House	18
		Zomeni Lion Hill Lodge	3

0   2
kilometres

Sagala Hills

Mombasa

spaced, tile-floored s/c tents, six s/c rooms and a pool. Hot water by boiler. BB Ksh8000

Manyatta Camp 4.5km from Voi town junction ☎020 2048954 or 0722 206998, ⊚voiwildlifelodge.com. Sharing the same large plot as the co-owned *Voi Wildlife Lodge* (see below), this is the more boutique, tented-camp side of the operation, with a view over a seasonal stream and a nominally more "bush" atmosphere, undermined by pumping music around the pool and restaurant and the paved floors and private plunge pools for each of the 24 tents. FB $240

Red Elephant Safari Lodge 4.3km from Voi town junction ☎0727 217511 or 0736 931180, ⊚red -elephant-lodge.com. Main "safari rooms" offer very basic, B&L-style comforts, with nets but no fans. The four "bush houses", facing the park fence and a waterhole, are bigger and much nicer ($36 extra). Reasonably pleasant, shady grounds, spoiled by a backyard-style, above-ground pool and an elementary pool area. FB $130

★ **Tsavo Lodge** 1.5km from Voi town junction ☎0720 423136 or 0721 328567, ⊚tsavocampsandlodges.com. Very good value s/c rooms (fans, nets, TVs) and s/c tents (lights and electric sockets), with as much of a safari feel from the architecture and pleasant, shady grounds as you could expect at this price. Electric showers. You can also camp here. Camping per party KSH2000, FB $90

Voi Wildlife Lodge 4.5km from Voi town junction ☎020 2048954 or 0722 206998, ⊚voiwildlifelodge .com. Industrial-sized lodge of 187 rooms, featuring acres of concrete, facing the park fence much as a beach resort faces onto the ocean. Spacious hotel rooms with verandas, nets and ceiling fans (no safes), and nominal surcharges for Luxury and Ratna rooms. There's wi-fi in the bar area (Ksh500/hr). Two pools. FB $210

Zomeni Lion Hill Lodge 4km from Voi town junction ☎020 8030828 or 0735 877431, ⊚lionhilllodge.com. Perched on a hilltop, this is a pleasant, modern boutique lodge with ten rooms and two tents (nets, floor fans, lots of tiling) and wonderful views from the dining area and most verandas. FB $160

EATING, DRINKING AND NIGHTLIFE

Adonai Café Next to Zion Plaza Guest House. Pleasant café/restaurant with a cute little terrace overlooking the street. Everything here is super-cheap – beans Ksh30, pancakes Ksh30, pepper steak Ksh180, masala chips Ksh90 – though they only have a fraction of what's on the menu. Daily 6.30am–9pm.

Club X-Tacy Across from Barclays Bank. The open-air terrace at the front is popular with local boozers and football fans for the TVs, somewhat cold beer and fried food. The dancefloor inside wakes up more at weekends with occasional live music (entry Ksh200). Open 24hr.

New Distarr Hotel Voi centre. Lively restaurant with

good service, doing tasty food, this is *the* place for burgers, curries and birianis (burger & chips Ksh220, chicken biriani Ksh280, beef curry and rice Ksh180). Daily 6am–11pm.

Silent Guest Resort Voi centre Slightly pricier than the norm, with more Western-style dishes, such as pepper steak and chips (Ksh400). Daily 7am–9pm.

Sky Baze Post office street, Voi centre. Decent local nightspot for cheap beer and music. Open 24hr.

★ **Swahili Dishes** Post office street. Does excellent, coastal-style rice and beans (Ksh100), goat biriani (Ksh200), bhajias (Ksh20) and the like, and they usually have fresh juices on the go (Ksh70).

Ngutuni Game Sanctuary

Southeast of Voi, tucked into the space between the boundary of Tsavo East National Park and the highway; main entrance 13km south of the north exit for Voi and 7km south of the south exit • Free but exclusive to overnight guests or lunch visitors; night drive with a ranger in your own vehicle $20/person • 30 square kilometres

The **Ngutuni Game Sanctuary** – a former ranch – has a good network of driveable trails criss-crossing the thorn bush. There's plenty of game here, too, including **elephants**, **lions** and large numbers of **buffalo**. If you have your own vehicle, you can usually take a ranger for a game drive: alternatively, ask the lodge management for a copy of their map of the sanctuary. While the sanctuary doesn't match Tsavo East or West for spectacle or a sense of wilderness, it makes for a good stopover between Nairobi and Mombasa, or an affordable base for exploring the area.

ACCOMMODATION   NGUTUNI

★ **Ngutuni Lodge** Signposted, 5km from the highway ☎043 2030747, ⊚bit.ly/Ngutuni. Good safari over-nighter that is popular with mid-market tour groups. Rooms are a decent size and very comfortable (they could possibly

do with a/c at this altitude, but the fans work well enough), with good bathrooms. Each has a balcony facing the waterhole, which is floodlit at night. The lodge prides itself on good cooking, and staff are friendly and helpful. FB $222

5

Sagala Game Sanctuary

20 square kilometres

Sagala Game Sanctuary is a Swiss-owned ranch of savanna and woodland, largely unfenced, Buffalo and oryx are two of their commoner species, and the area is home to more than 200 species of birds. The central core includes the attractively low-key and very inexpensive *Sagala Lodge*, where they organize excursions into the Sagala Hills as well as around the sanctuary.

ACCOMMODATION — SAGALA GAME SANCTUARY

★ **Sagala Lodge** 3km south of Ngutuni Lodge, on the west side of the highway ⓣ0770 427671 or 0724 567700, ⓦkenya-sagala-lodge.com. A really affordable safari option – or highway rest-stop – set in a shady patch of acacia woodland, this is an all-round good place. The simple rooms, each an individual *banda* with terrace, have nets, but no fans, and the generator is on from 6.30–10pm. You can also camp, with use of a bathroom. There's a game-watching platform, where you can kick back on a sofa with a pair of binoculars and scan the bush in the sanctuary across the fence. Guides are available for sanctuary drives (free to guests, tip expected). Finally, there's also a good pool (Ksh200 to non-guests). Lunch (which includes use of pool) costs Ksh750. Camping Ksh500 per person, BB Ksh5000

The Sagala Hills

Regular matatus run the 20km from Voi to Sagala village (1hr)

An unusual day-trip from Voi – with some lovely walking country largely unvisited by tourists – is the **Sagala Hills**, which rise just south of Voi. The village of **Sagala** is a small rural centre with a shop, a *hoteli* serving nice *chai* and chicken, and a bar opposite the football field. The **Wray Memorial Museum** (Ksh200) occupies Kenya's second-oldest church building, established in 1883 by Reverend Joseph Wray (for the oldest, see p.420), with nineteenth-century photos and other documents.

From Sagala, you'll need a local to guide you around – older children will be happy to oblige. A 45-minute walk takes you past a small bridge to the even smaller settlement of **Talio**, which has wonderful views of the Taita Hills, Mount Kasigau and the savanna below. From Talio, small paths lead off through the fields to the base of the hills where there are other little villages (allow an hour or two to get there, depending on the path). Visitors are rare, so be tactful, especially with your camera, and generous with your time.

ACCOMMODATION — THE SAGALA HILLS

You can **stay** in Sagala or in Talio, where you can either stay locally (someone will happily take Ksh500 to put you up) or pitch a tent somewhere – ask at the school.

Gethsemane Cottages Sagala village ⓣ043 2030705, ⓔgethsagal@yahoo.com. You wouldn't expect much in Sagala, but there's a nice veranda at this little cottage setup, and you have use of the kitchen if you want. BB Ksh2500

Maungu and the Marungu Hills

After Voi, the road veers across the relentless **Maungu Plains**, also known as the **Taru Desert**, a plateau of "wait-a-bit" thorn and occasional baobabs which forms another, though less significant, migratory corridor for wildlife passing between Tsavo East and the southern plains of Tsavo West. Scenically dreary for much of the year, the plains come alive with colour after heavy rains, and during May and June can be carpeted in flowers. The small road town of Maungu itself, 30km from the Voi-Nairobi (north) junction, has a couple of B&Ls.

ACCOMMODATION — MAUNGU AND THE MARUNGU HILLS

★ **Rock Side Camp** 10km from Maungu down a rough signposted track to the southwest ⓣ020 2041443 or 0751 014915, ⓦrocksidecamp.com. Popular with German visitors and in the shadow of the imposing "Kale 1" Rock (which you can climb – it takes about an hour), this offers good food and a pool. It's hosted by the owners, who live on site and proudly claim it has never closed in 26 years. Great views and remarkably good value, though it's worth paying a little extra for one of the newer, bigger chalets. FB $\overline{\$165}$

5

The Kasigau corridor and Rukinga Wildlife Sanctuary

No day visits, overnight pre-booked stays only (see Camp Tsavo, below) • 680 square kilometres, including Taita Ranch

Between Maungu and Mackinnon Road, tucked beyond the rocky hills of the Marungu Range, more than 2000 square kilometres on the south side of the highway comprises the **Kasigau corridor**, an important wildlife corridor between the Tsavo East and Tsavo West national parks. The area is the focus of a UN "REDD" project (Reducing Emissions from Deforestation and Forest Degradation) being run by the innovative Wildlife Works (ⓦwildlifeworks.com), based on Rukinga Ranch, in partnership with the local community. With more than 400 staff, the company runs **Rukinga Wildlife Sanctuary** and a carbon-neutral factory creating fashion clothing from organic cotton.

It's an impressive model for conservation: as well as employment opportunities from the factory and tourism, the 100,000 people around Rukinga are the first in Kenya to benefit from **carbon credits**, giving people a financial stake in the protection of wildlife and the safeguarding of their local environment.

Beyond the conservation and environmental benefits, the **wildlife experience** here is outstanding: despite the thickness of the bush, spotting elephants at Rukinga is usually easy (there are generally around 300, and the top count in recent years was 1640), and the sanctuary is full of other game, including buffalo, giraffe, lions and cheetahs.

ARRIVAL AND DEPARTURE   RUKINGA WILDLIFE SANCTUARY

By car Only 4WD vehicles are allowed to enter Rukinga Wildlife Sanctuary. To reach *Camp Tsavo*, turn right (southwest) at the brown, earthen "Wildlife Works" sign on the south side of Maungu, 800m south of the Tanzila

Jamia Mosque, just over the speed bumps; then from the boom gate, just up the track from here, it is 16km to *Camp Tsavo* (home to all visitor facilities, *bandas* and *Ndovu House*).

ACCOMMODATION

★ **Camp Tsavo** 17km south of Maungu (transport to the camp from Maungu is possible for an extra payment: arrange well in advance) ☎ 0752 511029, reservations in Diani ☎ 040 3202056, ⓦ bit.ly/CampTsavo, see map p.319. An unusual and very good-value natural history base, this former "Taita Discovery Centre" offers dorm beds and safari tents, s/c *bandas*, or rooms in the well-equipped and comfortable *Ndovu House*. Affable staff and guides, together with a great deal of wildlife in and around the

camp, including a delightful family of genets in *Ndovu House*, make the whole place a charmingly offbeat base. You can opt to participate in a variety of well-thought-out ecological and cultural activities lasting from an hour to several days, and ranging from game drives and night game drives to mountain biking, bush survival skills and village visits – or even have a go at making paper from elephant dung. Dorm bed or bed in safari tent FB $\overline{\$55}$, *banda* FB $\overline{\$75}$ per person, *Ndovu House* FB $\overline{\$100}$ per person

Mackinnon Road

Some 11km south of Tsavo East National Park's Buchuma Gate, the first place you might stop for refreshments is the long sprawl of **Mackinnon Road**, distinguished by its huge and beautiful **mosque** and the neighbouring burial place of Sayyed Baghali Shah Pir Padree – a holy man who worked on the railway – right alongside the railway track. By tradition, vehicles are supposed to hoot their horns in salutation as they pass the shrine.

Samburu, Mariakani and Mazeras

East of the small settlement of **Samburu** (no connection with the national reserve in northern Kenya of the same name), the land is peopled mostly by members of the large **Mijikenda** ethnic group, their distinctive, droopy, thatched cottages often replaced nowadays by more formal square ones, increasingly also whitewashed and tin-roofed in

5

the coastal manner. The **Duruma** Mijikenda of this district herd cattle, make charcoal and grow some sisal – there's little else they can do in such a dry region.

The tiny centre of **Maji ya Chumvi** ("salt water") and the growing Mombasa satellite and truckers' town of **Mariakani** ("place of the *mariaka*", the Kamba arrows used in nineteenth-century wars against the Maasai), with its huge steel-rolling mill, bring you closer to the coastal domain.

The coast mood really takes over at **Mazeras**, a largely Duruma town. From this point onwards, the landscape has a quite different cast, with its mango trees, bananas and cassava, and – encouraging for weary travellers – the sublime sight of thousands of **coconut palms**. The route from Mazeras to the north heads along a ridge through the Mijikenda back country (see p.420). The main road plunges on, down the scarp to the Indian Ocean and Mombasa.

ARRIVAL AND DEPARTURE	SAMBURU, MARIAKANI AND MAZERAS

BY CAR

If you're driving to or from the coast but looking to avoid the traffic of Mombasa and its crowded suburbs, there are alternative routes for 4WD vehicles.

To Kilifi and the north coast A short cut, along the C107, leads out of the centre of Mariakani, heading more or less due east for 19km through the rolling Mijikenda back country to Kaloleni (see p.422), and then for a further 35km northeast through pretty forest and farmland to rejoin the coastal highway a few kilometres south of Kilifi creek. You can also take the turning north from Mazeras to Kaloleni, via Rabai and Ribe (see p.420). Allow 2hr from Mariakani or Mazeras to Kilifi, more after heavy rain.

To Kwale and the south coast For Kinango, Kwale and/ or Diani Beach, turn off the highway at Samburu or Mariakani to take the back country route over the Shimba

Hills (see p.424). Allow 1hr 30min to Kinango, another hour to Kwale and 30min more to Diani Beach.

BY BUS AND MATATU

Coming by public transport from the Nairobi direction to the coast (or the reverse), you can skip Mombasa by asking to be dropped at Samburu, Mariakani or Mazeras.

To Kilifi and the north coast If your destination on the coast is Kilifi or further north, then you'll need to get a matatu to Kaloleni from either Mariakani or Mazeras, both of which see vehicles leaving all morning. Onward connections to Kilifi get fewer later in the day.

To Kwale and the south coast To do the Kinango "short cut" to the coast, avoiding Mombasa city, you're likely to have to spend a night in a cheap B&L in Samburu or Mariakani before getting one of the few daily matatus that leave very early for Kinango and Kwale (see p.425).

The Taita Hills

Heading west on the horribly mangled A23 **from Voi to Taveta** takes you through a very accessible but largely unvisited region with a fascinating and distinct culture – the **Taita Hills**. Despite the name, the hills don't have any real connection with the Taita Hills Wildlife Sanctuary, which lies on the rolling plains to the south of the A23 road.

From the junction at **Mwatate**, the C104 twists for 14km into precipitous and beautiful hills, striped with cliffs, waterfalls, intense cultivation and patches of thick forest. There's a high population density, reasonable prosperity and a strong sense of community up here. Most of the welcoming **Taita people** speak the Taita language, a member of the coastal Bantu family related to Swahili and Mijikenda.

Wundanyi

Regular matatus up from Voi pitch through the fertile chasms on the switchback road to the attractive little district capital of **WUNDANYI**. There's not much to the place – it's really just a main street and a side street – but conifer trees on the slopes, and a babbling brook running past Wundanyi's football field, reinforce the feeling of departure from the thorn bush and scrub on the plains below. Further enhancing that feeling, the locally notorious Shomoto Hill, from which Taita criminals were hurled to their deaths under traditional law, rises up to the west.

5

The Cave of skulls

1.5km outside town on the Mbale road, 400m beyond *Hebron Guest House* and 700m before *Mwasungia Scenery Guest House* (see below), hidden in a banana grove just below the road

The sense of suspended reality in Wundanyi is accentuated by **Mwanda** – the **cave of skulls**, one of many ancestor shrines in the hills (there's one for each clan). In the niche rest the skulls of nineteen Taita ancestors, exhumed from their graves. Rather than looking for it yourself and possibly making a cultural *faux pas*, ask one of the guesthouses to provide a guide. Traditionally, the shrine was an advice centre where life's perplexities were resolved by consultation with the dead, and where sacrifices were made in times of drought. Christianity has eroded some of the reverence that the Taita once had for these shrines (and traditional dances and rituals have almost disappeared), but they are left undisturbed nonetheless.

ARRIVAL AND DEPARTURE   WUNDANYI

By matatu There are direct connections with Voi (1–2hr) and Mombasa (3–4hr), most of them leaving Wundanyi in the early morning. For Taveta (allow at least 3hr), you'll have to change vehicles, down on the A23 at Mwatate

(around 30min–1hr).
By car It's a straightforward drive up to Wundanyi from the Voi–Taveta road. Allow 1hr to reach the town from Voi.

INFORMATION

Services Entering town, turn right at the T-junction just before the bridge, and, after passing the Shell station, the KCB (ATM) and the post office, take the first left around the back of the large football field. This leads to Barclays (ATM),

the *Paradise Hotel*, the helpful Jumwa Solutions Cybercafé (Ksh1/min), and the *Lavender Garden Hotel*. If you don't turn left, continuing up the hill brings you to the market and matatu stand on the next left.

ACCOMMODATION, EATING AND DRINKING

There's a limited number of places to **stay** and **eat**. You'll find street food on Wundanyi's big market days, Tues and Fri.

★ **Hebron Guest House/Taita Research Station** On the road to Mbale just out of town (at the bridge, turn right and cross the stream and take the right fork after 600m; it's 100m from the fork) ☎ 0723 058078. Very nice, clean and well run, in a peaceful location, this occasional venue for Finnish scientists (which explains the sauna: Ksh500 per session) offers dorm beds as well as single and double rooms, plus hearty meals of meat, rice, veg and fruit (Ksh500). Dorm bed __Ksh1000,__ room __Ksh2000__

Lavender Garden Hotel Overlooking the football field ☎ 0715 876473 or 0789 962577. This bright, mid-range hotel has good s/c rooms – the best in town – equipped with nets, TVs and nice bathrooms with electric showers. Prices are steep unless you're a resident (Ksh2400), so haggle hard and at least try to get a room at the front for sunset views from the balcony across the

valley to the local landmarks of Wesu Rock and Shomoto Hill, the old Taita execution spot. BB __$65__

Mwasungia Scenery Guest House On the Mbale road, 1.2km from the fork (1.8km from the bridge over the stream in town) ☎ 0729 554522 or 0734 403225. Recommended for its helpful owner and lovely location rather than for its slightly ramshackle facilities, this is the best place to settle into if you're interested in finding out more about the Taita people: the owner is knowledgeable, and can take you on walks around the hills to see waterfalls, skull caves and Shomoto Hill. Rooms are basic, and the house is shared with the family. Meals are available on request (prices negotiable). You can also camp in the orchard (negotiable rates). Room only __Ksh500__ per person

Paradise Hotel Opposite the Lavender garden. Busy local bar, recommended for tasty meals and a lively atmosphere. Open 24hr.

Taita Hills Wildlife Sanctuary

Entry is off the south side of the A23, signposted 15.5km west of the junction for Wundanyi in Mwatate • $30 • Night game drives with a guide and driver (9pm, 2hr-plus; $20) are a regular feature that is rarely available in KWS-managed national parks • 113 square kilometres

One place attracting major tourist traffic in this district, particularly visitors on fleeting air safaris from the coast, is **Taita Hills Wildlife Sanctuary**, which isn't in the Taita Hills at all, but in the hillocky lowlands 15km west of Mwatate on the Taveta road. Set up in

5

1973 by the Hilton hotel chain, the sanctuary is now owned and managed by Sarova Hotels, who successfully balance wildlife and human needs in an environment that, while not being fully natural, seems to work well for both.

For most of the year, the sanctuary is full of wildlife. There are more than fifty species of **large mammals** and three hundred species of birds here, and its small size means the rangers always have a good idea of where the key animals can be seen. It's not uncommon to spot two dozen species in a morning game drive, among them lions, cheetahs, large herds of elephant and buffalo, and all the other southern plains grazers. During the drier times of the year, when the animals are not dispersed, the water sources beneath *Salt Lick Lodge*, on the southern side of the sanctuary, provide waterhole game-viewing, including a very good ground-level hide, far better than you could hope to experience at *Treetops* or *The Ark* (see p.191).

ACCOMMODATION

TAITA HILLS WILDLIFE SANCTUARY

★ **Sarova Salt Lick Lodge** Inside the sanctuary ☎ 043 2030270 or 0728 608765, ⊚ sarovahotels.com. Built on stilts over a chain of waterholes, this looks from a distance like a clump of mushrooms sprouting from the bush. The semicircular rooms occupy turret-like, conical-roofed houses, linked by aerial walkways, their walls finished in mock-sandbag style, all in keeping with the area's World War I battle history. Architecture aside, remarkable animal-viewing is the hallmark of *Salt Lick*. As you sip your beer over the heads of elephants drinking from the waterhole below, you're literally within touching

distance of dozens of trunks. Granted, you're rarely sitting here alone (there's usually a good crowd of locals and tourists), but few lodges in Kenya offer this kind of access. Pachyphile heaven. FB **$315**

Sarova Taita Hills Lodge 500m from the road, just before the sanctuary gate, ☎ 043 2030540 or 0728 608765, ⊚ sarovahotels.com. Comfortable bush hotel whose attractive rooms have nets and fans. Ordinary but copious meals are complemented by a very good pool, and poolside animal-watching over the fence into the sanctuary. Good value for money. FB **$280**

The Voi–Taveta road and southern Tsavo West

The **A23 road** from Voi to Taveta more or less follows the old railway line. It's painfully rocky as far as Mwatate, and then improves slightly to corrugated *murram* as it forms a corridor through the southern arm of **Tsavo West National Park**, where drivers can keep up a decent speed, mostly in a cloud of orange dust.

At **Maktau**, national park administration offices and a scattering of *dukas* are about the limits of excitement. You might want to take a look at **Maktau Indian Cemetery** where a number of World War I combatants are commemorated.

Although technically you enter the park at Maktau and leave it again at **Mbuyuni**, you don't pay any fees to drive along this 37km corridor. You're very likely to see some game, especially in the rainy season, but there's nowhere worth stopping on the road itself until you reach Taveta.

If you want to drive into the main area of Tsavo West National Park, north of the road, the easiest turning is the one for **Ziwani Gate**, 72km west of Mwatate, 14km east of Taveta. It arrows north, mostly following the park boundary line, with wildlife much in evidence, for 20km, to arrive at Ziwani Gate on the right and *Voyager Ziwani Camp* (see p.348) on the left. This route into Tsavo West's "Developed Area" can be closed when heavy rains damage the Tsavo river bridge in the park.

Lumo Community Wildlife Sanctuary

Entry is off the south side of the A23, signposted 23.5km west of the junction for Wundanyi in Mwatate • $40 • ⊚ lumoconservancy.com • 460 square kilometres

Comprising Lualenyi Ranch, Miramba Communal Grazing Area and Ossa Group Ranch (hence LU-M-O), **Lumo Wildlife Sanctuary** is one of Kenya's newest and most successful community conservation initiatives. With *Lion's Bluff* lodge now fully operational, the area is a real draw for coast-based safaris – if only the route here from Voi wasn't quite so terrible.

More than four times the size of Taita Hills Sanctuary, Lumo shares its boundary, and visitors are able to do game drives in both areas. There are usually plenty of **elephants** to be seen, together with most of the other species of plains game common in the southern Kenyan parks. **Predators** tend to be elusive, but sightings of lion, cheetah and leopard are well noted and passed on – so you're unlucky to miss them if they're in the area. Night drives can sometimes include some real rarities, such as **aardwolf** and **serval**, of which Lumo has recorded melanistic – all black – individuals.

As well as mammals, Lumo is a bit of a paradise for ornithologists, with an estimated 400-plus species of **birds**, include rare endemics like the Taita apalis, Taita thrush and southern banded snake eagle. There's a resident ornithologist at *Lion's Bluff* who is just as happy going out with novice birders as he is with experienced enthusiasts.

ACCOMMODATION

LUMO SANCTUARY

Cheetah Campsite Lumo Community Wildlife Sanctuary, about 8km from the A23, ⓦ bit.ly /LumoCamping. Well-maintained campsite with showers, toilets, drinking water and firewood included in the rate, and the option of sleeping in a four-bed shelter under mosquito nets. Tents are available to rent, and campers can use the lodge restaurant and bar. You need to hire the services of the rangers while you are in camp (Ksh2000/24hr). Camping $20 per person, shelter $30 per person

★ **Lion's Bluff** Lumo Community Wildlife Sanctuary, about 8km from the A23 (steep in parts; 4WD required)

☏ 0717 555498 or 0722 782627, ⓦ lionsblufflodge .com, Nairobi reservations ⓦ advantage-ea.com. Formerly *Lion Rock Tsavo Camp*, this community-owned lodge, spectacularly sited at the end of a dramatic ridge, has stunning sunsets and sunrises and good views of Kilimanjaro in clear weather. Best feature: the comfortable double and twin tented *bandas* with jutting balconies, on platforms suspended from one side of the steep slope. Letdowns: flakey showers and school-dinner meals (Ksh1000). Nevertheless, non-seasonal rates make this superb value all year round. FB $270

Taveta

Connected to the rest of Kenya by a couple of rough roads and a railway that has had no trains for years, **TAVETA** is situated 4km from the Tanzanian border. It has a mixed population of Taveta, Taita, Maasai, Kamba, Kikuyu and Luo, and even some Makonde, who originally came from Mozambique and were brought to work the sisal estates in the 1930s. For a few moments' reflection, visit the **World War I cemetery** at the entrance to town, next to the post office. The only paved street in town crosses the old railway line and heads straight for the border post, but the town's real main street runs north from the paved road immediately west of the railway crossing.

ARRIVAL AND DEPARTURE

TAVETA

By bus and matatu There are normally plenty of buses and matatus connecting Voi and Taveta (3hr); several daily vehicles to/from Mombasa (5hr) and one or two early morning departures to/from Oloitokitok (4hr). Local vehicles are most frequent on market days: Wed and Sat in Taveta; Tues and Fri in Chumvini/Njukini north of Lake Chala; and Tues and Sat in Oloitokitok, far to the north, near the eastern end of Amboseli National Park.

By car If you're driving to Oloitokitok, 79km from Taveta (turn north off the A23 4km east of Taveta), note that the road can be very rough going, and can be impassable in the rains, even with a 4WD. Voi is 109km east of Taveta, and you should allow 2–3hr for the drive, depending on how fast

you speed over the very rough surface.

Onwards to Tanzania The Tanzanian border post is 3.5km from the customs and immigration control in Taveta – there's only a very small settlement on the Tanzanian side, right on the border itself; the first place of any size is Himo, 10km into Tanzania. If you're not driving, you can reach the Tanzanian side by *piki-piki*. From the Tanzanian side of the border, where there is decent tarmac, there are frequent vehicles to Moshi (37km; 40min) and Arusha (118km; 2hr). Moneychangers in Taveta's market, and at the Tanzanian border, exchange Tanzanian shillings for Kenyan shillings, but, as ever, beware of scams and be sure you know the rate (approximately Ksh1000 = Tsh18,400 = US$11.50).

5

INFORMATION

Services Taveta's only paved street has a Barclays bank (ATM) and Safaricom (internet access Ksh2/min).

ACCOMMODATION

Kuwako Bar 50m up the main street north of the Lake Challa Hotel. Magnificent, gaudy murals in its popular bar-restaurant, and dingy, rock-bottom rooms at matching prices. Ksh600

★ **Lake Challa Hotel** 400m past the market ☎ 043 5352240 or 0735 849170. Excellent-value s/c rooms – the

best in Taveta – around an internal courtyard, with nets, DSTV, fans and electric showers. They serve good food and have a relaxed TV bar. BB Ksh2200

Tripple J Paradise On the paved road to the border ☎ 0725 095220. Much inferior to the *Challa* but a good deal cheaper as well. BB Ksh1400

EATING AND DRINKING

The Gate Way Pub Just before the railway crossing. A good place to sink a cold beer and chew on some *nyama choma*, both at low prices. Daily 8am–10pm.

Sarara Hotel Next to the New Challa. The local *matoke* stew (Ksh140) is popular, though you might baulk at eating eight green bananas in one sitting, even if they are smothered with gravy. Daily 7am–8pm.

Lake Chala

A four-square-kilometre crater lake north of Taveta, **Lake Chala** has one shore in Kenya and the other in Tanzania. Very deep and remarkably blue, it is a bewitchingly beautiful landscape, completely unsuspected from the plains below. Chala is still paddled over by a few friendly fishermen in their dugouts and is spiritually significant, with **lake monster** stories part of local folklore. The lake is bilharzia-free and was also believed to be free of crocodiles. However, the death while swimming of a young British traveller in 2002, and the discovery of her body, missing an arm, points to the presence of crocodiles, and you are strongly advised not to swim here (though the Kenya sub-aqua club still runs regular diving trips here). While locals swear the crocodile responsible was killed a few years later, there's no reason to think the reptiles won't colonize the lake again. They are resourceful survivors, and have been known to trek overland for long distances.

ARRIVAL AND DEPARTURE   LAKE CHALA

By bus or matatu Local vehicles are most frequent on market days: Wed and Sat in Taveta; Tues and Fri in Chumvini/Njukini north of Lake Chala; and Tues and Sat in Oloitokitok, far to the north, near the eastern end of Amboseli National Park.

By car Lake Chala is just west of the road between Taveta and Amboseli. Exactly 7.4km north of the

junction outside Taveta (the junction is 3.6km east of the railway crossing), you'll find a stone cairn in a triangle of stones by the road, the start of the 1.3km motor track that scrapes over bare rock up the side of the crater to the rim (high-clearance 4WD essential). From the top, it's another 800m along the south rim to the ruins of the *Lake Challa Safari Lodge*.

ACCOMMODATION

Wild camping In the ruins of Lake Challa Safari Lodge. Slightly eerie environment in which you can camp free of charge (people come here from Nairobi), although there are no facilities and you'll need to bring drinking water. The

village of Chala, 4km north of the cairn on the road at the base of the hill, has the closest simple supplies. If you want to find out in advance if the lodge is being restored, contact the *Lake Challa Hotel* in Taveta, which has the same owner.

Lake Jipe

Between the Voi–Taveta road and **Lake Jipe**, 35km south of Taveta, old sisal plantations in various states of cultivation and abandonment (squatters have moved onto the former estate here) cover the flat lands, along with cotton and even coconuts. Lake Jipe straddles the Tanzania border, like Lake Chala. At its northern end, it's fed by Kilimanjaro's snowmelt, passing via Lake Chala's underground outlet, as well as by streams flowing to the south from the Pare Mountains, across the border in Tanzania. Unlike Chala, Lake Jipe's shores are flat and thickly carpeted in reed beds. Several villages along the northern shore make a living from fishing, while the southeastern shore lies inside the almost unvisited southern section of Tsavo West National Park.

The lakeshore

At **Mukwajoni**, the fishing village 2km north of the park gate, you'll find only fish and the most basic provisions, so bring supplies from Taveta. When exploring the bush around the lakeshore, you should keep a sharp eye out for **hippos**, especially between the park gate and the village. A feasible target for a couple of hours' walk is the pair of hills, **Vilima Viwili** ("Two Hills"), just outside the park boundary, about 2km east of the track.

Once at the lake, the track becomes confusing as it heads south towards Tsavo West National Park's **Jipe Gate**, where you can enter the park (see p.346). Keep as close to the lake as you can, as the gate is directly on the shore. The rangers here are friendly and have little to do; they also have a **boat** (negotiable rates) for a spot of crocodile- and hippo-spotting.

Map

ACCOMMODATION
Grogan's Castle	2
KWS Lake Jipe Bandas	3
Voyager Ziwani Camp	1

0 — 5 kilometres

63 Road junction number

LAKES CHALA & JIPE

ARRIVAL AND DEPARTURE
LAKE JIPE

By taxi or piki-piki If you don't have your own vehicle, get a taxi in Taveta for the day – Ksh6000 should cover it – or get a *piki-piki* (Ksh1000 each way).

By car Head east from Taveta along the Voi road, turning right 6.6km from Taveta railway crossing. The 25km road down to Lake Jipe runs straight over the flat land between the Voi road and the lake. It's an area prone to flood, and the cambered *murram* road can be very slippery when wet.

ACCOMMODATION

There's nowhere to stay in Mukwajoni, though someone may be happy to put you up for a small fee.

KWS Lake Jipe Bandas and public campsite Just inside Jipe Gate ☏0726 610508, ✉reservations@kws .go.ke. Toilets, showers, and three simple twin *bandas* with nets. Despite the sometimes vicious attentions of mosquitoes, this is a peaceful and rewarding spot, and a paradise for birders. Camping $̲1̲5̲, whole *banda* $̲5̲0̲

5

Grogan's Castle

Head east from Taveta along the Voi road, turning right 6.6km from Taveta railway crossing; the 800m track leading up to Grogan's Castle starts 6.8km down this murram road

Grogan's Castle, a white and red mansion on an isolated hill rising from the plain, deserves a little detour. This extraordinary residence was built during World War II by Ewart Grogan, one of the most influential early colonists (see p.591). His mixed reputation was founded on a walk from the Cape to Cairo, which he undertook in 1898, on a notorious public flogging that he carried out on three of his servants (nearly killing one of them), and on his wealth: his status was such that he was able to dictate terms to the governor of Kenya before he even arrived in the colony, and at the peak of his prosperity his holdings extended to more than 2500 square kilometres.

The "castle", which Grogan hoped would become a government agricultural training school (it never was), was run-down for decades, during which time it provided roosts for birds, bats and insects. It's an enigmatic building, part hacienda, part folly, with huge arched windows that catch every breeze. The enormous circular main lounge gives spectacular 360-degree views out towards Kilimanjaro and Lake Jipe. The current owners, the high-profile former Taveta MP, Basil Criticos, and his wife, have opened it as a quirky hotel and refurbishment is gradually taking place.

ACCOMMODATION AND EATING   GROGAN'S CASTLE

Grogan's Castle Hotel Grogan's Castle ☎ 0735 671006, Ⓦ kafafa.com/groganscastlekenya. This would-be country-house hotel is a mixed bag: the rooms are impressive, but they're not all s/c, and they cry out for the soft touches that would make them comfortable, while the shared bathrooms are fairly rudimentary. With too many odd smells, far too much unsavoury insect life and a jovially amateurish approach to management, Basil Fawlty seems to lurk behind every creaking door. On the other hand, the food is unexpectedly good, served *en groupe* at Grogan's colossal dining table. Stay for the meals, the location, the views and the sheer exuberance of Grogan's vision – but there's still a way to go before this place fulfils its potential, making it currently overpriced, even if you're a resident (Ksh14,000). FB **$300**

Amboseli National Park

$80 with Safari Card (see p.71) • ☎ 020 2433025, Ⓔ amboselinp@kws.go.ke, Ⓦ bit.ly/Amboseli • 392 square kilometres

Amboseli, the Maasai's "Place of Dust", is a small and very popular park, and often full of visitors. Scenically, however, it is redeemed by the stunning spectacle of **Kilimanjaro** towering over it and – in those clichéd but irresistible photos taken with telephoto lenses – appearing almost to fill the sky. In the right light, the snowy massif, washed coral and orange, is devastatingly beautiful. Sunrise and sunset are the most likely times to see the mountain, especially during the rainy season when the air is much clearer, but for the most part it remains tantalizingly shrouded in a thick shawl of cloud.

On the animal side, Amboseli is **elephant** country *par excellence*. You will see large herds, and some individuals with big tusks. Predators, apart from hyenas and jackals, are relatively scarce (lions are almost absent, thanks to the revenge wrought by the Maasai upon the expulsion of them and their herds from the park (see p.337), but good numbers of herbivores are present. In the dry season, most of the animals crowd into the impenetrable marshy areas and patches of acacia woodland where food plants are available. But during and shortly after the rains the picture is different, the animals more dispersed and the landscape greener.

In the dry season, Amboseli can seem a parched, unattractive place, with Kilimanjaro disappointingly hazed into oblivion. Heading straight for the park's centre at Ol Tukai, with its lodges, workers, filling station, fences and barriers, doesn't improve first impressions. During the rains, however, it all looks far more impressive, with the shallow and seasonal **Lake Amboseli** partially filled, and a number of other seasonal lakes and ponds – the temporary home of small flocks of flamingos, pelicans and other migratory species – scattered across the landscape.

Balloon flights are sometimes available at Amboseli, but no operators were up and running at the time of writing.

VISITING THE MAIN PARKS

The first realization of where you are in Kenya's **big parks** – among uncaptured, and for the most part unfenced, wild animals – can be truly arresting. It may take you a day or two to adjust, as your normal, human-centric view of the world is re-balanced towards an environment in which big creatures hunt, die, mate, feed and enjoy themselves all around you in a wilderness landscape not much changed in centuries. Which parks you choose to visit can seem at first like a pin-in-the-map decision: any of them can provide a store of amazing sight and sound impressions (see p.72).

Amboseli, **Tsavo West** and **Tsavo East**, all in southern Kenya, are the three most accessible parks, with ever-busy game lodges, well-worn trails, large numbers of tourists and big herds of elephant. Amboseli, with its picture-postcard backdrop of Mount Kilimanjaro and guaranteed elephants, is an instant draw, but the flat landscape and lack of tree cover means you may be sharing the stunning vistas with dozens of very noticeable safari vehicles. Tsavo East, in contrast, is so huge you can usually escape company completely, although its sheer size makes the same easy for the animals, too. Tsavo West is also huge, but better watered, allowing higher concentrations of wildlife in a varied landscape that includes hills, woodland springs and lava flows in the scenery changes. On the other hand, the bush and woodland landscape can make animal-viewing harder. The little-visited but highly recommended **Chyulu Hills National Park**, to the northeast of Amboseli, has spectacular walking country, two magnificent luxury lodges and a superb new self-catering lodge.

Maasai Mara has the most fabled reputation of Kenya's parks, with horizons of wildlife on every side in a rich, rolling landscape of grasslands and wooded streams. Although it is somewhat isolated in the southwest, it is well worth the effort and cost of getting there, especially if you can arrange your visit during the yearly **wildebeest migration**. This takes place over an eight- to ten-week period, roughly between early July and early November, and is usually at its most spectacular at the end of August.

North of Mount Kenya, on the fringes of Kenya's desert region, the adjoining national reserves of **Samburu** and **Buffalo Springs**, and, just to the east, **Shaba National Reserve** share the bounty of the Ewaso Nyiro River system. These reserves have a number of animal varieties not found in the southern parks, including northern races and species of giraffe, zebra, various antelope and ostrich. Each of the reserves is small, even compared with Amboseli, which lends an impression of great concentrations of animals and birds, especially in the dry season when water sources are magnets for the wildlife.

Over to the east of Mount Kenya, the Kenya Wildlife Service's rescue and relaunch of **Meru National Park**, which in the 1990s had fallen into the hands of bandits and poachers, has been an impressive piece of work. Verdant Meru is one of the country's most beautiful parks, and still relatively unvisited, despite having, among its few places to stay, some of the very best options in the country – at both the luxury and budget ends of the spectrum – and nowadays some of the best wildlife-viewing.

GETTING AROUND   THE PARKS

Read through the advice about safaris, and particularly **guides** (see p.78), before signing up for a safari. If you're **driving**, the numbered junctions ("#17", "#158" and so on) and clearly defined *murram* roads and tracks make most parts of the parks relatively easy to get around, so long as you have a map (though the painted numbers on some cairns are illegible and many maps are out of date). Don't ignore the **distances** involved, especially in the large parks: at 40km/h, the speed limit in all the parks and reserves, it can take a long time to make a few centimetres of progress on the map. If you set off somewhere, be sure you have time to get back to base by nightfall, as all the parks **close their gates** at 7pm, and you are not allowed to drive around after that time. If you are changing camp, inform the management at your destination about your movements. Except at the designated nature trails, or where there's an obvious parking area, you should stay in your vehicle all the time, even if you break down – rangers will eventually find you.

5

Ol Tukai

Ol Tukai is a central oasis of trees and vegetation, a kind of "human reserve", fenced off from the rest of the park, with lodges and elementary support services, that was formerly the focus of most of the park's human activity. Today, the accommodation at *Ol Tukai Lodge* itself is the saving grace here, for if the derelict appearance of the now-closed *Amboseli Lodge* weren't enough, the extraordinary elephant destruction of the trees in what was once a pleasant patch of woodland has to be seen to be believed. The Ol Tukai perimeter fence has been breached by the elephants in several places, and a whole avenue of acacias has been taken out by them.

Game drives

Small enough to explore easily in two or three game drives over a couple of days, Amboseli is mostly open country with good visibility. A good first stop is **Observation Hill**. Early in the morning, with Kilimanjaro a pervasive sky-filler to the south, the swamps of **Enkongo Narok**, replenished underground from the mountain top, are looped out in a brilliant emerald sash beneath. You can get out and walk around up here, and chat with the rangers posted on-site.

There's always a concentration of animals around the swamps and along the driveable tracks which follow their fringes. These marshes are permanent enough to keep **hippos** in Amboseli all year, and the park is also home to hundreds of **elephant** and **buffalo** and a raucous profusion of **birdlife**. **Lake Kioko**, between Lake Amboseli and Ol Tukai – most easily seen along the track between junctions #21 and #26 – is a particularly worthwhile oasis, and similarly **Olokenya swamp**, with its seasonal lakes north and east of Ol Tukai, is always worth slow exploration.

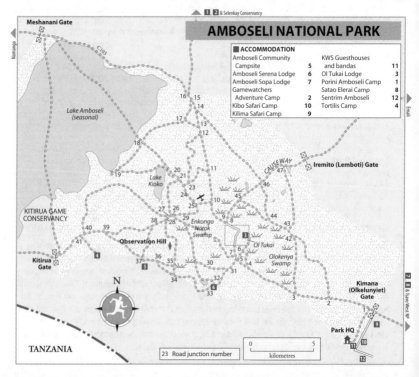

AMBOSELI NATIONAL PARK

■ ACCOMMODATION

Amboseli Community Campsite	**5**	KWS Guesthouses and bandas	**11**
Amboseli Serena Lodge	**6**	Ol Tukai Lodge	**3**
Amboseli Sopa Lodge	**7**	Porini Amboseli Camp	**1**
Gamewatchers Adventure Camp	**2**	Satao Elerai Camp	**8**
Kibo Safari Camp	**10**	Sentrim Amboseli	**12**
Kilima Safari Camp	**9**	Tortilis Camp	**4**

Meshanani Gate

Namanga

C103

Lake Amboseli (seasonal)

KITIRUA GAME CONSERVANCY

Kitirua Gate

Lake Kioko

Observation Hill

Enkongo Narok Swamp

Ol Tukai

Olokenya Swamp

CAUSEWAY

Iremito (Lemboti) Gate

Emali

Kimana (Olkelunyiet) Gate

Park HQ

N

TANZANIA

23	Road junction number

0   5
kilometres

▲ **1 2** & Selenkay Conservancy

AMBOSELI'S HISTORY

What is now Amboseli was part of the **Southern Maasai Reserve** at the turn of the last century. Then tourism arrived in the 1940s and the Amboseli Reserve was created as a wildlife sanctuary. Unlike Nairobi and Tsavo national parks, created at the same time and sparsely inhabited, Amboseli's swamps were used by the Maasai to water their herds and they saw no reason not to continue sharing the area with the wildlife and – if necessary – with the tourists. In 1961, the Maasai District Council at Kajiado was given control of the area. But the combined destructive capacities of cattle and tourists began to tell in the 1960s and a rising water table in the following decade brought poisonous alkali to the surface and decimated huge tracts of acacia woodland.

Kenyatta declared the 400-square-kilometre zone around the swamps (the present-day Amboseli) a **national park** in 1970 – a status that formally excluded the Maasai and their cattle, although in practical terms the park staff could do nothing to keep them out. Infuriated, the Maasai all but exterminated the park's magnificent long-horned black rhinos over the next few years, seizing on Amboseli's tourist emblem with a vengeance (the surviving rhinos were translocated). They also obliterated a good part of the lion population, which has still not recovered. Not until a piped water supply was set up for the cattle did the Maasai finally give up the land. For years, compromise appeared to be the order of the day, and, in the dry season, you'll see numerous herds of cattle and their herders encroaching well into the park unhindered, as they always did. Tensions rose in 2012, however, after a Maasai boy was killed by a buffalo and a number of animals, including elephants, were speared in retribution.

The **erosion** of Amboseli's grasslands by circling minibuses did a great deal of damage in the 1980s, turning it into a vehicle-clogged dustbowl that appealed little to animals or tourists. A concerted programme of environmental conservation, road-building and ditch-making was initiated, and this, combined with the toughest approach of any park to off-road driving (including fines and expulsions), has improved the situation enormously.

Lions are quite rare, but **cheetahs** are seen fairly frequently in the woods a little further south, and there are often dozens of **giraffe** among the acacias. Look out, too, for the beautifully formed, rapier-horned **fringe-eared oryx** antelope, and for **gerenuk**, stretching their long necks up to forage in the trees.

The open plains are scoured by **zebra** and haphazard, solitary **wildebeest**. The two species are often seen together – a good deal from the zebras' point of view because in a surprise attack the predator usually ends up with the less fleet-footed wildebeest. There are tail-flicking **gazelle** out here, too, of both species: the open country provides good protection against cheetah ambushes.

Maasai cultural bomas

Just outside the park, west of *Amboseli Serena Lodge* (between junctions #33 and #34) • From Ksh500 to $30/person, depending on your perceived ability to pay

Opinions are divided about the **Maasai cultural bomas**. After paying a fee, you get the right to take as many pictures as you want, and may be treated to a display of traditional dancing, while the Maasai get the right to pitch their curios at you with practised persistence. Try to ensure, at least, that your payment is going to the Maasai, and not to your driver (see box, p.358).

Selenkay Conservancy

Between Amboseli National Park and the Mombasa highway • Access exclusive to Gamewatchers clients and local Maasai; $200 return by road or $390 return by charter flight direct to the conservancy • 60 square kilometres

North of the park proper, but only easily accessed from it, with a driver-guide who knows the way, the **Selenkay Conservancy** is one of Kenya's pioneering community conservation success stories. Here, Gamewatchers Safaris, one of the country's most

5

KILIMANJARO'S GLACIERS

The most glorious views of **Kilimanjaro** are often on clear mornings during the rainy season. At these moments, when the dust in the air has been washed away and the clouds separate, the whole mountain seems to glow in the sky. Heavy rain often falls on the upper slopes in the form of snow, leaving a thick white topping and creating the impression that all is well with the atmosphere. It is of course an illusion: the glaciers are melting. The solid 10,000-year-old ice that rests on the peaks and once smothered the mountain with an icecap more than 20km across, has been steadily disappearing since Kilimanjaro was first seen by outsiders in the middle of the nineteenth century. Until the 1980s, the melting effect was slow, reducing the ice cover by about one third, but another third has vanished since then and glaciologists estimate the mountain will be ice-free by 2030.

---

environmentally sound safari operators, co-manages *Porini Amboseli Camp* (see opposite) with the local Maasai community. With a maximum of eighteen visitors, there are no time-serving, long-distance staff here: you're looked after by local warriors, generating direct income for their families.

Although the Selenkay (also spelled Selengei) area is bushy, with few stretches of open savanna, and wildlife is much less habituated to vehicles than in the park, the **game-viewing** can still be good, with predators frequently seen, as well as elephants, several species of antelope, and often the more infrequently observed mammals – there's a porcupine den close to the camp, for example. And the beauty of being here is the chance to go on game walks with your Maasai hosts, as often as you like. Down in a sandy area near the seasonal **Merueshi River**, they do sundowners and bush dinners, while their tree platform, near a waterhole, is a regular bush breakfast and sundowner spot, a favourite especially with younger visitors. It's about 4.5km from camp – a two-hour gentle walk, and they bring you back by vehicle if you prefer.

ARRIVAL AND DEPARTURE
AMBOSELI NATIONAL PARK

BY CAR

Most drive-in visitors to Amboseli use the beautifully smooth, fast and quiet Emali road, which takes you from the Mombasa highway to the eastern end of the park. Don't take the slower route from Nairobi that uses the A104 to Namanga. If you're coming from Arusha to Amboseli, however, you drive north towards Nairobi and turn right after the border at Namanga.

From Emali The C102, opened in 2010, swoops south through Maasai grazing concessions and mixed farmland towards Oloitokitok. Keep a look out, if the sky is clear, for the unmistakeable shape of Kilimanjaro on the horizon, often directly ahead. It's 59km from Emali to the junction for Iremito Gate and a further 21km on the gravel E397 to the gate itself: this is the fastest route to the centre of the park at Ol Tukai. Alternatively, it's 90km from Emali to the eastern, Kimana Gate, junction, and then 22km more on the gravel C103 road to Kimana Gate: this gives you the quickest access to camps outside the eastern gate.

From Namanga The 76km Namanga–Ol Tukai road is comfortable only at more than 60km/h, and very wearing once you're inside the park, where the well-enforced speed limit is 40km/h.

Between Amboseli and Tsavo West Many independent travellers connect Amboseli with Tsavo West on a

wildlife-viewing itinerary – the process is similar in both directions. From Amboseli, the C103 road leaves the park's east side at Kimana Gate (also known as Olkelunyiet Gate) and meets the C102 highway 22km east of the gate, and 5km south of the trading centre of Kimana. The junction for the continuation of the C103 east of the highway is well signposted just over 3km further south, but is often so badly washed away that it's not clear which route to take. As you head east, it quickly becomes a reasonably smooth *murram* road. Just under 13km from the highway you reach a GSU roadblock. There has been banditry in the area in the past, though not for many years, and as a result you have to travel on to Tsavo West's Chyulu Gate (66km from the junction, 53km from the checkpoint) either in convoy with an official vehicle, or escorted by an armed guard. The officers here process the daily convoys at 8.30am, 10am and 2.30pm. If you show up after 2.30pm they will organize an armed guard to sit in your vehicle (payment should not be necessary: you simply drop him at the other end).

BY BUS AND MATATU

In practice, budget travellers don't often try to reach Amboseli by public transport, but sign up for a cheap safari instead (seee p.117). Buses and matatus from Nairobi will only take you as far as Namanga on the west side, while buses and matatus from Nairobi or Mombasa will only get you as far as Kimana or Oloitokitok on the east side, from where you'll have to chance your luck with passing vehicles or, at a pinch, hop on a *piki-piki*. You'll need an equally flexible attitude if you want to get to Chyulu Gate, Tsavo West, as there are very few local matatus: be prepared for long waits in this area.

BY PLANE

There are daily Airkenya and SafariLink flights from Nairobi's Wilson Airport (2–3 daily; around 1hr; around $150 one way, $260 round trip) and flights on Mombasa Air Safari from Mombasa and Diani Beach to the park's only airstrip (daily; around 1hr 30min; around $360 one way, $480 round trip).

ACCOMMODATION

There are two reliable **lodges** and a luxury **tented camp** effectively inside the park, while a clutch of camps and lodges – some with much less certain credentials – has sprung up just outside the park, near Kimana Gate in the southeast. If you're booking a safari that includes a stay in that area, bear in mind that the park's $80 daily fee allows only one exit and re-entry per 24hr. This may restrict the number of game drives you do inside the park itself.

INSIDE THE PARK

Amboseli Community Campsite Just outside the park boundary at junction #37, accessible only via the park ☎ 0711 674435 or 0722 867394, ⊛ amboseli communitycampsite.com. The park's only real budget accommodation, on a fine, wooded site, though apart from warm sodas, a couple of toilets are the only facilities, and even water supplies can be unreliable. There are also eighteen *bandas* (actually two-person ridge tents, with floor mattresses and thatched roofs; these have no lighting, but there are bucket showers and European-style long-drop toilets and a kitchen/cooking area, with water provided in buckets. It pays to have a look around before choosing a *banda*, as they are scattered across a wide area. Own-tent camping or bed in *banda* $25 per person

Amboseli Serena Lodge Southern park area, near the Enkongo Narok swamp ☎ 0734 699838 or 0735 522361, ⊛ serenahotels.com. Always busy, but graciously managed, *Serena's* adobe-style architecture is well hidden behind a jungle of tropical plants and creepers. The 92 modestly sized rooms, adorned with animal murals, have built-in nets, ceiling fans, 24hr electricity and functional bathrooms with constant hot water. There's a large and inviting pool, good wildlife-viewing from the terraces and fairly priced petrol and diesel for sale. Ecotourism Kenya Silver Award. FB $370

KWS Guesthouses and bandas By the Park HQ, just inside the park, 2km south of Kimana Gate, reservations with KWS in Nairobi ☎ 0726 610 508, ⊜ reservations @kws.go.ke. The Kenya Wildlife Service manages two self-catering houses where you reserve the whole house – *Kilimanjaro Guest House* (six beds) and *Kibo Guest House* (four beds) – and five twin-bedded *bandas* (Nyati, Simba #1 and #2 and Chui #1 and #2). Bedding, warm water, firewood and security are provided (plus gas for cooking and generator electricity in the houses, and kerosene lighting in the *bandas*), but you need to bring everything else. *Kibo House* $200, *Kilimanjaro House* $150, whole *banda* $80

Ol Tukai Lodge Ol Tukai area ☎ 045 622275 or 0735 350005, ⊛ oltukailodge.com. Set among tall trees and lawns, *Ol Tukai Lodge* has stylish, rustic architecture, beautiful communal areas, and wooden cottages housing the fairly simple rooms, which have nets, and floor fans on request. Half the rooms look out beyond the low-key electric fence towards the Amboseli plains (rooms #1–48, "Elephant View"), and the rest look out towards Kilimanjaro (#49–80, "Mountain View"). There's a pleasant pool, and Maasai dances most evenings. Ecotourism Kenya Bronze Award. FB $443

Tortilis Camp Just outside the southern park boundary, accessible only via the park ☎ 020 2149913 or 0714 606960, ⊛ tortiliscamp.com. Set around a low hill, and named after the *Acacia tortilis* trees of the area, with stunning views of Kilimanjaro, this camp, surrounded by a sensitively low electric fence, is one of Cheli & Peacock's oldest. While not quite offering the same boutique feel as most of the others – it's a little larger and less informal – the seventeen tent-*banda* combinations are stylish enough. Perks include good meals on the terrace (they grow their own veg), a lovely pool, superb birdlife and waterhole game-viewing, plus drives into the neighbouring Kitirua Conservancy (fees included in rate). All guides are bronze or silver. Ecotourism Kenya Silver Award. Package $1180

SELENKAY CONSERVANCY

★ **Porini Amboseli Camp** 37km south of Emali, then 34km on bush tracks to the west: very difficult route to follow without a guide ☎ 020 7123129 or 020 7122504, ⊛ porini.com. Deep in the bush, shaded by acacias, this is an intimate and highly enjoyable experience, with nine very comfortable and spacious en-suite tents, each with a double and single bed, solar lighting, and full bathrooms with hot "safari showers" to order. Rates include day and night drives, bush walks, sundowners and a village visit unusual for being completely non-commercial – you won't be hassled to buy crafts all the time you're there. Apart from the manager and head chef, all the staff are Maasai

5

from the local community. Closed mid-April–May; no children under 8. Ecotourism Kenya Gold Award. Rates include conservancy fee. Package $870

Gamewatchers Adventure Camp About 5km from Porini Amboseli Camp ☎020 7123129 or 020 7122504, ⊛porini.com. Budget version of *Porini Amboseli*, with accommodation in small dome tents. The rest of the experience, however, with local guides and all activities – including game drives, game walks and a Maasai village visit – is the same as the more expensive base. Hosted by a silver guide from the local community. Rates include conservancy fee but, unusually, no drinks. Nightly rate based on a three-night stay, not including travel. Package $460

OUTSIDE KIMANA GATE

Amboseli Sopa Lodge 5km east of Kimana Gate ☎045 622334, ⊛sopalodges.com. Eighty-three spacious and comfortably furnished rooms, with no nets, fans or a/c, but in a very pleasant garden setting, with good views of Kilimanjaro and a pool. The lodge has no vehicles of its own, and acts as a base for safaris from the coast. Ecotourism Kenya Bronze Award. FB $314

Kibo Safari Camp 2km south of Kimana Gate ☎020 2672834 or 0721 380539, ⊛kibosafaricamp.com. The sixty-odd diminutive ridge tents here are getting old. It's not luxurious, but has a rough sort of charm, at least compared with neighbouring *Sentrim*, and the pool is a plus. FB Ksh28000

Kilima Safari Camp 500m east of Kimana Gate ☎020 6005072 or 0722 741161, ⊛madahotels.com. Owned by the operators of *Fig Tree Camp* in the Mara, this very different beast – a huge investment incorporating lofty public areas, a splendid pool and flamboyant "tent" and chalet designs – was opened in 2009. Too much furniture, uncomfortable beds and not enough shade on site may, hopefully, change with time – it has the potential to be a nice place. FB $630

Sentrim Amboseli 3.5km south of Kimana Gate ☎0733 852083 or 0722 207361, ⊛sentrim-hotels .com. Concrete, even green concrete, is still concrete. And this charmless, shadeless property has lots of it. Sixty identical tents with plywood furniture, each with a fan, electric socket, room safe and hotel-style bathroom. Pool. FB $240

ELERAI CONSERVATION AREA

★ **Satao Elerai Camp** Elerai conservation area, 10km southeast of Kimana Gate ☎020 2434600 or 0729 403566, ⊛sataoelerai.com. Like its sister camp in Tsavo East, Satao Elerai is a very comfortable, well-run, mid-range safari camp that isn't mass market, but isn't chic or small enough to be boutique. Great views of Kilimanjaro – when the mountain isn't being coy – are complemented by competent guiding (one silver and three bronze guides) in a private, game-rich community area of 20 square kilometres. Good food, with choices, and a nice pool make this excellent value for money. Ecotourism Kenya Silver Award. FB $490

Oloitokitok

With Kilimanjaro towering in front of you, the C102 slices across the plains, curves through the pretty, spring-fed oasis of Kimana and then climbs up to the Maasai country town of **OLOITOKITOK** at an altitude of 1700m. You'll pass through Oloitokitok, which is at the southern end of the C102 highway, 104km from Emali, if heading direct to Taveta from Nairobi or planning to cross the border to Tanzania via the foothills of Kilimanjaro. It's also a potential place from which to start a climb up the mountain.

Although it's ignored by 99 percent of tourist traffic, this one-street hill town is in a stunning location, closer to Kilimanjaro than anywhere else in Kenya – Kibo Peak is just 25km from Oloitokitok as the crow flies. It's a relaxed place to settle into if you're interested in finding out more about the Maasai, as this is their easternmost major centre. Markets happen on Tuesdays and Saturdays. There's a customs post on the north side of town (you'll be waved through unless you're going to **Tanzania**), but the actual border is 8km further south at Illasit, on the road to Taveta.

ARRIVAL AND DEPARTURE   OLOITOKITOK

By bus and matatu With the arrival of the new highway, there's always connections with Emali (2hr), but on market days (Tues & Sat) there's even more traffic, as well as more frequent services to Taveta (2hr). For transport direct to Nairobi (4–5hr), be prepared for an early start.

By car Oloitokitok's Oilibya petrol station always has fuel. Oloitokitok is 104km from Emali (around a 1hr 30min drive), and some 230km from Nairobi (around 3hr, depending on where you start from and the Nairobi traffic).

INFORMATION AND TOURS

Climbing Kilimanjaro You can arrange escorted Kilimanjaro climbs at *Kibo Slopes Cottages* from around $1500 for seven days. You will obviously need to be fit for the hike and have your papers in order (Tanzanian visa and yellow fever certificate).

Services KCB and Equity banks both change money (KCB has an ATM). There's a post office and several relatively pricey internet cafés – try KiliCyber (Mon–Sat 8am–5pm; Ksh3/min), beneath *Ntawuoh Lodge*.

ACCOMMODATION, EATING AND DRINKING

★ **Kibo Slopes Cottages** 700m down a track branching off the main road to the east, immediately south of the customs post (on the left side of the road if you're coming from the Emali direction) ☎0721 104149, ⓦ kibocottages.com. Superior to everywhere else in town, with very clean and tidy s/c rooms, some with good views, and four-bed cottages for the same price. There's a bar and restaurant (beef pasta and salad Ksh450, toasted cheese sandwich Ksh120) and pretty gardens, and it's a well-established base for climbing Kilimanjaro (see ⓦ kiboslopessafaris.com). BB **$62**

Safaris Guest House 100m from the Oilibya petrol station ☎0728 244514. Christian-run lodgings with nets, sockets and electric showers. Advertising it as "Posh self-contained rooms" is perhaps going too far, but the house is tidy, clean and well run. **Ksh800**

From Oloitokitok to Taveta

The tarmac continues invitingly south out of Oloitokitok to the Tanzanian border crossing and market town of **Illasit**, where it veers off to the south towards Moshi in Tanzania. The road that continues in a southeasterly direction to Taveta starts well, with graded grey gravel skirting the flanks of Kilimanjaro, at least as far as the dispersed centre of **Njukini-Chumvini**. From here to **Lake Chala**, however, it's in a poor state and often impassable after heavy rain, even with 4WD. From Chala to **Taveta** (see p.331) it's much better.

Much of the scenery along this route is beautiful, the landscape changing from scrubby cattle pasture to plots of sisal and maize – marking the end of Maasai territory – and patches of acacia woodland, cut by streams and dotted with swamp. There are only a few settlements, acting as market centres for Maasai and Taveta farmers, but **Rombo** is notable for its very fine mosque with its soaring minaret.

Chyulu Hills National Park

$20 (see p.72) • ☎ 020 2153433, ⓦ bit.ly/Chyulu, ⓔ chyulunp@kws.go.ke • 741 square kilometres

The **Chyulu Hills National Park**, which follows the spine of the geologically recent Chyulu Hills lava ridge – only formed around 500 years ago – is one of Kenya's least visited and least developed national parks. Aside from the wildlife and the glorious scenery (the hills took the role of the less impressive Ngong Hills for the filming of *Out of Africa*), the main attraction is **Leviathan Cave**, the world's second-longest lava tube. You can explore Leviathan from *Umani Springs* lodge (see p.323). **Wildlife** is present in great numbers, though what you'll see varies constantly: the plains between the C102 highway and the hills are often speckled with game, including giraffe, buffalo, eland, zebra and wildebeest. In the glades of the forested hills themselves you can see elephant and giant forest hog and even, in the park's northwestern corner, towards the Makedo Gate, around fifteen **black rhinos** living on the lava flow under constant KWS surveillance. The crest of the Chyulus is wreathed in mossy cloud forest, constantly watered by the clouds that make the landscapes here so ravishingly beautiful.

ARRIVAL AND DEPARTURE   CHYULU HILLS NATIONAL PARK

By car A high-clearance 4WD is required to get into the park. The easiest access is signposted off the south side of the Mombasa highway, 18.7km south of the Sikh Temple at

Makindu and 4km north of Kibwezi junction (around a 4hr drive from Nairobi). Alternatively, you can drive into the hills from *Ol Donyo Lodge* or *Campi ya Kanzi* (see p.342).

By air SafariLink flies from Nairobi Wilson via Tsavo West to *Ol Donyo Lodge* airstrip daily in the morning (1hr–1hr 30min; around $170 one way and $270 round trip), with a second afternoon flight in the high season.

GETTING AROUND

The park's **Makedo Gate** can be reached from Mbirikani 4km south of Emali on the C102 Emali–Oloitokitok road, while the Kibwezi Gate is reached from a junction 1.5km south of Kibwezi on the Nairobi–Mombasa road. You can also get into the park from either of the lodges, *Ol Donyo Lodge* or *Campi ya Kanzi*. Whichever way you go, you'll need to be in a sturdy **4WD** and preferably have a guide: the terrain inside the park is steep and hard going.

ACCOMMODATION

★ **Campi ya Kanzi** Southern end of the Chyulu Hills, 12km north of the C103 Amboseli–Tsavo West road on the Kuku group ranch ☎ 045 622516 or satellite +88 2164 3339831, ⊕ maasai.com. Passionately conceived, award-winning Maasai–Italian eco-collaboration of eight tented cottages and a stone-and-thatch central building, constructed without tree-felling, entirely powered from renewable sources, sourcing water with a huge rain-water catchment and using organic produce from their own garden, dairy cows and hens. Ecotourism Kenya Gold Award. Conservancy fee $150. Package $1300

★ **Ol Donyo Lodge** On the western flank of the Chyulus, 29km east of Mbirikani on the C102

☎ 020 6000457 or 020 6005108, ⊕ bit.ly/OlDonyo. Astonishingly chic bush lodge, consisting of ten extremely stylish and spacious suites in six separate lodges, all with roof terraces, outdoor showers, private views and eight with their own plunge pools (the lodge's water requirement – 20,000 litres brought up daily by tractor from Mbirikani – jars with the important work they do with the Maasailand Preservation Trust). Guests eat separately or together, sometimes with the owners, legendary safari pilot Richard Bonham and family. Included are guided walks and mountain biking, riding, day and night game drives (DSLR camera and lenses available for a supplement). Conservancy fee $100. Package. $1300

Tsavo West National Park

$65 with Safari Card (see p.71) • ☎ 0720 968527, ⊕ bit.ly/TsavoWest • 7065 square kilometres

The combined area of **Tsavo West and Tsavo East national parks** makes this by far the biggest wildlife reserve in Kenya, and one of the largest in the world, sprawling across 20,812 square kilometres of dry bush country. It's the same area as Wales, and two-and-a-half times bigger than Yellowstone National Park in the USA.

Of the two Tsavos, **Tsavo West**, encircled by roads and encroaching human populations, is the most visited and the most developed. Yet within its vast 7000 square kilometre extent, the popular part that receives nearly all visitors is a "mere" 1000 square kilometres, known as the **Developed Area**, located between the Tsavo River and the Mombasa highway. Here, a combination of magnificent landscapes and good access and facilities (*Kilaguni* and *Severin* both welcome casual visitors, and *Kilaguni* has fuel supplies) attracts visitors in large numbers, while the well-watered, volcanic soils support wooded grasslands and a great quantity and diversity of animal life – though it's not always easily seen.

The Developed Area

Across the hilly **Developed Area**, there's an unending succession of fantastic views across the plains, dotted with volcanic cones and streaked with forest at the water margins. When the animals are abundant, every turn in the track seems to bring you face to face with zebra, giraffe, huge herds of buffalo, casual prides of lions – descendants of the "man-eaters of Tsavo" (see p.322) – or methodical, strolling elephants, almost orange from the dust. An unusual species to look for is the beautiful and shy **lesser kudu** antelope – always, it seems, running away.

One large mammal you're less likely to see is the black rhino. In the 1960s, Tsavo had as many as nine thousand **black rhinos** – the biggest population in Africa. By 1981, they had been poached to barely one hundred individuals across Tsavo West and East

5

(see box, p.350). The situation today has improved, and about 65 of Tsavo West's eighty rhinos are now in the safety of the **Ngulia Rhino Sanctuary** (see below).

The little circuit that takes you around the foot of **Rhodesian Hill** is recommended too, and **Poacher's Lookout**, near *Severin*, is a very promising place for a quiet scan with binoculars. There's a thatched shelter on this prominent hilltop, where you can sit in the breeze. Note that the summit is 4.5km from junction #32, not 2km as marked.

Ngulia Rhino Sanctuary
At the eastern end of the developed area • Daily 4–6pm • Free

You may see one of the sanctuary's 65 **rhinos** if you drive around its thick bush for a while. You can always visit the holding pen in the middle of the sanctuary to inspect the latest arrivals. Another fifteen rhinos live free in the park itself, each one under constant surveillance.

Mzima Springs
500m south of junction #11, 48km from Mtito Andei and close to both Kilaguni Lodge and Severin Safari Camp

The biggest attraction in Tsavo West is **Mzima Springs**. This stream of crystal-clear water was made famous by Alan Root's 1983 film *Mzima: Portrait of a Spring*, which followed crocodiles and hippos in their underwater lives. It's a delightful, and popular, spot, so you're advised to arrive very early to avoid a possible tour-bus atmosphere. With luck, some of the night's animal visitors may still be around, while the luxuriant growth around the water reverberates noisily with birds and monkeys.

You can walk around freely, as elephants and predators rarely visit, and there are **KWS rangers** posted by the car park to look after you, but make sure you're not close to the

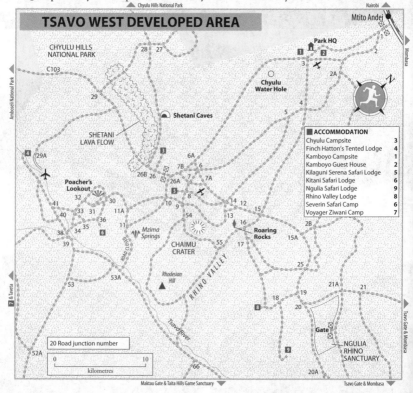

TSAVO WEST DEVELOPED AREA

CHYULU HILLS NATIONAL PARK

Chyulu Hills National Park

C103

Amboseli National Park

Nairobi

Mtito Andei

Mombasa

Park HQ

Chyulu Water Hole

Shetani Caves

SHETANI LAVA FLOW

Poacher's Lookout

Mzima Springs

CHAIMU CRATER

Rhodesian Hill

RHINO VALLEY

Roaring Rocks

Tsavo River

ACCOMMODATION

Chyulu Campsite	3
Finch Hatton's Tented Lodge	4
Kamboyo Campsite	1
Kamboyo Guest House	2
Kilaguni Serena Safari Lodge	5
Kitani Safari Lodge	6
Ngulia Safari Lodge	9
Rhino Valley Lodge	8
Severin Safari Camp	6
Voyager Ziwani Camp	7

Gate

NGULIA RHINO SANCTUARY

20 Road junction number

0   10
kilometres

Taveta

& Taita

Tsavo Gate & Mombasa

Maktau Gate & Taita Hills Game Sanctuary

Tsavo Gate & Mombasa

5

water's edge, where large crocodiles lurk. Equally be sure that you're not between a hippo and the water, especially early or late in the day, or during wet weather. They seem settled in their routine, content to snort and flounder en masse, but are notoriously irritable animals.

There are two large pools, connected by a rush of rapids and shaded by stands of date and raffia palms. The upper pool used to be the favoured **hippo** wallow, though in recent years they seem to prefer the lower pool. The springs' hippo population was cruelly hammered by the drought of 2009, during which the springs were the only source of water in the region, and the surrounding grasslands, on which the hippos graze at night, were reduced to a dustbowl as wildlife moved into the area. Despite the efforts of the KWS and local lodges to supply bales of hay, dozens of hippos starved to death. Their numbers are increasing again, but it will take years for them to recover fully.

At the side of the top pool, a circular underwater **viewing chamber** has been built at the end of a short pier. With luck (and it doesn't happen on every visit), you'll see the unforgettably comic tip-toeing of an underwater hippo, or the sinuous, streamlined stealth of a crocodile in motion, as well as the blue swirl of large fish.

Mzima Springs' water is filtered to aquarium transparency by the lava of the **Chyulu range**, just to the north of here: the porous rock absorbs the water like a sponge and gravity squeezes it out into the springs. A direct pipeline from Mzima to Mombasa, completed in 1966, is the source of most of the city's **drinking water**. Engineers devised a way of taking water from beneath the lava, but above the spring, preserving the area's integrity. There are one or two signs of the pipeline, but most are unobtrusive.

You don't have to be a botanist to enjoy Mzima's two **tree trails**, with examples of various trees labelled with their common uses and their English, local and botanical names. It's easy to spend a couple of hours in the area: try to sit for a while completely alone on the bank and you'll begin to piece together the ecological miracle of the place, as the mammals, birds and other creatures forget about your presence. And look out for **sycamore figs**, the spectacular tree that features in the extraordinary nature documentary *The Queen of Trees* (Mark Deeble & Victoria Stone, 2006; widely available on DVD) about the symbiotic relationship between the sycamore fig and the tiny fig wasp.

Game-viewing at the lodges

Kilaguni Serena Safari Lodge (see p.347) off junction 8, about 30km from Mtito Andei Gate **Severin Safari Camp** (see p.348) off junction #36, 8km from Mzima Springs

You may not be staying in the relative luxury of **Kilaguni Lodge** or **Severin Safari Camp**, but a visit to either can be highly rewarding, for the pleasure of sitting on the terrace with a cold beer, or having lunch (allow $25), while you watch the enthralling natural circus going on a few metres away. At acacia-shaded *Severin*, guests and wildlife are on exactly the same level, making the experience very intimate, while the **waterholes** at *Kilaguni*, spread beneath the panorama of the Chyulu Hills, are a well-known magnet for animal visitors.

At *Kilaguni*, dazzling **birds** hop everywhere, **agama lizards** skim along the walls (the miniature orange and blue dragons are the males in mating colours), **hyraxes** scamper between the tables, and **dwarf mongooses** are regular visitors. Out by the waterholes, scuffling **baboon troops**, several species of **antelope** and **gazelle**, **buffalo**, **zebra**, **giraffe** and **elephant** all provide a constant spectacle, with the possibility of the occasional kill adding tension. At dusk, **bats** swoop, while **genets**, **jackals** and **hyenas** lurk near the floodlights, drawn by the smell of dinner – though, thankfully, the lodge has stopped the practice of baiting them with meat scraps.

While *Kilaguni* is a dead cert for animal action, the much newer *Severin* is beginning to make a mark. The camp at *Severin*, far from dominating the landscape, seems to be absorbed by its environment, and there's nothing to stop the animals treating the whole camp as their own. Signs warn visitors not to stray off the paths, but you'll need little reminding, as families of **warthogs** trot past the terrace, **impala** and **giraffe** nibble audibly, and **lion kills** take place close to reception. Unlike *Kilaguni*, which is fenced, guests at *Severin* have to be escorted to and from their tents after dark.

5

Birding at Ngulia Safari Lodge

8km west of Tsavo Gate, 6.5km south of junction #18

Ngulia Safari Lodge is a stopover on the annual southern migration of hundreds of thousands of European **birds**, but the reasons for its attraction for the birds – apart from its isolated lights – aren't really known. Kenyan and overseas ornithologists and amateur birders gather at the end of November for a fortnight to identify and ring the birds that are trapped in mist nets (20,000 in 2008) to build up a picture of their migration routes. If you'd like to participate, contact the lodge or your national birdwatching organization for information.

Lava flows and caves

Shetani lava flow starts about 10km east of junction #29 and continues east for more than 1km – the caves are 5.5km up the high-clearance-only track that climbs the flank of the volcano, north of junction #26B; after 5km, start looking out on the right side of the track for an oil drum, and a fig tree that covers the entrance

The lava that purifies Mzima's water can be seen in black outcrops all around the Developed Area of Tsavo. The main park road from Amboseli to Chyulu Gate runs right across the spectacular **Shetani lava flow**. The eruption that spewed it out two hundred years ago was evidently a cataclysmic event for local people, and is still the focus of stories about fire and evil spirits (*shetani* means "devil" in Swahili). People are said to have been buried under the hot lava, and legend has it that their plaintive cries can be heard on certain nights. The local people appease the ghosts with offerings of food which, of course, are gone by daybreak.

At several places you're allowed out of your vehicle to explore the lava, which is brittle, honeycombed and unstable. After only two centuries, very few plants have yet taken hold. The **caves** are certainly worth investigation, and they sometimes contain the bones of various unlucky animals that have stumbled in and couldn't get out again. You'll need a powerful torch, however, to get very far.

Chaimu Crater

Nature trail 6km southeast of junction #9

At the foot of the extinct **Chaimu volcano**, you can leave your vehicle and climb up to the crater rim – a steep scramble through the scree that delivers magnificent views across the park. Although it doesn't look high, it can be surprisingly hard work and you shouldn't attempt it in the heat of the day. There are no rangers here, so you need to be acutely aware of your surroundings and watch out for large mammals.

ARRIVAL AND DEPARTURE   **TSAVO WEST NATIONAL PARK**

Nearly all visitors to Tsavo West come by private vehicle or on a road or air safari.

By bus and matatu There are no bus or matatu services into Tsavo West National Park itself. The small service town of Mtito Andei (see p.322), midway between Mombasa and Nairobi and walking distance from Mtito Andei Gate, is easily reached by public transport, but if you're hoping for a lift into the park, you're likely to be in for a long wait. It's not a good idea to be dropped at Tsavo Gate, the southern gate on the Mombasa highway located where the highway crosses the Tsavo River, as there is no settlement there, and again you could wait a very long time before getting a lift into the park.

By car Allow roughly 4hr to reach Mtito Andei from either Nairobi or Mombasa, depending on where you start from and the traffic at the time of departure. Coming from Mombasa, allow roughly 2–3hr to reach Tsavo Gate. Fill up before entering the park and take drinking water. *Kilaguni* lodge has a small filling station (daily 7am–4pm & 6–7pm; prices

about ten percent above the pump price in Mtito Andei). The information centre at Mtito Andei gate has interesting background about Tsavo West, as well as a small shop selling cold drinks: other gates have few if any facilities. Coming from the coast direction, the quickest access is Tsavo Gate, in the southeast of the Developed Area. Access via Chyulu Gate and Ziwani Gate (see p.330) is possible, but bear in mind the warning about the small Tsavo river bridge in the park, which is apt to be closed after heavy rains.

By plane There are at least daily flights from Nairobi Wilson on SafariLink and Airkenya to *Kilaguni* and/or *Finch Hatton's* airstrip, depending on demand (around 1hr; around $190 one way, $300 round trip). You can fly daily to the same airstrips from Mombasa and Diani Beach with Mombasa Air Safari (around 1hr 30min; around $360 one way, $480 round trip).

ROUGH DRIVING TIMES IN TSAVO WEST

From Mtito Andei gate: 1hr to *Kilaguni* or *Severin*; 1hr 30min to *Finch Hatton's*.
From Tsavo Gate: 40min to *Ngulia*, 1hr 30min to *Kilaguni* and *Severin*; 2hr to *Finch Hatton's*.
From Chyulu Gate: less than 20min to *Severin* or *Kilaguni*; 1hr 30min to *Ngulia*; *Finch Hatton's* is a turning, south, 15km west of Chyulu Gate.
From Ziwani Gate: 1hr 30min to *Severin* and *Kilaguni*; 2hr to *Finch Hatton's* or *Ngulia*.

5

GETTING AROUND

Once you're in the park, if you're driving yourself, you'll soon come to appreciate your dependency on the **marker cairns** at the numbered junctions. Unfortunately, at the time of writing, the signage in the park is woefully inadequate, with many numbers illegible and distances underestimated. A **GPS unit** or a **smart phone** is very useful. If you're planning to use any of the park roads south of the Tsavo River, be aware that the only bridges are between junctions #38 and #39 south of Severin, and between #55 and #65 near Rhino Valley. The road south of junction #11, at Mzima Springs, following the Mombasa pipeline, is closed.

ACCOMMODATION

A lack of modestly priced **accommodation** is less of an obstacle in Tsavo West than in most of the other main parks. As well as the two campsites in the Developed Area, there are several KWS-designated "special campsites" along the north bank of the Tsavo River – though remember these have no facilities of any kind and have to be organized in advance through KWS (see p.59). If you're not equipped to camp but can bring food supplies, there are mid-priced, self-catering options in the shape of the *bandas* at *Rhino Valley Lodge* and *Kitani Safari Lodge*, and the house rental at *Kamboyo House*, near the park headquarters.

CAMPSITES

Chyulu Campsite Just outside Chyulu Gate, 600m north of junction #26. Basic European-style toilets, running water for the showers and shacks for pitching your tent under (assuming it's a smallish dome tent). $15 per person
Kamboyo Campsite Just north of junction #3, near the park HQ not far from Mtito Andei Gate. Nice enough, with plenty of easy pitches under shady trees, and a promising-looking shower and squat toilet block. Unfortunately it has no water, so you need to bring your own. $15 per person

TENTED CAMPS AND LODGES

Finch Hatton's Tented Lodge 9km south of junction #29, 65km from Mtito Andei Gate ☎ 020 8030936 or 0716 021818, ⓦ finchhattons.com. With 31 tents (#1 to #7 are best) planted around springs and lakes full of hippos and crocs, this is named after the aristocrat who introduced royalty to the bush. Owner-managed, with flair, you're served multi-course dinners, on good china and linen, by befezzed waiters, as Mozart tinkles above the evening frog chorus. But it's not everybody's porcelain cup of tea – too big and fancy to call boutique, and not quite comfortable enough, with no nets. The dated snob appeal, and food that veers wildly from sublime to second rate, are solidly offset by large and well-built tents, and the site's truly remarkable natural environment – similar to Mzima Springs. There's free wi-fi around the bar and a good pool. Their own airstrip is 3km away. FB $645
Kamboyo Guest House 2km northeast of junction #3, by the park HQ and research centre ☎ 0726 610508,

ⓔ reservations@kws.go.ke. Well located, above a small waterhole, with views to the south from the large upstairs balcony and ground-floor veranda, this spacious, clean and decently furnished house has seven beds, firewood on demand, gas and electricity. The generator is usually on 8.30–11.30am, 2.30–5.30pm and 6.30–10.30pm. Whole house $200
Kilaguni Serena Safari Lodge Off junction #8, about 30km from Mtito Andei Gate ☎ 020 8030800 or 0734 699865, ⓦ serenahotels.com. Dating from 1962, the oldest park lodge in Kenya is a perennial favourite with many repeat visitors, as much as anything for its prime site and terrific wildlife ambience, with a spectacular panoramic overlook of two floodlit waterholes. There's a busy atmosphere and it's very often full, but standards are high for the price. The 56 rooms, in thatched cottages (most facing the wildlife action, with views towards the Chyulu Hills and Kili from the balconies), aren't big, but are well laid out, with nets, fans and power points. Modest pool. Ecotourism Kenya Silver Award. FB $310
★ **Kitani Safari Lodge** By Severin Safari Camp, off junction #36, 8km from Mzima Springs ☎ 020 2684247 or 0733 645444, ⓦ severinsafaricamp.com. The former *Kitani Bandas*, competently managed by *Severin*, comprises eight very comfortable twin or double self-catering *bandas*, with nets, free firewood, bathrooms, good kitchens with gas cookers, and electric sockets. *Banda* #3 has the best views, but all share the intimate connection with the Tsavo environment. Guests can go to the main camp to eat

5

or use the pool (you'll need to drive or call them to arrange transport). Whole *banda* $120

Ngulia Safari Lodge 48km west of Tsavo Gate, 6.5km south of junction #18 ☎ 043 2030140 or 0722 139393, ⊛ safari-hotels.com. Somewhat isolated in the more hilly eastern side of the park, this dated, 1970s-apartment-block-style hotel offers small rooms, with nets and floor fans but no other frills, but tremendous views over the plains far below. The two small waterholes by the terrace attract buffalo, but the immediate area has less wildlife appeal than the other lodges, for which compensation comes in the form of controversial, nightly leopard-baiting. Usually busy with minibus tours from Mombasa, it's well maintained, with a small pool, and casual visitors are welcome. FB $290

Rhino Valley Lodge 3.5km west of junction #18 ☎ 0725 517832, reservations ☎ 0721 328567, ⊛ tsavo campsandlodges.com. The location of the former *Ngulia Bandas*, nestled on the steep north slopes of Ngulia Hill, offers sweeping vistas from the terrace bar-restaurant and there's a waterhole opposite *bandas* #4, #5 and #6. But like *Ngulia Safari Lodge*, you don't get the concentrations of wildlife you find around *Kilaguni* or *Severin*. There are six *bandas* and a family room with fully equipped kitchens and eighteen more basic *bandas* with no kitchen. Electricity, powering sockets and fridges, is supplied from 6–11am and 5–8.30pm. Self-catering $110, FB $200

★ **Severin Safari Camp** Off junction #36, 8km from Mzima Springs ☎ 020 2684247 or 0733 645444, ⊛ severinsafaricamp.com. Enthusiastic, hands-on German management is responsible for the distinctive flavour of this very cool, thoughtfully conceived camp of tents and luxury *bandas*, sprawled on a flat, bushy plain, teeming with wildlife. Casual visitors are welcome for meals that are well out of the ordinary (try the cook-your-own hot stone grill with dipping sauces), the superb pool and the rejuvenating massage spa, all witnessed by a ceaseless parade of giraffe, antelope, warthogs and birdlife attracted by the camp's five waterholes. Bush walks and night drives possible. No network, but free wi-fi throughout. Tent #16 and *banda* #3 have the best views. Ecotourism Kenya Silver Award. FB $390

Voyager Ziwani Camp Just outside Ziwani Gate, about 40km south of the Developed Area, most easily reached from the Taveta–Voi road (see p.330) ☎ 020 2688982, ⊛ heritage-eastafrica.com. On a glorious site on the Sainte stream, dammed to create a hippo and crocodile pool, *Ziwani* has 25 recently refurbished tents on plinths under thatched roofs. Although a good hour's drive south of the park's main attractions (from which it is sometimes cut off when river floods wash away the crossing points over the Tsavo River), the local bonuses such as early-morning walks and night game drives more than compensate. FB $550

Tsavo East National Park

$65 with Safari Card (see p.71) • ⊛ bit.ly/TsavoEastNP • 13,747 square kilometres

Northeast of the highway, the railway, and the apparent natural divide that separates Kenya's northern and southern environments, lies **Tsavo East National Park**. Although it is the larger part of the combined Tsavo parks, the sector north of the **Galana River** has few tracks and is much less visited. South of the river, the great triangle of flat wilderness, with **Aruba Dam** in the middle, has become popular with safari operators, since it offers a pretty sure chance of seeing plenty of animals, in a very open environment, just half a day's drive from most coastal hotels.

Apart from some tumbled **crags and scarps** near Voi, and the rocky cleft of the Galana River (fed by the Tsavo and the Athi), Tsavo East is an uninterrupted **plain of bush**, dotted with the crazed shapes of baobab trees. It's a forbiddingly enormous reserve and at times over the last three decades has seemed an odd folly, especially since its northern area was closed to the public for many years due to the long war against elephant and rhino **poachers** (see box, p.350). Since the 1990s, this campaign has been largely won and the elephants are once again on the increase, their numbers swelled by a major KWS translocation operation that moved three hundred elephants to Tsavo East from Shimba Hills. Rhinos are still very rare in Tsavo East and numbers exceedingly hard to estimate but it's believed there may be about fifty individuals, mostly in the north, but occasionally seen south of the Galana, in the triangle between the Galana, the Mbololo stream and the highway. With the northern sector secure and rangers in place, the whole of Tsavo East was opened for tourism in 2006, though infrastructure north of the Galana is still basic.

With minibus safaris increasingly taking in Tsavo East, the emptiness of the park is no longer as overwhelming as it was, but the park's vastness means that for much of the

5

time, you will still have the pleasure of exploring the wilderness completely alone. It's easy to get away off the two or three beaten tracks, and you may find something special – a **serval** perhaps, or a **lesser kudu**. You are certain to see a lot of Tsavo East's delightfully colourful **elephants**, be they huge, dusty-red adults, or little chocolate babies fresh out of a mud bath.

Tsavo East's elephant orphans

Until a few years ago, the scarcity of mature bull and matriarch **elephants** was still noticeable after so many had been killed by poachers. These days, good-sized herds and large tuskers are increasingly common. As well as the KWS relocation of elephants from the coast, much of the hard work in re-establishing elephants in Tsavo East has been done by the **David Sheldrick Wildlife Trust**, based in Nairobi (see p.144). If you "adopt" an orphan (minimum $50; ⓦsheldrickwildlifetrust.org), you can make arrangements to visit the release facilities, either at the stockade near Voi Gate or the one near the Ithumba park headquarters in the far north.

Game drives along the Galana

The **Galana River** itself, with its fringing cordon of branching **doum palms**, creates a captivating backdrop, the sandy river bed often dotted with wildlife in the dry season. West of junction #110, above the confluence of the Tsavo and Athi rivers and the start of the Galana, is **Observation Hill**, while downstream, east of junction #160, are the gently spectacular **Lugard's Falls**, where you're allowed to park and clamber around the bizarrely eroded rocks. Even in relatively dry conditions, the

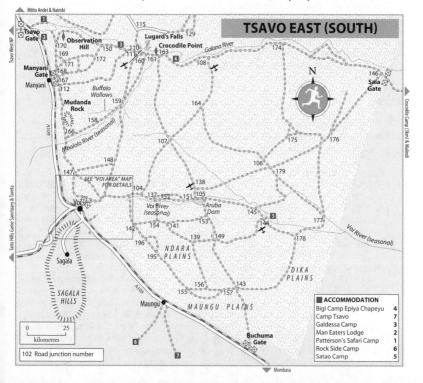

TSAVO EAST (SOUTH)

Mtito Andei & Nairobi

Tsavo Gate

Observation Hill

Lugard's Falls

Crocodile Point

Galana River

Manyani Gate

Manyani

Buffalo Wallows

Mudanda Rock

Mbololo River (seasonal)

SEE "VOI AREA" MAP FOR DETAILS

Voi

Voi River (seasonal)

Aruba Dam

Voi River (seasonal)

Sala Gate

Crocodile Camp (3km) & Malindi

NDARA PLAINS

DIKA PLAINS

Sagala

SAGALA HILLS

Maungu

MAUNGU PLAINS

Buchuma Gate

0   25
kilometres

102 Road junction number

ACCOMMODATION

Bigi Camp Epiya Chapeyu	4
Camp Tsavo	7
Galdessa Camp	3
Man Eaters Lodge	2
Patterson's Safari Camp	1
Rock Side Camp	6
Satao Camp	5

Talta Hills Game Sanctuary & Taveta

Tsavo West NP

Mombasa

5

falls, progressing from foaming rapids to narrow cascades gouged deep into the rock, are quite impressive.

A kilometre east of the falls, another short diversion takes you to **Crocodile Point**, something of a letdown as the crocs are hard to see unless you get up close, which you're no longer allowed to do. **Hippos** are easier to spot from the vantage point.

Game drives south of the Galana

Most **game drives** from the camps near the Galana River use the main dirt road along the south bank of the river as an introduction, and then strike south along the

THE TSAVO POACHING WARS

In Tsavo, as throughout the country, the question of how to manage the **elephants** is still paramount. While several other countries permit trophy hunting, it has been illegal in Kenya since the 1970s and the policy here is to hunt the poachers and allow the elephants to reach their own natural balance within the defined park territory. Zoologists are divided about whether there is an optimal elephant population for a park like Tsavo, especially as natural weather patterns and now climate change are so significant. The destruction by elephants of Tsavo East's fragile woodlands and ongoing human-elephant conflict in the farmlands around the perimeter (the park boundary is fenced around Voi) are perennial concerns.

Such questions have been submerged for many years by the overbearing problem of ivory **poaching**, which at one time looked like it would wipe out the elephants completely. In 1967, the combined Tsavo parks' elephant population was more than 30,000. It went down to 5300 in 1988, and today stands at around 12,000. Elephants are long-lived and intelligent animals with complex kinship patterns, and the social structure of the herds in many districts was badly distorted in the 1980s, with many older animals killed and too many inexperienced younger elephants unable to fend for themselves or to act as role models for infants. The poachers had changed too; they were no longer marginalized Kamba farmers killing an occasional elephant with an old gun or poisoned arrows, but a new breed of well-connected gangster, equipped with automatic weapons, wiping out whole family groups in a single attack.

The international **ivory trade moratoriums**, in place from 1989, stopped the ivory trade in its tracks, and had an immediate effect on the numbers of new elephant corpses being logged in Tsavo East. Equally dramatic was the unprecedented aggression with which the Kenyan parks authorities started carrying out their duties under the bluntly pragmatic new Director of the Kenya Wildlife Service, **Richard Leakey**, with poachers liable to be shot on sight.

The pressure from some countries to reopen the ivory trade has been strongly resisted by Kenya but this in turn has helped push the price of ivory past the $2000/kg mark. The turmoil in neighbouring **Somalia** is potentially a huge threat, with evidence that Al-Shabaab is using ivory and rhino horn to fund terrorist attacks.

Tsavo East's **black rhinos** are much further down the path to annihilation. Their number in Kenya is estimated at around 600 (compared to 330 in 1989, at the height of the poaching), a figure that is perhaps twenty percent of the total population of the species. More than 95 percent of Kenya's rhinos, most of them in Tsavo, were killed in the 1970s. This escalation was largely due to a major expansion of the market for rhino horn in China (where powdered horn is used in traditional medicine), and in **Yemen** where oil money put the rhino-horn dagger-handle, traditionally the prerogative of the rich, within reach of thousands of Yemeni men. Many tonnes of horns were smuggled out of Mombasa by dhow before the authorities made any effort to halt the trade.

Yet the savage groundwork in rhino extermination had been done long before. After World War II, the Makueni area southeast of Machakos was designated as a Kamba resettlement area, and the colonial Kenya Game Department sent in one J.A. Hunter to clear it of unwelcoming rhinos. He lived up to his name, shooting 1088 black rhinos.

Today there are around fifty black rhinos in Tsavo East, and there are breeding populations in a number of ranches and sanctuaries around the country, while the concept of **saving the rhino** has become a national cause. Nevertheless, as long as there's a market for the horn, with current values estimated at up to $50,000/kg, rhinos will remain under threat.

roads following tributary *luggas*, up into the higher bush country between the Galana and Voi rivers. Heading south from the Galana, any of the park roads from junctions #150, #111, #110, #161, #163, #108 or #174 can yield good results. **Buffalo Wallows Lugga** (junction #110, then #159) is often rewarding, with the chance of seeing a leopard, and plenty of birdlife. Lions, and occasionally cheetahs, can be seen along these water courses.

Some 20km further southwest, just north of junction #158, **Mudanda Rock** is particularly recommended. Resembling a scaled-down version of Australia's Uluru, it towers above a natural dam which, during the dry season, draws elephants in their hundreds.

Game-viewing near Voi

Starting out from the relatively busy Voi area (see p.323), the wooden margins of the **Voi River** often hide a profusion of wildlife, and this area is one of the most promising in the park. Try the **Ndololo Campsite** at junction #103 and the pretty **Kanderi Swamp loop** at #174. After rains, keep your windows up when driving through the tall grass and undergrowth, not only for security against large animals, but as a defence against the tsetse flies that may mistake your vehicle for a large animal.

Don't assume the flat expanses between **Buchuma Gate** and the seasonal Voi River will be devoid of interest. Try alternative routes to the main arteries – for example the remote loop across the **Dika plains** from junction #143 to Satao Camp, where elephants are often abundant and cheetahs not uncommon.

Aruba Dam

Until 2007, the most obvious focus in Tsavo East was the formerly beautiful **Aruba Dam** on the Voi River, the marshy fringes of which were an excellent spot for bird- and animal-watching, and where decrepit *Aruba Lodge* nestled in the trees on the north shore. Sadly, the area has been ruined by a large and obtrusive lodge constructed inside a large fenced compound, and it will be years, if ever, before the area recovers. For the last few years, the lake has been dry.

Visiting Tsavo East's northern sector

The park's **northern sector** is most easily accessed from Mtito Andei Gate East, but in the dry season it's also possible to reach the northern sector over the Galana river bed at junction #160, the only crossing point. Beware of mistaking mud for the smooth rock bed: unwitting drivers sometimes get stuck. On the western side of the northern sector lies a huge, ancient lava flow, in the shape of the **Yatta plateau**, stretching from Mtito Andei towards the Galana River, above the east bank of the Athi River.

ARRIVAL AND DEPARTURE   **TSAVO EAST NATIONAL PARK**

There is no public transport and no scheduled flights into the park itself. Unless you charter a plane (see p.138), you'll be driving into the park, though you could take a bus or matatu to one of the gates and try for a lift.

BY CAR
If you're going independently, fill up and take spare fuel and drinking water. Traffic and accidents can practically double the journey time, but assuming your trip along the Mombasa highway goes relatively smoothly, the journey from Nairobi might take 4hr (to Mtito Andei Gate) to 5hr (Voi Gate), and the trip from Mombasa 2hr (Buchuma Gate) to 4hr (Mtito Andei Gate). Distances inside Tsavo East are huge – think of it

as a small country – and there is little infrastructure, so help can be a long time coming. When choosing your route for game drives, try to avoid park roads that lead direct to major lodges: Sala Gate to Aruba, for example is horribly corrugated. Most of the gates have limited or zero facilities, although busy Buchuma gate has a decent-sized curio store and a reasonably good restaurant and bar.

From gates on the Mombasa road From north to

5

south: Mtito Andei Gate East gives access to the northern sector; Tsavo Gate is used for *Patterson's Camp* (30min); Manyani Gate for *Galdessa* (30min) and *Epiya Chapeyu* (1hr); Voi Gate (see p.324) for *Voi Safari Lodge* (15min), *Tarhi*, *Ndololo* (30mins), *Aruba* (1hr) and *Satao* (1hr 30min); and Buchuma Gate for *Aruba* or *Satao* if driving up from Mombasa (both 1hr 30min).

From Sala Gate On the east side of the park, Sala Gate is 105km due west of Malindi. The first 40km stretch over coral rock road surface is quite jarring, but the remaining 65km over red *murram* and gravel are mostly fairly smooth, though heavy rain can cause delays. Allow 3hr to reach the

gate, and be prepared to make a fixed 7am start from the police barrier outside Malindi. You are supposed to travel this route in convoy – although there no longer appears to be any security threat. Once at Sala Gate, it's a good 1hr 30min to *Epiya Chapeyu*, *Aruba* or *Satao*.

BY BUS AND MATATU

It's perfectly feasible to be dropped by a bus or matatu at one of the gates on the Mombasa highway, or in Voi, but getting a lift into the park is always difficult, and you still have the problem of getting around without your own vehicle. Voi Gate at the weekend is probably your best bet.

ACCOMMODATION

Tsavo East's **accommodation** options are more numerous and varied than you might expect. Our listings include most of those inside the park itself, but outside the park you'll find cheaper options, as well as one or two good lodges and tented camps, around Voi and off the Mombasa highway (see pp.324–327).

ITHUMBA AREA

David Sheldrick Trust Camp At Ithumba, northern sector, Nairobi reservations through ⓦsheldrick wildlifetrust.org. Four twin tents under thatched roofs, a communal area, and three staff. Expensive for a DIY park, and these visits are only available to sponsors (see p.144) by pre-arrangement. Self-catering, whole camp $\overline{\$550}$

SOUTH OF THE GALANA

Bigi Camp Epiya Chapeyu South bank of the Galana River, 12km west of junction #108, 10.5km east of junction #110 (Lugard's Falls) ⓞNo camp tel, ⓦepiya -chapeyu-camp.com, Nairobi reservations ⓞ20 3749796 or 0733 743210. Also known as *Bigi Camp*, this unstuffy, Italian-run camp (*Epiya Chapeyu* means "The man with the hat" in Waliangulu, in reference to the nearby rock on the Yatta plateau), in a lovely location close to the banks of the Galana River, has fourteen closely spaced tents. The better ones in the front row face the river, but they don't have nets or front decks. Not fancy, but extremely good value, and casual visitors are welcome for lunch (Ksh1500). FB $\overline{\$170}$

★ **Galdessa Camp** 4km north of junction #111 on the south bank of the Galana ⓞ0734 283810 or 040 3202217, ⓦgaldessa.com. This spectacular, Italian-owned boutique camp is stunningly conceived and located above the river. With a wonderful ambience, lavish and comfortably furnished *banda*-tents, good, hearty, Italian cooking and great attention to detail, it's by far Tsavo East's best camp. It's situated in one of the few areas of Tsavo East where you have a chance of spotting black rhino, and elephants are nearly always seen crossing the river here. One bronze guide. FB $\overline{\$520}$

KWS Ndololo Campsite Near the Kanderi swamp off junction #103, right next to *Ndololo Safari Camp*, 11km from the national park junction in Voi, reservations in Nairobi ⓞ0726 610508, ⓔreservations@kws.go.ke. Popular and well-shaded site with clean loos and showers,

a communal kitchen/food preparation area, and helpful askaris who will sell you firewood. $\overline{\$15}$ per person

Ndololo Safari Camp Near the Kanderi swamp off junction #103, 11km from the national park junction in Voi ⓞ0721 328567, ⓦtsavocampsand lodges.com. Forty closely spaced but spacious tents under makuti roofs, with tiled and solid-paved floors, small terraces, nets and decent plumbed-in bathrooms. Nothing fancy, but relatively good value. FB $\overline{\$200}$

Patterson's Safari Camp West bank of the Athi River, 9km from the Mombasa highway (take the turning to the east, directly opposite Tsavo Gate of Tsavo West national park, 400m north of the Tsavo bridge) ⓞ020 2021674 or 0723 752173, ⓦpattersonsafaricamp .com. With its eco-friendly architecture, decent tents and white sand underfoot, there's an intimate, tropical-island feel here and it offers great value for money. It's not a wildlife-rich area, but you'll see hippos, crocs and elephants and hear the full story of Col. Patterson and the man-eaters of Tsavo. FB $\overline{\$190}$

★ **Satao Camp** Off junction #144, around 45km from Voi or Buchuma Gate, and 60km from Sala Gate ⓞ043 2030204 or 020 2039571, ⓦsataocamp.com. *Satao* has a fine, low-key ambience, its thatch-covered, slightly old-fashioned tents ranged beneath big trees. The atmosphere will suit you if you want to relax in the bush and enjoy the wildlife – elephants, occasional lions and lots of plains game attracted to the waterhole. Solar-heated hot water evenings only. Transfers, two game drives and all drinks available as a "package" supplement of $150/person per day. Ecotourism Kenya Silver Award. One silver guide. FB $\overline{\$370}$

Sentrim Tsavo Camp Off junction #136, 16km from the national park junction in Voi ⓞNo camp tel, reservations through Sentrim ⓞ0722 207361 or 0733 852083, ⓦsentrimhotels.net. The former Tarhi Camp has a fenced but pleasant, partly wooded site.

Spacious faux-tents with solid floors and walls, cheap furniture and hotel-style bathrooms are gradually replacing old-style safari tents – there are also identical cottages for guests who want to lock themselves in from the wildlife. Generator power. Elephants are often seen from the dining area, which usually serves basic buffet meals. FB **$255**

Voi Safari Lodge On a rocky crag, 8km from the national park junction in Voi (4.5km from Voi Gate) ☎ 043 2030019, ⓦ safari-hotels.com. Not to be confused with the

brashly oversized *Voi Wildlife Lodge* outside the park (see p.325), this 53-room lodge is quite busy enough, and similar in many respects to its sister establishment, *Ngulia Safari Lodge* in Tsavo West (see p.348). Despite the shortcomings of its dated style (it first opened in 1967), this is a perennial favourite for its top location, its two floors of smallish rooms banking onto a tree-covered hill, its near-guaranteed game-viewing from the terrace and the magnificent panorama plunging to the horizon. Pool. FB **$290**

Narok

NAROK is the funnel through which the majority of road transport enters the Maasai Mara. It's a bumpy, hustly mess, but is the last guarantee of fuel, a cold drink or almost anything for more than 80km before you enter the reserve. If you arrive here after 5pm, you may well end up having to stay the night, as you won't have time to get into the reserve itself by nightfall (the gates close at 7pm).

Despite its touts and garish tourist bazaars full of carvings and beads, Narok is lively and interesting, always full of Maasai on shopping expeditions or doing business at the market. It might be worth calling in at the **Narok Maa Cultural Museum** (daily 9am–6pm; Ksh500; ⓦbit.ly/NarokMuseum) after the Kobil station, on the right as you come into town from Nairobi. But the space is badly maintained, and – short of simply making a goodwill donation – it's hard to justify the price tag for a few minutes in this dusty and largely empty room.

ARRIVAL AND DEPARTURE
NAROK

By car On a good day Narok is 2hr from Nairobi, once you've cleared the city traffic. There are several decent filling stations here with good repair facilities. Fill up, and check your spare jerrican: there are no full-service filling stations south of Narok.

By bus and matatu The main matatu stage is opposite Kenol on the southwest side of town. There are frequent

vehicles every day to and from Nairobi (3hr) and several vehicles a day along the C12 to Sekenani and Talek (villages by the Maasai Mara reserve gates of the same names; allow 2hr, and much longer after rain) and along the C13 to Mara Rianta (for Musiara Gate; allow 3hr, and again much longer after rain) and on to Lolgorien (4hr-plus) and Migori (5hr-plus), beyond the western side of the reserve.

INFORMATION

Banks Several banks in Narok have ATMs: KCB, on the north side of the main road (right, coming in from Nairobi), 300m west of Kobil and just before the museum; Barclays, on the south side of the main road, just past the museum; Equity, turn north (right) at the Hass petrol station, up the side street (400m on the left).

Internet There are several internet cafés, including Sky Apple Enterprises on the left, just before the Hass junction (Ksh1/min).

Market Narok's main market is on the north side of the town centre, to the right as you go through town towards the reserve.

ACCOMMODATION, EATING AND DRINKING

Naropil Restaurant Down the alley to the left of the museum. Very pleasant, shady outdoor restaurant serving a good variety of local dishes – a mix of stodge (chapatti, *ugali* and chips, Ksh100; chicken pilau Ksh300), a nice line in vegetarian options (mixed veg platter Ksh150) and cheap cold sodas (Ksh50). Daily 5am–10.30pm.

Seasons Hotel South side of the road as you enter Narok (left, coming from Nairobi) ☎ 0725 975687, ⓦ seasons hotelskenya.com. Surprisingly good hotel, much patronized by tour drivers, but considering its motto ("We give the most

for the least") a little pricey for what it offers: clean, well-maintained, smallish rooms with electric showers in reasonable bathrooms, plus the chance of a dip in a sometimes sparkling pool. Hearty, varied buffet meals (Ksh700). BB **$78**

Transit Hotel South side of the road as you enter Narok (400m past Seasons Hotel) ☎ 0722 257621 or 0725 608993. Less salubrious than *Seasons*, but further uphill and pleasantly breezy, with B&L-style rooms behind a travel-company-stickered foyer, and a popular, top-value bar-restaurant (selection from the hot buffet, Ksh300/plate). BB **Ksh1000**

5

Maasai Mara National Reserve

$80 (see p.72) • No single official website, but see ⓦ maratriangle.org, ⓦ bit.ly/MaasaiMaraNarok and ⓦ maasaimara.com • 1510 square kilometres

For a long list of reasons, **Maasai Mara** is the best animal reserve in Kenya. Set at nearly 2000m above sea level, the reserve is a great wedge of undulating **grassland** in the remote, sparsely inhabited southwest of the country, right up against the Tanzanian border and, indeed, an extension of the even bigger **Serengeti plains** in Tanzania. This is a land of short grass and croton bushes (Mara means "spotted", after the yellow crotons dotted on the plains), where the wind plays with the thick, green mantle after the rains and, nine months later, whips up dust devils from the baked surface. Maasai Mara's climate is relatively predictable, with ample rain, and the new grass supports an annual **wildebeest migration** of half a million animals from the dry plains of Tanzania.

At any time of year, the Mara has abundant wildlife. Whether you're watching the migration, a pride of lions hunting, a herd of elephants grazing in the marsh, or hyenas squabbling with vultures over the carcass of a buffalo, you are conscious all the time of being in a realm apart. To travel through the reserve in August or September, while the wildebeest are in possession, feels like being caught up in the momentum of a historic event. There are few places on earth where animals hold such dazzling sway.

With its plentiful vegetation and wildlife, the reserve's **ecosystem** might at first appear resilient to the effect of huge numbers of tourists. However, the Mara is the most visited wildlife area in Kenya, and the balance between increasing tourist numbers and wildlife can't be maintained indefinitely. Off-road driving kills the protective cover of vegetation and can create dust bowls that spread like sores through the effects of natural wind and water erosion and become muddy quagmires in the rains.

Human population increase is also a threat: the **animal numbers** in the Mara are still huge by comparison with most other parts of Africa, but the enormous herds of every species – not just wildebeest – that were here after independence are gone, as Kenya's population has quadrupled. With the land subdivided and sold off, the old ecosystem, in which the Maasai and their herds mingled with the wildlife, is beyond being challenged: local people no longer tolerate lions and hyenas near their homes, or buffalo where their children are walking to school, or elephants raiding their corn. The answer, in an imperfect world, is **wildlife conservancies** for the wildlife and ranching and settlement areas for people.

The reserve and the conservancies

In terms of structuring your visit, think of the national reserve in three parts. In the west you have the **Mara Triangle**, between the Mara River and the Oloololo Escarpment. This lush, green area is only accessible from Oloololo Gate in the north, or by crossing the Purungat Bridge in the far south. It's administered by the Mara Conservancy on behalf of Trans-Mara County Council based at Kilgoris (ⓦ maratriangle.org). The rest of the

---

HOW TO VISIT THE MAASAI MARA

The vast majority of visitors arrive in the Maasai Mara on pre-booked air or road **safari packages**, which can work out cheaper than making independent arrangements. If you're travelling on a budget, you'll have to accept that the reserve is not a cheap option and even organized **budget-camping safaris** (see p.117) can seem expensive. While it is just about possible to access the area by public transport (see p.362), and then camp or stay in budget establishments, the experience is likely to leave you wishing you'd saved a little more before coming here. There's also a third option if you can afford it; there's nothing to stop you **renting a vehicle**, ideally with an experienced driver-guide (see p.49), and visiting the region entirely independently, while staying at camps or lodges you've booked directly.

5

THE HISTORY OF THE MAASAI MARA

When the reserve was created, today's familiar scene of plentiful wildlife looked very different. Traditionally, the **Maasai** lived in some harmony with the wildlife, hunting only lion, as a ritual exercise, and, in times of famine, the beasts they called "wild cattle" – the eland and buffalo. When the first European **hunting safaris** made the Mara world-famous in the early years of the last century, the white hunters were ransacking a region recently deserted by the Maasai. Smallpox had ravaged the Maasai communities and rinderpest had torn through their cattle herds.

By 1961, the white hunters had brought the Mara's lion population down to nine, and the Maasai Mara was created as a game sanctuary to be administered by the Maasai District Council at Narok. In 2001, management of the **Mara Triangle** was handed over to the **Mara Conservancy**, a non-profit management company. Over the last decade, management of this area has been considerably better than in the rest of the reserve, with full transparency of gate receipts, major success against poachers, and improved road maintenance. Meanwhile, the management of the Narok side has been shambolic: the draft of a much mooted management plan for the whole reserve has been "under review" for years.

Outside the reserve proper to the north, most of the Maasai **group ranches** east of the Mara river have in recent years converted from pasturelands to wildlife conservancies, and all of them now have their own entry fees, usually levied by the camps and lodges where guests are staying and added to the bill. Safari operators and local community leaders have recently transformed much of the largest group ranch, Koiyaki, into the **Mara North**, **Olare Orok** and **Mara Naboisho** conservancies, and as the community-led (rather than tour operator-led) model for managing wildlife and tourism proves increasingly successful, the trend looks set to continue.

On the broader horizon, conservationists lobby for a trans-frontier park, that would link the Maasai Mara with Serengeti – like the Great Limpopo Transfrontier Park that encompasses South Africa's Kruger, Mozambique's Limpopo and Zimbabwe's Gonarezhou parks. Aside from securing the ecosystem, it would hugely benefit the safari industries of both countries. Given the present relations between them, however (there is no border crossing on the south side of the reserve), it feels like a pipedream.

national reserve, the **Narok side**, is administered by Narok County Council (💿 bit.ly/MaasaiMaraNarok) and consists of the **Musiara sector** in the north and the **Sekenani sector** in the centre and east. The Musiara sector, bounded by the Mara and Talek rivers, is the location of *Governor's Camp* and *Intrepids* and has some of the most photogenic wildebeest river crossings. The Sekenani sector, the largest portion of the reserve, is bordered by the Talek, Mara and Sand rivers, and has *Keekorok Lodge* – the oldest lodge in the reserve – in its centre.

Outside the reserve, roughly a dozen **conservancies**, **group ranches** and **private game ranches**, usually run in partnership with the local Maasai communities, offer wildlife-viewing that is often the equal of what you'll see in the reserve proper – increasingly reflected in their management practices, conservation work and prices. Some of them, including the Mara North and Mara Naboisho conservancies, only permit game drives for visitors staying at their camps and lodges, the aim being to limit visitor numbers and exclude drive-in minibus tours.

Game drives

The Maasai Mara is the one part of Kenya where the **concentrations of game** that existed in the nineteenth century can still be seen, even if it's true numbers have hugely diminished overall. The panorama sometimes resembles one of those wild-animal wall charts, where groups of unlikely-looking animal companions are forced into the artist's frame. You can see a dozen different species in one gaze: gazelle, zebra, giraffe, buffalo, topi, kongoni, wildebeest, eland, elephant, hyena, jackal, ostrich, and a pride of lions waiting for a chance. The most interesting areas, scenically and zoologically, tend to be westwards, signalled by the long ridge of the Oloololo Escarpment. If you only have a

5

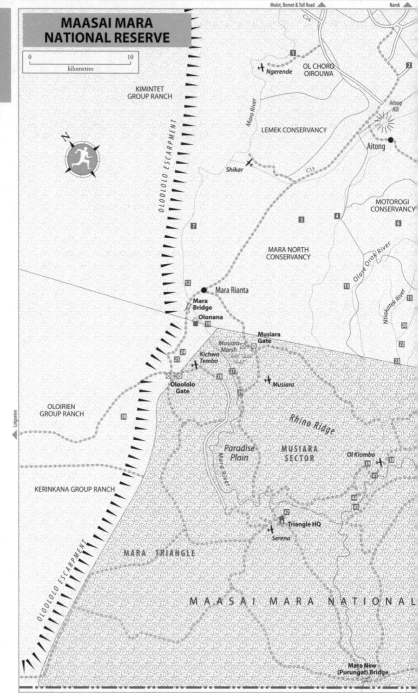

MAASAI MARA NATIONAL RESERVE

0 — 10
kilometres

Mulot, Bomet & Toll Road

Narok

C14

Ngerende

OL CHORO OIROUWA

2

Mara River

Aitong Hill

LEMEK CONSERVANCY

Aitong

KIMINTET GROUP RANCH

Shikar

C13

MOTOROGI CONSERVANCY

6

OLOOLOLO ESCARPMENT

7

5

4

MARA NORTH CONSERVANCY

Olare Orok River

13

15

Ntiakatek River

20

12

Mara Rianta

Mara Bridge

Olonana

Musiara Gate

22

23

Musiara Marsh

24

Kichwa Tembo

25

27

28

Musiara

OLOIRIEN GROUP RANCH

Olololo Gate

29

30

Rhino Ridge

Loigarien

Paradise Plain

Mara River

MUSIARA SECTOR

Ol Kiambo

39

38

KERINKANA GROUP RANCH

41

44

45

47

Triangle HQ

Serena

MARA TRIANGLE

OLOOLOLO ESCARPMENT

M A A S A I   M A R A   N A T I O N A L

Mara New (Purungat) Bridge

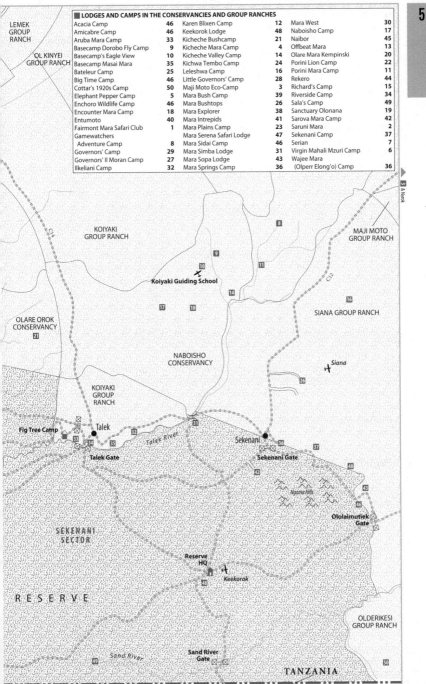

LODGES AND CAMPS IN THE CONSERVANCIES AND GROUP RANCHES

Acacia Camp	46	Karen Blixen Camp	12	Mara West	30
Amicabre Camp	46	Keekorok Lodge	48	Naboisho Camp	17
Aruba Mara Camp	33	Kicheche Bushcamp	21	Naibor	45
Basecamp Dorobo Fly Camp	9	Kicheche Mara Camp	4	Offbeat Mara	13
Basecamp's Eagle View	10	Kicheche Valley Camp	14	Olare Mara Kempinski	20
Basecamp Masai Mara	35	Kichwa Tembo Camp	24	Porini Lion Camp	22
Bateleur Camp	25	Leleshwa Camp	16	Porini Mara Camp	11
Big Time Camp	46	Little Governors' Camp	28	Rekero	44
Cottar's 1920s Camp	50	Maji Moto Eco-Camp	3	Richard's Camp	15
Elephant Pepper Camp	5	Mara Bush Camp	39	Riverside Camp	34
Enchoro Wildlife Camp	46	Mara Bushtops	26	Sala's Camp	49
Encounter Mara Camp	18	Mara Explorer	38	Sanctuary Olonana	19
Entumoto	40	Mara Intrepids	41	Sarova Mara Camp	42
Fairmont Mara Safari Club	1	Mara Plains Camp	23	Saruni Mara	2
Gamewatchers		Mara Serena Safari Lodge	47	Sekenani Camp	37
Adventure Camp	8	Mara Sidai Camp	46	Serian	7
Governors' Camp	29	Mara Simba Lodge	31	Virgin Mahali Mzuri Camp	6
Governors' Il Moran Camp	27	Mara Sopa Lodge	43	Wajee Mara	
Ilkeliani Camp	32	Mara Springs Camp	36	(Olperr Elong'o) Camp	36

day or two, and you're inside the reserve, you could do worse than spend most of your time here, near the **Mara River**.

It sometimes seems, however, that wherever there are animals there are **people** – in minibuses, in Land Cruisers, in rented Suzukis, often parked in ravenous, zoom-lens-touting packs around understandably irritable lions, leopards and cheetahs (the official limit is five vehicles around an animal at any one time). This popularity is highly seasonal, and can be overbearing around Christmas and during the migration, but it need not spoil your visit. If you aren't driving yourself, encourage your driver to explore new areas (obviously not off-road) and perhaps stress you'd rather experience the reserve in its totality than tick off animal species.

The animals

Big brunette **lions** are the best-known denizens of the Maasai Mara. Thirty years ago, as many as a thousand lions lived here, but their numbers have dropped hugely and there are now probably around 250 in the reserve, with perhaps another 150 in the conservancies, or around one in five of Kenya's estimated population. They are relatively easy to find, however, and there are usually several prides firmly in possession of their territories in the Musiara and Sekenani sectors, as well as in the Triangle. Instinctively, they use the Mara's river and stream meanders and many confluences as "lobster pots" to corner their prey in ambushes, and it is sometimes possible to watch them hunt, as they take very little notice of vehicles. The **Mara Predator Project**, run by Living With Lions, is creating an online ID database of the northern Mara prides. Lodge guides use the lions' facial whisker spots to identify individuals, and visitors are encouraged to get involved by reporting sightings at ⓦlivingwithlions.org/mara.

While lions seem to be lounging under every other bush, finding a **cheetah** is much harder (they can sometimes be seen on the *murram* mounds alongside the Talek–Sekenani road). These are usually solitary cats – slender, unobtrusive, somewhat shy and vulnerable to harassment by wildlife-watchers. Cases of cheetahs using vehicles as look-out hills – first noted only in the 1990s – have become common, as they lose their fear and adapt to close human scrutiny. Their natural hunting times are dawn and dusk, but some cheetahs prefer to hunt during the middle of the day, when the humans are shaded in the lodges. This is not a good time of day for the cheetah, which expends terrific energy in each chase and may have to give up if it goes on for more then thirty or forty seconds. When they move, cheetahs exhibit marvellous speed and agility and,

---

VISITING MAASAI VILLAGES

One diversion you're likely to be offered, especially if travelling on an organized safari, is a visit to a **Maasai** *enkang*, usually incorrectly called a *manyatta* (an *enkang* is an ordinary homestead, a *manyatta* a ceremonial bush camp). Forget about the authenticity of tribal life: this is the real world. Children and old people are sick, young men have moved to the towns, and everyone wants your money. Unprepared and uncomfortable, most visitors find the experience depressing or a bit of a rip-off, or both. You'll pay around $20/person if organized by your lodge, camp or safari driver, or around Ksh1000/person if you arrange it yourself, for the right to have a look around, peer inside some dwellings, and be on the receiving end of a determined sales pitch to get you to buy souvenirs. Because of the supposed sales opportunity, safari drivers have for decades paid a tiny fee to the headman of their chosen village and kept the bulk of the cash (the standard commission, hard as it is to believe, was 96 percent, or less than a dollar per visitor actually paid to the community). A number of initiatives are now changing this, however, and the best operators and camps have worked hard to make the experience less mercantile and more worthwhile for both parties. If you can forget any TV-documentary illusions, and actually sit down and talk to the Maasai (there will always be people who speak a little English), the experience can be transformed and full of interest and laughter.

if you're lucky enough to witness a kill, it's likely to take place in a cloud of dust a kilometre from where the chase began.

Leopards, are seen increasingly often in the daytime, and there are plenty of them. Leopard Gorge, in the Mara North Conservancy, is an obvious place to look. Their deep, grating roar at night – a grunt, repeated – is a sound which, once heard, you carry around with you.

Rangers are certain to know the current news about the **black rhinos** – every calf born is a victory – though finding them is often difficult. Check out the thickets of desert date trees (*Balanites*) near *Little Governors'* marsh, or Rhino Ridge, where one or two of the reserve's *faru* are sometimes obligingly positioned. There are also two **white rhinos** in the area, brought in from South Africa and living in the Ol Choro Oirouwa Rhino Sanctuary in the conservancy of the same name, close to *Mara Safari Club*. The sanctuary (ⓦolchorro.blogspot.com; $5 entry) is upstream along the Mara River, well to the north of the reserve.

Maasai Mara's other heavyweights are about in abundance. The Mara River surges with **hippo**, while big families of **elephant** traipse along the forested river and stream margins and spread out across the plains when there's plenty of vegetation to browse. The reserve is home to an estimated thousand or so elephants, with another five hundred living in the districts beyond its boundaries.

Among all these outstanding characters, the herds of humble grazers can quickly fade into the background. It's easy to become blasé when one of the much-hyped "big five" (elephant, rhino, buffalo, lion, leopard) isn't eyeballing you at arm's length – but those are the hunter's trophies and not necessarily the photographer's. **Warthog** families like rows of dismantled Russian dolls, **zebra** and **gazelle**, odd-looking **hartebeest** and slick, purple-flanked **topi** are all scattered with abandon across the scene. The topi are particularly characteristic of the Maasai Mara, being almost confined in Kenya largely to this reserve: there are always one or two in every herd standing sentry on a grass tussock or an old termite mound. Topi and **giraffe** – whose dream-like, slow-motion canter is one of the reserve's most beautiful and underrated sights – are often good pointers for predators in the vicinity: look closely at what they're watching.

The reserve used to have rare herds of **roan antelope** – swaggering, horse-sized animals with sweeping, curved horns, but they became extinct here in the 1970s, and today you'll only see them in Ruma National Park near Lake Victoria. The roans are just a standout example of a serious **decline** in the Mara's wildlife populations. Although the numbers are a constantly moving pattern, as animals move in and out of the counting zones used in aerial surveys, the long-term trend is very much down, with most species having lost at least half their Mara populations since the 1980s. Buffalo and giraffe have been particularly badly hit.

On a positive note, the surveys have concentrated on the reserve itself, and as community conservancies have replaced herding communities, so the wildlife has been moving into the much better managed areas beyond the reserve boundaries, all of which report increasing populations of wildlife. And **wild dogs** are back, reported from a number of conservancies.

The wildebeest migration

ⓦ wildebeestmigration.blogspot.com has information on the migration's progress and timings each year

It is the annual **wildebeest migration**, often billed as one of the seven natural wonders of the world, that has planted Maasai Mara so firmly in the popular imagination. The numbers are far down from their peaks of over a million wildebeest in the 1960s and 70s, but still an average of nearly half a million animals swell the Mara's sedentary population ever year.

With a lemming-like instinct, the herds gather in their hundreds of thousands in May and June on the withering plains of the Serengeti to begin the long journey northwards, following the scent of moisture and green grass in the Mara. They arrive in

5

July and August, streaming over the Sand River and into the Sekenani side of the reserve, gradually munching their way westwards towards the escarpment in a milling mass, and turning south again, back to the Serengeti, in October and November. Never the most graceful of animals, wildebeest seem to play up to their appearance with unpredictable behaviour; bucking like wild horses, springing like jack-in-the-boxes, or suddenly sprinting off through the herd for no apparent reason.

The **Mara River** is their biggest obstacle. Heavy rains falling up on the Mau Range where the river rises can produce a brown flood that claims thousands of animals as they try to cross. Like huge sheep (they are, in fact, most closely related to goats), the brainless masses swarm desperately to the banks and plunge in. Many are fatally injured on rocks and fallen branches; others are skewered by flailing legs and horns. With every surge, more bodies bob to the surface and float downstream. Heaps of bloated carcasses line the banks; injured and dying animals struggle in the mud, while vultures and marabou storks squat in glazed, post-prandial stupor.

The migration's full, cacophonous impact is awesomely melodramatic – both on the plains and at the deadly river crossings. This superabundance of meat accounts for the Mara's big lion population. Through it all, **spotted hyenas** scamper and loiter like psychopathic sheepdogs: a quarter of a million wildebeest **calves** are born in January and February before the migration, of which two out of three perish in the Mara without returning to the Serengeti.

THE MAASAI

After deep reflection on my people and culture, I have painfully come to accept that the Maasai must change to protect themselves, if not their culture. They must adapt to the realities of the modern world for the sake of their own survival. It is better to meet an enemy out in the open and to be prepared for him than for him to come upon you at home unawares.

Tepilit Ole Saitoti, writing in *Maasai* (Elm Tree Books/Abrams)

Of all Kenya's peoples, the **Maasai** have received the most attention. Often strikingly tall and slender, dressed in brilliant red cloth, with beads, metal jewellery and – for young men – long, ochred hairstyles, they have a reputation for ferocity fed by their somewhat arch superiority complex. Traditionally, they lived off milk and blood (extracted, by a close shot with a stumpy arrow, from the jugular veins of their live cattle), and they loved their herds more than anything else, rarely slaughtering a beast. They maintained rotating armies of spartan warriors – the **morani** – who killed lions as a test of manhood. And they opposed all interference and invasion with swift, implacable violence. The Maasai scorn of foreigners was absolute: they called the Europeans, who came swaddled in clothing, *iloridaa enjekat* or "those who confine their farts". They also derided African peoples who cultivated by digging the earth – the Maasai even left their dead unburied – while those who kept cattle were given grudging respect so long as they conceded that all the world's cattle were a gift from God to the Maasai, whose incessant cattle-raiding was thus righteous reclamation of stolen property. **Cattle** are still at the heart of Maasai society. There are dozens of names for different colours and patterns, and each animal among their three million is individually cherished.

Some of this noble savagery was undoubtedly exaggerated by Swahili and Arab slave and ivory traders, anxious to protect their routes from the Europeans. At the same time, something close to a **cult of the Maasai** has been around ever since Thomson walked *Through Maasai Land* (see p.590) in 1883. In the early years of the colony, Governor Delamere's obsession with the people and all things Maasai spawned a new term, "Maasai-itis", and with it a motley crop of romantic notions about their ancestors, alluding to ancient Egypt and Rome, and even to the lost tribes of Israel.

The Maasai have been assailed on all sides: by uplands farmers expanding from the north; by eviction from the tourist/conservation areas within the Maasai Mara boundaries; and by a climate of opposition to their traditional lifestyle from all around. Sporadically urged to grow

ARRIVAL AND DEPARTURE

BY AIR

Access is most straightforward by the scheduled daily air services on SafariLink (ⓦflysafarilink.com) and Airkenya (ⓦairkenya.com) from Nairobi. Unless otherwise noted, flights land at one or more of the nine airstrips in the reserve and adjoining conservancies, depending on passenger requirements, so flight times and the order of arrival vary. Every lodge and camp has a preferred airstrip and will transfer guests accordingly.

From Nairobi Flights (45min–1hr 30min; $200 each way including taxes, less in the low season) leave from Wilson Airport. Additional Mara flights include Governors Aviation (ⓦbit.ly/GovernorsAviation), which flies daily between Wilson and the Musiara Airstrip ($200 each way).

From Naivasha In the high season, SafariLink routes one southbound Nairobi flight a day via Naivasha (Naivasha–Mara around 40min; $226).

From Laikipia and Samburu In the high season, SafariLink and Airkenya fly to the Mara from Nanyuki/Lewa Downs/Loisaba/Samburu/Shaba (1–2hr; around $350;

southbound only).

From the coast Mombasa Air Safari (ⓦmombasaairsafari .com) flies to the Mara airstrips daily in the high season from Mombasa via Diani Beach (around 3hr; $330 one way, $440 return; same price from both airports), via Tsavo West and Amboseli, and from Malindi (2hr 15min; $330 one way, $440 return).

From Migori SafariLink flies daily in the high season between the Mara and Migori on the Tanzanian border (30min; $243 each way), avoiding hours of bumpy road travel for passengers visiting the Serengeti and the Mara on the same safari.

BY CAR

Although hard-surfaced roads are making gradual advances into the region, the final approaches to the reserve – and all the routes inside it and in the adjoining conservancies – still have a gravel or mud surface. If you decide to drive, give yourself plenty of time, use a 4WD vehicle, and check that you know the precise location and

---

crops, go to school, build permanent houses, and generally settle down and stop being a nuisance, the Maasai face an additional dilemma in squaring these edicts with the fickle demands of the **tourist industry** for traditional authenticity. Maasai dancing is *the* entertainment, while necklaces, gourds, spears, shields, *rungus* (clubs), busts (carved by Kamba carvers) and even life-sized wooden *morani*, to be shipped home in a packing case, are the stock-in-trade of the souvenir shops. For the Maasai themselves, the rewards are fairly scant. Few make much of a living selling souvenirs, but enterprising *morani* can do well by just posing for photos, and even better if they hawk themselves in Nairobi or down on the coast.

Many men persevere with the status of **warriorhood**, though modern Kenya makes few concessions to it. The *morani*, arrested for hunting lions and prevented from building *manyattas* for the *eunoto* transition in which they pass into elderhood, have kept most of the superficial marks of the warrior without being able to live the life fully. The ensemble of a cloth tied over one shoulder, together with spear, sword, club and braided hair, is still widely seen, and after circumcision, in their early days as warriors, young men can still be encountered out in the bush, hunting for birds to add to their elaborate, taxidermic headdresses. But there is considerable local frustration and, when the pasture is poor, the *morani* have little compunction about driving their herds into the reserve to compete with the wildlife.

With improved medical and veterinary facilities having eased the hardships of the traditional way of life, the Maasai have been expanding again, with **land** the biggest issue. The Maasai have still not fully come to terms with the idea of individual ownership of it, although the recent introduction of wildlife **community conservancies** run by Maasai Group Ranches with tourist industy partners seems at last to be providing a steady source of income.

The **lifestyle** is changing: education, MPs and elections, new laws and new projects, jobs and cash, all impinge on Maasai communities – with mixed results. The traditional Maasai staple diet of curdled milk and cow's blood has largely been replaced by *ugali*. Many Maasai have taken work in the tourist lodges and tented camps while others end up as security guards in Nairobi. For the majority, who continue to live semi-nomadic lives among a welter of constraints, the future would seem to hold little promise. But that stubborn cultural pride – the kind of hauteur that keeps a cattle-owner thoroughly impoverished in cash terms, while he counts his 220 beasts – may yet insulate the Maasai against the social upheavals that seem certain to rock the lives of many Kenyans in the twenty-first century. For further information, see ⓦmaasai-association.org.

5

final directions for your lodge or camp. Fuel In the reserve area is usually available at Talek village and sometimes at *Fig Tree*, *Keekorok*, *Sarova*, *Serena* and *Simba* lodges, but carry a full jerrican of spare fuel.

FROM SOUTHWEST KENYA AND TANZANIA

Entry is not permitted directly from Tanzania's Serengeti National Park into the Maasai Mara at the Maasai Mara reserve's Sand River Gate, and there are no other gates or routes between the two.

Via Lolgorien Most people coming from Tanzania cross the border at Sirari-Isebania and head north 20km to Suna-Migori, before turning east on the unsurfaced C13 road (see p.273) towards the Mara. Once you reach Lolgorien, 46km from Suna, the road is mostly good *murram* all the way through to the Mara, with turnings to the long-closed *Olkurruk Mara Lodge* after 65km and *Mara West Camp* after 66km. After 70km you reach the junction for the road down to Oloololo Gate. Keep going northeast and you cross the Mara River, climb up to the straggling settlement of Mara Rianta and then reach the turning down to the Musiara Gate.

FROM NAIROBI

From Nairobi, take the lower road to Naivasha, down the escarpment, turning left at the unpleasantly burgeoning truck stop of Mai Mahiu (allow 1–3hr to do this 50km to get here from Nairobi, depending on traffic and where you start from). The newly surfaced 92km road from Mai Mahiu to Narok is in excellent condition and shouldn't take more than an hour.

Via Narok to the Sekenani, Talek and Ololaimutiek gates Once through Narok, if you branch left onto the C12 highway 3.2km after the bridge in Narok town, the road makes its way south towards Sekenani Gate and the eastern section of the reserve. From the C12 junction, the first 23km are excellent tarmac, but at the end of that comes Kenya's most notorious road – the 58km to Sekenani Gate, on a mix of corrugated *murram* (which isn't too bad at a decent speed) and scraped older tarmac (where you're driving on rocky road foundations). In anything but a top-of-the-range 4WD, it's a miserably uncomfortable, 1hr 30min–2hr trial. You reach Talek Gate from Sekenani Gate by following the Talek River on a reasonable road for 18km. For Ololaimutiek Gate, turn left at the little junction settlement of Ngoswani (35km from the C12 junction, before you reach Sekenani Gate), then drive 16km southeast, before swinging right, to the south and southwest, reaching Ololaimutiek after approximately another 30km.

Via Narok to the Musiara and Oloololo gates For access to the western end of the reserve from Nairobi, you start by taking the decent B3 highway from Narok to Sotik. West of the C12 junction (3.2km west of the bridge at the bottom of the hill in Narok town), there are two main turnings south off the B3. The first is just past Ololulunga, 28km west of the C12 junction, signposted to *Fairmont Mara Safari Club*. This route goes via the small centres of Ngorengore and Lemek and becomes the rutted and often muddy C13. The second turning off the B3 is exactly 50km from the C12 junction, just south of Mulot. Here, a private toll road (Ksh500) takes you south, a few kilometres away from the east bank of the Mara river towards *Fairmont Mara Safari Club* and others outside the reserve, and ultimately joins the road from Kaboson (see below) and then the C13 at Aitong Hill. Unless you're advised differently as you approach the region, or when planning your trip, use the toll road if you can, in preference to the tortuous public road. 2km further west along the C13 from Aitong Hill, the road to Talek Gate (34.5km) forks south, via Aitong village, while the C13 continues for 25km straight across the plains to the Mara bridge. The turning for Musiara Gate is 3.7km before the bridge; the turning for Oloololo Gate is 5.8km after it.

FROM KISUMU, KERICHO OR KISII

Approaching the Maasai Mara from Kisumu, Kericho or Kisii (see p.277), all routes converge on the overgrown village of Bomet, with its three streets running around the back of the petrol station, a small market, a few meagre *hotelis* and *dukas*, a KCB (with ATM), a post office, and some very basic lodgings.

Via Bomet and Mulot on the B3 Southeast of Bomet, the surfaced B3 heads for Narok, crossing the headwaters of the Mara River. The easiest route into the reserve is via the toll road from the Mulot junction, a right (south) turning, 25km southeast of Bomet.

Via Bomet and Mulot on the C14 A shorter but rougher alternative is the unpaved C14 for Sigor and Kaboson. The first important turning for this route is right, exactly 4km after crossing the river on the south side of Bomet. After a further 19km, take the right fork to Kaboson, and 8km later, just outside Kaboson where the road turns west towards Kilgoris, turn left and drive another 10km on the C14 to cross the Mara River. You then join the C13 after a further 13km, by the prominent Aitong Hill.

BY BUS AND MATATU

There are a few **matatus** and **buses** making daily runs from Narok through the group ranches along the C13 via Mara Rianta to Lolgorien, and occasionally as far as Migori. Local matatus also run to Sekenani and Talek gates at least once each day. You're likely to see a good deal of plains game along the way – so long as you can see out of the window – so you could, at a pinch, get a flavour of the Mara district ecosystem without paying any reserve or conservancy fees. Hopping out en route, however, is inadvisable.

GETTING AROUND

Organized drives As well as the usual 2–3hr game drives ($70–100/person) available at most lodges and the larger tented-camps, you can often find $30–50/person game drives (depending on group size) at the budget camps near the eastern gates.

Vehicle rental You'll need a vehicle if you want to do a game drive independently, as there are no hop-on-hop-off tours of any kind. You may find someone with an old Land Rover or similar by asking around the villages at Talek, Sekenani or Ololaimutiek gates or in the neighbouring budget campsites. Expect to spend a minimum of $100 or $150/day to hire a serviceable van, pick-up or 4WD and a driver.

Roads and driving Graded roads, with improved surfaces and theoretically unbreachable banks and ditches alongside them to deter off-road driving, have been laid in various parts of the reserve, especially in the east. There is also a reasonable all-weather road from Talek Gate to Sekenani Gate, inside the reserve. During the rains, however, and for some weeks after, the western parts of the reserve can be treacherous. In many parts of the reserve and conservancies, it can be hard to know what is a road

and what is a set of wheel tracks leading nowhere. Apart from wanting to avoid off-road driving, it is easy to get lost. If you don't have a guide with you, it's a very good idea to have a GPS or a smart phone – the mobile network is good in many areas.

River crossings, bridges and fords The Mara Triangle and Narok sides of the reserve are effectively separated by the Mara River. Only two bridges span the Mara River: the Mara Bridge on the C13 road just outside the reserve in the north, and the Mara New Bridge (or Purungat Bridge) on the southern boundary, by the Tanzanian border. These bridges are the only points where you can cross the Mara, not counting the foot-passenger dinghy at *Little Governors*. On the Narok side of the reserve, crossings over the Talek are also limited. There are bridges by *Mara Simba*, west of Sekenani Gate, and at Talek Gate, and three fords – one near *Rekero*, one by Ol Kiombo airstrip, and one at *Intrepids*. After rains, the fords are often impassable for anything from a few hours to several days. In that event you have to drive around to the north to "Double Crossing", near the confluence of the Olare Orok and Ntiakatek rivers, where the two narrow fords are usually passable.

RESERVE & CONSERVANCY FEES

One of the advantages of visiting the Mara with a safari operator, rather than independently, is that they take charge of your national reserve and conservancy **fees**, adding the cost to your bill or including the charges in your accommodation rate. Most visitors staying in the reserve don't venture north into the conservancies and group ranches, while visitors staying in conservancy-based camps usually make just one, full-day trip into the reserve proper, especially during the migration, when some camps cover this cost themselves, usually including one reserve ticket per three-day stay. All tickets

---

BALLOON FLIGHTS

At around $450–500/person for the one-hour flight followed by breakfast with sparkling wine (it's never champagne, whatever the label says), **balloon safaris** are the ultimate safari treat – even watching the inflation and lift-off from the ground is spectacular. It's a highly enjoyable and very memorable experience, especially as you float above the trees along the Mara River, but photographic opportunities can be limited by low light, and the fact that you mostly fly quite high – so don't bank on every shot being a winner.

The flights take place in the usually calm conditions immediately after dawn, but if the wind is up, they don't fly at all and you get a refund. If you're not staying at a lodge or camp with a launch site, the operators will come and pick you up. After breakfast, you do a game drive on your way back to your lodge.

There seems no obvious reason why balloon flights in Kenya are about twice the price of almost everywhere else in the world: depending on your budget, you may want to leave your booking until the last minute, as two-for-one deals are sometimes available.

BALLOON OPERATORS

Adventures Aloft ⓦ adventuresaloftafrica.com. Flights from *Fig Tree Camp* (on the Talek, west of Talek Gate).
Balloon Safaris ⓦ bit.ly/BalloonSafaris. Flights from *Keekorok Lodge*.
Governors' Balloon Safaris Ltd ⓦ bit.ly/Gov

CampBalloons. Flights from *Little Governors' Camp*.
Hot Air Safaris ⓦ maraballooning.com. Flights from *Ilkeliani Camp*.
Transworld Kenya ⓦ bit.ly/TransworldBalloons. Flights from *Sarova Mara*, *Mara Serena* and *Fairmont Mara Safari Club*.

5

are valid 24hr from entry and the time of departure is, increasingly, closely monitored to ensure you pay again if you overstay. Remember, even if you're a shoestring camper, you are expected to pay reserve or conservancy fees, depending on which bit of grass (or dust) your tent is pitched on. There are a few properties where guests are not expected to pay fees unless they enter the reserve – right out side Talek Gate, for example – but don't count on this lasting indefinitely.

Reserve tickets Daily fees to visit the reserve are $80/person for 24hr if staying outside the reserve and $70 if staying inside the reserve. Payments for the Narok side are transferable to the Mara Triangle sector and vice versa. Mara Triangle entry points (Oloololo Gate, Mara New Bridge and Serena airstrip) take Visa credit and debit cards as well as cash. Entry points on the Narok side of the reserve (the gates at Musiara, Talek, Sekenani and Ololaimutiek, plus Musiara, Kichwa Tembo, Ol Kiombo and Keekorok airstrips) in theory only accept pre-paid Maasai Mara National Reserve charge cards, which can be obtained and loaded at certain branches of Equity Bank in Nairobi, Mombasa and Narok. This arrangement between Narok County Council and the bank has provoked a storm of protest from people at the gates who had been accustomed to dipping into the gate money, and there are signs that it may not last very long, with cash payments on the gates widely accepted as of late 2012 (see p.73).

Conservancy tickets These usually cost the same as, or a little more than, reserve tickets, and are not usually valid for the reserve itself (although some conservancies include a certain duration inside the reserve for each visitor). The four most active conservancies (Mara North, Olare Orok-Motorogi, Ol Kinyei and Naboisho) are exclusive to the guests in their lodges and camps, and include the fees in their daily rates.

ACCOMMODATION

When deciding **where to stay** in the Mara region, don't be unduly swayed by whether a lodge or camp is inside the **reserve proper**: the **conservancies** and **group ranches** outside the reserve have excellent wildlife-viewing and their own special features, and are often much less crowded than the busiest parts of the reserve. If you're visiting for the migration, at some point you're going to want to head towards the Mara River to try to witness one of the famous **wildebeest crossing points**. For this, accommodation on the western side of the reserve might be a good idea, and it tends to be at a premium at that time. There's a lot to be said, however, for camps that are far from others, such as *Offbeat Mara*, *Mara Porini*, *Naboisho* or *Sala's*, that give you those moments early in the morning when it's just you, the animals and the sun coming up over the plain.

Accommodation types The Mara region's hundred-plus lodges and camps, scattered across the national reserve and the adjoining conservancies, vary greatly in style, atmosphere and price: one person's sumptuous luxury will be another's garish opulence, while a place that seems delightfully informal and in keeping with the environment to one visitor may feel a bit plain and unpolished to another. "Getting what you pay for" seems to apply less in the Mara, where not all the most expensive camps are everything they're cracked up to be. It is worth taking the trouble to choose carefully and check things such as the camp's ecotourism rating (if any) and the number of KPSGA-qualified guides it has. Seasonal rates are very marked in the Mara, where the high season prices given here (July–Oct, during the migration) are often twice or more the low season rates (April–May).

What is included Regardless of how long you stay, all the lodges and camps, with the exception of the budget places outside the reserve, operate on at least full board (FB) basis, and their rates include all meals. They normally expect guests to arrive for lunch and leave after breakfast. Some provide a "package", which includes all meals and drinks, two or more game drives per day and other activities where available. The majority of guests on "package" will fly in, while most of those on full board will be on drive-in safaris, with a driver/guide accompanying them for the whole trip. Most of the camps and lodges on the conservancies include conservancy fees in their rates, whereas most places in the reserve itself exclude reserve fees.

Booking Reservations are essential, especially at popular times (Christmas/New Year and the July–Oct migration season). The mid-range to luxury lodges and tented camps vary greatly in price, and offer vastly different levels of service. There's nothing intrinsically cheaper about sleeping under canvas: the cheaper places are pack-'em-in lodges, while the most expensive establishments are boutique tented camps, often with rosters of bronze, silver and even gold guides among the staff. Except where noted, all the mainstream lodges and camps have vehicles and driver-guides on site. Unless otherwise stated, the prices given here do not include reserve or conservancy fees.

CAMPSITES

Independent campers at public or private campsites have to have two rangers per campsite on overnight security duty, at a cost of Ksh2000 each.

PUBLIC CAMPSITES

There are several reserve-managed public campsites,

5

CASUAL MEALS AND DRINKS

With all camps and lodges taking care of their clients' **food and drinks**, and the majority of visitors on organized safaris, pre-booked independent trips or doing DIY camping safaris, there are no independent **restaurants** in the Mara. As an independent visitor, or simply a safari client who wants to spend a few hours *not* game-watching, then if you head to one of the larger lodges or camps, you will normally be welcomed for breakfast, drinks, lunch or afternoon tea (dinner isn't an option inside the reserve, where night-driving is not allowed, though in theory it would be in the conservancies). It might be best to call a day ahead to check they can cater for you: smaller, hosted camps will usually decline because they won't have adequate supplies and wouldn't want you to intrude on their guests, while the big lodges (*Fig Tree*, *Keekorok*, *Sarova*, *Serena*, *Simba* and *Sopa*) will very likely be able to provide for you without advance notice.

charging $30/person per night (no booking possible; payment in cash). Most have only the most basic facilities, though firewood can usually be bought. You can expect some good-natured pestering by rangers and others, who will try to extract money by guiding you on game drives in your vehicle. Note that the Oloolo and Musiara gates have no nearby settlements (the village of Mara Rianta is a few kilometres to the north), while outside the Talek, Sekenani and Ololaimutiek gates, ramshackle "villages" of mabati houses, shops and bars have sprung up. The most remote of the reserve gates, Sand River Gate, has no settlement and very limited facilities.

Mara Conservancy Headquarters Near the Triangle's Iseiya headquarters by Mara Serena Safari Lodge. Despite being close to human activity, the *Iseiya* and *Elaui* campsites here have very limited facilities. $30 per person

Oloolo Gate At Oloolo Gate. Welcoming campsite run by the Mara Conservancy, with showers and toilets and wonderful views of the escarpment. You can drive to nearby Mara Rianta village for basic supplies. $30 per person

Sand River Gate At Sand River Gate. The best of the gate campsites, with toilets, water and firewood available and nicely located in a spot where animals come to drink at night. No nearby supplies. $30 per person

PRIVATE CAMPSITES

The Mara Triangle has eight private campsites in excellent locations, but with no facilities whatsoever. These are for exclusive use, and there's a Ksh10,000/week booking fee in addition to the $40/person daily fee (enquiries via ⓦ bit.ly /TriangleCamping). You can also book a private campsite in the greater Mara region through Campsite Bookings (ⓣ0733 602048 or 0733 239226, ⓦ campbookings.com), who manage seven campsites on the Talek, Olare Orok and Ntiakatek rivers, just outside the reserve. Like the private campsites in the reserve there's a weekly booking fee (in this case Ksh33,000) plus a Ksh2000/person per day camping fee. You need to bring all your requirements with you.

BUDGET TENTED CAMPS AND BANDA SITES

The following places are outside the Talek, Sekenani and Ololaimutiek gates and offer simple tents or basic *bandas* with beds and bedding, and usually the possibility of pitching your own tent, too. If the site is physically outside the national reserve boundary, you should only have to pay fees if you enter the reserve.

OLOLAIMUTIEK GATE

Acacia Camp Ololaimutiek Gate ⓣ0726 089107, reservations ⓣ020 2679110, ⓔ mara@acaciacamp .com, ⓦ bit.ly/AcaciaCampMara. A well-run place, owned by the South African *African Travel Company* and mostly catering for overland tours. There's a bar, and meals on request ($9), or use the cooking area. Two-bed ridge tents, with bedding, shared toilets and showers (hot water 5–9am & 5–9pm). Camping Ksh500 per person, twin tent $40

Amicabe Camp Ololaimutiek Gate ⓣ0727 642242 or 0727 633833, reservations in Nairobi ⓣ020 3182334, ⓦ amicabretravel.com. Pleasant site, with small tents with separate shower and toilet blocks. Limited bar and restaurant with a $20 per person per day supplement for FB. Camping per person $30, twin tent only $110

Big Time Camp Ololaimutiek Gate ⓣ0722 437936 or 0722 570722, ⓦ bigtimeholidays.co.ke. Busy and well looked after, with shady groves for the s/c tents, and an on-site bar-restaurant. FB $100

Enchoro Wildlife Camp Ololaimutiek Gate ⓣ0710 322787, ⓦ enchorowildlifecamp.com. A cut above the cheapest places near this gate, this Hostelling International affiliate is located in a shady site, with decent-sized, s/c ridge tents under shelters, and a bar-restaurant (meals Ksh700). Dorm beds FB $30, FB $120

Mara Sidai Camp Ololaimutiek Gate ⓣ0722 584290, ⓦ marasidaicamp.com. The best of the bunch near this gate, on a wooded site, with neat little ridge tents under shelters, and a small bar-restaurant (meals $15; beer Ksh200). FB $160

5

SEKENANI GATE

Mara Springs Camp 3km from Sekenani Gate above the Sekenani River ☎0722 511752, ⓦbit.ly /MaraSprings. Large site, with a number of options, including basic ridge tents, and permanent tents with built-in WC and shower, supplied with generator electricity. The ablutions blocks are basic, but quite clean. Bar-restaurant (meals to order $10). Camping $10, twin tent $60

Wajee Mara (Olperr Elong'o) Camp 1km north of Sekenani Gate, then 2km east ☎0713 938938, ⓦwajeemaracamp.com. A shady site with decent toilets and showers, good security, and ridge tents and cabins for those without their own equipment. Camping $10 per person, FB $80

TALEK GATE

★ **Aruba Mara Camp** East bank of the Talek, 100m from Talek Gate ☎0722 902369 or 0717 216455, ⓦaruba-safaris.com. Well-run German-Kenyan operation, offering terrific value for money (if you're happy being in the busy Talek area) in a variety of tents facing the reserve across the river. The shady DIY campsite has good ablutions and there's a bar-restaurant (breakfast Ksh500, dinner Ksh1000). Camping Ksh500, FB including two game drives $230

Riverside Camp Talek Gate ☎0720 218319 or 0735 700902, ⓦriversidecampmara.com. For the Mara, this offers excellent value, with neat s/c *bandas* (though no fans or nets), some with good river views, plus a dining room and bar. Camping $6, twin banda $64

LODGES AND CAMPS IN THE NATIONAL RESERVE

The accommodation inside the reserve includes affordable mainstream lodges such as *Mara Simba* and one of the most expensive camps in the region, *Explorer Mara*. Inevitably, key routes, river crossings and animal viewing spots can become crowded in the reserve, especially over Christmas and during the migration. Reserve fees of $80/person per 24hr are not included in the rates given.

THE MARA CONSERVANCY (MARA TRIANGLE)

★ **Little Governors' Camp** West bank of the Mara, in the Mara Triangle just upstream from Governor's Il Moran (Musiara Airstrip) ☎020 2734000, ⓦgovernors camp.com. Accessed from the Musiara sector by a rope-pulled boat across the Mara, and hidden in the trees, with wonderful birdwatching, this has seventeen tents, all facing an oxbow marsh of the Mara. There's no fence and plenty of animal action, with elephants, buffaloes and hippos keeping the *askaris* very busy. Balloon launch site. Many bronze guides. Ecotourism Kenya Bronze Award. FB $1118

Mara Serena Safari Lodge On a hilltop in the Mara Triangle, above the Mara River (Serena Airstrip) ☎050 22253 or 0734 699828, ⓦserenahotels.com. Located on a saddle overlooking the Mara River, close to the migration crossings, this lodge is intriguingly designed, based on a re-creation of two Maasai *enkangs*, with smallish but appealingly cellular, cave-like rooms with nets. Most have good views. Ecotourism Kenya Bronze Award. Pool. FB $1120

MUSIARA SECTOR

Governors' Camp East bank of the Mara, near Musiara Gate (Musiara Airstrip) ☎020 2734000, ⓦgovernors camp.com. Close to the fantastic game-viewing of the Musiara marsh, this large, busy, highly regarded operation (the main camp of the group) has 37 tents: 28 face the river and 9 face the plain, of which 6 are family-sized. Many bronze guides. Ecotourism Kenya Silver Award. FB $962

Governors' Il Moran Camp East bank of the Mara, just upstream from the main Governors' (Musiara Airstrip) ☎020 2734000, ⓦgovernorscamp.com. The ten huge, steel-framed tents, which all face the river (though unfortunately the camp footpath runs in front of tents #1–5), are old-fashioned and mounted on heavy concrete plinths, but they're more spacious and better furnished than the main camp. Closed April 10–May 31. FB $1244

Mara Bush Camp Close to Ol Kiombo Airstrip, on the banks of the Olare Orok ☎0728 025277, ⓦmarabushcamp.com. Run by the excellent Sunworld Safaris (see p.118) and operating mostly for the wildebeest

---

SECURITY IN THE MARA

With no towns in the region, **security** in the Mara is generally fairly good, though you should leave nothing of value unguarded, particularly in the budget camps at Talek, Sekenani and Ololaimutiek gates, or obviously if you are camping. You should perhaps be even more concerned about **baboons**. These sometimes intimidating monkeys are prone to grab anything that looks inviting, whether edible or not, and dash off with it to examine it later. You would be asking for trouble if you left your tent unguarded. If you can't be sure that the whole site is completely safe and supervised, then you'll need to leave an *askari* behind on an agreed fee to guard your tent while you're out on game drives. Or else pack up completely before you leave and lock your gear (minus any valuables) in your vehicle.

migration, this is a recommended, thirteen-tent seasonal camp, with nets and decks, offering great value for money, especially for keen photographers. Battery-charging in the lounge tent while the generator is on from 6.30–11pm. Bronze and silver guides. Closed Mar 20–July 9, Nov 16–Dec 19, Jan 7–31. FB $640

Mara Explorer North bank of the Talek River, just upstream from sister camp Mara Intrepids (Ol Kiombo Airstrip) ☎ 0717 204794, ✆ heritage-eastafrica.com. Upmarket sister of *Mara Intrepids*, this boutique camp is very peaceful, with seven double and three twin open-plan tents, all with decks facing the river, and open-air bathtubs. As it's unfenced, guests use radios to summon the *askaris* after dark. Generator until midnight (sockets in tents). Guests can use *Intrepids'* pool, with free transfers. Shares two silver and six bronze guides with *Intrepids*. Ecotourism Kenya Silver Award. Package $1610

Mara Intrepids North bank of the Talek, just downstream from sister camp Mara Explorer (Ol Kiombo Airstrip) ☎ 0727 523734, ✆ heritage -eastafrica.com. This shady camp of thirty tents (all with four-poster beds and nets) on a bluff overlooking the river is a perennial family favourite – the *huge* family tents have a double, a twin and a large living area (room for up to six). Popular activities clubs for children and teens, watchtower (very good for migration photos) and pool. FB rates include game drives but not drinks. Shares two silver and six bronze guides with *Explorer*. Ecotourism Kenya Silver Award. FB $1280

★ **Rekero** North bank of the Talek, close to its confluence with the Mara (Ol Kiombo Airstrip) ☎ 0702 964904, ✆ asiliaafrica.com. Seasonal camp of nine large tents, on the banks of the Talek in the middle of the reserve, used as a base by Disney's *African Cats* film crew. You rely on solar power (central battery-charging), kerosene lamps, filtered drinking water and bucket showers, and enjoy convivial evenings with fellow guests, guides and hosts (many bronze guides and four silver, including *Big Cat Diary*'s Jackson Looseiya), surrounded by the noises of the night. Ecotourism Kenya Silver Award. Closed April & May. Package $1400

SEKENANI SECTOR

Naibor 1km downstream from Rekero, on the Talek, close to its confluence with the Mara ☎ 020 2513147 or 0729 406582, ✆ naibor.com. Sumptuously comfortable permanent camp (with boutique offspring *Little Naibor* and *Naibor Wilderness*) on a densely wooded bend in the river,

---

CELEBRITY BIG CAT

Originally, it was **The Marsh Lions**, by Brian Jackman and Jonathan Scott, first published in 1982, that captured the public imagination with its tales of the characters in the Kichwa Tembo, Miti Mbili and Marsh prides living in the Musiara and Mara North areas. Given names like Notch, Scar and Shadow, the anthropomorphism provided a hook for readers into the lives of big cats that a traditional natural history account might have struggled to achieve. The makers of Disney's 1994 film **The Lion King**, who visited Kenya on safari during their research phase, seem to have had the same idea, keeping their movie grounded – as far as the cartoon world allows – in the lives of real animals, and making *The Lion King* into one of the biggest-grossing animations of all time.

Presenting real lion behaviour, while treating the cats as the subjects of a reality TV show – and later as celebrities – was the concept behind the BBC's **Big Cat Diary**, which started airing, more or less live, during the migration season of 1996. Feeding, and then indulging, a huge audience appetite, *Big Cat Diary* – later *Big Cat Live* – followed the fortunes of the Mara's lions, leopards and cheetahs and ran until 2008, becoming one of the network's most popular shows, regularly viewed by ten percent of the UK population. In the most recent feline film phenomenon, safari meets soap-opera in Disney's **African Cats**, a much hyped cinema release that blends remarkable documentary footage with a part-fictional storyline – the equivalent of *The Hills* or *The Only Way is Essex*, but with real manes.

Visitors to the Mara are no longer content with just seeing lions: they want their guides to track down their favourite TV cats, differentiating between the members of the Marsh pride and Notch and his sons, who all have their own online gossip forums and fan clubs. Such extreme anthropomorphism has conservation benefits – the Mara's big cats are recognized as important characters worthy of protection, not persecution, and the Mara guides themselves form attachments to particular cats, which builds tolerance for predators.

The intense fascination with the minutiae of the lives of a few individuals has clear benefits for the future survival of big cats in Kenya, especially in the most touristed areas. The risk is that it may divert attention away from the wider conservation story of Africa's lions, leopards and cheetahs that never have their own television show.

Naibor is immaculately located for migration-watchers (open-sided Land Cruisers) as well as birders and luxury-seekers. Lots of shade, figwood furniture and light canvas. Run largely on solar power. Massage and beauty therapy. No under-8s. Package $1370

Keekorok Lodge In the heart of the reserve's Sekenani sector (Keekorok Airstrip) ☎ 020 2345463, ⓦ sunafrica hotels.com. This 101-room lodge is the oldest in the reserve, dating from 1963. Although the smallish rooms and furnishings are showing their age, the Keekorok ecosystem adjusted long ago to the lodge's presence, and there's good game-viewing in the vicinity. The hippo bar and elephant deck, out on the boardwalk in the papyrus swamp, are a bonus. Good pool, and the best shop in the Mara. Ecotourism Kenya Bronze Award. One bronze and one silver guide. FB $440

Mara Simba Lodge South bank of the Talek River, 6km northwest of Sekenani Gate (Keekorok Airstrip) ☎ 0754 743021 or 0737 771199, ⓦ marasimba.com. Opened in 2005, this has 84 identical hotel-style rooms in blocks of four, with fans, all overlooking the river, and seventeen cabin-style "tents". Public areas are on decks ranged out over the Talek. Usually the busiest lodge in the Mara, with an international mix of guests, and in the low season the cheapest big lodge in the reserve itself by some margin. Pool. FB $575

Sala's Camp Far south of the Sekenani sector, at the confluence of the Sand and Keekorok rivers (Keekorok Airstrip) ☎ 020 5020888 or 0725 675830, ⓦ thesafari collection.com. Location is the real draw of Sala's. Far to the south of the reserve, hugging the edge of the Serengeti, it's the first camp to see the migration arrive and the last to see it leave. With just seven very comfortable tents, and no other camps in the area, it's exceptionally peaceful, and there's always a good communal group-dinner-campfire atmosphere, accentuated by the camp being unfenced. Closed May & Nov. Conservation fee of $45 (plus standard reserve fee). Package $1180

Sarova Mara Camp Off the main C12 entrance road, 2km inside Sekenani Gate (Keekorok Airstrip) ☎ 050 222386 or 0773 610405, ⓦ sarovahotels.com. The most accessible of the reserve's camps and lodges is well managed and always busy and welcoming, with plenty of nice touches, such as vegetarian options at every meal. The large pool and verdant gardens are fun, and it's worth seeking out James Ole Tira, the charming on-site elder and naturalist. FB $445

LODGES AND CAMPS IN THE CONSERVANCIES AND GROUP RANCHES

Camps and lodges in the conservancies and group ranches outside the reserve are able to offer guided walks and night drives. Not all do so, and night drives are being discouraged in some areas, though using red/orange lights is much less stressful for the animals than bright spotlights. Walking, however, although strictly a daytime activity, is highly recommended if you get the chance. You will need to sign a disclaimer, and will usually be accompanied by an armed guard. The conservancies are also the areas where horse-riding safaris, and occasional escorted cycling safaris, operate.

KIMINTET GROUP RANCH AND OLOOLOLO GAME RANCH

Carved out of the Kimintet Group Ranch, on the west bank of the Mara, the ten-square-kilometre private Oloololo Game Ranch adjoins the main reserve, with access to the Mara Triangle, via the Oloololo Gate, just minutes away. Oloololo is the subject of an ongoing dispute between its foreign owners and their Maasai partners and the rest of the Kimintet community. Ranch fees (but not national reserve fees) are included in overnight stays.

Bateleur Camp Adjoining Kichwa Tembo on Oloololo Game Ranch (Kichwa Tembo Airstrip) ☎ 020 2464745, ⓦ bit.ly/BateleurCamp. Discreetly fenced, situated on the fringe of a belt of African greenheart forest, with superb birdlife, this is more exclusive than its co-owned neighbour, but eye-wateringly expensive beyond reason. The eighteen very comfortable cabin-style "tents" come with huge bathrooms, tucked in two wings among the trees on either side of a small lap pool, each with a four-poster bed and an armchair-furnished deck overlooking the plains. Twenty bronze-level-or-above guides, including four female guides. Ecotourism Kenya Bronze Award. Package $2410

Kichwa Tembo Camp Adjoining Bateleur, on Oloololo Game Ranch (Kichwa Tembo Airstrip) ☎ 020 2464745, ⓦ bit.ly/KichwaTembo. Emerging from the trees at the foot of the Oloololo Escarpment, this long-established favourite has excellent food and, unusually, two female driver-guides. The modestly furnished, old-fashioned tents are a little basic for the price (luxury tents are $100 extra but much further away from the guests' area and pool), and have no electric sockets (battery-charging and wi-fi are available in the central area). It's great for children, however, with a lovely decked pool and large lawns facing the plains. Twenty bronze-level-or-above guides, including four female guides. Ecotourism Kenya Bronze Award. Package $800

Sanctuary Olonana West bank of the Mara on Kimintet Game Ranch (Kichwa Tembo Airstrip) ☎ 020 6950002 or 020 6950244, ⓦ bit.ly/Olonana. Lavishly appointed ecocamp, solar-powered, with comfortable public areas and huge tented rooms, with nets and spectacular views over the river. Olonana is unusual for the personal attention it pays to guests and the welcome extended to children. Pool and spa. Ecotourism Kenya Gold Award. Package $1800

5

MAJI MOTO GROUP RANCH
Northeast of the national reserve, stretching towards the Loita Hills , this 600-square-kilometre group ranch (no fees, free access) is the closest in the Mara ecosystem to Narok, making access to it much quicker and easier than to the national reserve: you're just a 3hr drive from Nairobi. (Conversely, if you want to visit the reserve from Maji Moto, it will be a full-day trip.) There has been little tourism or conservation development in this region, which includes the hill peaks of Lolula (2249m) and Olekijapi (2232m).

★ **Maji Moto Eco-Camp** Maji Moto Group Ranch ☎ 0716 430722 or 0773 689788, ⓦ majimotocamp .com. This is a unique small ecocamp in an inspiring hillside location, with just a few pitches for modest-sized dome tents that are erected – and furnished with comfy mattresses and bedding – only when clients are in camp. Slovene-Maasai owned and staffed by charming Maasai from the Maji Moto community, the key attraction here, as much as wildlife, is Maasai culture – understanding it and participating in it, with fun warrior training/play-fighting for willing participants, making it ideal for adventurous families. Limited solar power, no generator, kerosene lamps, simple meals, evening supply of hot water for bucket showers from the hot springs by donkey. Included: bush walks, mountain-bike rides, bathing in the springs. Excluded: game drives (on request, at extra cost). FB $180

MARA NABOISHO CONSERVANCY
The most recent conservancy in the Mara region, the 211-square-kilometre Mara Naboisho Conservancy (ⓦ maranaboisho.com) was formed, like Olare Orok and Ol Kinyei, out of former group ranches by persuading the 500-odd Maasai landowners to move out of their two hundred square kilometres, while hosting small numbers of high-paying safari-goers, employing Maasai staff and paying a monthly fee to every Maasai family based on bed-nights. You can see the success of Naboisho (which means "coming together" in Maa) in the huge populations of animals roaming the glorious landscapes here – elephants and giraffes everywhere and as many as 70 lions monitored by the innovative Mara-Naboisho Lion Project (ⓦ mnlp.org). The groundbreaking Koiyaki guiding school is based at Naboisho and is well worth a visit. There is as yet no airstrip for scheduled flights in the conservancy, and most transfers, from Siana or Ol Kiombo airstrips, take at least 1hr.

Basecamp Dorobo Fly Camp Above a tributary of the Talek, close to Basecamp's Eagle View (Naboisho Airstrip) ☎ 0733 333909, ⓦ basecampkenya.com. Minimal-footprint dome-tent camp in a grove of acacia trees, a short distance across the valley from Eagle's View, this is often used as a one-nighter by guests staying at the main lodge, or at Basecamp Mara on the Talek. Solar showers, bush meals, Maasai guards. FB $460

★ **Basecamp's Eagle View** Above a tributary of the Talek (Naboisho Airstrip) ☎ 0733 333909, ⓦ base campkenya.com. Formerly the training lodge for the Koiyaki Guiding School – a recommended nearby visit – the Basecamp foundation took over this stunningly sited, boutique ecolodge – formerly Basecamp Wilderness – and transformed it in 2012. Eight large tents and one family tent are ranged around the bluff with views on all sides, and there's a large dining area and a superb sundowner terrace. Package $930

★ **Encounter Mara Camp** Banks of the Olmorijo River (Naboisho Airstrip) ☎ 020 2034197, ⓦ encountermara .com. With dried-elephant-dung pathways and large, luxuriously furnished tents, this new and engagingly hosted camp lies in a prime game area. Group dining is a chance to relive days (and nights) of full-on game drives, plus bush walks. Their local village, Enooronkon, can happily be visited ($20) without any selling allowed. Package $1050

Kicheche Valley Camp Above the Moliband Stream (Naboisho Airstrip) ☎ 020 2493569, ⓦ kicheche.com. Tucked into a wooded corner of the conservancy, this is the most architecturally innovative of the Kicheche camps, with just six platform tents dotted across the hillside and a spacious lounge tent above a spring that draws animals all the time. Food is particularly good here – the manager is a trained chef. Power to room sockets 24hr. Closed April–May. Package $1260

★ **Naboisho Camp** (Naboisho Airstrip) ☎ 0702 964904, ⓦ asiliaafrica.com. The sister camp to Rekero, inside the reserve, this is the most luxurious of the Naboisho conservancy's handful of tented camps, with large tents, magnificent rainfall-shower outdoor bathrooms and hosted dining in the huge mess tent. Game walks are a standout feature (the manager is a top South African guide) and the game close to camp can be heart-stoppingly impressive, with lion kills and other encounters being frequent events. Expert local Maasai guides. Package $1600

MARA NORTH CONSERVANCY
The 320-square-kilometre Mara North Conservancy (MNC; ⓦ maranorth.com), northwest of the reserve, is classic savanna bush country, the land broken into ridges by bush-choked luggas, with high densities of game. The conservancy (part of the Koiyaki Group Ranch) is the home range of several much-studied lion prides, including the Acacia pride and the Gorge pride, named after the iconic Leopard Gorge, 5km northeast of Musiara Gate. The local Maasai landowners still have some grazing rights in the MNC and not all the camps and lodges in the conservancy are signed up to the agreement – meaning their guests are unable to do game drives here, but have to drive to the reserve on the C13 corridor. Entry to MNC is exclusively for MNC camp and lodge guests and the daily conservancy fees are included in rates.

5

Elephant Pepper Camp Off the C13 (Mara North Airstrip) **☎**0735 337630 or 0752 041885, **ⓦ**elephant peppercamp.com. In a dense grove of elephant pepper trees, with eight lovely tents pitched in two wings each side of the stylish central area, this is owned by boutique safari operator Cheli & Peacock, on a private lease of four square kilometres. The camp uses a non-permanent construction (no cement) for minimal impact and is entirely solar-powered; they have two silver and two bronze guides. Ecotourism Kenya Gold Award. Closed April–June 15. Package **$1420**

★ **Karen Blixen Camp** East bank of the Mara (Mara North Airstrip) **☎**0773 063863 or 020 3524215, **ⓦ**karenblixencamp.com. This innovative, Danish-owned unfenced camp has 22 tents along the river (home to forty hippos) or on raised platforms. Although the environment is still adjusting, the naturalistic grounds (all trees and bushes planted come from within a 5km radius), grey-water recycling and gas water-heaters for each tent are all promising signs. Tents have cooler-boxes and 24hr, solar-powered sockets. Small pool. Package **$1022**

★ **Kicheche Mara Camp** "Acacia Valley", on the west bank of the Olare Orok (Mara North Airstrip) **☎**020 2493569, **ⓦ**kicheche.com. Kicheche Mara, already one of the Mara ecosystem's standout camps, has migrated from its former habitat in Lemek Group Ranch to this wildlife-rich valley above a stream. There are eight comfortable and roomy tents, two of which can be family tents, with bucket showers to order. Like all the Kicheche camps, it's a perennial favourite with photographers, assisted by Kicheche's seven Mara-based guides, three of whom are silver. Closed April–May. Ecotourism Kenya Silver Award. Package **$1030**

★ **Offbeat Mara** On the Olare Orok stream in the middle of MNC (Musiara Airstrip) **☎**0704 909355 or 0704 909356, **ⓦ**offbeatsafaris.com. A hidden jewel in the Mara, this exceptional, boutique tented camp is unusually informal, unpretentious and enjoyable. The six reasonably sized tents are very private and surrounded by untramelled bush – no clipped lawns or electric fences here, nor any other vehicles around, just fantastic wildlife right in front of you. Charming hosts, outstanding staff, one bronze and two silver guides, and excellent, generous meals and wine. Package **$1180**

★ **Saruni Mara** Far to the north, past Aitong (Ngerende Airstrip) **☎**020 2694338 or 0735 950903, **ⓦ**saruni camp.com, Nairobi reservations **☎**020 6003090, **ⓦ**chelipeacock.com. One of the most stylish lodges in the Mara, with just six, roomy, breezy cottages overlooking a bird- and game-filled valley far to the north of the Mara plains, which you can see through a cleft in the hills. With very good food, free wi-fi, awesome showers and the "Masai Wellbeing Space" (free massage with each booking), this is a highly recommended base, especially if you're as happy doing local game walks as game drives. Two silver guides. Ecotourism Kenya Silver Award. Package **$1600**

Serian Spanning the Mara, 6km north of the C13 road (Mara North Airstrip) **☎**0735 922222 or 0735 566237, **ⓦ**serian.net; Nairobi reservations **☎**020 2663397, **ⓦ**africanterritories.co.ke. One of the region's most attractive and individual camps, with seven tents on the east bank and four more (called *Ngare Serian*) across the river via a splendid suspension bridge. The super-comfortable tents are dubbed "marquees" and bathrooms are daringly "adjoining" rather than en-suite. A private driver-guide for each tent is part of the package, as are stays in a nearby tree house and fly camp if required. With generator electricity only in public areas, and solar and kerosene in tents for lighting, this is a stylish lesson in how to create a beautiful and eco-friendly camp. Package **$1490**

OLARE OROK AND MOTOROGI CONSERVANCIES

The 133-square-kilometre Olare Orok Conservancy (OOC; **ⓦ**oocmara.com) is unusual for its highly focused Mara conservation work and the success of its community integration. It sets the benchmarks for sustainable Mara tourism – one tent per 700 acres (just under three square kilometres) and no more than twelve tents in a camp. Funds are channelled from visitors to the Maasai landowners, who also have access to the conservancy's grasslands during times of drought. Tusk Trust and the International Fund for Animal Welfare are both donors, and the wildlife-viewing is exceptional, with all the predators present and, with more than forty lions, some of the best lion-watching in the Mara ecosystem. Olare Orok joined with Motorogi in 2012 to form a single tourism and conservation area, managed by the same warden and rangers. A new eco-camp developed by Virgin boss Richard Branson, *Mahali Mzuri Camp* (**ⓦ**mahalimzuri.virgin.com), is set to open in Motorogi in 2013.

★ **Kicheche Bushcamp** Southeastern Olare Orok Conservancy (Ol Kiombo Airstrip) **☎**020 2493569, **ⓦ**kicheche.com. This extremely popular camp offers six luxurious tents, with huge bedrooms, built-in safari showers, and large, very private verandas – all furnished in a fresh, minimalist way. Luxury aside, it's the attentive management, superb food and top-class guiding from one of their silver or bronze guides that makes a stay here so special. Avid photographers appreciate the little touches like beanbags in the open-sided Land Cruisers, and the much prized ability of the driver-guides to always offer you just the right angle. With award-winning photographer Paul Goldstein the co-owner, it's perhaps no surprise. Ecotourism Kenya Silver Award. Closed April–May. Package **$1120**

Mara Plains Camp Ntiakatek River (Ol Kiombo Airstrip) **☎**020 6000457 or 020 6005108, **ⓦ**bit.ly /MaraPlains. Tucked into woodland, surrounded by open savanna, this has eight, elegant, hexagonal tents on decks (two facing the plains, six the river). These are soon to be greatly enlarged, in the same sumptuous style, to offer even more privacy and space. Superb views from the front of the camp go clear across the migration grazing grounds. Run by film and photography pros who share their expert knowledge. 24hr generator and tent sockets. Package $1950

Olare Mara Kempinski Banks of the Ntiakatek River (Ol Kiombo Airstrip) ☎020 2966000 or 0705 050501, ⓦolaremara.com, reservations through ⓦkempinski .com. Ambitious and fancy new tented, fenced camp, with lodge-like central areas and a good-size pool. Hardwood floors, decks with guard rails above the river bank and tiled bathrooms all make the huge, well-spaced tents feel more like hotel rooms, and the whole site is still somewhat raw and in need of shady trees. But the staff are particularly nice and it will suit you if you don't want any kind of "bush" experience. Pool. Package $1800

★ **Porini Lion Camp** Near the seasonal Ntiakatek River, OOC (Ol Kiombo Airstrip) ☎020 7123129 or 020 7122504, ⓦporini.com. Fine eco-camp managed in collaboration with the local Maasai community, in a brilliant game-viewing area particularly renowned for big cats. It's far from other camps, but close enough to the reserve to visit. The ten very spacious and airy tents are run as responsibly as possible, with full recycling, and the staff, all from the local community, are paid significantly higher wages than the norm. Guests eat together. Bronze and silver guides. Ecotourism Kenya Silver Award. Closed mid-April to end May. Package $1180

Richard's Camp By the Ntiakatek River (Ol Kiombo Airstrip) ☎0733 700014, ⓦrichardscamp.com, Nairobi reservations ☎0735 579999, ⓦscckenya.com. A very enjoyable, high-end bush camp, run by an energetic, fun-loving team, with eight tents, solar lighting, hot water by the big bucketful and battery-charging in the office. The owner Richard Roberts is a pilot, and his Cessna 180 or little yellow biplane are available for scenic flights over the Mara (or wherever you can afford). Five bronze guides. Closed May & Nov. Package $1340

OL CHORO OIROUWA CONSERVANCY

A private conservancy bounded by the Mara River, the 69-square-kilometre Ol Choro Oirouwa is a largely pristine area. It's away from the routes of most visitors, and while it's also off the wildebeest migration route, the relative absence of other tourist vehicles makes game drives very rewarding. There's a small white rhino sanctuary here (see p.359).

Fairmont Mara Safari Club East bank of the Mara, off the C14 (Ngerende Airstrip) ☎020 2265555, ⓦfairmont.com. Modish, rather formal tented camp, with fifty riverside tents, in shady grounds linked by

concrete paths. It's a peaceful base, with a beautiful public deck area and heated pool, and very large, tile-floored, rather-too-closely-spaced tents, with four-poster, netted beds and city-hotel amenities. Rates include two game drives, but no drinks or other extras. Heated pool. Wi-fi available. FB $799

OLDERIKESI GROUP RANCH

The remote Olderikesi group ranch has only one, spectacular, camp. The district is teeming with wildlife (including some huge lions), especially since the camp negotiated an agreement with the Maasai stakeholders in the area to create a "no cattle" zone around the camp in exchange for the community charges levied from visitors.

★ **Cottar's 1920s Camp** On Olderikesi GR, close to the Tanzanian border (Keekorok Airstrip) ☎0770 564911, ⓦcottars.com, Nairobi reservations ☎020 6003090, ⓦchelipeacock.com. The finely tuned colonial atmosphere (antiques, oriental carpets), organic kitchen gardens and ten huge, sumptuous tents are just the icing on the cake, for this is one of the best wildlife camps in Kenya, in a game-rich area, with a low human population density. The five-bedroom house is contemporary in style, and very private, so appeals to families. Exceptionally good vehicles, and the three gold guides are, naturally, outstanding. Pool. Package $2060

OL KINYEI CONSERVANCY

Created as recently as 2005, with just one camp from which the local group ranch members benefit substantially, the 67-square-kilometre Ol Kinyei was the Mara's first community-owned conservancy. Formed in partnership with Gamewatchers Safaris, it demonstrated that landowners could make a living from tourism, and the model has since been replicated all over the greater Mara region. Happily bypassed by the lines of vehicles driving between Narok and Sekenani Gate, this is an area in which guided walks and a good degree of cultural immersion are the norm. There are at least twenty lions in the conservancy, plus other cats and plenty of plains game.

Gamewatchers Adventure Camp About 5km from Porini Mara Camp (Naboisho Airstrip) ☎020 7123129 or 020 7122504, ⓦporini.com. Budget version of Porini Mara, with accommodation in small dome tents. The rest of the experience, with local guides and all activities including game drives, game walks, and a Maasai village visit, is the same as the more expensive base. Hosted by a silver guide from the local community. Rates include conservancy fee but not drinks. Three-night minimum stay. Package $460

★ **Porini Mara Camp** 5km west of the C12 road (Naboisho Airstrip) ☎020 7123129 or 020 7122504, ⓦporini.com. Like other *Porini* camps, in the Amboseli area and further west in the Mara – such as *Porini Lion* (see above) – this eco-camp is run in partnership with the local

5

community. The unfenced camp has just six very nice tents and a communal mess. Game walks are a popular feature and guests eat together, creating an intimate atmosphere that's a million miles from the Mara's mainstream lodges. Bronze and silver guides. Ecotourism Kenya Silver Award. Closed mid-April & May. Package $\overline{\$1120}$

OLOIRIEN GROUP RANCH

Most of the land of this huge group ranch lies west of the Oloololo Escarpment, far from the main areas of the reserve, and as a consequence the district is relatively little visited. To the south of the one, spectacularly sited, lodge lies the abandoned *Olkurruk Mara Lodge*, built to house Sidney Pollack and his actors Robert Redford and Meryl Streep during the filming of *Out of Africa* in 1985.

Mara West Crest of the Oloololo Escarpment, overlooking the Mara Triangle (Kichwa Tembo Airstrip) ☎0734 849293, ⓦmarawest.com, Nairobi reservations ⓦadvantage-ea.com. Perched to enjoy some of the best views over the Mara, this unusual, small and very good-value tented camp is a 20–30min drive from the Mara Triangle. Accommodation is in economy tents with shared bathrooms or very comfortable en-suite "tented chalets". FB $\overline{\$516}$

SIANA GROUP RANCH AND CONSERVANCY

The vast Siana Group Ranch stretches from Sekenani Gate to Ololaimutiek Gate and contains a great range of habitats, from shelving plains to forested hills, including the peak of Trevor (1904m) on the north side. Siana includes a number of budget camps and *banda* sites, especially near the gates, but the full involvement of the local Purko Maasai community has not yet properly started. The core Conservancy area being promoted by a number of camps is planned to be a 100-square-kilometre, minibus-free wildlife sanctuary.

Entumoto Accessed via Sekenani Gate, turning east immediately on entering the reserve (Keekorok Airstrip) ☎0713 400903 or 0737 981848, ⓦentumoto .com. New Swedish-Maasai collaboration in a tranquil, forested valley in the Ngama Hills, right on the border of the national reserve. The enormous platform tents, with acres of decking, ostentatious furnishings and built-in fireplaces, are ranged up the hill – in some cases a good 5min walk from the mess tent and lounge. Exceptionally good food, partly from an organic veg garden. Pool. Package $\overline{\$1260}$

★ **Leleshwa Camp** On a tributary of the Talek (Siana Airstrip) ☎0725 332839, ⓦleleshwacamp.com. Accessed from its parking area by a footbridge across the deep cleft of the densely wooded Ropile River, Leleshwa is enjoyably hosted, has tons of bush atmosphere, great food, top guiding and thousands of acres to explore, shared only

with other Leleshwa guests. The four standard tents (there are also two suites) are real tents, and large, without being self-consciously massive, and well furnished, with tiled bathrooms. There's lots of game in camp – escorts are essential after dark. Generator power. Closed May. Package $\overline{\$1390}$

Mara Bushtops On a 10-square-kilometre private game sanctuary on Siana GR, northeast of Sekenani Gate (Siana Airstrip) ☎020 2137862 or 733 490209, ⓦbit.ly/Bushtops. Highly regarded, and self-regarding, hotel-style lodge – based around the old home of Mara hunting and safari legend Glen Cottar – on a fine north-facing hillside, with a tremendous vista from the pool deck and the best wine cellar in the Mara. While being a natural honeymoon lodge, the Bushtops sanctuary has outstanding game, including regularly playing host to denning wild dogs. Five silver and three bronze guides. Personal room butlers. Free wi-fi and good network throughout. Package $\overline{\$1740}$

Mara Sopa Lodge Outside Ololaimutiek Gate (Siana Airstrip) ☎020 251 6160 or 020 2416485, ⓦsopalodges .com. Equalling *Keekorok* (see p.368) in size, this has a hundred rooms, all quite spacious and with pull-around nets. The public areas are impressive and there's a good pool overlooking the wooded valley but it's more of a resort than a game lodge. There's little wildlife to see from the lodge, even with binoculars, and it's a fair drive to the central parts of the reserve. Ecotourism Kenya Silver Award. FB $\overline{\$314}$

★ **Sekenani Camp** On the reserve boundary 6km southeast of Sekenani Gate (Keekorok Airstrip) ☎050 22454 or 0722 147810, ⓦsekenani-camp.com. Unusual and affordable camp, with a good atmosphere, on a ridge in the forest. Tents are all on raised platforms, accessed through tunnels cut through the trees, with bathrooms nicely illuminated by plastic sheeting in the *mabati* roofs above the tents. The area sees elephants, buffaloes and lots of birdlife. Well worth considering if you've been to the Mara before and want somewhere a little different. Pool. FB $\overline{\$500}$

TALEK AREA OF KOIYAKI GROUP RANCH

The mostly mainstream camps and lodges along the north bank of the Talek are often thought of as being inside the reserve. In fact they are all in the southernmost part of Koiyaki Group Ranch, which means that bush walks are possible – though the human pressures are such that there's not a lot of bush left in the area. Access into the reserve itself is easy via Talek gate and the Talek bridge, with the plains of the Sekenani sector and the confluence of the Talek and Mara rivers equally close.

★ **Basecamp Masai Mara** North bank of the Talek, close to Talek Gate (Ol Kiombo Airstrip) ☎0726 924196, ⓦbasecampkenya.com. This award-winning camp, one

5

MAASAI/MASAI – WHAT'S IN A NAME?

The spelling of the name "Maasai" can provoke passion among various authorities, with claims that there are different spellings for the people (Maasai) and the reserve (Masai Mara). In fact the spelling of the people and the reserve with one "a" preceded the first attempt to write down the Maa language, which uses standard international orthography for a long "a" (Ⓦbit.ly/MaaDictionary). The written form of the Maa language is still not much used, but the double-a spelling of the word Maasai is increasingly considered the standard form, even though the name was originally spelled most commonly with one "a".

of the Mara's most eco-friendly places to stay, runs on solar energy, uses composting toilets and recycles all waste. The twelve comfy tents with verandas, Kilgoris-grass-thatched roofs and open-air showers, seem to grow out of the environment. Ecotourism Kenya Gold Award. Two bronze guides and one silver. FB **$670**

Ilkeliani Camp North bank of the Talek looking out onto the Mara plains (Ol Kiombo Airstrip) ☎0733 258120 or 0704 084444, Ⓦilkeliani.com. Spacious and eco-friendly establishment with seventeen well-spaced tents along the river in a fifty-acre compound, with nature walks possible. Old-style tents (with sockets for battery-charging) are powered by solar panels and a rarely needed generator. FB **$440**

Samburu–Buffalo Springs National Reserves

$70 (see p.72) • samburucouncil.com/reserves.htm • 165 square kilometres

Up in the north of the country, in the hot, arid lowlands beneath Mount Kenya, **Samburu National Reserve** was set up around the richest stretch of the Ewaso Nyiro (or Uaso Ngiro) River in the late 1960s. Although the river usually stops flowing for a month or two around January, the combination of near-permanent water and forest shade on the banks draws plentiful wildlife in the dry season and maintains many of the less migratory species all year round.

While the wildlife spectacle doesn't always match that of the southern parks, the peace and scenic beauty of Samburu is unquestionable and, in the kind of mood swing which only an equatorial region can produce, the contrast with the fertile farming country of the Highlands just a few dozen kilometres to the south couldn't be more striking. In the background, the sharp hill of **Koitogor** rises in the middle of Samburu Reserve, making a useful reference point. And on the horizon, 30km to the north, looms the gaunt red block of **Ol Olokwe** mountain. **Buffalo Springs National Reserve**, the continuation of Samburu on the south side of the river, and **Shaba National Reserve**, further downstream to the east, are often treated as if they were just part of "Samburu". They remain distinct reserves with their own entrance fees, but will allow common game drives across them, which means you will only have to pay $70 once. That said, although it used to be very easy to cross from Samburu into Buffalo Springs over the bridge near the Samburu headquarters, the crossing is closed at the time of writing. The **bridge** was washed away in severe floods in 2010, rebuilt by the British Army and reopened with great ceremony, only to be washed away again in 2011. To get into Buffalo Springs or Samburu from the opposite side, you now have to go back to the highway and cross the bridge there, via Archer's Post – a 45km diversion to reach the other side of the bridge that takes around two hours without stopping to watch wildlife.

Adjoining Samburu to the north is the 95-square-kilometre **Kalama Community Wildlife Conservancy** ($90, including access to Samburu-Buffalo Springs, Ⓦnrt-kenya .org/kalama.html), of which a core 31 square kilometres is a crucial wildlife migration corridor, with just one, very high-end, boutique lodge, *Saruni Samburu* (see p.377). To the northwest of the reserves lies the **Westgate** (or West Gate) **Community Conservancy** ($50; Ⓦbit.ly/WestGate), which covers an even larger district of semi-arid grazing land, but has a very small core conservancy area of less than 10 square kilometres around the exclusive *Sasaab Lodge* (see p.377).

Isolated incidents of **banditry** still occur around Archer's Post and on the roads into the three reserves. Security is generally good, but if you're driving yourself, it's always worth having a chat with the police at the checkpoint just north of Isiolo.

Exploring Samburu–Buffalo Springs

Except during and immediately after the rains, scrubby bush country takes up most of the reserve district, but there are some large acacia thickets, especially in the eastern part of **Buffalo Springs**. The **springs** themselves are a welcome target: two pools of clear if weedy water, the smaller of which has been sanitized with concrete for the benefit of swimmers and, most of the time, the exclusion of crocodiles (be sure to check before jumping in). The larger one is the water supply for the town of Archer's Post. While looking out for crocs, you should also beware of lions, which sometimes rest under the bushes by the neighbouring natural waterhole.

The dry-country ecosystems are prone to large variations in animal populations as they move in search of water and grazing, which means that Samburu's **wildlife** can occasionally be disappointing. Some visitors, however, have tremendous luck and Samburu–Buffalo Springs can provide consistently excellent animal-watching. The best areas are often along the south side of the river in Buffalo Springs Reserve, opposite *Samburu Lodge*. Poaching wiped out the rhinos from here years ago, but **lions** are often seen.

Meanwhile, the locally burgeoning **elephant herds** have ruined some sections of the riverine forest. Various rare or more localized races and species compensate, though, and are often seen here in large numbers. Among these, the **reticulated giraffe** with its beautiful jigsaw marking, **Grevy's zebra** (the large, finely striped species that has a bushy mane and outsized ears), the **Somali ostrich**, which has blue rather than pink legs, and the **gerenuk**, the antelope that stands on its hind legs to reach foliage, are all common and conspicuous. Samburu's **birdlife** is diverse and prolific and includes the ferocious **martial eagle**, pygmy falcon, Egyptian goose and several species of hornbill.

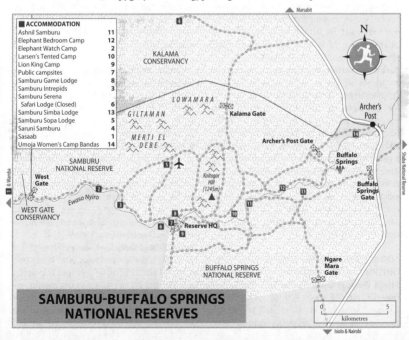

■ ACCOMMODATION	
Ashnil Samburu	11
Elephant Bedroom Camp	12
Elephant Watch Camp	2
Larsen's Tented Camp	10
Lion King Camp	9
Public campsites	7
Samburu Game Lodge	8
Samburu Intrepids	3
Samburu Serena Safari Lodge (Closed)	6
Samburu Simba Lodge	13
Samburu Sopa Lodge	5
Saruni Samburu	4
Sasaab	1
Umoja Women's Camp Bandas	14

SAMBURU–BUFFALO SPRINGS NATIONAL RESERVES

5

ARRIVAL AND DEPARTURE

SAMBURU–BUFFALO SPRINGS

If you're circling Mount Kenya, Samburu Reserve is close at hand, a couple of hours north of Nanyuki.

By bus and matatu Public transport runs down onto the hazy plain as far as Isiolo (see p.537) from where there are also regular services to Archer's Post. There is no public transport into the reserves, but you might be lucky with a lift, assuming you've made plans to stay somewhere or are going to camp near the reserve HQ. In practice, if you're visiting the reserves independently on a budget, you're better off making arrangements to do game drives at Archer's Post (see p.540) or one of the budget camps outside Samburu reserve.

By car The fast new road to Merille (see p.540) has reduced the rare instances of roadside banditry. Occasional episodes of inter-tribal conflict can still interrupt daily life in this region, but you are not likely to be required to wait at the

police checkpoint for an escort for the short continuation to the Ngare Mara Gate. Remember to fill up with fuel before leaving Isiolo. *Samburu Game Lodge* usually has supplies, sold at a twenty percent mark-up, and Archer's Post now has a filling station. You should be able to reach the lodges in Buffalo Springs in under an hour and the Samburu reserve HQ area in about an hour.

By plane Airkenya and SafariLink both fly from Nairobi to Samburu and Shaba (at least daily; 1–2hr depending on routing; about $200 each way, $340 round trip). In addition, depending on season and demand, Airkenya flies one way from Meru to Samburu (daily; 30min; $183) and both airlines fly one way from Samburu to Maasai Mara (daily; 1hr 30min–2hr; about $360).

ACCOMMODATION

There's an increasing range of **lodges** and **tented camps** in Samburu–Buffalo Springs, though in recent years they've often seemed too many for the number of visitors. In March 2010, the Ewaso Nyiro burst its banks and the floods swamped all the riverbank lodges and camps in Samburu and Buffalo Springs. Several have had to be largely rebuilt, and one – *Serena Samburu* – has still not reopened.

CAMPSITES

Samburu has several public campsites along the banks of the Ewaso Nyiro, near the bridge and park headquarters. All have very basic shared facilities, including long-drop toilets and cold showers. The baboons at the campsites are beyond being an amusement and you need to leave your tent under guard. The fact that baboons sometimes fall victim to crocs at the water's edge seems less distressing after you've been in the area for a day or two.

Park Headquarters campsites If you're camping on a budget, you will probably gravitate to one of the four campsites between the bridge and the park HQ. Two of the sites are nicer and located right on the river under shady trees close to the HQ (and a 5min walk from *Samburu Game Lodge*), while the two further sites, closer to the bridge, are set slightly back from the river and don't have a view. While these are not as nice, they do have small dome tents for rent ($20/day). You can use *Samburu Game Lodge's* restaurant and pool and, if you don't have a vehicle, you may even manage to get a lift around the reserve. You always have the option of booking yourself onto a morning or evening game drive on a lodge Land Cruiser ($70). **$30** per person

LODGES AND TENTED CAMPS

OUTSIDE SAMBURU RESERVE

Umoja Women's Camp Bandas River bank, 1.2km from the centre of Archer's Post (off the road to the reserve's Archer's Post Gate) ☎0721 659717, ⓦumojawomen.org. A delightfully different setup,

founded by the charismatic women's rights campaigner Rebecca Lolosoli as an offshoot of her village for abused women, this has six simple, simply furnished s/c *bandas* with nets, plumbed-in bathrooms and mains power, a shady bar-restaurant above the river (meals Ksh400–600) and an eight-seater vehicle with driver to rent for game drives ($200/day). Camping **Ksh800** per person, twin *banda* **Ksh3000**

SAMBURU NATIONAL RESERVE

Elephant Bedroom Camp River bank ☎0721 638197 or 020 234192, ⓦatua-enkop.com. Well-designed, beautifully furnished, light, airy tents (four doubles and eight twins), some with plunge pools. Very appealing, designer bush living. Four bronze guides. Package **$860**

★ **Elephant Watch Camp** River bank, west of the reserve ☎020 8048602 or 0713 037886 or 0708 688295, ⓦelephantwatchsafaris.com. Elephant specialist Oria Douglas-Hamilton's camp sits on the sandy river bank. The six superb, individually fitted-out and variously shaped tents have massive nets and rambling, open-air bathroom-shower-toilets (bucket showers). Two silver guides. Closed April & Nov. Package **$1360**

Larsen's Tented Camp River bank ☎0720 626367 or 020 2045835, ⓦwildernesslodges.co.ke. Twenty tents, on a fenced plot, all facing the river. Tents have wooden floors, with fans but no nets, and sockets, minibars, tea-making and safes. Electricity, supplied by a noisy generator, is turned off at midnight. There's a nice, open-air massage suite, looking across to Koitogor rather than the river, and a

5

pool. Comfortable, with outstanding service and good guiding from its five bronze guides, but also quite scruffy and in need of refurbishment. FB **$650**

Lion King Camp River bank, just west of the reserve HQ ☎0703 116469 or 0710 350782, ⓦlionking safariskenya.com. A simple and authentic tented camp, owner-managed by an adventurous Samburu ecosystem enthusiast. Game drives are available in the camp vehicle (3hr; $36 per person). If you aren't driving, you'll need to arrange for them to pick you up from Archer's Post when you book to stay. Drinks extra. FB **$200**

Samburu Game Lodge River bank, near the reserve HQ ☎020 2045835 or 0720 626366, ⓦwilderness lodges.co.ke. The oldest lodge in Samburu, on a heavily wooded broad bend of the river, this is very well sited, with great tree cover. The rooms in blocks and thatched chalets have nets and fans, and come with excellent views and no fence (the bank provides an adequate boundary along most of the river frontage). It's still popular, but very tired, and in need of an overhaul. Nice pool with shaded surrounds. Crocs are fed daily in front of the lodge. FB **$440**

★ **Samburu Intrepids** River bank, west of the reserves ☎064 30453 or 0722 795569, ⓦheritage-eastafrica.com. Built on stilt platforms (for when the river floods), in a dense riverside thicket, the pleasant, modestly sized tents here have good bathrooms and wooden floors. Double-sized family tents are also available. All tents are river-facing, and one is disabled-friendly. The fine, expansive, public deck areas reach over the river bank and are shot through with indigenous trees. Five bronze guides, and children's and teens' activities clubs. Good pool. Ecotourism Kenya Silver Award. FB **$720**

Samburu Sopa Lodge Away from the river, on the road to Kalama Conservancy ☎0721 258278, ⓦsopalodges .com. Popular and affordable lodge, with sixty simple, comfortable rooms in two crescents of fifteen semi-detached cottages curling around the waterhole, which draws wildlife regularly. It's pleasant and welcoming enough, with efficient and friendly staff and a sparkling blue pool. The main drawback is its location, on the thorny hillside, 5km from the river. Ecotourism Kenya Bronze Award. FB **$314**

BUFFALO SPRINGS NATIONAL RESERVE

Ashnil Samburu River bank, 12km from Ngare Mara Gate, ⓦashnilhotels.com. Thirty rather small, low tented chalets, with hot, single-layer canvas roofs, mini-safes and floor-standing fans, but no nets. Generator electricity. Pool. FB **$468**

Samburu Simba Lodge On a bluff, set back from the river ☎0729 407162, ⓦmarasimba.com. Ranged along a flood meander of the Ewaso Nyiro, this sprawling lodge was completed in 2010. Its seventy modern, high-ceilinged rooms are spread between seven huge villas. The result looks like a Californian residential development, an impression enhanced by the health club, satellite TV and two pools. FB **$575**

KALAMA CONSERVANCY

★ **Saruni Samburu** On a high cliff north of Samburu (8km north of Archer's Post, then through the Kalama Conservancy gate on the highway, and 11km to the west) ☎0714 606900, ⓦsarunisamburu.com, Nairobi reservations ☎020 6003090, ⓦchelipeacock.com. This sensuous rock-and-steel vision of an architect and designer, clinging to a bare, rocky col, is unlike anywhere else in the Samburu district. It's completely beguiling: sit and gaze at Mount Kenya far to the south, swim in the pool, and recharge your spiritual batteries. Package **$1380**

WESTGATE COMMUNITY CONSERVANCY

★ **Sasaab** North bank of the river, 15km west of Samburu reserve's West Gate ☎020 5020888 or 0725 675830, ⓦthesafaricollection.com (nearby airstrip can be used by SafariLink). Situated atop a high hill overlooking the Ewaso Nyiro, this lodge has breathtaking, uninterrupted views across the Northern Frontier District. With heavy Moroccan influences in its design, each of the nine lavish rooms has more than 100 square metres of space, and a private plunge pool. The lodge has a spa, and activities on the conservancy include camel rides, engaging village visits, walks and game drives, plus full-day drives into Samburu. One silver and one bronze guide. Closed Nov 16–Dec 16. Package **$1400**

Shaba National Reserve

$70 (see p.72) • ⓦsamburucouncil.com/reserves.htm • 239 square kilometres

On the other side of the Isiolo–Archer's Post road lies the **Shaba National Reserve**, where Joy Adamson experimented with the release of hand-reared leopards. Highly recommended, Shaba is much less visited than Samburu or Buffalo Springs. If you're driving, you're likely to enter the reserve at **Natorbe Gate** (6km from the A2 highway junction a couple of kilometres south of Archer's Post) on a road that rolls up and down through a **lava field**. The landscapes of Shaba are a lot more varied than you might expect, with the dramatic bulk of **Bodich** mountain rising behind the river to the north, and steep hills, culminating in **Shaba** peak, pressing in on the south.

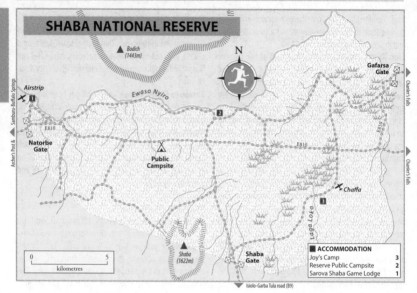

For animals, **Shaba** is quite the equal of its two neighbours, with lots of elephants, jackals, lions and plains game, including beautifully marked Grevy's zebra, reticulated giraffe and the gerenuk, which rarely if ever drinks, extracting water from morning dew on leaves. Scattered waterholes are the usual targets of visitors, who sometimes spend long periods just watching and waiting from their vehicles. Unusually, you are permitted to walk in various places in Shaba. The rangers at the gate can point out where. If you need fuel, you can usually get it at *Sarova Shaba Lodge*.

Chanler's Falls

You might consider venturing out of the reserve to the east to visit **Chanler's Falls**, 30km beyond Chanler's Falls (Gafarsa) Gate on the Ewaso Nyiro River. Double-check the security situation first with the rangers – there's no one here except Samburu herders.

ARRIVAL AND DEPARTURE   SHABA

By car, bus or matatu For driving to Shaba or trying to reach the reserve by public transport, the same details apply as for Samburu/Buffalo Springs (see p.376). The main entrance to the reserve, Natorbe Gate, is 1km south of Archer's Post and 1km north of Buffalo Springs Gate.

By plane You'll arrive on one of SafariLink's twice-daily flights from Nairobi Wilson (around $200 one way, $340 round trip) at *Sarova Shaba's* airstrip, just inside the reserve. Flight times vary, depending on the routing, averaging 1hr–1hr 30min.

ACCOMMODATION

★ **Joy's Camp** Southeast area of Shaba National Reserve ☎ 0725 957321 or 020 3513563, ⓦ joyscamp .com. Whatever you might feel about the late Ms Adamson (see p.380), who made her home here for a while, never has a camp been so aptly named. The palatial, Bedouin-style tents, gleaming with soft fabric and glass details, and perfectly spaced along a 1km stretch of buffalo-grazed marsh, seem to breathe relaxation. The birdlife is fantastic and the swimming pool, meals and generally chic ambience are sublime. When

you're ready to go game-watching, there are excellent guides – two bronze and two silver. The perfect honeymoon camp. Ecotourism Kenya Silver Award. Package $1220
Reserve public campsite 9km from Natorbe Gate, on the banks of the Ewaso Nyiro. There are two simple campsites in Shaba, neither with any facilities – this is the better of the pair. $30 per person
Sarova Shaba Game Lodge South bank of the Ewaso Nyiro at the western end of the reserve ☎ 064 30638 or

0728 603590, ⓦsarovahotels.com. Very attractively landscaped, with a superb swimming pool and streams running through public areas, but the fact that local herders were prevented from using the crystal-clear spring which feeds them jars a little (a well was dug for them instead). The eighty standard rooms have fans, but rotten old nets that don't really work (and you need them with all that water running around attracting the mosquitoes). Crocodile-feeding and viewing, daily at 7.30pm. Ecotourism Kenya Silver Award. FB $315

Meru National Park

$65 with Safari Card (see p.71) • ⓦ bit.ly/MeruNatPark • 870 square kilometres

You still don't see **Meru National Park** on many safari itineraries. Of the main parks covered in this chapter, it is the least visited and most unspoilt and pristine. Abundantly traversed by **streams** flowing into the Tana River on its southern boundary, and luxuriantly rained upon, the rolling **jungle** of tall grass, riverine forest and swamp is lent a hypnotic, other-worldly quality by wonderful stands of prehistoric-looking **doum palms**.

True, the **animals** aren't always as much in evidence here as they can be in some other Kenyan parks, though in recent years the wildlife numbers have been much improved, but the even more noticeable absence of minibuses and Land Cruisers more than compensates. After visiting some of the less bushy parks, where the animals can be spotted from far away, Meru's intimate, unusual landscape is quickly entrancing.

Kora National Park, and the three national reserves south and east of Meru – **Bisanadi**, **Mwingi** and **Rahole** – are all in the Land-Rover-expedition category, a total of 4500 square kilometres of scrub and semi-desert, and dense forest where they fringe the Tana River. Because of the history of poor security in the area (though there have been no recent incidents), you do need to check out the situation very carefully with KWS in Meru National Park if you're considering entering the Kora area.

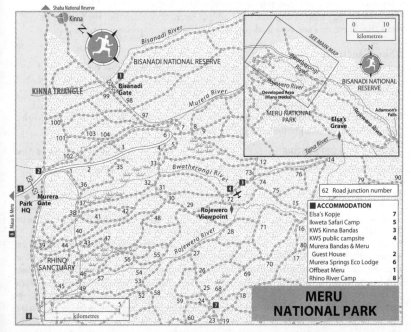

THE ADAMSONS

Meru is the area where the passionate animal lovers and recluses **George and Joy Adamson** (he a hunter turned game warden, she a gifted watercolourist and writer) released their most famous lioness **Elsa** back into the wild in the late 1950s – a story that became the bestselling book and film, *Born Free*. After the couple separated, the misanthropic Joy conducted a series of long-term experiments with orphaned cheetahs and leopards in Shaba National Reserve – years of dedicated, lonely work cut short by her murder in 1980. George, meanwhile, moved to **Kora National Park**, adjoining Meru, where he lived in the bush and continued to work with orphaned lions. He was also murdered, in 1989, by poachers.

Exploring the park

Meru's many tracks are all good gravel and most **junctions** have signposts and numbered cairns. A popular hook for a fairly long drive is the loop down to the grave of Elsa the lioness, on the banks of the Tana. And there are plenty of other enticing areas to investigate without going too far. Driving in through Murera Gate, for example, turn immediately sharp left up to the "**Kinna Triangle**", cross the Murera stream at junction #102 and pass a stupendous fig tree on your left. You then enter a beautiful area of thick vegetation, tall trees and high grass.

The Rojewero River

The **Rojewero River**, the largest of the park's twelve main streams, is an interesting watercourse: densely overgrown banks flash with birds and monkeys and dark waters ripple with hippos, crocs and freshwater turtles. Large and very visible herds of **elephant**, **buffalo** and **reticulated giraffe** are common, as are, in the more open areas, **gerenuk**, **Grevy's zebra** and **ostrich**. Predators were once scarce, though numbers seem to be on the up, and **lion** (which prey mainly on Meru's big herds of buffalo) and **cheetah** are increasingly seen, when they are not hidden in the long grass – the smaller grazers must have a nerve-wracking time of it here. Large numbers of **leopards** captured in the stock-raising lands of Laikipia have been released in the park in recent years, but these cats are wary and you have little chance of seeing them.

Rhino Sanctuary

On the right when you enter the park at Murera Gate • Free with national park ticket • 4WD only • 27 square kilometres

Meru's successful **rhino sanctuary** has been enlarged and is now protected by a fence and numerous rangers. The couple of dozen white rhinos are doing well, though the similar number of black rhinos suffer somewhat from tsetse flies. They're monitored around the clock and well habituated to visitors, so sightings can be outstanding, with plenty of time to take pictures at close quarters.

ARRIVAL AND DEPARTURE   MERU NATIONAL PARK

Getting to Meru is straightforward by air, or if you're driving. Public transport requires a bit more effort.

By plane Most visitors fly with Airkenya from Nairobi Wilson (daily; 1hr–1hr 30min; $241 each way). You can also fly with Airkenya *from* the park on to Samburu (daily 30min; $183), but not the other way round.

By car If you're driving from Nairobi, use the 225km route via Embu around the east side of Mount Kenya to Meru town (see p.183), allowing 4hr, then the straightforward route from Meru town via Maua to the park's Murera Gate (a further 72km, all tarmac; allow another 1hr to the park). Gradually, the highlands scene gives way to the lank grass, termite cathedrals and scattered trees and streams that

characterize the park's savanna. Fill your tank and jerrican at Maua (which has Barclays and KCB ATMs). There is usually fuel available about 5km outside the park on the Maua road as well.

By bus and matatu From Meru town there are frequent buses and matatus to Maua, 1hr into the Nyambeni Hills on a tarmac road, through steep tea terraces and plantations of *miraa*. From Maua, however, few matatus run the whole 30km stretch to the park gate, and although there's excellent budget accommodation in the park, you may find it hard to get there.

ACCOMMODATION AND EATING

Most drive-in visitors to the park head straight to one of the campsites, tented camps or *Elsa's Kopje* lodge. If it's late in the day, however, you might want to stay the night in the busy little *miraa*-trading centre of Maua.

MAUA

Maua Basin Hotel Signposted 300m off to the left as you arrive ☎0720 175415. The best option in Maua itself is a calm place with a choice of self-contained rooms in the "Museum" and "Basin" wings – the latter is the best choice, with more light. The hotel's *Hotsprings* restaurant has a long menu (Ksh300–500 for most dishes). BB Ksh3500

IN THE PARK

CAMPSITES AND KWS ACCOMMODATION

★ **KWS Kinna Bandas** Near the old park HQ ☎061 2303094 or 020 2109508, ✉reservations@kws.go.ke. On a shady site, the former *Bwatherongi Bandas* offers five s/c twin *bandas*, with very large rooms, nets and bathrooms, but no cooking facilities. The most appealing feature is the excellent swimming pool in the middle of the site, complete with recliners and cleaning robot. Whole *banda* $100

KWS public campsite Near the old park headquarters, 18km from the gate on a stretch of open ground running down to a wooded stream. There are toilet and shower blocks, and firewood is plentiful. $15 per person

KWS special campsite Dotted around the park, reservations in Nairobi ☎0726 610508, ✉reservations @kws.go.ke. None has any facilities except supplies of firewood, and you need to reserve ahead and pay a booking fee of Ksh7500. $30 per person

Murera Bandas & Meru Guest House By Murera Gate ☎061 2303094 or 020 2109508, ✉reservations@kws .go.ke. Four *bandas*, three with three beds (one double, one single in each) and one more luxurious twin, and a shared barbecue area. Larger groups can be accommodated in the nearby Meru Guest House, which sleeps five and has a kitchen. Triple *banda* $50, twin *banda* $70, whole guest house $120

LODGES AND TENTED CAMPS

★ **Elsa's Kopje** On Mughwango hill ☎020 6003090 or 0722 509387, ⊛elsaskopje.com. One of Kenya's best lodges, the charm of *Elsa's* is partly down to its stunning rocky hilltop location, with a 360-degree panorama that simply drives away cares. But the details are all spot-on, too

– excellent hosts, an infinity pool cleaved from the rock; birds, comical hyraxes and lizards everywhere; outrageously good food and wine; and completely delightful cottages, each open-fronted to let in the sky, with its own private deck among the shrubs and crags. Two silver and three bronze guides for bush walks and day and night game drives. Ecotourism Kenya Silver Award. Package $1400

Ikweta Safari Camp Just outside the park ☎0705 200050 or 0735 200050, ⊛ikwetasafaricamp.com. This comfortable camp offers affordable access to Meru National Park while maintaining an intimate feel, with just ten en-suite tents. The camp runs off mains electricity, has a pool and can arrange game drives into the park. FB Ksh12,600

Murera Springs Eco Lodge Outside Meru National Park ☎020 3876636, ⊛wildernessgetawaysea.com. This small and quirky ecolodge has just ten rooms, runs entirely on solar and offers meals made from home-grown ingredients. There is a refreshing pool and lounge area as well. FB $390

Offbeat Meru 1.3km east of junction #99 at the edge of the park in the Bisanadi National Reserve ☎0704 909355 or 0704 909356, ⊛offbeatsafaris.com. This traditional yet stylish and comfortable tented camp above the Bisanadi River is excellently run and a great base from which to explore the park. With only six tents (with flush toilets and bucket showers) the team's approach to safaris is flexible, and the communal dinners with other guests are sociable affairs. Activities are led by three knowledgeable guides, one silver and two bronze. Pool. Closed Apr 16–May 31 & Nov. Conservation fee $80. Package $880

★ **Rhino River Camp** By the Rhino Sanctuary, just outside the park ☎0732 809287 or 0732 985162, ⊛rhinorivercamp.com. New camp, built in 2010, nestling in the shade of dense forest, with eight private cottages, each with spacious, stylishly minimalist rooms with en-suite bathrooms and steel basin. Outside each cottage, the decking and private gazebo lends the camp a restful and appealingly Zen aesthetic. The pool and pool area are tucked into a canopied patch of forest by a stream, lending a jungly mood. One silver and three bronze guides who really know their stuff. Package $990

The Coast

LAMU WATERFRONT

The Coast

The coast is a world apart from "upcountry" Kenya and in many ways it feels like a different country. For a start, Mombasa, Kenya's second city, is a much easier place to enjoy than Nairobi. With its sun-scorched, colonnaded streets, this is the quintessential tropical port – steamy and unbelievably dilapidated – and it's fun to shop here, stroll the old city's alleys, or visit Fort Jesus. To the north and south of Mombasa there are superb beaches and a number of tourist resort areas, but nothing, as yet, highly developed in the Florida or Canary Islands sense. You can certainly enjoy yourself having a lazy time at a beach resort, but there's a lot more to the coast than recliners, swimming pools and buffet meals.

Most obviously, the beaches are the launch pad for one of the most beautiful **coral reefs** in the world. With rented equipment, you can do some spectacular dives, but even with a simple snorkel and mask, which are easily obtained, you can discover what really is another world. The two most spectacular areas are enclosed in **marine national parks**, around Watamu and Malindi, and at the island of Wasini.

The string of **islands** that runs up the coast – Wasini, Funzi, Chale, Lamu, Manda, Pate and Kiwaiyu – are all very much worth visiting. Apart from their beach and ocean attractions, most of them have some archeological interest, which is also a constant theme on the mainland: the whole coast is littered with the **ruins** of forts, mosques, tombs and even one or two whole towns. Some of these – including **Fort Jesus**, the old town of **Lamu** and the ruined city of **Gedi** – are already on the tourist circuit, but there are dozens that have hardly been cleared and make for compelling excursions if you're adventurous.

Islam has long been a major influence on the coast, and the traditional, annual fast is widely observed during the month of **Ramadan**, when no food or drinks are consumed during the hours of daylight. Visiting the coast at this time might leave a slightly

WATAMU

Highlights

❶ Fort Jesus Seven centuries of coastal history are on show in Mombasa's fascinating castle-museum. **See p.393**

❷ Tiwi Beach The reef is close to the shore here, and there are some excellent, low-key cottage developments. **See p.427**

❸ Kaya Kinondo Explore the first sacred forest to be opened to visitors with a knowledgeable community guide. **See p.433**

❹ Wasini A tiny, undeveloped island community, with wonderful diving and snorkelling. **See p.443**

❺ Arabuko Sokoke Forest East Africa's largest tract of indigenous coastal forest offers excellent guided walks and the chance to see monkeys and lots of birds and butterflies. **See p.450**

❻ Gedi Try to visit this lost city first thing in the morning or as the sun goes down, when the ruins are at their most atmospheric. **See p.452**

❼ Watamu The stunning bays, islets and casuarina-shaded beaches are matched by glorious coral gardens and good diving opportunities. **See p.454**

❽ Lamu A compelling, history-soaked city-state and UNESCO World Heritage Site, with no roads or vehicles. **See p.472**

HIGHLIGHTS ARE MARKED ON THE MAP ON P.386

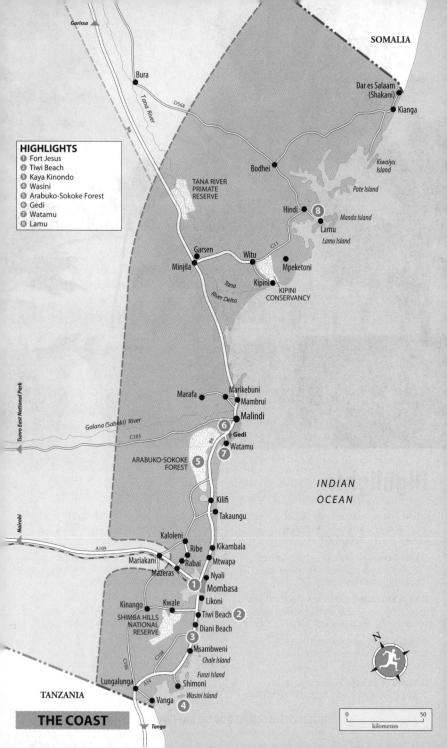

strange impression of a region where everyone is on night shift, but in practical terms it usually makes little difference. The end of Ramadan is marked by major **festivities**, as are several other Muslim holidays throughout the year (see p.67).

Resort areas

Plenty of visitors – perhaps the majority, in fact – treat the coast as their main destination in Kenya, combined with a short safari inland. There are four main, popular **resort areas**. First and foremost is the suburban district north of Mombasa island, often known as **North Coast**, around half an hour to an hour from Mombasa's Moi International airport; further north comes **Watamu**, about two hours from the airport; and lastly **Malindi**, another twenty minutes beyond Watamu. South of Mombasa, the main focus of the **South Coast** is Diani Beach, about an hour-and-a-half's drive from the airport on a good day (the ferry linking Mombasa to the south coast can delay you). Apart from the odd small development, the rest of the coast is little touched by tourism.

In many areas along the length of the coast, the sea is very shallow at low tide and in some places it's impossible to swim except at high tide. If you want to know about the tides during your visit, consult **tide tables** (see ⓦcoastweek.com/tides.htm). The protected lagoon inside the reef is free of currents and safe for swimming when the tide is high enough. Beyond the reef, however, conditions can be radically different. If you're planning to go beyond the reef – to dive or go deep-sea fishing, for example – always check that your boat has a useable life jacket for each passenger.

If you're on a shoestring budget, a word of warning: tempting as it can be, **sleeping out** on the beaches is nearly always unwise because of the danger of robbery. Although

---

ENVIRONMENT AND WILDLIFE

The hundreds of kilometres of sandy **beach** that fringe the low-lying coastal strip are backed by **dunes** and coconut palms, traversed by scores of streams and rivers. Flowing off the plateaus through tumbling jungle, these waterways meander across a narrow, fertile plain to the sea. In sheltered creeks, forests of **mangrove** trees cover vast areas and create a distinctive ecological zone of tidal mud flats.

Most of Kenya's **lowland forests** are on the coast and along the banks of the lower Tana River. The rainforests, all threatened by human incursion, include Witu forest near Lamu, the Mida-Gedi forest near Watamu, the Sabaki River Forest near Malindi, several forest fragments in the Shimba Hills, and the Ramisi River Forest on the southern coast. Several of the kaya sacred areas, such as Kaya Diani and Kaya Kinondo, are similar, although they're too small to have a rainforest microclimate. The most important area of natural forest is the **Arabuko Sokoke National Park**, south of Malindi. Arabuko-Sokoke is unique in that it comprises a largely unbroken block of 420 square kilometres of coastal forest, consisting of Brachystegia woodland (containing a huge variety of birdlife), dense Cynometra forest, and zones of mixed lowland rainforest that are very rich in plants, mammals and insects.

Wildlife on the coast is in keeping with the region's lush, intimate feel. The big game of upcountry Kenya is more or less absent (though Shimba Hills National Park southwest of Mombasa is an exception), but smaller creatures are abundant. **Monkeys** are especially common, with troops of baboons seen by the road, vervet and Sykes' monkeys frequently at home in hotel gardens, and spectacular Angolan colobus monkeys locally common in the forests behind Diani Beach. **Birdlife** is prolific – if you have even a mild interest you should bring binoculars. On the **reptile** front, snakes, those brilliant disguise artists, are rarely seen (except in a number of snake parks), but lizards skitter everywhere, including upside down on the ceiling at night, and bug-eyed chameleons waver across the road, sometimes making it to the other side. So do **giant millipedes**, up to 30cm long: these harmless scavengers have been nicknamed "Mombasa Express", after the famously slow train. **Insects** are here in full force, although thankfully efforts to eradicate mosquitoes are paying off, and most species, including the glorious **butterflies** of the Diani and Arabuko-Sokoke forests, are attractive participants in the coast's gaudy show.

there are one or two very remote areas where you might get away with it, you'll usually have to find a room or pitch your tent at one of the few campsites.

Seasons on the coast

This part of Kenya, with its monsoon climate, is the region most affected by the **seasons**. The somewhat unpredictable "long rains" between April and June are a much cheaper and quieter season than the rest of the year. While the beaches tend to be damp and the weather overcast during this low season (and some hotels close completely), you can make big savings on pre-booked holidays or, if you're travelling independently, reduce your accommodation costs by fifty percent or more. If you're diving, the **water clarity** is still reasonably good, at least at the start of the rains.

The **sea temperature** is warm to very warm all year round, averaging 25–30°C, but underwater visibility varies greatly, from as little as 5m between June and September to as much as 30m in December. The best overall months for weather and water visibility are usually October, November and March, though it can be very hot in March in the build-up to the long rains.

As for the Indian Ocean's **monsoon winds**, they always blow onshore: the dry, moderate *kaskazi* wind blows onto the beaches from the northeast from November to April; then the moister and stronger *kusi* blows in from the southeast from May to October. The changeover period is often very gusty. In this season large quantities of **seaweed** often sweep up onto the beach. In July, August and September there is generally quite a strong breeze, with choppy seas. From December to February, on the other hand, it's hot and dry, and much calmer.

ARRIVAL AND DEPARTURE   THE COAST

By plane Many visitors arrive at Moi International Airport (see p.398) in Mombasa. If you fly to Diani Beach, Mombasa, Malindi, Lamu or Kiwaiyu from Nairobi you'll save at least a day's travel. Note that it's only the flights to Mombasa and Diani Beach, with occasional views of Kilimanjaro, that are interesting in themselves. On the other hand, flying up to Lamu from Mombasa or Malindi offers stunning views over jungle and reef (see p.483).

By train When it was a reliable twice-daily service, the overnight train journey (see p.54) between Nairobi and Mombasa used to be a Kenyan travel highlight. While its infrequency (three times a week) and notorious

unreliability make it difficult to recommend unreservedly (elephants on the line and more mundane problems mean it's often hours late), it's a trip worth doing at least once.

By bus The constant stream of buses from Nairobi to Mombasa provides the cheapest transport, and you can stop anywhere en route if you want to explore. It's best to travel on a day bus rather than take a night bus, to reduce the chance of an accident on the very busy highway.

By car If you're driving, or you're in a rented vehicle with a driver, you'll be pleased to know that the highway is in good condition for its whole length, for the first time in decades (see p.318). Again, you're strongly advised to avoid driving after dark.

Mombasa

There's a sense of community and depth of history in **MOMBASA** that Nairobi lacks. Sleazy, hot and physically tropical in a way that could hardly be more different from the capital, Mombasa is the slightly indolent hub of the coast. Faded, flaking and occasionally charming, the city centre – neatly isolated by the sea from its suburbs – feels like a small town that was once great.

SECURITY IN MOMBASA

Although Mombasa isn't particularly intimidating, the Likoni ferry and the chaotic area around the junction of Jomo Kenyatta Avenue and Mwembe Tayari Road are two hotspots for occasional **pickpocketing** and bag snatching. It's also not unknown for pickpockets to stalk tourists along Moi Avenue and around Fort Jesus. Stay alert and you'll have no problems.

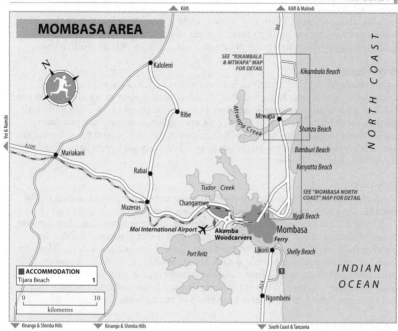

MOMBASA AREA

Kilifi

Kilifi & Malindi

NORTH COAST

Kaloleni

SEE "KIKAMBALA & MTWAPA" MAP FOR DETAIL

Kikambala Beach

Ribe

Mtwapa Creek

Mtwapa

Shanzu Beach

Voi & Nairobi

A109

Mariakani

Rabai

Bamburi Beach

Kenyatta Beach

Tudor Creek

Changamwe

SEE "MOMBASA NORTH COAST" MAP FOR DETAIL

Mazeras

Nyali Beach

Moi International Airport

Akamba Woodcarvers

Mombasa

Ferry

Port Reitz

Likoni

Shelly Beach

■ ACCOMMODATION
Tijara Beach **1**

INDIAN OCEAN

0 ——— 10
kilometres

Ngombeni

Kinango & Shimba Hills

Kinango & Shimba Hills

South Coast & Tanzania

6

While it's a chaotic city, the atmosphere, even in the commercial centre of what is one of Africa's busiest ports, is invariably relaxed and congenial. Rush hours, urgency and paranoia seem to be Nairobi's problems (as everyone here will tell you), not Mombasa's. And the gaping, marginal slums of many African cities hardly exist in Mombasa. It's true that **Miritini** and **Chomvu** and especially **Likoni** and **Changamwe** are burgeoning mainland suburbs that the municipality has more or less abandoned, but the brutalizing conditions of Nairobi's Kibera are absent.

Despite the palm trees, the sunshine and the happy languor, all is not bliss and perfection. **Street crime**, though it hardly approaches Nairobi's level, is still a problem, and you should be wary of displaying your valuables or accepting invitations to walk down dark alleys. But, as a general rule, Mombasa is a far less neurotic city than Nairobi. Even after dark, Mombasans can be seen taking a stroll, old men converse on the benches in Digo Road, and many shops stay open late.

Ethnically, Mombasa is perhaps even more diverse than Nairobi. The Asian and Arab influence is particularly pervasive, with fifty mosques and dozens of Hindu and Sikh temples lending a strongly oriental flavour. Still, the largest contingent speaks Swahili as a first language and it is the **Swahili civilization** that accounts for Mombasa's distinctive character. You'll see women wearing head-to-foot *buibuis* or brilliant *kanga* outfits, and men decked out in *kanzu* gowns and hip-slung *kikoi* wraps.

Arriving in Mombasa by plane or train in the morning, there's ample time, if you don't find the heat too much, to head straight out to the beaches – the nearest is Nyali Beach on the north coast mainland (see p.408). But you might want to spend a day or two in Mombasa itself, acclimatizing to the coast, catching the cadences of the coast's "pure Swahili", or *Kiswahili safi*, and looking around Kenya's most historic city.

Mombasa doesn't have a huge number of sights, but most visitors will want to check out its main one, Fort Jesus, in the shadow of which lies Mombasa's Old Town, still an atmospheric hive of narrow lanes, mosques and carved Swahili doorways. In the modern town centre, the tusks that feature on so many postcards are not wildly exciting, though fans of 1930s architecture might appreciate one or two of the buildings from that era on Digo Road. Further afield, there's a baobab forest (see p.398) and a seventeenth-century pillar tomb (see p.398) which are worth a visit.

Brief history

Mombasa is one of East Africa's oldest settlements and, so long as you aren't anticipating spectacular historical sites, it's a fascinating place to wander. The island has had a town on it, located somewhere between the present Old Town and Nyali Bridge, for at least 700 years, and there are enough documentary snippets from earlier times to guess that some kind of settlement has existed here for at least 2000 years. Mombasa's own optimistic claim to be 2500 years old comes from Roman and Egyptian adventure stories.

Early tales

Precisely what was going on before the Portuguese arrived is still hard to discern. **Ibn Battuta**, the roving fourteenth-century Moroccan, spent a relatively quiet night here in 1332 and declared the people of the town "devout, chaste and virtuous, their mosques strongly constructed of wood, the greater part of their diet bananas and fish". But another Arab traveller of a hundred years later found a less ordered society. "Monkeys have become the rulers of Mombasa since about 800 AH [1397 AD]," he wrote. "They even come and take the food from the dishes, attack men in their own homes and take away what they can find. When the monkeys enter a house and find a woman they hold congress with her. The people have much to put up with."

Early Portuguese visitors

Mombasa had considerably worse depredations to put up with after **Vasco da Gama**'s expedition, full of mercenary zeal, dropped anchor on Easter Saturday 1498. After courtesy gifts had been exchanged, relations suddenly soured and the fleet was prevented from entering the port. A few days later, richer by only one sheep and "large quantities of oranges, lemons and sugar cane", da Gama went off to try his crude diplomacy at Malindi, and found his first and lasting ally on the coast.

THE SHAPE OF THE CITY

Mombasa is an island, linked to the mainland by two causeways to the west, by a bridge to the north, and by a ferry to the south. You need to be prepared for poor first impressions: coming in by road over the Makupa Causeway from the airport or Nairobi, the erstwhile showcase Kenyatta Avenue is a shabby scene of crumbling facades and out-of-date hoardings, smothering the street from its beginning, via the triumphalist Independence Roundabout, to its final disintegration in the diesel-laden environment of the Mwembe Tayari bus parks.

At the city's heart, however, is the much more appealing **Old Town** – a lattice of lanes, mosques and cramped houses sloping gently down to the once-busy dhow harbour. **Fort Jesus**, an impressive reminder of Mombasa's complicated, bloody past, still overlooks the Old Town from where it once guarded the harbour entrance. It's now a national monument and museum. From the Old Town, clustered all around you, and mostly within easy walking distance, lies the whole expanse of downtown, **modern Mombasa**, with its wide streets and relative lack of high-rise buildings.

For **orientation** purposes, think of Digo Road, with the main market and GPO, as the city's spine: head up it to the north and you cross Nyali Bridge to the main Mombasa beach resorts; go down it to the south, as Nyerere Avenue, and you come to the Likoni ferry to the south coast mainland. East of Digo Road is the Old Town and one or two sedate streets of government offices. West of Digo Road you have, from north to south: Jomo Kenyatta Avenue, leading to the airport and the Nairobi highway; Haile Selassie Road, leading to the railway station; and Moi Avenue, Mombasa's main tourist strip, with its famous tusk arch, known simply as "the Tusks".

Mombasa was visited again in 1505 by a fourteen-strong Portuguese fleet. This time, the king of Mombasa had enlisted 1500 archers from the mainland and people stored arsenals of stone missiles on the rooftops in preparation for the expected **invasion** through the town's narrow alleys. The attack, pitching firearms against spears and poisoned arrows, was brutal and overwhelming. The town was squeezed on all sides and the king's palace (of which no trace remains) was seized. The king and most of the survivors slipped out of town into the palm groves which then covered most of Mombasa island, but 1513 Mombasans had been killed – as against five Portuguese.

The king attempted to save Mombasa by offering to become a vassal of Portugal, but the request was turned down, the Portuguese being unwilling to lose the chance to loot the town. The victors picked over the bodies in the courtyards and broke down the strongroom doors until the ships at anchor were almost overladen. Then, as a parting shot, they fired the town. The narrow streets and cattle stalls between the thatched houses produced a conflagration that razed Mombasa to the ground.

Portuguese occupation

In 1528, the Portuguese returned once again to wreck and plunder the new city that had been built on the ashes of the old. In the 1580s, it happened twice more. On the last occasion, in 1589, there was a frenzied **massacre** at the hands of the Portuguese on one side and – coincidentally – a marauding tribe of cannibal nomads from the interior called the Zimba on the other. The Zimba's unholy alliance with the Europeans came to a treacherous end at Malindi shortly afterwards, when the Portuguese, together with the townsfolk and three thousand Segeju archers, wiped them out.

Remarkably, only two years after this last catastrophe, Mombasa launched a major land expedition of its own against its old enemy, Malindi. The party was ambushed on the way by Malindi's Segeju allies, who themselves stormed and took Mombasa, later handing over the town to the Portuguese at Malindi. The Malindi corps transferred to Mombasa, the Malindi sheikh was grandly installed as sultan of the whole region, and the Portuguese set to work on **Fort Jesus**, dedicated in 1593.

Once completed, the fort became the focus of everything that mattered in Mombasa, changing hands a total of nine times between the early seventeenth century and 1875. The first takeover happened in 1631, in a **popular revolt** that resulted in the killing of every last Portuguese. But the Sultan, lacking support from any of the other towns under Portuguese domination, eventually had to desert the fort, and the Portuguese, waiting in Zanzibar, reoccupied it. They held it for the rest of the seventeenth century while consolidating their control of the Indian Ocean trade.

Omani rule

Meanwhile, the **Omani Arabs** were becoming increasingly powerful. As Dutch, English and French ships started to appear on the horizon, time was running out for the Portuguese trading monopoly. Efforts to bring settlers to their East African possessions failed, and they retreated more and more behind the massive walls of Fort Jesus. In 1696–98 Fort Jesus itself was besieged into submission by the Omanis who, with support from Pate and Lamu, had already taken the rest of the town. After 33 months almost all the defenders – the Portuguese corps and some 1500 Swahili loyalists – had died of starvation or plague.

Rapid disenchantment with the new Arab rulers spilled over in 1728 into a mutiny among the fort's African soldiers. The Portuguese were invited back – for a year. Then the fort was again besieged, and this time the Portuguese gave up quickly. They were allowed their freedom, and a number were said to have married and stayed in the town. But Portuguese power on the coast was shattered for ever.

The new Omani rulers were the **Mazrui** family, who soon declared themselves independent of Oman, outlawing slave-trading in Mombasa, and directly challenging the **Busaidi** family who had just seized power in the Arabian homeland.

6

British takeover

Intrigue in the Lamu Archipelago led to the Battle of Shela (see p.478) and Lamu's unwittingly disastrous invitation to the **Sultan of Oman**, Seyyid Said, to occupy its own fort. From here, and by now with **British** backing, the Busaidis went on to attack Mazrui Mombasa repeatedly in the 1820s.

There was a hiccup in 1824 when a British officer, **Captain Owen**, fired with enthusiasm for defeating the slave trade, extended British protection to Mombasa on his own account, despite official British support for the slave-trading Busaidis. Owen's

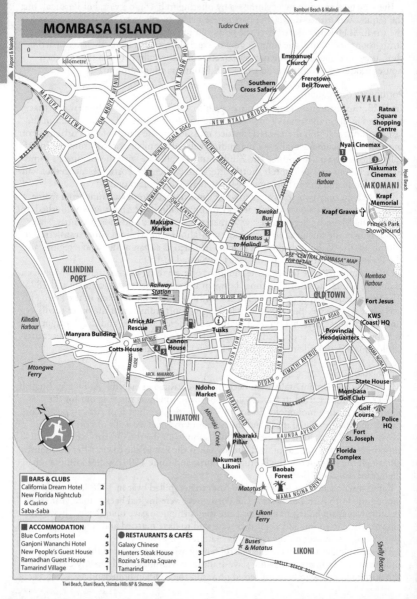

MOMBASA ISLAND

BARS & CLUBS
California Dream Hotel	2
New Florida Nightclub & Casino	3
Saba-Saba	1

ACCOMMODATION
Blue Comforts Hotel	4
Ganjoni Wananchi Hotel	5
New People's Guest House	3
Ramadhan Guest House	2
Tamarind Village	1

RESTAURANTS & CAFÉS
Galaxy Chinese	4
Hunters Steak House	3
Rozina's Ratna Square	1
Tamarind	2

Tiwi Beach, Diani Beach, Shimba Hills NP & Shimoni

"Protectorate" was a diplomatic embarrassment and – not surprisingly – did not last long. The Busaidi government was only installed when the Swahili "twelve tribes" of Mombasa fell into a dispute over the Mazrui succession and called in Seyyid Said, the Busaidi leader. In 1840, he moved his capital from Oman to Zanzibar and, with Mombasa firmly garrisoned, most of the coast was soon in his domain. Surviving members of the Mazrui family went to Takaungu near Kilifi and Gazi, south of Mombasa.

British influence was sharpened after their guns quelled the mutiny in 1875 of al-Akida, "an ambitious, unbalanced and not over-clever" commandant of Fort Jesus. Once British hegemony was established, they leased the **coastal strip** from the Sultan of Zanzibar and Fort Jesus became Mombasa's prison, which it remained until 1958. It was opened as a museum in 1962.

Independence on the coast

Mombasa has played a key role in Kenya's first fifty years of independence – as Kenya's second city and East and central Africa's most important port. Before independence, the coast had been leased by the British from the Sultan of Zanzibar, but the possibility of a federal union with the former Kenya Colony was soon buried by Jomo Kenyatta and the upcountry political elite of the 1960s. Since 1999, the Mombasa Republican Council, a group that claims "Pwani si Kenya" ("The Coast is not Kenya"), has campaigned for independence for the coast and against the marginalization of coastal interests by Nairobi. Their cause, however, has been tainted by its linkage with Islamic extremism which draws some of its support from the same well of deprivation. In August 2012, after a Muslim cleric was assassinated, there were riots in Mombasa as local youths fought street battles in poor quarters of the city centre with police brought down from Nairobi (see p.573).

Fort Jesus

Off Nkrumah Rd • Daily 8am–6pm • Ksh800, children Ksh400 • ☎ 042 2222425 or 0722 943999

For all its turbulent past, **Fort Jesus**, a classic European fortress of its age, is today a quiet museum-monument. Surprisingly spacious and tree-shaded inside its giant walls, it retains a lot of its original character, despite having been much repaired over the centuries. The curious angular construction was the design of an Italian architect and ensured that assailants trying to scale the walls would always be under crossfire from one of the bastions.

The best time to visit is probably first thing in the morning. Look out for the restored **Omani House**, in the far right corner as you enter the fort. Avoiding head contact with the lintel, climb up to the flat roof for a wonderful view over Mombasa. Interesting in their own way, too, are the uncomfortable-looking, wall-mounted **latrines**, overhanging the ditch just south of the Omani House, which would presumably have been closed in with mats. It is immediately obvious that Fort Jesus was not so much a building as a small, fortified town in its own right. The ruins of a church, storerooms, and possibly even shops are up at this end and, to judge by some accounts, the main courtyard was at times a warren of little dwellings. Captain Owen described it in 1824 as "a mass of indiscriminate ruins, huts and hovels, many of them built wherever space could be found but generally formed from parts of the ruins, matted over for roofs."

Most of the archeological interest is at the seaward end of the fort, where you'll find the **Hall of the Mazrui** with its beautiful stone benches and eighteenth-century inscription. A nearby room has been dedicated entirely to the display of a huge plaster panel of **wall paintings**, made with carbon and ochre by bored Portuguese sentries. Their subjects are fascinating: ships, figures in armour (including the captain of the fort wielding his baton), fish, and what seems to be a chameleon. Illiteracy precluded much writing but, oddly enough, there's nothing obscene either. The small **café** above the room with the wall paintings serves first-class lime juice, and the museum **restaurant**, behind the ticket office, has a lunch dish each day and various snacks.

Fort Jesus Museum

The **museum**, on the eastern side of the fort where the main soldiers' barracks block used to be, is small, but still manages to convey a good idea of the age and breadth of Swahili civilization, and also has a decent display of Mijikenda ethnography (see p.421). Most of the displays are of pottery, indigenous or imported, some from as far afield as China and some of it over a thousand years old. A number of private collections have contributed pieces and there's probably still a wealth of material in private hands. Look out for the big carved door taken from the Mazrui house in Gazi (p.439) and also the extraordinary whale vertebra used as a stool. The museum has a good exhibit on the long-term project to recover as much as possible from the wreck of the *Santo Antonio de Tanna*, which sank in 1697 while trying to break the prolonged Omani siege of the fort. Some seven thousand objects have already been brought to the surface, but the bulk of the ship itself remains nine fathoms deep in the harbour.

The Old Town

From Fort Jesus, the **Old Town** is an easy objective. While first impressions – of a quarter entirely devoted to gift and **curio shops** – are none too encouraging, the shops don't extend far into the Old Town. Further west, away from the fort, the stores are smaller, and correspondingly cheaper and less pretentious, with a couple of genuine antique shops along Kibokoni Road and the famous Noor Ala Noor cloth emporium on the corner of Old Kilindini Road and Mariakani Lane.

Mosques and other architecture

The Old Town is not, in fact, that old. Most buildings date from the nineteenth century, and though there may be foundations and even walls that go back many centuries, you'll get a clearer guide to the age of the town from its twenty or so **mosques**.

The **Mandhry Mosque** on Bachawy Road, founded in 1570, is officially the oldest in the city, and has a striking minaret, but it's rarely open to visitors. The **Basheikh Mosque** on Mwea Tabere Street, painted in green and white, is also acknowledged to be very old – "about 1300", they'll tell you, though this may be exaggerated. Entering the mosques – as long as they aren't locked – is usually all right for men if you're properly dressed (no shorts) and take your shoes off. Sometimes you may be expected to wash hands and feet. Women, however modestly dressed, will usually be politely refused.

DHOWS

Dhows are found in a variety of forms along the East African coast. The word is a generic Arabic term referring to the lateen-rigged vessels used in the Indian Ocean – a term which itself comes from the triangular, fore-and-aft "Latin" rigged sails of Roman vessels, in which the sail was suspended from a long yard mounted on the mast. Far from being based on ancient tradition, however, the highly manoeuvrable, dhow style of sailing rig in the Indian Ocean may have derived, secondhand, from Vasco da Gama's caravels that appeared in Mombasa at the end of the fifteenth century and had virtually the same setup. You can see similar vessels – feluccas – on the Nile.

Today, the large Kenyan trading dhows, known in Swahili as *jahazi*, are used less and less for transport and are more often bought up by tourist businesses. The *mashua* is a plank boat like a small *jahazi*, while the smaller *ngalawa* – double-outrigger dugout canoes with a small sail rigged high on the short mast – are the little boats which ferry passengers and whose captains normally potter about in the lagoon along the beaches, offering trips out to the reef.

DHOW CRUISES

Dhow cruises are an excellent way to get an insight into Mombasa's seafaring traditions – and see the city from some unusual angles.

Severin Book through your hotel ☎ 041 5485001, ⓦ severin-kenya.com. This German tour operator offers, among various excursions, evening dhow cruises on Tudor Creek ($99), followed by a son-et-lumière performance at Fort Jesus, and dinner in the courtyard of the fort. Any Mombasa or North Coast hotel will make a reservation for you.

Tamarind Cement Rd, Mkomani ☎ 041 471747, ⓦ tamarind.co.ke. The excellent *Tamarind* restaurant (see p.411) has outfitted two old *jahazis*, the *Nawalilkher* and the *Babulkher*, for Swahili seafood dinners under sail ($75), with a band in accompaniment.

6

Much of the other **architecture** in the Old Town is profoundly influenced by the Indian-style Zanzibari tastes of the Busaidi occupiers of the nineteenth century. This is particularly noticeable in the elegant fretwork **balconies** and shutters still maintained on a few houses, notably on **Ndia Kuu**. For older relics, you'll have to look further – there are a number of quite ancient tombs along the seafront, especially towards the northern end of the Old Town, some of which have pillars; this is the part of Mombasa considered to pre-date the Portuguese.

Returning south along the twisting **seafront road**, you come to the gigantic **Burhani Masjid** – the mosque of the Bohra community, renowned traders of Indian origin. In the unassuming setting of the Old Town, it is an imposingly massive edifice.

The Jain temple

Entrance on Langoni Rd • Daily 10am–12.30pm • Free

Heading up towards Digo Road, you might enjoy stopping by at the **Jain temple**. You have to remove shoes and anything made of leather. This sublime creation – intricate icing sugar outside, scrupulously clean and scented within and decorated in dozens of pastel shades – was only built in 1963. Jainism is an Indian religion, pre-dating but related to Buddhism, and commonest in Gujarat (original home of the majority of Kenyan Asians), which holds all life to be sacred. The temple interior is ornamentally magnificent: the painted figurines of deities in their niches are each provided with a drain so they can be easily showered down, while around the ceiling, exquisitely stylized pictures portray scenes from a human life, including a familiar snake temptation in a garden.

The dhow harbour

The **dhow harbour**, along the shores of the Old Town, is somewhat overrated. There are usually one or two boats in port but you can no longer expect to see dozens, let alone hundreds, of dhows, even at the end of the northeast monsoon in April, traditionally the peak time for arrivals: seasonal variations are less important now that the big *jahazis* have engines. Nor are you likely to have the opportunity to go aboard one of these exotic vessels, though a number of big dhows have been converted as dinner-cruise vessels (see above). Still, the area is an enjoyable place for a stroll, especially at weekends, when families dress up to go for a walk and children leap around in the sea below Fort Jesus.

Walks around Mombasa

Taking a walk, or a stroll, with plenty of cold-drink stops, is a time-honoured Mombasan diversion. You will probably want to see that immortal double pair of **elephant tusks** arching over Moi Avenue. To get to them, you have to run the gauntlet of curio booths that comes and goes, and sometimes almost hides the cool hideaway of **Uhuru Gardens**, with its Africa-shaped fountain. And when you reach the Tusks, you

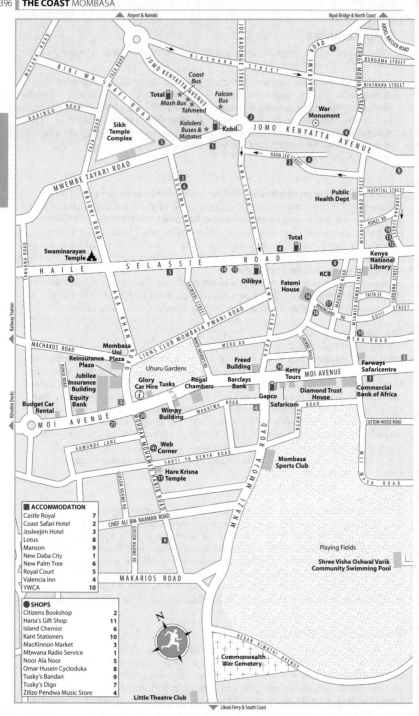

Airport & Nairobi   Nyali Bridge & North Coast

6

Railway Station

Kilindini Docks

War Monument

Public Health Dept

Kenya National Library

Swaminarayan Temple

Sikh Temple Complex

Coast Bus

Total

Mash Bus

Tahmeed

Falcon Bus

Kaloleni Buses & Matatus

Kobil

Total

Oilibya

KCB

Fatemi House

Mombasa Uni Plaza

Reinsurance Plaza

Jubilee Insurance Building

Equity Bank

Budget Car Rental

Glory Car Hire

Uhuru Gardens

Tusks

Regal Chambers

Freed Building

Ketty Tours

Barclays Bank

Gapco

Safaricom

Diamond Trust House

Commercial Bank of Africa

Farways Safaricentre

Wimpy Building

@ Web Corner

Hare Krisna Temple

Mombasa Sports Club

Playing Fields

Shree Visha Oshwal Varik Community Swimming Pool

MAKARIOS ROAD

Little Theatre Club

Commonwealth War Cemetery

Likoni Ferry & South Coast

■ ACCOMMODATION

Castle Royal	7
Coast Safari Hotel	2
Josleejim Hotel	3
Lotus	8
Manson	9
New Daba City	1
New Palm Tree	6
Royal Court	5
Valencia Inn	4
YWCA	10

● SHOPS

Citizens Bookshop	2
Haria's Gift Shop	11
Island Chemist	6
Kant Stationers	10
MacKinnon Market	3
Mbwana Radio Service	1
Noor Ala Noor	5
Omar Husein Cycloduka	8
Tusky's Bandari	9
Tusky's Digo	7
Zilizo Pendwa Music Store	4

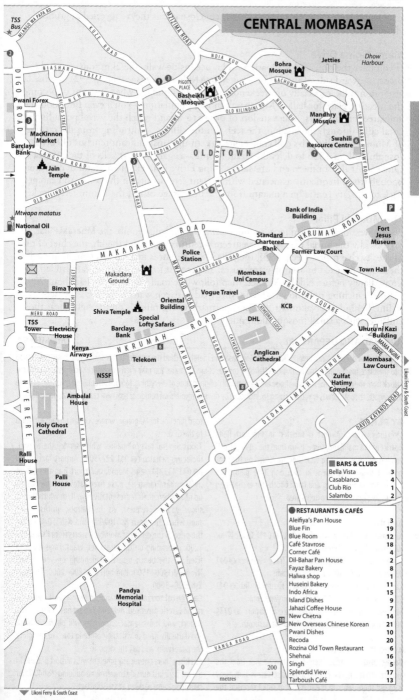

CENTRAL MOMBASA

6

TSS Bus

MLANGO WA PAPA RD

DIGO ROAD

KUZE ROAD

MTIITINA ROAD

NDIA KUU

LIWILI ROAD

BIASHARA STREET

NEHRU ROAD

KERICHO STREET

SAMBURU ROAD

WACHANSAMMEST

PIGOTT PLACE

MWEA TABERE ST.

Pwani Forex

MacKinnon Market

Barclays Bank

LANGONI ROAD

OLD KILINDINI ROAD

Jain Temple

OLD KILINDINI ROAD

BAMBIR ROAD

OLD KILINDINI RD

KIBOKONI STREET

NYERI STREET

Basheikh Mosque

Bohra Mosque

Jetties

Dhow Harbour

BACHUMA ROAD

NDIA KUU

Mandhry Mosque

Swahili Resource Centre

OLD TOWN

SIR MBARAK HINAWY ROAD

NDIA KUU

Bank of India Building

Standard Chartered Bank

Former Law Court

Fort Jesus Museum

Town Hall

Mtwapa matatus

National Oil

DIGO ROAD

MAKADARA ROAD

NKRUMAH ROAD

Police Station

MAKUTUBU ROAD

Mombasa Uni Campus

TREASURY SQUARE

Bima Towers

BALUCHI STREET

MERU ROAD

Makadara Ground

Shiva Temple

Oriental Building

Vogue Travel

MWAGGO ROAD

KCB

DHL

CATHEDRAL CLOSE

TSS Tower

Electricity House

Special Lofty Safaris

Barclays Bank

NKRUMAH ROAD

Kenya Airways

Telekom

NSSF

Ambalal House

Anglican Cathedral

KAUNDA AVENUE

NGOMENI LANE

CATHEDRAL ROAD

DHL

MVITA ROAD

Uhuru ni Kazi Building

MAMA NGINA DRIVE

Mombasa Law Courts

Zulfat Hatimy Complex

DEDAN KIMATHI AVENUE

DAVID KRANDA ROAD

NYERERE AVENUE

Holy Ghost Cathedral

Ralli House

Palli House

MIKINDANI ROAD

DEDAN KIMATHI AVENUE

KWALE ROAD

Pandya Memorial Hospital

VANGA ROAD

Likoni Ferry & South Coast

■ BARS & CLUBS

Bella Vista	3
Casablanca	4
Club Rio	1
Salambo	2

● RESTAURANTS & CAFÉS

Aleifiya's Pan House	3
Blue Fin	19
Blue Room	12
Café Stavrose	18
Corner Café	4
Dil-Bahar Pan House	2
Fayaz Bakery	8
Halwa shop	1
Huseini Bakery	11
Indo Africa	15
Island Dishes	9
Jahazi Coffee House	7
New Chetna	14
New Overseas Chinese Korean	21
Pwani Dishes	10
Recoda	20
Rozina Old Town Restaurant	6
Shehnai	16
Singh	5
Splendid View	17
Tarboush Café	13

0 — 200

metres

Likoni Ferry & South Coast

may regret your determination to view them close up, as they're revealed as grubby aluminium.

Mama Ngina Drive

If you have the time and inclination for an **oceanside walk**, the 2km route around the breezy, seaward side of the island along **Mama Ngina Drive** (see map, p.392) is a fine late afternoon walk, especially on weekends and public holidays, when it seems to become the meeting place for half of Mombasa's Indian population – you'll even find food stalls and street entertainers. There are lots of places to sit and watch the waves pounding the coral cliffs through the break in the reef. On the clifftop, protruding from the far side of Mombasa Golf Club's **golf course**, are the stumpy, insignificant remains of **Fort St Joseph**, built in 1826 to defend Mazrui Mombasa against the attacks of the Busaidi Omanis. At the southern end of Mama Ngina Drive is an extensive stand of enormous **baobab trees**, frequently associated with ancient settlements on the coast. You can get back to the city centre on a matatu from the busy stage east of the Likoni ferry dock.

The Mbaraki Pillar

To the west of the Likoni ferry roundabout is a huge pillar tomb, the **Mbaraki Pillar**. Supposedly the burial place of a seventeenth-century mainland sheikh, the chief of one of the "twelve tribes" (see p.393), the pillar's 8m height is impressive enough, but it is these days dwarfed by nearby warehouses. To get to it from the ferry area, turn left immediately before Ndoho Market, then follow the road round to the left about 200m, before branching right down a broad, dirt road between warehouses for a further 200m, behind the Nakumatt Likoni supermarket. The pillar is on the right, near the cliffside, with a small mosque alongside.

ARRIVAL AND DEPARTURE	MOMBASA

If you've never been to Africa before, flying into Mombasa and merely getting the transfer bus or taxi to your hotel throws you into the place more quickly than arriving in Nairobi's cosmopolitan embrace. You may even experience some level of **culture shock** from the poverty, the heat, the noise and the general upfront nature of everything. Mombasa remains a much easier place to navigate, though, however you are doing so, including by driving in your own vehicle or renting a car on arrival (see p.407).

BY PLANE

Moi International Airport is situated in the Port Reitz district of the mainland, some 10km from the city centre. If you haven't already got a visa, they are issued on the spot without delay – payment in cash only (see p.86). The airport has several ATMs, and bank booths for exchanging money just outside the customs area.

AIRLINES

Airkenya, Moi International Airport ☎041 3430217 or 0720 050940, ✆airkenya.com.

Fly540, Ground Floor, Mombasa Trade Centre ☎041 2319078 or 0710 540540, ✆fly540.com.

Kenya Airways, Electricity House, Nkrumah Rd ☎041 2227613 or 0734 105201, ✆kenya-airways.com.

Mombasa Air Safari, Moi International Airport ☎0734 400400 or 0734 500500, ✆mombasaairsafari.com.

AIRPORT TRANSPORT

Buses and matatus There is no bus service from the airport into town. The nearest matatu service is 1km away – to get there, walk to the first row of small shops at the

road junction for Magongo, where you can pick up a matatu to the GPO.

Taxis Several taxi companies which service the airport, including Kenatco (☎041 2227503), Airport Taxi SACCO (☎041 433211), and Mombasa Airport Transfers (✆bit .ly/MombasaTransfers), have fixed rates that are posted up near where their representatives wait, or which they'll show you on request. As in Nairobi, prices hover somewhere between Ksh100/km and Ksh150/km, and the price to the centre of Mombasa starts from Ksh1000–1200, depending on the street you want. Fares are also fixed for the beach resorts, depending on your hotel: Nyali Ksh1300–1500; Bamburi Ksh1800–2000; Mtwapa Ksh2500–3000.

Car rental You can also arrange to have a pre-booked car rental vehicle meet you. Avis and Budget have desks at the airport, and most rental companies will oblige, though you'll usually need to visit their office in town to complete the paperwork and pay the deposit.

Parking There's never any problem with airport parking in the car park just outside the terminal building (Ksh40/hr or safe, long-term parking at Ksh300/day).

DEPARTURE

If you're heading to Mombasa International Airport from the South Coast, be prepared for delays at the Likoni ferry which can easily add an hour to your journey time. Domestic departure tax is always included in the price of tickets, as is the international departure tax of $40 in the case of most airlines – though some charter companies (including Thomson/First Choice) exclude it, forcing the passenger to pay directly on departure.

Destinations Diani Beach/Ukunda (daily; 10min; one way $27); Lamu (daily; 1hr–1hr 30min; one way $107); Maasai Mara (daily; 2–3hr; one way $330, return $440) via Amboseli and Tsavo West (daily; 1–2hr; both one way $358, return $478); Malindi (daily; 30min; one way $47); Nairobi (6–7 daily; 1hr; one way from $60).

BY BUS

DESTINATIONS

Busia (2 daily; 15hr); Dar es Salaam (3 daily; 14–16hr), via Tanga (7hr); Garissa (2 daily; 8–10hr); Kisumu (9 daily; 14hr); Lamu via Kilifi and Malindi (6 daily; 7–8hr); Malaba (1 daily; 15hr); Malindi via Kilifi (approximately hourly; 1hr 30min); Nairobi (frequent, but especially around 7am and 7pm; 7–9hr).

BUS COMPANIES

Bus company booking offices are spread along Abdel Nasser Rd (for the north coast as far as Lamu) and Jomo Kenyatta Ave and Mwembe Tayari Rd (for Nairobi, the south coast and Tanzania). You can buy through-tickets to central and western Kenya on Coast and Mash, but all services go via Nairobi, usually requiring a change of buses. Competition on all routes is fierce, and some operators are more reputable than others. The safest is reckoned to be Mash, which has a good reputation for comfort, while there's little to choose between the bus companies running up and down the coast. For reasons of safety and comfort, the overnight journey to Nairobi isn't recommended.

Coast (Coast Air, Coastline, Coast Pekee) Mwembe Tayari Rd ☎ 041 3433166, ⓦ coastbus.com.

Destinations Nairobi (every morning and evening; Ksh1500–2200).

Falcon Jomo Kenyatta Ave, opposite Kobil ☎ 041 4900776.

Destinations Lamu (1 or more daily; Ksh1000); Malindi (1 or more daily; Ksh300).

Mash Mwembe Tayari Rd ☎ 041 2491955 or 041 3432471, ⓦ mash.ssanics.com.

Destinations Nairobi (every morning and evening; Ksh1500–2200).

Modern Coast Jomo Kenyatta Ave ☎ 041 2495812 or 020 2023776.

Destinations Nairobi (8.30am, 5pm; Ksh1600–2000).

Tahmeed Jomo Kenyatta Ave ☎ 0729 356561.

Destinations Dar es Salaam (6.30am; Ksh1800); Lamu (every morning; Ksh900).

Tawakal (Pwani Tawakal) Abdel Nasser Rd ☎ 0722 550111, ⓦ bit.ly/PwaniTawakal.

Destinations Lamu (every morning, Ksh1000), via Malindi (Ksh300).

TSS Abdel Nasser Rd ☎ 041 2221839.

Destinations Lamu (every morning, Ksh900), via Malindi (Ksh300).

BY TRAIN

Though the service now runs only three times a week and is often subject to long delays, the night train (see p.54) is a good way of travelling between Nairobi and Mombasa. Mombasa station sits at the west end of Haile Selassie Rd, 1km from the city's main north–south thoroughfare, Digo Rd. Swarms of taxis await the train's arrival – Ksh300–400 is the going rate between the station and any city-centre hotel.

Arrival The train leaves Nairobi at 7pm (Mon, Wed, Fri) arriving, in theory, Mombasa at 10am the next morning.

Departure The train for Nairobi leaves Mombasa at 7pm (Tues, Thurs & Sun), and arrives, in theory, at 9.30am the next day. However, don't count on making any further transport connections until at least the next afternoon. You can also disembark at around midnight in Voi, for Tsavo East National Park. It's best to buy tickets in person from the station when the train arrives. The station is open only on Tues, Thurs & Sun (☎ 0728 787294), roughly from 8am until the train departs.

BY MATATU

Matatus to the north coast beaches (Kenyatta, Bamburi and Shanzu), and on to Mtwapa, leave from opposite the Tusky's Digo supermarket at the end of Haile Selassie Ave and along the nearby area of Digo Rd as far as the GPO. Matatus going through to Malindi (in principle these don't drop or pick up until north of Mtwapa) congregate at the south end of Abdel Nasser Rd, near the junction with Mackawi Rd, by the mosque. Matatus for Kaloleni and Voi leave from the Kobil station at the junction of Mwembe Tayari Rd and Jomo Kenyatta Ave. If you're heading south of Mombasa, you'll need to get a matatu to the Likoni ferry (see below and p.400), and pick up onward transport on the other side.

Destinations Bamburi (frequent, 20–30min); Kaloleni (several, mornings and afternoons, 1hr 30min); Malindi (frequent, 2hr); Mazeras (frequent, 1hr); Mtwapa (frequent, 45min).

BY CAR

Driving into Mombasa Leave plenty of time to get into and out of Mombasa on the Nairobi road – traffic jams and hours of delays are becoming frequent between the island and Mazeras. Delays can also be bad over the Nyali bridge on the Malindi road, and while waiting for the Likoni ferry when coming from the south coast.

6

Parking If you're driving into the city, it is usually easy to find a parking space, though don't leave anything valuable in your vehicle, and don't leave it unguarded on the street overnight. Uniformed parking wardens patrol the streets, and will sell you a Ksh50 ticket which you display under your windscreen, entitling you to park as many times as you like over the course of the following 24hr. Beware of faded yellow "no parking" road markings on some kerbs: there are some corrupt wheel-clamping teams on the prowl, ready to take advantage of unwary visitors.

BY FERRY OR MATATU TO AND FROM LIKONI

The 24hr Likoni ferry connects the south coast to Mombasa island (10min; 4am–1am every 15min; 1am–4am hourly; pedestrians and cyclists free, cars Ksh90). T-shirted guards look out for pickpockets and security has greatly improved, but it's still wise to keep valuables tucked away and your car windows up. Rush hours can create long tailbacks of traffic waiting to cross in both directions, so leave plenty of time if you have a flight to catch. While main bus services use the ferry, if you're travelling by matatu, you change vehicles and cross on foot. The other ferry across Kilindini Creek, the Mtongwe ferry (daily 5–10am & 3–9pm), is a free commuter service, but only for foot passengers.

Matatu destinations from Likoni Diani Beach (occasional; 45min); Kwale (occasional, 40min); Lungalunga (occasional; 2hr); Msambweni (frequent; 1hr); Shimoni (occasional; 1hr 30min); Ukunda (frequent; 30min).

GETTING AROUND

With no municipal bus services, city transport comes down to **taxis** and more informal transport. Kenatco (☎041 2227503, ⊛kenatco.com), based in Ambalal House, Nkrumah Rd, runs a reliable 24hr taxi service with fixed prices. Most taxi fares on the island range from Ksh200 for a short hop to a top fare of abut Ksh400, depending on distance (cabs are all unmetered, so always agree the fare before setting off). Alternatively, choose between **matatus**, which run from the GPO to Nyali Bridge, Tudor Docks and the Likoni ferry (Ksh20–40 per hop, depending on distance); **tuk-tuks** (Ksh100–250 per ride for the whole vehicle, seating up to three plus luggage) or **piki-pikis**, motorbike taxis (usually Ksh100–200 on the island). Getting around the city centre **on foot** is easy enough, and sometimes faster than using transport, especially at rush hour.

INFORMATION

Tourist office Operated by the Mombasa and Coast Tourist Association, the tourist information office is on Moi Avenue, next to the Tusks (Mon–Fri 8am–5pm, Sat 9am–1pm; ☎041 2225428). Although offering little in material terms, the staff are helpful, and can advise you on transport and accommodation.

ACCOMMODATION

None of Mombasa's main resort hotels is located on the island, and barely any of the city's hotels are of international standard. Note that **water supplies** in Mombasa are unreliable, and many cheap places feature the telltale buckets and plastic basins which indicate that water sometimes has to be carried up. Even when the pipes are working, hot water is rare in budget hotels, but in this climate you're unlikely to miss it. Some places aiming for higher standards have the instant, electric showers that are widespread in the highlands. If you're travelling on a budget and don't mind staying on the north mainland, you might find the two **backpackers' hostels** in Nyali the best options (see p.409 and p.411). And if you want top-class comforts and service, then look at the *Tamarind*, also in Nyali, but a short journey from the city (see p.411).

CHEAP LODGINGS

Josleejim Hotel Duruma Rd ☎020 2038814 or 0735 318850; see map p.396. Sizeable, friendly place, with reasonable facilities, including safe parking. The s/c rooms, with nets, fans and clean sheets, make it good value for money. BB **Ksh1800**

New Daba City Mwembe Tayari Rd, next to Coast Bus ☎0722 472982; see map p.396. Clean and respectable cheapie with s/c rooms and nets but no hot water. Good value if you're counting the pennies. **Ksh1200**

New People's Guest House Abdel Nasser Rd, right by the main bus and matatu offices ☎0722 471032; see map p.392. Big, noisy, long-established, very male-dominated block, with good security and a busy *hoteli* on the ground floor. No frills, but handy if you're taking a morning bus to Lamu. **Ksh700**

Ramadhan Guest House Abdel Nasser Rd ☎0720 336979; see map p.392. A dependable, dirt-cheap option with airy, reasonably clean non s/c rooms with fans and nets. **Ksh500**

YWCA Corner of Kaunda Ave and Kiambu Ave ☎041 2229856 or 0727 806979, ✉ywcamsa@gmail.com; see map p.396. Pleasant ambience with good security and a cafeteria (6am–8pm), open to men (downstairs) as well as women (upstairs), and couples can share rooms, two of which are s/c. Best value for long stays, but book ahead (s/c twin rooms from Ksh16,520/month room only). No curfew, no guests in rooms. Additional one-off charges for all guests: Ksh200 admission fee and Ksh300 annual subscription. BB **Ksh2370**

HOTELS

Blue Comforts Hotel Archbishop Makarios Rd ☏ 041 2351111; see map p.392. Good-value standby with a shady breakfast terrace off the street at the front. All rooms have nets and fans, but upgrading to one with a/c and TV isn't worth the doubling in price. BB Ksh2000

Castle Royal Moi Ave ☏ 041 2220373 or 0720 843072, ⓦ sentrim-hotels.com; see map p.396. Mombasa's most venerable hotel, formerly the *Palace*, dating from 1909. Period on the outside, modern on the inside, with 68 a/c rooms with fan, DSTV and (in theory) wi-fi, and corridors open at both ends to allow a through breeze. All it lacks is a pool. BB $130

Coast Safari Hotel Raha Leo St ☏ 020 8017626 or 0717 357558; see map p.396. The former *Upcountry Guest House* is a cut above basic, with 41 fairly small, clean, well-maintained rooms, with fans, TV and nets, and a restaurant on the ground floor. Very convenient for long-distance buses. BB Ksh2400

Ganjoni Wananchi Hotel Archbishop Makarios Rd ☏ 0717 357790, ⓦ ganjoniwananchihotel.com; see map p.392. Popular, upcountry-style hotel, with busy bar and restaurant and competitively priced rooms with TV and fans (or a/c for a Ksh400 supplement). BB Ksh2800

★ **Lotus** Corner of Mvita Rd and Cathedral Rd ☏ 041 2313207 or 0722 612517, ⓦ lotushotelkenya.com; see map p.396. Located on a quiet corner not far from Fort Jesus, with a vaguely oriental feel, and overflowing with greenery, it's not surprising the plain but very neat, clean rooms with a/c and TV are often full. BB Ksh4500

Manson Mohdar Mohamed Habib Rd ☏ 041 2222419 or 0722 610615, ⓦ mansonhotel.com; see map p.396. Large, clean rooms of variable size in a seven-storey block, some with balconies, some with fans, others with a/c (Ksh600 extra). TV lounge and bar-restaurant on the ground floor. Secure, and good value. BB Ksh2700

★ **New Palm Tree** Nkrumah Rd ☏ 020 8025682 or 0732 334200, ⓦ newpalmtreehotel.com; see map p.396. Once quite a grand place, this still has bags of charm, despite the modernization that includes a cybercafé in the foyer (daily 9am–7pm, Ksh1/min). Alcohol is prohibited. Rooms are spacious and clean, with fans, a/c and nets. There's also a sunny first-floor courtyard. A good deal, and worth reserving. BB Ksh3500

Royal Court Haile Selassie Rd ☏ 041 2220932 or 0722 412867, ⓦ royalcourtmombasa.co.ke; see map p.396. Modern business-class hotel, close to the station, with good-sized rooms with spotless bathrooms, facing out over town. Rooftop bar-restaurant, plunge pool and gym. BB Ksh7550

Valencia Inn Haile Selassie Rd ☏ 041 2312399, ⓦ sanvalenciakenya.com; see map p.396. A relatively smart new conversion in a convenient, central location, with a/c, DSTV and wi-fi. Those rooms with a balcony at the front are worth the Ksh500 supplement. BB Ksh5000

EATING AND DRINKING

Mombasa is also well supplied with good, **cheap restaurants**. Especially if you're newly arrived from upcountry, they are one of the city's chief delights, as a discernible cuisine involving coconut, fish, chicken, rice and beans, and incorporating Asian flavours, begins to make an impression on your palate. Most places are open daily, but when there's a closure day it's usually a Monday. As well as proper restaurants, there are snacks and drinks to go in various parts of the city. During the day, for example, you can get green coconuts (drink the coconut water, then scoop out and eat the jelly-like flesh), sugar-cane juice freshly pressed from the cane, and cuplets of *kahawa thungu* (thick bitter coffee, usually flavoured with ginger or cardamom). After dark, by the bus stalls up Abdel Nasser Rd and along Jomo Kenyatta Ave and Mwembe Tayari Rd, as well as on other busy corners, you'll find what are effectively full meals for around Ksh100–200, including *nyama choma*, chapattis, spicy little chicken kebabs and freshly fried potato and cassava chips and crisps.

SNACK AND JUICE BARS

Aleifiya's Pan House just off Pigott Place, Old Town, next to Mbwana Radio Service music shop; see map p.396. Friendly little snack bar with cold drinks, fresh *maji ya miwa* (sugar-cane juice) and incredibly cheap *mahamri* (Ksh5), other snacks and simple dishes. Daily 6am–10pm.

★ **Dil-Bahar Pan House** corner of Digo Rd and Bungoma St; see map p.396. Indian snacks, *pan* (see box, p.403), excellent *chai* and good juices including melon, watermelon, and occasionally even custard apple. A calm refuge, or a place to read the paper. Daily 7am–9pm.

Fayaz Bakery Jomo Kenyatta Ave; see map p.396. A good range of cakes and biscuits, with decent brownies (Ksh45) and fruit muffins (Ksh60) as well as local specialities such as passion cake (Ksh60). Mon–Sat 9am–7.30pm (closed Fri noon–2.30pm), Sun 10am–2pm.

Halwa Shop Mackawi Rd; see map p.396. Fresh, gooey, intensely sweet and scented halwa is made here daily in the traditional way in a huge pan. Buy a little for a snack or a lot for presents (from Ksh500/kg). Hours vary with speed of business. Daily 9am–noon and 2–5pm.

Huseini Bakery Turkana St; see map.396. Nice selection of cakes and snacks, including their house speciality cookies – *nan khatai*, a light biscuit with nuts (from Ksh80/bag). Mon–Sat 9am–12.30pm & 2.30–7.30pm, closed Sun.

★ **Jahazi Coffee House** Ndia Kuu, Old Town ☏ 0725 896866 or 0726 409436; see map p.396. Beautifully decorated, joint Canadian-Kenyan venture in an eighteenth-century Old Town house, serving delicious spiced coffee with cardamom (Ksh100), *mahamri* and other snacks in a cool environment of cushions and carpets. Swahili lunch or dinner (Ksh800–1500), by advance order. Also serves as a cross-cultural rendezvous and book exchange. Daily 8am–6pm.

SWAHILI CUISINE

★ **Island Dishes** Kibokoni St; see map p.396. Wonderful Swahili dishes, including fish with coconut (from Ksh250), *mkate mayai* ("Swahili pizza" Ksh100) and several vegetarian options, plus juices from date to passion (Ksh50), with mango and chilli sauces on the table if you like it hot, or tamarind if you prefer it sweet and sour. Order items individually from the menu – don't be talked into a meal deal. Daily 8am–midnight.

Recoda Moi Ave, near the Tusks, ☎041 2223629; see map p.396. One of the oldest and most famous Swahili restaurants in Mombasa, relocated from the Old Town, and sadly stripped of most of its character. The food is good and cheap, but tends to be generic diner fare, much the same as you can find anywhere else in town – pilaus, birianis, chicken tikka, mostly in the Ksh250 region, and a few special Swahili dishes if you're lucky. Daily 6pm–midnight.

★ **Tarboush Café** Makadara Rd; see map p.396. Perennially busy grill and coast-style diner, its pavement terrace always crowded with a broad spectrum of locals and visitors. The beef *shawarma* pitta (Ksh220), chicken tikka (Ksh260) and beef *mishkaki* (Ksh230), are popular, and they do a good range of *naan* bread (Ksh60–100) and gorgeous juices. Daily 7am–late.

FAST FOOD AND HOTELIS

Blue Fin Meru Rd; see map p.396. Fish or chicken and chips (Ksh220–300), and other reasonably priced fry-ups such as Spanish omelette and chips (Ksh180), are the staples here, with *maru bhajia* (battered, spiced potatoes Ksh120/plate) a less common offering. Plus juices and daily specials. Mon–Sat 9.30am–8.30pm, closed Sun.

Blue Room Haile Selassie Rd ⊕ blueroomonline.com; see map p.396. Large, self-service food hall that's been a Mombasa institution with a devoted clientele for decades for its fans and clean tiled surfaces, and a menu dominated by burgers (from Ksh160) and pizzas (from Ksh320), plus a good range of chicken and beef dishes and quite a few vegetarian choices, plus home-made ice cream. Their free wi-fi (evenings only) is a bonus. Daily 8am–10pm.

★ **Corner Café** Corner of Jomo Kenyatta Ave and George Morura St; see map p.396. Popular and lively place, with tables on the pavement as well as inside the tiny premises, offering a small range of incredibly cheap and filling dishes and snacks, including pilau (Ksh120) and *sima na sukuma* (*ugali* and greens, Ksh60). Visit now, before the owner-manager changes it all. Daily 6am–9pm.

★ **Pwani Dishes** Turkana St; see map p.396. Cheap and cheerful diner, with lots of stews and basic Kenyan dishes in large servings at low prices. Try the coconut fish curry (Ksh160) or masala chips (Ksh150). Daily 7am–10pm.

INTERNATIONAL CUISINE

Galaxy Chinese Florida Complex, Mama Ngina Drive ☎020 2138611 or 0726 894002; see map p.392. Above the Florida club, this offers Cantonese and Hainanese seafood, but it's rather inconsistent and relatively pricey, with pan-fried whole fish Ksh800–1200/dish. Daily 11am–2.30pm & 6–11pm.

New Overseas Chinese Korean Moi Ave, 200m west of the Tusks ☎041 2230729 or 0724 101544; see map p.396. Good-value Cantonese and Korean cooking, focusing on seafood, with more expensive specialities including steamed crab, tuna fish *sashimi*, and *kimchi* (spicy pickled cabbage) soup, all at around Ksh500–800. Daily 11am–3pm & 5.30–11pm.

Rozina Old Town Restaurant, Africa Hotel Building, Mbarak Hinawy Rd ☎041 2312642 or 0722 411484; see map p.396. Located on the ground floor of a century-old house in the Old Town with a double-storey balcony, this restaurant has a long menu of Swahili and international dishes, including good seafood (coconut prawns Ksh800), a dozen grilled garlic oysters (Ksh500), jumbo T-bone steaks (Ksh1200), burgers and pizzas. Special Swahili coffee is brought in every evening. Daily 8am–10pm.

Splendid View Maungano Rd; see map p.396. Forget about the view of the *Splendid Hotel* (rather than a splendid view) and concentrate on the excellent house specialities – chicken biriani, garlic chicken and pili pili prawns, perhaps leaving room for a faluda for dessert. Count on Ksh500–1000/person. Mon–Fri 11am–2pm & 4.30–10.30pm, Sat 11am–2.30pm & 5.30–11pm, Sun 5–10.30pm.

INDIAN COOKING

Café Stavrose Maungano Rd; see map p.396. A small place that's been serving Indian snacks, tikka dishes and kebabs for years. Lunches around Ksh400. Mon–Fri 9am–7.30pm, Sat 9am–3pm, closed Sun.

Indo Africa Haile Selassie Rd ☎041 2317529 or 0721 743556; see map p.396. Although the decor here is notable for its absence, the food is reliably good, and not as fiercely spicy as the adjacent *New Chetna's*. Try the prawn or fish masala, jeera chicken or vegetarian *muttar paneer* – home-made cheese, cooked with peas. Allow around Ksh800/person. Daily (except Tues evening) noon–2.30pm & 7–10.30pm.

★ **New Chetna** Haile Selassie Rd ☎0770 010380; see map p.396. A long-time favourite for Indian sweets on the left, and tasty South Indian vegetarian dishes at low prices on

PAN SHOPS

Highly characteristic of Mombasa are the Indian **pan shops**, often doubling as tobacconists and corner shops. Worth trying at least once, *pan* is a natural digestive and stimulant that encourages salivation. Its main ingredient is chopped areca palm nut, flavoured with your choice of sweet spices and other ingredients, syrup, and white lime, from a display of dishes, all wrapped in a peppery-tasting, dark-green leaf from the betel vine, known as *pan* in Urdu and Hindi. Including ground tobacco is another option, but best avoided by novices. Pop the triangular parcel in your mouth and munch – it tastes as exotic and unlikely as it sounds – spitting out the copious juice as you go (note that *pan*, with or without tobacco, has various adverse effects on health). Two of the best *pan* counters in town are at the *Dil-Bahar Pan House* (see p.401) and the *New Chetna* restaurant (see p.402).

6

the right. On offer are well-made bhajias and other snacks and dishes (around Ksh120–200/plate) and a superb all-you-can-eat *thali* ("Please no sharing", Ksh350), but the food can be very hot, so treat with caution. Daily 8am–9pm.
Shehnai Fatemi House, Maungano Rd ☎041 2224801, ⓦrestaurantshehnai.com; see map p.396. Mughlai specialities with a good reputation (the restaurant has a *Chaîne des Rotisseurs* award), in a spacious and light interior with somewhat regal furniture. You're spoilt for choice: try *achar gosht* (mutton cooked in spices and

flavoured with pickles), or *machi tandoorwalli* (oven-baked marinated rock cod). Vegetarian meals around Ksh500, non-veg Ksh750. Tues–Sun noon–2pm & 7–10.30pm.
Singh Mwembe Tayari Rd ☎041 493283; see map p.396. A bit of a walk from the centre of town, but very close to all the long-distance buses and there's an a/c room to cool off. Well worth a visit for their extremely tasty, freshly prepared Punjabi curries, both meat and veg. Most mains under Ksh500. Tues–Sun noon–2.30pm & 7–10.30pm.

NIGHTLIFE

Mombasa doesn't have **bars** on every street corner, but there are one or two watering holes scattered around the city: the *Lotus Hotel* on Cathedral Rd (see p.401) is one of the nicest places in town for a civilized beer. There are several **nightclubs** on the island, too, though the busiest nightlife is in the resort area north of Mombasa, especially in Mtwapa (see p.418) and around Kenyatta Beach (see p.414). Most of the city clubs are free, but on popular nights (Wed, Fri & Sat), entry charges of Ksh100–300 are the norm. Long before the clubs get busy, a stroll around the generally safe Old Town will uncover one or two **coffee-sellers** serving black *kahawa* from traditional high-spouted jugs.

CLUBS AND LIVE MUSIC

Unless you want to be repeatedly accosted by prostitutes (or, if you're a woman, by men who are all convinced that they are the missing person in your life), it's best to visit most of the following clubs with at least a companion, if not in a group.
Bella Vista Next to Agip, on the corner of Moi Ave and Aga Khan Rd ☎041 2137010; see map p.396. Busy, local sports bar and restaurant (grills, pasta, salads; mains from Ksh600), Bella Vista attracted notoriety in 2012 when it was the subject of a grenade attack, but continues to be one of the most popular venues in the city centre. Loud rock and no single shots (doubles Ksh300) can make for a rowdy atmosphere, especially on Fri and Sat nights, but Sun daytimes are mellow, with people having brunch and listening to soul and R&B. Entry Ksh300 on disco nights. Daily 11am–4am.
California Dream Hotel Corner of Moi Ave and Liwatoni Rd ☎0721 485258; see map p.392. Formerly the alluringly named *Jam Rescue Hotel*, this has traditional Kikuyu and Swahili music on Wed, Fri and Sat nights. Beer Ksh150, sodas Ksh50, wine Ksh150. 24hr.

Casablanca Mnazi Moja Rd, just off Moi Ave; see map p.396. On the site of the old *Sunshine Club*, this draws a big mixed crowd to a lively terrace, and prostitutes gather here in force, especially upstairs. They can be a pain, or a laugh, depending on your mood. Relatively expensive drinks and food. 24hr.
Club Rio Baluchi St, Fri & Sat Ks100, other nights no charge; see map p.396. A symphony of pink cane furniture, this is central Mombasa's only DJ club. Wed, Fri and Sat nights are packed, and drinks tend to become more expensive as the night wears on, but other nights can be deserted. Live music, when there is some, is in the second-floor Calypso Bar. Generally hassle-free, and gay-friendly. 24hr.
New Florida Nightclub & Casino Mama Ngina Drive, overlooking the ocean, 2km from the city centre, ⓦfloridaclubskenya.com; see map p.392. This attempts to create a slick impression, with floor shows and glitter, but is similar in most respects to its Nairobi namesake (free until 7.30pm, then men Ksh300, women Ksh200 or free on Wed & Fri). The terrace above the ocean is a nice feature, as is keg beer, and there's a

6

pleasant little casino. DJs start around 7pm, with shows at 10pm and midnight. 24hr.

Saba-Saba Corner of Jomo Kenyatta Ave and Ronald Ngala Rd, through an unmarked entrance distinguished by the plants on the first-floor terrace; see map p.392. The bar at the front isn't very inspiring, but head out to the open terrace at the back, where the action is. There's often

live music, even in the day, and always a sweaty, local atmosphere. 24hr.

Salambo Moi Ave; see map p.396. By day a dozy bar with limited snacks, this comes to life at night as the city centre's only really local disco. On most nights there's a mix of Congolese sounds, soul and reggae, with midnight shows, acrobats, dancing and beauty contests. 24hr.

ARTS AND CULTURE

Cultural and artistic life in Mombasa is a bit limited. The **British Council** (First floor, Jubilee Insurance Building, Moi Ave ☎ 041 2223076, ⓦ britishcouncil.org) and **Alliance Française** (Freed Building, corner of Moi Ave and Kwa Shibu Rd ☎ 041 2225048, ⓦ afkenya.or.ke) occasionally sponsor events, but you can't guarantee anything. There's no equivalent of Nairobi's relatively flourishing arts and gallery scene.

Cinemas For a modern cinema experience, the closest and best cinema on the coast is the Nyali Cinemax over the bridge at Nyali Plaza, with four screens (map p.392).

Libraries Kenya National Library, Msanifu Kombo St (Mon–Thurs 8am–6.30pm, Fri 8am–4pm, Sat 8am–5pm); Fort Jesus Museum (archeology; Mon–Fri 8am–12.30pm & 2–4.30pm). The small a/c library at the British Council (First floor, Jubilee Insurance Building, Moi Ave; Mon–Thurs 7.45am–4.30pm, Fri 7.45am–1pm) has recent UK newspapers: temporary membership is available for Ksh200 per day (bring your passport).

Swahili Resource Centre Sir Mbarak Hinawy Rd; map p.396. Small a/c library, resource centre and research institute that offers one of the few avenues to exploring Swahili culture for casual interested visitors. Free entry. Mon–Fri 8.30am–4.30pm, Sat 9am–1pm.

Theatre The Little Theatre Club, Mnazi Moja Rd (☎ 041 2229258, ⓦ tiny.cc/LTCMombasa), was in the past mainly an outlet for amateur dramatics in the expat/settler community, but of late has been hosting productions by drama groups from all over the coastal region, as well as music performances. Seats around Ksh200–300.

SHOPPING

Mombasa is a good city for shopping, with a generally wide choice, and fewer hassles as you window-shop than in Nairobi. Once you know where to go for **crafts**, the business of buying **souvenirs** improves markedly. The usual rules apply when **bargaining** – don't start the ball rolling if you're not in the mood, and never offer a price you're not prepared to pay. If you want quite a few items, it's worth looking out for a well-stocked stall and then, as you reach one near-agreement after another with the stallholder, add a new item to your collection. This way you should be able to buy well-finished *vyondo* (sisal baskets) in the range of Ksh600–1000, small soapstone items for Ksh150–500, and simple bracelets and necklaces for around Ksh100 or less. It's much harder to estimate what you should pay for carvings as the price depends as much on the workmanship as on the size of the piece. Take a look in Haria's (see p.406) for an idea.

SOUVENIRS

The main tourist street is the stretch of Moi Ave between the Tusks and Digo Rd, and the pavement is periodically lined with souvenir stalls (their abundance fluctuates seasonally and with the fortunes of the tourist industry). Sisal baskets, soapstone, beadwork and fake ebony carvings make up most of what's on offer. Those at the Digo Rd end of Moi Ave tend to be the most aggressive at touting their wares, and getting past without stopping is not easy, while if you do halt, making cool decisions can be difficult. The line of stalls on Chembe Rd seems to be in something of a backwater, and they're more fun to deal with.

FABRICS

Mombasa is a good place to buy the coast's famous fabrics. Noor Ala Noor, on the corner of Old Kilindini Rd and Mariakani Lane, is an enjoyable shop. For the latest *kanga*

wrap designs check out the shops in Biashara St (especially the section between George Morura St and Digo Rd), where new designs are sold before they become available anywhere else in Kenya. It's worth checking prices in several shops before buying, and perhaps going in company so you can bargain for several lots at once (they are always sold in pairs and you should be looking to get a pair for around Ksh800). Woven *kikoi* wraps go for around Ksh600 each.

HOUSEHOLD GOODS

West of Mackawi Rd, Biashara St shifts from textiles to a less gaudy section of household goods – winnowing trays, coconut graters, palm bags, mats, spoons, furniture and the like – more mundane, but just as interesting to browse.

CRAFTS AND CARVINGS

Akamba Woodcarvers Village Near the airport;

FROM TOP FORT JESUS, MOMBASA (P.393); MOMBASA WATERFRONT >

6

coming from the airport, it's on the left about 300m before you reach Magongo Rd, the main road leading into the city ☎ 020 2654362, ⓦ akambahandicraftcoop .com; see map p.389. If you want to buy carvings, consider making a special trip to this enormous "woodcarvers' village". While it may appear that the art of woodcarving has been reduced here to not much more than a human conveyor belt, the village is in fact a cooperative, with willing members who are only too pleased to see visitors. Daily 8am–6pm.

★ **Haria's Gift Shop** Next to the Hare Krishna Temple, Mohdar Mohamed Habib Rd ☎ 011/2220198 or 0722 640 780; see map p.396. Displaced from Regal Chambers on Moi Ave as the rents rose, this remains the best place in Mombasa for crafts, and they accept credit cards. Haria's consistently offers good deals and you may even be able to get things here more cheaply than on the street. Mon–Sat 9am–6pm.

MARKETS

Mackinnon Market Digo Rd; map p.396. The city centre's main market has a splendid abundance of tropical fruit, including such exotics as jackfruit, soursops, custard apples and baobab seeds. Behind the market, there are several good sweet shops and a row of stores devoted to spices, coffee and tea. Daily 7am–6pm.

Makupa Market Corner of Majengo Rd and Salim Mwamganga Rd; map p.392. In the heart of the island's low-income housing district, this colourful, multipurpose market has a busy, almost rural atmosphere and is well worth a visit. Daily 7am–6pm.

MUSIC

Mombasa is as good a place as any to stock up on a few CDs or even cassettes. Prices are low: expect to pay between Ksh300 and Ksh1000 for a CD, depending on how legitimate the copy is.

Mbwana Radio Service Just off Pigott Place in the Old Town ☎ 041 2221550; map p.396. The best place for finding traditional Mijikenda music and Mombasa *taarab*, as well as traditional songs from the Wa-Bajuni people of Lamu district. Mon–Sat 8am–8pm.

Zilizo Pendwa Music Store Up an alley just off Raha Leo St ☎ 0722 728552; map p.396. Try this hole-in-the-wall shop for Kikuyu and other Kenyan sounds, as well as the ubiquitous gospel pop. Mon–Sat 7am–6.30pm.

SAFARIS FROM MOMBASA

Mombasa is important as a **safari hub**; the majority of safaris starting from the coast visit Tsavo East or Tsavo West. With a number of daily flights further afield, however, even the Maasai Mara is accessible for a short safari, though less than two nights isn't recommended. Expect to pay from around $300 for a two-day, one-night safari to Tsavo East, depending on the lodge or camp included and the size of your group. Air safaris to the Maasai Mara start at around $1000 for two nights, including the flight. Safaris should always include all transport and transfers, meals, park fees for the full duration of your stay, and a two- to three-hour game drive every morning and evening while in the park – be sure to do your research when you book (see p.76).

Kenya Wildlife Service Mama Ngina Drive, ☎ 020/2405089 (daily 6am–6pm). Point of issue and point of sale for National Park smartcards.

SAFARI OPERATORS AND TRAVEL AGENTS

African Quest Safaris Mezzanine floor, Palli House, Nyerere Ave ☎ 041 2227052 or 0722 410362, ⓦ african quest.co.ke; map p.396. Large operator offering competitively priced lodge safaris.

★ **Farways Safaricentre** Msanifu Kombo St ☎ 0733 773434 or 0734 855261, ⓔ farways@africaonline .co.ke; map p.396. Good value and very personal service from a small, long-established agent with an excellent network of operator contacts, including car rental, Zanzibar trips, accommodation bookings and safaris.

Glorious Safaris Nilnkatha Building, next to Bella Plaza, Nyali ☎ 041 476518 or 0733 239412, ⓦ glorious safaris.com; map p.408. Busy operator with strong British ties, offering competitively priced local excursions and safaris to Tsavo East and West.

Ketty Tours Ketty Plaza, Moi Ave ☎ 041 2229572 or 041 2312204, ⓦ kettytours.co.ke; see map p.396. Solid operator with good experience and a large rental fleet.

Pollman's Tours and Safaris Pollman's House, Malindi Rd, Bamburi, north of Mombasa ☎ 041 2014980 or 0721 786553, ⓦ pollmans.com; map p.408. One of the biggest operators (you'll see their vehicles everywhere), with reliable, mainstream safaris.

★ **Southern Cross Safaris** Southern Cross Centre, off Nyali Bridge (northbound, mainland side, immediate first exit on the left) ☎ 020 2434600, ⓦ southerncrosssafaris. com; map p.392. Highly respected operators and agents, with four bronze and ten silver guides and their own *Satao* camps.

★ **Special Lofty Safaris** 1st floor, Hassanali Building, Nkrumah Rd (first stairway east of Barclays Bank) ☎ 041 2220241 or 0722 412186, ⓦ lofty-tours.de; map p.396. Conscientious German-Kenyan operator running its own safaris. The main draw is experience and Land Cruisers, a more personal way of travelling than minibus.

Vogue Tours & Travel Nkrumah Rd, opposite DHL ☎ 0722 255096; map p.396. Professional travel agents worth visiting for cheap flights to Europe and Asia.

CAR AND BIKE RENTAL

Renting a car for an independent safari, prices tend to be a little cheaper in Mombasa than in Nairobi, especially if you deal with a local company. Most of the safari operators (see opposite) also rent vehicles with or without a driver. Expect to pay from around Ksh4000/day or Ksh25,000/week for a saloon car. Mombasa has bike tours but no bike rental, but Omar Husein Cycloduka, Haile Selassie Rd near Maungano Rd (Mon–Sat 8.30am–1pm & 2–6pm; ☎0770 112345), has a good selection for sale. Heavyweight roadsters with racks start from Ksh6000, while mountain bikes range between Ksh7500 and Ksh12,000.

Avis Mombasa Mombasa Car Hire, Ratna Square, Nyali ☎041 4470956 or at Moi International Airport ☎0736 750006, ⓦtiny.cc/AvisMombasa; map p.392.

Bike the Coast Go Kart Track, Bamburi ☎0722 873738, ⓦbikethecoast.com; map p.408. Small,

Swiss-owned operator specializing in half-day bicycle tours – an unusual and highly recommended option, although the tours that go inland require a bit of leg work.

Budget Budget Car Rental, Moi Ave ☎041 2220465 or at Moi International Airport ☎020 2386421, ⓦbudget .com; map p.396.

Distance Tours & Car Hire Wimpy Building, Moi Ave ☎0717 074056 or 0721 724 956579, ⓦdistancetours .com; map p.396. Centrally located fleet-owner with a good reputation.

Glory Car Hire Moi Ave, next to the Tourist Office ☎041 2221159, ⓦglorykenya.com; map p.396. Well-known company with good prices – saloons from around Ksh4000/ day.

Unik Car Hire & Safaris Ground floor, Fatemi House, Maungano Rd, off Haile Selassie Rd ☎041 2226310, ⓦunikcarhire.com; map p.396.

DIRECTORY

Banks There are one or more branches of each of the three main banks in the city centre, all with ATMs. Pwani Forex on Digo Rd (Mon–Fri 8.30am–5pm, Sat 8.30am–1pm) offers good exchange rates.

Consulates Germany, 2nd floor, Bank of India Building, Nkrumah Rd, ☎041 2228781, ⓔmombasa @germanconsul.com; Tanzania, 12th floor, TSS Tower, Nkrumah Rd ☎041 2228595, ⓔtancon@africaonline.co.ke (Mon–Fri 8am–3pm; visas $50 and two passport photos); UK c/o James Knight, Seaforth Shipping, 2nd floor, Cotts House, Moi Ave ☎041 2220023, ⓔJames.Knight -HonCon@fconet.fco.gov.uk (Mon–Fri 9am–2pm).

Golf Mombasa Golf Club ☎041 2228531 offers nine holes and costs Ksh1500. Alternatively, try Nyali Golf and Country Club (see p.409).

Hospitals & Emergencies Pandya Memorial Hospital, Dedan Kimathi Ave (☎041 2313577 or 0722 206424), is hygienic and efficient, and has an ambulance service, as does St John's Ambulance Service (☎041 2490625). Africa Air Rescue (AAR) Health Centre, Manyara Building, Mogadishu Rd, off the western end of Moi Ave (opposite Missions to Seamen), is open 24/7 (emergencies ☎041 2312405).

Immigration You can get visitor's pass extensions at the immigration office in the Zulfat Hatimy Complex, next to the Mombasa Law Courts on Dedan Kimathi Ave (☎041 2311745 or ☎041 2222676; see map p.396).

Internet access Try Web Corner on Mohdar Mohamed Habib Rd near the Tusks (Mon–Sat 8am–8.30pm, Sun 10am–7pm), among many others.

Mobile phones Safaricom's main customer centre on Moi Ave (Mon–Fri 8am–5.30pm, Sat 8.30am–2pm) is efficient and very helpful.

Pharmacies The staff at Diamond Arcade Pharmacy, Diamond Trust House, Moi Ave (Mon–Fri 8am–6pm, Sat 9am–2pm; ☎041 2316351), are helpful. Island Chemist, by *Josleejim Hotel* in Duruma Rd, is open late (Mon–Sat 8.30am–8.30pm, Sun 9am–8.30pm).

Supermarkets Nakumatt Likoni, Mbaraki Rd, near the Likoni ferry (open long hours), and Nakumatt Cinemax, Nyali (open 24hr); Tusky's Bandari, Haile Selassie Rd, and Tusky's Digo, Digo Rd (both Mon–Sat 7.30am–8.30pm, Sun 8am–7.30pm).

Swimming pools The Shree Visha Oshwal Varik Community swimming pool complex (daily 5.30am–7.30pm; Ksh300), off Nyerere Ave, is the best place to swim, with a good-sized lap pool, spring board and paddling pool.

Vaccinations For yellow fever, you first have to go to the Town Hall, Treasury Square, and pay (Ksh600), and then to the Public Health Department in Msanifu Kombo St, opposite the end of Hospital Rd (Mon–Fri 8am–4.30pm, closed lunchtime).

North of Mombasa

While the **north coast** is busier, brasher, and much less pastoral than the **south coast** (see p.422), the resorts are closer to the airport and Mombasa city and there are more targets for day-trips, though it's not as appealing if you simply want to stretch out on the beach. The resorts start with Nyali, just ten minutes' drive from the city centre.

6

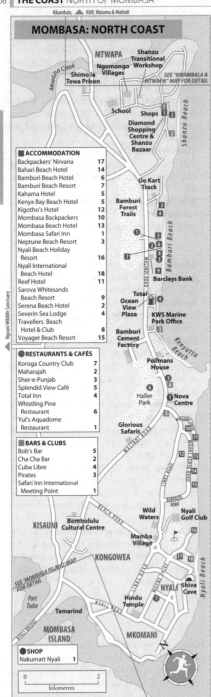

Kikambala, ▲ Kilifi, Watamu & Malindi

MOMBASA: NORTH COAST

MTWAPA

Shanzu Transitional Workshop

Ngomongo Villages

Shimo la Tewa Prison

Mtwapa Creek

SEE "KIKAMBALA & MTWAPA" MAP FOR DETAIL

School   Shops 1 2

Diamond Shopping Centre & Shanzu Bazaar

Shanzu Beach

Go Kart Track

Bamburi Forest Trails

Bamburi Beach

■ ACCOMMODATION
Backpackers' Nirvana	17
Bahari Beach Hotel	14
Bamburi Beach Hotel	6
Bamburi Beach Resort	7
Kahama Hotel	5
Kenya Bay Beach Hotel	5
Kigotho's Hotel	12
Mombasa Backpackers	10
Mombasa Beach Hotel	13
Mombasa Safari Inn	1
Neptune Beach Resort	3
Nyali Beach Holiday Resort	16
Nyali International Beach Hotel	18
Reef Hotel	11
Sarova Whitesands Beach Resort	9
Serena Beach Hotel	2
Severin Sea Lodge	4
Travellers' Beach Hotel & Club	8
Voyager Beach Resort	15

Barclays Bank

Total Ocean View Plaza

KWS Marine Park Office

Bamburi Cement Factory

Kenyatta Beach

Pollmans House

● RESTAURANTS & CAFÉS
Koroga Country Club	7
Maharajah	2
Sher-e-Punjab	3
Splendid View Café	5
Total Inn	4
Whistling Pine Restaurant	6
Yul's Aquadome Restaurant	1

Haller Park

Nova Centre

Glorious Safaris

■ BARS & CLUBS
Bob's Bar	5
Cha Cha Bar	2
Cuba Libre	4
Pirates	3
Safari Inn International Meeting Point	1

MALINDI ROAD

LINKS ROAD

MWAMBA ROAD

BARRACKS ROAD

KISAUNI

Bombolulu Cultural Centre

Wild Waters

Nyali Golf Club

Mamba Village

KONGOWEA

Nyali Beach

NYALI ROAD

BEACH ROAD

Shiva Cave

Hindu Temple

Port Tudor

Tamarind

NYALI ROAD

MOMBASA ISLAND

MKOMANI

NYALI BRIDGE

Nguuni Wildlife Sanctuary

● SHOP
Nakumatt Nyali	1

SEE "MOMBASA ISLAND" MAP FOR DETAIL

0   2
kilometres

Nyali

Nyali, the comfortable resort suburb of Mombasa on the north side of Tudor Creek, has a few minor items of interest – apart from some of the North Coast's main hotels. It was the site of **Johann Ludwig Krapf**'s first missionary toehold on the east coast (see p.420). Four years before Livingstone arrived in Africa, in May 1844, Krapf landed at Nyali with his wife and baby daughter to start work as the first missionary in what is now Kenya. His wife died of malaria on July 13, their baby the next day. The pathetic graves can be found on the seaward side of Cement Road, 700m south of the *Tamarind* restaurant (see p.411). Opposite the graves, on a small knoll, is the stone **Krapf Memorial** in a quiet, tended garden.

Freetown Bell

There's another reminder of Mombasa's history in the site of the **Freetown Bell**, at the Nyali Road junction. The bell was erected by the Society of Freed Slaves in the 1880s to warn the people of Freetown (named after Sir Bartle Frere, who founded the freed slave community here) of any impending attack by Arab slavers. The bell hung silently under its small stone arch until the 1920s when it was removed for safekeeping to the nearby Emmanuel Church (Freetown's parish church, erected in 1889), where it is still in use. The bell you see at the Nyali Road junction is a replica.

Nyali Beach

Nyali Beach is often crowded at weekends and holidays but, although fairly narrow, the sand is white and the palms offer some good shade. You can swim here until the tide is more than halfway out, but high tide can almost cover the beach, especially at the northern end – which does mean, however, that body-boarding is sometimes possible when the waves come in over the reef. The reef itself is a fair way out, and most people take a boat rather than try to swim. There are several points of access, but the easiest is by the entrance to *Nyali International Beach Hotel*.

Shiva Cave

One curiosity at the southern end of Nyali Beach is the so-called **Shiva Cave**, containing several *lingams* (phallic representations of the Hindu god Shiva) in the form of stalagmites, and a rock formation resembling the elephant-headed Hindu god Ganesh. The site was discovered by an Indian doctor, who treated a local farmer who had been attacked by a swarm of bees in the cave, after the farmer had found his cow rubbing her udders on the stalagmite – a set of circumstances rich with Hindu symbolism. The area, which includes a pleasant ledge overlooking the ocean, is maintained as a temple by the local Hindu Union, but visitors are welcome – remove your shoes first.

6

Mamba Village, Botanical Garden and Aquarium

Links Rd • Daily 8am–6.30pm • Ksh1000 • Horseriding is offered by the same organization further down Links Rd (beach rides Ksh1000, ☎041 3415778)

Behind Nyali Beach and the hotels, you can't miss **Mamba Village**. Nothing to do with venomous snakes, this is the biggest crocodile (*mamba*) farm in Kenya. Several pools in a former quarry are home to thousands of crocodiles at all stages of growth, alongside a freaks sideshow of congenitally deformed croc-lets. The overall effect – croco-burgers in the snack bar, five o'clock Pavlovian bell-ring feedings, and unlimited saurian souvenirs – is tacky, and the crocodile trail sits unhappily with the skin-farming half of the "village", which is not on show. Also part of the empire is the adjacent **Botanical Garden and Aquarium** and the Mamba International Nightclub.

Wild Waters

Links Rd • Slides open Tues–Fri 10am–6pm, Sat & Sun 11am–6pm, closed Mon; peak season daily 10am–10pm • Ksh1200, Ksh300 for non-sliders • ☎0726 337000, ⓦ wildwaterskenya.com

The fifteen slides at Wild Waters **waterpark** are a big hit with children and energetic adults. The bar, café and various amusements – including bumper cars, dry slides and gaming areas – are open until 10pm.

Nyali Golf and Country Club

Across the road from Mamba Village ☎041 471589 or 0722 414477

The enjoyable eighteen-hole course at **Nyali Golf and Country Club** is – despite stuffy indications to the contrary on the website – open to visitors. In addition to the golf, there's a swimming pool, squash and tennis, and a bar-restaurant.

ARRIVAL AND DEPARTURE   NYALI

A constant stream of matatus ferries passengers back and forth between the city centre and the Freretown junction, with some continuing south into Nyali. If you don't fancy cramming yourself inside and want a more door-to-door service, then tuk-tuks and boda-bodas are always available, as are conventional cabs.

ACCOMMODATION

Whether you're staying in one of the big Nyali hotels or not, all of them will arrange dhow trips and scuba and snorkelling excursions. In the evenings they put on bands, acrobat shows and other entertainments.

★ **Backpackers' Nirvana** Moyne Drive ☎0738 130386 or 0726 760460, ⓦ kenyabeds.com. A large private house with communal kitchen-lounge area, dorm room, one double room (with separate bathroom) and an appealing roof terrace that sleeps up to six. Run by a dog-loving, new age English expat, it's very low-key, friendly and informal. Free wi-fi. Dorm and roof beds BB Ksh1000, private double BB Ksh3000

Bahari Beach Hotel Mount Kenya Rd ☎041 4472822, ⓦ baharibeach.net. Built in 1971 and refurbished in 1997, this doesn't have much character and can feel stuffy. In common with most Nyali hotels, the rooms – which are reasonably spacious and have balconies – lack sea views. HB $200

Kigotho's Hotel Links Rd ☎0726 747050,

SWAHILI COASTAL CULTURE

For perhaps two thousand years, **foreign ideas** have been shaping the society, language, literature and architecture of the coast. Immigrants and traders from **Arabia**, **Persia** and **India** have been a subtle and gradual influence here. They would arrive each year in March or April on the northeast monsoon, stay for a few months, and return in September on the southerly monsoon.

Some, either by choice or mishap, would be left behind. Through intermarriage from the earliest times, a distinct ancient civilization called **Swahili** emerged. Swahili, a name thought to derive from the same Arabic root as *sahel*, meaning edge or coast, is also a Bantu language. Known to its speakers as **Kiswahili** (and correctly written kiSwahili), it is one of the most grammatically mainstream of the huge family of Bantu languages, and very typical of the family. Like all old languages used by trading peoples, Swahili contains strong clues about who its speakers mixed with – it's full of Arabic-derived words and peppered with others of Indian, Portuguese and English origin.

The Swahili are not a "tribe" in any definable sense – they are the result of a mixed heritage: families who can trace their roots to foreign shores in the distant past tend to claim superior social status. And, while Swahili culture is essentially **Muslim**, people's interpretation of their religion varies according to circumstance.

THE TOWNS

Like the Swahili language, it used to be thought that the **towns** of the coast began as Arab or even Persian trading forts. It is now known that Mombasa, Malindi, Lamu and a host of lesser-known settlements are essentially ancient African towns that have always tolerated immigration from overseas. With the odd exception, however, efforts to compromise their independence were met with violent resistance. When the Portguese arrived at the end of the fifteenth century, cultural memories of the Moorish occupation of their own country were still fresh. Accommodation to Islam was not on their agenda and, despite a long acquaintance with the coast, they never established an enduring colonial presence. They fared better in Goa on the Indian coast, further along the same monsoon trading route.

THE SLAVE INHERITANCE

Historically, **slavery** on the coast was quite different from the kind of slavery associated with the Atlantic slave trade. Although refugee and convict slaves were not uncommon, pawn-slavery was a more structured version of the institution. For example, the **Mijikenda** peoples (see p.421), who lived in the coastal hinterland, maintained close links with the coastal towns, trading their produce and providing armed forces when the towns were under threat, and receiving, in exchange, goods from overseas, especially cotton cloth and tools. As traders, the Swahili periodically accumulated surpluses of grain on the coast at times of severe drought inland. In exchange for famine relief, Mijikenda children or marginalized adults would then be taken to the towns by their relatives and fostered with Swahili families with whom they had links – to become pawns, or in effect domestic or farm slaves. Later, they married into their adoptive families, or paid off the debt and returned inland. But sometimes circumstances altered and, for various reasons, a small number of these indentured labourers were sold overseas, though the trade was always fairly insignificant.

When, in the late eighteenth century, the **slave trade** itself became a major aspect of commerce, and the available foreign goods (firearms, liquor and cloth) became irresistible, then any trace of trust in the old arrangements vanished. The weak and defenceless were captured and sold to slavers from the coast, often to end up on Dutch or French plantations in the Indian Ocean, or in Arabian households. And, with the domination of the Sultan of Oman on the coast in the early nineteenth century, and the large-scale migration of Arab families to East Africa, slaves from the far interior were increasingly set to work on their colonial coastal farms and plantations. When the British formally freed the slaves in 1907, they became a new social class in Swahili society.

---

❸ kigothohotel@yahoo.com. Although it's not on the beach, this is quite a nice place to stay, and good value for the area. The bright, quite spacious apartment-style rooms have fans (but no nets or a/c), plus a kitchenette with fridge and cooking facilities. There's an inexpensive bar and *nyama choma* on site, and a small pool. BB **Ksh6000**

★ **Mombasa Backpackers** Mwamba Drive ☎ 0701 561233, ⓦ mombasabackpackers.com. Large setup popular with NGOs and volunteers that often has a party atmosphere. There are well-thought-out dorms (three mixed, one female-only) with lock-up boxes, a bar-dining room and a very nice swimming pool set in a shady garden. Private non-s/c single and double rooms with fan and nets are also available in a house in the grounds. Camping Ksh500 per person, dorm beds Ksh1000, private rooms Ksh3000

Mombasa Beach Hotel Mount Kenya Rd ☎ 041 4471861 or 0722 203143, ⓦ safari-hotels.com. Despite the clumsy 1970s architecture, there's a good atmosphere here – largely the result of its shady, clifftop location and the fact that it attracts many more African guests than its competitors. Good staff and two pools (one huge, the other down near the beach) compensate for the rooms, which need a complete refit. HB Ksh240

Nyali Beach Holiday Resort Bungalows Rd ☎ 041 4472325 or 0725 849111, ⓦ nyalibeachresort.com. Mediterranean-style development right by the beach, with two pools. Most of the sixteen large, clean rooms, with a/c, nets and TVs, face both the pool and the beach, as do the self-catering apartments or "cottages". Restaurant, games room and safe parking. HB Ksh80

Nyali International Beach Hotel Bungalows Rd ☎ 020 2648100 or 0727 228344, ⓦ nyali-international .com. Pleasant and bustling, this is one of the coast's oldest hotels, dating from 1946, with two good pools, five

restaurants and extensive gardens. The standard Garden View rooms are okay, but only the marginally more expensive Sea View rooms have sea views; all of them need a refurb. HB Ksh100

Reef Hotel Mwamba Drive ☎ 041 471771, ⓦ reef hotelkenya.com. Once one of Nyali's best, this large and still-friendly 1972 resort is holding up, and even its peak-season prices are not excessive. Off-season, if you're not too fussy, it's even better value. There's a wide mix of guests and fairly basic food. HB Ksh182

★ **Tamarind Village** Cement Rd, Mkomani ☎ 041 474600 or 0725 959552, ⓦ tamarind.co.ke. Spacious, secure and extremely comfortable, serviced apartments, all privately owned and all with wonderful views across Tudor Creek to Mombasa island, the Old Town and the lights on Nyali Bridge. The *Tamarind* and *Harbour* restaurants are on hand, plus two swimming pools. Apartment only Ksh300

Voyager Beach Resort Barracks Rd ☎ 020 2103454, ⓦ heritage-eastafrica.com. With its impressive, ship-themed communal areas and generally high standards, this is easily the best hotel in Nyali and is very good value. But it's worth knowing this is also a very big hotel (232 rooms), with a fun-loving, largely British clientele enjoying three restaurants, four bars, nightly shows and 24hr snacks and drinks. It's not quiet, and the relentless nautical theme can be wearing. Facilities include tennis, a PADI diving school (the very good ⓦ buccaneerdiving.com) and all the watersports you'd expect. AI Ksh180

EATING AND DRINKING

Although growing in number, independent **restaurants**, **bars** and **clubs** are still a bit thin on the ground in Nyali: people tend to check out the other hotels, go into Mombasa, or explore further north (see p.414).

Hunters Steak House Cement Rd, Mkomani ☎ 041 474759. When you've had enough coconut fish curry, this is the place for an old-school meat fest, with the tenderest, and possibly most expensive, steaks on the coast (Ksh1600–2500). There's an a/c indoor area, plus garden tables. Wed–Mon 11.30am–2.30pm & 6.30–11pm.

Koroga Country Club Mvita Rd ☎ 0716 608080. The koroga principle is about bringing your friends and family to a place where all the necessary ingredients and cooking utensils are on hand – and then paying to cook the meal yourself. It seems a very male pastime (why can't you do that at home?), but it's popular in Kenya. Here, a watered-down version of koroga is also on offer – you order; they cook; you eat (it doubles as a restaurant, in other words). Well-prepared curries start from Ksh450, plus a few surprises like "fish drumsticks" (Ksh350). Expect a bill of

around Ksh1000 a head. If you want to do real koroga, call ahead – prawns Ksh1100/kg, rump steak Ksh1400/kg – and find a good spot in the lovely garden. Daily 11am–11pm.

Rozina's Ratna Sq ☎ 041 4470219 or 0724 984373. Like its Old Town sister establishment (p.402), *Ratna's* covers a range of tastes with nods to India, the UK and US as well as Swahili roots. Eat well for under Ksh1500. Daily 11am–10.30pm.

★ **Tamarind** Cement Rd, Mkomani ☎ 041 474600, ⓦ tamarind.co.ke. With a sublime location above Tudor Creek that offers great views across to Mombasa Old Town, this is unequivocally the best restaurant in Mombasa and one of the few places specializing in seafood and doing it really well. Tempting dishes and a pricey wine list mean you're unlikely to come away from dinner with change from Ksh4000 a head. Daily noon–2.30pm & 6–10pm.

From Nyali Bridge to Kenyatta Beach

Beyond the Freretown Bell and the junction for Nyali – always jostling with people trying to get transport to their shifts at the hotels – the main coast road, **Malindi Road**, ploughs through an area of burgeoning suburban growth. This is the Kenya coast that doesn't appear in the brochures: ignored by the resort developers because it's too far from the sea, the primitive living conditions and milling activity here can come as a shock if you're fresh off the plane. There are two very worthwhile visits in this area – **Bombolulu** and **Haller Park** – both of them recommended outings whether you're travelling independently or exploring from your beach hotel.

ARRIVAL AND DEPARTURE   FROM NYALI BRIDGE TO KENYATTA BEACH

Matatus from Mombasa GPO or Abdel Nasser Road come along this way, usually going as far as Mtwapa town on the other side of Mtwapa Creek before returning to the city.

EATING AND DRINKING

Whistling Pine Restaurant Haller Park · ☎ 041 5487464. Specializes in farmed game meat from Nguuni Wildlife Sanctuary. Daily 12.30–3pm & 7.30–10pm.

Bombolulu Workshops and Cultural Centre

Just off Malindi Rd, 3km north of Nyali Bridge · ⓦ bombolulu.org · **Workshops** Mon–Fri 8am–12.45pm & 2–5pm · Free **Showroom** Mon–Sat 8am–6pm · Free · **Cultural Centre** Mon–Sat 8am–5pm · Ksh900, including transport from nearby hotels

Bombolulu is a crafts training school and manufacturing centre, employing more than 150 disabled people, mostly polio victims, in its five handicraft workshops. The **jewellery workshop** is the programme's biggest money-spinner, with hundreds of original designs in metal and local materials, including old coins and seeds, exported to the US and Europe, where you'll come across them in charity gift catalogues. The shop is an excellent place to buy crafts, with somewhat lower prices than you'll find in the souvenir shops. There's also a **cultural centre**, incorporating re-creations of six tribal homesteads around a central restaurant and dancefloor, where traditional crafts, cooking and farming skills are demonstrated.

Haller Park

Malindi Rd, 5km north of Bombolulu · Daily 8am–5pm; Ksh800, children Ksh400 · ☎ 041 2101000 or 0722 410064, ⓦ haller.org.uk

Haller Park (also called Baobab Adventure and Bamburi Nature Park) is the outcome of an unusual attempt to rehabilitate a quarry. The Bamburi Cement Factory, whose giant kilns are visible from miles around, and whose familiar brown sacks are seen all over Kenya, has been scouring the land here for limestone since 1954. In 1971, it began a concentrated programme of tree-planting in an effort to rescue the disfigured landscape, putting a small-is-beautiful principle into conservation practice, making a modest, but terrifically successful, contribution in a land of huge wildlife parks. Later, as the project gained momentum, fish breeding was established, and large numbers of mammals and birds introduced, including several **hippos**. One of the hippos, **Owen**, is an orphan of the 2004 Indian Ocean tsunami, washed out to sea from his Sabaki River home, and later famously befriended here by **Mzee**, an elderly giant tortoise. Feeding time is 11am and 3pm for the giraffes, 4.30pm for the crocodiles, and 4.45pm for the hippos.

The footpaths twist through dense groves of casuarina, a tree known for its ability to withstand a harsh environment, across ground which is mostly below sea level, permanently moist with salty water percolating through the coral limestone rock. The fish-farming side of the operation experiments with different types of **tilapia**, a freshwater fish highly tolerant of brackish conditions, many tons of which now reach shops and restaurants every year, including the park's own restaurant.

Bamburi Forest Trails

Entrance on Malindi Rd, 4km north of Haller Park, opposite the turning for Bamburi Beach Hotel · Daily 8am–6pm · Ksh300, children Ksh150; bike rental Ksh300/hr

On a similar theme to Haller Park and also managed by Bamburi Cement, are the newer **Bamburi Forest Trails**. Intended mainly for joggers and cyclists, there are four looping tracks, and bicycles can be rented for use on the trails. There's also a Butterfly Pavilion.

Nguuni Sanctuary

5km inland • Pre-booked visits only, through Bamburi Forest Trails • ☎ 041 5485901, ⓦ thebaobabtrust.com

Nguuni Wildlife Sanctuary is the third of Bamburi Cement's sites, good for bird-spotting, and well known for its herds of farmed **eland** and **oryx antelope** and its ostrich farm. The sanctuary is also a fine birding area, with more than twenty ponds and lakes making it a diverse and attractive ecosystem.

6

North Coast beaches

Kenyatta and Bamburi beaches, together with Shanzu just to the north (see p.415), are the heart of the "North Coast". If you're out for the day, there should, in most cases, be little difficulty in visiting a hotel and using its facilities. The exceptions are the all-inclusive places, which naturally charge admission (usually around Ksh3000 for the day or evening, including lunch or dinner and all drinks). The beach itself is entirely public; it's the access to it which has been progressively restricted by the hotel developers. Either way, *Sarova Whitesands* (see p.414) and *Serena Beach* (see p.416) are the nicest hotels along this stretch.

Kenyatta and Bamburi beaches

Go-Kart Track and Bulldozing Area Tues–Sat 4–10pm; Sun 3–10pm • Karting Ksh1500/10min; bulldozing Ksh1700/30min •
☎ 0721 485247, ⓦ mombasa-gokart.com

Kenyatta Municipal Beach is almost the only beach in the country where you'll see droves of ordinary Kenyans by the seaside. There's a great family atmosphere here – and consequently little or no hassle. The beach goes far out at low tide, exposing plenty of coral pools and vast stretches of sand for undisturbed walks. There are sailing boats for rent and trips offered (check they have life jackets), and at the fringes under the low coconut trees pedlars sell ice creams and sodas, snacks and drinking coconuts, while others rent out inflated car inner tubes. For something different, try the Swiss-run **go-kart track** and **bulldozing arena** (yes, bulldozing) at the northern end of Bamburi, just off the main road.

Nearly thirty beach hotels throng the 6km shoreline that makes up **Bamburi beach**. The coconut-shaded sands tend to be buzzing with visitors and beach boys, but at least the sea is swimmable until the tide is more than halfway out and there are decent snorkelling spots towards the northern end, past Severin Sea Lodge – although a deep channel separates the reef from the shoreline all the way from Nyali to Shanzu.

ARRIVAL AND DEPARTURE
KENYATTA AND BAMBURI BEACHES

Matatus from Mombasa GPO or Abdel Nasser Road come along this way, usually going as far as Mtwapa town on the other side of Mtwapa Creek before returning to the city.

INFORMATION

Services There are three shopping centres along the main road from Nyali to Shanzu. The biggest is the Nova Centre, which includes a large Nakumatt supermarket, a good bookshop, Books First (with an internet café), various food and drink outlets, and Barclays and KCB ATMs. Should you need a doctor, Dr Buran (☎ 041 5485238) has a surgery here. Further north, Ocean View Shopping Plaza, next to the *Sai Rock* (former *Ocean View*) hotel, has a branch of the efficient Commercial Bank of Africa with an ATM, and Shaban Mini-Mart where you can change cash at good rates. The Bamburi shops just north of *Whitesands* include a small post office and another Barclays, again with an ATM.

ACCOMMODATION

Bamburi Beach Hotel Bamburi Beach, ☎ 041 5485611, ⓦ bamburibeachkenya.com. Unexceptional mid-sized resort hotel with a nice pool, but slow service. On the plus side, most rooms have sea views. Facilities include a PADI diving school, glass-bottomed boats, snorkelling, squash courts and a gym. Most guests are on AI. HB $213

Bamburi Beach Resort Malindi Rd, Bamburi Beach ☎ 020 2048275 or 0733 474482, ⓦ bamburiresort.com. Budget beach hotel just above the sands, with a cheap bar, a deck and pool. The airy, s/c rooms have a/c and nets, or you can self-cater. Discounts for longer stays. Room only $76

★ **Kahama Hotel** Malindi Rd, Bamburi Beach ☎ 041 5485395 or 0729 487446, ⓦ kahamahotel.co.ke. The former *Octopus Hotel*, just back from the beach, is pretty good all round for the price, with 32 decent, spacious rooms with nets and TVs and a nice pool. The *Pitcher and Butch* sports pub is located here, with regular music nights and live bands. The rates are a very good deal, though they bump them up about 300 percent at Christmas. BB Ksh3950

Kenya Bay Beach Hotel Malindi Rd, Bamburi Beach ☎ 041 5487600 or 0725 991500, ⓦ kenyabay .com. One of the old generation, but much better maintained than many others. Although it feels smaller than most Bamburi hotels, it still has 106 rooms (a/c, nets, TV, safe), very good staff and a good mix of nationalities. There's a watersports centre and free wi-fi in the lobby. BB $120

Neptune Beach Resort Off Malindi Rd, Bamburi Beach North ☎ 041 5485701, ⓦ neptunehotels.com. Refreshingly lacking in pretension, this is a fun package destination with excellent food, good staff, lots of activities

and watersports, and a cheerful atmosphere. BB $206

★ **Sarova Whitesands Beach Resort** Malindi Rd, Bamburi Beach ☎ 020 2128000, ⓦ sarovahotels.com. One of the biggest hotels in Kenya, with the longest seafront on the North Coast and not a *makuti* roof in sight. The grounds include extensive, interconnecting pools and busy restaurants, and the rooms all have nets, a/c, DSTV and large safes. You can do all the activities you'd expect, and there's wi-fi throughout. Underwent a major upgrade in 2012. BB $235

Severin Sea Lodge Off Malindi Rd, Bamburi Beach ☎ 041 2111805, ⓦ severin-kenya.com. Large, well-run resort hotel, with excellent sports and watersports and incredibly motivated staff. Rooms have the lot – a/c, TV, nets, safes and balconies. The *Imani Dhow* restaurant is a converted, beached Zanzibari *jahazi*. Great value for fifty weeks of the year: prices more than double over Christmas/ New Year. Eco-Tourism Kenya Bronze Award. HB $182

Travellers Beach Hotel & Club Malindi Rd, Bamburi Beach ☎ 041 5485121, ⓦ travellersbeach.com. Big, package-tour setup that crams a lot of rooms into the half-board *Beach* on one side and the all-inclusive *Club* on the other. You can swim into the lobby then slide out again, but you can't go on the beach at high tide, when it's submerged: four pools and lots of activities compensate. Dull gardens, and somewhat tenement-like room blocks, though the rooms are spacious and well appointed. They have a very good Indian restaurant, the *Sher-e-Punjab*. HB $300

EATING, DRINKING AND NIGHTLIFE

Apart from the hotel restaurants there are plenty of other eating and drinking places, most of which line the unpretty Mombasa–Malindi road. Most places offer free transport from nearby hotels.

Bob's Bar Birgis Complex, near Nova Centre ☎ 020 2021775 or 041 471000. Also known as *Murphy's Irish Pub*, this is a convivial place for a drink, with a mix of tourists and locals, flat screens for sports and good live music, usually on Thurs & Sun. 24hr.

Cuba Libre 200m north of Nova Centre, Malindi Rd, Bamburi Beach ☎ 0724 333209. Bar with live music (Wed & Sun from 6pm), plus an eclectic mix of food, from *nyama choma* to mulligatawny soup and guinea fowl in red wine sauce (mains around Ksh500–800). Drinks include a legit bottled version of palm wine. 24hr.

★ **Maharajah** Outside the Indiana Beach Hotel, Malindi Rd, Bamburi Beach ☎ 041 5485895. North Indian tandoori with a seafood twist – dishes include fish tikka or tandoori lobster, but there are plenty of chicken

options too. Curries and tandoori dishes around Ksh600, seafood Ksh1150. Daily 2–10.30pm.

Pirates Kenyatta Beach ☎ 041 5487119 or 0722 750277, ⓦ cemkenya.com/pirates. For many people, the main attraction on Kenyatta Beach is this combination of restaurant and breezy bar. The restaurant serves good, if not cheap, Mediterranean food, and the beach bar is the venue for popular nightly discos, with a mixed crowd and a variety of music. Daily 9.30am–late.

Sher-e-Punjab Travellers Beach Hotel, Malindi Rd, Bamburi Beach ☎ 041 5485121. Unusual among the hotel restaurants for having a reputation for style and quality. Vegetarian (paneer tikka, vegetable kebabs), chicken (jalfrezi, korma) and Mughlai (rogan josh, Mughlai birianis) dishes, and a very good-value Sun lunchtime

---

TURTLES

Several parts of Shanzu Beach, notably at *Serena Beach* hotel, are popular egg-laying sites for **sea turtles**. There are educational talks about these endangered marine reptiles at the hotel (Mon, 7pm), where the ban on motorized watersports is enforced (much of this sea area is a marine national park).

RESPONSIBLE SNORKELLING, DIVING AND FISHING

Coral reefs are the world's most fragile ecosystems. A reef is a living entity: every cluster of coral consists of thousands of individual organisms called polyps, constantly growing outwards as the older ones die and calcify and become covered in new growth. Solid though it seems, coral is extremely sensitive to sea temperature increases, and of course very vulnerable to physical damage by tourists or fishermen. When snorkelling, diving or fishing, it's worth bearing the following points in mind:

When mooring a boat, ensure you use established buoys, or drop anchor well away from the coral.

Dive and swim carefully, and never touch the coral. Even gentle abrasions can kill some polyps and coral suffocates if covered with silt or sand thrown up by a careless swipe of fins. If you wear fins, use them only in open water and use your hands to swim when near coral.

Don't feed the fish, as it may cause stress and encourages dependency. It also destabilizes the food chain and can cause some species to become aggressive (just like monkeys).

Don't collect souvenirs. Collecting shells, dead coral and starfish disrupts the ecosystem and is illegal in most countries, including Kenya – as is all trade in sea-turtle products. Getting caught when you arrive home can land you in serious trouble. Equally, buying marine souvenirs, rather than collecting them yourself, is no excuse, although they are widely for sale. Although the low is not enforced, selling shells is illegal.

Big-game fishing (the season runs Sept–March) reduces the population of natural predators, increasing the populations of their prey, in turn increasing pressure on organisms further down the food chain. Among the sports fishing fraternity, falling catch rates have spurred talk of introducing quotas. Happily, most boat charterers now operate a tag-and-release policy.

buffet, including vegetarian options. Count on Ksh1200–1500 a head. Daily 12.30–2.30pm & 7.30–10.30pm.

Total Inn By the Total garage, Ocean View Shopping Plaza, Malindi Rd. If you wondered where hotel staff can afford to eat, the answer is in places like this: basic African dishes and not a lobster in sight. Good conversations, and most items are less than Ksh100. Daily 7am–9pm.

Yul's Aquadome Restaurant Next to Bamburi Beach Hotel, Malindi Rd, Bamburi Beach. Very reliable spot, based at Yul's watersports centre, with one of the longest (and most consistently available) menus on the coast, and now more than twenty years old. Great pizzas and steaks, excellent boneless chicken and naan bread, and very good ice cream. Gets busy at weekends. Daily 9am–11pm.

Shanzu

At the northern end of the stretch of coast between Mombasa island and Mtwapa Creek, **Shanzu Beach** is dominated by exclusive (if not particularly upmarket) holiday clubs, although it does have a couple of other attractions, it's possible to swim even at fairly low tide, and there is very good snorkelling for much of the year.

Ngomongo Villages

1km east of Malindi Rd and copiously signposted • Daily 9am–5pm • Ksh700 • ☎ 041 5487063

Like Haller Park, the **Ngomongo Villages** are a reclamation project, but of a landfill site, rather than a quarry, and with a twist: as well as trees, it's been furnished with a collection of regional homesteads, complete with inhabitants in traditional dress, representing eight of Kenya's tribes. Don't expect authenticity, but you should be able to look forward to an enjoyable couple of hours in this ethnic theme park – though the occasional pestering for tips as you walk round makes it clear how dependent they are on getting regular visits by tourists. There are musicians and herbalists to, watch and talk to and hands-on activities like archery, Luo-style hook fishing, grain pounding and tree planting. It has an onsite restaurant.

Shanzu Transitional Workshop for Disabled Young Women

350m east of Ngomongo Villages • Mon–Sat 9am–6pm • ☎ 041 2223078

The **Shanzu Transitional Workshop for Disabled Young Women** is run by the Mombasa Girl Guides. Here, a group of women get on-the-job training in practical crafts skills, turning out a small selection of well-made clothes (including great Bermuda shorts), jewellery and leatherwork, all of which is for sale.

ARRIVAL AND INFORMATION SHANZU

By public transport Matatus for Shanzu from Mombasa GPO or Abdel Nasser Road usually go as far as Mtwapa town on the other side of Mtwapa Creek before returning to the city. Some pause at the junction of the Malindi Rd and Shanzu Rd, others turn down towards the coast proper and

drop and pick up at Shanzu shops.
Services Next to *Sonia Apartments*, in Shanzu, you'll find a large cluster of shops, including a cybercafé and the very good Kelele Record Shop, which sells local CDs.

ACCOMMODATION

Mombasa Safari Inn Shanzu Tourist Rd ☎0733 430996 or 0733 925736. One of the few cheapies in Shanzu, in the little "town centre" itself – friendly, and with modern s/c rooms. It has a popular outdoor bar and restaurant (see below). Room only **Ksh1450**

★ **Serena Beach Hotel** Shanzu Beach ☎041 3548771, ⓦserenahotels.com. Beautifully put together in a mélange of Moorish and Swahili designs, and very stylishly maintained, this is the standout proposition on

this stretch of coast, and indeed anywhere between Mombasa and Mtwapa. As in all *Serena* hotels, the standard rooms (all with a/c, DSTV, safes) are on the small side and drinks are pricey. There are lots of activities, most of them free to guests, including floodlit tennis and a/c squash courts, snorkelling, kayaking and sailing, and they take good care of children. PADI diving school. Eco-Tourism Kenya Bronze Award. HB **$289**

EATING, DRINKING AND NIGHTLIFE

Shanzu is pretty tacky when it comes to eating places and watering holes, with most places catering purely for a captive market of package tourists. Don't expect to find any ordinary Kenyan establishments.

Cha Cha Bar Past the entrance to the Serena. A pleasant and laidback outdoor bar-restaurant under a *makuti* roof, where you'll pay around Ksh800 for a main course or Ksh1500 for seafood. The working women here are less of a hassle than at other Shanzu venues, and there's occasional live music. Food daily until 11pm, bar open later.

Safari Inn International Meeting Point Shanzu Tourist Rd ☎0722 671475. A cheery bar and restaurant with good grills (main courses around Ksh800). The outdoor atmosphere is mellow, and it's open daily from 8am until the last customer leaves.

Mtwapa

Mtwapa Creek marks the edge of Greater Mombasa, where tropical suburbia, with its villas, supermarkets, clubs, restaurants – and poverty – is more or less left behind. North of here, the road heads with fewer distractions up to Kilifi, Watamu and Malindi.

The town of **MTWAPA** itself is in many ways the most distinctive of the road towns leading north out of Mombasa – and it's certainly the fastest growing. The most obvious reasons to pause here are **boats** and **big fish** – the beautiful **creek** is a focus for yacht owners and game fishermen – but there are also some good spots for eating, drinking and rambunctious nightlife. Plus, if you have a few hours to spare, don't overlook the fascinating **ruins of Jumba la Mtwana** and **Mtwapa Heritage Site** just north of the creek mouth.

Jumba la Mtwana

Daily 8am–6pm • Ksh500 • ⓦ museums.or.ke • The sign for the 3km access road is 2km north of Mtwapa Creek bridge; if you're travelling by public transport along the coast highway and are dropped off at the junction, you have a good chance of getting a lift down here

Well worth stopping for, and worth an excursion in its own right, are the ruins of **Jumba la Mtwana**. This national monument, one of three between Mombasa and Malindi, is the remains of a wealthy fourteenth- or fifteenth-century Swahili community. The phrase *jumba la mtwana* means "house of the slave", but the settlement has been deserted for some 500 years and probably had a different name in the past. It's a small site in an enchanting setting among baobabs and lawns, just above the beach; there's a small, single-room museum of photos and artefacts from the site; and a new restaurant, Monsoons (see p.419). This seems a strange place for a town, right on an open shore with no harbour, and it's possible the inhabitants were pushed here by raiding parties from inland groups, and relied on Mtwapa Creek as a safe anchorage for the overseas traders who would have visited yearly. Jumba is fortunate in having good water, but why it was deserted, and by whom, remains a mystery.

Compared with Gedi, further north (see p.452), Jumba's layout is simple. Though it lacks the eerie splendour of that much larger town, it must once have been a sizeable settlement; there were three mosques within the site and a fourth just outside. Most of the population would have lived in mud-and-thatch houses, which have long since disintegrated. In Swahili culture, building in stone (in fact, coral "rag" of different densities) has traditionally been used for mosques, and was the preserve of certain privileged people, principally the long-settled inhabitants of a town. Newcomers would almost always build in less durable materials appropriate to their shorter-term stake in the community.

The **people of Jumba** seem to have been very religious and hygienic – virtues that are closely associated in Islam. Cisterns and water jars, or at least the remains of them, are found everywhere among the ruined houses, and in most cases there are coral blocks nearby which would have been used to squat on while washing. The latrines are all stone-lined with long-drops. Of course, it is possible that the poorer people of Jumba lived in squalor in their mud huts, yet even the **House of Many Doors**, which seems to have been a fifteenth-century lodging house, provided guests with private washing and toilet facilities.

Mosque by the Sea

The best of Jumba's mosques is the **Mosque by the Sea**, which is right behind the beach itself, and shows evidence of a separate room for women, something which is only just becoming acceptable again in modern mosques. The cistern where worshippers washed is still intact, with coral foot-scrapers set nearby and a jumble of tombs behind the north wall, facing Mecca. One of these has a Koranic inscription carved in coral on a panel facing the sea and must have been the grave of an important individual: "Every soul shall taste death. You will simply be paid your wages in full on the Day of Resurrection. He who is removed from the fire and made to enter heaven, it is he who has won the victory. The earthly life is only delusion."

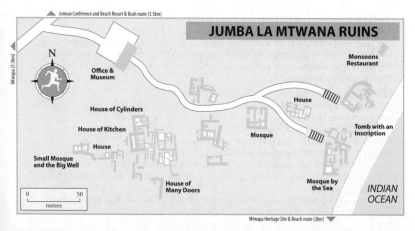

Jumba beach

Jumba Beach is a good place to while away an afternoon – in fact, late afternoon, when the atmosphere hangs among the ruins like cobwebs, is probably the best time to come. Strange but attractive **screw pines** grow in the sand, aerial-rooted like mangroves. It's a good spot for a swim and a picnic: there are toilets and showers by the ticket office.

Mtwapa Heritage Site

To the north of the creek mouth • ⓦ tinyurl.com/kjb2up • Easily reached on foot from Mtwapa town – take the track to the right by the huge baobab tree on the way down to the beach

If Jumba stoked your interest, you may be intrigued to visit the virtually unexcavated ruins at **Mtwapa Heritage Site** in the twelve acres of thick forest behind Mtwapa's tiny beach. Old Mtwapa dates from the twelfth century and scattered here are the remains of more than sixty houses, a mosque and a tomb. Although it's a gazetted monument (in other words, protected by law), there's no physical protection of the site, and its security looks uncertain. Meanwhile, enjoy the strange jungle ruins while you can: if you come down here soon after dawn, you'll also see plenty of monkeys, hornbills, monitor lizards and even dik-diks.

ACCOMMODATION

Beach Africa Maweni Beach, on the corner of the creek mouth and the ocean ☎ 0722 717629, ⓦ thebeach africa.org. German-owned campsite and very funky beach hostel site right above the sea, with camping and very basic *bandas*. It's a seasonally popular hangout spot, with food and cold drinks available (and the food can be very good), but inconsistent and quite cut off from Mtwapa town, which is too far to walk. It's signposted from Kenol station: take a piki-piki. Camping Ksh350 per person, dorm beds Ksh450, double room only Ksh1300

★ **Sweet Heart Lodge** East of the main road, just north of the market ☎ 0723 419452 or 0713 797902. Clean, properly managed and reasonably comfortable, this is the best B&L in Mtwapa, with s/c rooms with TV. BB Ksh2600

RESTAURANTS, BARS AND CLUBS

Bahnhof 300m north of the bridge on the west side of the road ☎ 0721 100638. Formerly German-, now British-owned sports bar, with big screens, pool tables, DJs and plenty of cold beer. It's usually heaving to the point of overflowing on a Saturday night, but always a good place to catch the local vibe. 24hr.

Casuarina Nomads 300m north of the bridge on the east side of the road ☎ 0724 374639. Although often full of prostitutes, the pleasant, *makuti*-roofed *Casuarina* is a perennial favourite among locals and more adventurous tourists and expats, with a good atmosphere, discos, occasionally traditional dancers at weekends, and good, chargrilled meat and seafood (from Ksh400) at all hours. 24hr.

★ **La Marina** On the north shore of the creek, east of the bridge ☎ 020 2434726 or 0723 223737, ⓦ lamarina -restaurant.com. Mtwapa's top restaurant, the former *Aquamarine* serves conventional meals on the creek shore – a very atmospheric spot for dinner (expect to spend

---

SWAHILI PROVERBS AND SAYINGS

The Swahili are renowned for the imagery, rhythm and complexity of their **proverbs**. *Kangas* always have some kind of adage printed on one side and these are often traditionally Swahili. The first one listed below is the one most often heard. For more *kanga* aphorisms, see ⓦ glcom.com/hassan/kanga.html.

Haraka, haraka: haina baraka – Haste, haste: there's no blessing in it.
Nyumba njema si mlango – A good house isn't (judged by) its door.
Mahaba ni haba, akili ni mali – Love counts for little, intelligence is wealth.
Faida yako ni hasara yangu – Your gain is my loss.
Haba na haba kujaza kibaba – Little by little fills the jug.
Kuku anakula sawa na mdomo wake – A chicken eats according to her beak.
Mungu alihlolandika, haliwezi kufutika – What God has written cannot be erased.
Heri shuka isiyo kitushi, kama shali njema ya mauwa – Better an honest loincloth than a fancy cloak (of shame).
Mke ni nguo, mgomba kupalilia – A wife means clothes (like) a banana plant means weeding.

around Ksh2000/head) and also offers "champagne dhow cruises", with a barbecue lunch or dinner and music and other entertainments. To get here, turn right at the signboard 550m north of the bridge, and head along the dirt track for 1.5km. Daily noon–10.30pm.

Lambada on the north side of Mtwapa, north of Casuarina ☎0722 726630. Industrial-strength mega-club – one of the coast's biggest – with pool, sunken dance floor and plastic-covered sofas. Theme nights and live music at weekends. 24hr.

★ **Monsoons** Jumba la Mtwana ruins ☎041 2012666 or 734 663370, ⊛letseat.at/Monsoons. Serving seafood by the seashore near the House of the Slave, this new establishment makes for a great excuse for a trip to the ruins. Good, Italian-styled mains from under Ksh1000, including linguine with crab and chilli (Ksh1000), various lobster dishes (from Ksh2000) or fillet steak (Ksh1300). Tues–Sun 11am–7pm.

Moorings On the north side of the creek, west of the bridge ☎041 5485045 or 0723 032536, ⊛themoorings .co.ke. This floating restaurant, in a fine, breezy location, is a good place for talk and tales – and to hook up with others, either in person or via the notice board. They have reasonably priced drinks and snacks, and a mainly seafood menu that vies with *La Marina* for quality – though it's less consistent. Main courses Ksh600–1200. To get here, turn left 300m north of the bridge. Tues–Sun 10am–midnight.

Kikambala

If you're staying in Mombasa or one of the North Coast resorts, the low-key resort area around **KIKAMBALA**, a few kilometres north of Mtwapa, is about as far as you'd want to come for a day-trip. Parts of the coastal strip here are still thickly forested and the beach itself is a glorious white expanse, though it's two to three kilometres from the highway. With the countryside here being very flat, the sea goes out for nearly a kilometre, and the lagoon isn't deep enough to swim in except at high tide. The Israeli-owned *Paradise Hotel* at Kikambala was the location of an al-Qaeda **suicide bombing** in 2002 in which sixteen people died, including two Israeli children and five members of a Giriama dance troupe. The tragic episode achieved notoriety when the hotel was rebuilt, but the dancers' families received scant compensation.

ARRIVAL AND DEPARTURE
KIKAMBALA

By public transport To reach Kikambala from Mombasa by public transport, Mtwapa-based matatus from Mombasa GPO or Abdel Nasser Road usually go only as far as Mtwapa town before returning to the city. From Mtwapa, you'll need to find another matatu going down towards the Kikambala hotels. Vehicles normally approach the beach properties from the northern access road, 7.4km north of Mtwapa Bridge (signposted for the *Sun'n'Sand Hotel*). Coming from the south, you can also cut down to the beach from the turning in Majengo, 5.3km north of Mtwapa Bridge, a sandy road that heads straight to the Jumuia Conference & Beach Resort. Such vehicles can be fairly infrequent, so the alternative would be to get to one of those junctions and then hop on a piki-piki or boda-boda.

ACCOMMODATION

The Kikambala **hotels** are virtually the last on the coast north of Mombasa until you reach Kilifi. There are few independent restaurants or bars at Kikambala, and most people stick to their hotels.

Jumuia Conference & Beach Resort Beachfront road, Kikambala (5.3km north of Mtwapa Bridge, then 3km along murram) ☎020 3548318 or 0710

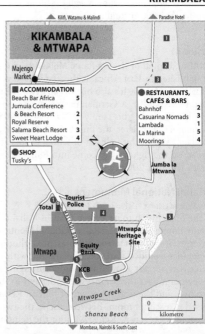

288043, @resortjumuia.com. Formerly known as *Kanamai*, this sprawling, pretty place under the coconuts, run by the National Christian Council of Kenya, has been comprehensively updated in recent years. The rooms, while not cutting-edge-elegant, are spacious and well furnished, with good fans and nets. Large pool. BB `Ksh3950`

Royal Reserve Beachfront road, Kikambala, just north of Jumuia ☎020 2057155 or 0722 205220, @royal reserve.net. Good-value, homely, a/c apartments, sleeping four to six, with nets, DSTV and kitchenettes, in a beachfront complex with pool and restaurant. There's a good feel here, and plenty of activities, but it's as divorced from the real Kenya as it's possible to be. Self-catering 4-bed apartment `$140`

Salama Beach Resort Beachfront road, Kikambala (just south of Jumuia) ☎0735 453253, @salama -beach-resort.com. Cool, attractive, German-owned bungalow-style hotel, right by the beach, with an infinity pool. Rooms have terraces and a/c (small supplement), and their *Maridadi* restaurant has a good rep. BB `$160`

Inland from Mombasa

MAZERAS is just a short hop up the hill from Mombasa. If you're coming from Nairobi, this small town marks the end of the long vistas of scrub; it's perched right on the edge of the steep scarp, amid bananas and coconuts. If you're travelling by road, it isn't a bad idea to break your journey here and savour the new atmosphere. The *hotelis* serve good, flavourful, coastal *chai* and there is a slightly unkempt **botanical garden** (daily 6am–6pm; free) on the Mombasa side of town, which makes a good break for the travel-weary. Across the highway (on the southwest side) and up the hill a little way is a **mission** and its century-old church, signs of an evangelical presence in the hills behind Mombasa that goes back, remarkably, over 150 years.

For historians of Methodism and the Church Missionary Society or, perhaps more likely, connoisseurs of palm wine, the **road to Kaloleni**, 22km north of Mazeras, is a required sidetrack (see map, p.389). It's a wonderfully scenic drive in its own right, looping through lush vales, with a wide panorama down to the coast to the east. Masses of **coconut trees** sway all around and, invariably, there are groups of flamboyantly dressed Mijikenda women walking along the roadside: leaving the highway you're instantly back in rural Kenya.

Rabai

RABAI, capital of the **Wa-Rabai Mijikenda** and site of the earliest Christian mission to be established in East Africa, is the first village you come to, 4.5km from Mazeras, on the road to Kaloleni. It's also one of only two Mijikenda villages still occupying its original *kaya* (see p.449). A German pastor, the Reverend **Johann Ludwig Krapf**, came here in 1846 after losing his family at Nyali (see p.408), and left his mark on the community when, 41 years later, the imposing **St Paul's church** was erected. The centre of the village, marked by a cluster of school rooms and sports fields, lies 500m off the main road on the right as you come into Rabai from Mazeras. For the church and museum, fork left after 200m.

Rabai National Monument
Opposite the entrance to St Paul's • Daily 8am–6pm • Ksh500

The first church to have been built in Rabai (1846–48), and the first church in Kenya, now houses the modest **Rabai National Monument**. Not the most exciting place in Kenya, it contains a few well-presented photographs but little else. The ticket, however, includes a guided tour and explanation, with visits to a full-scale replica of the *kaya* (tourists are not allowed to wander through the real one), and the village's nearby viewpoint over the countryside. Adjacent to the museum is the house where Krapf used to live, and the nearby cottage of Johann Rebmann, Krapf's proselytizing partner, is used as a school room. Between them, the two missionaries managed to explore a great deal of what is now Kenya without the demonstrations of firepower so many of their

THE MIJIKENDA PEOPLES

The principal people of the coastal hinterland region are the **Mijikenda** ("Nine Tribes"), a loose grouping whose Bantu languages are to a large extent mutually intelligible, and closely related to Swahili. They are believed to have arrived in their present homelands in the sixteenth or seventeenth century from a quasi-historical state called Shungwaya, which had undergone a period of intense civil chaos. This centre was probably located somewhere in the Lamu hinterland or in the southwest corner of present-day Somalia. According to oral tradition, the people who left it were the Giriama, the Digo, the Rabai, the Ribe, the Duruma, the Chonyi, the Jibana, the Kauma and the Kambe (not to be confused with the Kamba of the highlands around Machakos).

All these tribes now live in the coastal hinterland, the **Giriama** and the **Digo** being the largest and best-known. Like so many other Kenyan peoples, the Mijikenda had age-set systems that helped cut across the divisive groupings of clan and subclan to bind communities together. And these involved some fierce traditions: the installation of a new ruling elders' age-set, for example, required the killing and castration of a stranger. This, like most of the milder practices of tribal tradition, was abandoned in the early twentieth century.

The Mijikenda have always had a diverse **economy**. They were cultivators, long-distance traders, makers of palm wine (a Digo speciality now diffused all over Mijikenda-land), hunters, fishermen and herders – the Duruma especially and, at one time, the Giriama, were almost as fond of cows as the Maasai. They still maintain local market cycles. These are four-day weeks in the case of the Giriama: days one and two for labour, day three for preparation, and day four, called *Chipalata*, for the market.

Despite acquiring all the trappings of modern life along with most Kenyan peoples, the Mijikenda have been unusually successful at maintaining their cultural identity. They warred with the British in 1914 over the imposition of taxes and the demand for porters for World War I. And they have preserved a vigorous conservative tradition of adherence to their old beliefs in spirits and the power of their ancestors. While this is very apparent from the resurgence of interest in preserving their traditional sacred groves, or *kayas* (see p.449), and getting graveposts (*vigango*) returned from foreign collections, it's also notable in the relative ease with which you can pick up CDs of **traditional music**, especially in Mombasa: wonderful rhythms and some very delicate *chivoti* flute melodies.

If you're a little off the beaten track, are really interested and have time to spare, even casual enquiries will elicit invitations to **weddings** or **funerals**, where the old traditions – and music – are still very much the centrepieces, despite a veneer of Christianity or Islam. Many Mijikenda have found conversion to **Islam** helpful in their dealings with coastal traders and businessmen. The conversion seems to be the latest development in the growth of Swahili society, and that change is probably the biggest threat to Mijikenda cultural integrity.

successors thought necessary. Krapf worked out the grammar of the Swahili language and contributed a partial translation of the Bible (not published in full until 1890).

Ribe

RIBE (the main village of the Wa-Ribe Mijikenda) is more substantial than Rabai, but harder to get to. Some 7km northeast of Rabai, a road snakes up to the right from the deep valley floor: Ribe village – a few small shops and a basic bar-restaurant – is 1.5km along here.

Ribe cemetery

Fifteen minutes' walk from Ribe centre, through the *shambas* and dense undergrowth, is a tiny **cemetery**, regularly cleared of weeds and creepers, near the site of Ribe's Methodist mission, itself crumbled to its foundations and now completely overgrown. It isn't hard to find, and it's worth visiting if only to take a look at the pathetic graves of those few **missionaries** who struggled all the way here before succumbing in what must have been nearly impossible conditions. They were often very young: the Reverend Butterworth, whose carpentry skills ensured him a welcome arrival, died aged 23, just two months after coming ashore; they used his new tools to make the coffin. It isn't surprising that the cemetery faces out to sea: towards Mombasa, supplies, the mail and new settlers.

Kaloleni

The paved road from Mazeras comes to its end at **KALOLENI**. On the way, you pass through dense coconut groves where many of the trees have been initialled to avoid ownership disputes. The tapping of **palm wine** (*mnazi*), banned by the government, is still widely practised here, with the **Giriama** section of the Mijikenda leading the field. They call palm wine "the mother of the coconut", since tapping the trees for juice hinders formation of the nuts.

Tapping is done by cutting off the flower stem, binding it tightly and allowing the sap that would have produced new coconuts to collect in a container – usually a baobab pod – tied to the end. Here it ferments rapidly and has to be regularly collected. Variations in the local demand for *mnazi*, which is most often drunk at community gatherings like weddings and funerals, and in the coastal market for *copra* (the dried coconut flesh used in soap and oil manufacture), tend to influence the owners of trees in their decision whether to tap or to grow *copra*. You will see trees incised with step-notches (enabling the tapper to reach the top), that end several metres below the crown, indicating that a tree has been left for several years to develop coconuts.

Although, strictly speaking, illegal, **palm wine** is locally available up and down the coast. In Kaloleni, it usually comes in plastic mineral-water bottles, and costs about Ksh100 a litre. You drink it (discreetly) through a reed straw with a coconut-fibre filter.

ARRIVAL AND DEPARTURE
INLAND FROM MOMBASA

By bus and matatu There are frequent buses and matatus from Mombasa to Kaloleni via Rabai (from the Jomo Kenyatta/Mwembe Tayari junction) which makes this an easy day-trip away from the coast. If you arrive in Kaloleni before mid-afternoon, you'll be able to catch a matatu further north to Kilifi, and from there back to Mombasa or onwards to Malindi. Leaving Kaloleni, there are frequent buses and matatus back to Mombasa via Rabai and Mazeras, or to Mariakani, for Nairobi, and less frequent matatus north to Kilifi, 40km away (catch these at the bottom of the hill by the Kilifi junction).

By car and bike Note that there's only irregular fuel in Kaloleni, so fill up in Mombasa or Mariakani. The road from Kaloleni to Kilifi is particularly memorable for its scenes of local life in the coconut groves and forests – it's a great route to drive (see p.328) or cycle along, though sometimes difficult after heavy rain.

The South Coast

South of Mombasa, a continuous strip of beach runs between Likoni and Msambweni, backed by palms and broken once or twice by small rivers. Along the whole coast south from Mombasa to the Tanzanian border, there's just one highly developed resort area, **Diani Beach**. South of Diani, the coast is little known and, in most tour operators' minds at least, nobody stops again until they reach **Shimoni**. This is great news if you have the time to go searching out untrodden beaches. With your own vehicle, or on an organized trip, you can also visit the **Shimba Hills National Park** and the neighbouring **Mwaluganje Elephant Sanctuary**, either overnight or on an easy day-trip excursion.

Likoni and Ngombeni

The fact that you have to take the **Likoni ferry** (see p.400) to get to the south coast emphasizes its separation from Mombasa, and the queues and usual delays have tended to deter hotel developers a little. **LIKONI** itself is a busy suburb of Mombasa, straggling down the southbound road for nearly 5km. A coast road, served by

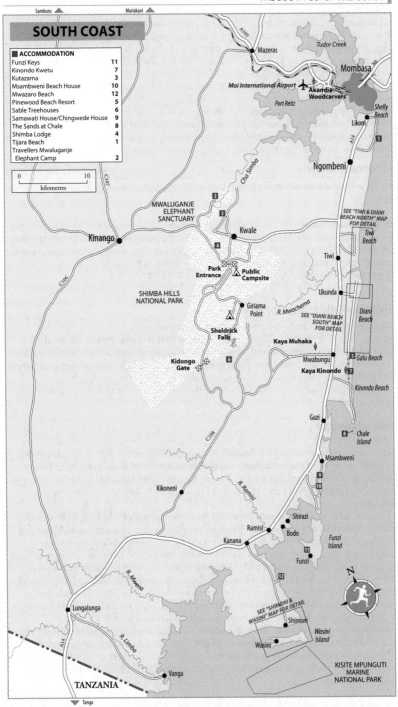

SOUTH COAST

ACCOMMODATION

Funzi Keys	11
Kinondo Kwetu	7
Kutazama	3
Msambweni Beach House	10
Mwazaro Beach	12
Pinewood Beach Resort	5
Sable Treehouses	6
Samawati House/Chingwede House	9
The Sands at Chale	8
Shimba Lodge	4
Tijara Beach	1
Travellers Mwaluganje Elephant Camp	2

0   10
kilometres

Samburu   Mariakani

Mazeras

Tudor Creek

Mombasa

A109

Moi International Airport   Akamba Woodcarvers

Port Reitz

Shelly Beach

C107

Likoni

Ngombeni

A14

Cha Simba

MWALUGANJE ELEPHANT SANCTUARY

SEE "TIWI & DIANI BEACH NORTH" FOR DETAIL

Kwale

Tiwi Beach

Kinango

Tiwi

Park Entrance   Public Campsite

Ukunda

SHIMBA HILLS NATIONAL PARK

R. Mwachema

Diani Beach

C106

Giriama Point

SEE "DIANI BEACH SOUTH" MAP FOR DETAIL

Kaya Muhaka

Sheldrick Falls

Galu Beach

Kidongo Gate

Kaya Kinondo

Mwabungu

Kinondo Beach

C108

Gazi

Chale Island

Msambweni

Kikoneni

R. Ramisi

Shirazi

Ramisi   Bodo

Funzi Island

Kanana

Funzi

Lungalunga

R. Mwena

R. Limba

SEE "SHIMONI & WASINI MAP FOR DETAIL

N

A14

Shimoni

Wasini Island

TANZANIA

Wasini

KISITE MPUNGUTI MARINE NATIONAL PARK

Tanga

6

infrequent matatus, runs around the creek mouth to the east (see "Mombasa Island" map, p.392), to **Shelly Beach**, facing the ocean. Named for its shells and once a popular local resort area, the beach is narrow and the sea here only feasible for swimming at high tide. With the closure of the big *Shelly Beach Hotel*, all the local alternatives have also closed.

A little further south, as you leave the outskirts of Likoni, a turning to the east down to the ocean at the straggling village of **Ngombeni** is the first of several sidetracks off the highway that enable people with their own vehicles to find private coves and beaches, many of them backed by patches of coastal forest. You need a 4WD vehicle and an adventurous spirit – and possibly GPS. It's surprising how uninhabited the immediate coastline is, and how many unspoilt beaches are waiting to be discovered.

ACCOMMODATION   LIKONI AND NGOMBENI

There is no resort development between Mombasa and Tiwi Beach, but private homes are popping up in one or two spots.

★**Tijara Beach Pungu** East of Ngomeni (5.5km from the Likoni ferry ramp, then 3km towards the sea) ☏020 2057701 or 0722 701701, ⓦtijarabeach .com. Idyllically located coastal hideaway, conveniently close to Mombasa but completely secluded and private, consisting of four, well-spaced, luxury cottages (fans, nets, sea breezes but no a/c), set in gardens around a shady pool. The virtually private beach, excellent snorkelling, birdlife and coral caves are a bonus. Free wi-fi. AI **$740**

Shimba Hills National Park

Daily 6.30am–6.30pm • $20 (see p.72) • ⓦkws.go.ke/shimba.html • 310 square kilometres

Kenya's most underrated wildlife refuge, **Shimba Hills National Park** is less than an hour's drive from Mombasa and, at 400m above sea level, wonderfully refreshing after the humidity on the coast (take some warm clothes). The hilly park of scattered jungle and grassland is comparatively little visited, which is all to the good. It has a wonderful game-viewing lodge and one of the best-situated camping and *banda* sites in the country.

Around the park

Although the park is famous for its thick **forest**, one of the easiest places to experience the forest is at *Shimba Lodge* (see opposite), rather than on a game drive. You can see most of the **primates** from the lodge, too – colobus, Sykes' and vervet monkeys, as well as bushbabies and greater galagos – and **leopards** range in the same area. Other predators are rare in Shimba Hills: the lions have gone, but you might see a **serval**.

You are likely to see **elephants**, especially from the vantage of Elephant Hill or at the nearby **Sheldrick Falls**, particularly if you go early in the day. There are armed guards at Elephant Hill who will escort you to the falls. It's a very pretty walk down a steep hillside, and then a partly wooded trail to the falls themselves, but quite a long hike back up again. Take drinking water, and swimming gear if you want to splash in the pool. Allow about three hours for the excursion. There were around six hundred elephants in Shimba until the translocation of half of them to Tsavo East in 2005. The remaining three hundred are still arguably more than Shimba can support: fortunately, the creation of the Mwaluganje Elephant Sanctuary (see p.426) has been a great success.

Buffalo are fairly common, as are **bushbuck** and several species of **duiker**. Look out also for the park's small herd of **Maasai giraffe**, the product of a tentative experiment. Although Shimba never had giraffe naturally, a few individuals were introduced in the 1990s, though the jury is still out on whether they can thrive here. **Ostriches** have also been introduced.

Shimba is best known for its indigenous herds of **sable antelope**, magnificent animals as big as horses, with great, sweeping horns. The park is their only habitat in Kenya. You may well see groups of chestnut-coloured females, but the territorial, jet-black males, for which the species is named, are more solitary and harder to find. If you have a guide he'll know where to look, but they're most commonly seen in the area overlooking the ocean, between the public campsite and Giriama Point.

ARRIVAL AND INFORMATION

SHIMBA HILLS NATIONAL PARK

6

Arrival and departure There are fairly frequent matatus to the small district capital of Kwale from the Likoni ferry dock, but no obvious way of visiting the park from there unless you're lucky with a lift. The park's main gate is 3km beyond Kwale, along the elephant-dunged *murram* road to Kigango. If you're driving, it's best to have a high-clearance 4WD to enter the park itself. You should get away with an ordinary car in dry weather, but some park roads may be too rough for it: the rangers at the gate will tell you. An adventurous alternative route, to the

park (or out of it) links Kwale with Shimoni via Kidongo Gate. For this you need GPS or a smartphone with Google Maps/Google Earth, and a high-clearance 4WD for the rocky crossing of the Ramisi River and several other tricky stretches.

Safaris The most straightforward option for visiting Shimba is on a safari from Mombasa or from the coast. Trips from most coast hotels and travel agents cost about $150 for a day-trip or $300 for an overnight trip including *Shimba Lodge* (see below).

ACCOMMODATION

Sable Valley Treehouses On the southeastern slopes below the park ☎0733 222420 and 0733 222428, ⓦadvantage-ea.com. A highly attractive place to stay in the Shimba Hills, offering very private, elevated rooms (just two among the trees), with your own staff, in a superb location. Package $668

★ **Shimba Lodge** ☎0722 200952 or 0722 207763, ⓦaberdaresafarihotels.com. One of the best things about the Shimba Hills, *Shimba*, like *Treetops* (see p.191), is a "tree-hotel", though superior in all respects to the original. Although the standard rooms, with nets, and shared showers and toilets, are very basic for a lodge, when there are bushbabies on the branch outside, a fish eagle in the trees opposite, and monitor lizards hunting by the lake below, you don't spare too much thought for luxuries. The best feature is the tree-level walkway, which runs for 100m to a platform high above

a small clearing where elephants often visit. After dark, spotlights illuminate bushbabies, hundreds of bats and a whirling hailstorm of jungle insects. It's a memorable evening – and the food is usually good. No children under 7. FB $400

Shimba Hills National Park Campsites The main public campsite of four in the park is located at one of the best vantage points in the park, about 3km from the main gate. The four, twin-bedded *bandas* here, *Sable Bandas* (☎0726 610508, ⓔreservations@kws.go.ke), are adequate, though the bedding, lamps, shower and nearby toilet are unreliable, and you need to treat the water. The setting, however, is sublime: a thickly forested bluff hundreds of metres above the coconut-crowded coastal plain. It's well worth spending the night up here just for the sunrise. Camping per person $15, twin *banda* $70

Kinango

Small and compact, with a couple of streets converging on a crossroads, Kinango is west of the Shimba Hills, some 52km on reasonably good *murram* from the Mombasa highway pit stop of Samburu (see p.328), a trip that takes about one-and-a-half hours in a 4WD vehicle. Kinango is an hour's drive from Kwale.

EATING AND DRINKING

KINANGO

Joymax Café On the Mariakani road, 200m from the central junction. A wholesome and extremely cheap *hoteli*

(*sima na sukuma*, Ksh45), with fine 360-degree murals and an English-speaking manageress. Daily 7am–10pm.

Kwale

Kwale is the capital of the district of the same name and quite a pleasant, bustling little hill town, with lots of shade and reasonable facilities, including ATMs and fuel.

6

THE DIGO

Most of the people who live along the southern coastal strip here are **Digo**, and their neat rectangular houses, made of dried mud and coral on a framework of wood, are a distinctive part of the lush roadside scene. Digo women tend to dress very colourfully in multiple kangas. Although they belong to the Mijikenda group of peoples, the Digo are unusual in traditionally having **matrilineal inheritance**: in other words they traced descent through the female line, so that a man would, on his death, pass his property on to his sister's sons rather than his own. It is an unusual system with interesting implications for the state of the family and the position of women. However, the joint assault of Islamic and European values over the last century has shifted the emphasis back towards the male line, and in many ways, women in modern Digo society have less freedom and autonomy than they had a hundred years ago. The site of one of the Digo's ancestral villages, a sacred forest at Kaya Kinondo, near Diani Beach, can be visited with a Digo guide (see p.433).

ARRIVAL AND DEPARTURE   KWALE

By bus and matatu There are matatus all day to Likoni (Ksh80) and Kombani (the junction for Tiwi and Ukunda; Ksh50). Occasionally matatus go to Kinango and from there to Mariakani and Samburu on the Mombasa-Nairobi highway. If you're driving, allow a good hour between Kinango and Kwale, especially after rain.

ACCOMMODATION

★ **Kutazama** On the Goloni ridge 6km north of Kwale ☎0723 4023433 or 0733 708309, ⊛kutazama.com. This owner-managed boutique lodge is a stunning place to stay, blending with the landscape and full of tribal artefacts. It has just two, very luxurious and secluded, guest villas, each with a deck and spa pool. Stunning views, walks in the area and a split-level infinity pool overlooking a great loop of the Cha Shimba River make this a perfect honeymoon hideaway. Package $850

★ **Kwale Golden Guesthouse** Town centre, on the north side of the tarmac ☎0722 326758. The best option in Kwale town, offering very clean, s/c rooms, with nets and ceiling fans (smaller rooms with no fans are a little cheaper). The breakfast included is a motel-style affair. BB Ksh2600

Mwaluganje Elephant Sanctuary

Northwest of Shimba Hills National Park; the main gate is beyond the Shimba Hills park entrance, 14km west of Kwale, then 2km along a signposted track to the right • $30 • ☎0722 343050

Mwaluganje Elephant Sanctuary, situated on the slopes of the privately owned Goloni Escarpment, is a remarkable success story of community ecotourism, created in 1995 to defuse conflict between the local Duruma farmers and the district's elephants, which had made a habit of trashing crops and killing farmers. After consultation between the local people, KWS and the Eden Wildlife Trust, 240 square kilometres were set aside for the sanctuary, separated along a third of its boundary from farmland with electric fencing, but with a corridor left open to Shimba Hills to keep the elephants' migration route open. The low-lying areas around the Manolo River are dominated by baobab, while thick brachystegia forest covers the escarpment's flanks, and harbours one of the densest concentrations of elephants in Africa. You're guaranteed to see elephants, and, in time, it's hoped that threatened species can be relocated here from other parts of Kenya. Other mammals are thin on the ground, but there's prolific birdlife.

ARRIVAL AND DEPARTURE   MWALUGANJE ELEPHANT SANCTUARY

You can get here on an organized tour with Travellers Beach Hotel in Bamburi (☎041 5485121) or with your own transport, enabling you to drive around the sanctuary.

ACCOMMODATION

Travellers Mwaluganje Elephant Camp Reservations through Travellers Beach Hotel in Bamburi ☎041 5485121, ⊛travellersbeach.com. Set along the shoulder of a low hill, facing a well-established elephant trail and waterhole, offering twenty twin-bedded tents under thatched roofs, each with bathrooms and electricity. It's not fancy, but the experience is fun. FB $220

Tiwi Beach

The first real magnet on the coast south of Mombasa is **Tiwi Beach**, which lies a couple of kilometres to the east of the main road. Popular among budget travellers having a bit of a splurge, Tiwi rates as genuine tropical paradise material and attracts lots of Kenya resident families down from Nairobi. The reef lies just offshore, and there are good snorkelling opportunities at high tide, especially at the northern end. With the exception of the large *Amani Tiwi Beach Resort* at its southern end, Tiwi is still cottage territory, with a handful of plots vying for business. The main drawbacks (though you might think they're advantages) are the relative isolation of the beach from Mombasa and Diani, and the lack of restaurants and bars outside the cottages and guesthouses. The clear pluses are fewer tourists and fewer beach boys. In the dry season, you can walk to the south end of Tiwi Beach and wade across the Mwachema River to Diani Beach and the strange Kongo Mosque, right next to the *Indian Ocean Beach Resort*.

ARRIVAL AND DEPARTURE
TIWI BEACH

Access roads If you're driving, there are two access roads down to Tiwi Beach from the main South Coast highway. The northern road (signposted for *Sand Island* and *Maweni & Capricho*) is a narrow sandy track some 17km from the Likoni ferry; the second, about 1.5km further south, has a bigger clump of signboards and is much wider. If you've been dropped at either junction by matatu, you're strongly advised not to walk, especially if you have luggage with you: the roads through the cashew woods have seen a number of robberies over the years. Waiting for a ride won't be a huge problem, certainly on the southern access road, where you should get a taxi (Ksh500) and can easily pick up a *piki-piki* (Ksh200–300). Alternatively, most of the beach properties will happily pick you up for free from the main road if you contact them in advance.

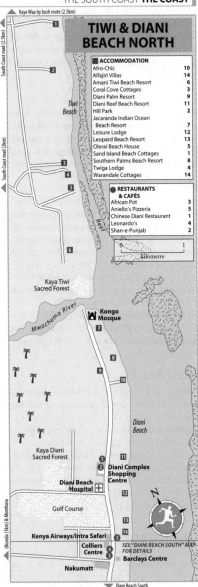

TIWI & DIANI BEACH NORTH

■ ACCOMMODATION

Afro-Chic	10
Alfajiri Villas	14
Amani Tiwi Beach Resort	6
Coral Cove Cottages	3
Diani Palm Resort	9
Diani Reef Beach Resort	11
Hill Park	2
Jacaranda Indian Ocean Beach Resort	7
Leisure Lodge	12
Leopard Beach Resort	13
Olerai Beach House	5
Sand Island Beach Cottages	1
Southern Palms Beach Resort	8
Twiga Lodge	4
Warandale Cottages	14

● RESTAURANTS & CAFÉS

African Pot	3
Aniello's Pizzeria	5
Chinese Diani Restaurant	1
Leonardo's	4
Shan-e-Punjab	2

ACCOMMODATION, EATING AND DRINKING

Seasons on Tiwi tend to reflect the school holidays of the regular, Kenya resident clients of most of the properties: at Christmas and Easter, and in July and August, advance booking is a very good idea. There isn't much in the real budget range, but the extra expense is well worth it if you choose carefully. It's tricky to stay in a self-catering cottage without your own vehicle, though some people manage on fruit and fish from vendors and the occasional lift to the shops. Self-catering cottages usually offer the services of a cook/housekeeper for Ksh800–1000/day.

6

Amani Tiwi Beach Resort Tiwi Beach ⓦamani tiwibeachresort.com. The beach's only large, tourist hotel, with more than 200 rooms and one of the longest pools in Kenya. It burned down in 2009 and reopened at the end of 2012. HB $\overline{\$180}$

★ **Coral Cove Cottages** Tiwi Beach ☎0722 732797, ⓦcoralcove.tiwibeach.com. Large, stand-alone cottages with good bathrooms and an attractive, palm-shaded beach, all bathed in a laidback mood provided by low-key but consistently helpful management. Dogs and cats, rescue parrots and a troop of vervet monkeys are all part of the atmosphere. The sea here is shallow, good for children, and favoured by egg-laying turtles. **Ksh5800**

Hill Park Tiwi Beach Tiwi Beach ☎040 3300012 or ☎0722 328365, ⓦhillparktiwibeach.com. The former *Maweni Beach, Capricho* and *Moonlight Bay* properties, amalgamated under a single management, include self-catering cottages and hotel rooms, a restaurant and a good pool and pool bar. *Maweni* has a variety of cottages with stunning sea views in beautiful gardens roamed by dik-diks; *Capricho* is slightly pricier, with well-designed vault-roofed cottages and plenty of cool space; and *Moonlight Bay* has four cottages and a restaurant. $\overline{\$110}$

★ **Olerai Beach House** Tiwi Beach ☎0707 705073 or 0722 512476, ⓦoffbeatsafaris.com. Delightful, very spacious family beach house with excellent staff, superb swimming pool and rock water slide, gardens, coral cave area for shady table-tennis sessions, and a virtually deserted beach front. Sleeps 8–12, either on self-catering basis, or all-inclusive with exceptionally good meals. Whole house self-catering $\overline{\$500}$, AI $\overline{\$600}$

★ **Sand Island Beach Cottages** Tiwi Beach ☎0722 395005, ⓦsandislandbeach.com. Well maintained if fairly rustic – though being seriously revamped by new managers – the six self-catering cottages at this former family home are all sea-facing. The long-established, shady site is very attractive, with the sand island exposed at low tide just metres across the lagoon, and safe swimming possible at all states of the tide. The ruins of old slave quarters stand in the grounds. Free wi-fi. $\overline{\$100}$

Twiga Lodge Tiwi Beach ☎040 3205126 or 0721 577614. Lively, secure and good value, this hostel and campsite trades on a reputation established in the 1970s, and is perennially popular with budget travellers and overlanders with their own vehicles. The budget rooms are simple but good-value (some have verandas), and the superior rooms, which cost twice as much, are big, bright and airy. You can also camp. There's a provisions shop; the bar-restaurant does decent meals from 8am–9pm; and the bar stays open as late as the last customer. Camping **Ksh300**, double **Ksh3000**

Diani Beach

Diani Beach ought to fulfil most dreams about the archetypal palm-fringed beach. The sand is soft and brilliantly white; the sea is turquoise and usually crystal-clear; the reef is a safe thirty-minute swim or a ten-minute boat ride away; and, arching overhead, the coconut palms create pools of cool shade and keep up a perpetual slow sway as the breeze rustles through their fronds. While competition for space always threatens to mar Diani's paradisal qualities, the 2008 downturn in tourism knocked out some of the hotels, while the droves of hustlers, or "beach boys", dwindled to a few relatively easily brushed-off diehards. Security has been tightened up, with *askaris* posted all the way along the beach outside every property, and tight security at hotel entrances.

BEACH BOYS AND SAFETY

Spending some peaceful time on the beach can sometimes seem virtually impossible because of the **hustlers** plying their wares, their camel rides, their boat trips, or just themselves. Fortunately, the problem has abated in recent years, but a few beach-boy pesterers, in theory all licensed in some way, still hang on. People have different ways of dealing with them. Ignoring their greetings is considered rude, and may well not deter them. One solution is to strike up a friendship of sorts with one beach boy, to buy at least something, or to go on a boat trip. Once you have a friend, and have done some business, you should find you can then use the beach with fewer hassles from the others. It's not so easy for single women, but the principle for most situations still applies – don't fight it. There is no need, incidentally, to feel physically threatened on the beach. Every hotel has its *askaris* (security guards) posted along the boundary between the hotel plot and the beach, and they usually stay alert to the slightest sign of trouble – which is rare indeed.

Running 300m behind the beach and separated from it by bush, the **Diani Beach road** feels – in the high season – like Kenya's number-one strip. Fortunately, forest and scrubby bush separate the road from the shore, although more of the **Diani Forest** disappears every year as one new plot after another is cleared.

Along Diani Beach

Enjoying yourself on Diani isn't difficult and there are plenty of activities on offer (see p.438). As on other beaches in Kenya, all of Diani Beach is open to the public, and there are **access paths**, some signposted, between many of the hotels: if you can't find one, you can always access the beach by visiting one of the hotels. If you're doing something that depends on having enough beach (football or volleyball) or sufficient sea depth (wind- or kitesurfing, or snorkelling in the lagoon), it's worth checking the **tides** (see p.387), as the lagoon often drops to ankle depth at low tide, while at high tide all but a thin strip of the beach is generally under water.

If you're on Diani Beach in early June, look out for the local community fundraiser, **Diani Rules** (ⓦdianirules.com), which you're liable to get roped into. From goat races to dhow races, Frisbee tournaments to volleyball, it's all grist to the mill and part of a three-day party that generally swirls around *Forty Thieves* beach bar and one or other of the hotels, usually raising money for Kwale District Eye Centre.

Kongo Mosque

At the far north end of the beach, at the mouth of the Mwachema River; it's most easily reached through the grounds of the Indian Ocean Beach Resort

For a short cultural excursion, visit the **Kongo Mosque**. Surrounded by venerable baobabs, the mosque sits beyond the *Indian Ocean Beach Resort*'s boundary fence and the inevitable *askari*. Also known as Diani Persian Mosque, the building is

DIANI BEACH SOUTH

● SHOPS	
KFI Supermarket	3
Shan-e-Punjab	
Supermarket	2
Shreegreeng	1

■ ACCOMMODATION	
Asha Cottage	7
Baobab Beach Resort	14
Chill at Sunset	22
Diani Campsite/	
Diani Backpackers	3
Diani Marine Village	10
Diani Sea Lodge	11
Diani Sea Resort	5
Flamboyant	8
Forest Dream Cottages	15
Kenyaways Kite Village	17
Kinondo Kwetu	20
LTI-Kaskazi Beach	2
Neptune Paradise	
Beach Resort	18
Neptune Palm Beach	19
Papillon Lagoon Reef	13
Pinewood Beach Resort	21
South Coast Backpackers	16
Stilts	9
Swahili Beach Hotel	1
The Sands at Nomad	12
Water Lovers	6
Wayside Beach	
Apartments	4

● RESTAURANTS & CAFÉS	
Ali Barbour's	
Cave Restaurant	8
Al Manara "Sails"	
Beach Bar & Restaurant	16
Aniello's Why Not	6
BBII	10
Café Wahnsinn	1
Chill at Sunset	17
Colobus Shade	14
Forty Thieves	
Beach Bar & Restaurant	7
Love Bakery	3
Lymingtons Bistro	4
Mr T Roof Garden	
Bar & Restaurant	18
Mwaepe Fisherman's	
Restaurant	13
Nomads Beach Bar &	
Red Pepper	12
Stilts	9
Sundowner	15
Tandoori Bay	11
Winds	5
Yibba Yabba	2

■ BARS & CLUBS	
Full Moon	1
Kim4Love	3
Shakatak	2

DIVING ON THE SOUTH COAST

Many hotels have **dive centres**, where you can do everything from a basic beginner lesson plus assisted dive (around €100) to a full course giving you an internationally recognized PADI qualification (€480 for the Open Water Diver). Before choosing a centre, take time to compare their equipment, and ask them about their environmental policy, safety procedures and general experience. They should at the very least have up-to-date PADI accreditation, and ideally be affiliated to Scuba Schools International (SSI). One of the oldest and best-established outfits, with an excellent reputation and good equipment, is **Diving the Crab** (☎0723 108108, ⓦdivingthecrab.com), who have several dive bases on Diani Beach. **Diani Marine**, who run the *Diani Marine Village*, also have an excellent reputation.

If you already have scuba certification, single dives cost around €75. If you're a complete novice, you can often take a free dip in the pool wearing diving equipment, to test your affinity – most people find breathing underwater curiously addictive. If you're qualified, but haven't dived for a while, you should take a pool check at one of the hotels' PADI schools, which is usually free of charge, before going out to sea.

enigmatic and disconcerting, the barrel-vaulted mosque with its five heavy wooden doors brooding like a huge tomb under the trees. Named after the former forest of the area, the mosque is thought to be the one remaining building – maybe the only stone one – of a Wa-Shirazi settlement here (see p.440) that grew up in the fourteenth or fifteenth century around the first safe anchorage south of Mombasa. If you want to have a close look, take photos, or even have a chance of going inside if you're suitably dressed, you should first introduce yourself to one of the elders who are usually sitting nearby. A small "donation for the upkeep of the mosque" is expected.

Diani Forest

For a walk, or a jog, head south along the Diani Beach road, which has more shade than the northern stretch. Towards the end of the tarmac surface are some wonderful patches of jungle, comprising the dwindling **Jadini** or more correctly **Diani Forest** ("Jadini", disappointingly, turns out to be an embellished acronym made from the initials of members of a white settler family who once owned most of the land around here). There's the almost obligatory snake park, but if you'd like to search for some animals in the wild rather than support this venture, then several of the tracks leading off inland will take you straight into magnificent areas of hardwood forest, alive with birds and butterflies, and rocking with vervet and colobus monkeys. The most impressive stands of forest are the isolated *kayas*, or **sacred groves**, of which there are at least three along the Diani Beach road: **Kaya Diani**, on the north side of the Leisure Lodge golf course (easy to drive or walk to the edge of the forest, and several trees have plaques proclaiming the grove's status); **Kaya Ukunda**, west of the entrance to *Diani Sea Lodge*; and **Kaya Kinondo**, south of *Pinewood Beach Resort*. Kinondo is the first *kaya* to be officially opened to visitors (see p.433).

The Colobus Trust

Colobus Cottage 6.8km south of Nakumatt • Mon–Sat 8am–5pm • Ksh500, under-12s free • ☎0711 479453, ⓦcolobustrust.org

Diani's **Angolan colobus monkeys**, whose population is estimated at around 1500, have come in for special attention since the early 1990s, as concern has mounted over land encroachment and deaths from speeding cars. The resultant campaign, spearheaded by the Wakuluzu Colobus Trust, has put up warning signs, speed bumps and ingenious wire, rope and wood "colobobridges" at known danger spots over the road, which the monkeys quickly learned to use. You can pick up more information at **Colobus Cottage** and learn about the Colobus Trust's active campaigns to halt illegal tree-felling by local hotel owners. If you have time and flexibility, they welcome volunteers here.

6

DIANI WILDLIFE

If you're a **birdwatcher**, Diani's hotel gardens offer spectacular entertainment, though the status of the Diani forest's threatened species is uncertain. Look out for southern banded snake-eagle, spotted ground-thrush, plain-backed sunbird and Fischer's turaco, all of which have been seen here, though the spotted ground-thrush not since the 1980s.

You're unlikely to come across **snakes**. Whether harmless green tree snakes, egg-eating snakes or pythons (the commonest species), or more rarely venomous mambas, those that get anywhere near the hotels tend to be bludgeoned to death by enthusiastic *askaris* who also use their sling shots to keep the local monkeys on the run.

The Diani Beach forest used to be the haunt of **leopards**, but they haven't been seen in this part of the coast for decades now. Venture into the woods at night, however, preferably with a guide, and you will see eyes in the dark – usually those of **bushbabies**.

The most iconic of Diani's wildlife are its rare Angolan colobus monkeys (see p.40). Of the other monkeys, **baboons** are most common, and can be quite aggressive. Their adopted diet of hotel leftovers means they've multiplied greatly, and are not afraid of humans, so keep your distance. Overly tame **Sykes' monkeys** are also becoming a nuisance: don't leave things on your hotel balcony.

ARRIVAL AND DEPARTURE
DIANI BEACH

By public transport If you're coming to Diani by public transport from Mombasa, first take the Likoni ferry and then catch a matatu for Diani Beach. If there are no direct matatus, get one to Ukunda (see p.439), and then take a connection down to the beach road.

By taxi From Mombasa, taxis cost around Ksh3500 to Ksh5000, depending on your final destination.

By plane Ukunda (Diani Beach) airstrip is right in the thick of things, less than ten minutes' drive from most hotels along the beach (just west of the beach road, 1.5km south of the junction). Taxis are always waiting (estimate a minimum

fare of Ksh500m and allow a total fare of Ksh150/km for more than 3km), but most hotels will include a free transfer if you've booked a room. There are daily flights to Nairobi with SafariLink (ⓦsafarilink-kenya.com) and Airkenya (ⓦairkenya.com) for $166 one way, $276 return , and to Tsavo West and Amboseli with Mombasa Air Safari (ⓦmombasaairsafari.com; $315 one way, $420 return); MAS also offers connections to Mombasa for its thrice-weekly services to Malindi ($67) and Lamu ($107). Fly540 are based 600m south of Nakumatt (☏0732 540559), while Kenya Airways are c/o Intra Safaris (see p.439).

GETTING AROUND

Car rental Try Glory Car Hire, Diani Beach Shopping Centre (☏0734 437536, ⓦgloryenya.com); Ketty Tours, Petro filling station (☏040 3203582, ⓦkettysafari.com), or Cool Auto Car Hire, in the parade of shops and offices south of Café Wahnsinn (☏0722 212558), which advertises vehicles

from under Ksh2000/day.

Taxis Most hotels have taxis in their forecourts, and there's a stand opposite Barclays Bank. Also, try Diani Beach Shopping Centre, where the chairman of the taxi drivers' association is based.

INFORMATION AND SERVICES

Diani has one or two good **tour operators and safari agents**, together with an increasingly heavy scattering of **shops** – including a big new Nakumatt supermarket, a Barclays Bank, plus several other **ATMs**, a **post office** and several **cybercafés** (see p.438).

ACCOMMODATION

Although there are some good **hotels** north of the Ukunda junction, the much longer beachfront to the south retains some flicker of the pre-hotel era, and this is where most of the remaining forest is. To the north, the scene is brasher and more despoiled. Some all-inclusives are open to casual visitors: you'll pay from Ksh1500 to Ksh2000 for a daytime wrist band, including lunch and all drinks and normal activities, and around Ksh2000 to Ksh3000 for the evening equivalent. **Budget accommodation** along the beach is sparse, although there are one or two places to camp. If you're with your family or in a group, renting a cottage is invariably better-value than taking hotel rooms, and gives you the chance to cook local food – or have it cooked for you. If you're self-catering, most places are regularly visited by fruit and fish vendors and someone to cook and look after the house or apartment for you is usually available for an additional Ksh1000 or so per day. The distances in the following listings are from the Ukunda junction on the Diani Beach road, next to Nakumatt.

CAMPING AND BUDGET ROOMS

Diani Campsite/Diani Backpackers 1.4km south ☎0716 234181, ⊛dianicampsite.com; map p.429. Once something of an institution when it was *Dan Trench's* (Trench was the elderly character who opened up Diani Beach in the 1960s), this site fell on hard times, but its new incarnation is a popular standby, with self-catering cottages, most with kitchens and nets, plus a pool and the busy *Winds* bar-restaurant. Campers can use cooking facilities. Camping with own tent Ksh400, camping with site tent with bed per person Ksh650, self-catering cottage Ksh3000

★ **South Coast Backpackers** 6.4km south of Nakumatt, then 500m inland ☎0715 629659 or 0715 614038, ⊛southcoastbackpackers.net; map p.429. The newest backpackers on the coast, this full-on party place occupies a surprisingly luxurious villa, with tropical gardens, a fine pool and plenty of fellow travellers to share the bar and restaurant. Camping Ksh650 per person, dorm bed Ksh1000, room only Ksh2500

★ **Stilts** 3km south, opposite Ali Barbour's Cave restaurant ☎0722 523278, ⊛stiltsdiani.com; map p.429. Just over the road from the beach, but right in the bush, with five non-s/c *bandas* on stilts, two s/c cottages with nets and fans, well-shaded pitches for camping, plenty of wildlife and a good bar-restaurant. Solar lighting in rooms and no electric sockets except in cottages – charge your batteries at the bar where there's also a personal safe for each guest. Camping Ksh300, treehouse Ksh2800, cottage Ksh3600

Wayside Beach Apartments 1.4km south, between the main road and the defunct Trade Winds hotel ☎0722 820913 or 0722 211133, ⊛kenyaurlaub .com; map p.429. Mediterranean-style, German-owned two- to six-bed self-catering apartments in a building around a good pool and bar-restaurant (breakast Ksh400), but not right on the beach. Ksh4500

HOTELS AND COTTAGES NORTH OF THE JUNCTION

AfroChic 2.3km north ☎0733 645564, ⊛elewana collection.com; map p.427. A large, Mediterranean-style house, with just ten cool and spacious rooms with balconies, each differently styled. While it's undoubtedly more chic than Afro, this is a comfortable, personable place to stay with top attention to detail and first-class food – as you'd expect at this price. It suits many honeymooners making a first trip to Kenya. Room safes, tea & coffee, DSTV, DVDs, free wi-fi. FB $680

Diani Reef Beach Resort 1.5km north ☎040 3202723 or 0733 682660, ⊛dianireef.com; map p.427. Built in the 1970s and revamped in 2005, complete with under-lobby aquarium, this is one of the largest hotels on the coast, on a steep stretch of beach, with three restaurants, five bars, and 143 rooms, all cool and comfortable, but with little to distinguish them but the size of their balconies. The two pools may not be the largest on the coast, but facilities are good, and include all watersports, a diving school, the *Evanes* casino, *Sins nightclub* and *Maya* spa. HB $245

Diani Palm Resort 2.4km north ☎040 3202523, ⊛dianipalmhotel.com; map p.427. Although on the landward side of the road, the beach is just 400m away, and

6

VISITING KAYA KINONDO

Kenya's first *kaya* or **Mijikenda sacred forest** (see box, p.449) to open to visitors is the Digo tribe's **Kaya Kinondo** (Mon–Sat 8am–5pm; Ksh1000; ☎0722 446916, ⊛kaya-kinondo-kenya .com), behind Kinondo Beach, at the southern end of Diani Beach. Kaya Kinondo was first inhabited by the Digo in 1560 and abandoned as a village site in 1880.

There's an interpretation centre by the entrance which is well worth spending fifteen minutes looking around before you set off on your forest walk. To enter the forest itself, you visit with a Digo guide from the centre (no independent wanderings allowed), wrapped in a *kaniki* (indigo-dyed calico sarong) that you will be loaned. Photography is encouraged (except at the grave sites near the centre), but you are expected to show deep respect for the impressive forest environment – which means no running around and no kissing and cuddling. Behave as if in a church or mosque and you won't go far wrong. As soon as you leave the sunlight and enter the cathedral-like gloom of the understorey, a hush tends to fall on proceedings, as you concentrate on stepping over the buttress roots of forest giants and avoiding contact with trailing creepers or ant-covered surfaces.

There's a more light-hearted side to the experience, in any case, as tree-hugging (transmit all your cares and fears to the tree) and stories of "herbal Viagra", aphrodisiac essences and cures for back pain in pregnant women are all part of the two-hour nature walk as you're accompanied, if you're lucky, by someone of seemingly limitless knowledge. The animals you'll see, apart from monkeys, are mostly smaller denizens of the undergrowth, but no less worth spying for that – fiery red squirrels, slow-flying shade-loving butterflies and giant millipedes and, possibly, an elephant shrew snuffling through the leaf litter with its probing proboscis.

6

this part-Swiss-managed hotel offers all the essentials, with less fuss and at far less expense than most of its neighbours. The 22 s/c rooms are fresh and clean (if a little basic), with nets, TV and fridge. There's a reasonably priced bar-restaurant and a good-sized pool. BB **Ksh5800**

Jacaranda Indian Ocean Beach Resort 3.4km north ☎0721 672111 or 0734 600922, ⊛jacarandahotels.com; map p.427. The northernmost property on Diani Beach, on a huge plot, opened in 1992 with – at the time – state-of-the-art, Lamu-style rooms. It still feels a little special, and is popular for weddings and honeymoons. The 100 rooms have cute, alcove bathrooms, fridges, safes and tea-making kits, and upstairs rooms incorporate balconies looking out across the baobab-studded gardens. The oceanfront rooms are worth the small supplement. On the down side, the pool is too shallow and rather exposed. HB **$420**

Leisure Lodge 1km north ☎041 2011131 or 0722 206968, ⊛leisurelodgeresort.com; map p.427. One of the earlier Diani hotels (1971) but slickly revamped, and in a striking location on low cliffs hollowed by bat-filled caves, above a fine, tree-shaded beach. Five pools soak up the guests from 170 rooms and there's a casino and an 18-hole golf course. Standard rooms lack sea views, but come with a/c, nets and DSTV. PADI diving school, windsurfing school and tennis. HB **$264**

Leopard Beach Resort 700m north ☎0733 202721 or 0724 255280, ⊛leopardbeachresort.com; map p.427. Once stylish, this big resort hotel, set in lush gardens with ponds and waterfalls, is still regularly updated. There's always a good atmosphere and generally decent food. Superior rooms and cottages have sea views, but overall the 158 rooms (plus new villas with private pools) vary a lot in standard. Steps lead down to the beach. One relatively modest pool. PADI diving school. HB **$265**

Southern Palms Beach Resort 2.7km north ☎040 3203721 or 0733 333366, ⊛southernpalmskenya.com; map p.427. Bright, welcoming package hotel, with a spring in its step. The average-sized rooms, with screened windows (no nets), TV, fridge and safe, are perhaps a bit blandly cosmopolitan (and top-floor rooms are a bit of a climb), but the overall, fun approach, with two enormous, 80m, freeform pools, four restaurants, five bars and a kids' club, makes it ideal for families. Windsurfing, floodlit tennis courts, squash, gym. HB **$250**

Warandale Cottages 600m north ☎0724 923585, ⊛warandale.com; map p.427. On the same plot as *Kijiji*, and sharing the pool, these six self-catering cottages are extremely pleasant, fresh and spacious. Three are sea-facing, others (cheaper) are set back among the trees, with the advantage of more likely bushbaby and monkey sightings. A daily cook/cleaner is included with each cottage. **Ksh7000**

HOTELS SOUTH OF THE JUNCTION

★ **Asha Cottage** 2km south ☎0723 644945 or 0727 624626, ⊛ashacottages.com; map p.429. Cool, light, airy, family-run, very private boutique guesthouse, right by the beach, with just five rooms with nets, fans and a/c, and water heated by solar panels. All have pool and sea views. They capture rainwater, separate and recycle all waste, and donate a percentage of income to community projects. Pool, and excellent seafood meals. No under-12s and normally no one-night stays. Wi-fi extra. HB **$240**

Baobab Beach Resort 5.9km south ☎020 2057093 or 0733 333303, ⊛baobab-beach-resort.com; map p.429. The 1970s *Robinson Club Baobab* is now an elegant and well-kept all-inclusive, part of the big TUI group, located at the southern end of Diani Beach on a coral rock promontory. With 239 rooms, including the 2008 *Maridadi* wing (much bigger rooms) and the separate *Kole Kole Resort* (south of the promontory), it's a busy place, on a sizeable plot – though sadly they have cleared much of the indigenous forest. It has a reputation for good food and is popular with Brits. Clients have access to all three parts of the resort. Diving the Crab PADI diving school. Eco-Tourism Kenya Bronze Award. *Kole Kole* closed April–June. AI **$250**

Chill at Sunset 12.4km south, on Kinondo Beach ☎0732 656225, ⊛chillatsunset.jimdo.com; map p.429. Relaxed and child-friendly German-Kenyan-run cottage-style hotel right on the beach, with safes, fridges and water dispensers in the rooms. It's far to the south of beach boy range, and has a popular beach bar and a good pool behind. BB **$180**

★ **Diani Marine Village** 3km south, right next to Forty Thieves ☎020 2650426 or 0707 629060, ⊛dianimarine.com; map p.429. A great-value dive base, and whether you're diving or not, the spacious rooms, with fans and nets (no a/c), a fine pool and pool snack bar, great breakfasts in the Kilimanjaro *banda* and free wi-fi make it well worth considering. They also have a number of self-catering villas. BB **$100**

Diani Sea Lodge 3.3km south ☎040 3203438 or 0711 387028, ⊛dianisea.com; map p.429. Large, German-owned, slightly downmarket, Mediterranean-style version of the jointly owned *Diani Sea Resort*. The rooms are a letdown: despite the good-sized double beds, a/c and frame-fitted nets, most are small, in bungalows set back in the gardens. Pool and children's pool, gym, tennis court, crazy golf, windsurfing and PADI diving school. Mainly German clientele. AI **$173**

Diani Sea Resort 1.9km south ☎040 3203438 or ☎0711 387028, ⊛dianisea.com; map p.429. Built in 1991 and much more cheerful than its sister hotel, with good service, nice staff and plenty of things to do. Again, most guests are German, many on long stays. Great pool, gym, tennis and squash courts, crazy golf, windsurfing and PADI diving school. AI **$200**

Flamboyant 2.8km south ☎040 3202033 or 0714 456130, ⓦdianibeachkenya.com; map p.429. Large family house, adapted as a stylish and comfortable hotel, sleeping twenty guests in a variety of a/c rooms with fans and nets. Free laundry and free wi-fi. There's a good pool, tennis and squash. Good for singles (no single supplement). BB $400

Forest Dream Cottages 5.5km south (and then 800m into the forest) ☎040 3300220 or 0714 293055, ⓦforestdream.com; map p.429. Funky, boutique "eco-resort" of makuti-roofed cottage rooms around communal lounge areas, set among the trees. While the rooms are fine, they're rather dark and don't have much style, but the whole place is enthusiastically well run and very committed to the protection of the Diani forest and its wildlife. Great for families. Solar water heating, nice pool, free bikes, tennis, volleyball and wi-fi. BB $145

Kenyaways Kite Village 7.5km south, on Galu Beach ☎0728 886821 or 0721 495876, ⓦthekenyaway .com; map p.429. A selection of nicely done, light, well-furnished rooms – including some larger and more deluxe ones – in and around this former family home, converted in 2008. The big thing here is kitesurfing (the h2O Extreme kite school is based here). There's a pool, and free wi-fi. Minimum 2 nights. BB $95

★ **Kinondo Kwetu** 12km south, on Kinondo beach ☎0710 251565 or 0710 898030, ⓦkinondo-kwetu .com; map p.429. Far south of Diani Beach proper, *Kinondo Kwetu* ("Our Home at Kinondo") mixes Scandinavian cool and Kenyan warmth in a beguiling combination, with lots of African art, sumptuous fabrics and dark wood, catering for a maximum of 38 guests. The breeze-cooled rooms, none of which locks (or needs to), have stylish, bright interiors; there's excellent cuisine, charming Swedish hosts, and almost nobody on the beach (though note the beach is narrow, the reef far out and the lagoon shallow at low tide). Free airport transfers, sauna, sports and non-motorized watersports, plus a PADI diving school and riding stables. Closed May & June. Al $1120

LTI-Kaskazi Beach 300m south ☎040 3203725 or 0715 400370, ⓦkaskazibeachhotel.com; map p.429. Well run and competitively priced, successfully balancing package-tour prices with a friendly atmosphere. While the rooms are ready for a refurb, the public areas are still stylish enough, decorated with Arabic motifs, white-tiled floors and tinkling fountains. There's also the sad little ruined seventeenth-century "Diani mosque" in the garden, which is basically just an old wall. HB $250

Neptune Paradise Beach Resort 8.5km south, on Galu Beach ☎040 3202350 or 040 3300046, ⓦneptunehotels.com; map p.429. Decent rooms in tightly packed rows of two-storey *bandas* (few with sea views), on a plot that requires lengthy, shadeless walks and has been extended seawards to the point where there is no

beach left at high tide. Reasonable facilities include two pools and a diving school. The co-owned *Neptune Palm Beach*, 200m to the south, is more luxurious. Al $250

Papillon Lagoon Reef 5.5km south ☎020 8092332 or ☎020 2331338, ⓦrexresorts.com; map p.429. Middle-market, mid-sized, mostly all-inclusive hotel, with 119 rooms and a good reputation for value-for-money stays, but inconsistent service and food. Rooms, of which 18 have sea views, are spacious, comfortable, with a/c and fans, useful safes (extra payment) and balconies. Free windsurfing and snorkelling for Al guests, and free diving demos available in the pleasant pool. Al $192

★ **Pinewood Beach Resort** 10.8km south, on Galu Beach ☎020 2080981 or 0723 957080, ⓦpinewood -village.com; map p.429. Well-managed, Mediterranean-style resort hotel on a quiet stretch of beach south of the main Diani strip, all set in pretty gardens. Take an ordinary room and eat in the restaurant, or a suite and get the services of your own chef thrown in. 58 rooms in cottages of two doubles upstairs and one suite downstairs, with great a/c, nets and safes. There's a good gym and the popular Aqualand watersports centre down on the beach. HB $247

★ **The Sands at Nomad** 4.8km south ☎040 3300269 or 0725 373888, ⓦthesandsatnomad.com; map p.429. Appealing hotel of cool, well-designed rooms and cottages (though standards and prices vary greatly: the nice sea-facing rooms and beach cottages are much more expensive) tucked among baobabs close to the shore, with 37 rooms and suites, and very personal service. There's a good beach bar and restaurant, the HQ of the Diving the Crab PADI diving school, a 5m-deep pool (good for dive training), and a kitesurfing school. Closed May & June. BB $225

Swahili Beach Hotel 100m south ☎020 2661708 or 0707 730753, ⓦswahilibeach.com; map p.429. This spectacular new resort development has 170 rooms – vaguely Mediterranean exteriors, Swahili chic interiors – in two-storey clusters around the landscaped grounds. The dauntingly austere lobby brings to mind an enormous mosque, while the cascading swimming pool – starting near reception and descending in seven tiers to the beach, embellished by fake rocks and imported palm trees – is pure Sun City. Opened in 2012, before it was finished, the jury is still out on service, food quality and attention to detail, but the rooms themselves are spacious and very comfortable. Huge spa, gym, HB $350

★ **Water Lovers Ocean View** 2.2km south ☎073 790535 or 0727 008840, ⓦwaterlovers.it; map p.429. Both friendly and trying to be eco-friendly, with six cottages and a villa, largely powered by solar panels, this boutique beach lodge lies in a coconut grove more or less on the seashore. The centrepiece is a small infinity pool above the sands. The Italian-slanted restaurant goes in for local produce and home cooking. BB $280

6

EATING AND DRINKING

The following listings, with distances given from the Ukunda junction, include some of the best, and best-value, places to eat. Finding food for **self-catering** is straightforward enough, with stalls along the beach road, fish and fruit vendors doing the rounds of most likely sites, and several supermarkets, including a new Nakumatt (see p.439).

RESTAURANTS AND CAFÉS

African Pot 300m north, ☎072 644707; map p.427. A pleasant bar serving cold beer and well-prepared Kenyan fare (kebabs Ksh200, avocado salad Ksh200, beef masala Ksh525, green banana in coconut sauce Ksh250), plus a pool table. Daily 7.30am–midnight.

★ **Ali Barbour's Cave Restaurant** 2.8km south ☎0714 456130, ⓦalibarbours.com; map p.429. Bizarrely built inside a 150,000-year-old coral cave, you enter the restaurant at ground level and descend a staircase. The lavish French and seafood menu (lobster bisque and chilli crab among the highlights) is well presented. Three courses from around Ksh3000. Daily 7–9.30pm.

Al Manara "Sails" Beach Bar and Restaurant 7.8km south ☎0716 863884; map p.429. Changing lunch menu of seafood or meat dishes, with starters around Ksh700 and mains from Ksh1200. Dinner is a huge, set menu, generally priced at Ksh1800–3000, depending on what's on it (call ahead). Daily lunch and dinner till late.

Aniello's Pizzeria Just south of Colliers Centre ☎0705 131156; map p.427. A reliable standby for wood-fired oven pizza (from Ksh450), pasta (around Ksh650) and meat and fish (from Ksh800). There's another branch of Aniello's – Aniello's Why Not; a snack bar with a shady terrace – pizzas, salads Ksh550, ice cream Ksh100/scoop – at Bahirini plaza (daily 7.30am–10.30pm). Daily 10am–11pm or later.

BBII 3.4km south (then 300m inland); map p.429. The place to come when you're tired of being a tourist, this is a nice local pub with outdoor tables, TV and a bar behind a cage in the approved fashion. Tuskers Ksh120, sodas Ksh40. Daily early to late.

Café Wahnsinn 600m south of Nakumatt; map p.429. With a huge menu, ranging from burger and chips (Ksh340) to pastas and grills (from Ksh500), and a live band most evenings, "Café Crazy" is always worth checking out. Beers Ksh170, wine Ksh200. Tues–Sun early until midnight.

Chill at Sunset 12.4km south, Kinondo Beach ☎0732 656225, ⓦchillatsunset.jimdo.com; map p.429. Lovely chill-out beach-bar-restaurant, with no menu: guests call or visit to order food in advance, and if they're staying in the rooms, they discuss lunch and dinner after breakfast. Main courses are usually Ksh1000, or more for prawns or lobster. Daily 8am–late.

Chinese Diani Restaurant Diani Complex Shopping Centre, 1.5km north ☎0720 418563; map p.427. Good Chinese restaurant, but fairly pricey (beef with oyster sauce Ksh650, special fried rice Ksh350). Free pick-up from hotels.

Daily 11.30am–2.30pm & 6–10.30pm.

Colobus Shade 6.4km south; map p.429. Right by Diani's main fish-landing jetty, a seafood-only beach restaurant set under a baobab tree, offering the catch of the day, with rice, potatoes, salad and chapatti (Ksh700) – and knockout service. Beer Ksh150 and even wine by the bottle from Ksh1000. Daily 9am–8pm.

★ **Forty Thieves Beach Bar & Restaurant** 2.8km south; map p.429. This famous local watering hole – bare feet, sand underfoot and loud voices – is a good place for a daytime drink and perfect in the evening when the beachfront is floodlit. Live band, roasts & curry buffet on Sundays; the second Tues of the month is tapas night. Dishes range from oysters (a dozen Ksh300) to big salads (Ksh500), pizzas (Ksh600) and grills. Beers Ksh300, wine Ksh200. Wed, Fri & Sat disco (Ksh300); English football and other sport on TV; quiz nights; pool tables. Daily 8am–late.

Leonardo's Colliers Centre ☎0720 501707; map p.427. Notable for the pair of ostentatious "Range Rovers" built from wood and leather and usually parked outside, this fancy Italian joint is all wood with a fabric roof. Pasta and pizza Ksh800–1000, other mains around Ksh1000, home-made ice creams Ksh200/scoop, plus good coffee. Charcoal-grilled meat and fish are prepared next to the pizza oven. Supervised children's play area. Daily 9.30am–11.30pm, last food orders 10.15pm.

Love Bakery Diani Shopping Centre; map p.429. Campaigning kind of bakery, with lots of delicious pastries, breads and pizza slices prepared from top-quality organic products, and posters proclaiming their virtues (most items Ksh200 or less). Mon–Sat 8.30am–6pm.

Lymingtons Bistro Diani Beach Shopping Centre ☎0720 900562; map p.429. Popular for breakfasts, grills and salads, with variations on a full English for Ksh600, burgers for Ksh500 and a wide variety of salads for Ksh700 or less. They have a bar, too. Daily 7am–9pm.

Mr T Roof Garden Bar & Restaurant 9.2km south, ☎0717 231076; map p.429. Although a little overpriced for the standard menu of tourist seafood and African dishes (main courses Ksh500–800), the breeze through the trees and convivial company keeps people coming back. Daily 8am–midnight.

Mwaepe Fisherman's Restaurant 6.4km south, ☎0723 791373; map p.429. A slightly fancier place than neighbouring Colobus Shade, and trading heavily on its location, but with exactly the same seafood offerings, from Ksh800. Daily 8am–8pm.

★ **Nomads Beach Bar & Restaurant** At Sands at Nomad, 4.8km south ☎0724 262426 or 0735 373888;

map p.429. Popular beach bar with snacks, pizzas, seafood and its famous Sunday lunch curry buffet, a real family affair, with regular live jazz or a one-man band. Part of the restaurant is devoted to excellent Japanese and Thai food – allow around Ksh3000 per person. Beach bar daily 6.30am–midnight, restaurant daily 7.30am–10.30pm.

Shan-e-Punjab Diani Complex Shopping Centre, 1.4km north ☎0786 03012; map p.427. This Punjabi restaurant and snack bar still features an open-air garden, serving vegetarian and non-vegetarian dishes. Very good value, with most dishes around Ksh400–700. Free transfers from anywhere in Diani. Daily 9am–11pm.

Stilts 3km south, opposite Ali Barbour's Cave restaurant; map p.429. The pleasant tree-level bar-restaurant at this popular backpackers' offers main dishes at Ksh400–700 (curries, steaks, fish), snacks and sandwiches and a daily local cuisine "money saver", such as beans and chapattis, for Ksh250. Mon–Sat 8am–8.30pm, Sun 8am–noon.

Sundowner 7km south ☎0725 498281; map p.429. A cheap and unpretentious restaurant and bar, serving good African dishes, curries (Ksh300–400) and seafood ("Maasai Fish" – breaded and fried fish fillet Ksh350) in a laidback atmosphere. Beers Ksh120. Daily 9am–late.

Tandoori Bay 3.5km south, opposite Diani Sea Lodge; map p.429. Popular all-day TV bar. Although they no longer serve food, the pool tables and regular disco make it a popular rendezvous. Tusker Ksh200, soda Ksh120. 24hr.

Winds 1.5km south, Diani Campsite; map p.429. Popular diner and TV bar at *Diani Campsite*. Fry-ups and sandwiches around the Ksh350 mark, as well as grills (Ksh500) and salads (Ksh400). Daily 7am–10pm.

★ **Yibba Yabba** 1km south, Diani Beach Shopping Centre ☎0788 319013 or 020 2335959, ⊕yibbayabba .com; map p.429. Friendly, English-run sports bar, pub-style restaurant serving a long menu of tasty dishes at fair prices (all-day breakfast Ksh750, club sandwiches Ksh550). Also offers a delivery service for several Diani restaurants. Free wi-fi. Daily 9am–midnight.

NIGHTLIFE

Giriama dancing is the big entertainment that is often touted. It's perhaps not something to go out of your way to find, but is fun if you happen upon it. A couple of professional troupes work the hotels, performing acrobatically to the accompaniment of superb drumming. You're also likely to happen across **Maasai dancers**, invariably the real thing, although they come from various locales. The guttural polyphonic singing is fascinating, though the performances usually end with a "Maasai market" where they sell overpriced (and not necessarily very Maasai) trinkets. More seldom seen are the **Taarab bands** (see p.579), who sometimes play in hotel dining rooms on special occasions or public holidays. All these entertainments are seasonal and you will find much less going on when it's quiet.

CLUBS

Apart from predictable hotel discos, there are several independent nightclubs along the road, each with its own idiosyncrasies, all with at least a trace of sleaze. Couples who visit will usually be ignored, but single men can expect lots of business-like propositions, and women without male partners will be constantly chatted up. None of the discos starts to warm up before 11pm. Entry prices range from free to Ksh300 depending on the season, the night and the entertainment in prospect.

Full Moon 600m south of Nakumatt; map p.429. The only major club in this part of Diani regularly hosts DJ nights and live music. Check it out during the day and it seems a little less intimidating at night. High season nightly until late, low season Thurs–Sat only.

★ **Kim4Love** 3.5km south of Nakumatt, on the beach, ☎0722 889844, ⊕kim4love.net; map p.429. Set amid the eerie ruins of the *Two Fishes* hotel, demolished by fire in 1999, this beach bar-restaurant comes alive on weekend afternoons when Kim – the "ambassador of love" – plays with his band to a relaxed crowd of "richest and poorest without boundaries". Great-value food (dishes Ksh200–400). Daily 8am–midnight or later at weekends.

Shakatak 3.5km south of the junction, opposite Diani Sea Lodge ⊕shakatak-kenya.com; map p.429. With a wooden dancefloor and air conditioning, this is a bit of a dive, but it does play the best music mix on the strip. You can eat here reasonably cheaply if you want. Beers are just Ksh200, wine Ksh250. Daily 7pm–4am.

GETTING AROUND DIANI BEACH AT NIGHT

To get around Diani Beach at night without your own vehicle, you'll have to rely mostly on **taxis**. Any restaurant or hotel will call one for you: they never take more than a few minutes, but always agree the price firmly before getting in. Ksh500 is about the lowest fare, with Ksh150/km being about right for journeys of more than a few kilometres. While everyone will warn you about walking on the beach at night, under a full moon it's a pleasure that's hard to resist. With no valuables, especially in a group, you're very unlikely to have any problems.

ACTIVITIES

Bicycle rental When you tire of the beach and the sea, or of just lying under the palm trees, you could rent a bicycle and go off exploring – from about Ksh500 per half-day. Bicycle rental outlets come and go: ask at your hotel. Diani Bikes, next to Ushago Food Court, rent out their yellow bicycles at negotiable rates (Ksh1200/day the usual figure quoted; ☎0713 959668, ⓦdianibikes.com). Quad Bikes are available from Excursion Quads (1.3km south of the junction; ☎0721 459258 or 0733 434475), starting at €60 for two hours, including hotel transfers. Choco's Biker Point, 6.8km south of Nakumatt (☎0706 629606; Mon–Sat 7.30am–6pm), has 150cc bikes from Ksh1500/day and nice bicycles from Ksh700/day.

Boat/canoe trips A trip to the reef on one of the outrigger canoes is highly recommended. The crews know all the good spots for snorkelling and it should cost you Ksh1000 to Ksh2000 for up to three hours of pottering about with a captain and one crew. One of the best areas is directly opposite Baobab Beach Resort, about 300m out towards the reef, where there is a cluster of coral heads. You can arrange a trip through any hotel reception, or directly

on the beach. There are a number of dhow-trip operators (see box below).

Golf 18-hole course at Leisure Lodge (see p.434).

Microlight flights 20–30min flights (one person plus the pilot) are available for scudding low over the reef and coastal jungle. Contact Coastal Microlights (ⓦcoastalmicrolights.com), who will collect you from your hotel – around $70 inclusive per person.

Snorkelling Most hotels also offer snorkelling gear (free to all-inclusive guests, or you can rent it for about Ksh500), and you can then float out across the lagoon towards the reef. You need to be a reasonably confident swimmer: there are no strong currents nor any real danger, but the reef is 600–1000m away and swimming back on the ebb tide can be tiring. A number of companies offer snorkelling trips (see box below).

Wind- and kitesurfing The sheltered lagoon behind the reef is ideal for windsurfing (Ksh1000/hr or often free to all-inclusive guests) and kitesurfing (one-day courses from $70). There are kite schools at the *Kenyaways* and *Sands at Nomad* hotels.

DIRECTORY

Banks and exchange Barclays by the Ukunda junction has a 24-hour ATM; KCB has an ATM at Nakumatt; Maritime Forex by the Petro filling station is open office hours.

Internet access Available at several places, of which the best is Hot Gossip on the upper tier of the rebuilt Diani Beach

Shopping Centre. Others include Top Africa, on the north side of Colliers Centre (Ksh5/min), and *Forty Thieves Cyber*, at the beach bar of the same name (daily 9am–9pm; Ksh6/min). For Safaricom dongle or Smartphone issues, visit the big new Safaricom service centre at Nakumatt, first floor.

DHOW, SNORKELLING, DOLPHIN AND WHALE SHARK TRIPS

Several **excursion operators** are based at Diani Beach. They pick you up from your hotel either for free or for a nominal extra charge. For the most part, the dhows are not under sail but are powered by on-board or outboard motors. All can be booked direct, or though your hotel. Always ensure there's a usable life jacket for each passenger.

★ **Charlie Claws** Office at Leopard Beach Hotel ☎0722 205156 or 0722 205155, ⓦwasini.com. Day-long dhow, snorkelling and dolphin-searching trips at Kisite Mpunguti Marine National Park, with a seafood lunch at their own restaurant at the northwest end of Wasini island, which also has a large, landscaped swimming pool. $125 including park fees, drinks, lunch, community visits and all equipment, with pick-up from north or south coast, or direct from Shimoni. Scuba-diving, if you're qualified or want to try, costs an additional $50 for one dive, or $80 for two. Usually closed May and June.

East African Whale Shark Trust Aqualand, next to Pinewood Beach Resort ☎0720 293156, ⓦgiantsharks.org. EAWST organize in-water, whale shark encounters, especially during the peak Feb–March whale shark season. Prices vary depending on

group size and duration, but expect around $150/person.

Paradise Divers Wasini Island ☎0736 277377, ⓦparadisediver.net. Well-managed, Hungarian-owned dive and boat operation with a basic tented camp and restaurant on the northeast corner of Wasini. They offer 7-day, 10-dive packages from $950.

★ **Pilli-Pipa Dhow Safaris** Colliers Centre ☎040 3203559 or 0722 244694, ⓦpillipipa.com. Small-group dhow day-trips to Kisite Marine Park for outstanding snorkelling (field guides, masks, snorkels and fins provided), with a late lunch of crab claws, good wine and Swahili food at a private house on the north side of Wasini island. Departures most days at 8.30am from Shimoni jetty. $125, including marine park fees, all equipment and transfers. Usually closed May and June. Daily 7am–6pm.

Medical services Dr Rekhi and Dr Raj (T 0735 223223 or 0722 569261), at the small, modern Diani Beach Hospital, next to Diani Complex Shopping Centre, are recommended. One of the best hospitals on the coast, they have an Outpatients department and a 24-hour pharmacy. Standard tourist consultation is Ksh2000. Emergency T 0700 999999.

Notice boards There are notice boards at most of the shopping centres, usually outside the supermarkets, or try *Yibba Yabba* at Diani Beach Shopping Centre.

Post office By the aiport entrance road, 1.4km south of Nakumatt.

Supermarkets The new Nakumatt, on the junction of the main Diani Road and the road to Ukunda, which opened in 2011, has decimated some of the smaller competition. Shreegreeng, behind the Petro filling station, is one of several alternatives, and Shan-e-Punjab Supermarket, 1.5km south of Nakumatt, is particularly good value for beer, wine and spirits (daily 9am–6pm).

Safari operators and agents There are various safari agents and operators in the shopping centres along the strip. The following are all worth checking out, although you should always be clear whether you are talking to the operator of the safari in question or simply an agent who is selling it. DM Tours & Safaris at Diani Beach Shopping Centre (T 0722 470382, W dmtours.net; Mon–Sat 8am–5pm) does well-organized safaris with landcruisers less than 4 years old, with a maximum of 4 passengers; Bush2Beach, Golf Villas, behind Diani Hospital (T 040 3202575 or 0722 411566, W beach2bushkenya.com), is expensive but highly regarded; Intra Safaris, Colliers Centre (T 040 3202630 or 0723 288189, W intrasafaris.com), are a well-established safari operator and airline agent; JT Safaris (aka "The Orange Hut"; T 040 3300299 or 0721 769771, W julius-safaris.com), 8.5km south of Nakumatt opposite Neptune Paradise Hotel, has a very good reputation, and is easily confused with Julius Thuvi Safaris, in the parade of shops and offices just south of Café Wahnsinn (T 0723 997495, W jtsafaris.com), and Juletabi Safaris in the Nakumatt building (T 0733 752365, W juletabisafaris.com).

6

Ukunda

Until a few years ago just a village on the highway, **UKUNDA** is now a scruffily burgeoning town and the main service centre for the Diani Beach resort hotels, strung out along the Likoni–Lungalunga road, with a post office, a number of banks with ATMs, several petrol stations, various places with internet access, and hundreds of *dukas*, kiosks and *hotelis*. Only marginally touched by tourism, except insofar as many of its residents work in the hotels, Ukunda has a life of its own. If your holiday isn't otherwise adventurous, it's worth a visit to see something of Kenya a little more authentic than the strip.

South to Shimoni

South of *Neptune Paradise Hotel* (see p.435), the Diani Beach road returns to gravel, although it continues in a driveable condition, past one or two secluded properties around Kinondo, and past Kaya Kinondo itself. There's little transport down here, so you're likely to be driving or walking. You get to a hard right-hand bend, then 100m later a sharp left turning for Chale Point. **Chale island** is 4km further south, and 300m offshore. The island, once an uninhabited beauty spot, was acquired in the early 1990s by a property developer, with the help of two local MPs, despite being public land and a gazetted Mijikenda *kaya*. The resulting resort, the largely Italian-patronized *Sands at Chale*, owned by *The Sands at Nomad* in Diani, angered local people and wiped out acres of natural vegetation. The owners claim the development has been sensitive, that only a third of the island has been built upon and that the other part is a nature reserve. If, instead of driving down to Chale Point you keep straight ahead, you emerge, after exactly 3km of slightly rough-and-ready coral rag road, onto the main highway down to Tanzania, at a point 13km south of Ukunda.

Gazi

Down the main coastal highway south of Ukunda, **GAZI** is next, a sleepy little village just off the road. It was once headquarters of the Mazrui leader **Sheikh Mbaruk ("Baruku") bin Rashid**, who acquired a reputation for torturing prisoners after half-suffocating them in the fumes of burning chillis. The story was perhaps intended to discredit him as he was the principal figure behind the **Mazrui Rebellion** of 1895, an uprising against British authority that saw Mbaruk flying a German flag at his house and supplying his men with arms donated by the Germans. The British had to send for troops from India and fighting continued for nine months before an Omani puppet regime was re-established and the rebels crushed. Mbaruk died in exile in German Tanganyika. Baruku's mansion is now a primary school, which you can look around out of school hours. More than 150 years old, it was obviously a very grand place – the heavy ceiling timbers show that it once had an upper storey – but it is now sadly neglected.

There are two turnings to Gazi, which lies between the road and the shore. The first is 3.1km from the Chale island/Diani South turning. The village itself lies back from a deep, mangrove-filled bay and has no beach to speak of. Gazi Beach, about 2km south of the village, is more promising. Local women in Gazi manage the **Gazi Women's Mangrove Boardwalk**, a 250m trail through the mangroves, which is worth visiting, especially for birdwatchers, as the modest donations support the community.

Msambweni

Continuing down the highway from Gazi, **MSAMBWENI** is a sizeable village with a famous leprosarium. The road to the beach goes through the village, following the coast for several kilometres before turning back to the highway. The beach is lovely – low cliffs and less uniformity than Diani – and there are no beach hassles down here, but the tide goes out for miles, with lots of rock pools, so it's not ideal for snorkelling or for most watersports.

Funzi island

If, instead of returning north to the main road from Msambweni, you follow the coastline, you eventually reach **Funzi island**, separated from the mainland by a narrow channel that you can walk across at low tide. Unlike exclusive Chale, you can easily camp on the island if equipped for a fair amount of self-sufficiency, and Diani operators (see p.438) run bird- and crocodile-watching day-trips here. The village of **Funzi** is at the southern end, about 6km from the mainland, and there are beaches and sections of reef scattered close to the forested shore on both sides of the island.

Shirazi

The tiny and very old settlement of **SHIRAZI**, also known as Kifunzi (which means "little Funzi"), sits on the shore, a short distance before Ramisi. Any of the tracks through the sugar fields on the left of the road will take you to the hamlet – a scattering of houses in the jungle and a small harbour among mangroves.

Like many villages on the coast, Shirazi is a backwater in every sense. The people cut a small quantity of *boriti* (mangrove poles), though much less than they used to; they fish; and they also grow produce in their garden plots, which are continually being raided by monkeys. But the setting is memorably exotic and worth the 2km detour from the main road. They may not have cold sodas at Shirazi, but they do have coconuts and tranquillity.

Just a couple of hundred metres south of Shirazi rests the enigmatic hulk of a Friday mosque, its *mihrab* still standing. Elders in Shirazi, who describe how earlier

---

THE WA-SHIRAZI

The people of Shirazi call themselves **Wa-Shirazi** and are the descendants of a once-important group of the Swahili-speaking people. During the fifteenth and sixteenth centuries, they ruled the coast from Tiwi to Tanga from their eight settlements on the shore, one of which is believed to have been this village. Around 1620, these towns were captured by the Wa-vumba, another Swahili group. The Wa-Shirazi, now scattered in pockets along the coast, speak a distinctive dialect of Swahili. Historians used to think that they originally emigrated from Shiraz, in Persia, but it now seems likely that very few of them have Persian ancestry and that the name was adopted for political reasons.

inhabitants were routed by the Maasai and fled to the Comoros Islands, remember when the mosque was still intact, though by the beginning of the twentieth century it had already been abandoned. The mosque is now surrounded by a modest tourist development, currently closed.

Ramisi

The coast highway passes through verdant regions of parkland, with borassus, doum and coconut palms (borassus palms are the ones with a bulge in the trunk, like pythons that have swallowed a goat) interspersed with swampy dells. Further south, the landscape becomes one of rolling fields of sugar cane, culminating in **Ramisi**, which was the coast's main sugar-producing area, until the closure of its factory.

6

CHALE ISLAND

Sands at Chale ☎040 3300269 or 0733 610455, ⓦthesandsatchaleisland.com. Owned by *The Sands at Nomad* in Diani, this angered local people and wiped out acres of natural vegetation. The owners claim only a third of the island has been built upon and that the other part is a nature reserve. Either way, there's a package feel to the resort which you wouldn't expect in the location, and the food is nowhere near as good as at the other *Sands*. You reach it by boat, or by tractor at low tide. But not without a reservation – the island has been well and truly privatized. FB $435

MSAMBWENI

Chingwede House Chelsoon, Msambweni Beach ☎0733 633332, ⓦtiny.cc/Chingwede. Fine self-catering house sleeping eight, sharing the same plot as *Samawati*. Whole house, self-catering. $340

★ **Msambweni Beach House** ☎020 3577093 or 0723 697346, ⓦmsambweni-beach-house.com. A fabulous boutique hotel, the pride of its Belgian owner-designer, rising from the edge of the highest cliffs on the

Kenyan coast above a remote beach complete with caves and a private dining area. *Msambweni*'s huge and inviting infinity pool is only matched by the opulence of the coolly palatial rooms and really superb food. Closed May. AI $700

Samawati House Chelsoon, Msambweni Beach ☎0722 818128, ⓦsamawati.co.ke. Beautiful house sleeping up to eight, with a large pool, sharing a big plot with *Chingwede House* on the palm-studded shore southeast of the village. Whole house, self-catering. $310

FUNZI ISLAND

Funzi Keys West coast of Funzi Island ☎0733 900 446 or 0733 900582, ⓦthefunzikeys.com. Attentively managed creek-shore resort accessible only by boat or charter flight, surrounded by sand spits and mangroves, and consisting of enormous, open-plan, stone and thatched cottages. Tons of Robinson Crusoe charm is the main appeal, though it seems overpriced when compared with similar hideaways and most activities, even non-motorized, cost extra. No ocean beach on site. Closed April 16–June 30. AI $610

Shimoni

In the 1980s, the US had its eye on **Wasini** – the rocky sliver of an island just offshore from the village of **Shimoni** – as a potential naval base. Fortunately the idea was shelved, and Shimoni, 14km down a picturesque sand and mud road from the highway, remains relatively untouched and fascinating. This is one of the world's most renowned game-fishing areas. The Pemba Channel (the Tanzanian island of Pemba lies 50km offshore) is considered one of the world's very best stretches of sea for hunting big fish: **marlin** weighing a quarter of a tonne (550 pounds) and **tiger sharks** close on half a tonne race through these waters, marlin at recorded speeds of more than 100km/h (60mph).

If you're driving down to Shimoni yourself it's worth calling at *Mwazaro Beach* (see p.443), which has to be one of the country's most eco-friendly establishments and welcomes casual visitors for meals or drinks. *Mwazaro*, which means "prayer place", is on a beautiful, lonely beach, opposite the delta of the Ramisi River, with forests of **mangroves** all around (eight of the nine species native to Africa can be found here and the owners of Mwazaro have replanted some ten square kilometres), excellent **snorkelling** at the nearby reef, and creek- and sea-trips available. Most visitors only pass

6

through little **Shimoni** itself when coming here for dhow trips to Wasini and the Kisite-Mpunguti Marine National Park, but it's worth an hour or two of your time.

If you can, try to be in Shimoni first thing: an auction takes place at the **fish auction house** by the jetty every morning. Depending on the night's catch, it can be an interesting event, as the seas in the Pemba Channel are rich in fish, though major captures like marlin and shark are rarely on the slab.

The Slave Caves

Daily guided tours 8.30am–6pm • Ksh400

The "**slave caves**" after which Shimoni was named (*shimo* means "cave" in Swahili) have achieved fame locally, if not much further afield, through the melodramatic warblings of Kenyan-born singer Roger Whittaker's song *Shimoni*, which was recorded in the caves. Based on the evidence of iron rings in the rocks, it's believed that they were used to store slaves prior to shipment to Zanzibar. Historians from the National Museums of Kenya are looking for further evidence, and with 5km of silted-up caverns to excavate they may have some way to go. These are caves into which you descend from ground level. Once you're down, shafts of sunlight pierce through holes in the forest floor to illuminate the stalactites and dangling lianas quite beautifully.

The ruined two-storey building opposite the caves ticket office was formerly the headquarters of the **Imperial British East African Company**, dating from 1885.

ARRIVAL AND DEPARTURE
SHIMONI

By matatu There are direct matatus from Likoni to Shimoni, but they can be infrequent, and tend to run mostly early in the morning. Vehicles for Lungalunga will drop you at the junction where you shouldn't have much trouble getting a lift.

By cargo dhows There is a possibility of getting a cargo dhow from Shimoni to Pemba (3hr; Ksh2000) and sometimes straight to Zanzibar (6hr; Ksh3000); if you've lined up a passage, you should report to the customs and immigration offices in Shimoni.

ACCOMMODATION

Betty's Camp 500m west of the village centre ☎0722 434709, ⓦbettys-camp.com. Aiming at the budget game-fishing market, this has a choice of small, stuffy, non-s/c ridge tents, with floor fans, or modest rooms with

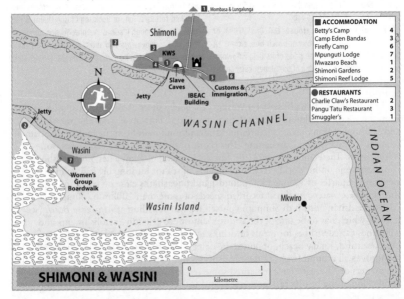

■1, Mombasa & Lungalunga

Shimoni

KWS

Slave Caves

Jetty

IBEAC Building

Customs & Immigration

WASINI CHANNEL

Jetty

Wasini

Women's Group Boardwalk

Wasini Island

Mkwiro

INDIAN OCEAN

■ ACCOMMODATION	
Betty's Camp	4
Camp Eden Bandas	3
Firefly Camp	6
Mpunguti Lodge	7
Mwazaro Beach	1
Shimoni Gardens	2
Shimoni Reef Lodge	5

● RESTAURANTS	
Charlie Claw's Restaurant	2
Pangu Tatu Restaurant	3
Smuggler's	1

SHIMONI & WASINI

0 — 1 kilometre

ceiling fans (2 small non-s/c, 1 large s/c) in a large, quaint rondavel, with a shared, breezy, top-floor lounge area. There's a pleasant little pool (a surprising Ksh750 for non-guests), but the whole place is hugely overpriced for the facilities and standards. BB **$188**

Camp Eden Bandas 300m west of the village centre ☎020 3549520 or 0722 277443, ✉reservations @kws.go.ke. Wonderful for naturalists and managed by the local Kenya Wildlife Service rangers, *Camp Eden* is a group of seven, airy and clean, if fairly rudimentary, *makuti*-roofed *bandas* in the forest; three of them s/c, four non-s/c (the latter have basins outside, but share squat loos and showers). There's mains electricity, but it's best to bring your own drinking water. You can also camp. Camping **$15**, *banda* **$50**

Firefly Camp 700m east of Shimoni village centre ☎0722 244694. Managed by the people who run Pilli-Pipa Dhow Safaris (see p.438), this gap year/voluntourism camp is frequently used by Camps International. When space is available, however (call to check), you can camp in this beautiful spot, with showers, toilets and basic cooking facilities available. Per person **Ksh500**

★ **Mwazaro Beach** 1km off the Shimoni road, 7.5km

from the highway ☎0722 711476 or 0722 961848, ⓦkeniabeach.com. "Where God makes holidays" is how the German owners describe this eco-resort at a Digo *kaya* where approval was sought and granted for the low-key, sustainable development of 11 *makuti* cottages and 4, more comfortable, coral rag rooms, all with fitted nets, and powered exclusively by wind and solar energy. It's a major kitesurf centre, and also serves excellent, Zanzibari set meals. HB **$125**

Shimoni Gardens 1.5km west of the village centre ☎0722 117900. Small, breezy rooms made of cane, reed and *makuti*, or sturdier stone-built cottages, not actually on the shore, but not too far away, with a bar and restaurant, plus a separate beach bar-restaurant closer to the shore, with a pool table and cold drinks (open 24hr), and its own boats for snorkelling and fishing expeditions. BB **Ksh4000**

Shimoni Reef Lodge 300m east of the village centre ☎0722 400476, ⓦshimonireeflodge.com. Aimed less at sport fishermen than at divers. Pleasant enough accommodation in ten whitewashed split-level cottages with separate bedroom and lounge areas, floor fans and nets, but rather average food. Salt-water pool. HB **$160**

EATING AND DRINKING

Smuggler's Just west of the slave caves ☎0721 398349. An upcountry-style bar-restaurant where you can usually get chicken, beef or goat, either stewed or roasted, sold by weight (beef fillet Ksh750/kg, goat Ksh600/kg), accompanied by rice, *ugali* or chapattis. They also sell juices and do good breakfasts. Daily early until late.

Wasini island and offshore

WASINI isn't far offshore, but there's no standard, cheap and simple way for tourists to reach the island. Only 5km long and 1km across, Wasini has about a thousand inhabitants, and is totally adrift from the mainstream of coastal life. There are no cars, nor any need for them: you can walk all the way around the island in a couple of hours on the narrow footpaths through the bush. With something of Lamu's cast about it, the island is completely undeveloped, and people tend to be conservative in dress – something you should be sensitive to while visiting (don't wander around in a swimming costume). The village of **Wasini**, an old Wa-vumba settlement, is built in and around its own ruins. It's a fascinating place to wander and there's even a small pillar tomb which still has its complement of inset Chinese porcelain. The **beach** in front of the village (and in fact the shores all round the island) – littered with shells, pottery shards, pieces of glass and scrap metal – are a beachcomber's paradise that you could explore for hours (though be wary of pocketing sea shells or any artefacts).

Behind the village is a bizarre area of long-dead **coral gardens**, raised out of the sea by changing sea levels, but still flooded by twice-monthly spring tides.

The boardwalk

Daily 8am–5pm • Ksh200

Walking along the **boardwalk**, built by a local women's group, with funds going towards education and healthcare in the village, through the coral grottoes, with birds and butterflies in the air, gives you the surreal impression that you're snorkelling on dry land. The ground is covered by a short swathe of sea grass – the tasty *mboga pwani* (sea vegetable) – and patrolled by fleets of small crabs with enormous right claws. Beyond the coral garden, the boardwalk continues into the mangroves, giving an excellent chance to visit an environment not usually easy to get into.

Mkwiro

The village of **MKWIRO**, at the eastern end of Wasini, is still largely a fishing village. The inhabitants have traditionally had little contact with Wasini village, but the arrival of a diving business means they are now also engaging with the tourist economy.

Kisite-Mpunguti Marine National Park

Park fee $20 • Ⓦ kws.org

Wasini has ideal conditions for **snorkelling**, with limpid water all around, and the waters offshore are the most likely area on Kenya's coast for seeing dolphins. Several operators (see p.438) run full-day trips in large dhows to the reefs around Kisite island, part of **Kisite-Mpunguti Marine National Park**, which is actually made up of Kisite National Park, which covers 11 square kilometres, and Mpunguti National Reserve, which has less protection and covers 28 square kilometres. The area is renowned for having some of the best snorkelling in Kenya. Similar trips, on a more ad hoc basis, can be arranged with boat captains at the dock in Shimoni: depending on the number in your party, demand on the day and the kind of vessel provided, the price for a three-hour trip could range from Ksh3000 to Ksh10,000, excluding park fees. You'll get the most out of the trip by getting down here as early as possible, adding lunch to the deal, and making a whole day of it. Always check that there are enough life jackets, and that they're usable.

The boats normally go out of the Wasini channel to the east, then turn south to pass the islets of **Mpunguti ya Chini** and **Mpunguti ya Juu** ("little" and "great" Mpunguti) on the port side. Some 5km further southwest, **Kisite Islet**, a coral-encircled rock about 100m long, is the usual destination and anchoring point. The best parts of the Kisite anchoring area are towards the outer edge of the main "coral garden". There are fish and sea creatures in abundance here, including angel fish, moray eels, octopuses, rock cod or grouper and some spectacularly large sea cucumbers up to 60cm long. At certain times of the year, however, the water is less clear, and repeated anchorings have destroyed much of the coral in at least one small area. Ask the crew if you'd like to try to find a better area: the **Mako Koke Reef**, the other main part of Kisite marine park, is about 4km further west. The KWS headquarters, by *Eden Bandas*, where you buy **park tickets**, has a good display of information about local marine wildlife.

ARRIVAL AND DEPARTURE   WASINI ISLAND AND OFFSHORE

The **snorkelling-cruise operators** take pre-booked lunchers across the channel in their boats (see box, p.438), but if you're not one of these, you'll have to **hire a motor boat** on the spot, at a price of Ksh1500 to Ksh3000 depending on your bargaining skills. Meanwhile, you'll see local people using **jahazi**, the sailing boat "matatus" that are really the same kind of vessel, and which, despite resentment from the tourist-boat captains, you should be able to use, too (Ksh100–500 depending on bargaining skills and luck).

ACCOMMODATION

Mpunguti Lodge Wasini Town ☏0722 566623. Commonly known as *Masood's*, this is a simple, rustic affair without electricity, though flush toilets and showers have been installed, some rooms are self-contained, and rainwater tanks provide sufficient water for most of the year. The family (Masood himself passed on a few years ago) have a collection of Wasini's old pottery and ceramics. FB **Ksh5000**

Paradise Divers Northeast corner of Wasini ☏0736 277377, Ⓦ paradisediver.net. Tents under *bandas* and restaurant, with long-stay packages and casual stays by the day available. Extra charges for ad hoc diving, snorkelling or boat trips as required. FB **$120**

EATING AND DRINKING

Charlie Claw's Restaurant Wasini Ⓦ wasini.com. This open-air restaurant, with a lovely pool, is the location at the western tip of Wasini where Charlie Claw's dhow excursions set down for a lavish seafood lunch. Lunch only, booked with excursion (see p.438).

Pangu Tatu Restaurant Wasini Ⓦ pillipipa.com. Pilli Pipa's seafood lunch base, set in a shady grove of hole-riddled old reef on the north shore of Wasini. Lunch only, booked with excursion (see p.438).

ONWARDS TO TANZANIA

If you want to get to Dar es Salaam on the same day, you'll need to be at the border post at Lungalunga by 9am. After completing formalities on the Kenyan side, take a matatu or taxi or walk the 6km to Horohoro on the Tanzanian side. By *dala dala* (matatu) the journey to Tanga takes two to three hours from Horohoro, where you may have to change vehicles for a further five-hour journey to Dar. There are moneychangers at both border posts, but ascertain the current rate before starting negotiations, and always check the notes carefully before handing yours over. If you're buying Tanzanian shillings with Kenyan, you usually get the best rate on the Tanzanian side, and in fact you'll get them at a better rate here than you will in Tanga or Dar.

Vanga

Kenya's southernmost settlement, **VANGA** is the largest coastal town to have been left alone by the tourist industry. There are odd matatus from Likoni and Ukunda, but no lodgings and no formal *hotelis*, so take supplies.

The big old house on the seafront is a nineteenth-century **British customs house**, in the care of the National Museums of Kenya. Many of the other houses in the village were constructed during **World War I** by General Paul von Lettow-Vorbeck, to billet troops he had recruited in German East Africa to fight the British. It is said that the cache of gold from which he paid them is buried under a baobab tree, but that it is cursed: several people are said to have defied the curse and not survived.

Assuming you haven't come in search of buried treasure, **dugout canoes** can be rented very cheaply for wobbly punting trips through the mangroves.

ARRIVAL AND DEPARTURE   VANGA

By car To get here you travel down one of the country's most beautiful roads, the quiet highway that swoops across green plains and baobab-dotted hillsides from the Shimoni junction to the border town of Lungalunga. Here, you'll need to stop to explain your movements to officials. Midway between the customs check and the immigration barrier you turn left to start the 17km *murram* road to Vanga. The track skims the Tanzanian border past *shambas* and tunnels through tall forest. Vanga itself is in the mangroves, approached along a causeway that regularly floods on the spring tide, despite the sea wall.

ACCOMMODATION

You should be able to find someone in the village who'll organize accommodation for you: you might even try to round up some palm wine and a goat and make a party of your visit.

From Kilifi to Malindi

Between Mtwapa Creek and **Malindi**, the landscape is a diverse collage. First, between Kikambala and Kilifi lies a major **sisal-growing** area, focused around the small town of **Vipingo**, which has just one or two *dukas* and *hotelis*, but not much else. As far as the eye can see, arrow-straight rows of fleshy-leafed, cactus-like sisal plants stretch in every direction, the remaining **baobab trees** standing out bizarrely. A few kilometres inland sits the new Vipingo Ridge golf resort (wvipingoridge.com).

Towards **Kilifi**, the road bucks through a hilly area and the baobabs grow more profusely amid the scrub. **Kilifi creek** and **Takaungu creek** are both stunning, the clash of blue water and green cliffs almost unnatural. As you approach the turning for **Watamu**, thick, jungly forest (the **Arabuko Sokoke National Park**) and mangrove swamp characterize the district around **Mida Creek**. Further north, there's a more populated zone of *shambas* and thicket as you approach **Malindi**.

There is lots of scope for **beach hunting** along this part of the coast. Malindi and, to some extent, Watamu have been developed, but Kilifi functions largely as a Giriama market centre and district capital, while Takaungu seems virtually unknown, a throwback to pre-colonial days. There's also superb snorkelling at the **marine national parks** at Watamu and Malindi – local divers reckon Watamu has the better coral, and Malindi better fish, but it's partly a matter of luck and your experience on the day. Lastly, the ruined town of **Gedi**, deep in the forest near Watamu, is one of the most impressive archeological sites in East Africa.

6

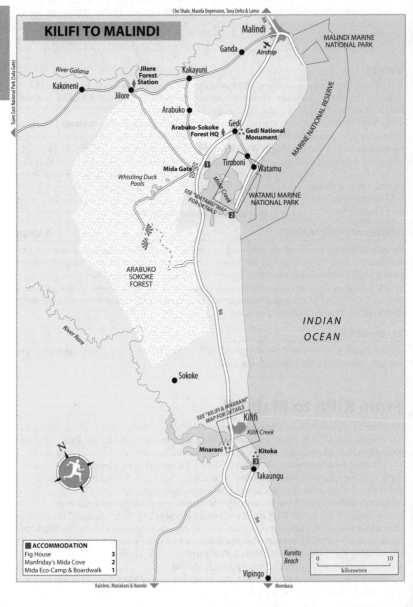

KILIFI TO MALINDI

Che Shale, Marafa Depression, Tana Delta & Lamu

Malindi

MALINDI MARINE
NATIONAL PARK

Ganda • Airstrip

River Galana

Jilore
Forest
Station

Kakayuni

Kakoneni

Jilore

Arabuko

MARINE NATIONAL RESERVE

Gedi
Arabuko-Sokoke
Forest HQ

Gedi National
Monument

Timboni

Mida Gate

Watamu

Tsavo East National Park (Sala Gate)

Whistling Duck
Pools

Mida Creek

SEE "WATAMU" MAP
FOR DETAILS

WATAMU MARINE
NATIONAL PARK

ARABUKO
SOKOKE
FOREST

INDIAN
OCEAN

River Rare

Sokoke

SEE "KILIFI & MNARANI"
MAP FOR DETAILS

Kilifi

Kilifi Creek

Mnarani

Kitoka

Takaungu

N

Kurvitu
Beach

0   10
kilometres

Vipingo

Kaloleni, Mariakani & Nairobi   Mombasa

BAOBAB STORIES

The **baobab**'s strange appearance has a number of explanations in Kenyan mythology. The most common one relates how the first baobab planted by God was an ordinary-looking tree, but it refused to stay in one place and wandered round the countryside. As a punishment, God planted it back again – upside down – and immobilized it.

Baobabs may live well over 2000 years, putting them among the longest-lived organisms that have ever existed. During a severe drought, their large green pods can be cracked open and the nuts made into a kind of flour. The resulting "hungry bread" is part of the common culture of the region. Even in normal times, they have their uses: the tangy white pith of the fruit is boiled with sugar to make a popular bright red sweet that you will see on sale at street stalls.

6

Takaungu

Ten kilometres south of Kilifi, there's a turn-off to the east to **TAKAUNGU**. Takaungu is enchanting – a quiet, composed village of whitewashed Swahili houses on a high bluff above **Takaungu Creek**, with a perfect, ocean-facing **beach**, situated 1km east of the village. There are three mosques and one or two small shops and *hotelis*, but no lodgings.

Takaungu Creek

Takaungu Creek is startlingly beautiful – sometimes, depending on the light, it's almost the colour of Blue Curacao – and absolutely transparent; the small swimming beach on the stream is covered at high tide, but you can still dive from the rocks. Upstream, the creek disappears between flanks of dense jungle. When you're ready to move on, the small, council-operated passenger ferry provides a slow, very cheap service across the narrow creek to the Kilifi side; from there, it's a 5km (90min) walk through the sisal fields to Kilifi bridge.

ARRIVAL AND DEPARTURE   TAKAUNGU

Although there are a couple of **matatus** most days from Mombasa direct to Takaungu, if you get dropped off at the turning by a Kilifi-bound vehicle, the chances of a lift down to Takaungu are relatively slim, but the **walk** (5km) is not too long.

ACCOMMODATION

If you want to stay in the village and you speak a little Swahili, people will put you up for a very reasonable price.

Fig House On the north side of the creek ☏0722/415447, ⍟fighousekenya.com. A beautiful self-catering hideaway (sleeps 8–11) with staff, pool and private tunnel to the creek shore – it's accessible by road from the Kilifi side. Whole house, self-catering **$700**

EATING

Food supplies are variable: women around the village will prepare food if you ask, and especially if you supply the ingredients. There's no produce market, but there's a small **fish market** by the creek – be there when the catch arrives to get the best of it.

Kilifi, Mnarani and the creek

Kenya's coastline was submerged in the recent geological past, resulting in the creation of the islands and drowned river valleys – the creeks – of today. **KILIFI**, a small but animated town, is on such a creek. When the Portuguese knew it, Kilifi's centre was on the south side of the creek and called **Mnarani** (still the name of the village on that side). Together with Kitoka on the north side of Takaungu Creek, and a settlement on the site of the present town of Kilifi, these three constituted the mini-state of Kilifi.

In recent decades, as the **Giriama** tribe of the Mijikenda (see p.421) has expanded, Kilifi has become one of their most important towns. Giriama women used to be quickly noticed by everyone for their unusual dress, incorporating a padded backside, although this is now only seen in rural areas. Older women still occasionally go topless but younger women invariably cover up, at least in town. The Mijikenda peoples, and the Giriama especially, are known as great sorcerers and practitioners of witchcraft, and Kilifi is still the frequent scene of accusations that sometimes reach the press.

There's little of **sightseeing interest** in Kilifi itself. The two main **mosques** – one a stumpy shed in the town centre, the other a newer and attractively minareted blue, green and white temple, the Masjid ul Noor, at the north junction – more or less sum up the sightseeing interest, but across the creek are the more interesting **Mnarani ruins**.

Mnarani ruins

Under the trees high above the water near the old ferry landing and then up a rather steep flight of steps • Daily 7am–6pm • Ksh500

The small site of the **Mnarani ruins** is archeologically famous mainly for the large number of inscriptions found on its masonry, all in a difficult form of monumental Arabic. They can be seen in several places, in particular in the well-preserved *mihrab* of the main mosque. Just behind this is a very tall octagonal white pillar tomb, which dominates the remains. In front of the mosque, a precipitous well plummets right down to creek level. A little way removed from the main mosque (signposted in front of the office), a smaller mosque is hidden away among the baobabs. As a whole, the site is pretty and quite photogenic, though if you're not a specialist its most memorable aspect is its superlative position.

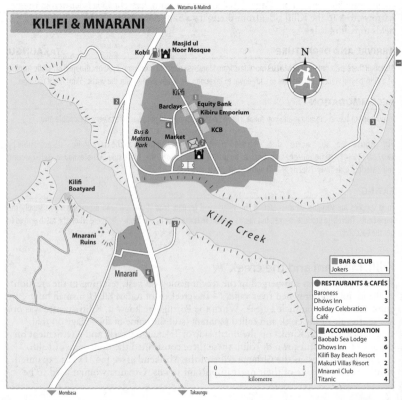

KILIFI & MNARANI

Watamu & Malindi

Masjid ul Noor Mosque

Kobil

Kilifi

Equity Bank
Kibiru Emporium

Barclays

KCB

Bus & Matatu Park

Market

Kilifi Boatyard

Mnarani Ruins

Kilifi Creek

Mnarani

Mombasa   Takaungu

0   1
kilometre

■ BAR & CLUB	
Jokers	1

● RESTAURANTS & CAFÉS	
Baroness	1
Dhows Inn	3
Holiday Celebration Café	2

■ ACCOMMODATION	
Baobab Sea Lodge	3
Dhows Inn	6
Kilifi Bay Beach Resort	1
Makuti Villas Resort	2
Mnarani Club	5
Titanic	4

THE MIJIKENDA KAYAS

Each Mijikenda tribe (see box, p.421) has a traditional **kaya** central settlement, a fortified village in the forest ranging from 12 acres to three square kilometres in extent, usually built on raised ground some distance from the coast, but sometimes right by the shore. Some Mijikenda peoples built only one *kaya* while others built secondary *kayas* or even whole clusters. The *kayas* are considered to be the dwelling places of ancestral spirits, although they are now sacred glades rather than fortified villages.

In theory, each *kaya* contains a *fingo* – a charm said to derive from the Mijikenda's ancestral home of Shungwaya. Most *fingo* have been lost or stolen for private collections of "primitive art" or loft-converters' ideas of interesting *objets d'art* – like the **grave posts** called *kigango* (*vigango* in the plural) that also used to be a feature of every *kaya*.

Today, many *kayas* are neglected, but they are still remembered and visited by tribal elders. Along with the belief in their sacred qualities comes a local conservation tradition: undisturbed and uncultivated, they represent a unique biological storehouse on the East African coast. A WWF-backed botanical research programme, the Coastal Forest Conservation Unit, run by the National Museums of Kenya, is slowly mapping out the *kaya* ecosystems. In 2008 the *kayas* were collectively inscribed as a **UNESCO World Heritage Site** (ⓦwhc.unesco .org/en/list/1231). More than twenty have so far been given legal status and paper protection, and elders are being encouraged to reassert their authority over them before property developers move in. There may be more than fifty altogether, though some could be so small that they will disappear under the bulldozer before anyone remembers them.

The first *kaya* to open to visitors is **Kaya Kinondo** on Diani Beach (see box, p.433).

The beaches

The **beaches** around Kilifi are mostly accessible only through private property, and the best are up on the open coast to the northeast of the town. Along this 10km tarred road, however, there are several fairly recent developments.

ARRIVAL AND DEPARTURE · KILIFI

The town is draped along the north side of the creek to the east of the bridge. If you're driving you'll probably pass it by. Even most bus and matatu travellers only see it from the inside of the vehicle while more fares are being picked up. But staying the night in Kilifi is a perfectly good plan and certainly better than arriving late in Malindi. There's no shortage of transport to Mombasa and Malindi. Northbound, most buses to Lamu and Garissa pass through around 8am.

SERVICES

Banks There are Barclays and KCB banks in town, both with ATMs; the post office is near the market.
Internet cafés There are several internet cafés, of which the one beneath the *Titanic Hotel* is the best bet (Mon–Sat 8am–5pm).

Shops Kilifi's Oloitipitip Market is always bursting with fresh fruit and vegetables, but good supermarkets are in short supply. Kibiru Emporium (daily) has a good range of wines and spirits, plus cold drinks.

ACCOMMODATION

Accommodation in Kilifi ranges from basic town lodgings to one or two pleasant resort hotels, including the very popular *Mnarani Club*.

KILIFI TOWN

Dhows Inn Mnarani, at the south side of the bridge ☎020 8088833 or 0722 375214. Popular boozer (beer Ksh130) and restaurant with big, clean, good-value s/c rooms in the garden, each with two large beds, fan, nets, and electric sockets. Good meals include stews and fried fish at around the Ksh350 mark. In the evening it's often quite lively, as are the neighbouring bars. BB Ksh2000
Makuti Villas Resort North side of the bridge, west of

the highway ☎041 7522371 or 0734 873704, ⓦmakutivillas.com. Budget tourist-class establishment, with 36 good-sized s/c rooms with nets and ceiling fans and good bathrooms, a pleasant pool and a warm welcome. Their pizzas are usually very good, too. BB $63
Mnarani Club South side of the creek, entrance near the bridge ☎041 7522318, ⓦmnarani.co.za. Comfortable package resort, overlooking Kilifi creek from expansive gardens, with a good international mix of clients,

decent food and good service and animation. There are two categories of rooms and it's worth paying a bit extra for the more spacious and breezy Creek rooms, with stable doors, windows on two sides, a/c and fridge. The views over the creek from the hotel's pool are glorious, and there's a private beach. HB **$181**

Titanic Town centre, reception at the back of the hotel at street level ☎041 7522370 or 0726 363437. This big central lodging house with the unpromising name offers a seemingly unlimited variety of rooms. Go for a room on the top floor if you want any kind of view, though they tend to be small up here. All have fans, TVs and good nets, and the better rooms are very spacious. Non-residents' rates are way overpriced, but highly negotiable. BB **Ksh4500**

KILIFI BEACH

Baobab Sea Lodge 3.2km along the coast road from the highway ☎041 7522570 or 0731 964016,

ⓦmadahotels.com. Attractively sited amid densely planted gardens and baobabs, in a pleasant position on a bluff above the shore, just north of the creek mouth at the south end of the beach. Tennis courts and a good pool with lots of shade, but no sea-swimming at low tide. The rooms, while simple, are spacious and attractively furnished, with a/c, good nets, fans, fridges and safes, but they lack sea views. FB **$165**

Kilifi Bay Beach Resort 6.5km along the coast road from the highway ☎041 7522264 or 0725 888560, ⓦmadahotels.com. The best of Kilifi's hotels, with a stunning location right down on the beach (the best rooms have stupendous sea views; all have balconies), mature tropical gardens with coconut palms, a freeform pool for when the tide is out, great four-poster beds, spacious *makuti*-roofed communal areas, good service and decent breakfasts. Diving and watersports can be arranged. FB **$215**

EATING AND DRINKING

Baroness Bar & Restaurant By the KCB bank. One of the town centre's relatively more upmarket venues, a popular place where local dishes are joined by the pepper steak with chips (Ksh400) and chicken curry (Ksh175). Daily 7am–11pm.

Dhows Inn Mnarani, at the south side of the bridge. Good meals, including stews and fried fish at around the Ksh350 mark. In the evening it's often quite lively, as are the neighbouring bars. Daily 7am–late.

Holiday Celebration Café On the ground-floor terrace of the Watergate Hotel. Busy diner serving up spaghetti and meat sauce (Ksh200), kebabs (Ksh60) and Spanish omelettes (Ksh120) to a hungry local clientele. Daily 6.30am–10pm.

Jokers Behind Equity Bank. A brand-new Italian-style internet café with free wi-fi and good juices (around

Ksh150), snacks and fresh cakes (Ksh100–200), run by the people at Makuti Villas. Daily 7.30am–9pm.

★ **Kilifi Boatyard** Kilifi creekshore, south side, accessible via a dirt road from the old main road, 1km inland, then 2km down a steep gravel road to the waterfront ☎020 3509505, ⓦkilifiboats.com. With fine views of the creek and the dramatic bridge, this informal bar-restaurant is popular with Kilifi's seaside-settler and sailing community, making it *the* place for making contacts if you have any ideas of Indian Ocean crewing, or want to make contacts for sea-fishing excursions. They turn out fresh and simple seafood dishes, including fish and chips, or crab samosas and full English breakfasts (dishes Ksh300–1000), and there's a notice board for exchanging news and trading kit. Daily 7.30am–6.30pm.

Arabuko Sokoke National Park

Whether driving or walking, head first for the Forest Visitor Centre, 1.5km south of the Watamu junction on the Malindi–Mombasa road • $20 • ⓦ kws.go.ke/arabuko.html

The cashew trees lining both sides of the road north of Kilifi soon give way to tracts of jungle where monkeys scatter across the road and hornbills plunge into the cover of the trees. This is the **Arabuko Sokoke National Park**, the largest patch of indigenous coastal forest in East Africa. At one time it would have covered most of the coastal hinterland behind the shoreline settlements, part of an ancient forest belt stretching from Mozambique to Somalia. There are some 400 square kilometres to explore here, though you'll need a vehicle, or a few days for some walking. A tiny part of the area (six square kilometres in the far north) was declared a national park in 1991.

The bans on cutting timber and clearing bush for agriculture aren't popular with **local residents**, many of whom see the forest as a useless waste of land. To combat this ill feeling, the Kenya Wildlife Service, National Museums of Kenya and a forest support group, the Friends of Arabuko Sokoke (ⓦwatamu.net/foasf.html), have pioneered a number of projects to make conservation worthwhile for the community, including

ARABUKO SOKOKE FOREST WILDLIFE

Beside **elephants** (usually evidenced by their dung), **Sykes' monkeys** and **yellow baboons**, the forest also shelters two rare species of mammal. The 35cm-high **Aders' duiker** is a shy miniature antelope that usually lives in pairs, and the extraordinary **golden-rumped elephant shrew** (see p.42), which has been adopted as the symbol of the forest, is a bizarre insectivore, about the size of a small cat, that resembles a giant mouse with an elongated nose, running on stilts. In one of those mystifyingly evolved animal relationships, it consorts with a small bird, the **red-capped robin chat**, which warns it of danger and in turn picks up insects disturbed by the shrew's snufflings. Your best chance of seeing a shrew is to look for its fluttering companion among the tangle of branches: the shrew will be close by. Elephant shrews can usually be seen (but not for long – they're very speedy) on the walk along the Nature Trail close to the Visitor Centre, or along the sandy tracks further inside the forest. You may also spot one darting across forest trails ahead of you. The exceedingly rare **Sokoke bush-tailed mongoose** is unlikely to put in an appearance – there have been no sightings since the mid-1980s.

The forest is also home to six globally threatened **bird species**, including the small **Sokoke scops owl**, which is found only in the red-soiled *Cynometra* section of the forest, and the **Sokoke pipit** – both very hard to spot, although guides can help locate them. The other endangered birds are the **Amani sunbird**, **Clarke's weaver**, the **East Coast akalat** and the **spotted ground thrush**, a migrant from South Africa. As well as its wealth of mammals and birds, the forest is, in Africa, second only to the Okavango Delta in Botswana for the diversity of its **frog** population, a fact very much in evidence after heavy rain.

butterfly farming (see p.454), a bee-keeping scheme in which villagers are given low-cost beehives to produce honey from forest flowers (it's sold at the Forest Visitor Centre), and the harvesting of medicinal plants under licence.

EXPLORING ARABUKO SOKOKE NATIONAL PARK

Guides The Forest Visitor Centre, 1.5km south of the Watamu junction on the Malindi–Mombasa road, has guides available to escort you and you can camp at the main site beside the Visitor Centre ($15) or, if you book ahead, stay in the Tree House ($15), a large platform in the branches, with enough space for a two-person dome tent. Walking in the forest is best in the morning or late afternoon, and although this isn't the Amazon, a degree of preparation is a good idea if you plan on venturing far down any of the tracks leading off the main road. The Visitor Centre maps are adequate for the main trails but a GPS unit would be helpful if you're venturing off the main trails (though the signal can be weak under the trees). Official ASF are available at the Visitor Centre (or booked in advance on ☎ 0734 994931). You can also book them for fantastic night walks, which would be impossible on your own.

Nature Trail A nature trail takes you from the Visitor Centre around the first part of the forest. After rain, this area is spectacularly adorned with the nests of foam-nest tree frogs. It takes most of a morning, but it's an easy walk

and makes an excellent introduction to the forest and its medicinal uses. Take water and insect repellent with you. Another easy walk is to the tree house, a viewing platform high up a tree by a former sand quarry, from which you get superb vistas over the forest.

Driving routes If you're short of time, there are several driving routes, ideally with 4WD, which are also suitable for bikes. The main route starts at the Mida entrance, 2km south of the Visitor Centre on the main Mombasa–Malindi road, and goes up to the viewpoint through *Brachystegia* forest – look out for the rare Amani sunbird on the way. From the viewpoint, which looks east over the forest to Mida Creek and the Indian Ocean, a walking track continues a further 2km to a second viewpoint that looks west onto *Cynometra* forest and a large, exposed escarpment. There are other paths along the western edge of Whistling Duck Pools, at the junction between the *Brachystegia* and *Cynometra* forest on the main driving track between the Mida entrance and the viewpoints. These ponds are a favourite haunt for white-faced whistling ducks, little grebe and open-billed storks, as well as the odd elephant.

Mida Creek

Although not part of Arabuko Sokoke Forest, **Mida Creek**, which extends inland from the coast to the main road, is an interesting and unusually accessible area of tidal mud, grassland and mangrove forest, and is popular with naturalists.

Mida Creek Mangrove Board Walk & Bird Hide

3km south of the Arabuko Sokoke visitor centre, and signposted about 1km off the main road • Ksh250, plus Ksh300 per hour for your guide (up to four visitors)

The main target in Mida Creek is **Mida Creek Mangrove Board Walk & Bird Hide**. You park at the little information hut, then pay your fees and are escorted out through the mangroves to commune with the tidal ecosystem for as long as you like. If you're a keen birder, you might want to check the tides before your visit (see p.387). The best time to see waders is as the tide comes in.

ACCOMMODATION

MIDA CREEK

★ **Mida Eco-Camp** Next to the board walk ☎0729 213042 or 0701 018320, ⓦmidaecocamp.com. This Giriama community project with private UK input is a charming and welcoming gem of a place. The handful of quirky rooms in various experimental formats (nets, shared toilets and showers, solar power, but no plug sockets in the rooms) is complemented by a blissfully relaxing, open-air tree-platform lounge area where everyone tends to congregate for a cold beer, while watching the sun go down. The community's Giriama dance troupe often performs in the evening. Meals are highly recommended (around Ksh700) and the staff, who all benefit directly from every guest, will go out of their way to look after you. They particularly welcome children. Camping **Ksh300**, BB **Ksh1800**

Manfriday's Mida Cove Mida Creek south shore, most easily reached by boat from Temple Point on the Watamu side (they will meet you there or at Malindi airport) ☎020 2335387 or 0721 388401, ⓦmanfridays.com. If you want Robinson-Crusoe-esque remoteness, without sacrificing your comforts, these four individually serviced villas around a pool above the beach at the mouth of Mida Creek will fit the bill. Room only **$140**

Gedi ruins

Ruins daily 7am–6pm • Ksh500 • **Nature trail and observation platform** daily 7am–6pm • Ksh100 • Any Mombasa- or Malindi-bound bus or matatu can drop you off at the Kobil station at Gedi junction, where the Malindi–Mombasa road meets the turn-off for Watamu; the junction is a ten-minute walk from the site, which is clearly signposted

Dense forest in the area may help to explain the enigma of **GEDI**. This large, thirteenth- to seventeenth-century Swahili town was apparently unknown to the Portuguese, despite the fact that they had a strong presence only 15km away in Malindi for nearly a hundred years, during a time when Gedi is judged to have been at the peak of its prosperity. Bafflingly, Gedi, sometimes spelled Gede, is not mentioned in any old Portuguese, Arabic or Swahili writings and it has to be assumed that as it was set back from the sea and deep in the forest its scale and significance were never noticed.

The **ruins** are confusing, eerie and hauntingly beautiful, especially in the late afternoon. Even if you're not that interested in visiting historical sites, don't miss this one. Forest has invaded the town over the three centuries since it was deserted, and baobabs and magnificent buttress-rooted trees tower over the dimly lit walls and arches.

Gedi has a sinister reputation and local people have always been uneasy about it. Since 1948, when it was opened to the public, it has collected its share of ghost stories and tales of inexplicable happenings. Some of this cultural baggage may derive from the supposed occupation of the ruins in the eighteenth century by the **Oromo** (probably ancestors of the Orma, who live along the Tana River). At the time, the violent and unsettled lifestyle of the Oromo was a major threat to the coastal communities. Even today, Gedi tingles spines easily, particularly if you are on your own. James Kirkman, the archeologist who first worked at the site, remembers: "when I first started to work at Gedi I had the feeling that something or somebody was looking out from behind the walls, neither hostile nor friendly but waiting for what he knew was going to happen."

The more time you spend at Gedi, the further you seem from an answer to its anomalies. The display of pottery shards from all over the world in the small **museum** shows that the town must have been actively trading with overseas merchants, yet it is 5km from the sea and 2km from Mida Creek; and the coastline has probably moved inland over the centuries, so it might previously have been even further away. At the time, with the supposed Oromo threat hanging over the district, sailing into Mida Creek would have been like entering a lobster pot. The reasons for Gedi's location remain thoroughly obscure and its absence from historical records grows more inexplicable the more you think about it.

The site

The **town** is typical of medieval Swahili settlements. It was walled, and originally covered just under a quarter of a square kilometre – some 45 acres. The majority of its estimated 2500 inhabitants probably lived in mud-and-thatch huts, on the southern, poorer side of town, away from Mecca. These have long been overwhelmed and dissolved by the jungle. The palace and the stone town were in the northern part of the settlement. When the site was reoccupied at the end of the sixteenth century – archeologists have established that there was a hiatus of about fifty years – a new inner wall was built, enclosing just this prestigious zone.

It's easy to spend hours at Gedi, and rewarding to walk down some of the well-swept paths through the thick jungle away from the main ruins. In the undergrowth, you catch spooky glimpses of other buildings still unexcavated. ASSETS, the Arabuko Sokoke Schools & Ecotourism Scheme (ⓦassets-kenya.org), has built a nature trail and an observation platform, high in a baobab overlooking the palace. With patience you may see a **golden-rumped elephant shrew** (see p.451). Gedi also has monkeys, bushbabies, tiny duiker antelope and, according to local legend, a huge, mournful, sheep-like animal that follows you like a shadow down the paths.

The Palace

The **Palace**, with its striking entrance porch, sunken courts and honeycomb of little rooms, is the most impressive single building. The concentration of **houses** outside its east wall is where most of Gedi's interesting finds were made and they are named accordingly: house of the scissors, house of the ivory box, house of the dhow (with a picture of a dhow on the wall). If you have been to Lamu, the tight layout of buildings and streets will be familiar, although in Gedi all the houses had just one storey.

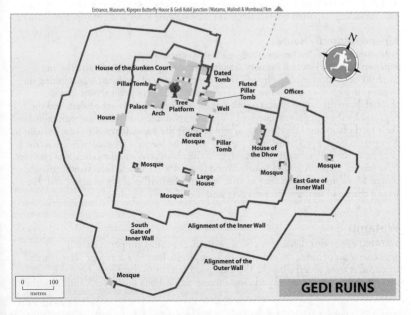

GEDI RUINS

6

As usual, sanitary arrangements are much in evidence: Gedi's toilets are all of identical design, and superior to the long-drops you still find in Kenya today. While many of the houses have been modified over the centuries, these bathrooms seem original. Look out for the **house of the sunken court**, one of the most elaborate dwellings, with its self-conscious emulation of the palace's courtyards.

As you walk around, watch out for the **ants** that have colonized many of the ruins, forming seething brown columns and gathering in enormous clumps. Be careful where you put your feet when stepping over walls and try not to stand on the walls themselves: they are very fragile.

The Great Mosque

Gedi's **Great Mosque**, one of seven on the site, was its Friday mosque, the mosque of the whole town. Compared with other ruined mosques on the coast, this one is very large and had a *minbar*, or pulpit, of three stone steps, rather than the usual wooden construction. Perhaps an inkling of the kind of people who worshipped here – they were both men and women – and their form of Islam, comes from the carving of a broad-bladed **spearhead** above the arch of the mosque's northeast doorway. Whoever they were, they were clearly not the "colonial Arabs" long believed by European classical scholars to have been the people of Gedi: it's hard to believe that Arabs would have made use of the spear symbol of East African pastoralists.

Tombs

Near the mosque is a good example of a **pillar tomb**. These are found all along the coast and are associated with men of importance – chiefs, sheikhs and senior community elders. The fact that this kind of grave is utterly alien to the rest of the Islamic world is further indication that coastal Islam was distinctly African for a long time. Such tombs aren't constructed any more, although there's one from the nineteenth century in Malindi. It looks as if the more recent waves of Arab immigration to the coast have tended to discourage what must have seemed to them an eccentric, even barbaric, style. The **dated tomb** close to the ticket office gives an idea of Gedi's age. Its epitaph reads 802 AH – or 1400 AD. Also by the office, the **museum** exhibits various finds from the site, including imported artefacts such as Chinese Ming vases and even Spanish scissors.

Kipepeo Butterfly House

By the entrance to Gedi ruins • Daily 8am–5pm • Ksh200 • ☎ 0719 671161, ⓦ kipepeo.org

Kipepeo Butterfly House & Farmers' Training Centre (*kipepeo* means "butterfly" in Swahili) helps local residents benefit from the proximity of the forest by exploiting the overseas market for exotic butterflies as preserved specimens and subjects in walk-through butterfly houses. Local people net the adult butterflies in the forest, and the eggs laid by the females are harvested. When hatched, the caterpillars are maintained on their food plants until they pupate, at which point the pupae (chrysalises) are brought to Kipepeo to be shipped to foreign customers, and the breeders are paid. Visitors to the centre can see the insects at various stages of their life cycle, and the centre also provides information on the Arabuko Sokoke Forest (see p.450), and sells local handicrafts and honey. Morning is the best time to visit, when the butterflies are most active and you have a chance of seeing them emerging, and their wings expanding.

Watamu

WATAMU can at first sight seem a bit superficial, consisting simply of a small agglomeration of hotels, a strip of beachfront private homes, a compact village shaded by coconut trees, and the beach. There are good reasons to come here, however, including the superb marine park, some interesting wildlife initiatives, youthful nightlife

(sporadically) and the beautiful beach itself. Watamu is comfortable with tourists, and despite tourism's high profile, there's a discernibly easier-going atmosphere here than at Diani, Malindi or along Mombasa's north coast. As most of the beach is within the marine park, KWS regulations tend to be more strictly enforced to keep hawkers away.

This is an exceptional shoreline, with three stunning bays – **Watamu Bay**, the **Blue Lagoon** and **Turtle Bay** – separated by raised coral cliffs and dotted with tiny, sculpted

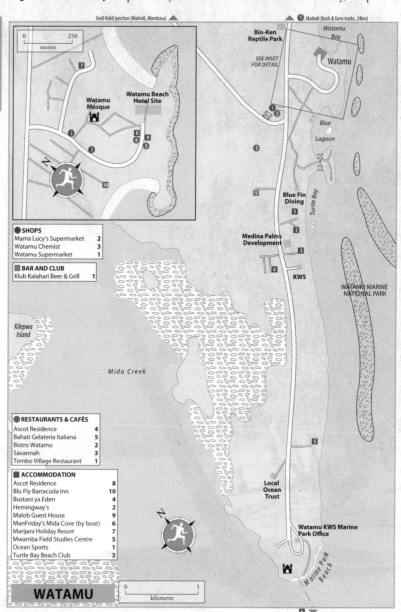

Gedi Kobil junction (Malindi, Mombasa) ▲

▲ ❶ Malindi (bush & farm tracks, 24km)

Watamu Bay

Bio-Ken Reptile Park

SEE INSET FOR DETAIL

Watamu

0 — 250
metres

Watamu Mosque

Watamu Beach Hotel Site

Blue Lagoon

Turtle Bay

Blue Fin Diving

Medina Palms Development

KWS

WATAMU MARINE NATIONAL PARK

Kilepwa Island

Mida Creek

Local Ocean Trust

Watamu KWS Marine Park Office

Marine Park Beach

WATAMU

0 — 1
kilometre

● **SHOPS**
Mama Lucy's Supermarket	2
Watamu Chemist	3
Watamu Supermarket	1

■ **BAR AND CLUB**
Klub Kalahari Beer & Grill	1

● **RESTAURANTS & CAFÉS**
Ascot Residence	4
Bahati Gelateria Italiana	5
Bistro Watamu	2
Savannah	3
Tembo Village Restaurant	1

■ **ACCOMMODATION**
Ascot Residence	8
Blu Fly Barracuda Inn	10
Bustani ya Eden	4
Hemingway's	2
Malob Guest House	9
ManFriday's Mida Cove (by boat)	6
Marijani Holiday Resort	7
Mwamba Field Studies Centre	5
Ocean Sports	1
Turtle Bay Beach Club	3

coral islets. Watamu is good for **diving** – and a good place to get qualified, with several diving schools. Out in the **Watamu Marine National Park**, when the visibility is good, the submerged crags of living coral gardens and their swirls of brilliant fish are still magically vivid, although like elsewhere they are suffering from contact damage and the steady rise in sea temperature.

Watamu Village

Watamu village is a weird mixture of unhurried fishing community and Europhile souvenir centre. The traditional rubs elbows with the pseudo-hip; Samburu and Maasai *morani* in full ochred splendour stand around waiting for photographers to approach them; and the worshippers wandering in and out of the large Jamia Mosque seem quite unfazed by it all.

Bio-Ken reptile park

Daily 10am–noon & 2–5pm • Ksh750 • ☏ 042 2332303, ⓦ bio-ken.com

About 1.3km north of the Gedi junction is a superb little **reptile park**, Bio-Ken, which houses a large collection of snakes, some lizards, plus a few tortoises, terrapins and the odd young crocodile. It's an interesting visit – they have some very impressive creatures here – and you'll be guided round by someone who actually knows a bit about reptiles as all the staff are well informed and one is a silver-level safari guide.

Watamu Marine National Park

Daily 6am–6pm • $15 • ⓦ kws.org

The **Watamu Marine National Park** stretches along the coast from the Blue Lagoon to Mida Creek. On the one hand, this **total exclusion zone** for fishermen has not been greeted with rhapsody by all local people. On the other, tourists come in large numbers and Watamu hasn't gone far wrong in identifying their needs. This is a highly rated **snorkelling** and **diving** territory, where the reef is reasonably close to shore, still mostly in good condition and the water crystal clear in the right season. Harmless **whale sharks** also occasionally visit the area, as do dolphins – a highlight for any diver. Boat trips can be arranged in quest of these, and it's become accepted practice to pay only a nominal charge for the trip if you're unsuccessful. Check the terms carefully before signing up with any of the dive operators (see p.460).

The coral gardens

If you've never taken a swim before in a shoal of coral fish, the spectacle can be breathtaking: every conceivable combination of colour and shape – and a few inconceivable ones – is represented. The ostentatious dazzle of some of them, especially the absurd parrot fish, can be simply hilarious. The most common destination is the "**coral gardens**", a kilometre or two offshore, where the boat drifts, suspended in five or six metres of scintillatingly clear water. Here, over a group of giant coral heads, where fish naturally congregate, you enter the unusual park. If you dive to the sea floor, you'll get an intense experience of sharing the undersea world with the fish and the coral. Watch out for the small, harmless octopuses that stay motionless until disturbed and then jet themselves across the sea bed – they're brilliant masters of disguise, altering their form and colour to match their surroundings. If such adventures aren't your forte, the glass bottoms of the boats provide an alternative view – but it's often a slightly murky and narrow one.

GETTING TO WATAMU MARINE NATIONAL PARK

Ocean Sports and Hemingway's (see p.459) both run glass-bottom boat snorkelling trips. Otherwise, you'll have to haggle with the boatmen along the beach, or outside the park headquarters and ticket office down at the south end of the Watamu road at Temple Point. Expect to pay around Ksh3000 per person (not including park fees) for a three-hour trip in a glass-bottomed boat combining the coral gardens with, at high tide, a trip along Mida Creek. Masks, snorkels and sometimes fins are provided, but remember to take plenty of sun cream.

Watamu beach

Watamu's **beach** is beautiful, with its coral outcrop islands within swimming distance of the hotel gardens. Although they mostly started as **fishing** and **diving** centres (see p.460), many of the hotels are getting involved with **community and environmental projects** that channel tourist excursion money into the local economy.

Local Ocean Trust: Turtle Rehab Centre

Mon–Fri 9.30am–12.30pm & 2.30–4.30pm, Sat 9.30am–noon • Ksh300 • ⊛ watamuturtles.com

Among environmental initiatives, one in which many hotels participate, and which individual tourists can contribute to, is the Watamu turtle watch scheme run by **Local Ocean Trust**. This project protects the eggs of threatened marine turtles from poaching by paying local people to guard nests. The same group also pays fishermen to hand in turtles that have got ensnared in fishing nets for treatment of their injuries and release back into the sea – anything from eight hundred to a thousand turtles every year. The **Turtle Rehab Centre** has some shady quarantine pools where you can usually "meet" recovering turtles.

August brings lots of sea grass to Watamu, and turtles mate and lay in the same month. The **eggs**, which are buried en masse on the beach in pits dug by the females with their flippers, and then covered in sand, take 60 to 75 days to incubate, so October and November are commonly the months when nests usually hatch. Watamu's turtles are mostly the green and hawksbill species. Despite extensive research and observation, it is still not known where the babies go after hatching. What is clear is that only one in a thousand survives to maturity.

Visitors can sponsor a turtle for release or a nest for guarding (you can see the nest sites if you walk down the Watamu peninsula towards Temple Point). The Local Ocean Trust is informed when nests that are being guarded start to hatch, so, if you contact them, you may be able to go and see the baby turtles scuttling down the sand like tiny clockwork toys. Mwamba Field Studies Centre (see opposite) is a good place to be based if you don't want to miss anything.

ARRIVAL AND DEPARTURE   WATAMU

By bus and matatu Getting to Watamu is easy, with frequent matatus making the run from Malindi. Buses and matatus ploughing up and down the coast highway will drop you at the Gedi junction, leaving you to walk, hitch a lift, wait for a local matatu, or take a *tuk-tuk* or cab for the last, dead-straight, 6km.

GETTING AROUND

By bike Bicycle rental is offered by a number of outlets, especially in high season when it gets quite competitive (Ksh500–1000 per day, depending on season and number of days). Bikes are a great way of getting to know Watamu, with the Gedi ruins and anywhere on the beach road easily reachable in thirty minutes or so.

SERVICES

Coming into Watamu itself, you pass the **post office** before reaching the beach road T-junction, along which matatus scud up and down all the time. Just north of the junction, if you continue up the beach road a little way past the turning for the supermarket, a road off to the right takes you into the village (the KCB bank, with **ATM**, is on the left). Watamu Chemist is open Mon–Sat 8am–8pm, Sun 8am–1pm. Watamu Supermarket and Mama Lucy's supermarket are both well stocked, but there's no big-name supermarket in town.

ACCOMMODATION

There are several accommodation options in the village itself – everything from humble B&Ls to a pleasant holiday hotel. If you have a tent, you can **camp** at *Ocean Sports*. Watamu's **beach hotels and lodgings** are a mixed bag. Several focus on watersports, with diving and game fishing the main activities. The big fishing competition in the first or second week of March can make accommodation scarce, but May and June usually see excellent low-season rates. Matatus usually only go as far south as *Turtle Bay*, where *piki-pikis* or *tuk-tuks* can be hired to take you further south.

VILLAGE ACCOMMODATION

Ascot Residence Village centre ☎042 2232326 or 0721 267761, ⊛ascotresidence.com. Good-value, two-room studios (sleeping four), with nets and fans but no a/c, and a large pool. The pleasant, breezy public areas get fairly lively in high season and there's a small casino/gaming room. Most guests are Italian. BB $75

Malob Guest House Near the entrance to the village ☎042 232260 or 0717 008101. Friendly lodgings off a small courtyard. The eight s/c rooms, with nets and fans, are clean enough, if a bit dark and dingy. Ksh1200

Marijani Holiday Resort North of the village ☎0735 258263, ⊛marjani-holiday-resort.com. Friendly, very informal German-run place, with fifteen, comfortable and good-value rooms (four-poster beds, nets, fans, fridges, spotless bathrooms) in two stylish houses. All rooms have fridges, some have kitchens. BB Ksh3000

BEACH HOTELS AND OTHER ACCOMMODATION

The following listings are arranged from north to south. Unless otherwise noted, they are all on the beach.

Blu Fly Barracuda Inn ☎042 232223 or 042 232522, ⊛blufly.it. Unusual hotel with impressive *makuti*-vaulted reception, well worth considering for its location on the shore of the Blue Lagoon, and its great views. Ground-floor rooms are more spacious – all have a/c – and there are tennis courts and a pool. Largely Italian guests. BB $180

★ **Ocean Sports** ☎034 195227 or 0724 389732, ⊛oceansports.net. Slightly macho place, whose reputation ("Open Shorts") has sailed before it for years. During holiday times it swarms with young Anglo-Kenyans doing their own thing, but the staff are great, as is the food, and it's right above the beach, with a great deck. All 44 rooms have nets, fans, a/c and safes and pleasantly rustic bathrooms, but foam mattresses on the beds are disappointing. There's an adjoining campsite plus tennis, squash, two pools, a PADI diving school and free wi-fi. Camping Ksh500, double Ksh12,800

Hemingway's ☎042 2332724, ⊛hemingways.co.ke. From Oct–April, landing big fish is high on the agenda here, but this is a really good mainstream hotel where the atmosphere tends towards the formal, though there's nothing much for children – or non-fishing adults. Deluxe rooms in the north wing are very nice, large with huge beds, a/c and sea views, but no TVs. Two pools. HB $360

★ **Turtle Bay Beach Club** ☎042 22332003 or 0721 830604, ⊛turtlebay.co.ke. Expertly run, all-inclusive holiday club, full of happy holidaymakers, mainly from the UK. Lots to do, lots to eat, and plenty of cheap booze. The gardens are cramped, but facilities include two pools, tennis, PADI diving and windsurfing schools, and free bicycles and watersports. Staff and management actively participate in local community and environmental initiatives – they have a silver rating from Ecotourism Kenya. AI $240

Bustani ya Eden West of the road, not on the beach ☎042 2332124 or 0787 576336. Plain, tidy, comfortable, s/c, chalet-style rooms, with fans and nets, attached to a locally renowned bar-restaurant, with reasonably priced seafood and African dishes. Free wi-fi. BB Ksh2500

★ **Mwamba Field Studies Centre** ☎020 335865, ⊛arocha.org. Formerly *Mrs Simpson's*, this guesthouse is now run by the Christian conservation group A Rocha, though it is open to all and is only evangelical about the environment. They have 14 beds in various clean, simple s/c rooms with nets, and camping pitches. Snorkelling gear, bird walks and turtle-watching are all available and it's close to the nearly deserted beach. Staying is on a FB basis only, including for campers, with all meals eaten communally. Camping per person Ksh1750, FB Ksh7000

EATING, DRINKING AND NIGHTLIFE

Ascot Residence Village centre ☎0721 267761. Caters mainly to Italian couples looking for a romantic dinner. The wood-fired pizza oven produces very authentic pizzas, and the wine list is moderately priced. Pizzas from Ksh500, seafood dishes from Ksh750. Daily 11.30am–2pm & 6–10pm.

★ **Bahati Gelateria Italiana** Watamu village ☎0724 079856. Outstandingly good home-made *gelati* and pastries in this very popular and polished Italian-run ice-cream parlour and snack-café that has grown from tiny beginnings to fill a whole block. Perfect for a dawn breakfast of hot croissants and cappuccino. Daily 5.30am–7pm.

Bistro Watamu By the supermarket. A popular stop-off for local *wazungu*, this serves very nice, freshly ground coffee (Ksh100), cakes (Ksh150), quiche slices (Ksh150), toasted sandwiches (Ksh220), and shakes and juices (Ksh100–200). Mon–Sat 8am–5pm.

Klub Kalahari Beer & Grill and Sky Gardens Signposted off the beach road. Lively bar and Watamu's best local nightspot, a great place to meet local people, with DJs in season and occasional live music. Daily 10am–late.

★ **Savannah** Down a track opposite the post office ☎0726287637 or 0721 845446. Family restaurant with strong Brit appeal, *Savannah* is a home-away-from-home "local" for many repeat visitors to Watamu, with darts and quizzes (plus a pool) to add to the draw of burgers (Ksh750), steaks (Ksh950), seafood platters and a monthly Sunday hog roast. Mid-July to April Tues–Sun 10am–midnight, May to mid-July Fri & Sat 6pm–midnight, Sun 10am–midnight.

6

Tembo Village Restaurant Signposted along the road to Bioken ☎0721 980840 or 0721 706468, ⓦtembovillage.com. Highly recommended restaurant at this small hotel, only open to visitors for dinner. The dinner menu offers a small range of seafood, grills and salads that changes daily. Allow Ksh2000 per person, without drinks. Daily 7–9pm.

DIVING

From October to March, when the water is clearest, the diving possibilities are extensive, with as many as sixteen diving sites off Watamu, compared with Malindi's five sites. **Turtle Reef**, a few hundred metres offshore, offers big shoals of surgeon and parrot fish around high coral heads. Further out, a popular site is **Moray Reef**, where at least one, very large moray eel has become used to visiting divers. Further north, a good spot for beginners is the shallow **Drummers Reef** site, where you can see blue-spotted rays, napoleon wrasse and scorpion fish, and, fairly often on the landward side, **turtles**. There are three dive centres at Watamu; the best plan is probably to visit all of them and make your own assessment of their competence and suitability. Remember that **marine park fees** are extra ($15 per day, payable at the KWS Marin Park office at the end of the beach road, or to your operator). If you're a qualified diver, each dive will cost around €30–40 including equipment, or somewhat less with your own equipment. There are reductions if you book a series of dives, and small supplements for night- and wreck-dives. If you haven't dived for a while, you should be asked to do a check-out dive (usually free) or a one-day refresher. If you're a beginner, you can do either a one-day, one-dive course (around €100), or opt for a PADI course of four dives over five days – leading to Open Water certification – for around €400.

DIVE OPERATORS

Aqua Ventures Based at Ocean Sports ☎042 2332420, ⓦdiveinkenya.com. Long-establised leading operator, with PADI Open Water certification for €460. BSAC Premier Centre (the only one in Kenya), used by the British army for dive training. Underwater digital camera hire at €30 per dive. **Blue Fin Diving** Next to Blue Bay Village ☎0722 261242, ⓦbluefindiving.com. Based in Watamu from Nov–April and Malindi from July–Nov, but offering diving year-round (from intro dives to PADI Open Water certification – €360) from many of Watamu's hotels.

Turtle Bay Beach Club See p.459 ☎0733 295487 or 0721 830604, ⓦturtlebay.co.ke/dive_centre.html, ⓦturtledive.com. Single dives for qualified divers with own equipment: €33; PADI Open Water certificate: €460.

FISHING

The **game-fishing** season runs from July to mid-April (there is no legal season as such, but few boats go out in the rough seas between May and July), with the main season for **billfish** – those with spikes on their snouts, including sailfish and black, striped and blue marlin – roughly November to mid-March. Other species commonly hooked include wahoo, kingfish, dorado, bonito, giant trevally and various sharks, including some big tiger sharks and bull sharks. If you're fishing between July and October, before the wind swings round, it's good to be aware that conditions can be rough – it's not for the faint-hearted. While some fish are caught for eating and invariably killed and sold by the crew (yellow fin tuna particularly), all captains have a policy of tag-and-release for sharks and billfish. The fish are tagged for migration research, and a $5 bounty paid for delivery of tags from recaptured fish. The biggest **sea-fishing centre** in Watamu is Hemingway's (see p.459). Watamu-based **independent boat owners** offer a day's fishing from around $700, usually for a group of four or five, with lunch and drinks included. They're normally prepared to be a little more flexible than Hemingway's on the question of what time you have to be back on shore.

TRIP PROVIDERS

Alleycat ☎020 2335871 or 0722 734788, ⓦalley catfishing.com. Full days from around $650–850 depending on season.
Hemingway's ☎042 2332277, ⓦhemingways.co .ke. Full-day trips from 6.30am–4.30pm for a maximum of four people, prices from $750–1100 depending on season.
Tarka Based at Ocean Sports ☎0722 282573, ⓔtarka @swiftmalindi.com. 10-hour day-trips from $650–900 depending on season.

Malindi and around

When Vasco da Gama's fleet arrived at **MALINDI** in 1498, it met an unexpectedly warm welcome. The king of Malindi had presumably heard of Mombasa's attempts to sabotage the fleet a few days earlier and, no friend of Mombasa himself, he was swift to ally himself with the powerful and dangerous Portuguese. Until they finally subdued

Mombasa nearly one hundred years later, Malindi was the Portuguese centre of operations on the East African coast. Once Fort Jesus was built, Malindi's ruling family was invited to transfer their power base there, which they did, and for many years Malindi was virtually a ghost town as its aristocrats lived it up in Mombasa under Portuguese protection.

Malindi's reputation for **hospitality** to strangers has stuck, and so has the suggestion of sell-out. It has an amazingly salacious reputation, and although there was a slump in German tourism after the first AIDS-awareness crisis in the 1980s, a quick glance in some of the bars suggests that the sex safari is back in full swing, now dominated by Italians. As a growing zone for the cultivation of Euros, Malindi is slipping towards cultural anonymity: it can't seem to make up its mind whether it wants to be a Mombasa or a Lamu. While its old centre clings on to some Swahili character, it lacks Lamu's self-contained tranquillity. And although it makes a good base for visits to Gedi and the Arabuko Sokoke Forest, and for a trip to Lamu, it remains unashamedly geared towards beach tourism.

Consequently, whether you enjoy Malindi or not depends a little on how highly you rate the unsophisticated parts of Kenya, and whether you appreciate a fully fledged resort town for its facilities or loathe it for its tackiness. It also depends on when you're here. During December and January, the town can sometimes be a bit nightmarish, with everything African seeming to recede behind the swarms of window-shopping tourists and Suzuki jeeps.

Fortunately, Malindi has some important saving graces. Number one is the **coral reef** south of the town centre. The combined Malindi/Watamu Marine National Park and Reserve encloses some of the best stretches on the coast, and the Malindi fish have become so used to humans that they swarm in front of your mask like a kaleidoscopic snowstorm. Malindi is also a **game-fishing** centre with regular competitions, and it's also something of a surfing, windsurfing and kitesurfing resort, too. Good-sized rollers steam into the bay through the long break in the reef, opposite the town, between June and late September, whipped up by the southerly monsoon (*kusi*) wind. The surfing isn't world class, but it's fun, and good enough for boogie boards.

Despite the heavy reliance on tourism, Malindi still has some interest as a Kenyan town with an ancient history, and a few places of interest other than its beach and reef. An interesting old Swahili quarter, one or two archeological and historical sites, a busy market, shops, *hotelis* and plenty of lodgings all balance out the tourist boutiques, beauty salons and real-estate agencies. As for the **Italian influence**, the new resident expats have brought the town riches that nowhere else in Kenya can boast – and some of the best pizzas, pasta and ice cream in the whole of Africa – even if the suspiciously dormant state of some Italian businesses makes you wonder how legitimate they all are.

Malindi town

Malindi was first opened up by settlers as a seaside resort in the 1930s, at a time when ocean air, "sea level and sanity" were considered the proper antidote to the grind of

---

SEA AND WATER CONDITIONS IN MALINDI

Malindi's shoreline can get very windy around September, and during June, July and November the beach becomes covered in **seaweed** – many hotels clear their beachfronts daily, though the seaweed is clean and perfectly harmless, and in fact prevents erosion of the beach (clearing it is prohibited within the limits of the marine park). It's also worth knowing that the headland of **Vasco da Gama Point** marks a locally important division. To the north, the sea water is often reddish-brown and cloudy – full of the soil erosion brought down by the Sabaki River, especially after rain – and, to the south, the Marine Park encloses a zone of often aquarium-clear water.

making a living in the highlands. The last of a sun-wrinkled generation from a bygone area can still be seen strolling on **Lamu Road**, which though increasingly built up with little malls and new developments is happily still shaded by big trees. Lamu Road is set far back from the **seafront**, however, which you can't see from the town centre.

Today, taking a walk into town is still the main pastime, and not without its idiosyncratic rewards. The old part of Malindi is a half-hour diversion: interesting enough, even though there's nothing specific to see and few of the buildings date from

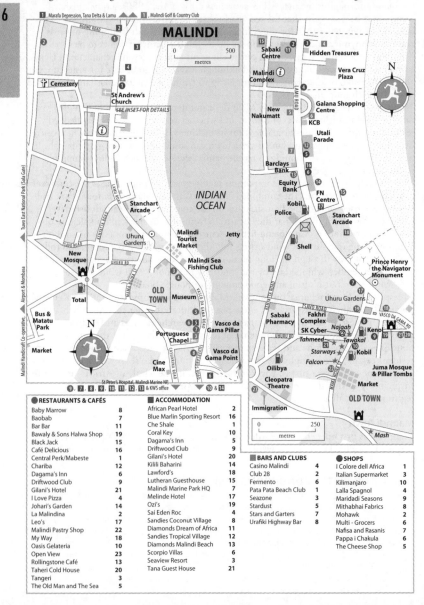

MALINDI

INDIAN OCEAN

● RESTAURANTS & CAFÉS	
Baby Marrow	8
Baobab	7
Bar Bar	11
Bawaly & Sons Halwa Shop	19
Black Jack	15
Café Delicious	16
Central Perk/Mabeste	1
Chariba	12
Dagama's Inn	6
Driftwood Club	9
Gilani's Hotel	21
I Love Pizza	4
Johari's Garden	14
La Malindina	2
Leo's	17
Malindi Pastry Shop	22
My Way	18
Oasis Gelateria	10
Open View	23
Rollingstone Café	13
Taheri Cold House	20
Tangeri	3
The Old Man and The Sea	5

■ ACCOMMODATION	
African Pearl Hotel	2
Blue Marlin Sporting Resort	16
Che Shale	1
Coral Key	10
Dagama's Inn	5
Driftwood Club	9
Gilani's Hotel	20
Kilili Baharini	14
Lawford's	18
Lutheran Guesthouse	15
Malindi Marine Park HQ	7
Melinde Hotel	17
Ozi's	19
Sai Eden Roc	4
Sandies Coconut Village	8
Diamonds Dream of Africa	11
Sandies Tropical Village	12
Diamonds Malindi Beach	13
Scorpio Villas	6
Seaview Resort	3
Tana Guest House	21

■ BARS AND CLUBS	
Casino Malindi	4
Club 28	2
Fermento	6
Pata Pata Beach Club	1
Seazone	3
Stardust	5
Stars and Garters	7
Urafiki Highway Bar	8

● SHOPS	
I Colore dell Africa	1
Italian Supermarket	3
Kilimanjaro	10
Lalla Spagnol	4
Maridadi Seasons	9
Mithabhai Fabrics	8
Mohawk	2
Multi - Grocers	6
Nafisa and Rasanis	7
Pappa i Chakula	6
The Cheese Shop	5

6

MALINDI'S BEACHES

The beach near the town centre, several hundred metres east of Lamu Road, is windswept and less appealing than you might imagine. For more of a seaside atmosphere, the seafront **Vasco da Gama Road** further south is pleasant, especially in the late afternoon. For the real McCoy, beach-wise, you need to go further south of the town centre to the aptly named **Silversands Beach**, complete with its reef-fringed lagoon, palm trees and inevitable beach boys.

---

before the second half of the nineteenth century. But the juxtaposition of the workaday business of the old town with the *mzungu*-mania only a couple of minutes' walk away on Lamu Road produces a schizophrenic atmosphere that perfectly epitomizes Malindi.

Malindi's **archeological sites** are fairly scant. The two **pillar tombs** in front of the Juma (Friday) Mosque on the waterfront are fine upstanding examples of the genre, though the shorter one is only nineteenth century. This being Malindi, their appearance is sometimes described as "circumcised", though Islamic scholars on the coast do not of course accept the phallic label applied by foreigners.

Malindi's most notable monuments are Portuguese, the most recent bequest being the ugly 1959 **Monument to Prince Henry the Navigator** on the seaward side of Uhuru Gardens. It looks a little more impressive if you walk around the other side and notice the Portuguese red cross on the front of the sail.

The town museum

Daily 8am–6pm • Ksh500, including same-day entry to Portuguese Chapel and Vasco da Gama Cross

A nineteenth-century trader's shop on the waterfront – the **House of Columns** – was opened as the town **museum** in 2004. With a preserved coelacanth fish downstairs, and some photographs of archeological sites on the coast upstairs – plus a good series of wall posters explaining Vasco da Gama and the Portuguese period on the coast – there is not quite enough to justify the entry fee on its own. The occasional temporary exhibition is a bonus, and the fee does include entry to Malindi's two Portuguese sites.

Portuguese monuments

Both daily 8am–6pm • Ksh500, including same-day entry to museum

The **Vasco da Gama Pillar,** far out on a coral outcrop on Vasco da Gama Point, and dating from 1499, makes a good target for a stroll. Once threatened by coastal erosion, the outcrop has been reinforced and the pillar itself – a typical Portuguese *padrao*, or standard, of its era that would have carried the Portuguese coat of arms – is regularly whitewashed.

The **Portuguese Chapel** on Vasco da Gama Road is a tiny cube of a church now covered with *makuti*, whose foundations were laid in the sixteenth century on the site of a Portuguese burial ground. There are a number of old burial sites in the grounds as well as more recent graves with inscriptions.

Malindi Marine National Park

Daily 6am–6pm • $15 • Boat trips: you should find a little room for discussion but won't be able to knock down prices much below the current going rate of Ksh3000 (excluding park fees) for two hours, especially at peak seasons; in fact your outing may be somewhat curtailed if you bargain too ruthlessly • Glass-bottomed boats Ksh3000–5000 for two hours • ⓦ kws.org • Six square kilometres

Trips out to the **marine park** can be arranged with the boat-trip salesmen who make their rounds of the beaches and hotels most mornings. Alternatively, make your own way down to the park office and very pretty beach at **Casuarina Point**, 5km from town, where you can choose your boat and captain. Be sure to check out the condition of masks and snorkels, and insist on a set for each member of the party. Fins, assuming they have any that fit you, are not likely to be up to much.

The national park takes in the loveliest areas of coral garden, between 1km and 4km offshore, and the trip is worth every shilling you finally agree on. The **snorkelling** itself is sublime and, especially if this is your first time snorkelling, is an unforgettable experience. Look out for the unusual weedy scorpionfish, an array of beautiful sea horses and the bizarre-looking Spanish dancer – a huge and colourful sea slug. Unless you have a mortal fear of snorkelling, don't bother with the **glass-bottomed boats**, which generally have small, not very clear windows.

The Marafa Depression

Ksh1000 community fee • To get to Marafa, take the road out of Malindi heading north, turn left on the other side of the Galana (Sabaki) bridge and from there go via Marikebuni and Magarini (about 80km round trip); alternatively, a handful of matatus run to Marafa village every day, or you could hire a cab and negotiate the price – between Ksh5000 and Ksh10,000; to get to the gorge itself, fork right at the end of Marafa village, and the canyon is about 500m along on the left, hidden until you're right at its edge

Northwest of Malindi, the **Marafa Depression** is the remains of a large sandstone ridge, now reduced by wind, rain and floodwater to a series of gorges, where steep gullies and narrow arêtes alternately eat into or jut from the main ridge wall. The colours of the exposed sandstone range from off-white through pale pink and orange to deep crimson, all capped by the rich tawny topsoil. It's particularly dramatic at sunset.

"Hell's Kitchen" is the common nickname for this impressive landscape, though the locals call it Nyari – "the place broken by itself" – and tell numerous moralizing stories about its dark origins. The main one sets the word of a monotheistic, all-powerful deity against traditional wisdom, and tells how the people of a village that once stood here were warned by God about a forthcoming miraculous event. They were commanded to move out, and all did so, except one old woman, who refused to believe such nonsense. The village and the old lady disappeared a short while later, leaving Nyari.

At the lip of the gorge, it's easy to descend the steep path to the bottom, where you can count on spending an hour or two exploring the natural architecture of what looks like an early *Star Trek* set.

ARRIVAL AND DEPARTURE
MALINDI AND AROUND

BY BUS AND MATATU

If you're arriving from Mombasa, you'll end up at the main bus station and matatu area, about ten minutes' walk south of town along the Mombasa road; a taxi to the centre shouldn't cost more than Ksh400, or Ksh1000 to the furthest beach hotels (half that for a *tuk-tuk*). Leaving Malindi, there are frequent services to Gedi, Watamu, Kilifi and Mombasa, and infrequent local matatus and buses for points inland from the main bus station and matatu park. In addition, some matatus for Watamu leave from the town centre by the old market in Mama Ngina Road. Coming from Lamu or Garissa, you'll be dropped by the bus companies' booking offices in the town centre between the market and the high street. Bus services to Lamu start off from Mombasa, and pass by their Malindi booking offices in the centre of town by the old market at around 9am or 11pm each day, reaching the Mokowe jetty for the short crossing to Lamu approximately 5–6 hours later; tickets cost Ksh600–700. It's advisable to buy your ticket for Lamu the day before – otherwise you may have an exceedingly uncomfortable standing-up experience to look forward to. Tawakal is the current market leader and runs two to six services daily.

Bus companies Companies travelling to Lamu include Falcon (☎042 2130850), Najaah (no tel.) Simba Coach (no tel.) Starways (☎0729 000266 or 0721 144117), Tahmeed (☎0724 898998 or 0722 502740), Tawakal (☎042 2131832 or 0722 550111) and TSS (no tel.).

BY PLANE

Malindi airport is barely 3km south of the town centre and you can walk into Malindi in half an hour. Matatus heading to the main stage (halfway between the airport and the town centre) will pick you up on the main road just outside the airport; otherwise, taxis charge around Ksh1000 to most beach hotels, or Ksh400–500 into town. If you need to park at the airport, you can do so safely (Ksh40/hr).

Airlines Kenya Airways, Utalii Parade (☎042 2120237 or ☎0723 786314, ☻kenya-airways.com), flies daily to/from Nairobi JKIA (1hr) in high season and a reduced schedule in low season; Airkenya, Sabaki Centre, Lamu Rd (☎042 2120411 or ☎0713 981490 ☻airkenya.com), operates daily flights to Nairobi Wilson (45min) in high season and on Wed, Fri and Sun in low season; Fly540, North Coast Travel Services, opposite the FN Centre, Lamu Rd (☎042 2130312 or ☎ 042 2120370, ☻fly540.com), flies daily to Nairobi JKIA; Mombasa Air Safari, Southern Sky Safaris, Malindi Complex (☎042 2130547 or 0734 400400, ☻mombasaairsafari.com), flies most days to/from Lamu (30min), Mombasa (35min) and Maasai Mara (90min; $400); Aeronav Air Service, Malindi Airport (☎0722 210570 or 020 8032185), offer charter services and run a daily scheduled flight to Maasai Mara in the high season (90min; $365).

GETTING AROUND

Car rental There are no full-service car rental firms in Malindi. Try Glory Car Hire, Tours and Safaris at Multi-Grocer Shopping Centre (☎0711 374797 or 0734 007777), which offers self-drive saloons from around Ksh4000/day. Otherwise, private taxi and 4WD owners will meet your requirements: ask your hotel front desk. Prices for saloons with driver start from Ksh5000/day around town.

Taxis Baobab Taxis (☎042 2130499) has fixed rates posted opposite the Portuguese Chapel on the baobab tree that serves as its HQ. *Tuk-tuks* are cheaper, *boda-bodas* cheaper still.

INFORMATION AND SERVICES

Tourist office On Lamu Road, at the very back of the Malindi Complex building, on the first floor (Mon–Fri 8am–12.30pm & 2–4.30pm; ☎042 2120747 or 042 2120689). Staff don't have much in the way of information, but are the people to contact if you have a serious complaint about a hotel, safari operator or restaurant.

Banks Barclays, Equity, KCB and Standard Chartered banks all have 24hr ATMs.

Internet access SK Cyber on Uhuru Road (daily 8am–noon & 1–8pm), opposite *Tana Guest House*.

ACCOMMODATION

There's plenty of accommodation on offer, though over Christmas room availability can be tight. The cheap town lodgings also fill up in high season, during Maulidi and at the end of Ramadan. Tourist establishments usually vary their prices seasonally by up to fifty percent, and many close during May and part or all of June. You can **camp** in the KWS compound near the Marine Park office.

BUDGET ROOMS AND CAMPING

Dagama's Inn Vasco da Gama Rd, on the seafront ☎0706 350401. A variety of rooms, some s/c, simple but clean, with nets. Best are the two front rooms overlooking the beach, with a balcony. Ksh1000

Gilani's Hotel Vasco da Gama Rd, on the seafront ☎042 2120307 or 0722 646872. Above the restaurant there are seven s/c rooms, some of which have four-poster beds with nets and fans, balconies and sea views, making this good budget value. No hot water. BB Ksh1800

Lutheran Guesthouse Lamu Rd, town centre ☎0723 766278. Set in a large garden, with double, triple and quad rooms (clean and mosquito-netted with fans, two s/c), plus two self-catering bungalows, each for four people (Ksh40,000/month). There's a no-alcohol policy. BB Ksh1800

Malindi Marine Park HQ 5km south of the town centre ☎042 2120845 or 020 6000800, ✉reservations @kws.go.ke. The Marine Park HQ's new, twin-bedded, non-s/c, self-catering *bandas* are good value and worth considering if you want to do a lot of snorkelling in the marine park. You can also camp, but either way you'll need to be self-sufficient to stay there – much easier if you have a vehicle. Camping $15, *bandas* $50

★ **Ozi's** Vasco da Gama Rd, on the seafront ☎042 2120218 or 0720 218947, ✉bit.ly/ozismalindi. Very secure, friendly and popular with travellers, *Ozi's* is arranged around a central courtyard. None of the rooms is s/c, though all have ceiling fans, and the shared showers and toilets are clean. It's next to the Juma mosque, so you may be woken by the early prayer call. Free laundry. BB Ksh2000

Tana Guest House Uhuru Rd. While basic, the *Tana* is well kept and very cheap, with nets and fans, and is handy for buses to Lamu. Rooms in the main block (s/c and non-s/c) can be hot, but there are slightly dearer, "special self-contained" rooms around a quiet courtyard at the back. Good, busy ground-floor *hoteli* with plenty of choice. Room only Ksh800

HOTELS IN THE TOWN CENTRE AND NORTH

North of town, all the upmarket hotels have pools, but the beach is some 500m east of Lamu Road and relatively little used. Watersports are very limited at most of these hotels: with no reef offshore, there's no snorkelling, and the current makes windsurfing only feasible if you're experienced. One exception is the excellent *Che Shale*, a 30min drive from Malindi, north of Mambrui.

African Pearl Lamu Rd ☎0725 131956, ✇african pearl.com. Ten spacious rooms in a characterful – if verging on tired – older house decorated with garish paintings, plus four self-catering cottages with kitchens, and a fully equipped gym. The best rooms are comfortable and have large verandas (some are a/c too). Good pool, free wi-fi and a bar-restaurant (with *nyama choma*) at the front near the road. Good value if you choose one of the best rooms. BB Ksh3500, self-catering cottage Ksh5000

Blue Marlin Sporting Resort Lamu Rd ☎020 3509906. Reasonably comfortable and stylish, and very affordable, complex of 31 furnished apartments in the heart of town. If you want to be right in the thick of things, this is ideal. $75

★ **Che Shale** 24km north of Malindi, and 6km off the main road (transfer Ksh2500 from town) ☎0722 230931, ✇cheshale.com. Literally on the beach – and what a beach – this is one of Kenya's best mid-budget beach bases, opened in 1978, but now reinvented as a kitesurfing centre. With just five s/c, palm-mat and wood *bandas*, sand underfoot and cool owner-manager hosts, staff and fellow guests, this is the archetypal beach hideaway. The separate *Kajama bandas*, 200m north, are the non-s/c, non-electric, budget option. Closed mid-April to June 30. HB Kajama $125, HB Che Shale $240

Lawford's Lamu Rd ☎042 2121265, ⊛malindikey .com. Owned by the Italian *Coral Key*, this renovated Malindi institution, set in spacious palm-filled gardens, has been transformed. All the rooms are suites, done out in a confident, European design, with powerful a/c, safes, TV, cool bathrooms and designer beds. Two pools, and very well-equipped pampering from Lawford's Spa. BB $100

Melinde Hotel Off Lamu Rd ☎042 2120019, ⊛melindehotel.com. The former *Palm Garden*, completely made over, has 20 cool and unusually spacious rooms, funkily decorated in white and gold – though the bathrooms tend to be very dark – with fan (or a/c for a small supplement) and free wi-fi. Extremely good value – at these prices you might ugrade to a suite for Ksh1500 extra. BB Ksh3400

Sai Eden Roc Lamu Rd ☎042 2120480, ⊛edenrochotel.co.ke. Large old package-tour place, with huge and largely untended gardens stretching several hundred metres down to the dunes and beach. Friendly if somewhat disorganized management and mostly German guests. Rooms with a/c, or smaller rooms with fans. BB Ksh8000

Seaview Resort Lamu Rd ☎042 2130427 or 0735 432371, ⊛seaviewresortmalindi.com. Low-key development in a pleasant, wooded setting. The big rooms, with a/c, fans and TV, are quite nicely done, and there's a pool. Self-catering cottages are also available (sleeping up to 4). Good value. Self-catering Ksh7200, BB Ksh7500, self-catering cottage $70

HOTELS SOUTH OF THE TOWN

Protected by reefs, this is where the greatest development has taken place in the last few years, with one resort hotel after another reaching almost down to Casuarina Point. Most are Italian-owned or managed, and Italian visitors comprise the majority of guests. Taxis shouldn't cost more

than Ksh1000 from town to Casuarina Point, or Ksh400 to the *Driftwood*, and less by *tuk-tuk*. Distances are from Uhuru Gardens in town.

Coral Key 2km south, on Silversands Rd ☎042 2130717 or 0722 207319, ⊛malindikey.com. Huge Italian-run resort, with more than 200 rooms on three neighbouring plots, but not all a/c. Nine pools, and a good Italian restaurant and pizzeria. Activities include tennis, a climbing wall and a disco every Friday. BB $140

★ **Driftwood Club** 2.7km south, on Silversands Rd ☎042 2120155 or 0721 724489, ⊛driftwoodclub .com. With a deserved and very long-established reputation among the local Anglo-Kenyan community for its excellent food and service, the *Driftwood* is highly recommended – though expensive for non-residents. As well as garden rooms with a/c and nets, there are two luxury a/c cottages sharing a private pool, and three, a/c, self-catering villas. Facilities include a modest pool and free wi-fi. Rates are non-seasonal, except for a Christmas/New Year supplement. BB $249

Kilili Baharini 4km south, on Casuarina Rd ☎0770 206500 or 0702 999566, ⊛kililibaharini.com. Rather a classy setup, with rooms organized in small enclaves, each group clustered around its own pool. There's also a bigger main pool. The a/c rooms are fresh, with tasteful Swahili-style furniture. Big on massage treatments and very popular with Italian visitors. BB $240

Sandies and Diamonds Resorts 3km south, on Casuarina Rd ☎042 2120444, 0722 209485 or 0720 607075, ⊛planhotel.com. Stretched along 500m of shoreline, this is an Italian-slanted holiday complex, encompassing three different hotels, ranging from the cheapish and cheerful *Sandies Coconut Village* to the pricey *Diamonds Dream of Africa*, via *Sandies Tropical Vilage*. *Tropical Village* has over 100 rooms; the others 100 rooms between them. Guests can use the extensive facilities across all four. AI $260

★ **Scorpio Villas** 1km south, on Vasco da Gama Rd, not directly on the beach ☎042 2120194 or 0700 437680, ⊛scorpio-villas.com. Small-scale, Italian-owned "village", in a plot dense with tropical vegetation, rebuilt since a fire in 2007. The 48 a/c rooms with nets, DSTV, fridges and safes are characterful, with Swahili-style four-poster beds. Three pools and its own, semi-private beach area. Remarkably good value. BB Ksh8000

EATING AND DRINKING

Malindi Market is celebrated for fruit and vegetables – second, on the coast, only to Mombasa's. Malindi's speciality is smoked sailfish, absolutely delicious and often available as a starter. Cheese is available from The Cheese Shop in Utalii Parade on Lamu Road (Mon–Sat 8am–9pm), from the Italian supermarket at the Sabaki Centre (Mon–Sat 9am–1pm & 4–7pm), and from Pappa i Chakula (Mon–Sat 8.30am–12.30pm & 2–6pm), a little Italian deli at the back of the Multi-Grocer shopping centre, which also has fresh pasta, olives and salami. If you're driving south, 8km from Malindi town centre is Retief Farm Shop, on the left (daily, informal hours), which sells several varieties of fresh mangoes at bargain prices, plus dried mango and Arabuko Sokoke honey.

HOTELIS AND CHEAP RESTAURANTS

Baobab Vasco da Gama Rd, on the seafront next to the Portuguese Chapel. Moderately priced curries, Italian and African dishes (mostly from Ksh700), and pricey prawns and lobsters (from Ksh1200). Popular as much for its food as for the cheap, cold beer (Ksh150) and sweeping views over the beach and fishing boats. Daily 7am–11pm.

★ **Bawaly and Sons Halwa Shop** In the town centre near Uhuru Gardens. Long-established spot, famous for its fragrant version of the gooey jelly sweet (from Ksh500/kg). The minimum order is 250g, but you can eat a small amount on the spot and have the rest wrapped up to take away. Tiny cups of spiced *kahawa* come free. Daily 8.30am–12.15pm & 3–5.45pm.

Black Jack Bar & Restaurant Off Lamu Rd behind the Melinde Hotel. A relaxed outdoor TV bar doing *nyama choma* with *ugali* (Ksh300) and cheap beer (Ksh130). Daily 10am–midnight.

Café Delicious Kenyatta Rd. A small diner with a pleasant, shady terrace, serving fried breakfasts (Ksh140), snacks and basic cheap meals, plus cold sodas. Mon–Sat 7am–7pm.

Central Perk (aka Mabeste) Lamu Rd. Irrelevantly named pool bar and *hoteli* with a good variety of cheap snacks and fried food and beers for Ksh140. Open 24 hours.

Chariba Lamu Rd. Popular *hoteli* for good-value fry-ups and upcountry dishes including *sukuma* for Ksh50 and *chai* for Ksh30. Mon–Sat 6am–10pm.

Dagama's Inn Vasco da Gama Rd, on the seafront ☎0706 350401. Basic *hoteli* menu, plus curries from Ksh250, seafood from Ksh350 and steaks from Ksh450. Can be good when busy but it's always best to order in advance. Daily 7am–10pm.

Gilani's Vasco da Gama Rd, on the seafront ☎0722 646872. Wide-ranging offerings, many of which are available in high season, including chicken and fish dishes from Ksh400, pizzas from Ksh350, even bruschetta (Ksh100) and salads (from Ksh200). Daily 7am–11pm.

★ **Johari's Garden** In the garden of the FN Centre Building, through a passage from Lamu Rd behind Equity Bank ☎0722 318170. Cool hideaway that's always busy with upcountry folks enjoying excellent-value, large portions of well-prepared, fresh Kikuyu dishes, including beef stew with *mataha* (Ksh230). Lovely fresh passion juice. Daily 6am–9pm.

Leo's Lamu Rd. Very popular café/snack bar/cocktail lounge, doing panini from Ksh300, good coffees from Ksh100–250 and cocktails from Ksh400. Mon–Sat 8am–10pm.

Malindi Pastry Shop Mama Ngina St, near the market. Not what you'd expect to find here – a decent bakers and patisserie, with a big variety of tempting home-made cakes (from Ksh30) and cookies (from Ksh90/pack).

Daily 8am–noon & 3–8pm.

Oasis Gelateria Silversands Rd, 1.8km from Uhuru Gardens. This big snack bar is very good – as much for its delicious omelettes and espresso as for the forty flavours of ice cream. Daily: high season 8am–midnight; low season 3–11pm.

Open View Bar and Restaurant By the Total roundabout. One of Malindi's biggest and best-value *nyama choma* joints (beef Ksh450/kg), with mostly outside seating. No shortage of company, and they never run out of beer, but the place can be noisy and fumey until the traffic has died down. Open 24 hours.

Rollingstone Café Lamu Rd. Good value, centrally located, shady and perfect for people-watching. Snacks and fast(ish) food, mostly for Ksh100 or less. Mon–Sat 7am–10pm.

★ **Taheri Cold House** Fakhri Complex, Tsavo Rd. A great spot for juices, snacks and cheap meals. Try the chicken tikka (Ksh200), shish kebab (Ksh150) or "Zanzibari mix" – vegetable-based snacks in your choice of sauce (Ksh160). Reliably cold sodas, too. Tues–Thurs 7.30am–8.30pm, Fri–Sun 7.30am–11pm.

UPMARKET RESTAURANTS

★ **Baby Marrow** Vasco da Gama Rd, near the Portuguese Chapel ☎0727 581682. One of Malindi's best restaurants, *Baby Marrow* aims for Italian bush elegance. Starters include smoked sailfish, and mains feature lots of crab and lobster dishes (Ksh1000–2000), and meat dishes for around Ksh1000. Daily 11am–2pm & 6–11pm.

Bar Bar Sabaki Centre, Lamu Rd ☎0719 5162812. A little piece of Italy in Kenya, with authentic and tasty pizzas and pasta (most from Ksh800), and pricier meat and seafood dishes (most from Ksh1000), rounded off with excellent espresso. 7am–11pm.

★ **Driftwood Club** Silversands beach ☎042 2120155. Always a good place to eat, with seafood making a very strong showing (oysters, smoked sailfish and excellent sashimi are always available). The Friday BBQ (from Ksh500 per item), Sunday curry lunch buffet (Ksh1600) and Thursday Mongolian night (all you can eat for Ksh1450) are worth planning around. Daily noon–3pm & 7–10pm.

I Love Pizza Vasco da Gama Rd, on the seafront ☎042 2120672. Well-established seafront place with a pleasant terrace, though in the daytime the traffic can be offputting. The pizzas (from Ksh800) and pasta dishes (from Ksh450) are fine, though they push their more expensive seafood (seafood platter for two, for example, Ksh2000), which is also good. Beware: prices don't include taxes. Daily 11am–3pm & 6–11pm.

★ **La Malindina** Off Lamu Rd, at the back of town ☎042 2131449 or 042 2120045. Specializing in, and only serving, seafood, a typical set meal (Ksh4000) at this gourmet restaurant starts with seafood salad with fish carpaccio, followed by spaghetti *fruits de mer*, then a choice of crab, lobster or prawns, dessert and coffee. Non-seafood tastes can be catered for, with notice. Most wines (Italian and South African) range from Ksh2000–4000. Closed May & June. One service daily, at 8.45 for 9pm.

★ **My Way** Vasco da Gama Rd, on the seafront near the tourist market ☏ 042 2120709. With a kitchen supervised by its owner-manager, this multipurpose open-air restaurant, sports bar and music venue has locals and tourists gravitating for good chicken and pizzas, Kikuyu dishes, big screens, free wi-fi and the pool table. Very reasonable prices (pizzas from Ksh400, steaks from Ksh450, *mataha* Ksh120, pilau Ksh150, beers Ksh150). Daily 9am–11pm.

★ **The Old Man and The Sea** Vasco da Gama Rd, on the seafront ☏ 042 2131106 or 0734/645567. Consistently good, professionally managed Moorish-style

restaurant specializing in seafood (which they know how to do perfectly – the giant tiger prawns are famous: Ksh1600), with some vegetarian dishes and steaks (from Ksh600). For such excellent food – expect a bill of around Ksh2000–3000 per person, plus drinks – it's great value for money. Prices don't include taxes. Daily 12.30–2.30pm & 7–10.30pm.

Tangeri Vasco da Gama Rd, opposite the Seafishing Club ☏ 042 2131420 or 0725 482857. It's all about atmosphere here – Arabian nights meets Italian romance. At dinner, the best tables are on the balcony, high above the street. The menu is mostly Italian-curated seafood – sashimi (Ksh800), pastas (from Ksh800), and risotto by advance order (from Ksh1200). Litres of house wine (Ksh1000) are a good deal. Closed mid-April–mid-July. Daily 7.30–11.30pm.

NIGHTLIFE

After dark, especially in high season, Malindi's clubs and bars throb with action and, regardless of your gender, status or, increasingly, even your age, you're unlikely to avoid being propositioned, and not necessarily by a sex worker. Entry charges are rare unless entertainment has been laid on. Beers at most places are Ksh200-plus, with a glass of house wine Ksh300-plus.

Casino Malindi Lamu Rd. With free entry to anyone gambling, it's almost worth playing a few hands just to watch the grim-looking Italian bosses tending their novice Kenyan croupiers. Good steaks, too. Daily 9am–5am.

Club 28 Lamu Rd, adjacent to Eden Roc Hotel. This smaller, mostly outdoor club gets busy later, and is usually considered the last place to visit – it can be heaving at 4am. Open 24 hours.

Fermento Galana Shopping Centre. Air-conditioned disco-bar with affordable drinks. You take a ticket and pay your bill on departure. High season Tues–Sun 8pm–late; low season Wed, Fri, Sat 8pm–late.

★ **Pata Pata Beach Club** On the beach, north side of town ⊛ patapatakenya.com. Mediterranean-style super club – part-covered, part-outdoors – with a capacity of 4000, an 18,000-watt sound system, two bars, two dance-floors, comfy sofas and garden seating, foam guns, lights and a freeform dance pool. And very unhappy neighbours who may yet get it closed down, justifiably, for environmental infringements. Entry Ksh300. High season

daily 9pm–6am; low season Sat only 9pm–6am.

Seazone Vasco da Gama Rd, next to the Portuguese chapel. Strongly upcountry-flavoured bar and snack-restaurant, with cheap beers, pool table and music, usually reggae. Daily 9am–1am.

★ **Stardust** Lamu Rd, opposite Galana Shopping Centre. Often the busiest club in town, especially in high season, when half of Malindi – Italians and Kenyans alike – seem to be here waggling their backsides in time to 1980s cheese. Open 24 hours, partly closed in low season.

Stars and Garters Lamu Rd, next to Barclays Bank. Brash and busy *makuti*-roofed complex, especially popular for the flat-screen TVs showing English football. Good range of snacks, and fuller meals too, including pasta, seafood and grills. There's a disco most evenings and live music more often than anywhere else in town. Open 24 hours.

Urafiki Highway Bar Kenyatta Rd. Cheerful, cheap and unpretentious local bar with tables inside and out (warm beers Ksh120) and not a tourist in sight. Open 24 hours.

CRAFTS AND SHOPPING

There are two main crafts markets to head for when you're in the buying mood. Most obvious is the main **tourist crafts market** (daily 8am–6pm) on the seashore below the old town. Naturally, if you stray down here you'll be pounced upon, and leaving without buying anything isn't easy. On the other hand, you can also leave with all sorts of little free gifts if you strike the right bargain. The other area is the **Malindi Handicraft Co-operative** (daily 8am–6.30pm), 2.5km west of the main market and matatu stage on the Mombasa road, where you can watch and freely photograph the woodcarvers at work, but there's no bargaining at the shop. Alternatively, for more expensive crafts and the possibility of browsing unhurriedly, try one of the **upmarket shops** along Lamu Road, just to the north of Uhuru Gardens. Prices tend to be high, but visits are useful for checking comparative values.

SHOPS

I Colore dell Africa Lamu Rd. Large, Italian gifts-and-interiors shop with a great variety of attractive items from East Africa, Europe and the Far East.

Kilimanjaro Mama Ngina Rd. With a pleasing range of dried goods and spices displayed across the counter, this is the shop to secure those aromatic souvenirs at regular prices.

Lalla Spagnol Lamu Rd, just north of the Galana shopping centre. High-end interior design and furnishings, including lots of owner-made and owner-commissioned stuff from Lamu and the Far East.

Maridadi Seasons Old Town ⓦmaridadiseasons.com. Sales of nearly all the well-priced sisal baskets, beaded bags, sandals, belts and leatherwork in this shop support

crafts makers from the community.

Mithabhai Fabrics Shop Mama Ngina Rd, next to Kenol. With a good selection of fabrics sold by the metre plus a great range of kikois and kangas, this is one of Malindi's best cloth outlets.

Mohawk Lamu Rd, opposite the Sabaki Centre. Two shops: on the left, nice beaded designer sandals, bags, cushions, ladies' clothes, accessories and jewellery; on the right, tableware, furnishings, wall hangings, mirrors and knick-knacks.

Nafisa and Rasanis At the southern end of Lamu Rd, on the corner near Uhuru Gardens. Lots of top-quality crafts and *objets d'art* in these two shops, and their neighbours, including old Lamu silver and jewellery as well as more familiar items available on the street.

ACTIVITIES

Board-based watersports – **surfing**, **windsurfing** and **kitesurfing** – and **diving** and **snorkelling** are Malindi's touristic *raison d'être*. Unfortunately, diving is somewhat marred by the Galana (Sabaki) River's outpouring of thousands of tonnes of prime red topsoil from the upcountry plateaus. The cloudy water prevents any coral growing north of Vasco da Gama Point and the sea in this north part of Malindi is muddy-brown from November to January. The good diving and snorkelling season, in the coastal area starting from Vasco da Gama Point southwards, lasts only from July to October. During the April to June long rains, it's low season and not great for clarity, while between November and March, silt makes the water too murky, and the larger hotels usually organize daily excursions for their guests to dive or snorkel in Watamu.

SNORKELLING

Seasonal variations aside, with your own gear you can snorkel in the lagoon, or snorkel out to the inside edge of the reef anywhere north of the marine park. At the park boundary at Casuarina Point the reef hugs the shore, and it runs north to its conclusion off Vasco da Gama Point, where it's more than 900m from the beach. If you find conditions not as good as you'd hoped, it's easy to check out nearby Watamu (see p.460). Some local divers believe Watamu's coral is superior, but Malindi has a greater diversity of fish.

SURFING

Malindi Bay is the main surfing beach (June to the end of September, when the swell is on), and surfboards are available from some of the tourist hotels in town. The beach here is a good 5–10min walk from the road. There are several public access points (see map, p.462), and some hotels will allow use of their beach access for a small fee, which means you can use their pool and leave your things on their guarded premises.

KITESURFING

Malindi is one of the world's kitesurfing hotspots. Learning

at *Che Shale*, (see p.465), the beach lodge which is partly responsible for the development of the sport, costs €340 for a three-day (9-hour) residential course, on top of your accommodation. The best seasons for this are January to April and July to mid-October.

DIVE CENTRES AND DIVING SCHOOLS

There are two main dive centres in Malindi, and you should probably visit them both before deciding which one to use. Remember marine park fees are extra ($15 per day). The Watamu account (see p.460) has more general advice and information.

Blue-Fin Based at Tropical Beach Resort ☎0722 261242, ⓦbluefindiving.com. Based in Malindi from July–Nov and in Watamu from Nov–April, but offering diving year-round (from intro dives to PADI Open Water certification – €360) from many of Malindi's hotels.

Upinde Based at Mariposa Restaurant south along the beach from Scorpio Villas ☎0723 962123 or 0735 418570, ⓦupindediving.com. One-day introduction courses and five-day PADI Open Water qualification courses – €330.

DIRECTORY

Cinema Cleopatra Theatre, by the big Total roundabout, screens English premiership football matches.

Golf Malindi Golf and Country Club (☎042 2120404) features an unusual eleven-hole (fifteen-tee) course

behind the dunes on the north side of town.

Honorary Consuls The Italian honorary consul (the only diplomatic representative in Malindi; Mon–Fri 9am–noon ☎0722 825392 or emergencies ☎0722 224750) has an office in the Sabaki Centre, behind *Bar Bar*.

Hospital The Italian-run St Peter's Hospital on Casuarina Rd (☎ 042 2120086 or 0735 601304) is well run and has an ambulance service.

Immigration Get your visitor's permit extended in the offfice opposite Cleopatra Theatre (☎ 042 2120149).

Kenya Wildlife Service Casuarina Point (daily 6am–6pm). Point of issue and point of sale for National Park smartcards.

Pharmacy Sabaki Pharmacy (daily 8am–9pm), Kenyatta Rd, at the corner of Tsavo Rd.

Supermarkets There are several small places in the shopping arcades up Lamu Rd in the town centre, the best – with the widest range – being Multi-Grocers. The new Nakumatt on Lamu Rd trumps them all.

Travel agents A good scattering along Lamu Rd and the seafront all offer similar services, including safaris to Tsavo East and as far as Maasai Mara. In town, try Southern Sky Safaris, Malindi Complex (☎ 042 2130547), or *Ozi's Guest House*, whose owner runs African Concept (☻ africanconcept .co.ke). At the airport, check out Allamanda Safaris (☎ 0721 251461, ☻ allamandasafaris.com).

The Tana Delta

North out of Malindi, the **road to Lamu** sets off as a tarmac highway, crosses the Sabaki (Galana) River and passes one or two resort developments and the anachronistic little seaside town of **MAMBRUI**, with its pretty mosque, semi-ruined pillar tomb and the unusual spectacle of cows on the beach. The idyllic kitesurfing base of *Che Shale* (see p.465) is further up the coast on the south side of the **Ras Ngomeni peninsula**. About 60km north of Malindi, you leave the *shambas* and scattered homesteads behind and enter the bush of the **Tana Delta**, with the road arrowing straight across the flat, gentle landscape, brown and arid, or grey-green and swampy, depending on the season.

The former ferry-crossing town of **Garsen** has been sidelined by the tarmac **New Garsen Causeway**, which sweeps over the Tana River 7km to the south of the flyblown town before petering out into a dirt track after you reach Witu. If you want to break your journey, Garsen has a KCB bank with an ATM and, in season, some of the best and cheapest mangoes in Kenya.

Between the river and the end of the trip, the scenery can pall, but if you're on the bus, the journey is always enlivened by the other passengers and by stops at various small Tana delta towns and villages. Occasional flashes of colour – the sky-blue cloaks of **Orma** herders or the red, black and white of shawled **Somali** women – break up the journey, along with wonderful **birdlife** and some **big game**, too: especially giraffe and antelope (notably waterbuck), and even the odd elephant if you look hard enough. The road passes right through the recently created **Kipini sanctuary** (see opposite).

Note that parts of this area were severely affected by ethnic violence in 2012 (see p.472), and some governments were warning travellers to avoid it.

Tana River National Primate Reserve

40km north of Garsen, straddling the Tana River • $20 • ☻ bit.ly/TanaRiverNR • If you're driving, the Mchelelo track to the river is the one to use, though it's not signposted from the road; if you want to try to visit the reserve using public transport, you need to allow time for unforeseen delays: buses heading from Malindi to Garissa occasionally stop in Mnazini village, just outside the southern end of the reserve, or can drop you on the highway at one of the two turnings, Hara village or the KWS signpost, where you could wait for a lift or walk (5–10km) • 170 square kilometre

The **Tana River National Primate Reserve** is a refuge for two of Kenya's rarest and most beautiful monkeys, the **Tana River red colobus** and the **Tana River mangabey**. This is a remote area, with little in the way of supplies, so you'll need to call ahead and bring provisions with you. The forest is magically beautiful, cool and dark, with huge, buttress-rooted trees, and surprisingly restricted in extent, often spreading less than 1km away from the riverbank.

Mnazini is a fine, coastal-style village beneath mango trees. There are no lodgings, but *hotelis* will take you in for the night once you've cleared your stay with the sub-chief and the headman. The shops have basic provisions, as do those in Wenje and Hara.

Nobody in the area knows the Tana River National Primate Reserve by that name. Locals all refer to **Mchelelo**, the site of the primate research headquarters on the west bank of the Tana. There is a basic self-service tent available to rent from KWS at the research camp (see below), but few other facilities.

Wildlife

Although little is laid on for the few visitors who come, you may well be given a detail of armed rangers on the anti-poaching force to accompany you as you walk the trails looking for **red colobus** and **crested mangabey monkeys**. Continued human encroachment on the forest, which is increasingly split into small intact zones, threatens both species, and the colobus very rarely leave the trees, limiting them to whichever patch they find themselves in.

Your chances of seeing both kinds of monkey are good, and the other highlights of the reserve are mostly avian: the superb birdlife includes goliath heron, Pel's fishing owl, southern banded snake eagle and the exceedingly rare Tana River cisticola, not to mention vast numbers of Palaearctic migrants in season. **Mammals** in the reserve, apart from the rare primates, include blue monkeys, baboons, Grevy's and Burchell's zebra, oryx, lesser kudu, and even lions, giraffe and buffalo. On the east side of the park you can see elephants, and there's also a small seasonal population of the endangered Hunter's hartebeest, or hirola. If you're interested in making a boat trip on the sluggish river, dodging the large numbers of hippos and crocodiles, you're likely to find local Pokomo boatmen willing to take you.

TANA RIVER NATIONAL PRIMATE RESERVE

Hola & Garissa
Wenje
Tana River
Airstrip
Hara
Makere
Reserve HQ
KWS Signpost
Mchelelo Camp
Tana River
BAOMO TRACK
Baomo
Nkano
Kitere
MNAZINI TRACK
Mnazini
Garsen, Malindi & Lamu

0 2 kilometres

N

ACCOMMODATION   **MCHELELO**

★ **Mchelelo Research Camp** Tana River National Primate Reserve, enquiries through KWS in Nairobi ☎ 0726 610508, ✉ reservations@kws.go.ke. One large frame tent, partly mosquito-proofed, under a thatched *banda* in the forest, with a plumbed-in bathroom, is the setting for a truly do-it-yourself experience where you share facilities with research primatologists. Depending on workload, the zoologists may be able to help you see the forest monkeys or organize trips in the area. Bring bedding and all your food and drink requirements. The camp kitchen is at your disposal, but the scientists come first. Camping per person **$15**

Kipini and around

If you have a 4WD vehicle and a fair amount of patience, the trip to Lamu can be stretched over several days, with time to explore the fascinating region around the Tana Delta. This area includes the dune-shrouded coast and the small town of **Kipini**, with the Swahili ruins of **Ungwana**, **Shaka** and **Mwana** along the shore to the east, within a few kilometres. If you're interested in exploring down here, try to see the warden of the museum at Fort Jesus for further information. These sites were partially excavated in the 1970s and 1980s, but have since largely returned to bush and jungle. Ungwana is the most impressive, with an unusual mosque with two *mihrabs* and strange tombs with cruciform markings.

As yet almost wholly untouched by tourism, a visit to the district around the fishing village of **Kipini** at the mouth of the Tana and the larger market centre of **Witu**, 21km inland, repays the slight effort of getting here and finding somewhere to stay. **Kipini** was once the headquarters of Tana River District, before that title was shifted to Hola at the

6

TROUBLE IN THE DELTA

Despite progress at the micro level with initiatives like those of *Delta Dunes Lodge* and the Lower Tana Delta Trust, the threats to the Tana Delta region seem to be accumulating (see ⓦ tanariver delta.org). After the failure of a highly damaging irrigation and rice-growing project in the 1990s, the latest, environmentally disastrous, idea is a gigantic biofuel project, that would carpet more than 200 square kilometres of bush and flood land with sugar-cane plantations for cheap ethanol – plans that may not be entirely prevented by the delta being recently put under international protection as Kenya's sixth Ramsar Site – a wetlands area of global importance. Competition for scarce resources is also pitching communities against each other: in 2012, more than 100 people from the pastoralist Orma and farming Pokomo communities were killed in alternate raids on each other's villages, sparked by disputes over water and grazing rights (see p.574). Travel advisories warned against visiting the region, though no foreign visitors were affected.

---

time of independence. Nowadays, its former importance is evident only in a mixed population of Orma, Pokomo, Bajun, Somali and Swahili, who get by on fishing, small-scale farming and some herding.

Kipini Wildlife and Botanical Conservancy

Northeast of Kipini • No fees; contact the conservancy in advance • ⓦ kipiniconservancy.org

The Kipini Wildlife and Botanical Conservancy is a former ranch – the Nairobi Cattle Ranch – that failed, largely because of tsetse fly, and has now been reborn as a wildlife sanctuary. The people of the area, traditional hunter-gatherers, the **Boni**, are now mostly subsistence farmers. The conservancy is still in its infancy, but the intention is to create a viable natural resource, modelled on the former ranches of Laikipia. As you'll see if you stop off here, the area is full of **wildlife**, including elephants, giraffe, buffalo, lesser kudu, hirola, lions, the odd dugong in the creeks and, they claim, hunting dogs.

ARRIVAL AND DEPARTURE   KIPINI AND AROUND

By public transport To get to Kipini by public transport, leave the Lamu bus at Witu, where there's a connecting matatu to the village (most buses heading for Lamu or Malindi pass through Witu during the morning). Village *hotelis* serve delicious *dalasini* cinnamon tea.

ACCOMMODATION

Kipini has no formal lodgings, but you should be able to stay with a local family for a few hundred shillings. Alternatively, you could stay in Witu itself (again, no formal lodgings), and rent a bicycle locally for getting around.

Delta Dunes On the bush-covered sand dunes near the ocean, midway across the Delta's width ☎ 0721 322745 or 0723 538930, ⓦ deltadunes.co.ke. It's possible to stay near the delta mouth at the highly appealing, castaway-style *Delta Dunes*, where there are six *bandas* made from driftwood, mangrove poles and *makuti*. Stays include all meals and drinks, boat trips, fishing, game and bird walks and village visits. Delta Dunes works with thirteen thousand local people – Orma herders and Pokomo farmers – through the community's Lower Tana Delta Trust, and a proportion of income from guests goes direct to community bank accounts. Conservancy fee $60. Closed May & June . Package **$1100**

Kipini Tana River Lodge Kipini on the north bank of the Tana's mouth, enquiries through Coral Key in Malindi (see p.466) ⓦ malindikey.com. A remote bush and beach lodge close to the ocean, this comprises seven simple bungalows and two slightly fancier "suites", all with nets, fans, generator electricity and verandas. It's a great getaway for birders and people who like messing about in boats. Package **$350**

The Lamu Archipelago

A cluster of desert islands tucked into Kenya's north coast, **Lamu** and its neighbours have a special appeal that many visitors find irresistible. Together they form a separate spectrum of Swahili culture, a world apart from the beaches of Mombasa and Malindi.

To a great extent the islands are anachronisms: there are still almost no motor vehicles, and life moves at the pace of a **donkey** or a **dhow**. Yet there have been considerable changes over the centuries and Lamu itself is now changing faster than ever. Because of its special status in the Islamic world as a much-respected centre of **religious teaching**, Saudi aid has poured into the island: the hospital, schools and religious centres are all supported by it. At the same time, Lamu's tourist economy has opened up far beyond the budget travellers of the 1970s. Foreign investors are eagerly sought and new **guesthouses** and **boutique hotels** go up every year, especially in Shela, which has more space to expand than Lamu town. Islanders are ambivalent about the future. A new **port** is quite likely (see p.476), although it would contribute to the destruction of Lamu's historic character.

6

The damage that would be done goes further than spoiling the tranquillity. The Lamu archipelago is one of the most important sources for knowledge about pre-colonial Africa. **Archeological sites** indicate that towns have existed on these islands for at least 1200 years. The dunes behind Lamu beach, for example, are said to conceal the remains of long-deserted settlements. And somewhere close by on the mainland, perhaps just over the border in Somalia, archeologists expect one day to uncover the ruins of Shungwaya, the town that the nine tribes that comprise the Mijikenda people claim as their ancestral home. The whole region is an area where there is still real continuity between history and modern life.

Lamu island itself, most people's single destination, still has plenty to recommend it, despite the inevitable sprouting of satellite dishes, cybercafés and souvenir shops. It has the archipelago's best beach and its two main towns, Lamu and Shela. **Manda island**, directly opposite, is little visited except as Lamu's gateway to the outside world (the airstrip), though its own beach is beautiful and there are several delightful places to stay. **Pate island**, accessible by dhow or motorboat, but completely off the tourism radar, makes a fascinating excursion if you have a week or more in the area.

Lamu island

Perhaps best left until the end of your stay in Kenya, **LAMU** may otherwise precipitate a change in your plans as you're lulled into a slow rhythm in which days and weeks pass by unheeded and objectives get forgotten. The deliciously lazy atmosphere is, for many people, the best worst-kept secret on the coast. All the senses get a full work-out here, so that actually *doing* anything is sometimes a problem. You can spend hours on a roof or veranda just watching the town go by, feeling its mood swing effortlessly through its well-worn cycles – from prayer call to prayer call, from tide to tide, and from dawn to dusk.

If this doesn't hit the right note for you, you might actually rather hate Lamu: hot, dirty and boring are adjectives that have been applied by sane and pleasant people. You can certainly improve your chances of liking Lamu by not coming here at the tail end

---

SECURITY IN THE LAMU ARCHIPELAGO

In 2011, two separate events sparked intense media attention questioning the **safety** of tourism in the Lamu archipelago. In September, bandits raided a British couple's banda at *Kiwayu Safari Village* on a remote beach on the mainland facing the northern tip of Kiwaiyu island. The man was shot dead and his wife kidnapped – she was released six months later after a ransom was paid. In October an elderly French expatriate was kidnapped from her home on the island of Manda. She died soon afterwards due to her fragile state of health.

Foreign governments issued **travel advisories** warning against travel in the area, and security measures in the archipelago were significantly heightened. At the time of this book going to press, early 2013, British travel advice still warned against travel to Kiwaiyu island and the mainland areas north of Pate within 60km of the Somalian border. Pate, Manda and Lamu islands are not included in the warnings and, with greatly increased marine surveillance, are considered as safe as the rest of the coast.

of the dry season, when the town's gutters are blocked with refuse, the courtyard gardens wilt under the sun and the heat is sapping.

Lamu is something of a **myth** factory. Conventionally labelled an "Arab trading town", it is actually one of the last viable remnants of the **Swahili civilization** that was the dominant cultural force along the coast until the arrival of the British. In the 1960s, Lamu's unique blend of beaches, gentle Islamic ambience, funky old town and a host population well used to strangers was a recipe which took over where Marrakesh left off, and it acquired a reputation as Kenya's Kathmandu; the end of the African hippie trail and a stopover on the way to India. Shaggy foreigners were only allowed to visit on condition they stayed in lodgings and didn't camp on the beach.

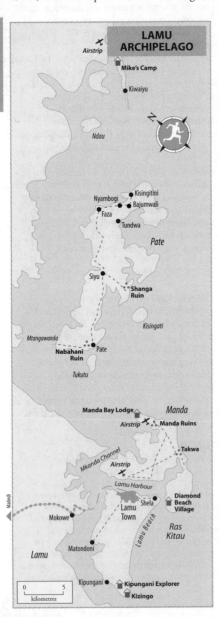

LAMU ARCHIPELAGO

Not many people want to camp out these days. The proliferation of guesthouses in the heart of **Lamu town** encourages an ethos that is more interactive than hippie-escapist. Happily, visitors and locals cross paths enough to avoid any tedium – though for women travelling without men, this can itself become tedious (see p.484). Having said that, there can hardly be another town in the world as utterly unthreatening as Lamu. Leave your room at midnight for a breath of air and you can stroll up a hushed Harambee Avenue, or tread up the darkest of alleys, and fear absolutely nothing. It's an exhilarating experience.

If you want to spend all your time on the **beach**, then staying in **Shela** is the obvious solution, and there's an ever-growing range of quite stylish possibilities there, though hardly anywhere really inexpensive.

Fewer people see the **interior** of Lamu island itself, which is a pity, as it's a pretty, if rather inhospitable area. Much of it is patched into *shambas* with the herds of cattle, coconut palms, mango and citrus trees that still provide the bulk of Lamu's wealth. The two villages you might head for here are **Matondoni**, on the north shore of the island, by the creek, and **Kipungani**, on the western side.

Brief history

The undeniably **Arab** flavour of Lamu is not nearly as old as the town itself. It derives from the later nineteenth

FESTIVALS ON LAMU ISLAND

Maulidi, a week-long celebration of Muhammad's birth (see p.67), sees the entire town involved in processions and dances, and draws in pilgrims from all over East Africa and the Indian Ocean. For faithful participants, the Lamu Maulidi is so laden with *baraka* (blessings) that some say two trips to Lamu are worth one to Mecca in the eyes of God. If you can possibly arrange it, this is the occasion to be in Lamu, but unless you make bookings, you'll need to arrive at least a week in advance to have any hope of getting a room. The other principal festival of the year is the **Lamu Cultural Festival** held in November to promote Swahili culture and heritage. With donkey and dhow racing, swimming, dancing and traditional craft displays, including carving, dhow-building, embroidery and henna decoration – all of it fairly competitive – the festival engages the town for the best part of a week.

century when the **Omanis**, and to some extent the **Hadhramis** from what is now Yemen, held sway in the town. The first British representatives in Lamu found themselves among pale-skinned, slave-owning Arab rulers, and the cultural and racial stereotypes that were propagated have never completely disappeared.

Lamu was established on its present site by the fourteenth century, but there have been people living on the island for much longer than that. The fresh-water supplies beneath Shela made the island attractive to refugees from the mainland and people have been escaping here for two thousand years or more. It was also one of the earliest places on the coast to attract settlers from the Persian Gulf and there were almost certainly people here from Arabia and southwest Asia even before the foundation of Islam.

In 1505, Lamu was visited by a heavily armed **Portuguese** man-of-war and the king of the town quickly agreed to pay the first of many cash tributes as protection money. For the next 180 years Lamu was nominally under Portuguese rule, though the Portuguese favoured Pate as a place to live. In the 1580s, the **Turkish** fleet of Amir Ali Bey threatened Portuguese dominance, but superior firepower and relentless savagery kept them out, and Lamu, with little in the way of an arsenal, had no choice but to bend with the wind – losing a king now and then to the Portuguese executioners – until the Omanis arrived with fast ships and a serious bid for lasting control.

The rise and fall of Lamu

By the end of the seventeenth century, Lamu's Portuguese predators were vanquished and for nearly 150 years it had a revitalizing breathing space. This was its **Golden Age**, when Lamu became a republic, ruled over by the *Yumbe*, a council of elders who deliberated in the palace (now a ruined plot in the centre of town), with only the loosest control imposed by their Omani overlords. This was the period when most of the big houses were built and when Lamu's classic architectural style found its greatest expression. Arts and crafts flourished and business along the waterfront made the town a magnet throughout the Indian Ocean. Huge ocean-going dhows rested half the year in the harbour, taking on ivory, rhino horn, mangrove poles and cereals. There was time to compose long poems and argue about language, the Koran and local politics. Lamu became the northern coast's **literary and scholastic focus**, a distinction inherited from Pate.

For a brief time, Lamu's star was in the ascendant in all fields. There was even a famous victory in the **Battle of Shela** in 1812. A combined Pate-Mazrui force landed at Shela with the simple plan of capturing Lamu – not known for its resolve in battle – and finishing the construction of the fort which the Nabahanis from Pate had begun a few years earlier. To everyone's surprise, particularly the Lamu defenders, the tide had gone out and the invaders were massacred as they tried to push their boats off the beach. Appalled at the overkill and expecting a swift response from the Mazruis in Mombasa, Lamu sent to Oman itself for Busaidi protection and threw away independence forever. Had the eventual outcome of this panicky request been foreseen, the Lamu *Yumbe* might have reconsidered. Seyyid Said, Sultan of Oman, was more than happy to send a garrison to complete and occupy Lamu's fort – and from this toehold in Africa, he went on to smash the Mazrui rebels in Mombasa (see p.391), taking the entire coast and moving his own sultanate to Zanzibar.

Lamu gradually sank into economic collapse towards the end of the nineteenth century as Zanzibar and Mombasa grew in importance. In a sense, it has been stagnating ever since. The building of the Uganda railway from Mombasa and the abolition of slavery did nothing to improve matters for Lamu in economic terms, and its decline has kept up with the shrinking population. However, the **resettlement programme** on the nearby mainland and – in recent years – a much safer road from Malindi has led to a revived upcountry commercialism taking root around the market square.

In March 2012, the government initiated a massive US$20 billion infrastructure development project 16km north of Lamu, the Lamu Port-South Sudan-Ethiopia Transport Corridor (LAPSSET). This, which would be the continent's largest ever civil engineering project, would see a pipeline built to deliver oil from South Sudan to a new refinery near Lamu island, alongside the building of a giant tanker terminal, more than 1700km of new highways and railways to South Sudan and Ethiopia, and three new airports and tourist resorts in Lamu, Isiolo and Lake Turkana. Unsurprisingly, the plans have met resistance from local groups, and many are sceptical that the project will ever be fully realized.

Lamu town

Perhaps surprisingly for so laidback a corner of Kenya, there's no shortage of things to do in **LAMU TOWN**. A UNESCO World Heritage Site, it's unendingly fascinating to stroll through, with few monuments but hundreds of ancient houses, arresting street scenes and cool corners to sit and rest. And the **museum** outshines all others in Kenya bar the National Museum in Nairobi.

Initially confusing, Lamu town is not the random clutter of houses and alleys it appears. The town is divided into two main parts – long-established Mkomani in the north and still-expanding Langoni in the south. This north-south division is found in most Swahili towns and reflects the importance of Mecca, which is due north of Lamu. The town is divided further into forty *mitaa* or **wards**, roughly corresponding to the blocks in a modern city. The names of these suggest a great deal about how the town once looked. Kinooni ("whetstone corner") boasts to this day a heavy block of stone on the corner for sharpening swords, reputedly imported from Oman, and Utakuni ("main market") ward still has a row of shops, even though most of the buildings on this north side of town are now purely residential.

Very few towns in sub-Saharan Africa have kept their original **town plan** so intact (Timbuktu in West Africa is another), and Lamu's history is sufficiently documented, and its architecture well enough preserved, to give you a good idea of how the town developed. The other main division, apart from Mkomani and Langoni, is between the **waterfront** buildings and the town behind, separated by **Usita wa Mui**, now Harambee Avenue (actually a narrow alley for the most part). Until around 1830, this was the waterfront, but the pile of accumulated rubbish in the harbour had become large enough by the time the fort was finished to consider reclaiming it, and, gradually, those who could afford to, built on it. The **fort** lost its pre-eminent position and Lamu, from the sea, took on a different aspect, which included Indian styles such as arches, verandas and shuttered windows.

VISITING LAMU'S MAIN SIGHTS

While the National Museums of Kenya has tried to impose a charge of Ksh3000 to visit Lamu's four main sights (the museum, the fort, the house museum and the German post office museum), there's not a great deal of take-up at that price and most visitors pay separately. It's another good reason to take out temporary membership of the Kenya Museum Society (see p.110) if you're in Nairobi.

DHOW CRUISE, LAMU (P.483) >

When discovering Lamu for yourself, you shouldn't get lost too easily if you remember that **Harambee Avenue** runs parallel to and fifty metres behind the waterfront, and that streets leading into town all run slightly uphill.

Lamu Museum

On the waterfront promenade • Daily 8am–6pm • Ksh500 • The museum can arrange guided tours to archeological sites on Manda and Pate islands: contact the curator, Salim Bunu ☎ 0722 730002 or 042 4633073, or email via the Nairobi headquarters (see p.110) • ⊕ museums.or.ke

The one place you should definitely count on devoting an hour or so to is **Lamu Museum**. The house, built in 1891 on the waterfront, once served as a British colonial government residence. Of Kenya's regional museums, this is the one that best lives up to its name. There's no need to fill spare rooms here with game trophies and trivia; the region's history provides more than enough material.

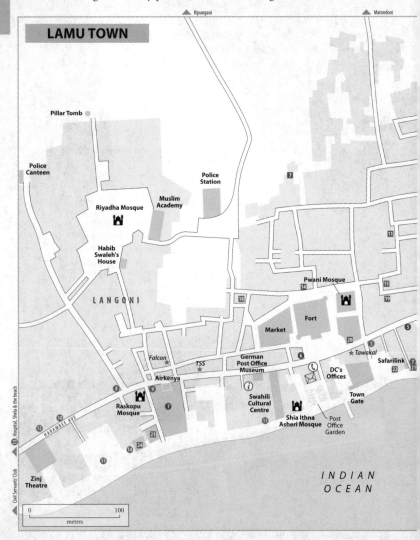

As you enter, there's a large aerial photo of the town for a fascinating bird's-eye insight. Elsewhere, exhibitions of **Swahili culture** – architecture, boats and boat-building, and domestic life – are displayed. There are also rooms devoted to the non-Swahili peoples of the mainland: farmers like the **Pokomo**, **Orma** cattle herders and **Boni** hunters. Two magnificent ceremonial **siwa horns**, one in ivory from Pate, the other from Lamu itself, and made of brass, are the prize exhibits – probably the oldest-surviving musical instruments in sub-Saharan Africa.

Lamu Fort Museum

Harambee Ave • Daily 8am–6pm • Ksh500

The **fort**, which was begun in 1809 and completed in 1821, seems oddly stranded in its modern-day position, deprived of its role as defender of the waterfront. It served as a

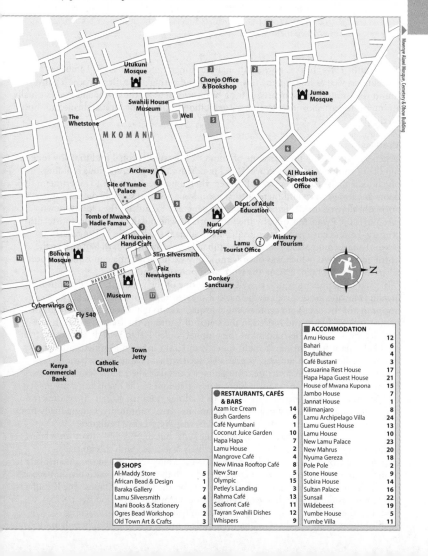

ACCOMMODATION	
Amu House	12
Bahari	6
Baytulkher	4
Café Bustani	3
Casuarina Rest House	17
Hapa Hapa Guest House	21
House of Mwana Kupona	15
Jambo House	7
Jannat House	1
Kilimanjaro	8
Lamu Archipelago Villa	24
Lamu Guest House	13
Lamu House	10
New Lamu Palace	23
New Mahrus	20
Nyuma Gereza	18
Pole Pole	2
Stone House	9
Subira House	14
Sultan Palace	16
Sunsail	22
Wildebeest	19
Yumbe House	5
Yumbe Villa	11

RESTAURANTS, CAFÉS & BARS	
Azam Ice Cream	14
Bush Gardens	6
Café Nyumbani	1
Coconut Juice Garden	10
Hapa Hapa	7
Lamu House	2
Mangrove Café	4
New Minaa Rooftop Café	8
New Star	5
Olympic	15
Petley's Landing	3
Rahma Café	13
Seafront Café	11
Tayran Swahili Dishes	12
Whispers	9

SHOPS	
Al-Maddy Store	5
African Bead & Design	1
Baraka Gallery	7
Lamu Silversmith	4
Mani Books & Stationery	6
Ogres Bead Workshop	2
Old Town Art & Crafts	3

6

SWAHILI STONE ARCHITECTURE

Lamu's **stone houses** are perfect examples of architecture appropriate to its setting. The basic design is an open box shape enclosing a large courtyard, around the inner walls of which are set inward-facing rooms on two or three floors, the top floor forming an open roof terrace with a *makuti* roof. The rooms are thus long and narrow, their ceilings supported by close-set timbers or mangrove poles (*boriti*). Most had exquisite carved doors at one time, though in all but a few dozen homes these have been sold off to pay for upkeep. Many also had *zidaka*, plasterwork niches in the walls to give an illusion of extended space, which are now just as rare. Bathroom arrangements are ingenious, with fish kept in the large water storage cisterns to eat mosquito larvae. In parts of Lamu these old houses are built so close together you could step over the street from one roof to another.

The private space inside Lamu's houses is barely distinguishable from the public space outside. The noises of the town percolate into the interiors, encouraged by the constant flow of air created by the narrow coolness of the dark streets and the heat which accumulates on upper surfaces exposed to the sun.

prison until 1984, but it's now a national monument and open as the **Lamu Fort Museum**, as well as housing the town's **library** and acting as a gallery space. It's always fun to walk round the ramparts, getting bird's-eye views of the town, and there's usually an interesting art show or a **temporary exhibition** of photos or local archeological finds on display.

Mosques

When you start checking out some of Lamu's 23 **mosques**, you'll find that any tone of rigid conformity you might expect is lacking. Most are simple, spacious buildings, as much local men's clubs as places of prayer. There's no special reason to enter them; their doors are always open and there's little to see. Male visitors, suitably dressed, are normally allowed inside; female visitors are generally excluded. The oldest-known mosque is the **Pwani Mosque**, by the fort, parts of which date back to the fourteenth century. Lamu's current Friday mosque is the **Jumaa**, the big one in Pangahari ("sword-sharpening place") ward. Unfortunately, the **Mwenye Alawi Mosque**, at the north end of town, which was once Lamu's only exclusively female mosque, has been taken over by the men, leaving the women to pray at home.

The star of Lamu's mosques, as well as being one of the youngest, is the sumptuous **Riyadha Mosque** located well to the back of the town, in Langoni. Built at the beginning of the twentieth century, the mosque has brought about a radical shift in Lamu's style of Islam, and indeed in the status of Lamu in the Islamic world. It was founded by a sharif, a descendant of the prophet, called **Habib Swaleh**, who came from the Hadramaut (present-day Yemen) to settle in Lamu in the mid-nineteenth century. His house, close by the mosque, is acknowledged with a plaque, but is basically a simple wattle-and-daub structure, containing a caretaker's bed and a few old papers. Habib Swaleh and his group introduced a new freedom to the five-times-daily prayers, with singing, tambourines and spontaneous readings from the Koran. They attracted a large following, particularly from the slave and ex-slave community, but gradually from all social spheres, even the aristocratic families with long Lamu pedigrees.

Some of the other mosques later adopted the style, but the Riyadha, apart from being Lamu's largest mosque, is still the one most closely associated with this kind of inspirational worship. Non-Muslim men who visit while worship is in session are likely to be invited in and encouraged to sit cross-legged with the rest of the assembly. Any sense of stale ritual is far removed: the atmosphere is light, the music infectious. The Riyadha is also famous as the spiritual home of Lamu's annual **Maulidi** celebration (see p.475).

Next to the Riyadha is the big, square **Muslim Academy** – a major teaching establishment, and, like the Riyadha itself and so much else in Lamu, heavily under

Saudi patronage. Both men and women are allowed to have a look around, but there's very little to see. More interesting are some of the students, who come from all over the Islamic world.

Tombs

After the fort, the only other national monument in Lamu (though you may not believe it when you see it) is the fluted **pillar tomb** behind Riyadha Mosque. This may date from as far back as the fourteenth century, and the occasional visit by a tourist might persuade the families in the neighbourhood that it's worth preserving; it can only be a matter of time before it leans too far and collapses on a passing child. In the middle of town, by a betel vine plot, is another tomb, that of **Mwana Hadie Famau**, a local woman of the fifteenth or sixteenth century. This has been walled up and has lost the porcelain-embedded pillars that would once have stood at each corner.

Swahili House Museum

West of Harambee Ave • Daily 8am–6pm• Ksh500, children Ksh250

The **Swahili House Museum** in Mkomani is an eighteenth-century house that's been restored to an approximation of its original appearance. Unfortunately, the guided tour (included in the entrance fee) is brief and the house is very small, consisting only of a small courtyard, two sleeping galleries, two toilets and an upstairs kitchen and roof.

The Donkey Sanctuary

On the waterfront • ⓦ thedonkeysanctuary.org.uk

The **Donkey Sanctuary** is funded by a UK-based animal charity. They'll show you round in the morning and are always happy to receive donations, which they use for free veterinary care of animals that are otherwise sometimes literally worked to death. More than animal-lovers, they have had a significant impact economically, too, with their twice-yearly donkey de-worming programme in the Lamu archipelago.

The cemetery and around

Heading north out of town, through the wards of Tundani ("fruit-picking place") and Weyoni ("donkey racetrack"), you reach the **cemetery**. This is the goal of many religious processions and strolling up there makes an interesting twenty-minute short

---

TRADITION AND MORALITY IN LAMU

A number of **old photographs** on display in the museum belie pronouncements about "unchanging Lamu". The women's cover-all black **buibui**, for example, turns out to be a fashion innovation introduced comparatively recently from southern Arabia. It wasn't worn in Lamu much before the 1930s when, ironically, a degree of emancipation encouraged women of all classes to adopt the high-status styles of purdah. In earlier times, high-born women would appear in public entirely hidden inside a tent-like canopy called a **shiraa**, which had to be supported by slaves; the abolition of slavery at the beginning of the twentieth century marked the demise of this odd fashion.

Outsiders have tended to get the wrong end of the stick about Swahili seclusion. While women are undoubtedly heavily restricted in their public lives, in private they have considerable freedom. The notion of **romantic love** runs deep in Swahili culture. Love affairs, divorces and remarriage are the norm, and the buibui is perhaps as useful to women in disguising their liaisons as it is to their husbands in preventing them.

All this comes into focus a little when wandering through the alleys. You may even bump into some of Lamu's **transvestite** community – cross-dressing men whose lifestyle, which derives from Oman, is accepted and long established. In fact, the more you explore, the more you realize that the town's conventional image is like the walls of its houses – a severe facade concealing an unrestrained interior.

walk. You then come out by the slaughterhouse and rubbish dumps, populated by marabou storks. In the inlet behind them, several large **dhows** and smaller boats are moored. Many are rotting, but one or two are quite new, even unfitted. If you have dreams of owning a dhow (they make great houseboats), you're looking at around $10,000 for a 12m hull. The price depends largely on the time required to build it – two years isn't unusual.

Shela

6

SHELA was once a thriving, self-contained community: Shela's people trace their ancestry back to Manda island and speak a dialect of Swahili quite distinct from that of Lamu town. After the demise of slavery, however, and the coming of the Europeans, it was in limbo for decades; then, post-independence, it found itself midway between rural decline and upmarket tourist boom. Since the turn of the century that balance has definitively altered: the tourists have won. Most of the fine old houses have been bought by foreigners and converted into ravishing holiday homes, decked in bougainvillea. But, since becoming a UNESCO World Heritage Site in 2001, there has also been a surge in new building, sending multi-floored luxury homes and boutique hotels up above the palms. In global terms, the boom is still small-scale, but intense enough to have already overshadowed the historical buildings in the village centre.

It's possible to catch a local boat from Lamu to Shela for Ksh150 per person (30–40min), or you can charter a water taxi from the Shela jetty or Peponi beach for around Ksh600 (10min). Check with *Bush Gardens Restaurant* on Lamu waterfront for departure times and locations of the shared boats.

Friday Mosque

Behind Peponi Hotel

One of Shela's few historical sights is the strange and much-photographed **Friday Mosque**, built in 1829, which stands out for its unusual, rocket-shaped minaret and once stood high above every other building. Not any more. If you're suitably dressed, you can ask to visit and may even be able to go to the top.

Shela beach and sand dunes

A usually deserted 12km sickle of white sand, backed by empty **sand dunes**, Lamu's **beach** is the real thing; you half-expect Robinson Crusoe to come striding out of the heat haze. Unprotected by a reef, the sea here has some motion to it, and it is one of the few places on the coast where, at certain times of the year, you can body-surf (August is probably best). Unfortunately, women may find that wanderers along the beach can be a nuisance, muggings are not unheard of, and there have been incidents of rape, so stay within shouting distance of other sunbathers and preferably go to the beach in company.

All that said, the **sun** is a more likely assailant. There's absolutely no cover and you'll often find that the wind is too strong for erecting a sunshade. Ordinary sunscreen cream is available in town. Coconut oil, also sold in town, is used by some people to avoid drying out, but you need a deep tan to begin with, otherwise your skin will fry.

Matondoni

MATONDONI is the most talked-about destination on Lamu apart from Shela and the beach, but in truth, it's not wildly exciting and its fame as the district's principal dhow-building centre seems misplaced. However, the one-hour walk there is a fine one if you start early (the soft sand track isn't fun in blazing sunshine). A sane, enjoyable alternative is to go by **donkey**: fix up a beast through your guesthouse reception, or you can take one of the sand dhows on its trip from Lamu jetty to Matondoni, get some lunch and walk back, following the telephone wires.

DHOW TRIPS

Where the hotel hustlers left off after you settled in, the dhow-ride men take up the challenge. You'll be persistently hassled until you agree to go on a trip and then, as if the word's gone out, you'll be left alone. The fact is your face quickly becomes familiar to anyone whose livelihood depends upon tourists. Dhow trips are usually a lot of fun and, all things considered, very good value. The simplicity of Swahili sailing is delightful, using a single lateen sail that can be set in virtually any position and never seems to obstruct the view. Sloping past the mangroves, with their primeval-looking tangle of roots at eye level, hearing any number of squeaks and splashes from the small animals and birds that live among them, is quite a serene pleasure.

There are limitless possibilities for dhow trips, though only a short menu of possibilities is usually offered. The cheapest trip is a slow sail across Lamu harbour and up Takwa "river", fishing as you go, followed by a barbecue on the beach at **Manda island**, then back to town. This might commence with some squelching around in the mud under the mangroves, digging for huge bait-worms. If the trip is timed properly with the tides, you can include a visit to **Takwa ruins**, or, for rather more money, you can stay the night on the beach behind the ruins and come back the next day. This is usually done around full moon. Takwa has to be approached from the landward side up the creek, and this can only be done at high tide. A further variation has you sailing south through Lamu harbour, past the headland at Shela and out towards the ocean for some **snorkelling** over the reefs on the southwest corner of Manda around **Kinyika rock**. Snorkel and mask are normally provided, but bringing your own is obviously much better. Although all dhows should carry enough useable life jackets, this is particularly essential if you're venturing beyond the reef, where the seas can be very rough and accidents happen all too often.

The **price** you pay will depend on how many are in your party, where you want to go, for how long, and how much work it's going to be for the crew. Agree on the price beforehand (a full day with lunch starts from around Ksh1200 per person) and pay up afterwards, although some captains may ask you for a small deposit to buy food. Be clear on who is supplying food and drink, apart from any fish you might catch.

Cameras are easily damaged on dhow trips, so wrap them up well in a plastic bag. And take the clothes and drinks you'd need for a 24-hour spell in the Sahara – you'll burn up and dry out otherwise. The Promise Ahadi Dhow Operators Collective (☎072 3650807), on the waterfront in Lamu Town, or Shela Marine (☎072 5003411) in Shela organize recommended dhow trips.

Kipungani

If you really want to look around the whole island, proceed from Matondoni to **KIPUNGANI**, one hour's walk from the end of the beach (4hr from Shela village). This is the halfway mark on the round-the-island walk; the whole trip takes eight or nine hours at least. It is useful to know the state of the tides for the stretch from Matondoni to Kipungani, as you can take a direct route through the mangroves at low tide (but don't get caught out).

ARRIVAL AND DEPARTURE

LAMU ISLAND

By plane Planes land on Manda island, across the harbour directly opposite the town. If you're staying a few days only and then flying out, it's a very good idea to go straight to the appropriate airline office on arrival to reconfirm your return seat. The short boat trip from the airstrip (Ksh100 to Lamu Town) gives you a wonderful introductory panorama of Lamu's nineteenth-century waterfront. There are currently four airlines connecting Lamu with Kiwaiyu, Malindi, Mombasa and Nairobi – unfortunately, Kenya Airways, under *Casuarina Guesthouse* (☎042 4632040–1), has cancelled its Lamu service; however, there are plans to resume when the Manda airstrip has completed its new runway. SafariLink, next to *Sunsail Hotel* (☎ 042 4632211;

daily 8am–5pm, early closing on Sun), has daily flights to Wilson Airport, Nairobi (4pm; $175). But no service April–June and only four days a week Nov–Dec 15. Airkenya on Harambee Avenue in Langoni (☎042 4633445 or ☎042 4633063; daily 8am–5pm), has daily flights to Nairobi Wilson (3.40pm; $179 or $342 return). Fly540 (☎042 4632054; Mon–Fri 8am–noon & 2–5pm, Sat 8am–noon) flies daily direct to Nairobi JKIA (Sun 4.20pm; $197), and via Malindi (Mon–Sat 11.55am, Sun 3pm; $72), while Mombasa Air Safari (bookings care of SafariLink) flies three times weekly to Mombasa ($107) via Malindi ($67).

By bus The bus companies running daily from Lamu to Mombasa via Malindi are Falcon, Tahmeed, Tawakal and

6

TSS. Buses depart from Mokowe jetty on the mainland, starting at 7am, and run every hour; the first *mtaboti* ferries leave Lamu Town at 6–6.30am to connect. Buy tickets (about Ksh600 to Mombasa) the day before or earlier to be sure of a seat – the booking office is on Harambee Ave (booking office hours generally daily 8.30am–12.30pm, 2.30–4.30pm & 7–8.30pm). Tawakal (☏042 4033380) is the fastest, costs a little more (Mombasa Ksh800) than the others and sells out more quickly. It also runs more services, until late morning or early afternoon (usually 7am, 11am and 1pm).

From the mainland The bus trip or drive to Lamu ends at Mokowe dock, on the mainland, where a chugging *mtaboti*

(motorboat taxi, Ksh100) takes you around the creek for the 30min ride to the town. The *mtabotis* are timed to coincide with the buses, though there are other less frequent services throughout the day. Grab your luggage, ignore the touts pulling you every which way, and jump on the boat which seems fullest – they all go to Lamu. Don't be misled by anyone trying to sell you a *mtaboti* charter; just wait for the next public *mtaboti* with everyone else. Alternatively, you can take a fast boat for Ksh150, or charter either for Ksh1500–2000. If you drive up, remove all your valuables and leave your vehicle in the car park where it should be safe (tipping the *askari* beforehand may improve security further).

INFORMATION

Tourist Information Office (☏042 4633132; Mon–Fri 7.30am–12.30pm & 2–4.30pm) is at the north end of town on the waterfront, next to *Lamu House*.

Beach boy hustlers and guides Once you're at the harbour, you'll inevitably be met by a bevy of beach boy hustlers offering to take your baggage and guide you to a hotel. Some work for hotels or guesthouses and are just trying to fill rooms; some think they may get lucky with a quick tip for helping you; others genuinely want to be your guide for the duration of your stay. It's difficult to avoid these characters and they certainly won't allow you to stand around on the quayside looking at your map, so it's best to

know in advance how to get to your preferred destination from the jetty. As usual, firmness, smiles and robust clarity are the best course. If you don't want a guide, be quite clear about that, and if they follow you anyway, explain what has happened to the hotel receptionist. The whole palaver is usually over very quickly as they turn their attentions to the next boatload of arrivals. If you need a guide in Lamu – and they can be useful and informative – your best bet is to ask other travellers to recommend one, or visit the Tourist Office and be sure your guide has a proper ID card. You'll need to tell any guide you engage which places you would like to visit and agree a fee: Ksh800 per day is about right.

ACCOMMODATION

LAMU TOWN

The better lodgings are generally those on the waterfront or those with a height advantage; places on Harambee Avenue tend to be suffocatingly hot. In December, January, July and August, and particularly during Maulidi, room availability can be tight, so book ahead if you can. Between April and June, you may find some places closed. Room prices depend on the season as well as your bargaining skills – haggling is possible at most lodgings, even those places charging eye-watering sums. The size of your group, how long you intend to stay and when you will actually pay are all useful bargaining chips. Unless the town is heaving with visitors, you shouldn't have any problem getting a discount. If you like the place, aim to agree a rate for the duration of your stay and then pay daily. As well as hotels and guesthouses, it's often possible to rent private houses by the week or month. The quantity and standard of furnishing varies, but there's always a kitchen and usually a cook and cleaner. Visit ☏ lamu.org for a wide variety of the options in Lamu, Manda and Shela; if you're already in town, put the word out that you're interested in finding a house, and they'll find you.

Amu House ☏0723 170973. Extremely attractive and welcoming, this is a restored, American-owned stone house with newer rooms added on top, built in the same style and offering really good value. The doubles and triples

are airy, with large bathrooms. Dinner available upon request. BB Ksh1500

Bahari ☏0721 903835, ☏mbisha@hoymail.com. Basic but spacious s/c rooms on several floors, around a cool, plant-filled courtyard. A little rough around the edges but features include amusingly tokenistic "four-poster" beds, nets and fans, and most rooms have a fridge. The excellent rooftop terrace is a good place to meet travellers with its newly renovated restaurant. Haggle hard. BB Ksh2500

★ **Baytulkher** ☏0725 617996, ☏baytulkher @talktalk.net. Decorated in funky, bright colours, with naïve paintings, this is a beautiful, well-lit, airy house, with spacious s/c rooms, bathrooms you can enjoy (rather than want to leave quickly) and lots of quiet corners for rest and contemplation. The huge top-floor "suite" opens on all sides, and has great views. BB Ksh6500

Café Bustani ☏0722 859594, ☏lamuchonjo@yahoo .com. One very nice, s/c, top-floor room, with good ventilation, Swahili four-posters with nets and fan and a large bathroom. Terraces close to the room, and they do good coffee, juices and smoothies. BB Ksh2400

Casuarina Rest House ☏042 4633123 or 0722 915746, ☏kaluc36@yahoo.com. A warren of rooms on the seafront, with nets and fans, in a nice position, but very basic. Okay if you're prepared to put up with rudimentary comforts and security. Two rooms are s/c. BB Ksh1500

Hapa Hapa Guest House ☎0712 526215. Behind the popular eating place of the same name, this has one big double room at the front, with fan but rather poor ventilation. BB Ksh2500

House of Mwana Kupona ☎0735 980848. Owned by Nairobi-based expats, the home of the famous nineteenth-century female poet Mwana Kupona is rented as a whole house, with a shared kitchen, two large, secure rooms, plus several other, pleasant, more flexible rooms with double beds. BB Ksh8000

★ **Jambo House** ☎0713 411714, ⓦjambohouse .com. A homely guesthouse run by an attentive world-traveller. Bedrooms are cosy and clean, and there's an airy upstairs terrace. Free wi-fi. BB Ksh2800

Jannat House ☎0720 289897, ⓦjannathouse.com. Atmospheric, Swedish-owned boutique hotel with fifteen, s/c and non-s/c, rooms (nets and fans), a very nice, small pool, a bar-restaurant and a dhow, *Jannat*. Arranged around a heavily planted courtyard with much of its original decoration (*zidaka* stuccowork niches and furniture) still intact, plenty of terraces with comfy chairs and lovely views over the town. BB $105

★ **Kilimanjaro** ☎0721 141924, ⓔinfo@kilamanjaro lamu.com. Managed by a personable local DJ, this is a very good choice, with a nice chill-out scene on the rooftop and a popular Sunday jazz breakfast. The kitchen is available if you want to self-cater. The penthouse with the big double bed is best, and the same price as the six other rooms. BB $48

Lamu Archipelago Villa ☎0721 108650. The s/c rooms here aren't that great – just a bit too small, and rather plain – but the position, right on the waterfront, is a plus. The rooms at the front are by far the better ones. BB Ksh2500

Lamu Guest House ☎042 4633338. An old house right in the heart of things, which has been owned by the same Indian family for seven generations. It's inevitably somewhat hot and stuffy given its location, but the ceilings are high and there are nets and fans; a few of the rooms are s/c. The rates are dirt cheap, with an emphasis on the dirt. BB Ksh700

★ **Lamu House** ☎042 4633491, ⓦlamuhouse.com. A stunning conversion, based on two traditional houses, Salama and Azania, each with five s/c suites with private terrace, really comfortable beds and superb bathrooms. Rooms downstairs can be a little dark: ideally get one upstairs at the front. There are also two cool, white courtyards with plunge pools, and a decent swimming pool as well. Rates include daily transfers to the Lamu House beach club on Manda. Excellent on-site restaurant and bar run by a charming Belgian restaurateur. BB $200

New Mahrus ☎0720 574446, ⓦmahrushotel.com. Although not on the waterfront, this rambling old place, with its own creaking, run-down charm, has a great

location by the square, looking across to the fort. It's one of the cheapest places in town, with single, non-s/c rooms for just Ksh400, but rooms could be cleaner and security is rather uncertain. The upper rooms, facing the square, are best. BB Ksh1000

★ **Nyuma Gereza** ☎0722 721232, ⓦnyumagereza hotel.blogspot.com. Located behind the fort, and personably run by its devoutly Muslim owner (no alcohol or beach boys in rooms), this excellent conversion has ten s/c rooms with fans and nets, and guests have use of a kitchen but no fridge. BB Ksh1800

Pole Pole Guest House ☎042 4633344. Getting a bit run-down, but still pleasant, and very good value, especially if you're used to B&Ls. It has a fantastic roof terrace with a bird's-eye view from the roof, one of the highest in town. Nets and fans in most rooms. Ksh1200

Stone House ☎0736 699417 or 0722 528377, ⓦstonehousehotellamu.com. A well-run hotel in middle of town with plenty of lounging spaces on each floor and a wonderful oceanview rooftop restaurant. BB $80

★ **Subira House** ☎0726 916686, ⓔinfo@subirahouse .net. Built for the Sultan of Zanzibar, this palace-turned-boutique-hotel directly behind the Lamu Fort features breezy lounging galleries throughout its three-storeys, decorated in authentic Lamu style. Rooms are clean, private and spacious with strong eco-values from the friendly and helpful Swedish owners. The restaurant features light and healthy meals with produce from their organic farm. BB €76

★ **Sultan Palace** ☎0728 991280. Dramatic, tall house, next to and (surprisingly) owned by *Petley's*, with four large rooms, each with two or three large beds. Steep stairs lead up to a splendid, top-floor lounge area under the *makuti* eves. BB Ksh5000

Sunsail ☎042 4632065 or 0722 666303, ⓦsunsail hotel.co.ke. Situated in the old stone "Mackenzie" trader's house on the waterfront, the rooms here have high ceilings and smart tiled bathrooms, but this doesn't compensate for their small size – and only the two at the front have sea views. Unfortunately the roof terrace is enclosed. Still, reasonable value for money. BB Ksh3000

★ **Wildebeest** ☎0723 687408 or ☎0712 851499, ⓔwildebeeste@hotmail.com. Fascinating, old, gallery-cum-apartments, with a hair-raising multiplicity of steep, Escher-like staircases, owned by a Lamu artist-caretaker, and stuffed with artwork and bric-a-brac. Breakfast and other meals available. Exceptional value. BB Ksh8000

Yumbe House ☎042 4633101 or 0725 352117. A cut above the average lodging, this has ten, mostly quite spacious, s/c rooms, including some good-value singles, all with fans, nets and fridge (a nice touch), above a well-planted courtyard. The top room is easily the best. Check when booking as you may be put up at *Yumbe Villa*, their annexe, a few minutes' walk away, which is not as nice. BB Ksh3200

6

6

SHELA

While Shela can be a hedonistic place to pass a few days, it doesn't offer the thrill of staying among the mosques and street life of Lamu town itself. In addition, the price of rooms here can be up to twice what they would be in town, and there are few restaurants aside from those in the hotels. In addition to hotels and guesthouse rooms, though, there are now more than twenty self-catering houses to rent, with prices starting at around $200/night. For more information, contact Lamu Retreats (☎020 600482, ⊛lamuretreats.com) or Lamu Homes & Safaris (☎020 4446384, ⊛lamuhomes.com).

Banana House 200m inaland from the waterfront ☎0721 275538, ⊛bananahouse-lamu.com. A wellness centre offering yoga and ayurvedic cuisine. The well-maintained houses are run by Banana and his lovely Dutch wife. The penthouse rooms have excellent ocean views, while the garden space and pool are great for meeting other travellers. BB **€115**

Fatuma's Tower In the village ☎0722 277138, ⊛fatumastower.com. A truly enchanting garden experience set in the back of the village in a spacious self-contained compound among frangipanis and a restored tower building. Furnished with antiques and featuring a yoga hall, library and penthouse suite. The Acacia Suite has a great view and is the best value for money. BB **€95**

Island Hotel Back of the village, near the sand dunes ☎042 4633290 or 0712 670961. An older-style place, with spacious, attractively furnished rooms, all with nets on frames and instant showers, and a restful atmosphere. Rooms 16 and 17 are especially appealing – almost open-air, like sleeping on the roof but in privacy and comfort. The *Barracuda* rooftop restaurant is good and reasonably priced, but doesn't have an alcohol licence. Sometimes closes May to mid-June. BB **Ksh4500**

Jannatan In the centre of Shela ☎0711 972590 or 0722 729219. Big place with a good, deep pool, though unshaded. However, it's essentially just a modern hotel, even with the fake *zidaka*-style ceilings. Seventeen rooms on five floors, so there are good views from the top – just no atmosphere. BB **Ksh4000**

★ **Kijani House** On the waterfront north of Shela ☎0202 435700 or 0725 545264, ⊛kijani-lamu.com. Comfortable and pretty, environmentally conscious Swiss-owned hotel, with eleven beautifully done rooms (with solar-heated showers, fans, frame nets and safes) around tropical gardens, and their own fruit farm close by. There are also two small pools, a restaurant serving Italian-style set menus, and a bar with a nice range of Italian and South African wines. Closed May & June. BB **€175**

Peponi On the beach, 100m south of Shela Jetty ☎0733 203082 or 0722 203082, ⊛peponi-lamu .com. Shela's main beachfront focus, where everyone stops in for a cold drink, *Peponi* is fabulously situated, and offers superb food (some would say the best on Lamu). But if

you're staying – and it's quite expensive for what you get – pay the extra for rooms in the main house, as the standard rooms in chalets across the lawn are not that special. Good pool. Closed May & June. BB **€215**

★ **Pwani Guest House** Behind Peponi ☎0712 506778, ⊛lamu.org. Stylish, roomy house; the three doubles and two singles (all s/c) offer various options, but all are a good deal, by Shela standards, with their old furniture, antique stucco work and soft light. Breakfast and dinner are served on the rooftop terrace, which has beautiful sea views. BB **Ksh5000**

★ **Shella Bahari Guest House** On the waterfront 100m north of Peponi ☎042 4632046 or 0722 901643, ⊛shellabahari.co.ke. You pay a premium for the location here, right next to the water. The five rooms, all s/c and different rates, are simple but nicely done and there's an excellent restaurant downstairs. BB **Ksh8000**

Shella Royal House 100m inland from the waterfront ☎0721 341770, ✉shella@wildernessgetawaysea .com. A bright and breezy place, with yellow floors and stairs. The rooms, all with mahogany four-posters, are of varying standards. There's a great swing bed on the roof terrace, perfect for lounging, with a 360-degree view, and a fabulous "honeymoon room" on the top floor. BB **Ksh9000**

Stopover On the waterfront, south of Kijani House ☎0720 127222, ⊛lamu.org. Five simple, but nicely done, s/c rooms directly on the seafront near the dhow harbour, all opening out onto balconies with sea views. There's a ground-floor restaurant overlooking the sea, serving great fish curries. The three first-floor rooms can be rented out as a self-catering apartment with kitchen facilities. BB **Ksh5000**

KIZINGONI BEACH

Kipungani Explorer Near Kizingoni Beach ☎020 2103454, ⊛heritage-eastafrica.com. A delightful "desert island" complex of fourteen simple mat-and-*makuti* thatch *bandas* up on the beach, with a bar and restaurant decorated with driftwood and the products of beachcombings. The food is superb, the views over the sands and channel are exceptional, and the welcome, service and sense of blissful isolation are everything you could ask for. Excursions, windsurfing and snorkelling trips are all on offer, and there's a pool, too. If you don't want to walk or ride, you can get there direct from Lamu town by speedboat (30min), or more slowly by dhow. Closed Easter–June. FB **$380**

SOUTHWEST LAMU

★ **Kizingo** On the southwest tip of the island ☎0733 954770 or 0722 901544, ⊛kizingo.com. A secluded eco-lodge, created in partnership with nearby Kipungani village. There are six thatched *bandas* nestled among the sand dunes, each with perfect sea views, and the food

---

DINNER AT HOME

If you spend any time in Lamu, you'll probably run into someone offering you a "genuine" **Swahili dinner** at home. At its best, this is a great way of seeing how the majority of Lamu's inhabitants live, and the food can be delicious. On the other hand, the price demanded at the end (which, like everything in Lamu, depends mainly on how hard you haggle and your perceived ability to pay) might not necessarily be any cheaper than eating in a decent restaurant. As in a restaurant, you should pay after your meal, not before.

6

served up at the restaurant is wonderfully fresh. From November to April you can swim with wild bottlenose dolphins, and between November and June turtles lay eggs on the beach; the owners will take guests to watch the newborn turtles make their way into the ocean. If you want to rent a house in this remote part of Lamu, there are now several lavish, new beachfront properties on a 24-acre private stretch between *Kizingo* and *Kipungani Explorer*. Check out w kizingonibeach.com for more details. Closed May & June. FB **$400**

EATING AND DRINKING

There are enough restaurants and passable *hotelis* in Lamu to enable you to eat out twice a day for a week without going back to your first port of call. A fine balance has been achieved between what is demanded and what can be supplied: yoghurt, fruit salad, pancakes, milkshakes and puréed fruit juices have become Lamu specialities. Superb lobster and crab dishes, oysters, snapper and delicious steaks of swordfish, barracuda and shark are also on many menus – it's a nice change to find a fishing town where you can actually eat seafood relatively affordably. Upcountry staples – beans, curries, pilau, steak, chicken, chips, eggs, even *ugali* – are available from a number of ordinary *hotelis* crowded along Harambee Avenue, particularly in Langoni. Also along Harambee Avenue, you'll find tiny mutton kebabs and cakes on sale at night; they cost next to nothing and are usually delicious. Prices are fairly standard, Ksh80 to Ksh150 for shakes and juices, depending on size, and Ksh500 to Ksh700 for full meals. Cheaper places, that don't go out of their way to attract tourists, serve meals for Ksh150 to Ksh250.

SNACK BARS AND LOCAL HOTELIS

Azam Ice Cream On the waterfront in Langoni. Lamu's only ice-cream parlour, with a half-decent selection of flavours. Daily 9.30am–1.30pm & 4–10pm.

Coconut Juice Garden Harambee Ave. Good juices and shakes, blended as you wish – combinations include passion and pawpaw, and a sublime coconut and banana. Mon–Sat 7am–6pm.

Rahma Café Harambee Ave. Popular local teashop and *hoteli*.

Tayran Swahili Dishes Harambee Ave, Langoni. Locals squeeze together at shared tables in this tiny chop house to eat fried fish, beans, samosas and *mandaazi*.

RESTAURANTS AND TRAVELLERS' CAFÉS

★ **Bush Gardens** On the waterfront, Mkomani ☏ 0712 521633. Competing for the same business as *Hapa Hapa* (see below) but more upmarket, this seafood and kebab place has a popular following and a charming proprietor. The food varies from average to first-rate (the grilled garlic fish is magnificent) and prices are reasonable – shakes Ksh50–100, fish around Ksh450. Daily 7am–10pm.

Café Nyumbani Harambee Ave, opposite *Lamu House* ☏ 0721 151304. Popular first-floor restaurant for breakfasts, lunches and dinners, with a wide variety of prices and dishes (mains Ksh250–1000). The speciality is barbecued seafood in garlic and tamarind sauce. You have to call or text several hours in advance (or the day before) to order food, but it's well worth it. Daily 7am–10pm.

Hapa Hapa On the waterfront, Mkomani. ☏ 0712 526215. Popular, central seafront rendezvous – the food is inexpensive, generally good, and occasionally excellent. And then there are the famous pint jugs of freshly pressed juices, shakes and smoothies. A good place to people-watch, or just daydream. Daily 7.30am–10pm.

Mangrove Café Next to Petley's ☏ 0722 471266. Popular travellers' café serving up freshly squeezed juices and snacks. Daily 6am–9pm.

Lamu House On the waterfront, Mkomani ☏ 042 4633491, w lamuhouse.com. With its terrace cleverly tucked away behind a low wall, eating here is more relaxing than in some of the more exposed restaurants. Although not cheap, it's not as expensive as you might imagine (Ksh2000 for three courses, without drinks), and the seafood dishes are invariably fragrant and well prepared. Daily 7am–10pm.

New Minaa Rooftop Café Just off Harambee Ave, Langoni ☏ 0722 661907. A pleasant roof-terrace restaurant that's also a good place to mingle with the locals. Serves good fried fish, beans in coconut and chapattis. Daily 6am–10pm.

★ **New Star** Harambee Ave, Langoni ☏ 0722 105033. Under a dilapidated roof, this Lamu institution (35 years and still going strong) is one of the few restaurants catering equally to travellers and locals, and one of the cheapest in town, with tasty stew and rice for Ksh120. Especially good for breakfast before an early-morning walk to the beach.

MARKETS AND SELF-CATERING

If you enjoy doing your own cooking (several lodgings have kitchens you can use), a whole new world starts to open up. The produce market in front of the fort – run for the most part by upcountry women – has everything you'll need, with separate sections for meat, fish, and fruit and vegetables. For fish and shellfish, get there very early: by 9am all the interesting stock has been sold. Lamu has wonderful fruit and is famous for its enormous, aromatic mangoes, but you should also try the unusually sweet, juicy grapefruit. While you're here, you might also find one of Lamu's traditional exports, betel, the green vine you see trailing out of all the empty plots in town. The sweet, hot-tasting leaves are wrapped around other ingredients, including white lime and betel nut, which stains the teeth red, to make *pan* which you chew (see p.403). For something sweet, try the halwa shop on Harambee Avenue in Langoni, and there's a good bakery facing the right side of the fort.

Daily 5.30am–10.30pm.

Olympic On the waterfront, Langoni ☎ 0728 667692. Popular, long-established beachfront place with colourful and homely decor for fresh juices, snacks and rice and fish-based meals. Excellent seafood menu specializing in Indian sauces. Daily 8am–10pm.

Seafront Café On the waterfront, Langoni. This travellers' restaurant offers coconut fish or beans, rice, pilau and *karanga*, though standards are variable. Daily 9.30am–midnight.

★ **Whispers** Harambee Ave, Langoni ☎ 042 4632024. If you need a break from the local joints on the waterfront this coffee shop and book/antique store offers real espressos, wonderful cakes, smoothies, pizzas, pastas and salads that are hard to resist. Unless, that is, you're really counting the pennies – a snack and a coffee can cost Ksh600. Has a deli section and does takeaways, though portions tend to be on the small side. Usually closed May & June. Daily 9am–9pm.

BARS AND CLUBS

There's usually a disco, sometimes with a Ksh50 or Ksh100 entrance, on Fri & Sat at the *Civil Servants' Club*, about 1km south of the GPO (entrance on the waterfront).

Petley's Landing On the waterfront, below the hotel of the same name. The only stand-alone bar in town is a horrible, noisy music bar, and has nothing to do with its namesake. Daily noon till late.

SHOPPING

Woodcarving shops are mostly found in Mkomani, along the waterfront and in Harambee Avenue. Model dhows, chests, furniture and *siwa* horns are all attractive but bulky. Beautifully hand-carved safari chairs are also a hassle to carry, but the prices make them worth acquiring. Wooden trays are an opportunity to have something lighter and useful that also shows off Lamu craftsmanship. If you have something in mind, and a day or two in hand, you can always order a particular piece or design. Some of the shops selling jewellery and trinkets have genuinely old and interesting pieces: look out especially for tiny lime caskets in silver, earlobe plugs in buffalo horn or silver, and old coins. A number of tailors along Harambee Avenue will run up shirts, trousers, shorts and skirts very cheaply in a day or so. The easiest way to end up with something that fits is to provide a model garment for them to copy. Langoni is the place to hunt out pairs of printed ladies' *kangas* and men's woven *kikoi* wraps.

African Bead and Leather Design Near the arch in Mkomani. Sourced from a community workshop near the *Tamarind* in Mombasa, they have leather bags, beadwork and beaded sandals, and handmade fashion.

Baraka Gallery Harambee Ave, Langoni. Even if it's expensive, the wares here are so diverse and attractive – from silver and glass jewellery to intricate basketware, leather goods and paper crafts – that it's a must-visit for souvenir hunters. Daily 9am–1pm & 3.30–7.30pm.

Lamu Silversmith On Harambee Ave just up from the *Lamu Guest House*. Long-established and recommended silver craftsmen who will design to order.

Ogres Bead Workshop Just off Harambee Ave, Mkomani. Run by two brothers from Nairobi, this workshop sells wonderful handmade jewellery. Custom pieces made to order.

Old Town Art and Crafts Mkomani. Big shop of carvings, paintings and jewellery – the sort of stuff you don't easily find elsewhere in Lamu. Like an upcountry souvenir emporium, but in a relaxed atmosphere.

DIRECTORY

Bank KCB, on the waterfront (Mon–Fri 9am–3pm, Sat 9–11am), has an ATM. There is also an ATM in Shela

Books and newspapers Mani Books & Stationers, near the fort, sells newspapers and magazines. For a selection of books, visit the offices of Lamu Chonjo magazine, at *Café Bustani* in Mkomani, near the Swahili House Museum.

Cinema The Zinj Theatre on Harambee Ave in Langoni screens international and Bollywood films. It also occasionally screens live English Premiership or European Champions League football matches.

Henna painting A number of women around town offer henna designs for hands and feet, for which you can expect to pay around Ksh1000 for both hands or both feet. The best women have portfolios of designs to choose from – you'll see them in one or two shop fronts and private doorways. If done properly, your hands or feet will be bound in cloth for twelve hours and the design should stay for up to six months, or a year on nails.

Internet access Cyberwings, next to *Petley's*, has webcams (daily 9am–9pm, sometimes closed around 1–2pm; Ksh1.50/min); *New Mahrus Hotel*, first floor (Ksh2/min, Ksh100/hr); Bustani Café (daily 8am–7pm; free wi-fi).

Hospital The Saudi-funded hospital, out in the direction of Shela (☎042 4633012), attracts patients from a huge part of northeastern Kenya. There are also several private clinics – ask around.

Library The town library (Mon–Fri 8am–12.30pm &

2–5.30pm, Sat 10am–noon; ☎042 4633201) is on the top floor of the fort. It has a surprisingly good collection, with lots on Lamu, as well as a sixteenth-century Koranic manuscript.

Speedboat charter Not exactly in keeping with the spirit of Lamu's lifestyle, it certainly gets you from A to B effectively, but drinks diesel fuel and is thus expensive. You can hire a boat via the Promise Ahadi Dhow Operators Collective in Lamu Town (☎0723 650807). Rates are around Ksh8000 to Pate, Ksh10,000 to Faza and Ksh15,000 to Kiwaiyu. In Shela, *Shela Marine* (☎0725 003411) offers a similar service at similar prices.

Supermarkets/general stores Al Maddy Store, Harambee Ave (daily 9am–12.30pm & 5–10pm in theory, but often shuts earlier), or Bagdam Store, Harambee Ave (Mon–Sat 8.15am–12.30pm & 4–10pm, Sun 8.15am–12.30pm).

Swahili lessons Being suffused in Swahili culture, Lamu is a good place to learn the language – the Tourist Information Centre (see p.484) can put you in touch with a teacher. Alternatively, ask at the Department of Adult Education on Harambee Ave or at Lamu Museum.

Tide tables Check out *Coast Week* or, if you can get online, ⓦlamu.org/tide-table.

Visa extensions Immigration office in the District Commissioner's (DC's) offices on the waterfront.

Manda Island

Practically within shouting distance of Lamu town, **Manda** – with next to no fresh water – was only recently almost uninhabited but is now the site of several new luxury homes and a couple of boutique resorts. Aside from the allure of the pristine beach, it is also the site of the main airstrip on the islands, and the location of the old ruined town of **Takwa** (favourite destination of the dhow-trip operators). Significant archeologically for the ruins of Takwa and Manda, the north side of the island is also the location of the fabulous *Manda Bay* lodge (see p.490).

Manda ruins

You can walk from *Manda Bay* to the nearby **Manda ruins**, just fifteen minutes away. The population of this town is estimated to have been around three thousand. It's a fascinating, barely excavated site, with baobabs poking through the old walls. The remnants include the *mihrab*, and most of the walls, of a sizeable mosque. Watch out for **snakes** – the island has a diverse variety.

Takwa ruins

Daily 8am–6pm • Ksh500 • A thirty-minute boat ride from Lamu

Whether you make a flying visit to **Takwa** or sleep out on the beach behind it, the site is well worth seeing. A flourishing town in the sixteenth and seventeenth centuries, it was deserted (as usual, no one knows why), and is in many respects reminiscent of Gedi (see p.452). As at other sites, toilets and bathrooms figure prominently in the architecture. In Islam, cleanliness is so close to godliness as to almost signify it – the Takwans must have been a devout community. The doors of all the houses face north towards Mecca, as does the main street with the **mosque** at the end of it. The mosque is interesting for the pillar at one end, which suggests it was built on a tomb site (that of a founder of the town perhaps), and for the simple lines of its *mihrab*, so different from the ornate curlicues of later designs. Another impressive **pillar tomb** stands alone, just outside the town walls, its date translating to about 1683, and it still occasionally attracts pilgrims from Shela (some of whom claim their ancestry lies in Takwa), who come here to pray for rain.

Takwa has been thoroughly cleared but, in order to preserve it for the future, hardly excavated at all. What has been found, however, suggests an industrious and healthy community, living in an easily defensible position with a wall all around the town, the ocean on one side behind the dunes, and mangroves on the other. Despite this, they appear to have left in a panic and, as usual, there's ample room for conjecture about why. Part of the great appeal of Kenya's ruined towns lies in the open debate that still continues about who, precisely, their builders and citizens were, and why they so often left in such evident haste. And there's always the fascinating possibility that old Swahili manuscripts will turn up to explain it all.

ARRIVAL AND DEPARTURE   MANDA ISLAND

Local **boats** run between Lamu jetty and Manda beach for Ksh400. For departure times check with *Diamond Beach Village* on Manda or *Bush Gardens Restaurant* on Lamu Town waterfront.

ACCOMMODATION AND EATING

Carla's Beach Hut At Ras Kitau ⓦlamu.org. Back-to-basics two-bedroom thatched-roof *banda*, just steps from the ocean. Facilities are minimal (take food and water), but the setting is magnificent. **€50**

★ **Diamond Beach Village** On the southern arm of Manda, facing Shela ☎0720 915001, ⓦdiamond beachvillage.com. Far more affordable than the *Majlis* next door, offering simple self-contained *bandas*, a beach bar/restaurant with woodfired pizza oven, a rather wacky treehouse in a baobab, sound environmental principles, and a superb beachfront location. Great social setting with weekly Sunday pizza and movie nights. They have evening electricity and pride themselves on great food and strong Bloody Marys. Closed April 15–June 30. BB **$145**

Lamu House Beach Bar & Restaurant Down the beach from the Majlis Resort, facing Shela. If Robinson Crusoe had a sophisticated palate, he would live here. Rising out of the sand, the beach club serves up ice-cold drinks and great seafood all in a lovely beach picnic setup, complete with watersports, beach chairs and showers. The

weekly Sunday brunches are not to be missed. Three courses from Ksh1500.

The Majlis Resort Down the beach from Diamond Beach Village, facing Shela ☎0773 777066, ⓦmajlis resorts.com. A series of exclusive beachfront luxury villas and suites catering to high rollers and European aristocracy. The beach bar and restaurant serves up some excellent fine dining, and the second floor bar in the main building is perfect spot to watch the sunset while sipping on an overpriced margarita. FB **€540**

★ **Manda Bay** At the northwestern tip of Manda Island ☎0722 203329 or 0722 203109, ⓦmandabay .com. This exclusive beach camp of palm mat, wood and *makuti bandas* in an extravagantly beautiful setting is the perfect honeymoon retreat. When you're not participating in every conceivable watersport, or taking a sundowner trip on the lodge's own enormous dhow, you can swing in your hammock and be entertained by a huge variety of birds (there are bird baths outside every *banda*). FB **$1000**

Pate Island

Only two hours by ferry from Lamu, totally unaffected by tourism and rarely visited, **Pate island** has some of the most impressive ruins anywhere on the coast and a clutch of old Swahili settlements which, at different times, have been as important as Lamu or more so. There are few places on the coast as memorable.

Pate is mostly low-lying and almost surrounded by mangrove swamps; no two maps of it ever agree (ours shows only the permanent dry land, not the ever-changing mangrove forests that surround it in the shallow sea; see p.474), so getting on and off the island requires deft awareness of the tides. Its remoteness, coupled with a lack of information and limited transport on the island, deters travellers. In truth, though, Pate is not a difficult destination, and is an easier island to walk around than Lamu, with none of that island's exhausting soft sand.

It's wise to take **water** with you (five litres if possible), as Pate's supplies are unpredictable and often very briny. Most islanders live on home-produced **food** and staples brought from Lamu and, although there are a few small shops on the island, it's a good idea to have some emergency provisions (which also make useful gifts if required). **Mosquitoes** and flies are a serious menace on Pate, especially during the long rains. The shops sell mosquito coils but it's also worth carrying some repellent for use during the day.

Brief history

According to its own **history**, the *Pate Chronicle*, Pate was founded in the early years of Islam with the arrival of Arabian immigrants. This mini-state is supposed to have lasted until the thirteenth century, when another group of dispossessed Arab rulers – the **Nabahani** – arrived. The story may have been embellished by time, but archeological evidence does support the existence of a flourishing port on the present site of Pate as early as the ninth century. Probably by the fifteenth century the town exerted a considerable influence on most of the quasi-autonomous settlements along the coast, including Lamu.

The first **Portuguese** visitors were friendly, trading with the Pateans for the multicoloured silk cloth for which the town had become famous, and they also introduced gunpowder, which enabled wells to be easily excavated, a fact which must have played a part in Pate's rising fortunes. During the sixteenth century, a number of Portuguese merchants settled and married in the town, but as Portugal tightened its grip and imposed taxes, relations quickly deteriorated. There were repeated uprisings and reprisals until, by the middle of the seventeenth century, the Portuguese had withdrawn to the security of Fort Jesus in Mombasa. Even today, though, several families in Pate are said to be Wa-reno (from the Portuguese *reino*, "kingdom"), meaning of Portuguese descent.

During the late seventeenth and eighteenth centuries, having thrown out the old rulers and avoided domination by new invaders like the Omani Arabs, Pate underwent a **cultural rebirth** and experienced a flood of creative activity similar to Lamu's. The two towns had a lively relationship, and were frequently in a state of war. At some time during the Portuguese period, Pate's harbour had started to silt up and the town began to use Lamu's, which must have caused great difficulties. In addition, Pate was ruled by a Nabahani king who considered Lamu part of his realm. The disastrous Battle of Shela of 1812 (see p.478) marked the end of Lamu's political allegiance to Pate and the end of Pate as a city-state.

Pate town

From the dock at Mtangawanda there's more than one route to Pate town. The old path, a narrow **footpath** through thick bush, the *ndia ya Pate*, or "path to Pate", is the one old people will show you, and once on the trail it's easy to follow. You cross a broad, tidal "desert", pockmarked with fiddler crab holes, then climb a slight rise to drop through thicker bush, and arrive after an hour on the edge of town. However, since the dredging of the Mkanda channel, Patean labourers have been working at enlarging the dock at Mtangawanda, and a tractor and trailer, carrying a barrel of fresh water for concrete-mixing, follows a new **motorable road** back and forth throughout the day, and will usually give you a lift.

Despite its small size, **PATE** could hardly be described as a village. Yet, reduced to the status of sub-location, its only link with government an assistant chief, its sole provision a primary school, the town is today a mere shadow of its former self. But at least its inhabitants are said to remain the richest on the island, thanks to their cash crop, **tobacco**, possibly introduced by the Portuguese and certainly grown here longer than anywhere else on the coast.

After Lamu, Pate comes as a series of surprises. There's no electricity, no alcohol and, apart from the tractor, a handful of matatus and a few motorbikes, very few vehicles. The town plan is pretty much the same – a maze of narrow streets and high-walled houses – but here the streets are made of earth, and the houses are built of coral and dried mud, unplastered and somehow forbidding. The overall layout is confusing, with little slope, as in Lamu, to help your orientation. Pateans do, in fact, refer to the "upper" and "lower" parts of town – Kitokwe and Mitaaguu respectively. The lower part is down near the town dock, which is only briefly underwater at high tide. If you arrive from Mtangawanda in the "upper" part of town – reputedly poorer and less friendly – you're likely to be struck immediately by the *Wapate* – the **people**, and notably the women. Brilliant, determined ladies, with short, bushy hair and rows of gold earrings, stare out directly, unhidden by *buibuis*. If you speak any Swahili, you're likely to find the dialect here unrecognizable. *Wazungu* are rare and, after Lamu's characteristic studied repose (well, beach boys aside), Pate is arrestingly upfront in its dealings with foreigners.

The Nabahani ruins

Boys will guide you around the ruins for a small payment, but don't expect anyone to take you at night; although it's very beautiful in a full moon, you'll have to go alone because the locals are afraid of the *djinn* and ghosts living there • Check with the museum in Lamu Town to hire a local guide for Ksh500 (☎ 0722 730002)

More layers are peeled off Pate's enigmatic exterior when you start to explore the ruins of the **Nabahani** town just outside the modern one. The walls, roofless buildings, tombs, mosques and unidentifiable structures, stretched across several acres, are fascinating, the more so perhaps because this isn't an "archeological site" in the commonly expected mould. Farmers cultivate tobacco and other crops in the stony fields between the walls.

Most impressive are the **Mosque with Two Mihrabs**, a nearby house that still has a facing of beautiful *zidaka* (niches) on one wall, and the remains of a sizeable mansion. This last building, you'll be told, is a **Portuguese house**. Certainly, the worn-down stumps of bottle glass projecting from the top of one of its walls do lend it a curiously European flavour, and in the plaster on another wall are scratched two very obvious galleons. Its ceiling slots are square for timbers rather than round for *boriti*, as elsewhere in the ruins.

Shards of pottery and household objects lie in the rubble everywhere, but many of the interiors of the buildings are so clogged with tangled roots and vegetation that getting in is almost impossible. It is worth persevering, however: the sense of personal discovery is exciting.

Many of the walls and buildings have already been demolished to obtain lime for tobacco cultivation. Without weighty financial backing, it's hard to see how the National Museums of Kenya could preserve the remains of old Pate as well as compensate the farmers. Gradually, tragically, it is all returning to the soil.

Siyu

The walk from Pate to **Siyu** is a slightly tricky 8km, or you can take a matatu from Pate (Ksh100). Having set off in the correct direction, you will find the first half-hour fairly straightforward; if in doubt, bear right. You come to a crossroads (easily missed unless you look backwards) and turn right. This narrow red-dirt path soon broadens into a track known as the *barabara ya gari* (the "motor highway"); it takes you to a normally dry tidal inlet where you veer left a little before continuing straight on through thick bush for another hour to reach Siyu. Wherever the bush on either side is high enough you may come across gigantic spiders' webs strung across the path. The spiders are brightly coloured, non-hairy, and merely waiting for insects, but they are nevertheless intimidating. Fortunately, they have the sense to build their webs high up and well out of the way.

Siyu is even less well documented than Pate. Still less accessible by sea, the town was a flourishing and unsuspected centre of Islamic scholarship from the seventeenth to the nineteenth century and apparently something of a **sanctuary** for Muslim intellectuals and craftsmen. While Lamu, Pate and other trading towns were engaged in political rivalry and physical skirmishing, Siyu never had its heart in commerce or maritime activities, and never attracted much Portuguese attention. Instead, there was enormous devotion to **Koran-copying**, **book-making**, **text illumination**, and cottage industries like the **woodcarving** and **leatherwork** for which it's still famous locally. Siyu **sandals** are said to be absolutely the best (though plastic flip-flops have forced almost all the makers out of business), and Siyu **carved doors** are among the most beautiful of all Swahili doors, with distinctive guilloche patterns and inlays of ground shell.

The sources of wealth and stability for Siyu's flowering are a little mysterious, but the town's agricultural base obviously supported it well and it was probably the largest settlement on the island in the early nineteenth century, with up to thirty thousand inhabitants. In 1873, the British vice-consul in Zanzibar could still describe Siyu as "the pulse of the whole district".

These days you wouldn't know it. Fewer than four thousand people live here, and signs of the old brilliance are hard to find. Siyu lost its independence and presumably much of its artistic flair when the Sultan of Zanzibar's Omani troops first occupied the fort in 1847 – though it was twenty years before the Omanis were able to hold it for more than a brief spell.

Most of Siyu's houses today conform to the "open-box" plan typical of the Kenyan coast: yellowish mud with a ridged *makuti* roof, open at each end. These houses stand, each on its own, with no real streets to connect them, so that although it's larger than Pate, Siyu feels far more like a village. The cultural isolation of these communities from each other, a separateness which continues to this day, is easily appreciated after arriving in Siyu from Pate. There are still few *buibuis* here, but there's much less jewellery in evidence and the atmosphere is altogether less severe.

Siyu Fort

Built in the early nineteenth century (no one knows for sure by whom), **Siyu Fort** is the town's most striking building and indeed, in purely monumental terms, the most imposing building anywhere in the Lamu archipelago. Substantially renovated, it is one of the few surviving traces of the glory days. It's freely accessible, though watch out for dangers like the well and the unstable walls. Around the outskirts of Siyu on the south side are a number of quite impressive **tombs**. The big domed tomb with porcelain niches dates from 1853.

Shanga ruins

Shanga is on the south coast of the island, about an hour's walk from Siyu • Expect to pay around Ksh1000 for a guide

You'll need the help of a good guide if you hope to visit the ruins of **SHANGA**, a large Swahili town at least 1000 years old, which would be almost impossible to find unaided. You literally have to hack your way through the undergrowth when you arrive at the ruins. The most impressive sight is the white pillar tomb, eminently phallic, which you come to first. The very large Friday mosque nearby and a second mosque nearer the sea are only the most obvious of innumerable other remains in every direction.

Excavations at Shanga have revealed a walled site of 12 acres with five access gates and a cemetery outside the walls containing 340 stone tombs. There was even a sea wall. Inside the town, 130 houses were surveyed, together with what looks to have been a palace similar in some respects to the one at Gedi. Shanga is believed to have been occupied from the ninth to the fourteenth centuries and, in a pattern that may sound familiar, no very convincing reasons have been found for its abandonment, nor for why it was never mentioned by travellers and traders of the time.

A limited amount of work has been done to restore some of the plaster in a set of *zidaka* wall niches and on the fluted pillar tomb, but on the whole the excavations only seem to have encouraged the jungle. Getting from one ruin to the next isn't easy. Dangerously camouflaged **wells**, and **snakes**, both of which are common, enliven the Shanga experience. If you walk on down to the sea – and assuming you have a certain capacity for hardship in paradise – there's a beautiful **beach** and some ideal camping spots. Perhaps needless to say, you would need to be completely self-reliant, and preferably in a group.

6

Faza

From **Siyu to Faza** the walk is shorter than from Pate to Siyu and more interesting, through waist-high grass, fertile *shambas* and sections of bush. It takes about two hours, but you'll need guidance, at least as far as the airstrip which was inherited from a 1980s oil-prospecting venture. From there it's straightforward. An hour or so out of Siyu, you reach the first *shambas*. Note that it's now also possible to travel from Mtangawanda to Faza by matatu (Ksh200).

Faza itself is almost an island, surrounded by tidal flats and mangroves. A secondary school, health centre, police station (with nothing to do) and even a post office have made Faza the most important settlement on Pate island. There's even a Land Rover ambulance donated by Saudi Arabia. Fishing is the commonest occupation, with much of the catch going to a cold room at Kisingitini, from where it's shipped to Mombasa.

As a contemporary Kenyan rural centre, Faza makes an interesting place to walk around and you're almost certain to have plenty of time to fill before the boat leaves. A fine evening stroll takes you across the mud on the concrete causeway to the thickets on the "mainland", where the island's expanding secondary school is located. The other villages on the island, all fairly modern and bunched together, lie within a forty-minute walk of Faza: **Kisingitini**, **Bajumwali**, **Tundwa**, and the closest, **Nyambogi**. Due to the recent fire that destroyed most of the homes, the village now features rows of tin-roofed homes that lack the charm of its previous historic structures.

Faza's ruins

Archeologically, **Faza** has less to offer than its neighbours. It was one of the most defiant Swahili towns over any attempts to usurp its independence, and was razed by the Pate army after a dispute over water rights in the fifteenth century, and again by the Portuguese in 1586 after collaborating with the Turkish fleet of Amir Ali Bey. On this occasion, the entire population was massacred and the head of Faza's king was taken to Goa in a barrel of salt to be paraded triumphantly in the streets. Faza's unfortunate history may partly account for its relative lack of ruins, but one success is commemorated in the **tomb** of Seyyid Hamed bin Ahmed al-Busaidy, commander-in-chief of the Sultan of Zanzibar's forces, who met his death in 1844 under a hail of arrows. His grave or *kaburi*, with a long epitaph, lies just outside the town.

There are several ruined mosques around Faza, including the very crumbled **Kunjanja** mosque. The ruins of the eighteenth-century **Mbwarashally**, or **Shala Fatani** mosque, merit a visit, however. Now theoretically protected by the National Museums of Kenya, most of the mosque is a pile of rubble. Its *mihrab*, however, turns out to incorporate exquisite and unusual heart motifs, including the Islamic creed, or *shahada*, inscribed within an inverted heart shape.

ARRIVAL AND DEPARTURE
PATE ISLAND

By mtaboti water taxi A water taxi (Ksh250) departs from the municipal jetty in Lamu every day except Friday for Pate island's main dock at Mtangawanda (a quiet spot on the island's southwest tip), which takes two to three hours, then Faza (another hour) and finally Kisingitini (another half-hour). The boats usually leave about an hour before high tide. Since the dredging of the Mkanda channel, between Manda and the mainland, they can reach Mtangawanda at any state of the tide, but getting close enough to Faza and Kisingitini still requires careful timing. Pate town lies in the southeast corner of the island at the head of a creek so shallow that it's difficult to get up there even in a flat-bottomed boat at high tide.

By boat Rather than taking the *mtaboti* water taxi, you could choose to take a dhow to Pate. Alternatively, if you have less time but can afford to spend a lot more, you might look into taking a speedboat (see p.489), which would enable you to reach Pate town direct, at high tide, in less than half an hour (Ksh10,000). But timing is critical, only small boats can make it at all, and you have to wait until the next high tide to get out of Pate creek again – unless the speedboat captain goes round to Mtangawanda or Siyu, leaving you to walk. The obvious plan, having walked from Mtangawanda dock to Pate town (allow at least an hour), is then to walk through Siyu to Faza, returning to Lamu by ferry from there. The walk from Pate town to Faza can be done in a day if tides force an early start.

ACCOMMODATION

Accommodation is rarely a problem (normally, you'll be invited to stay by someone almost as soon as you arrive in a village), but as there are no proper lodgings, an insect-proof **tent** is a useful back-up. If you plan on spending several days on Pate, and especially if you're interested in the archeology of the region, you should ask at Lamu Museum and Lamu Fort for **advice**.

Kiwaiyu

From Faza you're within striking distance of the desert island retreat of **Kiwaiyu** (also spelt Kiwayu). The island is a long strip of sand dunes, held in place with low scrub and the odd tree and fronted on the ocean side by a superb beach. The village of **Kiwaiyu**, near the southern end of the island, has limited provisions at a couple of shops. Twenty minutes' walk to the south, you reach a private fishing lodge on the high southern tip of the island. From here, the empty, ocean-facing beach, with the reef close offshore, is just a scramble down the sandy hillside. There are one or two first-class **snorkelling** spots off this southern tip of the island, with huge coral heads and a multitude of fish. Ask for precise directions, as it's possible to spend hours looking and still miss them. For something a little different, ask your captain on the boat over about a fantastic little hut in a baobab tree where travellers can spend the night. Your captain will make you the most amazing fresh fish, grilled on the back of the dhow over charcoal. Prices for the trip (including food) will vary according to each captain, but expect to pay a minimum of Ksh12,000 per night for up to six guests.

Since the tragic events of September 2011 (see box, p.473) and the Kenyan military incursion into Somalia, *Kiwaiyu Safari Village* (the luxury beach lodge on the mainland facing the northern tip of the island that was the location of the first kidnapping) has been closed and tourism to the island has dropped off – check the latest security advice before travelling here.

ARRIVAL AND DEPARTURE KIWAIYU

By boat Kiwaiyu is about an hour from Faza by *mtaboti*, if you can find one. A group dhow charter in Lamu is probably more realistic: you can charter a small dhow for four or five days for Ksh5000 to Ksh8000 a day. That should include breakfast and dinner for a small group, snorkelling and fishing gear, and plenty of fresh water. You can expect to spend at least 24 hours on the journey in each direction, depending on wind, tides and the skill of the crew. The experience of sailing, the nights under the stars, and the company of the Swahili crew are altogether highly recommended. A one-way speedboat (2–3hr) from Lamu will cost Ksh10,000–12,000.

By plane Air Lamu and SafariLink offer charter services to Kiwaiyu. Airkenya flights from Nairobi and SafariLink flights from Nairobi via Lamu were suspended at the time of writing.

ACCOMMODATION

Champali Camp On a mangrove creek within the Kiunga Marine National Marine Reserve at the southern end of Kiwaiyu ☎0723 487145, ✉info @champalicamp.co.ke, ⊛champali.co.ke. This self-catering camp offers stylishly decorated *bandas*. The camp is staffed, but there are no hosts so you have the place to yourselves. It is much more affordable than *Mike's Camp* and ideal for large groups of up to ten. Closed May–July. Conservation fee $15 per person. Whole camp **Ksh28000**

★ **Mike's Camp** About 2km north of Kiwaiyu village ☎0733 963813 or 0733 583627, ⊛mikescamp kiwayu.com. A group of seven spacious, comfortably furnished *bandas* of palm mats and wood, planted on the crest of the island to catch the breeze. The camp, run by the completely laidback and affable Mike Kennedy, is only accessible up the inside channel between Kiwaiyu and the mainland at high tide. Their little shop sells articles made by local people from recycled odds and ends, and they also have possibly the coldest beers in Kenya and brand-new diving equipment: there's fantastic coral right off the beach down on the ocean side. Rather wonderfully, *Mike's* is run entirely on wind power. Closed May & June. FB **$360**

The North

GIRAFFES, LAIKIPIA

The North

There is one half of Kenya about which the other half knows nothing and seems to care even less.

Negley Farson, Last Chance in Africa

You rarely think of deserts in Kenya, but the North – more than half the country – is an arid zone, most of it cinder-dry for ten months of the year. The old "Northern Frontier District" remains one of the most exciting and adventurous parts of Africa: a vast tract of territory, crisscrossed by ancient migration routes, and still tramped by nomadic Samburu, Boran, Rendille, Gabbra, Turkana and Somali herders. Unfortunately, it also has a dangerous reputation, with livestock-rustling and tribal feuding widespread, while banditry, and the spillover from Somalia's civil conflict, make it too risky to visit northeastern Kenya – the whole area east of the Isiolo–Marsabit–Moyale road. By contrast, the vast territories to the north and west of Mount Kenya, including Lake Turkana and the beautiful Laikipia region, are safe – if still adventurous – areas to visit.

7

The most obvious attraction in northern Kenya is the **Laikipia plateau**, a region of hilly savanna, northwest of Mount Kenya. Second in wildlife density only to the Maasai Mara, Laikipia boasts more endangered species than anywhere else in the country (including Kenya's biggest population of black rhino) alongside some very successful examples of mixed ranching and conservation, and some very upmarket boutique lodges and camps.

While Laikipia is increasingly popular for high-end fly-in safaris, the classic travel target in the far north is the wonderful jade splash of **Lake Turkana**. The lake's islands, prehistoric sites and, in recent years, the Lake Turkana Festival, are major attractions to add to the strong appeal of the adventurous journey to the lakeshore.

Although **Moyale** is little more than Kenya's border town with Ethiopia, the remote road north to the frontier runs past fascinating **Marsabit National Park**, with its misty, highland forests rising above the desert. Looking east, not many people take the long road to **Garissa** or use the Tana River route to reach the coast, but as long as the Tana River route remains relatively safe, it's a recommended alternative to joining the heavy traffic on the Mombasa highway.

In terms of **climate**, although the landscape is parched for most of the year, when the **rains** do come (usually around May) they can have a dramatic effect, bringing torrents of water along the ravines and *luggas* (watercourses) and tearing away bridges and concrete fords with a violence that has to be seen to be believed. Flood waters often sweep over the plains to leave an ooze of mud and, within twenty-four hours, new

Highlights

❶ Laikipia eco-lodges Visiting one of the game sanctuaries in this high plains region is one of the best ways to see some of Kenya's surviving black rhinos and other rare wildlife. **See p.506**

❷ Walk with baboons Pay a visit to a habituated baboon troop accompanied by an informative primate researcher. **See p.508**

❸ Track wild dogs Extremely rare and elusive wild dogs are making a comeback in Kenya and can be seen quite frequently in the North, especially on some of the Laikipia ranches, where they are carefully monitored. **See p.510**

❹ Central Island National Park Totally untouched volcanic sanctuary in the middle of Lake Turkana, where Nile crocodiles breed. A memorable boat trip from the lake's western shore. **See p.518**

❺ Maralal The most scruffily picturesque town in Kenya, with a wild atmosphere and an annual camel-racing tournament in August. **See p.520**

❻ Lake Turkana Festival On the eastern shore of shimmering Lake Turkana, this annual, three-day tribal jamboree offers remarkable cross-cultural encounters. **See p.529**

❼ Marsabit Remote highland oasis in the northern deserts with a fascinating cultural mix and close to Marsabit National Park with its superb crater lakes, elephants and birdlife. **See p.544**

HIGHLIGHTS ARE MARKED ON THE MAP ON P.500

shoots. In these conditions, you can easily get stranded. However, if your plans are flexible, being up north during the rains is an exciting time to explore.

GETTING AROUND

With its high-end lodges attracting luxury safari travellers, most parts of Laikipia are commonly accessed by scheduled **light aircraft services** to the airfields at Nanyuki, Lewa Downs and Loisaba. If you're travelling by land any further north, the layout of the routes radiating north from the Central Highlands means you'll need to make a decision about which of them to use, since there are few east–west routes linking the north–south arteries. The road network limits you to **four main possibilities**: the direct route from Kitale to the west shore of Lake Turkana at Kalokol; the other direct route from Maralal to the east shore at Loiyangalani; the route that passes close to the Mathews Range north of Samburu and joins the route to Loiyangalani; and the route via Marsabit and North Horr that also reaches Loiyangalani – eventually.

By car If you're driving in the north, good mechanical know-how and having enough water and fuel should be your priorities, since you'll need to be almost self-sufficient. It's best to have a sturdy 4WD, and while you might manage in a Suzuki or something similar in the dry season, in the rains it's absolutely essential to have a very rugged vehicle such as a Land Rover or a Land Cruiser.

By bus or matatu Bus and matatu services are patchy at best, while informal rides with trucks can work out, but are exhausting and very unpredictable. Where information is available it's included in the "Arrival and departure" sections throughout this chapter.

Laikipia

Northwest of Mount Kenya, **Laikipia District** (ⓦlaikipiatourism.com) is a vast plateau of more than 9000 square kilometres encompassing much of the transitional land

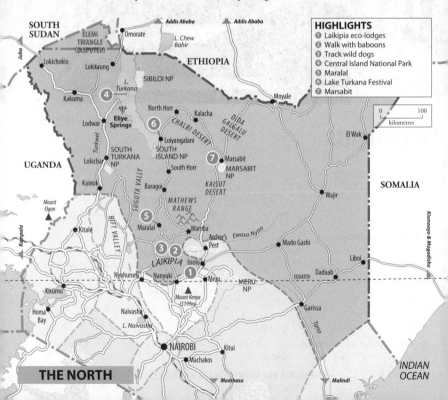

HIGHLIGHTS
1. Laikipia eco-lodges
2. Walk with baboons
3. Track wild dogs
4. Central Island National Park
5. Maralal
6. Lake Turkana Festival
7. Marsabit

WILDLIFE IN LAIKIPIA

Laikipia is increasingly recognized as one of the jewels in Kenya's safari crown. The district contains a wealth of endangered species, including **black rhinos**, whose world population is between three thousand and four thousand, nearly six hundred of them in Kenya. Of those, half are in Laikipia. As browsers rather than grazers, black rhinos don't interfere with cattle pasture, and do well in the same environment so long as the bush isn't cleared. Apart from the rhinos, more than two thousand **elephants** still undertake a seasonal migration during the long rains from Laikipia northwards into the Samburu rangelands. The district also supports an estimated 25 percent of the world's remaining population of **Grevy's zebra**, a species fast disappearing in its other habitats in Ethiopia. There are also several elusive packs of **African wild dogs**.

In Laikipia, wildlife tends to be more closely managed than in the national parks. Rhinos, for example, are individually monitored by assigned rangers, while predators are often radio-collared to enable them to be tracked. Recently, some conservancies have experimented with SIM-card-tagging problem elephants so that rangers receive a text on their mobiles when they stray into farmlands. The solutions may seem unnatural, but they're working, and visitors are often encouraged to participate – in radio-tracking wild dogs, for example. For further information, check out the excellent website of the Laikipia Wildlife Forum (Ⓦ laikipia.org), the body that coordinates the region's various interest groups and visitor facilities. The very useful guidebook, *Laikipia: A Natural History Guide*, is available on the site as a free download.

7

between the well-watered central highlands to the south and the semi-desert grazing steppe of the Samburu in the north. On the face of it, Laikipia is not an obvious destination and the few roads that cross it are mostly poor and sometimes impassable in the rains. It straddles the increasingly blurred divisions between Samburu and Kalenjin pastoralists and Kikuyu agriculturalists, which has led periodically to **ethnic violence**. It also remains the focus of a century-old land dispute between the Laikipiak Maasai and white ranchers.

At the same time, while competition with wildlife has increased, there is now widespread cooperation between local people and ranchers, resulting in some of Kenya's most encouraging conservation success stories and making Laikipia one of the best regions in Kenya to see **wildlife**. There are no national parks or reserves here – all the conservation initiatives are undertaken privately or in the voluntary sector – and yet community land is managed in ways that respect traditional lifestyles while meeting the needs of wildlife and producing revenues from tourism. As tourist numbers grow, indigenously owned group ranches are also beginning to work independently to achieve the same ends.

Ol Pejeta Conservancy

Daily 7am–7pm • $68 day visit or $63 overnight visit (overnight fee included in most stays; see exceptions under "Accommodation") • Ⓦ olpejetaconservancy.org • 365 square kilometres

For immersion in the Laikipia ecosystem, **Ol Pejeta Conservancy**, just a few kilometres west of Nanyuki (see p.178), is a good place to start. Formerly a cattle ranch belonging to the Lonrho corporation, it is now owned by Fauna and Flora International (Ⓦ fauna-flora.org) and run as a not-for-profit business. Consisting mostly of rolling grasslands and acacia thicket, with boreholes providing ample water, it contains some of Laikipia's greatest concentrations of mammals, including all the big plains game.

The ranch combines wildlife management with running the world's largest herd of Boran cattle – the breed considered to be the best beef producer for Africa. The cattle are kept in mobile *bomas* at night to protect them from predators, and the cattle-wildlife combination is judged to be a model of integrated ranching and conservation, as cattle-grazing stimulates new pasture for the wildlife, while the surrounding communities benefit from slaughtering facilities and stock improvement for their own herds.

The Eastern sector of Ol Pejeta is the oldest part of the reserve, formerly the Sweetwaters Rhino Sanctuary (now seamlessly incorporated into the rest of Ol Pejeta), one inhabitant of which, a black rhino bull called **Morani**, was tame enough to be fed by visitors and became an icon for Ol Pejeta's conservation work. Morani died in 2008, and a successor, a blind black rhino called **Baraka**, is steadily being introduced to close encounters with tourists in Morani's special square-kilometre paddock. Apart from Baraka, it's hard to see **black rhinos**, of which there are around eighty roaming through Ol Pejeta, as they stay well away from the tracks, seeking out good browsing in the thickets.

You will much more easily spot the conservancy's less timid and even larger **southern white rhinos** as they tank their way through the bush in search of pasture. Four **northern white rhinos**, the last of their subspecies, were moved to Ol Pejeta from a zoo in the Czech Republic in 2009 after the remaining wild individuals were poached to extinction in northern DRC. They are closely protected in a 30-square-kilometre sanctuary, and the aim is to breed them with the southern white rhinos and then select for northern white traits and steadily preserve the characteristics of the subspecies.

7

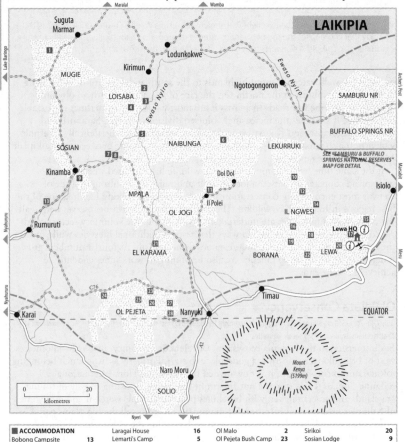

■ ACCOMMODATION		Laragai House	16	Ol Malo	2	Sirikoi	20
Bobong Campsite	13	Lemarti's Camp	5	Ol Pejeta Bush Camp	23	Sosian Lodge	9
Borana Lodge	19	Lewa House	17	Ol Pejeta House	26	Suyian Soul	7
Bush Adventures Camp	14	Lewa Safari Camp	18	Pelican House	27	Sweetwaters Tented Camp	28
El Karama Eco-Lodge	21	Lewa Wilderness	15	Porini Rhino Camp	24	Tassia Lodge	10
Il Ngwesi Eco Lodge	12	Loisaba Wilderness	4	Sabuk Lodge	3	Twala Cultural	
Kicheche Laikipia Camp	25	Mutamaiyu House	1	The Sanctuary at		Village Campsite	11
Laikipia Wilderness	8	Ngare Ndare Tree Platform	22	Ol-Lentille	6		

Chimpanzee Sanctuary

Daily 9–10.30am & 3–4.30pm • Free

Ol Pejeta also contains a **chimpanzee sanctuary**, with chimps from the Jane Goodall Institute in Burundi, and confiscated pets and bushmeat-trade orphans from other parts of Africa. The one-square-kilometre haven, unique in Kenya – a country that has had no wild chimps in historical times – protects more than forty of the great apes in two troops; a younger troop on the west side of the Ewaso Nyiro River, and an older troop, that visitors can view, on the east side. This is strictly an animal refuge, supported by a number of charities and individuals at a cost of more than $4000 a year per chimp. The chimps, all of which have suffered varying degrees of psychological trauma, are given contraceptive medication to prevent them from breeding, and fed on a daily supply of fruit and vegetables supplied by the rangers. As the crazier of the chimps smash sticks against the electric fence to the amusement of visitors, it all feels sadly institutionalized, despite the relative space and freedom, and may leave you wondering what connection, if any, it has with the long-term conservation of this highly endangered species.

7

ARRIVAL AND INFORMATION

OL PEJETA CONSERVANCY

There are **flights** to Nanyuki airport on SafariLink or Airkenya, with onward transfers organized by Ol Pejeta. Approaching **by road**, turn left just south of the "Equator" signs on the way into Nanyuki (west; signposted "Ol Pejeta House 20km, Sweetwaters 15km") for the 13km drive to Rongai Gate.

ACCOMMODATION

Unless otherwise specified, all accommodation rates include Ol Pejeta's $63 nightly conservation fee.

Camping sites ☎0752 325379 or 0707 187141, ⓦolpejetaconsservancy.org. Ol Pejeta offers four camping sites available on an exclusive, pre-booked basis only – Hippo Hide and Ewaso on the banks of the Ewaso Nyiro River, Mura Donga in an area of thick vegetation, and Ngobit on the banks of the Ngobit River. When you add up the costs, this isn't budget camping, but toilets, firewood and water are provided. Daily fee whole site Ksh5000 plus conservation fee $63 per person and camping Ksh1500 per person.

★ **Kicheche Laikipia Camp** ☎020 2493569, ⓦkicheche.com. Opened in 2009 in a remote stretch of bush, on a gentle slope above a broad, seasonal waterhole, this is the first *Kicheche* camp outside the Mara, offering six very comfortable spacious tents with stylish extra touches – plants, rugs, wooden bathroom furniture, excellent food and wine – and warm, enthusiastic and experienced hosts. Lion-tracking drives available, submitting data to predator researchers. Closed April & May. Package $1020

Ol Pejeta Bush Camp ☎0734 445283 or 0721 242361, ⓦinsidersafrica.com (Nairobi reservations ☎020 6003090, ⓦchelipeacock.com). Six comfortable tents on the banks of the Ewaso Nyiro, including one big family tent, with solar lighting, local community guides and lots of game walks. Salt scattered on the opposite bank often brings rhinos at night. Excellent for photographers. Closed May & Nov; AI $920, package $1020

Ol Pejeta House ☎062 2032409 or 0736 515151,

ⓦserenahotels.com. Bursting with design novelties, original art and flawed magnificence, this is arms tycoon Adnan Khashoggi's former holiday retreat, comprising the flamboyant and monster-bedded "Mr Khashoggi's Room" and "Mrs Khashoggi's Room", plus two upper guest rooms (1 dbl, 1 twin), and a cottage with two large suites. Giraffes stalk the gardens and there are two pools. Daily conservation fee $63. FB $510

Pelican House ☎0701 496177 or 0752 325379, ⓦolpejetaconsservancy.org. A beautifully renovated traditional highlands thatched farm cottage with views of a nearby dam, sleeping six people in three double rooms (or up to ten using four extra single beds). Amenities include a garden and veranda, generator, kitchen (fridge-freezer, gas cooker), all bedding and towels, plus the services of a housekeeper/cook and *askari*. Daily conservation fee $63. Whole house Ksh29,000

★ **Porini Rhino Camp** ☎020 7123129 or 0722 509200, ⓦporini.com. A simple and unfussy low-impact bush camp, consisting of six very spacious tents erected along a *lugga*. Everything here is run on entirely sustainable principles, with safari showers, solar power throughout and all non-biodegradable waste returned to Nairobi. Excellent staff and guides. Closed mid-April to end of May. Eco-Tourism Kenya Silver Award. Package including flights from Nairobi, based on obligatory minimum two nights, $1245 per night

Sweetwaters Tented Camp ☎062 2032409 or 0734

699852, Ⓦ serenahotels.com. The most affordable camp in Ol Pejeta, with 100 beds, a small pool and decent and varied food on a flat but very wheelchair-accessible site. All the tents (some older and simpler, some newer, more spacious and luxurious) face the electric-fence-protected

waterhole. Most tents face Mt Kenya (be up by 6.45am for photos), but with its hotel-like public areas and night lights shining from Nanyuki's flower farms, this is not the place if you want to be deep in the bush. Conservation fee $63. FB **$370**

EATING AND DRINKING

Morani's Restaurant Morani Information Centre enclosure Ⓣ 0706 160114, Ⓦ bit.ly/MoranisRestaurant. Ol Pejeta's first and only restaurant outside the camps and lodges. Grab a snack or drink (shakes and smoothies

Ksh300, beers Ksh200, wine Ksh350) or choose from all-day breakfasts, burgers, salads and daily specials from around Ksh600. Daily 8am–6pm.

Eastern Laikipia

In the far southeast of Laikipia lies the former cattle ranch of **Lewa Downs**, one of the earliest ranches to convert to wildlife conservation and now largely incorporated into the **Lewa Wildlife Conservancy**. A little to the north of Lewa – and in much wilder country – are the locally owned group ranches of **Il Ngwesi** and **Lekurruki**, while bordering Lewa to the west is an exemplary game-and-cattle ranch, **Borana**.

Lewa Wildlife Conservancy

Entrance via the Matunda gate on the west side of the Timau–Isiolo road, 4km from the Meru junction, from where it's 8km along an earth road to the Wildlife Conservancy headquarters; entry by 4WD only • $90 • Ⓦ lewa.org • 250 square kilometres

Lewa Wildlife Conservancy, fenced all around and carefully managed, is conservation as a business. As well as the high daily fees, the revenue from the café and gift shop (closed Sun) and expensive accommodation all help to support the **Northern Rangelands Trust**, partnering Lewa with local communities.

Lewa incorporates the former Ngare Sergoi Rhino Sanctuary, set up by the owners in 1983, and the entire area is now home to more than 65 black and 50 white rhinos. This grassland environment, a mixture of open plains, scrub bush and woodland in the valleys, is one area in Kenya where sightings of black rhinos are the norm rather than a special event. In addition, there are some 350 Grevy's zebra, accounting for more than a tenth of the world's remaining wild population, and, unusually, a population of rare semi-aquatic sitatunga antelope in Lewa swamp.

The well-organized annual **Lewa Marathon** (see p.69), in June, has been run on the conservancy since 1999 to raise funds for conservation and development in Kenya, and now attracts more than a thousand international entrants.

Il Ngwesi Group Ranch

Scheduled flights to Lewa Downs, then a 90min transfer; alternatively, the ranch is also reachable by driving via Nanyuki and Lewa HQ • No casual entry (conservation fees included in overnight stays) • Ⓣ 020 2033122, Ⓦ ilngwesi.com

While Lewa is surrounded by a fence, the group ranches northwest of Lewa Downs are traditional, unfenced community land, incorporating fixed and transient communities, grazing herds and substantial wildlife. In both areas, you'll get the most out of the experience if you get out into the bush **on foot**, with armed guides.

Foremost among these areas is the six-thousand-strong Laikipiak Maasai community of **Il Ngwesi Group Ranch**, a 145-square-kilometre slab of wilderness, adjoining Lewa to the south, bounded by the Ngare Ndare and Tinga rivers to the east and north, and by the dramatic hills of the **Mukogodo Forest** to the west. Options included in most stays include night drives, bush walks, riverside breakfasts, hikes in the Mukogodo forest and visits to Il Ngwesi's rhino sanctuary, where the first transplant from Lewa, a black rhino male called Omni, is tame enough for very close encounters through the wire.

Lekurruki Group Ranch

Scheduled flights to Lewa Downs, then a 2hr 30min transfer; alternatively, the ranch is also reachable by driving via Lewa HQ • $60 • ⓦ nrt-kenya.org/lekurruki.html • 240 square kilometres

Like Il Ngwesi, the **Lekurruki Group Ranch** is superb wildlife territory, but even wilder and hillier. Adjoining Il Ngwesi's north side, the ranch assures a migration corridor between the Samburu and Buffalo Springs reserves to the north and the Il Ngwesi and Lewa conservancies to the south, although animals can be hard to spot. The Tusk Trust has trained two dozen rangers to patrol the no-grazing areas of the ranch where the wildlife has pre-eminence – there's no mixed herding and wildlife conservation model here. The ranch's *Tassia Lodge* is a good two hours' drive from Lewa HQ, although it's better to allow three.

Borana Ranch

Drive through Timau towards Meru and turn left after 500m; Borana Lodge (see p.506) is 20km further, via the small centre of Ethi • $80 • ⓦ borana.co.ke • 142 square kilometres

The **Borana Ranch** is a settler farm that has evolved into a model of twenty-first-century holistic land management. Like Ol Pejeta, Borana has successfully integrated farming with conservation by allowing intensive short-term livestock grazing of managed areas, followed by long periods of recovery and game grazing. The ranch mixes **beef production** from a two-thousand-strong herd of Boran cattle with **wool production** and textile and leather manufacture (a company called Hide and Sheep Ltd employing disabled members of the local community), along with **rare species conservation** and **high-end tourism** for a maximum of 32 visitors at any one time.

Working closely with Lewa Conservancy, the plan is to open the fence-line between the two areas to enable the Lewa rhinos to wander even more freely. Borana currently has around three hundred **elephants** (twelve matriarchs with collars so that tabs can be kept on where they are) and four prides of **lions** (again, with a radio-collared lioness in each pride). They also monitor **wild dogs**, **hyenas** and **cheetahs** and have stable populations of all three.

For visitors, apart from the chance to participate in game and wildlife management, the big activity at Borana is **riding**, allowing you to get very close to wildlife that would naturally shy away from vehicles or visitors on foot. Most of the thoroughbreds here are not really for beginners but perfect for experienced equestrians – although, on the eastern side of the ranch, they have a stable of children's and novice mounts too. As well as **walking**, another hugely enjoyable option here is **mountain biking**. Most activities are included in the accommodation packages.

Ngare Ndare Forest

Drive through Timau towards Meru and turn left after 500m; Ngare Ndare Forest gate is 12km further on, via the small centre of Ethi • ⓦ bit.ly/NgareNdare

Wedged between the foothills of Mount Kenya and Lewa Wildlife Conservancy, **Ngare Ndare Forest** is a fine stretch of indigenous forest, with a limited number of trails and a campsite. The tree-level **canopy walkway** looks precarious, but it's proving very popular with local urbanites, especially from Nanyuki, as a way of reconnecting with nature without exposing themselves to mud, thorns or the possibility of meeting large animals at ground level. Rangers ensure the safety of visitors.

ARRIVAL AND DEPARTURE   EASTERN LAIKIPIA

Most people fly up to the Lewa area, either on a scheduled service to Lewa HQ's Lewa Downs airfield (at least daily from Nairobi, 1hr 15min; sometimes also from Maasai Mara, 1hr 45min), or by charter to the airstrips at *Il Ngwesi* or *Tassia Lodge*. If you drive up, Lewa HQ is about 4hr from Nairobi. If you're driving beyond Lewa, ensure you leave 2hr to get from Lewa HQ to *Il Ngwesi*, and three hours to reach *Tassia Lodge*. It can be quicker to drive via Borana Ranch (see above), but check with them first. The tracks are rough in parts and hard to follow: a smart phone, GPS unit, or, better still, a guide, is very useful.

ACCOMMODATION

Unless otherwise specified, all accommodation rates include the relevant daily conservancy fees.

LEWA

Lewa House 8km north of Lewa HQ ☏ 0710 781303, ⓦ lewahouse.com (Nairobi reservations ☏ 020 6000457, ⓦ bush-and-beyond.com). Rustic but elegant, this is Lewa's top residence, with three large cottages (with one double and one twin room) and four single-room cottages. Game-watching includes day and night drives, and game walks. There are also beautiful gardens, a pool overlooking the waterhole and solar power. Mobile network available. Closed Apr & Nov. Package **$1700**

Lewa Safari Camp On the west side of the conservancy ☏ 020 2618711 or 0720 499425 (Nairobi reservations ☏ 020 6003090, ⓦ chelipeacock.com). Formerly known as *Lerai Tented Camp*, this is the most affordable, relatively speaking, of the Lewa options: twelve well-spaced, homely and very comfortably furnished tents, some with fine views. The main lodge building is thatched cedar, with a lounge overlooking a floodlit waterhole where rhino and elephant come to drink. Service is usually excellent and there's a pool. Eco-Tourism Kenya Bronze Award. Package **$1320**

Lewa Wilderness Eastern side of Lewa ☏ 0723 273668, ⓦ lewawilderness.com (Nairobi reservations ☏ 020 6000457, ⓦ bush-and-beyond.com). The former home of the Craig family, who came to Lewa in the 1920s, with a pre-war English-country-house atmosphere, congenial hosts and staff, superior cooking (often using ingredients from the organic garden), infinity pool, and accommodation in eight cottages. Riding is available at the large stables. Closed April, May & Nov. Package **$1700**

★ **Sirikoi** Centre of Lewa, by Sirikoi Swamp, 5km west of Lewa HQ ☏ 0706 160176 or 0722 334566, ⓦ sirikoi .com. The most upmarket of the Lewa properties, this superb game camp has four huge luxury tents on wooden platforms, plus a cottage sleeping four and a house sleeping six (both for exclusive use), all nestled among acacias near a permanent swamp bursting with wildlife day and night. Day and night game drives, game walks and bush meals are all included. No under-5s in tents. Package **$1830**

IL NGWESI

Bush Adventures Camp Il Ngwesi Group Ranch ☏ 0724 301095, ⓦ bush-adventures.com. Far from the lavish tented camps of the Mara, *Bush Adventures* offers an experience that is much more integrated into the local environment, and particularly the local Laikipiak Maasai culture. You stay here to experience life in the bush and learn the ways of a warrior, with a full schedule of real training. The camp of comfortable but modest tents, with solar-powered hot water, is set high on the river bank. No

sockets for charging and limited mobile network. No under-5s. Three-night minimum stay. Package **$1130**

★ **Il Ngwesi Eco Lodge** Il Ngwesi Group Ranch (local reservations Laipha House, Nanyuki ☏ 020 2033122, ⓦ ilngwesi.com; Nairobi reservations ⓦ lets-go-travel .net). A much lauded eco-lodge, owned and managed by the local Maasai community, perched along a ridge facing a game-rich valley. Uniquely, *all* the proceeds go to the local community. The six spacious, raised, open-fronted *bandas* incorporate twisting branches and wonderful views, while *bandas* #1 and #5 have star-beds which can be pulled out onto their decks. There's a small infinity pool. Guaranteed wildlife, including elephants, seen daily at the waterhole. Eco-Tourism Kenya Silver Award. FB **$770**

LEKURRUKI GROUP RANCH

★ **Tassia Lodge** Lekurruki Group Ranch ☏ 0725 972923 or 0727 049489, ⓦ tassiasafaris.com. This beautifully sited lodge overlooks a scenic valley where you have a good chance of spotting elephants. There are just six rooms, emerging seemingly organically from the landscape, a naturally formed swimming pool nestled in the rocks, and exceptionally good and varied food, including plenty of salads and vegetarian options. Activities include game walks; overnight, camel-assisted fly-camping; and paragliding with expert guidance (bring your own equipment). No TV, no network, no internet – the whole idea is to completely escape all that. Eco-Tourism Kenya Silver Award. Closed April & Nov. Package **$1020**

BORANA

Borana Lodge Central Borana ranch ☏ 0715 579999, ⓦ borana.co.ke or tiny.cc/Scc. A *Responsible Tourism Award* winner, built in 1992 in a hilly area with dramatic views in every direction, *Borana* has eight immaculate, well-spaced cottages of cedar, thatch and stone, with fireplaces (at 2000m, you'll often need a fire). The lodge overlooks a waterhole-dam where elephants sometimes swim, and close-up views from the hide are possible. The infinity pool is sited high, with awe-inspiring views. Closed Nov. Package **$1380**

★ **Laragai House** Northern Borana, 8km north of Borana Lodge ☏ 0715 579999, ⓦ borana.co.ke (Nairobi reservations through ⓦ tiny.cc/Scc). Perched in an extraordinary site on the edge of an escarpment looking north, this house of almost palatial proportions has a large, heated pool, a waterhole-dam 400m down the hillside and stunning views all around. There's a superb sound system in the lounge, and you get excellent meals and service. It's perfect for a luxury house party, which is just as well as you

have to take the whole property (minimum six people, maximum 16). Package $1380

NGARE NDARE FOREST

Ngare Ndare Tree Platform Just south of Borana Ranch in the Ngare Ndare Forest ☎ tel ⊛ bit.ly /NgareNdare. The showcase forest campsite for a recently established elephant corridor, allowing elephants to migrate freely between the slopes of Mount Kenya and the plains of Laikipia. Built 7m up a *mugumu* tree, the platform can be used as a lounge and observation point while you camp on the ground, or alternatively free-standing tents can be erected on the platform itself. No facilities, but support rangers and *askaris* are available. Camping $20 per person

Central Laikipia

A great chunk of land in central Laikipia, on the east side of the Ewaso Nyiro, is now managed as the **Naibunga Conservancy**, covering more than 170 square kilometres and comprising swathes of conservation land ceded by eight community-owned group ranches in the area: **Il Motiok**, **Kijabe**, **Koija**, **Kuri-Kuri**, **Morupusi**, **Nkiloriti**, **Tiemamut** and **Il Polei**. There is, as yet, a limited range of places to stay, though several of the group ranches are encouraging wild camping with guides (further details at ⊛ laikipia.org).

Privately owned ranches northwest of Nanyuki include El Karama, Ol Jogi and Mpala. **El Karama**, a settler ranch since the early 1960s, covers nearly sixty square kilometres and as well as being a working ranch with a herd of unusual Sahiwal cattle also provides a home for Grevy's zebra, plenty of elephants, reticulated giraffe, leopards, at least one pride of lions and – occasionally – wild dogs, among many other species.

Mpala Ranch and Conservancy, owned by the American Mpala Wildlife Foundation, ranges across two hundred square kilometres and incorporates a state-of-the-art wildlife and environmental research centre. However, there is no accommodation on the ranch for tourist visitors.

Ol Jogi is a 270-square-kilometre ranch owned by the art-dealing and horse-racing Wildenstein family, where KWS staff and US government vets are engaged in a long-term project to extract **gerenuk** semen for captive breeding.

Il Polei Group Ranch: Walking with Baboons

Walks last about 2hr and normally cost $20 per person in a group of up to four • Call Jonathan Rana on ☎ 0724 943948, ⊛ baboonsrus.com

An interesting new community activity at Twala Cultural Village, near Il Polei, is **Walking with Baboons**, a chance for visitors to overturn some of the popular myths and prejudices that our species holds for this less cultured, but no less social, primate. In the early morning or at dusk you go out with a guide trained by the Uaso Ngiro Baboon Project to observe a habituated troop at close quarters on their rocky sleeping ledges. You'll learn about the importance of avoiding eye contact and the subtlety of baboon family and social life. It's a fascinating and highly recommended experience, and the money goes to support local community projects.

ARRIVAL AND DEPARTURE   CENTRAL LAIKIPIA

The main central Laikipia road goes northwest from Nanyuki, passing the turning (on the left after 9km) to Rumuruti and Nyahururu, then continues, still paved, via the small centres of **Jua Kali** and **Naibor** and turns into dirt road after 25km, where the track to **Il Polei** and **Dol-Dol** heads off to the right. Having passed the turnings for El Karama (left, 33km, at the "El K" stone, then a further 9km to reach the headquarters and lodge) and Ol Jogi Ranch (right, 39km), the road crosses the big metal bridge over the Ewaso Nyiro after 47km, immediately passing the turning for Mpala Ranch and then, after 77km, reaching Sosian Ranch (see p.510).

ACCOMMODATION

Unless otherwise specified, all accommodation rates include the relevant daily conservancy or conservation fees.

★ **El Karama Eco-Lodge** 42km northwest of Nanyuki ☎ 0726 875953 (send an SMS first), ⊛ laikipiasafaris .com. An exceptionally nice and affordable set-up on the banks of the Ewaso Nyiro River, with four comfy s/c *bandas* and two cottages. You can camp, self-cater or be pampered on a full-board basis (drinks extra). Excellent day and night game drives and game walks with experienced, armed guide-ranger are included in the price, and there are delicious, hearty meals, using ranch produce. Limited mobile network, and free wi-fi at the lodge's art gallery/office. The whole lodge is exclusively solar-powered. Camping (when available): whole campsite for up to five campers Ksh10,000, conservation fee $40 per person, package $320

★ **Laikipia Wilderness** Ol Doinyo Lemboro Ranch, 50km north of Nanyuki, past Mpala Ranch ☎ 0727 804926, ⓦ laikipia-wilderness.com. Opened in 2012, this new tented camp is run by a couple with a great deal of experience. The east-facing tents are perched high above the Ewaso Narok River, and the area teems with wildlife, including elephants, leopards and wild dogs. Activities include game walks, day and night game drives, river tubing, rock scrambling and fishing. Package $980

Lemarti's Camp In Koija Group Ranch, above the Ewaso Nyiro River near its confluence with the Ewaso Narok ☎ 0733 638147, ⓦ lemartiscamp.com. Low-impact, fig-tree-shaded, boutique camp of five luxurious riverside tents, with decks and open-air bathrooms, all solar-powered, created by a white Kenyan fashion designer and her Samburu husband – after whom the camp is named. Child-friendly Samburu chic is the prevailing ethic, with bush walks and plenty of Samburu activities included, and optional game drives (extra) across the river in Mpala Ranch. Package $1680

The Sanctuary at Ol-Lentille Ol-Lentille Conservancy, Kijabe Group Ranch ⓦ ol-lentille.com (Nairobi reservations ☎ 020 6000457, ⓦ bush-and-beyond.com). Spectacular all round, and truly remote, this Maasai-owned lodge (with strong local community links) is Laikipia's most expensive address: four houses, each sleeping two to six and with its own staff, guide and 4WD. Most activities, including riding, quad-bikes and game drives (relatively limited wildlife but occasional wild dogs), are included, but simply relaxing and soaking up the peaceful environment – there's a good pool and spa – is a large part of the appeal. Package $1990

Twala Cultural Village Campsite Near Il Polei town, 43km from Nanyuki along the Dol-Dol road (no phone). Simple if rather expensive campsite with water, firewood, showers and toilets. This is the place to hook up for the "Walking with Baboons" experience (see opposite). Walking with the Maasai and their cattle and walking with plants are also possible ($10 each walk). Camping $30 per person

Northwestern Laikipia

The ranches to the **west of the Ewaso Nyiro** are the most remote of the Laikipia range lands and include large tracts of country that are still not open to the public or easily visited, including some very big private and corporate landholdings such as author Kuki Gallman's **Ol Ari Nyiro Laikipia Wildlife Conservancy** (ⓦ gallmannkenya.org).

Loisaba Community Trust

120km from Nanyuki, 110km from Nyahururu • $80 • ⓦ loisaba.com • 250-square-kilometres

The **Loisaba** is a private ranch-cum-game sanctuary with a 2500 herd of Boran cattle, stretching from the bush-covered slopes and valleys near the river to high, flat grasslands in the west, bordering Mugie Ranch. The lodge's array of activities, arranged through the *Loisaba Wilderness* lodge (see p.510), includes camel rides, mountain-biking, quad-biking (from which all revenue goes to a local education trust), balloon trips, helicopter flights and river-rafting.

Mugie Ranch

Based around the junction of the Rumuruti–Maralal road with the road to Lake Baringo • $60 ($30 if visiting for less than 4hr) • Minimum 24hr pre-booking required • ☎ 0722 903179, ⓦ mugie.org

Mugie Ranch covers two hundred square kilometres, of which the former Mugie Rhino Sanctuary accounted for nearly half. Unfortunately, the market for rhino horn was such that there were repeated incidents of poaching, even with a 36-man protection team from KWS. The whole group of black rhinos was relocated in 2012, some to Nairobi National Park and some to form a new population in Ruma National Park, near Lake Victoria. The ranch is still recommended, easily accessed direct from the Rumuruti–Maralal road, and provides sanctuary to a number of rare species, including Grevy's zebra and Jackson's hartebeest.

Ol Malo Wildlife Conservancy

Scheduled flights to Loisaba (or Nanyuki plus charter flight to Ol Malo airstrip), or a 3hr-plus drive from Nanyuki • $80 • W olmalo.org •
20 square kilometres

At the northernmost ranch in northwestern Laikipia, the privately owned **Ol Malo**, elephants and leopards are seen right below the lodge almost every day. Formerly a cattle ranch, and by all accounts not a very well managed one, it is now a thriving willdlife sanctuary with a wide range of species.

Sosian Ranch

28km north of Rumuruti (at Kinamba village, bear right under the open boom gate; after 5.5km you reach a sign on a stone; the ranch HQ
and *Sosian Lodge* are 1.5km further on) • $90 • W sosian.com • 100 square kilometres

The **Sosian Ranch** has superb wildlife, with all the large mammals you would expect, bar rhinos, including a resident, breeding pack of wild dogs. The ranch does active work in predator research, collaborating with neighbouring Mpala Ranch, and guests at the lodge can easily go out tracking the dogs, which can be highly rewarding, especially on foot. Sightings aren't guaranteed, but they're frequent enough to make them a likely possibility.

ARRIVAL AND DEPARTURE   NORTHWESTERN LAIKIPIA

By plane There are several airstrips for charter flights, but most visitors use the SafariLink scheduled service to Loisaba airstrip (no service April 1—June 15 & Nov 1—Dec 15). Destinations include Kiwayu and Lamu (1 daily; change in Nairobi), Maasai Mara (1 daily; 1hr 45min) and Nairobi (1 daily; 1hr).

By road Some of the ranches are tough to reach by road, especially those down towards the Ewaso Nyiro River, such as Loisaba, Sabuk and Ol Malo. Route coverage is given from Nyahururu via Rumuruti to Maralal (see p.520), from where these ranches and lodges are most easily accessed if you're driving.

ACCOMMODATION

Unless otherwise specified, all accommodation rates include the relevant daily conservation or conservancy fees.
If you're on any kind of budget, *Bobong* at *Ol Maisor Ranch* is a good – in fact your only – choice.

Bobong Campsite Ol Maisor Ranch, 18km north of Rumuruti, on a bluff just west of the road, 300m after the blue shipping container ☎ 020 2033179, 0735 243075 or 0722 936177 (send an SMS first), ✉ olmaisor@africaonline.co.ke. Deliberately low-key and child-friendly campsite, boasting fantastic views over the Laikipia plains, a small pool and a jungle gym. Activities range from bird walks along the Ewaso Narok River and Turkana cultural village visits to camel rides and longer camel safaris (Ksh3000/day or part-day), while animal orphans are always around and the daily life of the family farm is part of the appeal. As well as camping space there are also fully equipped and furnished self-catering s/c *bandas* (with one double bed and one single). Camping Ksh500 per person; *bandas* Ksh5000
Loisaba Wilderness Loisaba Community Trust ☎ 062 2031072 or 0705 202375, W loisaba.com (Nairobi reservations ☎ 020 6003090, W chelipeacock.com). Energetic and enthusiastic, the multi-award-winning *Loisaba* is as much about getting the adrenaline flowing as it is about watching kudu or tracking wild dogs, with a vast range of activities on offer. The set-up includes a seven-room hotel-style lodge set in manicured gardens with staggering views towards Mount Kenya, two fully staffed houses and two star-bed sites: *Loisaba Starbeds* above a

dam and the even better community-run *Koija Starbeds* on the east bank of the river (both fun but relatively basic and similarly expensive). Wi-fi in the lounge. Eco-Tourism Kenya Bronze Award. Package $1560
Mutamaiyu House Mugie conservancy, 10km northwest of the Baringo junction ☎ 062 2031235 or 0722 903179, W mugie.org. Expansive and gracious Swiss- and German-owned country house, decorated with tribal art, surrounded by African olives (*mutamaiyu*) and beautifully tended gardens, with a heated pool, in a relatively gentle, hilly landscape. As in most of the lodges in northwestern Laikipia, the wildlife is not just out in the bush, but encountered on the paths, in your outdoor shower, or on the way to dinner: warriors always accompany guests when anything dangerous is nearby. Four cottages are also available. Wi-fi throughout. Closed Jan & May—June. Package $1010
Ol Malo ☎ 062 2032715 or 0721 630686, W olmalo .com (Nairobi reservations ☎ 020 6000457, W bush -and-beyond.com). A *Responsible Tourism Award*-winning family-owned lodge commanding a vantage point high above the valley of the Ewaso Nyiro. Guest rooms, annexed off the main building, feature window glass (most Laikipia rooms are open-fronted) and are big on polished stone and wood. The more recent *Ol Malo House* (sleeps 12) is similar,

but with a kitsch, animal theme in the coloured-cement decor. Closed April, May & Nov. Package **$1700**

★ **Sabuk Lodge** Sabuk Conservancy, west bank of the Ewaso Nyiro ⓦsabuklodge.com (reservations ☎020 2663397, ⓦafricanterritories.com). Intimate and compellingly sited lodge, bursting with character, built on the edge of a remote gorge through which the Ewaso Nyiro permanently rushes and where elephants frequently cross. There are six spacious cottages, including one with its own plunge pool, while camel-assisted walking safaris (from a few hours to several nights) can be included in your stay at no extra cost. Warmly and intelligently hosted by a highly experienced safari guide, it's great for children and serves superb food. Two-night minimum stay. Package **$1510**

★ **Sosian Lodge** Near Kinamba ☎0704 909357, ⓦsosian.com (reservations ☎0704 909355, ⓦoffbeat safaris.com). Built in 1920, abandoned in the 1990s and completely restored as a riding and ecotourism base in 2002, *Sosian* is peaceful, roomy and supremely relaxing, with well-designed furniture in the seven rooms, charming hosts, excellent guides (one bronze, one silver) and delicious meals (the chef, with 27 years' experience, relies greatly on the lodge's own garden produce). Patchy mobile network. Closed May & Nov. Package **$1280**

Suyian Soul Suyian Ranch, north bank of the Ewaso Narok ☎0722 397860 (send an SMS first), ⓦsuyian.com (Nairobi reservations ☎020 4447151, ⓦuniglobelets gotravel.com). Just half an hour's drive from the Loisaba airstrip, this simple eco-camp, near a spring and salt lick, on a century-old ranch of more than 170 square kilometres, is unusual in its commitment to the environment. It relies entirely on solar energy and is built exclusively with materials found on the ranch, where the family have reared livestock for nearly a century. Package **$880**

Turkana

Straddling the Ethiopian border at its northern end, **Lake Turkana** stretches south for 250km, bisecting Kenya's rocky deserts like a turquoise sickle, hemmed in by sandy wastes and black-and-brown volcanic ranges. The water, a glassy, milky blue one minute, can become slate-grey and choppy or a glaring emerald green the next. Turkana's **climate** is extremely hot and dry for ten months of the year, and very humid during the rains. The lake is notorious for its strong easterly winds and the squalls whipped up are the cause of most accidental deaths on the lake, rather than hippos or crocodiles.

ECOLOGY AND WILDLIFE OF LAKE TURKANA

Lake Turkana is the biggest permanent desert lake in the world, a UNESCO World Heritage Site with a shoreline longer than the whole of Kenya's sea coast. Yet 10,000 years ago its surface was 150m higher than today. It spread south as far as the now desolate Suguta Valley and fed the headwaters of the Nile. Today it has been reduced to a mere sliver of its former expanse. A gigantic natural sump, with rivers flowing in but no outlets, it loses a staggering 3m of water through **evaporation** from its surface each year (nearly a centimetre every day). As a result, the lake water is quite alkaline – although you can just about drink it, and it's not hostile to all aquatic life.

Turkana's **water level** is subject to wild fluctuations. From the mid-1980s to 1997, the level receded steadily, leaving parts of the former shoreline more than 8km from the lake. But heavy El Niño rains in 1998 led to a 6m rise in the lake level in less than a year. Fish stocks recovered and former fishing communities rediscovered their vocation. Since then, however, the level has fallen again, the lakeshore receding by as much as 1km in some places. The massive Gilgel Gibe III dam under construction on Ethiopia's Omo River – Lake Turkana's biggest source – poses a huge threat to the lake and may lower the water surface by up to 10m with a rise in salinity that would threaten fish stocks and wildlife and the livelihoods of thousands of people. The Friends of Lake Turkana, who are active in opposing the dam, have a highly recommended website (ⓦfriendsoflaketurkana.org).

The prehistoric connection with the Nile accounts for the presence of enormous **Nile perch** (some weighing more than 100kg) and Africa's biggest population of **Nile crocodiles** – some 10,000 to 22,000 of them. Turkana is one of the few places where you can still see great stacks of crocs basking on sand banks. There is a profusion of **birdlife**, too, including European migrants seen most spectacularly on their way home between March and May. **Hippos**, widely hunted and starved out of many of their former lakeshore haunts through lack of grazing, manage to hang on in fairly large numbers, though you won't see many unless you go out of your way.

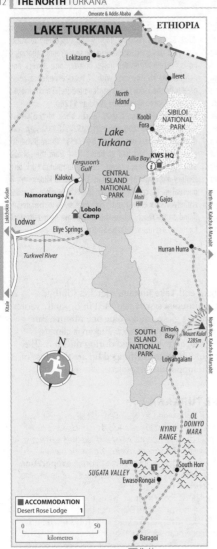

LAKE TURKANA

Omorate & Addis Ababa

ETHIOPIA

Lokitaung

Ileret

North Island

Koobi Fora

SIBILOI NATIONAL PARK

Lake Turkana

Ferguson's Gulf

Allia Bay · KWS HQ

Kalokol

CENTRAL ISLAND NATIONAL PARK

Namoratunga

Moiti Hill

Gajos

Lodwar

Lobolo Camp

Eliye Springs

Turkwel River

Hurran Hurra

Lokichokio & Sudan

Kitale

North Horr, Kalacha & Marsabit

SOUTH ISLAND NATIONAL PARK

Elmolo Bay

Mount Kulal 2285m

Loiyangalani

North Horr, Kalacha & Marsabit

N

OL DOINYO MARA

NYIRU RANGE

Tuum

South Horr

SUGATA VALLEY

Ewaso Rongai

■ ACCOMMODATION
Desert Rose Lodge   1

0 ——— 50
kilometres

Baragoi

Maralal

7

The lake was discovered for the rest of the world only in 1888 by the Hungarian explorer **Count Samuel Teleki de Szék** and his Austrian co-expeditionary **Ludwig von Höhnel**. They named it Lake Rudolf after their patron, the Crown Prince of Austria. Later, it became eulogized as the "Jade Sea" in travel writer John Hillaby's book (see p.589) about his camel trek. The name "Turkana" only came into being during the wholesale Kenyanization of place names in the 1970s. By then, it had also been dubbed the "Cradle of Mankind", the site of revelatory fossil discoveries in the field of **human evolution**. Apart from a couple of basic lodges and one or two windy campsites, the tourist infrastructure is nil, while only a single paved road reaches the region, stretching from Kitale to Lodwar (in dire condition) and on to Lokichokio. Turkana's fortunes may be changing, however: in 2012, vast reserves of oil were discovered near the town of Lokichar, a development that promises to bring infrastructure and investment to Turkana. What effect this will have on this isolated region remains to be seen. Turkana's **traditional cultures** are still very much a vibrant part of the scene, wherever you travel: the people you're most likely to encounter are **Turkana** (p.516) on the western and southern shores, **Samburu** (p.520) south of Loiyangalani, **Elmolo** (p.533) to the north of Loiyangalani, and **Gabbra** (p.543) further east. The Turkana and Samburu are pastoralists, who hold their cattle in great reverence; the Gabbra herd camels; while the Elmolo are traditionally property-less hunters and fishers.

ARRIVAL AND DEPARTURE   TURKANA

The only scheduled air service to Turkana is Fly540's daily **flight** from Nairobi JKIA's domestic terminal to Lodwar (see p.514), and in the absence of any high-quality camps or lodges in the region there are currently no air safaris. To get to this remote desert lake **overland** you have three main options: sign up for one of the limited number of organized camping safaris; take the matatus and lorries that transport goods and people north from the urban hubs in the Kenya highlands; or drive yourself. Relatively few visitors drive, though Turkana is becoming more popular with 4WD fans, especially as the roads gradually improve. There are three **road routes** to Lake Turkana described below: one to the western shore starting in Kitale, and two to the eastern shore – from Maralal and from Marsabit (the latter very remote). There is no route connecting the east and west shores (the volcanic Sugata Valley forming a blazing hot barrier) and no ferries on the lake itself either – Lake Turkana's only shipping is government-owned or private.

TURKANA TOURS

If driving isn't an option, the obvious solution is to sign up with one of the few operators offering **Turkana camping safaris**, costing around $1000 for a week-long trip. Most people thoroughly enjoy these trips, coming back loaded with amazing souvenirs and photographs, and stories of weird and wonderful encounters – although drawbacks include the brevity and fixed itinerary of the trips. Turkana camping safaris traditionally head for the eastern shore of Lake Turkana, travelling from Maralal to Loiyangalani.

Gametrackers ⓦ gametrackersafaris.com (see p.118). The best company, using converted trucks for large groups and Land Cruisers for small groups.

Their regular Turkana camping trips via the Chalbi Desert (departing Fri & Wed) are unique and highly recommended.

Via Kitale and Lodwar The western approach, from Kitale to Lodwar, is the one used by most independent travellers without their own vehicles. For transport, there's a choice of buses or lorries. Whichever way you do it, the road is diabolical, though there are plans to re-pave it within the next few years to accommodate traffic to the new oil fields. The best part of the journey is the beginning, covered in Chapter 4 (see p.293). The last ATM before you reach Lodwar is at Makutano (see p.293), where it is also a good idea to fill up with fuel, though you should be able to find that further north at Ortum.

Via Maralal and Loiyangalani The journey up to Samburu-land en route to Lake Turkana is a good deal shorter in distance than that to the west shore, but it's still a two-day drive from Nairobi, normally with an overnight stop in Maralal. If driving, you'll need a high-clearance 4WD, a couple of spare tyres and extra fuel. During the rainy season you could be held up for a day or more at several points waiting for swollen luggas to subside, but the route north of Maralal has been partly improved in recent years. Travelling north of Maralal without your own vehicle may require patience since there's little public transport and you may have to hitchhike for rides.

Via Marsabit and Loiyangalani It's also possible to travel independently from Isiolo to Loiyangalani via Marsabit and North Horr, but be prepared to wait a long time for lifts, first from Isiolo to Marsabit, and then on to North Horr. Gametrackers (see above) use this route on their northbound Turkana Truck trip via the Chalbi Desert.

The A1 road to Lodwar

From Kitale, the **A1 road to Lodwar** heads north over the **Cherangani Hills**. After climbing over the **Marich Pass** (see p.293), you leave the hill country and drop onto the plain, passing from Pokot into Turkana territory when you cross the Turkwel River just before **Kainuk** – an occasional flashpoint for inter-communal violence that lies 130km north of Kitale and 170km south of Lodwar. The change of scenery here is dramatic, but it's hard to extract much of scenic interest from the thorny wilderness of the **Turkana Plains** beyond – although if you're travelling by bus or lorry the regular stops to pick up increasingly wild-looking passengers maintain gently heightening expectations as you head north.

Nasalot National Reserve

20km west of Kainuk off the A1 Kitale–Lodwar road (no public transport) • Daily 6am–6pm • $20

From Kainuk you can detour to the small **Nasalot National Reserve**, which bounds the northern slopes of the mountains and the southern fringes of the south Turkana plains. From the gate, 6km off the Lodwar road (signposted on the left, west), the winding paved route drops several hundred metres into the heat, with plunging precipices and spectacular views all round, to the **Turkwel Gorge** and **hydroelectric dam**.

As the reserve is mostly covered with thick bush, **spotting animals** isn't all that easy, and you'd be unusually fortunate to see any of the reserve's lions and leopards. The elephants here, though larger than their southern cousins, hide themselves pretty well, and your best chance of seeing them is on the paved road at dawn or dusk.

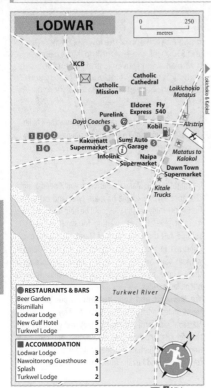

LODWAR

0   250
metres

KCB

Catholic Mission

Catholic Cathedral

Loikichokio Matatus

Eldoret Fly Express 540

Purelink

Daya Coaches

@

Kobil

Airstrip

Kakumatt Supermarket

Sumi Auto Garage

Matatus to Kalokol

Infolink

Naipa Supermarket

Dawn Town Supermarket

Kitale Trucks

Turkwel River

N

RESTAURANTS & BARS

Beer Garden	2
Bismillahi	1
Lodwar Lodge	4
New Gulf Hotel	5
Turkwel Lodge	3

ACCOMMODATION

Lodwar Lodge	3
Nawoitorong Guesthouse	4
Splash	1
Turkwel Lodge	2

& Kitale

South Turkana National Reserve

20km north of Nasalot, then 10km east off the A1 Kitale–Lodwar road • $20 • 📞 0724 954745

The **South Turkana National Reserve** lacks Nasalot's scenic grandeur, but is where the elephants migrate to between March and July. The lack of infrastructure (including much in the way of roads) makes it more challenging to explore, particularly since the reserve is over ten times the size of Nasalot. Wildlife, if you manage to spot it, includes giraffes, buffalo and crocodiles, which can sometimes be seen napping on the banks of the Kerio River.

Lodwar

For most Kenyans, mention of **LODWAR** conjures up remote and outlandish images of the badlands, an aberrant place where anything could befall you. The Turkana District capital is, to put it mildly, a wild town, and somewhat unformed and incongruous in this searing wilderness. During the 1980s it became Kenya's desert boomtown, the lake's fishing, the possibility of oil discoveries and the new road from Kitale all encouraging inward migration. While **Turkana people** have always predominated, **Luo** and **Luhya** also arrived in search of opportunities. With the exhaustion of farming country in the south, Lodwar and the area around it became increasingly attractive to pioneers and cowboys of all sorts. But this expansion has now fizzled out and Lodwar has returned to being a dusty frontier town.

Despite the heat and the dust, some people find the rough, frontier atmosphere of Lodwar exhilarating, but there's not a lot to do. If you have the time and energy, you can **hike** up one of the hills behind the town (the guides from *Nawoitorong Guesthouse* are best; see opposite), from where the view stretches for many kilometres. For **handicrafts**, you'll find good woven baskets on sale at the *Nawoitorong Guesthouse*. You might also want to pick up a pair of **5000-mile shoes** – flip-flops (thongs) made from old truck tyres – which are comfortable, virtually unbreakable, and can be purchased for around Ksh300 in the streets behind *Salama Hotel*.

ARRIVAL AND DEPARTURE
LODWAR

By plane By far the most comfortable way in and out of Lodwar is by air. Fly540 flies daily between Lodwar and Nairobi JKIA (2hr; Ksh12,540) via Kitale (40min; Ksh6740), leaving Lodwar at 11.40am; their office is on the main street next to the Eldoret Express office (📞0713 161297; daily 8am–5pm).

By bus From Kitale, a couple of buses leave for Lodwar in the morning (the first at around 9am); more leave between 2pm and 6pm, travelling in the evening to beat the heat.

Buses generally take 10–12hr to shudder and jolt along the 285km of crumbling asphalt laid in the early 1980s, though the journey will be shortened dramatically once the road improves. From Lodwar, buses to Kitale gather in the main street around *Salama Hotel*, and always leave in the evening, around 5–7pm. The one daily bus to Nairobi, run by Daya Coaches, leaves at 6.30pm from its office next to the *Salama Hotel*.

Destinations Kitale (3 daily; 10–12hr); Lokichokio (1 daily;

4hr); Nairobi (1 daily; 18hr).

By matatu Matatus for Kitale leave from the main stage in the centre of town, near the buses, but vehicles for Lokichokio and Kalokol have their own stage on the east side of town opposite the Oilibya filling station.

Destinations Lokichokio (3–5 daily; 4hr); Kalokol (2–3 daily; 1hr 30min).

Hitchhiking To hitchhike from Lodwar to Kitale, head in the morning to the roundabout at the eastern end of the main street, where you can flag down a lorry heading south. Local lads may also offer to help you find a vehicle for a small tip, but it's advisable to find out the going rate in advance if you think the driver will want paying (allow up to Ksh1200 to Kitale). Be aware, however, that Turkana bandits have been known to attack lorries along this road; some drivers choose to hire a guard – often just a local tribesman with a uniform and a gun – which seems to solve the problem. In any case, it's worth checking the security situation before you set out. Heading north from Kitale, there are always a few lorries bound for Lokichokio and the South Sudan border, and finding a vehicle is not too difficult. Make sure you take plenty of water for this trip, as delays and breakdowns are all too common and people are expected to fend for themselves.

INFORMATION

Services There's a KCB bank with an ATM, and a post office, both in the town centre. For internet access try Purelink (daily 8am–7pm; Ksh2/min) or Inforlink (daily 7am–9pm; Ksh1/min), both in the town centre.

ACCOMMODATION

With the exception of *Nawoitorong Guesthouse*, most of Lodwar's accommodation is tucked away behind a clutch of popular bars, which can make for a colourful stay. None of the following has hot water as such, although the supply is invariably tepid rather than cold, especially by evening time.

Lodwar Lodge ☎ 0728 007512. This popular hotel offers rows of quiet, spacious *bandas* behind a busy bar area, but be prepared for a bit of local colour; there are also cheaper s/c rooms in an adjacent concrete block. BB **Ksh90**

★ **Nawoitorong Guesthouse** 1km south over the Turkwel bridge, then 1.5km east ☎ 020 8018407. Part of the Turkana Women's Conference Centre, a cooperative set up in 1984 by four women who began baking bread together, *Nawoitorong* is made of local materials, is partly solar-powered, and uses profits to promote Turkana women's education. The non-s/c rooms in the main compound are spotless and have great mosquito nets but lack privacy and can be noisy; the three s/c cottages (Ksh2000) are better but more expensive. There's also excellent food. By far the best place to stay in Lodwar, but some way out of town. BB **Ksh1500**

Splash ☎ 0735 512229 or 0714 140164. Clean, friendly and relatively secure, offering s/c rooms with fans and nets, all named for African countries and regions, although it can be a bit of a party place and is consequently often noisy at night. Good breakfasts (Ksh150) and other food available (order in advance), and cold beer, plus secure parking in a gated compound at the back. BB **Ksh1500**

Turkwel Lodge ☎ 0712 689861. The most presentable of the town-centre lodgings, with clean s/c rooms with nets and ceiling fans, plus a few tidy cottages in the back. The rooms are reasonably quiet, and there's a good bar and restaurant out front. BB **Ksh1050**

EATING AND DRINKING

For **food** supplies the two main supermarket/grocery stores, Naipa (Mon–Sat 8.30am–8pm, Sun 11am–7.30pm) and Kakumatt (daily 7am–9pm), will fulfil most of your needs.

Beer Garden One of Lodwar's few discos, with DJs spinning a mix of Kenyan music and reggae and determined regulars partying well into the small hours. Fri & Sat 5pm–late.

Bismillahi Clean and cheap, with attentive service. Enjoy *nyama choma*, pilau, *mboga*, chapattis and cold sodas from the terrace out front, from where you can watch Lodwar's local characters drift by. Mains from Ksh70. Daily 24hr.

Lodwar Lodge ☎ 0728 007512. Large, convivial outdoor bar and terrace that serves as a magnet for local men during football matches; on game days the place gets packed, but at other times it's a nice spot to shoot some pool. Daily 7.30am–11pm.

New Gulf Hotel Opposite the Oilibya petrol station, near the Loki stage. Cavernous place serving tea, chapattis, *mandaazi* and all the usual staples for around Ksh60. Daily 6am–6pm.

Turkwel Lodge ☎ 0712 689861. Good, solid meals, with a focus on meats cooked every way you could imagine (Ksh230 for a quarter chicken). There's also some pleasant outdoor seating for drinkers. Daily 6am–11pm.

7

7

THE TURKANA

Until a few decades ago, the **Turkana**, the main people of the western shore of the lake, had very little contact with the outside world, or even with the Republic of Kenya. Turkana people did not traditionally wear clothing, though the women wear several tiers of beads around their necks and, if married, a metal band too. Turkana men are rarely seen without their *akichalong*, a small wooden headrest, like a stool, which they recline on at any opportunity. Many still wear a wide bracelet on their wrists called an *aberait*, which is in fact a weapon. Although it's usually covered with a leather guard, the edge of the *aberait* is razor-sharp, and can be wielded in a fight like a slashing knife, while leaving the hands free.

Linguistically, the Turkana are related to the Maa-speaking Samburu and Maasai. Indeed, along the northwest shore of the lake, the people are probably an old mixture of Turkana and Samburu, although, like the Luo (also distantly related by language), the Turkana did not traditionally practise circumcision. They moved east from their old homeland around the present-day borders of Sudan and Uganda in the seventeenth century. The desolate region between the lake and the Ugandan border that they now occupy is barely habitable land, and their daily struggle for existence has profoundly influenced the shape of their society and, inevitably, helped create the funnel into modern Kenya that Lodwar, with its road, has become.

The Turkana are more individualistic than most Kenyan peoples and they show a disregard for the ties of clan and family that must have emerged through repeated famines and wars. Some anthropologists have suggested that loyalty to particular **cattle brands** is a more important indicator of identity than blood ties or lineage. Although essentially **pastoralists**, always on the move to the next spot of grazing, the Turkana, with characteristic pragmatism, have scorned the taboo against fish so prevalent among herders, and **fishing** is a viable option that is increasingly popular. They also grow crops when they can get seeds and when there's adequate rainfall. Often the rains fail, notably during the prolonged drought of the early 1980s, which took a terrible toll on Turkana children. The situation eased up until 2007, when, again, a prolonged drought set in. Although the rains have been good for the past few years, life here is still very much a matter of day-to-day survival, supplemented here and there by food aid.

Turkana **bellicosity** is infamous in Kenya (Turkana migrants to the towns of the south are frequently employed as *askaris*). Relations with their neighbours – especially the Merille to the north of the lake, the Samburu to the south, and the Pokot to the southwest – have often been openly aggressive. British forces were engaged in the gradual conquest of the Turkana – the usual killings, livestock raids and property destruction – and they succeeded, at some cost, in eventually disarming them of their guns in the 1920s. But the Merille, meanwhile, were obtaining arms from Abyssinia's imperial government, and they took advantage of the Turkana's defenceless position. When war was declared by Italian-held Abyssinia in 1940, the British rearmed the Turkana, who swiftly exacted a savage revenge on the Merille. They were later disarmed again. Since then, the Turkana have fallen victim to heavily armed Toposa raiders from Sudan, who are thought to have killed as many as ten thousand Turkana in the far north. But a tribal peace pact signed in 2011 seems to be holding, and the region is relatively quiet at the moment.

Turkana **directness** is unmistakeable in all their dealings with *wazungu*. They are, for example, resolute and stubborn bargainers, while offers of relatively large sums for photos often leave them stone cold – not necessarily from any mystical fear of the camera, but because of a shrewd estimation of what the market will stand, and hence, presumably, of their own reputation.

The western lakeshore

Fringed by swaying palm trees and teeming with wildlife, the windswept **western lakeshore** feels like an oasis in this sun-baked region, and is certainly the most obvious focus of a trip to Turkana. It is, however, fairly inaccessible – many of the attractions in the area are difficult (if not impossible) to reach by public transport, and roads between them are few. Still, these wild, windswept beaches are hard to beat for their end-of-the-world appeal, and the sense that you've got the vast desert lake all to yourself.

Kalokol

Ferguson's Gulf is the only easily accessible place to head for on the lakeshore, accessed via the village of **KALOKOL**. Kalokol has a surprising amount of hassle for such a small place, although its main appeal is as an especially good place for buying **Turkana crafts**: wonderful (but far too big to transport) baskets, rich-smelling, oiled head stools (*akichalong*), ostrich-shell necklaces, and an array of snuff and tobacco horns made of cow horn (traditionally) or pieces of plastic piping.

ARRIVAL, ACCOMMODATION AND EATING   KALOKOL

Several **matatus** make the 60km trip every day from Lodwar. When you've had enough, take a matatu back to Lodwar, but don't leave it till too late in the afternoon; the last one leaves no later than 2pm. Alternatively, you could try **hitchhiking** out of Kalokol – far from guaranteed, though vehicles occasionally go all the way through to Kitale. Kalokol has only one basic **place to stay**, and while **food** supplies have improved a little with the opening of a few *dukas*, it's not a bad idea to bring at least some fruit with you from Lodwar.

Lake Turkana Guest House ☎0713 679687, ✉lake turkanaguesthouse@yahoo.com. Cheap, friendly and near the matatu stage, though the non-s/c rooms are spartan and rather cramped. The restaurant in front serves decent fried meat and pilau (mains around Ksh100). Room only Ksh700

Fried fish ladies Piles of cheap and delicious fried lake fish are usually available at least once a day at one of the houses in Kalokol. Ksh100 will pay for more than enough for one person. Ask around.

Ferguson's Gulf

Kalokol is about 3km from the shallow waters of **Ferguson's Gulf**: just follow the river course as it drains east. Hanging out by the lake here is fascinating, with the constantly mutating background of the western shore across the bay, as well as the closer prospect of Turkana fishermen, hundreds of species of birds, and the occasional glimpse of crocodile or hippo on the water's surface. From a distance, the activity at the water's edge seems silent since the wind whips all sound away, lending the whole scene a slightly dream-like quality.

Down on the shore you can talk with the children who follow you everywhere, and who often speak good English. If you make friends, you can be taken looking for snakes (be careful), to see *tembo* brewing (always by women) or, if you're lucky, to a dance. Teenagers' and children's dances happen several times a week, but they're best when there's a full moon: the boys tie cans of stones to their ankles and pretend to ignore the girls' flirting.

THE DANCING STONES OF NAMORATUNGA

During the journey between Lodwar and Kalokol, look out for the **standing stones of Namoratunga**, 15km southwest of Kalokol some 50m off on the south side of the road. They're easy to miss, being only a small cluster of metre-high cylindrical stones, but the Turkana are in the habit of balancing small rocks on top of them, so you'll know them when you see them. Like a miniature Stonehenge, the pillars are a spiritual focus and the scene of a major annual gathering of Turkana clans, usually in December. The stones pre-date the arrival of the Turkana, but little is known about them, even by the people themselves (the name "namoratunga" is used by Turkana to describe any standing stone site). One theory is that the stones were aligned with the positions of important stars in Eastern Cushitic astronomy and were used to determine the dates of ritual ceremonies. Some people call them "dancing stones", following a legend that told of a tribe dancing on the site, who were turned to stone by the ridicule of a group of new arrivals, the Turkana. More plausible reasons for their existence might be the concentration of haematite and copper ore around the site, the smelting of which (for making weapons) has historically had ritual significance. Uphill from the stones you'll find several raised rock cairns covering ancient graves, some perfectly delineated with larger regular stones. It's a fascinating site, and all rather mysterious.

When you're tired of wandering around, being mobbed by toddlers, watching the fishermen paddling out on their waterlogged rafts, and the pied kingfishers hovering and plunging over the shallows, you might consider having a **swim**. People may tell you it's safe, but going in is always a risk because of crocodiles.

Central Island National Park

Accessible from Eliye Springs or Ferguson's Gulf (round trip Ksh15,000–18,000 including petrol) • Daily 6am–6pm • $20 • ⓦ bit.ly/CentralIsland • Camp wild on the beach with your own equipment ($15; no facilities whatsoever) • Five square kilometres

A trip to the **Central Island National Park** is highly recommended, and the park warden or one of his rangers will normally accompany you. Make sure, however, that the boat you go in is thoroughly lake-worthy, equipped with life jackets, and that the crew know what they are doing – vicious squalls can blow up fast and it's more than 9km to the island. This is one of two island national parks in the lake (the other is the less accessible South Island), which, together with Sibiloi National Park on the northeast shore of the lake, are a UNESCO World Heritage Site. Central Island is a unique triple volcano poking gauntly out of the water. Most of the island is taken up by two crater lakes (a third has dried up) hidden behind its rocky shores. One of the lakes is the only known habitat of an ancient species of tilapia, a reminder of the time when Lake Turkana was connected to the Nile. The island is also the nesting ground for big colonies of water birds but, like some African Galapagos, it really belongs to the reptiles. Crocodiles breed here in the largest concentration in Africa, and at the right time of year (usually April and May) you can witness the newly hatched baby crocs breaking out of the nests and sprinting with loud squeaks down to the crater lake where they'll pass their first season. The vegetation is scant, but some of the sheltered lees are overgrown with thick grass and bushes for a short period each year, and the nests are dug beneath this foliage.

Eliye Springs

Eliye Springs, 66km east of Lodwar, used to be *the* place for travellers on the lakeshore and it still attracts the occasional overland truck and 4WD weekenders. It may be difficult to reach, but Eliye Springs readily compensates for the hassles of the journey – a paradisal place with rustling *doum* palms watered by hot springs, gorgeous views, and nothing to do except lounge about and enjoy the lakeside ambience.

ARRIVAL AND ACCOMMODATION   **ELIYE SPRINGS**

Getting there and back is the main problem, as there's **no public transport**. You can rent a vehicle with a driver for the day, at around Ksh7000 (4WD advisable as the trail gets very sandy towards the end). Alternatively, it's possible to walk along the lakeshore from Ferguson's Gulf – hire a guide (Ksh3000), load up with water and follow the lake south for 45km. A night walk by moonlight is best, but watch out for crocodiles.

Eliye Springs Camp & Lodge ☎0703 891810 or 0731 108296, ⓦ eliyespringsresort.com. The only real place to stay in Eliye Springs, this laidback lakeside resort offers a range of accommodation for all budgets. At the top end are luxurious Turkana *bomas* ($215), but simple *manyattas* are also available, or you can just pitch your tent among the palms. The lodge also rents boats for tours and fishing trips. Camping Ksh600 per person; *manyattas* $15

Lobolo Camp About 25km south of Kalokol, on the shore ☎0713 250155. This high-end place in another lakeshore oasis should reopen in summer 2013.

Lokichokio

The border town of **Lokichokio** (also spelled Lokichoggio and often just called Loki) is an unremittingly dry and rocky place, and even more of a cowboy town than Lodwar. During the civil war in southern Sudan Loki was something of a boom town; as the main UN aid centre, it was packed with an eclectic mix of international fixers, haggard relief workers, businessmen, doctors, pilots, nurses and missionaries. But when South Sudan gained its independence in 2011, the UN moved on to Juba. Most of Loki's upscale lodges have now closed down, those that are left are slowly rotting away, and the dusty streets have been reclaimed by Turkana herdsmen and their goats.

The road to Lokichokio passes the huge refugee camp at **Kakuma**, 144km northwest of Lodwar, which follows the banks of the Tarach *lugga* for nearly 10km. Set up for Sudanese refugees, this sprawl of huts and shacks is now being used for the overspill of Somali refugees from Dadaab camp in eastern Kenya. Kakuma has food and basic lodgings (and usually fuel), but nothing to warrant a stopover.

ARRIVAL AND DEPARTURE — LOKICHOKIO

By plane ALS (office at the airstrip ☎ 0727 666222) has reliable flights to Nairobi (daily at 4pm; 1hr 30min; from $210 one-way) and Rumbek in South Sudan (Mon, Wed, Fri at 10.30am; 1hr 30min; from $249 one-way).

Overland to South Sudan You can get a visa for $100 at the GoSS (Government of South Sudan) border post at NadaPal (daily 8am–4pm), where you'll also need to show your yellow fever certificate. Before leaving Kenya, you must first formally exit the country by getting stamped out at the immigration office in Loki: it's near the barracks on the Juba road just across the *lugga* on the north side of town (daily 8am–5pm). If you're entering Kenya, this is where you get your Kenyan visa ($50).

INFORMATION

Services There's a KCB bank with an ATM off the Lopiding road, and a post office at the north end of town, off the Juba road opposite the immigration office.

ACCOMMODATION AND EATING

748 Camp Lopiding road, 500m south of town ☎ 0720 772335, ✆ 748airservices.com. One of the last of Loki's once numerous luxury camps, this landscaped compound is overpriced and reeks of abandonment. But the roomy *bandas* are still in good shape, the garden is attractive and there's even a tiny gym. You can get burgers and steaks at the bar/restaurant for around Ksh600. FB $70

Ana Hotel Ejokonoi On the Lodwar road, 100m before the Makuti Guesthouse ☎ 0726 996045. Charming little café run by a local women's group, serving Kenyan staples alongside pasta (Ksh150), pancakes and sandwiches. Order two days in advance and they can even whip up a pizza. Daily 6.30am–9pm.

Makuti Guesthouse Town centre, on the main Lodwar road opposite the Sunbird ☎ 0735 199217. Clean, good-sized non-s/c rooms with nets and fans, all facing onto a brightly painted courtyard. The main drawback is the raucous bar out front, though it's a good place to grab some *nyama choma* or goat stew (around Ksh150). Room only Ksh800

Sunbird Town centre, on the main Lodwar road opposite the Makuti ☎ 0708 325173. Run by a Christian family, this quiet guesthouse has clean, non s/c rooms with fans and nets and doesn't allow alcohol on the premises, which makes it a perfect place to escape the noisy bars across the street. Room only Ksh800

Samburu-land

Samburu-land is the vast stretch of country to the southeast of Lake Turkana inhabited for the last three to four hundred years by the traditionally nomadic Samburu people, who are very closely related to the Maasai, and speak the same language, Maa. The easiest way to explore the region is to take an organized safari (see p.117), but if your budget is tight, and you have time, a flexible attitude and don't want a spoon-fed adventure, you'll get the maximum exposure to the area by travelling completely independently and without your own vehicle.

The C77 road to Maralal

Rumuruti (onomatopoeic Maa for "mosquito") is the first town you come to. Though fairly insignificant these days – it merely marks the end of the paved road from Nyahururu and the central highlands (see p.195) – this former Maasai stronghold of western Laikipia (see p.509) was settled by British soldiers after World War I and many of their ranches still exist. There's some very good game country in the vicinity, so you might want to stay nearby, for example at Bobong Campsite (see p.510).

Suguta Marmar, 15km north of the Baringo junction, and 20km south of Kisima,

THE SAMBURU

The **Samburu** are historically close to the Maasai. Their languages are nearly the same (both Maa) and culturally they are virtually indistinguishable to an outsider. Both came from the region around present-day northwest Turkana in the seventeenth century. The Samburu turned east, establishing themselves in the mountain pastures and spreading across to the plains; the Maasai continued south.

Improvements in health and veterinary care over the last century have swelled the Samburu population and the size of their herds. Many in the driest areas of their range in the northeast have turned to camel herding as a better insurance against drought than cattle. Since livestock is the basis of relations between in-laws (through the giving of "bride wealth" from the husband to his wife's family), having camel herds has disrupted patterns of marriage and initiation into new generations because camel herds increase more slowly than cattle herds. Memories, recording every transaction over successive generations, are phenomenal (the Samburu have only begun to acquire writing in the last four or five decades).

The Samburu age-set system, like many others in Africa, is a complicated arrangement to which a number of anthropologists have devoted lifetimes of investigation. Essentially it's a **gerontocracy** (rule by old men), and the polygamous elders are assured, by the system they manipulate, of having the first choice of young women to marry. The promiscuous and jingoistic – but, by Samburu reckoning, still juvenile – warriors are forced to wait, usually until their thirties, before initiation into elderhood and subsequent marriage and fatherhood bring them a measure of real respect. In turn, they perpetuate the system on their own sons, who have everything to gain by falling in line and much to lose if they withdraw their stake in the tradition – perhaps by going to Nairobi or the coast to look for work.

For **women** the situation is very different. They are married at 15 or 16, immediately after the still widely performed operation of clitoridectomy and before they have much chance to rebel. But they may continue affairs with their *morani* boyfriends, the unmarried juniors of their new, much older husbands. This polygamy in itself seems to be an important motivating force for the whole generation system. For the warriors and their girlfriends, there's a special young people's language – a vocabulary of conspiratorial songs and idioms – which has to be modified with the initiation of every age-set, so that it's kept secret from the elders.

This highly intricate system is now beginning to collapse in many areas, with a widespread disruption of pre-colonial ways; even the circumcision initiation of boys to warriorhood is less of a mass ceremony. While herds are still the principal criterion of wealth, people in some areas are turning to agriculture. There are enormous problems for such initiatives, especially when there's no aid or government support, but they do show that the standard stereotypes don't always fit. As for the *morani* warriors, opportunities for cattle-raiding and lion-killing have diminished with more efficient policing of their territories, although there are still frequent clashes with the Turkana on their northern borders. For some, tourist hunting has taken over: *morani* in full rig, striding past the beach hotels, looking for sales opportunities or liaisons, are no longer an unusual sight.

marks the boundary between Central Province and the Rift Valley, although there's little more than a livestock auction yard, a basic checkpoint and a few cheap *hotelis*.

Maralal

Some of the Laikipia settlers who ended up around Rumuruti would have dearly liked to set themselves up around the cool, conifer-draped highlands of **MARALAL**. But even before British administrators made this the district capital, Maralal had been a spiritual focus for the **Samburu people** and, despite some dithering, the colonial administrators didn't accede to the settlers' demands.

Maralal is a peculiar town, spread with abandon around a depression in the hills. Samburu people trudge its dusty streets – creating a brilliant collage of skins, blankets, beads, brass and iron, and giving the town a special smell, too, of sour milk, fat and cattle. You'll see warriors in full rig on bicycles; warriors with braided hair and bracelets, but wearing jeans and singlets; women decked with flanges of necklaces; old

MARALAL INTERNATIONAL CAMEL DERBY

The Maralal International **Camel Derby** (🌐yarecamelcamp.co.ke) makes for a strange weekend during the second week of August. Anyone can enter, or just watch, as dozens of competitors from East Africa, Europe, China, Australia and South Africa battle it out over 12km amateur and 42km semi-professional stages. There is also a tie-in with the Kenya Amateur Cycling Association, which organizes mountain-bike and amateur cycling races. The events are based at the *Yare Camel Camp* (see p.523), where you can get more details.

men with sticks; and young men carrying old rifles. The main town-centre watering hole is the *Buffalo Hotel*: the place sets itself up for Wild West comparisons and the climate is appropriate – unbelievably dusty, almost always windy and, at 2220m, sharp enough at night for log fires. All it needs is coyotes – and even there hyenas fill the role with their nocturnal whooping.

A notable resident of Maralal until 1994 was the travel writer and Arabist **Wilfred Thesiger**, who had made the town his home and had adopted a number of orphaned boys. Thesiger made his name with his accounts of the Shia Arabs of southern Iraq and the Bedu of the Arabian peninsula, and followed up these achievements with several books on Kenya, notably *My Kenya Days*. Among the Samburu he found equally congenial companions for his old age.

Kenyatta House

West of the town centre • Daily 8am–5pm • Free, but donations accepted

If you neglect to visit the liberally signposted **Kenyatta House**, don't fret. The fact that Kenyatta was detained here in 1961 before his final release doesn't really improve the interest of this unexceptional and almost empty bungalow. In a way it seems a pity that it's a slightly unloved national monument and not some family's home.

Maralal National Sanctuary

Maralal Safari Lodge, 2km southwest from the town centre • Daily 24hr • Free

Although in theory, the **Maralal National Sanctuary** covers more than 200 square kilometres to the west and north of Maralal, in practice almost all of it is now farmed or grazed, leaving just a couple of square kilometres around *Maralal Safari*

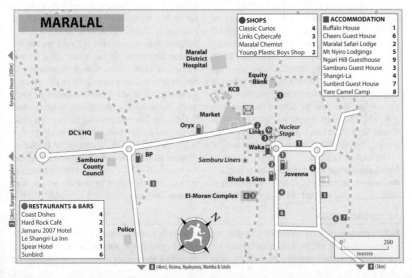

THE YOUNG PLASTIC BOYS' CO-OPERATIVE SELF-HELP GROUP

Arriving in Maralal, you'll invariably attract a flock of (often annoying) "**guides**" offering evening excursions to see traditional dancing in nearby *manyattas*, or else visits to local Samburu witch doctors and blacksmiths and Turkana villages. Use your judgement before accepting, making it absolutely clear how much you are prepared to pay. Recent visitors have reported relatively non-commercial and very worthwhile excursions.

An attempt to tame the guides by organizing them into disciplined groups is the **Young Plastic Boys' Co-operative Self-Help Group**, named after the street children who used to make dolls and trinkets using plastic bags and cartons. They have now progressed, under the guidance of the KWS and various NGOs, to carving and selling woodcrafts, spears and other souvenirs. Their shop is near the market, and sells a decent range of Pokot, Turkana, Rendille and Samburu crafts (or items inspired by those cultures), and they should also be able to sort you out with a reliable guide, should you need one, and advise on onward travel if you're having difficulties. If you want to look further for crafts, seek out a Plastic Boys offshoot, Classic Curios, a little crafts shop opposite the *Jamaru Restaurant*.

Lodge (see opposite) where plains wildlife is fairly common. You can sit on their terrace, or in the bar-restaurant, and watch a succession of wildlife from the sanctuary and nearby Yamo Forest, including zebra, baboon, warthog and impala – and, less often, eland, buffalo and hyena – file up the hill to the concrete waterhole a few metres away.

ARRIVAL AND DEPARTURE   MARALAL

Most matatus, and the few larger buses that serve Maralal, congregate in the centre of town between the market and what would be the main roundabout if the traffic observed it. The main bus/matatu companies are Nucleur (sic), Samburu Liners and Roots Culture. They all have ticket kiosks in the area.

GETTING TO MARALAL

From Nyahururu The easiest route to Maralal, the C77 rolls up from Nyahururu via Rumuruti. The road is tarmac as far as Rumuruti, and then poor-quality *murram* to Maralal. Regular buses serve this route from Nyahururu (10 daily; 4hr; Ksh500) with 2–3 connections daily to Nairobi (7hr; Ksh400).

From Isiolo and Wamba A second route to Maralal is the A2 from Isiolo past Archer's Post, then west along the C79 past the turn for Wamba, where it becomes the C78. Buses connect Maralal with both Wamba (5 daily; 3hr; Ksh500) and Isiolo (3 daily; 5hr; Ksh900). Despite some bad corrugations, scenically the C79/78 has everything to recommend it, including some magnificent desert buttes and sweeping views over the valley of the Ewaso Nyiro River, which flows east through the Samburu National Reserve. Some 176km from Isiolo and 86km from Wamba you reach flyblown little Kisima, at the junction with the C77 Rumuruti–Maralal road.

From Lake Baringo A third possible route to Maralal is the lonely but reasonable *murram* road from Lake Baringo, which in its earlier stages has some breathtaking

viewpoints back over the lake and fascinating Pokot villages on the way.

NORTH TO LAKE TURKANA

There's a once-daily bus north of Maralal to Baragoi (4hr), but no regular public transport beyond there, so if you're not driving, hitchhiking is usually the only way to Loiyangalani. It's best not to go to Baragoi without a confirmed lift on to Loiyangalani. In Maralal, you may find transport with private vehicles at *Yare Camel Camp* or *Maralal Safari Lodge*, but both places are inconveniently far from the centre and your chances of scoring a lift are higher if you stay in town and spread the word at the petrol stations that you're looking for a lift in a lorry. Gametrackers' Turkana safari (see p.513) reaches Maralal most Friday evenings, and if there's room you might persuade the driver to give you a lift, for a fee. Members of the Plastic Boys Group (see above) can also be helpful. If you're driving, note that Maralal is the last place where you can rely on supplies of beer, petrol and diesel (around ten percent more expensive here than in the towns to the south).

ACCOMMODATION

Buffalo House Town centre (no phone). Ultra-basic and a shadow of its former self, this centrally located boozer is just the thing if you're counting every penny, with

single-bedded rooms around a small courtyard and dubious shared showers and loos. The rooms (all non-s/c) are possibly the cheapest in Kenya, and definitely the cheapest in this book. Room only Ksh200

★ **Cheers Guest House** Town centre ☎0722 655877. Forty-five clean rooms, with decent bathrooms, TV and nets (and 24hr hot water – in theory – from a boiler). The three second-floor "executive" rooms (Ksh600 extra) are the breeziest and equipped with instant showers. They also have a laundry service and a busy breakfast room and restaurant on the ground floor (full English Ksh350). BB Ksh1550

Maralal Safari Lodge 2km southwest of the centre ☎0720 924523 or 0724 906327, ⊚tiny.cc/MaralalSL. This place has seen much better days – although you could have said the same thing decades ago – and despite the pretty gardens and genial staff it really is now on its last legs. Even so, it's hard not to like this decrepit pile, with its weather-beaten cabins like an old-style ski lodge, steeply pitched roofs and interiors fitted out in solid cedar. Instant showers are mounted over original metal bathtubs; the unreasonably pricey meals take hours to arrive (order the day before); and the small pool is defunct. However, regardless of what your passport says, you will automatically qualify for residents' rates – and are expected to further negotiate a final price. BB Ksh9700

Mt Nyiro Lodgings Town centre (no phone). Very basic, but clean, in a little block of s/c rooms. Take room #1 at the top, which gets the best breeze. Safe parking. Hot water mornings only. Room only Ksh800

Ngari Hill Guesthouse 3km east of Maralal on a hilltop on the road to the Karisia Hills ☎020 2011609 or 0735 228649, ⊚ngarihill.com. Filling a much-needed gap in town, this brand-new guesthouse with cottages and "tented rooms" offers the most comfortable accommodation in Maralal, though it's not convenient if you don't have your own transport. Camping Ksh500 per person, BB Ksh7000

★ **Samburu Guest House** Opposite the Police

housing on the way into town from the south ☎020 2374919 or 0704 846184, ⊚samburuguesthouse.com. The new best lodging in town – giving the *Sunbird* some competition – with decent, clean rooms, outward-facing windows, flatscreen TVs, bathrooms that work and safe parking in the courtyard. Room #10, at the front, with two big beds, is the best in the house. Downstairs, the restaurant (daily 7am–9pm; no bar) is supplied by enthusiastic kitchen staff. Wi-fi throughout – in theory. BB Ksh2000

Shangri-La El-Moran complex ☎0726 912525. The most interesting thing about the Samburu-owned *Shangri-La* is that each of the 21 rooms is named after one of the 21 generations of Samburu warriors who have been initiated since 1705. The tidy rooms are otherwise dull and a bit dark, but remarkably good-value, with instant showers, TV and nets. You can tear into some roast meat at the *Choma gardens* out back, and wash it down in the *Shangri-La Bar*. BB Ksh900

★ **Sunbird Guest House** Town centre ☎0720 654567. A lovely retreat from the hustle of town, this has fantastically clean, fresh rooms, with electricity, all charmingly and reassuringly well managed, with a wholesome *hoteli* attached for the wholesome clients they prefer to welcome. Great value. BB Ksh1200

Yare Camel Camp 4km down the Isiolo road ☎0722 333674, ⊚yarecamelcamp.co.ke. Maralal's main tourist centre, with some pleasant thatched *bandas*, a decent campsite, a well-stocked bar and a hard-working kitchen (order well in advance). Slightly ramshackle, but cosy and well looked after, and the little cabins, although quite overpriced on paper, have electricity and hot water – and unless you're here for the camel derby (see p.521), you can always bargain a much better rate. Activities include camel rides ($3/hour) and guided walks in the district ($25/day). Camping Ksh400 per person, BB $48

7

EATING AND DRINKING

Maralal has several decent **places to eat**, as well as the usual run of cheap and filling *hotelis*. A night spent in the town's numerous **bars** can be exhilarating, infuriating and silly, but rarely dangerous. Until the *Buffalo* Hotel (the town's former leading watering hole) is sold and reinvented as a flatscreen sports bar (yet to arrive in town), the best bars are at the *Yare Camel Camp* (daily 9am–midnight), which still sometimes heaves with Samburu pool players and drinkers, and the less frequented *Maralal Safari Lodge* (daily 10am–7pm).

Coast Dishes Town centre. Friendly local restaurant run by folks from Mombasa ("The neighbourhood will never be the same again" they proclaim in large letters on their facade) with Al Jazeera English on the TV, selling cheap and filling rice-based dishes – *mchele*, *pilau* and especially *katakata* (*KK* – only Ksh80), plus chapattis and *mahamri*. Eat and drink for Ksh200. Daily 6.30am–8.30pm.

Hard Rock Café Town centre. Excellent little place with cheap food including samosas, and meat-and-carb dishes such as pilau (Ksh90), chapatti and stew (Ksh150) and chapatti and beans (Ksh100, and friendly owners, who are

generous with advice on travel in the region. Daily 7am–9pm.

★ **Shangri-La Inn** Town centre. This one-time upmarket restaurant in Maralal's first "mall" still maintains a certain style, but at super-competitive prices, with a full English breakfast for Ksh200, continental breakfast Ksh100, masala chips Ksh100 and Spanish omelette Ksh40. Daily 6am–10pm

Spear Hotel Town centre. Reliable and popular *hoteli*, with a great atmosphere, widescreen TV, breakfasts, and a good list of filling dishes, including beef and rice (Ksh150) and *nyama*

choma (half a kilo of beef for Ksh180). Daily 6am–10pm.

★ **Sunbird** Town centre. Smart *hoteli* with an outdoor garden area. Order ahead for meals, which are good value

and well prepared, mostly fried dishes (around Ksh250/ plate). They don't have a bar, but will fetch beer, which can normally only be served with food. Daily 6.30am–9pm.

DIRECTORY

Banks Maralal is the last place to get cash en route to Lake Turkana – at the KCB or Equity banks (both in the town centre, both with ATMs), at *Yare Camel Camp* or at *Maralal Safari Lodge.*

Internet Links Cybercafé, town centre (Mon–Sat 8am–7.30pm, Sun 2–7.30pm; Ksh2/min).

Pharmacy *Maralal Chemist,* town centre (Mon–Sat 8am–6pm).

The Mathews Range

In the context of the vast spaces of the north, the **Mathews Range** – named after the Welshman General Lloyd Mathews, one-time commander-in-chief of the Sultan of Zanzibar's army – is virtually on Maralal's doorstep. The range, most of which is a forest reserve, is impressively wild hill country, with Mathew Peak (Ol Doinyo Lenkiyo) rising to 2375m. Lower down, the mountains are heavily cloaked in forest and thick bush; unusual vegetation includes "living fossil" cycad plants, giant cedars and podocarpus. Among the plentiful animal life are forest buffalo and outstanding butterflies.

Wamba

Matatus run between Maralal and Wamba (usually 3 daily; 3hr) and between Isiolo and Wamba (5 daily; 3hr)

To visit the Mathews, unless your main aim is to stay at *Sarara Camp* (see opposite), your most promising first target is **WAMBA**, a one-street town 5km off the C78/79 highway, roughly midway between Maralal and Isiolo. Wamba's main focus and chief claim to fame is the large, modern Catholic **hospital** on the way into town, which has the best medical facilities in northern Kenya. The town is also increasingly in the spotlight for its annual Namunyak Safaricom **marathon**, held the weekend before the race at Lewa (see p.504).

The big mountain you can see to the southeast of the town is **Warges** (2688m, 9km from Wamba as the crow flies), a southern outlier of the Mathews. Guides from Wamba will take you up there, though they'll stress how full of wild animals it is and how much their lives (not yours of course) are at risk.

The Kitich area

The main continuation from Wamba is towards the luxury **Kitich Camp** and the nearby KWS campsite (check with the KWS in Wamba that it's still open before travelling there). If you're **on foot** and heading for the campsite, find a guide in Wamba and set off cross-country, direct to **Ngelai** (the location of *Kitich*'s local airstrip), crossing several *luggas*. You'll see almost nobody on the way. The distance is about 30km and it's an exhausting day's walk. Ngelai has a Lutheran mission (2km out of the centre to the north) and a single shop, which may put you up for the night if you can't make the final 8km to the KWS campsite before nightfall.

If you're **driving** to Kitich Camp or the KWS campsite (4WD esssential, and note that there's no fuel along the way and normally none for sale at *Kitich*), set off out of Wamba towards Barsaloi (also spelled Parsaloi) along a rough road that commences 500m from the Maralal–Isiolo junction at the start of the Wamba access road. You drive 13km north towards Barsaloi, then turn right and do a further 17km to Ngelai, following the yellow stones. Some 6km past Ngelai, you fork left to ford the **Ngeng River**. With the mountains looming all around, this is the way into the heart of the Mathews. The KWS campsite is a couple of kilometres up the track on the other side of the Ngeng River, and *Kitich Camp* is some 4km further. This is first-rate **walking** and exploring country for hardy travellers (there is no public transport), but unless you are staying at *Kitich Camp* you need to be fully self-sufficient. Wherever you go, you'll need a guide to escort you. This is a very game-rich area with elephants everywhere, buffaloes, hyenas, leopards and many other creatures. You really have to watch yourself, especially if you go down near the river. It's a lot of fun, but take care.

Namunyak Wildlife Conservation Trust

Accessible by charter flight from Nanyuki to Sarara's airstrip or by road along the A2 to Sereolipi (97km north of Isiolo), then turning left and – *luggas* permitting – heading a further 32km along a bush track • $80 • ✆ tiny.cc/Namunyak • 340 square kilometres

The community-managed **Namunyak Wildlife Conservation Trust** forms a great stretch of rugged bush and forest, supported by the Tusk Trust. Here, with Warges rearing behind, is one of the north's best tented camps, *Sarara Camp*, and the only one to be found in the vast wilderness area of Namunyak. While game can be hard to spot – you might see klipspringer, Chandler's mountain reedbuck, elephant and (very rarely) leopard – the conservancy has rich pickings for birders, with Kenya's largest nesting colony of Rüppell's vultures and frequent sightings of Gambaga flycatcher, shining sunbird, tiny cisticola and stone partridge.

ACCOMMODATION AND EATING

THE MATHEWS RANGE

WAMBA

There are a few *dukas*, though they offer little in the way of fresh food beyond basic fruit and vegetables.

Saudia Lodge Wamba centre. One of the few B&Ls in town with clean and pleasant rooms, and pretty good value for the price. Room only Ksh800

Imani Bar & Restaurant Wamba centre. Serves the usual limited range of stews (from Ksh120) and a reasonable *githeri* (Ksh80), plus warm beers, to a grateful local crowd. Daily 7am–late.

NAMUNYAK WILDLIFE CONSERVATION TRUST

★ **Sarara Camp** Between the Isiolo–Marsabit road and Wamba ✆ sararacamp.com (Nairobi reservations ✆ 020 6000457, ✆ bush-and-beyond.com). A community-owned tented camp run by an experienced safari-business family, *Sarara*'s six tents – all rustic Africa luxury – have great outdoor loos-with-a-view and open-air showers. Go out with the guides (all bronze, but highly experienced) on drives and walks, or relax in the natural-rock infinity pool overlooking the waterhole and wait for the animals to come to you. Photographers will love the hide – perfect for viewing elephants that often come in droves. Closed April 15–May 31 & Oct 15–Dec 15. Package $1530

KITICH CAMP AREA

KWS campsite Close to Kitich camp (no phone; ask around in Wamba). Pleasant and shady, with showers and toilet, and water available from the nearby pools. Note that there's no food available at the campsite and, while you can fish in the river, there's a limit to how much catfish a person can stand. $15 per person

Kitich Camp Mathews forest ✆ +8821 643330048

CAMEL SAFARIS IN THE NORTH

Samburu camel herders drive their beasts to grazing all over this part of Kenya, and a number of small safari operators can offer the experience of walking with them along routes that depend on your time and budget. You can occasionally ride a camel, too, though the experience is far from comfortable, and most camels are not used to it. You will see a fair amount of wildlife, but the main point is to experience the magnificent desert and mountain landscapes in the area, and to understand something of Samburu culture (see p.520) through the stories and background you will learn along the way from the herders who accompany you.

Karisia Walking Safaris Tumaren Ranch, near Kimanjo, 80km southeast of Maralal ✆ 061 2309402 (Nairobi office ✆ 020 2064434 or 0721 836792), ✆ karisia.com. All-inclusive camel-assisted walking safaris in the Karisia Hills and Mathews Range, from $338/day.

Ol Maisor Camels Bobong Campsite, north of Rumuruti (see p.510) ✆ 020 2033179, 0735 243075 or 0722 936177 (send an SMS first), ✉ olmaisor@africaonline.co.ke. Camel-assisted walking safaris as far north as Lake Turkana. All-inclusive (including a "modicum" of beer and wine), from Ksh10,000 per person per day.

Wild Frontiers Naro Moru (see p.166) ✆ +8821 643334103 (satellite), ✆ wildfrontierskenya.com. Camel-assisted walking safaris, with one or two riding camels always available. Prices depend on requirements.

(satellite) ⓦkitichcamp.com (Nairobi reservations ☎020 6003090, ⓦchelipeacock.com). Nestled unobtrusively on the river bank beneath towering giant figs, and recently reopened for visitors after years on the back burner, *Kitich* is one of Kenya's most legendary locations, with six generously sized canvas tents and huge open-air, stone showers. The camp is exclusively solar-powered, and it's silver-rated by Ecotourism Kenya. The very personally hosted style, with the main activity being game walks in the forested hills, leaves a lasting impression of a remote and beautiful wilderness, and there are some fine excursions, including short walks up the valley to some deep rock pools where you can swim. Closed April 1–June 15 & Nov 1–Dec 15. Package ⚡**$920**

North to Loiyangalani

Until recently considered a day-long slog – at least – the **road from Maralal to Loiyangalani** has been graded and much improved: "somewhat bumpy" is about the worst description you could currently apply. It's about a five-hour drive in a 4WD.

The first stretch of the road north from Maralal climbs higher into the Podocarpus forests of the **Maralal national sanctuary**, before dropping down across the Lopet Plateau to the Elbarta Plains, 15km east of the scorching Suguta Valley. Settlements from here on are few but evenly scattered. The first two – **Morijo** and, 20km north, **Marti** – each have basic *chai* kiosks, one or two Somali-run stores, a mission and a police station.

Losiolo Escarpment

20km north of Maralal then a 6km detour through Poror, past a large wheat-farming project, to the edge of the escarpment • Ksh350/person to enter the area • Ksh300–600 to camp, depending on your bargaining skills

The Rift Valley is, by its nature, bordered from end to end by vertiginous escarpments and each one seems more impressive than the last. But the dramatic, scimitar edge of **Losiolo** is not just an escarpment; it's a colossal amphitheatre dropping down to the Suguta Valley, 2000m below. Try to get here very early in the morning while the air is still clear.

Baragoi

BARAGOI lies on the northern fringes of the barren Elbarta Plains, 37km north of Marti. Watered only occasionally by run-off from the Samburu Hills and Ndoto Mountains – the *lugga* that skirts the town is dry for much of the year – this is normally a blistering, unforgiving land, dotted here and there with sun-bleached cattle bones. First settled in the 1930s, Baragoi retains its original function as the region's major livestock market, attracting both Samburu from the southeast and Turkana from the northwest, for whom the town is one marker on the once invisible boundary – now usually considered to be the road – between their much disputed grazing lands.

On the northwest side of town is the **livestock market**. It's a gentle, unhurried affair where old men with gnarled hands and ostrich plumes in their hair play *ngiles* (or *mbau*) with stones and seeds on "boards" carved out of the bone-dry earth as they wait for business to arrive. Here, Samburu deal with Rendille and Turkana, some of whom spend up to seven days walking their livestock from Lake Turkana. In turn Samburu trek southeast for five or six days to reach Isiolo, where they aim to resell their animals at a profit.

If the herder is a **courting** age warrior (a *moran* in Samburu or a *lmoli* in Turkana), Isiolo is also where he buys the beads and bangles he needs in order to get a bride. Once back home, he presents the girl with the gifts and hosts a dance to mime and sing the attributes of the animals that will form his "bride wealth" (see box, p.520) and provide the future family with their means of survival. The young herder is expected to build the confidence of a bride-to-be by representing his beasts favourably and, to this end, he selects a single castrated bull, camel or goat, which he then mimics, gesturing to indicate its size, colour, the shape of its horns, even its temperament. There's a comical side, too, for even the poorest herder, trying his luck with a billy goat with lopsided horns, has to dance to attract a spouse, raising a few smiles with a self-deprecating parody of his goat.

Courtship dances are held frequently in the *manyattas* on the outskirts of town. They are wild and hugely enjoyable events, where you'll certainly be made welcome – though cameras are generally not acceptable.

ARRIVAL AND INFORMATION | BARAGOI AND AROUND

One daily **matatu** links Baragoi with Maralal but there are no matatus to Loiyangalani. If you're heading north, you'll have to line up a lift with a supply truck or a mission 4WD – ask at the lodgings and *hotelis*. The police station on the north side of town is helpful in finding likely drivers, but be prepared to wait all day. If you're **driving**, The Star filling station usually has fuel at about twenty percent markup on usual prices, and the *jua kali* repair yard on the south side of the main street has a generator for pumping tyres.

INFORMATION

Services Baragoi has no ATM or forex bureau, although there is a post office on the main street. For **internet**

access, try Digitech Computer Services on the main street (Ksh5/Mb).

ACCOMMODATION AND EATING

Morning Star Guest House Main street, town centre 0725 440974. The best place to stay in Baragoi, this B&L, owned by Paramount Chief Letelen Lenatorono, is very basic – no running water – but the non-s/c rooms are reasonably clean and there's a bar-restaurant on the ground floor. Room only **Ksh600**

Promise Bar A two-minute walk west of the town

centre. Nothing out of the ordinary, but with its fridge full of cold Tuskers (Ksh130) and nicely reggae-fied Samburu atmosphere, this is the standout choice among Baragoi's various watering holes. Daily 24hr.

Tawakal Hotel Main street, town centre. The best *hoteli* in town, with *nyama karanga* for Ksh200 and pilau at Ksh150. Daily dawn to mid-evening.

Mount Nyiru

From Baragoi, which marks the end of the forbidding Elbarta Plains, the road climbs into mountain country where the peaks are fantastically green if there's been rain and even the plains can be covered in a blanket of grass and wild flowers. Rising up ahead on the left is **Mount Nyiru** (also known as the Nyiru Range), a sheer stack of rugged mountains, partly swathed in thick forest, from which giant rocks jut, through which water gushes along steep ravines, and near the top of which perches one of Kenya's most remote and beguiling luxury lodges, **Desert Rose**.

To get here, some 16km north of Baragoi, there's a track to the left, at a T-junction indicated by a pockmarked gas cylinder and a slightly alarming handpainted sign, declaring "Tuum Parish – Land of Peace", showing an AK47 with a red cross through it. This track heads west for 10km then forks (left to Tuum, right to *Desert Rose* and Mount Nyiru). For the lodge, you drive a further 13km, passing through the cool, pretty settlement of **Ewaso Rongai** with its thick covering of huge acacia and fig trees, nestled deep in the valley, then climb a final 2km up a track cut partly through the bed rock and at times so steep and narrow it tests the nerve of even experienced 4WD drivers. The views en route to the track's end, at the high eyrie of *Desert Rose Lodge* – perched on the steep slopes of Mount Nyiru among crags and euphorbias – are magnificent.

ACCOMMODATION AND EATING | MOUNT NYIRU

★ **Desert Rose Lodge** Mount Nyiru, 24km from the Baragoi–South Horr road 0716 575942, desertrosekenya.com (Nairobi reservations 020 3864831, africanterritories.co.ke). Exhilarating to reach (by airstrip, helipad or mountain road), amid the towering landscapes of Mount Nyiru, and deeply relaxing

once you've arrived, this remote and beautiful lodge has five open-plan cottages and does wholesome meals with a bit of zing (home-grown fruit and veg). Unique in Kenya, it's perfect for children and teens, with its pool, local walks and natural waterslide. Patchy wi-fi. Open all year. Package **$1160**

South Horr

Camel hire from Ksh1000/camel per day, plus guide (from Ksh1000/day) and guard/porter fees (from Ksh700/day)

There's a positive jungle all year round at the oasis village of **SOUTH HORR** (*horr* means "flowing water"), the largest settlement between Baragoi and Loiyangalani, wedged tightly between the Nyiru and Ol Doinyo Mara mountains. With its pleasantly somnolent atmosphere, ample shade and relaxed Samburu camel herders lounging under the trees with their beasts, this is a great place to bunk down for a night or three,

SAMBURU DANCE PERFORMANCES

Around South Horr, you are likely to have the mixed pleasure of **Samburu dancing**, especially if you're on an organized safari. Payment of around Ksh1000 allows you to take as many pictures of the dancers as you want. Scepticism is briefly swamped by the hour-long jamboree that follows. A troupe of *morani* goes through an informal dance programme, flirtatiously threatening the audience with whoops and pounces. Young women and girls join in – sometimes with the evident disapproval of older Samburu onlookers – to be mock-propositioned with whisks of the men's ochre hairdos. Meanwhile, there's the constant offering of necklaces, trinkets, spears, tobacco pouches and more photo poses, to be negotiated individually with those who are too old or too young to dance. It's best not to worry about the fleeting illusion of "authenticity" on these occasions, but to accept them for what they are: vivid, funny, dynamic entertainment.

and making friends with local Samburu is easy. It's also a good place from which to set our for a **walk with camels** for a few hours or a few days.

The **mountain forest** around South Horr hides lots of wildlife and bursts with birds and butterflies, though unfortunately, many of the elephants and buffaloes have been poached. You can be guided by Samburu *morani* up the lower slopes of Nyiru and Ol Doinyo Mara, or, more ambitiously, on the stiff hike up to the peak of **Mount Nyiru**, with its stunning views over Lake Turkana. If you're thinking of doing any more daring expeditions in the region, be careful if you're embarking on anything way off the beaten track. Many local men who like to sell themselves as **guides** have led surprisingly sheltered lives and they don't know the desert like the backs of their hands any more than you do. Real knowledge and experience are sought after, and more expensive, so give yourself plenty of time and try to make contacts in advance, contacting a camel safari operator if possible (see p.525).

ACCOMMODATION AND EATING   SOUTH HORR

In South Horr itself, there's a choice of one or two basic B&Ls, and a few cheap *hotelis*. You can get cold drinks at *Arsenal Inn*, and sometimes beer.

Forest Department Campsite South side of the village, up a rough trail to the west of the road 1km south of the centre. Long-drop toilets, an *askari*, and a river that provides drinking water (once you've purified it), bathing spots and a means to wash the dust out of your clothes. Camping Ksh300 per person

Kurungu Teiyo Camp 7.5km north of the sharp left (north) turn on the road through South Horr (on the right, marked by a large concrete sign). No phone. Community camp on the Teiyo River, well shaded with fine old trees. Camping Ksh500 per person

Samburu Sports Center and Guest Lodge North side of the village (marked by a large stone sign on the right), 700m north of where the road through the village turns sharp left ☎0720 334561 or 0724 832088, ⓦsafari sportscamp.com Run by a born-again Christian Samburu couple in partnership with US missionaries, this offers a variety of *bandas*, a range of sports facilities and home-grown produce. All-round fantastic value and free internet, although no alcohol is sold or allowed. HB Ksh2000

From South Horr to the lake

After South Horr, the track winds down between the Nyiru Range to the west and the Ol Doinyo Mara mountains to the east, and for some 40km it stays fast with a sandy surface. Eventually it opens onto a featureless plain of black lava, where the going is much rockier and the gaunt massif of **Mount Kulal** dominates the northern horizon.

Both Samburu and Turkana live in, and move across, this area. The numerous **stone circles** and **cairns** around here are the remains of settlements and burial sites, which you'll come to recognize all over the region. Most distinctive are the low semicircular constructions, which you'll see in use as you approach the lake: these serve as shelters against the viciously hot wind that blows almost incessantly off the flanks of Kulal. The burial cairns are not as ancient as they may appear, as traditionally neither the Turkana nor Samburu buried their dead, but instead simply left the bodies out in the open for wild animals to eat. The more important members of the community, such as blacksmiths and respected elders, were sometimes buried under cairns, or were left in a hut whose door would be walled up. The site would be abandoned and never used again for human habitation. Since independence and the arrival of Christian missions, however, both Turkana and Samburu are now obliged to bury their dead.

As the road drops away in front, **Lake Turkana** suddenly appears, usually as a stunning vista of shot blues and greens, with the black, castellated silhouette of South Island hanging as if suspended between lake and sky. Descending a little further along a rocky stretch of road – known to drivers as The Staircase, part of which has now been concreted – you reach several bays. People have gone swimming here in the past, but crocodiles make this really inadvisable. You pass a few frail and temporary fishing settlements, seemingly stranded among the rocks, and, an hour or so later, reach Loiyangalani.

Loiyangalani

LOIYANGALANI – "the place of the trees" – is a small community far from metropolitan Kenya, a vague agglomeration of grass huts, mud huts, tin shacks, a police station, a school, a few campsites, and a handful of simple tourist lodges. The land around is mostly barren and stony, scattered with the bones of livestock, with palm trees and acacias clustered around the settlement's life source, a **warm spring** of fresh water.

LAKE TURKANA FESTIVAL

Visit Loiyangalani in May or June, and you'll find the annual **Lake Turkana Festival** (Ⓦ lake turkanafestival.com and Ⓦ museums.or.ke) taking place. Initiated in 2008 by the German embassy and coordinated by National Museums of Kenya, members of the ten main peoples of the northwest – Borana, Burji, Dassanech, El Molo, Gabbra, Konso, Rendille, Samburu, Turkana and Wata – gather in their thousands, in finest traditional garb, to dance and sing.

But the festival is as much about **reconciliation** as it is about partying. It brings together tribes who have frequently fought over grazing rights and have bitter histories of conflict and mutually exclusive world views. It's a memorable experience to wander down Loiyangalani's main street – renamed Festival Avenue for the occasion – and see a group of Samburu warriors in their best beads and hair being appraised by their opposite numbers from the Turkana community, and then see a cluster of Dassanech girls from the far north, being admired by two Borana elders.

After two days of sponsors' presentations, development forums, and impromptu rehearsals at various locations around Loiyangalani, the high point of the festival comes on the **third afternoon**. Everyone troops out to the festival grounds (a flat piece of desert, with a useful rocky ridge on one side that gives local kids a good vantage point) and – after a series of suitably verbose speeches by various politicians finally ends – each tribe's festival troupe takes it in turn to present their culture through music and dance.

It's not a huge event, which means you can get as close to the action as you want. There's a marquee and seating – first come, first served – but it's just as much fun to wander through the crowds of locals and participants, visit the **ethnic houses** at the edge of the arena that each troupe has built, and enjoy an atmosphere of unrestrained goodwill. The festival is also a photographer's dream. Everyone takes pictures of everyone (including locals, with their mobiles, of tourists), and for the occasion, nobody minds or dreams of asking for payment.

As the sun goes down, the performances shift from vivid dance and song to message-driven drama, then a fashion show in traditional costume, and then a disco, capped by a famous local singer. In 2012, the activist popster Eric Wainaina got a huge response from the very receptive audience, with traditionally clad Turkana and Samburu women trying out their moves on the dancefloor while adoring fans took to the stage to sing along.

Festival events (all free) are held at various sites around Loiyangalani. If you want to attend, book accommodation and transport as early as possible, as the festival's growth may outstrip Loiyangalani's ability to manage the number of visitors attending.

Festival Ground ▲ | ☐ AIC Mission, Desert Museum, ▲ Elmolo Bay, North Horr & Sibiloi National Park

☐ ACCOMMODATION
Kifaru Lodging 2
Malabo Resort 1
Mama Changa's 5
Mosaretu Camp 4
Oasis Lodge 3
Palm Shade Camp 6

● RESTAURANTS & BARS
Bamboo Fast Food 2
Cold Drink Hotel 3
Mpaso Bar 2
Nameless Hoteli 1

200 metres

LOIYANGALANI

Catholic Mission

The village – it's barely a town – came into being in the early 1960s with the arrival of the Italian mission to the **Elmolo** people and the first incarnation of *Oasis Lodge* (built in 1958). Somali raiders ransacked both establishments in 1965 – incidents reprised in some of the later scenes in Fernando Meirelles' film *The Constant Gardener*, which were shot here and made the town look like Darfur – but since then they have been left alone.

The original people of the area are the El Molo, a small group who live by hunting and fishing on the southeastern lakeshore, but there has been so much reconciliation of previously warring groups in the area, and intermarriage, that a new ethnic group – the so-called **Elmosaretu**, or El Molo, Samburu, Rendille and Turkana – is often cited as being the "tribe" of the district, and people proudly remind visitors of the annual Lake Turkana Festival (see box, p.529) and the peaceful progress being made here. The mission, too, is thriving as its net of influence reaches out to most of Loiyangalani's more permanent inhabitants, especially the children who attend the school.

For all its apparent drabness, Loiyangalani is far from dull. When you've had enough of haggling in what passes for the high street for artefacts and fantastic quartz, onyx, amethyst and other semi-precious stones collected from Kulal, as well as the odd fossil fish vertebra, you can stroll around the south side of the village to the mission and school. You'll inevitably pick up a cluster of teenagers eager to practise their English. Swahili has never made much impact in this part of Kenya and English is the usual teaching medium. Education is perhaps the most positive of the major influences, including tourism, state interference and Christianity, that pressurize local customs and traditions.

Desert Museum

4km north of Loiyangalani • Daily 8am–6pm • Ksh500

Loiyangalani's Italian-funded **Desert Museum** is a purpose-built, crescent-shaped exhibition space in a fine location overlooking the lake. Although it displays photos about the eight different tribes of the north, and clearly deserves support, what is on offer – an information centre, essentially – is much too limited in scope for the entry price.

Loiyangalani beach

2km west of Loiyangalani

Loiyangalani's **beach** is a grubby strip of gravel. People do swim here, and during the annual Lake Turkana Festival (see box, p.529) one morning is usually devoted to boat races and other events. Crocodiles rarely venture this close to town, but never say never. The beach has other potential dangers too: many of the loose stones on the shore shelter scorpions and carpet vipers. A scorpion sting isn't too serious but a viper bite can be dangerous if not treated.

ARRIVAL AND INFORMATION   LOIYANGALANI

There is no regular ground transport or flights to Loiyangalani. You'll need to put the word around in the village and visit the lodge and the camps to see if any vehicles are going your way. There is no petrol station and you should bring all the fuel you need. In an emergency, supplies are available in small quantities.

Services Loiyangalani has a post office in the town centre and a reasonable mobile network, but there is no ATM or forex bureau.

GOD'S WORK

The **Loiyangalani mission**, while changing the structure of traditional society through conversions to Catholicism (particularly sweeping among the Elmolo), is at the same time helping to make local people sufficiently independent to resist unwanted change and to make choices about their future, by helping to set up income-generating schemes such as shops, boats and the service station. Some of the Italian missionaries are extremely open and informative and the chance to talk to them may well arise if you're around for a few days. For non-Christians, however, the whole concept of missionaries and their work can be difficult to swallow. For all their schools and clinics, it's difficult to escape the feeling that the local people – for so long "untouched" by the outside world – managed very well with their original beliefs and traditions, which underpinned their society, cosmology and relationships. With Christianity now ascendant, the old structures are breaking down fast and some risk being lost completely. And by preferring to convert children, rather than their more obstinate parents, the deeper morality of the well-meaning missionaries is questionable at best.

ACCOMMODATION

7

Wherever you stay in Loiyangalani, be prepared for **wind and dust**: it just never stops. Campers, in particular, tend to struggle, because pegs get yanked out and everything blows away. Nights can be noisy too, with palm fronds crashing together overhead. Accommodation fills up during the festival, so **book** well in advance. For **meals and drinks**, there are one or two grocery stores and very elementary *hotelis* along the main street, but *Cold Drink Hotel*, the best known, is more of a TV hall these days and the camps or lodge are a better bet for meals and drinks.

Kifaru Lodging Loiyangalani centre (no phone). Also known as *Rhino Camp* (*kifaru* meaning rhino), this very basic central camp, with small *bandas* protected by elementary security, has long-drop loos and an erratic water supply. You'll be lucky to get much in the way of bedding for your foam mattress. Room only **Ksh600**

Malabo Resort North side of town, east of the airstrip ☎0724 705800, ⓦbit.ly/Malabo. Brand-new place, still being finished at the time of writing, with spacious round s/c *bandas*. While the infrastructure is sound, the shadeless setting leaves something to be desired and it's quite overpriced. Good sunset views. BB **Ksh4000**

Mama Changa's Behind Cold Drink Hotel. Eighteen clean, non s/c rooms with nets, a simple outdoor shower (sun-heated water until mid-evening) and a fairly hygienic pit latrine. The ladies here will cook for you if you provide the ingredients (Ksh100 each). Room only **Ksh1000**

Mosaretu Camp Loiyangalani centre ⓦbit.ly /Mosaretu. Run by the Mosaretu Women's Group and offering camping as well as traditional *bandas* under the palm trees, with mosquito nets and mattresses. Facilities include toilets, showers, a curio shop and a shared kitchen. Camping **Ksh300** per person; *bandas* **Ksh1000**

Oasis Lodge Loiyangalani centre ☎0729 954672, ⓦoasis-lodge.com. German-run lodge of 18 fairly basic, twin-bedded chalet-style rooms, that tries to be exclusive, and certainly charges as if it were. Although conceived as a fishing lodge, they don't always have a boat available, and their 4WD vehicle hire – another facility – is also barely operational (one small Datsun, seating four, $200/day). The views from the bar-restaurant and their two pools are the main draws (Ksh500 daily entrance fee to casual visitors allows use of the pools). Meals are largely set menus (breakfast Ksh1500, lunch and dinner Ksh2000). Soda Ksh250, beer Ksh250, wine Ksh1500 bottle. FB **$240**

★ **Palm Shade Camp** Loiyangalani centre ☎0726 714768. This well-kept, shady site with 11 reasonably cool non s/c *bandas* with nets is worth booking, especially during the festival. The very decent shared European toilets and adequate shared showers are supplied direct from the warm springs, decent meals (Ksh400) are available and the water (Ksh100/litre), sodas (Ksh70) and beers (Ksh160) are sometimes even cold. There's also a generator till late evening and a charging point by the dining area. Camping **Ksh500** per person; *bandas* **Ksh2000**

EATING AND DRINKING

Loiyangalani doesn't have a single establishment you could honestly call a restaurant. During the Lake Turkana Festival, some of the places below turn a faster trade than usual, but for most of the year food that's ready to serve is the exception rather than the rule. Most places can offer chapattis, rice, meat and sometimes fish – eventually – but you may find providing extra raw ingredients to the cook – tomatoes, potatoes, garlic and carrots, for example – is the best way to be sure of a good meal. They'll make a vegetable stew or cook them to order for a small fee. During the festival, the camps or lodge can be a better bet for (more expensive) meals and drinks.

7

LOIYANGALANI DANCES

In the evenings, dances often take place around Loiyangalani – informal, energetic, pogo-style performances for fun, that are always worth checking out. Track them down by the booming sound of collective larynxes. At Loiyangalani it's often the girls who ask the boys to dance, and you're welcome to join in. As usual, no cameras are allowed unless permission is expressly given and paid for (usually Ksh1000/person).

Bamboo Fast Food Main street, north side, opposite Cold Drink Hotel. "Fast" is purely relative: they only cook to order and don't have a menu to choose from, but you can certainly eat reasonably well here for Ksh300. And they do boast a large fridge which comes on in the morning and by sunset is providing cold water and sodas (but no beer; it's a Muslim establishment). Daily 7am–8pm.

Cold Drink Hotel Main street, south side. There's always food available here (good pancakes, for example, Ksh150), but cold drinks can't be guaranteed. Daily early until late.

Mpaso Bar 20m behind Bamboo Fast Food. Mpaso ("The Lake") sells pleasingly cold Tuskers and stays open late – although as the evening wears on some of the clientele can become a nuisance, especially to female customers. Daily mid-morning to 11pm.

Nameless hoteli Main street, towards the lake, on the north side of the road across from Kifaru Lodging. Go for a breakfast of *mandaazi* and chai and order lunch or dinner in advance. They do excellent lake fish, and will gladly make a vegetable stew if you provide the raw ingredients. Expect to pay around Ksh200 for breakfast and Ksh300 for lunch or dinner. Daily 7am–8pm.

Elmolo Bay

8km north of Loiyangalani • Ksh1000/person paid to the headman, which includes permission to take photos

The last viable community of Elmolo people (see box opposite) lives at **ELMOLO BAY**. During the week, many children are at school in Loiyangalani; they come home at the weekend, which is the best time to visit. There are two very small villages – **Layeni** 8km north of Loiyangalani, facing an island 500m offshore, and **Komote**, 4km further north, on the other side of the bay, where there is a church. Which of the two villages you visit depends on whom you hook up with in Loiyangalani, and their contacts. Visiting independently isn't encouraged: the Elmolo like to be advised by mobile that visitors are expected.

Impromptu dances start and little hands are slipped engagingly into yours for a walk around the low, grass huts. If you have a digital camera you'll be extremely popular with the village children, eager to look at their image on screen. You will also be shown the "market", a stall in the centre of the village displaying beadwork, belts, fertility dolls and gourds which you're invited to buy. It's a novel, disturbing experience that contrives to be stage-managed and voyeuristic at the same time. Because of their friendliness, their small number and the increased interest shown in them, the Elmolo risk being taken advantage of by tourists. However, the usual rules apply: ask before you take pictures and be generous with your time and your wallet. Incidentally, don't get worried when a mother hands you her child, then asks for money; she's not selling her offspring, but simply wants you to sponsor the child's education with a large wad of cash.

If you're taken over to the island facing Layeni, you should see **crocodiles** if you walk softly and approach the far shore cautiously. On the stern, rocky beaches on the western side, the remains of Elmolo fish picnics and old camps, even the occasionally virtually fossilized hippo tusk, can be found everywhere.

South Island National Park

$20 • Ⓦ kws.go.ke • 39 square kilometres

If you want to visit the Unesco World Heritage Site of **South Island National Park**, you should first ask about a trip at *Oasis Lodge* (see p.531), but spread the word and you may find a much cheaper means of getting there. It's a 30km round trip, so the weather needs to be fair. Although the warden doesn't always grant permission to camp there for the night, if you get the chance, it's one of the weirdest places to stay: its volcanic vents, rising some 300m above lake level, give out a ghostly luminous glow that has long put off local fishermen from venturing there.

Mount Kulal

It's a tough trip, but you could make a stab at climbing **Mount Kulal** (2285m), comprising two summits joined by a narrow and dicey ridge. The climb itself, once you're on the right track, is straightforward enough, but talk to some gem-hunters in town who should be able to guide you up for a negotiable fee. Note that, although Kulal seems to tower over Loiyangalani (its summit is more than 1900m above the lake), two days is barely enough to walk to the base and back, and the summit is 25km east of Loiyangalani as the crow flies. Factor in wind, dust and heat and you can see why you'd be well advised to get transport as far up the mountain as possible before you start climbing (expect to bargain hard, and end up paying Ksh12,000–15,000 for a day's vehicle hire with driver). The views from the top are fabulous, with the lake on

---

THE ELMOLO

The people of Loiyangalani with the best claim to being its original inhabitants are the **Elmolo**. The Elmolo call themselves *el-Des*, but their usual name comes from the Samburu *loo molo onsikirri*, "the people who eat fish". They once inhabited South Island, but now occupy a few clusters of grass huts on the torrid shores 8km north of Loiyangalani. Most of the six hundred-strong community lives here, partly by fishing and the occasional heroic crocodile or hippo hunt (officially banned), and partly by cash receipts from tourist visitors.

The Elmolo are enigmatic. At the time of Teleki's discovery of the lake, they spoke a **Cushitic** language, the family of languages to which Somali and Rendille belong. Recent linguistic research on historical migrations points to their having arrived on the shores of Lake Turkana at a very early time – perhaps more than 2000 years ago. They seem to have no tradition of livestock herding, which might have been kept up if they had turned, like the Turkana, to fishing as a supplement. Today they speak the Samburu dialect of Maa (the last Elmolo-speaker died in 1998) and have started to intermarry with the Samburu. This, as well as the mission's influence, has been quite significant in raising their numbers (from fewer than 200 fifty-odd years ago) but also in diluting their cultural identity. Once strictly monogamous, polygamy isn't uncommon now, and they also send many children to the school in Loiyangalani as weekly boarders. On the slope, right behind the village, looms the fairly recent Catholic church.

All this signals the final curtain for a culture and history that has been largely ignored or denied. The conventional wisdom about hunter-gatherers in Kenya is that they are often the descendants of pastoralists who lost their herds. But if the Elmolo are, as some say, pastoral Rendille who took to fishing in order to survive, then it's strange that they have never tried to replace their herds. For without herds, they could never hope to pay bride wealth for wives from their non-fishing neighbours in the traditional way. A better explanation, and one favoured by the Elmolo themselves, is that their people have always been fishermen and hunters and that pressures from other tribes, particularly the Turkana, had pushed them almost to the point of annihilation.

By the end of the twentieth century, the Elmolo fishing culture was rubbing off on other ethnic groups and even the Samburu had started to eat fish. As long ago as 1972, Peter Matthiessen wrote in *The Tree Where Man was Born*:

The Samburu and Turkana may linger for weeks at a time as guests of the Llo-molo, who have plenty of fish and cannot bear to eat with all these strangers hanging around looking so hungry. Other tribes, the Llo-molo say, know how to eat fish better than they know how to catch them … "We have to feed them," one Llo-molo says, "so that they will feel strong enough to go away."

The Elmolo are a charming and hospitable people, and how they survive in their chosen environment is hard to imagine. They are slightly smaller than the other peoples of the area, but the bowed legs that are supposed to be the characteristic result of their diet seem to be confined to the older people – you might have thought all that fish would give them strong bones.

one side and the searing Chalbi Desert on the other, and birdwatchers have the added incentive of a rare species of **white-eye** peculiar to the mountain. Bring all the water you'll need, as there are no supplies on the mountain.

Sibiloi National Park

Between Lake Turkana and Ethiopian border • $20 • ⓦ sibiloi.com, ⓦ bit.ly/Sibiloi • Possibly the best way of visiting the fossil sites is by timing your trip to coincide with a field school organized by the National Museums of Kenya in tandem with Rutgers University in the USA (approximately mid-June to the end of July; ⓦ koobifora.rutgers.edu) • 1571 square kilometres

Sibiloi National Park, a huge area stretching inland from Lake Turkana's northeast shore, provides, with its surprisingly abundant wildlife and famous **fossil sites**, a powerful incentive to continue further north. The so-called **Camp Turkana**, near the shore just south of Alia Bay, is the administrative centre marking the park's southern boundary and is where you'll find the KWS park headquarters. The National Museums of Kenya research base camp at **Koobi Fora**, the headland halfway up the park's coast (ⓦkfrp .com), is 30km further north. Koobi Fora is said to be a Gabbra corruption of Commiphora – the thorny bush of the region.

The fossils

Sibiloi was created to protect the sites of numerous remarkable **hominin fossil** finds that have been made since 1968 by Richard Leakey's, and latterly Kamoya Kimeu's, teams from the University of Nairobi. The rock desert and arid bush that makes up the park is an exceptional source because many of the fossils are found on the surface, blown clean by the never-ending wind. The finds set back the dates of intelligent, cooperative, tool-making behaviour among hominins further and further all the time. Most of the species concerned, however, are assumed to have died out, and the crucial discoveries that will link humankind to our prehuman ancestors have yet to be made. One striking find made at Sibiloi in 1972 was the skull labelled "1470", first thought to be of a *Homo habilis* ("Handy man") and then renamed *Homo rudolfensis* ("Rudolf man"), which is about 1.9 million years old. Although quite different from other species of early human-like primates, with its large brain and big, flat face, Rudolf man may yet be shown to be a direct ancestor of modern *Homo sapiens*. As more and more hominin discoveries are made at Sibiloi and on the other side of Lake Turkana (where excavations have yielded the earliest *australopithecine* yet discovered, *Australopithecus anamensis*, dated to between 4.2 and 3.9 million years), the evolutionary theories continue to flesh out.

Wildlife

At times, Sibiloi National Park has a wealth of **wildlife**. Indeed, until the 1930s, there were large numbers of elephant living here. Rainless years, ivory hunters and, especially, increases in the herds of livestock contributed to their demise. But lion, cheetah, hyena, both kinds of zebra (the ordinary Grant's and the finer-striped, taller Grevy's), giraffe, ostrich, Grant's gazelle, topi, kudu and gerenuk all occur here. Because of their protection from hunters, hippos and crocodiles are also numerous. The tree cover is minimal: the only trees you might see are in the petrified forest of stone trunks, at the **Sibiloi Fossil Forest**, a few kilometres east of the park headquarters – reminders of the lush vegetation of the lakeshore in prehistoric times.

Koobi Fora Museum

Koobi Fora Base Camp • Daily 8am–6pm • Ksh500 • ⓦ museums.or.ke; daily 8am–6pm

The small **Koobi Fora Museum**, where hominin fossils were formerly displayed alongside dioramas of prehistoric life, is well worth a visit while you're in the area – though they've moved the valuable remains to Nairobi and less impressive bones now make up most of the exhibits. Nearby, however, are several *in situ* fossil presentations, displayed exactly as they were unearthed, and left in the ground: of a prehistoric crocodile, a two-million-year-old elephant – estimated to have been as much as 6m in height – and a gigantic prehistoric tortoise as big as a small dinghy, that apparently died on its back, unable to right itself.

ARRIVAL AND DEPARTURE

SIBILOI NATIONAL PARK

By local truck or supply vehicle Vehicles heading up from Loiyangalani or Marsabit are rare and you could wait a week or more.

By 4WD A day's drive should get you from Loiyangalani to the park headquarters at Alia Bay. Driving along the Loiyangalani-North Horr road, turn north after some 45km. From here, a desolate track heads more or less due north for 40km to the settlement of Hurran Hurra, where a left turn should bring you to the camel watering-point and settlement of Gajos, another 40km northwest. Another left here (heading west, then northwest) begins the 15km gentle descent to the lake and the national park HQ. Leaving the park northwards,

driving to Ileret and the unmarked Ethiopian border is straightforward. If you want to drive into Ethiopia here, you have to report to immigration at Omorate, just as if you were coming from Lokitaung on the west side of the lake.

By plane or boat Apart from chartering a plane from Nairobi's Wilson airport (see p.138), an alternative way of getting to Sibiloi is by boat from Ferguson's Gulf on the lake's western shore, near Kalokol (p.517). There's an infrequent National Museums supply boat from here. Expect to pay anything from Ksh20,000 to Ksh30,000 for the round trip, and probably no less if you choose not to return to the western shore.

ACCOMMODATION

Allia Bay Guesthouse KWS park headquarters, Allia Bay ☎0735 815601 (Nairobi reservations ☎0726 610508, ⊛kws.go.ke). A three-room self-catering cottage sleeping five, with solar electricity, bathroom, lounge and functional kitchen. Whole house $100

KWS Campsites Near the KWS park HQ, Allia Bay ☎0735 815601 (Nairobi reservations ☎0726 610508, ⊛kws.go.ke). There's a choice of three sites, one by the lake and two inland, but there are no facilities – you'll have to be entirely self-sufficient. Camping $15 per person

Koobi Fora Bandas Research Base Camp, Koobi Fora (Nairobi reservations ☎020 8164134, ⊛museums .or.ke). These simple dorms with nets and shared European loos and showers can be used except in June and July when they're full of American research students. Dorm beds Ksh1000

Museum Bandas 3km southeast of the Research Base Camp, Koobi Fora, 300m from the shore (Nairobi reservations ☎020 8164134, ⊛museums.or.ke). Basic *bandas* in a remote spot, with three single beds each, shared showers, toilets and kitchen. Room only Ksh1000

The northeast

Travel in northeastern Kenya has a special quality. For much of the time, the normal stimuli – passing scenery, animals, people and fleetingly witnessed events – are replaced with a massive open sky, shimmering greenish-brown earth, and, just occasionally, a speck of movement. It might be some camels, a pair of ostriches, or perhaps a family moving somewhere with their donkeys. It's a sparse, absorbingly simple landscape, and not the least of its attractions is the restful absence of hassle and shove, and a solitude hardly found anywhere else.

GETTING AROUND

NORTHEASTERN KENYA

Although the distances are huge, northeastern Kenya has a relatively restricted travel circuit because two-thirds of it is effectively an off-limits "orange zone" (see box, p.537)). From **Isiolo** the most popular route simply goes north to **Marsabit** and **Marsabit National Park**. Most people who visit **Moyale** are going on to Ethiopia, or arriving from there; while **Garissa** provides an interesting route to the coast that is marginally outside the "orange zone".

You can also head northwest from Marsabit to **Lake Turkana**, via North Horr and some of the country's remotest districts; or do the reverse, leaving the more frequented route from Maralal to Lake Turkana and heading east to Marsabit. The region gets little tourism, because what appear to be major roads on the map often turn out to be rough – and at times almost indiscernible – tracks.

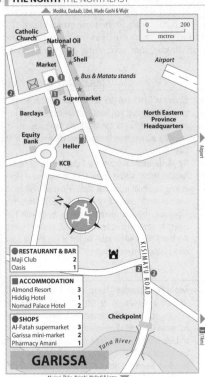

RESTAURANT & BAR
| Maji Club | 2 |
| Oasis | 1 |

ACCOMMODATION
Almond Resort	3
Hiddig Hotel	1
Nomad Palace Hotel	2

SHOPS
Al-Fatah supermarket	3
Garissa mini-market	2
Pharmacy Amani	1

GARISSA

Garissa

Some 390km east of Nairobi, on the route to Somalia, **GARISSA** is the capital of North Eastern Province, sprawling out widely across the plains, east of the bridge across the Tana River. It's the furthest east you can safely go towards Somalia without an armed escort: indeed, with its access road checkpoints and busy military presence it's long been considered the safest town in Kenya, and, despite gun and grenade attacks on churches in 2012, attributed to Al-Shabaab, it remains a relatively laidback town, with next to no hustle.

While at times the well-surfaced streets, offices and NGO presence make it feel a little like the offspring of Nairobi and Mombasa, a visit to the teeming market will remind you that you're in a largely Somali town – and reckoned to be Kenya's hottest (the thermometer rarely leaves the 32–37°C range during the day). Apart from the lively **central market**, which has some particularly nice merchants' courtyards on the eastern side, there are few other attractions, though the huge Wednesday **livestock market** is one.

Still, several surprisingly good hotels, and the other services here, make it a very likely stopover if you're travelling in the region.

ARRIVAL AND DEPARTURE

GARISSA

By buses/matatu There's a stream of vehicles daily between Garissa and Nairobi, with most Nairobi-bound buses terminating in Eastleigh's busy 12th Street. Transport south along the Tana, and onto Malindi and Mombasa, is more intermittent. Taking buses north or east is highly inadvisable.

Destinations Hola (2 daily; 3hr; Ksh400); Malindi (2 daily; 8hr; Ksh800); Mombasa (2 daily; 11hr; Ksh1100); Nairobi (10 daily; 7hr; Ksh700).

By car The A3 highway to Nairobi is fast and smooth for much of its length, with just one nasty section of potholed surface about 60km west of Garissa. Driving down the Tana on the B8 is a different matter, and you're best off with a

4WD with good suspension, plenty of fuel and two spare tyres. From the Garissa–Hola T-junction (13km west of the bridge), the road south is badly potholed at irregular intervals, but long good stretches mean a 40km/h average speed is possible. The road is particularly bad south of the Bura junction for 40km, where you'll make better speed off the road, on the sidetracks, than on it. The first 30km south of the Hola junction (where work extending north from Malindi has reached) is good tarmac. Thereafter, it's a mixture of re-surfacing and road-building as you pass the Garsen junction and the junction for Witu and Mokowe (Lamu). You can do Garissa–Malindi in five hours, but six is more comfortable.

INFORMATION

Services The KCB, Barclays and Equity banks have ATMs. There are no chain supermarkets, but Al-Fatah, beneath the *Hiddig Hotel*, is reasonable, while the friendly *Garissa mini-market* imports goods from the UK and is also a bit cheaper.

Pharmacy Amani (0725 580260; daily 6am–10pm) offers a wide range of medical services, including malaria tests (Ksh100).

TRAVEL IN THE NORTHEAST: A WARNING

Northeastern Kenya has long had a reputation for lawlessness, but what was sometimes dismissed as the exaggerations and ignorance of "down-country" Kenyans acquired a more brutal reality in the 1990s, which continues to this day.

Since the flight of **Somalia**'s dictator Siad Barre in 1991, and that country's anarchic disintegration into warring fiefdoms, northeastern Kenya has borne the full brunt of Somalia's desperate refugee crisis, with increasingly violent bandits targeting commercial vehicles, foreign aid workers and refugee camps.

The northeast is also home to **pastoralist tribes** who frequently engage in livestock rustling and clash over grazing and water rights. All this has been made more volatile by the prolonged drought in the region. You can be sure of one thing: there are more people than ever before with little to their names but guns and ammunition.

We've endeavoured to note the current security situation for all parts of this chapter, but as the lifetime of this guide extends to 2016, and the situation can change quickly, you are strongly advised to seek advice on the ground before travelling anywhere covered in the following pages. If you're driving in this region, ask advice everywhere you go and always stop at police checkpoints and ask them about the road ahead. You may sometimes be asked to travel in convoy, or to take an armed police officer as an escort to your next stop.

The main **no-go area** at the time of writing is the entire region of northeast Kenya east of the A2 Isiolo–Marsabit–Moyale road and north of the A3 Thika–Garissa road (but not including those roads themselves, and not including Shaba National Reserve or Meru National Park, both of which are safe). Wajir and Mandera, fascinating and remote as they are, are too close to the Somalia border to contemplate visiting at present.

7

ACCOMMODATION AND EATING

Garissa's **hotels** offer great value for money. Most don't bother to provide hot water, figuring guests will rarely want it. As for **meals**, finding tasty pilau or pasta is easy enough, although many establishments are dry, and neither sell, nor permit the consumption of, alcohol.

Almond Resort Signposted on the right, 1km along Lamu Rd ☎046 2102268 or 0711 829899, ⓦalmond -resort.com. With 80 rooms, each with DSTV, decent nets and free wi-fi (but no fans), this is a strong rival for *Nomad Palace*, and the huge, inviting pool (Ksh500 for non-guests) might just clinch it if you have your own transport. There's a large a/c option too, though as usual no bar (the neighbouring police mess substitutes). BB Ksh4500

Hiddig Hotel Opposite the Post Office ☎046 2102303 or 0720 963377. Simple but respectable rooms with a/c, fans, nets and DSTV in a convenient, central part of town, very close to shops and restaurants. BB Ksh2500

Maji Welfare & Sports Association Club Kisimayu Rd, opposite the Nomad Palace. Compared with the average

upcountry bar, this is very sedate and not particularly sporty, with outdoor tables and TVs and sodas at Ksh70, beers at Ksh150. Daily 8am–11pm.

★ **Nomad Palace Hotel** Kisimayu Rd ☎046 2103245 or 0715 294300, ⓦnomadpalacehotel.com. With a/c, fans, nets and DSTV in its comfortable rooms, plus free wi-fi, this large, mid-range place is the choice of NGOs and officials, and does good food in the shady courtyard (pizza from Ksh400, *mishkaki* Ksh300). They don't serve alcohol, but the *Maji Club* is one minute away across the street. Great value. BB Ksh3000

Oasis Near the bus stages. This recommended *hoteli* has all the staples: get your fix of *mandaazi*, *chai* and *karanga na chapatti* (Ksh180). Daily 6.30am–10pm.

Isiolo

ISIOLO – the northeast's most important town and the hub for travel to Marsabit and Moyale – is a frontier in every respect. The **Somali influence** here is noticeable everywhere in the northeast, and Isiolo is one of their most important towns in Kenya. It was here that many veteran Somali soldiers from World War I were settled: having been recruited in Aden and Kismayu, they gave up their nomadic lifestyle to become livestock dealers and retail traders.

The town is a real **cultural kaleidoscope**, with Boran, Meru, Samburu and some Turkana inhabitants, as well as the Somalis. To someone newly arrived from Nanyuki or Meru, the upland towns seem ordinary in comparison. Women from the irrigated *shambas* around Isiolo sell cabbages, tomatoes and carrots in the busy market; cattle owners, nomadic camel traders and merchants exchange greetings and the latest news from Nairobi and Moyale; in the livestock market, goats scamper through the alleys, while hawkers stroll along the road raising their Somali swords and strings of bangles to the minibuses heading up to reserves. And, in the shade, energetic *miraa*-chewing and hanging around are the major occupations. *Miraa* has a long history in Somali culture; the Nyambeni Hills, where most of the Kenyan crop is grown, are just 30km away (p.182).

The town is lively and welcoming, relatively safe and generally hassle-free, though it has become outrageously scruffy and litter-strewn in recent years. And when the tourist season is in full swing, with vehicles driving through to Samburu and the other reserves, it can seem as if you can't take a step here without being approached to buy something. If you're staying the night it's worth getting up early enough to have a chance of seeing the distinctive silhouette of **Mount Kenya** rising directly above the main A2 highway through town, 60km to the south.

ARRIVAL AND DEPARTURE
ISIOLO

By bus or matatu For southbound matatus it's best to be at the market stage before sunrise – last departures at 6am are not unheard of for some destinations. For matatus heading north to Wamba, Archer's Post and Merille, the same time applies at their stages around Equity Bank. You can book bus tickets at their stages and offices the evening before.

Destinations Archer's Post (many daily; 30min; Ksh150); Maralal (3 daily; 5hr; Ksh900); Marsabit (daily with Liban and/or Moyale Express: 6hr; Ksh1200); Merille (several

daily; 3hr; Ksh500); Meru (many daily; 1hr; Ksh200); Nairobi (several daily; 5–6hr; Ksh600–900); Moyale (several weekly; 18hr-plus; Ksh1500); Nanyuki (many daily; 2hr; Ksh300); Maua, for Meru National Park (several daily; 2hr 30min; Ksh400); Wamba (5 daily; 3hr; Ksh500).

By truck or hitchhiking There are usually trucks at least daily up to Marsabit and 2–3 times weekly to Moyale. Most take passengers, charging Ksh800 to Marsabit and Ksh1500 to Moyale, with supplements to ride in the cab (journey

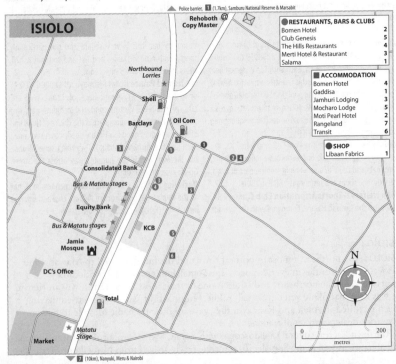

Police barrier, **1** (1.7km), Samburu National Reserve & Marsabit

Rehoboth
Copy Master

ISIOLO

RESTAURANTS, BARS & CLUBS	
Bomen Hotel	2
Club Genesis	5
The Hills Restaurants	4
Merti Hotel & Restaurant	3
Salama	1

ACCOMMODATION	
Bomen Hotel	4
Gaddisa	1
Jamhuri Lodging	3
Mocharo Lodge	5
Moti Pearl Hotel	2
Rangeland	7
Transit	6

SHOP	
Libaan Fabrics	1

Northbound Lorries

Shell

Barclays

Oil Com

Consolidated Bank

Bus & Matatu stages

Equity Bank

Bus & Matatu stages

KCB

Jamia Mosque

DC's Office

Total

N

Market

Matatu Stage

0   200
metres

7 (10km), Nanyuki, Meru & Nairobi

times unpredictable). For Samburu, Buffalo Springs and Shaba National Reserves (see p.374), Isiolo is the town through which nearly all road safari tourists pass.

By car The days of Isiolo being a bottleneck for cars waiting to join police convoys appear to be over, thanks to the fast new A2 highway that sweeps north through Archer's Post and on to Merille, 137km north of Isiolo. Even the gravel road from Merille to Marsabit has recently been graded, meaning the whole drive can be done in half a day. At the time of writing, early 2013, convoys were not being used for most vehicles.

INFORMATION

Services There are branches of KCB, Barclays, Consolidated and Equity banks, all with ATMs. For internet access try Rehoboth Copy Master (Mon–Fri 8am–6pm, Sat 8.30am–6pm; Ksh1.50/min).

ACCOMMODATION

Isiolo has some reasonable, mid-range **hotels** and some very cheap basic lodgings. You can **camp** at the *Gaddisa*, which has Isiolo's only pool, and in the gardens of the pleasant *Rangeland Hotel*.

★ **Bomen Hotel** Off the A2 highway, central Isiolo ☎064 52389 or 0705 309448. The busiest place in town: clean, polite and serving good lunchtime buffets in its restaurant. Rooms lack fans but are s/c and have nets, TVs and electric showers. The breezy top-floor suites are relatively good value for Ksh1000 extra. Free wi-fi (in theory). BB **Ksh3500**

Gaddisa 2km up the Garba Tula road (turn right at the police barrier) ☎0724 201115 or 0735 646370, ⍟gaddisa .com. Dutch-owned country hotel on the outskirts of town, still open after many years despite often seeming nearly empty. The seven rooms, facing onto the garden, are decent, clean and comfortable, and the huge, deep pool is operational. It's a good overlanders' base and also offers day-trips to Samburu National Reserve in a seven-seater Land Cruiser ($200). Camping **Ksh500** per person; BB **Ksh4500**

★ **Jamhuri Lodging** Off the A2 highway, central Isiolo ☎0722 384544. Newly renovated, clean, courteous, mellow (no alcohol or prostitutes allowed) and incredibly cheap, although rooms are non-s/c (there are s/c rooms for Ksh50 more in their building around the corner). Hot water mornings only. The nets are a bit perfunctory and/or badly hung, but the instant showers look safer than usual. Secure parking in the compound. Room only **Ksh450**

Mocharo Lodge Off the A2 highway, central Isiolo ☎064 2385. With excellent security, top-floor "suites", with TV and nets, and a good dining room downstairs, this is very good value for money. Safe parking in courtyard. BB **Ksh1500**

Moti Pearl Hotel A2 Highway, central Isiolo ☎064 52400 or 0725 800820, ⍟moti.co.ke. Although shiny and new, this aspiring "pearl of Isiolo" is too lacking in atmosphere to be really appealing. The balconies are good, but apart from the functional breakfast room, there's nowhere to eat or hang out and alcohol is neither served nor tolerated. BB **Ksh3500**

Rangeland 10km south of Isiolo ☎0720 060038 or 0721 434353 ⍟rangelandhotels.com. Set in pleasant grounds, around which hyraxes scamper, the s/c rooms in the eight garden cottages are decent value, with nets but no other extras. A little above the average B&L, this is a popular out-of-town drinking spot, and tends to be noisy in the evenings. Camping **Ksh500** per person; BB **Ksh2500**

Transit Off the A2 highway, central Isiolo ☎0723 362669. Simple, clean rooms with nets and fans but old-style showers (hot water mornings only), and not as good as *Mocharo*, which it competes with. Forty-eight rooms, comfy enough, but overpriced. BB **Ksh2500**

EATING AND DRINKING

Most of the Somali *hotelis* provide excellent **food**, day and night. You'll see pasta (usually spaghetti) appearing quite prominently on menus – one of the better Italian bequests to the Somalis.

Bomen Hotel Off the A2 highway, central Isiolo ☎064 52225 or 0705 309448. Ground-floor bar and restaurant, doing grills (most dishes Ksh300–400) and beer (Ksh100). Popular outdoor *nyama choma* grill. Daily 6am–11pm or later.

Club Genesis Off the A2 highway, central Isiolo. Busy bar and *nyama choma* joint, catering primarily to upcountry clients, and vibrating with deafening reggae by night. Daily 24hr.

The Hills Restaurants A2 highway, central Isiolo ☎0711 502609. Bustling bar, restaurant (pancakes Ksh50,

quarter chicken Ksh250) and *nyama choma* barbecue (beef Ksh500/kg), offering beers at Ksh130 and wine from Ksh600/bottle. Daily 5.30am–11pm.

Merti Hotel & Restaurant A2 highway, central Isiolo. Very good owner-run *hoteli* offering lots of staples – spaghetti (Ksh180), *ugali na sukuma* (Ksh70) and so on – at competitive prices and with half-portions of most dishes available. Daily 5.30am–10pm.

Salama A2 highway, central Isiolo. Friendly and popular place, recommended for an early breakfast or the very good spaghetti with gravy. Daily 6am–10pm.

SHOPPING

Isiolo is one of the best places to buy copper, brass and aluminium **bracelets**, costing around Ksh50 for simple ones, and from Ksh100 for the heavier, more complicated designs assuming you bargain effectively (starting prices are much higher). Short "**Somali swords**" in red leather scabbards are also much in evidence. The lads who mob you near the markets will invariably offer to guide you to one of the few blacksmiths in town to watch the fascinating process of twisting the wires for the bangles. Profits come from buying rough bangles, then polishing and selling them. If you go, you're generally expected to make a purchase and tip a few shillings to the young man. For their part, women offer small **wooden dolls** with woven hair, which in the past were given to young girls as both toys and fertility charms. If you're interested in buying local **fabrics**, *Libaan Fabrics* (daily 9am–9pm), between the A2 main road and the *Bomen Hotel*, offers a well-priced range of two-piece sets and large, ornately woven *gutina* cloths, with silver thread and tassles.

To Marsabit and North Horr

At one time, no matter what speed you travelled, this was a fantastically uncomfortable trip, with rocks, ruts and corrugations that knocked the daylights out of most vehicles and could shake smaller cars almost literally to bits. That picture may return in the future, but as of the end of 2012, the road **from Isiolo to Marsabit** was beautifully surfaced as far as **Merille**, on the southern fringe of Losai National Reserve, 137km north of Isiolo. The Chinese road builders reached there in July 2011, since when they've turned their attentions elsewhere, and it's not clear when they will come back to do the remaining 125km to Marsabit. However, even that stretch was properly graded in 2012, allowing an average speed of at least 50km/h, and making the whole journey from Isiolo to Marsabit quite feasible in about four hours in a private 4WD.

Archer's Post

35km north of Isiolo • Fuel is available at the Safaris Oil petrol station • Gate for Samburu National Reserve (see p.374)

Driving north from Isiolo, and passing over the occasionally dry, occasionally flooded Ewaso Nyiro River and through a police barrier, you hit the agglomeration of shiny-roofed shacks, rows of *dukas* and a scattering of cheap lodgings and *hotelis* that is **ARCHER'S POST**. This is as far north as you'll easily get by matatu, although the odd vehicle continues to Laisamis.

Ol Olokwe

North of Archer's Post, the road veers northwest and for thirty minutes the great mesa of **Ol Olokwe Mountain** (also known as Ol Doinyo Sabache) spreads massively across the horizon in front of you. If you're travelling independently with your own vehicle, you'll be in a position to climb it. If you want to have a crack at this, take the Wamba road and stop at the first village, Lerata; find the General Store and start asking for the Namunyak Conservancy manager (see p.525). You can climb Ol Olokwe in a day from Lerata with a crack-of-dawn start. Costs will include the $20 conservation fee plus whatever you negotiate for your guide – Ksh1000 for the day is about right, or more if you're in a group.

Ol Olokwe to Marsabit

For an hour north of Ol Olokwe you speed through a Wild West landscape of rearing mountains and endless bush. At the hamlet of Sereolipi, 62km from Archer's Post, there's a turning left, for Sarara Camp (see p.525). Look out for the **Cat and Mouse mesas** to the east of the road, and stay alert for **wildlife** by the road, or on it: ostriches, elephants, various antelope, zebra and giraffe can all be seen and they're not yet too familiar with fast-moving vehicles on a smooth highway.

Where the tarmac finishes, at the bridge over the **Merille lugga**, you start crossing the flat **Kaisut Desert** and plough through the **Losai National Reserve** in a cloud of dust – scrubby bush like the rest of the scenery around here. The desert settlement of **Laisamis** isn't much of a break – a windblown strew of tin-roofed huts, offering sodas

and chai to travellers. The **approach to Marsabit**, however, is unmistakeable. The road begins to climb and suddenly you're on a hilly island in the desert, a region of multiple volcanic craters, lush meadows and forest. The branches of the trees on the steep slopes are disguised by swathes of Spanish moss, looking at first glance like algae-covered rocks in shades of grey and green.

Marsabit

MARSABIT is a surprise. It's hard to prepare yourself, after the flat dust lands, for this fascinating hill oasis – in the desert but not of it. Rising a thousand metres above the surrounding plains, **Mount Marsabit**, or *Saku*, as it is known by locals, is permanently green, well watered by the clouds that form and disperse over it in a daily cycle. The high forest is usually mist-covered until late morning, the trees a characteristic tangle of foliage and lianas.

The town is the capital of the largest administrative district in the country, as well as a major meat- and livestock-trading centre, its rough roads either dusty or churned with mud. Small and intimate in feel, the lively cultural mix in the main market area is the biggest buzz: transient **Gabbra** herdsmen and **Boran** with their prized short-horn cattle, women in the printed shawls and chiffon wraps of **Somali** costume rubbing elbows with ochre-daubed **Rendille** wearing skins, high stacks of beads and wire, and fantastic braided hairstyles. There are government workers here, too, from other parts of Kenya, and a scattering of **Ethiopian immigrants** (mainly Burji) and refugees. For some Marsabit background, try Mude Dae Mude's novel *The Hills are Falling* (1979), now out of print, but you might still find a copy in Nairobi.

Hill and crater walks

There are several excursions you can do from Marsabit in a few hours. An easy short walk, for example, takes you up to a big, wind-powered **generator** on a hill just west of the town. A slightly longer hike goes up to the **VOK transmitter** behind the town, a route that passes through lush forest and offers magnificent panoramas of the whole district from the top.

The closest sizeable crater to Marsabit town is **Gof Redo**, about 5km north of the centre, in the fork of the roads to Moyale and North Horr. Either drive or walk out along the North Horr road until you see tracks branching off right after about 500m. If you have a vehicle you can drive most of the way to the base of the crater itself: head for the low col about 1.5km ahead: the gentler west side of the crater wall rises up here. There are some *manyattas* on the southwest rim, and you should be able to hire a guide quite easily if you want to scramble down inside for an hour or two. The crater is quite a favoured hideout for greater kudu.

MARSABIT

RESTAURANTS & BARS

Mountain Bar & Restaurant	1
New Saku B&L	2

ACCOMMODATION

Camp Henry	2
Chicho Hotel	4
Jeyjey Centre	3
KWS Ahmed Public Campsite	6
Marsabit Lodge	5
Pastoral Centre Guest House	1

The Singing Wells

A popular local walk goes to the "**singing wells**" near Ulanula (also known as Hula-Hula), a conical peak to the west of the Isiolo road, about 6km

PEOPLES OF THE NORTHEAST

Identities in the northeast can be confusing to foreigners. The largest group are the **Boran**, part of the **Oromo peoples** (formerly called Galla, an Amhara term of abuse), whose homeland was near the Bale Mountains in Ethiopia, from where they suddenly exploded out, in all directions, in the sixteenth century. The pastoral Boran developed and flourished in what is now southern Ethiopia, but Menelik's conquest of the area and the oppressive Amhara regime caused some of them to move down to the lowlands of northern Kenya, a much less suitable region for their cattle. The first Boran arrived in Marsabit only in 1921.

Similarly, the **Burji** are recent Ethiopian immigrants to the region between Marsabit and Moyale – an agricultural people who were encouraged to move south by colonial administrators in the 1930s who wanted more crops grown in the district. The Burji took quickly to Western education and trade, and as a result dominated Marsabit politically in the first decade after independence. There's traditionally little love lost between the nomadic Boran and the settled Burji.

At around the time of the Oromo expansion, another group of people – the forefathers of the Gabbra – arrived in northern Kenya, causing havoc in the region, only to be themselves pressured by the ensuing expansion of **Muslim Somalis** from the east. The ancestors of the **Gabbra** became "Boranized" to the extent that they changed their language and adopted Boran customs. Although most Boran and Gabbra, especially those who adopted a more sedentary life, have adopted Somali styles in dress and culture, they eschew Islam, preferring their own religions.

The **Rendille**, whose homeland is to the northwest of Marsabit, look and act like Samburu, with whom they are frequently allied; they speak a language close to Somali but have non-Muslim religious beliefs. They normally herd camels rather than cattle and, to a great extent, continue to roam the deserts, facing the prospect of settling down without any enthusiasm at all and visiting Marsabit only for vital needs or a brief holiday.

In Marsabit itself, distinctions other than superficial ones were becoming increasingly hard to apply by the 1990s, as people intermarried, sent more children to school, and absorbed new ideas from Nairobi – and from Christian missionaries. Still, language and religious beliefs remain significant in deciding who does what and with whom. Outside the town individual tribal identities are as strong – and potentially bloody – as ever. Since the massacre in 2005 at Turbi (a remote village 150km north of Marsabit), when Boran warriors attacked Gabbra villagers during a flare-up of customary inter-tribal cattle rustling, and killed sixty people, Marsabit has seen a deep chill in relations between the different peoples.

from town. These are less exotic than they sound, but they're still a good excuse to explore. Leaving Marsabit, you cross two bridges, then turn left and climb 200–300m up a narrow, tangled ravine. A concrete holding-tank, visible from the road, gives the place away. Behind it are two natural wells, the first with a wooden trough in front, the second longer and apparently deeper, containing a fluctuating depth of brown, frog-filled water. A silent pump house stands by.

The **singing** is done not by the wells but by the Boran herders who use them. When the water is low, human chains are formed to get it out with luxuriantly leaking leather buckets, and singing helps the work. At the driest times of the year you may be lucky and witness this, but try to get here early. Animals are usually driven to the wells after dawn; if you don't have a vehicle it's a brisk 75-minute walk from town. Go out there in the late afternoon, though, and you should get a lift back with one of the day's vehicles up from Isiolo.

ARRIVAL AND DEPARTURE   MARSABIT

By plane MAF (Mission Aviation Fellowship) operates flights from Nairobi Wilson to Marsabit and back, once or twice a week, usually on Tues and/or Fri mornings. When seats are available the going rate is Ksh10,000 one-way.

By bus or truck Buses (the older Liban and more modern Moyale Express) connect Moyale, Marsabit, Isiolo and Nairobi more or less daily, sometimes running more than one service.

Marsabit–Nairobi is a 12hr trip (Ksh2000). If you're moving on from Marsabit by any available means, you'll find that one or two trucks usually spend the night in Marsabit, en route from Moyale or Isiolo. The best place to wait for a lift south to Isiolo (going rate: Ksh800 in the back, Ksh1400 in the cab) is at the police checkpoint on the Isiolo road 3.5km from the Shell station. For a lift to Moyale (same prices), ask at the petrol stations or around the JeyJey Centre. Transport along the Lake Turkana road (Maikona, Kalacha, North Horr, Loiyangalani, Sibiloi National Park) is rare, with only a few vehicles each day – and sometimes none – and very little in the way of goods vehicles. Ask at the camps and hotels.

By car For servicing and parts, the best store is the ASM petrol station and garage. With the improvement of the A2 highway from Marsabit to Merille (125km), and the surfacing of its continuation to Isiolo (see p.539), vehicles travel faster and security seems to have improved. Safety may deteriorate again, however, during the lifetime of this

edition, so always ask about the road ahead as you pass through police checkpoints. As of late 2012, private vehicles were travelling freely – unescorted and not in convoys – between Marsabit and Isiolo and Marsabit and Loiyangalani. The route from Marsabit to Loiyangalani via North Horr and Kalacha is rough in parts, but feasible in all weathers – though you'll need GPS and/or a guide as passenger in one or two places where the route is unclear. When it's dry, most vehicles shoot across the Chalbi desert – not possible after rain when the floodwaters cover huge areas. Allow a full day and make an early start.

INFORMATION

Services There are KCB and Equity banks, both with ATMs. Marsabit has a post office and there's reasonable mobile

network in town, though it's very patchy in the national park.

ACCOMMODATION, EATING AND DRINKING

There's a fair spread of cheap accommodation in town – plus the tourist lodge in the national park. Wherever you choose, ask about **hot water** before moving in, as nights can get chilly (by some accounts, *Marsabit* means "place of cold") and lukewarm showers are no fun here. Moreover, in recent years, Marsabit has experienced terrible problems with water supplies. To **camp**, most people head for *Camp Henry*, but you can also camp just inside the national park's main gate (though you have to pay park fees). The best place to eat is the *JeyJey Centre*.

★ **Camp Henry** Signposted off the north side of the Isiolo road, 2km west of the Shell station, then 1.4km north ☎ 020 8004392 or 0735 420819, ✉ dommann @africaonline.co.ke. Excellent campsite, popular with self-catering overlanders, run by a Swiss former volunteer and Marsabit resident of 35 years and his wife, with shady pitches, clean showers and toilets. There's also a fine turf-roofed dorm bunkhouse (Samburu-hut-meets-Swiss-chalet) with four single beds and two twin bunks, with bedding. The shared rondavel-lounge has a fridge and there's a BBQ with free firewood. Camping **Ksh300** per person; dorm beds **Ksh400**

Chicho Hotel Behind the post office ☎ 069 2102846 or 0706 153827, ⊕ chichohotel.com. A recent addition to Marsabit's lodgings, this is the boutique offering, with five cute, somewhat cramped s/c rooms, fitted out with flat-screen DSTVs, electric showers, wi-fi (Marsabit's first hot spot), plus a pleasant dining room for breakfast and snacks. BB **Ksh3000**

JeyJey Centre Isiolo–Moyale road ☎ 0728 808802. Pleasant, well run and generally clean, though getting shabby in parts, *JeyJey* has 30 rooms, mostly non s/c

(Ksh200 extra for s/c with squat loo), with a decent restaurant (spaghetti bolognaise Ksh200, beef stew & chapatti Ksh240) but no bar. It's owned by former Saku MP Jarso Falana, who sometimes trucks water in from far away to supply guests. Room only **Ksh800**

Mountain Bar & Restaurant Between the Shell station and post office. Friendly die-hards' drinking den, with sodas at Ksh80 and beers for Ksh150, but no evidence of food. Daily 8am–11pm.

New Saku Bar Next door to Mountain Bar. Similar in most respects to its neighbour, if a little more restrained, this is largely an evening haunt and sometimes fills with drivers en route to Moyale or Isiolo. Daily 9am–10pm.

Pastoral Centre Guest House Signposted off the north side of the Isiolo road, 1.8km west of the Shell station, then 500m north ☎ 020 2059329 or 020 2356417. Clean, quiet and secure accommodation, with a chapel, pleasant grounds and accommodation in new s/c single rooms (no doubles), plus dorms with shared showers and toilets. Simple meals are included, and beers or sodas can be obtained if requested. HB **Ksh1750** per person

Marsabit National Park

The main (Ahmed) gate is at the edge of town, past the bank and the District Commissioner's office • $20 • ⊕ bit.ly/Marsabit • 1554 square kilometres

Having made the long journey to Marsabit, you'll certainly want to get into **Marsabit National Park**. The forest is wild and dense and the two crater lakes idyllically beautiful, although between the nearly impenetrable forests of the peaks and the stony scrub desert at the base of the mountain, you'll need a little luck for sightings. This is a rewarding park, but one where you have to look hard and your animal count will very much depend on the season of your visit. Good rains can encourage the grazers off the mountain and out into the temporarily lush desert, and predators will follow.

Except during the long rains (March to June), there's a good chance you'll see some of the long-tusked Marsabit **elephants**, relatives of the park's former inhabitant, the famous Ahmed – a particularly huge and well-endowed "big tusker" to whom Kenya's founding president Jomo Kenyatta gave "presidential protection" after seeing him, with elephant guards tracking him day and night – ironically, since Kenyatta's family were implicated in some of Kenya's biggest ivory smuggling scandals. Ahmed is, nonetheless, impressively replicated in fibreglass in the National Museum in Nairobi. His replacement, Mohammed, whose tusks were estimated at a cool 45kg each, has also gone to the elephant's graveyard. Elephants are tremendous wanderers, sometimes strolling into town, causing pandemonium. More problematically, the people of Marsabit have been encouraged to cultivate around the base of the mountain, thus creating a barrier to the elephants' free movement and unintentionally providing them with free lunches.

As well as big tuskers, the park is renowned for its **greater kudu**, and there's a wide range of other wildlife, plus amazing **birdlife**: almost four hundred species have been recorded, including 52 different birds of prey. Very rare **lammergeiers** (bearded vultures) are thought to nest on the sheer cliffs of Gof Bongole, the largest crater, which has a driveable track around its 10km rim. Marsabit is also something of a **snake** sanctuary, with some very large cobras – this isn't a place to go barefoot or in sandals.

7

ARRIVAL AND DEPARTURE   MARSABIT NATIONAL PARK

The park isn't visited that often and you may be in for a long wait if you want a lift around its forest tracks, but government officers and soldiers garrisoned in town do drive up to *Marsabit Lodge* fairly frequently. This short trip, with the view over the first lake – Gof Sokorte Dika – and its forested rim, is a lot better than nothing. You might also be able to convince an **armed ranger** to escort you on foot as far as the first lake (a Ksh1000 payment should be enough). This is a wonderful walk through the forest, with clouds of butterflies and the occasional mouth-drying encounter with buffalo or elephant. Don't attempt to **drive in the park** without 4WD, as many of the roads are steep and tend to be ridiculously muddy.

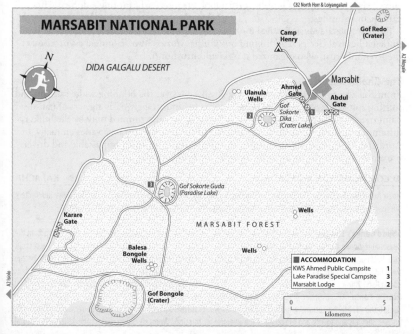

MARSABIT NATIONAL PARK

C82 North Horr & Loiyangalani

Gof Redo (Crater)

Camp Henry

A2 Moyale

DIDA GALGALU DESERT

Ulanula Wells

Ahmed Gate

Marsabit

Abdul Gate

Gof Sokorte Dika (Crater Lake)

Gof Sokorte Guda (Paradise Lake)

Wells

MARSABIT FOREST

Karare Gate

Balesa Bongole Wells

Wells

Gof Bongole (Crater)

A2 Isiolo

ACCOMMODATION
KWS Ahmed Public Campsite	1
Lake Paradise Special Campsite	3
Marsabit Lodge	2

0   5
kilometres

ACCOMMODATION

KWS Ahmed public campsite Near Ahmed gate, 100m down the hairpin to the left of the ranger's house ☎ 0722 393335; map p.545. This is a wonderfully shaded spot, somewhat overrun with baboons. $15 per person

Lake Paradise Special Campsite Deep in the forest at Lake Paradise (Gof Sokorte Guda) ☎ 0722 393335 (Nairobi reservations ☎ 0726 610508, ⓦ kws.go.ke); map p.545. A stunning, dark pool for much of the year, Lake Paradise has a wonderful KWS "special campsite" on its crater rim, where lion, leopard and the rare and shaggy striped hyena are all seen and heard from time to time. It requires an accompanying ranger and a Ksh7500 reservation fee which entitles you to stay for up to a week. No facilities —you need to bring everything. $30 per person

★ **Marsabit Lodge** On the shore of Gof Sokorte Dika ☎ 020 2695260 or 0728 324932, ⓦ marsabit lodge.com; map p.545. Outstanding views and the exquisite peace and beauty of its location, with wildlife converging at the lake and eagles swooping through the trees, compensate for the fairly rudimentary comforts (for a tourist-class lodge) and rather spooky emptiness. The lodge was semi-closed for years but has had a facelift and provides all the essentials, including electric showers and clean sheets, so long as you don't expect luxury or style. There's a bar, veranda and dining room (serving adequate, filling meals), a generator in the mornings and evenings, and very nice staff. HB Ksh8700

Maikona

MAIKONA, 90km from Marsabit on the road to North Horr, is a friendly Gabbra settlement on the fringes of the Chalbi Desert, with the last fresh water for 35km and a thriving daily market for goats and cattle. As with all the villages up here, keep your camera out of sight, and ask permission if you want to take **photographs**: belief in the camera's evil eye is prevalent.

Kalacha

The springs of **Kalacha Goda** are the *raison d'être* for the small town of **KALACHA**. If you drive through the village, you'll find them on the southwest side of the sprawling settlement, usually surrounded by hundreds of camels. While you're here, the **Kalacha Catholic Church** (unmissable in the "centre" of town, on the east side of the road; free entry; Mass 9am Sunday) is well worth a look, its interior beautifully adorned with Ethiopian paintings.

The first **Kalacha Music Festival** took place in April 2012, on similar lines to the Lake Turkana Festival (see p.529). To find out if it has turned into an annual event, contact the Kivulini Trust, who organized it (ⓦ kivulinitrust.org).

The Chalbi Desert

From Kalacha to North Horr, the track streaks out over the blinding white saltpans and shifting soft sands of the **Chalbi Desert**, ducks behind straggly oasis clusters of half-dead palm trees, and finally loses itself in a vast orange expanse rimmed only by the hulks of distant mountains. There are many routes and the best path to take varies annually. In April and May when the rains come, the desert routes are often impassable and drivers use a more northerly, rocky route to avoid the flooded plains.

ACCOMMODATION AND EATING   KALACHA

Tropic Air's **Kalacha Camp**, a community collaboration 2.5km southwest of the AIC mission, has closed down indefinitely, but may reopen during the lifetime of this edition. Note that there is little to no mobile signal in Kalacha.

Abudo Ganya's Lodge 500m west of the AIC mission. Reasonable *banda* camp (run by the twin brother of the local MP Chachu Ganya), with food available to order. Sadly their AIC-style swimming pool is not functioning. Whole *banda* Ksh1000

Acacia Camp AIC (African Inland Church) Mission compound ⓔ kalachastation@gmail.com. With its shady pitches, showers and toilets, and the bonus of the inventive

"tank" swimming pool supplied by a wind pump from the borehole, this is better than you have any right to expect out in these northern badlands. They have a full-service garage for emergency repairs, and services in their church, with its stained-glass windows, on Sun at 9am. Camping Ksh500 per person

Chalbi Safari Resort 1km southwest of the AIC mission. Women's group project specializing in cultural dances. Small *bandas* and meals available to order. *Banda* Ksh500

Kalacha Camp Kalacha ☎0722 207300 or 0711 311479, ⓦkalacha.org. The best accommodation in the area, with comfortable, twin-bedded s/c *bandas* and a small swimming pool, close to a communal mess area. Package $400

North Horr

NORTH HORR, when you finally reach it, is a welcome haven (although searingly hot), with a handful of *dukas* and *hotelis*, a busy Catholic mission and a number of NGOs, including the base of VSF Germany, the veterinarian support group working with pastoralists.

From here on down to Loiyangalani, the route – rarely much more than a set of wheel tracks – shifts between sandy *luggas* liable to flood and crunchy, black lava plains, as it skirts the northern flanks of Mount Kulal. The views, when you crest the ridge, looking down over Lake Turkana far away, can be spellbinding.

ACCOMMODATION AND EATING   North Horr

Catholic Mission Guest House North Horr centre ☎0720 959708. Simple non s/c twin rooms, with shared shower and toilet. Room only Ksh500 per person

Midland Entertainment North Horr centre, opposite the New Mandera. When you really need a cold drink, this has one of North Horr's most reliably stocked fridges. Daily 7am–9pm.

New Mandera Tourist Hotel North Horr centre ☎0716 628080. Rooms available at the back of the compound, with no nets or refinements. *Chai, chapattis,* cold sodas, pilau and spaghetti are always available at rock-bottom prices, as are genuinely helpful family and friends to guide you on your way. Room only Ksh150

To Moyale and Ethiopia

From Marsabit, the **journey to Moyale**, which straddles the Ethiopian border, takes upwards of ten hours, depending on the vehicle. For the first three of these you descend from the mountain's greenery past spectacular craters – **Gof Choba** is the whopper on the left – to the forbidding black moonscape of the **Dida Galgalu Desert**.

Dida Galgalu means "plains of darkness", according to one old story told by Boran pastoralists. Another account derives it from Galgalu, a woman buried here after she died of thirst trying to cross it. The road arrows north for endless kilometres, then cuts east across watercourses and through bushier country beneath high crags on the Ethiopian frontier. En route, you pass the turning to the small village of **Sololo** on the Ethiopian border, arrestingly sited between soaring peaks that can be climbed for stunning views over the northern plains and Ethiopian highlands.

There are some magnificent, towering **termite mounds** along the northern part of the route. They're a sight that seems quintessentially African, yet one that can quickly be taken for granted, like leafless trees in a northern winter. As the kilometres roll away, the day-long 250km from Marsabit to Moyale is resolved in just a few bends and a

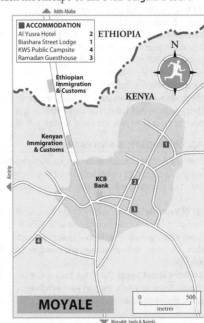

▲ Addis Ababa

■ ACCOMMODATION
Al Yusra Hotel	2
Biashara Street Lodge	1
KWS Public Campsite	4
Ramadan Guesthouse	3

ETHIOPIA

Ethiopian Immigration & Customs

KENYA

Kenyan Immigration & Customs

KCB Bank

Airstrip

MOYALE

0   500
metres

▼ Marsabit, Isiolo & Nairobi

7

couple of minor scenery changes. Over distances that would take days to cover on foot you can see where you have been and where you are going – a still, vast landscape seemingly echoed in the pastoralists' conservatism.

Towards the end of the journey, the road bends south, then doubles north again and winds up through the settlements of Burji farmers – an agricultural people who emigrated from Ethiopia early in the twentieth century (see box, p.543) – past their beautifully sculpted houses and sparse fields, to Moyale.

Moyale

Straddling the Ethiopian border, **MOYALE** makes Marsabit look like a metropolis. Though the town is growing rapidly, the centre is small enough to walk around in fifteen minutes. You'll find several sandy streets, a pretty mosque, a few *dukas*, a bar, a camel-tethering ground, two petrol stations (one of which occasionally belies its defunct appearance), a big police station, a fairly large market area, two banks with ATMs, and an incredibly slow post office. Moyale is not much to write home about in fact, and there's not a lot to do except wander around, perhaps try some camel milk (very rich and creamy) and pass the time of day with everyone else, with or without the aid of *miraa*, universally popular in the northeast (see p.184).

The most interesting aspect of Moyale is its **architecture** – at least, the good number of traditionally built houses that are still standing. The Boran build in several styles, including circular mud-and-thatch huts, but in town the houses are rectangular, made of mud and dung on a wood frame, with a flat or slightly tilted roof projecting 1–2m to form a porch, supported by sturdy posts and tree trunks. The roof is up to 50cm thick, a fantastic accretion of dried mud, sticks, scrap and vegetation. Chickens and goats get up there, improving the roof's fertility, and every time it rains another layer of insulating herbage springs up. As a result, the houses are cool while the outside temperature hovers above 30°C for most of the year.

ARRIVAL AND DEPARTURE   MOYALE

By bus Liban bus and the faster and more comfortable Moyale Express connect Moyale with Marsabit and Isiolo daily (the Moyale Express continues to Nairobi). Moyale to Marsabit is generally a 9–10hr trip (Ksh1500), with the continuation to Isiolo taking another 6hr (Ksh1200) and Nairobi a further 5hr (Ksh800).

By truck If there's no bus, or the bus is full, goods trucks are usually available to get you as far as Marsabit, where there's more transport. Expect to pay around Ksh800–1000 riding on top or in the back, and several hundred shillings

more to get a seat in the cab.

By car If you've just crossed the border from Ethiopia, you'll be pleased to know that roads south towards Nairobi are better than they've been for years, though the section as far as Marsabit will still test your vehicle. Depending on inter-ethnic tensions in the Moyale area and banditry incidents on the road, you may have to travel in convoy, but this security measure seems to be on the wane as the improved roads encourage more – and faster – traffic.

ACCOMMODATION AND EATING

There's no shortage of **accommodation**, but finding anything above the very low budget category is tricky – and the local *hotelis* and bars are equally basic when it comes to **meals and drinks**. The water in Moyale can be briny at times, and it's worth bringing as much drinking water with you as you can.

★ **Al Yusra Hotel** Town centre (it's the unmissable orange building by the hospital) ☎0722 257028. Finally, Moyale joins the rest of Kenya – a proper hotel with clean, s/c rooms with hot showers and breakfast. BB **Ksh3000**

Biashara Street Lodge Out of the town centre (no phone). A new, very clean and quiet place with showers, but inconveniently located. Room only **Ksh400**

KWS Public Campsite West side of Moyale. The Kenya Wildlife Service campsite on the west side of town has showers and toilets but no other facilities. You're likely to run into other overland travellers here. Camping **Ksh500** per person

Ramadan Guesthouse Near the mosque (no phone). Very clean and in a relatively quiet area, but usefully close to the town centre. Room only **Ksh400**

Into Ethiopia

Even if you're not intending to travel in **Ethiopia** (and if you haven't got a visa already, you won't be able to do so), the most interesting prospect in Moyale is to cross the valley into Kenya's neighbouring state and spend a few hours there. For Kenyans and Ethiopians, the border is an open one. For foreigners wanting to have a short look around, this is sometimes permitted even without a visa: you'll need to persuade the Ethiopian immigration officers that an hour or two in their country would make your day – and you will certainly have to leave your passport with them for safekeeping.

Ethiopian Moyale is larger than its Kenyan counterpart and somewhat more prosperous, with piped water, and a long-established electricity supply. In town, there are lots of simple stores, and plenty of eating places. You can pay for everything in Kenyan shillings. The market buzzes colourfully with camels and goats, piles of spices, flour and vegetables. Otherwise, life here seems much the same as over the border, but easier. As a back-door view of Ethiopia, however, it is no more representative than the other side of town is of Kenya.

7

SAMBURU WOMAN

Contexts

History

Kenya's pre-colonial past is still the subject of endless conjecture, and it can be difficult for the traveller to make much sense of it – especially since the physical record in ancient architecture is virtually nonexistent upcountry. On the coast, settlement ruins, old documents and the Islamic tradition help to convey the past. What follows, up to the colonial period, is a much condensed overview, intended to pull together the historical accounts of individual peoples that are given throughout the Guide. More emphasis is given here to the history of the last hundred years or so.

The cradle of humankind

Kenya is quite likely to be the place where human beings first evolved. Some of the oldest fossils of **ancestral hominins** have been found in the Tugen Hills, and the remains of what are thought to be our later ancestors were discovered on the shores of Lake Turkana. Even so, concrete evidence of the origins of humanity remains scant, and new finds could easily turn the latest theories upside down.

The East African **Rift Valley** is ideal territory for the search for human origins: volcanic eruptions have repeatedly showered thick layers of ash and cinders over fossil beds, building up strata that can be reliably used to compare ages. The **Leakey** family has been instrumental in much of the work that has been done. Olduvai Gorge in Tanzania was the first major site to disclose evidence of human prehistory, and Louis Leakey and his wife, Mary, worked there from the 1930s. Their son, Richard, went on to explore the Turkana region and found even older fossils, putting Kenya under the scientific spotlight. A suggestion in support of the "cradle of humankind" idea is that the Rift Valley's very formation – a major event on the earth's crust, which began some twenty million years ago – could have been the environmental spark that was the catalyst for human evolution.

In 2000, the Tugen Hills yielded finds from around six million years ago of a hitherto unknown species named *Orrorin tugenensis*. It was possibly the **first hominin** – that is to say, the first known specimen of a creature on our side of the evolutionary divide between humans and the modern-day great apes – although *Sahelanthropus tchadensis*, discovered in Chad in 2002, is another possible contender. The *O. tugenensis* remains were of a creature that was still an ape, but one that walked upright on two legs. Specimens have also been found in Kenya of the hominins known as **australopithecines**, which seem to have appeared around 4.2 million years ago. Samples of *Australopithecus anamensis*, the earliest known australopithecine, were unearthed on the east side of Lake Turkana in 1965. Examples of later australopithecines have also been found in Kenya, but it is no longer thought that these were our direct ancestors. Evidence that they were not comes in the form of **fossil skull 1470** (its catalogue

20 million years ago	6 million years ago	4.2 million years ago
Rift Valley formed	Earliest human ancestors live in Tugen Hills	Australopithecines inhabit Rift Valley

number), discovered by Bernard Ngeneo in 1972 and now in the National Museum in Nairobi (see p.112). Dated at 1.9 million years old, it was first believed to be an example of *Homo habilis* ("Handy man") and later renamed *Homo rudolfensis*. It proved that the earliest members of our genus, *Homo*, had co-existed with the later australopithecines.

Almost as important was the discovery in 1984 of the nearly complete 1.6-million-year-old skeleton of 12-year-old "**Turkana Boy**", a member of the later species *Homo erectus* ("Upright man"), the immediate ancestor of the human species, found at Nariokotome on the western shore of Lake Turkana. It was probably *Homo erectus* who developed **speech** and discovered how to make **fire**, while improving enormously on the **tool-making** efforts of *Homo habilis*. **Olorgasailie** and **Kariandusi** are two "hand axe" sites, probably belonging to *Homo erectus*, which have been used within the last five hundred thousand years. And it was *Homo erectus* who, if the "cradle" theory is right, spread the humanoid gene pool to Asia, Europe and the rest of Africa, where, over the next few hundred thousand years, *Homo sapiens* emerged on the scene.

Early inhabitants: up to 1600

Real history begins with *Homo sapiens*, living as **hunter-gatherers**. Numbering probably fewer than a hundred thousand, living in small units of several families, and either staying in one place for generations or moving through the country according to the dictates of the seasons, these earliest human inhabitants of Kenya may have been related to the ancestors of present-day Pygmy and Khoisan (Bushmen) peoples, and probably spoke "click" languages similar to those of today's Khoisan peoples of southern Africa and Tanzania.

The earliest distinct migration to Kenya was of **Cushitic**-speaking people from the Ethiopian Highlands who are thought to have arrived some time between 9000 BC and 1000 BC. Occasional hunters and gatherers themselves, they were also livestock herders and farmers. Over the centuries, they filled the areas that were too dry for a purely subsistence way of life. They also absorbed many of the previous inhabitants through inter-marriage. Having herds and cultivating land brought up questions of ownership, inheritance and water rights, and an elaboration of social institutions and customs to deal with them. The Cushites had a strong material culture, using stone, particularly obsidian, to produce beautiful arrowheads, knives and axes, as well as producing a range of pottery utensils. They also left evidence of their settlements in burial cairns and living sites at places like Hyrax Hill, near Nakuru. The same people may have built the irrigation works still used today along the Elgeyo Escarpment, west of Lake Baringo. For the most part, the earliest Cushites were absorbed by peoples who came later, and whose new languages they adopted. The changes were not all one-sided, however: **circumcision** and **clitoridectomy** (so-called female circumcision), practised by the early Cushites, became important cultural rituals for many of the peoples who succeeded and absorbed them. The **Somali** and **Rendille** of the northeast are the main groups still speaking Cushitic languages, although their arrival in Kenya was more recent. Today, only the Boni speak a language related to the Southern Cushitic of the first farmers and herders, although the Boni themselves are hunter-gatherers.

1.9 million years ago	1.6 million years ago	2000 BC
Direct human ancestor, "Handy man", lives on east shores of Lake Turkana	Direct human ancestor, "Upright man", lives on west shores of Lake Turkana	Cushitic-speaking peoples appear in Kenya

HUNTER-GATHERERS IN KENYA

Remnant hunter-gatherer groups still live in remote parts of Kenya – the **Boni** on the mainland near Lamu, the **Sanye** along the Tana River, the **El Molo** on the shores of Lake Turkana, and the **Okiek** and **Dorobo** in parts of the Highlands – but the languages they now speak have mostly been adopted from neighbouring peoples. The hunting and gathering way of life has persisted in the cultural memories of most Kenyan peoples, and some of the groups who still practise it may have been offshoots from farming or herding communities that broke up during droughts.

For present-day Kenya, the most important arrivals began to reach the country in the first few centuries AD. From the northwest and the headwaters of the Nile came the **Nilotic**-speaking ancestors of the so-called **Kalenjin** peoples; from the west and south came speakers of **Bantu** languages (see p.602), forebears of today's **Kikuyu**, **Gusii**, **Kamba** and **Mijikenda**, among others.

Along with their languages, the new arrivals brought technological innovations, including **iron** working. Iron had enabled the Bantu to spread from the Nigeria/Cameroon area across central Africa, clearing the virgin forests and hoeing the ground for their crops. Eastwards, they encountered new Asian food crops – bananas, yams and rice – some of which arrived in East Africa by way of the Indonesian colonization of Madagascar. This new diversity of foods helped people to settle permanently in chosen regions. The Kalenjin peoples consolidated in the western highlands. The Bantu were particularly successful and, as their broad economic base took hold across the southern half of Kenya, their languages quickly spread. Herding, hunting, fishing and gathering were important supplements to the agricultural mainstay, while trade conducted with their exclusively pastoral or hunter-gatherer neighbours, especially in iron tools, carried their influence further. By about 1000 AD, Kenya's Stone-Age technology had been largely replaced by an Iron-Age one and, as human domination of the country increased, the beginnings of real specialization in agriculture and herding set in among the different tribes.

Down on the **coast**, Bantu immigrants mixed, over several hundred years, with the Cushitic-speaking inhabitants and with a continuous trickle of settlers from Arabia and the Persian Gulf. With the advent of Islam, this mélange gradually gave rise to a distinct culture and civilization – **Swahili** – speaking a Bantu language laced with foreign vocabulary. The Swahili (see p.410) were Kenya's link with the rest of the world, trading animal skins, ivory, agricultural produce and slaves in exchange for cloth, metals, ceramics, grain, ghee and sugar, with ships from the Middle East, India and even China. The Swahili were the first Kenyans to acquire firearms. They were also the first to write their language (in the Arabic script) and the first to develop complex, stratified communities based on town and countryside.

Later arrivals: 1600–1885

New **American crops** – corn, cassava and tobacco – spread through Kenya after the Portuguese arrived on the coast in the early sixteenth century. They hugely increased the country's population capacity, while enabling a greater degree of permanent settlement and providing new trade goods.

200 AD	500 AD	1000 AD	1100
Nilotic-speaking ancestors of Kalenjin arrive in Kenya from the north	Bantu-speaking peoples arrive from the west	Iron-Age culture replaces Stone-Age culture throughout Kenya	Swahili culture established on coast

At about this time, a pastoral **Nilotic**-speaking people, distantly related to the earlier Kalenjin arrivals, began a migration from the northwest. These were the first **Luo**-speakers who, some generations earlier, had left their homeland (around Wau in southern Sudan) for economic reasons: in the alternately flooded and parched flatlands around the Nile, unusual conditions could be catastrophic and forced communities to flee. The Luo ancestors were always on the move, herding, planting, hunting or fishing. Politically, they had a fairly complex organization, as, for months on end, while the Nile flooded, communities would be stranded in concentration along the low ridges. Several good years might be followed by drought, and population pressure then forced less dominant groups to go off in search of water and pasture. The overall trend was southwards. Groups of migrants picked up other, non-Luo-speakers on the way, gradually assimilating them through intermarriage and language change, always drawing attention with the impressive regalia and social standing of their *ruoth* – the Luo kings.

On the shores of Lake Victoria, where the Luo finally settled, sleeping sickness is thought to have wiped out many of their herds. But they were pragmatic, resourceful people, whose background of mixed farming and herding during the era of migration supported them. They turned to agriculture and, increasingly, to fishing.

Another Nilotic, pastoral people, the **Turkana** appeared in Kenya later in the seventeenth century. Linguistically closer to the Maasai Nilotes, they seem to have shared the Luo resilience to economic hardship and they, too, have more recently turned to fishing. Also like the Luo, and almost unique among Kenyan peoples, they have never practised circumcision.

The arrival of the Maasai

The Maa-speakers – **Maasai** and **Samburu** – were the last major group to arrive in Kenya, and their rise and fall had far-reaching effects on neighbouring peoples. Moving southwards from the upper Nile valley, from the beginning of the seventeenth century, they expanded swiftly thanks to their nomadic pastoral lifestyle, transforming within a few generations from an obscure group into a dominant force in the region. Culturally, they borrowed extensively from their neighbours, especially the Nandi-speaking **Kalenjin** peoples. **Nandi** words and Kalenjin cultural values were adopted, including circumcision, the age-set system and some ancient (originally probably Cushitic) taboos against eating fish and certain wild animals. It's likely that much of the "traditional" Maasai appearance also owes something to these contacts. The Maasai migration was rapid. Their cattle were periodically herded south and other peoples raided en route to enlarge the herds: by 1800, they were widely established in the Rift Valley and on the plains, everywhere between Lake Turkana and Kilimanjaro. In response to Maasai dominance, many of the Bantu peoples adopted their styles and customs. Initiation by genital mutilation, probably already practised by most Bantu-speakers, was imbued with a new significance – especially for the Kikuyu – by intermarriage and close, if not always peaceable, relations with the Maasai.

Severe **droughts** in the nineteenth century pushed the Maasai further and further afield in search of new pastures, bringing them into conflict, and trade, with other peoples. Drought, disease and rinderpest epidemics (which killed off their cattle) were also responsible for a series of **Maasai civil wars** in the second half of the nineteenth century that disrupted the trading networks that had been set up between the coast and the

1500	Around 1500	Around 1650	Around 1680
Nilotic-speaking ancestors of Luo arrive from the north	American crops first appear in Kenya	Nilotic-speaking Turkana arrive from the north	Maasai and Samburu arrive from the north

interior. These were mainly controlled by Swahili, Mijikenda, Kamba and Kikuyu traders. Dutch, English and French goods were finding their way upcountry, and American interests were already being served during this period, as white calico cloth (still called *amerikani* today) became a major item of profit. In the slave trade's last throes, slaves were exported from western Kenya and Uganda to the coast and even to the Persian Gulf.

Largely in response to slavery and widespread fighting, the first **missionaries** installed themselves upcountry (the earliest went inland from Mombasa in 1846). Throughout this period, the Maasai disrupted travel in their territories, attacking Swahili slavers, Bantu traders and explorer-missionaries alike. The Maasai *morani* were specifically trained for raiding – a kind of guerrilla warfare – but, while their reputation lived on, they were bitterly divided among themselves and not organized on anything like a tribal scale.

By the end of the nineteenth century, with the European invasion of Africa in full swing, the Maasai, who could have been the imperialists' most intractable enemies, were unable to retaliate effectively. The **Nandi** of the western highlands, the main people of the Kalenjin group, had begun to take the Maasai's place as Kenya's most feared adversaries, and put up the stiffest resistance. They were organized to the extent of having a single spiritual leader, the *orkoiyot*, who ruled what was in effect a theocracy. Their war of attrition against the British delayed advances for a number of years. But the Nandi did not have the territorial advantage that would have helped the Maasai, and the assassination of their *orkoiyot*, Koitalel, by the British, destroyed their military organization.

On the coast, the **Sultanate of Oman**, which had ousted the Portuguese from Mombasa in 1698, ruled the whole region between Lamu and Mozambique, and made Zanzibar its capital in 1840. Oman was already under British influence, and officially a British protectorate, when the country split in 1856; Zanzibar, including what is now the coast of Kenya, became a sultanate in its own right. Coastal history is covered in more detail in Chapter 6 (see p.390).

The "Scramble for Africa"

All Kenya's peoples resisted colonial domination to some degree. In the first twenty years of British attempts to rule the region, tens of thousands were killed in ugly massacres and manhunts, and many more were made homeless. Administrators – whose memoirs (see p.591) are the most revealing background for that period – all differed in their ideas of the ultimate purpose of their work and the best means of imposing British authority.

British interests in East Africa at the close of the nineteenth century had sprung from the European power struggle and the "Scramble for Africa". The 1885 **Berlin Conference** chopped the continent into arbitrary spheres of influence. Germany was awarded what was to become Tanganyika; Britain got Kenya and Uganda. In 1886, formal agreements were drawn up and Kilimanjaro was ceded to Victoria's grandson, the Kaiser, giving each monarch a snowcapped, equatorial mountain.

Uganda was the focus of British interest, since Kenya – decimated by drought, locusts, rinderpest and civil war – seemed largely a deserted wasteland. And Uganda was strategically important for **control of the Nile** – which had long been a British preoccupation. But rivalry wasn't far beneath the seemingly amicable surface and Germany clearly had Uganda earmarked too. The country needed to be properly

1840	1790s–1880s	1846	1870s
Sultanate of Oman rules coast	Thousands of slaves transported from coast to Middle East and Persian Gulf	First European missionaries arrive in Kenya	Maasai civil wars

garrisoned and supplied, and Kenya was the necessary base from which to do that.

In 1888, the British government granted permission for commercial operations in Uganda to the **Imperial British East Africa Company** (IBEAC), which, for sea access, leased a wide swath of southern Kenya from the Sultan of Zanzibar. The British also authorized the IBEAC to administer Uganda and that section of Kenya on their behalf. The company officers – mostly young and totally inexperienced English clerks – established a series of trading forts at fifty-mile intervals in a line connected by a rough ox-track leading from Mombasa into Uganda. Machakos, Murang'a and Mumias all began as IBEAC stations.

The IBEAC eventually went bankrupt, however, having failed to establish any kind of administration, and in 1895 the British government stepped into the breach, declared a **protectorate** over Uganda and Kenya and decided to build a **railway** from Kenya's coast to its interior. This classic, valedictory piece of Victorian engineering took six years to complete and cost the lives of hundreds of Indian labourers. Financially, the "lunatic line" (as it came to be called) it was a commitment that grew out of all proportion to the likely returns and continued to grow long after the last rail was laid. But its completion transformed the future of East Africa. From now on, the supply lines were secure and the interior only a month's journey from Europe by ship and rail. Suddenly, the prospects for developing the cool, fertile Kenya highlands looked much more attractive than the distant unknowns of Uganda and its powerful kingdoms.

More immediately, the railway physically divided the **Maasai** at a time when they were not united, and moreover were moving into alliances with the British. Their grazing lands, together with the regions of the **Kalenjin** peoples and the **Kikuyu** on the lower slopes of the highlands, were to become the heartland of the white settler colony.

The Kenya colony

Many people in Edwardian Britain saw Kenya as a land of opportunity: a new New Zealand, or even a Jewish homeland (a party of Zionists was actually escorted around Kenya but declined the offer). It was Sir Charles Eliot, the Protectorate's second governor, who was the main mover behind the **settlement scheme**. While some colonialists urged consideration for the "rights of natives", the growing clamour of voices claiming the support of British taxpayers – who had met the bill for the railway – outweighed any altruism. Eliot's extravagant reports on the potential of British East Africa were published, and government policy was thereafter directed towards getting the settlers in and making the railway pay. And so a trickle of landless aristocrats, middle-class adventurers, big-game hunters, ex-servicemen and Afrikaners (the farming land was also advertised in South Africa) began travelling up the line. Using ox-wagons to get to the tracts of bush they had leased, they started their farms from scratch. Lord Delamere, governor himself for a time, was their biggest champion. In the years leading up to World War I, the trickle of settlers became a flood, and by 1916 the area "alienated" to **European settlers** had risen to 15,000 square kilometres of the best land. The so-called "**White Highlands**" were mostly on the slopes of Mount Kenya and the Aberdare Range, but also in the Rift Valley where the Maasai had been pushed out and Kikuyu labourers – known as squatters – were encouraged to migrate to work on the European farms. Imported livestock was hybridized with hardy, local breeds; coffee,

1885	1888	1895–1901	1916	1900s
Berlin Conference carves up Africa for the European powers	Imperial British East Africa Company founded	"Lunatic line" built from Mombasa to Lake Victoria	European settlers flood into Kenya	Land and labour laws enacted, including a hut tax

tea, sisal and pineapples were introduced and thrived; European crops flourished and cereals soon covered vast areas.

Nearly half the land worth farming was now in the hands of settlers, but it had become clear that it was far from empty of local inhabitants. Colonial invasion had occurred at a low point in the fortunes of Kenya's peoples and, unprepared for the scale of the incursion, they had been swiftly pushed aside into "native reserves" or became squatters without rights. As populations recovered, serious land shortages set in. The British appointment of "chiefs" – whose main task was to collect a tax on every hut – had the effect of diverting grievances against colonial policy onto these early collaborators and laying the foundations of a class structure in Kenyan society. Without a money economy, employment was the only means available to pay taxes and, effectively, a system of forced labour had been created. The whole apparatus quickly became entrenched in a series of **land and labour laws**. A poll tax was added to the hut tax; all African men were compelled to register to facilitate labour recruitment; squatters on alienated land were required to pay rent, through labour; and cash cropping on African plots was discouraged or banned (coffee licences, for example, were restricted to white farmers). The highlands were strictly reserved for white settlement, while land not owned by Europeans became Crown Land, its African occupants "tenants at will" of the Crown and liable to summary eviction.

Asians, too, were excluded from the highlands. While the leader of Kenya's Indians, **A.M. Jeevanjee**, had called for the transformation of Kenya into the "America of the Hindu", the proposal never came near consideration by the British. Barred from farming on any scale – except in the far west, where they developed sugar cane as an important crop – Indians concentrated on the middle ground, setting up general stores (*dukas*) across the country, investing in small industries and handling services.

World War I
World War I had a number of profound effects, although there were comparatively few battles in Kenya itself. Some 200,000 African porters and soldiers were conscripted and sent to Tanganyika (German East Africa), where 50,000 of them died. **General von Lettow Vorbeck**, the German commander, waged a dogged campaign against British forces despite the fact that his own were vastly outnumbered. Kenyan troops were deeply influenced by the experience. They had seen Europeans at war with each other; they had experienced European fallibility, and witnessed the kind of organization used to overcome it.

Sir Edward Northey, governor of Kenya at the time of armistice, pushed his **Soldier Settlement Scheme** through without difficulty. Its aim, to increase revenue by doubling the settler population in Kenya to nine thousand, seemed promising enough to a government sapped by war. But the Soldier Settlement Scheme was bitterly resented by Africans, particularly those who had fought alongside the soldiers and were now excluded from their gains.

Early nationalism and reaction
Political associations sprang up among ex-servicemen and those with a mission-school education: the Kikuyu Association, the Young Kikuyu Association and the Young Kavirondo Association. **Harry Thuku**, secretary of the Young Kikuyus, realized its

Around 1892	**1914–18**	**1918**	**1920**
Jomo Kenyatta born in Kiambu, north of Nairobi	200,000 African porters conscripted to serve in World War I	Soldier settlement scheme devised to double settler population to 9000	Kenya officially becomes a British Colony

potential and re-formed it as the East Africa Association in order to recruit on a nationwide basis. The hated registration law by which every African was obliged to carry a pass – the *kipande* – was a prime grievance, but tax reduction, introduction of land title deeds and wage increases were demanded as well. Alliances were built up with associations of embittered Indians and 1921 saw a year of protests and rallies. These culminated in Thuku's detention and the shooting by police of 25 demonstrators at a mass rally calling for his release. He remained in detention for eleven years.

The Indian constituency eventually secured two seats (nominated, not elected) on the Legislative Council. Africans, meanwhile, remained landless, disenfranchised and, like the Indians, racially segregated from the white community. As the settlers became established, they began to contribute appreciably to the income of the colony (which Kenya had officially become in 1920). Most of them seem to have believed that they were the founders of what would be a long and glorious era of white dominion. Indeed settler self-government, along Canadian or South African lines, was a declared aim. African demands were hardly heeded by the authorities, but the Colonial Office was in a difficult position over the **Indians**, who were already British subjects with the rights and privileges of Indians on the subcontinent and whose demands for equal rights they had trouble in refuting. Tentative proposals to give them voting rights, allow unrestricted immigration from India and abolish segregation caused indignation among the settlers. Their **Convention of Associations**, already arguing the case for white home rule, formed a "Vigilance Committee" which worked out detailed military plans for rebellion, including the kidnapping of the governor and the deportation of the Indians. Sensing a crisis, the Colonial Office drew up a white paper and a grudging settlement was reached that allowed five Indians and one Arab to be elected to the Legislative Council (the colony's local government), alongside eleven Europeans.

Although the "paramountcy of native interests" was reiterated in the Colonial Office's 1923 **Devonshire Declaration** (a government green paper designed to forestall the political demands of Indian settlers), Africans were in reality still denied any equality before the law. A system of **de facto apartheid** was being practised, and it was in this climate in the 1920s and 1930s that, floating above their economic troubles, the settlers had their heyday – the **Happy Valley life** so appallingly and fascinatingly depicted in *White Mischief* (see p.593) and other books.

Education, Kenyatta and the Kikuyu

The opportunities available to Africans came almost entirely through **mission schools** at first. Again, there was conflict between government and settlers on the question of **education**. The Colonial Office was committed, on paper at least, to the general development of the country for all its inhabitants, while the white farmers were on the whole adamant that raising educational standards could only lead to trouble. A crude form of Swahili had become the language of communication between Africans and Europeans. But the teaching of English was a controversial issue that hardliners foresaw eventually rebounding on government and settlers alike. In frustration, the Kikuyu set up self-help **independent schools** in the 1930s, primarily in order to teach their own children English.

Whether barring access to English education would ultimately have made any difference is debatable, but by the late 1930s there were already enough educated Africans to pose the beginnings of a serious challenge to white supremacy. One of these

1921	1921	1923–39	1928
Political associations form to protest taxes, lack of land title deeds and low wages	Police shoot dead 25 political protestors	Kenya Colony's "Happy Valley" heyday	Jomo Kenyatta joins the Kikuyu Central Association

was Kamau wa Ngengi, who later adopted the name **Jomo Kenyatta**. Born some time between 1889 and 1895 near Kiambu, just north of Nairobi, and educated at the Scottish Mission Centre in nearby Thogoto, Kenyatta adopted his name from the traditional beaded belt (*kenyatta*) he always wore.

After Thuku's imprisonment and the bloodshed at Nairobi in 1921, the East African Association was dissolved and was succeeded by the **Kikuyu Central Association** (**KCA**), which Kenyatta – by now a government employee in Nairobi – joined in 1924. The KCA was the spearhead of nationalism and lobbied hard for tax reductions, a return of alienated land, and the election of African representatives on the Legislative Council. It also protested against missionary efforts to outlaw **female circumcision**, on the grounds that the Church was attempting to undermine Kikuyu culture. This last conflict led to a leadership crisis in the KCA and for a number of years threatened to swamp other issues.

Kenya survived the 1929 stock market crash and the resulting global **depression** as the colonial government became increasingly committed to the struggling settlers it was now bailing out. Exports fell catastrophically, coffee planting by non-whites was still prohibited and the tax burden continued to be placed squarely on Africans. Faced with this crisis, even some of the settlers began to accept that large-scale changes were in order. Just as awareness was growing that the economy could not survive indefinitely unless Africans were given more of a chance to participate, Kenya was thrown into World War II.

World War II

Perhaps not surprisingly, soldiers were easily recruited into the **King's African Rifles** when Italian-held Ethiopia (then Abyssinia) declared war on Kenya in 1940. Volunteers wanted money, education and a chance to see the world; conscripts, filling the quotas assigned to their chiefs, faced a life at home or on the native reserve that was no better than enlisting. Propaganda immediately succeeded in casting Hitler's image as the embodiment of all racist evil. Some Africans thought the war, once won, would improve their position in Kenya. They were partly right. Military campaigns in Ethiopia and Burma owed much of their success to African troops, and during the war their efforts were glowingly praised by Allied commanders.

On the soldiers' return, a new awareness, more profound than that felt by those returning from World War I, came upon them. The white tribes of Europe had fought the war on the issue of self-determination; the message wasn't lost on Africans. Yet still, in almost every other sphere of life, they were demeaned and humiliated. The KCA had been banned at the outbreak of war, allegedly for supporting the Italian fascists, and African political life was subdued. Real change, for 99 percent of the population, was still a dream.

Kenya's food-exporting economy had done well out of the war and it was clear the colony could make a major contribution to Britain's recovery. The postwar Labour government encouraged economic expansion without going far enough to include Africans among the beneficiaries. Industrialization gathered momentum and there was a rapid growth of towns. There was also further promotion of **white immigration** – a new influx of European settlers arrived soon after the war – and greater power was given to the settlers on the Legislative and Executive Councils. Population growth and intense pressure on land in the rural areas – especially among the Kikuyu in the Central Highlands – led to severe disruptions of traditional community life as people were shunted into the reserves or else left their villages to search for work in the towns, while

1929	1939–45	1944	1945
Wall Street crash and global depression leads to catastrophic fall in Kenya's exports	World War II: Kenyans fight for the British in Ethiopia and Burma	Eliud Mathu appointed as first African member of the legislative council	Jomo Kenyatta attends Pan-African Congress in Manchester

recently arrived European settlers created farms and plantations on the land from which they had been removed. On the political front, militant **trade unionism**, dominated by ex-servicemen, gradually usurped the positions of those African leaders who had been prepared to work with the government.

Postwar African politics

A single African member, Eliud Mathu, was appointed to the Legislative Council in 1944. More significant, however, was the formation in 1944 of the **Kenya African Union** (**KAU**), a consultative group of leaders and spokesmen, whose first president was Harry Thuku, set up with the governor's approval to liaise with Mathu.

Kenyatta had spent most of the period between 1929 and 1946 in Britain, though there were stays in Russia where he studied revolutionary theory at an institute for colonial subjects. He initially went to London with a petition from the KCA about land grievances, and continued to work as a KCA campaigner until the organization was banned, while also studying anthropology under Bronisław Malinowski at the London School of Economics, writing his homage to the Kikuyu people, *Facing Mount Kenya*, and participating in the Fifth Pan-African Congress, in Manchester, immediately after the war in 1945. Kenyatta's **return to Kenya** in September 1946 coincided with an escalating uproar about land rights, and the successful, well-travelled and highly networked Kenyatta received an enthusiastic welcome. The return home of the leading light in the small world of Kenyan postwar politics signalled a real departure for African political rights and the birth of a new current of nationalism. The KAU, which Kenyatta joined in 1947, was transformed into an active political party – and ran straight into conflict with itself. The radicals within the party wanted sweeping changes in land ownership, equal voting rights and abolition of the pass law, under which all black Kenyans were restricted in their movements and forced to carry an internal passport and obey the pass law restricting their movements. The moderates were for negotiation, educational improvement, multiracial progress and a gradual shift of power. They were not convinced that their best interests lay in confronting the British head-on; they had all achieved considerable ambitions within the settler economy. Kenyatta, elected KAU president in 1948, was ambitious himself, and the Europeans mistrusted his intentions and rumour-mongered about his personal life and his communist connections.

Despite Kenyatta's efforts to steer a middle course, the KAU became increasingly radical and Kikuyu-dominated. While Kenyatta angled to give the party a multi-tribal profile to appease the settlers, he also managed to sacrifice some moderates in the leadership for the sake of party unity. There were defections as well: several radicals joined an underground movement and took oaths of allegiance against the British. Oath-taking groups emerged secretly all around the Central Highlands and, in 1951, a Central Committee was organized by key KAU members in Nairobi, Fred Kubai and Bildad Kaggia, to coordinate insurgent activities.

The Mau Mau Rebellion

The Central Committee began murdering its opponents and attacking white-owned property in what became known as the **Mau Mau Rebellion**. The origin of the name is obscure (it may derive from *muma*, a traditional Kikuyu oath), but the insurgents never

1945–48	1947	1951	August 1952
Postwar European immigration encouraged	Jomo Kenyatta becomes leader of Kenya African Union	Mau Mau oath-taking becomes widespread	Curfew imposed in parts of Nairobi

used it, calling themselves the **Land and Freedom Army** (**LFA**). The British accused Kenyatta of involvement, but this seems unlikely, although the insurgents used his name in their propaganda to justify their attacks. The LFA consisted largely of young men from the rural periphery of towns like Nyeri, Fort Hall (Murang'a) and Nairobi, and membership was overwhelmingly Kikuyu.

In August 1952, following arson attacks on the homes of people who had refused to take the Mau Mau oath, the government imposed a curfew on three districts of Nairobi. In October, **Chief Waruhiu wa Kungu**, the government's most senior African official, was murdered in Nairobi after making a speech condemning the Mau Mau and in response the British reacted by declaring a **State of Emergency** and arresting any suspected insurgents. Within ten days, they had detained nearly four thousand people.

Kenyatta had played a delicate political game, condemning strikes and even oath taking, but ready to seize on any chance to exploit the situation. Now, in October 1952, he and other KAU leaders were arrested and interned for their supposed part in the uprising. The Governor arranged for the bribing of a witness to give false evidence against Kenyatta. Meanwhile, tens of thousands of squatters in the Rift Valley were sacked by the white farmers and drifted home, where many took Mau Mau oaths. Thousands of **British troops** were sent to Kenya and a **Kikuyu Home Guard** formed to combat the Mau Mau, but the hardcore guerrillas fled from their villages and lived off the jungle for months on end, launching surprise attacks at night. They also relied on considerable support from Kikuyu homesteads for supplies, intelligence reports and stolen weapons.

By early 1953, the rebels were becoming more daring. In January they murdered a settler family, the Rucks, including their 6-year-old son, and in March, a party of 83 insurgents raided **Naivasha police station**, releasing 173 detainees and seizing a large quantity of weaponry. Almost simultaneously, a force of around a thousand insurgents attacked the village of **Lari**, northwest of Nairobi, whose residents were largely Kikuyus loyal to the colonial regime, many of them Home Guard members. The insurgents burned down their homes and hacked to death more than eighty people. The following day, Home Guard reprisal killings of Mau Mau sympathizers in the district topped one hundred, killed in a series of mass shootings.

The British now declared "**Special Areas**" in which anyone who failed to stop when challenged would be shot, and "**Prohibited Areas**" – including the Aberdare range and Mount Kenya – in which all Africans would be shot on sight. In April 1954 they put Nairobi under military control, rounding up all the city's Kikuyu residents and detaining seventeen thousand of them, before extending the operation to other Kikuyu areas. By the end of the year, there were 77,000 prisoners, held in more than fifty British **concentration camps** throughout the country, where they were subject to arbitrary acts of brutality and murder at the hands of British troops. At one point, a third of the entire male adult Kikuyu population was being held in detention. Under emergency powers, a policy of "**villagization**" was also enforced: by the end of 1955, more than a million people – almost the entire Kikuyu population – had been forcibly resettled in villages policed by guards and fenced with barbed wire.

British atrocities

At its height, in 1953–54, the insurgency consisted of some fifteen thousand guerrillas, but little by little the British hunted them down. By September 1956, only around five

October 1952	March 1953	1953
State of Emergency declared and Kenyatta arrested	Homes burned and more than eighty Kikuyu loyal to the British massacred by insurgents at Lari	Aberdare range and Mount Kenya declared "Protected areas" in which any Africans were shot on sight

thousand remained. The **end of the revolt** came in October 1956 with the capture and execution of **Dedan Kimathi**, the LFA's commander-in-chief. The State of Emergency nonetheless continued until 1960, when it was abandoned after news emerged in the press that British troops had bludgeoned detainees at **Hola** detention camp in March 1959, killing eleven and injuring sixty, sparking outrage in Britain.

During the Mau Mau uprising, insurgents murdered 32 white settlers and around 2000 Kenyan civilians, while fifty British troops lost their lives. In response, the British hanged 1090 rebels – more than in any other colonial uprising – and claimed to have killed around 11,000 guerrillas, destroying much of the documentation about the detention camps before independence. Evidence that has come to light since the turn of the century, however (see p.593 and p.594), suggests that British forces killed more than 50,000 people, and perhaps as many as 100,000. The evidence also shows that torture was a widespread tool of interrogation: thousands of detainees and villagers were subjected to gross human rights abuses while being screened and questioned, ranging from mutilation to rape, many of which resulted in death.

No British officials, nor any of the settlers who were also involved, have yet been prosecuted for atrocities committed during the Emergency. Nor has Britain yet paid any compensation or made any formal apology. Finally, in 2012, after years of representations, three elderly victims of torture during the Mau Mau period won the right to sue the UK government for reparations.

Independence: Uhuru

With the Emergency over, the KAU leaders still at liberty set about exploiting the European fear of a repeat episode. Anything that now delayed the fulfilment of African nationalist aspirations could be seen as fuel for another revolt. There was no longer any question of a South African-style, white-dominated independence. Settlers, mindful of the preparations for independence taking place in other African countries, began rallying to the cry of multiracialism in a vain attempt to secure what looked like a very shaky future.

At the 1960 Lancaster House Conference in London, called to discuss Kenya's future, African representatives won a convincing victory by pushing through measures to give them majorities in the Legislative Council and the Council of Ministers. The members of these bodies, all nominated by the colonial authorities, included **Tom Mboya**, the prominent and charismatic Luo trade unionist, and the radical politician **Oginga Odinga** (another Luo), as well as **Daniel Arap Moi** and the Mijikenda leader **Ronald Ngala**. A new constitution was drawn up and the right of access for all races to the "White Highlands" was confirmed. The declaration promised that "Kenya was to be an African country": the path to independence was guaranteed; British Prime Minister Harold Macmillan said as much in his "**Wind of Change**" speech to the South African parliament at the time the Lancaster House Conference was meeting. The settlers perceived a "calamitous betrayal", with universal franchise and African-dominated independence expected within a few years.

Minority tribal associations, meanwhile, foresaw troubles ahead if the Kikuyu/Luo elite achieved independence for Kenya at the cost of the smaller constituencies. In 1960, the Kenya African National Union (**KANU**) was formed, dominated by the

1954	1955	October 1956	March 3 1959
77,000 prisoners held by the British in concentration camps	Most Kikuyu forced out of homes and interned in camps	Mau Mau leader Dedan Kimathi captured and executed	Hola massacre: eleven detainees bludgeoned to death by British troops

Kikuyu and Luo politicians who had campaigned most prominently against British colonial rule. Soon after, a second, more moderate party, the Kenya African Democratic Union (**KADU**), was created, with Britain's help, to federate the minority, largely rural-based political associations in a broad defensive alliance against Kikuyu/ Luo domination. One of KADU's leading members was Daniel Arap Moi.

Elections were held in 1961, KANU emerging with nineteen seats against KADU's eleven. But KANU refused to form a government until Kenyatta was released from the house arrest in Maralal that followed his seven-year jail term. A temporary coalition government was formed, composed of KADU, European and Asian members. Kenyatta was duly released and, six months later, a member resigned his seat, making room for him on the Legislative Council. In 1962, Kenyatta became Minister for Constitutional Affairs and Economic Planning – a wide portfolio – in a new coalition government formed out of the KADU alliance and KANU. Despite a second London conference to try to reach an agreement about the federal constitution demanded by KADU, the question was left in the air.

Independence elections the following year seemed to answer the constitutional question: KANU emerged with an even greater lead and a mandate for a non-federal structure. On June 1 – **Madaraka Day** – Kenyatta became Kenya's first prime minister. And on December 12, 1963, control of foreign affairs was handed over and Kenya became formally **independent**.

The Kenyatta years: harambee

It was barely sixty years since the pioneer settlers had arrived. Many of them had panicked, sold up and left before independence, but others decided to stay under an **African government**. Despite his years in detention, Kenyatta turned out to have more consideration for their interests than could have been foreseen. He held successful meetings with settlers in his home village; his bearded, genial image and conciliatory speeches assuring them of their rights and security quickly earned him wide international support and the respected title Mzee (Elder). Many Europeans retained important positions in the administration and judiciary.

Milton Obote and Julius Nyerere, leaders of newly independent Uganda and Tanzania, held talks with Kenyatta on setting up an **East African Community** to share railways, aviation, telecommunications and customs. The union was formally inaugurated in 1967. There was a mood of optimism: it looked very much as if Kenya had succeeded against all the odds.

But there were urgent issues to contend with, among which **land reform** and the rehabilitation of freedom fighters and detainees were the most pressing. Large tracts of European land were bought up by the government and a programme to provide small plots to landless peasants was rapidly instigated. Political questions loomed large as well. On December 12, 1964, Kenya became a republic, its head of state no longer the Queen, but rather President Kenyatta. KADU was dissolved "in the interests of national unity" and its leaders absorbed into the ruling KANU party, making Kenya a de facto one-party state. For the sake of "national security", British troops were kept on, initially to quell a revolt of ethnic Somalis in the northeast and an army mutiny in Nairobi. A defence treaty has kept a British force at Nanyuki ever since.

July–Dec 1959	January 1960	1960	1961
All "villagization" and detention camps closed and prisoners released	Harold Macmillan gives "Wind of Change" speech	The Kenya African National Union, a political party dominated by the Kikuyu and Luo elite, is formed	Jomo Kenyatta freed from house arrest

There was heavy emphasis on **harambee** (pulling together), endorsed by Kenyatta at all his public appearances. *Harambee* meetings became a unique national institution: fund-raising events at which – in a not untraditional way – donations were made by local notables and politicians towards self-help education and health programmes. During the 1960s and 1970s, hundreds of *harambee* schools were built and equipped in this way. But the ostentatious gifts, and particularly the guaranteed press coverage the next day with donors listed in order of value, sometimes reduced the *harambee* vision of community development to an exercise in patronage and competitive status seeking.

On the **economic front**, the first decade of independence saw remarkable changes and rapid growth. The settlers' fairly broad-based crop-exporting economy was a powerful springboard for development, and not difficult to transfer to African control. While many large landholdings were sold *en bloc* to African investors, smaller farmers began to contribute significantly to export earnings through coffee, tea, pyrethrum and fruit. Industrialization proceeded at a slower pace: Kenya's mineral resources are limited and the country relies heavily on oil imports. **Foreign investment** wasn't especially beneficial, as investors were given wide freedoms to import equipment and technical skills and to re-export much of the profit.

The resettlement programme was abandoned in 1966, its objectives "largely attained". But many peasants, having been squatters on European farms, were now "illegal squatters" on private African land. Thousands migrated to the towns where unemployment was already a serious problem. Kenya was becoming a class-divided society. **Growth**, rather than a radical redistribution of wealth, was the government's main concern. Although by 1970 more than two-thirds of the European mixed farming lands were occupied by some fifty thousand Africans, and the overall standard of living had improved considerably, income disparities were greater than ever. **Kikuyu domination** was strongly resented by other groups, although it was perhaps inevitable that the people who had lost most and suffered most under British rule should expect to receive the most benefits from independence.

Political opposition

It was in this climate that KANU's leadership split. **Oginga Odinga**, the party vice president, resigned in 1966 to form the socialist **Kenya People's Union (KPU)** and 29 MPs joined him. The ex-guerrilla Bildad Kaggia became deputy head of the KPU and a vocal agitator for poorer Kikuyu. Kenyatta and Mboya closed ranks in KANU and prepared for political conflict. KPU was anti-capitalist and in favour of non-alignment, while KANU – led in this respect by Tom Mboya – stressed the need for close ties with the West and for economic conditions that would attract foreign investment. It was the last time in independent Kenya that clearly contrasting party policies were to be given a proper airing, although the KPU's stand was denounced as divisive, and the party was barely tolerated for three years, its members harassed and detained by the security forces, its activities obstructed by new legislation and constitutional amendments.

In KANU, Odinga's post of vice president was taken, briefly, by Joseph Murumbi and then, with behind-the-scenes encouragement from the British (keen to avoid a radical in the job), by Daniel Arap Moi. Odinga had strong, grassroots support in the Luo and Gusii districts of western Kenya. But Tom Mboya's supporters came from an even broader base, including many poor Kikuyu. By the end of the 1960s, speculation was

1962	June 1 1963	Dec 12 1963
Elections give a mandate to KANU for a non-federal structure	Kenya achieves self-government (Madaraka Day) under Prime Minister Jomo Kenyatta	Kenya takes control of its foreign affairs, regaining its independence, while Queen Elizabeth II remains formal head of state

mounting about whether he would be able to take over the presidency on Kenyatta's death. As the Mzee's right-hand man he was widely tipped to succeed – a possibility that alarmed Kenyatta's more high-profile Kikuyu supporters. In July 1969, Mboya was gunned down by a Kikuyu assassin in central Nairobi. No high-level complicity in the murder was ever brought to light, but Mboya's death was a devastating blow to Kenya's fragile stability, setting off shock waves along both class and tribal divisions. There was widespread fighting and rioting between Kikuyu and Luo, fuelled by years of rivalry and growing feelings of Luo exclusion from government. During a visit by Kenyatta to Kisumu – where he attended a public meeting at which Odinga and his supporters were present – hostility against his entourage was so great that police opened fire, killing at least ten demonstrators.

The KPU was immediately banned and Odinga detained without trial. Although the constitution continued to guarantee the right to form opposition parties, non-KANU nominations to parliament were, in practice, forbidden. There was a resurgence of oath taking among Kikuyu, Meru and Embu, pledging to maintain the Kikuyu hold on power. The Kikuyu contingent in the army was strengthened and a new force of shock troops, the **General Service Unit** (**GSU**), was recruited under Kikuyu officers; independent of police and army, it was to act as an internal security force. In the early 1970s, Kikuyu control – of the government, the administration, business interests and land – gripped tighter and tighter.

Kenyatta's closing years

Internationally, Kenya was seen as one of the safest **African investments** – a model of stability only too happy to allow the multinational corporations access to its resources and markets. The development of the tourist industry helped give the country a positive profile, and, in comparison with most other African countries, some still fighting for independence and others beset by civil war or paralyzed by drought, Kenya's future looked healthy enough. But in achieving record economic growth, foreign interests often seemed to crush indigenous ones. An elite of profiteers – nicknamed the **wabenzi** after the Mercedes Benzes they favoured – extracted enormous bribes out of transactions with foreign companies. Nepotism was blatant and Kenyatta himself was rumoured to be one of the richest men in the world. For the majority of Kenyan people, life was hardly any better than before independence. Students poured out of the secondary schools with few prospects of using their qualifications; population increase was the highest in the world; and, most damaging of all, land distribution was still grossly unfair in a society where land to grow subsistence crops was the basic means of survival.

In 1975, in the first ever explicit public attack on the Kikuyu monopoly of power, the radical populist MP **J.M. Kariuki** warned that Kenya could become a country of "ten millionaires and ten million beggars". He was arrested for his pains then released and, some weeks later, found murdered in the Ngong Hills. A massive turnout at his funeral was followed by angry **student demonstrations**. "Kariuki's death", wrote the then outspoken *Weekly Review*, "instils in the minds of the public the fear of dissidence, the fear to criticize, the fear to stand out and take an unconventional public stance." In the following years, a number of other MPs were detained, and the issue of landlessness ceased to be one that many people were prepared to shout about.

Dec 12 1964	1965	1966
Kenya becomes a republic (Jamhuri Day) in the British Commonwealth, its head of state now President Jomo Kenyatta	KADU party dissolved and Kenya becomes a de facto one-party state	KANU splits, with Vice President Oginga Odinga resigning to form the socialist, non-aligned Kenya People's Union

Kenyatta retreated into dictatorial seclusion, propped up by close Kikuyu cronies. As parliament, and even the cabinet, took an increasingly passive role in decision-making, the pronouncements from the Mzee's "court" began to be accompanied by vague suggestions that threats to his government were being made by unspecified foreign powers. By 1977, the **East African Community** had ceased to function. Delayed elections, hostility towards socialist Tanzania, further detentions and growing allegations of corruption formed the sullen backdrop to **Kenyatta's death**, in bed, on August 28, 1978.

Kenya under Moi: nyayo

The passing of the Mzee took Kenya by surprise. There was a nationwide outpouring of grief and shock, but for many, also a sense of relief, and anticipation that the future might better reflect the ideals of twenty years earlier. Vice President Daniel Arap Moi smoothly assumed power and gathered popular support with moves against corruption in the civil service, his stand against tribal nepotism (he himself was from the minority Kalenjin), and the release of all Kenyatta's political prisoners.

But the honeymoon was short. In the first year or two of his presidency, Moi's **nyayo** (footsteps) philosophy of "peace, love and unity" in the wake of Kenyatta found wide appeal, and his apparent honesty and outspoken attacks against tribalism impressed many, making him friends abroad. But economic management was weak, and the failure to make any adjustments in economic policy in favour of the rural and urban poor caused growing resentment at home. Oginga Odinga and other ex-KPU MPs were prevented from standing in the 1979 elections. Student protests began again and the closing of the university became an annual event. On the international scene, the whole Indian Ocean region became strategically important with the fall of the Shah of Iran and the Soviet invasion of Afghanistan, and Kenya developed close ties with the USA.

On Sunday August 1, 1982 – three months after constitutional amendments were pushed through to make Kenya officially a one-party state (to prevent Oginga Odinga registering the new Kenya Socialist Alliance party) – sections of the Kenya Air Force attempted a **military coup**. Without support in the other armed forces, however, the coup was easily put down by the army and the GSU, who killed scores of perceived coup supporters. The coup attempt heralded a new clampdown on students and "dissidents", such as Oginga Odinga, who was placed under house arrest.

Despite Moi's efforts to throttle all dissent, the groundswell of resentment continued to grow. An opposition group, **Mwakenya** (a Swahili acronym for Union of Nationalists to Liberate Kenya), attracted attention through its pamphlets calling for the replacement of the Moi government, new democratic freedoms and an end to corruption and Western influence. Hundreds of people, and sometimes their defence lawyers, were arrested. A 1987 **Amnesty International** report condemned Kenya's human rights record, as detainees died in custody and prisoners were routinely tortured and kept in waterlogged cells beneath Nyayo House in Nairobi. Public meetings of more than five people were banned, and all dissent, even within KANU, was crushed.

The path to multiparty democracy

In February 1990 **Robert Ouko**, the Luo foreign minister favoured by the West and widely viewed as a potential successor to the presidency, was murdered, sparking off a

July 1969	July 1969	July 1969
KANU party leader-in-waiting, Jomo Kenyatta's charismatic right-hand man and Luo trade unionist, Tom Mboya, is assassinated	During President Kenyatta's visit to Kisumu, police kill ten demonstrators protesting at Luo exclusion from government	The KPU is banned and Oginga Odinga detained without trial

RICHARD LEAKEY AND THE KENYA WILDLIFE SERVICE

Although now internationally renowned as a wildlife conservationist, **Richard Leakey** rose to prominence as a paleontologist from the shadows of his eminent parents Mary and Louis Leakey, publishing several books and eventually becoming head of the National Museums of Kenya in Nairobi.

In 1989, facing an international outcry over the poaching of elephants and the serious impact that was having on the tourist industry, President Moi hired Leakey to take charge of the newly formed **Kenya Wildlife Service** (KWS). Leakey's first move was a characteristically bold one: he invited the world's press to watch Moi ignite Kenya's US$3 million stockpile of confiscated **ivory** – producing the most memorable photo opportunity of the Moi presidency. He went on, with Moi's support, to create anti-poaching units and briefed them to shoot to kill any poachers in the parks. The World Bank and other donors were so impressed that they gave more than US$140 million in grants. The poaching stopped, elephants and rhinos were saved from the brink of extinction, and Kenya's international image was partially restored.

But Leakey's success went too far for some local politicians, particularly in Maasai-land. His confrontational approach to the balance of human and animal needs in the parks – all humans out – infuriated many. And he seemed incorruptible: the KWS had dried up completely as a source of patronage.

In June 1993, on a routine flight at the controls of his Cessna plane, Leakey crashed, losing both legs in the accident. Foul play was suspected, but not proven. Within months he was walking on artificial limbs, anxious to get back to work. But there had been a mood change in his employers. Noah Ngala, tourism minister at the time, announced that evidence of corruption and mismanagement had been unearthed at the KWS. No more bitter irony could be imagined. Leakey resigned and was replaced by the less trenchant David Western, an advocate of human–animal coexistence. Western was sacked in 1998 after falling out with government over their corrupt interference at Lake Nakuru and Tsavo West national parks and Leakey was reinstated, only to leave again to join the government itself.

Since the turn of the century, the increasingly militarized KWS has been run by a succession of appointees, each one determined to be seen as hard on poachers, but caught between government interference, the eloquent conservation lobby and the demands of the tourist industry.

week of nationwide **rioting**, most violent in Ouko's home town of Kisumu. Public opposition to the government mounted, and a Nairobi pro-democracy rally on July 7 (**Saba Saba** – Swahili for 7/7, as the event came to be known) degenerated into a riot, leading to dozens of deaths in street battles with armed police.

Moi blamed "hooligans and drug addicts" for the Saba Saba riots, and the government came down hard on journalists, stifling local newspapers and accusing the foreign press, particularly the BBC, of mischief-making. Relations with the international community plummeted. Against the prevailing, post-Cold War trend in Africa, Moi's stubborn resistance to multiparty democracy riled his overseas backers. He seemed barely aware of the new global consensus and the hard reassessment of aid distribution taking place among the rich countries.

In 1991, the steady build-up of an opposition lobby became so powerful it could no longer be dismantled. Oginga Odinga – effectively Kenya's elder statesman – set up the **Forum for the Restoration of Democracy (FORD)** in association with his son **Raila Odinga**

March 2 1975	August 28 1978	1978
Outspoken Kikuyu commentator J.M. Kariuki is murdered after criticizing the nepotism and corruption of the ruling elite	The Mzee (respected elder) President Jomo Kenyatta dies	Vice-President Daniel Arap Moi succeeds as President and releases all political prisoners

---

RELIGION IN KENYA

Indigenous religion (mostly based around the idea of a supreme god and intercession between the living and the spirit worlds by deceased ancestors) survives as an inclusive belief system only in remote areas of northern Kenya, among the remaining Okiek (or Ndorobo) hunter-gatherers in a few forests, and to some extent among pastoralists like the Maasai. While it is continually under threat from Christian missionaries, its influence over the lives of many nominally Christian or Muslim Kenyans remains powerful.

Varieties of **Catholicism** and **Protestantism** are dominant in the Highlands and westwards, and are increasingly pervasive elsewhere. In the Rift Valley and the far west, especially towards Lake Victoria, there are many minor Christian sects and churches – more than a thousand denominations in all – often based around the teachings of local prophets and preachers.

The moderate **Ismaili Muslim** sect is an influential Asian constituency with powerful business interests, led by the Aga Khan, whose Aga Khan Foundation is a major development agency in Kenya, investing in schools, hospitals and the tourist industry – it owns Serena Hotels.

Otherwise, broad-based, non-fundamentalist **Sunni Islam** dominates the coast and northeast, and is the fastest-growing religion in the country. Many towns have several mosques, of which one usually serves as the focal Friday mosque for the whole community. Kenyan Muslims tend to be moderate, but responses to the Kenyan armed forces' Somalia campaign (see p.573) suggest that there are enough extremists to cause serious problems.

Hindu and **Sikh** temples are found in most large towns, and there are also adherents of **Jainism** and the **Baha'i** faith.

---

and the influential Law Society chairman, **Paul Muite**. FORD quickly attracted government opponents from all quarters. Meanwhile, **John Troon**, the ex-Scotland Yard policeman hired by Moi to investigate Ouko's murder, revealed that the greatest suspicion fell on the president's closest advisor Nicholas Biwott, and his internal security chief, Hezekiah Oyugi, both of whom were sacked, arrested and later released "for lack of evidence", but not reinstated. Major donor nations subsequently suspended balance-of-payment support to Kenya, pending economic and political reforms. Moi got the message. Within days he announced there would be multiparty elections for the next parliament and a free vote for the presidency at the end of 1992.

The 1992 elections

FORD found the transformation from opposition lobby group to **political party** hard to manage. It extended a welcome to every ex-KANU minister who made the leap, and with elections approaching, the party promptly split into three ethnic factions, each with its own presidential candidate, and none with any clear party ideology. Dozens were killed and thousands made homeless in tribal violence in the Rift Valley, mainly between indigenous Kalenjin people who supported Moi, and migrant farmers and traders from central Kenya.

Using a combination of fraud, ballot-stuffing, manipulation of electoral rules, physical prevention of opposition candidates from presenting nomination papers, printing money to buy off the voters, and changing the polling date at the last minute, Moi made sure that he and his party won the **1992 election**. But for the first time there was also an elected multiparty opposition (even though there were few declared policies in the air), including the three FORD factions, and the Democratic Party (DP) under

1979	May 1982	Aug 1 1982	February 1984
Oginga Odinga and other opposition activists prevented from standing in elections	Constitutional amendments make Kenya officially a one-party state	Attempted coup by Kenya Air Force violently suppressed by army and GSU	Wagalla massacre of up to 3000 Degodia Somalis in Wajir

former Vice President Mwai Kibaki, who came third in the presidential poll behind Moi and Odinga. KANU had almost no MPs from Kikuyu or Luo areas.

The 1997 elections

Several years of economic slowdown followed, with strikes by teachers and nurses, mass demonstrations for constitutional reform and the breakdown of relations with the International Monetary Fund (IMF). Senior figures in the main opposition parties agreed to work together, with a single presidential candidate for the **1997 elections**, the economist and career politician Mwai Kibaki. **Richard Leakey** (see p.567) coordinated the alliance and raised funds. By June 1997, the opposition, and particularly students, were howling for reforms in advance of the elections. Police stormed Nairobi University to stop a rally commemorating the 1990 Saba Saba demonstrations and left more than a dozen dead, while brutally putting down protests that had broken out around the country.

For the rest of the year, repression alternated with promises of reform, punctuated by a series of national strikes. Mombasa erupted in violence in August 1997, when two police stations were attacked, six policemen killed, weapons stolen and dozens of upcountry people later killed and thousands more expelled by armed gangs who terrorized the district of **Likoni**. Notices circulated "reclaiming" the coast for its indigenous inhabitants, and demanding that the largely Kikuyu newcomers return to their home districts. In November 1997, finally parliament removed some of the legislation restricting freedom of movement and speech.

Elections were held in December, and the vote, predictably, split along ethnic lines. Mwai Kibaki's DP did well in the Kikuyu areas; Raila Odinga's National Development Party (NDP) took most of Luo-land; and Moi's KANU was widely endorsed on the coast and in the Rift Valley and north, securing Moi the presidency against second-placed Kibaki.

AL-QAEDA IN KENYA

On the morning of August 7, 1998, a van containing 800kg of TNT exploded in the parking lot behind the **US embassy** in Nairobi. In the embassy itself – the terrorists' intended target – some forty people, twelve of them Americans, perished; but the brunt of the blast was borne by the adjacent four-storey Ufundi Cooperative House. The resulting carnage led to 218 deaths and more than five thousand people injured, nearly all of them Kenyans, and property damage estimated at around $500 million. It is widely suspected that local **Al-Qaeda** operatives were responsible for the attack, as well as the bombing of the US embassy in Dar es Salaam, just a few minutes later.

Before the December 2002 elections, Kenya's tourist industry was shaken by an Al-Qaeda suicide bomb attack on the Israeli-owned *Paradise Hotel* at Kikambala that killed sixteen people, simultaneous with a failed attempt to shoot down an Israel-bound charter flight leaving Mombasa.

With the emergence of the **Al-Shabaab** jihadist organization in Somalia and their declared alliance with Al-Qaeda in 2010, Kenya faces even more serious threats across the porous Somali border and potentially at home, too, although there is little evidence of significant home-grown support for their aims.

1987	1989	Feb 1990	July 7 1990
Amnesty International report condemns Kenya's human rights record	Kenya's stockpile of ivory is burned in a PR stunt organized by KWS director Richard Leakey	Murder of Luo foreign minister Robert Ouko sparks widespread rioting	Saba Saba riots in Nairobi lead to dozens of deaths in battles with police

Moi's final term

The aftermath of the elections saw discussion on constitutional reform getting under way, with Moi bringing opposition figures on side. Raila Odinga was made chair of the constitutional reform committee and Richard Leakey was appointed as cabinet secretary with special responsibility for combating corruption. In June 2001, KANU and Odinga's NDP joined together in a formal coalition, Odinga joining the cabinet as energy minister.

With elections approaching in 2002, Odinga dissolved the NDP, which merged into KANU, a move that Moi hoped would bring Luo voters over to the party. The opposition also did some merging, when twelve groups joined to form the National Alliance Party of Kenya (**NAK**). Meanwhile the elderly Moi decided to back Uhuru Kenyatta as KANU's presidential candidate. Kenyatta was widely seen as a figurehead who would front a new regime on Moi's behalf, and Moi's backing of him particularly annoyed Raila Odinga, who had hoped to be the party's candidate. He and a number of other KANU grandees resigned their ministerial posts and set up a "Rainbow Alliance" within the party, opposed to Kenyatta's candidacy. In October they left KANU and formed the Liberal Democratic Party (LDP), which joined with the NAK to form the **National Rainbow Coalition** (**NARC**), with a single presidential candidate, Mwai Kibaki. NARC won a landslide victory in the December **2002 elections**, and KANU was turfed out of government for the first time since independence.

Kenya under Kibaki

Kibaki took up the presidency with an empty promise: **constitutional reform** within one hundred days. The biggest wrangle involved the proposed post of prime minister, which Odinga, apparently following a secret deal, saw as his. Part of the problem was that NARC was a loose alliance of politicians and ethnic blocs, and it soon began to fragment without Moi as a common opponent to unite it.

A constitutional convention was set up at the **Bomas of Kenya** conference centre in April 2003, but in a **draft constitution** passed in June 2005 the original Bomas proposals were shot through with amendments tabled in parliament, most notable among them the provision that the post of prime minister be in the president's gift. While the amendments also included a radical shake-up of Kenya's **land laws**, including proposals that women should have the right to inherit land and that foreigners should not be able to own land, Odinga and several other cabinet ministers campaigned for a "no" vote (represented by an orange) to the proposed constitution, which went to the country in a **referendum** in November 2005, resulting in a two-to-one rejection of the proposed constitution. His plans thwarted, Kibaki dismissed his entire cabinet, and then re-appointed them all, with the exception of Odinga and his senior followers, the Orange Team, who moved over to join KANU in opposition, marking the death of the NARC coalition. Constitutional reform was left in the air.

In other fields, Kibaki's reform ideas fared better. In 2003, his administration introduced **free primary education** for all, bringing schooling to 1.5 million more children, although the move was beset by logistical problems, teacher shortages, and a fall in schools' performance, with private schools dominating exam league tables. Post-Moi, the **press** was largely freer, although in an infamous raid in 2006, masked

Dec 1992	July 7 1997	Nov 1997	Dec 1997
Ethnic violence precedes first multi-party elections, and President Moi is re-elected	Police kill dozens of students during rally commemorating Saba Saba killings	Parliament lifts some restrictions on freedom of speech	Second multi-party elections result in another victory for Moi, to a backdrop of ethnic violence in the Rift Valley

ETHNIC VIOLENCE AND KENYA'S ELECTIONS

For years, any reference to **multiparty politics** by KANU leaders was accompanied by dire warnings of the bloody consequences for tribal harmony of such a system. Once the government was forced into a corner on the issue by foreign aid donors, the prophecy was quickly realized. Ethnic allegiances swamped the new political order before it had even consolidated, so that the opposition parties were unable to formulate policies and election strategies that were free of ethnic considerations.

For decades, the Rift Valley and other normally unproductive areas had been the destination for **migrants** from the Kikuyu, Kamba and Gusii tribes, who bought up marginal farmlands and tried to apply their farming techniques among the local Kalenjin and Maa-speakers while benefiting from local aid and subsistence initiatives. Victims of the early attacks in Rift Valley Province described organized gangs of youths terrorizing non-Kalenjin homesteads and villages, while local police arrived too late to do anything or just stood by.

In **electioneering** terms, the violence usually proved counterproductive, as the government lost more votes from disgust with their inaction than it gained from forcing opposition voters out of marginal KANU constituencies. Probably the aim was simply to demonstrate to the world at large that multipartyism in Africa leads to tribal violence. In this – to the Moi government's lasting shame – it succeeded.

The violence consisted of the looting of property, the theft of livestock, the burning of houses, and the beating up or killing of anyone who got in the way of the perpetrators. Their message was "Get off our land", and thousands of victims moved to refugee camps outside Eldoret, Nanyuki and other towns. During the 1990s, at least three thousand people were killed in violence between different language groups in the Rift Valley, western Kenya and on the coast, and at least three hundred thousand were displaced in **ethnic cleansing**. The violence would build up in the run-up to the elections and, in late 1992 and 1997 (and to a lesser extent in 2002), tensions ran high in traditional flashpoints.

As the results came in after the **2007 presidential elections**, both Raila Odinga and Mwai Kibaki declared victory, but it was Kibaki's swearing in on December 30 that sparked an instant, violent reaction across the country. Gangs of non-Kikuyu, Odinga supporters rampaged in the Rift Valley, in Kisumu and on the coast, attacking Kikuyu homes and businesses, killing men, women and children and, in an attack that received wide media coverage, burning a church in Eldoret sheltering fleeing Kikuyus, killing 35 people. There were running battles in Nairobi's slums between club- and machete-wielding youths of different tribes. By the end of January 2008, when talks brokered by former UN secretary-general Kofi Annan were finally under way, more than 1300 people had been killed and more than half a million displaced. The majority of the victims were Kikuyu, but other tribes were the targets of Kikuyu reprisal attacks and the police shot dead more than 100 demonstrators and looters. Unlike previous bouts of politically inspired ethnic violence, most of which had taken place in rural areas, the **2007–2008 clashes** were intense, and took place largely in towns, where foreign media were able to relay the unfolding carnage as it happened.

---

policemen stormed the offices of the Standard media group (which includes KTN TV, owned by the Moi family), burning papers, smashing equipment and seizing tapes, allegedly at the behest of President Kibaki's outspoken wife, who was being linked to drug-trafficking among other scandals.

The IMF and the World Bank resumed lending to Kenya in 2003 after the new government set up a five-year **Economic Recovery Strategy**, with a commitment to

August 7 1998	Dec 2002	2003	Nov 2005
Al-Qaeda bomb attack on US Embassy in Nairobi kills 263 and injures 5000	Opposition removes KANU from power, winning a landslide election victory with Mwai Kibaki	Free primary education introduced for all	Proposed new constitution put to the country in a referendum and rejected in protest at powers vested in the president

fighting corruption while opening up to privatization. The anti-corruption campaigner **John Githongo** was appointed Permanent Secretary for Government and Ethics, reporting directly to Kibaki. But high-level **corruption** continued virtually unabated. In 2005, the then British High Commissioner Sir Edward Clay memorably accused "gluttonous" officials of "vomiting on the shoes of donors" in a "looting spree" that had cost Kenya hundreds of millions of dollars. The scandal, which largely focused on the security industry, came to be known as **Anglo-Leasing** (the name of one of the companies involved) – a web of scams in which government money was paid to non-existent companies or for bogus or massively inflated contracts. Githongo took his job seriously and uncovered so much sleaze that when he presented his findings to the president, they were met with indignation rather than approval. He received death threats and had to flee into exile in the UK.

Public support for Kibaki's new Party of National Unity (**PNU**) government was wearing very thin as the country prepared for the 2007 elections, in which Kibaki was the PNU's candidate and Odinga, representing the Orange Democratic Movement (the successor party to the constitutional referendum's "no" vote), his rival. Throughout the Rift Valley, western Kenya and on the coast there was outright hostility to what was perceived to be a "Mount Kenya Mafia" running the country. The violent response to the elections, rigged by a government bent on staying in power, almost led to the break-up of Kenya itself in the **tribal clashes** of 2007 to 2008 (see p.571).

The Grand Coalition: 2008–2013

The **Grand Coalition** that eventually emerged from the electoral and societal wreckage of the clashes was led by **Mwai Kibaki**, who retained the presidency, and his ODM opponent, **Raila Odinga**, who became prime minister. Their bloated government, consisting of twenty highly paid ministers from each party grouping, attempted to buy off all competing interest groups by giving every senior politician a cabinet job.

The **police** and their paramilitary wing, the General Service Unit (**GSU**), continued to behave as if answerable to no one. While the eyes of the world saw unarmed youths gunned down by police officers during the post-election violence, far more dangerous targets were also being disposed of. In Nairobi's Mathare district and other slum areas in the Highlands, hundreds of alleged "Mungiki thugs" were shot (see p.159), and on Mount Elgon in the far west, in a local war that saw little coverage outside Kenya (see p.297), hundreds of people from the Sabaot sub-tribe of the Kalenjin were killed, tortured or raped. In an embarrassingly public humiliation in 2009, the administration was lambasted by the UN Special Rapporteur on Extrajudicial, Summary or Arbitrary Executions, **Philip Alston**, for its poor human rights record. Two weeks after Alston's speech, two human rights activists were shot dead in a traffic jam in Nairobi in broad daylight. Student demonstrations in response to the killings resulted in more casualties, from police bullets.

The prospect that politicians accused of crimes against humanity during the 2007–2008 post-election clashes and other internal conflicts might face prosecution at the International Criminal Court in The Hague alarmed the Kibaki–Odinga alliance. In the end, four key figures closely linked to the violence (two from the Kalenjin community, and two Kikuyu), including **William Ruto** and Kenya's richest man, son of

2005	Dec 2007–Feb 2008	April 2008
Government-appointed "anti-corruption czar" John Githongo flees Kenya after pointing the finger at President Kibaki	Rigged elections spark widespread violence, with more than 1300 people killed and half a million displaced	"Grand Coalition" government formed after months of negotiation, initially brokered by Kofi Annan

Kenya's founding president, **Uhuru Kenyatta** were informed that they were to be charged. Their trials are likely to take several years to complete.

Kenya's **new constitution**, driven through as a result of Kofi Annan's post-election mediation work, was finally enacted in August 2010 after a 67 percent "yes" vote in a second referendum. Among its many progressive features, the constitution makes a clear **separation of powers** between the executive, the legislature and the judiciary, devolves powers to 47 new **counties**, provides for a **bill of rights**, and guarantees **freedom of expression**. Critically for the 2013 elections, it also includes an **integrity chapter** for leaders, which should rule out anyone charged with a crime from running for president. But that depends on the newly independent judiciary making clear rulings, which in turn hangs on the **Commission for the Implementation of the Constitution** (CIC), already sitting for more than two years, making faster progress.

Al-Shabaab and trouble on the coast

Events, as ever, tend to overtake plans, and the **kidnappings** of aid workers and tourists in September and October 2011 precipitated a military intervention by Kenya's armed forces (the KDF) into southern Somalia – **Operation Linda Nchi** ("Protect the Country") – and had major repercussions for Kenya's tourist industry. Who the abductors were – Al-Shabaab Islamist terrorists, Somali pirates, local bandits or a combination – is still unclear. A British woman, whose husband was murdered when she was kidnapped near Kiwaiyu island, was released seven months later after her family paid a ransom. A French woman in poor health, kidnapped from her winter home on Manda island, died from lack of medication while being held.

The **war in Somalia** between the KDF and Al-Shabaab was showing no sign of coming to an early conclusion as this book went to press in early 2013. The KDF, having captured Somalia's second city, Kismayo, from Al-Shabaab, appeared to be prepared to dig in. Security in the Lamu archipelago was reinforced and foreign governments soon lifted their advisories cautioning against visiting Lamu, Manda and Pate, but the general security climate wasn't doing the tourist industry any favours. Meanwhile Al-Shabaab, uprooted from its former bases, staged a series of ad hoc **gun and grenade attacks** through 2012, with the presumed support of at least some Kenyan sympathizers, on defenceless targets including churches, bars, shops and transport parks, mostly in northeastern Kenya and low-income districts of Nairobi.

As the March 2013 elections approached, Kenya's tensions over Somalia began to emerge in local politics and power struggles, especially on the coast. A radical Muslim preacher, **Aboud Rogo**, implicated in fundraising for Al-Shabaab, was murdered in a drive-by shooting north of Mombasa in August 2012 – the fifth Islamist to be murdered or to have disappeared in Mombasa in 2012. The killers' identity was unclear, but Rogo's murder sparked three days of riots in poor districts of the city, resulting in several deaths and a further dampening down of the tourist industry – although resort areas were unaffected.

Parts of the coast were already tense because of the government's reaction to the **Mombasa Republican Council** (MRC), a separatist group who campaign under the slogan "Pwani si Kenya" ("The Coast is not Kenya") and whose aim is a coastal state independent from Kenya. The MRC, which maintains that its secessionist demands have a legitimate basis dating from colonial times, was banned in 2010, but the ban

2009	**2010**	**Aug 2010**	**April 2011**
United Nations representative Philip Alston lambasts government for extra-judicial killings	Widespread floods follow 2009's crippling droughts and bring death and destruction	New constitution approved in referendum after long consultative process	Six key figures, including two presidential candidates, named by ICC in The Hague in connection with 2008 post-election violence

WOMEN'S RIGHTS AND FGM

Women's groups flourish across the country, but tend to be concerned more with improvement of incomes, education, health and nutrition than social or political emancipation. The government-sponsored Maendeleo ya Wanawake Organization (MYWO) started to help women at a very basic level in the 1950s. It now encourages economic independence and, with a nominal annual membership fee, almost every woman in Kenya can belong. The umbrella group teaches basic literacy, family planning and nutrition, and is also working hard to abolish the practice of ritual **female genital mutilation** (FGM). This is carried out as a rite of passage on a significant proportion of Kenyan girls, and is more prevalent in some ethnic groups (the Gusii and the Maasai, for example, where it may still affect up to fifty percent) than others. Unsurprisingly, it is more common in rural areas and among uneducated communities. Kenya is a signatory to the UN's Human Rights Convention, which proscribes FGM, and the government promised in 1990 to ban the practice, but it was finally outlawed only in 2011. Women's groups are trying to persuade rural communities to accept a mutilation-free "alternative rite of passage", with some success.

was lifted by the High Court in Mombasa in July 2012 in a move intended to encourage the MRC to join the political process. It is a positive sign that, despite worries about sectarianism, Kenya's resurgent judiciary felt able to legitimize a pressure group some of whose members have been accused of violent intimidation of non-coastal communities.

If the judges are beginning to show their mettle, their authority is barely taken seriously by those in power – largely because it isn't translated into action by the **police**, whose institutional moral bankruptcy has driven generations of Kenyans to despair. After more than a hundred people were killed and thousands displaced in a month of orchestrated inter-ethnic raids and massacres in the **Tana Delta** in late 2012, ostensibly over access to water, a junior government minister, Dhadho Godana, charged with inciting Pokomo violence against the cattle-herding Orma for political ends, was sacked from his post, but released on bail. Meanwhile, the police did not question the Minister of Internal Security, Yusuf Hajji, allegedly complicit in inciting the Orma against the Pokomo.

Into the future

In the run-up to the **2013 elections** the country was on tenterhooks, with the frontrunner by a narrow margin the former coalition prime minister **Raila Odinga**. One prospective presidential candidate who was ruled out was the former Internal Security Minister **George Saitoti**, a broadly respected political survivor of Kikuyu parentage who had grown up in Maasailand, and who died in a crash in a badly maintained police helicopter near Nairobi in June 2012. Nevertheless, with a freshly minted and widely endorsed democratic constitution, and most of the country united against the terrorist threat from Somalia, there appeared to be a broad national commitment to ensuring a major outbreak of electoral violence did not happen again, even if serious local conflicts, especially where pastoralists share land with farmers, have become almost commonplace.

Kenya's prospects in the second decade of the twenty-first century would look

Sep 2011	Oct 2011	2012	July 2012
Two tourists kidnapped and one killed in two incidents in the Lamu archipelago	Kenya Defence Force (KDF) enters Somalia to combat Al-Shabaab terrorists	Attacks by presumed Islamist terrorists kill dozens in north-eastern towns and low-income districts of Nairobi and Mombasa	Separatist coastal group the MRC is legalized by Mombasa High Court

doubtful even if the country had a healthy environment and a strong economy. Kenya has been hugely affected by **climate change**, and in recent years crippling cycles of **drought and flooding** have seen millions of Kenyans in the north and east needing food aid.

Kenya's **poverty gap** increases every year – it's especially pronounced in the populous central highlands – and steep price rises for essential commodities such as flour, milk and sugar have seen many urban Kenyans struggling to keep up with **inflation** and meet basic daily needs – or to have any sense that their lives are changing for the better. Meanwhile, most politicians – and much of the country's educated and comfortably-off elite – continue to mouth platitudes about growth, development, and Rome not being built in a day, and about a long-term wish-list called **Vision 2030**. This includes grandiose plans for vast infrastructural developments in the north, including a high-speed railway and oil pipeline between South Sudan and Lamu, which have so far delivered nothing but kickbacks to government ministers and civil servants from grotesquely expensive "feasibility studies". In 2012, the British company Tullow Oil made a discovery of potentially commercially viable **oil reserves** in Turkana, but there are no immediate plans for extracting them.

Kenya's **future** seems increasingly uncertain; the combination of human and natural challenges almost overwhelming; the old spectres of corruption and tribalism still shockingly dynamic, never mind being vanquished; and the problems of landlessness, unemployment and poverty looming larger than ever. From the outside, the outlook doesn't appear bright. Kenyans are anticipating the next five years of government with some nervousness. But most would argue that the worst is probably over and things must get better eventually. If this endearing, ingrained optimism isn't borne out by real progress, by respect for the rule of law and adherence by the country's leaders to their own, hard-won new constitution, then increasing numbers of moderate Kenyans may turn to other means to make the changes they want.

Aug 2012	Aug 2012	Oct 2012
Assassination of Muslim preacher in Mombasa sparks three days of rioting in city centre	Raids between Pokomo and Orma communities in the Tana Delta kill more than 100 and leave thousands displaced	Elderly victims of torture during Mau Mau period win right to sue the UK government; KDF capture southern Somali city of Kismayo

Music

The music of Kenya is less well known abroad than that of a number of other African countries, but its home-grown vitality is there if you listen, and Nairobi's audiences and recording facilities have long been a draw for musicians from all over east and central Africa, bringing a Pan-African musical flavour to the city.

All the people of Kenya have **traditional musical cultures**, some of which have survived more intact than others – with the majority of Kenyans nowadays being Christian, gospel music has all but obliterated traditional music in many areas. Among the Kikuyu and the Kalenjin, for example, traditional music is almost extinct, and elsewhere, to hear anything at all, you need time, patience and local people's trust before being allowed to witness what can still be very sacred events. Kenyan **gospel** itself has been going through a transformation. On the one hand it's not the uplifting soulful version associated with African American churches in the United States, but neither is it any longer simply the tinny, synthesized, homogeneous beats of a few years ago. It still includes the choirs of the churches, both urban and rural, but modern gospel now mirrors every kind of pop music within Kenya.

As for **popular music**, there is no single identifiable genre of "Kenyan pop", but rather a number of styles that borrow freely and cross-fertilize with one another. Within Kenya's extremely widespread **benga** style, many musicians perform most of their songs in one of Kenya's indigenous languages. Other musicians, especially those playing rumba styles, aim at a broad national audience and thus perform in **Swahili**; the big-name bands can usually muster large crowds in sprawling, ethnically diverse towns like Nairobi, Nakuru or Mombasa. Others offer a local variant of the **Congolese** sound, with lyrics in **Lingala**, a Congolese language, understood by few people in Kenya. Meanwhile, **international pop sounds** such as R&B, hip-hop, reggae, ragga and dancehall have taken a more prominent role in Kenya's pop music sound, especially among the younger Kenyans.

A good complement to this music overview can be found at ⊕eastafricanmusic.com, a website put together by the author of this article, that features biographies of several musicians, articles on the Kenyan scene over the years and lists of recommended albums.

Traditional music

Music has traditionally been used to accompany ceremonies, events and **rites of passage**, from celebrations at a baby's birth to songs of adolescence and warriorhood, and from marriage, harvests and solar and lunar cycles to festivities, religious events and death. The oldest of Kenya's musical traditions is **ngoma**, a term which, in most Bantu languages of Kenya, refers to a specific kind of drum and a related dance; *ngoma* is nowadays used generally to describe all the facets of a musical performance, including the accompanying dances.

Although an inter-ethnic *ngoma* called *beni* ("band") emerged on the coast at the beginning of the twentieth century and spread inland (you can still witness this anachronistic, marching-band form on special occasions in Lamu), *ngoma* music today is essentially ethnic, related to a specific language group and using the respective vernacular and local dance rhythms. *Ngoma* also provides most of the music used during the life-cycle festivities (birth, initiation and circumcision, marriage and death), whether in the town or the country. Look out for recordings by Luhya *sukuti* groups, the *sukuti* being the central drum of these ensembles.

The following is a brief tribe-by-tribe rundown of more easily encountered traditional music and instruments. Obviously, there's much more available if you know where to search and what to ask for: essential **reading** for this is George Senoga-Zake's *Folk Music of Kenya* (Uzima Press, Nairobi). Other books about Kenyan music are thin on the ground, though most bookshops stock some school textbooks on music, some of which provide a handy introduction to the subject. You can usually find a few CDs of traditional music locally – and even the odd cassette – though it may take a little perseverance. Another source of background on traditional music, with audio clips, is ✪bluegecko.org.

Kamba and Chuka

The **Kamba** are best known for their skill at drumming, but this tradition has sadly now all but disappeared. To find any musicians, you'll have to go well off the beaten track in Ukambani. Start in the big town of Machakos and then move on to Kitui. Like the music of the Kamba, Chuka music from the east side of Mount Kenya is drumming genius and, sadly, equally near-extinct.

Bajuni

The **Bajuni** are a small ethnic group living in the Lamu Archipelago and on the nearby mainland, and are known musically for a recording of an epic women's work song called *Mashindano Ni Matezo*. One of only a very few easily available recordings of women singing traditionally in Kenya, it features counterpoint singing that gradually becomes hypnotic, punctuated by metallic rattles and supported by subdued drumming. You can find it in Lamu, Kilifi or Mombasa.

Boran

The **Boran**, who live between Marsabit and the Ethiopian border, have a rich musical tradition. Some Arab influence is readily discernible, as are more typically North African rhythms; most distinctive is their use of the *chamonge* calabash guitar, nowadays a large cooking pot loosely strung with metal wires. Recordings are difficult to obtain; ask in Isiolo or Marsabit.

Gusii

Gusii music is perhaps Kenya's oddest. The favoured instrument is the *obokano*, an enormous, deep-voiced version of the Luo *nyatiti* lyre, which at times can sound like roaring thunder. They also use the ground bow, essentially a large hole dug in the ground over which an animal skin is tightly pegged. The skin has a small hole cut in the centre, into which a single-stringed bow is placed and plucked: the sound defies description. Ask around in Kisii and you should be able to pick up recordings easily enough.

Luhya

Luhya music has a clear Bantu flavour, easily discernible in the pre-eminence of drums. Of these, the *sukuti* is best known, sometimes played in ensembles, and still used in rites of passage such as circumcision. Recordings are easily available in Kakamega and Kitale, and in some of the shops around River Road in Nairobi.

Luo

The **Luo** are best known as the originators of *benga* (see p.580). Their most distinctive musical instrument is the *nyatiti*, a double-necked eight-string lyre with a skin resonator which is also struck on one neck with a metal ring tied to the toe. It produces a tight, resonant sound, and is used to generate hypnotic, sometimes remarkably complex, rhythms. The instrument was used in the fields to relieve workers' tiredness, the music typically beginning at a moderate pace and quickening progressively, the musician singing over the sound. Look out also for recordings of *onand* (accordion) and *orutu* (a single-stringed fiddle).

Maasai

The nomadic lifestyle of the **Maasai** tends to preclude the carrying of large instruments, and as a result their music is one of the most distinctive in Kenya, characterized by a total lack of instruments and by some astonishing polyphonic multi-part singing. This can be call-and-response, and sometimes women are included in the chorus, but the most famous form is the songs of the warriors or *morani*, where each man sings part of a rhythm, more often than not from his throat (rather like a grunt), which together with the calls of his companions creates a pattern of rhythms. The songs are usually competitive (expressed through the singers alternately leaping as high as they can) or bragging – about how the singer killed a lion, or rustled cattle from a neighbouring community. The Maasai have retained much of their traditional culture, so singing is still very much used in traditional ceremonies, most spectacularly in the *eunoto* circumcision ceremony in which boys are initiated into manhood to begin their ten- to fifteen-year stint as *morani*.

Most tourists staying in big coastal hotels or in game park lodges in Amboseli and Maasai Mara will have a chance to sample Maasai music in the form of groups of *morani* playing at the behest of hotel management. Recordings can be difficult to find, though there is an excellent US website on Maasai music, ⓦ laleyio.com, with audio clips, and a CD available to order.

Mijikenda

The **Mijikenda** of the coast have a prolific musical tradition which has survived Christian conversion, and is readily available on tape throughout the coastal region. Performances can occasionally be seen in the larger hotels. Most of the music available is from the Giriama section of the Mijikenda, who live inland of Malindi. Like the Kamba, the Mijikenda are superb drummers and athletic dancers. The music is generally light and overlaid with complex rhythms, impossible not to dance to. Look out also for the *kiringongo* music of the Chonyi people, which features the xylophone (an instrument otherwise unknown in Kenya).

Samburu

Despite having been discovered by tourists and authors of coffee-table books, the only recordings of **Samburu** music are tracks on occasional compilations. Like their Maasai cousins, whose singing it closely resembles, Samburu music includes no instruments – at least in theory. In practice, they do play small pipes, and also a kind of guitar with a box resonator and loose metal strings – which seems to be related to the *chamonge* of the Boran. But these are played purely for pleasure, or to soothe a crying baby, and are thus not deemed "music" by Samburu. Listen out also for the sinuously erotic rain songs sung by women in times of drought. For recordings, ask around in Maralal.

Turkana

Until the 1970s, the **Turkana** were one of Kenya's remotest tribes, and in large part they're still untouched by Christian missionaries. Their traditional music is based loosely on a call-and-response pattern. The main instrument is a kudu antelope horn with or without finger holes, but most of their music is entirely vocal. A rarity to listen out for are the women's rain songs, sung to the god Akuj during times of drought. Traditional music is still played on ceremonial occasions but finding cassettes is extremely difficult; it's a question of asking around in Loiyangalani. You're usually welcome to join performances in Loiyangalani for a small fee.

Popular music

Until the mid-1990s, the defining elements of Kenyan popular music had always been the interplay of guitars, with prominent solos, and the **cavacha** rhythm – a kind of *clavé* beat, popularized in the mid-1970s by Congolese groups such as Zaiko Langa Langa and

Orchestra Shama Shama. While rapid-fire percussion, usually on the snare or high hat, continues to underlie a great sweep of Kenyan music, it's worth noting that the scene is very different to that of only ten or fifteen years ago; the ranks of the older generation of pop musicians have thinned quickly in recent years, with a huge number of experienced younger musicians having died from AIDS-related illnesses. The effects have been devastating, not only in the loss of creative talent, but because with these musicians goes the living memory of the evolution of Kenyan music in its historical context.

The arrival of the guitar

From the early 1950s on, with the coming of recording and broadcasting, the introduction of new instruments and the more widespread use of the **guitar**, an acoustic guitar-based music developed as accompaniment to songs sung in **Swahili**. A basis for Swahili-language popular music had already been laid by the *beni* groups

TAARAB MUSIC

Taarab (or *tarab/tarabu*), the main popular music of the coastal Swahili people, has a long tradition in the festive life of the Swahili, especially at weddings, and is also the general music of entertainment of the coastal communities. Many of the lead singers and bandleaders of *taarab* groups are women, almost unique in Kenyan traditional music. Furthermore, the music has strong Arabic/Islamic overtones in instrumentation, especially in the haunting vocals. While the Indian harmonium was (and still is) the main *taarab* instrument in the Lamu Archipelago, earlier *taarab* groups in Mombasa used the full Arabian orchestra, including the lute-like *oud* and violins. Today, the main instruments are guitar and electronic organ or synthesizer, and either an Indian harmonium or a small electronic organ/piano, plus a variety of local, Arabian or Indian drums. Indian movies, with their strong musical component, are very popular on the coast, and this has led to many of the features of Indian music being absorbed into *taarab*.

On Lamu island, the old centre of Swahili culture, most weddings today are served by a few amateur *taarab* groups, with professional groups bussed up from Mombasa only for more well-to-do marriages. The **Zein Musical Party**, now based in Mombasa, is the heir of Lamu's *taarab* tradition. Zein l'Abdin was born in Lamu and hails from a family in which the Swahili arts were highly valued. Together with the Swahili poet Sheikh Nabhany, Zein has unearthed a number of poems, dating back to the nineteenth century, which he includes in his repertoire. But Zein isn't just a fabulous singer and composer; he also ranks as the finest *oud* player in East Africa and is well known throughout the Islamic world.

Maulidi Musical Party, **Juma Bhalo** and **Zuhura & Party** have, for more than three decades, been Mombasa's main wedding favourites. Singers Maulidi Juma and Juma Bhalo are at ease both with traditional Swahili wedding songs and the Hindi-style songs so characteristic of Mombasa *taarab*, with Swahili words set to tunes from the latest Bollywood movies. Maulidi Musical Party are the archetypal Mombasa ensemble, their sound being based on a keyboard, with fills by accordion, guitar, bass and percussion, and many rhythms rooted in local *ngoma* traditions. In Maulidi's group, Mohamed Shigoo's keyboard work stands out as especially original, with a strong flavour of harmonium (which he used to play earlier in his career) and *nzumari* (a local double-reed horn) and backed by the distinctive voice of female singer **Malika** until her emigration to the USA. Mombasa's main remaining female star is the enchanting **Zuhura Swaleh**, whose energetic songs have a firm base in the local *chakacha* rhythms and lyrics.

With Zein, Maulidi and Zuhura now well into their 60s, and their voices having suffered from the strain of non-stop singing for six hours at weddings, they are mostly heard on local radio stations or can be bought on street CDs – or even audiocassettes. But the audience is looking for new stars: a relatively recent appearance on the scene is **Yusuf Mohamed "Tenge"**, who follows in the steps of Maulidi and Juma Bhalo. More recently **Prince Adio**, son of Mohamed Shigoo, has created some waves in linking *taarab* musical sensibilities and poetry with modern sequencing techniques, arriving at a mix of styles that is close to Tanzanian bongo flava and Swahili hip-hop.

flourishing in East African towns during the first half of the twentieth century. *Beni* songs, as well as the new guitar songs, featured the strong and critical social commentary so beloved of Kenyans. The songs were usually in the form of a short story and sometimes commented on an actual political or social topic, or perhaps recounted a personal experience of the musician. Romantic lyrics from this time are almost non-existent, even in songs dealing with men and women.

The guitar styles themselves developed out of different instrumental techniques and musical perceptions, but they were influenced by the records available at the time, mainly from other parts of Africa. Kenyan musicians of the period cite as important inspirations the finger-picking style of **Jean Bosco Mwenda** and **Losta Abelo**, both from Katanga (now Shaba Province in the Democratic Republic of Congo), and **George Sibanda**, from Bulawayo in Zimbabwe. From this period, the notables of Kenya's acoustic guitar styles were **John Mwale**, **George Mukabi** (directly out of the Luhya *sukuti* tradition) and **Isaya Mwinamo**.

The 1960s saw the introduction of **electric guitars** as well as larger groups of three to four guitars. Finger-picking guitarists from western Kenya and the smoother, driving, electric-guitar sound of groups like **Equator Sound Band** (Equator was a leading record label of the time), featuring the songs of **Daudi Kabaka**, **Fadhili William**, **Nashil Pichen** and **Peter Tsotsi**, dominated the airwaves and the record stores. Daudi Kabaka reigned as the "King of Twist", the twist being essentially a fast version of the South African rhythm found in songs such as "The Lion Sleeps Tonight". Into the 1970s, while Kabaka's African Eagles and others continued to play their brands of Swahili music, many top Kenyan groups, such as the Ashantis, Air Fiesta and the Hodi Boys, were playing Congolese covers and international pop, especially soul music, in the Nairobi clubs.

Benga and other modern styles

In the 1970s, a number of musicians began to define the direction of an emerging form, **benga**, which more than any other Kenyan music became Kenya's most characteristic pop sound. Although it originated with the Luo people of western Kenya, practically all the Kenyan guitar bands play variants of it, and today most of the regional or ethnic pop groups refer generally to their music as *benga*.

As a pop style, *benga* actually dates back to the 1950s, when musicians began adapting traditional dance rhythms and the sounds of the *nyatiti* and *orutu* to the acoustic guitar and later to electric instruments. During its heyday in the 1970s and into the 1980s, *benga* music dominated Kenya's recording industry and was very popular even in west and southern Africa.

By any standard, the most famous *benga* group is **Shirati Jazz**, led by D.O. (Daniel Owino) Misiani. Born in Shirati, Tanzania, just south of the Kenyan border, he has been playing *benga* since the mid-1960s and is still going strong. His style is characterized by soft, flowing and melodic two-part vocal harmonies, a very active, pulsating bass line that derives at least in part from traditional *nyatiti* and drum rhythms, and stacks of invigorating guitar work, the lead alternating with the vocal.

Other important *benga* artists include the pioneering **Colella Mazee** and **Ochieng Nelly** – either together or separately in various incarnations of **Victoria Jazz** and the **Victoria Kings** – as well as **George Ramogi** and his Continental Luo Sweet Band. The mid-1990s also saw the emergence of **Okatch Biggy** (Elly Otieno Okatch), **Heka Heka**, and **Prince Jully** (Julius Okumu) with the **Jolly Boys Band**. Today Heka Heka (and various offshoots of it) and the Jolly Boys have continued to flourish, moving into new, more risqué territory. After Prince Jully's death in 1997, Jully's wife, Lillian Auma, began fronting the Jolly Boys as Princess Jully, and the response has been phenomenal. She draws enthusiastic crowds wherever she performs.

One Luo name which doesn't fit neatly under the *benga* banner is **Ochieng Kabaselleh** with his Luna Kidi Band. Kabaselleh's songs were mostly in Luo, but sometimes with a liberal seasoning of Swahili and English. Likewise, the melodies and harmonies are from the *benga* realm, but the rhythm, guitar work and horns suggest influences from the Congolese/Swahili-dominated sound. Kabaselleh, who languished in prison for several years for "subversion" in the 1980s, returned to the music world with a flood of new releases in the 1990s and died in 1998.

A related group, set up by Kabaselleh in the late 1970s with several of his brothers, continues today as **Bana Kadori**. Originally brought together as a recording group, they are now an active performing band, their music running from Kabaselleh's hybrid *benga*-rumba style to mainstream *benga*. This *benga*-rumba style became increasingly popular in the first decade of this century with **Musa Juma** and his Limpopo International Band. Still rooted in Luo melodies and harmonies, the syncopated *benga* bass lines have given way to smoother, flowing rumba, with great commercial success in the pop music wars. After the release of his sixth CD in 2010, Musa Juma toured the US, but died in 2011. The uniquely Kenyan rumba style of *benga*, which originated with Ochieng Kabaselleh and was institutionalized by Musa Juma, continues to be played today by popular practitioners such as Igwe Prezda Bandasonn and his Patrons Musica, Johnny Junior with B-V Band, and Owilo Mike's Ja-Mnazi Africa.

Luhya

Many of Kenya's famous guitarists and vocalists come from the Luhya highlands just to the north of Lake Victoria and Luo-land. This was the ancestral home of early finger-picking guitarists like **John Mwale** and **George Mukabi**, as well as the late **Daudi Kabaka** and another twist proponent still active in the music business, **John Nzenze**. While these musicians cultivated broad appeal through the use of Swahili lyrics, other Luhya musicians stayed closer to their home areas linguistically as well as musically. In *benga* style, **Sukuma bin Ongaro** is famous for his humorous social commentaries. Even if you can't understand the language, his music is great to dance to and, of course, has some super guitar licks.

Shem Tube is a Luhya vocalist/guitarist whose music straddles both past and present – though it's his past which has given him a following in Europe, thanks to a vintage compilation in the *omutibo* style featuring his group **Abana ba Nasery** (The Nursery Boys). Coming together as a trio in the early 1960s, Abana ba Nasery used traditional Luhya rhythms and melody lines, but their two-guitar line-up and three-part vocal harmonies, with rhythms scraped from the neck ridges of an old Fanta bottle, presaged elements of modern Kenyan pop. Although they've never earned enough money to buy their own electric guitars and amps, Abana ba Nasery have had a string of local hits as an electric band under the stage names Mwilonje Jazz and Super Bunyore Band.

Kikuyu

As Kenya's largest ethnic group, the Kikuyu-speaking people of Central Province and Nairobi are a major market force in Kenya's music industry. Perhaps because of this large "built-in" audience, few Kikuyu musicians have tried to cross over into the national Swahili or English-language markets.

Kikuyu pop has a traditional melodic structure, quite distinct from the Luo and Luhya traditions of western Kenya. Most often the songs incorporate elements of *benga* and *cavacha*, but it's not unusual for there to be a dose of country and western, reggae or Congolese *soukous*. From the 1970s into the 1990s the indisputable king of Kikuyu pop was **Joseph Kamaru**, who, over the course of his career, carved out something of a musical empire, including a large band and dancers, two music stores and a recording studio. Still going strong in 1993, Kamaru shocked his fans by announcing that he had been "born again" and retired from music performance to devote his efforts to evangelism and gospel music promotion – a precursor to a much larger shift to gospel music in Kenyan society and the music business.

At least a part of the void left by Kamaru was filled by Jane Nyambura, one of very few female headliners in Kikuyu pop. Known simply as **Queen Jane**, she was a staunch advocate of the inclusion of traditional folk forms and local languages within contemporary pop, an approach which limited her radio exposure, but didn't stop her and four of her brothers and sisters from making their living from her band. Her death in 2010, while only in her mid-40s, was a huge blow for Kikuyu music fans and *benga* fans generally. It remains to be seen if one of the newer *benga* stars can fill the void: **Joyce wa Mamaa** (Joyce Wanjiku Njoki) is off to a solid start with her "Menya Wari Wakwa" album.

Kamba

Kamba pop music is firmly entrenched in the *benga/cavacha* camp, though it has distinctive features of its own. One is the delicate, flowing rhythm guitar, often reminiscent of the old carousel calliope that underlies many arrangements. While the primary guitar plays chords in the lower range, the second guitar, often in a high register, plays a fast pattern of fills. This is discernible in many of the recordings of the three most famous Kamba groups; the **Kalambya Boys** and **Kalambya Sisters**, **Peter Mwambi and his Kyanganga Boys** and **Les Kilimambogo Brothers Band**. With socially relevant lyrics, intricate guitar weaves and a solid dance-beat backing, Les Kilimambogo Brothers Band began recording in Swahili and achieved widespread popularity in Kenya, though their career was brought to an end by the death of leader **Kakai Kilonzo** in 1987. These days, a new generation of musicians is drawing the limelight away from the old guard, with **Ken wa Maria** dominating the Kamba market.

Congolese

Congolese musicians have been making musical waves in Kenya since the late 1950s, but it wasn't until the mid-1970s, after the passing of the American soul craze, that music from Congo began to dominate the city nightclubs. One of the first Congolese musicians to settle in Kenya during this period was **Baba Gaston**, who had already been in the business for twenty years when he arrived in Nairobi with his group Baba National in 1975. A prolific musician, he stole the scene until his retirement in 1989. Following Gaston, such groups as **Super Mazembe**, **Les Mangelepa** (some of Gaston's own musicians), as well as **Samba Mapangala** and an early version of his **Orchestra Virunga** took hold in the city. This period is still regarded as the golden age of Lingala music in Kenya and it flourishes locally with plenty of CD reissues in the shops.

Congolese music remains popular in various clubs in Nairobi and Kenya's big towns. In fact, some of the musicians of this golden period can be found performing today in successor bands to Mazembe and Mangelepa. But it's the more recent Congolese outfits who have regular gigs around Nairobi; groups like **Rhumba Japan**, **Bilenge Musica** and **SP Band**.

In both Congolese and Swahili popular music, **rumba** has always been a major ingredient. Songs typically open with a slow-to-medium rumba that ambles through the verses, backed by a light percussion of gentle congas, snare and high hat. Then, three or four minutes into the song there's a transition – or more often a hiatus. It's goodbye to verses and rolling rumba as a much faster rhythm, known as the *sebene* in Congo, highlighting the instrumental parts, especially solo guitar and brass, takes over with a vengeance. Swahili music over the last thirty years has been particularly faithful to this two-part structure, although today, both Swahili and Congolese musicians often dispense with the slow portion altogether.

Swahili bands: the Tanzanian influence

Kenya's own brand of **Swahili pop** music has its origin in the Tanzanian pop styles of the 1970s, though the Kenyan variety has followed a separate evolutionary path from the Tanzanian mainstream. In addition to the stylistic features it shares with the Congolese sound (light, high-hat-and-conga percussion and a delicate two/three-guitar interweave),

SWAHILI POP LYRICS

These are two songs you're almost certain to hear, sooner of later, regardless of where you stay or how you travel.

JAMBO BWANA

by Teddy Kalanda Harrison

Jambo, jambo Bwana	Greetings, greetings Bwana
Habari gani?	How are you doing?
Nzuri sana	Very well
Wageni, mwakaribishwa	Visitors, you are all welcomed
Kenya yetu	In our Kenya
Hakuna matata	There are no problems
Kenya ni nchi nzuri	Kenya's a beautiful country
Hakuna matata	There are no problems
Nchi ya kupendeza	A pleasing country
Hakuna matata	There are no problems
Nchi ya maajabu	A country of wonders
Hakuna matata	There are no problems
Nchi yenye amani	A country of peace
Hakuna matata	There are no problems

MALAIKA

Authorship disputed, first popularized by Fadhili William

Malaika, nakupenda malaika	Angel, I love you angel
Malaika, nakupenda malaika	Angel, I love you angel
Nami nifanyeje, kijana mwenzio?	And me, what shall I, your boyfriend, do?
Nashindwa na mali sina wee	If I weren't struggling for money
Ningekuoa malaika	I would marry you angel
Nashindwa na mali sina wee	If I weren't struggling for money
Ningekuoa malaika	I would marry you angel
Pesa zasumbuwa roho yangu	Money is the source of my heartache
Pesa zasumbuwa roho yangu	Money is the source of my heartache
Nami nifanyeje, kijana mwenzio?	And me, what shall I, your boyfriend, do?
Nashindwa na mali sina wee	If I weren't struggling for money
Ningekuoa malaika	I would marry you angel
Nashindwa na mali sina wee	If I weren't struggling for money
Ningekuoa malaika	I would marry you angel
Kidege, hukuwaza kidege	Little bird, I'm always dreaming of you, little bird
Kidege, hukuwaza kidege	Little bird, I'm always dreaming of you, little bird
Nami nifanyeje, kijana mwenzio?	And me, what shall I, your boyfriend, do?
Nashindwa na mali sina wee	If I weren't struggling for money
Ningekuoa malaika	I would marry you angel
Nashindwa na mali sina wee	If I weren't struggling for money
Ningekuoa malaika	I would marry you angel

the Kenyan Swahili sound is instrumentally sparse, allowing the bass to fill in gaps, often in syncopated rhythms. While the Congolese musicians are famous for their vocals and their intricate harmonies, Swahili groups are renowned for their demon guitarists and crisp, clear guitar interplay. Trumpets and saxes are common in recorded arrangements but usually omitted in club performances because of the extra expense.

One of the first Tanzanian groups to migrate to Kenya was **Arusha Jazz**, the predecessor of what is now the legendary **Simba Wanyika Original** ("Simba Wanyika" means "Lion of the Savanna"). Founded by Wilson Peter Kinyonga and his brothers George and William, the group began performing in Mombasa in 1971. In 1975, with Tanzanian recruit Omar Shabani on rhythm and Kenyan Tom Malanga on bass, the brothers shifted to Nairobi where, over a twenty-year period, they were favourites of the city's club scene and made scores of recordings. They broke up in the 1990s after the deaths of George and Wilson Kinyonga.

The **Wanyika** name is also famous in East Africa for several bands that emerged from Simba Wanyika Original. The group's first big split occurred in 1978 when the core of supporting musicians around the Kinyonga brothers left to form **Les Wanyika**. Under the leadership of Tanzanian lead guitarist John Ngereza, they remained one of Nairobi's top bands – distinguished by imaginative compositions and arrangements, a lean sound and the delicious blend of Professor Omari's rhythm guitar with John Ngereza's lead and Tom Malanga's bass – right up to Ngereza's death in 2000 (Omari had died in 1998) when the group broke up.

Another important figure in the Wanyika story is Tanzania-born **Issa Juma**, who quickly established a name for himself in Kenya as a premier vocalist in the early days of Les Wanyika. Issa formed Super Wanyika in 1981 and over the next few years had a series of hits featuring half a dozen other variations on the Wanyika names. One of the most prolific artists of the 1980s, he was perhaps the most versatile and creative of the Swahili artists in his willingness to take his music in different directions. His recorded output features many numbers that were a kind of fusion of Swahili rumba and *benga*, but isn't limited to this.

Foremost among other Tanzanians and Kenyans performing in the Swahili style are the **Maroon Commandos**. Members of the Kenyan Army, the Commandos are one of the oldest performing groups in the country. They first came together in 1970 and were initially mainly a covers band playing Congolese hits, but by 1977 they had become a strong force in the Swahili style with the huge Taita-language hit "Charonyi Ni Wasi". The Commandos have proven themselves quite experimental at times, mingling Swahili and *benga* styles and occasionally adding a keyboard and innovative guitar effects. Most recently, the Commandos have updated their sound to match the intensity of the *sebenes* of the Congolese groups; that fast-moving instrumental climax that builds over the last half of the song. Currently, the only serious proponents of the Swahili rumba sound aside from the Maroon Commandos are **Abdul Muyonga and Everest Kings**.

Perhaps the last of Kenya's great Swahili rumba bands was the late Twahir Mohamed's **Golden Sounds Band**, whose songs adhered to the complex evolutionary structure of the genre, but also featured a much denser vocal and instrumental sound.

Tourist and international pop

Where Kenyan pop meets the tourist industry, at the coastal resorts around Mombasa, bands can make a living just playing hotel gigs. These bands typically feature highly competent musicians, relatively good equipment and a fairly polished sound. The best of them are worth catching, typically playing an eclectic selection of old Congolese rumba tunes as warm-ups, popular international covers, a few Congolese favourites of the day, greatest hits from Kenya's past, and some original material that leans heavily towards the American/Euro pop sound, but with lyrics relating to local topics.

The most successful Kenyan group in this field has been the oddly named **Them Mushrooms**, now renamed **Uyoga** (Swahili for "mushroom"). The band managed to graduate from the coastal hotel circuit when they moved to Nairobi in 1987, but their music lives on at the coast, in particular their crowning achievement, the tourist anthem "Jambo Bwana". While Uyoga are proud to take credit for this insidiously infectious bit of fluff, they have shown over their long career that they have serious musical intentions, having been involved in a series of highly successful and diverse collaborations, including with one of the earliest of Kenyan guitar pioneers, **Fundi Konde**, *taarab* star Malika and the Kikuyu singer Queen Jane. Since 1993, the band have returned to their reggae roots.

Uyoga's long-time counterpart in the hotel circuit, **Safari Sound**, have the distinction of having made Kenya's bestselling album ever in *The Best of African Songs*, a veritable greatest hits of hotel classics with songs such as "Malaika", a beautiful composition about ill-starred love (see box, p.583), that has been covered by everyone from Harry Belafonte and Miriam Makeba to Angelique Kidjo.

The evolving scene

In the early 1990s, the Kenyan music business was at a low point. Piracy and diminishing sales meant that, as a business, recorded music was hardly worth the effort – and the music that was being produced at the time hardly seemed worth buying anyway. By the mid-1990s, however, a number of factors had set the stage for a radical departure from the styles of previous generations. For one thing, Kenya experienced the rise of commercial **FM radio**, which helped acquaint Kenyans with reggae, ragga, house, dancehall, hip-hop and R&B from abroad. Also around this time, **new technology** made recording much more affordable, and a new breed of independent Kenyan producer began to emerge. New groups were formed, performing in styles inspired largely by music from abroad, but adding local elements in language, subject matter and sometimes melody and instrumentation. **Tedd Josiah**, **Bruce Odhiambo** and **Suzanne and Gido Kibukosya** were among the producers who were instrumental in shepherding along these new artists, often with quite different musical intentions, from hip-hop covers of African pop classics to gospel balladry.

Eric Wainaina, who brought together an innovative mix of Kenyan pop sounds with American soft-rock influences, was one of the stars of this new generation of Kenyan musicians, especially in the turbulent early years of multi-party democracy, when his lyrics about corruption and poverty resonated across the country. Some of the best material of the late 1990s was showcased on two CDs put together by Tedd Josiah, *Kenyan: The First Chapter* and *Kenyan: The Second Chapter*. Notable from the first of these is **Kalamashaka's** "Tafsiri Hii", the trio's trendsetting Swahili hip-hop song addressing the reality of street life. *The Second Chapter* introduced the duo **Gidigidi Majimaji**, perhaps the most innovative and successful of Kenya's new breed of music stars, blending clever lyrics, African rhythms and instruments and contemporary hip-hop.

In much the same way that Josiah's *Chapters* CDs introduced a host of new artists to radio and the public, the production house known as **Ogopa Deejays** released three compilations featuring acts who have become fixtures of the Kenyan pop charts, including **Redsan**, **Kleptomaniax**, **Wahu**, **Big Pin**, **Mr Lenny** and the late **E-Sir**. Much of the early Ogopa sound was characterized as *kapuka*, a style built on a mixture of Kenyan hip-hop, ragga and house. It was a commercial sound that got plenty of airplay, and *kapuka* artists were often featured at corporate-sponsored events and festivals. As all this was playing out several years back, Kenyan **hip-hop** artists were quick to make a distinction between their music and *kapuka*, criticizing the latter for its shallowness and lack of meaningful social content. They argued that a great many *kapuka* practitioners never experienced the hardships of the poor in the urban slums, and their love songs and party music represented the rich boys and girls of the middle class. And indeed, one of the biggest of today's stars is the wealthy rapper **CMB Prezzo**, who likes to brag about his good fortune. Always the showman, Prezzo makes a point of arriving at concerts with a well-dressed entourage in flashy cars. He even hired a helicopter to airdrop him into a music awards ceremony, scoring points for brazen style – but no awards. However, his 2012 runner-up finish on the **Big Brother Africa StarGame** TV show has done him well in keeping his stock high.

Similar in sound to *kapuka* but lyrically deeper, the hip-hop genre known as **genge**, promoted by production house Calif Records, aims to be music for the masses, and indeed Calif artistes **Jua Cali** and **Nonini** have scored some massive hits in recent years. While the *genge/kapuka* rivalry didn't quite match the East Coast–West Coast hip-hop wars of the 1990s in the US, it does parallel the outcome in that, today, hip-hop is firmly established as one of the dominant commercial genres of Kenyan pop, and you don't have to look far to find some entertaining rivalries among artists – for example the ongoing dialogue in the media between Prezzo and Jaguar.

On the contemporary Kenyan scene, there is still no single genre that could represent a "Kenyan sound". There are multiple sounds, some of them quite engaging and well developed but having nothing particularly Kenyan about them. **Camp Mulla**, for example, is a Nairobi-based hip-hop group topping the charts with English rap, packaged in R&B and dance beats; very much a soulful, international, urban "bubblegum" hip-hop sound. There is nothing really local about it except that the younger Kenyan audience loves it. Similarly, in a pop-rock vein, there are some really excellent bands, perhaps a little more closely tied to African pop genres, but essentially competing on the international market with indie bands of all genres. A few of the recent standouts have been groups like **Sauti Sol**, **Tim** (Ennovator) **Rimbui's Ma3**, and **Eric Wainaina and the Best Band in Africa**. Each of these groups features soulful, vocally rich melodies and harmonies and a clean, light, often finger-picking, acoustic guitar sound – occasionally with some African guitar embellishments – and usually delivered with a mix of Swahili and English lyrics.

Just a Band also have another polished international sound – this time, a fusion of house, electronica and R&B. They won the 2008 Kisima award for Best Urban Fusion category. Fusion is the operative word for a great many of the current pop headliners. **Daddy Owen**, one of the top gospel stars, has made a name for himself doing *kapungala*, the combination of *kapuka* and Congolese Lingala. **Dan "Chizi" Aceda** bills himself as the Crown Prince of Benga, putting a *benga* take on R&B, house, reggae and other genres, while James Jozee and Susan Wanjiru, as **Gogosimo**, bring a contemporary coastal sound merging international pop with local sounds like the *chakacha* rhythm or the easy-listening so-called *bango* style, with mellow sax, popularized by Joseph Ngala.

Traditional instruments have returned in several pop forms. Drawing on Luo traditions, the group **Kenge Kenge** combines *orutu* fiddle, flute, horn, vocal harmonies and lively percussion on traditional Luo drums. Their high-energy music guarantees a packed house any night of the week. Taking these Luo musical elements in a different direction, *ohangla* musicians such as **Tony Nyadundo** and **Osogo Winyo** combine traditional percussion with keyboard, harmonica and drum kit for an updated version of the music formerly reserved for funerals, country beer parties, and celebrations such as for the birth of twins. This is must-see entertainment when live in its full social context, though it's less compelling for non-Luo-speakers listening on CD.

Another segment of Kenya's new music scene includes musicians looking to their roots for ways to reshape contemporary pop. **Yunasi**, **Kayamba Afrika** (and their offshoots) and US-based **Jabali Afrika** emphasize rich vocal harmonies blended with traditional African percussion and stringed instruments, along with guitar, bass and keyboards. **Nairobi City Ensemble** takes a slightly different approach in their album *Kalapapla*. The group begins with what they term "authentic melodies" from traditional roots but makes the sound contemporary with modern instruments, guest rappers, and the thoughtful use of traditional stringe instruments like the Luo *nyatiti* and *orutu*. Singer-songwriter and guitarist **Suzzana Owiyo** deserves special mention for her innovative approach to bringing the melodies and instruments of her traditional Luo culture into modern pop. All these efforts attract great critical interest and, despite being largely ignored by Kenyan radio and most under-30s, have resulted in financial support from cultural exchange organizations like the Alliance Française and the Goethe-Institut, and invitations to the artists to perform in music festivals across Africa and overseas.

Finally, **gospel** is probably be the most popular music in Kenya today. While not a music genre in itself but more a category – songs with a religious message – gospel eflects and borrows from most of today's popular music styles. **Juliani**, for example, was once part of the **Ukoo Flani** hip-hop collective but has branched out on his own with soulful rap to become one of Kenya's major gospel stars, with a message that is not only religious but also touches on social and environmental causes. Others, like best-seller **Emmy Kosgei**, have a choral flavour and South African sound, while **Daddy Owen** has built on Congolese rumba.

Kenya's ever-expanding musical universe is ripe for exploration – or even participation if you're a musician. If you want to learn more, most of the artists mentioned can be heard on YouTube, Reverbnation, SoundCloud and Spotify.

Discography

Music shops throughout Kenya will have CDs by many of the following artists. Online music stores also carry an increasing range of tracks. You can usually find a few CDs of **traditional music** locally, though you may have to persevere a little to find someone who sells them. **Kentunes** is the first dedicated Kenyan music online store (wkentunes.com).

★ **Golden Sounds Band** *Swahili Rumba* (Naxos World, US). Led by the brilliant saxophonist/arranger Twahir Mohamed, Golden Sounds played rumba music in the tradition of the Wanyika bands and Maroon Commandos. Repeated hearings are required before you really begin to appreciate everything this album offers, in the evolutionary development of musical motifs over tracks lasting around eight minutes apiece.

★ **Issa Juma and Super Wanyika Stars** *World Defeats the Grandfathers: Swinging Swahili Rumba 1982–1986* (Stern's Africa, UK). With his big voice, accompanied by great guitar solos, the deep-voiced Tanzanian led the third, more rockin', incarnation of the "Wanyika" groups to a string of hits. If this one brings you back demanding more, you're in luck: there's a follow-up online-only album, *World Defeats the Grandfathers, Vol. 2.*

H.N. Ochieng Kabaselleh & the Lunna Kidi Band *Sanduku ya Mapendo and Achi Maria* (Equator Heritage Sounds, US). From the area around Lake Victoria, Kabaselleh was one Kenyan bandleader whose music always stood apart – an interesting mix of Luo *benga*, Swahili rumba and Congolese influences, exemplified by these two collections of Kabaselleh's double-A-sided singles from the 1980s.

Kakai Kilonzo *Best of Kakai Vols 1 & 2* (Shava Musik, Germany). From the mid-1970s until his death in 1987, Kakai was at the top of the Kamba music scene in Kenya, with catchy Swahili lyrics and a tight *benga* sound. This is a fine compilation of vinyl singles from the 1980s which usually featured one song split between the A- and B-sides, but which here have been neatly stitched back together.

Fundi Konde *Fundi Konde Retrospective Vol 1, 1947–56* (RetroAfric, UK). Full of enticing, vintage Kenyan pop. Imagine a vocal line like a mellow, two-part "Chattanooga Choo Choo", add a smooth, jazzy electric guitar, bass and clarinet, and you have the ingredients for the typical Konde track. Konde's heyday was the 1950s, but he was rediscovered in the 1990s through his collaboration with Them Mushrooms.

★ **Les Wanyika** *Paulina: The Best of Professor Omari Shabani and John Ngereza* (Tamasha, Kenya). Les Wanyika were the last of the great Swahili rumba bands in the "Wanyika" lineage, dating back to the early 1970s, and this album is a gem, bringing together some of their finest material. The eloquent interplay of the guitars of John Ngereza and Professor Omari is stunning.

★ **Samba Mapangala & Virunga** *African Classics* (Sheer Sound). From the mid-1970s to the early 1990s, Virunga were one of Kenya's most exciting groups, while Samba Mapangala is still a favourite in East Africa despite having relocated to the USA. Each song is like a ten-minute story, exploring different combinations of rhythm, melody and harmony. This collection pulls together some of the best tracks of Samba's thirty-years-plus under the Virunga name, with classics such as "Malako", "Yembele" and "Sungura". For those who'd like to hear Samba's present-day sound, his 2011 release, *Maisha Ni Matumu* (Virunga Records), provides some first-rate dance numbers in a rumba sampler.

Maroon Commandos *Shika Kamba* (Sound Africa, Kenya). Tilting a little more towards the Congolese rumba sound in this release, the Maroon Commandos are still a great sound as Kenya's longest-running rumba group.

Collela Mazee and Victoria B Kings Band *Jessica* (Equator Heritage Sounds). Classic Luo *benga* music of the late 1970s and early 1980s: a pounding beat, pulsing bass and brilliant guitars, each track ending with a luscious guitar solo.

D.O. Misiani & Shirati Band *The King of History* (Stern's Africa, UK), *Benga Blast!* (Earthworks/Stern's, UK) and *Piny Ose Mer/The World Upside Down* (GlobeStyle, UK). Daniel Owino Misiani was one of the founding fathers of *benga* music and these are three fine examples of his work, the first two in glorious mono; the latter, a special recording for the GlobeStyle label in 1989.

John Amutabi Nzenze & Friends Angelike Twist (Equator Heritage Sounds). A pioneering figure in Kenyan music, Nzenze started his recording career as a teen back in the 1950s. This compilation beautifully highlights his contribution to the acoustic finger-picking guitar styles of the 1950s and the electric "twist" style that followed in the 1960s.

★ **Ayub Ogada** En Mana Kuoyo (Real World, UK). Sounding every bit as fresh and engaging as when first released in 1993, Ayub Ogada takes traditional Luo instruments and melodies in a new direction. This enthralling, low-key, largely acoustic album has beautiful melodies and captivating rhythms, featuring Ogada on the eight-stringed nyatiti lyre.

★ **Orchestra Super Mazembe** Giants of East Africa (Earthworks/Stern's, UK). Congolese group Super Mazembe played the dance halls and bars of Kenya for nearly thirty years before their demise. In songs such as "Kasongo" and "Shauri Yako", they exemplified the definitive sound of Congolese rumba in East Africa. Mazembe's early 1980s LP, Kaivaska, kindled much of the early enthusiasm for African music in the UK and Europe. This collection includes five of the best songs off Kaivaska, including "Kasongo" and "Shauri Yako".

Suzzana Owiyo Mama Africa (ARC Music, UK). This debut from a talented singer-songwriter is a delightful mix of traditional instruments, Owiyo's acoustic guitar and electric sounds with a few rough edges. Yamo Kudho (Blu Zebra Kenya) picks up where Mama Africa left off, in a more polished, tighter package, delivering sublime melodies with a bright acoustic sound and mixing in traditional Luo orutu oporo (horn) and percussion. Her third CD, My Roots (Kirkelig kulturverksted), is a superb production with plenty of Luo "roots" from traditional to innovative fusion numbers.

Eric Wainaina Sawa Sawa (Wainaina/Kaufmann Prod USA/Kenya). Originally part of the Five Alive singing group of the mid-1990s, Wainaina went off to the USA to study music. Spanning a broad range of styles, from up-tempo African dance rhythms to ballads and smooth jazz, and including "Nchi ya Kitu Kidogo" (Nation of a Little Something), decrying, with great humour, the way bribery has permeated Kenyan society. For Swahili-speakers, there were comic interludes from the Kenyan stand-up troupe Redykyulass. Wainaina followed up with the meticulously produced modern pop album, Twende Twende (Enkare, Kenya), and, from 2011, Eric's Love + Protest with The Best Band in Africa.

COMPILATIONS

★ **Kenya Dance Mania** (Earthworks/Stern's, UK). An excellent introduction to Kenya's various styles. Dance Mania includes some classics of the 1970s and 1980s, such as Les Wanyika's "Sina Makosa" and Maroon Commandos' evergreen hit "Charonyi Ni Wasi".

★ **Kilio cha Haki** (UpToYouToo, Netherlands). Its title translating as "Cry for Justice", this album was the outcome of a month-long recording project initiated by a Dutch foundation, bringing together 38 talents from Nairobi's slums to create innovative hip-hop. The excellent notes transcribe and translate the poignant Swahili lyrics. Proceeds go towards local development.

The Nairobi Beat: Kenyan Pop Music Today (Rounder, USA). A cross section of mid-1980s Kenyan pop put together by Doug Paterson, showcasing some of the best examples of regional benga styles: Luo, Kikuyu, Kamba and Luhya, plus a couple of Swahili and Congolese dance tunes for good measure.

★ **The Rough Guide to the Music of Kenya** (World Music Network, UK). A sampling of the many styles of Kenyan popular music, including the guitar-centric benga and Swahili rumba styles, taarab from the coastal region, current-day "traditional" sounds, and the shifting sounds of the younger generation (including Gidigidi Majimaji's "Ting Badi Malo").

Zanzibara 2: 1965–1975 (Buda Musique, France). A delightful collection of taarab music recorded by Mombasa's Mzuri Records. Features songs by the likes of Zuhura Swaleh, Zein l'Abdin and Maulidi Juma.

Written and researched by Doug Paterson (🌐 eastafricanmusic.com), with contributions from Jens Finke on traditional music (🌐 bluegecko.org) and Werner Graebner on taarab (🌐 jahazi-media.com).

Books

Literacy has massively improved in Kenya in recent decades and more than ninety percent of Kenyans can now read. Although a number of Kenyan authors have written in indigenous languages, English still predominates: check out the excellent blogs and websites (see p.66 and p.134). Locally printed books are sometimes very cheap, and offer insights into Kenyan life you wouldn't otherwise find. The Africa Book Centre (ⓦafricabookcentre. com) is a good source of print editions, and Kwani? (ⓦkwani.org) is Kenya's best literary website. Titles marked ★ are particularly recommended.

COFFEE-TABLE BOOKS

Mohamed Amin *Cradle of Mankind and Portrait of Kenya.* Stunning photographs of the Lake Turkana region by the award-winning maverick photo-journalist, killed in the Comoros plane hijack in 1997.

Yann Arthus-Bertrand *Kenya from the Air.* Superb images of the country from the eagle's viewpoint.

★ **Mitsuaki Iwago** *Serengeti: Natural Order on the African Plain.* Simply the best volume of wildlife photography ever assembled, this makes most glossies look feeble. If you're trying to persuade someone to visit East Africa – or if any aesthetic argument were needed to preserve the parks and animals – this is the book to use.

★ **David Keith Jones** *Shepherds of the Desert.* Brilliant photos, many in black and white, with a text more lucid and less superficial than most glossies, although the book concerns itself only with northern Kenya.

Nigel Pavitt *Kenya: A Country in the Making 1880–1940.* A much-admired production in Kenya itself, where many people – particularly Euro-Kenyan settler families – feel a connection to one or more of the 720 digitally restored photos in this sumptuous tome.

Brian Jackman and Jonathan Scott *The Marsh Lions.* Painstakingly researched and devotedly written study of the big cats and other animals around the Musiara Marsh in the Maasai Mara Reserve.

Jonathan Scott and Angela Scott *Stars of Big Cat Diary.* Valedictory volume for fans of the hit BBC series.

Tepilit Ole Saitoti and Carol Beckwith *Maasai.* The Maasai coffee-table book, with exquisite staged portraits of Maasai culture (and even Beckwith's camera can't disguise the tourist souvenirs in the background). Variably interesting, chauvinistic text, which plays the cult value of the Maasai for all it's worth.

TRAVEL AND GENERAL ACCOUNTS

★ **David Bennum** *Tick Bite Fever.* Full of acid wit, this memoir by a British newspaper journalist about growing up in an expat household in the 1970s offers an amusingly dry alternative to more cloying accounts.

Bill Bryson *Bill Bryson's Africa Diary.* A very brief but typically engaging little book recounting Bryson's travels around Kenya learning about the work of Care International. All profits go to the charity.

Bartle Bull *Safari: A Chronicle of Adventure.* A great, macho slab of a book, chronicling the history of the hunting safari, jammed with photos – grotesque but utterly compelling.

John Hillaby *Journey to the Jade Sea.* An obvious one to read before a trip to Lake Turkana, Hillaby's account of his walk in the early 1960s was an adventure "for the hell of it", as he wrote, complete with tall stories and madcap incompetence.

Adharanand Finn *Running with the Kenyans: Discovering the Secrets of the Fastest People on Earth.* The journalist and runner spent several months living in Iten with his young family – an inspiring work for aspiring world-beaters.

★ **Corinne Hofmann** *The White Masai.* Ridiculed and revered in equal measure, a Swiss woman's account of her extended love affair with a Samburu man, and her life in Barsaloi in the early 1990s.

J. Ludwig Krapf *Travel, Researches and Missionary Labours during an Eighteen Years Residence in Eastern Africa.* Fascinating account of travels to "Mombaz" and "Tzawo" among other localities: Krapf was the first missionary in Kenya, and the first European to set eyes on Mount Kenya.

★ **Peter Matthiessen** *The Tree Where Man Was Born.* Wanderings and musings in Kenya and northern Tanzania, first published in 1972. Enthralling for its detail on nature, society, culture and prehistory, and beautifully written, this is a gentle, appetizing introduction to the land and its people.

George Monbiot *No Man's Land.* A journey through Kenya and Tanzania, providing a shocking exposé of Maasai dispossession and trenchant criticism of the wildlife conservation movement.

Cynthia Moss *Elephant Memories: Thirteen Years in the Life of an Elephant Family*. A fascinating, moving account of her work in Amboseli by one of the world's leading authorities on the social life of the elephant.

Dervla Murphy *The Ukimwi Road*. Murphy's early 1990s bike ride from Kenya to Zimbabwe becomes – for her – a trip through lands lost to AIDS and neo-colonialism.

★ **Shiva Naipaul** *North of South*. First published in 1978, this classic account of Naipaul's life and travels in East Africa is caustic but always readable and sometimes hilarious.

Barack Obama *Dreams from My Father: A Story of Race and Inheritance*. Describing a 1988 journey during which the future 44th president of the USA spent five weeks visiting his father's family in Kenya – hanging out in Nairobi, going to the Mara, and visiting his father's grave in Kogelo.

Joyce Poole *Coming of Age with Elephants*. Deeply sympathetic account of studying the social and sexual behaviour of elephants in Amboseli alongside Cynthia Moss.

Keith B. Richburg *Out of America: A Black Man Confronts Africa*. Nairobi bureau chief for the *Washington Times* from 1991–94, Richburg discovered that he was American, not African, and preferred it that way.

Rick Ridgeway *The Shadow of Kilimanjaro*. The American adventurer and film-maker took a walk in 1997 through the bush from Kilimanjaro to Mombasa – mostly through Tsavo West and East, along the Tsavo-Galana River. Robust, readable and full of passionate enthusiasm for the wild country and the wildlife.

Wilfred Thesiger *My Kenya Days*. The account of thirty years in northern Kenya by a very strange man indeed – an old Etonian noble savage, wedded to his own ego and a reactionary, glamour-laden view of his tribal companions.

Joseph Thomson *Through Masai Land: A Journey Of Exploration Among The Snow-Clad Volcanic Mountains And Strange Tribes Of Eastern Equatorial Africa*. First published in 1885, these two volumes detail Thomson's African journeys of exploration and demonstrate his early eco-consciousness and sensitivity to the peoples he visited.

SPECIALIST GUIDES

ARTS

Susan Denyer *African Traditional Architecture*. Useful and interesting, with hundreds of photos (most of them old) and detailed line drawings.

Frank Willett *African Art*. An accessible volume; good value, with a generous ratio of illustrations to text.

Geoffrey Williams *African Designs from Traditional Sources*. A designer's and enthusiast's sourcebook.

WILDLIFE

Ann Birnie & Tim Noad *Trees of Kenya: An Illustrated Field Guide*. A very useful handbook, covering 300 of Kenya's most common native and exotic species.

Michael Blundell *Field Guide to the Wild Flowers of East Africa*. Botanical companion in the Collins series.

Adam Scott Kennedy *Birds of the Masai Mara* and *Animals of the Masai Mara*. Outstandingly photographed field guides to more than 200 species of birds, 65 mammals and 17 reptiles by a naturalist who has spent years hunting images.

★ **Jonathan Kingdon** *The Kingdon Pocket Guide to African Mammals*. The definitive handbook, abridged to this game-viewing format, with identification illustrations and distribution maps.

Cynthia Moss, Harvey Croze and Phyllis C Lee (eds) *The Amboseli Elephants: A Long-term Perspective on a Long-lived Mammal*. Beautifully produced, moving and highly readable round-up of the Amboseli Elephant Research Project's three decades of work.

Dave Richards *A Photographic Guide to the Birds of East Africa*. Ideal if you're a holiday birder, with more than 300 photos.

Chris Stuart and Tilde Stuart *Field Guide to the Larger Mammals of Africa*. Beautifully illustrated and well-edited field guide published in 2006.

Nigel Wheatley *Where to Watch Birds in Africa*. Tight structure and plenty of useful detail make this a must-have for serious birdwatchers. Includes 25 pages on Kenya.

Zimmerman, Turner and Pearson *Birds of Kenya & Northern Tanzania*. Weighty and comprehensive coverage for the serious birder, also available in a more portable paperback edition.

CLIMBING AND DIVING GUIDES

Iain Allan *The Mountain Club of Kenya Guide to Mount Kenya and Kilimanjaro*. For fully equipped alpinism, this is indispensable.

Anton Koornhof *The Dive Sites of Kenya and Tanzania*. Highly recommended, with detailed, beautifully illustrated text on every major site.

Andrew Wielochowski *Mount Kenya 1:50,000 Map and Guide*. Covers just the mountain itself, and includes technical information if you're scaling Nelion and Batian.

Helmut Debelius *Indian Ocean Reef Guide*. Field guide to all the main species of fish and invertebrates, with excellent identification photos.

ESSAYS

Wahome Mutahi *How to be a Kenyan*. A satirical view of Kenyan life by one of the country's most popular newspaper columnists. Painfully funny, and close to the bone.

Renato Kizito Sesana *Father Kizito's Notebook*. Kenyan life from the Catholic perspective of Father Kizito's weekly columns in the *Sunday Nation*. Full of insights into the struggle to survive that Kenyans call life, infused with humour and compassion.

COLONIAL WRITERS AND BIOGRAPHIES

★ **Isak Dinesen (Karen Blixen)** *Out of Africa*. First published in 1937, Blixen (Dinesen was a nom de plume) describes her life on her Ngong Hills coffee farm between the wars. It's an intense read – lyrical, introspective, sometimes obnoxiously and intricately racist, but worth pursuing and never superficial, unlike Sydney Pollack's film. Blixen's *Letters from Africa 1914–1931*, translated by Anne Born, gives posthumous insights.

Elspeth Huxley *The Flame Trees of Thika: Memories of an African Childhood* and *The Mottled Lizard*. Based on her own childhood, from a prolific author who also wrote numerous works on colonial history and society, including *White Man's Country*, a biography of the settlers' doyen, Lord Delamere, and *Out in the Midday Sun: My Kenya* – both as readable, and, to be fair, as predictable, as any. Her last book, *Nine Faces of Kenya*, is a somewhat dewy-eyed anthology of colonial East African ephemera. More interesting is the collection of her mother's letters, *Nellie: Letters from Africa*, which includes compelling coverage of the Mau Mau years from the pen of a likeably eccentric settler.

Beryl Markham *West with the Night*. Markham made the first east–west solo flight across the Atlantic. This is her only book about her life in the interwar Kenya colony, drawing together adventures, landscapes and contemporary figures.

★ **Richard Meinertzhagen** *Kenya Diary 1902–1906*. The haunting day-to-day narrative of a young British officer in the protectorate. Meinertzhagen's brutal descriptions of "punitive expeditions" are chillingly matter-of-fact and make the endless tally of his wildlife slaughter pale inoffensively by comparison. As a reminder of the savagery that accompanied the British intrusion (Meinertzhagen is notorious as the murderer of the Nandi chief, Koitalel), and a stark insight into the complex mind of one of its perpetrators, this is disturbing, but highly recommended. Good photos, too.

Edward Paice *Lost Lion of Empire: The Life of Ewart Grogan DSO, 1876–1976*. Fascinating biography of one of the Kenya colony's most rumbustious movers and shakers.

Paul Sullivan *Kikuyu District: The Edited Letters of Francis Hall 1892–1901*. The fascinating monthly letters home of one of the earliest officers in the East Africa Protectorate, stationed at what is now Murang'a, in the Central Highlands, are an easier read than Meinertzhagen's diary.

Judith Thurman *Isak Dinesen: The Life of a Storyteller*. A revisionist biography that was much used as a source for Sydney Pollack's *Out of Africa* film.

Sarah Wheeler *Too Close to the Sun: The Life and Times of Denys Finch Hatton*. Stylishly written biography of the colony's coolest dude, the enigmatic lover of Karen Blixen, who died at the controls of his plane in 1931.

KENYAN FICTION IN ENGLISH

Chinua Achebe and C.L. Innes (eds) *African Short Stories*. A collection that treats its material geographically, including

Kenyan stories from Jomo Kenyatta, Grace Ogot, Ngugi and a spooky offering (*The Spider's Web*) from Leonard Kibera.

NGUGI WA THIONG'O

Ngugi wa Thiong'o, the dominant figure of modern Kenyan literature, currently lives in the USA: although his books in English are no longer banned in Kenya, his political sympathies are unwelcome. Ngugi's work is art serving the revolution – didactic, brusque, graphic and unsentimental. He writes in Kikuyu, then translates his work into English. Powerful themes – exploitation, betrayal, cultural oppression, the imposition of Christianity, loss of and search for identity – drive the stories along urgently.

Disillusioned with English, Ngugi's first work in Kikuyu, in collaboration with Ngugi wa Mirii, was the play *Ngahiika Ndeenda* (*I Will Marry When I Want*), and its public performance by illiterate peasants at the Kamiriithu Cultural Centre in Limuru got him detained for a year.

For a first dip into Ngugi, try *Secret Lives* for short stories, *Weep Not, Child* for a brief but glowing early novel, or, for the mature Ngugi, *Petals of Blood* – a richly satisfying detective story that is at the same time a saga of wretchedness and struggle. Other novels include *The River Between*, on the old Kikuyu society and the coming of the Europeans; *A Grain of Wheat*, about the eve of independence; *Devil on the Cross* (originally written in detention on scraps of toilet paper); and *Matigari* ("The Patriots"). *Matigari*, first published in Kikuyu in 1986, had a remarkable effect in the Central Highlands. Rumours circulated that a man was spreading militant propaganda against the government of Daniel Arap Moi. The police even tried to track him down, before realizing he was a fictional character and confiscating all copies of the book.

His epic, satirical novel, *The Wizard of the Crow*, was his last work of fiction, published in 2006 to huge acclaim, before he started to write autobiographically about his childhood: *Dreams in a Time of War* (2010) and *In the House of the Intepreter* (2012). Ngugi's contribution to Kenyan literature is enormous, and delving in is rewarding, if not always easy.

Thomas Akare *The Slums*. A bleaker read than Meja Mwangi (see below), but also more humane. The dialogue melds seamlessly into the narrative; there are no doubts about the authentic rhythms of Kenyan English here, but much is assumed to be understood and there's much that won't be, unless perhaps you're sitting under a 25-watt light bulb in a River Road B&L.

Charlotte H. Bruner (ed) *Unwinding Threads: Writing by Women in Africa*. The East Africa contributions feature Kenyan writers Charity Waciuma and the excellent Grace Ogot, whose *The Rain Came* is a bewitching mystery myth, combining traditional Luo tales with her own fiction in a perplexingly Western form.

John Kiriamiti *My Life in Crime*. This racy autobiographical account, penned in prison by a professional robber, was so successful that the author went on to write two novels (*Son of Fate* and *The Sinister Trophy*) plus an account of his time as a villain told from his fiancée's point of view (*My Life with a Criminal: Millie's Story*).

Charles Mangua *Son of Woman*. Mangua tells the tale of a son of a prostitute and his misadventures: hard-bitten and cynical, but still engaging.

Ali Mazrui *The Trial of Christopher Okigbo*. A clever novel of ideas from the US-based political scientist, now in his 80s, who always infuriates both critics and supporters of Kenya.

★**Meja Mwangi** *Going Down River Road*; *Carcass for Hounds*; *Kill Me Quick*. Popular author Meja Mwangi is lighter and more accessible than Ngugi, his fiction infused with the absurdities of urban Nairobi slum life. *Going Down River Road* is his best-known work – perfect for reading *in situ*, with convincing scenes, chaotic action and sharp dialogue. Mwangi was shortlisted for the Commonwealth Writers' Prize with *Striving for the Wind* (1992), which is set in a rural rather than urban location.

★**Ngugi wa Thiong'o** *Decolonising the Mind: The Politics of Language in African Literature*. Ngugi, who writes in Kikuyu as well as English, has long been closely associated with attempts to move Kenyan literature and African literature in general towards expression in the readers' mother tongues (see box, p.591).

M.G. Vassanji *The In-between World of Vikram Lall*. Remarkable epic of multiple alienations and the power of corruption in a world of competing moralities. Lall is the chief protagonist, a Ugandan Asian exiled to Canada having been named Kenya's most corrupt man.

★**Binyavanga Wainaina** *Discovering Home*. A collection of short stories, including the title piece that won him the 2002 Caine Prize for African Writing. Wainaina takes Kenyan humour, tragedy, and especially the meaning of home for diaspora Kenyans, and mounts them in a beautiful frame. His latest, *One Day I Will Write About This Place*, is a beautifully written coming-of-age tale.

KENYAN POETRY

The oldest form of written poetry in Kenya is from the coast. **Swahili poetry** reads beautifully even if you don't understand the words. Written for at least 300 years, and sung for a good deal longer, it's one of Kenya's most enduring art forms. An *Anthology of Swahili Poetry* has been compiled and rather woodenly translated by **Ali A. Jahadmy**, but some of Swahili's best-known classical compositions from the Lamu Archipelago are included, with pertinent background. There's a more enjoyable anthology of romantic and erotic verse, *A Choice of Flowers*, with **Jan Knappert's** idiosyncratic translations and interpretations, and the same linguist's *Four Centuries of Swahili Verse*, which expounds and creatively interprets at much greater length.

Upcountry poetry in the sense of written verse is a recent form (though oral folk literature was often relayed in the context of music, rhythm and dance). *The Penguin Book of Modern African Poetry*, edited by Gerald Moore, is hefty and diverse, with a good selection of Kenyan contributions.

KENYA IN FOREIGN FICTION

★**Justin Cartwright** *Masai Dreaming*. A compelling novel that juxtaposes a film-maker's vision of Maasai-land with the barbarities of the Holocaust, linked by the tapes of a Jewish anthropologist.

Nicholas Drayson *A Guide to the Birds of East Africa*. Somewhat after the style of McCall Smith's *The No.1 Ladies' Detective Agency* – but with more substance – Drayson's gently satirical lark among Nairobi's Asian community is a readable introduction to the lighter side of contemporary life in the capital – and a delight for birders.

★**Adam Foulds** *The Broken Word*. Moving, gripping and beautifully crafted novella-length prose poem about a young recruit swept up in the hunt for Mau Mau guerrillas.

Jeremy Gavron *Moon*. Vivid short novel about a white boy growing up on a farm during the Mau Mau uprising.

Martha Gellhorn *The Weather in Africa*. Three absorbing novellas, each dealing with aspects of the Europe–Africa relationship, set on the slopes of Kilimanjaro, in the "White Highlands" of Kenya and on the tourist coast north of Mombasa.

David Lambkin *The Hanging Tree*. A human-nature-through-the-ages saga which makes a good yarn – in fact, several yarns.

★**John Le Carré** *The Constant Gardener*. The spymaster turns his hand to a whodunit set in Kenya, in which a campaigner against the misdeeds of Big Pharma is murdered. A brilliantly crafted story (though oddly unconvincing in its portrayal of expat society), turned into a multi-Oscar-winning movie by Fernando Meirelles.

Barbara Wood *Green City in the Sun*. A sprawling saga, in which, among a slew of fizzing plot lines, a settler family comes into conflict with a Kikuyu medicine woman. One of the few credible novels about the realities of colonial Kenya by a *mzungu* writer.

HISTORY AND PEOPLES

Jeffrey A. Fadiman *When We Began There Were Witchmen*. Recounts the story of the Meru people from their mythical origins in Shungwaya in northeastern Kenya to the decimation of Meru culture by a tiny handful of missionaries and colonial administrators.

Terry Hirst *The Struggle for Nairobi*. A sort of "Nairobi for Beginners" that manages to make town planning (or the lack of it) fascinating, bringing together a mass of otherwise hard-to-get information about the city's growth.

Jomo Kenyatta *Facing Mount Kenya*. A traditional, anthropological monograph, written from the rather conservative functionalist perspective, but, uniquely for its era, by a member of the society in question – in this case, the Kikuyu. This is one of the few scholarly works ever written on traditional Kikuyu culture, and as interesting for the insights it offers on Kenyatta as for its quite readable content.

Maxon and Ofcansky *Historical Dictionary of Kenya*. An A to Z of Kenya's history (including an extensive bibliography) from a reliable series that covers nearly every African country.

Thomas Spear and Richard Waller (eds) *Being Maasai*. Articles about Maasai identity – a subtle and interesting field, and vital reading for anyone concerned with the ethnic politics of modern Kenya.

KENYA IN AFRICAN HISTORY

GENERAL AFRICAN HISTORY

Guy Arnold *Africa: a Modern History*. A huge reference history of the continent, from 1960 up until 2000, that places Kenya in context and succinctly ticks all the boxes linking present conditions with past causes.

★ **Richard Dowden** *Africa: Altered States, Ordinary Miracles*. The wealth of experience and engagement of Dowden – respected journalist and director of the Royal African Society – come through in this collection of extended essays, including a brilliant encapsulation of Kenya's downward spiral of greed and corruption.

Christopher Hibbert *Africa Explored: Europeans in the Dark Continent 1769–1889*. Entertaining read, devoted in large part to the "discovery" of East and Central Africa.

★ **Alan Moorehead** *The White Nile*. A riveting account of the search for the source and European rivalries for control in the region.

Roland Oliver and J.D. Fage *A Short History of Africa*. Dated, but still a good introduction.

Thomas Pakenham *The Scramble for Africa*. The story of the European rush to exploit Africa in the name of commerce, Christianity and civilization in the last two decades of the nineteenth century.

COASTAL HISTORY

★ **G.S.P. Freeman-Grenville** *The East African Coast*. Fascinating, vivid and often extraordinary – a series of accounts from the first century to the nineteenth.

Sarah Mirza *Three Swahili Women: Life Histories from Mombasa, Kenya*. Three histories of ritual, three women's lives. Born between 1890 and 1920 into different social backgrounds, these biographies document enormous changes from the most important of neglected viewpoints.

★ **James de Vere Allen** *Swahili Origins: Swahili Culture and the Shungwaya Phenomenon*. The life work of a challenging and readable scholar.

PROTECTORATE AND COLONIAL KENYA

Chloe Campbell *Race and Empire: Eugenics in Colonial Kenya*. Disconcertingly readable, scholarly work that shows how deeply the possibilities raised by eugenics were part of the pre-1939 colonial project in Kenya and how quickly they were shelved after the horrors of World War II.

★ **James Fox** *White Mischief*. Investigative romp through the events surrounding the notorious unsolved murder of Lord Errol, one of Kenya's most aristocratic settlers, at Karen in 1941. Well told and highly revealing of British Kenyan society of the time. Michael Radford's 1987 film version is equally enjoyable.

Charles Miller *The Lunatic Express: An Entertainment in Imperialism*. The story of the Uganda railway. Miller narrates the drama of one of the great feats of Victorian engineering – as bizarre and as madly magnificent as any Wild West epic – adding weight with a broad historical background of East Africa from the year dot. The same author's very readable *The Battle for the Bundu* follows a little-known corner of World War I as fought out on the plains of Tsavo between British Kenya and German Tanganyika.

THE MAU MAU REBELLION

★ **David Anderson** *Histories of the Hanged: Testimonies from the Mau Mau Rebellion in Kenya*. Previously published as *Britain's Dirty War in Kenya*, this deeply researched study concludes that the British response to Mau Mau was unnecessarily harsh and of doubtful legality, and that many Mau Mau trials were flawed.

Caroline Elkins *Britain's Gulag: The Brutal End of Empire in Kenya*. Pulitzer prize-winning study of Britain's network of Mau Mau detention camps. Less dispassionate and more one-sided than *Histories of the Hanged* (Elkins spends little time discussing Mau Mau atrocities), Elkins has been accused of exaggeration. But this book is nevertheless a shocking indictment of British methods, and provides strong support for the legal cases that some survivors have lodged.

Tabitha Kanogo *Squatters and the Roots of Mau Mau 1905–63*. Delves into the early years of the "White Highlands" to show how resistance, and the conditions for revolt, were built into the relations between the settler land-grabbers and the peasant farmers and herders ("squatters") they usurped. Strong on the role of women in the Mau Mau movement.

J.M. Kariuki *Mau Mau Detainee: The Account by a Kenya African of His Experience in Detention Camps*. A remarkably forbearing account of life and death in the detention camps, Kariuki's vision for the future of Kenya and his loyalty to Kenyatta have a special irony after his assassination in 1975.

★ **David Throup** *Economic and Social Origins of Mau Mau*. An examination of the story from the end of World War II, covering the colonial mentality and differences in efficiency between peasant cash-cropping and more wasteful plantation agriculture.

POST INDEPENDENCE

Jean Davison *Voices from Mutira: Change in the Lives of Rural Gikuyu Women 1910–1995*. Moving and particularly interesting for the attitudes it documents on bride price and FGM.

Charles Hornsby *Kenya: A History Since Independence*. A detailed survey of Kenya's first half-century of nationhood that balances cold analysis of contemporary failures against the unpromising historical context out of which they emerged.

Joseph Karimi and Philip Ochieng *The Kenyatta Succession*. Worth tracking down and a good read about how the clique surrounding Kenyatta planned to seize power when he died, murdering Moi in the process. By good fortune, Kenyatta died in the wrong place: the Mzee's cronies would have been far worse than Moi.

Salim Lone *War and Peace in Kenya*. Major new account of the Orange Democratic Movement and Raila Odinga's role in the 2007–8 elections by the UN's former director of news and media and Odinga's former director of communications.

Tom Mboya *The Challenge of Nationhood*. The vision of Kenya's best-loved statesman – and a Luo – assassinated in 1969 for looking like a popular successor to Kenyatta.

Miguna Miguna *Peeling Back the Mask: A Quest for Justice in Kenya*. This book by the former prime minister's senior adviser, sacked in 2011, dishes the dirt about Raila Odinga and the Grand Coalition and caused a storm in Kenya when it was launched in Nairobi in 2012.

★ **Michaela Wrong** *It's Our Turn to Eat: The Story of a Kenyan Whistle Blower*. "To eat" is a Kenyan euphemism for helping yourself to what doesn't belong to you – what those in power have been doing since independence. British journalist Michaela Wrong's jaw-dropping account narrates the story of what happened when anti-corruption czar John Githongo tried to do his job.

Language

Surprisingly, perhaps, Swahili is one of the easiest languages to learn. It's pronounced exactly as it's written, with the stress nearly always on the penultimate syllable. And it's satisfyingly regular, so even with limited knowledge you can make yourself understood and construct simple sentences.

In Kenya, you'd rarely be stuck without Swahili, but it makes a huge difference to your perceptions if you try to speak it. People are delighted if you make the effort (though they'll also tend to assume you understand more than you do) and for travels further afield in East Africa, and especially in Tanzania, some knowledge of Swahili is a very useful backup. Don't forget that for many Kenyans Swahili is another foreign language they get by in, like English.

The language has spread widely from its coastal origins to become the lingua franca of East Africa and it has tended to lose its richness and complexity as a result. Upcountry, it is often spoken as a second language with a minimum of grammar. On the coast, you'll hear it spoken with tremendous panache: oratorical skills and punning (to which it lends itself with great facility) are much appreciated. Swahili is a Bantu language, and in fact one of the more mainstream of the family, but it has incorporated thousands of foreign words, the majority of them Arabic, but including Portuguese and English. Far more of this Arabic inheritance and borrowing is preserved on the coast. The "standard" dialect is derived from Zanzibar Swahili, the dialect the early missionaries learned and first transcribed into the Roman alphabet. **Written Swahili** is still not completely uniform, and you'll come across slight variations in spelling, particularly on menus.

Swahili language books and courses

There are several published language **courses** around. *Teach Yourself Swahili* by Joan Russell is an excellent book and CD, with practical Swahili that you can use from the beginning. *Kiswahili kwa Kitendo* ("Swahili by Action", by Sharifa Zawawi) is the best bet if you find ordinary grammars indigestible. The free online resource Mwana Simba (Ⓦmwanasimba .online.fr/E_TABLE.htm) includes grammar as well as an extensive dictionary. As for **phrasebooks**, try the pocket-sized *Rough Guide Swahili Dictionary Phrasebook*, which includes links to MP3 files to practise your pronunciation at Ⓦtinyurl.com/yhwqwyn.

Swahili pronunciation

Once you get the hang of voicing every syllable and remember that each vowel is a syllable and that nothing is silent, **pronunciation** is easy. However, odd-looking combinations of consonants are often pronounced as one, double-length syllable. **Mzee**, for example, is pronounced "mz-ay-ay" (rhyming with "hey") and **shauri** (troubles, problem) is pronounced "sha-oo-ri" while **mgonjwa** (ill) has just two syllables "mgo-njwa".

You'll often come across an "**m**" where it looks out of place: this letter can precede any other. That is because it's a noun prefix (usually replaced in the plural with "wa-" or "mi-"), as in **mtoto** (child; plural **watoto**) or **mti** (tree; plural **miti**). Just add a bit of an "m" sound at the beginning; "mm-toto". If you say "um-toto" or "ma-toto" you'll be misunderstood. "Ng" followed by an apostrophe makes a sound like the "ng" in banger, not Bangor (try saying "banger" without the "ba", and then use it in a word like **ng'ombe** – cow or beef). Without the apostrophe, the ng is like two separate letters as in "finger" (as in **nguo** – garment, clothes).

For memorizing, it often helps to ignore the first letter or syllable. Thousands of nouns, for example, start with "ki" (singular) and "vi" (plural), and they're all in the same noun class.

A as in Arthur

B as in bed

C doesn't exist on its own

CH as in church, but often sounds like a "t", a "dj" or a "ky"

D as in donkey

DJ like the "j" in pyjamas

DH like a cross between dhow and thou

E between the "e" in Edward and "ai" in ailing

F as in fan

G as in good

GH at the back of the throat, like a gargle or a French "r"

H as in harmless

I like the "e" in evil

J as in jug

K as in kiosk, sometimes like soft "t" or "ch"

KH like the "ch" in loch

L as in lullaby, but often pronounced like an "r"

M as in Martian

N as in nonsense

NG as in finger or hunger, with a clear "g" sound

NG' as in wrong or banger, with no "g" sound

O as in orange, never as in "open" or "do"

P as in penguin

Q doesn't exist (except in early Romanized texts; now "k")

R as in rapid

S as in Samson

T as in tiny

TH as in thanks, never as in "them"

U as in lute

V as in victory

W as in wobble

X doesn't exist

Y as in you

Z as in zero

Swahili words and phrases

The words and phrases listed here are all in common usage, but Swahili (like English) is far from being a homogeneous language, so don't be surprised if you sometimes get some funny looks. And, for lack of space for explanation, there are a number of apparent inconsistencies; just ignore them unless you intend to learn the language seriously. These phrases should at least make you understood.

GREETINGS AND TERMS OF ADDRESS

Tourists are greeted with **Jambo?** or more correctly **Hujambo?** (a multipurpose greeting, meaning "Things?" or "Problems?"). If you don't speak any Swahili, replying **Jambo** is fine, but if you want to make an effort, say **Sijambo** ("No problems") and continue with one of the following:

News?	Habari?	Very (a common emphasis)	Sana
Your news?	Habari yako?		
What news?	Habari gani?	Mister	Bwana (pl. mabwana)
Good, thanks	Nzuri	Addressing an adult woman	Mama
How goes?	Mambo?		
Well, thanks	Nzuri	Addressing an old lady	Bibi
What's up?	Vipi?		
Cool, sweet	Safi	Addressing an old man	Babu
Cool, excellent	Fiti		
Hello? Anyone in?	Hodi!	Youth, teenager	Kijana (pl. vijana)
Come in! Welcome! (also said on offering something)	Karibu	Child	Mtoto (pl. watoto)
		What's your name?	Jina lako nani?
Goodbye to one/many	Kwaheri/ni	White, European	-zungu (eg mzungu white person; wazungu, white people)
Thank you to one/many	Asante/ni		

BASICS

My name is/ I am called	Jina langu/Nina itwa	I am from ...	Ninatoka
		I am staying (at/in)	Ninakaa
Where are you from?	Unatoka wapi?	See you!	Tutaonana!
Where are you staying?	Unakaa wapi?	Yes, that's right	ndiyo

No	hapana; siyo; la (Arabic, heard mostly on the coast)	who?	nani?
		what?	nini?
I don't understand	Sifahamu/Sielewi	which?	gani?
I don't speak Swahili, but	Sisemi kiswahili, lakini	true	kweli
		and/with	na
How do you say ... in Swahili	Unasemaje kwa kiswahili ...?	or	au
		isn't it?	siyo?
Could you repeat that?	Sema tena	I'm English (or British)/Scottish/	Mimi ni mwingereza/ mskochi/mwelsh/
Speak slowly	Sema pole pole	Welsh/Irish/	muairish
I don't know	Sijui	American/	/mwamerika/
where (is)?	wapi?	Canadian/	mkanada/
here	hapa	Australian/	mwaustralia/
when?	lini?	a New Zealander/	mnyuziland/
now	sasa	Kenyan	mkenya
soon	sasa hivi		
why?	kwa nini?		
because	kwa sababu	The plurals for nationalities begin with "**Wa-**" instead of "**M-**".	
but	lakini		

SIGNS AND COMMON PHRASES

Danger	Hatari!	And two phrases you're more likely to hear than to ever say	
Warning	Angalia!/Onyo!		
Fierce dog!	Mbwa mkali!	Take a picture of me!	Piga picha mimi!
No entry!	Hakuna njia	Help the poor!	Saidia maskini!

ADJECTIVES AND IDIOMS

good (with a prefix at the front)	-zuri	problems, hassles	wasiwasi, matata
		friend	rafiki
bad (ditto)	-baya	sorry, pardon	samahani
big	-kubwa	It's nothing	Si kitu
small	-dogo	Excuse me, let me through	Hebu
a lot of	-ingi		
other/another	-ingine	What's up?	Namna gani?
not bad	si mbaya	If God wills it (heard often on the coast)	Inshallah
OK, right, fine	sawa		
fine, cool	safi		
completely	kabisa	please	tafadhali (rare upcountry and not heard much on the coast either)
thing(s)	kitu (vitu)		
No problem	Hakuna wasiwasi/ Hakuna matata		

DAILY NEEDS

Where can I sleep?	Naweza kulala wapi?	I'm hungry	Nina njaa
Can I stay here?	Naweza kulala hapa?	I'm thirsty	Nina kiu
		Is there any ...?	Iko ...? or Kuna ...?
room(s)	chumba (vyumba)	Yes there is ...	Iko ... or Kuna ...
bed(s)	kitanda (vitanda)	No there isn't any	Haiko ... or Hakuna ...
chair(s)	kiti (viti)	How much?	Ngapi?
table(s)	meza	money	pesa
toilet, bathroom	choo, bafu	What price ...?	Bei gani ...?
men, women	wanaume, wanawakea	How much is ...?	Pesa ngapi ...?
washing water	maji ya kuosha	I want...	Nataka ...
hot/cold water	maji moto/baridi	I don't want ...	Sitaki ...

Give me/Bring me (can I have?)	Nipe/Niletee	bank	benki
		post office	posta
again/more	tena	café, restaurant	hoteli
enough	tosha/basi	telephone	simu
expensive	ghali sana	cigarettes	sigara
cheap (also "easy")	rahisi	I'm ill	Mimi mgonjwa
fifty cents	sumni	doctor	daktari
Reduce the price, come down a little!	Punguza kidogo!	hospital	hospitali
		police	polisi
shop	duka	tip, bribe	chai

TRAVEL AND DIRECTIONS

travel	kusafiri	Where are you going?	Unaenda wapi?
journey	safari	To where?	Mpaka wapi?
bus(es)	bas, basi/mabasi	From where?	Kutoka wapi?
car(s), vehicle/s	gari (magari)	How many kilometres?	Kilometa ngapi?
taxi	teksi		
bicycle	baiskeli	This road, it goes to ...?	Barabara hii, ni njia ya ...?
train	treni		
plane	ndege	I'm going to...	Nenda ...
boat/ship	chombo/meli	Move along, squeeze up a little	Songa!/Songa kidogo
petrol	petroli		
road, path	njia/ndia	Let's go, carry on	Twende, endelea
highway	barabara	straight ahead	moja kwa moja
on foot/walking	kwa miguu	right	kulia
When does it leave?	Inaondoka lini?	left	kushoto
When will we arrive?	Tutafika lini?	up	juu
slowly	pole pole	down	chini
fast, quickly	haraka	I want to get off here	Nataka kushuka hapa
Wait!/Hang on a moment!	Ngoja!/Ngoja kidogo!		
Stop!	Simama!	The car has broken down	Gari imevunjika

TIME, CALENDAR AND NUMBERS

What time is it?	Saa ngapi?	this month	mwezi huu
four o'clock	saa nne (ie 4hr past dawn or dusk, in other words 10am or 10pm)	Monday	jumatatu
		Tuesday	jumanne
		Wednesday	jumatano
		Thursday	alhamisi
quarter past	na robo	Friday	ijumaa
half past	na nusu	Saturday	jumamosi
quarter to	kasa robo	Sunday	jumapili
minutes	dakika	1	moja
daytime	mchana	2	mbili
night-time	usiku	3	tatu
dawn	alfajiri	4	nne
morning	asubuhi	5	tano
early	mapema	6	sita
yesterday	jana	7	saba
today	leo	8	nane
tomorrow	kesho	9	tisa
last week/this week/next week	wiki iliopita/wiki hii/ wiki ijayo	10	kumi
		11	kumi na moja
this year	mwaka huu	12	kumi na mbili

20	ishirini	80	themanini
21	ishirini na moja	90	tisini
30	thelathini	100	mia moja
40	arobaini	121	mia moja na ishirini
50	hamsini		na moja
60	sitini	1000	elfu
70	sabini		

Menu and food terms

The lists below should be adequate for translating most Swahili menus and explaining what you want, though bear in mind that spelling may vary.

BASICS

barafu	ice	mboga	vegetables
baridi	cold	mchuzi	sauce
chakula	food	meza	table
chemka	boiled	mkate	bread
choma	roast	moto	hot
chumvi	salt	nusu	half
chupa	bottle	nyama	meat
hesabu	bill	piripiri	pepper
ingine	more, another	sahani	plate
kaanga	fried	samaki	fish
kijiko	spoon	siagi	butter, margarine
kisu	knife	sukari	sugar
maji	water, juice	uma	fork
matunda	fruit	yai (mayai)	egg(s)
maziwa	milk		

SNACKS

"bitings"	pre-dinner snacks		flavoured with spices, known as mahamri on the coast
chapatti	unleavened, flat wheat bread, baked on a hot plate or in an oven (tandoor)	maziwalala	yoghurt (literally "milk asleep")
halwa	gelatinous sweetmeat, like Turkish delight	mkate mayai	"egg-bread"; soft thin dough wrapped around fried egg and minced meat
keki	cake		
kachumbari	tomato, onion and coriander relish	samosa	deep-fried triangular case of chopped meat and vegetables
kitumbuo	deep-fried rice bread		
mandaazi	deep-fried sweet dough, sometimes	tosti/slice	slice of bread

DISHES

frigisi	chicken giblets	kata-kata	("half-half") a mix of whatever is available, usually including spaghetti, beans, rice, goat meat and shredded cabbage and carrot
githeri	Kikuyu dish of beans and corn, sometimes with meat		
irio/kienyeji/mataha	potato, cabbage and beans mashed together	kima	mince

koroga	(literally "to stir" or "cook" in Swahili) a meal style, rather than a dish: you buy the ingredients at a koroga restaurant and cook them in the garden with the equipment provided	pilau	rice with spices and meat
		sukuma wiki	boiled green leaves, usually a kind of spinach
		ugali/sima	cornmeal boiled to a solid porridge with water, occasionally milk; yellow ugali is considered inferior to white but is more nutritious
matoke	green banana, usually boiled and mashed		
mboga	vegetables usually potatoes, carrots and onions in meaty gravy		
mchele	plain white rice	uji	porridge or gruel made of millet; good for chilly mornings
michicha	spinach cooked with onions and tomatoes	wali	rice with added fat and spices (almost pilau)
mukimo	pumpkin leaf and potato mash, with corn		

MEAT

kondo	lamb	ng'ombe	beef
kuku	chicken	nguruwe	pork
mbuzi	goat	nyama choma	roast meat
mushkaki	kebab; small pieces of grilled, marinated meat on or off the skewer	steki	steak, grilled meat

FRUIT

limau	lime	nazi	coconuts
machungwa	oranges	ndimu	lemon
madafu	green coconuts	ndizi	bananas
maembe	mangos	papai	papaya/pawpaw
mastafeli	soursops	parachichi	avocado
matopetope	custard apples	pera	guava
nanasi	pineapple	sandara	mandarins

VEGETABLES

maharagwe	red kidney beans, often cooked with coconut	ndizi	bananas or plantains
		nyanya	tomatoes (also means grandmother)
mahindi	corn	sukuma wiki	greens, usually kale or collard greens
mbaazi	pigeon peas, small beans		
		viazi	potatoes
mtama	millet	vitunguu	onions
muhogo	cassava		

DRINKS

busaa	maize beer	mabziwalala	fermented milk/almost yoghurt
chai, chai kavu, chai strungi	tea, black tea, strongly spiced tea		
		kahawa	coffee
changa'a	hootch, illegal spirits	bia, tembo	beer
mnazi	coconut palm wine	pombe	booze
muratina	porridgey Kikuyu honey and millet beer		

Swahili animal names

Animal is **mnyama** (plural **wanyama**) but the names of most species are the same in singular and plural.

Aardvark	Muhanga	**Kudu**	Tandala
Baboon	Nyani	**Leopard**	Chui
Bat-eared fox	Bweha masigio	**Lion**	Simba
Bird (also means plane)	Ndege	**Lizard**	Mjusi
		Mongoose	Nguchiro
Buffalo	Nyati	**Monkey (usually Sykes' monkey)**	Kima
Bushbaby	Komba		
Cane rat	Ndeze	**Oribi**	Taya
Caracal	Simbamangu	**Oryx**	Choroa
Cat	Paka	**Ostrich**	Mbuni
Cheetah	Duma	**Otter**	Fisi maji
Chimpanzee	Soko	**Pangolin**	Kakukuona
Civet	Fungo	**Pig, hog**	Nguruwe
Colobus monkey	Mbega	**Porcupine**	Nungu
Crocodile	Mamba	**Ratel**	Nyegere
De Brazza's monkey	Kalasinga	**Reedbuck**	Tohe
Dog	Mbwa	**Rhinoceros**	Faru
Duiker	Nsya	**Roan antelope**	Korongo
Eland	Pofu	**Rock hyrax**	Pimbi
Elephant	Ndovu	**Sable antelope**	Pala hala
Elephant shrew	Sange	**Serval**	Mondo
Genet	Kanu	**Shark**	Papa
Gerenuk	Swala twiga	**Snake**	Nyoka
Giraffe	Twiga	**Springhare**	Kamandegere
Grant's gazelle	Swala granti	**Steinbok, grysbok**	Dondoo
Ground squirrel	Kindi	**Suni antelope**	Paa
Hare, rabbit	Sunguru	**Thomson's gazelle**	Swala tomi
Hartebeest	Kongoni	**Topi**	Nyamera
Hedgehog	Kalunguyeye	**Tortoise**	Kobe
Hippopotamus	Kiboko	**Tree hyrax**	Pembere
Horse, ass	Punda	**Vervet monkey**	Tumbili
Hunting dog	Mbwa mwitu	**Warthog**	Ngiri
Hyena	Fisi	**Waterbuck**	Kuru
Impala	Swala pala	**Wild cat**	Paka pori
Insect, bug	Mdudu	**Wildebeest**	Nyumbu
Jackal	Bweha	**Zebra**	Punda milia
Klipspringer	Mbuzi mawe		

Regional languages

Kenya's many languages are grouped into related clusters, comparable to Romance and Germanic languages in Europe. "Bantu", a word coined by twentieth-century linguists, derives from the common stem for "person" – ntu – and the plural prefix – ba – found in most of the six hundred contemporary Bantu languages across Africa. Look out for the way names vary with context: Mkamba, for example, refers to a Kamba person, Wakamba to Kamba people and Kikamba to the Kamba language. The following brief word lists are intended only for introductions and as a springboard for communication. If you'll be spending time in a particular linguistic region, you may be surprised at how difficult it is to track down useable primers and phrasebooks for these languages.

KENYA'S MAIN LANGUAGE GROUPS

Bantu-speaking
Western Bantu: Luhya, Gusii, Kuria
Central Bantu: Kamba, Kikuyu, Embu, Meru, Mbere, Tharaka
Coastal Bantu: Swahili, Mijikenda, Segeju, Pokomo, Taita, Taveta

Cushitic-speaking
Southern Cushitic: Boni
Eastern Cushitic: Somali, Rendille, Orma, Boran, Gabbra ("Oromo" is often used collectively for all four languages)

Nilotic-speaking
Lake-River Nilotic: Luo
Plains Nilotic: Maasai and Samburu (Maa-speakers), Turkana, Teso, Njemps, Elmolo
Highland Nilotic: Kalenjin (Nandi and its dialects), Marakwet, Pokot, Tugen, Kipsigis, Elkony

KALENJIN (RIFT VALLEY)

Hi, hello	Chamgei	1	Akenge
Sleep well	Rui komie	2	Aena
Goodbye	Sai sere	3	Somok
Thank you	Kongoe	4	Angwan
Good	Kararan	5	Mut
Yes	Uoi	6	Lo
No	Adja	7	Tisap
How are you?	I amu ne?	8	Sisit
Fine	Misi	9	Sokol
I am hungry	Ama rubet!	10	Taman

KAMBA (UKAMBANI, EAST OF NAIROBI)

How are you (sing.)?	Wimuseo?	Goodbye/go well (staying, pl.)	Endai noseo
Fine (sing.)	Nikuseo		
How are you (pl.)?	Mwiaseo?	1	Imwe
Fine (pl.)	Twiaseo	2	Ile
How are things?	Maundu mailye ata?	3	Itatu
Things are well	Maundu ni maseo	4	Inya
No problem /nothing wrong	Aiyie	5	Itano
		6	Thanthatu
Goodbye (leaving, sing.)	Tiwa noseo	7	Muonza
Goodbye (leaving, pl.)	Tiwai na useo	8	Nyanya
Goodbye/go well (staying, sing.)	Enda noseo	9	Kenda
		10	Ikumi

KIKUYU (CENTRAL HIGHLANDS)

How are things?	Kweruo atia?	1	Imwe
Fine!	Ni kuega!	2	Igiri
Are you well? (pl.)	Wi mwega/Muri ega?	3	Ithatu
		4	Inya
Response ("Nothing wrong")	Asha, ndi mwega	5	Ithano
		6	Ithathatu
Goodbye (when you're leaving)	Tigwo na wega	7	Mugwanja
		8	Inyanya
Goodbye (when you're staying)	Thii na wega	9	Kenda
		10	Ikumi

LUHYA (KAKAMEGA & WESTERN KENYA)

Good morning	Vushele (boo-sher-ae)	1		Indala
Hello, Good afternoon	Mulembe (moo-rem-bae)	2		Zivili
Good evening	Vwakhila (wah-hee-ra)	3		Vizaka
Responses	Vushele muno,	4		Zinee
	Mulembe muno,	5		Ziranu
	Vwakhila muno	6		Zisasava
How are you?	Karina?	7		Saba
Well, very well	Malahi (ma-lay-ee),	8		Munane
	Malahi sana	9		Tisa
Thank you	Urio muno (or-e-om-ono)	10		Likhomi
Goodbye	Vulahi (vu-lay-ee)			

LUO (LAKE VICTORIA)

How do you do?	Iriyo nade?	5		Abich
Response	Ariyo maber!	6		Auchiely
Thank you	Erokamano	7		Abiriyo
1	Achiel	8		Aboro
2	Ariyo	9		Ochiko
3	Adek	10		Apar
4	Angwen			

MAA (MAASAI)

Greetings to a man	Lo murrani! Supa!	3		Okuni
Response	Ipa!	4		Oonguan
Greetings to a woman	Na kitok! Takuenya!	5		Imiet
Response	Iko!	6		Ile
Thank you (very much!)	Ashe (naleng!)	7		Oopishana
		8		Isiet
Goodbye!	Sere!	9		Ooudo
1	Obo	10		Tomon
2	Aare			

Glossary

These words – not all of them Swahili – are all in common usage. Remember, however, that plural forms often have different beginnings.

Age-set/age grade Generation who have passed through rites of passage together, often including people of widely differing chronological ages

Administration Police (AP) Paramilitary police force, often stationed in areas of ethnic conflict

ASK Agricultural Society of Kenya

Askari Policeman, security guard, soldier

Banda Any kind of hut, usually round and thatched

Bangi, Bhang Marijuana

Baobab Species of tree whose trunk retains water

Barabara Main road

Bau Traditional calculation game of pebbles and holes

Boarding & Lodging (B&L) Cheap guesthouse

Boda-boda Bicycle taxi

Boma A fort or defensive stockade, often used to mean a small village or cluster of huts

Boriti Mangrove poles, used on the coast for building and exported to the Gulf states for the same purpose

Buibui The black cover-all cloak and scarf of Swahili women

Bwana Mister, a polite form of address

Chai Not just tea, but also the common term for a tip, or more often a small bribe or persuasion

Choo Toilet (pronounced "cho")

Day & Night Club Low-budget, 24-hour bar and occasional music club

Duka Shop, store

Duka la dawa Chemist

Enkang Maasai village

FORD Forum for the Restoration of Democracy, opposition political party

Fundi Mechanic, craftsman, expert

Gari Car

Gema The ethnic grouping of Gikuyu (Kikuyu), Embu and Meru

GK Government of Kenya

General Service Unit (GSU) Paramilitary security unit reporting directly to the president

Group ranch Community-owned grazing area with title deeds, rather than traditional rights

Harambee "Pull together" – the ideology of peaceable community development espoused by Jomo Kenyatta. Harambee meetings are local fund-raising gatherings for schools, clinics, etc.

Hoteli Small restaurant, tea shop or café

Jamhuri Republic

Jiko Kitchen or cooker

Jua kali "Hot sun" – open-air car repairer's yard or small workshop

Kanga Printed cotton sheet used as a wrap, often incorporating a motto

Kanisa Church

KBC Kenya Broadcasting Corporation

KPSGA Kenya Professional Safari Guides Association

KWS Kenya Wildlife Service

Kikoi Brightly coloured woven cloth

Laibon Maasai spiritual leader, with the status of regional headman

Lugga/Laga Dry river valley (usually in the north)

Mabati Corrugated-iron roofing sheets

Maendeleo Progress, development

Madaraka Independence

Magendo Corruption, bribery, abuse of power

Majimboism The creation of federal blocks in formerly heterogeneous regions – these days associated with ethnic cleansing

Makonde Beautifully worked Tanzanian woodcarving, typically in ebony and representing entwined spirit families

Makutano Junction

Makuti Palm-leaf roof common on the coast

Malaika Angel

Malaya Prostitute

Mama Common term of address for married women

Manamba Matatu tout, "turnboy"

Manyatta Temporary cattle camp, often loosely used for a village (Maasai)

Maskini The poor, beggars (Saidia maskini! "Help the poor!")

Matatu Shared minibus

Mbenzi Member of the rich elite (presumed to have a Mercedes; plural wabenzi)

Mbuyu Baobab (Swahili)

Mgeni Guest, tourist (pl. wageni)

Mgunga Acacia or gum Arabic tree (Swahili)

Miraa Qat, a natural stimulant

Mkenya Kenyan (pl. wakenya)

Mkoko Mangrove

Moran Man in the warrior age group of Maasai or Samburu (pl. morani)

Msikiti Mosque

Mtalii Tourist (pl. watalii)

Mtoto Child (pl. watoto)

Mungiki Anti-establishment Kikuyu youth cult that violently rejects Western values

Mungu God

Murram Red or black clay soil, usually referring to a road

Mwananchi Person, peasant, worker (pl. wananchi)

Mzee Old man – "the Mzee" is Kenyatta

Mzungu White person (pl. wazungu)

NCCK National Christian Council of Kenya

NDP National Development Party, mainly Luo

Ngai Supreme god of the Kikuyu and other groups

NGO Non-governmental organization

Nyama Animal, game, meat

Ngoma Dancing, drumming, party, celebration

Njia Road, path

Nyayo "Footsteps" – the follow-in-his-footsteps philosophy of post-Kenyatta Kenya propounded by President Moi

Panga Multipurpose short machete carried everywhere in the countryside

Pesa Money, cash

Pombe Booze

Rondavel Round hut or small house (see banda)

SACCO Savings and credit co-operative (or credit union) – popular in rural areas for providing a shared-ownership matatu for transport, income and credit

Safari Journey of any kind, but in the modern sense a trip of one or more days to see animals

Shamba Small farm, plot

Sista Informal term of address to young woman

Slum Any area of poor housing (no pejorative connotation)

Soda Fizzy drink, but also a euphemism for a tip

Soja Soldier, watchman, guard

Stage Matatu stand

Syce Groom or stable hand

Uhuru Freedom, independence

Ukimwi AIDS

Ulaya Europe

Upcountry An adjective defining the lands and culture of the interior, notably the highlands, as distinct from the coast

Wageni See mgeni

Wananchi See mwananchi

Watu Literally "people", but often used slightly disparagingly by expats and Anglo-Kenyans, especially when referring to their staff

Wazungu See mzungu

Small print and index

A ROUGH GUIDE TO ROUGH GUIDES

Published in 1982, the first Rough Guide – to Greece – was a student scheme that became a publishing phenomenon. Mark Ellingham, a recent graduate in English from Bristol University, had been travelling in Greece the previous summer and couldn't find the right guidebook. With a small group of friends he wrote his own guide, combining a highly contemporary, journalistic style with a thoroughly practical approach to travellers' needs.

The immediate success of the book spawned a series that rapidly covered dozens of destinations. And, in addition to impecunious backpackers, Rough Guides soon acquired a much broader readership that relished the guides' wit and inquisitiveness as much as their enthusiastic, critical approach and value-for-money ethos.

These days, Rough Guides include recommendations from budget to luxury and cover more than 200 destinations around the globe, as well as producing an ever-growing range of eBooks and apps.

Visit **roughguides.com** to see our latest publications.

Rough Guide credits

Editors: James Smart and Emma Gibbs
Layout: Pradeep Thapliyal and Nikhil Agarwal
Cartography: Rajesh Chhibber
Picture editor: Tim Draper
Proofreader: Jan McCann
Managing editor: Keith Drew
Assistant editor: Dipika Dasgupta
Production: Charlotte Cade
Cover design: Nicole Newman, Dan May, Pradeep Thapliyal

Editorial assistant: Olivia Rawes
Senior pre-press designer: Dan May
Design director: Scott Stickland
Travel publisher: Joanna Kirby
Digital travel publisher: Peter Buckley
Operations coordinator: Helen Blount
Publishing director (Travel): Clare Currie
Commercial manager: Gino Magnotta
Managing director: John Duhigg

Publishing information

This tenth edition published May 2013 by
Rough Guides Ltd,
80 Strand, London WC2R 0RL
11, Community Centre, Panchsheel Park,
New Delhi 110017, India
Distributed by the Penguin Group
Penguin Books Ltd,
80 Strand, London WC2R 0RL
Penguin Group (USA)
375 Hudson Street, NY 10014, USA
Penguin Group (Australia)
250 Camberwell Road, Camberwell,
Victoria 3124, Australia
Penguin Group (NZ)
67 Apollo Drive, Mairangi Bay, Auckland 1310,
New Zealand
Penguin Group (South Africa)
Block D, Rosebank Office Park, 181 Jan Smuts Avenue,
Parktown North, Gauteng, South Africa 2193
Rough Guides is represented in Canada by Tourmaline
Editions Inc. 662 King Street West, Suite 304, Toronto,
Ontario M5V 1M7
Printed in Malaysia by Vivar Printing Sdn Bhd

Help us update

We've gone to a lot of effort to ensure that the tenth edition of **The Rough Guide to Kenya** is accurate and up-to-date. However, things change – places get "discovered", opening hours are notoriously fickle, restaurants and rooms raise prices or lower standards. If you feel we've got it wrong or left something out, we'd like to know, and if you can remember the address, the price, the hours, the phone number, so much the better.

Please send your comments with the subject line "**Rough Guide Kenya Update**" to ✉ mail@uk.roughguides .com. We'll credit all contributions and send a copy of the next edition (or any other Rough Guide if you prefer) for the very best emails.

Find more travel information, connect with fellow travellers and book your trip on ⓦ roughguides.com

Acknowledgements

Richard Trillo: First, to my patient and tireless driver Ndolo Kaleli – never fazed, whether facing city *askaris* in Nairobi or a breakdown in the Chalbi Desert – thank you for the journeys updating this tenth edition. Equally first, to my family – Teresa and Alex who stayed behind this time, and roped-in assistants David and Phoebe, and my brother Robert – all my thanks for sharing the wild dogs and the warrior training, and the knocks, mud and dust, and for delivering your views on the good, the bad and the unprintable.

Many thanks for assistance and information to Race Tavasi Masumba and her team at Kenya Wildlife Service in Nairobi and to KWS wardens Kitavi Kaloki at Amboseli, Fred Omengo at Lake Nakuru, Collins Omondi at Tsavo West and Dickson Too at Marsabit.

I am very grateful to Chris McIntyre, founder of Expert Africa, for his unstinting support for our new Kenya travel programme, and to my Expert Africa colleagues Ellie Dunkels and Liz Wollen for being such good mentors and for making invaluable contributions to this edition from their recent trips to Kenya.

My grateful thanks still go to Jeremy Torr for the English Cycles mountain bike that got me round Kenya on the first edition and for the help from Rosie Mercer, Jackie Switzer and the Khans in Kisii. Also for work on previous editions, my continuing thanks go to Emma Gregg, Daniel Jacobs, Jens Finke, Okigbo Ojukwu and Nana Luckham, and for the music article to Doug Paterson, Werner Graebner and Jens Finke.

On this edition, huge thanks to my contributors Ayako Bertolli and Hilary Heuler, my editors James Smart, Gavin Thomas and Emma Gibbs, picture researchers Wilf Matos and Tim Draper and the Rough Guides design, layout and cartography teams. Special thanks to film-maker Lottie Gross for her very helpful input – and inspiration (if any were needed) to keep exploring the north; to Matthew Teller for being a storm-force Twitterer and generous source of news and connections; to Nigel Watt, Brenda Skinner and colleagues at North South Travel; and to my old Rough Guides mates Mark Ellingham and Martin Dunford.

For various combinations of friendship, information, help, hospitality and good ideas, my grateful thanks to: Jacques-Fabrice of aux4vents.com in Loiyangalani (who fixed our alternator twice…), Bryan Adkins of Wildlife Works, Juliet Agg-Manning, Alnavaz Amlani of Camp Kipipiri, Eddie Anderson of AIC Kalacha, Father Anthony of North Horr (who spent a day fixing our alternator for the third time), Hilary Atkins, Suleiman Bakar and colleagues at Kaya Kinondo, Jonathan Bending of Colobus Cottages, Phillipa Bengough of Tropic Air, Richard Bielby of the FCO travel advice unit, Roman and Neva Biondic and Sankale Ntutu and staff of Maji-Moto Eco Camp, Sara Blackburn of the Mara Predator Project, Caroline Blake and Taffeta Gay of Bannister Blake, Anselmo Blake of Mombasa Backpackers, Florence Bouchou of Forty Thieves, Sally Broom of Tripbod, John Buckley and Anu Vohora of SafariLink, Kerin Larby of Bush & Beyond, Annabelle and Steve Carey at Laikipia Wilderness, Joe and Gillian Charleson of Leleshwa, Stefano Cheli and team at Cheli and Peacock, Anton & Emma Childs, James Christian and Kerry Glen of Karisia, Damian & Elizabeth Cook of E-Tourism Frontiers, Calvin Cottar, Peter Coventry at Yibba Yabba, Deepa Darbar of Exclusive African Treasures, Dominique de Bonis Cosgrove of Asha Cottage, Nick and Jenni Demille, Alan & Sue Dixson and Angela Njehia of Uniglobe Let's Go Travel, Asgar (Ozi) Dossaji

in Malindi, Alex Flixman of Tropical Ice, Daniel Floren at Shimoni, Felicity Fowkes of Mida Ecocamp, Mary and David Furnivall, Linda Gaymer of Crescent Island, Marta Anna Gloserova of KenyaBuzz, Sophie and Murray Grant at El Karama, Jake Grieves-Cook and Mohanjeet Brar of Gamewatchers/Porini Camps, Vanessa Hahne and Astrid Cantauw of Severin, Abdallah Haji and Alex Mwikya of Marsabit Lodge, Antonia Hall of Tassia, Neil Hargreaves of Mara North Conservancy, Jitu Haria of Haria's Gift Shop, Papu Haroon of ManFridays Mida Cove, Paul Harrison in Mtwapa, Alan and Lynita Harris at Wildebeest Eco Camp, Theresa Heasman of Karibuni Lodge, Emma Hedges of Desert Rose, Mohammed Hersi at Sarova, Natalie Hoare for sharing the snake walk, Martin Housman at Roving Rovers, Andrew Jones at Maralal Safari Lodge, Shadrack Kahindi of Glorious Safaris, Paula Kahumbu, campaigning naturalist extraordinaire, for sharing the Ngong Road Forest walk, Fred Kaigua of KATO, Prudence Kambe at the Tamarind, Alnoor Kanji at Pinewood, Mohez Karmali and team at Concorde Car Hire, Will Knocker and family at Silole, Silas Koiyaren Kitonga and Laura Alessandrini of Bush Adventures, Chris Koller of Peponi Divers, Sharon Kyungu at National Museums of Kenya, Tess Longfield of Longfield PR, Laura Loyola at Tana River Primate Reserve, George Makwattah of Kambua Guest House, Ian and Larissa Manson Hart at Tijara Beach, Jackson Mbai of Kwale Golden Guest House, Greg Monson and team at Kicheche, Agostino Moru of Lake Turkana Festival, Lucy Moss of Dovetail, Jackson Mutua of Mara Sidai Camp, Pamela Muyeshi of Amaica, Hellen Ndeto of Acacia Camp, Dr Joseph Ogutu for sobering Mara wildlife information, Riccardo Orizio of Saruni, Patricia Ouko of Integritour, Dipesh Pabari of Camps International, Moshi Perera and Neelma Maru of Sankara, John and Amanda Perrett of Ol Maisor, Sally Peters at Kenya Airways, Anne Powys at Suyian Soul, Isabelle Quesada at Che Shale, Emma Redfern at DARE Kenya, Daniela Resenterra and Natalie Schofield at KTB, Gill and Garry Richardson at Kutazama, Anthea Rowan of Sand Island, Torben Rune and team at Southern Cross Mombasa, Rainie Samuels and Phil Tilley at Acacia Camp Swara Plains, Ian James Saunders of the African Environmental Film Foundation, Angela Sheldrick of the David Sheldrick Wildlife Trust, Gerdi Simon of Aruba Safaris, Monika Solanki for stories of Mombasa and Makindu, Mark Somen and Shamim Ehsani of Tribe, Stefano Soro of Planhotel, Samantha Spooner at the Nation, Esther Stoll of Turtle Bay Dive Centre, Dr Shirley Strum and team at Walking with Baboons, Roger Sylvester at the Driftwood, Lesley Symons of Backpackers' Nirvana, Dr Wolfgang Thome for non-stop information, Carla and Simon of Miti Mingi Guest House for sharing the CBD at night, Ida and Filip Trygg-Andersson of Kinondo Kwetu, Cynthia Walley of &Beyond, Kathrine Webb of Rift Valley Adventures, Matthew (safaritalk.com) Wilkinson, Verity Williams of Sabuk, Piers Winkworth and Charlotte Outram of Offbeat and Rachel Wood and staff at Olerai Beach House.

Ayako Bertolli would like to thank: Johann, Gilles and Fiammetta Turle, Christina and Paul Aarts, Tutti, Abdalla M Ahmed, Lucas Ndeto, Johann Jenson, Joshua Koskei, Petra Allmendinger and Tony Mugambi

ABOUT THE AUTHOR

Richard Trillo is the Kenya Programme Manager at Expert Africa, a UK tour operator specialising in tailor-made trips to East and southern Africa. For many years he was Director of Communications at Rough Guides, and as well as the Rough Guide to Kenya he is the author of the Rough Guide to West Africa and co-author of Rough Guides' First-Time Africa. He has travelled widely in Africa on every kind of budget and, since first visiting Kenya in 1981, he has travelled the length and breadth of the country many times. He has a master's degree in anthropology and African linguistics from the School of Oriental and African Studies, London University, but his first passion was wildlife – his childhood ambition to be a zoologist was thwarted by total impatience with chemistry. He lives in remote suburbia with his wife, Teresa Driver, and their transient offspring.
www.richardtrillo.com

Readers' letters

Thanks to all the readers who have taken the time to write in with comments and suggestions (and apologies if we've inadvertently omitted or misspelt anyone's name):

Paula Alvarado, Selma Aniere, Lucy Badham-Thornhill, Jeff Bagg, Susana Barbas, Jonathan Bending, Cindy Bradley, Marjolein de Bruin, Catherine Cain, Carter Calhoun, Monty Cassino, Andrew Cates, Lucie Červinková, Chambi Chachage, Sushil Chauhan, Susan Church, Norman & Margaret Conroy, Dany Cuyt, Alpha Danani, Nicholas Daniels, Zissa Davidson, Brook Driver, Emily Dunning, Julie Erskine, Frauke Felsch, Michael Freeman, Danny Friedrich, Linda Gaymer, Zen Geb, Tine Geenen, Lion Lepalo Gideon, Agata Gorecka, Bryan Harris, Theresa Heasman, Susan Henry, Vicky Hill, Peter Hills, Abraham Imbai, Johann Jenson, Carol Johnson, Mark Johnson, Alnoor Kanji, Gwen Kidera, Angela Kilenyi, Karom Kimani, Professor Mary C King, James Kirkaldy, Anna Klug, Vally Kovary, Marisa Lassman, Ben Leed, Rick LeVert, Emese Liliom, Lindsay Kennaway, Karoma Kimani, Ann Lipson, Sam Lovell, Colin Macbeth, Lori Mace, Andrea Maggi, Mariella Mallia, Pam Mandel, Rhys Mansell, Melanie Mauthner, Jennifer Maxwell-Dyer, Camilla Le May, Chris Mbogo, Bryan Medcalf, Pamela Michel, Thomas E Morgan, Sarah Morris, Alessio Mortelliti, Natalie Moss, John Mulholland, David Murdoch, Michael O'Hanlon, Etienne Oliff, Fred Omengo, Patricia Ouko, Hazel Peal, Jolene Plocka, Nikos Pocock, Brandon Potter, Helene Rainik, Deepa S Rao, Adam Rector, Elin Reitehaug, Anne Rose, John Round-Turner, Hassan Sachedina, Professor G Michael Schneider, James Schofield, Anoop Shahi, Philip Shaw, John G Smith, Morgan Smith, Marike Splint, Arnold Starosczyk, Alen Sterzaj, Balthasar Strunz, Paul Sullivan, Julie Syrad, Raymond Tremain, Ingrid Vee, Tiffany Venning, Anna Vinnars, Amy Walker, Ben Wallingford, Pyly Wanjiru, Ewa Wicatakala, Joan Willson, May Wong, Hayley Wood, Tracy Woodward, Kai Xue and Jayne Yeung.

Photo credits

All photos © Rough Guides except the following:
(Key: t-top; c-centre; b-bottom; l-left; r-right)

Index

Maps are marked in grey

O

P

Q

R

Map symbols

The symbols below are used on maps throughout the book

=====	Major road (mostly paved)	🏛	Park HQ	🐚	Rainforest
-----	Minor road (mostly unpaved)	⊠	Gate	⊠	Post office
⌃⌃	Mountain or hill range	𝌰	Campsite	P	Parking
▲	Mountain peak	⊙	Monument	⛪	Monastery
⋘	Escarpment	✈	Airport	✡	Synagogue
⅔	Cliff	✕	Airstrip	☪	Mosque
⅏	Viewpoint	∴	Ruin	▲	Temple
☼	Crater	★	Bus or matatu stop	⊡	Church
⌒	Cave	🏬	Petrol station	▨	Building
⚮	Waterfall	⊞	Hospital	◯	Stadium
↯	Marshland	@	Internet access	✝ ⊞	Christian cemetery
⋀⋀	Spring	ⓘ	Information office	▨	Park/reserve
◆	Point of interest	©	Telephone	▨	Beach
🕯	Lighthouse	⌒	Arch	▨	Glacier
⊼	Picnic area	🌳	Forest	▨	Mangrove
↳	Golf course	🌴	Baobabs	▨	Muslim cemetery
⌂	Lodge	🌴	Palms	▨	Coral reef

Listings key

- ▪ Accommodation
- ● Restaurants/Café
- ▪ Bars & Club
- ● Shop

Published in 1982, the first Rough Guide – to Greece – was a student scheme that became a publishing phenomenon. Mark Ellingham, a recent graduate in English from Bristol University, had been travelling in Greece the previous summer and couldn't find the right guidebook. With a small group of friends he wrote his own guide, combining a highly contemporary, journalistic style with a thoroughly practical approach to travellers' needs.

The immediate success of the book spawned a series that rapidly covered dozens of destinations. And, in addition to impecunious backpackers, Rough Guides soon acquired a much broader and older readership that relished the guides' wit and inquisitiveness as much as their enthusiastic, critical approach and value-for-money ethos.

These days, Rough Guides feature recommendations from shoestring to luxury and cover more than 200 destinations around the globe. Our ever-growing team of authors and photographers is spread all over the world, particularly in Europe, the US and Australia.

Rough Guides now number around 200 titles, including Pocket city guides, inspirational coffee-table books and comprehensive country and regional titles, plus technology guides from iPods to Android. As well as print books, we publish groundbreaking apps and eBooks for every major digital device.

Visit ⓦ roughguides.com to see our latest publications.

Rough Guide travel images are available for commercial licensing at ⓦ roughguidespictures.com.

1982 The First *Rough Guide to Greece* – written and researched by Mark Ellingham, John Fisher and Nat Jansz – is published, shortly followed by Spain and Portugal **1983** *Amsterdam* – written by Martin Dunford – is published **1986** The first Rough Guides' offices set up in Kennington, South London **1987** Rough Guides set up as independent company **1989** BBC2 commission a Rough Guides TV series presented by Magenta Devine and Sankha Guha

1990 Rough Guides first published in the US under the name The Real Guides **1994** The first Reference titles – *World Music*, *Classical Music* and *The Internet* – are published • World Music Network starts selling Rough Guides compilation CDs **1995** roughguides.com is launched **1997** New York office set up

2001 First eBooks launched **2002** Rough Guides moves to Penguin headquarters at 80 Strand, London • Delhi office established • Rip-proof city maps series launched **2003** New colour sections added to the guides • First commissioned photographic shoots take place **2004** The *Rough Guide to a Better World* published in association with DFID **2006** First full-colour Rough Guide – *World Party* – is published • **2007** 25s series launched in honour of the 25th anniversary • *Make the Most of Your Time on Earth* becomes best-selling RG and is nominated in Richard and Judy Book Club awards **2008** A new RG TV series is broadcast on Channel 5 **2009** The first hardback picture book – *Earthbound* – featuring our commissioned photography goes on sale

2010 All guides are printed on FCO approved paper **2011** The new full-colour Pocket Guides series is launched • The first city guide iPhone/iPad apps are released **2012** Rough Guides' travel books are relaunched in time for our 30th anniversary, using full colour throughout • The first Rough Guide eBooks made specifically for the iPad go on sale **2013** roughguides.com is relaunched

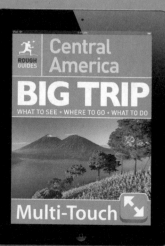

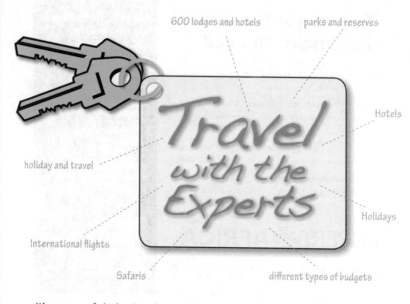

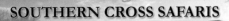

SOUTHERN CROSS SAFARIS
Connoisseur Safaris

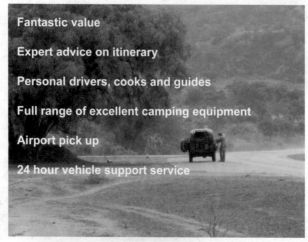

Offbeat Safaris

More than 20 years of experience in operating bespoke Kenyan safaris from vehicle, foot & horseback.

Combine this with Indian Ocean beaches and we truly offer holidays of a lifetime....

Offbeat Meru Camp | Sosian | Deloraine House | Offbeat Mara Camp | Offbeat Riding Safaris | Olerai Beach House

www.offbeatsafaris.com

Driftwood
Malindi - Kenya

Overlooking the shimmering blue waters of the Indian Ocean, the Driftwood is a small, charming hotel on the beautiful Kenyan coast. This unique experience combines stylish accommodation and excellent food with an informal ambience unmatched on Kenya's coast.

For reservations contact: The Driftwood Beach Club,
Mobile: +254 721 724489, +254 734 747133. Email: reservations@driftwoodclub.com

EXPLORE

EXPERIENCE

ESCAPE

Talk to an expert: call the author...

I first went to Kenya in 1981 at the end of an independent overland trip through Africa. We spent six months there, taking buses, matatus and the train (which still ran twice daily) grabbing lifts and cycling all over the country. On our very first safari – camping in the Maasai Mara – we watched in awe as hordes of wildebeest surged up the riverbank towards us, and huge crocs thrashed around in the brown waters.

We camped on the shores of Lake Naivasha, with hippos thundering past our tent at night, stayed in a cheap hostel called Beautiful House in the back streets of Lamu, and had our first experience of snorkelling over the coral gardens of the Indian Ocean.

I went back a few years later to research this Rough Guide – the first practical guide to Kenya – and I've since been back countless times to update the guide, write articles and go on family safaris. Our first trip with the children – Alex aged 4 and David aged 5 months – started with a Christmas Eve drive to the Mara, in heavy rain. Our most recent trip, with David now 20 and Phoebe 17, featured warrior training, Tiwi Beach and the Chyulu Hills.

Although I've been all over Kenya, there's always a host of new experiences to try each time I return. I'm currently fizzing with enthusiasm for the Lake Turkana Festival, the conservancies of the Mara, the wildlife sanctuaries of southern Kenya and Laikipia, the green spaces of Nairobi and some hidden gems along the coast.

I'm happy to admit it – I'm a Kenya travel addict. Now I've joined the award-winning Expert Africa to pass on my knowledge and experience through the safari programme we've created.

I'm on hand to discuss Expert Africa's unusually diverse range of camps and lodges in Kenya, and help you plan the perfect trip. Chat through your ideas with me or one of my expert colleagues on the numbers below. Or email me at richard.trillo@expertafrica.com and I'll get straight back to you.

Richard Trillo

Z922697

HE ROUGH GUIDE TO

Kenya

itten and researched by

chard Trillo

h additional contributions by

Ayako Bertolli, Hilary Heuler and Doug Paterson

ROUGH
GUIDES

roughguides.com